Virgin

FORMULA 1 RECORD FILE

BRUCE SMITH

First published in Great Britain in 2000 by
Virgin Books
an imprint of Virgin Publishing Ltd
Thames Wharf Studios
Rainville Road
London W6 9HA

A catalogue record for this book is available from the British Library.

ISBN 0 7535 0461 8

Designed by Roger Kohn
Typeset by Bruce Smith
Printed and bound by
Mackays of Chatham plc, Chatham, Kent

CONTENTS

CONTENTS

INTRODUCTION

FORMULA 1 RECORD FILE

If you are a Formula 1 aficionado then you may well know basic facts like: Riccardo Patrese has made the most Grands Prix starts or that Alain Prost has recorded the most wins in Formula 1. But whether you follow the sport with a passion or passing interest, you probably won't know which driver has come second the most, or which driver has recorded the most retirements from a race. Well the answers to posers such as these and many, many more can be found within the pages that follow. Apart from these interesting teasers there is a lot more practical information covering the first 50 years of the FIA Formula 1 Championship. Race results, grid position, driver and team records and a whole host more make this perhaps the most comprehensive Formula 1 stats book ever published. Certainly, it's great value for money and I hope that it will accompany you to races you may attend or to the arm of your favourite chair when you are settling in to watch the next big race.

As with the *Formula 1 Pocket Annual*, I welcome feedback from readers with suggestions and ideas for inclusion in future editions of the *Formula 1 Record File*. I can be reached via email, fax or through my PO Box details, which are given below.

The information herein is taken from the extensive computer database I have developed down the years, which I believe to be about as error-free as possible. However, I am a realist and would appreciate hearing from anyone who spots any errors that have crept into this book; anyone doing so will receive a credit in the next edition.

Finally, because of the way the sport has developed in the past 50 years, I have set out some general rules of engagement and these are listed below.

CONTACT DETAILS

email: SmithBruce@Hotmail.com

Address: PO Box 382, St Albans, Herts, AL2 3JD

Web site: www.formula-1.co.uk

RACE STARTS

What determines whether a driver has made a Grand Prix start? The rules have been a bit hazy down the years and this has led to discrepancies in various statistics quoted in the media. Perhaps the most famous of these is the total quoted for four-time World Champion Alain Prost, who has either 199 or 200 Grands Prix starts, depending on your source.

For the purpose of this book, Prost has 199 starts, and the rules governing this, and other total calculations, are as follows:

A driver who takes the grid for the start, from which the race is then run, is credited with a start.

Restarts – a driver who does not make the grid for the restart of a race, which is then run, even though he may have made the first start, is not classified as making a start.

Formation laps – a driver who lines up on the grid for the race but then suffers an accident or problem on the formation lap which means he is unable to make the race start, is not classified as having made a start. (If the race start is aborted and the driver then successfully rejoins the restart, this counts as a start.) This is where the confusion arises over Alain Prost (and more recently Damon Hill) as both had a dns because they both retired on the formation lap.

Indy 500 – starts include the Indianapolis races that were part of the World Championship in the first decade of the sport. Not all reference sources do this and as such this can lead to more discrepancies in totals. For example, Ascari started 32 Grands Prix. However, one of these was the Indy 500 and therefore some references may list him as having competed in 31.

Occasionally F1 cars were joined in Grands Prix by F2 cars, which ran as part of a concurrent event. These drivers are credited with Grands Prix starts, even though they were not awarded points.

There are, of course, grey areas in these rules, although these mainly come from races prior to the 1990s. In such cases the original race classification is adhered to. For example, Mike Thackwell suffered a shunt at the first start of the 1980 Canadian Grand Prix and did not make the restart. He was recorded as a retirement in the official race results. However, by application of the rules, he was technically a dns. It may be the fact that he effectively became the youngest driver to have participated in a Formula 1 Grand Prix that led to the original decision. Where possible, any murky areas are identified at relevant points in the Record File.

As far as the race results go, I have endeavoured to list drivers who registered a dns wherever possible. However, they are only listed if the driver had actually qualified for the race as determined by the fact that he obtained a grid position in qualifying. However, if a driver has never actually qualified for a race then he has not been afforded an individual entry in the drivers section. Reserve entries are not listed.

Due to the high number of drivers who often failed to qualify or pre-qualify for the early GPs, these have not been listed. However, those drivers who did not qualify due to the 107% qualification rule have been listed at the appropriate points in the latter races of the 1990s.

SHARED DRIVES

In the early years (1950-61) of the FIA Championship, cars were occasionally 'shared' by drivers. Thus it was quite possible for one driver to start a race and another to finish it using the same car. Equally, drivers occasionally 'gave up' their car to another better-placed driver. Take, for instance, the 1951 French Grand Prix. Luigi Fagioli gave up his leading drive to Juan Manual Fangio and both are registered as winning the race – such were the rules in those formative years. Accordingly Fangio is normally quoted as having 24 wins from his 51 races, even though two of these came from shared drives. The Grands Prix Results section indicates shared drives where they occurred by (S) after the starting driver's name and a full list of these can be found under the heading Shared Drives which starts on page 345.

Some drivers also made their debut as a Grand Prix driver by taking over a car from another driver. For example, Jo Bonnier took over from Luigi Villoresi during the 1956 Italian Grand Prix, but his first starting drive was in 1957. Because of the definition assigned to determining whether a driver has started a race or not, the 1956 drive is not listed as a 'start'. If you wish to include these then you should also take note of the aforementioned list in the Shared Drives section. However, in most cases a bracketed total is provided to indicate the total including shared drives, where the driver did not start the race, and as such would have been credited with the start.

In later years points were not awarded for shared drivers, but occasionally they were used tactically to help one championship contender finish ahead of his rivals, therefore pushing them down the points list. Jim Clark did this in the 1964 US race at Watkins Glen in a bid to finish ahead of his championship rivals Surtees and Hill.

INDY 500

As already mentioned, results from the Indianapolis 500 races that formed part of the early World Championship are listed.

It is normal in Champ Car (previously Cart) to classify everyone with a position, regardless of whether they retired or not. Positions are determined by the number of laps completed. This is of course not the case in Formula 1 and the normal F1 method of classification is adhered to for Indy 500 Grands Prix. Note also that driver statistics include these World Championship results.

NAMING CONVENTIONS

In most parts of this Record File, drivers are identified simply by their surname. However, where several drivers have the same surnames then their initial is used after the surname to identify them. For example:

Fittipaldi,E.
Fittipaldi,C.

Where drivers have like forenames then the entire forename is listed after the surname. For example:

Stewart,Jackie
Stewart,Jimmy

GRAND PRIX KEY

Various keys to abbreviations can be found at the relevant points throughout this book. However, the abbreviations used to represent Grands Prix are consistent and are detailed below:

Arg	Argentina	Ita	Italy
Aus	Australia	Jap	Japan
Aut	Austria	Mal	Malaysia
Bel	Belgium	Mex	Mexico
Bra	Brazil	Mon	Monaco
Can	Canada	Mor	Morocco
CP	Caesar's Palace	NZ	New Zealand
Dal	Dallas	Pac	Pacific
Esp	Spain	Pes	Pescara
Eur	Europe	Por	Portugal
Fin	Finland	SA	South Africa
Fra	France	San	San Marino
GB	Great Britain	Swi	Switzerland
Ger	Germany	US	United States
Hol	Holland	USAE	USA (East)
Hun	Hungary	USAW	USA (West)

ACKNOWLEDGEMENTS

Special thanks go to Jonathan Taylor at Virgin Books for his help in establishing this Record File concept and Mark Webb for his help in producing this book.

RACE
RESULTS

GRANDS PRIX RACE SUMMARY

GPNo	Year	No	Grand Prix	Circuit	Date	Winner	Pole	Fastest Lap
1	1950	1	British	Silverstone	13 May 50	Farina	Farina	Farina
2	1950	2	Monaco	Monte Carlo	21 May 50	Fangio	Fangio	Fangio
3	1950	3	Indy 500	Indianapolis	30 May 50	Parsons	Faulkner	Holland
4	1950	4	Swiss	Bremgarten	4 Jun 50	Farina	Fangio	Farina
5	1950	5	Belgian	Spa	18 Jun 50	Fangio	Fangio	Farina
6	1950	6	French	Reims	2 Jul 50	Fangio	Fangio	Fangio
7	1950	7	Italian	Monza	3 Sep 50	Farina	Fangio	Fangio
8	1951	1	Swiss	Bremgarten	27 May 51	Fangio	Fangio	Fangio
9	1951	2	Indy 500	Indianapolis	29 May 51	Wallard	Nalon	Wallard
10	1951	3	Belgian	Spa	17 Jun 51	Farina	Fangio	Fangio
11	1951	4	French	Reims	1 Jul 51	Fagioli & Fangio	Fangio	Fangio
12	1951	5	British	Silverstone	14 Jul 51	Gonzalez,J.	Gonzalez,J.	Farina
13	1951	6	German	Nurburgring	29 Jul 51	Ascari	Ascari	Fangio
14	1951	7	Italian	Monza	16 Sep 51	Ascari	Fangio	Farina
15	1951	8	Spanish	Pedrables	28 Oct 51	Fangio	Ascari	Fangio
16	1952	1	Swiss	Bremgarten	18 May 52	Taruffi	Farina	Taruffi
17	1952	2	Indy 500	Indianapolis	30 May 52	Ruttman	Agabashian	Vukovich
18	1952	3	Belgian	Spa	22 Jun 52	Ascari	Ascari	Ascari
19	1952	4	French	Rouen	6 Jul 52	Ascari	Ascari	Ascari
20	1952	5	British	Silverstone	19 Jul 52	Ascari	Farina	Ascari
21	1952	6	German	Nurburgring	3 Aug 52	Ascari	Ascari	Ascari
22	1952	7	Dutch	Zandvoort	17 Aug 52	Ascari	Ascari	Ascari
23	1952	8	Italian	Monza	7 Sep 52	Ascari	Ascari	Ascari & Gonzalez,J.
24	1953	1	Argentine	Buenos Aires	18 Jan 53	Ascari	Ascari	Ascari
25	1953	2	Indy 500	Indianapolis	30 May 53	Vukovich	Vukovich	Vukovich
26	1953	3	Dutch	Zandvoort	7 Jun 53	Ascari	Ascari	Villoresi
27	1953	4	Belgian	Spa	21 Jun 53	Ascari	Fangio	Gonzalez,J.
28	1953	5	French	Reims	5 Jul 53	Hawthorn	Ascari	Fangio
29	1953	6	British	Silverstone	18 Jul 53	Ascari	Ascari	Ascari & Gonzalez,J.
30	1953	7	German	Nurburgring	2 Aug 53	Farina	Ascari	Ascari
31	1953	8	Swiss	Bremgarten	23 Aug 53	Ascari	Fangio	Ascari
32	1953	9	Italian	Monza	13 Sep 53	Fangio	Ascari	Fangio
33	1954	1	Argentine	Buenos Aires	17 Jan 54	Fangio	Farina	Gonzalez,J.
34	1954	2	Indy 500	Indianapolis	31 May 54	Vukovich	McGrath	McGrath
35	1954	3	Belgian	Spa	20 Jun 54	Fangio	Fangio	Fangio
36	1954	4	French	Reims	4 Jul 54	Fangio	Fangio	Herrmann
37	1954	5	British	Silverstone	17 Jul 54	Gonzalez,J.	Fangio	Ascari, Behra, Fangio, Gonzalez,J.Hawthorn, Marimon & Moss
38	1954	6	German	Nurburgring	1 Aug 54	Fangio	Fangio	Kling
39	1954	7	Swiss	Bremgarten	22 Aug 54	Fangio	Gonzalez,J.	Fangio
40	1954	8	Italian	Monza	5 Sep 54	Fangio	Fangio	Gonzalez,J.
41	1954	9	Spanish	Pedrables	24 Oct 54	Hawthorn	Ascari	Ascari
42	1955	1	Argentine	Buenos Aires	16 Jan 55	Fangio	Gonzalez,J.	Fangio
43	1955	2	Monaco	Monte Carlo	22 May 55	Trintignant	Fangio	Fangio
44	1955	3	Indy 500	Indianapolis	30 May 55	Sweikert	Hoyt	Vukovich
45	1955	4	Belgian	Spa	5 Jun 55	Fangio	Castelotti	Fangio

GRANDS PRIX RACE SUMMARY

GPNo	Year	No	Grand Prix	Circuit	Date	Winner	Pole	Fastest Lap
46	1955	5	Dutch	Zandvoort	19 Jun 55	Fangio	Fangio	Mieres
47	1955	6	British	Aintree	16 Jul 55	Moss	Moss	Moss
48	1955	7	Italian	Monza	1 Sep 55	Fangio	Fangio	Moss
49	1956	1	Argentine	Buenos Aires	22 Jan 56	Musso & Fangio	Fangio	Fangio
50	1956	2	Monaco	Monte Carlo	13 May 56	Moss	Fangio	Fangio
51	1956	3	Indy 500	Indianapolis	30 May 56	Flaherty	Flaherty	Russo,P.
52	1956	4	Belgian	Spa	3 Jun 56	Collins	Fangio	Moss
53	1956	5	French	Reims	1 Jul 56	Collins	Fangio	Fangio
54	1956	6	British	Silverstone	14 Jul 56	Fangio	Moss	Moss
55	1956	7	German	Nurburgring	5 Aug 56	Fangio	Fangio	Fangio
56	1956	8	Italian	Monza	2 Sep 56	Moss	Fangio	Moss
57	1957	1	Argentine	Buenos Aires	13 Jan 57	Fangio	Moss	Moss
58	1957	2	Monaco	Monte Carlo	19 May 57	Fangio	Fangio	Fangio
59	1957	3	Indy 500	Indianapolis	30 May 57	Hanks	O'Connor	Rathmann,J.
60	1957	4	French	Rouen	7 Jul 57	Fangio	Fangio	Musso
61	1957	5	British	Aintree	20 Jul 57	Brooks & Moss	Moss	Moss
62	1957	6	German	Nurburgring	4 Aug 57	Fangio	Fangio	Fangio
63	1957	7	Pescara	Pescara	18 Aug 57	Moss	Fangio	Moss
64	1957	8	Italian	Monza	8 Sep 57	Moss	Lewis Evans	Brooks
65	1958	1	Argentine	Buenos Aires	19 Jan 58	Moss	Fangio	Fangio
66	1958	2	Monaco	Monte Carlo	18 May 58	Trintignant	Brooks	Hawthorn
67	1958	3	Dutch	Zandvoort	26 May 58	Moss	Lewis Evans	Moss
68	1958	4	Indy 500	Indianapolis	30 May 58	Bryan	Rathmann,D.	Bettenhausen
69	1958	5	Belgian	Spa	15 Jun 58	Brooks	Hawthorn	Hawthorn
70	1958	6	French	Reims	6 Jul 58	Hawthorn	Hawthorn	Hawthorn
71	1958	7	British	Silverstone	19 Jul 58	Collins	Moss	Hawthorn
72	1958	8	German	Nurburgring	3 Aug 58	Brooks	Hawthorn	Moss
73	1958	9	Portuguese	Oporto	14 Aug 58	Moss	Moss	Hawthorn
74	1958	10	Italian	Monza	7 Sep 58	Brooks	Moss	Hill,P.
75	1958	11	Moroccan	Casablanca	19 Oct 58	Moss	Hawthorn	Moss
76	1959	1	Monaco	Monte Carlo	10 May 59	Brabham,J.	Moss	Brabham,J.
77	1959	2	Indy 500	Indianapolis	30 May 59	Ward	Thompson	Thomson
78	1959	3	Dutch	Zandvoort	31 May 59	Bonnier	Bonnier	Moss
79	1959	4	French	Reims	5 Jul 59	Brooks	Brooks	Moss
80	1959	5	British	Aintree	18 Jul 59	Brabham,J.	Brabham,J.	Moss & McLaren
81	1959	6	German	Berlin	2 Aug 59	Brooks	Brooks	Brooks
82	1959	7	Portuguese	Monsanto	23 Aug 59	Moss	Moss	Moss
83	1959	8	Italian	Monza	13 Sep 59	Moss	Moss	Hill,P.
84	1959	9	US	Sebring	12 Dec 59	McLaren	Moss	Trintignant
85	1960	1	Argentine	Buenos Aires	7 Feb 60	McLaren	Moss	Moss
86	1960	2	Monaco	Monte Carlo	29 May 60	Moss	Moss	McLaren
87	1960	3	Indy 500	Indianapolis	30 May 60	Rathmann,J.	Sachs	Rathmann,J.
88	1960	4	Dutch	Zandvoort	6 Jun 60	Brabham,J.	Moss	Moss
89	1960	5	Belgian	Spa	19 Jun 60	Brabham,J.	Brabham,J.	Brabham,J., Hill,P. & Ireland
90	1960	6	French	Reims	3 Jul 60	Brabham,J.	Brabham,J.	Brabham,J.
91	1960	7	British	Silverstone	16 Jul 60	Brabham,J.	Brabham,J.	Hill,G.
92	1960	8	Portuguese	Oporto	14 Aug 60	Brabham,J.	Surtees	Surtees

GRANDS PRIX RACE SUMMARY

GPNo	Year	No	Grand Prix	Circuit	Date	Winner	Pole	Fastest Lap
93	1960	9	Italian	Monza	4 Sep 60	Hill,P.	Hill,P.	Hill,P.
94	1960	10	US	Riverside	20 Nov 60	Moss	Moss	Brabham,J.
95	1961	1	Monaco	Monte Carlo	14 May 61	Moss	Moss	Ginther & Moss
96	1961	2	Dutch	Zandvoort	22 May 61	von Trips	Hill,P.	Clark
97	1961	3	Belgian	Spa	18 Jun 61	Hill,P.	Hill,P.	Ginther
98	1961	4	French	Reims	2 Jul 61	Baghetti	Hill,P.	Hill,P.
99	1961	5	British	Aintree	15 Jul 61	von Trips	Hill,P.	Brooks
100	1961	6	German	Nurburgring	6 Aug 61	Moss	Hill,P.	Hill,P.
101	1961	7	Italian	Monza	10 Sep 61	Hill,P.	Von Trips	Baghetti
102	1961	8	US	Watkins Glen	8 Oct 61	Ireland	Brabham,J.	Brabham,J.
103	1962	1	Dutch	Zandvoort	20 May 62	Hill,G.	Surtees	McLaren
104	1962	2	Monaco	Monte Carlo	3 Jun 62	McLaren	Clark	Clark
105	1962	3	Belgian	Spa	17 Jun 62	Clark	Hill,G.	Clark
106	1962	4	French	Rouen	8 Jul 62	Gurney	Clark	Hill,G.
107	1962	5	British	Aintree	21 Jul 62	Clark	Clark	Clark
108	1962	6	German	Nurburgring	5 Aug 62	Hill,G.	Gurney	Hill,G.
109	1962	7	Italian	Monza	16 Sep 62	Hill,G.	Clark	Hill,G.
110	1962	8	US	Watkins Glen	7 Oct 62	Clark	Clark	Clark
111	1962	9	South African	East London	29 Dec 62	Hill,G.	Clark	Clark
112	1963	1	Monaco	Monte Carlo	26 May 63	Hill,G.	Clark	Surtees
113	1963	2	Belgian	Spa	9 Jun 63	Clark	Hill,G.	Clark
114	1963	3	Dutch	Zandvoort	23 Jun 63	Clark	Clark	Clark
115	1963	4	French	Reims	30 Jun 63	Clark	Clark	Clark
116	1963	5	British	Silverstone	20 Jul 63	Clark	Clark	Surtees
117	1963	6	German	Nurburgring	4 Aug 63	Surtees	Clark	Surtees
118	1963	7	Italian	Monza	8 Sep 63	Clark	Surtees	Clark
119	1963	8	US	Watkins Glen	6 Oct 63	Hill,G.	Hill,G.	Clark
120	1963	9	Mexican	Mexico City	27 Oct 63	Clark	Clark	Clark
121	1963	10	South African	East London	28 Dec 63	Clark	Clark	Gurney
122	1964	1	Monaco	Monte Carlo	10 May 64	Hill,G.	Clark	Hill,G.
123	1964	2	Dutch	Zandvoort	24 May 64	Clark	Gurney	Clark
124	1964	3	Belgian	Spa	14 Jun 64	Clark	Gurney	Gurney
125	1964	4	French	Rouen	28 Jun 64	Gurney	Clark	Brabham,J.
126	1964	5	British	Brands Hatch	11 Jul 64	Clark	Clark	Clark
127	1964	6	German	Nurburgring	2 Aug 64	Surtees	Surtees	Surtees
128	1964	7	Austrian	Zeltweg	23 Aug 64	Bandini	Hill,G.	Gurney
129	1964	8	Italian	Monza	6 Sep 64	Surtees	Surtees	Surtees
130	1964	9	US	Watkins Glen	4 Oct 64	Hill,G.	Clark	Clark
131	1964	10	Mexican	Mexico City	25 Oct 64	Gurney	Clark	Clark
132	1965	1	South African	East London	1 Jan 65	Clark	Clark	Clark
133	1965	2	Monaco	Monte Carlo	30 May 65	Hill,G.	Hill,G.	Hill,G.
134	1965	3	Belgian	Spa	13 Jun 65	Clark	Hill,G.	Clark
135	1965	4	French	Clermont Ferrand	27 Jun 65	Clark	Clark	Clark
136	1965	5	British	Silverstone	10 Jul 65	Clark	Clark	Hill,G.
137	1965	6	Dutch	Zandvoort	18 Jul 65	Clark	Hill,G.	Clark
138	1965	7	German	Nurburgring	1 Aug 65	Clark	Clark	Clark
139	1965	8	Italian	Monza	12 Sep 65	Stewart,Jackie	Clark	Clark
140	1965	9	US	Watkins Glen	3 Oct 65	Hill,G.	Hill,G.	Hill,G.

GRANDS PRIX RACE SUMMARY

GPNo	Year	No	Grand Prix	Circuit	Date	Winner	Pole	Fastest Lap
141	1965	10	Mexican	Mexico City	24 Oct 65	Ginther	Clark	Gurney
142	1966	1	Monaco	Monte Carlo	22 May 66	Stewart,Jackie	Clark	Bandini
143	1966	2	Belgian	Spa	12 Jun 66	Surtees	Surtees	Surtees
144	1966	3	French	Reims	3 Jul 66	Brabham,J.	Bandini	Bandini
145	1966	4	British	Brands Hatch	16 Jul 66	Brabham,J.	Brabham,J.	Brabham,J.
146	1966	5	Dutch	Zandvoort	24 Jul 66	Brabham,J.	Brabham,J.	Hulme
147	1966	6	German	Nurburgring	2 Aug 66	Brabham,J.	Clark	Surtees
148	1966	7	Italian	Monza	4 Sep 66	Scarfiotti	Parkes	Scarfiotti
149	1966	8	US	Watkins Glen	2 Oct 66	Clark	Brabham,J.	Surtees
150	1966	9	Mexican	Mexico City	25 Oct 66	Surtees	Surtees	Ginther
151	1967	1	South African	Kyalami	2 Jan 67	Rodriguez,P.	Brabham,J.	Hulme
152	1967	2	Monaco	Monte Carlo	7 May 67	Hulme	Brabham,J.	Clark
153	1967	3	Dutch	Zandvoort	4 Jun 67	Clark	Hill,G.	Clark
154	1967	4	Belgian	Spa	18 Jun 67	Gurney	Clark	Gurney
155	1967	5	French	Le Mans	2 Jul 67	Brabham,J.	Hill,G.	Hill,G.
156	1967	6	British	Silverstone	15 Jul 67	Clark	Clark	Hulme
157	1967	7	German	Nurburgring	6 Aug 67	Hulme	Clark	Gurney
158	1967	8	Canadian	Mosport Park	27 Aug 67	Brabham,J.	Clark	Clark
159	1967	9	Italian	Monza	10 Sep 67	Surtees	Clark	Clark
160	1967	10	US	Watkins Glen	1 Oct 67	Clark	Hill,G.	Hill,G.
161	1967	11	Mexican	Mexico City	22 Oct 67	Clark	Clark	Clark
162	1968	1	South African	Kyalami	1 Jan 68	Clark	Clark	Clark
163	1968	2	Spanish	Jarama	12 May 68	Hill,G.	Amon	Beltoise
164	1968	3	Monaco	Monte Carlo	26 May 68	Hill,G.	Hill,G.	Attwood
165	1968	4	Belgian	Spa	9 Jun 68	McLaren	Amon	Surtees
166	1968	5	Dutch	Zandvoort	23 Jun 68	Stewart,Jackie	Amon	Beltoise
167	1968	6	French	Rouen	7 Jul 68	Ickx	Rindt	Rodriguez,P.
168	1968	7	British	Brands Hatch	20 Jul 68	Siffert	Hill,G.	Siffert
169	1968	8	German	Nurburgring	4 Aug 68	Stewart,Jackie	Ickx	Stewart,Jackie
170	1968	9	Italian	Monza	8 Sep 68	Hulme	Surtees	Oliver
171	1968	10	Canadian	St Jovite	22 Sep 68	Hulme	Rindt	Siffert
172	1968	11	US	Watkins Glen	6 Oct 68	Stewart,Jackie	Andretti,Mario	Stewart,Jackie
173	1968	12	Mexican	Mexico City	3 Nov 68	Hill,G.	Siffert	Siffert
174	1969	1	South African	Kyalami	2 Jan 69	Stewart,Jackie	Brabham,J.	Stewart,Jackie
175	1969	2	Spanish	Montjuich Park	4 May 69	Stewart,Jackie	Rindt	Rindt
176	1969	3	Monaco	Monte Carlo	18 May 69	Hill,G.	Stewart,Jackie	Stewart,Jackie
177	1969	4	Dutch	Zandvoort	21 Jun 69	Stewart,Jackie	Rindt	Stewart,Jackie
178	1969	5	French	Clermont Ferrand	6 Jul 69	Stewart,Jackie	Stewart,Jackie	Stewart,Jackie
179	1969	6	British	Silverstone	19 Jul 69	Stewart,Jackie	Rindt	Stewart,Jackie
180	1969	7	German	Nurburgring	3 Aug 69	Ickx	Ickx	Ickx
181	1969	8	Italian	Monza	7 Sep 69	Stewart,Jackie	Rindt	Beltoise
182	1969	9	Canadian	Mosport Park	20 Sep 69	Ickx	Ickx	Ickx & Brabham,J.
183	1969	10	US	Watkins Glen	5 Oct 69	Rindt	Rindt	Rindt
184	1969	11	Mexican	Mexico City	19 Oct 69	Hulme	Brabham,J.	Ickx
185	1970	1	South African	Kyalami	7 Mar 70	Brabham,J.	Stewart,Jackie	Surtees & Brabham,J.
186	1970	2	Spanish	Jarama	19 Apr 70	Stewart,Jackie	Brabham,J.	Brabham,J.

GPNo	Year	No	Grand Prix	Circuit	Date	Winner	Pole	Fastest Lap
187	1970	3	Monaco	Monte Carlo	10 May 70	Rindt	Stewart,Jackie	Amon
188	1970	4	Belgian	Spa	7 Jun 70	Rodriguez,P.	Stewart,Jackie	Rindt
189	1970	5	Dutch	Zandvoort	21 Jun 70	Rindt	Rindt	Ickx
190	1970	6	French	Clermont Ferrand	5 Jul 70	Rindt	Ickx	Brabham,J.
191	1970	7	British	Brands Hatch	18 Jul 70	Rindt	Rindt	Brabham,J.
192	1970	8	German	Hockenheim	2 Aug 70	Rindt	Ickx	Ickx
193	1970	9	Austrian	Osterreichring	16 Aug 70	Ickx	Rindt	Ickx & Regazzoni
194	1970	10	Italian	Monza	6 Sep 70	Regazzoni	Ickx	Regazzoni
195	1970	11	Canadian	St Jovite	20 Sep 70	Ickx	Stewart,Jackie	Regazzoni
196	1970	12	US	Watkins Glen	4 Oct 70	Fittipaldi,E.	Ickx	Ickx
197	1970	13	Mexican	Mexico City	25 Oct 70	Ickx	Regazzoni	Ickx
198	1971	1	South African	Kyalami	6 Mar 71	Andretti,Mario	Stewart,Jackie	Andretti,Mario
199	1971	2	Spanish	Montjuich Park	18 Apr 71	Stewart,Jackie	Ickx	Ickx
200	1971	3	Monaco	Monte Carlo	23 May 71	Stewart,Jackie	Stewart,Jackie	Stewart,Jackie
201	1971	4	Dutch	Zandvoort	20 Jun 71	Ickx	Ickx	Ickx
202	1971	5	French	Paul Ricard	4 Jul 71	Stewart,Jackie	Stewart,Jackie	Stewart,Jackie
203	1971	6	British	Silverstone	17 Jul 71	Stewart,Jackie	Regazzoni	Stewart,Jackie
204	1971	7	German	Nurburgring	1 Aug 71	Stewart,Jackie	Stewart,Jackie	Cevert
205	1971	8	Austrian	Osterreichring	15 Aug 71	Siffert	Siffert	Siffert
206	1971	9	Italian	Monza	5 Sep 71	Gethin	Amon	Pescarolo
207	1971	10	Canadian	Mosport Park	19 Sep 71	Stewart,Jackie	Stewart,Jackie	Hulme
208	1971	11	US	Watkins Glen	3 Oct 71	Cevert	Stewart,Jackie	Ickx
209	1972	1	Argentine	Buenos Aires	23 Jan 72	Stewart,Jackie	Reutemann	Stewart,Jackie
210	1972	2	South African	Kyalami	4 Mar 72	Hulme	Stewart,Jackie	Hailwood
211	1972	3	Spanish	Jarama	1 May 72	Fittipaldi,E.	Ickx	Ickx
212	1972	4	Monaco	Monte Carlo	14 May 72	Beltoise	Fittipaldi,E.	Amon
213	1972	5	Belgian	Nivelles	4 Jun 72	Fittipaldi,E.	Fittipaldi,E.	Beltoise
214	1972	6	French	Clermont Ferrand	2 Jul 72	Stewart,Jackie	Amon	Amon
215	1972	7	British	Brands Hatch	15 Jul 72	Fittipaldi,E.	Ickx	Stewart,Jackie
216	1972	8	German	Nurburgring	30 Jul 72	Ickx	Ickx	Ickx
217	1972	9	Austrian	Osterreichring	13 Aug 72	Fittipaldi,E.	Fittipaldi,E.	Hulme
218	1972	10	Italian	Monza	10 Sep 72	Fittipaldi,E.	Ickx	Ickx
219	1972	11	Canadian	Mosport Park	24 Sep 72	Stewart,Jackie	Revson	Stewart,Jackie
220	1972	12	US	Watkins Glen	8 Oct 72	Stewart,Jackie	Stewart,Jackie	Stewart,Jackie
221	1973	1	Argentine	Buenos Aires	28 Jan 73	Fittipaldi,E.	Regazzoni	Fittipaldi,E.
222	1973	2	Brazilian	Interlagos	11 Feb 73	Fittipaldi,E.	Peterson	Fittipaldi,E. & Hulme
223	1973	3	South African	Kyalami	3 Mar 73	Stewart,Jackie	Hulme	Fittipaldi,E.
224	1973	4	Spanish	Montjuich Park	29 Apr 73	Fittipaldi,E.	Peterson	Peterson
225	1973	5	Belgian	Zolder	20 May 73	Stewart,Jackie	Peterson	Cevert
226	1973	6	Monaco	Monte Carlo	3 Jun 73	Stewart,Jackie	Stewart,Jackie	Fittipaldi,E.
227	1973	7	Swedish	Anderstorp	17 Jun 73	Hulme	Peterson	Hulme
228	1973	8	French	Paul Ricard	1 Jul 73	Peterson	Stewart,Jackie	Hulme
229	1973	9	British	Silverstone	14 Jul 73	Revson	Peterson	Hunt
230	1973	10	Dutch	Zandvoort	29 Jul 73	Stewart,Jackie	Peterson	Peterson
231	1973	11	German	Nurburgring	5 Aug 73	Stewart,Jackie	Stewart,Jackie	Pace
232	1973	12	Austrian	Osterreichring	19 Aug 73	Peterson	Fittipaldi,E.	Pace
233	1973	13	Italian	Monza	9 Sep 73	Peterson	Peterson	Stewart,Jackie

GRANDS PRIX RACE SUMMARY

GPNo	Year	No	Grand Prix	Circuit	Date	Winner	Pole	Fastest Lap
234	1973	14	Canadian	Mosport Park	23 Sep 73	Revson	Peterson	Fittipaldi,E.
235	1973	15	US	Watkins Glen	7 Oct 73	Peterson	Peterson	Hunt
236	1974	1	Argentine	Buenos Aires	13 Jan 74	Hulme	Peterson	Regazzoni
237	1974	2	Brazilian	Interlagos	27 Jan 74	Fittipaldi,E.	Fittipaldi,E.	Regazzoni
238	1974	3	South African	Kyalami	30 Mar 74	Reutemann	Lauda	Reutemann
239	1974	4	Spanish	Jarama	28 Apr 74	Lauda	Lauda	Lauda
240	1974	5	Belgian	Nivelles	12 May 74	Fittipaldi,E.	Regazzoni	Hulme
241	1974	6	Monaco	Monte Carlo	26 May 74	Peterson	Lauda	Peterson
242	1974	7	Swedish	Anderstorp	9 Jun 74	Scheckter,J.	Depailler	Depailler
243	1974	8	Dutch	Zandvoort	23 Jun 74	Lauda	Lauda	Peterson
244	1974	9	French	Dijon	7 Jul 74	Peterson	Lauda	Scheckter,J.
245	1974	10	British	Brands Hatch	20 Jul 74	Scheckter,J.	Lauda	Lauda
246	1974	11	German	Nurburgring	4 Aug 74	Regazzoni	Lauda	Scheckter,J.
247	1974	12	Austrian	Osterreichring	18 Aug 74	Reutemann	Lauda	Regazzoni
248	1974	13	Italian	Monza	8 Sep 74	Peterson	Lauda	Pace
249	1974	14	Canadian	Mosport Park	22 Sep 74	Fittipaldi,E.	Fittipaldi,E.	Lauda
250	1974	15	US	Watkins Glen	6 Oct 74	Reutemann	Reutemann	Pace
251	1975	1	Argentine	Buenos Aires	12 Jan 75	Fittipaldi,E.	Jarier	Hunt
252	1975	2	Brazilian	Interlagos	26 Jan 75	Pace	Jarier	Jarier
253	1975	3	South African	Kyalami	1 Mar 75	Scheckter,J.	Pace	Pace
254	1975	4	Spanish	Montjuich Park	27 Apr 75	Mass	Lauda	Andretti,Mario
255	1975	5	Monaco	Monte Carlo	11 May 75	Lauda	Lauda	Depailler
256	1975	6	Belgian	Zolder	25 May 75	Lauda	Lauda	Regazzoni
257	1975	7	Swedish	Anderstorp	8 Jun 75	Lauda	Brambilla	Lauda
258	1975	8	Dutch	Zandvoort	22 Jun 75	Hunt	Lauda	Lauda
259	1975	9	French	Paul Ricard	6 Jul 75	Lauda	Lauda	Mass
260	1975	10	British	Silverstone	19 Jul 75	Fittipaldi,E.	Pryce	Regazzoni
261	1975	11	German	Nurburgring	3 Aug 75	Reutemann	Lauda	Regazzoni
262	1975	12	Austrian	Osterreichring	17 Aug 75	Brambilla	Lauda	Brambilla
263	1975	13	Italian	Monza	7 Sep 75	Regazzoni	Lauda	Regazzoni
264	1975	14	US	Watkins Glen	5 Oct 75	Lauda	Lauda	Fittipaldi,E.
265	1976	1	Brazilian	Interlagos	25 Jan 76	Lauda	Hunt	Jarier
266	1976	2	South African	Kyalami	6 Mar 76	Lauda	Hunt	Lauda
267	1976	3	US West	Long Beach	28 Mar 76	Regazzoni	Regazzoni	Regazzoni
268	1976	4	Spanish	Jarama	2 May 76	Hunt	Hunt	Mass
269	1976	5	Belgian	Zolder	16 May 76	Lauda	Lauda	Lauda
270	1976	6	Monaco	Monte Carlo	30 May 76	Lauda	Lauda	Regazzoni
271	1976	7	Swedish	Anderstorp	13 Jun 76	Scheckter,J.	Scheckter,J.	Andretti,Mario
272	1976	8	French	Paul Ricard	4 Jul 76	Hunt	Hunt	Lauda
273	1976	9	British	Brands Hatch	18 Jul 76	Lauda	Lauda	Lauda
274	1976	10	German	Nurburgring	1 Aug 76	Hunt	Hunt	Scheckter,J.
275	1976	11	Austrian	Osterreichring	15 Aug 76	Watson	Hunt	Hunt
276	1976	12	Dutch	Zandvoort	29 Aug 76	Hunt	Peterson	Regazzoni
277	1976	13	Italian	Monza	12 Sep 76	Peterson	Laffite	Peterson
278	1976	14	Canadian	Mosport Park	3 Oct 76	Hunt	Hunt	Depailler
279	1976	15	US East	Watkins Glen	10 Oct 76	Hunt	Hunt	Hunt
280	1976	16	Japanese	Fuji	24 Oct 76	Andretti,Mario	Andretti,Mario	Hasemi
281	1977	1	Argentine	Buenos Aires	9 Jan 77	Scheckter,J.	Hunt	Hunt

GRANDS PRIX RACE SUMMARY

GPNo	Year	No	Grand Prix	Circuit	Date	Winner	Pole	Fastest Lap
282	1977	2	Brazilian	interlagos	23 Jan 77	Reutemann	Hunt	Hunt
283	1977	3	South African	Kyalami	5 Mar 77	Lauda	Hunt	Watson
284	1977	4	US West	Long Beach	3 Apr 77	Andretti,Mario	Lauda	Lauda
285	1977	5	Spanish	Jarama	8 May 77	Andretti,Mario	Andretti,Mario	Laffite
286	1977	6	Monaco	Monte Carlo	22 May 77	Scheckter,J.	Watson	Scheckter,J.
287	1977	7	Belgian	Zolder	5 Jun 77	Nilsson	Andretti,Mario	Nilsson
288	1977	8	Swedish	Anderstorp	19 Jun 77	Laffite	Andretti,Mario	Andretti,Mario
289	1977	9	French	Dijon	3 Jul 77	Andretti,Mario	Andretti,Mario	Andretti,Mario
290	1977	10	British	Silverstone	16 Jul 77	Hunt	Hunt	Hunt
291	1977	11	German	Hockenheim	31 Jul 77	Lauda	Scheckter,J.	Lauda
292	1977	12	Austrian	Osterreichring	14 Aug 77	Jones	Lauda	Watson
293	1977	13	Dutch	Zandvoort	28 Aug 77	Lauda	Andretti,Mario	Lauda
294	1977	14	Italian	Monza	11 Sep 77	Andretti,Mario	Hunt	Andretti,Mario
295	1977	15	US East	Watkins Glen	2 Oct 77	Hunt	Hunt	Peterson
296	1977	16	Canadian	Mosport Park	9 Oct 77	Scheckter,J.	Andretti,Mario	Andretti,Mario
297	1977	17	Japanese	Fuji	23 Oct 77	Hunt	Andretti,Mario	Scheckter,J.
298	1978	1	Argentine	Buenos Aires	15 Jan 78	Andretti,Mario	Andretti,Mario	Villeneuve,G.
299	1978	2	Brazilian	Rio de Janeiro	29 Jan 78	Reutemann	Peterson	Reutemann
300	1978	3	South African	Kyalami	4 Mar 78	Peterson	Lauda	Andretti,Mario
301	1978	4	US West	Long Beach	2 Apr 78	Reutemann	Reutemann	Jones
302	1978	5	Monaco	Monte Carlo	7 May 78	Depailler	Reutemann	Lauda
303	1978	6	Belgian	Zolder	21 May 78	Andretti,Mario	Andretti,Mario	Peterson
304	1978	7	Spanish	Jarama	4 Jun 78	Andretti,Mario	Andretti,Mario	Andretti,Mario
305	1978	8	Swedish	Anderstorp	17 Jun 78	Lauda	Andretti,Mario	Lauda
306	1978	9	French	Paul Ricard	2 Jul 78	Andretti,Mario	Watson	Reutemann
307	1978	10	British	Brands Hatch	16 Jul 78	Reutemann	Peterson	Lauda
308	1978	11	German	Hockenheim	30 Jul 78	Andretti,Mario	Andretti,Mario	Peterson
309	1978	12	Austrian	Osterreichring	13 Aug 78	Peterson	Peterson	Peterson
310	1978	13	Dutch	Zandvoort	27 Aug 78	Andretti,Mario	Andretti,Mario	Lauda
311	1978	14	Italian	Monza	10 Sep 78	Lauda	Andretti,Mario	Andretti,Mario
312	1978	15	US East	Watkins Glen	1 Oct 78	Reutemann	Andretti,Mario	Jarier
313	1978	16	Canadian	Montreal	8 Oct 78	Villeneuve,G.	Jarier	Jones
314	1979	1	Argentine	Buenos Aires	21 Jan 79	Laffite	Laffite	Laffite
315	1979	2	Brazilian	Interlagos	4 Feb 79	Laffite	Laffite	Laffite
316	1979	3	South African	Kyalami	3 Mar 79	Villeneuve,G.	Jabouille	Villeneuve,G.
317	1979	4	US West	Long Beach	8 Apr 79	Villeneuve,G.	Villeneuve,G.	Villeneuve,G.
318	1979	5	Spanish	Jarama	29 Apr 79	Depailler	Laffite	Villeneuve,G.
319	1979	6	Belgian	Zolder	13 May 79	Scheckter,J.	Laffite	Villeneuve,G.
320	1979	7	Monaco	Monte Carlo	27 May 79	Scheckter,J.	Scheckter,J.	Depailler
321	1979	8	French	Dijon	1 Jul 79	Jabouille	Jabouille	Arnoux
322	1979	9	British	Silverstone	14 Jul 79	Regazzoni	Jones	Regazzoni
323	1979	10	German	Hockenheim	29 Jul 79	Jones	Jabouille	Villeneuve,G.
324	1979	11	Austrian	Osterreichring	12 Aug 79	Jones	Arnoux	Arnoux
325	1979	12	Dutch	Zandvoort	26 Aug 79	Jones	Arnoux	Villeneuve,G.
326	1979	13	Italian	Monza	9 Sep 79	Scheckter,J.	Jabouille	Regazzoni
327	1979	14	Canadian	Montreal	30 Sep 79	Jones	Jones	Jones
328	1979	15	US East	Watkins Glen	7 Oct 79	Villeneuve,G.	Jones	Piquet
329	1980	1	Argentine	Buenos Aires	13 Jan 80	Jones	Jones	Jones

GRANDS PRIX RACE SUMMARY

GPNo	Year	No	Grand Prix	Circuit	Date	Winner	Pole	Fastest Lap
330	1980	2	Brazilian	Interlagos	27 Jan 80	Arnoux	Jabouille	Arnoux
331	1980	3	South African	Kyalami	1 Mar 80	Arnoux	Jabouille	Arnoux
332	1980	4	US West	Long Beach	30 Mar 82	Piquet	Piquet	Piquet
333	1980	5	Belgian	Zolder	4 May 80	Pironi	Jones	Laffite
334	1980	6	Monaco	Monte Carlo	18 May 80	Reutemann	Pironi	Reutemann
335	1980	7	French	Paul Ricard	29 Jun 80	Jones	Laffite	Jones
336	1980	8	British	Brands Hatch	13 Jul 80	Jones	Pironi	Pironi
337	1980	9	German	Hockenheim	10 Aug 80	Laffite	Jones	Jones
338	1980	10	Austrian	Osterreichring	17 Aug 80	Jabouille	Arnoux	Arnoux
339	1980	11	Dutch	Zandvoort	31 Aug 80	Piquet	Arnoux	Arnoux
340	1980	12	Italian	Imola	14 Sep 80	Piquet	Arnoux	Jones
341	1980	13	Canadian	Montreal	28 Sep 80	Jones	Piquet	Pironi
342	1980	14	US East	Watkins Glen	5 Oct 80	Jones	Giacomelli	Jones
343	1981	1	US West	Long Beach	15 Mar 81	Jones	Patrese	Jones
344	1981	2	Brazilian	Rio de Janeiro	29 Mar 81	Reutemann	Piquet	Surer
345	1981	3	Argentine	Buenos Aires	12 Apr 81	Piquet	Piquet	Piquet
346	1981	4	San Marino	Imola	3 May 81	Piquet	Villeneuve,G.	Villeneuve,G.
347	1981	5	Belgian	Zolder	17 May 81	Reutemann	Reutemann	Reutemann
348	1981	6	Monaco	Monte Carlo	31 May 81	Villeneuve,G.	Piquet	Jones
349	1981	7	Spanish	Jarama	21 Jun 81	Villeneuve,G.	Laffite	Jones
350	1981	8	French	Dijon	5 Jul 81	Prost	Arnoux	Prost
351	1981	9	British	Silverstone	18 Jul 81	Watson	Arnoux	Arnoux
352	1981	10	German	Hockenheim	2 Aug 81	Piquet	Prost	Jones
353	1981	11	Austrian	Osterreichring	16 Aug 81	Laffite	Arnoux	Laffite
354	1981	12	Dutch	Zandvoort	30 Aug 81	Prost	Prost	Jones
355	1981	13	Italian	Monza	13 Sep 81	Prost	Arnoux	Reutemann
356	1981	14	Canadian	Montreal	27 Sep 81	Laffite	Piquet	Watson
357	1981	15	Caesar's Pal.	Las Vegas	17 Oct 81	Jones	Reutemann	Pironi
358	1982	1	South African	Kyalami	23 Jan 82	Prost	Arnoux	Prost
359	1982	2	Brazilian	Rio de Janeiro	21 Mar 82	Prost	Prost	Prost
360	1982	3	US West	Long Beach	4 Apr 82	Lauda	de Cesaris	Lauda
361	1982	4	San Marino	Imola	25 Apr 81	Pironi	Arnoux	Pironi
362	1982	5	Belgian	Zolder	9 May 82	Watson	Prost	Watson
363	1982	6	Monaco	Monte Carlo	23 May 82	Patrese	Arnoux	Patrese
364	1982	7	US	Detroit	6 Jun 82	Watson	Prost	Prost
365	1982	8	Canadian	Montreal	13 Jun 82	Piquet	Pironi	Pironi
366	1982	9	Dutch	Zandvoort	3 Jul 82	Pironi	Arnoux	Warwick
367	1982	10	British	Brands Hatch	18 Jul 82	Lauda	Rosberg	Henton
368	1982	11	French	Paul Ricard	25 Jul 82	Arnoux	Arnoux	Patrese
369	1982	12	German	Hockenheim	8 Aug 82	Tambay	Pironi	Piquet
370	1982	13	Austrian	Osterreichring	15 Aug 82	de Angelis	Piquet	Piquet
371	1982	14	Swiss	Dijon	29 Aug 82	Rosberg	Prost	Prost
372	1982	15	Italian	Monza	12 Sep 82	Arnoux	Andretti,Mario	Arnoux
373	1982	16	Caesar's Pal.	Las Vegas	25 Sep 82	Alboreto	Prost	Alboreto
374	1983	1	Brazilian	Rio de Janeiro	13 Mar 83	Piquet	Rosberg	Piquet
375	1983	2	US West	Long Beach	27 Mar 83	Watson	Tambay	Lauda
376	1983	3	French	Paul Ricard	17 Apr 83	Prost	Prost	Prost
377	1983	4	San Marino	Imola	1 May 83	Tambay	Arnoux	Patrese

GRANDS PRIX RACE SUMMARY

GPNo	Year	No	Grand Prix	Circuit	Date	Winner	Pole	Fastest Lap
378	1983	5	Monaco	Monte Carlo	15 May 83	Rosberg	Prost	Piquet
379	1983	6	Belgian	Spa	22 May 83	Prost	Prost	de Cesaris
380	1983	7	US	Detroit	5 Jun 83	Alboreto	Arnoux	Watson
381	1983	8	Canadian	Montreal	12 Jun 83	Arnoux	Arnoux	Tambay
382	1983	9	British	Silverstone	16 Jul 83	Prost	Arnoux	Prost
383	1983	10	German	Hockenheim	7 Aug 83	Arnoux	Tambay	Arnoux
384	1983	11	Austrian	Osterreichring	14 Aug 83	Prost	Tambay	Prost
385	1983	12	Dutch	Zandvoort	28 Aug 83	Arnoux	Piquet	Arnoux
386	1983	13	Italian	Monza	11 Sep 83	Piquet	Patrese	Piquet
387	1983	14	European	Brands Hatch	25 Sep 83	Piquet	de Angelis	Mansell
388	1983	15	South African	Kyalami	15 Oct 83	Patrese	Tambay	Piquet
389	1984	1	Brazilian	Rio de Janeiro	25 Mar 84	Prost	de Angelis	Prost
390	1984	2	South African	Kyalami	7 Apr 84	Lauda	Piquet	Tambay
391	1984	3	Belgian	Zolder	29 Apr 84	Alboreto	Alboreto	Arnoux
392	1984	4	San Marino	Imola	6 May 84	Prost	Piquet	Piquet
393	1984	5	French	Dijon	20 May 84	Lauda	Tambay	Prost
394	1984	6	Monaco	Monte Carlo	3 Jun 84	Prost	Prost	Senna
395	1984	7	Canadian	Montreal	17 Jun 84	Piquet	Piquet	Piquet
396	1984	8	Detroit	Detroit	24 Jun 84	Piquet	Piquet	Warwick
397	1984	9	Dallas	Dallas	8 Jul 84	Rosberg	Mansell	Lauda
398	1984	10	British	Brands Hatch	22 Jul 84	Lauda	Piquet	Lauda
399	1984	11	German	Hockenheim	5 Aug 84	Prost	Prost	Prost
400	1984	12	Austrian	Osterreichring	19 Aug 84	Lauda	Piquet	Lauda
401	1984	13	Dutch	Zandvoort	26 Aug 84	Prost	Prost	Arnoux
402	1984	14	Italian	Monza	9 Sep 84	Lauda	Piquet	Lauda
403	1984	15	European	Nurburgring	7 Oct 84	Prost	Piquet	Alboreto & Piquet
404	1984	16	Portuguese	Estoril	21 Oct 84	Prost	Piquet	Lauda
405	1985	1	Brazilian	Rio de Janeiro	7 Apr 85	Prost	Alboreto	Prost
406	1985	2	Portuguese	Estoril	21 Apr 85	Senna	Senna	Senna
407	1985	3	San Marino	Imola	5 May 85	de Angelis	Senna	Alboreto
408	1985	4	Monaco	Monte Carlo	19 May 85	Prost	Senna	Alboreto
409	1985	5	Canadian	Montreal	16 Jun 85	Alboreto	de Angelis	Senna
410	1985	6	US	Detroit	23 Jun 85	Rosberg	Senna	Senna
411	1985	7	French	Paul Ricard	7 Jul 85	Piquet	Rosberg	Rosberg
412	1985	8	British	Silverstone	21 Jul 85	Prost	Rosberg	Prost
413	1985	9	German	Nurburgring	4 Aug 85	Alboreto	Fabi,T.	Lauda
414	1985	10	Austrian	Osterreichring	18 Aug 85	Prost	Prost	Prost
415	1985	11	Dutch	Zandvoort	25 Aug 85	Lauda	Piquet	Prost
416	1985	12	Italian	Monza	8 Sep 85	Prost	Senna	Mansell
417	1985	13	Belgian	Spa	15 Sep 85	Senna	Prost	Prost
418	1985	14	European	Brands Hatch	6 Oct 85	Mansell	Senna	Laffite
419	1985	15	South African	Kyalami	19 Oct 85	Mansell	Mansell	Rosberg
420	1985	16	Australian	Adelaide	3 Nov 85	Rosberg	Senna	Rosberg
421	1986	1	Brazilian	Rio de Janeiro	23 Mar 86	Piquet	Senna	Piquet
422	1986	2	Spanish	Jerez	13 Apr 86	Senna	Senna	Mansell
423	1986	3	San Marino	Imola	27 Apr 86	Prost	Senna	Piquet
424	1986	4	Monaco	Monte Carlo	11 May 86	Prost	Prost	Prost

GRANDS PRIX RACE SUMMARY

GPNo	Year	No	Grand Prix	Circuit	Date	Winner	Pole	Fastest Lap
425	1986	5	Belgian	Spa	25 May 86	Mansell	Piquet	Prost
426	1986	6	Canadian	Montreal	15 Jun 86	Mansell	Mansell	Piquet
427	1986	7	US	Detroit	22 Jun 86	Senna	Senna	Piquet
428	1986	8	French	Paul Ricard	6 Jul 86	Mansell	Senna	Mansell
429	1986	9	British	Brands Hatch	13 Jul 86	Mansell	Piquet	Mansell
430	1986	10	German	Hockenheim	27 Jul 86	Piquet	Rosberg	Berger,G.
431	1986	11	Hungarian	Hungaroring	10 Aug 86	Piquet	Senna	Piquet
432	1986	12	Austrian	Osterreichring	17 Aug 86	Prost	Fabi,T.	Berger,G.
433	1986	13	Italian	Monza	7 Sep 86	Piquet	Fabi,T.	Fabi,T.
434	1986	14	Portuguese	Estoril	21 Sep 86	Mansell	Senna	Mansell
435	1986	15	Mexican	Mexico City	12 Oct 86	Berger,G.	Senna	Piquet
436	1986	16	Australian	Adelaide	26 Oct 86	Prost	Mansell	Piquet
437	1987	1	Brazilian	Rio de Janeiro	12 Apr 87	Prost	Mansell	Piquet
438	1987	2	San Marino	Imola	3 May 87	Mansell	Senna	Fabi,T.
439	1987	3	Belgian	Spa	17 May 87	Prost	Mansell	Prost
440	1987	4	Monaco	Monte Carlo	30 May 87	Senna	Mansell	Senna
441	1987	5	US	Detroit	21 Jun 87	Senna	Mansell	Senna
442	1987	6	French	Paul Ricard	5 Jul 87	Mansell	Mansell	Piquet
443	1987	7	British	Silverstone	12 Jul 87	Mansell	Piquet	Mansell
444	1987	8	German	Hockenheim	26 Jul 87	Piquet	Mansell	Mansell
445	1987	9	Hungarian	Hungaroring	9 Aug 87	Piquet	Mansell	Piquet
446	1987	10	Austrian	Osterreichring	16 Aug 87	Mansell	Piquet	Mansell
447	1987	11	Italian	Monza	6 Sep 87	Piquet	Piquet	Senna
448	1987	12	Portuguese	Estoril	20 Sep 87	Prost	Berger,G.	Berger,G.
449	1987	13	Spanish	Jerez	27 Sep 87	Mansell	Piquet	Berger,G.
450	1987	14	Mexican	Mexico City	18 Oct 87	Mansell	Mansell	Piquet
451	1987	15	Japanese	Suzuka	1 Nov 87	Berger,G.	Berger,G.	Prost
452	1987	16	Australian	Adelaide	15 Nov 87	Berger,G.	Berger,G.	Berger,G.
453	1988	1	Brazilian	Rio de Janeiro	3 Apr 88	Prost	Senna	Berger,G.
454	1988	2	San Marino	Imola	1 May 88	Senna	Senna	Prost
455	1988	3	Monaco	Monte Carlo	15 May 88	Prost	Senna	Senna
456	1988	4	Mexican	Mexico City	29 May 88	Prost	Senna	Prost
457	1988	5	Canadian	Montreal	12 Jun 88	Senna	Senna	Senna
458	1988	6	US	Detroit	19 Jun 88	Senna	Senna	Prost
459	1988	7	French	Paul Ricard	3 Jul 88	Prost	Prost	Prost
460	1988	8	British	Silverstone	10 Jul 88	Senna	Berger,G.	Mansell
461	1988	9	German	Hockenheim	24 Jul 88	Senna	Senna	Nannini
462	1988	10	Hungarian	Hungaroring	7 Aug 88	Senna	Senna	Prost
463	1988	11	Belgian	Spa	28 Aug 88	Senna	Senna	Berger,G.
464	1988	12	Italian	Monza	11 Sep 88	Berger,G.	Senna	Alboreto
465	1988	13	Portuguese	Estoril	25 Sep 88	Prost	Prost	Berger,G.
466	1988	14	Spanish	Jerez	2 Oct 88	Prost	Senna	Prost
467	1988	15	Japanese	Suzuka	30 Oct 88	Senna	Senna	Senna
468	1988	16	Australian	Adelaide	13 Nov 88	Prost	Senna	Prost
469	1989	1	Brazilian	Rio de Janeiro	26 Mar 89	Mansell	Senna	Patrese
470	1989	2	San Marino	Imola	23 Apr 89	Senna	Senna	Prost
471	1989	3	Monaco	Monte Carlo	7 May 89	Senna	Senna	Prost
472	1989	4	Mexican	Mexico City	28 May 89	Senna	Senna	Mansell

GRANDS PRIX RACE SUMMARY

GPNo	Year	No	Grand Prix	Circuit	Date	Winner	Pole	Fastest Lap
473	1989	5	US	Phoenix	4 Jun 89	Prost	Senna	Senna
474	1989	6	Canadian	Montreal	18 Jun 89	Boutsen	Prost	Palmer
475	1989	7	French	Paul Ricard	9 Jul 89	Prost	Prost	Gugelmin
476	1989	8	British	Silverstone	16 Jul 89	Prost	Senna	Mansell
477	1989	9	German	Hockenheim	30 Jul 89	Senna	Senna	Senna
478	1989	10	Hungarian	Hungaroring	13 Aug 89	Mansell	Patrese	Mansell
479	1989	11	Belgian	Spa	27 Aug 89	Senna	Senna	Prost
480	1989	12	Italian	Monza	10 Sep 89	Prost	Senna	Prost
481	1989	13	Portuguese	Estoril	24 Sep 89	Berger,G.	Senna	Berger,G.
482	1989	14	Spanish	Jerez	1 Oct 89	Senna	Senna	Senna
483	1989	15	Japanese	Suzuka	22 Oct 89	Nannini	Senna	Prost
484	1989	16	Australian	Adelaide	5 Nov 89	Boutsen	Senna	Nakajima
485	1990	1	US	Phoenix	11 Mar 90	Senna	Berger,G.	Berger,G.
486	1990	2	Brazilian	Interlagos	25 Mar 90	Prost	Senna	Berger,G.
487	1990	3	San Marino	Imola	13 May 90	Patrese	Senna	Nannini
488	1990	4	Monaco	Monte Carlo	27 May 90	Senna	Senna	Senna
489	1990	5	Canadian	Montreal	10 Jun 90	Senna	Senna	Berger,G.
490	1990	6	Mexican	Mexico City	24 Jun 90	Prost	Berger,G.	Prost
491	1990	7	French	Paul Ricard	8 Jul 90	Prost	Mansell	Mansell
492	1990	8	British	Silverstone	15 Jul 90	Prost	Mansell	Mansell
493	1990	9	German	Hockenheim	29 Jul 90	Senna	Senna	Boutsen
494	1990	10	Hungarian	Hungaroring	12 Aug 90	Boutsen	Boutsen	Patrese
495	1990	11	Belgian	Spa	26 Aug 90	Senna	Senna	Prost
496	1990	12	Italian	Monza	9 Sep 90	Senna	Senna	Senna
497	1990	13	Portuguese	Estoril	23 Sep 90	Mansell	Mansell	Patrese
498	1990	14	Spanish	Jerez	30 Sep 90	Prost	Senna	Patrese
499	1990	15	Japanese	Suzuka	21 Oct 90	Piquet	Senna	Patrese
500	1990	16	Australian	Adelaide	4 Nov 90	Piquet	Senna	Mansell
501	1991	1	US	Phoenix	10 Mar 91	Senna	Senna	Alesi
502	1991	2	Brazilian	Interlagos	24 Mar 91	Senna	Senna	Mansell
503	1991	3	San Marino	Imola	28 Apr 91	Senna	Senna	Berger,G.
504	1991	4	Monaco	Monte Carlo	12 May 91	Senna	Senna	Prost
505	1991	5	Canadian	Montreal	2 Jun 91	Piquet	Patrese	Mansell
506	1991	6	Mexican	Mexico City	16 Jun 91	Patrese	Patrese	Mansell
507	1991	7	French	Magny Cours	7 Jul 91	Mansell	Patrese	Mansell
508	1991	8	British	Silverstone	14 Jul 91	Mansell	Mansell	Mansell
509	1991	9	German	Hockenheim	28 Jul 91	Mansell	Mansell	Patrese
510	1991	10	Hungarian	Hungaroring	11 Aug 91	Senna	Senna	Gachot
511	1991	11	Belgian	Spa	25 Aug 91	Senna	Senna	Moreno
512	1991	12	Italian	Monza	8 Sep 91	Mansell	Senna	Senna
513	1991	13	Portuguese	Estoril	22 Sep 91	Patrese	Patrese	Mansell
514	1991	14	Spanish	Barcelona	29 Sep 91	Mansell	Berger,G.	Patrese
515	1991	15	Japanese	Suzuka	20 Oct 91	Berger,G.	Berger,G.	Senna
516	1991	16	Australian	Adelaide	3 Nov 91	Senna	Senna	Berger,G.
517	1992	1	South African	Kyalami	1 Mar 92	Mansell	Mansell	Mansell
518	1992	2	Mexican	Mexico City	22 Mar 92	Mansell	Mansell	Berger,G.
519	1992	3	Brazilian	Interlagos	5 Apr 92	Mansell	Mansell	Patrese
520	1992	4	Spanish	Barcelona	3 May 92	Mansell	Mansell	Mansell

GRANDS PRIX RACE SUMMARY

GPNo	Year	No	Grand Prix	Circuit	Date	Winner	Pole	Fastest Lap
521	1992	5	San Marino	Imola	17 May 92	Mansell	Mansell	Patrese
522	1992	6	Monaco	Monte Carlo	31 May 92	Senna	Mansell	Mansell
523	1992	7	Canadian	Montreal	14 Jun 92	Berger,G.	Senna	Berger,G.
524	1992	8	French	Magny Cours	5 Jul 92	Mansell	Mansell	Mansell
525	1992	9	British	Silverstone	12 Jul 92	Mansell	Mansell	Mansell
526	1992	10	German	Hockenheim	26 Jul 92	Mansell	Mansell	Patrese
527	1992	11	Hungarian	Hungaroring	16 Aug 92	Senna	Patrese	Mansell
528	1992	12	Belgian	Spa	30 Aug 92	Schumacher,M.	Mansell	Schumacher,M.
529	1992	13	Italian	Monza	13 Sep 92	Senna	Mansell	Mansell
530	1992	14	Portuguese	Estoril	27 Sep 92	Mansell	Mansell	Senna
531	1992	15	Japanese	Suzuka	25 Oct 92	Patrese	Mansell	Mansell
532	1992	16	Australian	Adelaide	8 Nov 92	Berger,G.	Mansell	Schumacher,M.
533	1993	1	South African	Kyalami	14 Mar 93	Prost	Prost	Prost
534	1993	2	Brazilian	Interlagos	28 Mar 93	Senna	Prost	Schumacher,M.
535	1993	3	European	Donington Park	11 Apr 93	Senna	Prost	Senna
536	1993	4	San Marino	Imola	25 Apr 93	Prost	Prost	Prost
537	1993	5	Spanish	Barcelona	9 May 93	Prost	Prost	Schumacher,M.
538	1993	6	Monaco	Monte Carlo	23 May 93	Senna	Prost	Prost
539	1993	7	Canadian	Montreal	13 Jun 93	Prost	Prost	Schumacher,M.
540	1993	8	French	Magny Cours	4 Jul 93	Prost	Hill,D.	Schumacher,M.
541	1993	9	British	Silverstone	11 Jul 93	Prost	Prost	Hill,D.
542	1993	10	German	Hockenheim	25 Jul 93	Prost	Prost	Schumacher,M.
543	1993	11	Hungarian	Hungaroring	15 Aug 93	Hill,D.	Prost	Prost
544	1993	12	Belgian	Spa	29 Aug 93	Hill,D.	Prost	Prost
545	1993	13	Italian	Monza	12 Sep 93	Hill,D.	Prost	Hill,D.
546	1993	14	Portuguese	Estoril	26 Sep 93	Schumacher,M.	Hill,D.	Hill,D.
547	1993	15	Japanese	Suzuka	24 Oct 93	Senna	Prost	Prost
548	1993	16	Australian	Adelaide	7 Nov 93	Senna	Senna	Hill,D.
549	1994	1	Brazilian	Interlagos	27 Mar 94	Schumacher,M.	Senna	Schumacher,M.
550	1994	2	Pacific	Aida	17 Apr 94	Schumacher,M.	Senna	Schumacher,M.
551	1994	3	San Marino	Imola	1 May 94	Schumacher,M.	Senna	Hill,D.
552	1994	4	Monaco	Monte Carlo	15 May 94	Schumacher,M.	Schumacher,M.	Schumacher,M.
553	1994	5	Spanish	Barcelona	29 May 94	Hill,D.	Schumacher,M.	Schumacher,M.
554	1994	6	Canadian	Montreal	12 Jun 94	Schumacher,M.	Schumacher,M.	Schumacher,M.
555	1994	7	French	Magny Cours	3 Jul 94	Schumacher,M.	Hill,D.	Hill,D.
556	1994	8	British	Silverstone	10 Jul 94	Hill,D.	Hill,D.	Hill,D.
557	1994	9	German	Hockenheim	31 Jul 94	Berger,G.	Berger,G.	Coulthard
558	1994	10	Hungarian	Hungaroring	14 Aug 94	Schumacher,M.	Schumacher,M.	Schumacher,M.
559	1994	11	Belgian	Spa	28 Aug 94	Hill,D.	Barrichello	Hill,D.
560	1994	12	Italian	Monza	11 Sep 94	Hill,D.	Alesi	Hill,D.
561	1994	13	Portuguese	Estoril	25 Sep 94	Hill,D.	Berger,G.	Coulthard
562	1994	14	European	Jerez	16 Oct 94	Schumacher,M.	Schumacher,M.	Schumacher,M.
563	1994	15	Japanese	Suzuka	6 Nov 94	Hill,D.	Schumacher,M.	Hill,D.
564	1994	16	Australian	Adelaide	13 Nov 94	Mansell	Mansell	Schumacher,M.
565	1995	1	Brazilian	Interlagos	26 Mar 95	Schumacher,M.	Hill,D.	Schumacher,M.
566	1995	2	Argentine	Buenos Aires	9 Apr 95	Hill,D.	Coulthard	Schumacher,M.
567	1995	3	San Marino	Imola	30 Apr 95	Hill,D.	Schumacher,M.	Berger,G.
568	1995	4	Spanish	Catalunya	14 May 95	Schumacher,M.	Schumacher,M.	Hill,D.

GRANDS PRIX RACE SUMMARY

GPNo	Year	No	Grand Prix	Circuit	Date	Winner	Pole	Fastest Lap
569	1995	5	Monaco	Monte Carlo	28 May 95	Schumacher,M.	Hill,D.	Alesi
570	1995	6	Canadian	Montreal	12 Jun 95	Alesi	Schumacher,M.	Schumacher,M.
571	1995	7	French	Magny Cours	2 Jul 95	Schumacher,M.	Hill,D.	Schumacher,M.
572	1995	8	British	Silverstone	10 Jul 95	Herbert	Hill,D.	Hill,D.
573	1995	9	German	Hockenheim	30 Jul 95	Schumacher,M.	Hill,D.	Schumacher,M.
574	1995	10	Hungarian	Hungaroring	13 Aug 95	Hill,D.	Hill,D.	Hill,D.
575	1995	11	Belgian	Spa	27 Aug 95	Schumacher,M.	Berger,G.	Coulthard
576	1995	12	Italian	Monza	10 Sep 95	Herbert	Coulthard	Berger,G.
577	1995	13	Portuguese	Estoril	24 Sep 95	Coulthard	Coulthard	Coulthard
578	1995	14	European	Nurburgring	1 Oct 95	Schumacher,M.	Coulthard	Schumacher,M.
579	1995	15	Pacific	Aida	17 Oct 95	Schumacher,M.	Coulthard	Schumacher,M.
580	1995	16	Japanese	Suzuka	29 Oct 95	Schumacher,M.	Schumacher,M.	Schumacher,M.
581	1995	17	Australian	Adelaide	13 Nov 95	Hill,D.	Hill,D.	Hill,D.
582	1996	1	Australian	Melbourne	10 Mar 96	Hill,D.	Villeneuve,J.	Villeneuve,J.
583	1996	2	Brazilian	Interlagos	31 Mar 96	Hill,D.	Hill,D.	Hill,D.
584	1996	3	Argentine	Beunos Aires	7 Apr 96	Hill,D.	Hill,D.	Alesi
585	1996	4	European	Nurburgring	28 Apr 96	Villeneuve,J.	Hill,D.	Hill,D.
586	1996	5	San Marino	Imola	5 May 96	Hill,D.	Schumacher,M.	Hill,D.
587	1996	6	Monaco	Monte Carlo	19 May 96	Panis	Schumacher,M.	Alesi
588	1996	7	Spanish	Catalunya	2 Jun 96	Schumacher,M.	Hill,D.	Schumacher,M.
589	1996	8	Canadian	Montreal	16 Jun 96	Hill,D.	Hill,D.	Villeneuve,J.
590	1996	9	French	Magny Cours	30 Jun 96	Hill,D.	Schumacher,M.	Villeneuve,J.
591	1996	10	British	Silverstone	14 Jul 96	Villeneuve,J.	Hill,D.	Villeneuve,J.
592	1996	11	German	Hockenheim	28 Jul 96	Hill,D.	Hill,D.	Hill,D.
593	1996	12	Hungarian	Hungaroring	11 Aug 96	Villeneuve,J.	Schumacher,M.	Hill,D.
594	1996	13	Belgian	Spa	25 Aug 96	Schumacher,M.	Villeneuve,J.	Berger,G.
595	1996	14	Italian	Monza	8 Sep 96	Schumacher,M.	Hill,D.	Schumacher,M.
596	1996	15	Portuguese	Estoril	22 Sep 96	Villeneuve,J.	Hill,D.	Villeneuve,J.
597	1996	16	Japanese	Suzuka	13 Oct 96	Hill,D.	Villeneuve,J.	Villeneuve,J.
598	1997	1	Australian	Melbourne	9 Mar 97	Coulthard	Villeneuve,J.	Frentzen
599	1997	2	Brazilian	Interlagos	30 Mar 97	Villeneuve,J.	Villeneuve,J.	Villeneuve,J.
600	1997	3	Argentine	Buenos Aires	13 Apr 97	Villeneuve,J.	Villeneuve,J.	Berger,G.
601	1997	4	San Marino	Imola	27 Apr 97	Frentzen	Villeneuve,J.	Frentzen
602	1997	5	Monaco	Monte Carlo	11 May 97	Schumacher,M.	Frentzen	Schumacher,M.
603	1997	6	Spanish	Catalunya	25 May 97	Villeneuve,J.	Villeneuve,J.	Fisichella
604	1997	7	Canadian	Montreal	15 Jun 97	Schumacher,M.	Schumacher,M.	Coulthard
605	1997	8	French	Magny Cours	29 Jun 97	Schumacher,M.	Schumacher,M.	Schumacher,M.
606	1997	9	British	Silverstone	13 Jul 97	Villeneuve,J.	Villeneuve,J.	Schumacher,M.
607	1997	10	German	Hockenheim	27 Jul 97	Berger,G.	Berger,G.	Berger,G.
608	1997	11	Hungarian	Hungaroring	10 Aug 97	Villeneuve,J.	Schumacher,M.	Frentzen
609	1997	12	Belgian	Spa	24 Aug 97	Schumacher,M.	Villeneuve,J.	Villeneuve,J.
610	1997	13	Italian	Monza	7 Sep 97	Coulthard	Alesi	Hakkinen
611	1997	14	Austrian	A1 Ring	21 Sep 97	Villeneuve,J.	Villeneuve,J.	Villeneuve,J.
612	1997	15	Luxembourg	Nurburgring	28 Sep 97	Villeneuve,J.	Hakkinen	Frentzen
613	1997	16	Japanese	Suzuka	12 Oct 97	Schumacher,M.	Villeneuve,J.	Frentzen
614	1997	17	European	Jerez	26 Oct 97	Hakkinen	Villeneuve,J.	Frentzen
615	1998	1	Australian	Melbourne	8 Mar 98	Hakkinen	Hakkinen	Hakkinen
616	1998	2	Brazilian	Interlagos	29 Mar 98	Hakkinen	Hakkinen	Hakkinen

GRANDS PRIX RACE SUMMARY

GPNo	Year	No	Grand Prix	Circuit	Date	Winner	Pole	Fastest Lap
617	1998	3	Argentine	Buenos Aires	12 Apr 98	Schumacher,M.	Coulthard	Wurz
618	1998	4	San Marino	Imola	26 Apr 98	Coulthard	Coulthard	Schumacher,M.
619	1998	5	Spanish	Catalunya	10 May 98	Hakkinen	Hakkinen	Hakkinen
620	1998	6	Monaco	Monte Carlo	24 May 98	Hakkinen	Hakkinen	Hakkinen
621	1998	7	Canadian	Montreal	7 Jun 98	Schumacher,M.	Coulthard	Schumacher,M.
622	1998	8	French	Magny Cours	28 Jun 98	Schumacher,M.	Hakkinen	Coulthard
623	1998	9	British	Silverstone	12 Jul 98	Schumacher,M.	Hakkinen	Schumacher,M.
624	1998	10	Austrian	A1 Ring	26 Jul 98	Hakkinen	Fisichella	Coulthard
625	1998	11	German	Hockenheim	2 Aug 98	Hakkinen	Hakkinen	Coulthard
626	1998	12	Hungarian	Hungaroring	16 Aug 98	Schumacher,M.	Hakkinen	Schumacher,M.
627	1998	13	Belgian	Spa	30 Aug 98	Hill,D.	Hakkinen	Schumacher,M.
628	1998	14	Italian	Monza	13 Sep 98	Schumacher,M.	Schumacher,M.	Hakkinen
629	1998	15	Luxembourg	Nurburgring	27 Sep 98	Hakkinen	Schumacher,M.	Hakkinen
630	1998	16	Japanese	Suzuka	1 Nov 98	Hakkinen	Schumacher,M.	Schumacher,M.
631	1999	1	Australian	Melbourne	7 Mar 99	Irvine	Hakkinen	Schumacher,M.
632	1999	2	Brazilian	Interlagos	11 Apr 99	Hakkinen	Hakkinen	Hakkinen
633	1999	3	San Marino	Imola	2 May 99	Schumacher,M.	Hakkinen	Schumacher,M.
634	1999	4	Monaco	Monte Carlo	16 May 99	Schumacher,M.	Hakkinen	Hakkinen
635	1999	5	Spanish	Barcelona	30 May 99	Hakkinen	Hakkinen	Schumacher,M.
636	1999	6	Canadian	Montreal	13 Jun 99	Hakkinen	Schumacher,M.	Irvine
637	1999	7	French	Magny Cours	27 Jun 99	Frentzen	Barrichello	Coulthard
638	1999	8	British	Silverstone	11 Jul 99	Coulthard	Hakkinen	Hakkinen
639	1999	9	Austrian	A1 Ring	25 Jul 99	Irvine	Hakkinen	Hakkinen
640	1999	10	German	Hockenheim	1 Aug 99	Irvine	Hakkinen	Coulthard
641	1999	11	Hungarian	Hungaroring	15 Aug 99	Hakkinen	Hakkinen	Coulthard
642	1999	12	Belgian	Spa	29 Aug 99	Coulthard	Hakkinen	Hakkinen
643	1999	13	Italian	Monza	12 Sep 99	Frentzen	Hakkinen	Schumacher,R.
644	1999	14	European	Nurburgring	26 Sep 99	Herbert	Frentzen	Hakkinen
645	1999	15	Malaysian	Sepang	17 Oct 99	Irvine	Schumacher,M.	Schumacher,M.
646	1999	16	Japanese	Suzuka	31 Oct 99	Hakkinen	Schumacher,M.	Schumacher,M.

GRANDS PRIX RACE LISTINGS

A complete summary of every Grand Prix race to have been run as part of the FIA Championship from 1950 to 1999 follows. Each race is treated identically and the listings are straightforward to follow. During the 1950s and the 1970s the race fields were often quite extensive. In a number of races it has been impossible to fit the complete starting grid on the page or to continue it in the column opposite. Where this is the case a + sign has been placed after the last grid entry. To find the rest of the grid make a note of the Grand Prix No at the top of the column and then locate this in the GRID COMPLETION DETAILS section of the book which starts on page 349.

Located at the end of the listings you can also find details of shared drives (page 345) and those races that had a specific F2 starting grid (348).

British

GRAND PRIX No: 1
DATE: May 13, 1950
VENUE: Silverstone
POLE LAP: Farina, 1m 50.8s
FASTEST LAP: Farina, 1m 50.6s

Pn	Driver	Car	Laps	Time/Reason
1	Farina	Alfa Romeo	70	2h 13m 23.6s
2	Fagioli	Alfa Romeo	70	2h 13m 26.2s
3	Parnell,R.	Alfa Romeo	70	2h 14m 15.6s
4	Giraud-Cabantous	Talbot	68	
5	Rosier	Talbot	68	
6	Gerard	ERA	67	
7	Harrison	ERA	67	
8	Etancelin	Talbot	65	
9	Hampshire	Maserati	64	
10	Fry (S)	Maserati	64	
11	Claes	Talbot	64	
12	Fangio	Alfa Romeo	61	oil pipe
uc	Kelly	Alta	57	
r	Bira	Maserati	48	fuel feed
r	Murray	Maserati	43	engine
r	Crossley	Alta	42	transmission
r	de Graffenried	Maserati	35	con rod
r	Chiron	Maserati	23	clutch
r	Martin	Talbot	7	oil pressure
r	Walker,P. (S)	ERA	4	gearbox
r	Johnson,L.	ERA	1	supercharger

STARTING GRID:

1 Farina
2 Fagioli
3 Fangio
4 Parnell,R.
5 Bira
6 Giraud-Cabantous
7 Martin
8 de Graffenried
9 Rosier
10 Walker,P.
11 Chiron
12 Johnson,L.
13 Gerard
14 Etancelin
15 Harrison
16 Hampshire
17 Crossley
18 Murray
19 Kelly
20 Fry
21 Claes

Monaco

GRAND PRIX No: 2
DATE: May 21, 1950
VENUE: Monte Carlo
POLE LAP: Fangio, 1m 50.2s
FASTEST LAP: Fangio, 1m 51.0s

Pn	Driver	Car	Laps	Time/Reason
1	Fangio	Alfa Romeo	100	3h 13m 18.7s
2	Ascari	Ferrari	99	
3	Chiron	Maserati	98	
4	Sommer	Ferrari	97	
5	Bira	Maserati	95	
6	Gerard	ERA	94	
7	Claes	Talbot	94	
r	Villoresi	Ferrari	62	rear axle
r	Etancelin	Talbot	35	oil pipe
r	Gonzalez,J.	Maserati	0	fire
r	Farina	Alfa Romeo	0	accident
r	Fagioli	Alfa Romeo	0	accident
r	Rosier	Talbot	0	accident
r	Manzon	Simca-Gordini	0	accident
r	de Graffenried	Maserati	0	accident
r	Trintignant	Simca-Gordini	0	accident
r	Harrison	ERA	0	accident
r	Rol	Maserati	0	accident
r	Schell	Cooper-JAP	0	accident
dns	Pian	Maserati		accident
dns	Whitehead,P.	Ferrari		engine

STARTING GRID:

1 Fangio
2 Farina
3 Gonzalez,J.
4 Etancelin
5 Fagioli
6 Villoresi
7 Ascari
8 Chiron
9 Sommer
10 Rosier
11 Manzon
12 de Graffenried
13 Trintignant
14 Harrison
15 Bira
16 Gerard
17 Rol
18 Claes
18 Pian
19 Schell
20 Whitehead,P.

Indianapolis 500

GRAND PRIX No:	3
DATE:	May 30, 1950
VENUE:	Indianapolis
POLE LAP:	Faulkner, 1m 06.992s
FASTEST LAP:	Holland, 1m 09.8s

Pn	Driver	Car	Laps	Time/Reason
1	Parsons	Kurtis Kraft	138	2h 46m 56.0s
2	Holland	Deidt	137	
3	Rose	Deidt	137	
4	Green	Kurtis Kraft	137	
5	Chitwood (S)	Kurtis Kraft	136	
6	Wallard	Moore	136	
7	Faulkner	Kurtis Kraft	135	
8	Connor	Lesovsky	135	
9	Russo,P.	Nichels	135	
10	Flaherty	Kurtis Kraft	135	
11	Fohr	Marchese	133	
12	Carter	Stevens	133	
13	Hellings	Kurtis Kraft	132	
14	McGrath	Kurtis Kraft	131	accident
15	Ruttman	Lesovsky	130	
16	Hartley	Langley	128	
17	Davies	Ewing	128	
18	McDowell,J.	Kurtis Kraft	128	
19	Brown,Walt	Kurtis Kraft	127	
20	Webb	Maserati	126	
21	Hoyt	Kurtis Kraft	125	
22	Ader	Rae	123	
23	Holmes	Olson	123	accident
24	Rathmann,J.	Wetteroth	122	
r	Banks (S)	Maserati	112	oil line
r	Schindler	Snowberger	111	universal joint
r	Levrett (S)	Adams	108	oil pressure
r	Agabashian	Kurtis Kraft	64	oil line
r	Jackson	Kurtis Kraft	52	supercharger
r	Hanks	Kurtis Kraft	42	oil pressure
r	Bettenhausen	Deidt	30	wheel bearing
r	Rathmann,D.	Watson	25	stalled
r	Dinsmore	Kurtis Kraft	10	oil leak

STARTING GRID:

1 Faulkner
2 Agabashian
3 Rose
4 Connor
5 Parsons
6 McGrath
7 Dinsmore
8 Bettenhausen +

Swiss

GRAND PRIX No:	4
DATE:	June 4, 1950
VENUE:	Bremgarten
POLE LAP:	Fangio, 2m 42.1s
FASTEST LAP:	Farina, 2m 41.6s

Pn	Driver	Car	Laps	Time/Reason
1	Farina	Alfa Romeo	42	2h 02m 53.7s
2	Fagioli	Alfa Romeo	42	2h 02m 54.1s
3	Rosier	Talbot	41	
4	Bira	Maserati	40	
5	Bonetto	Maserati-Milan	40	
6	de Graffenried	Maserati	40	
7	Pagani	Maserati	39	
8	Schell	Talbot	39	
9	Chiron	Maserati	39	
10	Claes	Talbot	39	
11	Branca	Maserati	35	
r	Fangio	Alfa Romeo	32	valve
r	Etancelin	Talbot	24	gearbox
r	Martin	Talbot	18	accident
r	Sommer	Ferrari	18	suspension
r	Villoresi	Ferrari	8	transmission
r	Ascari	Ferrari	3	oil pipe
r	Giraud-Cabantous	Talbot	0	accident

STARTING GRID:

1 Fangio
2 Farina
3 Fagioli
4 Villoresi
5 Ascari
6 Etancelin
7 Giraud-Cabantous
8 Bira
9 Martin
10 Rosier
11 de Graffenried
12 Bonetto
13 Sommer
14 Claes
15 Pagani
16 Chiron
17 Branca
18 Schell

Belgian

GRAND PRIX No: 5
DATE: June 18, 1950
VENUE: Spa-Francorchamps
POLE LAP: Fangio, 4m 37.0s
FASTEST LAP: Farina, 4m 34.1s

Pn	Driver	Car	Laps	Time/Reason
1	Fangio	Alfa Romeo	35	2h 47m 26s
2	Fagioli	Alfa Romeo	35	2h 47m 40s
3	Rosier	Talbot	35	2h 49m 45s
4	Farina	Alfa Romeo	35	2h 51m 31s
5	Ascari	Ferrari	34	
6	Villoresi	Ferrari	33	
7	Levegh	Talbot	33	
8	Claes	Talbot	32	
9	Crossley	Alta	30	
10	Branca	Maserati	29	
r	Chaboud	Talbot	21	
r	Sommer	Talbot	19	engine
r	Etancelin	Talbot	14	overheating
r	Giraud-Cabantous	Talbot	1	engine

STARTING GRID:

1 Farina
2 Fangio
3 Fagioli
4 Villoresi
5 Sommer
6 Ascari
7 Etancelin
8 Rosier
9 Giraud-Cabantous
10 Levegh
11 Chaboud
12 Crossley
13 Branca
14 Claes

French

GRAND PRIX No: 6
DATE: July 2, 1950
VENUE: Reims
POLE LAP: Fangio, 2m 30.6s
FASTEST LAP: Fangio, 2m 35.6s

Pn	Driver	Car	Laps	Time/Reason
1	Fangio	Alfa Romeo	64	2h 57m 52.8s
2	Fagioli	Alfa Romeo	64	2h 58m 18.5s
3	Whitehead,P.	Ferrari	61	
4	Manzon	Simca-Gordini	61	
5	Etancelin (S)	Talbot	59	
6	Pozzi (S)	Talbot	56	
7	Farina	Alfa Romeo	55	fuel pump
8	Giraud-Cabantous	Talbot	52	
r	Levegh	Talbot	36	engine
r	Bonetto	Maserati-Milan	14	engine
r	Claes	Talbot	11	overheating
r	Rosier	Talbot	10	overheating
r	Parnell,R.	Maserati	9	engine
r	Rol	Maserati	6	engine
r	Chiron	Maserati	6	engine
r	Hampshire	Maserati	5	engine
r	Sommer	Talbot	4	engine
r	Gonzalez,J.	Maserati	3	engine
dns	Chaboud	Lago-Talbot		

STARTING GRID:

1 Fangio
2 Farina
3 Fagioli
4 Etancelin
5 Giraud-Cabantous
6 Sommer
7 Rol
8 Gonzalez,J.
9 Levegh
10 Parnell,R.
11 Chaboud
12 Hampshire
13 Manzon
14 Chiron
15 Pozzi
16 Rosier
17 Claes
18 Bonetto
19 Whitehead,P.

Italian

GRAND PRIX No:	7
DATE:	September 3, 1950
VENUE:	Monza
POLE LAP:	Fangio, 1m 58.6s
FASTEST LAP:	Fangio, 2m 00.0s

Pn	Driver	Car	Laps	Time/Reason
1	Farina	Alfa Romeo	80	2h 51m 17.4s
2	Serafini	Ferrari	80	2h 52m 36.0s
3	Fagioli	Alfa Romeo	80	2h 52m 53.0s
4	Rosier	Talbot	75	
5	Etancelin	Talbot	75	
6	de Graffenried	Maserati	72	
7	Whitehead,P.	Ferrari	72	
r	Murray	Maserati	56	gearbox
r	Harrison	ERA	51	radiator
r	Sommer	Talbot	48	gearbox
r	Mairesse,G.	Talbot	42	
r	Rol	Maserati	39	
r	Taruffi	Alfa Romeo	34	valve
r	Levegh	Talbot	29	
r	Fangio	Alfa Romeo	23	gearbox
r	Claes	Talbot	22	overheating
r	Ascari	Ferrari	21	engine
r	Biondetti	Ferrari-Jaguar	17	engine
r	Louveau	Talbot	16	
r	Comotti	Maserati-Milan	15	
r	Chiron	Maserati	13	oil pressure
r	Trintignant	Simca-Gordini	13	water pipe
r	Sanesi	Alfa Romeo	11	engine
r	Manzon	Simca-Gordini	7	transmission
r	Bira	Maserati	1	engine
r	Pietsch	Maserati	0	engine

STARTING GRID:

1	Fangio	13	Rosier
2	Ascari	14	Louveau
3	Farina	15	de Graffenried
4	Sanesi	16	Whitehead,P.
5	Fagioli	17	Chiron
6	Serafini	18	Levegh
7	Taruffi	19	Harrison
8	Sommer	20	Claes
9	Rol	21	Murray
10	Manzon	22	Biondetti
11	Mairesse,G.	23	Comotti
12	Trintignant	24	Pietsch

Swiss

GRAND PRIX No:	8
DATE:	May 27, 1951
VENUE:	Bremgarten
POLE LAP:	Fangio, 2m 35.9s
FASTEST LAP:	Fangio, 2m 51.1s

Pn	Driver	Car	Laps	Time/Reason
1	Fangio	Alfa Romeo	42	2h 07m 53.6s
2	Taruffi	Ferrari	42	2h 08m 48.9s
3	Farina	Alfa Romeo	42	2h 09m 13.0s
4	Sanesi	Alfa Romeo	41	
5	de Graffenried	Alfa Romeo	40	
6	Ascari	Ferrari	40	
7	Chiron	Maserati	40	
8	Moss	HWM	40	
9	Rosier	Talbot	39	
10	Etancelin	Talbot	39	
11	Fischer	Ferrari	39	
12	Schell	Maserati	38	
13	Whitehead,P.	Ferrari	36	accident
14	Claes	Talbot	35	
15	Mairesse,G.	Talbot	31	
r	Louveau	Talbot	30	accident
r	Abeccassis	HWM	22	magneto
r	Giraud-Cabantous	Talbot	13	ignition
r	Villoresi	Ferrari	12	accident
r	Gonzalez,J.	Talbot	9	oil pump
r	Hirt	Veritas	0	fuel pump

STARTING GRID:

1	Fangio	12	Etancelin
2	Farina	13	Gonzalez,J.
3	Villoresi	14	Moss
4	Sanesi	15	Giraud-Cabantous
5	de Graffenried	16	Hirt
6	Taruffi	17	Schell
7	Ascari	18	Claes
8	Rosier	19	Chiron
9	Whitehead,P.	20	Abeccassis
10	Fischer	21	Mairesse,G.
11	Louveau		

Indianapolis 500

GRAND PRIX No:	9
DATE:	May 29, 1951
VENUE:	Indianapolis
POLE LAP:	Nalon, 1m 05.935s
FASTEST LAP:	Wallard, 1m 07.260s

Pn	Driver	Car	Laps	Time/Reason
1	Wallard	Kurtis Kraft	200	3h 57m 38.05s
2	Nazaruk	Kurtis Kraft	200	3h 59m 25.31s
3	McGrath (S)	Kurtis Kraft	200	4h 00m 29.42s
4	Linden	Sherman	200	4h 02m 18.06s
5	Ball	Schroeder	200	4h 02m 30.27s
6	Banks	Moore	200	4h 03m 18.02s
7	Forberg	Kurtis Kraft	193	
8	Carter	Deidt	180	
r	Bettenhausen	Deidt	178	spun off
r	Nalon	Kurtis Kraft	151	stalled
r	Force	Kurtis Kraft	142	engine
r	Hanks	Kurtis Kraft	135	engine
r	Schindler	Kurtis Kraft	129	engine
r	Rose	Deidt	126	accident
r	Faulkner	Kuzma	123	crankshaft
r	Davies	Pawl	110	rear axle
r	Agabashian	Kurtis Kraft	109	clutch
r	Scarborough	Kurtis Kraft	100	front axle
r	Mackey	Kurtis Kraft	97	clutch
r	Stevenson	Marchese	93	fire
r	Parsons	Kurtis Kraft	87	magneto
r	Green	Kurtis Kraft	80	engine
r	Ruttman	Kurtis Kraft	78	crankshaft
r	Dinsmore	Schroeder	73	overheating
r	Miller	Kurtis Kraft	56	ignition
r	Brown,Walt	Kurtis Kraft	55	magneto
r	Ward	Bromme	34	oil line
r	Griffith	Kurtis Kraft	30	rear axle
r	Vukovich	Trevis	29	oil tank
r	Connor	Lesovsky	29	driveshaft
r	Hellings	Deidt	18	engine
r	McDowell,J.	Maserati	15	fuel tank
r	James,Joe	Watson	8	driveshaft

STARTING GRID:

1 Nalon
2 Wallard
3 McGrath
4 Carter
5 Rose
6 Ruttman
7 Nazaruk
8 Parsons
9 Bettenhausen
10 Green
11 Agabashian
12 Hanks
13 Brown,Walt
14 Faulkner
15 Scarborough
16 Schindler
17 Banks
18 Griffith
19 Stevenson
20 Vukovich
21 Connor
22 Force
23 Hellings
24 Forberg
25 Ward
26 McDowell,J.
27 Davies
28 Miller
29 Ball
30 James,Joe
31 Linden
32 Dinsmore
33 Mackey

Belgian

GRAND PRIX No:	10
DATE:	June 17, 1951
VENUE:	Spa-Francorchamps
POLE LAP:	Fangio, 4m 25.0s
FASTEST LAP:	Fangio, 4m 22.1s

Pn	Driver	Car	Laps	Time/Reason
1	Farina	Alfa Romeo	36	2h 45m 46.2s
2	Ascari	Ferrari	36	2h 48m 37.2s
3	Villoresi	Ferrari	36	2h 50m 08.1s
4	Rosier	Talbot	34	
5	Giraud-Cabantous	Talbot	34	
6	Pilette,A.	Talbot	33	
7	Claes	Talbot	33	
8	Levegh	Talbot	32	
9	Fangio	Alfa Romeo	32	
r	Chiron	Maserati	27	piston
r	Sanesi	Alfa Romeo	11	radiator
r	Taruffi	Ferrari	8	rear axle
r	Etancelin	Talbot	0	transmission

STARTING GRID:

1 Fangio
2 Farina
3 Villoresi
4 Ascari
5 Taruffi
6 Sanesi
7 Rosier
8 Giraud-Cabantous
9 Chiron
10 Etancelin
11 Claes
12 Pilette,A.
13 Levegh

French

GRAND PRIX No:	11
DATE:	July 1, 1951
VENUE:	Reims
POLE LAP:	Fangio, 2m 25.7s
FASTEST LAP:	Fangio, 2m 27.8s

Pn	Driver	Car	Laps	Time/Reason
1	Fagioli (S)	Alfa Romeo	77	3h 22m 11.0s
2	Gonzalez,J. (S)	Ferrari	77	3h 23m 09.2s
3	Villoresi	Ferrari	74	
4	Parnell,R.	Ferrari	73	
5	Farina	Alfa Romeo	73	
6	Chiron	Talbot	71	
7	Giraud-Cabantous	Talbot	71	
8	Chaboud	Talbot	69	
9	Mairesse,G.	Talbot	66	
10	Sanesi	Alfa Romeo	58	
11	Fangio	Alfa Romeo	55	
r	Claes	Talbot	53	accident
r	Rosier	Talbot	42	rear axle
r	Etancelin	Talbot	36	inlet manifold
r	Gordini	Simca-Gordini	26	valve gear
r	Schell	Maserati	23	overheating
r	Trintignant	Simca-Gordini	10	valve
r	Ascari	Ferrari	9	gearbox
r	Simon	Simca-Gordini	6	engine
r	Manzon	Simca-Gordini	2	engine
r	Marimon	Maserati-Milan	1	piston
r	de Graffenried	Maserati	0	transmission
r	Whitehead,P.	Ferrari	0	gasket

STARTING GRID:

1	Fangio	13	Rosier
2	Farina	14	Chaboud
3	Ascari	15	Marimon
4	Villoresi	16	de Graffenried
5	Sanesi	17	Gordini
6	Gonzalez,J.	18	Trintignant
7	Fagioli	19	Mairesse,G.
8	Chiron	20	Whitehead,P.
9	Parnell,R.	21	Simon
10	Etancelin	22	Schell
11	Giraud-Cabantous	23	Manzon
12	Claes		

British

GRAND PRIX No:	12
DATE:	July 14, 1951
VENUE:	Silverstone
POLE LAP:	Gonzalez,J., 1m 43.4s
FASTEST LAP:	Farina, 1m 44.0s

Pn	Driver	Car	Laps	Time/Reason
1	Gonzalez,J.	Ferrari	90	2h 42m 18.2s
2	Fangio	Alfa Romeo	90	2h 43m 09.2s
3	Villoresi	Ferrari	88	
4	Bonetto	Alfa Romeo	87	
5	Parnell,R.	BRM	85	
6	Sanesi	Alfa Romeo	84	
7	Walker,P.	BRM	84	
8	Shawe-Taylor	ERA	84	
9	Whitehead,P.	Ferrari	83	
10	Rosier	Talbot	83	
11	Gerard	ERA	82	
12	Hamilton	Talbot	81	
13	Claes	Talbot	80	
14	Farina	Alfa Romeo	75	fire
uc	Kelly	Alta	75	
r	Ascari	Ferrari	55	gearbox
r	Fotheringham-Parker	Maserati	45	oil pipe
r	Murray	Maserati	44	valve spring
r	Chiron	Talbot	40	brakes
r	James,John	Maserati	22	radiator

STARTING GRID:

1	Gonzalez,J.	13	Chiron
2	Fangio	14	Claes
3	Farina	15	Murray
4	Ascari	16	Fotheringham-Parker
5	Villoresi	17	James,John
6	Sanesi	18	Kelly
7	Bonetto	19	Walker,P.
8	Whitehead,P.	20	Parnell,R.
9	Rosier		
10	Gerard		
11	Hamilton		
12	Shawe-Taylor		

German

GRAND PRIX No:	13
DATE:	July 29, 1951
VENUE:	Nurburgring
POLE LAP:	Ascari, 9m 55.8s
FASTEST LAP:	Fangio, 9m 55.8s

Pn	Driver	Car	Laps	Time/Reason
1	Ascari	Ferrari	20	3h 23m 03.3s
2	Fangio	Alfa Romeo	20	3h 23m 33.8s
3	Gonzalez,J.	Ferrari	20	3h 27m 42.3s
4	Villoresi	Ferrari	20	3h 28m 53.5s
5	Taruffi	Ferrari	20	3h 30m 52.4s
6	Fischer	Ferrari	19	
7	Manzon	Simca-Gordini	19	
8	Rosier	Talbot	19	
9	Levegh	Talbot	18	
10	Swaters	Talbot	18	
11	Giraud-Cabantous	Talbot	17	accident
12	Claes	Talbot	17	
r	Trintignant	Simca-Gordini	12	engine
r	Bonetto	Alfa Romeo	11	magneto
r	Hamilton	Talbot	11	oil pressure
r	Simon	Simca-Gordini	11	engine
r	Pietsch	Alfa Romeo	11	accident
r	Farina	Alfa Romeo	7	overheating
r	Etancelin	Talbot	3	gearbox
r	Branca	Maserati	3	engine
r	Chiron	Talbot	2	engine
r	de Graffenried	Maserati	1	engine
dns	Murray	Maserati		accident

STARTING GRID:

1	Ascari	13	Chiron
2	Gonzalez,J.	14	Trintignant
3	Fangio	15	Rosier
4	Farina	16	de Graffenried
5	Villoresi	17	Branca
6	Taruffi	18	Claes
7	Pietsch	19	Levegh
8	Fischer	20	Hamilton
9	Manzon	21	Etancelin
10	Bonetto	22	Swaters
11	Giraud-Cabantous	23	Murray
12	Simon		

Italian

GRAND PRIX No:	14
DATE:	September 16, 1951
VENUE:	Monza
POLE LAP:	Fangio, 1m 53.2s
FASTEST LAP:	Farina, 1m 56.5s

Pn	Driver	Car	Laps	Time/Reason
1	Ascari	Ferrari	80	2h 42m 39.3s
2	Gonzalez,J.	Ferrari	80	2h 43m 23.9s
3	Bonetto (S)	Alfa Romeo	79	
4	Villoresi	Ferrari	79	
5	Taruffi	Ferrari	78	
6	Simon	Simca-Gordini	74	
7	Rosier	Talbot	73	
8	Giraud-Cabantous	Talbot	72	
9	Rol	OSCA	67	
r	Fangio	Alfa Romeo	38	piston
r	Manzon	Simca-Gordini	29	engine
r	Trintignant	Simca-Gordini	29	piston
r	Chiron	Talbot	22	ignition
r	Levegh	Talbot	9	engine
r	Swaters	Talbot	7	overheating
r	Farina	Alfa Romeo	6	lubrication
r	Claes	Talbot	4	scavenge pump
r	de Graffenried	Alfa Romeo	1	supercharger
r	Whitehead,P.	Ferrari	1	piston
r	Landi	Ferrari	1	transmission
dns	Parnell,R.	BRM		engine
dns	Richardson	BRM		no licence

STARTING GRID:

1	Fangio	12	Trintignant
2	Farina	13	Manzon
3	Ascari	14	Giraud-Cabantous
4	Gonzalez,J.	15	Rosier
5	Villoresi	16	Landi
6	Taruffi	17	Chiron
7	Bonetto	18	Rol
8	Parnell,R.	19	Whitehead,P.
9	de Graffenried	20	Levegh
10	Richardson	21	Claes
11	Simon	22	Swaters

Spanish

GRAND PRIX No:	15
DATE:	October 28, 1951
VENUE:	Pedrables
POLE LAP:	Ascari, 2m 10.59s
FASTEST LAP:	Fangio, 2m 16.93s

Pn	Driver	Car	Laps	Time/Reason
1	Fangio	Alfa Romeo	70	2h 46m 54.10s
2	Gonzalez,J.	Ferrari	70	2h 47m 48.38s
3	Farina	Alfa Romeo	70	2h 48m 39.64s
4	Ascari	Ferrari	68	
5	Bonetto	Alfa Romeo	68	
6	de Graffenried	Alfa Romeo	66	
7	Rosier	Talbot	64	
8	Etancelin	Talbot	63	
9	Manzon	Simca-Gordini	63	
10	Godia	Maserati	60	
r	Villoresi	Ferrari	47	ignition
r	Simon	Simca-Gordini	47	engine
r	Claes	Talbot	36	accident
r	Taruffi	Ferrari	29	wheel
r	Trintignant	Simca-Gordini	24	engine
r	Grignard	Talbot	22	engine
r	Giraud-Cabantous	Talbot	6	accident
r	Chiron	Talbot	3	rocker
r	Bira	OSCA	0	engine
dns	Jover	Maserati		engine

STARTING GRID:

1	Ascari	11	Trintignant
2	Fangio	12	Chiron
3	Gonzalez,J.	13	Etancelin
4	Farina	14	Giraud-Cabantous
5	Villoresi	15	Claes
6	de Graffenried	16	Godia
7	Taruffi	17	Grignard
8	Bonetto	18	Jover
9	Manzon	19	Bira
10	Simon	20	Rosier

Swiss

GRAND PRIX No:	16
DATE:	May 18, 1952
VENUE:	Bremgarten
POLE LAP:	Farina, 2m 47.5s
FASTEST LAP:	Taruffi, 2m 49.1s

Pn	Driver	Car	Laps	Time/Reason
1	Taruffi	Ferrari	62	3h 01m 46.1s
2	Fischer	Ferrari	62	3h 04m 23.3s
3	Behra	Gordini	61	
4	Wharton	Frazer Nash	60	
5	Brown,A.	Cooper-Bristol	59	
6	de Graffenried	Maserati-Plate	58	
7	Hirt	Ferrari	56	
8	Brandon	Cooper-Bristol	55	
r	Bira	Simca-Gordini	51	engine
r	Simon (S)	Ferrari	50	magneto
r	Schell	Maserati-Plate	30	engine
r	Moss	HWM	23	withdrew
r	Macklin	HWM	23	withdrew
r	Manzon	Gordini	19	cooling damper
r	Farina	Ferrari	16	magneto
r	Collins	HWM	12	driveshaft
r	Abeccassis	HWM	13	driveshaft
r	Ulmen	Veritas	3	fuel tank
r	Stuck,H.	AFM	3	piston
r	Rosier	Ferrari	2	accident
r	de Terra	Simca-Gordini	0	magneto

STARTING GRID:

1	Farina	12	Macklin
2	Taruffi	13	Wharton
3	Manzon	14	Stuck,H.
4	Simon	15	Brown,A.
5	Fischer	16	Ulmen
6	Collins	17	Brandon
7	Behra	18	Schell
8	de Graffenried	19	Hirt
9	Moss	20	Rosier
10	Abeccassis	21	de Terra
11	Bira		

Indianapolis 500

GRAND PRIX No: 17
DATE: May 30, 1952
VENUE: Indianapolis
POLE LAP: Agabashian, 1m 05.212s
FASTEST LAP: Vukovich, 1m 06.600s

Pn	Driver	Car	Laps	Time/Reason
1	Ruttman	Kuzma	200	3h 52m 41.88s
2	Rathmann,J.	Kurtis Kraft	200	3h 56m 44.21s
3	Hanks	Kurtis Kraft	200	3h 58m 53.48s
4	Carter	Lesovsky	200	3h 59m 30.21s
5	Cross	Kurtis Kraft	200	4h 01m 22.08s
6	Bryan	Kurtis Kraft	200	4h 02m 06.23s
7	Reece	Kurtis Kraft	200	
8	Connor	Kurtis Kraft	200	
9	Griffith	Kurtis Kraft	200	
10	Parsons	Kurtis Kraft	200	
11	McGrath	Kurtis Kraft	200	
12	Rigsby	Watson	200	
13	James,Joe	Kurtis Kraft	200	
14	Schindler	Stevens	200	
15	Fonder	Sherman	197	
16	Johnson,E.	Trevis	193	
17	Vukovich	Kurtis Kraft	191	steering
18	Stevenson	Kurtis Kraft	187	
19	Banks	Lesovsky	184	
20	Ayulo	Lesovsky	184	
21	McDowell,J.	Kurtis Kraft	182	
r	Webb	Bromme	162	oil pressure
r	Ward	Kurtis Kraft	130	oil pressure
r	Bettenhausen	Deidt	93	oil pressure
r	Nalon	Kurtis Kraft	84	supercharger
r	Sweikert	Kurtis Kraft	77	differential
r	Agabashian	Kurtis Kraft	71	supercharger
r	Hartley	Kurtis Kraft	65	exhaust
r	Scott	Kurtis Kraft	49	driveshaft
r	Miller	Kurtis Kraft	41	supercharger
r	Ascari	Ferrari	40	wheel
r	Ball	Stevens	34	gear case
r	Linden	Kurtis Kraft	20	oil pump

STARTING GRID:

1 Agabashian
2 Linden
3 McGrath
4 Nalon
5 Hanks
6 Carter
7 Ruttman
8 Vukovich +

Belgian

GRAND PRIX No: 18
DATE: June 22, 1952
VENUE: Spa-Francorchamps
POLE LAP: Ascari, 4m 37.0s
FASTEST LAP: Ascari, 4m 54.0s

Pn	Driver	Car	Laps	Time/Reason
1	Ascari	Ferrari	36	3h 03m 46.8s
2	Farina	Ferrari	36	3h 05m 41.5s
3	Manzon	Gordini	36	3h 08m 14.7s
4	Hawthorn	Cooper-Bristol	35	
5	Frere	HWM	34	
6	Brown,A.	Cooper-Bristol	34	
7	de Tornaco	Ferrari	33	
8	Claes	Simca-Gordini	33	
9	Brandon	Cooper-Bristol	33	
10	Bira	Simca-Gordini	32	
11	Macklin	HWM	32	
12	Laurent	HWM	32	
13	Legat	Veritas	31	
14	O'Brien	Simca-Gordini	30	
15	Gaze	HWM	30	
r	Montgomerie-Charrington	Aston-Butter.	16	misfiring
r	Behra	Gordini	13	accident
r	Taruffi	Ferrari	13	accident
r	Wharton	Frazer Nash	10	accident
r	Rosier	Ferrari	5	transmission
r	Collins	HWM	2	driveshaft
r	Moss	ERA	0	gudgeon pin

STARTING GRID:

1 Ascari
2 Farina
3 Taruffi
4 Manzon
5 Behra
6 Hawthorn
7 Wharton
8 Frere
9 Brown,A.
10 Moss
11 Collins
12 Brandon
13 de Tornaco
14 Macklin
15 Montgomerie-Charrington
16 Gaze
17 Rosier
18 Bira
19 Claes
20 Laurent
21 Legat
22 O'Brien

French

GRAND PRIX No: 19
DATE: July 6, 1952
VENUE: Rouen
POLE LAP: Ascari, 2m 14.8s
FASTEST LAP: Ascari, 2m 17.3s

Pn	Driver	Car	Laps	Time/Reason
1	Ascari	Ferrari	76	3h 00m 0.0s
2	Farina	Ferrari	76	
3	Taruffi	Ferrari	75	
4	Manzon	Gordini	74	
5	Trintignant	Gordini	72	
6	Collins	HWM	70	
7	Behra	Gordini	70	
8	Etancelin	Maserati	70	
9	Macklin	HWM	70	
10	Giraud-Cabantous	HWM	68	
11	Fischer (S)	Ferrari	66	
12	Comotti	Ferrari	63	
r	Bira	Gordini	56	rear axle
r	Hawthorn	Cooper-Bristol	50	ignition
r	de Graffenried (S)	Maserati-Plate	33	brakes
r	Whitehead,P.	Alta	25	clutch
r	Rosier	Ferrari	16	engine
r	Claes	Simca-Gordini	14	con rod
r	Schell	Maserati-Plate	6	gearbox
r	Carini	Ferrari	1	head gasket

STARTING GRID:

1	Ascari	11	Schell
2	Farina	12	de Graffenried
3	Taruffi	13	Whitehead,P.
4	Behra	14	Macklin
5	Manzon	15	Hawthorn
6	Trintignant	16	Comotti
7	Bira	17	Fischer
8	Collins	18	Etancelin
9	Rosier	19	Carini
10	Giraud-Cabantous	20	Claes

British

GRAND PRIX No: 20
DATE: July 19, 1952
VENUE: Silverstone
POLE LAP: Farina, 1m 50.0s
FASTEST LAP: Ascari, 1m 52.0s

Pn	Driver	Car	Laps	Time/Reason
1	Ascari	Ferrari	85	2h 44m 11.0s
2	Taruffi	Ferrari	84	
3	Hawthorn	Cooper-Bristol	83	
4	Poore	Connaught	83	
5	Thompson	Connaught	82	
6	Farina	Ferrari	82	
7	Parnell,R.	Cooper-Bristol	82	
8	Salvadori	Ferrari	82	
9	Downing	Connaught	82	
10	Whitehead,P.	Ferrari	81	
11	Bira	Gordini	81	
12	Whitehead,G.	Alta	80	
13	Fischer	Ferrari	80	
14	Claes	Simca-Gordini	79	
15	Macklin	HWM	79	
16	McAlpine	Connaught	79	
17	Schell	Maserati-Plate	78	
18	Bianco	Maserati	77	
19	de Graffenried	Maserati-Plate	76	
20	Brandon	Cooper-Bristol	76	
21	Crook	Frazer Nash	75	
22	Collins	HWM	72	misfiring
23	Brown,A.	Cooper-Bristol	69	
r	Hamilton	HWM	43	engine
r	Moss	ERA	35	cylinder head
r	Trintignant	Gordini	21	gearbox
r	Gaze	HWM	19	head gasket
r	Murray	Cooper-Bristol	13	spark plugs
r	Manzon	Gordini	8	clutch
r	Hirt	Ferrari	2	brakes
r	Cantoni	Maserati	0	brakes
dns	Aston	Aston-Butter.		

STARTING GRID:

1	Farina	6	Parnell,R.
2	Ascari	7	Hawthorn
3	Taruffi	8	Poore
4	Manzon	9	Thompson
5	Downing	10	Bira

+

German

GRAND PRIX No:	21
DATE:	August 3, 1952
VENUE:	Nurburgring
POLE LAP:	Ascari, 10m 04.4s
FASTEST LAP:	Ascari, 10m 05.1s

Pn	Driver	Car	Laps	Time/Reason
1	Ascari	Ferrari	18	3h 06m 13.3s
2	Farina	Ferrari	18	3h 06m 27.4s
3	Fischer,R.	Ferrari	18	3h 13m 23.4s
4	Taruffi	Ferrari	17	
5	Behra	Gordini	17	
6	Laurent	Ferrari	16	
7	Riess	Veritas	16	
8	Ulmen	Veritas	16	
9	Niedermayr	AFM	15	
10	Claes	HWM	15	
11	Klenk	Veritas	14	
12	Klodwig	BMW	14	
r	Manzon	Gordini	8	lost wheel
r	Heeks	AFM	6	
r	Gaze	HWM	5	gearbox
r	Balsa	BMW	4	
r	Brudes	Veritas	4	engine
r	Bechem	BMW	4	spark plugs
r	Cantoni	Maserati	3	rear axle
r	Krause	BMW	2	
r	Schoeller	Ferrari	2	shock absorber
r	Aston	Aston-Butter	1	oil pressure
r	Carini	Ferrari	1	brakes
r	Pietsch	Veritas	1	gearbox
r	Helfrich	Veritas	1	
r	Frere	HWM	1	de Dion tube
r	Peters	Veritas	1	
r	Trintignant	Gordini	1	gearbox
dq	Bonetto	Maserati	1	push start
r	Bianco	Maserati	0	
dns	Krakau	AFM-BMW		
dns	Fischer,L.	AFM-BMW		

STARTING GRID:

1	Ascari	6	Fischer
2	Farina	7	Pietsch
3	Trintignant	8	Klenk
4	Manzon	9	Heeks
5	Taruffi	10	Bonetto

+

Dutch

GRAND PRIX No:	22
DATE:	August 17, 1952
VENUE:	Zandvoort
POLE LAP:	Ascari, 1m 46.5s
FASTEST LAP:	Ascari, 1m 49.8s

Pn	Driver	Car	Laps	Time/Reason
1	Ascari	Ferrari	90	2h 53m 28.5s
2	Farina	Ferrari	90	2h 54m 08.6s
3	Villoresi	Ferrari	90	2h 55m 02.9s
4	Hawthorn	Cooper-Bristol	88	
5	Manzon	Gordini	87	
6	Trintignant	Gordini	87	
7	Hamilton	HWM	85	
8	Macklin	HWM	84	
9	Landi (S)	Maserati	83	
10	Wharton	Frazer Nash	76	rear axle
11	Moss	ERA	72	engine
uc	Van der Lof	HWM	70	
r	Downing	Connaught	26	oil pressure
r	de Tornaco	Ferrari	18	valve
r	Frere	Simca-Gordini	14	gearbox
r	Behra	Gordini	9	carburettor
r	Flinterman	Maserati	6	differential
r	Bianco	Maserati	3	rear axle

STARTING GRID:

1	Ascari	10	Hamilton
2	Farina	11	Frere
3	Hawthorn	12	Bianco
4	Villoresi	13	Downing
5	Trintignant	14	Van der Lof
6	Behra	15	Flinterman
7	Wharton	16	Landi
8	Manzon	17	de Tornaco
9	Macklin	18	Moss

Italian

GRAND PRIX No:	23
DATE:	September 7, 1952
VENUE:	Monza
POLE LAP:	Ascari, 2m 05.1s
FASTEST LAP:	Ascari & Gonzalez,J., 2m 06.1s

Pn	Driver	Car	Laps	Time/Reason
1	Ascari	Ferrari	80	2h 50m 45.6s
2	Gonzalez,J.	Maserati	80	2h 51m 47.4s
3	Villoresi	Ferrari	80	2h 52m 49.8s
4	Farina	Ferrari	80	2h 52m 57.0s
5	Bonetto	Maserati	79	
6	Simon	Ferrari	79	
7	Taruffi	Ferrari	77	
8	Landi	Maserati	76	
9	Wharton	Cooper-Bristol	76	
10	Rosier	Ferrari	75	
11	Cantoni	Maserati	75	
12	Poore	Connaught	74	
13	Brandon	Cooper-Bristol	73	
14	Manzon	Gordini	71	
15	Brown,A.	Cooper-Bristol	68	
r	Moss	Connaught	60	push rod
r	Bianco	Maserati	46	mechanical
r	Behra	Gordini	42	valve
uc	Hawthorn	Cooper-Bristol	38	
r	Rol	Maserati	23	engine
r	Trintignant	Gordini	4	valve gear
r	McAlpine	Connaught	3	rear suspension
r	Fischer	Ferrari	2	engine
r	Bayol	OSCA	0	gearbox

STARTING GRID:

1	Ascari	13	Bonetto
2	Villoresi	14	Fischer
3	Farina	15	Wharton
4	Trintignant	16	Rol
5	Gonzalez,J.	17	Rosier
6	Taruffi	18	Landi
7	Manzon	19	Poore
8	Simon	20	Brandon
9	Moss	21	Brown,A.
10	Bayol	22	McAlpine
11	Behra	23	Cantoni
12	Hawthorn	24	Bianco

Argentine

GRAND PRIX No:	24
DATE:	January 18, 1953
VENUE:	Buenos Aires
POLE LAP:	Ascari, 1m 55.4s
FASTEST LAP:	Ascari, 1m 48.4s

Pn	Driver	Car	Laps	Time/Reason
1	Ascari	Ferrari	97	3h 01m 04.6s
2	Villoresi	Ferrari	96	
3	Gonzalez,J.	Maserati	96	
4	Hawthorn	Ferrari	96	
5	Galvez	Maserati	96	
6	Behra	Gordini	94	
7	Trintignant (S)	Gordini	91	
8	Barber,J.	Cooper-Bristol	90	
9	Brown,A.	Cooper-Bristol	87	
r	Manzon	Gordini	67	lost wheel
r	Fangio	Maserati	35	prop shaft
r	Bonetto	Maserati	32	transmission
r	Farina	Ferrari	31	accident
r	Menditeguy	Gordini	24	gearbox
r	Birger	Simca-Gordini	22	crownwheel and pinion
r	Schwelm-Cruz	Cooper-Bristol	20	lost wheel

STARTING GRID:

1	Ascari	9	Galvez
2	Fangio	10	Menditeguy
3	Villoresi	11	Behra
4	Farina	12	Brown,A.
5	Gonzalez,J.	13	Schwelm-Cruz
6	Hawthorn	14	Birger
7	Trintignant	15	Bonetto
8	Manzon	16	Barber,J.

Indianapolis 500

GRAND PRIX No:	25
DATE:	May 30, 1953
VENUE:	Indianapolis
POLE LAP:	Vukovich, 1m 05.032s
FASTEST LAP:	Vukovich, 1m 06.240s

Pn	Driver	Car	Laps	Time/Reason
1	Vukovich	Kurtis Kraft	200	3h 53m 01.7s
2	Cross	Kurtis Kraft	200	3h 56m 32.56s
3	Hanks (S)	Kurtis Kraft	200	3h 57m 13.24s
4	Agabashian (S)	Kurtis Kraft	200	3h 57m 40.91s
5	McGrath	Kurtis Kraft	200	4h 00m 51.33s
6	Daywalt	Kurtis Kraft	200	4h 01m 11.88s
7	Rathmann,J. (S)	Kurtis Kraft	200	
8	McCoy	Stevens	200	
9	Bettenhausen (S)	Kuzma	196	accident
10	Davies	Kurtis Kraft	193	
11	Nalon	Kurtis Kraft	191	accident
12	Scarborough (S)	Kurtis Kraft	190	
13	Ayulo	Kuzma	184	engine
14	Bryan	Schroeder	183	
15	Holland (S)	Kurtis Kraft	177	magneto
16	Ward (S)	Kurtis Kraft	177	rear axle
17	Faulkner (S)	Kurtis Kraft	176	
r	Teague	Kurtis Kraft	169	oil leak
r	Webb (S)	Kurtis Kraft	166	oil leak
r	Sweikert	Kuzma	151	radius rod
r	Nazaruk	Turner	146	driveshaft
r	Flaherty	Kurtis Kraft	115	accident
r	Hoyt (S)	Kurtis Kraft	107	overheating
r	Carter	Lesovsky	94	ignition
r	Russo,P.	Kurtis Kraft	89	magneto
r	Parsons	Kurtis Kraft	86	crankshaft
r	Freeland	Watson	76	accident
r	Hartley	Kurtis Kraft	53	accident
r	Stevenson	Kuzma	42	fuel leak
r	Niday	Kurtis Kraft	30	magneto
r	Scott	Bromme	14	oil leak
r	Thomson	Del Roy	6	ignition
r	Linden	Stevens	3	accident

STARTING GRID:

1 Vukovich	5 Linden
2 Agabashian	6 Bettenhausen
3 McGrath	7 Hoyt
4 Ayulo	8 Parsons +

Dutch

GRAND PRIX No:	26
DATE:	June 7, 1953
VENUE:	Zandvoort
POLE LAP:	Ascari, 1m 51.1s
FASTEST LAP:	Villoresi, 1m 52.8s

Pn	Driver	Car	Laps	Time/Reason
1	Ascari	Ferrari	90	2h 53m 35.8s
2	Farina	Ferrari	90	2h 53m 46.2s
3	Bonetto (S)	Maserati	89	
4	Hawthorn	Ferrari	89	
5	de Graffenried	Maserati	88	
6	Trintignant	Gordini	87	
7	Rosier	Ferrari	86	
8	Collins	HWM	84	
9	Moss	Connaught	83	
r	Villoresi	Ferrari	67	throttle
r	McAlpine	Connaught	64	engine
r	Schell	Gordini	60	transmission
uc	Claes	Connaught	52	
r	Fangio	Maserati	36	rear axle
r	Mieres	Gordini	28	transmission
r	Gonzalez,J.	Maserati	22	rear axle
r	Wharton	Cooper-Bristol	18	suspension
r	Salvadori	Connaught	13	valve
r	Macklin	HWM	7	throttle

STARTING GRID:

1 Ascari	11 Salvadori
2 Fangio	12 Trintignant
3 Farina	13 Bonetto
4 Villoresi	14 McAlpine
5 Gonzalez,J.	15 Macklin
6 Hawthorn	16 Collins
7 de Graffenried	17 Claes
8 Rosier	18 Wharton
9 Moss	19 Mieres
10 Schell	

Belgian

GRAND PRIX No:	27
DATE:	June 21, 1953
VENUE:	Spa-Francorchamps
POLE LAP:	Fangio, 4m 30.0s
FASTEST LAP:	Gonzalez,J., 4m 34.0s

Pn	Driver	Car	Laps	Time/Reason
1	Ascari	Ferrari	36	2h 48m 30.3s
2	Villoresi	Ferrari	36	2h 51m 18.5s
r	Claes (S)	Maserati	36	accident
3	Marimon	Maserati	35	
4	de Graffenried	Maserati	35	
5	Trintignant	Gordini	35	
6	Hawthorn	Ferrari	35	
7	Schell	Gordini	33	
8	Rosier	Ferrari	33	
9	Wacker	Gordini	32	
10	Frere	HWM	30	
uc	Pilette,A.	Connaught	29	
r	Macklin	HWM	18	engine
r	Farina	Ferrari	15	engine
r	Fangio	Maserati	12	engine
r	Gonzalez,J.	Maserati	11	accelerator
r	Behra	Gordini	8	head gasket
r	Collins	HWM	3	clutch
r	Berger,Georges	Simca-Gordini	2	engine
r	Legat	Veritas	0	transmission

STARTING GRID:

1	Fangio	13	Rosier
2	Ascari	14	Behra
3	Gonzalez,J.	15	Wacker
4	Farina	16	Collins
5	Villoresi	17	Macklin
6	Marimon	18	Pilette,A.
7	Hawthorn	19	Legat
8	Trintignant	20	Berger,Georges
9	de Graffenried		
10	Claes		
11	Frere		
12	Schell		

French

GRAND PRIX No:	28
DATE:	July 5, 1953
VENUE:	Reims
POLE LAP:	Ascari, 2m 41.2s
FASTEST LAP:	Fangio, 2m 41.1s

Pn	Driver	Car	Laps	Time/Reason
1	Hawthorn	Ferrari	60	2h 44m 18.6s
2	Fangio	Maserati	60	2h 44m 19.6s
3	Gonzalez,J.	Maserati	60	2h 44m 20.4s
4	Ascari	Ferrari	60	2h 44m 23.2s
5	Farina	Ferrari	60	2h 44m 26.2s
6	Villoresi	Ferrari	60	2h 45m 34.5s
7	de Graffenried	Maserati	58	
8	Rosier	Ferrari	56	
9	Marimon	Maserati	55	
10	Behra	Gordini	55	
11	Gerard	Cooper-Bristol	55	
12	Claes	Connaught	53	
13	Collins	HWM	52	
14	Giraud-Cabantous	HWM	50	
15	Chiron	OSCA	43	
r	Bonetto	Maserati	41	engine
r	Moss	Cooper-Alta	37	clutch
r	Bira	Connaught	28	differential
r	Bayol	OSCA	17	engine
r	Wharton	Cooper-Bristol	16	bearings
r	Trintignant	Gordini	15	transmission
r	Macklin	HWM	8	clutch
r	Mieres	Gordini	3	rear axle
r	Schell	Gordini	3	con rod
r	Salvadori	Connaught	1	ignition

STARTING GRID:

1	Ascari	14	Wharton
2	Bonetto	15	Bayol
3	Villoresi	16	Macklin
4	Fangio	17	Collins
5	Gonzalez,J.	18	Giraud-Cabantous
6	Farina	19	Salvadori
7	Hawthorn	20	Schell
8	Marimon	21	Claes
9	de Graffenried	22	Behra
10	Rosier	23	Trintignant
11	Bira	24	Mieres
12	Gerard	25	Chiron
13	Moss		

British

GRAND PRIX No: 29
DATE: July 18, 1953
VENUE: Silverstone
POLE LAP: Ascari, 1m 48.0s
FASTEST LAP: Ascari & Gonzalez,J., 1m 50.0s

Pn	Driver	Car	Laps	Time/Reason
1	Ascari	Ferrari	90	2h 50m 00s
2	Fangio	Maserati	90	2h 51m 00s
3	Farina	Ferrari	88	
4	Gonzalez,J.	Maserati	88	
5	Hawthorn	Ferrari	87	
6	Bonetto	Maserati	82	
7	Bira	Connaught	82	
8	Wharton	Cooper-Bristol	80	
9	Stewart,Jimmy	Cooper-Bristol	79	accident
10	Whitehead,P.	Cooper-Alta	79	
11	Rosier	Ferrari	78	
r	Rolt	Connaught	70	half shaft
r	Villoresi	Ferrari	66	rear axle
r	Marimon	Maserati	65	engine
r	Brown,A.	Cooper-Bristol	61	fan belt
r	Collins	HWM	56	accident
r	Fairman	HWM	53	clutch
r	Salvadori	Connaught	50	suspension
r	de Graffenried	Maserati	33	clutch
r	Macklin	HWM	30	clutch
r	Behra	Gordini	29	fuel pump
r	Stewart,Ian	Connaught	25	engine
r	Trintignant	Gordini	14	rear axle
r	Hamilton	HWM	14	clutch
r	Gerard	Cooper-Bristol	8	suspension
r	Schell	Gordini	5	magneto
r	Crook	Cooper-Bristol	0	fuel feed
r	McAlpine	Connaught	0	split hose

STARTING GRID:

1 Ascari
2 Gonzalez,J.
3 Hawthorn
4 Fangio
5 Farina
6 Villoresi
7 Marimon
8 Trintignant
9 Schell
10 Rolt
11 Wharton
12 Macklin
13 McAlpine
14 Whitehead,P.
15 Stewart,Jimmy
16 Bonetto +

German

GRAND PRIX No: 30
DATE: August 2, 1953
VENUE: Nurburgring
POLE LAP: Ascari, 9m 59.8s
FASTEST LAP: Ascari, 9m 56.0s

Pn	Driver	Car	Laps	Time/Reason
1	Farina	Ferrari	18	3h 02m 25.0s
2	Fangio	Maserati	18	3h 03m 29.0s
3	Hawthorn	Ferrari	18	3h 04m 08.6s
4	Bonetto	Maserati	18	3h 11m 13.6s
5	de Graffenried	Maserati	17	
6	Moss	Cooper-Alta	17	
7	Swaters	Ferrari	17	
8	Ascari	Ferrari	17	
9	Herrmann	Veritas	17	
10	Rosier	Ferrari	17	
11	Nuckey	Cooper-Bristol	16	
12	Helfrich	Veritas	16	
13	McAlpine	Connaught	16	
14	Krause	BMW	16	
r	Villoresi (S)	Ferrari	15	engine
r	Brown,A.	Cooper-Bristol	15	engine
uc	Klodwig	BMW	15	
uc	Seidel	Veritas	14	
r	Marimon	Maserati	13	suspension
r	Claes	Connaught	11	
r	Barth	EMW	11	
r	Karch	Veritas	10	
r	Heeks	Veritas	8	
r	Behra	Gordini	7	gearbox
r	Schell	Gordini	6	head gasket
r	Bira	Connaught	6	rocker
r	Fitzau	AFM	3	
r	Adolff	Ferrari	2	
r	Bechem	AFM	2	
r	Bauer	Veritas	1	
r	Salvadori	Connaught	0	rocker
r	Trintignant	Gordini	0	differential
r	Stuck,H.	AFM	0	
r	Loof	Veritas	0	fuel pump

STARTING GRID:

1 Ascari
2 Fangio
3 Farina
4 Hawthorn
5 Trintignant
6 Villoresi +

Swiss

GRAND PRIX No: 31
DATE: August 23, 1953
VENUE: Bremgarten
POLE LAP: Fangio, 2m 40.1s
FASTEST LAP: Ascari, 2m 41.3s

Pn	Driver	Car	Laps	Time/Reason
1	Ascari	Ferrari	65	3h 01m 34.40s
2	Farina	Ferrari	65	3h 02m 47.33s
3	Hawthorn	Ferrari	65	3h 03m 10.36s
4	Fangio (S)	Maserati	64	
5	Lang	Maserati	62	
6	Villoresi	Ferrari	62	
7	Wharton	Cooper-Bristol	62	
r	Landi	Maserati	54	gearbox
uc	Scherrer	HWM	49	
uc	de Terra	Ferrari	48	
r	de Graffenried	Maserati	47	camshaft
r	Marimon	Maserati	45	oil pipe
r	Trintignant	Gordini	43	rear axle
r	Behra	Gordini	36	oil pressure
r	Bonetto (S)	Maserati	28	valve
r	Macklin	HWM	28	valve
r	Hirt	Ferrari	16	oil leak
r	Frere	HWM	1	con rod
r	Rosier	Ferrari	0	accident
r	Swaters	Ferrari	0	accident

STARTING GRID:

1 Fangio
2 Ascari
3 Farina
4 Trintignant
5 Marimon
6 Villoresi
7 Hawthorn
8 de Graffenried
9 Wharton
10 Bonetto
11 Lang
12 Behra
13 Swaters
14 Rosier
15 Macklin
16 Frere
17 Hirt
18 Scherrer
19 de Terra
20 Landi

Italian

GRAND PRIX No: 32
DATE: September 13, 1953
VENUE: Monza
POLE LAP: Ascari, 2m 02.7s
FASTEST LAP: Fangio, 2m 04.6s

Pn	Driver	Car	Laps	Time/Reason
1	Fangio	Maserati	80	2h 49m 45.9s
2	Farina	Ferrari	80	2h 49m 47.3s
uc	Ascari	Ferrari	79	accident
3	Villoresi	Ferrari	79	
4	Hawthorn	Ferrari	79	
5	Trintignant	Gordini	79	
6	Bonetto	Maserati	77	out of fuel
7	Mieres	Gordini	77	
8	Mantovani (S)	Maserati	76	
9	Marimon	Maserati	75	accident
10	Maglioli	Ferrari	75	
11	Schell	Gordini	75	
12	Chiron	OSCA	72	
13	Bira	Maserati	72	
14	de Graffenried	Maserati	70	engine
15	Brown,A.	Cooper-Bristol	70	
16	Moss	Cooper-Alta	70	
uc	Stuck,H.	AFM	67	
uc	Giraud-Cabantous	HWM	67	
uc	Rosier	Ferrari	65	
uc	Fairman	HWM	61	
uc	Wharton	Cooper-Bristol	57	
uc	McAlpine	Connaught	56	
r	Carini	Ferrari	40	mechanical
r	Salvadori	Connaught	33	throttle
r	Landi	Maserati	18	piston
r	Bayol	OSCA	17	mechanical
r	Fitch	HWM	14	engine
r	Claes	Connaught	7	fuel pipe
r	Macklin	HWM	5	engine

STARTING GRID:

1 Ascari
2 Fangio
3 Farina
4 Marimon
5 Villoresi
6 Hawthorn
7 Bonetto
8 Trintignant
9 de Graffenried
10 Moss
11 Maglioli
12 Mantovani +

Argentine

GRAND PRIX No: 33
DATE: January 17, 1954
VENUE: Buenos Aires
POLE LAP: Farina, 1m 44.8s
FASTEST LAP: Gonzalez,J., 1m 48.2s

Pn	Driver	Car	Laps	Time/Reason
1	Fangio	Maserati	87	3h 00m 55.8s
2	Farina	Ferrari	87	3h 02m 14.8s
3	Gonzalez,J.	Ferrari	87	3h 02m 56.8s
4	Trintignant	Ferrari	86	
5	Bayol	Gordini	85	
6	Schell	Maserati	84	
7	Bira	Maserati	83	
8	de Graffenried	Maserati	83	
9	Maglioli	Ferrari	82	
dq	Hawthorn	Ferrari		push start
dq	Behra	Gordini		push start
r	Marimon	Maserati	5	accident
r	Mieres	Maserati		engine
r	Daponte	Maserati		oil pressure
r	Loyer	Gordini		oil pressure
r	Rosier	Ferrari	2	accident
dns	Musso	Maserati		engine
dns	Menditeguy	Maserati		engine

STARTING GRID:

1 Farina
2 Gonzalez,J.
3 Fangio
4 Hawthorn
5 Trintignant
6 Marimon
7 Musso
8 Mieres
9 Menditeguy
10 Bira
11 Schell
12 Maglioli
13 de Graffenried
14 Rosier
15 Bayol
16 Loyer
17 Behra
18 Daponte

Indianapolis 500

GRAND PRIX No: 34
DATE: May 31, 1954
VENUE: Indianapolis
POLE LAP: McGrath, 1m 03.815s
FASTEST LAP: McGrath, 1m 04.040s

Pn	Driver	Car	Laps	Time/Reason
1	Vukovich	Kurtis Kraft	200	3h 49m 17.27s
2	Bryan	Kuzma	200	3h 50m 27.26s
3	McGrath	Kurtis Kraft	200	3h 50m 36.97s
4	Ruttman (S)	Kurtis Kraft	200	3h 52m 09.90s
5	Nazaruk	Kurtis Kraft	200	3h 52m 41.85s
6	Agabashian	Kurtis Kraft	200	3h 53m 04.83s
7	Freeland	Phillips	200	
8	Russo,P. (S)	Kurtis Kraft	200	
9	Crockett	Kurtis Kraft	200	
10	Niday	Stevens	200	
11	Cross (S)	Kurtis Kraft	200	
12	Stevenson (S)	Kuzma	199	
13	Ayulo	Kuzma	197	
14	Sweikert	Kurtis Kraft	197	
15	Carter (S)	Kurtis Kraft	196	
16	McCoy	Kurtis Kraft	194	
17	Reece	Pankratz	194	
18	Elisian (S)	Stevens	193	
19	Armi (S)	Kurtis Kraft	193	
r	Hanks (S)	Kurtis Kraft	191	spun off
r	O'Connor	Kurtis Kraft	181	spun off
r	Ward (S)	Pawl	172	stalled
r	Hartley (S)	Kurtis Kraft	168	clutch
r	Thomson (S)	Nichels	165	stalled
r	Linden (S)	Nichels	165	torsion bar
r	Hoyt	Kurtis Kraft	130	engine
r	Daywalt	Kurtis Kraft	111	accident
r	Rathmann,J. (S)	Kurtis Kraft	110	accident
r	Bettenhausen	Kurtis Kraft	105	bearings
r	Webb (S)	Bromme	104	fuel pump
r	Duncan (S)	Schroeder	101	brake cylinder
r	Parsons	Kurtis Kraft	79	engine
r	Homeier	Kurtis Kraft	74	accident

STARTING GRID:

1 McGrath
2 Daywalt
3 Bryan
4 Thomson
5 Stevenson
6 Freeland
7 Reece
8 Carter +

Belgian

GRAND PRIX No:	35
DATE:	June 20, 1954
VENUE:	Spa-Francorchamps
POLE LAP:	Fangio, 4m 22.1s
FASTEST LAP:	Fangio, 4m 25.5s

Pn	Driver	Car	Laps	Time/Reason
1	Fangio	Maserati	36	2h 44m 42.4s
2	Trintignant	Ferrari	36	2h 45m 06.6s
3	Moss	Maserati	35	
4	Hawthorn (4)	Ferrari	35	
5	Pilette,A.	Gordini	35	
6	Bira	Maserati	35	
7	Mantovani	Maserati	34	
r	Frere	Gordini	13	engine
r	Farina	Ferrari	13	ignition
r	Behra	Gordini	11	suspension
r	Marimon	Maserati	2	valve
r	Swaters	Ferrari	0	engine
r	Gonzalez,J.	Ferrari	0	oil pipe
r	Mieres	Maserati	0	fire

STARTING GRID:

1	Fangio	8	Pilette,A.
2	Gonzalez,J.	9	Moss
3	Farina	10	Frere
4	Marimon	11	Mantovani
5	Hawthorn	12	Mieres
6	Trintignant	13	Bira
7	Behra	14	Swaters

French

GRAND PRIX No:	36
DATE:	July 4, 1954
VENUE:	Reims
POLE LAP:	Fangio, 2m 29.4s
FASTEST LAP:	Herrmann, 2m 32.9s

Pn	Driver	Car	Laps	Time/Reason
1	Fangio	Mercedes	61	2h 42m 47.9s
2	Kling	Mercedes	61	2h 42m 48.0s
3	Manzon	Ferrari	60	
4	Bira	Maserati	60	
5	Villoresi	Maserati	58	
6	Behra	Gordini	56	
r	Frere	Gordini	50	rear axle
r	Trintignant	Ferrari	35	piston
r	Rosier	Ferrari	27	engine
r	Marimon	Maserati	27	gearbox
r	Mieres	Maserati	24	piston
r	Wharton	Maserati	19	transmission
r	Schell	Maserati	19	fuel pump
r	Herrmann	Mercedes	16	engine
r	Salvadori	Maserati	14	transmission
r	Gonzalez,J.	Ferrari	12	engine
r	Macklin	HWM	9	engine
r	Berger,Georges	Gordini	8	valve
r	Hawthorn	Ferrari	8	engine
r	Pollet	Gordini	8	engine
r	Ascari	Maserati	0	engine

STARTING GRID:

1	Fangio	12	Manzon
2	Kling	13	Rosier
3	Ascari	14	Villoresi
4	Gonzalez,J.	15	Macklin
5	Marimon	16	Wharton
6	Bira	17	Behra
7	Herrmann	18	Pollet
8	Hawthorn	19	Frere
9	Trintignant	20	Berger,Georges
10	Salvadori	21	Schell
11	Mieres		

British

GRAND PRIX No: 37
DATE: July 17, 1954
VENUE: Silverstone
POLE LAP: Fangio, 1m 45.0s
FASTEST LAP: Ascari, Behra, Fangio, Gonzalez,J., Hawthorn, Marimon & Moss, 1m 50.0s

Pn	Driver	Car	Laps	Time/Reason
1	Gonzalez,J.	Ferrari	90	2h 56m 14.0s
2	Hawthorn	Ferrari	90	2h 57m 24.0s
3	Marimon	Maserati	89	
4	Fangio	Mercedes	89	
5	Trintignant	Ferrari	87	
6	Mieres	Maserati	87	
7	Kling	Mercedes	87	
8	Wharton	Maserati	86	
9	Pilette,A.	Gordini	86	
10	Gerard	Cooper-Bristol	85	
11	Beauman	Connaught	84	
12	Schell	Maserati	83	
13	Marr	Connaught	82	
r	Moss	Maserati	79	transmission
uc	Thorne	Connaught	78	
r	Whitehouse	Connaught	63	fuel system
r	Behra	Gordini	54	suspension
r	Salvadori	Maserati	53	gearbox
r	Bira (S)	Maserati	44	accident
uc	Gould	Cooper-Bristol	44	
r	Villoresi	Maserati	40	con rod
r	Riseley-Prichard	Connaught	40	accident
r	Parnell,R.	Ferrari	25	water jacket
r	Ascari	Maserati	20	valve
r	Bucci	Gordini	17	accident
r	Collins	Vanwall	16	head gasket
r	Manzon	Ferrari	15	engine
r	Whitehead,P.	Cooper-Alta	4	oil pipe
r	Rosier	Ferrari	2	engine
r	Brandon	Cooper-Bristol	2	
dns	Brown,A.	Cooper-Bristol		

STARTING GRID:

1	Fangio	6	Kling
2	Gonzalez,J.	7	Salvadori
3	Hawthorn	8	Trintignant
4	Moss	9	Wharton
5	Behra	10	Bira

+

German

GRAND PRIX No: 38
DATE: August 1, 1954
VENUE: Nurburgring
POLE LAP: Fangio, 9m 50.1s
FASTEST LAP: Kling, 9m 55.1s

Pn	Driver	Car	Laps	Time/Reason
1	Fangio	Mercedes	22	3h 45m 45.8s
2	Gonzalez,J. (S)	Ferrari	22	3h 47m 22.3s
3	Trintignant	Ferrari	22	3h 50m 54.4s
4	Kling	Mercedes	22	3h 51m 52.3s
5	Mantovani	Maserati	22	3h 54m 36.3s
6	Taruffi	Ferrari	21	
7	Schell	Maserati	21	
8	Rosier	Ferrari	21	
9	Manzon	Ferrari	20	
10	Behra	Gordini	20	
r	Bira	Maserati	18	steering
r	Lang	Mercedes	10	spun off
r	Bucci	Gordini	8	lost wheel
r	Helfrich	Klenk-Meteor	8	engine
r	Herrmann	Mercedes	7	fuel pipe
r	Frere	Gordini	4	lost wheel
r	Hawthorn	Ferrari	3	rear axle
r	Mieres	Maserati	2	fuel tank
r	Moss	Maserati	1	big end
r	Pilette,A.	Gordini	0	suspension
dns	Marimon	Maserati		fatal accident
dns	Villoresi	Maserati		withdrew
dns	Wharton	Maserati		withdrew

STARTING GRID:

1	Fangio	13	Taruffi
2	Hawthorn	14	Schell
3	Moss	15	Mantovani
4	Herrmann	16	Bucci
5	Gonzalez,J.	17	Mieres
6	Frere	18	Rosier
7	Trintignant	19	Bira
8	Marimon	20	Pilette,A.
9	Behra	21	Helfrich
10	Villoresi	22	Wharton
11	Lang	23	Kling
12	Manzon		

Swiss

GRAND PRIX No: 39
DATE: August 22, 1954
VENUE: Bremgarten
POLE LAP: Gonzalez,J., 2m 39.5s
FASTEST LAP: Fangio, 2m 39.7s

Pn	Driver	Car	Laps	Time/Reason
1	Fangio	Mercedes	66	3h 00m 34.5s
2	Gonzalez,J.	Ferrari	66	3h 01m 32.3s
3	Herrmann	Mercedes	65	
4	Mieres	Maserati	64	
5	Mantovani	Maserati	64	
6	Wharton	Maserati	64	
7	Maglioli	Ferrari	61	
8	Swaters	Ferrari	58	
r	Kling	Mercedes	38	fuel system
r	Trintignant	Ferrari	32	engine
r	Hawthorn	Ferrari	30	oil pump
r	Schell	Maserati	22	oil pump
r	Moss	Maserati	21	oil pump
r	Wacker	Gordini	9	transmission
r	Behra	Gordini	7	clutch
r	Bucci	Gordini	0	fuel pump

STARTING GRID:

1	Gonzalez,J.	9	Mantovani
2	Fangio	10	Bucci
3	Moss	11	Maglioli
4	Trintignant	12	Mieres
5	Kling	13	Schell
6	Hawthorn	14	Behra
7	Herrmann	15	Wacker
8	Wharton	16	Swaters

Italian

GRAND PRIX No: 40
DATE: September 5, 1954
VENUE: Monza
POLE LAP: Fangio, 1m 59.0s
FASTEST LAP: Gonzalez,J., 2m 00.8s

Pn	Driver	Car	Laps	Time/Reason
1	Fangio	Mercedes	80	2h 47m 47.9s
2	Hawthorn	Ferrari	79	
3	Maglioli (S)	Ferrari	78	
4	Herrmann	Mercedes	77	
5	Trintignant	Ferrari	75	
6	Wacker	Gordini	75	
7	Collins	Vanwall	75	
8	Rosier	Maserati	74	
9	Mantovani	Maserati	74	
10	Moss	Maserati	71	
11	Daponte	Maserati	70	
r	Ascari	Ferrari	48	valve
r	Villoresi	Maserati	42	clutch
r	Kling	Mercedes	36	accident
r	Mieres	Maserati	34	suspension
r	Musso	Maserati	32	transmission
r	Manzon	Ferrari	16	engine
r	Gonzalez,J.	Ferrari	16	gearbox
r	Bucci	Gordini	13	transmission
r	Behra	Gordini	2	engine

STARTING GRID:

1	Fangio	11	Trintignant
2	Ascari	12	Behra
3	Moss	13	Maglioli
4	Kling	14	Musso
5	Gonzalez,J.	15	Manzon
6	Villoresi	16	Collins
7	Hawthorn	17	Bucci
8	Herrmann	18	Wacker
9	Mantovani	19	Daponte
10	Mieres	20	Rosier

Spanish

GRAND PRIX No: 41
DATE: October 24, 1954
VENUE: Pedrables
POLE LAP: Ascari, 2m 19.10s
FASTEST LAP: Ascari, 2m 20.4s

Pn	Driver	Car	Laps	Time/Reason
1	Hawthorn	Ferrari	80	3h 13m 52.1s
2	Musso	Maserati	80	3h 15m 05.3s
3	Fangio	Mercedes	79	
4	Mieres	Maserati	79	
5	Kling	Mercedes	79	
6	Godia	Maserati	76	
7	Rosier	Maserati	74	
8	Wharton	Maserati	74	
9	Bira	Maserati	68	
r	Mantovani	Maserati	58	accident
r	de Graffenried (S)	Maserati	57	engine
r	Herrmann	Mercedes	50	fuel injection
r	Trintignant	Ferrari	47	gearbox
r	Pollet	Gordini	37	mechanical
r	Schell	Maserati	28	rear axle
r	Moss	Maserati	19	oil pump
r	Behra	Gordini	16	mechanical
r	Swaters	Ferrari	15	engine
r	Ascari	Lancia	9	clutch
r	Villoresi	Lancia	1	brakes
r	Manzon	Ferrari	1	engine

STARTING GRID:

1	Ascari	12	Kling
2	Fangio	13	Godia
3	Hawthorn	14	Wharton
4	Schell	15	Bira
5	Villoresi	16	Pollet
6	Moss	17	Manzon
7	Musso	18	Behra
8	Trintignant	19	Swaters
9	Herrmann	20	Rosier
10	Mantovani	21	de Graffenried
11	Mieres		

Argentine

GRAND PRIX No: 42
DATE: January 16, 1955
VENUE: Buenos Aires
POLE LAP: Gonzalez,J., 1m 43.1s
FASTEST LAP: Fangio, 1m 48.3s

Pn	Driver	Car	Laps	Time/Reason
1	Fangio	Mercedes	96	3h 00m 38.6s
2	Gonzalez,J. (S)	Ferrari	96	3h 02m 08.2s
3	Farina (2)	Ferrari	94	
4	Herrmann (S)	Mercedes	94	
5	Mieres	Maserati	91	
6	Schell (S)	Maserati	88	
7	Musso (S)	Maserati	83	
r	Bucci (S)	Maserati	54	fuel pressure
r	Mantovani (S)	Maserati	54	mechanical
r	Iglesias	Gordini	38	transmission
r	Trintignant	Ferrari	36	valve
r	Castellotti (S)	Lancia	35	accident
r	Moss	Mercedes	29	fuel vaporisation
r	Uria	Maserati	22	fuel pressure
r	Ascari	Lancia	21	accident
r	Bayol	Gordini	7	transmission
r	Villoresi	Lancia	1	fuel pipe
r	Behra	Maserati	1	accident
r	Kling	Mercedes	1	accident
r	Birger	Gordini	1	accident
r	Menditeguy	Maserati	1	accident

STARTING GRID:

1	Gonzalez,J.	12	Castellotti
2	Fangio	13	Menditeguy
3	Ascari	14	Trintignant
4	Behra	15	Bayol
5	Farina	16	Mieres
6	Kling	17	Iglesias
7	Schell	18	Musso
8	Moss	19	Mantovani
9	Birger	20	Bucci
10	Herrmann	21	Uria
11	Villoresi		

Monaco

GRAND PRIX No:	43
DATE:	May 22, 1955
VENUE:	Monte Carlo
POLE LAP:	Fangio, 1m 41.1s
FASTEST LAP:	Fangio, 1m 42.4s

Pn	Driver	Car	Laps	Time/Reason
1	Trintignant	Ferrari	100	2h 58m 09.7s
2	Castellotti	Lancia	100	2h 58m 30.0s
3	Behra (S)	Maserati	99	
4	Farina	Ferrari	99	
5	Villoresi	Lancia	99	
6	Chiron	Lancia	95	
7	Pollet	Gordini	91	
8	Perdisa (S)	Maserati	86	spun off
9	Taruffi (S)	Ferrari	86	
r	Moss	Mercedes	81	spun off
r	Ascari	Lancia	80	accident
r	Schell	Ferrari	67	engine
r	Mieres	Maserati	64	rear axle
r	Bayol	Gordini	63	rear axle
r	Fangio	Mercedes	49	transmission
r	Manzon	Gordini	38	gearbox
r	Simon	Mercedes	24	valve
r	Hawthorn	Vanwall	22	throttle linkage
r	Rosier	Maserati	8	fuel tank
r	Musso	Maserati	7	transmission

STARTING GRID:

1	Fangio	11	Perdisa
2	Ascari	12	Hawthorn
3	Moss	13	Manzon
4	Castellotti	14	Farina
5	Behra	15	Taruffi
6	Mieres	16	Bayol
7	Villoresi	17	Rosier
8	Musso	18	Schell
9	Trintignant	19	Chiron
10	Simon	20	Pollet

Indianapolis 500

GRAND PRIX No:	44
DATE:	May 30, 1955
VENUE:	Indianapolis
POLE LAP:	Hoyt, 1m 04.265s
FASTEST LAP:	Vukovich, 1m 03.670s

Pn	Driver	Car	Laps	Time/Reason
1	Sweikert	Kurtis Kraft	200	3h 53m 59.53s
2	Bettenhausen (S)	Kurtis Kraft	200	3h 56m 43.11s
3	Davies	Kurtis Kraft	200	3h 57m 31.89s
4	Thomson	Kuzma	200	3h 57m 38.44s
5	Faulkner (S)	Kurtis Kraft	200	3h 59m 16.66s
6	Linden	Kurtis Kraft	200	3h 59m 57.47s
7	Herman	Kurtis Kraft	200	
8	O'Connor	Kurtis Kraft	200	
9	Daywalt	Kurtis Kraft	200	
10	Flaherty	Kurtis Kraft	200	
11	Carter	Kuzma	197	
12	Weyant	Kurtis Kraft	196	
13	Johnson,E.	Trevis	196	
14	Rathmann,J.	Epperly	191	
r	Freeland	Phillips	178	transmission
r	Niday	Kurtis Kraft	170	accident
r	Cross	Kurtis Kraft	168	engine
r	Templeman	Trevis	142	transmission
r	Hanks	Kurtis Kraft	134	transmission
r	Andrews	Schroeder	120	fuel pump
r	Parsons	Kurtis Kraft	119	magneto
r	Russo,E.	Pawl	112	ignition
r	Crawford,R.	Kurtis Kraft	111	engine
r	Bryan	Kuzma	90	fuel pump
r	Vukovich	Kurtis Kraft	56	fatal accident
r	McGrath	Kurtis Kraft	54	magneto
r	Keller	Kurtis Kraft	54	accident
r	Ward	Kuzma	53	accident
r	Boyd	Kurtis Kraft	53	accident
r	Elisian	Kurtis Kraft	53	stalled
r	Hoyt	Stevens	40	oil leak
r	Agabashian	Kurtis Kraft	39	spun off
r	Reece	Pankratz	10	engine

STARTING GRID:

1	Hoyt	5	Vukovich
2	Bettenhausen	6	Hanks
3	McGrath	7	Faulkner
4	Agabashian	8	Linden

+

Belgian

GRAND PRIX No:	45
DATE:	June 5, 1955
VENUE:	Spa-Francorchamps
POLE LAP:	Castelotti, 4m 18.1s
FASTEST LAP:	Fangio, 4m 20.6s

Pn	Driver	Car	Laps	Time/Reason
1	Fangio	Mercedes	36	2h 39m 29.0s
2	Moss	Mercedes	36	2h 39m 37.1s
3	Farina	Ferrari	36	2h 41m 09.5s
4	Frere	Ferrari	36	2h 42m 54.5s
5	Mieres (S)	Maserati	35	
6	Trintignant	Ferrari	35	
7	Musso	Maserati	34	
8	Perdisa	Maserati	33	
9	Rosier	Maserati	33	
r	Kling	Mercedes	21	oil pipe
r	Castellotti	Lancia	16	gearbox
r	Hawthorn	Vanwall	8	gearbox
r	Behra	Maserati	3	accident
dns	Claes	Maserati		engine

STARTING GRID:

1	Castellotti	8	Frere
2	Fangio	9	Hawthorn
3	Moss	10	Trintignant
4	Farina	11	Perdisa
5	Behra	12	Rosier
6	Kling	13	Mieres
7	Musso	14	Claes

Dutch

GRAND PRIX No:	46
DATE:	June 19, 1955
VENUE:	Zandvoort
POLE LAP:	Fangio, 1m 40.0s
FASTEST LAP:	Mieres, 1m 40.9s

Pn	Driver	Car	Laps	Time/Reason
1	Fangio	Mercedes	100	2h 54m 23.8s
2	Moss	Mercedes	100	2h 54m 24.1s
3	Musso	Maserati	100	2h 55m 20.9s
4	Mieres	Maserati	99	
5	Castellotti	Ferrari	97	
6	Behra	Maserati	97	
7	Hawthorn	Ferrari	97	
8	da Silva Ramos	Gordini	92	
9	Rosier	Maserati	92	
10	Pollet	Gordini	90	
11	Claes	Ferrari	88	
r	Trintignant	Ferrari	64	gearbox
r	Manzon	Gordini	43	transmission
r	Gould	Maserati	23	accident
r	Kling	Mercedes	21	spun off
r	Walker,P.	Maserati	2	wheel bearing

STARTING GRID:

1	Fangio	9	Castellotti
2	Moss	10	Walker,P.
3	Kling	11	Manzon
4	Musso	12	Pollet
5	Hawthorn	13	Rosier
6	Behra	14	da Silva Ramos
7	Mieres	15	Gould
8	Trintignant	16	Claes

British

GRAND PRIX No:	47
DATE:	July 16, 1955
VENUE:	Aintree
POLE LAP:	Moss, 2m 00.4s
FASTEST LAP:	Moss, 2m 00.4s

Pn	Driver	Car	Laps	Time/Reason
1	Moss	Mercedes	90	3h 07m 21.2s
2	Fangio	Mercedes	90	3h 07m 21.3s
3	Kling	Mercedes	90	3h 08m 33.0s
4	Taruffi	Mercedes	89	
5	Musso	Maserati	89	
6	Hawthorn (6)	Ferrari	87	
7	Sparken	Gordini	81	
8	Macklin	Maserati	79	
9	Wharton (S)	Vanwall	72	
r	Trintignant	Ferrari	59	overheating
r	Mieres	Maserati	47	piston
r	Brabham,J.	Cooper-Bristol	30	valve
r	McAlpine	Connaught	30	oil pipe
r	Collins	Maserati	29	clutch
r	da Silva Ramos	Gordini	26	engine
r	Gould	Maserati	21	brakes
r	Salvadori	Maserati	19	gearbox
r	Rolt (S)	Connaught	18	throttle
r	Marr	Connaught	17	accident
r	Castellotti	Ferrari	16	transmission
r	Simon	Maserati	15	gearbox
r	Schell	Vanwall	13	accelerator
r	Behra	Maserati	9	oil pipe
r	Manzon	Gordini	4	transmission

STARTING GRID:

1	Moss	13	Trintignant
2	Fangio	14	Rolt
3	Behra	15	Wharton
4	Kling	16	Macklin
5	Taruffi	17	McAlpine
6	Mieres	18	da Silva Ramos
7	Schell	19	Marr
8	Simon	20	Salvadori
9	Musso	21	Gould
10	Castellotti	22	Sparken
11	Manzon	23	Collins
12	Hawthorn	24	Brabham,J.

Italian

GRAND PRIX No:	48
DATE:	September 1, 1955
VENUE:	Monza
POLE LAP:	Fangio, 2m 46.5s
FASTEST LAP:	Moss, 2m 46.9s

Pn	Driver	Car	Laps	Time/Reason
1	Fangio	Mercedes	50	2h 25m 04.4s
2	Taruffi	Mercedes	50	2h 25m 05.1s
3	Castellotti	Ferrari	50	2h 25m 50.6s
4	Behra	Maserati	50	2h 29m 01.0s
5	Menditeguy	Maserati	49	
6	Maglioli	Ferrari	49	
7	Mieres	Maserati	48	
8	Trintignant	Ferrari	47	
9	Fitch	Maserati	46	
r	Hawthorn	Ferrari	38	gearbox
r	Kling	Mercedes	32	gearbox
r	Musso	Maserati	31	gearbox
r	Gould	Maserati	31	sump
r	Moss	Mercedes	27	engine
r	Pollet	Gordini	26	engine
r	da Silva Ramos	Gordini	23	fuel pump
r	Collins	Maserati	22	suspension
r	Schell	Vanwall	7	de Dion tube
r	Lucas	Gordini	7	engine
r	Wharton	Vanwall	0	fuel injection
dns	Farina	Lancia		
dns	Villoresi	Lancia		

STARTING GRID:

1	Fangio	12	Maglioli
2	Moss	13	Schell
3	Kling	14	Hawthorn
4	Castellotti	15	Trintignant
5	Farina	16	Menditeguy
6	Behra	17	Wharton
7	Mieres	18	da Silva Ramos
8	Villoresi	19	Pollet
9	Taruffi	20	Fitch
10	Musso	21	Gould
11	Collins	22	Lucas

Argentine

GRAND PRIX No: 49
DATE: January 22, 1956
VENUE: Buenos Aires
POLE LAP: Fangio, 1m 42.5s
FASTEST LAP: Fangio, 1m 45.3s

Pn	Driver	Car	Laps	Time/Reason
1	Musso (S)	Lancia-Ferrari	98	3h 00m 03.7s
2	Behra	Maserati	98	3h 00m 28.1s
3	Hawthorn	Maserati	96	
4	Landi (S)	Maserati	92	
5	Gendebien	Lancia-Ferrari	91	
6	Uria (S)	Maserati	88	
r	Moss	Maserati	81	engine
r	Collins	Lancia-Ferrari	58	accident
r	Piotti	Maserati	57	accident
r	Menditeguy	Maserati	42	half- shaft
r	Castellotti	Lancia-Ferrari	40	gearbox
r	Gonzalez,J.	Maserati	24	valve
r	Fangio	Lancia-Ferrari	22	fuel pump

STARTING GRID:

1	Fangio	8	Hawthorn
2	Castellotti	9	Collins
3	Musso	10	Gendebien
4	Behra	11	Landi
5	Gonzalez,J.	12	Piotti
6	Menditeguy	13	Uria
7	Moss		

Monaco

GRAND PRIX No: 50
DATE: May 13, 1956
VENUE: Monte Carlo
POLE LAP: Fangio, 1m 44.0s
FASTEST LAP: Fangio, 1m 44.4s

Pn	Driver	Car	Laps	Time/Reason
1	Moss	Maserati	100	3h 00m 32.9s
2	Collins	Lancia-Ferrari	100	3h 00m 39.0s
3	Behra	Maserati	99	
4	Fangio (S)	Lancia-Ferrari	94	
5	da Silva Ramos	Gordini	93	
uc	Manzon	Gordini	90	transmission
6	Bayol (S)	Gordini	88	
7	Perdisa	Maserati	86	
8	Gould	Maserati	85	
r	Rosier	Maserati	72	engine
r	Castellotti	Lancia-Ferrari	14	clutch
r	Trintignant	Vanwall	10	overheating
r	Schell	Vanwall	1	accident
r	Musso	Lancia-Ferrari	1	accident
dns	Hawthorn	BRM		engine
dns	Brooks	BRM		engine

STARTING GRID:

1	Fangio	9	Collins
2	Moss	10	Hawthorn
3	Castellotti	11	Bayol
4	Behra	12	Manzon
5	Schell	13	Brooks
6	Trintignant	14	da Silva Ramos
7	Perdisa	15	Rosier
8	Musso	16	Gould

Indianapolis 500

GRAND PRIX No:	51
DATE:	May 30, 1956
VENUE:	Indianapolis
POLE LAP:	Flaherty, 1m 01.815s
FASTEST LAP:	Russo,P., 1m 02.320s

Pn	Driver	Car	Laps	Time/Reason
1	Flaherty	Watson	200	3h 53m 28.84s
2	Hanks	Kurtis Kraft	200	3h 53m 49.29s
3	Freeland	Phillips	200	3h 54m 59.07s
4	Parsons	Kuzma	200	3h 56m 54.48s
5	Rathmann,D.	Kurtis Kraft	200	3h 57m 50.65s
6	Sweikert	Kuzma	200	3h 59m 03.83s
7	Veith	Kurtis Kraft	200	
8	Ward	Kurtis Kraft	200	
9	Reece	Lesovsky	200	
10	Griffith	Stevens	199	
11	Hartley	Kuzma	196	
12	Agabashian	Kurtis Kraft	196	
13	Christie	Kurtis Kraft	196	
14	Keller	Kurtis Kraft	195	
15	Johnson,E.	Kuzma	195	
16	Garrett	Kuzma	194	
17	Dinsmore	Kurtis Kraft	191	
18	O'Connor	Kurtis Kraft	187	
19	Bryan	Kuzma	185	
r	Rathmann,J.	Kurtis Kraft	175	engine
r	Tolan	Kurtis Kraft	173	mechanical
r	Bettenhausen	Kurtis Kraft	160	accident
r	Elisian (23)	Kurtis Kraft	160	brakes
r	Daywalt	Kurtis Kraft	134	accident
r	Turner	Kurtis Kraft	131	mechanical
r	Andrews	Kurtis Kraft	94	transmission
r	Linden	Kurtis Kraft	90	oil leak
r	Herman	Kurtis Kraft	74	accident
r	Crawford,R.	Kurtis Kraft	49	accident
r	Boyd	Kurtis Kraft	35	oil leak
r	Ruttman	Kurtis Kraft	22	spun off
r	Thomson	Kuzma	22	spun off
r	Russo,P.	Kurtis Kraft	21	accident

STARTING GRID:

1	Flaherty	6	Parsons
2	Rathmann,J.	7	Agabashian
3	O'Connor	8	Russo,P.
4	Rathmann,D.	9	Linden
5	Bettenhausen	10	Sweikert +

11	Ruttman	23	Veith
12	Boyd	24	Turner
13	Hanks	25	Christie
14	Elisian	26	Freeland
15	Ward	27	Herman
16	Daywalt	28	Keller
17	Crawford,R.	29	Garrett
18	Thomson	30	Griffith
19	Bryan	31	Tolan
20	Andrews	32	Johnson,E.
21	Reece	33	Dinsmore
22	Hartley		

Belgian

GRAND PRIX No:	52
DATE:	June 3, 1956
VENUE:	Spa-Francorchamps
POLE LAP:	Fangio, 4m 09.8s
FASTEST LAP:	Moss, 4m 14.7s

Pn	Driver	Car	Laps	Time/Reason
1	Collins	Lancia-Ferrari	36	2h 40m 00.3s
2	Frere	Lancia-Ferrari	36	2h 41m 51.6s
3	Perdisa (S)	Maserati	36	2h 43m 16.9s
4	Schell	Vanwall	35	
5	Villoresi	Maserati	34	
6	Pilette,A.	Lancia-Ferrari	33	
7	Behra	Maserati	33	
8	Rosier	Maserati	33	
r	Fangio	Lancia-Ferrari	23	transmission
r	Trintignant	Vanwall	10	engine
r	Scotti	Connaught	10	oil pressure
r	Moss	Maserati	9	lost wheel
r	Castellotti	Lancia-Ferrari	9	transmission
r	Gould	Maserati	2	gearbox
r	Godia	Maserati	0	accident
dns	Hawthorn	Maserati		withdrew

STARTING GRID:

1	Fangio	9	Perdisa
2	Moss	10	Rosier
3	Collins	11	Villoresi
4	Behra	12	Scotti
5	Castellotti	13	Hawthorn
6	Schell	14	Godia
7	Trintignant	15	Gould
8	Frere	16	Pilette,A.

French

GRAND PRIX No: 53
DATE: July 1, 1956
VENUE: Reims
POLE LAP: Fangio, 2m 23.3s
FASTEST LAP: Fangio, 4m 25.8s

Pn	Driver	Car	Laps	Time/Reason
1	Collins	Lancia-Ferrari	61	2h 34m 23.4s
2	Castellotti	Lancia-Ferrari	61	2h 34m 23.7s
3	Behra	Maserati	61	2h 35m 53.3s
4	Fangio	Lancia-Ferrari	61	2h 35m 58.5s
5	Perdisa (S)	Maserati	59	
6	Rosier	Maserati	58	
7	Godia	Maserati	57	
8	da Silva Ramos	Gordini	57	
9	Manzon	Gordini	56	
10	Hawthorn (S)	Vanwall	56	
11	Pilette,A.	Gordini	55	
r	Simon	Maserati	45	mechanical
r	Taruffi	Maserati	38	mechanical
r	Gendebien	Lancia-Ferrari	37	clutch
r	Villoresi	Maserati	21	brakes
r	de Portago	Lancia-Ferrari	19	gearbox
r	Trintignant	Bugatti	17	throttle
r	Moss	Maserati	11	gear lever
r	Schell	Vanwall	5	engine
dns	Chapman	Vanwall		accident

STARTING GRID:

1	Fangio	11	Gendebien
2	Castellotti	12	Rosier
3	Collins	13	Perdisa
4	Schell	14	da Silva Ramos
5	Chapman	15	Manzon
6	Hawthorn	16	Taruffi
7	Behra	17	Godia
8	Moss	18	Trintignant
9	de Portago	19	Pilette,A.
10	Villoresi	20	Simon

British

GRAND PRIX No: 54
DATE: July 14, 1956
VENUE: Silverstone
POLE LAP: Moss, 1m 41.0s
FASTEST LAP: Moss, 1m 43.2s

Pn	Driver	Car	Laps	Time/Reason
1	Fangio	Lancia-Ferrari	101	2h 59m 47.0s
2	de Portago (S)	Lancia-Ferrari	100	
3	Behra	Maserati	99	
4	Fairman	Connaught	98	
5	Gould	Maserati	97	
6	Villoresi	Maserati	96	
7	Perdisa	Maserati	95	
8	Godia	Maserati	94	
9	Manzon	Gordini	94	
10	Moss	Maserati	93	rear axle
11	Castellotti (S)	Lancia-Ferrari	92	
12	Gerard	Cooper-Bristol	88	
r	Schell	Vanwall	86	fuel pipe
r	Titterington	Connaught	74	con rod
r	da Silva Ramos	Gordini	71	rear axle
r	Trintignant	Vanwall	69	fuel line
r	Collins	Lancia-Ferrari	63	oil pressure
r	Salvadori	Maserati	58	fuel system
r	Brooks	BRM	39	accident
r	Rosier	Maserati	23	magneto
r	Hawthorn	BRM	23	universal joint
r	Halford	Maserati	22	piston
r	Maglioli	Maserati	21	gearbox
r	Scott-Brown	Connaught	16	axle
r	Emery	Emeryson	12	ignition
r	Brabham,J.	Maserati	3	mechanical
r	Flockhart	BRM	1	engine
r	Gonzalez,J.	Vanwall	0	driveshaft

STARTING GRID:

1	Moss	10	Scott-Brown
2	Fangio	11	Titterington
3	Hawthorn	12	de Portago
4	Collins	13	Behra
5	Schell	14	Gould
6	Gonzalez,J.	15	Perdisa
7	Salvadori	16	Trintignant
8	Castellotti	17	Flockhart
9	Brooks	18	Manzon

+

German

GRAND PRIX No:	55
DATE:	August 5, 1956
VENUE:	Nurburgring
POLE LAP:	Fangio, 9m 51.2s
FASTEST LAP:	Fangio, 9m 41.6s

Pn	Driver	Car	Laps	Time/Reason
1	Fangio	Lancia-Ferrari	22	3h 38m 43.7s
2	Moss	Maserati	22	3h 39m 30.1s
3	Behra	Maserati	22	3h 46m 22.0s
4	Godia	Maserati	20	
dq	Halford	Maserati	20	push start
5	Rosier	Maserati	19	
uc	Volonterio	Maserati	16	
r	Milhoux	Gordini	15	engine
r	de Portago (S)	Lancia-Ferrari	14	accident
r	Villoresi	Maserati	13	engine
r	Schell	Maserati	12	overheating
r	Musso (S)	Lancia-Ferrari	12	accident
r	Collins	Lancia-Ferrari	8	fuel leak
r	Castellotti	Lancia-Ferrari	5	magneto
r	Maglioli	Maserati	3	steering
r	Gould	Maserati	3	oil pressure
r	Salvadori	Maserati	2	rear suspension
r	Manzon	Gordini	0	suspension
r	Scarlatti	Ferrari	0	mechanical
dns	Perdisa	Maserati		accident
dns	Pilette,A.	Gordini		accident

STARTING GRID:

1	Fangio	12	Schell
2	Collins	13	Gould
3	Castellotti	14	Rosier
4	Moss	15	Manzon
5	Musso	16	Godia
6	Perdisa	17	Scarlatti
7	Maglioli	18	Pilette,A.
8	Behra	19	Volonterio
9	Salvadori	20	Villoresi
10	de Portago	21	Milhoux
11	Halford		

Italian

GRAND PRIX No:	56
DATE:	September 2, 1956
VENUE:	Monza
POLE LAP:	Fangio, 2m 42.6s
FASTEST LAP:	Moss, 2m 45.5s

Pn	Driver	Car	Laps	Time/Reason
1	Moss	Maserati	50	2h 23m 41.3s
2	Collins (S)	Lancia-Ferrari	50	2h 23m 47.0s
3	Flockhart	Connaught	49	
4	Godia	Maserati	49	
5	Musso	Lancia-Ferrari	48	steering
6	Fairman	Connaught	47	
7	Piotti	Maserati	47	
8	de Graffenried	Maserati	46	
9	Fangio (S)	Lancia-Ferrari	46	
10	Simon	Gordini	45	
11	Gerini	Maserati	42	
r	Maglioli (S)	Maserati	42	steering
uc	Salvadori	Maserati	41	
r	Schell	Vanwall	31	transmission
r	Behra	Maserati	23	magneto
r	Halford	Maserati	15	engine
r	Trintignant	Vanwall	12	rear suspension
r	Taruffi	Vanwall	11	suspension
r	Castellotti	Lancia-Ferrari	8	puncture
r	Manzon	Gordini	6	gearbox
r	Villoresi (S)	Maserati	6	engine
r	de Portago	Lancia-Ferrari	5	puncture
r	Leston	Connaught	5	torsion bar
r	da Silva Ramos	Gordini	2	engine
dns	von Trips	Lancia-Ferrari		accident

STARTING GRID:

1	Fangio	14	Salvadori
2	Castellotti	15	Piotti
3	Musso	16	Fairman
4	Taruffi	17	Gerini
5	Behra	18	Godia
6	Moss	19	de Graffenried
7	Collins	20	Leston
8	Villoresi	21	da Silva Ramos
9	de Portago	22	Halford
10	Schell	23	Manzon
11	Trintignant	24	Flockhart
11	von Trips	25	Simon
13	Maglioli		

Argentine

GRAND PRIX No:	57
DATE:	January 13, 1957
VENUE:	Buenos Aires
POLE LAP:	Moss, 1m 42.6s
FASTEST LAP:	Moss, 1m 44.7s

Pn	Driver	Car	Laps	Time/Reason
1	Fangio	Maserati	100	3h 00m 55.9s
2	Behra	Maserati	100	3h 01m 14.2s
3	Menditeguy	Maserati	99	
4	Schell	Maserati	98	
5	Gonzalez,J. (S)	Lancia-Ferrari	98	
6	Perdisa (S)	Lancia-Ferrari	98	
7	Bonnier	Maserati	95	
8	Moss	Maserati	93	
9	de Tomaso	Ferrari	91	
10	Piotti	Maserati	90	
r	Castellotti	Lancia-Ferrari	75	hub shaft
r	Hawthorn	Lancia-Ferrari	34	clutch
r	Musso	Lancia-Ferrari	30	clutch
r	Collins	Lancia-Ferrari	26	clutch

STARTING GRID:

1	Moss	8	Menditeguy
2	Fangio	9	Schell
3	Behra	10	Gonzalez,J.
4	Castellotti	11	Perdisa
5	Collins	12	de Tomaso
6	Musso	13	Bonnier
7	Hawthorn	14	Piotti

Monaco

GRAND PRIX No:	58
DATE:	May 19, 1957
VENUE:	Monte Carlo
POLE LAP:	Fangio, 1m 42.7s
FASTEST LAP:	Fangio, 1m 45.6s

Pn	Driver	Car	Laps	Time/Reason
1	Fangio	Maserati	105	3h 10m 12.8s
2	Brooks	Vanwall	105	3h 10m 38.0s
3	Gregory	Maserati	103	
4	Lewis-Evans	Connaught	102	
5	Trintignant	Lancia-Ferrari	100	
6	Brabham,J.	Cooper-Climax	100	
r	von Trips (S)	Lancia-Ferrari	95	engine
r	Scarlatti (S)	Maserati	64	oil leak
r	Flockhart	BRM	59	timing gear
r	Menditeguy	Maserati	50	accident
r	Bueb	Connaught	46	fuel tank
r	Schell	Maserati	22	suspension
r	Gould	Maserati	9	accident
r	Hawthorn	Lancia-Ferrari	3	accident
r	Collins	Lancia-Ferrari	3	accident
r	Moss	Vanwall	3	accident

STARTING GRID:

1	Fangio	9	von Trips
2	Collins	10	Gregory
3	Moss	11	Flockhart
4	Brooks	12	Gould
5	Hawthorn	13	Lewis-Evans
6	Trintignant	14	Scarlatti
7	Menditeguy	15	Brabham,J.
8	Schell	16	Bueb

Indianapolis 500

GRAND PRIX No:	59
DATE:	May 30, 1957
VENUE:	Indianapolis
POLE LAP:	O'Connor, 1m 02.522s
FASTEST LAP:	Rathmann,J., 1m 02.750s

Pn	Driver	Car	Laps	Time/Reason
1	Hanks	Epperly	200	3h 41m 14.25s
2	Rathmann,J.	Epperly	200	3h 41m 35.71s
3	Bryan	Kuzma	200	3h 43m 28.25s
4	Russo,P.	Kurtis Kraft	200	3h 44m 11.10s
5	Linden	Kurtis Kraft	200	3h 44m 28.55s
6	Boyd	Kurtis Kraft	200	3h 45m 49.55s
7	Teague	Kurtis Kraft	200	
8	O'Connor	Kurtis Kraft	200	
9	Veith	Phillips	200	
10	Hartley	Lesovsky	200	
11	Turner	Kurtis Kraft	200	
12	Thomson	Kuzma	199	
13	Christie	Kurtis Kraft	197	
14	Weyant	Kuzma	196	
15	Bettenhausen	Kurtis Kraft	195	
16	Parsons	Kurtis Kraft	195	
17	Freeland	Kurtis Kraft	192	
r	Reece	Kurtis Kraft	182	throttle
r	Edmunds	Kurtis Kraft	170	spun off
r	Tolan	Kuzma	138	clutch
r	Herman	Dunn	111	accident
r	Agabashian	Kurtis Kraft	107	fuel leak
r	Sachs	Kuzma	105	fuel pump
r	Magill	Kurtis Kraft	101	accident
r	Johnson,E.	Kurtis Kraft	93	wheel bearing
r	Cheesbourg	Kurtis Kraft	81	fuel leak
r	Keller	Kurtis Kraft	75	accident
r	Daywalt	Kurtis Kraft	53	accident
r	Elisian	Kurtis Kraft	51	timing gear
r	Ward	Lesovsky	27	supercharger
r	Ruttman	Watson	13	engine
r	Russo,E.	Kurtis Kraft	0	accident
r	George	Kurtis Kraft	0	accident

STARTING GRID:

1 O'Connor
2 Sachs
3 Ruttman
4 Agabashian
5 Boyd
6 Reece
7 Elisian
8 Keller
9 George
10 Russo,P.
11 Thomson
12 Linden
13 Hanks
14 Hartley
15 Bryan
16 Veith
17 Parsons
18 Magill
19 Turner
20 Johnson,E.
21 Freeland
22 Bettenhausen
23 Cheesbourg
24 Ward
25 Weyant
26 Russo,E.
27 Edmunds
28 Teague
29 Daywalt
30 Herman
31 Tolan
32 Rathmann,J.
33 Christie

French

GRAND PRIX No:	60
DATE:	July 7, 1957
VENUE:	Rouen
POLE LAP:	Fangio, 2m 21.5s
FASTEST LAP:	Musso, 2m 22.5s

Pn	Driver	Car	Laps	Time/Reason
1	Fangio	Maserati	77	3h 07m 46.4s
2	Musso	Lancia-Ferrari	77	3h 08m 37.2s
3	Collins	Lancia-Ferrari	77	3h 09m 52.4s
4	Hawthorn	Lancia-Ferrari	76	
5	Schell	Maserati	70	
6	Behra	Maserati	69	
7	MacDowell,M.	Cooper-Climax	68	
r	Lewis-Evans	Vanwall	30	steering
r	Menditeguy	Maserati	30	engine
r	Salvadori	Vanwall	25	valve
r	MacKay-Fraser	BRM	24	transmission
r	Trintignant	Lancia-Ferrari	23	magneto
r	Gould	Maserati	4	rear axle
r	Brabham,J.	Cooper-Climax	4	accident
r	Flockhart	BRM	2	accident

STARTING GRID:

1 Fangio
2 Behra
3 Musso
4 Schell
5 Collins
6 Salvadori
7 Hawthorn
8 Trintignant
9 Menditeguy
10 Lewis-Evans
11 Flockhart
12 MacKay-Fraser
13 Brabham,J.
14 Gould
15 MacDowell,M.

British

GRAND PRIX No: 61
DATE: July 20, 1957
VENUE: Aintree
POLE LAP: Moss, 2m 00.2s
FASTEST LAP: Moss, 1m 59.2s

Pn	Driver	Car	Laps	Time/Reason
1	Brooks/Moss	Vanwall	90	3h 06m 37.8s
2	Musso	Lancia-Ferrari	90	3h 07m 03.4s
3	Hawthorn	Lancia-Ferrari	90	3h 07m 20.6s
4	Trintignant (S)	Lancia-Ferrari	88	
5	Salvadori	Cooper-Climax	85	
6	Gerard	Cooper-Bristol	82	
7	Lewis-Evans	Vanwall	82	
r	Brabham,J.	Cooper-Climax	74	clutch
uc	Bueb	Maserati	71	
r	Behra	Maserati	68	clutch
r	Collins	Lancia-Ferrari	52	radiator
r	Moss (S)	Vanwall	50	engine
r	Fangio	Maserati	48	engine
r	Fairman	BRM	47	engine
r	Leston	BRM	44	engine
r	Schell	Maserati	38	water pump
r	Menditeguy	Maserati	34	transmission
r	Bonnier	Maserati	17	transmission
dns	Gould	Maserati		accident

STARTING GRID:

1	Moss	11	Menditeguy
2	Behra	12	Leston
3	Brooks	13	Brabham,J.
4	Fangio	14	Gould
5	Hawthorn	15	Salvadori
6	Lewis-Evans	16	Fairman
7	Schell	17	Bonnier
8	Collins	18	Gerard
9	Trintignant	19	Bueb
10	Musso		

German

GRAND PRIX No: 62
DATE: August 4, 1957
VENUE: Nurburgring
POLE LAP: Fangio, 9m 25.6s
FASTEST LAP: Fangio, 9m 17.4s

Pn	Driver	Car	Laps	Time/Reason
1	Fangio	Maserati	22	3h 30m 38.3s
2	Hawthorn	Lancia-Ferrari	22	3h 30m 41.9s
3	Collins	Lancia-Ferrari	22	3h 31m 13.9s
4	Musso	Lancia-Ferrari	22	3h 34m 15.9s
5	Moss	Vanwall	22	3h 35m 15.8s
6	Behra	Maserati	22	3h 35m 16.8s
7	Schell	Maserati	22	3h 37m 25.8s
8	Gregory	Maserati	21	
9	Brooks	Vanwall	21	
10	Scarlatti	Maserati	21	
11	Halford	Maserati	21	
12	Barth	Porsche	21	
13	Naylor	Cooper-Climax	20	
14	de Beaufort	Porsche	20	
15	Marsh	Cooper-Climax	17	
r	Herrmann	Maserati	14	chassis
r	Maglioli	Porsche	13	engine
r	Godia	Maserati	11	steering
r	Salvadori	Cooper-Climax	11	suspension
r	Lewis-Evans	Vanwall	10	gearbox
r	Brabham,J.	Cooper-Climax	6	transmission
r	England	Cooper-Climax	4	distributor
r	Gibson	Cooper-Climax	3	steering
r	Gould	Maserati	2	rear axle

STARTING GRID:

1	Fangio	13	Scarlatti
2	Hawthorn	14	Salvadori
3	Behra	15	Maglioli
4	Collins	16	Halford
5	Brooks	17	Naylor
6	Schell	18	Brabham,J.
7	Moss	19	Gould
8	Musso	20	de Beaufort
9	Lewis-Evans	21	Godia
10	Gregory	22	Marsh
11	Herrmann	23	England
12	Barth	24	Gibson

Pescara

GRAND PRIX No:	63
DATE:	August 18, 1957
VENUE:	Pescara
POLE LAP:	Fangio, 9m 44.6s
FASTEST LAP:	Moss, 9m 44.6s

Pn	Driver	Car	Laps	Time/Reason
1	Moss	Vanwall	18	2h 59m 22.7s
2	Fangio	Maserati	18	3h 02m 36.6s
3	Schell	Maserati	18	3h 06m 09.5s
4	Gregory	Maserati	18	3h 07m 39.2s
5	Lewis-Evans	Vanwall	17	
6	Scarlatti	Maserati	17	
7	Brabham,J.	Cooper-Climax	15	
r	Halford	Cooper-Climax	10	transmission
r	Godia	Maserati	10	engine
r	Musso	Lancia-Ferrari	9	oil tank
r	Bonnier	Maserati	7	overheating
r	Salvadori	Cooper-Climax	3	accident
r	Behra	Maserati	3	oil pipe
r	Piotti	Maserati	0	engine
r	Gould	Maserati	0	accident
r	Brooks	Vanwall	0	engine

STARTING GRID:

1	Fangio	9	Bonnier
2	Moss	10	Scarlatti
3	Musso	11	Gould
4	Behra	12	Godia
5	Schell	13	Piotti
6	Brooks	14	Halford
7	Gregory	15	Salvadori
8	Lewis-Evans	16	Brabham,J.

Italian

GRAND PRIX No:	64
DATE:	September 8, 1957
VENUE:	Monza
POLE LAP:	Lewis-Evans, 1m 42.4s
FASTEST LAP:	Brooks, 1m 43.7s

Pn	Driver	Car	Laps	Time/Reason
1	Moss	Vanwall	87	2h 35m 03.9s
2	Fangio	Maserati	87	2h 35m 45.1s
3	von Trips	Lancia-Ferrari	85	
4	Gregory	Maserati	84	
5	Scarlatti (S)	Maserati	84	
6	Hawthorn	Lancia-Ferrari	83	
7	Brooks	Vanwall	82	
8	Musso	Lancia-Ferrari	82	
9	Godia	Maserati	81	
10	Gould	Maserati	78	
11	Simon (S)	Maserati	72	
r	Collins	Lancia-Ferrari	61	valve
r	Behra	Maserati	49	overheating
r	Lewis-Evans	Vanwall	48	engine
r	Halford	Maserati	46	engine
r	Schell	Maserati	33	oil pipe
r	Bonnier	Maserati	30	overheating
r	Piotti	Maserati	2	engine

STARTING GRID:

1	Lewis-Evans	10	Hawthorn
2	Moss	11	Gregory
3	Brooks	12	Scarlatti
4	Fangio	13	Bonnier
5	Behra	14	Halford
6	Schell	15	Godia
7	Collins	16	Simon
8	von Trips	17	Piotti
9	Musso	18	Gould

Argentine

GRAND PRIX No:	65
DATE:	January 19, 1958
VENUE:	Buenos Aires
POLE LAP:	Fangio, 1m 42.0s
FASTEST LAP:	Fangio, 1m 41.8s

Pn	Driver	Car	Laps	Time/Reason
1	Moss	Cooper-Climax	80	2h 19m 33.7s
2	Musso	Ferrari	80	2h 19m 36.4s
3	Hawthorn	Ferrari	80	2h 19m 46.3s
4	Fangio	Maserati	80	2h 20m 26.7s
5	Behra	Maserati	78	
6	Schell	Maserati	77	
7	Menditeguy	Maserati	76	
8	Godia	Maserati	75	
9	Gould	Maserati	71	
r	Collins	Ferrari	0	rear axle

STARTING GRID:

1	Fangio	6	Menditeguy
2	Hawthorn	7	Moss
3	Collins	8	Schell
4	Behra	9	Godia
5	Musso	10	Gould

Monaco

GRAND PRIX No:	66
DATE:	May 18, 1958
VENUE:	Monte Carlo
POLE LAP:	Brooks, 1m 39.8s
FASTEST LAP:	Hawthorn, 1m 40.6s

Pn	Driver	Car	Laps	Time/Reason
1	Trintignant	Cooper-Climax	100	2h 52m 27.9s
2	Musso	Ferrari	100	2h 52m 48.1s
3	Collins	Ferrari	100	2h 53m 06.7s
4	Brabham,J.	Cooper-Climax	97	
5	Schell	BRM	91	
r	von Trips	Ferrari	90	engine
6	Allison	Lotus-Climax	90	
r	Bonnier	Maserati	71	accident
r	Hill,G.	Lotus-Climax	69	engine
r	Salvadori	Cooper-Climax	55	gearbox
r	Hawthorn	Ferrari	46	fuel pump
r	Moss	Vanwall	37	engine
r	Behra	BRM	27	brakes
r	Scarlatti	Maserati	26	engine
r	Brooks	Vanwall	21	spark plugs
r	Lewis-Evans	Vanwall	11	steering

STARTING GRID:

1	Brooks	9	Collins
2	Behra	10	Musso
3	Brabham,J.	11	von Trips
4	Salvadori	12	Schell
5	Trintignant	13	Allison
6	Hawthorn	14	Scarlatti
7	Lewis-Evans	15	Hill,G.
8	Moss	16	Bonnier

Dutch

GRAND PRIX No:	67
DATE:	May 26, 1958
VENUE:	Zandvoort
POLE LAP:	Lewis-Evans, 1m 37.1s
FASTEST LAP:	Moss, 1m 38.5s

Pn	Driver	Car	Laps	Time/Reason
1	Moss	Vanwall	75	2h 04m 49.2s
2	Schell	BRM	75	2h 05m 37.1s
3	Behra	BRM	75	2h 06m 31.5s
4	Salvadori	Cooper-Climax	74	
5	Hawthorn	Ferrari	74	
6	Allison	Lotus-Climax	73	
7	Musso	Ferrari	73	
8	Brabham,J.	Cooper-Climax	73	
9	Trintignant	Cooper-Climax	72	
10	Bonnier	Maserati	71	
11	de Beaufort	Porsche	69	
r	Scarlatti	Maserati	51	rear axle
r	Lewis-Evans	Vanwall	45	valve
r	Hill,G.	Lotus-Climax	41	gasket
r	Collins	Ferrari	32	spun off
r	Gregory	Maserati	16	engine
r	Brooks	Vanwall	13	rear axle

STARTING GRID:

1	Lewis-Evans	10	Collins
2	Moss	11	Allison
3	Brooks	12	Musso
4	Behra	13	Hill,G.
5	Brabham,J.	14	Gregory
6	Hawthorn	15	Bonnier
7	Schell	16	Scarlatti
8	Trintignant	17	de Beaufort
9	Salvadori		

Indianapolis 500

GRAND PRIX No:	68
DATE:	May 30, 1958
VENUE:	Indianapolis
POLE LAP:	Rathmann,D., 1m 01.655s
FASTEST LAP:	Bettenhausen, 1m 02.370s

Pn	Driver	Car	Laps	Time/Reason
1	Bryan	Epperly	200	3h 44m 13.8s
2	Amick,G.	Epperly	200	3h 44m 41.45s
3	Boyd	Kurtis Kraft	200	3h 45m 23.75s
4	Bettenhausen	Epperly	200	3h 45m 45.60s
5	Rathmann,J.	Epperly	200	3h 45m 49.45s
6	Reece	Watson	200	3h 46m 30.75s
7	Freeland	Phillips	200	
8	Larson	Watson	200	
9	Johnson,E.	Kurtis Kraft	200	
10	Cheesbourg	Kurtis Kraft	200	
11	Keller	Kurtis Kraft	200	
12	Parsons	Kurtis Kraft	200	
13	Tolan	Kuzma	200	
r	Christie	Kurtis Kraft	189	spun off
r	Wilson,D.	Kuzma	151	fire
r	Foyt	Kuzma	148	spun off
r	Magill	Kurtis Kraft	136	red flagged
r	Russo,P.	Kurtis Kraft	122	throttle
r	Templeman	Kurtis Kraft	116	brakes
r	Ward	Lesovsky	93	magneto
r	Garrett	Kurtis Kraft	80	magneto
r	Sachs	Kuzma	68	transmission
r	Thomson	Kurtis Kraft	52	steering
r	Weyant	Dunn	38	accident
r	Turner	Lesovsky	21	fuel pump
r	Veith	Kurtis Kraft	1	accident
r	Rathmann,D.	Watson	0	accident
r	Elisian	Watson	0	accident
r	O'Connor	Kurtis Kraft	0	fatal accident
r	Goldsmith	Kurtis Kraft	0	accident
r	Unser,J.	Kurtis Kraft	0	accident
r	Sutton	Kurtis Kraft	0	accident
r	Bisch	Kuzma	0	accident

STARTING GRID:

1	Rathmann,D.	6	Parsons
2	Elisian	7	Bryan
3	Reece	8	Boyd
4	Veith	9	Bettenhausen
5	O'Connor	10	Turner +

Belgian

GRAND PRIX No:	69
DATE:	June 15, 1958
VENUE:	Spa-Francorchamps
POLE LAP:	Hawthorn, 3m 57.1s
FASTEST LAP:	Hawthorn, 3m 58.3s

Pn	Driver	Car	Laps	Time/Reason
1	Brooks	Vanwall	24	1h 37m 06.3s
2	Hawthorn	Ferrari	24	1h 37m 27.0s
3	Lewis-Evans	Vanwall	24	1h 40m 07.2s
4	Allison	Lotus-Climax	24	1h 41m 21.8s
5	Schell	BRM	23	
6	Gendebien	Ferrari	23	
7	Trintignant	Maserati	23	
8	Salvadori	Cooper-Climax	23	
9	Bonnier	Maserati	22	
10	de Filippis	Maserati	22	
r	Godia	Maserati	21	engine
r	Brabham,J.	Cooper-Climax	16	gasket
r	Hill,G.	Lotus-Climax	12	engine
r	Musso	Ferrari	5	accident
r	Behra	BRM	5	engine
r	Collins	Ferrari	5	overheating
r	Seidel	Maserati	3	engine
r	Gregory	Maserati	0	engine
r	Moss	Vanwall	0	valve
r	Kavanagh	Maserati		engine

STARTING GRID:

1	Hawthorn	11	Lewis-Evans
2	Musso	12	Allison
3	Moss	13	Salvadori
4	Collins	14	Bonnier
5	Brooks	15	Hill,G.
6	Gendebien	16	Trintignant
7	Schell	17	Seidel
8	Brabham,J.	18	Godia
9	Gregory	19	de Filippis
10	Behra	20	Kavanagh

French

GRAND PRIX No:	70
DATE:	July 6, 1958
VENUE:	Reims
POLE LAP:	Hawthorn, 2m 21.7s
FASTEST LAP:	Hawthorn, 2m 24.9s

Pn	Driver	Car	Laps	Time/Reason
1	Hawthorn	Ferrari	50	2h 03m 21.3s
2	Moss	Vanwall	50	2h 03m 45.9s
3	von Trips	Ferrari	50	2h 04m 21.0s
4	Fangio	Maserati	50	2h 05m 51.9s
5	Collins	Ferrari	50	2h 08m 46.2s
6	Brabham,J.	Cooper-Climax	49	
7	Hill,P.	Maserati	49	
8	Bonnier	Maserati	48	
9	Gerini	Maserati	47	
10	Ruttman	Maserati	45	
11	Behra	BRM	39	fuel pump
12	Schell	BRM	39	overheating
13	Lewis-Evans (S)	Vanwall	38	engine
uc	Salvadori	Cooper-Climax	37	
r	Godia	Maserati	28	accident
r	Trintignant	BRM	23	oil pipe
r	Brooks	Vanwall	15	gearbox
r	Hill,G.	Lotus-Climax	11	engine
r	Musso	Ferrari	9	fatal accident
r	Shelby	Maserati	8	engine
r	Allison	Lotus-Climax	6	engine

STARTING GRID:

1	Hawthorn	12	Brabham,J.
2	Musso	13	Hill,P.
3	Schell	14	Salvadori
4	Collins	15	Gerini
5	Brooks	16	Bonnier
6	Moss	17	Shelby
7	Trintignant	18	Ruttman
8	Fangio	19	Hill,G.
9	Behra	20	Allison
10	Lewis-Evans	21	von Trips
11	Godia		

British

GRAND PRIX No: 71
DATE: July 19, 1958
VENUE: Silverstone
POLE LAP: Moss, 1m 39.4s
FASTEST LAP: Hawthorn, 1m 40.8s

Pn	Driver	Car	Laps	Time/Reason
1	Collins	Ferrari	75	2h 09m 04.2s
2	Hawthorn	Ferrari	75	2h 09m 28.4s
3	Salvadori	Cooper-Climax	75	2h 09m 54.8s
4	Lewis-Evans	Vanwall	75	2h 09m 55.0s
5	Schell	BRM	75	2h 10m 19.0s
6	Brabham,J.	Cooper-Climax	75	2h 10m 27.4s
7	Brooks	Vanwall	74	
8	Trintignant	Cooper-Climax	73	
9	Shelby	Maserati	72	
r	von Trips	Ferrari	59	engine
r	Bonnier	Maserati	49	gearbox
r	Gerini	Maserati	43	gearbox
r	Burgess	Cooper-Climax	40	clutch
r	Moss	Vanwall	25	engine
r	Allison	Lotus-Climax	21	engine
r	Bueb	Connaught	19	gearbox
r	Behra	BRM	19	puncture
r	Stacey	Lotus-Climax	19	overheating
r	Hill,G.	Lotus-Climax	17	overheating
r	Fairman	Connaught	7	engine

STARTING GRID:

1	Moss	11	von Trips
2	Schell	12	Trintignant
3	Salvadori	13	Bonnier
4	Hawthorn	14	Hill,G.
5	Allison	15	Shelby
6	Collins	16	Burgess
7	Lewis-Evans	17	Bueb
8	Behra	18	Gerini
9	Brooks	19	Fairman
10	Brabham,J.	20	Stacey

German

GRAND PRIX No: 72
DATE: August 3, 1958
VENUE: Nurburgring
POLE LAP: Hawthorn, 9m 14.0s
FASTEST LAP: Moss, 9m 09.2s

Pn	Driver	Car	Laps	Time/Reason
1	Brooks	Vanwall	15	2h 21m 15.0s
2	Salvadori	Cooper-Climax	15	2h 24m 44.7s
3	Trintignant	Cooper-Climax	15	2h 26m 26.2s
4	von Trips	Ferrari	15	2h 27m 31.3s
5	McLaren	Cooper-Climax	15	2h 27m 41.3s
6	Barth	Porsche	15	2h 27m 47.4s
7	Burgess	Cooper-Climax	15	2h 28m 14.3s
8	Marsh	Cooper-Climax	15	2h 28m 24.9s
9	Hill,P.	Ferrari	15	2h 29m 00.5s
10	Allison	Lotus-Climax	13	
11	Bueb	Lotus-Climax	13	
r	Hawthorn	Ferrari	11	engine
r	Collins	Ferrari	10	fatal accident
r	Schell	BRM	8	brakes
r	Seidel	Cooper-Climax	8	suspension
r	Hill,G.	Lotus-Climax	4	oil pipe
r	Behra	BRM	3	suspension
r	Goethals	Cooper-Climax	3	fuel pump
r	Herrmann	Maserati	3	engine
r	Moss	Vanwall	3	magneto
r	de Beaufort	Porsche	3	mechanical
r	Gibson	Cooper-Climax	2	mechanical
r	Brabham,J.	Cooper-Climax	0	accident
r	Naylor	Cooper-Climax	0	fuel pump
r	Bonnier	Maserati	0	accident

STARTING GRID:

1	Hawthorn	14	Marsh
2	Brooks	15	de Beaufort
3	Moss	16	Bueb
4	Collins	17	Seidel
5	von Trips	18	Gibson
6	Salvadori	19	Brabham,J.
7	Trintignant	20	Herrmann
8	Schell	21	Bonnier
9	Behra	22	Hill,G.
10	Hill,P.	23	Goethals
11	Burgess	24	Allison
12	McLaren	25	Naylor
13	Barth		

Portuguese

GRAND PRIX No: 73
DATE: August 14, 1958
VENUE: Oporto
POLE LAP: Moss, 2m 34.21s
FASTEST LAP: Hawthorn, 2m 32.37s

Pn	Driver	Car	Laps	Time/Reason
1	Moss	Vanwall	50	2h 11m 27.8s
2	Hawthorn	Ferrari	50	2h 16m 40.6s
3	Lewis-Evans	Vanwall	49	
4	Behra	BRM	49	
5	von Trips	Ferrari	49	
6	Schell	BRM	49	
7	Brabham,J.	Cooper-Climax	48	
8	Trintignant	Cooper-Climax	48	
r	Shelby	Maserati	47	accident
9	Salvadori	Cooper-Climax	46	
r	Brooks	Vanwall	36	accident
r	Hill,G.	Lotus-Climax	25	accident
r	Allison	Maserati	15	mechanical
r	Bonnier	Maserati	9	driver ill
r	de Filippis	Maserati	6	mechanical

STARTING GRID:

1 Moss
2 Hawthorn
3 Lewis-Evans
4 Behra
5 Brooks
6 von Trips
7 Schell
8 Brabham,J.
9 Trintignant
10 Shelby
11 Salvadori
12 Hill,G.
13 Allison
14 Bonnier
15 de Filippis

Italian

GRAND PRIX No: 74
DATE: September 7, 1958
VENUE: Monza
POLE LAP: Moss, 1m 40.5s
FASTEST LAP: Hill,P., 1m 42.9s

Pn	Driver	Car	Laps	Time/Reason
1	Brooks	Vanwall	70	2h 03m 47.8s
2	Hawthorn	Ferrari	70	2h 04m 12.0s
3	Hill,P.	Ferrari	70	2h 04m 16.1s
4	Gregory (S)	Maserati	69	
5	Salvadori	Cooper-Climax	62	
6	Hill,G.	Lotus-Climax	62	
7	Allison	Lotus-Climax	61	
r	de Filippis	Maserati	57	con rod
r	Cabianca	Maserati	51	engine
r	Behra	BRM	42	brakes
r	Herrmann	Maserati	32	valve
r	Lewis-Evans	Vanwall	30	overheating
r	Trintignant	Cooper-Climax	24	gearbox
r	Moss	Vanwall	17	gearbox
r	Bonnier	BRM	14	fire
r	Gendebien	Ferrari	4	de Dion tube
r	Gerini	Maserati	2	mechanical
r	Shelby	Maserati	1	mechanical
r	Schell	BRM	0	accident
r	von Trips	Ferrari	0	accident
r	Brabham,J.	Cooper-Climax	0	accident

STARTING GRID:

1 Moss
2 Brooks
3 Hawthorn
4 Lewis-Evans
5 Gendebien
6 von Trips
7 Hill,P.
8 Behra
9 Schell
10 Bonnier
11 Gregory
12 Hill,G.
13 Trintignant
14 Salvadori
15 Brabham,J.
16 Allison
17 Shelby
18 Herrmann
19 Gerini
20 Cabianca
21 de Filippis

Moroccan

GRAND PRIX No: 75
DATE: October 19, 1958
VENUE: Casablanca
POLE LAP: Hawthorn, 2m 23.1s
FASTEST LAP: Moss, 2m 22.5s

Pn	Driver	Car	Laps	Time/Reason
1	Moss	Vanwall	53	2h 09m 15.0s
2	Hawthorn	Ferrari	53	2h 10m 39.8s
3	Hill,P.	Ferrari	53	2h 10m 40.6s
4	Bonnier	BRM	53	2h 11m 01.8s
5	Schell	BRM	53	2h 11m 48.8s
6	Gregory	Maserati	52	
7	Salvadori	Cooper-Climax	51	
8	Fairman	Cooper-Climax	50	
9	Herrmann	Maserati	50	
10	Allison	Lotus-Climax	49	
11	Brabham,J.	Cooper-Climax	49	
12	McLaren	Cooper-Climax	48	
13	Gerini	Maserati	48	
14	la Caze	Cooper-Climax	48	
15	Guelfi	Cooper-Climax	48	
16	Hill,G.	Lotus-Climax	45	
r	Lewis-Evans	Vanwall	41	fatal accident
r	Picard	Cooper-Climax	30	accident
r	Brooks	Vanwall	29	engine
r	Gendebien	Ferrari	29	accident
r	Bridger	Cooper-Climax	29	accident
r	Behra	BRM	26	engine
r	Seidel	Maserati	15	accident
r	Flockhart	BRM	15	camshaft
r	Trintignant	Cooper-Climax	9	engine

STARTING GRID:

1	Hawthorn	14	Salvadori
2	Moss	15	Flockhart
3	Lewis-Evans	16	Allison
4	Behra	17	Gerini
5	Hill,P.	18	Herrmann
6	Gendebien	19	Brabham,J.
7	Brooks	20	Seidel
8	Bonnier	21	McLaren
9	Trintignant	22	Bridger
10	Schell	23	la Caze
11	Fairman	24	Picard
12	Hill,G.	25	Guelfi
13	Gregory		

Monaco

GRAND PRIX No: 76
DATE: May 10, 1959
VENUE: Monte Carlo
POLE LAP: Moss, 1m 39.6s
FASTEST LAP: Brabham,J., 1m 40.4s

Pn	Driver	Car	Laps	Time/Reason
1	Brabham,J.	Cooper-Climax	100	2h 55m 51.3s
2	Brooks	Ferrari	100	2h 56m 11.7s
3	Trintignant	Cooper-Climax	98	
4	Hill,P.	Ferrari	97	
5	McLaren	Cooper-Climax	96	
r	Salvadori	Cooper-Maser.	83	transmission
r	Moss	Cooper-Climax	81	transmission
r	Flockhart	BRM	64	brakes
r	Schell	BRM	48	fuel tank
r	Bonnier	BRM	44	accident
r	Behra	Ferrari	24	engine
r	Hill,G.	Lotus-Climax	21	fire
r	Gregory	Cooper-Climax	6	transmission
r	Halford	Lotus-Climax	1	accident
r	Allison	Ferrari	1	accident
r	von Trips	Porsche	1	accident

STARTING GRID:

1	Moss	9	Schell
2	Behra	10	Flockhart
3	Brabham,J.	11	Gregory
4	Brooks	12	von Trips
5	Hill,P.	13	McLaren
6	Trintignant	14	Hill,G.
7	Bonnier	15	Allison
8	Salvadori	16	Halford

Indianapolis 500

GRAND PRIX No:	77
DATE:	May 30, 1959
VENUE:	Indianapolis
POLE LAP:	Thompson, 1m 01.683s
FASTEST LAP:	Thomson, 1m 01.890s

Pn	Driver	Car	Laps	Time/Reason
1	Ward	Watson	200	3h 40m 49.20s
2	Rathmann,J.	Watson	200	3h 41m 12.48s
3	Thomson	Lesovsky	200	3h 41m 39.85s
4	Bettenhausen	Epperly	200	3h 42m 36.25s
5	Goldsmith	Epperly	200	3h 42m 55.60s
6	Boyd	Epperly	200	3h 44m 06.23s
7	Carter	Kurtis Kraft	200	
8	Johnson,E.	Kurtis Kraft	200	
9	Russo,P.	Kurtis Kraft	200	
10	Foyt	Kuzma	200	
11	Hartley	Kuzma	200	
12	Veith	Moore	200	
13	Herman	Dunn	200	
14	Daywalt	Kurtis Kraft	200	
15	Arnold	Kurtis Kraft	200	
16	McWithey	Kurtis Kraft	200	
r	Sachs	Kuzma	182	spun off
r	Keller	Kuzma	163	engine
r	Flaherty	Watson	162	accident
r	Rathmann,D.	Watson	150	fire
r	Cheesbourg	Kuzma	147	magneto
r	Freeland	Kurtis Kraft	136	magneto
r	Crawford,R.	Elder	115	accident
r	Branson	Phillips	112	torsion bar
r	Christie	Kurtis Kraft	109	engine
r	Grim	Kurtis Kraft	85	magneto
r	Turner	Christensen	47	fuel tank
r	Weyant	Kurtis Kraft	45	accident
r	Larson	Kurtis Kraft	45	accident
r	Magill	Sutton	45	accident
r	Amick,R.	Kurtis Kraft	45	accident
r	Sutton	Lesovsky	34	accident
r	Bryan	Epperly	1	engine

STARTING GRID:

1 Thomson
2 Sachs
3 Rathmann,J.
4 Rathmann,D.
5 Grim
6 Ward
7 Veith
8 Johnson,E.
9 Hartley
10 Branson
11 Boyd
12 Carter
13 Daywalt
14 Turner
15 Bettenhausen
16 Goldsmith
17 Foyt
18 Flaherty
19 Larson
20 Bryan
21 Arnold
22 Sutton
23 Herman
24 Christie
25 Freeland
26 Amick,R.
27 Russo,P.
28 Keller
29 Weyant
30 Cheesbourg
31 Magill
32 Crawford,R.
33 McWithey

Dutch

GRAND PRIX No:	78
DATE:	May 31, 1959
VENUE:	Zandvoort
POLE LAP:	Bonnier, 1m 36.0s
FASTEST LAP:	Moss, 1m 36.6s

Pn	Driver	Car	Laps	Time/Reason
1	Bonnier	BRM	75	2h 05m 26.8s
2	Brabham,J.	Cooper-Climax	75	2h 05m 41.0s
3	Gregory	Cooper-Climax	75	2h 06m 49.8s
4	Ireland	Lotus-Climax	74	
5	Behra	Ferrari	74	
6	Hill,P.	Ferrari	73	
7	Hill,G.	Lotus-Climax	73	
8	Trintignant	Cooper-Climax	73	
9	Allison	Ferrari	71	
10	de Beaufort	Porsche	68	
r	Moss	Cooper-Climax	62	gearbox
r	Schell	BRM	46	engine
r	Brooks	Ferrari	42	oil leak
r	Shelby	Aston Martin	25	engine
r	Salvadori	Aston Martin	3	overheating

STARTING GRID:

1 Bonnier
2 Brabham,J.
3 Moss
4 Behra
5 Hill,G.
6 Schell
7 Gregory
8 Brooks
9 Ireland
10 Shelby
11 Trintignant
12 Hill,P.
13 Salvadori
14 de Beaufort
15 Allison

French

GRAND PRIX No: 79
DATE: July 5, 1959
VENUE: Reims
POLE LAP: Brooks, 2m 19.4s
FASTEST LAP: Moss, 2m 22.8s

Pn	Driver	Car	Laps	Time/Reason
1	Brooks	Ferrari	50	2h 01m 26.5s
2	Hill,P.	Ferrari	50	2h 01m 54.0s
3	Brabham,J.	Cooper-Climax	50	2h 03m 04.2s
4	Gendebien	Ferrari	50	2h 03m 14.0s
5	McLaren	Cooper-Climax	50	2h 03m 14.2s
6	Flockhart	BRM	50	2h 03m 32.2s
7	Schell	BRM	47	
dq	Moss	BRM	42	push start
8	Scarlatti	Maserati	41	
9	de Beaufort	Maserati	40	
10	d'Orey	Maserati	40	
uc	Trintignant	Cooper-Climax	36	
r	Behra	Ferrari	31	piston
r	Salvadori	Cooper-Maser.	20	piston
r	Gurney	Ferrari	19	radiator
r	Ireland	Lotus-Climax	13	wheel bearing
r	Burgess	Cooper-Maser.	13	engine
r	Gregory	Cooper-Climax	9	driver exhaustion
r	Hill,G.	Lotus-Climax	7	radiator
r	Davis	Cooper-Maser.	6	oil pipe
r	Bonnier	BRM	6	head gasket

STARTING GRID:

1 Brooks
2 Brabham,J.
3 Hill,P.
4 Moss
5 Behra
6 Bonnier
7 Gregory
8 Trintignant
9 Schell
10 McLaren
11 Gendebien
12 Gurney
13 Flockhart
14 Hill,G.
15 Ireland
16 Salvadori
17 Davis
18 d'Orey
19 Burgess
20 de Beaufort
21 Scarlatti

British

GRAND PRIX No: 80
DATE: July 18, 1959
VENUE: Aintree
POLE LAP: Brabham,J., 1m 58.0s
FASTEST LAP: Moss & McLaren, 1m 57.0s

Pn	Driver	Car	Laps	Time/Reason
1	Brabham,J.	Cooper-Climax	75	2h 30m 11.6s
2	Moss	BRM	75	2h 30m 33.8s
3	McLaren	Cooper-Climax	75	2h 30m 34.0s
4	Schell	BRM	74	
5	Trintignant	Cooper-Climax	74	
6	Salvadori	Aston Martin	74	
7	Gregory	Cooper-Climax	73	
8	Stacey	Lotus-Climax	71	
9	Hill,G.	Lotus-Climax	70	
10	Bristow	Cooper-Borg.	70	
11	Taylor,H.	Cooper-Climax	69	
12	Ashdown	Cooper-Climax	69	
13	Bueb	Cooper-Borg.	69	
r	Shelby	Aston Martin	68	magneto
r	d'Orey	Maserati	56	accident
r	Flockhart	BRM	53	spun off
r	Fairman	Cooper-Climax	37	gearbox
r	Bonnier	BRM	37	throttle
r	Burgess	Cooper-Maser.	31	gearbox
r	Herrmann	Cooper-Maser.	20	gearbox
r	Piper	Lotus-Climax	19	head gasket
r	Naylor	JBW-Maserati	17	transmission
r	Taylor,M.	Cooper-Climax	15	transmission
r	Brooks	Vanwall	12	misfiring

STARTING GRID:

1 Brabham,J.
2 Salvadori
3 Schell
4 Trintignant
5 Gregory
6 Shelby
7 Moss
8 McLaren
9 Hill,G.
10 Bonnier
11 Flockhart
12 Stacey
13 Burgess
14 Naylor
15 Fairman
16 Bristow
17 Brooks
18 Bueb
19 Herrmann
20 d'Orey
21 Taylor,H.
22 Piper
23 Ashdown
24 Taylor,M.

German

GRAND PRIX No: 81

DATE: August 2, 1959

VENUE: Berlin

POLE LAP: Brooks, 2m 05.9s

FASTEST LAP: Brooks, 2m 04.5s

Pn	Driver	Car	Laps	Time/Reason
1	Brooks	Ferrari	60	2h 09m 31.6s
2	Gurney	Ferrari	60	2h 10m 33.2s
3	Hill,P.	Ferrari	60	2h 10m 36.7s
4	Trintignant	Cooper-Climax	59	
5	Bonnier	BRM	58	
6	Burgess	Cooper-Maser.	56	
uc	Schell	BRM	49	pushed over line
r	McLaren	Cooper-Climax	36	clutch
r	Herrmann	BRM	36	accident
r	Gregory	Cooper-Climax	23	engine
r	Brabham,J.	Cooper-Climax	15	clutch
r	Hill,G.	Lotus-Climax	10	oil radiator
r	Ireland	Lotus-Climax	7	gearbox
r	Allison	Ferrari	2	clutch
r	Moss	Cooper-Climax	1	gearbox

STARTING GRID:

1	Brooks	9	McLaren
2	Moss	10	Hill,G.
3	Gurney	11	Herrmann
4	Brabham,J.	12	Trintignant
5	Gregory	13	Ireland
6	Hill,P.	14	Allison
7	Bonnier	15	Burgess
8	Schell		

Portuguese

GRAND PRIX No: 82

DATE: August 23, 1959

VENUE: Monsanto

POLE LAP: Moss, 2m 02.89s

FASTEST LAP: Moss, 2m 05.07s

Pn	Driver	Car	Laps	Time/Reason
1	Moss	Cooper-Climax	62	2h 11m 55.1s
2	Gregory	Cooper-Climax	62	2h 12m 01.6s
3	Gurney	Ferrari	61	
4	Trintignant	Cooper-Climax	60	
5	Schell	BRM	59	
6	Salvadori	Aston Martin	59	
7	Flockhart	BRM	59	
8	Shelby	Aston Martin	58	
9	Brooks	Ferrari	57	
10	Cabral	Cooper-Maser.	56	
r	McLaren	Cooper-Climax	38	transmission
r	Brabham,J.	Cooper-Climax	23	accident
r	Bonnier	BRM	10	engine
r	Hill,P.	Ferrari	5	accident
r	Hill,G.	Lotus-Climax	5	accident
r	Ireland	Lotus-Climax	3	gearbox

STARTING GRID:

1	Moss	9	Schell
2	Brabham,J.	10	Brooks
3	Gregory	11	Flockhart
4	Trintignant	12	Salvadori
5	Bonnier	13	Shelby
6	Gurney	14	Cabral
7	Hill,P.	15	Hill,G.
8	McLaren	16	Ireland

Italian

GRAND PRIX No: 83
DATE: September 13, 1959
VENUE: Monza
POLE LAP: Moss, 1m 39.7s
FASTEST LAP: Hill,P., 1m 40.4s

Pn	Driver	Car	Laps	Time/Reason
1	Moss	Cooper-Climax	72	2h 04m 05.4s
2	Hill,P.	Ferrari	72	2h 04m 52.1s
3	Brabham,J.	Cooper-Climax	72	2h 05m 17.9s
4	Gurney	Ferrari	72	2h 05m 25.0s
5	Allison	Ferrari	71	
6	Gendebien	Ferrari	70	
7	Schell	BRM	70	
8	Bonnier	BRM	70	
9	Trintignant	Cooper-Climax	70	
10	Shelby	Aston Martin	70	
11	Davis	Cooper-Maser.	68	
12	Scarlatti	Cooper-Climax	68	
13	Flockhart	BRM	67	
14	Burgess	Cooper-Maser.	67	
15	Cabianca	Maserati	64	
r	Salvadori	Aston Martin	44	engine
r	McLaren	Cooper-Climax	22	engine
r	Fairman	Cooper-Maser.	18	piston
r	Ireland	Lotus-Climax	14	brakes
r	Hill,G.	Lotus-Climax	1	engine
r	Brooks	Ferrari	0	piston

STARTING GRID:

1	Moss	12	Scarlatti
2	Brooks	13	Trintignant
3	Brabham,J.	14	Ireland
4	Gurney	15	Flockhart
5	Hill,P.	16	Burgess
6	Gendebien	17	Salvadori
7	Schell	18	Davis
8	Allison	19	Shelby
9	McLaren	20	Fairman
10	Hill,G.	21	Cabianca
11	Bonnier		

US

GRAND PRIX No: 84
DATE: December 12, 1959
VENUE: Sebring
POLE LAP: Moss, 3m 00.0s
FASTEST LAP: Trintignant, 3m 05.0s

Pn	Driver	Car	Laps	Time/Reason
1	McLaren	Cooper-Climax	42	2h 12m 35.7s
2	Trintignant	Cooper-Climax	42	2h 12m 36.3s
3	Brooks	Ferrari	42	2h 15m 36.6s
4	Brabham,J.	Cooper-Climax	42	2h 17m 33.0s
5	Ireland	Lotus-Climax	39	
6	von Trips	Ferrari	38	
7	Blanchard	Porsche	38	
r	Salvadori	Cooper-Maser.	23	transmission
r	Allison	Ferrari	23	clutch
r	Ward	Kurtis Kraft	20	clutch
r	de Tomaso	Cooper-Osca	13	brakes
r	Hill,P.	Ferrari	8	clutch
r	d'Orey	TM Maserati	6	oil leak
r	Schell	Cooper-Climax	5	clutch
r	Constantine	Cooper-Climax	5	head gasket
r	Moss	Cooper-Climax	4	gearbox
r	Stacey	Lotus-Climax	1	clutch
r	Said	Connaught	0	accident
dns	Cade	Maserati		engine

STARTING GRID:

1	Moss	11	Salvadori
2	Brabham,J.	12	Stacey
3	Schell	13	Said
4	Brooks	14	de Tomaso
5	Trintignant	15	Constantine
6	von Trips	16	Blanchard
7	Allison	17	d'Orey
8	Hill,P.	18	Cade
9	Ireland	19	Ward
10	McLaren		

Argentine

GRAND PRIX No:	85
DATE:	February 7, 1960
VENUE:	Buenos Aires
POLE LAP:	Moss, 1m 36.9s
FASTEST LAP:	Moss, 1m 38.9s

Pn	Driver	Car	Laps	Time/Reason
1	McLaren	Cooper-Climax	80	2h 17m 49.5s
2	Allison	Ferrari	80	2h 18m 15.8s
3	Trintignant (S)	Cooper-Climax	80	2h 18m 26.4s
4	Menditeguy	Cooper-Maser.	80	2h 18m 42.8s
5	von Trips	Ferrari	79	
6	Ireland	Lotus-Climax	79	
7	Bonnier	BRM	79	
8	Hill,P.	Ferrari	77	
9	Rod. Larreta	Lotus-Climax	77	
10	Gonzalez,J.	Ferrari	77	
11	Bonomi	Cooper-Maser.	76	
12	Gregory	Behra-Porsche	76	
13	Munaron	Maserati	72	
14	Estefano	Maserati	70	
r	Schell	Cooper-Climax	63	fuel pump
r	Brabham,J.	Cooper-Climax	42	gearbox
r	Moss	Cooper-Climax	40	suspension
r	Hill,G.	BRM	37	overheating
r	Stacey	Lotus-Climax	24	driver exhaustion
r	Chimeri	Maserati	23	driver exhaustion
r	Creus	Maserati	16	driver exhaustion
r	Scarlatti	Maserati	10	overheating

STARTING GRID:

1	Moss	12	Menditeguy
2	Ireland	13	McLaren
3	Hill,G.	14	Stacey
4	Bonnier	15	Rodriguez Larreta
5	von Trips	16	Gregory
6	Hill,P.	17	Bonomi
7	Allison	18	Scarlatti
8	Trintignant	19	Munaron
9	Schell	20	Estefano
10	Brabham,J.	21	Chimeri
11	Gonzalez,J.	22	Creus

Monaco

GRAND PRIX No:	86
DATE:	May 29, 1960
VENUE:	Monte Carlo
POLE LAP:	Moss, 1m 36.3s
FASTEST LAP:	McLaren, 1m 36.2s

Pn	Driver	Car	Laps	Time/Reason
1	Moss	Lotus-Climax	100	2h 53m 45.5s
2	McLaren	Cooper-Climax	100	2h 54m 37.6s
3	Hill,P.	Ferrari	100	2h 54m 47.4s
4	Brooks	Cooper-Climax	99	
5	Bonnier	BRM	83	
6	Ginther	Ferrari	70	
7	Hill,G.	BRM	66	accident
8	von Trips	Ferrari	61	clutch
9	Ireland	Lotus-Climax	56	engine
r	Gurney	BRM	44	suspension
dq	Brabham,J.	Cooper-Climax	40	push start
r	Salvadori	Cooper-Climax	29	overheating
r	Stacey	Lotus-Climax	23	engine
r	Surtees	Lotus-Climax	17	transmission
r	Bristow	Cooper-Climax	17	gearbox
r	Trintignant	Cooper-Maser.	4	gearbox

STARTING GRID:

1	Moss	9	Ginther
2	Brabham,J.	10	Hill,P.
3	Brooks	11	McLaren
4	Bristow	12	Salvadori
5	Bonnier	13	Stacey
6	Hill,G.	14	Gurney
7	Ireland	15	Surtees
8	von Trips	16	Trintignant

Indianapolis 500

GRAND PRIX No:	87
DATE:	May 30, 1960
VENUE:	Indianapolis
POLE LAP:	Sachs, 1m 01.395s
FASTEST LAP:	Rathmann,J., 1m 01.590s

Pn	Driver	Car	Laps	Time/Reason
1	Rathmann,J.	Watson	200	3h 36m 11.36s
2	Ward	Watson	200	3h 36m 24.11s
3	Goldsmith	Epperly	200	3h 39m 18.58s
4	Branson	Phillips	200	3h 39m 19.28s
5	Thomson	Lesovsky	200	3h 39m 22.65s
6	Johnson,E.	Trevis	200	3h 40m 21.88s
7	Ruby	Watson	200	
8	Veith	Meskowski	200	
9	Tinglestad	Trevis	200	
10	Christie	Kurtis Kraft	200	
11	Amick,R.	Epperly	200	
12	Carter	Kuzma	200	
13	Homeier	Kuzma	200	
14	Hartley	Kurtis Kraft	196	
15	Stevenson	Watson	196	
16	Grim	Meskowski	194	
17	Templeman	Kurtis Kraft	191	clutch
r	Hurtubuise	Christensen	185	engine
r	Bryan	Epperly	152	fuel pump
r	Ruttman	Watson	134	rear axle
r	Sachs	Ewing	132	magneto
r	Freeland	Kurtis Kraft	129	magneto
r	Bettenhausen	Watson	125	engine
r	Weiler	Epperly	103	accident
r	Foyt	Kurtis Kraft	90	clutch
r	Russo,E.	Kurtis Kraft	84	accident
r	Boyd	Epperly	77	engine
r	Force	Kurtis Kraft	74	brakes
r	McWithey	Epperly	60	brakes
r	Sutton	Watson	47	engine
r	Rathmann,D.	Watson	42	brakes
r	Herman	Ewing	34	clutch
r	Wilson,D.	Kurtis Kraft	11	magneto

STARTING GRID:

1	Sachs	6	Ruttman
2	Rathmann,J.	7	Johnson,E.
3	Ward	8	Branson
4	Rathmann,D.	9	Stevenson
5	Sutton	10	Bryan

+

Dutch

GRAND PRIX No:	88
DATE:	June 6, 1960
VENUE:	Zandvoort
POLE LAP:	Moss, 1m 33.2s
FASTEST LAP:	Moss, 1m 33.8s

Pn	Driver	Car	Laps	Time/Reason
1	Brabham,J.	Cooper-Climax	75	2h 01m 47.2s
2	Ireland	Lotus-Climax	75	2h 02m 11.2s
3	Hill,G.	BRM	75	2h 02m 43.8s
4	Moss	Lotus-Climax	75	2h 02m 44.9s
5	von Trips	Ferrari	74	
6	Ginther	Ferrari	74	
7	Taylor,H.	Cooper-Climax	70	
8	de Beaufort	Cooper-Climax	69	
r	Stacey	Lotus-Climax	57	transmission
r	Hill,P.	Ferrari	54	engine
r	Bonnier	BRM	54	engine
r	Clark	Lotus-Climax	42	transmission
r	Trintignant	Cooper-Maser.	39	gearbox
r	Gurney	BRM	11	brakes
r	Bristow	Cooper-Climax	9	engine
r	McLaren	Cooper-Climax	8	universal joint
r	Brooks	Cooper-Climax	4	gearbox
dns	Gregory	Cooper-Maser.		dispute
dns	Daigh	Scarab		dispute
dns	Salvadori	Aston Martin		dispute
dns	Reventlow	Scarab		dispute

STARTING GRID:

1	Moss	12	Ginther
2	Brabham,J.	13	Hill,P.
3	Ireland	14	Taylor,H.
4	Bonnier	15	von Trips
5	Hill,G.	16	Gregory
6	Gurney	17	Trintignant
7	Bristow	18	de Beaufort
8	Stacey	19	Daigh
9	McLaren	20	Salvadori
10	Brooks	21	Reventlow
11	Clark		

Belgian

GRAND PRIX No:	89
DATE:	June 19, 1960
VENUE:	Spa-Francorchamps
POLE LAP:	Brabham,J., 3m 50.0s
FASTEST LAP:	Brabham,J., Hill,P. & Ireland, 3m 51.9s

Pn	Driver	Car	Laps	Time/Reason
1	Brabham,J.	Cooper-Climax	36	2h 21m 37.3s
2	McLaren	Cooper-Climax	36	2h 22m 40.6s
3	Gendebien	Cooper-Climax	35	
4	Hill,P.	Ferrari	35	
uc	Hill,G.	BRM	35	engine
5	Clark	Lotus-Climax	34	
6	Bianchi	Cooper-Climax	28	
r	Stacey	Lotus-Climax	24	fatal accident
r	Mairesse,W.	Ferrari	23	transmission
r	von Trips	Ferrari	22	transmission
r	Bristow	Cooper-Climax	19	fatal accident
r	Daigh	Scarab	16	engine
r	Bonnier	BRM	14	engine
r	Ireland	Lotus-Climax	13	accident
r	Gurney	BRM	4	engine
r	Brooks	Cooper-Climax	2	gearbox
r	Reventlow	Scarab	1	engine
dns	Moss	Lotus-Climax		injured

STARTING GRID:

1	Brabham,J.	10	Clark
2	Brooks	11	von Trips
3	Moss	12	Gurney
4	Hill,P.	13	Mairesse,W.
5	Gendebien	14	McLaren
6	Hill,G.	15	Bianchi
7	Bonnier	16	Reventlow
8	Ireland	17	Stacey
9	Bristow	18	Daigh

French

GRAND PRIX No:	90
DATE:	July 3, 1960
VENUE:	Reims
POLE LAP:	Brabham,J., 2m 16.8s
FASTEST LAP:	Brabham,J., 2m 17.5s

Pn	Driver	Car	Laps	Time/Reason
1	Brabham,J.	Cooper-Climax	50	1h 57m 24.9s
2	Gendebien	Cooper-Climax	50	1h 58m 13.2s
3	McLaren	Cooper-Climax	50	1h 58m 16.8s
4	Taylor,H.	Cooper-Climax	49	
5	Clark	Lotus-Climax	49	
6	Flockhart	Lotus-Climax	49	
7	Ireland	Lotus-Climax	43	
8	Halford	Cooper-Climax	40	engine
9	Gregory	Cooper-Maser.	37	
10	Burgess	Cooper-Maser.	36	
r	von Trips	Ferrari	31	transmission
r	Hill,P.	Ferrari	29	transmission
r	Bonnier	BRM	22	engine
r	Bianchi	Cooper-Climax	18	transmission
r	Gurney	BRM	17	engine
r	Munaron	Cooper-Ferrari	15	transmission
r	Mairesse,W.	Ferrari	14	transmission
r	Brooks	Vanwall	7	vibration
r	Trintignant	Cooper-Maser.	0	accident
r	Hill,G.	BRM	0	accident
dns	Ginther	Scarab		engine

STARTING GRID:

1	Brabham,J.	12	Clark
2	Hill,P.	13	Taylor,H.
3	Hill,G.	14	Brooks
4	Ireland	15	Bianchi
5	Mairesse,W.	16	Halford
6	von Trips	17	Gregory
7	Gurney	18	Trintignant
8	Flockhart	19	Munaron
9	McLaren	20	Ginther
10	Bonnier	21	Burgess
11	Gendebien		

British

GRAND PRIX No: 91
DATE: July 16, 1960
VENUE: Silverstone
POLE LAP: Brabham,J., 1m 34.6s
FASTEST LAP: Hill,G., 1m 34.4s

Pn	Driver	Car	Laps	Time/Reason
1	Brabham,J.	Cooper-Climax	77	2h 04m 24.6s
2	Surtees	Lotus-Climax	77	2h 05m 14.2s
3	Ireland	Lotus-Climax	77	2h 05m 54.2s
4	McLaren	Cooper-Climax	76	
5	Brooks	Cooper-Climax	76	
6	von Trips	Ferrari	75	
7	Hill,P.	Ferrari	75	
8	Taylor,H.	Cooper-Climax	74	
9	Gendebien	Cooper-Climax	74	
10	Gurney	BRM	74	
11	Trintignant	Aston Martin	72	
12	Piper	Lotus-Climax	72	
13	Naylor	JBW-Maserati	72	
14	Hill,G.	BRM	71	accident
15	Gregory	Cooper-Maser.	71	
16	Munaron	Cooper-Ferrari	68	
17	Clark	Lotus-Climax	68	
r	Bianchi	Cooper-Climax	60	magneto
r	Bonnier	BRM	59	suspension
r	Daigh	Cooper-Climax	56	overheating
r	Burgess	Cooper-Maser.	56	engine
r	Fairman (S)	Cooper-Climax	44	fuel pump
r	Salvadori	Aston Martin	44	steering
r	Greene	Cooper-Maser.	12	overheating

STARTING GRID:

1	Brabham,J.	13	Salvadori
2	Hill,G.	14	Gregory
3	McLaren	15	Fairman
4	Bonnier	16	Taylor,H.
5	Ireland	17	Bianchi
6	Gurney	18	Naylor
7	von Trips	19	Daigh
8	Clark	20	Burgess
9	Brooks	21	Trintignant
10	Hill,P.	22	Greene
11	Surtees	23	Piper
12	Gendebien	24	Munaron

Portuguese

GRAND PRIX No: 92
DATE: August 14, 1960
VENUE: Oporto
POLE LAP: Surtees, 2m 25.56s
FASTEST LAP: Surtees, 2m 27.53s

Pn	Driver	Car	Laps	Time/Reason
1	Brabham,J.	Cooper-Climax	55	2h 19m 00.03s
2	McLaren	Cooper-Climax	55	2h 19m 58.00s
3	Clark	Lotus-Climax	55	2h 20m 53.26s
4	von Trips	Ferrari	55	2h 20m 58.84s
dq	Moss	Lotus-Climax	50	drove in wrong direction
5	Brooks	Cooper-Climax	49	
6	Ireland	Lotus-Climax	48	
7	Gendebien	Cooper-Climax	46	
r	Cabral	Cooper-Maser.	37	gearbox
r	Surtees	Lotus-Climax	36	radiator
r	Hill,P.	Ferrari	29	accident
r	Gurney	BRM	24	engine
r	Gregory	Cooper-Maser.	21	gearbox
r	Hill,G.	BRM	8	gearbox
r	Bonnier	BRM	6	engine

STARTING GRID:

1	Surtees	9	von Trips
2	Gurney	10	Hill,P.
3	Brabham,J.	11	Gregory
4	Moss	12	Brooks
5	Hill,G.	13	Bonnier
6	McLaren	14	Gendebien
7	Ireland	15	Cabral
8	Clark		

Italian

GRAND PRIX No:	93
DATE:	September 4, 1960
VENUE:	Monza
POLE LAP:	Hill,P., 2m 41.4s
FASTEST LAP:	Hill,P., 2m 43.6s

Pn	Driver	Car	Laps	Time/Reason
1	Hill,P.	Ferrari	50	2h 21m 09.2s
2	Ginther	Ferrari	50	2h 23m 36.8s
3	Mairesse,W.	Ferrari	49	
4	Cabianca	Cooper-Ferrari	48	
5	von Trips	Ferrari	48	(F2 car)
6	Herrmann	Porsche	47	(F2 car)
7	Barth	Porsche	47	(F2 car)
8	Drogo	Cooper-Climax	45	(F2 car)
9	Seidel	Cooper-Climax	44	
10	Gamble	Behra-Porsche	41	(F2 car)
r	Naylor	JBW-Maserati	41	gearbox
r	Thiele	Cooper-Maser.	32	gearbox
r	Munaron	Cooper-Ferrari	27	oil pipe
r	Scarlatti	Cooper-Maser.	26	throttle
r	Wilson,V.	Cooper-Climax	23	sump (F2 car)
r	Owen	Cooper-Climax	1	accident

STARTING GRID:

1 Hill,P.
2 Ginther
3 Mairesse,W.
4 Cabianca
5 Scarlatti
6 von Trips
7 Naylor
8 Munaron
9 Thiele
10 Herrmann
11 Owen
12 Barth
13 Seidel
14 Gamble
15 Drogo
16 Wilson,V.

US

GRAND PRIX No:	94
DATE:	November 20, 1960
VENUE:	Riverside
POLE LAP:	Moss, 1m 54.4s
FASTEST LAP:	Brabham,J., 1m 56.2s

Pn	Driver	Car	Laps	Time/Reason
1	Moss	Lotus-Climax	75	2h 28m 52.2s
2	Ireland	Lotus-Climax	75	2h 29m 30.2s
3	McLaren	Cooper-Climax	75	2h 30m 14.2s
4	Brabham,J.	Cooper-Climax	74	
5	Bonnier	BRM	74	
6	Hill,P.	Cooper-Climax	74	
7	Hall	Lotus-Climax	73	
8	Salvadori	Cooper-Climax	73	
9	von Trips	Cooper-Maser.	72	
10	Daigh	Scarab	70	
11	Lovely	Cooper-Ferrari	69	
12	Gendebien (S)	Cooper-Climax	69	
13	Drake	Maserati	68	
14	Taylor,H.	Cooper-Climax	68	
15	Trintignant	Cooper-Maser.	66	
16	Clark	Lotus-Climax	61	
r	Hill,G.	BRM	34	gearbox
r	Burgess	Cooper-Maser.	29	ignition
r	Naylor	JBW-Maserati	20	engine
r	Gurney	BRM	18	overheating
r	Flockhart	Cooper-Climax	11	transmission
r	Brooks	Cooper-Climax	6	spun off
r	Surtees	Lotus-Climax	4	accident

STARTING GRID:

1 Moss
2 Brabham,J.
3 Gurney
4 Bonnier
5 Clark
6 Surtees
7 Ireland
8 Gendebien
9 Brooks
10 McLaren
11 Hill,G.
12 Hall
13 Hill,P.
14 Taylor,H.
15 Salvadori
16 von Trips
17 Naylor
18 Daigh
19 Trintignant
20 Lovely
21 Flockhart
22 Drake
23 Burgess

Monaco

GRAND PRIX No:	95
DATE:	May 14, 1961
VENUE:	Monte Carlo
POLE LAP:	Moss, 1m 39.1s
FASTEST LAP:	Ginther & Moss, 1m 36.3s

Pn	Driver	Car	Laps	Time/Reason
1	Moss	Lotus-Climax	100	2h 45m 50.1s
2	Ginther	Ferrari	100	2h 45m 53.7s
3	Hill,P.	Ferrari	100	2h 46m 31.4s
4	von Trips	Ferrari	98	accident
5	Gurney	Porsche	98	
6	McLaren	Cooper-Climax	95	
7	Trintignant	Cooper-Maser.	95	
8	Allison	Lotus-Climax	93	
9	Herrmann	Porsche	91	
10	Clark	Lotus-Climax	89	
r	Surtees	Cooper-Climax	68	fuel pump
r	Bonnier	Porsche	59	fuel pump
r	Brooks	BRM-Climax	54	engine
r	May	Lotus-Climax	41	gearbox
r	Brabham,J.	Cooper-Climax	38	engine
r	Hill,G.	BRM-Climax	11	fuel pump
dns	Ireland	Lotus-Climax		injured

STARTING GRID:

1 Moss
2 Ginther
3 Clark
4 Hill,G.
5 Hill,P.
6 von Trips
7 McLaren
8 Brooks
9 Bonnier
10 Ireland
11 Gurney
12 Surtees
13 Herrmann
14 May
15 Allison
16 Trintignant
17 Brabham,J.

Dutch

GRAND PRIX No:	96
DATE:	May 22, 1961
VENUE:	Zandvoort
POLE LAP:	Hill,P., 1m 35.7s
FASTEST LAP:	Clark, 1m 35.5s

Pn	Driver	Car	Laps	Time/Reason
1	von Trips	Ferrari	75	2h 01m 52.1s
2	Hill,P.	Ferrari	75	2h 01m 53.0s
3	Clark	Lotus-Climax	75	2h 02m 05.2s
4	Moss	Lotus-Climax	75	2h 02m 14.3s
5	Ginther	Ferrari	75	2h 02m 14.4s
6	Brabham,J.	Cooper-Climax	75	2h 03m 12.2s
7	Surtees	Cooper-Climax	75	2h 03m 18.8s
8	Hill,G.	BRM-Climax	75	2h 03m 21.9s
9	Brooks	BRM-Climax	74	
10	Gurney	Porsche	74	
11	Bonnier	Porsche	73	
12	McLaren	Cooper-Climax	73	
13	Taylor,T.	Lotus-Climax	73	
14	de Beaufort	Porsche	72	
15	Herrmann	Porsche	72	

STARTING GRID:

1 Hill,P.
2 von Trips
3 Ginther
4 Moss
5 Hill,G.
6 Gurney
7 Brabham,J.
8 Brooks
9 Surtees
10 Clark
11 Bonnier
12 Herrmann
13 McLaren
14 Taylor,T.
15 de Beaufort

Belgian

GRAND PRIX No: 97
DATE: June 18, 1961
VENUE: Spa-Francorchamps
POLE LAP: Hill,P., 3m 59.3s
FASTEST LAP: Ginther, 3m 59.8s

Pn	Driver	Car	Laps	Time/Reason
1	Hill,P.	Ferrari	30	2h 03m 03.8s
2	von Trips	Ferrari	30	2h 03m 04.5s
3	Ginther	Ferrari	30	2h 03m 23.3s
4	Gendebien	Ferrari	30	2h 03m 49.4s
5	Surtees	Cooper-Climax	30	2h 04m 30.6s
6	Gurney	Porsche	30	2h 04m 34.8s
7	Bonnier	Porsche	30	2h 05m 50.9s
8	Moss	Lotus-Climax	30	2h 06m 59.4s
9	Lewis	Cooper-Climax	29	
10	Gregory	Cooper-Climax	29	
11	de Beaufort	Porsche	28	
12	Clark	Lotus-Climax	24	
13	Brooks	BRM-Climax	24	
r	Hill,G.	BRM-Climax	23	oil leak
r	Trintignant	Cooper-Maser.	22	transmission
r	Bandini	Cooper-Maser.	19	oil pressure
r	Brabham,J.	Cooper-Climax	11	engine
r	Bianchi	Lotus-Climax	9	oil pipe
r	Ireland	Lotus-Climax	9	engine
r	McLaren	Cooper-Climax	8	fuel system
r	Mairesse,W.	Lotus-Climax	7	engine

STARTING GRID:

1	Hill,P.	12	Gregory
2	von Trips	13	Lewis
3	Gendebien	14	de Beaufort
4	Surtees	15	McLaren
5	Ginther	16	Clark
6	Hill,G.	17	Bandini
7	Brooks	18	Ireland
8	Moss	19	Mairesse,W.
9	Bonnier	20	Trintignant
10	Gurney	21	Bianchi
11	Brabham,J.		

French

GRAND PRIX No: 98
DATE: July 2, 1961
VENUE: Reims
POLE LAP: Hill,P., 2m 24.9s
FASTEST LAP: Hill,P., 2m 27.1s

Pn	Driver	Car	Laps	Time/Reason
1	Baghelti	Ferrari	52	2h 14m 17.5s
2	Gurney	Porsche	52	2h 14m 17.6s
3	Clark	Lotus-Climax	52	2h 15m 18.6s
4	Ireland	Lotus-Climax	52	2h 15m 27.8s
5	McLaren	Cooper-Climax	52	2h 15m 59.3s
6	Hill,G.	BRM-Climax	52	2h 15m 59.4s
7	Bonnier	Porsche	52	2h 17m 32.9s
8	Salvadori	Cooper-Climax	51	
9	Hill,P.	Ferrari	50	
10	Taylor,H.	Lotus-Climax	49	
11	May	Lotus-Climax	48	
12	Gregory	Cooper-Climax	43	
13	Trintignant	Cooper-Maser.	42	
14	Burgess	Lotus-Climax	42	
r	Ginther	Ferrari	40	oil pressure
r	Moss	Lotus-Climax	30	suspension
r	Mairesse,W.	Lotus-Climax	25	fuel system
r	Scarlatti	de Tomaso-Osca	24	engine
r	de Beaufort	Porsche	22	engine
r	Bianchi	Lotus-Climax	21	clutch
r	von Trips	Ferrari	17	engine
r	Brabham,J.	Cooper-Climax	13	oil pressure
r	Collomb	Cooper-Climax	6	engine
r	Brooks	BRM-Climax	3	overheating
r	Surtees	Cooper-Climax	3	suspension
r	Lewis	Cooper-Climax	3	overheating

STARTING GRID:

1	Hill,P.	12	Baghelti
2	von Trips	13	Bonnier
3	Ginther	14	Brabham,J.
4	Moss	15	Salvadori
5	Clark	16	Gregory
6	Hill,G.	17	de Beaufort
7	Surtees	18	Lewis
8	McLaren	19	Bianchi
9	Gurney	20	Mairesse,W.
10	Ireland	21	Collomb
11	Brooks	22	May

+

British

GRAND PRIX No: 99
DATE: July 15, 1961
VENUE: Aintree
POLE LAP: Hill,P., 1m 58.8s
FASTEST LAP: Brooks, 1m 57.8s

Pn	Driver	Car	Laps	Time/Reason
1	von Trips	Ferrari	75	2h 40m 53.6s
2	Hill,P.	Ferrari	75	2h 41m 39.6s
3	Ginther	Ferrari	75	2h 41m 40.4s
4	Brabham,J.	Cooper-Climax	75	2h 42m 02.2s
5	Bonnier	Porsche	75	2h 42m 09.8s
6	Salvadori	Cooper-Climax	75	2h 42m 19.8s
7	Gurney	Porsche	74	
8	McLaren	Cooper-Climax	74	
9	Brooks	BRM-Climax	73	
10	Ireland	Lotus-Climax	72	
11	Gregory	Cooper-Climax	71	
12	Bandini	Cooper-Maser.	71	
13	Maggs	Lotus-Climax	69	
14	Burgess	Lotus-Climax	69	
15	Greene	Gilby-Climax	69	
16	de Beaufort	Porsche	69	
r	Clark	Lotus-Climax	62	oil leak
uc	Seidel	Lotus-Climax	58	
dq	Fairman	Ferguson-Clim.	56	push start
r	Bianchi	Lotus-Climax	45	gearbox
r	Moss	Lotus-Climax	44	brakes
r	Hill,G.	BRM-Climax	43	engine
r	Baghelti	Ferrari	27	spun off
r	Marsh	Lotus-Climax	25	engine
r	Surtees	Cooper-Climax	23	transmission
r	Parnell,T.	Lotus-Climax	12	clutch
r	Lewis	Cooper-Climax	7	handling
r	Ashmore	Lotus-Climax	7	engine
r	Taylor,H.	Lotus-Climax	5	accident
r	Natili	Cooper-Maser.	0	engine

STARTING GRID:

1	Hill,P.	9	Brabham,J.
2	Ginther	10	Surtees
3	Bonnier	11	Hill,G.
4	von Trips	12	Gurney
5	Moss	13	Salvadori
6	Brooks	14	McLaren
7	Ireland	15	Lewis
8	Clark	16	Gregory +

German

GRAND PRIX No: 100
DATE: August 6, 1961
VENUE: Nurburgring
POLE LAP: Hill,P., 8m 55.2s
FASTEST LAP: Hill,P., 8m 57.8s

Pn	Driver	Car	Laps	Time/Reason
1	Moss	Lotus-Climax	15	2h 18m 12.4s
2	von Trips	Ferrari	15	2h 18m 33.8s
3	Hill,P.	Ferrari	15	2h 18m 34.9s
4	Clark	Lotus-Climax	15	2h 19m 29.5s
5	Surtees	Cooper-Climax	15	2h 20m 05.5s
6	McLaren	Cooper-Climax	15	2h 20m 53.8s
7	Gurney	Porsche	15	2h 21m 35.0s
8	Ginther	Ferrari	15	2h 23m 35.5s
9	Lewis	Cooper-Climax	15	2h 23m 36.1s
10	Salvadori	Cooper-Climax	15	2h 30m 23.9s
11	Maggs	Lotus-Climax	14	
12	Burgess	Cooper-Climax	14	
13	Herrmann	Porsche	14	
14	de Beaufort	Porsche	14	
15	Marsh	Lotus-Climax	13	
16	Mairesse,W.	Ferrari	13	accident
17	Ashmore	Lotus-Climax	13	
r	Trintignant	Cooper-Maser.	12	engine
r	Collomb	Cooper-Climax	11	engine
r	Bandini	Cooper-Maser.	9	engine
r	Brooks	BRM-Climax	6	engine
r	Bonnier	Porsche	4	engine
r	Seidel	Lotus-Climax	2	steering
r	Ireland	Lotus-Climax	1	fire
r	Hill,G.	BRM-Climax	1	accident
r	Brabham,J.	Cooper-Climax	0	accident

STARTING GRID:

1	Hill,P.	13	Mairesse,W.
2	Brabham,J.	14	Ginther
3	Moss	15	Salvadori
4	Bonnier	16	Ireland
5	von Trips	17	de Beaufort
6	Hill,G.	18	Lewis
7	Gurney	19	Bandini
8	Clark	20	Marsh
9	Brooks	21	Trintignant
10	Surtees	22	Maggs
11	Herrmann	23	Seidel
12	McLaren	24	Burgess +

Italian

GRAND PRIX No:	101
DATE:	September 10, 1961
VENUE:	Monza
POLE LAP:	Von Trips, 2m 46.3s
FASTEST LAP:	Baghetti, 2m 48.4s

Pn	Driver	Car	Laps	Time/Reason
1	Hill,P.	Ferrari	43	2h 03m 13.0s
2	Gurney	Porsche	43	2h 03m 44.2s
3	McLaren	Cooper-Climax	43	2h 05m 41.4s
4	Lewis	Cooper-Climax	43	2h 05m 53.4s
5	Brooks	BRM-Climax	43	2h 05m 53.4s
6	Salvadori	Cooper-Climax	42	
7	de Beaufort	Porsche	41	
8	Bandini	Cooper-Maser.	41	
9	Trintignant	Cooper-Maser.	41	
10	Parnell,T.	Lotus-Climax	40	
11	Taylor,H.	Lotus-Climax	39	
12	Pirocchi	Cooper-Maser.	38	
r	Moss	Lotus-Climax	36	wheel
r	Ginther	Ferrari	23	engine
r	Starrabba	Lotus-Maserati	19	engine
r	Bonnier	Porsche	14	suspension
r	Vaccarella	de Tomaso-Con.	13	engine
r	Baghelti	Ferrari	13	engine
r	Rodriguez,R.	Ferrari	13	engine
r	Gregory	Lotus-Climax	11	suspension
r	Hill,G.	BRM-Climax	10	engine
r	Brabham,J.	Cooper-Climax	8	engine
r	Naylor	JBW-Climax	6	engine
r	Fairman	Cooper-Climax	5	engine
r	Ireland	Lotus-Climax	4	chassis
r	Surtees	Cooper-Climax	2	accident
r	Seidel	Lotus-Climax	1	engine
r	Bussinello	de Tomaso-Osca	1	engine
r	Lippi	de Tomaso-Osca	1	engine
r	Clark	Lotus-Climax	1	accident
r	von Trips	Ferrari	1	fatal accident
r	Ashmore	Lotus-Climax	0	accident

STARTING GRID:

1	von Trips	6	Baghelti
2	Rodriguez,R.	7	Clark
3	Ginther	8	Bonnier
4	Hill,P.	9	Ireland
5	Hill,G.	10	Brabham,J. +

US

GRAND PRIX No:	102
DATE:	October 8, 1961
VENUE:	Watkins Glen
POLE LAP:	Brabham,J., 1m 17.0s
FASTEST LAP:	Brabham,J., 1m 18.2s

Pn	Driver	Car	Laps	Time/Reason
1	Ireland	Lotus-Climax	100	2h 13m 45.8s
2	Gurney	Porsche	100	2h 13m 50.1s
3	Brooks	BRM-Climax	100	2h 14m 34.8s
4	McLaren	Cooper-Climax	100	2h 14m 43.8s
5	Hill,G.	BRM-Climax	99	
6	Bonnier	Porsche	98	
7	Salvadori	Cooper-Climax	96	engine
8	Clark	Lotus-Climax	96	
9	Penske	Cooper-Climax	96	
10	Ryan	Lotus-Climax	95	
11	Sharp	Cooper-Climax	93	
12	Gendebien	Lotus-Climax	92	
r	Ruby	Lotus-Climax	75	magneto
r	Hall	Lotus-Climax	75	fuel leak
r	Moss	Lotus-Climax	58	engine
r	Brabham,J.	Cooper-Climax	57	engine
r	Gregory	Lotus-Climax	23	gearbox
r	Hansgen	Cooper-Climax	14	accident
r	Surtees	Cooper-Climax	0	engine

STARTING GRID:

1	Brabham,J.	11	Gregory
2	Hill,G.	12	Salvadori
3	Moss	13	Ryan
4	McLaren	14	Hansgen
5	Clark	15	Gendebien
6	Brooks	16	Penske
7	Gurney	17	Sharp
8	Ireland	18	Hall
9	Surtees	19	Ruby
10	Bonnier		

Dutch

GRAND PRIX No: 103
DATE: May 20, 1962
VENUE: Zandvoort
POLE LAP: Surtees, 1m 32.5s
FASTEST LAP: McLaren, 1m 34.4s

Pn	Driver	Car	Laps	Time/Reason
1	Hill,G.	BRM	80	2h 11m 02.1s
2	Taylor,T.	Lotus-Climax	80	2h 11m 29.3s
3	Hill,P.	Ferrari	80	2h 12m 23.2s
4	Baghelti	Ferrari	79	
5	Maggs	Cooper-Climax	78	
6	de Beaufort	Porsche	76	
7	Bonnier	Porsche	75	
8	Rodriguez,R.	Ferrari	73	spun off
9	Ginther	BRM	71	accident
10	Lewis	Cooper-Climax	70	
11	Clark	Lotus-Climax	70	
r	Ireland	Lotus-Climax	61	spun off
r	Gregory	Lotus-Climax	54	gearbox
uc	Seidel	Emeryson-Clim.	52	
r	Gurney	Porsche	47	gearbox
r	McLaren	Cooper-Climax	21	gearbox
r	Salvadori	Lola-Climax	11	withdrew
r	Surtees	Lola-Climax	8	suspension
r	Brabham,J.	Lotus-Climax	3	accident
r	Pon	Porsche	2	spun off

STARTING GRID:

1	Surtees	11	Rodriguez,R.
2	Hill,G.	12	Baghelti
3	Clark	13	Bonnier
4	Brabham,J.	14	de Beaufort
5	McLaren	15	Maggs
6	Ireland	16	Gregory
7	Ginther	17	Salvadori
8	Gurney	18	Pon
9	Hill,P.	19	Lewis
10	Taylor,T.	20	Seidel

Monaco

GRAND PRIX No: 104
DATE: June 3, 1962
VENUE: Monte Carlo
POLE LAP: Clark, 1m 35.4s
FASTEST LAP: Clark, 1m 35.5s

Pn	Driver	Car	Laps	Time/Reason
1	McLaren	Cooper-Climax	100	2h 46m 29.7s
2	Hill,P.	Ferrari	100	2h 46m 31.0s
3	Bandini	Ferrari	100	2h 47m 53.8s
4	Surtees	Lola-Climax	99	
5	Bonnier	Porsche	93	
6	Hill,G.	BRM	92	engine
7	Mairesse,W.	Ferrari	90	pressure
r	Brabham,J.	Lotus-Climax	77	suspension
r	Ireland	Lotus-Climax	63	fuel pump
r	Clark	Lotus-Climax	55	clutch
r	Salvadori	Lola-Climax	44	suspension
r	Maggs	Cooper-Climax	43	gearbox
r	Taylor,T.	Lotus-Climax	24	oil leak
r	Ginther	BRM	0	accident
r	Gurney	Porsche	0	accident
r	Trintignant	Lotus-Climax	0	accident

STARTING GRID:

1	Clark	9	Hill,P.
2	Hill,G.	10	Bandini
3	McLaren	11	Surtees
4	Mairesse,W.	12	Salvadori
5	Gurney	13	Ginther
6	Brabham,J.	14	Taylor,T.
7	Trintignant	15	Bonnier
8	Ireland	16	Maggs

Belgian

GRAND PRIX No:	105
DATE:	June 17, 1962
VENUE:	Spa-Francorchamps
POLE LAP:	Hill,G., 3m 57.0s
FASTEST LAP:	Clark, 3m 55.6s

Pn	Driver	Car	Laps	Time/Reason
1	Clark	Lotus-Climax	32	2h 07m 32.3s
2	Hill,G.	BRM	32	2h 08m 16.4s
3	Hill,P.	Ferrari	32	2h 09m 38.8s
4	Rodriguez,R.	Ferrari	32	2h 09m 38.9s
5	Surtees	Lola-Climax	31	
6	Brabham,J.	Lotus-Climax	30	
7	de Beaufort	Porsche	30	
8	Trintignant	Lotus-Climax	30	
9	Bianchi	Lotus-Climax	29	
10	Siffert	Lotus-Climax	29	
r	Taylor,T.	Lotus-Climax	25	accident
r	Mairesse,W.	Ferrari	25	accident
r	Ginther	BRM	22	transmission
r	Maggs	Cooper-Climax	21	gearbox
r	McLaren	Cooper-Climax	19	oil pressure
uc	Campbell-Jones	Lotus-Climax	16	
r	Gregory	Lotus-BRM	12	withdrew
r	Ireland	Lotus-Climax	8	suspension
r	Baghelti	Ferrari	3	ignition
dns	Gurney	Lotus-BRM		car not ready

STARTING GRID:

1	Hill,G.	11	Surtees
2	McLaren	12	Clark
3	Taylor,T.	13	de Beaufort
4	Hill,P.	14	Baghelti
5	Ireland	15	Brabham,J.
6	Mairesse,W.	16	Trintignant
7	Rodriguez,R.	17	Siffert
8	Gregory	18	Bianchi
9	Ginther	19	Campbell-Jones
10	Maggs	20	Gurney

French

GRAND PRIX No:	106
DATE:	July 8, 1962
VENUE:	Rouen
POLE LAP:	Clark, 2m 14.8s
FASTEST LAP:	Hill,G., 2m 16.9s

Pn	Driver	Car	Laps	Time/Reason
1	Gurney	Porsche	54	2h 07m 35.5s
2	Maggs	Cooper-Climax	53	
3	Ginther	BRM	52	
4	McLaren	Cooper-Climax	51	
5	Surtees	Lola-Climax	51	
6	de Beaufort	Porsche	51	
7	Trintignant	Lotus-Climax	50	
8	Taylor,T.	Lotus-Climax	48	
9	Hill,G.	BRM	44	
r	Bonnier	Porsche	42	gearbox
r	Clark	Lotus-Climax	33	suspension
r	Lewis	Cooper-Climax	27	brakes
r	Salvadori	Lola-Climax	20	oil pressure
r	Gregory	Lotus-BRM	14	ignition
r	Brabham,J.	Lotus-Climax	10	suspension
r	Siffert	Lotus-BRM	5	clutch
r	Ireland	Lotus-Climax	1	wheel

STARTING GRID:

1	Clark	10	Ginther
2	Hill,G.	11	Maggs
3	McLaren	12	Taylor,T.
4	Brabham,J.	13	Trintignant
5	Surtees	14	Salvadori
6	Gurney	15	Siffert
7	Gregory	16	Lewis
8	Ireland	17	de Beaufort
9	Bonnier		

British

GRAND PRIX No:	107
DATE:	July 21, 1962
VENUE:	Aintree
POLE LAP:	Clark, 1m 53.6s
FASTEST LAP:	Clark, 1m 55.0s

Pn	Driver	Car	Laps	Time/Reason
1	Clark	Lotus-Climax	75	2h 26m 20.8s
2	Surtees	Lola-Climax	75	2h 27m 10.0s
3	McLaren	Cooper-Climax	75	2h 28m 05.6s
4	Hill,G.	BRM	75	2h 28m 17.6s
5	Brabham,J.	Lotus-Climax	74	
6	Maggs	Cooper-Climax	74	
7	Gregory	Lotus-Climax	74	
8	Taylor,T.	Lotus-Climax	74	
9	Gurney	Porsche	73	
10	Lewis	Cooper-Climax	72	
11	Settember	Emeryson-Clim.	71	
12	Burgess	Cooper-Climax	71	
13	Ginther	BRM	70	
14	de Beaufort	Porsche	69	
15	Chamberlain	Lotus-Climax	64	
16	Ireland	Lotus-Climax	61	
r	Hill,P.	Ferrari	46	ignition
r	Salvadori	Lola-Climax	34	ignition
r	Bonnier	Porsche	26	crownwheel and pinion
r	Seidel	Lotus-BRM	10	brakes
r	Shelly	Lotus-Climax	5	overheating

STARTING GRID:

1	Clark	12	Hill,P.
2	Surtees	13	Maggs
3	Ireland	14	Gregory
4	McLaren	15	Lewis
5	Hill,G.	16	Burgess
6	Gurney	17	de Beaufort
7	Bonnier	18	Shelly
8	Ginther	19	Settember
9	Brabham,J.	20	Chamberlain
10	Taylor,T.	21	Seidel
11	Salvadori		

German

GRAND PRIX No:	108
DATE:	August 5, 1962
VENUE:	Nurburgring
POLE LAP:	Gurney, 8m 47.2s
FASTEST LAP:	Hill,G., 10m 12.2s

Pn	Driver	Car	Laps	Time/Reason
1	Hill,G.	BRM	15	2h 38m 45.3s
2	Surtees	Lola-Climax	15	2h 38m 47.8s
3	Gurney	Porsche	15	2h 38m 49.7s
4	Clark	Lotus-Climax	15	2h 39m 27.4s
5	McLaren	Cooper-Climax	15	2h 40m 04.9s
6	Rodriguez,R.	Ferrari	15	2h 40m 09.1s
7	Bonnier	Porsche	15	2h 43m 22.6s
8	Ginther	BRM	15	2h 43m 45.4s
9	Maggs	Cooper-Climax	15	2h 43m 52.1s
10	Baghelti	Ferrari	15	2h 47m 00.0s
11	Burgess	Cooper-Climax	15	2h 47m 00.6s
12	Siffert	Lotus-Climax	15	2h 47m 03.8s
13	de Beaufort	Porsche	15	2h 47m 57.1s
14	Walter	Porsche	14	
15	Vaccarella	Porsche	14	
16	Bianchi	ENB-Maserati	14	
r	Lewis	Cooper-Climax	10	
r	Brabham,J.	Brabham-Climax	8	throttle
r	Hill,P.	Ferrari	8	shock absorber
r	Greene	Gilby-BRM	7	suspension
r	Trintignant	Lotus-Climax	3	gearbox
r	Bandini	Ferrari	3	accident
r	Salvadori	Lola-Climax	3	gearbox
r	Schiller	Lotus-BRM	3	oil pressure
r	Collomb	Cooper-Climax	2	gearbox
r	Taylor,T.	Lotus-Climax	0	accident

STARTING GRID:

1	Gurney	12	Hill,P.
2	Hill,G.	13	Baghelti
3	Clark	14	Walter
4	Surtees	15	Vaccarella
5	McLaren	16	Burgess
6	Bonnier	17	Siffert
7	Ginther	18	Bandini
8	de Beaufort	19	Greene
9	Salvadori	20	Schiller
10	Rodriguez,R.	21	Lewis
11	Trintignant	22	Collomb

Italian

GRAND PRIX No:	109
DATE:	September 16, 1962
VENUE:	Monza
POLE LAP:	Clark, 1m 40.35s
FASTEST LAP:	Hill,G., 1m 42.3s

Pn	Driver	Car	Laps	Time/Reason
1	Hill,G.	BRM	86	2h 29m 08.4s
2	Ginther	BRM	86	2h 29m 38.2s
3	McLaren	Cooper-Climax	86	2h 30m 06.2s
4	Mairesse,W.	Ferrari	86	2h 30m 06.6s
5	Baghelti	Ferrari	86	2h 30m 39.7s
6	Bonnier	Porsche	85	
7	Maggs	Cooper-Climax	85	
8	Bandini	Ferrari	84	
9	Vaccarella	Lotus-Climax	84	
10	de Beaufort	Porsche	81	
11	Hill,P.	Ferrari	81	
12	Gregory	Lotus-BRM	77	
r	Gurney	Porsche	66	
r	Rodriguez,R.	Ferrari	63	engine
r	Ireland	Lotus-Climax	45	suspension
r	Surtees	Lola-Climax	42	engine
r	Salvadori	Lola-Climax	41	engine
r	Taylor,T.	Lotus-Climax	25	transmission
r	Settember	Emeryson-Clim.	18	overheating
r	Trintignant	Lotus-Climax	17	electrical
r	Clark	Lotus-Climax	12	transmission

STARTING GRID:

1 Clark
2 Hill,G.
3 Ginther
4 McLaren
5 Ireland
6 Gregory
7 Gurney
8 Surtees
9 Bonnier
10 Mairesse,W.
11 Rodriguez,R.
12 Maggs
13 Salvadori
14 Vaccarella
15 Hill,P.
16 Taylor,T.
17 Bandini
18 Baghelti
19 Trintignant
20 de Beaufort
21 Settember

US

GRAND PRIX No:	110
DATE:	October 7, 1962
VENUE:	Watkins Glen
POLE LAP:	Clark, 1m 15.8s
FASTEST LAP:	Clark, 1m 15.0s

Pn	Driver	Car	Laps	Time/Reason
1	Clark	Lotus-Climax	100	2h 07m 13.0s
2	Hill,G.	BRM	100	2h 07m 22.2s
3	McLaren	Cooper-Climax	99	
4	Brabham,J.	Brabham-Climax	99	
5	Gurney	Porsche	99	
6	Gregory	Lotus-BRM	99	
7	Maggs	Cooper-Climax	97	
8	Ireland	Lotus-Climax	96	
9	Penske	Lotus-Climax	96	
10	Schroeder	Lotus-Climax	93	
11	Sharp	Cooper-Climax	91	
12	Taylor,T.	Lotus-Climax	85	
13	Bonnier	Porsche	79	
r	Ginther	BRM	34	engine
r	Trintignant	Lotus-Climax	31	brakes
r	Mayer	Cooper-Climax	30	engine
r	Surtees	Lola-Climax	18	oil line
r	de Beaufort	Porsche	8	accident

STARTING GRID:

1 Clark
2 Ginther
3 Hill,G.
4 Gurney
5 Brabham,J.
6 McLaren
7 Gregory
8 Taylor,T.
9 Bonnier
10 Maggs
11 Mayer
12 Penske
13 de Beaufort
14 Sharp
15 Ireland
16 Schroeder
17 Trintignant
18 Surtees

South African

GRAND PRIX No:	111
DATE:	December 29, 1962
VENUE:	East London
POLE LAP:	Clark, 1m 29.3s
FASTEST LAP:	Clark, 1m 31.0s

Pn	Driver	Car	Laps	Time/Reason
1	Hill,G.	BRM	82	2h 08m 03.3s
2	McLaren	Cooper-Climax	82	2h 08m 53.1s
3	Maggs	Cooper-Climax	82	2h 08m 53.6s
4	Brabham,J.	Brabham-Climax	82	2h 08m 57.1s
5	Ireland	Lotus-Climax	81	
6	Lederle	Lotus-Climax	78	
7	Ginther	BRM	78	
8	Love	Cooper-Climax	78	
9	Johnstone	BRM	76	
10	Pieterse	Lotus-Climax	71	
11	de Beaufort	Porsche	70	
r	Serrurier	LDS-Alfa	62	radiator
r	Clark	Lotus-Climax	61	oil leak
r	Salvadori	Lola-Climax	56	fuel tank
r	Harris	Cooper-Alfa	31	engine
r	Surtees	Lola-Climax	26	engine
r	Taylor,T.	Lotus-Climax	11	transmission

STARTING GRID:

1	Clark	10	Lederle
2	Hill,G.	11	Salvadori
3	Brabham,J.	12	Love
4	Ireland	13	Pieterse
5	Surtees	14	Serrurier
6	Maggs	15	Harris
7	Ginther	16	de Beaufort
8	McLaren	17	Johnstone
9	Taylor,T.		

Monaco

GRAND PRIX No:	112
DATE:	May 26, 1963
VENUE:	Monte Carlo
POLE LAP:	Clark, 1m 34.3s
FASTEST LAP:	Surtees, 1m 34.5s

Pn	Driver	Car	Laps	Time/Reason
1	Hill,G.	BRM	100	2h 41m 49.7s
2	Ginther	BRM	100	2h 41m 54.3s
3	McLaren	Cooper-Climax	100	2h 42m 02.5s
4	Surtees	Ferrari	100	2h 42m 03.8s
5	Maggs	Cooper-Climax	98	
6	Taylor,T.	Lotus-Climax	98	
7	Bonnier	Cooper-Climax	94	
r	Clark	Lotus-Climax	78	accident
r	Brabham,J.	Lotus-Climax	77	gearbox
r	Ireland	Lotus-BRM	40	accident
r	Mairesse,W.	Ferrari	37	transmission
r	Trintignant	Lola-Climax	34	engine
r	Gurney	Brabham-Climax	25	crownwheel and pinion
r	Hall	Lotus-BRM	20	gearbox
r	Siffert	Lotus-BRM	3	engine

STARTING GRID:

1	Clark	9	Taylor,T.
2	Hill,G.	10	Maggs
3	Surtees	11	Bonnier
4	Ginther	12	Siffert
5	Ireland	13	Hall
6	Gurney	14	Trintignant
7	Mairesse,W.	15	Brabham,J.
8	McLaren		

Belgian

GRAND PRIX No: 113
DATE: June 9, 1963
VENUE: Spa-Francorchamps
POLE LAP: Hill,G., 3m 54.1s
FASTEST LAP: Clark, 3m 58.1s

Pn	Driver	Car	Laps	Time/Reason
1	Clark	Lotus-Climax	32	2h 27m 47.6s
2	McLaren	Cooper-Climax	32	2h 32m 41.6s
3	Gurney	Brabham-Climax	31	
4	Ginther	BRM	31	
5	Bonnier	Cooper-Climax	30	
6	de Beaufort	Porsche	30	
r	Maggs	Cooper-Climax	27	spun off
r	Settember	Scirocco-BRM	25	spun off
r	Surtees	Ferrari	18	engine
r	Bianchi	Lola-Climax	17	spun off
r	Hill,G.	BRM	17	gearbox
r	Hall	Lotus-BRM	16	spun off
r	Siffert	Lotus-BRM	16	spun off
r	Hill,P.	ATS (Italy)	13	transmission
r	Brabham,J.	Brabham-Climax	11	electrical
r	Amon	Lola-Climax	9	oil leak
r	Ireland	BRP-BRM	8	gearbox
r	Baghelti	ATS (Italy)	7	gearbox
r	Mairesse,W.	Ferrari	6	engine
r	Taylor,T.	Lotus-Climax	4	oil pressure

STARTING GRID:

1	Hill,G.	11	Taylor,T.
2	Gurney	12	Hall
3	Mairesse,W.	13	Bonnier
4	Maggs	14	Siffert
5	McLaren	15	Amon
6	Brabham,J.	16	Bianchi
7	Ireland	17	Hill,P.
8	Clark	18	de Beaufort
9	Ginther	19	Settember
10	Surtees	20	Baghelti

Dutch

GRAND PRIX No: 114
DATE: June 23, 1963
VENUE: Zandvoort
POLE LAP: Clark, 1m 31.6s
FASTEST LAP: Clark, 1m 33.7s

Pn	Driver	Car	Laps	Time/Reason
1	Clark	Lotus-Climax	80	2h 08m 13.07s
2	Gurney	Brabham-Climax	79	
3	Surtees	Ferrari	79	
4	Ireland	BRP-BRM	79	
5	Ginther	BRM	79	
6	Scarfiotti	Ferrari	78	
7	Siffert	Lotus-BRM	77	
8	Hall	Lotus-BRM	77	
9	de Beaufort	Porsche	75	
r	Hill,G.	BRM	69	engine
r	Brabham,J.	Brabham-Climax	67	chassis
uc	Taylor,T.	Lotus-Climax	66	
uc	Bonnier	Cooper-Climax	56	
r	Amon	Lola-Climax	28	water pump
r	Baghelti	ATS (Italy)	17	ignition
r	Hill,P.	ATS (Italy)	15	wheel
r	Maggs	Cooper-Climax	13	overheating
r	McLaren	Cooper-Climax	6	gearbox
r	Mitter	Porsche	1	clutch

STARTING GRID:

1	Clark	11	Scarfiotti
2	Hill,G.	12	Amon
3	McLaren	13	Hill,P.
4	Brabham,J.	14	Gurney
5	Surtees	15	Baghelti
6	Ginther	16	Mitter
7	Ireland	17	Siffert
8	Bonnier	18	Hall
9	Maggs	19	de Beaufort
10	Taylor,T.		

French

GRAND PRIX No: 115
DATE: June 30, 1963
VENUE: Reims
POLE LAP: Clark, 2m 20.2s
FASTEST LAP: Clark, 2m 21.6s

Pn	Driver	Car	Laps	Time/Reason
1	Clark	Lotus-Climax	53	2h 10m 54.3s
2	Maggs	Cooper-Climax	53	2h 11m 59.2s
3	Hill,G.	BRM	53	2h 13m 08.2s
4	Brabham,J.	Brabham-Climax	53	2h 13m 09.5s
5	Gurney	Brabham-Climax	53	2h 13m 27.7s
6	Siffert	Lotus-BRM	52	
7	Amon	Lola-Climax	51	
8	Trintignant	Lotus-Climax	50	
9	Ireland	BRP-BRM	49	
10	Bandini	BRM	45	
11	Hall	Lotus-BRM	45	
r	McLaren	Cooper-Climax	42	electrical
r	Taylor,T.	Lotus-Climax	41	crownwheel and pinion
uc	Hill,P.	Lotus-BRM	34	
uc	Bonnier	Cooper-Climax	32	
r	Gregory	Lotus-BRM	30	gearbox
r	Surtees	Ferrari	12	fuel pump
r	Settember	Scirocco-BRM	5	wheel
r	Ginther	BRM	4	radiator
dns	Scarfiotti	Ferrari		injured
dns	Arundell	Lotus-Climax		withdrew

STARTING GRID:

1 Clark
2 Hill,G.
3 Gurney
4 Surtees
5 Brabham,J.
6 McLaren
7 Taylor,T.
8 Maggs
9 Ireland
10 Siffert
11 Bonnier
12 Ginther
13 Hill,P.
14 Scarfiotti
15 Trintignant
16 Arundell
17 Amon
18 Hall
19 Gregory
20 Settember
21 Bandini

British

GRAND PRIX No: 116
DATE: July 20, 1963
VENUE: Silverstone
POLE LAP: Clark, 1m 34.4s
FASTEST LAP: Surtees, 1m 36.0s

Pn	Driver	Car	Laps	Time/Reason
1	Clark	Lotus-Climax	82	2h 14m 09.6s
2	Surtees	Ferrari	82	2h 14m 35.4s
3	Hill,G.	BRM	82	2h 14m 47.2s
4	Ginther	BRM	81	
5	Bandini	BRM	81	
6	Hall	Lotus-BRM	80	
7	Amon	Lola-Climax	80	
8	Hailwood	Lotus-Climax	78	
9	Maggs	Cooper-Climax	78	
10	de Beaufort	Porsche	76	
11	Gregory	Lotus-BRM	75	
12	Anderson	Lola-Climax	75	
13	Campbell-Jones	Lola-Climax	74	
r	Siffert	Lotus-BRM	66	gearbox
r	Bonnier	Cooper-Climax	65	oil pressure
r	Gurney	Brabham-Climax	59	engine
r	Raby	Gilby-BRM	59	gearbox
r	Burgess	Scirocco-BRM	36	ignition
r	Brabham,J.	Brabham-Climax	27	engine
dq	Ireland	BRP-BRM	26	push start
dq	Taylor,T.	Lotus-Climax	23	push start
r	Settember	Scirocco-BRM	20	ignition
r	McLaren	Cooper-Climax	7	engine

STARTING GRID:

1 Clark
2 Gurney
3 Hill,G.
4 Brabham,J.
5 Surtees
6 McLaren
7 Maggs
8 Bandini
9 Ginther
10 Taylor,T.
11 Ireland
12 Bonnier
13 Hall
14 Amon
15 Siffert
16 Anderson
17 Hailwood
18 Settember
19 Raby
20 Burgess
21 de Beaufort
22 Gregory
23 Campbell-Jones

German

GRAND PRIX No:	117
DATE:	April 4, 1963
VENUE:	Nurburgring
POLE LAP:	Clark, 8m 45.8s
FASTEST LAP:	Surtees, 8m 47.0s

Pn	Driver	Car	Laps	Time/Reason
1	Surtees	Ferrari	15	2h 13m 06.8s
2	Clark	Lotus-Climax	15	2h 14m 24.3s
3	Ginther	BRM	15	2h 15m 51.7s
4	Mitter	Porsche	15	2h 21m 18.3s
5	Hall	Lotus-BRM	14	
6	Bonnier	Cooper-Climax	14	
7	Brabham,J.	Brabham-Climax	14	
8	Taylor,T.	Lotus-Climax	14	
r	Siffert	Lotus-BRM	10	transmission
uc	Collomb	Lotus-Climax	10	
r	de Beaufort	Porsche	9	lost wheel
r	Maggs	Cooper-Climax	7	engine
r	Gurney	Brabham-Climax	6	gearbox
r	Cabral	Cooper-Climax	6	gearbox
r	Burgess	Scirocco-BRM	5	steering
r	Settember	Scirocco-BRM	5	accident
r	McLaren	Cooper-Climax	3	accident
r	Amon	Lola-Climax	2	accident
r	Hill,G.	BRM	2	gearbox
r	Mairesse,W.	Ferrari	1	accident
r	Ireland	Lotus-BRM	0	accident
r	Bandini	BRM	0	accident

STARTING GRID:

1	Clark	12	Bonnier
2	Surtees	13	Gurney
3	Bandini	14	Amon
4	Hill,G.	15	Mitter
5	McLaren	16	Hall
6	Ginther	17	de Beaufort
7	Mairesse,W.	18	Taylor,T.
8	Brabham,J.	19	Burgess
9	Siffert	20	Cabral
10	Maggs	21	Collomb
11	Ireland	22	Settember

Italian

GRAND PRIX No:	118
DATE:	September 8, 1963
VENUE:	Monza
POLE LAP:	Surtees, 1m 37.3s
FASTEST LAP:	Clark, 1m 38.9s

Pn	Driver	Car	Laps	Time/Reason
1	Clark	Lotus-Climax	86	2h 24m 19.6s
2	Ginther	BRM	86	2h 25m 54.6s
3	McLaren	Cooper-Climax	85	
4	Ireland	BRP-BRM	84	engine
5	Brabham,J.	Brabham-Climax	84	
6	Maggs	Cooper-Climax	84	
7	Bonnier	Cooper-Climax	84	
8	Hall	Lotus-BRM	84	
9	Trintignant	BRM	83	
10	Hailwood	Lola-Climax	82	
11	Hill,P.	ATS (Italy)	79	
12	Anderson	Lola-Climax	79	
r	Spence	Lotus-Climax	73	oil pressure
r	Gurney	Brabham-Climax	64	fuel feed
uc	Baghelti	ATS (Italy)	63	
r	Hill,G.	BRM	59	clutch
r	Siffert	Lotus-BRM	40	oil pressure
r	Bandini	Ferrari	37	gearbox
r	Gregory	Lotus-BRM	26	engine
r	Surtees	Ferrari	16	engine
dns	Amon	Lola-Climax		injured

STARTING GRID:

1	Surtees	12	Gregory
2	Hill,G.	13	Maggs
3	Clark	14	Hill,P.
4	Ginther	15	Amon
5	Gurney	16	Siffert
6	Bandini	17	Hall
7	Brabham,J.	18	Hailwood
8	McLaren	19	Anderson
9	Spence	20	Trintignant
10	Ireland	21	Baghelti
11	Bonnier		

US

GRAND PRIX No:	119
DATE:	October 6, 1963
VENUE:	Watkins Glen
POLE LAP:	Hill,G., 1m 13.4s
FASTEST LAP:	Clark, 1m 14.5s

Pn	Driver	Car	Laps	Time/Reason
1	Hill,G.	BRM	110	2h 19m 22.1s
2	Ginther	BRM	110	2h 19m 54.6s
3	Clark	Lotus-Climax	109	
4	Brabham,J.	Brabham-Climax	108	
5	Bandini	Ferrari	106	
6	de Beaufort	Porsche	99	
7	Broeker	Stebro-Ford	88	
8	Bonnier	Cooper-Climax	85	
r	Surtees	Ferrari	82	engine
r	Hall	Lotus-BRM	76	
r	McLaren	Cooper-Climax	74	fuel feed
r	Siffert	Lotus-BRM	56	gearbox
r	Ward	Lotus-BRM	44	gearbox
r	Maggs	Cooper-Climax	44	engine
r	Gurney	Brabham-Climax	42	chassis
r	Rodriguez,P.	Lotus-Climax	36	engine
r	Taylor,T.	Lotus-Climax	24	ignition
r	Gregory	Lola-Climax	14	overheating
r	Sharp	Lotus-BRM	6	tappet
r	Hill,P.	ATS (Italy)	4	oil pump
r	Baghelti	ATS (Italy)	0	oil pump

STARTING GRID:

1	Hill,G.	12	Bonnier
2	Clark	13	Rodriguez,P.
3	Surtees	14	Siffert
4	Ginther	15	Hill,P.
5	Brabham,J.	16	Hall
6	Gurney	17	Ward
7	Taylor,T.	18	Sharp
8	Gregory	19	de Beaufort
9	Bandini	20	Baghelti
10	Maggs	21	Broeker
11	McLaren		

Mexican

GRAND PRIX No:	120
DATE:	October 27, 1963
VENUE:	Mexico City
POLE LAP:	Clark, 1m 58.8s
FASTEST LAP:	Clark, 1m 58.1s

Pn	Driver	Car	Laps	Time/Reason
1	Clark	Lotus-Climax	65	2h 09m 52.1s
2	Brabham,J.	Brabham-Climax	65	2h 11m 33.2s
3	Ginther	BRM	65	2h 11m 46.8s
4	Hill,G.	BRM	64	
5	Bonnier	Cooper-Climax	62	
6	Gurney	Brabham-Climax	62	
7	Sharp	Lotus-BRM	61	
8	Hall	Lotus-BRM	61	
9	Siffert	Lotus-BRM	59	
10	de Beaufort	Porsche	58	
r	Solana	BRM	57	engine
r	Hill,P.	ATS (Italy)	39	suspension
r	Bandini	Ferrari	35	engine
r	McLaren	Cooper-Climax	29	engine
r	Rodriguez,P.	Lotus-Climax	25	suspension
r	Gregory	Lola-Climax	25	suspension
r	Taylor,T.	Lotus-Climax	18	engine
dq	Surtees	Ferrari	18	push start
r	Baghelti	ATS (Italy)	10	fuel system
r	Amon	Lotus-BRM	8	engine
r	Maggs	Cooper-Climax	7	engine

STARTING GRID:

1	Clark	12	Taylor,T.
2	Surtees	13	Maggs
3	Hill,G.	14	Gregory
4	Gurney	15	Hall
5	Ginther	16	Sharp
6	McLaren	17	Hill,P.
7	Bandini	18	de Beaufort
8	Bonnier	19	Amon
9	Siffert	20	Rodriguez,P.
10	Brabham,J.	21	Baghelti
11	Solana		

South African

GRAND PRIX No:	121
DATE:	December 28, 1963
VENUE:	East London
POLE LAP:	Clark, 1m 28.9s
FASTEST LAP:	Gurney, 1m 29.1s

Pn	Driver	Car	Laps	Time/Reason
1	Clark	Lotus-Climax	85	2h 10m 36.9s
2	Gurney	Brabham-Climax	85	2h 11m 43.7s
3	Hill,G.	BRM	84	
4	McLaren	Cooper-Climax	84	
5	Bandini	Ferrari	84	
6	Bonnier	Cooper-Climax	83	
7	Maggs	Cooper-Climax	82	
8	Taylor,T.	Lotus-Climax	81	
9	Love	Cooper-Climax	80	
10	de Beaufort	Porsche	79	
11	Serrurier	LDS-Alfa	78	
12	Blokdyk	Cooper-Maser.	77	
r	Brabham,J.	Brabham-Climax	71	spun off
uc	Niemann	Lotus-Ford	66	
r	de Klerk	Alfa Special	53	gearbox
r	Prophet	Brabham-Ford	48	oil pressure
r	Ginther	BRM	43	transmission
r	Surtees	Ferrari	43	engine
r	Pieterse	Lotus-Climax	3	engine
r	Tingle	LDS-Alfa	2	transmission
dns	Driver	Lotus-BRM		accident

STARTING GRID:

1 Clark
2 Brabham,J.
3 Gurney
4 Surtees
5 Bandini
6 Hill,G.
7 Ginther
8 Taylor,T.
9 McLaren
10 Maggs
11 Bonnier
12 Pieterse
13 Love
14 Prophet
15 Niemann
16 de Klerk
17 Tingle
18 Serrurier
19 Blokdyk
20 de Beaufort
21 Driver

Monaco

GRAND PRIX No:	122
DATE:	May 10, 1964
VENUE:	Monte Carlo
POLE LAP:	Clark, 1m 34.0s
FASTEST LAP:	Hill,G., 1m 33.9s

Pn	Driver	Car	Laps	Time/Reason
1	Hill,G.	BRM	100	2h 41m 19.5s
2	Ginther	BRM	99	
3	Arundell	Lotus-Climax	97	
4	Clark	Lotus-Climax	96	engine
5	Bonnier	Cooper-Climax	96	
6	Hailwood	Lotus-BRM	96	
7	Anderson	Brabham-Climax	86	
8	Siffert	Lotus-BRM	78	
r	Hill,P.	Cooper-Climax	70	suspension
r	Bandini	Ferrari	67	gearbox
r	Gurney	Brabham-Climax	61	gearbox
r	Trintignant	BRM	53	driver exhaustion
r	Brabham,J.	Brabham-Climax	29	fuel injection
r	McLaren	Cooper-Climax	17	oil leak
r	Surtees	Ferrari	14	gearbox
r	Taylor,T.	BRP-BRM	7	fuel leak
dns	Ireland	Lotus-BRM		injured

STARTING GRID:

1 Clark
2 Brabham,J.
3 Hill,G.
4 Surtees
5 Gurney
6 Arundell
7 Bandini
8 Ginther
9 Hill,P.
10 McLaren
11 Bonnier
12 Anderson
13 Trintignant
14 Taylor,T.
15 Hailwood
16 Siffert
17 Ireland

Dutch

GRAND PRIX No:	123
DATE:	May 24, 1964
VENUE:	Zandvoort
POLE LAP:	Gurney, 1m 31.2s
FASTEST LAP:	Clark, 1m 32.8s

Pn	Driver	Car	Laps	Time/Reason
1	Clark	Lotus-Climax	80	2h 07m 35.4s
2	Surtees	Ferrari	80	2h 08m 29.0s
3	Arundell	Lotus-Climax	79	
4	Hill,G.	BRM	79	
5	Amon	Lotus-BRM	79	
6	Anderson	Brabham-Climax	78	
7	McLaren	Cooper-Climax	78	
8	Hill,P.	Cooper-Climax	76	
9	Bonnier	Brabham-BRM	76	
10	Baghelti	BRM	74	
11	Ginther	BRM	64	
r	Hailwood	Lotus-BRM	57	crownwheel
uc	Siffert	Brabham-BRM	55	
r	Brabham,J.	Brabham-Climax	44	ignition
r	Bandini	Ferrari	25	fuel injection
r	Gurney	Brabham-Climax	23	steering wheel
r	de Beaufort	Porsche	8	engine
dns	Maggs	BRM		accident

STARTING GRID:

1	Gurney	10	Bandini
2	Clark	11	Anderson
3	Hill,G.	12	Bonnier
4	Surtees	13	Amon
5	McLaren	14	Hailwood
6	Arundell	15	Maggs
7	Brabham,J.	16	Baghelti
8	Ginther	17	de Beaufort
9	Hill,P.	18	Siffert

Belgian

GRAND PRIX No:	124
DATE:	June 14, 1964
VENUE:	Spa-Francorchamps
POLE LAP:	Gurney, 3m 50.9s
FASTEST LAP:	Gurney, 3m 49.2s

Pn	Driver	Car	Laps	Time/Reason
1	Clark	Lotus-Climax	32	2h 06m 40.5s
2	McLaren	Cooper-Climax	32	2h 06m 43.9s
3	Brabham,J.	Brabham-Climax	32	2h 07m 28.6s
4	Ginther	BRM	32	2h 08m 39.1s
5	Hill,G.	BRM	31	out of fuel
6	Gurney	Brabham-Climax	31	out of fuel
7	Taylor,T.	BRP-BRM	31	
8	Baghelti	BRM	31	
9	Arundell	Lotus-Climax	28	
10	Ireland	BRP-BRM	28	
dq	Revson	Lotus-BRM	27	push start
r	Siffert	Brabham-BRM	13	engine
r	Hill,P.	Cooper-Climax	13	engine
r	Bandini	Ferrari	11	engine
r	Pilette,A.	Scirocco-Clim.	10	engine
r	Bonnier	Brabham-BRM	7	driver ill
r	Amon	Lotus-BRM	3	engine
r	Surtees	Ferrari	3	engine
dns	Maggs	BRM		engine
dns	Anderson	Brabham-Climax		ignition

STARTING GRID:

1	Gurney	11	Amon
2	Hill,G.	12	Taylor,T.
3	Brabham,J.	13	Siffert
4	Arundell	14	Bonnier
5	Surtees	15	Hill,P.
6	Clark	16	Ireland
7	McLaren	17	Baghelti
8	Ginther	18	Maggs
9	Bandini	19	Anderson
10	Revson	20	Pilette,A.

French

GRAND PRIX No: 125
DATE: June 28, 1964
VENUE: Rouen
POLE LAP: Clark, 2m 09.6s
FASTEST LAP: Brabham,J., 2m 11.4s

Pn	Driver	Car	Laps	Time/Reason
1	Gurney	Brabham-Climax	57	2h 07m 49.1s
2	Hill,G.	BRM	57	2h 08m 13.2s
3	Brabham,J.	Brabham-Climax	57	2h 08m 14.0s
4	Arundell	Lotus-Climax	57	2h 08m 59.7s
5	Ginther	BRM	57	2h 10m 01.2s
6	McLaren	Cooper-Climax	56	
7	Hill,P.	Cooper-Climax	56	
8	Hailwood	Lotus-BRM	56	
9	Bandini	Ferrari	55	
10	Amon	Lotus-BRM	53	
11	Trintignant	BRM	52	
12	Anderson	Brabham-Climax	50	
r	Ireland	BRP-BRM	31	spun off
r	Clark	Lotus-Climax	31	engine
r	Surtees	Ferrari	6	engine
r	Taylor,T.	BRP-BRM	6	brakes
r	Siffert	Brabham-BRM	4	engine

STARTING GRID:

1	Clark	10	Hill,P.
2	Gurney	11	Ireland
3	Surtees	12	Taylor,T.
4	Arundell	13	Hailwood
5	Brabham,J.	14	Amon
6	Hill,G.	15	Anderson
7	McLaren	16	Trintignant
8	Bandini	17	Siffert
9	Ginther		

British

GRAND PRIX No: 126
DATE: July 11, 1964
VENUE: Brands Hatch
POLE LAP: Clark, 1m 38.1s
FASTEST LAP: Clark, 1m 38.8s

Pn	Driver	Car	Laps	Time/Reason
1	Clark	Lotus-Climax	80	2h 15m 07.0s
2	Hill,G.	BRM	80	2h 15m 09.8s
3	Surtees	Ferrari	80	2h 16m 27.6s
4	Brabham,J.	Brabham-Climax	79	
5	Bandini	Ferrari	78	
6	Hill,P.	Cooper-Climax	78	
7	Anderson	Brabham-Climax	78	
8	Ginther	BRM	77	
9	Spence	Lotus-Climax	77	
10	Ireland	BRP-BRM	77	
11	Siffert	Brabham-BRM	76	
12	Baghelti	BRM	76	
13	Gurney	Brabham-Climax	75	
14	Taylor,J.	Cooper-Ford	56	
r	Bonnier	Brabham-BRM	46	brakes
r	Revson	Lotus-BRM	43	engine
r	Raby	Brabham-BRM	37	wheel
r	Maggs	BRM	37	gearbox
r	Taylor,T.	Lotus-BRM	22	driver ill
r	Hailwood	Lotus-BRM	16	oil line
r	Amon	Lotus-BRM	9	clutch
r	McLaren	Cooper-Climax	6	gearbox
r	Gardner	Brabham-Ford	0	accident
dns	Attwood	BRM		withdrew

STARTING GRID:

1	Clark	13	Spence
2	Hill,G.	14	Ginther
3	Gurney	15	Hill,P.
4	Brabham,J.	16	Siffert
5	Surtees	17	Raby
6	McLaren	18	Taylor,T.
7	Anderson	19	Gardner
8	Bandini	20	Taylor,J.
9	Bonnier	21	Baghelti
10	Ireland	22	Revson
11	Amon	23	Maggs
12	Hailwood	24	Attwood

German

GRAND PRIX No: 127
DATE: August 2, 1964
VENUE: Nurburgring
POLE LAP: Surtees, 8m 38.4s
FASTEST LAP: Surtees, 8m 39.0s

Pn	Driver	Car	Laps	Time/Reason
1	Surtees	Ferrari	15	2h 12m 04.8s
2	Hill,G.	BRM	15	2h 13m 20.4s
3	Bandini	Ferrari	15	2h 16m 57.6s
4	Siffert	Brabham-BRM	15	2h 17m 27.9s
5	Trintignant	BRM	14	engine
6	Maggs	BRM	14	
7	Ginther	BRM	14	
8	Spence	Lotus-Climax	14	
9	Mitter	Lotus-Climax	14	
10	Gurney	Brabham-Climax	14	
r	Amon	Lotus-BRM	12	suspension
r	Brabham,J.	Brabham-Climax	11	crownwheel/pinion
r	Bucknum	Honda	11	spun off
r	Revson	Lotus-BRM	10	accident
r	Clark	Lotus-Climax	7	engine
r	McLaren	Cooper-Climax	4	engine
r	Anderson	Brabham-Climax	4	suspension
r	Barth	Cooper-Climax	3	clutch
r	Baghelti	BRM	2	throttle
r	Hill,P.	Cooper-Climax	1	engine
r	Hailwood	Lotus-BRM	0	engine
r	Bonnier	Brabham-BRM	0	ignition
dns	de Beaufort	Brabham-BRM		fatal accident

STARTING GRID:

1	Surtees	13	Hailwood
2	Clark	14	Trintignant
3	Gurney	15	Anderson
4	Bandini	16	Maggs
5	Hill,G.	17	Spence
6	Brabham,J.	18	Revson
7	McLaren	19	Mitter
8	Hill,P.	20	Barth
9	Amon	21	Baghelti
10	Siffert	22	Bucknum
11	Ginther	23	de Beaufort
12	Bonnier		

Austrian

GRAND PRIX No: 128
DATE: August 23, 1964
VENUE: Zeltweg
POLE LAP: Hill,G., 1m 09.84s
FASTEST LAP: Gurney, 1m 10.56s

Pn	Driver	Car	Laps	Time/Reason
1	Bandini	Ferrari	105	2h 06m 18.2s
2	Ginther	BRM	105	2h 06m 24.4s
3	Anderson	Brabham-Climax	102	
4	Maggs	BRM	102	
5	Ireland	BRP-BRM	102	
6	Bonnier	Brabham-Climax	101	
7	Baghelti	BRM	96	
8	Hailwood	Lotus-BRM	95	
9	Brabham,J.	Brabham-Climax	76	
r	Rindt	Brabham-BRM	58	steering
r	Hill,P.	Cooper-Climax	58	accident
r	Gurney	Brabham-Climax	47	suspension
r	McLaren	Cooper-Climax	43	engine
r	Spence	Lotus-Climax	41	transmission
r	Clark	Lotus-Climax	40	transmission
r	Taylor,T.	BRP-BRM	21	suspension
r	Siffert	Brabham-BRM	18	spun off
r	Surtees	Ferrari	8	suspension
r	Amon	Lotus-Climax	7	engine
r	Hill,G.	BRM	5	distributor

STARTING GRID:

1	Hill,G.	11	Ireland
2	Surtees	12	Siffert
3	Clark	13	Rindt
4	Gurney	14	Anderson
5	Ginther	15	Baghelti
6	Brabham,J.	16	Taylor,T.
7	Bandini	17	Amon
8	Spence	18	Hailwood
9	McLaren	19	Maggs
10	Bonnier	20	Hill,P.

Italian

GRAND PRIX No:	129
DATE:	September 6, 1964
VENUE:	Monza
POLE LAP:	Surtees, 1m 37.4s
FASTEST LAP:	Surtees, 1m 38.8s

Pn	Driver	Car	Laps	Time/Reason
1	Surtees	Ferrari	78	2h 10m 51.8s
2	McLaren	Cooper-Climax	78	2h 11m 57.8s
3	Bandini	Ferrari	77	
4	Ginther	BRM	77	
5	Ireland	BRP-BRM	77	
6	Spence	Lotus-Climax	77	
7	Siffert	Brabham-BRM	77	
8	Baghelti	BRM	77	
9	Scarfiotti	Ferrari	77	
10	Gurney	Brabham-Climax	75	
11	Anderson	Brabham-Climax	75	
12	Bonnier	Brabham-Climax	74	
13	Revson	Lotus-BRM	72	
r	Brabham,J.	Brabham-Climax	59	engine
r	Clark	Lotus-Climax	27	engine
r	Cabral	ATS (Italy)	24	engine
r	Trintignant	BRM	21	engine
r	Bucknum	Honda	12	brakes
r	Hailwood	Lotus-BRM	4	engine
r	Hill,G.	BRM	0	clutch
dns	Rudaz	Cooper-Climax		piston

STARTING GRID:

1	Surtees	12	Bonnier
2	Gurney	13	Ireland
3	Hill,G.	14	Anderson
4	Clark	15	Baghelti
5	McLaren	16	Scarfiotti
6	Siffert	17	Hailwood
7	Bandini	18	Revson
8	Spence	19	Cabral
9	Ginther	20	Rudaz
10	Bucknum	21	Trintignant
11	Brabham,J.		

US

GRAND PRIX No:	130
DATE:	October 4, 1964
VENUE:	Watkins Glen
POLE LAP:	Clark, 1m 12.65s
FASTEST LAP:	Clark, 1m 12.70s

Pn	Driver	Car	Laps	Time/Reason
1	Hill,G.	BRM	110	2h 16m 38.0s
2	Surtees	Ferrari	110	2h 17m 08.5s
3	Siffert	Brabham-BRM	109	
4	Ginther	BRM	107	
5	Hansgen	Lotus-Climax	107	
6	Taylor,T.	BRP-BRM	106	
7	Spence	Lotus-Climax	102	
8	Hailwood	Lotus-BRM	101	
r	Gurney	Brabham-Climax	69	oil pressure
uc	Sharp	Brabham-BRM	65	
r	Bandini	Ferrari	58	engine
r	Clark	Lotus-Climax	54	fuel injection
r	Bucknum	Honda	50	overheating
r	Amon	Lotus-BRM	47	engine
r	Bonnier	Brabham-Climax	37	wheel
r	McLaren	Cooper-Climax	26	engine
r	Brabham,J.	Brabham-Climax	14	engine
r	Hill,P.	Cooper-Climax	4	ignition
r	Ireland	BRP-BRM	2	gear lever

STARTING GRID:

1	Clark	11	Amon
2	Surtees	12	Siffert
3	Gurney	13	Ginther
4	Hill,G.	14	Bucknum
5	McLaren	15	Taylor,T.
6	Spence	16	Hailwood
7	Brabham,J.	17	Hansgen
8	Bandini	18	Sharp
9	Bonnier	19	Hill,P.
10	Ireland		

Mexican

GRAND PRIX No:	131
DATE:	October 25, 1964
VENUE:	Mexico City
POLE LAP:	Clark, 1m 57.24s
FASTEST LAP:	Clark, 1m 58.37s

Pn	Driver	Car	Laps	Time/Reason
1	Gurney	Brabham-Climax	65	2h 09m 50.32s
2	Surtees	Ferrari	65	2h 10m 59.26s
3	Bandini	Ferrari	65	2h 10m 59.95s
4	Spence	Lotus-Climax	65	2h 11m 12.18s
5	Clark	Lotus-Climax	64	engine
6	Rodriguez,P.	Ferrari	64	
7	McLaren	Cooper-Climax	64	
8	Ginther	BRM	64	
9	Hill,P.	Cooper-Climax	63	engine
10	Solana	Lotus-Climax	63	
11	Hill,G.	BRM	63	
12	Ireland	BRP-BRM	61	
13	Sharp	Brabham-BRM	60	
r	Amon	Lotus-BRM	45	gearbox
r	Brabham,J.	Brabham-Climax	44	engine
r	Hailwood	Lotus-BRM	11	overheating
r	Siffert	Brabham-BRM	10	fuel pump
r	Bonnier	Brabham-Climax	9	suspension
r	Taylor,T.	BRP-BRM	5	overheating

STARTING GRID:

1	Clark	11	Ginther
2	Gurney	12	Amon
3	Bandini	13	Siffert
4	Surtees	14	Solana
5	Spence	15	Hill,P.
6	Hill,G.	16	Ireland
7	Brabham,J.	17	Hailwood
8	Bonnier	18	Taylor,T.
9	Rodriguez,P.	19	Sharp
10	McLaren		

South African

GRAND PRIX No:	132
DATE:	January 1, 1965
VENUE:	East London
POLE LAP:	Clark, 1m 27.2s
FASTEST LAP:	Clark, 1m 27.6s

Pn	Driver	Car	Laps	Time/Reason
1	Clark	Lotus-Climax	85	2h 06m 46.0s
2	Surtees	Ferrari	85	2h 07m 15.0s
3	Hill,G.	BRM	85	2h 07m 17.8s
4	Spence	Lotus-Climax	85	2h 07m 40.4s
5	McLaren	Cooper-Climax	84	
6	Stewart,Jackie	BRM	83	
7	Siffert	Brabham-BRM	83	
8	Brabham,J.	Brabham-Climax	81	
9	Hawkins	Brabham-Ford	81	
10	de Klerk	Alfa Special	79	
11	Maggs	Lotus-BRM	77	
12	Gardner	Brabham-BRM	75	
13	Tingle	LDS-Alfa	73	
14	Prophet	Brabham-Ford	71	
r	Bandini	Ferrari	66	electrical
uc	Anderson	Brabham-Climax	50	
r	Bonnier	Brabham-Climax	42	transmission
r	Rindt	Cooper-Climax	39	electrical
r	Love	Cooper-Climax	20	transmission
r	Gurney	Brabham-Climax	11	ignition

STARTING GRID:

1	Clark	11	Stewart,Jackie
2	Surtees	12	Anderson
3	Brabham,J.	13	Maggs
4	Spence	14	Siffert
5	Hill,G.	15	Gardner
6	Bandini	16	Hawkins
7	Bonnier	17	de Klerk
8	McLaren	18	Love
9	Gurney	19	Prophet
10	Rindt	20	Tingle

Monaco

GRAND PRIX No: 133
DATE: May 30, 1965
VENUE: Monte Carlo
POLE LAP: Hill,G., 1m 32.5s
FASTEST LAP: Hill,G., 1m 31.7s

Pn	Driver	Car	Laps	Time/Reason
1	Hill,G.	BRM	100	2h 37m 39.6s
2	Bandini	Ferrari	100	2h 38m 43.6s
3	Stewart,Jackie	BRM	100	2h 39m 21.5s
4	Surtees	Ferrari	99	out of fuel
5	McLaren	Cooper-Climax	98	
6	Siffert	Brabham-BRM	98	
7	Bonnier	Brabham-Climax	97	
8	Hulme	Brabham-Climax	92	
9	Anderson	Brabham-Climax	85	
r	Hawkins	Lotus-Climax	79	accident
r	Attwood	Lotus-BRM	43	accident
r	Brabham,J.	Brabham-Climax	42	engine
r	Bucknum	Honda	32	gearbox
r	Gardner	Brabham-BRM	28	engine
r	Hailwood	Lotus-BRM	11	gearbox
r	Ginther	Honda	0	transmission

STARTING GRID:

1	Hill,G.	9	Anderson
2	Brabham,J.	10	Siffert
3	Stewart,Jackie	11	Gardner
4	Bandini	12	Hailwood
5	Surtees	13	Bonnier
6	Attwood	14	Hawkins
7	McLaren	15	Bucknum
8	Hulme	16	Ginther

Belgian

GRAND PRIX No: 134
DATE: June 13, 1965
VENUE: Spa-Francorchamps
POLE LAP: Hill,G., 3m 45.4s
FASTEST LAP: Clark, 4m 12.9s

Pn	Driver	Car	Laps	Time/Reason
1	Clark	Lotus-Climax	32	2h 23m 34.8s
2	Stewart,Jackie	BRM	32	2h 24m 19.6s
3	McLaren	Cooper-Climax	31	
4	Brabham,J.	Brabham-Climax	31	
5	Hill,G.	BRM	31	
6	Ginther	Honda	31	
7	Spence	Lotus-Climax	31	
8	Siffert	Brabham-BRM	31	
9	Bandini	Ferrari	30	
10	Gurney	Brabham-Climax	30	
11	Rindt	Cooper-Climax	29	
12	Bianchi	BRM	29	
13	Ireland	Lotus-BRM	27	
r	Attwood	Lotus-BRM	26	spun off
r	Gregory	BRM	12	fuel pump
r	Bucknum	Honda	9	engine
r	Bonnier	Brabham-Climax	8	ignition
r	Surtees	Ferrari	5	ignition
r	Gardner	Brabham-BRM	2	ignition
dns	Anderson	Brabham-Climax		withdrew

STARTING GRID:

1	Hill,G.	11	Bucknum
2	Clark	12	Spence
3	Stewart,Jackie	13	Attwood
4	Ginther	14	Rindt
5	Gurney	15	Bandini
6	Surtees	16	Ireland
7	Bonnier	17	Bianchi
8	Siffert	18	Gardner
9	McLaren	19	Anderson
10	Brabham,J.	20	Gregory

French

GRAND PRIX No: 135
DATE: June 27, 1965
VENUE: Clermont-Ferrand
POLE LAP: Clark, 3m 18.3s
FASTEST LAP: Clark, 3m 18.9s

Pn	Driver	Car	Laps	Time/Reason
1	Clark	Lotus-Climax	40	2h 14m 38.4s
2	Stewart,Jackie	BRM	40	2h 15m 04.7s
3	Surtees	Ferrari	40	2h 17m 11.9s
4	Hulme	Brabham-Climax	40	2h 17m 31.5s
5	Hill,G.	BRM	39	
6	Siffert	Brabham-BRM	39	
7	Spence	Lotus-Climax	39	
8	Bandini	Ferrari	36	spun off
r	Anderson	Brabham-Climax	30	spun off
r	McLaren	Cooper-Climax	23	suspension
r	Bonnier	Brabham-Climax	21	ignition
r	Amon	Lotus-BRM	20	fuel system
r	Ireland	Lotus-BRM	18	gearbox
r	Gurney	Brabham-Climax	16	engine
r	Ginther	Honda	9	ignition
r	Bucknum	Honda	4	engine
r	Rindt	Cooper-Climax	3	accident

STARTING GRID:

1 Clark
2 Stewart,Jackie
3 Bandini
4 Surtees
5 Gurney
6 Hulme
7 Ginther
8 Amon
9 McLaren
10 Spence
11 Bonnier
12 Rindt
13 Hill,G.
14 Siffert
15 Anderson
16 Bucknum
17 Ireland

British

GRAND PRIX No: 136
DATE: July 10, 1965
VENUE: Silverstone
POLE LAP: Clark, 1m 30.8s
FASTEST LAP: Hill,G., 1m 32.2s

Pn	Driver	Car	Laps	Time/Reason
1	Clark	Lotus-Climax	80	2h 05m 25.4s
2	Hill,G.	BRM	80	2h 05m 28.6s
3	Surtees	Ferrari	80	2h 05m 53.0s
4	Spence	Lotus-Climax	80	2h 06m 05.0s
5	Stewart,Jackie	BRM	80	2h 06m 40.0s
6	Gurney	Brabham-Climax	79	
7	Bonnier	Brabham-Climax	79	
8	Gardner	Brabham-BRM	78	
9	Siffert	Brabham-BRM	78	
10	McLaren	Cooper-Climax	77	
11	Raby	Brabham-BRM	73	
12	Gregory	BRM	70	
13	Attwood	Lotus-BRM	63	
14	Rindt	Cooper-Climax	62	
r	Ireland	Lotus-BRM	41	engine
r	Rhodes	Cooper-Climax	38	ignition
r	Anderson	Brabham-Climax	33	gearbox
r	Hulme	Brabham-Climax	29	alternator
r	Ginther	Honda	26	ignition
r	Bandini	Ferrari	2	engine

STARTING GRID:

1 Clark
2 Hill,G.
3 Ginther
4 Stewart,Jackie
5 Surtees
6 Spence
7 Gurney
8 Bandini
9 Hulme
10 McLaren
11 Rindt
12 Gardner
13 Bonnier
14 Ireland
15 Attwood
16 Anderson
17 Siffert
18 Gregory
19 Raby
20 Rhodes

Dutch

GRAND PRIX No: 137
DATE: July 18, 1965
VENUE: Zandvoort
POLE LAP: Hill,G., 1m 30.7s
FASTEST LAP: Clark, 1m 30.6s

Pn	Driver	Car	Laps	Time/Reason
1	Clark	Lotus-Climax	80	2h 03m 59.1s
2	Stewart,Jackie	BRM	80	2h 04m 07.1s
3	Gurney	Brabham-Climax	80	2h 04m 12.1s
4	Hill,G.	BRM	80	2h 04m 44.2s
5	Hulme	Brabham-Climax	79	
6	Ginther	Honda	79	
7	Surtees	Ferrari	79	
8	Spence	Lotus-Climax	79	
9	Bandini	Ferrari	79	
10	Ireland	Lotus-BRM	78	
11	Gardner	Brabham-BRM	77	
12	Attwood	Lotus-BRM	77	
13	Siffert	Brabham-BRM	55	
r	Rindt	Cooper-Climax	48	oil pressure
r	McLaren	Cooper-Climax	36	crownwheel/pinion
r	Bonnier	Brabham-Climax	16	ignition
r	Anderson	Brabham-Climax	11	overheating

STARTING GRID:

1	Hill,G.	10	Siffert
2	Clark	11	Gardner
3	Ginther	12	Bandini
4	Surtees	13	Ireland
5	Gurney	14	Rindt
6	Stewart,Jackie	15	Bonnier
7	Hulme	16	Anderson
8	Spence	17	Attwood
9	McLaren		

German

GRAND PRIX No: 138
DATE: August 1, 1965
VENUE: Nurburgring
POLE LAP: Clark, 8m 22.7s
FASTEST LAP: Clark, 8m 24.1s

Pn	Driver	Car	Laps	Time/Reason
1	Clark	Lotus-Climax	15	2h 07m 52.4s
2	Hill,G.	BRM	15	2h 08m 08.3s
3	Gurney	Brabham-Climax	15	2h 08m 13.8s
4	Rindt	Cooper-Climax	15	2h 11m 22.0s
5	Brabham,J.	Brabham-Climax	15	2h 12m 33.6s
6	Bandini	Ferrari	15	2h 13m 01.0s
7	Bonnier	Brabham-Climax	15	2h 13m 50.9s
8	Gregory	BRM	14	
r	Surtees	Ferrari	11	gearbox
r	Siffert	Brabham-BRM	9	engine
r	Attwood	Lotus-BRM	8	water pipe
r	Mitter	Lotus-Climax	8	water pipe
r	Spence	Lotus-Climax	8	driveshaft
r	McLaren	Cooper-Climax	7	gearbox
r	Hulme	Brabham-Climax	5	fuel leak
r	Amon	Lotus-BRM	3	ignition
r	Hawkins	Lotus-Climax	3	oil leak
r	Stewart,Jackie	BRM	2	suspension
r	Gardner	Brabham-BRM	0	gearbox
dns	Anderson	Brabham-Climax		accident

STARTING GRID:

1	Clark	11	Siffert
2	Stewart,Jackie	12	Mitter
3	Hill,G.	13	Hulme
4	Surtees	14	Brabham,J.
5	Gurney	15	Anderson
6	Spence	16	Amon
7	Bandini	17	Attwood
8	Rindt	18	Gardner
9	Bonnier	19	Gregory
10	McLaren	20	Hawkins

Italian

GRAND PRIX No: 139
DATE: September 12, 1965
VENUE: Monza
POLE LAP: Clark, 1m 35.9s
FASTEST LAP: Clark, 1m 36.4s

Pn	Driver	Car	Laps	Time/Reason
1	Stewart,Jackie	BRM	76	2h 04m 52.8s
2	Hill,G.	BRM	76	2h 04m 56.1s
3	Gurney	Brabham-Climax	76	2h 05m 09.3s
4	Bandini	Ferrari	76	2h 05m 09.3s
5	McLaren	Cooper-Climax	75	
6	Attwood	Lotus-BRM	75	
7	Bonnier	Brabham-Climax	74	
8	Rindt	Cooper-Climax	74	
9	Ireland	Lotus-BRM	74	
r	Clark	Lotus-Climax	63	fuel pump
r	Spence	Lotus-Climax	62	ignition
r	Vaccarella	Ferrari	58	
r	Bussinello	BRM	58	
r	Ginther	Honda	56	
r	Hulme	Brabham-Climax	46	suspension
r	Gardner	Brabham-BRM	45	engine
r	Siffert	Brabham-BRM	43	gearbox
r	Geki	Lotus-Climax	37	crownwheel/pinion
r	Surtees	Ferrari	34	clutch
r	Bucknum	Honda	27	engine
r	Gregory	BRM	22	gearbox
r	Baghelti	Brabham-Climax	12	engine
r	Bassi	BRM	8	engine

STARTING GRID:

1	Clark	13	Attwood
2	Surtees	14	Bonnier
3	Stewart,Jackie	15	Vaccarella
4	Hill,G.	16	Ireland
5	Bandini	17	Ginther
6	Bucknum	18	Gardner
7	Rindt	19	Baghelti
8	Spence	20	Geki
9	Gurney	21	Bussinello
10	Siffert	22	Bassi
11	McLaren	23	Gregory
12	Hulme		

US

GRAND PRIX No: 140
DATE: October 3, 1965
VENUE: Watkins Glen
POLE LAP: Hill,G., 1m 11.25s
FASTEST LAP: Hill,G., 1m 11.90s

Pn	Driver	Car	Laps	Time/Reason
1	Hill,G.	BRM	110	2h 20m 36.1s
2	Gurney	Brabham-Climax	110	2h 20m 48.6s
3	Brabham,J.	Brabham-Climax	110	2h 21m 33.6s
4	Bandini	Ferrari	109	
5	Rodriguez,P.	Ferrari	109	
6	Rindt	Cooper-Climax	108	
7	Ginther	Honda	108	
8	Bonnier	Brabham-Climax	107	
9	Bondurant	Ferrari	106	
10	Attwood	Lotus-BRM	101	
11	Siffert	Brabham-BRM	99	
12	Solana	Lotus-Climax	95	
13	Bucknum	Honda	92	
r	Stewart,Jackie	BRM	12	suspension
r	McLaren	Cooper-Climax	11	oil pressure
r	Clark	Lotus-Climax	11	engine
r	Ireland	Lotus-BRM	9	driver ill
r	Spence	Lotus-Climax	9	engine

STARTING GRID:

1	Hill,G.	10	Bonnier
2	Clark	11	Siffert
3	Ginther	12	Bucknum
4	Spence	13	Rindt
5	Bandini	14	Bondurant
6	Stewart,Jackie	15	Rodriguez,P.
7	Brabham,J.	16	Attwood
8	Gurney	17	Solana
9	McLaren	18	Ireland

Mexican

GRAND PRIX No:	141
DATE:	October 24, 1965
VENUE:	Mexico City
POLE LAP:	Clark, 1m 56.17s
FASTEST LAP:	Gurney, 1m 55.84s

Pn	Driver	Car	Laps	Time/Reason
1	Ginther	Honda	65	2h 08m 32.1s
2	Gurney	Brabham-Climax	65	2h 08m 35.0s
3	Spence	Lotus-Climax	65	2h 09m 32.3s
4	Siffert	Brabham-BRM	65	2h 10m 26.5s
5	Bucknum	Honda	64	
6	Attwood	Lotus-BRM	64	
7	Rodriguez,P.	Ferrari	62	
8	Bandini	Ferrari	62	
r	Hill,G.	BRM	56	engine
r	Solana	Lotus-Climax	55	ignition
r	Bonnier	Brabham-Climax	43	suspension
r	Rindt	Cooper-Climax	39	ignition
r	Brabham,J.	Brabham-Climax	38	oil leak
r	Stewart,Jackie	BRM	35	clutch
r	Bondurant	Lotus-BRM	29	suspension
r	McLaren	Cooper-Climax	25	gearbox
r	Clark	Lotus-Climax	8	engine
dns	Ireland	Lotus-BRM		driver sacked

STARTING GRID:

1	Clark	10	Bucknum
2	Gurney	11	Siffert
3	Ginther	12	Bonnier
4	Brabham,J.	13	Ireland
5	Hill,G.	14	Rodriguez,P.
6	Spence	15	McLaren
7	Bandini	16	Rindt
8	Stewart,Jackie	17	Attwood
9	Solana	18	Bondurant

Monaco

GRAND PRIX No:	142
DATE:	May 22, 1966
VENUE:	Monte Carlo
POLE LAP:	Clark, 1m 29.9s
FASTEST LAP:	Bandini, 1m 29s

Pn	Driver	Car	Laps	Time/Reason
1	Stewart,Jackie	BRM	100	2h 33m 10.5s
2	Bandini	Ferrari	100	2h 33m 50.7s
3	Hill,G.	BRM	99	
4	Bondurant	BRM	95	
r	Ginther	Cooper-Maser.	80	driveshaft
uc	Ligier	Cooper-Maser.	75	
uc	Bonnier	Cooper-Maser.	73	
r	Clark	Lotus-Climax	60	suspension
r	Rindt	Cooper-Maser.	56	engine
r	Siffert	Brabham-BRM	35	clutch
r	Spence	Lotus-BRM	34	suspension
r	Brabham,J.	Brabham-Repco	17	gearbox
r	Surtees	Ferrari	16	transmission
r	Hulme	Brabham-Climax	15	driveshaft
r	McLaren	McLaren-Ford	9	oil leak
r	Anderson	Brabham-Climax	3	engine

STARTING GRID:

1	Clark	9	Ginther
2	Surtees	10	McLaren
3	Stewart,Jackie	11	Brabham,J.
4	Hill,G.	12	Spence
5	Bandini	13	Siffert
6	Hulme	14	Bonnier
7	Rindt	15	Ligier
8	Anderson	16	Bondurant

Belgian

GRAND PRIX No:	143
DATE:	June 12, 1966
VENUE:	Spa-Francorchamps
POLE LAP:	Surtees, 3m 38.0s
FASTEST LAP:	Surtees, 4m 18.7s

Pn	Driver	Car	Laps	Time/Reason
1	Surtees	Ferrari	28	2h 09m 11.3s
2	Rindt	Cooper-Maser.	28	2h 09m 53.4s
3	Bandini	Ferrari	27	
4	Brabham,J.	Brabham-Repco	26	
5	Ginther	Cooper-Maser.	25	
uc	Ligier	Cooper-Maser.	24	
uc	Gurney	Eagle-Climax	23	
r	Bondurant	BRM	0	accident
r	Bonnier	Cooper-Maser.	0	accident
r	Clark	Lotus-Climax	0	accident
r	Hill,G.	BRM	0	accident
r	Hulme	Brabham-Climax	0	accident
r	Siffert	Cooper-Maser.	0	accident
r	Spence	Lotus-BRM	0	accident
r	Stewart,Jackie	BRM	0	accident
dns	McLaren	McLaren-Seren.		bearings
dns	Arundell	Lotus-BRM		engine

STARTING GRID:

1	Surtees	10	Clark
2	Rindt	11	Bondurant
3	Stewart,Jackie	12	Ligier
4	Brabham,J.	13	Hulme
5	Bandini	14	Siffert
6	Bonnier	15	Gurney
7	Spence	16	McLaren
8	Ginther	17	Arundell
9	Hill,G.		

French

GRAND PRIX No:	144
DATE:	July 3, 1966
VENUE:	Reims
POLE LAP:	Bandini, 2m 07.8s
FASTEST LAP:	Bandini, 2m 11.3s

Pn	Driver	Car	Laps	Time/Reason
1	Brabham,J.	Brabham-Repco	48	1h 48m 31.3s
2	Parkes	Ferrari	48	1h 48m 40.8s
3	Hulme	Brabham-Repco	46	
4	Rindt	Cooper-Maser.	46	
5	Gurney	Eagle-Climax	45	
6	Taylor,J.	Brabham-BRM	45	
7	Anderson	Brabham-Climax	44	
8	Amon	Cooper-Maser.	44	
uc	Ligier	Cooper-Maser.	42	
r	Rodriguez,P.	Lotus-Climax	40	oil line
uc	Bandini	Ferrari	37	
uc	Bonnier	Brabham-Climax	32	
r	Hill,G.	BRM	13	engine
r	Siffert	Cooper-Maser.	10	fuel system
r	Spence	Lotus-BRM	8	clutch
r	Surtees	Cooper-Maser.	5	fuel system
r	Arundell	Lotus-BRM	3	gearbox

STARTING GRID:

1	Bandini	10	Spence
2	Surtees	11	Ligier
3	Parkes	12	Anderson
4	Brabham,J.	13	Rodriguez,P.
5	Rindt	14	Gurney
6	Siffert	15	Taylor,J.
7	Amon	16	Arundell
8	Hill,G.	17	Bonnier
9	Hulme		

British

GRAND PRIX No: 145
DATE: July 16, 1966
VENUE: Brands Hatch
POLE LAP: Brabham,J., 1m 34.5s
FASTEST LAP: Brabham,J., 1m 37.0s

Pn	Driver	Car	Laps	Time/Reason
1	Brabham,J.	Brabham-Repco	80	2h 13m 13.4s
2	Hulme	Brabham-Repco	80	2h 13m 23.0s
3	Hill,G.	BRM	79	
4	Clark	Lotus-Climax	79	
5	Rindt	Cooper-Maser.	79	
6	McLaren	McLaren-Seren.	78	
7	Irwin	Brabham-Climax	78	
8	Taylor,J.	Brabham-BRM	76	
9	Bondurant	BRM	76	
10	Ligier	Cooper-Maser.	75	
11	Lawrence	Cooper-Ferrari	73	
uc	Siffert	Cooper-Maser.	70	
uc	Anderson	Brabham-Climax	70	
r	Surtees	Cooper-Maser.	66	transmission
r	Bonnier	Brabham-Climax	42	clutch
r	Arundell	Lotus-BRM	31	gearbox
r	Stewart,Jackie	BRM	16	engine
r	Spence	Lotus-BRM	14	oil leak
r	Gurney	Eagle-Climax	8	engine
r	Taylor,T.	Shannon-Clim.	0	engine

STARTING GRID:

1	Brabham,J.	11	Siffert
2	Hulme	12	Irwin
3	Gurney	13	McLaren
4	Hill,G.	14	Bondurant
5	Clark	15	Bonnier
6	Surtees	16	Taylor,J.
7	Rindt	17	Ligier
8	Stewart,Jackie	18	Taylor,T.
9	Spence	19	Lawrence
10	Anderson	20	Arundell

Dutch

GRAND PRIX No: 146
DATE: July 24, 1966
VENUE: Zandvoort
POLE LAP: Brabham,J., 1m 28.1s
FASTEST LAP: Hulme, 1m 30.6s

Pn	Driver	Car	Laps	Time/Reason
1	Brabham,J.	Brabham-Repco	90	2h 20m 32.5s
2	Hill,G.	BRM	89	
3	Clark	Lotus-Climax	88	
4	Stewart,Jackie	BRM	88	
5	Spence	Lotus-BRM	87	
6	Bandini	Ferrari	87	
7	Bonnier	Cooper-Maser.	84	
8	Taylor,J.	Brabham-BRM	84	
9	Ligier	Cooper-Maser.	84	
r	Siffert	Cooper-Maser.	79	engine
r	Anderson	Brabham-Climax	72	suspension
r	Surtees	Cooper-Maser.	43	electrical
r	Hulme	Brabham-Repco	36	ignition
r	Arundell	Lotus-BRM	27	ignition
r	Gurney	Eagle-Climax	26	oil line
r	Parkes	Ferrari	10	accident
r	Rindt	Cooper-Maser.	2	accident
dns	McLaren	McLaren-Seren.		engine

STARTING GRID:

1	Brabham,J.	10	Surtees
2	Hulme	11	Siffert
3	Clark	12	Spence
4	Gurney	13	Bonnier
5	Parkes	14	McLaren
6	Rindt	15	Anderson
7	Hill,G.	16	Arundell
8	Stewart,Jackie	17	Ligier
9	Bandini	18	Taylor,J.

German

GRAND PRIX No: 147
DATE: August 2, 1966
VENUE: Nurburgring
POLE LAP: Clark, 8m 16.5s
FASTEST LAP: Surtees, 8m 49.0s

Pn	Driver	Car	Laps	Time/Reason
1	Brabham,J.	Brabham-Repco	15	2h 27m 03.0s
2	Surtees	Cooper-Maser.	15	2h 27m 47.4s
3	Rindt	Cooper-Maser.	15	2h 29m 35.6s
4	Hill,G.	BRM	15	2h 33m 44.4s
5	Stewart,Jackie	BRM	15	2h 35m 31.9s
6	Bandini	Ferrari	15	2h 37m 59.4s
7	Gurney	Eagle-Climax	15	
8	Beltoise	Matra-Ford	14	(F2 car)
9	Hahne	Matra-BRM	14	(F2 car)
10	Schlesser,J.	Matra-Ford	14	(F2 car)
11	Herrmann	Brabham-Ford	14	(F2 car)
12	Arundell	Lotus-BRM	14	
r	Spence	Lotus-BRM	12	alternator
r	Clark	Lotus-Climax	11	accident
r	Lawrence	Cooper-Ferrari	10	suspension
r	Scarfiotti	Ferrari	9	electrical
r	Parkes	Ferrari	9	accident
r	Hulme	Brabham-Repco	8	ignition
r	Rodriguez,P.	Lotus-Ford	7	engine (F2 car)
r	Rees	Brabham-Ford	4	engine (F2 car)
r	Bonnier	Cooper-Maser.	4	clutch
r	Courage	Lotus-Ford	3	accident (F2 car)
r	Bondurant	BRM	3	engine
r	Ahrens	Brabham-Ford	3	gearbox (F2 car)
r	Anderson	Brabham-Climax	2	transmission
r	Ickx	Matra-Ford	0	accident (F2 car)
r	Taylor,J.	Brabham-BRM	0	fatal accident
dns	Mitter	Lotus-Ford		injured
dns	Moser	Brabham-Ford		engine

STARTING GRID:

1	Clark	9	Rindt
2	Surtees	10	Hill,G.
3	Stewart,Jackie	11	Mitter
4	Scarfiotti	12	Bondurant
5	Brabham,J.	13	Bonnier
6	Bandini	14	Spence
7	Parkes	15	Anderson
8	Gurney	16	Hulme

+

Italian

GRAND PRIX No: 148
DATE: September 4, 1966
VENUE: Monza
POLE LAP: Parkes, 1m 31.3s
FASTEST LAP: Scarfiotti, 1m 32.4s

Pn	Driver	Car	Laps	Time/Reason
1	Scarfiotti	Ferrari	68	1h 47m 14.8s
2	Parkes	Ferrari	68	1h 47m 20.6s
3	Hulme	Brabham-Repco	68	1h 47m 20.6s
4	Rindt	Cooper-Maser.	67	
5	Spence	Lotus-BRM	67	
6	Anderson	Brabham-Climax	66	
7	Bondurant	BRM	65	
8	Arundell	Lotus-BRM	63	
9	Geki	Lotus-Climax	63	
uc	Baghelti	Ferrari	59	
r	Clark	Lotus-BRM	58	gearbox
r	Siffert	Cooper-Maser.	46	engine
r	Bandini	Ferrari	33	ignition
r	Surtees	Cooper-Maser.	31	fuel leak
r	Ginther	Honda	16	accident
r	Gurney	Eagle-Weslake	7	engine
r	Brabham,J.	Brabham-Repco	7	oil leak
r	Stewart,Jackie	BRM	5	fuel leak
r	Bonnier	Cooper-Maser.	3	throttle
r	Hill,G.	BRM	0	engine

STARTING GRID:

1	Parkes	11	Hill,G.
2	Scarfiotti	12	Bonnier
3	Clark	13	Arundell
4	Surtees	14	Spence
5	Bandini	15	Anderson
6	Brabham,J.	16	Baghelti
7	Ginther	17	Siffert
8	Rindt	18	Bondurant
9	Stewart,Jackie	19	Gurney
10	Hulme	20	Geki

US

GRAND PRIX No:	149
DATE:	October 2, 1966
VENUE:	Watkins Glen
POLE LAP:	Brabham,J., 1m 08.42s
FASTEST LAP:	Surtees, 1m 09.67s

Pn	Driver	Car	Laps	Time/Reason
1	Clark	Lotus-BRM	108	2h 09m 40.1s
2	Rindt	Cooper-Maser.	107	
3	Surtees	Cooper-Maser.	107	
4	Siffert	Cooper-Maser.	105	
5	McLaren	McLaren-Ford	105	
6	Arundell	Lotus-Climax	101	
r	Ireland	BRM	96	alternator
uc	Ginther	Honda	81	
r	Spence	Lotus-BRM	74	ignition
r	Bucknum	Honda	58	engine
uc	Bonnier	Cooper-Maser.	57	
r	Brabham,J.	Brabham-Repco	55	engine
r	Stewart,Jackie	BRM	53	engine
r	Hill,G.	BRM	52	crownwheel/pinion
r	Bandini	Ferrari	34	engine
r	Hulme	Brabham-Repco	18	oil pressure
r	Gurney	Eagle-Weslake	13	clutch
r	Rodriguez,P.	Lotus-BRM	13	starter
dq	Bondurant	Eagle-Climax	5	push start

STARTING GRID:

1	Brabham,J.	11	McLaren
2	Clark	12	Spence
3	Bandini	13	Siffert
4	Surtees	14	Gurney
5	Hill,G.	15	Bonnier
6	Stewart,Jackie	16	Bondurant
7	Hulme	17	Ireland
8	Ginther	18	Bucknum
9	Rindt	19	Arundell
10	Rodriguez,P.		

Mexican

GRAND PRIX No:	150
DATE:	October 25, 1966
VENUE:	Mexico City
POLE LAP:	Surtees, 1m 53.18s
FASTEST LAP:	Ginther, 1m 53.75s

Pn	Driver	Car	Laps	Time/Reason
1	Surtees	Cooper-Maser.	65	2h 06m 35.40s
2	Brabham,J.	Brabham-Repco	65	2h 06m 43.22s
3	Hulme	Brabham-Repco	64	
4	Ginther	Honda	64	
5	Gurney	Eagle-Climax	64	
6	Bonnier	Cooper-Maser.	63	
7	Arundell	Lotus-BRM	61	
8	Bucknum	Honda	60	
r	Rodriguez,P.	Lotus-Climax	48	crownwheel and pinion
r	McLaren	McLaren-Ford	39	engine
r	Siffert	Cooper-Maser.	32	suspension
r	Rindt	Cooper-Maser.	31	suspension
r	Ireland	BRM	27	transmission
r	Stewart,Jackie	BRM	25	oil leak
r	Bondurant	Eagle-Weslake	23	fuel feed
r	Hill,G.	BRM	17	engine
r	Solana	Cooper-Maser.	8	overheating
r	Clark	Lotus-BRM	8	gearbox
dns	Spence	Lotus-BRM		accident

STARTING GRID:

1	Surtees	11	Siffert
2	Clark	12	Spence
3	Ginther	13	Bonnier
4	Brabham,J.	14	Bucknum
5	Rindt	15	McLaren
6	Hulme	16	Solana
7	Hill,G.	17	Ireland
8	Rodriguez,P.	18	Arundell
9	Gurney	19	Bondurant
10	Stewart,Jackie		

South African

GRAND PRIX No:	151
DATE:	January 2, 1967
VENUE:	Kyalami
POLE LAP:	Brabham,J., 1m 28.3s
FASTEST LAP:	Hulme, 1m 29.9s

Pn	Driver	Car	Laps	Time/Reason
1	Rodriguez,P.	Cooper-Maser.	80	2h 05m 45.9s
2	Love	Cooper-Climax	80	2h 06m 12.3s
3	Surtees	Honda	79	
4	Hulme	Brabham-Repco	78	
5	Anderson	Brabham-Climax	78	
6	Brabham,J.	Brabham-Repco	76	
uc	Charlton	Brabham-Climax	67	
uc	Botha	Brabham-Climax	60	
r	Tingle	LDS-Climax	56	accident
r	Courage	Lotus-BRM	51	fuel system
r	Gurney	Eagle-Climax	44	suspension
r	Siffert	Cooper-Maser.	41	engine
r	Rindt	Cooper-Maser.	38	engine
r	Spence	BRM	31	oil line
r	Bonnier	Cooper-Maser.	30	engine
r	Clark	Lotus-BRM	22	engine
r	Hill,G.	Lotus-BRM	6	accident
r	Stewart,Jackie	BRM	2	engine

STARTING GRID:

1	Brabham,J.	10	Anderson
2	Hulme	11	Gurney
3	Clark	12	Bonnier
4	Rodriguez,P.	13	Spence
5	Love	14	Tingle
6	Surtees	15	Hill,G.
7	Rindt	16	Siffert
8	Charlton	17	Botha
9	Stewart,Jackie	18	Courage

Monaco

GRAND PRIX No:	152
DATE:	May 7, 1967
VENUE:	Monte Carlo
POLE LAP:	Brabham,J., 1m 27.6s
FASTEST LAP:	Clark, 1m 29.5s

Pn	Driver	Car	Laps	Time/Reason
1	Hulme	Brabham-Repco	100	2h 34m 34.3s
2	Hill,G.	Lotus-BRM	99	
3	Amon	Ferrari	98	
4	McLaren	McLaren-BRM	97	
5	Rodriguez,P.	Cooper-Maser.	96	
6	Spence	BRM	96	
r	Bandini	Ferrari	81	fatal accident
r	Courage	BRM	64	spun off
r	Clark	Lotus-Climax	42	suspension
r	Surtees	Honda	32	engine
r	Siffert	Cooper-Maser.	31	engine
r	Rindt	Cooper-Maser.	14	gearbox
r	Stewart,Jackie	BRM	14	crownwheel/pinion
r	Gurney	Eagle-Weslake	4	fuel system
r	Servoz-Gavin	Matra-Ford F2	1	fuel system
r	Brabham,J.	Brabham-Repco	0	engine

STARTING GRID:

1	Brabham,J.	9	Siffert
2	Bandini	10	McLaren
3	Surtees	11	Servoz-Gavin
4	Hulme	12	Spence
5	Clark	13	Courage
6	Stewart,Jackie	14	Amon
7	Gurney	15	Rindt
8	Hill,G.	16	Rodriguez,P.

Dutch

GRAND PRIX No: 153
DATE: June 4, 1967
VENUE: Zandvoort
POLE LAP: Hill,G., 1m 24.60s
FASTEST LAP: Clark, 1m 28.08s

Pn	Driver	Car	Laps	Time/Reason
1	Clark	Lotus-Ford	90	2h 14m 45.1s
2	Brabham,J.	Brabham-Repco	90	2h 15m 08.7s
3	Hulme	Brabham-Repco	90	2h 15m 10.8s
4	Amon	Ferrari	90	2h 15m 12.4s
5	Parkes	Ferrari	89	
6	Scarfiotti	Ferrari	89	
7	Irwin	Lotus-BRM	88	
8	Spence	BRM	87	
9	Anderson	Brabham-Climax	86	
10	Siffert	Cooper-Maser.	83	
r	Surtees	Honda	72	throttle
r	Stewart,Jackie	BRM	50	brakes
r	Rindt	Cooper-Maser.	40	suspension
r	Rodriguez,P.	Cooper-Maser.	39	gearbox
r	Hill,G.	Lotus-Ford	10	engine
r	Gurney	Eagle-Weslake	8	fuel system
r	McLaren	McLaren-BRM	1	accident

STARTING GRID:

1 Hill,G.
2 Gurney
3 Brabham,J.
4 Rindt
5 Rodriguez,P.
6 Surtees
7 Hulme
8 Clark
9 Amon
10 Parkes
11 Stewart,Jackie
12 Spence
13 Irwin
14 McLaren
15 Scarfiotti
16 Siffert
17 Anderson

Belgian

GRAND PRIX No: 154
DATE: June 18, 1967
VENUE: Spa-Francorchamps
POLE LAP: Clark, 3m 28.1s
FASTEST LAP: Gurney, 3m 31.9s

Pn	Driver	Car	Laps	Time/Reason
1	Gurney	Eagle-Weslake	28	1h 40m 49.4s
2	Stewart,Jackie	BRM	28	1h 41m 52.4s
3	Amon	Ferrari	28	1h 42m 29.4s
4	Rindt	Cooper-Maser.	28	1h 43m 03.3s
5	Spence	BRM	27	
6	Clark	Lotus-Ford	27	
7	Siffert	Cooper-Maser.	27	
8	Anderson	Brabham-Climax	26	
9	Rodriguez,P.	Cooper-Maser.	25	engine
10	Ligier	Cooper-Maser.	25	
uc	Scarfiotti	Ferrari	24	
r	Brabham,J.	Brabham-Repco	14	engine
r	Hulme	Brabham-Repco	13	engine
r	Bonnier	Cooper-Maser.	9	engine
r	Hill,G.	Lotus-Ford	2	clutch
r	Irwin	BRM	0	engine
r	Surtees	Honda	0	engine
r	Parkes	Ferrari	0	accident

STARTING GRID:

1 Clark
2 Gurney
3 Hill,G.
4 Rindt
5 Amon
6 Stewart,Jackie
7 Brabham,J.
8 Parkes
9 Scarfiotti
10 Surtees
11 Spence
12 Bonnier
13 Rodriguez,P.
14 Hulme
15 Irwin
16 Siffert
17 Anderson
18 Ligier

French

GRAND PRIX No:	155
DATE:	July 2, 1967
VENUE:	Le Mans
POLE LAP:	Hill,G., 1m 36.2s
FASTEST LAP:	Hill,G., 1m 36.7s

Pn	Driver	Car	Laps	Time/Reason
1	Brabham,J.	Brabham-Repco	80	2h 13m 21.3s
2	Hulme	Brabham-Repco	80	2h 14m 10.8s
3	Stewart,Jackie	BRM	79	
4	Siffert	Cooper-Maser.	77	
5	Irwin	BRM	76	engine
6	Rodriguez,P.	Cooper-Maser.	76	
uc	Ligier	Cooper-Maser.	68	
r	Amon	Ferrari	47	throttle
r	Gurney	Eagle-Weslake	40	fuel system
r	Rindt	Cooper-Maser.	33	engine
r	McLaren	Eagle-Weslake	25	ignition
r	Clark	Lotus-Ford	22	crownwheel/pinion
r	Anderson	Brabham-Climax	16	ignition
r	Hill,G.	Lotus-Ford	13	crownwheel/pinion
r	Spence	BRM	9	transmission

STARTING GRID:

1	Hill,G.	9	Irwin
2	Brabham,J.	10	Stewart,Jackie
3	Gurney	11	Siffert
4	Clark	12	Spence
5	McLaren	13	Rodriguez,P.
6	Hulme	14	Anderson
7	Amon	15	Ligier
8	Rindt		

British

GRAND PRIX No:	156
DATE:	July 15, 1967
VENUE:	Silverstone
POLE LAP:	Clark, 1m 25.3s
FASTEST LAP:	Hulme, 1m 27.0s

Pn	Driver	Car	Laps	Time/Reason
1	Clark	Lotus-Ford	80	1h 59m 25.6s
2	Hulme	Brabham-Repco	80	1h 59m 38.4s
3	Amon	Ferrari	80	1h 59m 42.2s
4	Brabham,J.	Brabham-Repco	80	1h 59m 47.4s
5	Rodriguez,P.	Cooper-Maser.	79	
6	Surtees	Honda	78	
7	Irwin	BRM	77	
8	Hobbs	BRM	77	
9	Rees	Cooper-Maser.	76	
10	Ligier	Brabham-Repco	76	
r	Anderson	Brabham-Climax	67	engine
r	Hill,G.	Lotus-Ford	64	engine
r	Spence	BRM	43	ignition
r	Gurney	Eagle-Weslake	33	clutch
r	Moser	Cooper-ATS	28	oil pressure
r	Rindt	Cooper-Maser.	26	engine
r	Stewart,Jackie	BRM	19	transmission
r	McLaren	Eagle-Weslake	13	engine
r	Siffert	Cooper-Maser.	9	engine
r	Bonnier	Cooper-Maser.	0	engine

STARTING GRID:

1	Clark	11	Spence
2	Hill,G.	12	Stewart,Jackie
3	Brabham,J.	13	Irwin
4	Hulme	14	Hobbs
5	Gurney	15	Rees
6	Amon	16	Anderson
7	Surtees	17	Siffert
8	Rindt	18	Bonnier
9	Rodriguez,P.	19	Moser
10	McLaren	20	Ligier

German

GRAND PRIX No:	157
DATE:	August 6, 1967
VENUE:	Nurburgring
POLE LAP:	Clark, 8m 04.1s
FASTEST LAP:	Gurney, 8m 15.1s

Pn	Driver	Car	Laps	Time/Reason
1	Hulme	Brabham-Repco	15	2h 05m 55.7s
2	Brabham,J.	Brabham-Repco	15	2h 06m 34.2s
3	Amon	Ferrari	15	2h 06m 34.7s
4	Surtees	Honda	15	2h 08m 21.4s
5	Bonnier	Cooper-Maser.	15	2h 14m 37.8s
6	Ligier	Brabham-Repco	14	
7	Irwin	BRM	13	
8	Rodriguez,P.	Cooper-Maser.	13	
r	Gurney	Eagle-Weslake	12	transmission
r	Siffert	Cooper-Maser.	11	fuel system
r	Hill,G.	Lotus-Ford	7	suspension
r	Hahne	Lola-BMW	6	suspension
r	Stewart,Jackie	BRM	5	crownwheel/pinion
r	Rindt	Cooper-Maser.	4	steering
r	Clark	Lotus-Ford	4	suspension
r	McLaren	Eagle-Weslake	3	oil line
r	Spence	BRM	2	crownwheel and

STARTING GRID:

1	Clark	10	Rodriguez,P.
2	Hulme	11	Spence
3	Stewart,Jackie	12	Siffert
4	Gurney	13	Hill,G.
5	McLaren	14	Hahne
6	Surtees	15	Irwin
7	Brabham,J.	16	Bonnier
8	Amon	17	Ligier
9	Rindt		

Canadian

GRAND PRIX No:	158
DATE:	August 27, 1967
VENUE:	Mosport Park
POLE LAP:	Clark, 1m 22.4s
FASTEST LAP:	Clark, 1m 23.1s

Pn	Driver	Car	Laps	Time/Reason
1	Brabham,J.	Brabham-Repco	90	2h 40m 40.0s
2	Hulme	Brabham-Repco	90	2h 41m 41.9s
3	Gurney	Eagle-Weslake	89	
4	Hill,G.	Lotus-Ford	88	
5	Spence	BRM	87	
6	Amon	Ferrari	87	
7	McLaren	McLaren-BRM	86	
8	Bonnier	Cooper-Maser.	85	
9	Hobbs	BRM	85	
10	Attwood	Cooper-Maser.	84	
11	Fisher	Lotus-BRM	81	
r	Clark	Lotus-Ford	68	ignition
r	Wietzes	Lotus-Ford	68	ignition
r	Stewart,Jackie	BRM	64	throttle
uc	Pease	Eagle-Climax	47	
r	Irwin	BRM	17	spun off
r	Rindt	Cooper-Maser.	3	ignition
dns	Siffert	Cooper-Maser.		starter

STARTING GRID:

1	Clark	10	Spence
2	Hill,G.	11	Irwin
3	Hulme	12	Hobbs
4	Amon	13	Siffert
5	Gurney	14	Attwood
6	McLaren	15	Bonnier
7	Brabham,J.	16	Pease
8	Rindt	17	Wietzes
9	Stewart,Jackie	18	Fisher

Italian

GRAND PRIX No:	159
DATE:	September 10, 1967
VENUE:	Monza
POLE LAP:	Clark, 1m 28.5s
FASTEST LAP:	Clark, 1m 28.5s

Pn	Driver	Car	Laps	Time/Reason
1	Surtees	Honda	68	1h 43m 45.0s
2	Brabham,J.	Brabham-Repco	68	1h 43m 45.2s
3	Clark	Lotus-Ford	68	1h 44m 08.1s
4	Rindt	Cooper-Maser.	68	1h 44m 41.6s
5	Spence	BRM	67	
6	Ickx	Cooper-Maser.	66	
7	Amon	Ferrari	64	
r	Hill,G.	Lotus-Ford	58	engine
r	Baghelti	Lotus-Ford	50	engine
r	Siffert	Cooper-Maser.	50	accident
r	McLaren	McLaren-BRM	46	engine
r	Bonnier	Cooper-Maser.	46	overheating
r	Stewart,Jackie	BRM	45	engine
r	Hulme	Brabham-Repco	30	overheating
r	Ligier	Brabham-Repco	26	engine
r	Irwin	BRM	16	fuel system
r	Scarfiotti	Eagle-Weslake	5	engine
r	Gurney	Eagle-Weslake	4	engine

STARTING GRID:

1	Clark	10	Scarfiotti
2	Brabham,J.	11	Rindt
3	McLaren	12	Spence
4	Amon	13	Siffert
5	Gurney	14	Ickx
6	Hulme	15	Bonnier
7	Stewart,Jackie	16	Irwin
8	Hill,G.	17	Baghelti
9	Surtees	18	Ligier

US

GRAND PRIX No:	160
DATE:	October 1, 1967
VENUE:	Watkins Glen
POLE LAP:	Hill,G., 1m 05.48s
FASTEST LAP:	Hill,G., 1m 06.00s

Pn	Driver	Car	Laps	Time/Reason
1	Clark	Lotus-Ford	108	2h 03m 13.2s
2	Hill,G.	Lotus-Ford	108	2h 03m 19.5s
3	Hulme	Brabham-Repco	107	
4	Siffert	Cooper-Maser.	106	
5	Brabham,J.	Brabham-Repco	104	
6	Bonnier	Cooper-Maser.	101	
7	Beltoise	Matra-Ford F2	101	
r	Surtees	Honda	96	alternator
r	Amon	Ferrari	95	engine
r	Stewart,Jackie	BRM	72	fuel system
r	Ickx	Cooper-Maser.	45	overheating
r	Ligier	Brabham-Repco	43	engine
r	Irwin	BRM	41	engine
r	Spence	BRM	35	engine
r	Rindt	Cooper-Maser.	33	engine
r	Gurney	Eagle-Weslake	24	suspension
r	McLaren	McLaren-BRM	16	water pipe
r	Solana	Lotus-Ford	7	ignition

STARTING GRID:

1	Hill,G.	10	Stewart,Jackie
2	Clark	11	Surtees
3	Gurney	12	Siffert
4	Amon	13	Spence
5	Brabham,J.	14	Irwin
6	Hulme	15	Bonnier
7	Solana	16	Ickx
8	Rindt	17	Ligier
9	McLaren	18	Beltoise

Mexican

GRAND PRIX No:	161
DATE:	October 22, 1967
VENUE:	Mexico City
POLE LAP:	Clark, 1m 47.56s
FASTEST LAP:	Clark, 1m 48.13s

Pn	Driver	Car	Laps	Time/Reason
1	Clark	Lotus-Ford	65	1h 59m 28.70s
2	Brabham,J.	Brabham-Repco	65	2h 00m 54.06s
3	Hulme	Brabham-Repco	64	
4	Surtees	Honda	64	
5	Spence	BRM	63	
6	Rodriguez,P.	Cooper-Maser.	63	
7	Beltoise	Matra-Ford F2	63	
8	Williams	Ferrari	63	
9	Amon	Ferrari	62	
10	Bonnier	Cooper-Maser.	61	
11	Ligier	Brabham-Repco	61	
12	Siffert	Cooper-Maser.	59	engine
r	McLaren	McLaren-BRM	44	oil pressure
r	Irwin	BRM	32	oil leak
r	Stewart,Jackie	BRM	23	engine
r	Hill,G.	Lotus-Ford	17	transmission
r	Solana	Lotus-Ford	12	suspension
r	Gurney	Eagle-Weslake	3	radiator

STARTING GRID:

1	Clark	10	Siffert
2	Amon	11	Spence
3	Gurney	12	Stewart,Jackie
4	Hill,G.	13	Rodriguez,P.
5	Brabham,J.	14	Beltoise
6	Hulme	15	Irwin
7	Surtees	16	Williams
8	McLaren	17	Bonnier
9	Solana	18	Ligier

South African

GRAND PRIX No:	162
DATE:	January 1, 1968
VENUE:	Kyalami
POLE LAP:	Clark, 1m 21.6s
FASTEST LAP:	Clark, 1m 23.7s

Pn	Driver	Car	Laps	Time/Reason
1	Clark	Lotus-Ford	80	1h 53m 56.6s
2	Hill,G.	Lotus-Ford	80	1h 54m 21.9s
3	Rindt	Brabham-Repco	80	1h 54m 27.0s
4	Amon	Ferrari	78	
5	Hulme	McLaren-BRM	78	
6	Beltoise	Matra-Ford F2	77	
7	Siffert	Cooper-Maser.	77	
8	Surtees	Honda	75	
9	Love	Brabham-Repco	75	
uc	Pretorius	Brabham-Climax	70	
r	Gurney	Eagle-Weslake	57	overheating
r	Ickx	Ferrari	51	oil tank
r	Bonnier	Cooper-Maser.	46	overheating
r	Stewart,Jackie	Matra-Ford	43	engine
r	Tingle	LDS-Repco	34	overheating
r	van Rooyen	Cooper-Climax	21	engine
r	Rodriguez,P.	BRM	19	fuel overheating
r	Brabham,J.	Brabham-Repco	16	engine
r	de Adamich	Ferrari	13	accident
r	Spence	BRM	7	fuel overheating
r	Redman	Cooper-Maser.	4	engine
r	Charlton	Brabham-Repco	3	crownwheel/pinion
r	Scarfiotti	Cooper-Maser.	2	water pipe

STARTING GRID:

1	Clark	13	Spence
2	Hill,G.	14	Charlton
3	Stewart,Jackie	15	Scarfiotti
4	Rindt	16	Siffert
5	Brabham,J.	17	Love
6	Surtees	18	Beltoise
7	de Adamich	19	Bonnier
8	Amon	20	van Rooyen
9	Hulme	21	Redman
10	Rodriguez,P.	22	Tingle
11	Ickx	23	Pretorius
12	Gurney		

Spanish

GRAND PRIX No:	163
DATE:	May 12, 1968
VENUE:	Jarama
POLE LAP:	Amon, 1m 27.9s
FASTEST LAP:	Beltoise, 1m 28.3s

Pn	Driver	Car	Laps	Time/Reason
1	Hill,G.	Lotus-Ford	90	2h 15m 20.1s
2	Hulme	McLaren-Ford	90	2h 15m 36.0s
3	Redman	Cooper-BRM	89	
4	Scarfiotti	Cooper-BRM	89	
5	Beltoise	Matra-Ford	81	
r	McLaren	McLaren-Ford	77	oil leak
r	Surtees	Honda	74	gearbox
r	Siffert	Lotus-Ford	62	transmission
r	Amon	Ferrari	57	fuel system
r	Courage	BRM	52	fuel system
r	Rodriguez,P.	BRM	27	accident
r	Ickx	Ferrari	13	ignition
r	Rindt	Brabham-Repco	10	oil pressure
dns	Brabham,J.	Brabham-Repco		engine

STARTING GRID:

1	Amon	8	Ickx
2	Rodriguez,P.	9	Rindt
3	Hulme	10	Siffert
4	McLaren	11	Courage
5	Beltoise	12	Scarfiotti
6	Hill,G.	13	Redman
7	Surtees	14	Brabham,J.

Monaco

GRAND PRIX No:	164
DATE:	May 26, 1968
VENUE:	Monte Carlo
POLE LAP:	Hill,G., 1m 28.2s
FASTEST LAP:	Attwood, 1m 28.1s

Pn	Driver	Car	Laps	Time/Reason
1	Hill,G.	Lotus-Ford	80	2h 00m 32.3s
2	Attwood	BRM	80	2h 00m 34.5s
3	Bianchi	Cooper-BRM	76	
4	Scarfiotti	Cooper-BRM	76	
5	Hulme	McLaren-Ford	73	
r	Surtees	Honda	16	gearbox
r	Rodriguez,P.	BRM	16	accident
r	Courage	BRM	11	chassis
r	Beltoise	Matra	11	accident
r	Siffert	Lotus-Ford	11	crownwheel/pinion
r	Gurney	Eagle-Weslake	9	engine
r	Rindt	Brabham-Repco	8	accident
r	Brabham,J.	Brabham-Repco	7	suspension
r	Servoz-Gavin	Matra-Ford	3	transmission
r	Oliver	Lotus-Ford	0	accident
r	McLaren	McLaren-Ford	0	accident

STARTING GRID:

1	Hill,G.	9	Rodriguez,P.
2	Servoz-Gavin	10	Hulme
3	Siffert	11	Courage
4	Surtees	12	Brabham,J.
5	Rindt	13	Oliver
6	Attwood	14	Bianchi
7	McLaren	15	Scarfiotti
8	Beltoise	16	Gurney

Belgian

GRAND PRIX No:	165
DATE:	June 9, 1968
VENUE:	Spa-Francorchamps
POLE LAP:	Amon, 3m 28.6s
FASTEST LAP:	Surtees, 3m 30.5s

Pn	Driver	Car	Laps	Time/Reason
1	McLaren	McLaren-Ford	28	1h 40m 02.1s
2	Rodriguez,P.	BRM	28	1h 40m 14.2s
3	Ickx	Ferrari	28	1h 40m 41.7s
4	Stewart,Jackie	Matra-Ford	27	
5	Oliver	Lotus-Ford	26	transmission
6	Bianchi	Cooper-BRM	26	
7	Siffert	Lotus-Ford	25	engine
8	Beltoise	Matra	25	
r	Courage	BRM	21	engine
r	Hulme	McLaren-Ford	17	transmission
r	Surtees	Honda	10	suspension
r	Amon	Ferrari	7	radiator
r	Redman	Cooper-BRM	6	accident
r	Rindt	Brabham-Repco	5	engine
r	Brabham,J.	Brabham-Repco	5	throttle
r	Attwood	BRM	5	water pipe
r	Hill,G.	Lotus-Ford	5	transmission
r	Bonnier	McLaren-BRM	0	wheel

STARTING GRID:

1	Amon	10	Redman
2	Stewart,Jackie	11	Attwood
3	Ickx	12	Bianchi
4	Surtees	13	Beltoise
5	Hulme	14	Hill,G.
6	McLaren	15	Oliver
7	Courage	16	Bonnier
8	Rodriguez,P.	17	Rindt
9	Siffert	18	Brabham,J.

Dutch

GRAND PRIX No:	166
DATE:	June 23, 1968
VENUE:	Zandvoort
POLE LAP:	Amon, 1m 23.54s
FASTEST LAP:	Beltoise, 1m 45.91s

Pn	Driver	Car	Laps	Time/Reason
1	Stewart,Jackie	Matra-Ford	90	2h 46m 11.3s
2	Beltoise	Matra	90	2h 47m 45.2s
3	Rodriguez,P.	BRM	89	
4	Ickx	Ferrari	88	
5	Moser	Brabham-Repco	87	
6	Amon	Ferrari	85	
7	Attwood	BRM	85	
8	Bonnier	McLaren-BRM	82	
9	Hill,G.	Lotus-Ford	81	spun off
uc	Oliver	Lotus-Ford	80	
r	Gurney	Eagle-Weslake	63	throttle
r	Siffert	Lotus-Ford	55	gearbox
r	Courage	BRM	51	spun off
r	Surtees	Honda	50	alternator
r	Rindt	Brabham-Repco	39	ignition
r	Brabham,J.	Brabham-Repco	22	spun off
r	McLaren	McLaren-Ford	19	accident
r	Hulme	McLaren-Ford	10	engine
r	Bianchi	Cooper-BRM	9	accident

STARTING GRID:

1	Amon	11	Rodriguez,P.
2	Rindt	12	Gurney
3	Hill,G.	13	Siffert
4	Brabham,J.	14	Courage
5	Stewart,Jackie	15	Attwood
6	Ickx	16	Beltoise
7	Hulme	17	Moser
8	McLaren	18	Bianchi
9	Surtees	19	Bonnier
10	Oliver		

French

GRAND PRIX No: 167
DATE: July 7, 1968
VENUE: Rouen
POLE LAP: Rindt, 1m 56.1s
FASTEST LAP: Rodriguez,P., 2m 11.5s

Pn	Driver	Car	Laps	Time/Reason
1	Ickx	Ferrari	60	2h 25m 40.9s
2	Surtees	Honda	60	2h 27m 39.5s
3	Stewart,Jackie	Matra-Ford	59	
4	Elford	Cooper-BRM	58	
5	Hulme	McLaren-Ford	58	
6	Courage	BRM	57	
7	Attwood	BRM	57	
8	McLaren	McLaren-Ford	56	
9	Beltoise	Matra	56	
10	Amon	Ferrari	55	
11	Siffert	Lotus-Ford	54	
uc	Rodriguez,P.	BRM	53	
r	Rindt	Brabham-Repco	45	fuel tank
r	Brabham,J.	Brabham-Repco	15	fuel system
r	Servoz-Gavin	Cooper-BRM	14	accident
r	Hill,G.	Lotus-Ford	14	transmission
r	Schlesser,J.	Honda	2	fatal accident
dns	Oliver	Lotus-Ford		accident

STARTING GRID:

1	Rindt	10	Rodriguez,P.
2	Stewart,Jackie	11	Oliver
3	Ickx	12	Siffert
4	Hulme	13	Attwood
5	Amon	14	Brabham,J.
6	McLaren	15	Courage
7	Surtees	16	Servoz-Gavin
8	Beltoise	17	Schlesser,J.
9	Hill,G.	18	Elford

British

GRAND PRIX No: 168
DATE: July 20, 1968
VENUE: Brands Hatch
POLE LAP: Hill,G., 1m 28.9s
FASTEST LAP: Siffert, 1m 29.7s

Pn	Driver	Car	Laps	Time/Reason
1	Siffert	Lotus-Ford	80	2h 01m 20.3s
2	Amon	Ferrari	80	2h 01m 24.7s
3	Ickx	Ferrari	79	
4	Hulme	McLaren-Ford	79	
5	Surtees	Honda	78	
6	Stewart,Jackie	Matra-Ford	78	
7	McLaren	McLaren-Ford	77	
8	Courage	BRM	72	
r	Rindt	Brabham-Repco	55	fuel system
r	Rodriguez,P.	BRM	52	engine
uc	Moser	Brabham-Repco	52	
r	Oliver	Lotus-Ford	43	transmission
r	Widdows	Cooper-BRM	34	ignition
r	Elford	Cooper-BRM	26	engine
r	Hill,G.	Lotus-Ford	26	transmission
r	Beltoise	Matra	11	engine
r	Attwood	BRM	10	radiator
r	Gurney	Eagle-Weslake	8	fuel system
r	Bonnier	McLaren-BRM	7	engine
r	Brabham,J.	Brabham-Repco	0	engine

STARTING GRID:

1	Hill,G.	11	Hulme
2	Oliver	12	Ickx
3	Amon	13	Rodriguez,P.
4	Siffert	14	Beltoise
5	Rindt	15	Attwood
6	Gurney	16	Courage
7	Stewart,Jackie	17	Elford
8	Brabham,J.	18	Widdows
9	Surtees	19	Moser
10	McLaren	20	Bonnier

German

GRAND PRIX No:	169
DATE:	August 4, 1968
VENUE:	Nurburgring
POLE LAP:	Ickx, 9m 04.0s
FASTEST LAP:	Stewart,Jackie, 9m 36.0s

Pn	Driver	Car	Laps	Time/Reason
1	Stewart,Jackie	Matra-Ford	14	2h 19m 03.2s
2	Hill,G.	Lotus-Ford	14	2h 23m 06.4s
3	Rindt	Brabham-Repco	14	2h 23m 12.6s
4	Ickx	Ferrari	14	2h 24m 58.4s
5	Brabham,J.	Brabham-Repco	14	2h 25m 24.3s
6	Rodriguez,P.	BRM	14	2h 25m 28.2s
7	Hulme	McLaren-Ford	14	2h 25m 34.2s
8	Courage	BRM	14	2h 26m 59.6s
9	Gurney	Eagle-Weslake	14	2h 27m 16.9s
10	Hahne	Lola-BMW	14	2h 29m 14.6s
11	Oliver	Lotus-Ford	13	
12	Ahrens	Brabham-Repco	13	
13	McLaren	McLaren-Ford	13	
14	Attwood	BRM	13	
r	Amon	Ferrari	11	accident
r	Beltoise	Matra	8	accident
r	Bianchi	Cooper-BRM	6	fuel tank
r	Siffert	Lotus-Ford	6	ignition
r	Surtees	Honda	3	ignition
r	Elford	Cooper-BRM	0	accident

STARTING GRID:

1	Ickx	11	Hulme
2	Amon	12	Beltoise
3	Rindt	13	Oliver
4	Hill,G.	14	Rodriguez,P.
5	Elford	15	Brabham,J.
6	Stewart,Jackie	16	McLaren
7	Surtees	17	Ahrens
8	Courage	18	Hahne
9	Siffert	19	Bianchi
10	Gurney	20	Attwood

Italian

GRAND PRIX No:	170
DATE:	September 8, 1968
VENUE:	Monza
POLE LAP:	Surtees, 1m 26.07s
FASTEST LAP:	Oliver, 1m 26.50s

Pn	Driver	Car	Laps	Time/Reason
1	Hulme	McLaren-Ford	68	1h 40m 14.8s
2	Servoz-Gavin	Matra-Ford	68	1h 41m 43.2s
3	Ickx	Ferrari	68	1h 41m 43.4s
4	Courage	BRM	67	
5	Beltoise	Matra	66	
6	Bonnier	McLaren-BRM	64	
r	Siffert	Lotus-Ford	58	suspension
r	Brabham,J.	Brabham-Repco	56	oil pressure
r	Hobbs	Honda	42	engine
r	Stewart,Jackie	Matra-Ford	42	engine
r	Oliver	Lotus-Ford	38	transmission
r	McLaren	McLaren-Ford	34	oil leak
r	Rindt	Brabham-Repco	33	engine
r	Rodriguez,P.	BRM	22	engine
r	Gurney	Eagle-Weslake	19	engine
r	Hill,G.	Lotus-Ford	10	wheel
r	Surtees	Honda	8	accident
r	Amon	Ferrari	8	accident
r	Bell	Ferrari	4	fuel system
r	Elford	Cooper-BRM	2	accident
dns	Andretti,Mario	Lotus-Ford		Excluded - raced in US

STARTING GRID:

1	Surtees	12	Oliver
2	McLaren	13	Gurney
3	Amon	14	Servoz-Gavin
4	Ickx	15	Hobbs
5	Hill,G.	16	Rodriguez,P.
6	Stewart,Jackie	17	Brabham,J.
7	Hulme	18	Courage
8	Bell	19	Beltoise
9	Siffert	20	Bonnier
10	Rindt	21	Elford
11	Andretti,Mario		

Canadian

GRAND PRIX No: 171
DATE: September 22, 1968
VENUE: St Jovite
POLE LAP: Rindt, 1m 33.8s
FASTEST LAP: Siffert, 1m 35.1s

Pn	Driver	Car	Laps	Time/Reason
1	Hulme	McLaren-Ford	90	2h 27m 11.2s
2	McLaren	McLaren-Ford	89	
3	Rodriguez,P.	BRM	88	
4	Hill,G.	Lotus-Ford	86	
5	Elford	Cooper-BRM	86	
6	Stewart,Jackie	Matra-Ford	83	
r	Beltoise	Matra	77	gearbox
r	Amon	Ferrari	72	transmission
r	Servoz-Gavin	Matra-Ford	71	accident
uc	Bianchi	Cooper-BRM	56	
r	Pescarolo	Matra	54	oil pressure
r	Rindt	Brabham-Repco	39	engine
r	Oliver	Lotus-Ford	32	transmission
r	Brabham,J.	Brabham-Repco	31	exhaust
r	Siffert	Lotus-Ford	29	oil leak
r	Gurney	McLaren-Ford	29	radiator
r	Courage	BRM	22	gearbox
r	Brack	Lotus-Ford	18	transmission
r	Surtees	Honda	10	gearbox
r	Bonnier	McLaren-BRM	0	fuel system
dns	Ickx	Ferrari		injured
dns	Pease	Eagle-Climax		engine

STARTING GRID:

1	Rindt	12	Rodriguez,P.
2	Amon	13	Servoz-Gavin
3	Siffert	14	Ickx
4	Gurney	15	Courage
5	Hill,G.	16	Beltoise
6	Hulme	17	Elford
7	Surtees	18	Bonnier
8	McLaren	19	Bianchi
9	Oliver	20	Pescarolo
10	Brabham,J.	21	Brack
11	Stewart,Jackie	22	Pease

US

GRAND PRIX No: 172
DATE: October 6, 1968
VENUE: Watkins Glen
POLE LAP: Andretti,Mario, 1m 04.20s
FASTEST LAP: Stewart,Jackie, 1m 05.22s

Pn	Driver	Car	Laps	Time/Reason
1	Stewart,Jackie	Matra-Ford	108	1h 59m 20.3s
2	Hill,G.	Lotus-Ford	108	1h 59m 45.0s
3	Surtees	Honda	107	
4	Gurney	McLaren-Ford	107	
5	Siffert	Lotus-Ford	105	
6	McLaren	McLaren-Ford	103	
r	Courage	BRM	93	suspension
r	Hulme	McLaren-Ford	92	accident
r	Bianchi	Cooper-BRM	88	clutch
r	Brabham,J.	Brabham-Repco	77	engine
r	Rindt	Brabham-Repco	73	engine
r	Elford	Cooper-BRM	71	engine
r	Rodriguez,P.	BRM	66	suspension
r	Bonnier	McLaren-BRM	62	engine
r	Amon	Ferrari	59	water pump
r	Beltoise	Matra	44	transmission
r	Unser,B.	BRM	35	engine
r	Andretti,Mario	Lotus-Ford	32	clutch
r	Bell	Ferrari	14	engine
dns	Oliver	Lotus-Ford		accident
dns	Pescarolo	Matra		engine

STARTING GRID:

1	Andretti,Mario	12	Siffert
2	Stewart,Jackie	13	Beltoise
3	Hill,G.	14	Courage
4	Amon	15	Bell
5	Hulme	16	Oliver
6	Rindt	17	Elford
7	Gurney	18	Bonnier
8	Brabham,J.	19	Unser,B.
9	Surtees	20	Bianchi
10	McLaren	21	Pescarolo
11	Rodriguez,P.		

Mexican

GRAND PRIX No: 173
DATE: November 3, 1968
VENUE: Mexico City
POLE LAP: Siffert, 1m 45.22s
FASTEST LAP: Siffert, 1m 44.23s

Pn	Driver	Car	Laps	Time/Reason
1	Hill,G.	Lotus-Ford	65	1h 56m 44.0s
2	McLaren	McLaren-Ford	65	1h 58m 03.3s
3	Oliver	Lotus-Ford	65	1h 58m 24.6s
4	Rodriguez,P.	BRM	65	1h 58m 25.0s
5	Bonnier	Honda	64	
6	Siffert	Lotus-Ford	64	
7	Stewart,Jackie	Matra-Ford	64	
8	Elford	Cooper-BRM	63	
9	Pescarolo	Matra	62	
10	Brabham,J.	Brabham-Repco	59	oil pressure
r	Servoz-Gavin	Matra-Ford	57	ignition
r	Gurney	McLaren-Ford	28	suspension
r	Courage	BRM	25	engine
r	Bianchi	Cooper-BRM	21	engine
r	Surtees	Honda	17	overheating
r	Amon	Ferrari	16	transmission
r	Solana	Lotus-Ford	14	broken wing
r	Beltoise	Matra	10	suspension
r	Hulme	McLaren-Ford	10	suspension
r	Ickx	Ferrari	3	ignition
r	Rindt	Brabham-Repco	2	ignition

STARTING GRID:

1	Siffert	12	Rodriguez,P.
2	Amon	13	Beltoise
3	Hill,G.	14	Oliver
4	Hulme	15	Ickx
5	Gurney	16	Servoz-Gavin
6	Surtees	17	Elford
7	Stewart,Jackie	18	Bonnier
8	Brabham,J.	19	Courage
9	McLaren	20	Pescarolo
10	Rindt	21	Bianchi
11	Solana		

South African

GRAND PRIX No: 174
DATE: January 2, 1969
VENUE: Kyalami
POLE LAP: Brabham,J., 1m 20.0s
FASTEST LAP: Stewart,Jackie, 1m 21.6s

Pn	Driver	Car	Laps	Time/Reason
1	Stewart,Jackie	Matra-Ford	80	1h 50m 39.1s
2	Hill,G.	Lotus-Ford	80	1h 50m 57.9s
3	Hulme	McLaren-Ford	80	1h 51m 10.9s
4	Siffert	Lotus-Ford	80	1h 51m 28.3s
5	McLaren	McLaren-Ford	79	
6	Beltoise	Matra-Ford	78	
7	Oliver	BRM	77	
8	Tingle	Brabham-Repco	73	
uc	de Klerk	Brabham-Repco	67	
r	Rindt	Lotus-Ford	43	fuel system
r	Surtees	BRM	39	engine
r	Rodriguez,P.	BRM	37	water leak
r	Amon	Ferrari	33	engine
r	Brabham,J.	Brabham-Ford	31	handling
r	Andretti,Mario	Lotus-Ford	31	gearbox
r	Love	Lotus-Ford	30	ignition
r	Ickx	Brabham-Ford	19	ignition
r	van Rooyen	McLaren-Ford	11	brakes

STARTING GRID:

1	Brabham,J.	10	Love
2	Rindt	11	Beltoise
3	Hulme	12	Siffert
4	Stewart,Jackie	13	Ickx
5	Amon	14	Oliver
6	Andretti,Mario	15	Rodriguez,P.
7	Hill,G.	16	de Klerk
8	McLaren	17	Tingle
9	van Rooyen	18	Surtees

Spanish

GRAND PRIX No: 175
DATE: May 4, 1969
VENUE: Montjuich Park
POLE LAP: Rindt, 1m 25.7s
FASTEST LAP: Rindt, 1m 28.3s

Pn	Driver	Car	Laps	Time/Reason
1	Stewart,Jackie	Matra-Ford	90	2h 16m 54.0s
2	McLaren	McLaren-Ford	88	
3	Beltoise	Matra-Ford	87	
4	Hulme	McLaren-Ford	87	
5	Surtees	BRM	84	
6	Ickx	Brabham-Ford	83	suspension
r	Rodriguez,P.	BRM	72	engine
r	Amon	Ferrari	56	engine
r	Brabham,J.	Brabham-Ford	51	engine
r	Siffert	Lotus-Ford	30	engine
r	Rindt	Lotus-Ford	19	accident
r	Courage	Brabham-Ford	18	engine
r	Hill,G.	Lotus-Ford	8	accident
r	Oliver	BRM	0	oil line

STARTING GRID:

1	Rindt	8	Hulme
2	Amon	9	Surtees
3	Hill,G.	10	Oliver
4	Stewart,Jackie	11	Courage
5	Brabham,J.	12	Beltoise
6	Siffert	13	McLaren
7	Ickx	14	Rodriguez,P.

Monaco

GRAND PRIX No: 176
DATE: May 18, 1969
VENUE: Monte Carlo
POLE LAP: Stewart,Jackie, 1m 24.6s
FASTEST LAP: Stewart,Jackie, 1m 25.1s

Pn	Driver	Car	Laps	Time/Reason
1	Hill,G.	Lotus-Ford	80	1h 56m 59.4s
2	Courage	Brabham-Ford	80	1h 57m 16.7s
3	Siffert	Lotus-Ford	80	1h 57m 34.0s
4	Attwood	Lotus-Ford	80	1h 57m 52.3s
5	McLaren	McLaren-Ford	79	
6	Hulme	McLaren-Ford	78	
7	Elford	Cooper-Maser.	74	
r	Ickx	Brabham-Ford	48	suspension
r	Stewart,Jackie	Matra-Ford	22	transmission
r	Beltoise	Matra-Ford	20	transmission
r	Amon	Ferrari	16	transmission
r	Moser	Brabham-Ford	15	transmission
r	Rodriguez,P.	BRM	15	engine
r	Surtees	BRM	9	accident
r	Brabham,J.	Brabham-Ford	9	accident
r	Oliver	BRM	0	accident

STARTING GRID:

1	Stewart,Jackie	9	Courage
2	Amon	10	Attwood
3	Beltoise	11	McLaren
4	Hill,G.	12	Hulme
5	Siffert	13	Oliver
6	Surtees	14	Rodriguez,P.
7	Ickx	15	Moser
8	Brabham,J.	16	Elford

Dutch

GRAND PRIX No:	177
DATE:	June 21, 1969
VENUE:	Zandvoort
POLE LAP:	Rindt, 1m 20.85s
FASTEST LAP:	Stewart,Jackie, 1m 22.94s

Pn	Driver	Car	Laps	Time/Reason
1	Stewart,Jackie	Matra-Ford	90	2h 06m 42.1s
2	Siffert	Lotus-Ford	90	2h 07m 06.6s
3	Amon	Ferrari	90	2h 07m 12.6s
4	Hulme	McLaren-Ford	90	2h 07m 19.3s
5	Ickx	Brabham-Ford	90	2h 07m 19.8s
6	Brabham,J.	Brabham-Ford	90	2h 07m 52.9s
7	Hill,G.	Lotus-Ford	88	
8	Beltoise	Matra-Ford	87	
9	Surtees	BRM	87	
10	Elford	McLaren-Ford	84	
r	Moser	Brabham-Ford	54	steering
r	McLaren	McLaren-Ford	24	suspension
r	Rindt	Lotus-Ford	16	transmission
r	Courage	Brabham-Ford	12	clutch
r	Oliver	BRM	9	gearbox

STARTING GRID:

1	Rindt	9	Courage
2	Stewart,Jackie	10	Siffert
3	Hill,G.	11	Beltoise
4	Amon	12	Surtees
5	Ickx	13	Oliver
6	McLaren	14	Moser
7	Hulme	15	Elford
8	Brabham,J.		

French

GRAND PRIX No:	178
DATE:	July 6, 1969
VENUE:	Clermont-Ferrand
POLE LAP:	Stewart,Jackie, 3m 00.6s
FASTEST LAP:	Stewart,Jackie, 3m 02.7s

Pn	Driver	Car	Laps	Time/Reason
1	Stewart,Jackie	Matra-Ford	38	1h 56m 47.4s
2	Beltoise	Matra-Ford	38	1h 57m 44.5s
3	Ickx	Brabham-Ford	38	1h 57m 44.7s
4	McLaren	McLaren-Ford	37	
5	Elford	McLaren-Ford	37	
6	Hill,G.	Lotus-Ford	37	
7	Moser	Brabham-Ford	36	
8	Hulme	McLaren-Ford	35	
9	Siffert	Lotus-Ford	34	
r	Amon	Ferrari	30	engine
r	Rindt	Lotus-Ford	22	driver ill
r	Courage	Brabham-Ford	21	bodywork
r	Miles	Lotus-Ford	1	fuel system

STARTING GRID:

1	Stewart,Jackie	8	Hill,G.
2	Hulme	9	Siffert
3	Rindt	10	Elford
4	Ickx	11	Courage
5	Beltoise	12	Miles
6	Amon	13	Moser
7	McLaren		

British

GRAND PRIX No: 179
DATE: July 19, 1969
VENUE: Silverstone
POLE LAP: Rindt, 1m 20.8s
FASTEST LAP: Stewart,Jackie, 1m 21.3s

Pn	Driver	Car	Laps	Time/Reason
1	Stewart,Jackie	Matra-Ford	84	1h 55m 55.6s
2	Ickx	Brabham-Ford	83	
3	McLaren	McLaren-Ford	83	
4	Rindt	Lotus-Ford	83	
5	Courage	Brabham-Ford	83	
6	Elford	McLaren-Ford	82	
7	Hill,G.	Lotus-Ford	82	
8	Siffert	Lotus-Ford	81	
9	Beltoise	Matra-Ford	78	
10	Miles	Lotus-Ford	75	
r	Rodriguez,P.	Ferrari	61	engine
r	Amon	Ferrari	45	gearbox
r	Hulme	McLaren-Ford	27	ignition
r	Oliver	BRM	19	transmission
r	Bonnier	Lotus-Ford	6	engine
r	Bell	McLaren-Ford	5	suspension
r	Surtees	BRM	1	suspension

STARTING GRID:

1	Rindt	10	Courage
2	Stewart,Jackie	11	Elford
3	Hulme	12	Hill,G.
4	Ickx	13	Oliver
5	Amon	14	Miles
6	Surtees	15	Bell
7	McLaren	16	Bonnier
8	Rodriguez,P.	17	Beltoise
9	Siffert		

German

GRAND PRIX No: 180
DATE: August 3, 1969
VENUE: Nurburgring
POLE LAP: Ickx, 7m 42.1s
FASTEST LAP: Ickx, 7m 43.8s

Pn	Driver	Car	Laps	Time/Reason
1	Ickx	Brabham-Ford	14	1h 49m 55.4s
2	Stewart,Jackie	Matra-Ford	14	1h 50m 53.1s
3	McLaren	McLaren-Ford	14	1h 53m 17.0s
4	Hill,G.	Lotus-Ford	14	1h 53m 54.2s
5	Siffert	Lotus-Ford	12	suspension
6	Beltoise	Matra-Ford	12	suspension
r	Hulme	McLaren-Ford	11	transmission
r	Oliver	BRM	11	sump
r	Rindt	Lotus-Ford	10	ignition
r	Bonnier	Lotus-Ford	4	fuel tank
r	Courage	Brabham-Ford	1	accident
r	Elford	McLaren-Ford	0	accident
r	Andretti,Mario	Lotus-Ford	0	accident
dns	Surtees	BRM		suspension
dns	Hahne	BMW		withdrew
dns	Quester	BMW		withdrew
dns	Mitter	BMW		fatal accident

STARTING GRID:

1	Ickx	10	Beltoise
2	Stewart,Jackie	11	Andretti,Mario
3	Rindt	12	Oliver
4	Siffert	13	Bonnier
5	Hulme	14	Surtees
6	Elford	15	Hahne
7	Courage	16	Quester
8	McLaren	17	Mitter
9	Hill,G.		

Italian

GRAND PRIX No:	181
DATE:	September 7, 1969
VENUE:	Monza
POLE LAP:	Rindt, 1m 25.48s
FASTEST LAP:	Beltoise, 1m 25.20s

Pn	Driver	Car	Laps	Time/Reason
1	Stewart,Jackie	Matra-Ford	68	1h 39m 11.26s
2	Rindt	Lotus-Ford	68	1h 39m 11.34s
3	Beltoise	Matra-Ford	68	1h 39m 11.43s
4	McLaren	McLaren-Ford	68	1h 39m 11.45s
5	Courage	Brabham-Ford	68	1h 39m 44.70s
6	Rodriguez,P.	Ferrari	66	
7	Hulme	McLaren-Ford	66	
8	Siffert	Lotus-Ford	64	engine
9	Hill,G.	Lotus-Ford	63	transmission
10	Ickx	Brabham-Ford	61	oil pressure
uc	Surtees	BRM	60	
r	Oliver	BRM	48	oil pressure
r	Moser	Brabham-Ford	9	fuel leak
r	Brabham,J.	Brabham-Ford	6	fuel line
r	Miles	Lotus-Ford	3	engine

STARTING GRID:

1	Rindt	9	Hill,G.
2	Hulme	10	Surtees
3	Stewart,Jackie	11	Oliver
4	Courage	12	Rodriguez,P.
5	McLaren	13	Moser
6	Beltoise	14	Miles
7	Brabham,J.	15	Ickx
8	Siffert		

Canadian

GRAND PRIX No:	182
DATE:	September 20, 1969
VENUE:	Mosport Park
POLE LAP:	Ickx, 1m 17.4s
FASTEST LAP:	Ickx & Brabham,J., 1m 18.1s

Pn	Driver	Car	Laps	Time/Reason
1	Ickx	Brabham-Ford	90	1h 59m 25.7s
2	Brabham,J.	Brabham-Ford	90	2h 00m 11.9s
3	Rindt	Lotus-Ford	90	2h 00m 17.7s
4	Beltoise	Matra-Ford	89	
5	McLaren	McLaren-Ford	87	
6	Servoz-Gavin	Matra-Ford	84	
7	Lovely	Lotus-Ford	81	
8	Brack	BRM	80	
r	Hill,G.	Lotus-Ford	42	engine
r	Siffert	Lotus-Ford	40	transmission
r	Miles	Lotus-Ford	40	gearbox
r	Rodriguez,P.	Ferrari	37	oil pressure
r	Stewart,Jackie	Matra-Ford	32	accident
dq	Pease	Eagle-Climax	22	too slow
r	Surtees	BRM	15	engine
r	Courage	Brabham-Ford	13	fuel leak
r	Cordts	Brabham-Climax	10	oil leak
r	Hulme	McLaren-Ford	9	distributor
r	Oliver	BRM	2	engine
r	Moser	Brabham-Ford	0	accident

STARTING GRID:

1	Ickx	11	Miles
2	Beltoise	12	Oliver
3	Rindt	13	Rodriguez,P.
4	Stewart,Jackie	14	Surtees
5	Hulme	15	Servoz-Gavin
6	Brabham,J.	16	Lovely
7	Hill,G.	17	Pease
8	Siffert	18	Brack
9	McLaren	19	Cordts
10	Courage	20	Moser

US

GRAND PRIX No: 183
DATE: October 5, 1969
VENUE: Watkins Glen
POLE LAP: Rindt, 1m 03.62s
FASTEST LAP: Rindt, 1m 04.34s

Pn	Driver	Car	Laps	Time/Reason
1	Rindt	Lotus-Ford	108	1h 57m 56.8s
2	Courage	Brabham-Ford	108	1h 58m 43.8s
3	Surtees	BRM	106	
4	Brabham,J.	Brabham-Ford	106	
5	Rodriguez,P.	Ferrari	101	
6	Moser	Brabham-Ford	98	
uc	Servoz-Gavin	Matra-Ford	92	
r	Hill,G.	Lotus-Ford	90	accident
r	Ickx	Brabham-Ford	77	engine
r	Eaton	BRM	76	engine
r	Beltoise	Matra-Ford	72	engine
r	Hulme	McLaren-Ford	52	gearbox
r	Stewart,Jackie	Matra-Ford	35	engine
r	Lovely	Lotus-Ford	25	transmission
r	Oliver	BRM	23	engine
r	Andretti,Mario	Lotus-Ford	3	suspension
r	Siffert	Lotus-Ford	3	fuel system
dns	McLaren	McLaren-Ford		engine

STARTING GRID:

1	Rindt	10	Brabham,J.
2	Hulme	11	Surtees
3	Stewart,Jackie	12	Rodriguez,P.
4	Hill,G.	13	Andretti,Mario
5	Siffert	14	Oliver
6	McLaren	15	Servoz-Gavin
7	Beltoise	16	Moser
8	Ickx	17	Lovely
9	Courage	18	Eaton

Mexican

GRAND PRIX No: 184
DATE: October 19, 1969
VENUE: Mexico City
POLE LAP: Brabham,J., 1m 42.90s
FASTEST LAP: Ickx, 1m 43.05s

Pn	Driver	Car	Laps	Time/Reason
1	Hulme	McLaren-Ford	65	1h 54m 08.8s
2	Ickx	Brabham-Ford	65	1h 54m 11.4s
3	Brabham,J.	Brabham-Ford	65	1h 54m 47.3s
4	Stewart,Jackie	Matra-Ford	65	1h 54m 55.8s
5	Beltoise	Matra-Ford	65	1h 55m 47.3s
6	Oliver	BRM	63	
7	Rodriguez,P.	Ferrari	63	
8	Servoz-Gavin	Matra-Ford	63	
9	Lovely	Lotus-Ford	62	
10	Courage	Brabham-Ford	61	
11	Moser	Brabham-Ford	60	fuel leak
r	Surtees	BRM	53	gearbox
r	Rindt	Lotus-Ford	21	suspension
r	Eaton	BRM	6	gearbox
r	Siffert	Lotus-Ford	4	accident
r	Miles	Lotus-Ford	3	fuel system

STARTING GRID:

1	Brabham,J.	9	Surtees
2	Ickx	10	Miles
3	Stewart,Jackie	11	Oliver
4	Hulme	12	Moser
5	Siffert	13	Servoz-Gavin
6	Rindt	14	Rodriguez,P.
7	Beltoise	15	Lovely
8	Courage	16	Eaton

South African

GRAND PRIX No: 185
DATE: March 7, 1970
VENUE: Kyalami
POLE LAP: Stewart,Jackie, 1m 19.3s
FASTEST LAP: Surtees & Brabham,J., 1m 20.8s

Pn	Driver	Car	Laps	Time/Reason
1	Brabham,J.	Brabham-Ford	80	1h 49m 34.6s
2	Hulme	McLaren-Ford	80	1h 49m 42.7s
3	Stewart,Jackie	March-Ford	80	1h 49m 51.7s
4	Beltoise	Matra	80	1h 50m 47.7s
5	Miles	Lotus-Ford	79	
6	Hill,G.	Lotus-Ford	79	
7	Pescarolo	Matra	78	
8	Love	Lotus-Ford	78	
9	Rodriguez,P.	BRM	76	
10	Siffert	March-Ford	75	
11	de Klerk	Brabham-Ford	75	
r	Charlton	Lotus-Ford	73	ignition
r	Rindt	Lotus-Ford	72	engine
r	Surtees	McLaren-Ford	60	engine
r	Ickx	Ferrari	59	engine
r	Eaton	BRM	58	engine
r	Servoz-Gavin	March-Ford	57	engine
r	Courage	de Tomaso-Ford	38	accident
r	McLaren	McLaren-Ford	38	engine
r	Andretti,Mario	March-Ford	25	overheating
r	Stommelen	Brabham-Ford	22	engine
r	Oliver	BRM	21	gearbox
r	Amon	March-Ford	13	overheating

STARTING GRID:

1 Stewart,Jackie
2 Amon
3 Brabham,J.
4 Rindt
5 Ickx
6 Hulme
7 Surtees
8 Beltoise
9 Siffert
10 McLaren
11 Andretti,Mario
12 Oliver
13 Charlton
14 Miles
15 Stommelen
16 Rodriguez,P.
17 Servoz-Gavin
18 Pescarolo
19 Hill,G.
20 Courage
21 de Klerk
22 Love
23 Eaton

Spanish

GRAND PRIX No: 186
DATE: April 19, 1970
VENUE: Jarama
POLE LAP: Brabham,J., 1m 23.9s
FASTEST LAP: Brabham,J., 1m 24.3s

Pn	Driver	Car	Laps	Time/Reason
1	Stewart,Jackie	March-Ford	90	2h 10m 58.2s
2	McLaren	McLaren-Ford	89	
3	Andretti,Mario	March-Ford	89	
4	Hill,G.	Lotus-Ford	89	
5	Servoz-Gavin	March-Ford	88	
r	Surtees	McLaren-Ford	75	gearbox
r	Brabham,J.	Brabham-Ford	60	engine
r	Stommelen	Brabham-Ford	42	engine
r	Pescarolo	Matra	33	engine
r	Beltoise	Matra	31	engine
r	Amon	March-Ford	9	engine
r	Hulme	McLaren-Ford	9	ignition
r	Rindt	Lotus-Ford	9	ignition
r	Rodriguez,P.	BRM	3	withdrew
r	Ickx	Ferrari	0	accident
r	Oliver	BRM	0	accident
dns	Courage	de Tomaso-Ford		accident

STARTING GRID:

1 Brabham,J.
2 Hulme
3 Stewart,Jackie
4 Beltoise
5 Rodriguez,P.
6 Amon
7 Ickx
8 Courage
9 Rindt
10 Pescarolo
11 Oliver
12 McLaren
13 Surtees
14 Servoz-Gavin
15 Hill,G.
16 Andretti,Mario
17 Stommelen

Monaco

GRAND PRIX No: 187
DATE: May 10, 1970
VENUE: Monte Carlo
POLE LAP: Stewart,Jackie, 3m 28.0s
FASTEST LAP: Amon, 3m 27.4s

Pn	Driver	Car	Laps	Time/Reason
1	Rindt	Lotus-Ford	80	1h 54m 36.6s
2	Brabham,J.	Brabham-Ford	80	1h 54m 59.7s
3	Pescarolo	Matra	80	1h 55m 28.0s
4	Hulme	McLaren-Ford	80	1h 56m 04.9s
5	Hill,G.	Lotus-Ford	79	
6	Rodriguez,P.	BRM	78	
7	Peterson	March-Ford	78	
8	Siffert	March-Ford	76	fuel injection
r	Amon	March-Ford	60	suspension
uc	Courage	de Tomaso-Ford	58	
r	Stewart,Jackie	March-Ford	57	engine
r	Oliver	BRM	42	engine
r	Beltoise	Matra	21	crownwheel/pinion
r	McLaren	McLaren-Ford	19	suspension
r	Surtees	McLaren-Ford	14	oil pressure
r	Ickx	Ferrari	11	transmission

STARTING GRID:

1 Stewart,Jackie
2 Amon
3 Hulme
4 Brabham,J.
5 Ickx
6 Beltoise
7 Pescarolo
8 Rindt
9 Courage
10 McLaren
12 Peterson
12 Siffert
13 Surtees
14 Oliver
15 Rodriguez,P.
16 Hill,G.

Belgian

GRAND PRIX No: 188
DATE: June 7, 1970
VENUE: Spa-Francorchamps
POLE LAP: Stewart,Jackie, 1m 24.0s
FASTEST LAP: Rindt, 1m 23.2s

Pn	Driver	Car	Laps	Time/Reason
1	Rodriguez,P.	BRM	28	1h 38m 09.9s
2	Amon	March-Ford	28	1h 38m 11.0s
3	Beltoise	Matra	28	1h 39m 53.6s
4	Giunti	Ferrari	28	1h 40m 48.4s
5	Stommelen	Brabham-Ford	28	1h 41m 41.7s
6	Pescarolo	Matra	27	battery
7	Siffert	March-Ford	26	fuel pressure
8	Ickx	Ferrari	26	
uc	Peterson	March-Ford	20	
r	Hill,G.	Lotus-Ford	19	engine
r	Brabham,J.	Brabham-Ford	18	clutch
r	Stewart,Jackie	March-Ford	13	engine
r	Miles	Lotus-Ford	12	gearbox
r	Rindt	Lotus-Ford	10	engine
r	Oliver	BRM	6	engine
r	Courage	de Tomaso-Ford	3	oil pressure
r	Bell	Brabham-Ford	0	gearbox

STARTING GRID:

1 Stewart,Jackie
2 Rindt
3 Amon
4 Ickx
5 Brabham,J.
6 Rodriguez,P.
7 Stommelen
8 Giunti
9 Peterson
10 Siffert
11 Beltoise
12 Courage
13 Miles
14 Oliver
15 Bell
16 Hill,G.
17 Pescarolo

Dutch

GRAND PRIX No: 189
DATE: June 21, 1970
VENUE: Zandvoort
POLE LAP: Rindt, 1m 18.50s
FASTEST LAP: Ickx, 1m 19.23s

Pn	Driver	Car	Laps	Time/Reason
1	Rindt	Lotus-Ford	80	1h 50m 43.4s
2	Stewart,Jackie	March-Ford	80	1h 51m 13.4s
3	Ickx	Ferrari	79	
4	Regazzoni	Ferrari	79	
5	Beltoise	Matra	79	
6	Surtees	McLaren-Ford	79	
7	Miles	Lotus-Ford	78	
8	Pescarolo	Matra	78	
9	Peterson	March-Ford	78	
10	Rodriguez,P.	BRM	77	
11	Brabham,J.	Brabham-Ford	76	
uc	Hill,G.	Lotus-Ford	71	
r	Cevert	March-Ford	31	engine
r	Eaton	BRM	26	oil tank
r	Oliver	BRM	23	engine
r	Courage	de Tomaso-Ford	22	fatal accident
r	Siffert	March-Ford	22	engine
r	Gethin	McLaren-Ford	18	accident
r	Gurney	McLaren-Ford	2	engine
r	Amon	March-Ford	1	clutch

STARTING GRID:

1	Rindt	11	Gethin
2	Stewart,Jackie	12	Brabham,J.
3	Ickx	13	Pescarolo
4	Amon	14	Surtees
5	Oliver	15	Cevert
6	Regazzoni	16	Peterson
7	Rodriguez,P.	17	Siffert
8	Miles	18	Eaton
9	Courage	19	Gurney
10	Beltoise	20	Hill,G.

French

GRAND PRIX No: 190
DATE: July 5, 1970
VENUE: Clermont-Ferrand
POLE LAP: Ickx, 2m 58.22s
FASTEST LAP: Brabham,J., 3m 00.75s

Pn	Driver	Car	Laps	Time/Reason
1	Rindt	Lotus-Ford	38	1h 55m 57.0s
2	Amon	March-Ford	38	1h 56m 04.6s
3	Brabham,J.	Brabham-Ford	38	1h 56m 41.8s
4	Hulme	McLaren-Ford	38	1h 56m 42.7s
5	Pescarolo	Matra	38	1h 57m 16.4s
6	Gurney	McLaren-Ford	38	1h 57m 16.7s
7	Stommelen	Brabham-Ford	38	1h 58m 17.2s
8	Miles	Lotus-Ford	38	1h 58m 44.2s
9	Stewart,Jackie	March-Ford	38	1h 59m 06.6s
10	Hill,G.	Lotus-Ford	37	
11	Cevert	March-Ford	37	
12	Eaton	BRM	36	
13	Beltoise	Matra	35	fuel system
14	Giunti	Ferrari	35	
uc	de Adamich	McLaren-Alfa	29	
r	Siffert	March-Ford	23	accident
r	Peterson	March-Ford	17	crownwheel and
r	Ickx	Ferrari	16	engine
r	Rodriguez,P.	BRM	6	gearbox
r	Oliver	BRM	5	engine

STARTING GRID:

1	Ickx	11	Giunti
2	Beltoise	12	Oliver
3	Amon	13	Cevert
4	Stewart,Jackie	14	Stommelen
5	Brabham,J.	15	de Adamich
6	Rindt	16	Siffert
7	Hulme	17	Gurney
8	Pescarolo	18	Miles
9	Peterson	19	Eaton
10	Rodriguez,P.	20	Hill,G.

British

GRAND PRIX No:	191
DATE:	July 18, 1970
VENUE:	Brands Hatch
POLE LAP:	Rindt, 1m 24.8s
FASTEST LAP:	Brabham,J., 1m 25.9s

Pn	Driver	Car	Laps	Time/Reason
1	Rindt	Lotus-Ford	80	1h 57m 02.0s
2	Brabham,J.	Brabham-Ford	80	1h 57m 34.9s
3	Hulme	McLaren-Ford	80	1h 57m 54.6s
4	Regazzoni	Ferrari	80	1h 57m 56.8s
5	Amon	March-Ford	79	
6	Hill,G.	Lotus-Ford	79	
7	Cevert	March-Ford	79	
8	Fittipaldi,E.	Lotus-Ford	78	
9	Peterson	March-Ford	72	
uc	Lovely	Lotus-Ford	69	
r	Gurney	McLaren-Ford	60	oil pressure
r	Rodriguez,P.	BRM	58	accident
r	Oliver	BRM	54	engine
r	Stewart,Jackie	March-Ford	52	clutch
r	Surtees	Surtees-Ford	51	oil pressure
r	Pescarolo	Matra	41	accident
r	Beltoise	Matra	24	wheel
r	Andretti,Mario	March-Ford	21	suspension
r	Siffert	March-Ford	19	suspension
r	Miles	Lotus-Ford	15	engine
r	Eaton	BRM	10	oil pressure
r	Ickx	Ferrari	6	transmission
dns	Stommelen	Brabham-Ford		accident
dns	de Adamich	McLaren-Alfa R.		fuel tank
dns	Redman	de Tomaso-Ford		wheel

STARTING GRID:

1	Rindt	14	Peterson
2	Brabham,J.	15	Cevert
3	Ickx	16	Rodriguez,P.
4	Oliver	17	Eaton
5	Hulme	18	Amon
6	Regazzoni	19	de Adamich
7	Miles	20	Surtees
8	Stewart,Jackie	21	Siffert
9	Andretti,Mario	22	Fittipaldi,E.
10	Stommelen	23	Hill,G.
11	Beltoise	24	Lovely
12	Gurney	25	Redman
13	Pescarolo		

German

GRAND PRIX No:	192
DATE:	August 2, 1970
VENUE:	Hockenheim
POLE LAP:	Ickx, 1m 59.5s
FASTEST LAP:	Ickx, 2m 00.5s

Pn	Driver	Car	Laps	Time/Reason
1	Rindt	Lotus-Ford	50	1h 42m 00.3s
2	Ickx	Ferrari	50	1h 42m 01.0s
3	Hulme	McLaren-Ford	50	1h 43m 22.1s
4	Fittipaldi,E.	Lotus-Ford	50	1h 43m 55.4s
5	Stommelen	Brabham-Ford	49	
6	Pescarolo	Matra	49	
7	Cevert	March-Ford	49	
8	Siffert	March-Ford	47	engine
9	Surtees	Surtees-Ford	46	engine
r	Hill,G.	Lotus-Ford	37	engine
r	Amon	March-Ford	34	engine
r	Regazzoni	Ferrari	30	engine
r	Miles	Lotus-Ford	24	engine
r	Stewart,Jackie	March-Ford	20	engine
r	Andretti,Mario	March-Ford	15	gearbox
r	Peterson	March-Ford	11	engine
r	Rodriguez,P.	BRM	7	ignition
r	Oliver	BRM	5	engine
r	Brabham,J.	Brabham-Ford	4	oil line
r	Beltoise	Matra	4	suspension
r	Gethin	McLaren-Ford	3	throttle

STARTING GRID:

1	Ickx	12	Brabham,J.
2	Rindt	13	Fittipaldi,E.
3	Regazzoni	14	Cevert
4	Siffert	15	Surtees
5	Pescarolo	16	Hulme
6	Amon	17	Gethin
7	Stewart,Jackie	18	Oliver
8	Rodriguez,P.	19	Peterson
9	Andretti,Mario	20	Hill,G.
10	Miles	21	Beltoise
11	Stommelen		

Austrian

GRAND PRIX No:	193
DATE:	August 16, 1970
VENUE:	Osterreichring
POLE LAP:	Rindt, 1m 39.23s
FASTEST LAP:	Ickx & Regazzoni, 1m 40.4s

Pn	Driver	Car	Laps	Time/Reason
1	Ickx	Ferrari	60	1h 42m 17.3s
2	Regazzoni	Ferrari	60	1h 42m 17.9s
3	Stommelen	Brabham-Ford	60	1h 43m 45.2s
4	Rodriguez,P.	BRM	59	
5	Oliver	BRM	59	
6	Beltoise	Matra	59	
7	Giunti	Ferrari	59	
8	Amon	March-Ford	59	
9	Siffert	March-Ford	59	
10	Gethin	McLaren-Ford	59	
11	Eaton	BRM	58	
12	de Adamich	McLaren-Alfa	57	
13	Brabham,J.	Brabham-Ford	56	
14	Pescarolo	Matra	56	
15	Fittipaldi,E.	Lotus-Ford	55	
r	Hulme	McLaren-Ford	30	engine
r	Surtees	Surtees-Ford	27	engine
r	Schenken	de Tomaso-Ford	25	engine
r	Rindt	Lotus-Ford	21	engine
r	Moser	Bellasi-Ford	13	radiator
r	Andretti,Mario	March-Ford	13	accident
r	Stewart,Jackie	March-Ford	7	fuel pipe
r	Miles	Lotus-Ford	4	brakes
r	Cevert	March-Ford	0	engine

STARTING GRID:

1	Rindt	13	Pescarolo
2	Regazzoni	14	Oliver
3	Ickx	15	de Adamich
4	Stewart,Jackie	16	Fittipaldi,E.
5	Giunti	17	Stommelen
6	Amon	18	Andretti,Mario
7	Beltoise	19	Schenken
8	Brabham,J.	20	Siffert
9	Cevert	21	Gethin
10	Miles	22	Rodriguez,P.
11	Hulme	23	Eaton
12	Surtees	24	Moser

Italian

GRAND PRIX No:	194
DATE:	September 6, 1970
VENUE:	Monza
POLE LAP:	Ickx, 1m 24.14s
FASTEST LAP:	Regazzoni, 1m 25.20s

Pn	Driver	Car	Laps	Time/Reason
1	Regazzoni	Ferrari	68	1h 39m 06.9s
2	Stewart,Jackie	March-Ford	68	1h 39m 12.6s
3	Beltoise	Matra	68	1h 39m 12.7s
4	Hulme	McLaren-Ford	68	1h 39m 13.0s
5	Stommelen	Brabham-Ford	68	1h 39m 13.3s
6	Cevert	March-Ford	68	1h 40m 10.3s
7	Amon	March-Ford	67	
8	de Adamich	McLaren-Alfa	61	
uc	Gethin	McLaren-Ford	60	
r	Oliver	BRM	36	engine
r	Peterson	March-Ford	35	engine
r	Brabham,J.	Brabham-Ford	31	accident
r	Ickx	Ferrari	25	clutch
r	Eaton	BRM	21	overheating
r	Schenken	de Tomaso-Ford	17	engine
r	Pescarolo	Matra	14	engine
r	Giunti	Ferrari	14	fuel system
r	Rodriguez,P.	BRM	12	engine
r	Siffert	March-Ford	3	engine
r	Surtees	Surtees-Ford	0	electrical
dns	Rindt	Lotus-Ford		fatal accident
dns	Hill,G.	Lotus-Ford		withdrew
dns	Miles	Lotus-Ford		withdrew
dns	Fittipaldi,E.	Lotus-Ford		withdrew

STARTING GRID:

1	Ickx	13	de Adamich
2	Rodriguez,P.	14	Peterson
3	Regazzoni	15	Beltoise
4	Stewart,Jackie	16	Gethin
5	Giunti	17	Hill,G.
6	Oliver	18	Pescarolo
7	Siffert	19	Amon
8	Brabham,J.	20	Miles
9	Hulme	21	Stommelen
10	Surtees	22	Schenken
11	Cevert	23	Eaton
12	Rindt	24	Fittipaldi,E.

Canadian

GRAND PRIX No:	195
DATE:	September 20, 1970
VENUE:	St Jovite
POLE LAP:	Stewart,Jackie, 1m 31.5s
FASTEST LAP:	Regazzoni, 1m 32.2s

Pn	Driver	Car	Laps	Time/Reason
1	Ickx	Ferrari	90	2h 21m 18.4s
2	Regazzoni	Ferrari	90	2h 21m 33.2s
3	Amon	March-Ford	90	2h 22m 16.3s
4	Rodriguez,P.	BRM	89	
5	Surtees	Surtees-Ford	89	
6	Gethin	McLaren-Ford	88	
7	Pescarolo	Matra	87	
8	Beltoise	Matra	85	
9	Cevert	March-Ford	85	
10	Eaton	BRM	85	
uc	Schenken	de Tomaso-Ford	79	
uc	Hill,G.	Lotus-Ford	77	
r	de Adamich	McLaren-Alfa	68	oil pressure
uc	Peterson	March-Ford	65	
r	Hulme	McLaren-Ford	58	flywheel
r	Brabham,J.	Brabham-Ford	56	oil leak
uc	Oliver	BRM	52	
r	Stewart,Jackie	Tyrrell-Ford	31	stub axle
r	Stommelen	Brabham-Ford	22	steering
r	Siffert	March-Ford	21	engine

STARTING GRID:

1	Stewart,Jackie	11	Gethin
2	Ickx	12	de Adamich
3	Regazzoni	13	Beltoise
4	Cevert	14	Siffert
5	Surtees	15	Hulme
6	Amon	16	Peterson
7	Rodriguez,P.	17	Schenken
8	Pescarolo	18	Stommelen
9	Eaton	19	Brabham,J.
10	Oliver	20	Hill,G.

US

GRAND PRIX No:	196
DATE:	October 4, 1970
VENUE:	Watkins Glen
POLE LAP:	Ickx, 1m 03.07s
FASTEST LAP:	Ickx, 1m 02.74s

Pn	Driver	Car	Laps	Time/Reason
1	Fittipaldi,E.	Lotus-Ford	108	1h 57m 32.8s
2	Rodriguez,P.	BRM	108	1h 58m 09.2s
3	Wisell	Lotus-Ford	108	1h 58m 18.0s
4	Ickx	Ferrari	107	
5	Amon	March-Ford	107	
6	Bell	Surtees-Ford	107	
7	Hulme	McLaren-Ford	106	
8	Pescarolo	Matra	105	
9	Siffert	March-Ford	105	
10	Brabham,J.	Brabham-Ford	105	
11	Peterson	March-Ford	104	
12	Stommelen	Brabham-Ford	104	
13	Regazzoni	Ferrari	101	
14	Gethin	McLaren-Ford	100	
r	Stewart,Jackie	Tyrrell-Ford	82	oil leak
r	Hill,G.	Lotus-Ford	72	clutch
r	Cevert	March-Ford	62	lost wheel
r	Schenken	de Tomaso-Ford	61	suspension
r	Bonnier	McLaren-Ford	50	water pipe
r	Beltoise	Matra	27	handling
r	Hutchinson	Brabham-Ford	21	fuel tank
r	Oliver	BRM	14	engine
r	Eaton	BRM	10	engine
r	Surtees	Surtees-Ford	6	flywheel

STARTING GRID:

1	Ickx	13	Bell
2	Stewart,Jackie	14	Eaton
3	Fittipaldi,E.	15	Peterson
4	Rodriguez,P.	16	Brabham,J.
5	Amon	17	Cevert
6	Regazzoni	18	Beltoise
7	Oliver	19	Stommelen
8	Surtees	20	Schenken
9	Wisell	21	Gethin
10	Hill,G.	22	Hutchinson
11	Hulme	23	Siffert
12	Pescarolo	24	Bonnier

Mexican

GRAND PRIX No:	197
DATE:	October 25, 1970
VENUE:	Mexico City
POLE LAP:	Regazzoni, 1m 41.86s
FASTEST LAP:	Ickx, 1m 43.11s

Pn	Driver	Car	Laps	Time/Reason
1	Ickx	Ferrari	65	1h 53m 28.4s
2	Regazzoni	Ferrari	65	1h 54m 13.8s
3	Hulme	McLaren-Ford	65	1h 54m 14.3s
4	Amon	March-Ford	65	1h 54m 15.4s
5	Beltoise	Matra	65	1h 54m 18.5s
6	Rodriguez,P.	BRM	65	1h 54m 53.1s
7	Oliver	BRM	64	
8	Surtees	Surtees-Ford	64	
9	Pescarolo	Matra	61	
uc	Wisell	Lotus-Ford	56	
r	Brabham,J.	Brabham-Ford	52	engine
r	Stewart,Jackie	Tyrrell-Ford	33	suspension
r	Gethin	McLaren-Ford	27	engine
r	Stommelen	Brabham-Ford	15	fuel system
r	Cevert	March-Ford	8	engine
r	Hill,G.	Lotus-Ford	4	overheating
r	Siffert	March-Ford	3	engine
r	Fittipaldi,E.	Lotus-Ford	1	engine

STARTING GRID:

1	Regazzoni	10	Gethin
2	Stewart,Jackie	11	Pescarolo
3	Ickx	12	Wisell
4	Brabham,J.	13	Oliver
5	Amon	14	Hulme
6	Beltoise	15	Surtees
7	Rodriguez,P.	16	Siffert
8	Hill,G.	17	Stommelen
9	Cevert	18	Fittipaldi,E.

South African

GRAND PRIX No:	198
DATE:	March 6, 1971
VENUE:	Kyalami
POLE LAP:	Stewart,Jackie, 1m 17.8s
FASTEST LAP:	Andretti,Mario, 1m 20.3s

Pn	Driver	Car	Laps	Time/Reason
1	Andretti,Mario	Ferrari	79	1h 47m 35.5s
2	Stewart,Jackie	Tyrrell-Ford	79	1h 47m 56.4s
3	Regazzoni	Ferrari	79	1h 48m 06.9s
4	Wisell	Lotus-Ford	79	1h 48m 44.9s
5	Amon	Matra	78	
6	Hulme	McLaren-Ford	78	
7	Redman	Surtees-Ford	78	
8	Ickx	Ferrari	78	
9	Hill,G.	Brabham-Ford	77	
10	Peterson	March-Ford	77	
11	Pescarolo	March-Ford	77	
12	Stommelen	Surtees-Ford	77	
13	de Adamich	March-Alfa	73	
r	Fittipaldi,E.	Lotus-Ford	57	engine
r	Surtees	Surtees-Ford	55	gearbox
r	Cevert	Tyrrell-Ford	45	accident
r	Ganley	BRM	41	driver ill
r	Rodriguez,P.	BRM	32	overheating
r	Siffert	BRM	30	overheating
r	Charlton	Brabham-Ford	30	engine
r	Love	March-Ford	29	gearbox
r	Pretorius	Brabham-Ford	21	engine
r	Gethin	McLaren-Ford	6	fuel leak
r	Bonnier	McLaren-Ford	4	suspension
r	Soler-Roig	March-Ford	4	engine

STARTING GRID:

1	Stewart,Jackie	14	Wisell
2	Amon	15	Stommelen
3	Regazzoni	16	Siffert
4	Andretti,Mario	17	Redman
5	Fittipaldi,E.	18	Pescarolo
6	Surtees	19	Hill,G.
7	Hulme	20	Pretorius
8	Ickx	21	Love
9	Cevert	22	de Adamich
10	Rodriguez,P.	23	Bonnier
11	Gethin	24	Ganley
12	Charlton	25	Soler-Roig
13	Peterson		

Spanish

GRAND PRIX No:	199
DATE:	April 18, 1971
VENUE:	Montjuich Park
POLE LAP:	Ickx, 1m 25.9s
FASTEST LAP:	Ickx, 1m 25.1s

Pn	Driver	Car	Laps	Time/Reason
1	Stewart,Jackie	Tyrrell-Ford	75	1h 49m 03.4s
2	Ickx	Ferrari	75	1h 49m 06.8s
3	Amon	Matra	75	1h 50m 01.5s
4	Rodriguez,P.	BRM	75	1h 50m 21.3s
5	Hulme	McLaren-Ford	75	1h 50m 30.4s
6	Beltoise	Matra	74	
7	Cevert	Tyrrell-Ford	74	
8	Gethin	McLaren-Ford	73	
9	Schenken	Brabham-Ford	72	
10	Ganley	BRM	71	
11	Surtees	Surtees-Ford	67	
uc	Wisell	Lotus-Ford	58	
r	Fittipaldi,E.	Lotus-Ford	53	suspension
r	Pescarolo	March-Ford	53	rear wing
r	Andretti,Mario	Ferrari	50	engine
r	Soler-Roig	March-Ford	46	fuel pipe
r	de Adamich	March-Alfa	26	transmission
r	Peterson	March-Ford	24	ignition
r	Regazzoni	Ferrari	12	engine
r	Stommelen	Surtees-Ford	8	fuel pressure
r	Siffert	BRM	5	gearbox
r	Hill,G.	Brabham-Ford	4	steering

STARTING GRID:

1	Ickx	12	Cevert
2	Regazzoni	13	Peterson
3	Amon	14	Fittipaldi,E.
4	Stewart,Jackie	15	Hill,G.
5	Rodriguez,P.	16	Wisell
6	Beltoise	17	Ganley
7	Gethin	18	de Adamich
8	Andretti,Mario	19	Stommelen
9	Hulme	20	Soler-Roig
10	Siffert	21	Schenken
11	Pescarolo	22	Surtees

Monaco

GRAND PRIX No:	200
DATE:	May 23, 1971
VENUE:	Monte Carlo
POLE LAP:	Stewart,Jackie, 1m 23.2s
FASTEST LAP:	Stewart,Jackie, 1m 22.2s

Pn	Driver	Car	Laps	Time/Reason
1	Stewart,Jackie	Tyrrell-Ford	80	1h 52m 21.3s
2	Peterson	March-Ford	80	1h 52m 46.9s
3	Ickx	Ferrari	80	1h 53m 14.6s
4	Hulme	McLaren-Ford	80	1h 53m 28.0s
5	Fittipaldi,E.	Lotus-Ford	79	
6	Stommelen	Surtees-Ford	79	
7	Surtees	Surtees-Ford	79	
8	Pescarolo	March-Ford	77	
9	Rodriguez,P.	BRM	76	
10	Schenken	Brabham-Ford	76	
r	Siffert	BRM	58	oil pipe
r	Beltoise	Matra	47	crownwheel/pinion
r	Amon	Matra	45	crownwheel/pinion
r	Regazzoni	Ferrari	24	accident
r	Gethin	McLaren-Ford	22	accident
r	Wisell	Lotus-Ford	21	suspension
r	Cevert	Tyrrell-Ford	5	accident
r	Hill,G.	Brabham-Ford	1	accident

STARTING GRID:

1	Stewart,Jackie	10	Surtees
2	Ickx	11	Regazzoni
3	Siffert	12	Wisell
4	Amon	13	Pescarolo
5	Rodriguez,P.	14	Gethin
6	Hulme	15	Cevert
7	Beltoise	16	Stommelen
8	Peterson	17	Fittipaldi,E.
9	Hill,G.	18	Schenken

Dutch

GRAND PRIX No: 201
DATE: June 20, 1971
VENUE: Zandvoort
POLE LAP: Ickx, 1m 17.42s
FASTEST LAP: Ickx, 1m 34.95s

Pn	Driver	Car	Laps	Time/Reason
1	Ickx	Ferrari	70	1h 56m 20.1s
2	Rodriguez,P.	BRM	70	1h 56m 28.1s
3	Regazzoni	Ferrari	69	
4	Peterson	March-Ford	68	
5	Surtees	Surtees-Ford	68	
6	Siffert	BRM	68	
7	Ganley	BRM	66	
8	van Lennep	Surtees-Ford	65	
9	Beltoise	Matra	65	
10	Hill,G.	Brabham-Ford	65	
11	Stewart,Jackie	Tyrrell-Ford	65	
12	Hulme	McLaren-Ford	63	
uc	Pescarolo	March-Ford	62	
uc	Barber,S.	March-Ford	60	
uc	Gethin	McLaren-Ford	60	
r	Soler-Roig	March-Ford	57	engine
r	Schenken	Brabham-Ford	38	suspension
r	Cevert	Tyrrell-Ford	29	accident
dq	Stommelen	Surtees-Ford	18	push start
dq	Wisell	Lotus-Ford	16	reversed into pits
r	Nanni	March-Alfa	7	accident
r	Walker,D.	Lotus-Turbine	5	accident
r	Andretti,Mario	Ferrari	4	fuel system
r	Amon	Matra	1	accident

STARTING GRID:

1	Ickx	13	Peterson
2	Rodriguez,P.	14	Hulme
3	Stewart,Jackie	15	Pescarolo
4	Regazzoni	16	Hill,G.
5	Amon	17	Soler-Roig
6	Wisell	18	Andretti,Mario
7	Surtees	19	Schenken
8	Siffert	20	Nanni
9	Ganley	21	van Lennep
10	Stommelen	22	Walker,D.
11	Beltoise	23	Gethin
12	Cevert	24	Barber,S.

French

GRAND PRIX No: 202
DATE: July 4, 1971
VENUE: Paul Ricard
POLE LAP: Stewart,Jackie, 1m 50.71s
FASTEST LAP: Stewart,Jackie, 1m 54.09s

Pn	Driver	Car	Laps	Time/Reason
1	Stewart,Jackie	Tyrrell-Ford	55	1h 46m 41.7s
2	Cevert	Tyrrell-Ford	55	1h 47m 09.8s
3	Fittipaldi,E.	Lotus-Ford	55	1h 47m 15.8s
4	Siffert	BRM	55	1h 47m 18.9s
5	Amon	Matra	55	1h 47m 22.8s
6	Wisell	Lotus-Ford	55	1h 47m 57.7s
7	Beltoise	Matra	55	1h 47m 58.6s
8	Surtees	Surtees-Ford	55	1h 48m 06.6s
9	Gethin	McLaren-Ford	54	
10	Ganley	BRM	54	
11	Stommelen	Surtees-Ford	53	
12	Schenken	Brabham-Ford	50	oil pressure
13	Mazet	March-Ford	50	
uc	Max	March-Ford	46	
r	Pescarolo	March-Ford	44	gearbox
r	Hill,G.	Brabham-Ford	34	oil pipe
r	de Adamich	March-Alfa	31	engine
r	Rodriguez,P.	BRM	27	ignition
r	Regazzoni	Ferrari	20	accident
r	Peterson	March-Alfa	19	engine
r	Hulme	McLaren-Ford	15	ignition
r	Ickx	Ferrari	4	engine
r	Soler-Roig	March-Ford	3	fuel pump

STARTING GRID:

1	Stewart,Jackie	13	Surtees
2	Regazzoni	14	Schenken
3	Ickx	15	Wisell
4	Hill,G.	16	Ganley
5	Rodriguez,P.	17	Fittipaldi,E.
6	Siffert	18	Pescarolo
7	Cevert	19	Gethin
8	Beltoise	20	de Adamich
9	Amon	21	Soler-Roig
10	Stommelen	22	Max
11	Hulme	23	Mazet
12	Peterson		

British

GRAND PRIX No: 203
DATE: July 17, 1971
VENUE: Silverstone
POLE LAP: Regazzoni, 1m 18.1s
FASTEST LAP: Stewart,Jackie, 1m 19.9s

Pn	Driver	Car	Laps	Time/Reason
1	Stewart,Jackie	Tyrrell-Ford	68	1h 31m 31.5s
2	Peterson	March-Ford	68	1h 32m 07.6s
3	Fittipaldi,E.	Lotus-Ford	68	1h 32m 22.0s
4	Pescarolo	March-Ford	67	
5	Stommelen	Surtees-Ford	67	
6	Surtees	Surtees-Ford	67	
7	Beltoise	Matra	66	
8	Ganley	BRM	66	
9	Siffert	BRM	66	
10	Cevert	Tyrrell-Ford	65	
11	Nanni	March-Ford	65	
12	Schenken	Brabham-Ford	63	transmission
uc	Wisell	Lotus-Turbine	57	
uc	de Adamich	March-Alfa	56	
r	Gethin	McLaren-Ford	53	engine
r	Ickx	Ferrari	51	engine
r	Regazzoni	Ferrari	48	oil pressure
r	Amon	Matra	35	engine
r	Hulme	McLaren-Ford	32	engine
r	Bell	Surtees-Ford	23	suspension
r	Beuttler	March-Ford	21	oil pressure
r	Charlton	Lotus-Ford	1	engine
r	Oliver	McLaren-Ford	0	accident
r	Hill,G.	Brabham-Ford	0	accident

STARTING GRID:

1	Regazzoni	13	Charlton
2	Stewart,Jackie	14	Gethin
3	Siffert	15	Beltoise
4	Fittipaldi,E.	16	Hill,G.
5	Peterson	17	Pescarolo
6	Ickx	18	Surtees
7	Schenken	19	Wisell
8	Hulme	20	Beuttler
9	Amon	21	Nanni
10	Cevert	22	Oliver
11	Ganley	23	Bell
12	Stommelen	24	de Adamich

German

GRAND PRIX No: 204
DATE: August 1, 1971
VENUE: Nurburgring
POLE LAP: Stewart,Jackie, 7m 19.0s
FASTEST LAP: Cevert, 7m 20.1s

Pn	Driver	Car	Laps	Time/Reason
1	Stewart,Jackie	Tyrrell-Ford	12	1h 29m 15.7s
2	Cevert	Tyrrell-Ford	12	1h 29m 45.8s
3	Regazzoni	Ferrari	12	1h 29m 52.8s
4	Andretti,Mario	Ferrari	12	1h 31m 20.7s
5	Peterson	March-Ford	12	1h 31m 44.8s
6	Schenken	Brabham-Ford	12	1h 32m 12.3s
7	Surtees	Surtees-Ford	12	1h 32m 34.7s
8	Wisell	Lotus-Ford	12	1h 35m 47.4s
9	Hill,G.	Brabham-Ford	12	1h 35m 52.7s
10	Stommelen	Surtees-Ford	11	
11	Elford	BRM	11	
12	Nanni	March-Alfa	10	
r	Fittipaldi,E.	Lotus-Ford	8	oil leak
r	Siffert	BRM	6	suspension
r	Amon	Matra	6	accident
r	Gethin	McLaren-Ford	5	accident
r	Pescarolo	March-Ford	5	suspension
dq	Beuttler	March-Ford	3	wrong way into pits
r	Hulme	McLaren-Ford	3	fuel leak
r	de Adamich	March-Alfa	2	fuel injection
r	Ganley	BRM	2	engine
r	Ickx	Ferrari	1	accident

STARTING GRID:

1	Stewart,Jackie	12	Stommelen
2	Ickx	13	Hill,G.
3	Siffert	14	Ganley
4	Regazzoni	15	Surtees
5	Cevert	16	Amon
6	Hulme	17	Wisell
7	Peterson	18	Elford
8	Fittipaldi,E.	19	Gethin
9	Schenken	20	de Adamich
10	Pescarolo	21	Nanni
11	Andretti,Mario	22	Beuttler

Austrian

GRAND PRIX No: 205

DATE: August 15, 1971

VENUE: Osterreichring

POLE LAP: Siffert, 1m 37.44s

FASTEST LAP: Siffert, 1m 38.47s

Pn	Driver	Car	Laps	Time/Reason
1	Siffert	BRM	54	1h 30m 23.9s
2	Fittipaldi,E.	Lotus-Ford	54	1h 30m 28.0s
3	Schenken	Brabham-Ford	54	1h 30m 43.7s
4	Wisell	Lotus-Ford	54	1h 30m 55.8s
5	Hill,G.	Brabham-Ford	54	1h 31m 12.3s
6	Pescarolo	March-Ford	54	1h 31m 48.4s
7	Stommelen	Surtees-Ford	54	1h 32m 01.3s
8	Peterson	March-Ford	53	
9	Oliver	McLaren-Ford	53	
10	Gethin	BRM	52	
11	Marko	BRM	52	
12	Nanni	March-Alfa	51	
uc	Beuttler	March-Ford	47	
r	Cevert	Tyrrell-Ford	42	engine
r	Stewart,Jackie	Tyrrell-Ford	35	stub axle
r	Ickx	Ferrari	31	engine
r	Lauda	March-Ford	19	handling
r	Surtees	Surtees-Ford	12	engine
r	Regazzoni	Ferrari	8	engine
r	Ganley	BRM	5	ignition
r	Hulme	McLaren-Ford	4	engine
dns	Bonnier	McLaren-Ford		fuel leak

STARTING GRID:

1	Siffert	12	Stommelen
2	Stewart,Jackie	13	Pescarolo
3	Cevert	14	Ganley
4	Regazzoni	15	Nanni
5	Fittipaldi,E.	16	Gethin
6	Ickx	17	Marko
7	Schenken	18	Surtees
8	Hill,G.	19	Beuttler
9	Hulme	20	Bonnier
10	Wisell	21	Lauda
11	Peterson	22	Oliver

Italian

GRAND PRIX No: 206

DATE: September 5, 1971

VENUE: Monza

POLE LAP: Amon, 1m 22.40s

FASTEST LAP: Pescarolo, 1m 23.80s

Pn	Driver	Car	Laps	Time/Reason
1	Gethin	BRM	55	1h 18m 12.60s
2	Peterson	March-Ford	55	1h 18m 12.61s
3	Cevert	Tyrrell-Ford	55	1h 18m 12.69s
4	Hailwood	Surtees-Ford	55	1h 18m 12.78s
5	Ganley	BRM	55	1h 18m 13.21s
6	Amon	Matra	55	1h 18m 44.96s
7	Oliver	McLaren-Ford	55	1h 19m 37.43s
8	Fittipaldi,E.	Lotus-Turbine	54	
9	Siffert	BRM	53	
10	Bonnier	McLaren-Ford	51	
r	Hill,G.	Brabham-Ford	47	gearbox
uc	Jarier	March-Ford	47	
r	Beuttler	March-Ford	41	engine
r	Pescarolo	March-Ford	40	suspension
r	de Adamich	March-Alfa	33	engine
r	Regazzoni	Ferrari	17	engine
r	Ickx	Ferrari	15	engine
r	Stewart,Jackie	Tyrrell-Ford	15	engine
r	Nanni	March-Alfa	11	electrical
r	Moser	Bellasi-Ford	5	suspension
r	Schenken	Brabham-Ford	5	suspension
r	Marko	BRM	3	engine
r	Surtees	Surtees-Ford	3	engine
dns	Stommelen	Surtees-Ford		accident

STARTING GRID:

1	Amon	13	Oliver
2	Ickx	14	Hill,G.
3	Siffert	15	Surtees
4	Ganley	16	Beuttler
5	Cevert	17	Hailwood
6	Peterson	18	Fittipaldi,E.
7	Stewart,Jackie	19	Nanni
8	Regazzoni	20	de Adamich
9	Schenken	21	Bonnier
10	Pescarolo	22	Moser
11	Gethin	23	Stommelen
12	Marko	24	Jarier

Canadian

GRAND PRIX No: 207
DATE: September 19, 1971
VENUE: Mosport Park
POLE LAP: Stewart,Jackie, 1m 15.3s
FASTEST LAP: Hulme, 1m 43.5s

Pn	Driver	Car	Laps	Time/Reason
1	Stewart,Jackie	Tyrrell-Ford	64	1h 55m 12.9s
2	Peterson	March-Ford	64	1h 55m 51.2s
3	Donohue	McLaren-Ford	64	1h 56m 47.8s
4	Hulme	McLaren-Ford	63	
5	Wisell	Lotus-Ford	63	
6	Cevert	Tyrrell-Ford	62	
7	Fittipaldi,E.	Lotus-Ford	62	
8	Ickx	Ferrari	62	
9	Siffert	BRM	61	
10	Amon	Matra	61	
11	Surtees	Surtees-Ford	60	
12	Marko	BRM	60	
13	Andretti,Mario	Ferrari	60	
14	Gethin	BRM	59	
15	Eaton	BRM	59	
16	Nanni	March-Ford	57	
uc	Beuttler	March-Ford	56	
uc	Lovely	Lotus-Ford	55	
r	Stommelen	Surtees-Ford	26	overheating
r	Beltoise	Matra	15	accident
r	Barber,S.	March-Ford	13	oil pressure
r	Regazzoni	Ferrari	7	accident
r	Hill,G.	Brabham-Ford	2	accident
r	Schenken	Brabham-Ford	1	ignition
dns	Ganley	BRM		accident
dns	Craft	Brabham-Ford		engine
dns	Pescarolo	March-Ford		accident

STARTING GRID:

1	Stewart,Jackie	11	Beltoise
2	Siffert	12	Ickx
3	Cevert	13	Andretti,Mario
4	Fittipaldi,E.	14	Surtees
5	Amon	15	Hill,G.
6	Peterson	16	Gethin
7	Wisell	17	Schenken
8	Donohue	18	Regazzoni
9	Ganley	19	Marko
10	Hulme	20	Nanni +

US

GRAND PRIX No: 208
DATE: October 3, 1971
VENUE: Watkins Glen
POLE LAP: Stewart,Jackie, 1m 42.642s
FASTEST LAP: Ickx, 1m 43.470s

Pn	Driver	Car	Laps	Time/Reason
1	Cevert	Tyrrell-Ford	59	1h 43m 52.0s
2	Siffert	BRM	59	1h 44m 32.1s
3	Peterson	March-Ford	59	1h 44m 36.1s
4	Ganley	BRM	59	1h 44m 48.7s
5	Stewart,Jackie	Tyrrell-Ford	59	1h 44m 52.0s
6	Regazzoni	Ferrari	59	1h 45m 08.4s
7	Hill,G.	Brabham-Ford	58	
8	Beltoise	Matra	58	
9	Gethin	BRM	58	
10	Hobbs	McLaren-Ford	58	
11	de Adamich	March-Alfa	57	
12	Amon	Matra	57	
13	Marko	BRM	57	
14	Cannon	BRM	56	
15	Hailwood	Surtees-Ford	54	accident
16	Bonnier	McLaren-Ford	54	out of fuel
17	Surtees	Surtees-Ford	54	
uc	Barber,S.	March-Ford	52	
uc	Fittipaldi,E.	Lotus-Ford	49	
uc	Lovely	Lotus-Ford	49	
r	Ickx	Ferrari	48	electrical
r	Hulme	McLaren-Ford	47	accident
r	Schenken	Brabham-Ford	40	engine
r	Craft	Brabham-Ford	29	suspension
r	Pescarolo	March-Ford	22	engine
r	Posey	Surtees-Ford	14	engine
r	Nanni	March-Ford	10	wheel
r	Wisell	Lotus-Ford	5	accident
r	Revson	Tyrrell-Ford	0	clutch

STARTING GRID:

1	Stewart,Jackie	10	Beltoise
2	Fittipaldi,E.	11	Peterson
3	Hulme	12	Ganley
4	Regazzoni	13	Surtees
5	Cevert	14	Hailwood
6	Siffert	15	Schenken
7	Ickx	16	Marko
8	Amon	17	Posey
9	Wisell	18	Hill,G. +

Argentine

GRAND PRIX No:	209
DATE:	January 23, 1972
VENUE:	Buenos Aires
POLE LAP:	Reutemann, 1m 12.46s
FASTEST LAP:	Stewart,Jackie, 1m 13.66s

Pn	Driver	Car	Laps	Time/Reason
1	Stewart,Jackie	Tyrrell-Ford	95	1h 57m 58.8s
2	Hulme	McLaren-Ford	95	1h 58m 24.8s
3	Ickx	Ferrari	95	1h 58m 58.2s
4	Regazzoni	Ferrari	95	1h 59m 05.5s
5	Schenken	Surtees-Ford	95	1h 59m 07.9s
6	Peterson	March-Ford	94	
7	Reutemann	Brabham-Ford	93	
8	Pescarolo	March-Ford	93	
9	Ganley	BRM	93	
10	Marko	BRM	93	
11	Lauda	March-Ford	93	
r	Fittipaldi,E.	Lotus-Ford	59	suspension
r	Cevert	Tyrrell-Ford	59	gearbox
r	Wisell	BRM	58	water hose
r	Revson	McLaren-Ford	49	engine
r	Andretti,Mario	Ferrari	20	engine
r	Hill,G.	Brabham-Ford	11	fuel pump
r	de Adamich	Surtees-Ford	10	fuel metering unit
dq	Walker,D.	Lotus-Ford	8	illegal repairs
r	Gethin	BRM	1	oil pipe
r	Soler-Roig	BRM	1	accident

STARTING GRID:

1	Reutemann	12	Ganley
2	Stewart,Jackie	13	de Adamich
3	Revson	14	Pescarolo
4	Hulme	15	Hill,G.
5	Fittipaldi,E.	16	Wisell
6	Regazzoni	17	Gethin
7	Cevert	18	Marko
8	Ickx	19	Walker,D.
9	Andretti,Mario	20	Soler-Roig
10	Peterson	21	Lauda
11	Schenken		

South African

GRAND PRIX No:	210
DATE:	March 4, 1972
VENUE:	Kyalami
POLE LAP:	Stewart,Jackie, 1m 17.0s
FASTEST LAP:	Hailwood, 1m 18.9s

Pn	Driver	Car	Laps	Time/Reason
1	Hulme	McLaren-Ford	79	1h 45m 49.1s
2	Fittipaldi,E.	Lotus-Ford	79	1h 46m 03.2s
3	Revson	McLaren-Ford	79	1h 46m 14.9s
4	Andretti,Mario	Ferrari	79	1h 46m 27.6s
5	Peterson	March-Ford	79	1h 46m 38.1s
6	Hill,G.	Brabham-Ford	78	
7	Lauda	March-Ford	78	
8	Ickx	Ferrari	78	
9	Cevert	Tyrrell-Ford	78	
10	Walker,D.	Lotus-Ford	78	
11	Pescarolo	March-Ford	77	
12	Regazzoni	Ferrari	77	
13	Stommelen	March-Ford	77	
14	Marko	BRM	76	
15	Amon	Matra	76	
16	Love	Surtees-Ford	73	accident
17	Pace	March-Ford	73	
uc	Ganley	BRM	70	
uc	de Adamich	Surtees-Ford	69	
uc	Gethin	BRM	65	
r	Beltoise	BRM	60	engine
r	Stewart,Jackie	Tyrrell-Ford	44	gearbox
r	Hailwood	Surtees-Ford	28	suspension
r	Reutemann	Brabham-Ford	27	fuel line
r	Schenken	Surtees-Ford	8	engine
r	Charlton	Lotus-Ford	1	fuel pump
dns	Ferguson	Brabham-Ford		engine

STARTING GRID:

1	Stewart,Jackie	11	Beltoise
2	Regazzoni	12	Revson
3	Fittipaldi,E.	13	Amon
4	Hailwood	14	Hill,G.
5	Hulme	15	Reutemann
6	Andretti,Mario	16	Ganley
7	Ickx	17	Charlton
8	Cevert	18	Gethin
9	Peterson	19	Walker,D.
10	Schenken	20	de Adamich +

Spanish

GRAND PRIX No: 211
DATE: May 1, 1972
VENUE: Jarama
POLE LAP: Ickx, 1m 18.43s
FASTEST LAP: Ickx, 1m 21.01s

Pn	Driver	Car	Laps	Time/Reason
1	Fittipaldi,E.	Lotus-Ford	90	2h 03m 41.2s
2	Ickx	Ferrari	90	2h 04m 00.2s
3	Regazzoni	Ferrari	89	
4	de Adamich	Surtees-Ford	89	
5	Revson	McLaren-Ford	89	
6	Pace	March-Ford	89	
7	Fittipaldi,W.	Brabham-Ford	88	
8	Schenken	Surtees-Ford	88	
9	Walker,D.	Lotus-Ford	87	out of fuel
10	Hill,G.	Brabham-Ford	86	
11	Pescarolo	March-Ford	86	
r	Stewart,Jackie	Tyrrell-Ford	69	accident
r	Amon	Matra	65	gearbox
r	Gethin	BRM	65	engine
r	Cevert	Tyrrell-Ford	64	ignition
r	Hulme	McLaren-Ford	47	gearbox
r	Ganley	BRM	37	engine
r	Wisell	BRM	24	accident
r	Andretti,Mario	Ferrari	23	engine
r	Hailwood	Surtees-Ford	19	electrical
r	Peterson	March-Ford	15	fuel leak
r	Stommelen	March-Ford	15	accident
r	Beltoise	BRM	8	gearbox
r	Lauda	March-Ford	6	differential
r	Soler-Roig	BRM	6	accident

STARTING GRID:

1	Ickx	14	Fittipaldi,W.
2	Hulme	15	Hailwood
3	Fittipaldi,E.	16	Pace
4	Stewart,Jackie	17	Stommelen
5	Andretti,Mario	18	Schenken
6	Amon	19	Pescarolo
7	Beltoise	20	Ganley
8	Regazzoni	21	Gethin
9	Peterson	22	Soler-Roig
10	Wisell	23	Hill,G.
11	Revson	24	Walker,D.
12	Cevert	25	Lauda
13	de Adamich		

Monaco

GRAND PRIX No: 212
DATE: May 14, 1972
VENUE: Monte Carlo
POLE LAP: Fittipaldi,E., 1m 11.43s
FASTEST LAP: Amon, 1m 12.12s

Pn	Driver	Car	Laps	Time/Reason
1	Beltoise	BRM	80	2h 26m 54.7s
2	Ickx	Ferrari	80	2h 27m 32.9s
3	Fittipaldi,E.	Lotus-Ford	79	
4	Stewart,Jackie	Tyrrell-Ford	78	
5	Redman	McLaren-Ford	77	
6	Amon	Matra	77	
7	de Adamich	Surtees-Ford	77	
8	Marko	BRM	77	
9	Fittipaldi,W.	Brabham-Ford	77	
10	Stommelen	March-Ford	77	
11	Peterson	March-Ford	76	
12	Hill,G.	Brabham-Ford	76	
13	Beuttler	March-Ford	76	
14	Walker,D.	Lotus-Ford	75	
15	Hulme	McLaren-Ford	74	
16	Lauda	March-Ford	74	
17	Pace	March-Ford	72	
uc	Cevert	Tyrrell-Ford	70	
r	Pescarolo	March-Ford	58	accident
r	Regazzoni	Ferrari	51	accident
r	Hailwood	Surtees-Ford	48	accident
r	Ganley	BRM	47	accident
r	Schenken	Surtees-Ford	31	accident
dq	Gethin	BRM	27	reversed into pits
r	Wisell	BRM	16	engine

STARTING GRID:

1	Fittipaldi,E.	14	Walker,D.
2	Ickx	15	Peterson
3	Regazzoni	16	Wisell
4	Beltoise	17	Marko
5	Gethin	18	de Adamich
6	Amon	19	Hill,G.
7	Hulme	20	Ganley
8	Stewart,Jackie	21	Fittipaldi,W.
9	Pescarolo	22	Lauda
10	Redman	23	Beuttler
11	Hailwood	24	Pace
12	Cevert	25	Stommelen
13	Schenken		

Belgian

GRAND PRIX No:	213
DATE:	June 4, 1972
VENUE:	Nivelles
POLE LAP:	Fittipaldi,E., 1m 21.4s
FASTEST LAP:	Beltoise, 1m 40.0s

Pn	Driver	Car	Laps	Time/Reason
1	Fittipaldi,E.	Lotus-Ford	85	1h 44m 06.7s
2	Cevert	Tyrrell-Ford	85	1h 44m 33.3s
3	Hulme	McLaren-Ford	85	1h 45m 04.8s
4	Hailwood	Surtees-Ford	85	1h 45m 18.7s
5	Pace	March-Ford	84	
6	Amon	Matra	84	
7	Revson	McLaren-Ford	83	
8	Ganley	BRM	83	
9	Peterson	March-Ford	83	
10	Marko	BRM	83	
11	Stommelen	March-Ford	83	
12	Lauda	March-Ford	82	
13	Reutemann	Brabham-Ford	81	
14	Walker,D.	Lotus-Ford	79	
r	Hill,G.	Brabham-Ford	72	suspension
uc	Pescarolo	March-Ford	59	
r	Regazzoni	Ferrari	57	accident
r	de Adamich	Surtees-Ford	55	engine
r	Nanni	Tecno	53	accident
r	Ickx	Ferrari	46	fuel injection
r	Beuttler	March-Ford	31	transmission
r	Fittipaldi,W.	Brabham-Ford	27	gearbox
r	Gethin	BRM	26	fuel pump
r	Beltoise	BRM	14	overheating
r	Schenken	Surtees-Ford	10	overheating

STARTING GRID:

1	Fittipaldi,E.	14	Peterson
2	Regazzoni	15	Ganley
3	Hulme	16	Hill,G.
4	Ickx	17	Gethin
5	Cevert	18	Fittipaldi,W.
6	Beltoise	19	Pescarolo
7	Revson	20	Stommelen
8	Hailwood	21	Schenken
9	Reutemann	22	Beuttler
10	de Adamich	23	Marko
11	Pace	24	Nanni
12	Walker,D.	25	Lauda
13	Amon		

French

GRAND PRIX No:	214
DATE:	July 2, 1972
VENUE:	Clermont-Ferrand
POLE LAP:	Amon, 2m 53.4s
FASTEST LAP:	Amon, 2m 53.9s

Pn	Driver	Car	Laps	Time/Reason
1	Stewart,Jackie	Tyrrell-Ford	38	1h 52m 21.5s
2	Fittipaldi,E.	Lotus-Ford	38	1h 52m 49.2s
3	Amon	Matra	38	1h 52m 53.4s
4	Cevert	Tyrrell-Ford	38	1h 53m 10.8s
5	Peterson	March-Ford	38	1h 53m 18.3s
6	Hailwood	Surtees-Ford	38	1h 53m 57.6s
7	Hulme	McLaren-Ford	38	1h 54m 09.6s
8	Fittipaldi,W.	Brabham-Ford	38	1h 54m 46.6s
9	Redman	McLaren-Ford	38	1h 55m 17.0s
10	Hill,G.	Brabham-Ford	38	1h 55m 21.0s
11	Ickx	Ferrari	37	
12	Reutemann	Brabham-Ford	37	
13	Nanni	Ferrari	37	
14	de Adamich	Surtees-Ford	37	
15	Beltoise	BRM	37	
16	Stommelen	March-Ford	37	
17	Schenken	Surtees-Ford	36	
18	Walker,D.	Lotus-Ford	34	gearbox
r	Beuttler	March-Ford	33	out of fuel
uc	Depailler	Tyrrell-Ford	33	
r	Wisell	BRM	24	gear linkage
r	Pace	March-Ford	18	engine
r	Marko	BRM	8	driver injury
r	Lauda	March-Ford	3	transmission
dns	Pescarolo	March-Ford		accident
dns	Gethin	BRM		accident
dns	Bell	Tecno		damaged chassis
dns	Charlton	Lotus-Ford		car not ready

STARTING GRID:

1	Amon	10	Hailwood
2	Hulme	11	Pace
3	Stewart,Jackie	12	Pescarolo
4	Ickx	13	de Adamich
5	Schenken	14	Beltoise
6	Marko	15	Redman
7	Cevert	16	Fittipaldi,W.
8	Fittipaldi,E.	17	Stommelen
9	Peterson	18	Depailler

British

GRAND PRIX No: 215
DATE: July 15, 1972
VENUE: Brands Hatch
POLE LAP: Ickx, 1m 22.2s
FASTEST LAP: Stewart,Jackie, 1m 24.0s

Pn	Driver	Car	Laps	Time/Reason
1	Fittipaldi,E.	Lotus-Ford	76	1h 47m 50.2s
2	Stewart,Jackie	Tyrrell-Ford	76	1h 47m 54.3s
3	Revson	McLaren-Ford	76	1h 49m 02.7s
4	Amon	Matra	75	
5	Hulme	McLaren-Ford	75	
6	Merzario	Ferrari	75	
7	Peterson	March-Ford	74	accident
8	Reutemann	Brabham-Ford	73	
9	Lauda	March-Ford	73	
10	Stommelen	March-Ford	71	
11	Beltoise	BRM	70	
12	Fittipaldi,W.	Brabham-Ford	69	suspension
13	Beuttler	March-Ford	69	
r	Schenken	Surtees-Ford	63	suspension
r	Cevert	Tyrrell-Ford	60	accident
r	Walker,D.	Lotus-Ford	58	suspension
r	Ickx	Ferrari	48	oil pressure
r	Hill,G.	Brabham-Ford	47	accident
r	Pace	March-Ford	39	differential
r	Oliver	BRM	36	suspension
r	Hailwood	Surtees-Ford	30	gearbox
r	Charlton	Lotus-Ford	21	gearbox
r	Nanni	Tecno	9	accident
r	Pescarolo	Williams-Ford	7	accident
r	Gethin	BRM	5	engine
r	de Adamich	Surtees-Ford	3	accident
dns	Migault	Connew-Ford		suspension

STARTING GRID:

1	Ickx	11	Hulme
2	Fittipaldi,E.	12	Cevert
3	Revson	13	Pace
4	Stewart,Jackie	14	Oliver
5	Schenken	15	Walker,D.
6	Beltoise	16	Gethin
7	Hailwood	17	Amon
8	Peterson	18	Nanni
9	Merzario	19	Lauda
10	Reutemann	20	de Adamich +

German

GRAND PRIX No: 216
DATE: July 30, 1972
VENUE: Nurburgring
POLE LAP: Ickx, 7m 07.0s
FASTEST LAP: Ickx, 7m 13.6s

Pn	Driver	Car	Laps	Time/Reason
1	Ickx	Ferrari	14	1h 42m 12.3s
2	Regazzoni	Ferrari	14	1h 43m 00.6s
3	Peterson	March-Ford	14	1h 43m 19.0s
4	Ganley	BRM	14	1h 44m 32.5s
5	Redman	McLaren-Ford	14	1h 44m 48.0s
6	Hill,G.	Brabham-Ford	14	1h 45m 11.9s
7	Fittipaldi,W.	Brabham-Ford	14	1h 45m 12.4s
8	Beuttler	March-Ford	14	1h 47m 23.0s
9	Beltoise	BRM	14	1h 47m 32.5s
10	Cevert	Tyrrell-Ford	14	1h 47m 56.0s
11	Stewart,Jackie	Tyrrell-Ford	13	accident
12	Merzario	Ferrari	13	
13	de Adamich	Surtees-Ford	13	
14	Schenken	Surtees-Ford	13	
15	Amon	Matra	13	
uc	Pace	March-Ford	11	
r	Pescarolo	March-Ford	10	accident
r	Fittipaldi,E.	Lotus-Ford	10	gearbox
r	Hulme	McLaren-Ford	8	engine
r	Hailwood	Surtees-Ford	8	suspension
r	Reutemann	Brabham-Ford	6	crownwheel/pinion
r	Stommelen	March-Ford	5	electrical
r	Walker,D.	Lotus-Ford	5	oil tank
r	Bell	Tecno	4	engine
r	Charlton	Lotus-Ford	3	driver ill
r	Lauda	March-Ford	3	oil tank
r	Wisell	BRM	3	engine

STARTING GRID:

1	Ickx	11	Pace
2	Stewart,Jackie	12	Schenken
3	Fittipaldi,E.	13	Beltoise
4	Peterson	14	Stommelen
5	Cevert	15	Hill,G.
6	Reutemann	16	Hailwood
7	Regazzoni	17	Wisell
8	Amon	18	Ganley
9	Pescarolo	19	Redman
10	Hulme	20	de Adamich +

Austrian

GRAND PRIX No:	217
DATE:	August 13, 1972
VENUE:	Osterreichring
POLE LAP:	Fittipaldi,E., 1m 35.97s
FASTEST LAP:	Hulme, 1m 38.32s

Pn	Driver	Car	Laps	Time/Reason
1	Fittipaldi,E.	Lotus-Ford	54	1h 29m 16.7s
2	Hulme	McLaren-Ford	54	1h 29m 17.8s
3	Revson	McLaren-Ford	54	1h 29m 53.2s
4	Hailwood	Surtees-Ford	54	1h 30m 01.4s
5	Amon	Matra	54	1h 30m 02.3s
6	Ganley	BRM	54	1h 30m 17.9s
7	Stewart,Jackie	Tyrrell-Ford	54	1h 30m 25.8s
8	Beltoise	BRM	54	1h 30m 38.1s
9	Cevert	Tyrrell-Ford	53	
10	Lauda	March-Ford	53	
11	Schenken	Surtees-Ford	52	
12	Peterson	March-Ford	52	
13	Gethin	BRM	51	
14	de Adamich	Surtees-Ford	51	
15	Stommelen	March-Ford	48	
uc	Pace	March-Ford	46	
uc	Nanni	Tecno	45	
r	Hill,G.	Brabham-Ford	35	fuel metering unit
r	Fittipaldi,W.	Brabham-Ford	30	brake pipe
r	Beuttler	March-Ford	23	fuel metering unit
r	Migault	Connew-Ford	22	suspension
r	Ickx	Ferrari	19	fuel pressure
r	Reutemann	Brabham-Ford	13	fuel metering unit
r	Regazzoni	Ferrari	12	fuel pressure
r	Walker,D.	Lotus-Ford	6	engine
dns	Pescarolo	March-Ford		accident

STARTING GRID:

1	Fittipaldi,E.	12	Hailwood
2	Regazzoni	13	de Adamich
3	Stewart,Jackie	14	Hill,G.
4	Revson	15	Fittipaldi,W.
5	Reutemann	16	Gethin
6	Amon	17	Stommelen
7	Hulme	18	Pace
8	Schenken	19	Walker,D.
9	Ickx	20	Cevert
10	Ganley	21	Beltoise
11	Peterson	22	Lauda +

Italian

GRAND PRIX No:	218
DATE:	September 10, 1972
VENUE:	Monza
POLE LAP:	Ickx, 1m 35.65s
FASTEST LAP:	Ickx, 1m 36.30s

Pn	Driver	Car	Laps	Time/Reason
1	Fittipaldi,E.	Lotus-Ford	55	1h 29m 58.4s
2	Hailwood	Surtees-Ford	55	1h 30m 12.9s
3	Hulme	McLaren-Ford	55	1h 30m 22.2s
4	Revson	McLaren-Ford	55	1h 30m 34.1s
5	Hill,G.	Brabham-Ford	55	1h 31m 04.0s
6	Gethin	BRM	55	1h 31m 20.3s
7	Andretti,Mario	Ferrari	54	
8	Beltoise	BRM	54	
9	Peterson	March-Ford	54	
10	Beuttler	March-Ford	54	
11	Ganley	BRM	52	
12	Wisell	BRM	51	
13	Lauda	March-Ford	50	
r	Ickx	Ferrari	45	electrical
r	Amon	Matra	37	brakes
r	de Adamich	Surtees-Ford	32	brakes
r	Schenken	Surtees-Ford	20	suspension
r	Surtees	Surtees-Ford	19	fuel vaporisation
r	Fittipaldi,W.	Brabham-Ford	19	suspension
r	Regazzoni	Ferrari	16	accident
r	Pace	March-Ford	15	accident
r	Reutemann	Brabham-Ford	14	suspension
r	Cevert	Tyrrell-Ford	13	engine
r	Nanni	Tecno	6	engine
r	Stewart,Jackie	Tyrrell-Ford	0	clutch

STARTING GRID:

1	Ickx	13	Hill,G.
2	Amon	14	Cevert
3	Stewart,Jackie	15	Fittipaldi,W.
4	Regazzoni	16	Beltoise
5	Hulme	17	Ganley
6	Fittipaldi,E.	18	Pace
7	Andretti,Mario	19	Surtees
8	Revson	20	Lauda
9	Hailwood	21	de Adamich
10	Wisell	22	Schenken
11	Reutemann	23	Nanni
12	Gethin	24	Peterson
		25	Beuttler

Canadian

GRAND PRIX No: 219
DATE: September 24, 1972
VENUE: Mosport Park
POLE LAP: Revson, 1m 13.6s
FASTEST LAP: Stewart,Jackie, 1m 15.7s

Pn	Driver	Car	Laps	Time/Reason
1	Stewart,Jackie	Tyrrell-Ford	80	1h 43m 16.9s
2	Revson	McLaren-Ford	80	1h 44m 05.1s
3	Hulme	McLaren-Ford	80	1h 44m 11.5s
4	Reutemann	Brabham-Ford	80	1h 44m 17.6s
5	Regazzoni	Ferrari	80	1h 44m 23.9s
6	Amon	Matra	79	
7	Schenken	Surtees-Ford	79	
8	Hill,G.	Brabham-Ford	79	
9	Pace	March-Ford	78	fuel pressure
10	Ganley	BRM	78	
11	Fittipaldi,E.	Lotus-Ford	78	
12	Ickx	Ferrari	76	
13	Pescarolo	March-Ford	73	
r	Wisell	Lotus-Ford	64	fuel line
uc	Beuttler	March-Ford	59	
dq	Peterson	March-Ford	54	pushed car
r	Cevert	Tyrrell-Ford	50	gearbox
r	Gethin	BRM	25	suspension
uc	Barber,S.	March-Ford	24	
r	Beltoise	BRM	20	oil cooler
r	Brack	BRM	20	accident
r	Fittipaldi,W.	Brabham-Ford	4	gearbox
r	de Adamich	Surtees-Ford	1	gearbox
dq	Lauda	March-Ford	0	push start
dns	Bell	Tecno		accident

STARTING GRID:

1	Revson	14	Ganley
2	Hulme	15	de Adamich
3	Peterson	16	Wisell
4	Fittipaldi,E.	17	Hill,G.
5	Stewart,Jackie	18	Pace
6	Cevert	19	Lauda
7	Regazzoni	20	Beltoise
8	Ickx	21	Pescarolo
9	Reutemann	22	Barber,S.
10	Amon	23	Brack
11	Fittipaldi,W.	24	Beuttler
12	Gethin	25	Bell
13	Schenken		

US

GRAND PRIX No: 220
DATE: October 8, 1972
VENUE: Watkins Glen
POLE LAP: Stewart,Jackie, 1m 40.481s
FASTEST LAP: Stewart,Jackie, 1m 41.644s

Pn	Driver	Car	Laps	Time/Reason
1	Stewart,Jackie	Tyrrell-Ford	59	1h 41m 45.4s
2	Cevert	Tyrrell-Ford	59	1h 42m 17.6s
3	Hulme	McLaren-Ford	59	1h 42m 22.9s
4	Peterson	March-Ford	59	1h 43m 07.9s
5	Ickx	Ferrari	59	1h 43m 08.5s
6	Andretti,Mario	Ferrari	58	
7	Depailler	Tyrrell-Ford	58	
8	Regazzoni	Ferrari	58	
9	Scheckter,J.	McLaren-Ford	58	
10	Wisell	Lotus-Ford	57	
11	Hill,G.	Brabham-Ford	57	
12	Posey	Surtees-Ford	57	
13	Beuttler	March-Ford	57	
14	Pescarolo	March-Ford	57	
15	Amon	Matra	57	
16	Barber,S.	March-Ford	57	
17	Hailwood	Surtees-Ford	56	accident
18	Revson	McLaren-Ford	54	ignition
uc	Lauda	March-Ford	49	
r	Pace	March-Ford	48	fuel system
r	Gethin	BRM	47	engine
r	Ganley	BRM	44	engine
r	Walker,D.	Lotus-Ford	44	engine
r	Fittipaldi,W.	Brabham-Ford	43	engine
r	Beltoise	BRM	40	ignition
r	Redman	BRM	34	engine
r	Reutemann	Brabham-Ford	31	engine
r	de Adamich	Surtees-Ford	25	suspension
r	Schenken	Surtees-Ford	22	suspension
r	Fittipaldi,E.	Lotus-Ford	17	suspension
r	Bell	Tecno	8	overheating
dns	Surtees	Surtees-Ford		no engine

STARTING GRID:

1	Stewart,Jackie	7	Amon
2	Revson	8	Scheckter,J.
3	Hulme	9	Fittipaldi,E.
4	Cevert	10	Andretti,Mario
5	Reutemann	11	Depailler
6	Regazzoni	12	Ickx

+

Argentine

GRAND PRIX No: 221
DATE: January 28, 1973
VENUE: Buenos Aires
POLE LAP: Regazzoni, 1m 10.54s
FASTEST LAP: Fittipaldi,E., 1m 11.22s

Pn	Driver	Car	Laps	Time/Reason
1	Fittipaldi,E.	Lotus-Ford	96	1h 56m 18.2s
2	Cevert	Tyrrell-Ford	96	1h 56m 22.9s
3	Stewart,Jackie	Tyrrell-Ford	96	1h 56m 51.4s
4	Ickx	Ferrari	96	1h 57m 00.8s
5	Hulme	McLaren-Ford	95	
6	Fittipaldi,W.	Brabham-Ford	95	
7	Regazzoni	BRM	93	
8	Revson	McLaren-Ford	92	
9	Merzario	Ferrari	92	
10	Beuttler	March-Ford	90	suspension
r	Jarier	March-Ford	84	gearbox
r	Beltoise	BRM	79	engine
uc	Ganley	Williams-Ford	79	
r	Peterson	Lotus-Ford	67	oil pressure
r	Lauda	BRM	66	oil pressure
r	Reutemann	Brabham-Ford	16	gearbox
r	Pace	Surtees-Ford	10	suspension
r	Hailwood	Surtees-Ford	10	transmission
r	Nanni	Williams-Ford	0	engine

STARTING GRID:

1	Regazzoni	11	Revson
2	Fittipaldi,E.	12	Fittipaldi,W.
3	Ickx	13	Lauda
4	Stewart,Jackie	14	Merzario
5	Peterson	15	Pace
6	Cevert	16	Nanni
7	Beltoise	17	Jarier
8	Hulme	18	Beuttler
9	Reutemann	19	Ganley
10	Hailwood		

Brazilian

GRAND PRIX No: 222
DATE: February 11, 1973
VENUE: Interlagos
POLE LAP: Peterson, 2m 30.5s
FASTEST LAP: Fittipaldi,E. & Hulme, 2m 35.0s

Pn	Driver	Car	Laps	Time/Reason
1	Fittipaldi,E.	Lotus-Ford	40	1h 43m 55.6s
2	Stewart,Jackie	Tyrrell-Ford	40	1h 44m 09.1s
3	Hulme	McLaren-Ford	40	1h 45m 42.0s
4	Merzario	Ferrari	39	
5	Ickx	Ferrari	39	
6	Regazzoni	BRM	39	
7	Ganley	Williams-Ford	39	
8	Lauda	BRM	38	
9	Nanni	Williams-Ford	38	
10	Cevert	Tyrrell-Ford	38	
11	Reutemann	Brabham-Ford	38	
12	Bueno	Surtees-Ford	36	
r	Beltoise	BRM	23	electrical
r	Beuttler	March-Ford	17	overheating
r	Pace	Surtees-Ford	8	suspension
r	Hailwood	Surtees-Ford	6	gearbox
r	Jarier	March-Ford	5	gearbox
r	Peterson	Lotus-Ford	5	wheel
r	Fittipaldi,W.	Brabham-Ford	5	overheating
r	Revson	McLaren-Ford	2	gearbox

STARTING GRID:

1	Peterson	11	Fittipaldi,W.
2	Fittipaldi,E.	12	Revson
3	Ickx	13	Lauda
4	Regazzoni	14	Hailwood
5	Hulme	15	Jarier
6	Pace	16	Ganley
7	Reutemann	17	Merzario
8	Stewart,Jackie	18	Nanni
9	Cevert	19	Beuttler
10	Beltoise	20	Bueno

South African

GRAND PRIX No: 223
DATE: March 3, 1973
VENUE: Kyalami
POLE LAP: Hulme, 1m 16.28s
FASTEST LAP: Fittipaldi,E., 1m 17.10s

Pn	Driver	Car	Laps	Time/Reason
1	Stewart,Jackie	Tyrrell-Ford	79	1h 43m 11.1s
2	Revson	McLaren-Ford	79	1h 43m 35.6s
3	Fittipaldi,E.	Lotus-Ford	79	1h 43m 36.1s
4	Merzario	Ferrari	78	
5	Hulme	McLaren-Ford	77	
6	Follmer	Shadow-Ford	77	
7	Reutemann	Brabham-Ford	77	
8	de Adamich	Surtees-Ford	77	
9	Scheckter,J.	McLaren-Ford	75	engine
10	Ganley	Williams-Ford	73	
11	Peterson	Lotus-Ford	73	
r	Pace	Surtees-Ford	69	accident
uc	Keizan	Tyrrell-Ford	67	
uc	Jarier	March-Ford	66	
uc	Cevert	Tyrrell-Ford	66	
uc	Beuttler	March-Ford	65	
r	Fittipaldi,W.	Brabham-Ford	52	gearbox
r	Pretorius	Williams-Ford	35	overheating
r	Lauda	BRM	26	engine
r	Oliver	Shadow-Ford	14	engine
r	Beltoise	BRM	4	clutch
r	Charlton	Lotus-Ford	3	accident
r	Ickx	Ferrari	2	accident
r	Regazzoni	BRM	2	accident
r	Hailwood	Surtees-Ford	2	accident

STARTING GRID:

1	Hulme	14	Oliver
2	Fittipaldi,E.	15	Merzario
3	Scheckter,J.	16	Stewart,Jackie
4	Peterson	17	Fittipaldi,W.
5	Regazzoni	18	Jarier
6	Revson	19	Ganley
7	Beltoise	20	de Adamich
8	Reutemann	21	Follmer
9	Pace	22	Keizan
10	Lauda	23	Beuttler
11	Ickx	24	Pretorius
12	Hailwood	25	Cevert
13	Charlton		

Spanish

GRAND PRIX No: 224
DATE: April 29, 1973
VENUE: Montjuich Park
POLE LAP: Peterson, 1m 21.8s
FASTEST LAP: Peterson, 1m 23.8s

Pn	Driver	Car	Laps	Time/Reason
1	Fittipaldi,E.	Lotus-Ford	75	1h 48m 18.7s
2	Cevert	Tyrrell-Ford	75	1h 49m 01.4s
3	Follmer	Shadow-Ford	75	1h 49m 31.8s
4	Revson	McLaren-Ford	74	
5	Beltoise	BRM	74	
6	Hulme	McLaren-Ford	74	
7	Beuttler	March-Ford	74	
8	Pescarolo	March-Ford	73	
9	Regazzoni	BRM	69	
10	Fittipaldi,W.	Brabham-Ford	69	
11	Nanni	Williams-Ford	69	
12	Ickx	Ferrari	69	
r	Reutemann	Brabham-Ford	65	transmission
r	Ganley	Williams-Ford	62	fuel system
r	Peterson	Lotus-Ford	56	gearbox
r	Stewart,Jackie	Tyrrell-Ford	46	brakes
r	Lauda	BRM	27	tyres
r	Hill,G.	Shadow-Ford	26	brakes
r	Hailwood	Surtees-Ford	24	oil pipe
r	Oliver	Shadow-Ford	23	engine
r	de Adamich	Brabham-Ford	17	lost wheel
r	Pace	Surtees-Ford	13	transmission

STARTING GRID:

1	Peterson	12	Fittipaldi,W.
2	Hulme	13	Oliver
3	Cevert	14	Follmer
4	Stewart,Jackie	15	Reutemann
5	Revson	16	Pace
6	Ickx	17	de Adamich
7	Fittipaldi,E.	18	Pescarolo
8	Regazzoni	19	Beuttler
9	Hailwood	20	Nanni
10	Beltoise	21	Ganley
11	Lauda	22	Hill,G.

Belgian

GRAND PRIX No: 225
DATE: May 20, 1973
VENUE: Zolder
POLE LAP: Peterson, 1m 22.46s
FASTEST LAP: Cevert, 1m 25.42s

Pn	Driver	Car	Laps	Time/Reason
1	Stewart,Jackie	Tyrrell-Ford	70	1h 42m 13.4s
2	Cevert	Tyrrell-Ford	70	1h 42m 45.3s
3	Fittipaldi,E.	Lotus-Ford	70	1h 44m 16.2s
4	de Adamich	Brabham-Ford	69	
5	Lauda	BRM	69	
6	Amon	Tecno	67	
7	Hulme	McLaren-Ford	67	
8	Pace	Surtees-Ford	66	
9	Hill,G.	Shadow-Ford	65	
10	Regazzoni	BRM	63	accident
11	Beuttler	March-Ford	63	accident
r	Jarier	March-Ford	60	accident
r	Beltoise	BRM	56	engine
r	Fittipaldi,W.	Brabham-Ford	45	engine
r	Peterson	Lotus-Ford	42	accident
r	Revson	McLaren-Ford	33	accident
r	Ganley	Williams-Ford	16	accident
r	Reutemann	Brabham-Ford	13	accident
r	Follmer	Shadow-Ford	13	throttle
r	Oliver	Shadow-Ford	11	accident
r	Nanni	Williams-Ford	6	engine
r	Ickx	Ferrari	6	oil pump
r	Hailwood	Surtees-Ford	4	accident

STARTING GRID:

1	Peterson	13	Hailwood
2	Hulme	14	Lauda
3	Ickx	15	Amon
4	Cevert	16	Jarier
5	Beltoise	17	Nanni
6	Stewart,Jackie	18	de Adamich
7	Reutemann	19	Fittipaldi,W.
8	Pace	20	Beuttler
9	Fittipaldi,E.	21	Ganley
10	Revson	22	Oliver
11	Follmer	23	Hill,G.
12	Regazzoni		

Monaco

GRAND PRIX No: 226
DATE: June 3, 1973
VENUE: Monte Carlo
POLE LAP: Stewart,Jackie, 1m 27.5s
FASTEST LAP: Fittipaldi,E., 1m 28.1s

Pn	Driver	Car	Laps	Time/Reason
1	Stewart,Jackie	Tyrrell-Ford	78	1h 57m 44.3s
2	Fittipaldi,E.	Lotus-Ford	78	1h 57m 45.6s
3	Peterson	Lotus-Ford	77	
4	Cevert	Tyrrell-Ford	77	
5	Revson	McLaren-Ford	76	
6	Hulme	McLaren-Ford	76	
7	de Adamich	Brabham-Ford	75	
8	Hailwood	Surtees-Ford	75	
9	Hunt	March-Ford	73	engine
10	Oliver	Shadow-Ford	72	
11	Fittipaldi,W.	Brabham-Ford	71	fuel system
r	Jarier	March-Ford	67	gearbox
r	Hill,G.	Shadow-Ford	61	suspension
r	Merzario	Ferrari	58	oil pressure
r	Reutemann	Brabham-Ford	46	gearbox
r	Ickx	Ferrari	44	transmission
r	Ganley	Williams-Ford	40	transmission
r	Beltoise	BRM	39	accident
r	Purley	March-Ford	31	fuel system
r	Pace	Surtees-Ford	30	transmission
r	Nanni	Williams-Ford	30	transmission
r	Lauda	BRM	24	gearbox
r	Amon	Tecno	22	overheating
r	Regazzoni	BRM	15	brakes
r	Beuttler	March-Ford	3	engine
dns	Follmer	Shadow-Ford		accident

STARTING GRID:

1	Stewart,Jackie	12	Amon
2	Peterson	13	Hailwood
3	Hulme	14	Jarier
4	Cevert	15	Revson
5	Fittipaldi,E.	16	Merzario
6	Lauda	17	Pace
7	Ickx	18	Hunt
8	Regazzoni	19	Reutemann
9	Fittipaldi,W.	20	Follmer
10	Ganley	21	Nanni
11	Beltoise	22	Beuttler

Swedish

GRAND PRIX No:	227
DATE:	June 17, 1973
VENUE:	Anderstorp
POLE LAP:	Peterson, 1m 23.810s
FASTEST LAP:	Hulme, 1m 26.146s

Pn	Driver	Car	Laps	Time/Reason
1	Hulme	McLaren-Ford	80	1h 56m 46.1s
2	Peterson	Lotus-Ford	80	1h 56m 50.1s
3	Cevert	Tyrrell-Ford	80	1h 57m 00.7s
4	Reutemann	Brabham-Ford	80	1h 57m 04.1s
5	Stewart,Jackie	Tyrrell-Ford	80	1h 57m 12.1s
6	Ickx	Ferrari	79	
7	Revson	McLaren-Ford	79	
8	Beuttler	March-Ford	78	
9	Regazzoni	BRM	77	
10	Pace	Surtees-Ford	77	
11	Ganley	Williams-Ford	77	
12	Fittipaldi,E.	Lotus-Ford	76	gearbox
13	Lauda	BRM	75	
14	Follmer	Shadow-Ford	74	
r	Beltoise	BRM	57	engine
r	Oliver	Shadow-Ford	50	suspension
r	Hailwood	Surtees-Ford	41	handling
r	Jarier	March-Ford	38	throttle
r	Hill,G.	Shadow-Ford	16	ignition
r	Fittipaldi,W.	Brabham-Ford	0	accident
dns	Wisell	March-Ford		suspension

STARTING GRID:

1	Peterson	12	Regazzoni
2	Cevert	13	Fittipaldi,W.
3	Stewart,Jackie	14	Wisell
4	Fittipaldi,E.	15	Lauda
5	Reutemann	16	Pace
6	Hulme	17	Oliver
7	Revson	18	Hill,G.
8	Ickx	19	Follmer
9	Beltoise	20	Jarier
10	Hailwood	21	Beuttler
11	Ganley		

French

GRAND PRIX No:	228
DATE:	July 1, 1973
VENUE:	Paul Ricard
POLE LAP:	Stewart,Jackie, 1m 48.37s
FASTEST LAP:	Hulme, 1m 50.99s

Pn	Driver	Car	Laps	Time/Reason
1	Peterson	Lotus-Ford	54	1h 41m 36.5s
2	Cevert	Tyrrell-Ford	54	1h 42m 17.4s
3	Reutemann	Brabham-Ford	54	1h 42m 23.0s
4	Stewart,Jackie	Tyrrell-Ford	54	1h 42m 23.5s
5	Ickx	Ferrari	54	1h 42m 25.4s
6	Hunt	March-Ford	54	1h 42m 59.1s
7	Merzario	Ferrari	54	1h 43m 05.7s
8	Hulme	McLaren-Ford	54	1h 43m 06.1s
9	Lauda	BRM	54	1h 43m 22.3s
10	Hill,G.	Shadow-Ford	53	
11	Beltoise	BRM	53	
12	Regazzoni	BRM	53	
13	Pace	Surtees-Ford	51	
14	Ganley	Williams-Ford	51	
15	von Opel	Ensign-Ford	51	
16	Fittipaldi,W.	Brabham-Ford	50	throttle
r	Scheckter,J.	McLaren-Ford	42	accident
r	Fittipaldi,E.	Lotus-Ford	41	accident
r	Hailwood	Surtees-Ford	29	oil leak
r	de Adamich	Brabham-Ford	27	transmission
r	Wisell	March-Ford	19	overheating
r	Follmer	Shadow-Ford	16	fuel pressure
r	Pescarolo	March-Ford	15	overheating
r	Jarier	March-Ford	7	transmission
r	Oliver	Shadow-Ford	0	clutch

STARTING GRID:

1	Stewart,Jackie	13	de Adamich
2	Scheckter,J.	14	Hunt
3	Fittipaldi,E.	15	Beltoise
4	Cevert	16	Hill,G.
5	Peterson	17	Lauda
6	Hulme	18	Pace
7	Jarier	19	Fittipaldi,W.
8	Reutemann	20	Follmer
9	Regazzoni	21	Oliver
10	Merzario	22	Wisell
11	Hailwood	23	Pescarolo
12	Ickx	24	Ganley
		25	von Opel

British

GRAND PRIX No: 229
DATE: July 14, 1973
VENUE: Silverstone
POLE LAP: Peterson, 1m 16.3s
FASTEST LAP: Hunt, 1m 18.6s

Pn	Driver	Car	Laps	Time/Reason
1	Revson	McLaren-Ford	67	1h 29m 18.5s
2	Peterson	Lotus-Ford	67	1h 29m 21.3s
3	Hulme	McLaren-Ford	67	1h 29m 21.5s
4	Hunt	March-Ford	67	1h 29m 21.9s
5	Cevert	Tyrrell-Ford	67	1h 29m 55.1s
6	Reutemann	Brabham-Ford	67	1h 30m 03.2s
7	Regazzoni	BRM	67	1h 30m 30.2s
8	Ickx	Ferrari	67	1h 30m 35.9s
9	Ganley	Williams-Ford	66	
10	Stewart,Jackie	Tyrrell-Ford	66	
11	Beuttler	March-Ford	65	
12	Lauda	BRM	63	
13	von Opel	Ensign-Ford	61	
r	Fittipaldi,W.	Brabham-Ford	44	oil pipe
r	Fittipaldi,E.	Lotus-Ford	36	transmission
r	Watson	Brabham-Ford	36	fuel system
r	Hill,G.	Shadow-Ford	24	suspension
r	Amon	Tecno	6	fuel pressure
r	McRae	Williams-Ford	0	throttle
r	Beltoise	BRM	0	accident
r	de Adamich	Brabham-Ford	0	accident
r	Follmer	Shadow-Ford	0	accident
r	Hailwood	Surtees-Ford	0	accident
r	Mass	Surtees-Ford	0	accident
r	Pace	Surtees-Ford	0	accident
r	Scheckter,J.	McLaren-Ford	0	accident
r	Williamson	March-Ford	0	accident
r	Oliver	Shadow-Ford	0	accident
dns	Purley	March-Ford		accident

STARTING GRID:

1	Peterson	9	Lauda
2	Hulme	10	Regazzoni
3	Revson	11	Hunt
4	Stewart,Jackie	12	Hailwood
5	Fittipaldi,E.	13	Fittipaldi,W.
6	Scheckter,J.	14	Mass
7	Cevert	15	Pace
8	Reutemann	16	Purley +

Dutch

GRAND PRIX No: 230
DATE: July 29, 1973
VENUE: Zandvoort
POLE LAP: Peterson, 1m 19.47s
FASTEST LAP: Peterson, 1m 20.31

Pn	Driver	Car	Laps	Time/Reason
1	Stewart,Jackie	Tyrrell-Ford	72	1h 39m 12.5s
2	Cevert	Tyrrell-Ford	72	1h 39m 28.3s
3	Hunt	March-Ford	72	1h 40m 15.5s
4	Revson	McLaren-Ford	72	1h 40m 21.6s
5	Beltoise	BRM	72	1h 40m 25.8s
6	van Lennep	Williams-Ford	70	
7	Pace	Surtees-Ford	69	
8	Regazzoni	BRM	68	
9	Ganley	Williams-Ford	68	
10	Follmer	Shadow-Ford	67	
11	Peterson	Lotus-Ford	66	gearbox
uc	Hill,G.	Shadow-Ford	56	
r	Hailwood	Surtees-Ford	52	electrical
r	Lauda	BRM	51	fuel pump
r	Hulme	McLaren-Ford	31	engine
r	Fittipaldi,W.	Brabham-Ford	27	accident
r	Amon	Tecno	22	fuel pressure
r	Reutemann	Brabham-Ford	9	burst tyre
r	Purley	March-Ford	8	stopped to help
r	Williamson	March-Ford	7	fatal accident
r	Beuttler	March-Ford	2	electrical
r	Fittipaldi,E.	Lotus-Ford	2	driver ill
r	Oliver	Shadow-Ford	1	accident
dns	von Opel	Ensign-Ford		suspension

STARTING GRID:

1	Peterson	13	Fittipaldi,W.
2	Stewart,Jackie	14	von Opel
3	Cevert	15	Ganley
4	Hulme	16	Fittipaldi,E.
5	Reutemann	17	Hill,G.
6	Revson	18	Williamson
7	Hunt	19	Amon
8	Pace	20	van Lennep
9	Beltoise	21	Purley
10	Oliver	22	Follmer
11	Lauda	23	Beuttler
12	Regazzoni	24	Hailwood

German

GRAND PRIX No: 231
DATE: August 5, 1973
VENUE: Nurburgring
POLE LAP: Stewart,Jackie, 7m 07.8s
FASTEST LAP: Pace, 7m 11.4s

Pn	Driver	Car	Laps	Time/Reason
1	Stewart,Jackie	Tyrrell-Ford	14	1h 42m 03.0s
2	Cevert	Tyrrell-Ford	14	1h 42m 04.6s
3	Ickx	McLaren-Ford	14	1h 42m 44.2s
4	Pace	Surtees-Ford	14	1h 42m 56.8s
5	Fittipaldi,W.	Brabham-Ford	14	1h 43m 22.9s
6	Fittipaldi,E.	Lotus-Ford	14	1h 43m 27.3s
7	Mass	Surtees-Ford	14	1h 43m 28.2s
8	Oliver	Shadow-Ford	14	1h 43m 28.7s
9	Revson	McLaren-Ford	14	1h 44m 14.8s
10	Pescarolo	March-Ford	14	1h 44m 25.5s
11	Stommelen	Brabham-Ford	14	1h 45m 41.7s
12	Hulme	McLaren-Ford	14	1h 45m 41.7s
13	Hill,G.	Shadow-Ford	14	1h 45m 52.0s
14	Hailwood	Surtees-Ford	13	
15	Purley	March-Ford	13	
16	Beuttler	March-Ford	13	
r	Reutemann	Brabham-Ford	7	engine
r	Regazzoni	BRM	7	engine
r	Follmer	Shadow-Ford	5	accident
r	Beltoise	BRM	4	gearbox
r	Lauda	BRM	1	accident
r	Peterson	Lotus-Ford	0	ignition
dns	Ganley	Williams-Ford		accident

STARTING GRID:

1	Stewart,Jackie	13	Fittipaldi,W.
2	Peterson	14	Fittipaldi,E.
3	Cevert	15	Mass
4	Ickx	16	Stommelen
5	Lauda	17	Oliver
6	Reutemann	18	Hailwood
7	Revson	19	Ganley
8	Hulme	20	Beuttler
9	Beltoise	21	Hill,G.
10	Regazzoni	22	Follmer
11	Pace	23	Purley
12	Pescarolo		

Austrian

GRAND PRIX No: 232
DATE: August 19, 1973
VENUE: Osterreichring
POLE LAP: Fittipaldi,E., 1m 34.98s
FASTEST LAP: Pace, 1m 37.29s

Pn	Driver	Car	Laps	Time/Reason
1	Peterson	Lotus-Ford	54	1h 28m 48.8s
2	Stewart,Jackie	Tyrrell-Ford	54	1h 28m 57.8s
3	Pace	Surtees-Ford	54	1h 29m 35.4s
4	Reutemann	Brabham-Ford	54	1h 29m 36.7s
5	Beltoise	BRM	54	1h 30m 10.4s
6	Regazzoni	BRM	54	1h 30m 27.2s
7	Merzario	Ferrari	53	
8	Hulme	McLaren-Ford	53	
9	van Lennep	Williams-Ford	52	
10	Hailwood	Surtees-Ford	49	
11	Fittipaldi,E.	Lotus-Ford	48	fuel pipe
uc	Ganley	Williams-Ford	44	
r	Jarier	March-Ford	37	engine
r	von Opel	Ensign-Ford	34	fuel pressure
r	Fittipaldi,W.	Brabham-Ford	31	fuel system
r	Hill,G.	Shadow-Ford	28	suspension
r	Follmer	Shadow-Ford	23	crownwheel and pinion
r	Stommelen	Brabham-Ford	21	wheel bearing
r	Oliver	Shadow-Ford	9	fuel leak
r	Cevert	Tyrrell-Ford	6	suspension
r	Hunt	March-Ford	3	fuel system
r	Beuttler	March-Ford	0	oil cooler
r	Revson	McLaren-Ford	0	clutch
dns	Amon	Tecno		no engine
dns	Lauda	BRM		injury

STARTING GRID:

1	Fittipaldi,E.	13	Beltoise
2	Peterson	14	Regazzoni
3	Hulme	15	Hailwood
4	Revson	16	Fittipaldi,W.
5	Reutemann	17	Stommelen
6	Merzario	18	Oliver
7	Stewart,Jackie	19	von Opel
8	Pace	20	Follmer
9	Hunt	21	Ganley
10	Cevert	22	Hill,G.
11	Beuttler	23	Amon
12	Jarier	24	van Lennep
		25	Lauda

Italian

GRAND PRIX No:	233
DATE:	September 9, 1973
VENUE:	Monza
POLE LAP:	Peterson, 1m 34.80s
FASTEST LAP:	Stewart,Jackie, 1m 35.30s

Pn	Driver	Car	Laps	Time/Reason
1	Peterson	Lotus-Ford	55	1h 29m 17.0s
2	Fittipaldi,E.	Lotus-Ford	55	1h 29m 17.8s
3	Revson	McLaren-Ford	55	1h 29m 45.8s
4	Stewart,Jackie	Tyrrell-Ford	55	1h 29m 50.2s
5	Cevert	Tyrrell-Ford	55	1h 30m 03.2s
6	Reutemann	Brabham-Ford	55	1h 30m 16.8s
7	Hailwood	Surtees-Ford	55	1h 30m 45.7s
8	Ickx	Ferrari	54	
9	Purley	March-Ford	54	
10	Follmer	Shadow-Ford	54	
11	Oliver	Shadow-Ford	54	
12	Stommelen	Brabham-Ford	54	
13	Beltoise	BRM	54	
14	Hill,G.	Shadow-Ford	54	
15	Hulme	McLaren-Ford	53	
uc	Ganley	Williams-Ford	44	
r	Beuttler	March-Ford	34	gearbox
r	Lauda	BRM	33	accident
r	Regazzoni	BRM	30	ignition
r	Pace	Surtees-Ford	17	burst tyre
r	van Lennep	Williams-Ford	13	overheating
r	von Opel	Ensign-Ford	9	overheating
r	Fittipaldi,W.	Brabham-Ford	5	brakes
r	Merzario	Ferrari	1	suspension
dns	Hunt	March-Ford		accident

STARTING GRID:

1	Peterson	14	Ickx
2	Revson	15	Lauda
3	Hulme	16	Fittipaldi,W.
4	Fittipaldi,E.	17	von Opel
5	Pace	18	Regazzoni
6	Stewart,Jackie	19	Oliver
7	Merzario	20	Ganley
8	Hailwood	21	Follmer
9	Stommelen	22	Hill,G.
10	Reutemann	23	van Lennep
11	Cevert	24	Purley
12	Beuttler	25	Hunt
13	Beltoise		

Canadian

GRAND PRIX No:	234
DATE:	September 23, 1973
VENUE:	Mosport Park
POLE LAP:	Peterson, 1m 13.697s
FASTEST LAP:	Fittipaldi,E., 1m 15.496s

Pn	Driver	Car	Laps	Time/Reason
1	Revson	McLaren-Ford	80	1h 59m 04.1s
2	Fittipaldi,E.	Lotus-Ford	80	1h 59m 36.8s
3	Oliver	Shadow-Ford	80	1h 59m 38.6s
4	Beltoise	BRM	80	1h 59m 40.6s
5	Stewart,Jackie	Tyrrell-Ford	79	
6	Ganley	Williams-Ford	79	
7	Hunt	March-Ford	78	
8	Reutemann	Brabham-Ford	78	
9	Hailwood	Surtees-Ford	78	
10	Amon	Tyrrell-Ford	77	
11	Fittipaldi,W.	Brabham-Ford	77	
12	Stommelen	Brabham-Ford	76	
13	Hulme	McLaren-Ford	75	
14	Schenken	Williams-Ford	75	
15	Merzario	Ferrari	75	
16	Hill,G.	Shadow-Ford	73	
17	Follmer	Shadow-Ford	73	
18	Pace	Surtees-Ford	72	wheel
uc	Jarier	March-Ford	71	
uc	von Opel	Ensign-Ford	68	
r	Lauda	BRM	62	transmission
r	Scheckter,J.	McLaren-Ford	32	accident
r	Cevert	Tyrrell-Ford	32	accident
r	Beuttler	March-Ford	20	engine
r	Peterson	Lotus-Ford	16	suspension
r	Gethin	BRM	5	oil pump

STARTING GRID:

1	Peterson	12	Hailwood
2	Revson	13	Follmer
3	Scheckter,J.	14	Oliver
4	Reutemann	15	Hunt
5	Fittipaldi,E.	16	Beltoise
6	Cevert	17	Hill,G.
7	Hulme	18	Stommelen
8	Lauda	19	Pace
9	Stewart,Jackie	20	Merzario
10	Fittipaldi,W.	21	Beuttler
11	Amon	22	Ganley +

US

GRAND PRIX No: 235
DATE: October 7, 1973
VENUE: Watkins Glen
POLE LAP: Peterson, 1m 39.657s
FASTEST LAP: Hunt, 1m 41.652s

Pn	Driver	Car	Laps	Time/Reason
1	Peterson	Lotus-Ford	55	1h 41m 15.8s
2	Hunt	March-Ford	55	1h 41m 16.5s
3	Reutemann	Brabham-Ford	55	1h 41m 38.7s
4	Hulme	McLaren-Ford	55	1h 42m 06.0s
5	Revson	McLaren-Ford	55	1h 42m 36.2s
6	Fittipaldi,E.	Lotus-Ford	55	1h 43m 03.7s
7	Ickx	Williams-Ford	54	
8	Regazzoni	BRM	54	
9	Beltoise	BRM	54	
10	Beuttler	March-Ford	54	
11	Jarier	March-Ford	53	accident
12	Ganley	Williams-Ford	53	
13	Hill,G.	Shadow-Ford	53	
14	Follmer	Shadow-Ford	53	
15	Oliver	Shadow-Ford	51	
16	Merzario	Ferrari	51	
uc	Fittipaldi,W.	Brabham-Ford	48	
r	Scheckter,J.	McLaren-Ford	39	suspension
r	Mass	Surtees-Ford	35	engine
r	Lauda	BRM	35	fuel pump
r	Hailwood	Surtees-Ford	34	suspension
r	Pace	Surtees-Ford	32	suspension
r	Watson	Brabham-Ford	7	engine
dq	Redman	Shadow-Ford	5	push start
r	von Opel	Ensign-Ford	0	throttle slides
dns	Cevert	Tyrrell-Ford		fatal accident
dns	Stewart,Jackie	Tyrrell-Ford		withdrew
dns	Amon	Tyrrell-Ford		withdrew

STARTING GRID:

1	Peterson	11	Scheckter,J.
2	Reutemann	12	Merzario
3	Fittipaldi,E.	13	Amon
4	Cevert	14	Redman
5	Hunt	15	Beltoise
6	Stewart,Jackie	16	Regazzoni
7	Hailwood	17	Mass
8	Revson	18	Jarier
9	Hulme	19	Hill,G.
10	Pace	20	Ganley

+

Argentine

GRAND PRIX No: 236
DATE: January 13, 1974
VENUE: Buenos Aires
POLE LAP: Peterson, 1m 50.78s
FASTEST LAP: Regazzoni, 1m 52.10

Pn	Driver	Car	Laps	Time/Reason
1	Hulme	McLaren-Ford	53	1h 41m 02.0s
2	Lauda	Ferrari	53	1h 41m 11.3s
3	Regazzoni	Ferrari	53	1h 41m 22.4s
4	Hailwood	McLaren-Ford	53	1h 41m 33.8s
5	Beltoise	BRM	53	1h 41m 53.9s
6	Depailler	Tyrrell-Ford	53	1h 42m 54.5s
7	Reutemann	Brabham-Ford	52	out of fuel
8	Ganley	March-Ford	52	out of fuel
9	Pescarolo	BRM	52	
10	Fittipaldi,E.	McLaren-Ford	52	
11	Edwards	Lola-Ford	51	
12	Watson	Brabham-Ford	49	
13	Peterson	Lotus-Ford	48	
r	Hill,G.	Lola-Ford	45	overheating
r	Robarts	Brabham-Ford	35	gearbox
r	Ickx	Lotus-Ford	35	transmission
r	Stuck,H-J.	March-Ford	31	clutch
r	Migault	BRM	31	engine
r	Scheckter,J.	Tyrrell-Ford	25	overheating
r	Pace	Surtees-Ford	21	engine
r	Merzario	Williams-Ford	19	engine
r	Hunt	March-Ford	11	overheating
r	Mass	Surtees-Ford	10	engine
r	Revson	Shadow-Ford	1	accident
r	Jarier	Shadow-Ford	0	accident
dns	von Opel	Ensign-Ford		handling

STARTING GRID:

1	Peterson	13	Merzario
2	Regazzoni	14	Beltoise
3	Fittipaldi,E.	15	Depailler
4	Revson	16	Jarier
5	Hunt	17	Hill,G.
6	Reutemann	18	Mass
7	Ickx	19	Ganley
8	Lauda	20	Watson
9	Hailwood	21	Pescarolo
10	Hulme	22	Robarts
11	Pace	23	Stuck,H-J.
12	Scheckter,J.	24	Migault

+

Brazilian

GRAND PRIX No: 237
DATE: January 27, 1974
VENUE: Interlagos
POLE LAP: Fittipaldi,E., 2m 32.97s
FASTEST LAP: Regazzoni, 2m 36.05s

Pn	Driver	Car	Laps	Time/Reason
1	Fittipaldi,E.	McLaren-Ford	32	1h 24m 37.1s
2	Regazzoni	Ferrari	32	1h 24m 50.6s
3	Ickx	Lotus-Ford	31	
4	Pace	Surtees-Ford	31	
5	Hailwood	McLaren-Ford	31	
6	Peterson	Lotus-Ford	31	
7	Reutemann	Brabham-Ford	31	
8	Depailler	Tyrrell-Ford	31	
9	Hunt	March-Ford	31	
10	Beltoise	BRM	31	
11	Hill,G.	Lola-Ford	31	
12	Hulme	McLaren-Ford	31	
13	Scheckter,J.	Tyrrell-Ford	31	
14	Pescarolo	BRM	30	
15	Robarts	Brabham-Ford	30	
16	Migault	BRM	30	
17	Mass	Surtees-Ford	30	
r	Watson	Brabham-Ford	27	clutch
r	Stuck,H-J.	March-Ford	24	transmission
r	Jarier	Shadow-Ford	22	brakes
r	Merzario	Williams-Ford	20	throttle
r	Revson	Shadow-Ford	11	overheating
r	Ganley	March-Ford	9	engine
r	Edwards	Lola-Ford	3	rear wing
r	Lauda	Ferrari	3	engine

STARTING GRID:

1	Fittipaldi,E.	14	Scheckter,J.
2	Reutemann	15	Watson
3	Lauda	16	Depailler
4	Peterson	17	Beltoise
5	Ickx	18	Hunt
6	Revson	19	Jarier
7	Hailwood	20	Ganley
8	Regazzoni	21	Hill,G.
9	Merzario	22	Pescarolo
10	Mass	23	Migault
11	Hulme	24	Robarts
12	Pace	25	Edwards
13	Stuck,H-J.		

South African

GRAND PRIX No: 238
DATE: March 30, 1974
VENUE: Kyalami
POLE LAP: Lauda, 1m 16.58s
FASTEST LAP: Reutemann, 1m 18.16s

Pn	Driver	Car	Laps	Time/Reason
1	Reutemann	Brabham-Ford	78	1h 42m 40.96s
2	Beltoise	BRM	78	1h 43m 14.90s
3	Hailwood	McLaren-Ford	78	1h 43m 32.10s
4	Depailler	Tyrrell-Ford	78	1h 43m 25.20s
5	Stuck,H-J.	March-Ford	78	1h 43m 27.20s
6	Merzario	Williams-Ford	78	1h 43m 37.00s
7	Fittipaldi,E.	McLaren-Ford	78	1h 43m 49.40s
8	Scheckter,J.	Tyrrell-Ford	78	1h 43m 51.50s
9	Hulme	McLaren-Ford	77	
10	Brambilla	March-Ford	77	
11	Pace	Surtees-Ford	77	
12	Hill,G.	Lola-Ford	77	
13	Scheckter,I.	Lotus-Ford	76	
14	Keizan	Tyrrell-Ford	76	
15	Migault	BRM	75	
16	Lauda	Ferrari	74	engine
17	Robarts	Brabham-Ford	74	
18	Pescarolo	BRM	72	
19	Charlton	McLaren-Ford	71	
r	Regazzoni	Ferrari	65	oil pressure
r	Watson	Brabham-Ford	54	fuel pipe
r	Ickx	Lotus-Ford	31	brakes
r	Hunt	Hesketh-Ford	13	transmission
r	Mass	Surtees-Ford	11	accident
r	Driver	Lotus-Ford	6	clutch
r	Peterson	Lotus-Ford	2	accident
r	Belso	Williams-Ford	0	clutch

STARTING GRID:

1	Lauda	11	Beltoise
2	Pace	12	Hailwood
3	Merzario	13	Watson
4	Reutemann	14	Hunt
5	Fittipaldi,E.	15	Depailler
6	Regazzoni	16	Peterson
7	Stuck,H-J.	17	Mass
8	Scheckter,J.	18	Hill,G.
9	Hulme	19	Brambilla
10	Ickx	20	Charlton +

Spanish

GRAND PRIX No:	239
DATE:	April 28, 1974
VENUE:	Jarama
POLE LAP:	Lauda, 1m 18.44s
FASTEST LAP:	Lauda, 1m 20.83s

Pn	Driver	Car	Laps	Time/Reason
1	Lauda	Ferrari	84	2h 00m 29.6s
2	Regazzoni	Ferrari	84	2h 01m 05.2s
3	Fittipaldi,E.	McLaren-Ford	83	
4	Stuck,H-J.	March-Ford	82	
5	Scheckter,J.	Tyrrell-Ford	82	
6	Hulme	McLaren-Ford	82	
7	Redman	Shadow-Ford	81	
8	Depailler	Tyrrell-Ford	81	
9	Hailwood	McLaren-Ford	81	
10	Hunt	Hesketh-Ford	81	
11	Watson	Brabham-Ford	80	
12	Pescarolo	BRM	80	
13	Pace	Surtees-Ford	78	
14	Schenken	Trojan-Ford	76	spun off
uc	Jarier	Shadow-Ford	73	
r	Hill,G.	Lola-Ford	43	engine
r	Merzario	Williams-Ford	37	accident
r	Mass	Surtees-Ford	35	gearbox
r	Migault	BRM	27	engine
r	Ickx	Lotus-Ford	26	brakes
r	Peterson	Lotus-Ford	23	engine
r	Amon	Amon-Ford	22	brakes
r	von Opel	Brabham-Ford	14	oil leak
r	Reutemann	Brabham-Ford	12	accident
r	Beltoise	BRM	2	engine
dns	Brambilla	March-Ford		accident

STARTING GRID:

1	Lauda	12	Beltoise
2	Peterson	13	Jarier
3	Regazzoni	14	Stuck,H-J.
4	Fittipaldi,E.	15	Pace
5	Ickx	16	Watson
6	Reutemann	17	Depailler
7	Merzario	18	Hailwood
8	Hulme	19	Mass
9	Scheckter,J.	20	Hill,G.
10	Brambilla	21	Pescarolo
11	Hunt	22	Redman +

Belgian

GRAND PRIX No:	240
DATE:	May 12, 1974
VENUE:	Nivelles
POLE LAP:	Regazzoni, 1m 09.82s
FASTEST LAP:	Hulme, 1m 11.31s

Pn	Driver	Car	Laps	Time/Reason
1	Fittipaldi,E.	McLaren-Ford	85	1h 44m 20.6s
2	Lauda	Ferrari	85	1h 44m 20.9s
3	Scheckter,J.	Tyrrell-Ford	85	1h 45m 06.2s
4	Regazzoni	Ferrari	85	1h 45m 12.6s
5	Beltoise	BRM	85	1h 45m 28.6s
6	Hulme	McLaren-Ford	85	1h 45m 31.1s
7	Hailwood	McLaren-Ford	84	
8	Hill,G.	Lola-Ford	83	
9	Brambilla	March-Ford	83	
10	Schenken	Trojan-Ford	83	
11	Watson	Brabham-Ford	83	
12	Edwards	Lola-Ford	82	
13	Jarier	Shadow-Ford	82	
14	van Lennep	Williams-Ford	82	
15	Schuppan	Ensign-Ford	82	
16	Migault	BRM	82	
17	Pilette,T.	Brabham-Ford	81	
18	Redman	Shadow-Ford	80	engine
r	Ickx	Lotus-Ford	72	overheating
r	Pryce	Token-Ford	66	suspension
r	Reutemann	Brabham-Ford	62	fuel system
r	Peterson	Lotus-Ford	56	fuel leak
r	Larrousse	Brabham-Ford	53	tyres
r	Mass	Surtees-Ford	53	suspension
r	Depailler	Tyrrell-Ford	53	brakes
r	Pace	Surtees-Ford	50	wheel
r	von Opel	Brabham-Ford	49	oil pressure
r	Hunt	Hesketh-Ford	45	suspension
r	Merzario	Williams-Ford	29	transmission
r	Pescarolo	BRM	12	accident
r	Stuck,H-J.	March-Ford	6	clutch

STARTING GRID:

1	Regazzoni	7	Beltoise
2	Scheckter,J.	8	Pace
3	Lauda	9	Hunt
4	Fittipaldi,E.	10	Stuck,H-J.
5	Peterson	11	Depailler
6	Merzario	12	Hulme +

Monaco

GRAND PRIX No:	241
DATE:	May 26, 1974
VENUE:	Monte Carlo
POLE LAP:	Lauda, 1m 26.3s
FASTEST LAP:	Peterson, 1m 27.9s

Pn	Driver	Car	Laps	Time/Reason
1	Peterson	Lotus-Ford	78	1h 58m 03.7s
2	Scheckter,J.	Tyrrell-Ford	78	1h 58m 32.5s
3	Jarier	Shadow-Ford	78	1h 58m 52.6s
4	Regazzoni	Ferrari	78	1h 59m 06.8s
5	Fittipaldi,E.	McLaren-Ford	77	
6	Watson	Brabham-Ford	77	
7	Hill,G.	Lola-Ford	76	
8	Edwards	Lola-Ford	75	
9	Depailler	Tyrrell-Ford	74	
r	Pescarolo	BRM	62	gearbox
r	Ickx	Lotus-Ford	34	engine
r	Lauda	Ferrari	32	ignition
r	Hunt	Hesketh-Ford	27	transmission
r	Hailwood	McLaren-Ford	11	accident
r	Reutemann	Brabham-Ford	5	accident
r	Migault	BRM	4	accident
r	Schuppan	Ensign-Ford	4	accident
r	Stuck,H-J.	March-Ford	3	accident
r	Brambilla	March-Ford	0	accident
r	Beltoise	BRM	0	accident
r	Schenken	Trojan-Ford	0	accident
r	Pace	Surtees-Ford	0	accident
r	Redman	Shadow-Ford	0	accident
r	Merzario	Williams-Ford	0	accident
r	Hulme	McLaren-Ford	0	accident
dns	Mass	Surtees-Ford		no spares

STARTING GRID:

1	Lauda	12	Hulme
2	Regazzoni	13	Fittipaldi,E.
3	Peterson	14	Merzario
4	Depailler	15	Brambilla
5	Scheckter,J.	16	Redman
6	Jarier	17	Mass
7	Hunt	18	Pace
8	Reutemann	19	Ickx
9	Stuck,H-J.	20	Hill,G.
10	Hailwood	21	Migault
11	Beltoise	22	Watson

+

Swedish

GRAND PRIX No:	242
DATE:	June 9, 1974
VENUE:	Anderstorp
POLE LAP:	Depailler, 1m 24.758s
FASTEST LAP:	Depailler, 1m 27.262s

Pn	Driver	Car	Laps	Time/Reason
1	Scheckter,J.	Tyrrell-Ford	80	1h 58m 31.4s
2	Depailler	Tyrrell-Ford	80	1h 58m 31.8s
3	Hunt	Hesketh-Ford	80	1h 58m 34.7s
4	Fittipaldi,E.	McLaren-Ford	80	1h 59m 24.9s
5	Jarier	Shadow-Ford	80	1h 59m 47.8s
6	Hill,G.	Lola-Ford	79	
7	Edwards	Lola-Ford	79	
8	Belso	Williams-Ford	79	
9	von Opel	Brabham-Ford	79	
10	Brambilla	March-Ford	79	engine
11	Watson	Brabham-Ford	77	
r	Lauda	Ferrari	69	suspension
r	Wisell	March-Ford	59	suspension
r	Hulme	McLaren-Ford	56	suspension
r	Mass	Surtees-Ford	53	suspension
r	Reutemann	Brabham-Ford	29	oil leak
r	Ickx	Lotus-Ford	27	oil pressure
r	Regazzoni	Ferrari	23	gearbox
r	Pace	Surtees-Ford	14	handling
r	Kinnunen	Surtees-Ford	8	engine
r	Peterson	Lotus-Ford	8	transmission
r	Hailwood	McLaren-Ford	5	fuel leak
r	Beltoise	BRM	2	engine
r	Roos	Shadow-Ford	1	gearbox
r	Pescarolo	BRM	0	fire
dns	Merzario	Williams-Ford		driver ill

STARTING GRID:

1	Depailler	12	Hulme
2	Scheckter,J.	13	Beltoise
3	Lauda	14	Watson
4	Regazzoni	15	Hill,G.
5	Peterson	16	Wisell
6	Hunt	17	Brambilla
7	Ickx	18	Edwards
8	Jarier	19	Pescarolo
9	Fittipaldi,E.	20	von Opel
10	Reutemann	21	Belso
11	Hailwood	22	Mass

+

Dutch

GRAND PRIX No:	243
DATE:	June 23, 1974
VENUE:	Zandvoort
POLE LAP:	Lauda, 1m 18.31s
FASTEST LAP:	Peterson, 1m 21.44s

Pn	Driver	Car	Laps	Time/Reason
1	Lauda	Ferrari	75	1h 43m 00.4s
2	Regazzoni	Ferrari	75	1h 43m 08.6s
3	Fittipaldi,E.	McLaren-Ford	75	1h 43m 30.6s
4	Hailwood	McLaren-Ford	75	1h 43m 31.6s
5	Scheckter,J.	Tyrrell-Ford	75	1h 43m 34.6s
6	Depailler	Tyrrell-Ford	75	1h 43m 51.9s
7	Watson	Brabham-Ford	75	1h 44m 14.3s
8	Peterson	Lotus-Ford	73	
9	von Opel	Brabham-Ford	73	
10	Brambilla	March-Ford	72	
11	Ickx	Lotus-Ford	71	
12	Reutemann	Brabham-Ford	71	
dq	Schuppan	Ensign-Ford	68	illegal tyre
r	Hulme	McLaren-Ford	65	ignition
r	Migault	BRM	59	gearbox
r	Merzario	Williams-Ford	54	gearbox
r	Edwards	Lola-Ford	36	fuel system
r	Jarier	Shadow-Ford	27	clutch
r	Beltoise	BRM	18	gearbox
r	Hill,G.	Lola-Ford	16	clutch
r	Pescarolo	BRM	14	handling
r	Mass	Surtees-Ford	8	cv joint
r	Hunt	Hesketh-Ford	1	accident
r	Stuck,H-J.	March-Ford	0	accident
r	Pryce	Shadow-Ford	0	accident

STARTING GRID:

1 Lauda
2 Regazzoni
3 Fittipaldi,E.
4 Hailwood
5 Scheckter,J.
6 Hunt
7 Jarier
8 Depailler
9 Hulme
10 Peterson
11 Pryce
12 Reutemann
13 Watson
14 Edwards
15 Brambilla
16 Beltoise
17 Schuppan
18 Ickx
19 Hill,G.
20 Mass
21 Merzario
22 Stuck,H-J.
23 von Opel
24 Pescarolo
25 Migault

French

GRAND PRIX No:	244
DATE:	July 7, 1974
VENUE:	Dijon
POLE LAP:	Lauda, 58.79s
FASTEST LAP:	Scheckter,J., 1m 00.00s

Pn	Driver	Car	Laps	Time/Reason
1	Peterson	Lotus-Ford	80	1h 21m 55.0s
2	Lauda	Ferrari	80	1h 22m 15.4s
3	Regazzoni	Ferrari	80	1h 22m 22.9s
4	Scheckter,J.	Tyrrell-Ford	80	1h 22m 23.1s
5	Ickx	Lotus-Ford	80	1h 22m 32.6s
6	Hulme	McLaren-Ford	80	1h 22m 33.2s
7	Hailwood	McLaren-Ford	79	
8	Depailler	Tyrrell-Ford	79	
9	Merzario	Williams-Ford	79	
10	Beltoise	BRM	79	
11	Brambilla	March-Ford	79	
12	Jarier	Shadow-Ford	79	
13	Hill,G.	Lola-Ford	78	
14	Migault	BRM	78	
15	Edwards	Lola-Ford	77	
16	Watson	Brabham-Ford	76	
r	Fittipaldi,E.	McLaren-Ford	27	engine
r	Reutemann	Brabham-Ford	24	handling
r	Mass	Surtees-Ford	4	clutch
r	Pescarolo	BRM	0	clutch
r	Pryce	Shadow-Ford	0	accident
r	Hunt	Hesketh-Ford	0	accident

STARTING GRID:

2 Peterson
1 Lauda
3 Pryce
4 Regazzoni
5 Fittipaldi,E.
6 Hailwood
7 Scheckter,J.
8 Reutemann
9 Depailler
10 Hunt
11 Hulme
12 Jarier
13 Ickx
14 Watson
15 Merzario
16 Brambilla
17 Beltoise
18 Mass
19 Pescarolo
20 Edwards
21 Hill,G.
22 Migault

British

GRAND PRIX No: 245
DATE: July 20, 1974
VENUE: Brands Hatch
POLE LAP: Lauda, 1m 19.70s
FASTEST LAP: Lauda, 1m 21.1s

Pn	Driver	Car	Laps	Time/Reason
1	Scheckter,J.	Tyrrell-Ford	75	1h 43m 02.2s
2	Fittipaldi,E.	McLaren-Ford	75	1h 43m 17.5s
3	Ickx	Lotus-Ford	75	1h 44m 03.7s
4	Regazzoni	Ferrari	75	1h 44m 09.4s
5	Lauda	Ferrari	74	
6	Reutemann	Brabham-Ford	74	
7	Hulme	McLaren-Ford	74	
8	Pryce	Shadow-Ford	74	
9	Pace	Brabham-Ford	74	
10	Peterson	Lotus-Ford	73	
11	Watson	Brabham-Ford	73	
12	Beltoise	BRM	72	
13	Hill,G.	Lola-Ford	69	
14	Mass	Surtees-Ford	68	
r	Pescarolo	BRM	64	engine
uc	Migault	BRM	63	
r	Hailwood	McLaren-Ford	57	spun off
r	Jarier	Shadow-Ford	45	suspension
r	Stuck,H-J.	March-Ford	36	accident
r	Depailler	Tyrrell-Ford	35	engine
r	Merzario	Williams-Ford	25	engine
r	Brambilla	March-Ford	17	fuel pressure
r	Schenken	Trojan-Ford	6	suspension
r	Hunt	Hesketh-Ford	2	suspension
r	Gethin	Lola-Ford	0	driver discomfort

STARTING GRID:

1 Lauda
2 Peterson
3 Scheckter,J.
4 Reutemann
5 Pryce
6 Hunt
7 Regazzoni
8 Fittipaldi,E.
9 Stuck,H-J.
10 Depailler
11 Hailwood
12 Ickx
13 Watson
14 Migault
15 Merzario
16 Jarier
17 Mass
18 Brambilla
19 Hulme
20 Pace
21 Gethin
22 Hill,G.
23 Beltoise
24 Pescarolo
25 Schenken

German

GRAND PRIX No: 246
DATE: August 4, 1974
VENUE: Nurburgring
POLE LAP: Lauda, 7m 00.80s
FASTEST LAP: Scheckter,J., 7m 11.10s

Pn	Driver	Car	Laps	Time/Reason
1	Regazzoni	Ferrari	14	1h 41m 35.0s
2	Scheckter,J.	Tyrrell-Ford	14	1h 42m 25.7s
3	Reutemann	Brabham-Ford	14	1h 42m 58.3s
4	Peterson	Lotus-Ford	14	1h 42m 59.2s
5	Ickx	Lotus-Ford	14	1h 43m 00.0s
6	Pryce	Shadow-Ford	14	1h 43m 53.1s
7	Stuck,H-J.	March-Ford	14	1h 44m 33.7s
8	Jarier	Shadow-Ford	14	1h 45m 00.9s
9	Hill,G.	Lola-Ford	14	1h 45m 01.4s
10	Pescarolo	BRM	14	1h 45m 52.7s
11	Bell	Surtees-Ford	14	1h 46m 52.7s
12	Pace	Brabham-Ford	14	1h 48m 01.3s
13	Brambilla	March-Ford	14	1h 50m 18.1s
14	Ashley	Token-Ford	13	
15	Hailwood	McLaren-Ford	12	accident
r	Hunt	Hesketh-Ford	11	gearbox
r	Mass	Surtees-Ford	10	engine
r	Depailler	Tyrrell-Ford	5	suspension
r	Merzario	Williams-Ford	5	throttle
r	Beltoise	BRM	4	transmission
r	Schuppan	Ensign-Ford	4	gearbox
r	Fittipaldi,E.	McLaren-Ford	2	suspension
r	Laffite	Williams-Ford	2	suspension
r	Watson	Brabham-Ford	1	suspension
r	Lauda	Ferrari	0	accident
dq	Hulme	McLaren-Ford	0	restarted in T-car after accident

STARTING GRID:

1 Lauda
2 Regazzoni
3 Fittipaldi,E.
4 Scheckter,J.
5 Depailler
6 Reutemann
7 Hulme
8 Peterson
9 Ickx
10 Mass
11 Pryce
12 Hailwood
13 Hunt
14 Watson
15 Beltoise
16 Merzario
17 Pace
18 Jarier
19 Hill,G.
20 Stuck,H-J. +

Austrian

GRAND PRIX No:	247
DATE:	August 18, 1974
VENUE:	Osterreichring
POLE LAP:	Lauda, 1m 35.40s
FASTEST LAP:	Regazzoni, 1m 37.22s

Pn	Driver	Car	Laps	Time/Reason
1	Reutemann	Brabham-Ford	54	1h 28m 44.7s
2	Hulme	McLaren-Ford	54	1h 29m 27.6s
3	Hunt	Hesketh-Ford	54	1h 29m 46.3s
4	Watson	Brabham-Ford	54	1h 29m 54.1s
5	Regazzoni	Ferrari	54	1h 29m 57.8s
6	Brambilla	March-Ford	54	1h 29m 58.5s
7	Hobbs	McLaren-Ford	53	
8	Jarier	Shadow-Ford	52	
9	Quester	Surtees-Ford	51	
10	Schenken	Trojan-Ford	50	
11	Stuck,H-J.	March-Ford	48	suspension
12	Hill,G.	Lola-Ford	48	
uc	Ashley	Token-Ford	46	
r	Peterson	Lotus-Ford	45	transmission
r	Ickx	Lotus-Ford	43	accident
r	Depailler	Tyrrell-Ford	42	accident
r	Pace	Brabham-Ford	41	fuel leak
r	Fittipaldi,E.	McLaren-Ford	37	engine
uc	Laffite	Williams-Ford	37	
r	Merzario	Williams-Ford	24	fuel pressure
r	Pryce	Shadow-Ford	22	spun off
r	Beltoise	BRM	21	engine
r	Lauda	Ferrari	16	engine
r	Stommelen	Lola-Ford	14	accident
r	Scheckter,J.	Tyrrell-Ford	8	engine

STARTING GRID:

1	Lauda	14	Depailler
2	Reutemann	15	Stuck,H-J.
3	Fittipaldi,E.	16	Pryce
4	Pace	17	Hobbs
5	Scheckter,J.	18	Beltoise
6	Peterson	19	Schenken
7	Hunt	20	Brambilla
8	Regazzoni	21	Hill,G.
9	Merzario	22	Ickx
10	Hulme	23	Jarier
11	Watson	24	Ashley
12	Laffite	25	Quester
13	Stommelen		

Italian

GRAND PRIX No:	248
DATE:	September 8, 1974
VENUE:	Monza
POLE LAP:	Lauda, 1m 33.16s
FASTEST LAP:	Pace, 1m 34.20s

Pn	Driver	Car	Laps	Time/Reason
1	Peterson	Lotus-Ford	52	1h 22m 56.6s
2	Fittipaldi,E.	McLaren-Ford	52	1h 22m 57.4s
3	Scheckter,J.	Tyrrell-Ford	52	1h 23m 21.3s
4	Merzario	Williams-Ford	52	1h 24m 24.3s
5	Pace	Brabham-Ford	51	
6	Hulme	McLaren-Ford	51	
7	Watson	Brabham-Ford	51	
8	Hill,G.	Lola-Ford	51	
9	Hobbs	McLaren-Ford	51	
10	Pryce	Shadow-Ford	50	
11	Depailler	Tyrrell-Ford	50	
r	Regazzoni	Ferrari	40	engine
r	Lauda	Ferrari	31	engine
r	Ickx	Lotus-Ford	30	throttle
r	Stommelen	Lola-Ford	24	suspension
r	Laffite	Williams-Ford	21	engine
r	Jarier	Shadow-Ford	19	engine
r	Brambilla	March-Ford	16	accident
r	Schenken	Trojan-Ford	14	gearbox
r	Reutemann	Brabham-Ford	11	gearbox
r	Stuck,H-J.	March-Ford	10	engine
r	Pescarolo	BRM	3	engine
r	Hunt	Hesketh-Ford	2	engine
r	Migault	BRM	0	gearbox
r	Beltoise	BRM	0	electrical

STARTING GRID:

1	Lauda	13	Brambilla
2	Reutemann	14	Stommelen
3	Pace	15	Merzario
4	Watson	16	Ickx
5	Regazzoni	17	Laffite
6	Fittipaldi,E.	18	Stuck,H-J.
7	Peterson	19	Hulme
8	Hunt	20	Schenken
9	Jarier	21	Hill,G.
10	Depailler	22	Pryce
11	Beltoise	23	Hobbs
12	Scheckter,J.	24	Migault
		25	Pescarolo

Canadian

GRAND PRIX No:	249
DATE:	September 22, 1974
VENUE:	Mosport Park
POLE LAP:	Fittipaldi,E., 1m 13.188s
FASTEST LAP:	Lauda, 1m 13.659s

Pn	Driver	Car	Laps	Time/Reason
1	Fittipaldi,E.	McLaren-Ford	80	1h 40m 26.1s
2	Regazzoni	Ferrari	80	1h 40m 39.2s
3	Peterson	Lotus-Ford	80	1h 40m 40.6s
4	Hunt	Hesketh-Ford	80	1h 40m 41.8s
5	Depailler	Tyrrell-Ford	80	1h 41m 21.5s
6	Hulme	McLaren-Ford	79	
7	Andretti,Mario	Parnelli-Ford	79	
8	Pace	Brabham-Ford	79	
9	Reutemann	Brabham-Ford	79	
10	Koinigg	Surtees-Ford	78	
11	Stommelen	Lola-Ford	78	
12	Donohue	Penske-Ford	78	
13	Ickx	Lotus-Ford	78	
14	Hill,G.	Lola-Ford	77	
15	Laffite	Williams-Ford	74	
16	Mass	Surtees-Ford	72	
uc	Amon	BRM	70	
r	Lauda	Ferrari	67	accident
r	Pryce	Shadow-Ford	65	engine
r	Watson	Brabham-Ford	61	suspension
uc	Beltoise	BRM	60	
r	Scheckter,J.	Tyrrell-Ford	48	brakes
r	Jarier	Shadow-Ford	46	transmission
r	Merzario	Williams-Ford	40	handling
r	Wietzes	Brabham-Ford	33	engine
r	Stuck,H-J.	March-Ford	12	fuel pressure

STARTING GRID:

1	Fittipaldi,E.	12	Mass
2	Lauda	13	Pryce
3	Scheckter,J.	14	Hulme
4	Reutemann	15	Watson
5	Jarier	16	Andretti,Mario
6	Regazzoni	17	Beltoise
7	Depailler	18	Laffite
8	Hunt	19	Merzario
9	Pace	20	Hill,G.
10	Peterson	21	Ickx
11	Stommelen	22	Koinigg +

US

GRAND PRIX No:	250
DATE:	October 6, 1974
VENUE:	Watkins Glen
POLE LAP:	Reutemann, 1m 38.978s
FASTEST LAP:	Pace, 1m 40.608s

Pn	Driver	Car	Laps	Time/Reason
1	Reutemann	Brabham-Ford	59	1h 40m 21.4s
2	Pace	Brabham-Ford	59	1h 40m 32.2s
3	Hunt	Hesketh-Ford	59	1h 41m 31.8s
4	Fittipaldi,E.	McLaren-Ford	59	1h 41m 39.2s
5	Watson	Brabham-Ford	59	1h 41m 47.2s
6	Depailler	Tyrrell-Ford	59	1h 41m 49.0s
7	Mass	Surtees-Ford	59	1h 41m 51.5s
8	Hill,G.	Lola-Ford	58	
9	Amon	BRM	57	
10	Jarier	Shadow-Ford	57	
11	Regazzoni	Ferrari	55	
12	Stommelen	Lola-Ford	54	
uc	Peterson	Lotus-Ford	52	fuel line
uc	Wilds	Ensign-Ford	50	
uc	Pryce	Shadow-Ford	47	
r	Scheckter,J.	Tyrrell-Ford	44	fuel line
r	Merzario	Williams-Ford	43	electrical
r	Lauda	Ferrari	38	suspension
r	Laffite	Williams-Ford	31	wheel
r	Donohue	Penske-Ford	27	suspension
r	Dolhem	Surtees-Ford	25	withdrew
r	Brambilla	March-Ford	21	fuel system
r	Koinigg	Surtees-Ford	9	fatal accident
r	Ickx	Lotus-Ford	7	suspension
dq	Schenken	Lotus-Ford	6	started illegally
r	Hulme	McLaren-Ford	4	engine
dq	Andretti,Mario	Parnelli-Ford	3	push start

STARTING GRID:

1	Reutemann	11	Laffite
2	Hunt	12	Amon
3	Andretti,Mario	13	Depailler
4	Pace	14	Donohue
5	Lauda	15	Merzario
6	Scheckter,J.	16	Ickx
7	Watson	17	Hulme
8	Fittipaldi,E.	18	Pryce
9	Regazzoni	19	Peterson
10	Jarier	20	Mass +

Argentine

GRAND PRIX No:	251
DATE:	January 12, 1975
VENUE:	Buenos Aires
POLE LAP:	Jarier, 1m 49.21s
FASTEST LAP:	Hunt, 1m 50.91s

Pn	Driver	Car	Laps	Time/Reason
1	Fittipaldi,E.	McLaren-Ford	53	1h 39m 26.29s
2	Hunt	Hesketh-Ford	53	1h 39m 32.20s
3	Reutemann	Brabham-Ford	53	1h 39m 43.35s
4	Regazzoni	Ferrari	53	1h 40m 02.08s
5	Depailler	Tyrrell-Ford	53	1h 40m 20.54s
6	Lauda	Ferrari	53	1h 40m 45.94s
7	Donohue	Penske-Ford	52	
8	Ickx	Lotus-Ford	52	
9	Brambilla	March-Ford	52	
10	Hill,G.	Lola-Ford	52	
11	Scheckter,J.	Tyrrell-Ford	52	
12	Pryce	Shadow-Ford	51	transmission
13	Stommelen	Lola-Ford	51	
14	Mass	McLaren-Ford	50	
r	Pace	Brabham-Ford	46	engine
r	Merzario	Williams-Ford	44	
r	Andretti,Mario	Parnelli-Ford	27	driveshaft
r	Wilds	BRM	24	oil pump
r	Peterson	Lotus-Ford	15	brakes
r	Laffite	Williams-Ford	15	gearbox
r	Fittipaldi,W.	Fittipaldi-Ford	12	accident
dq	Watson	Surtees-Ford	6	illegal repairs
dns	Jarier	Shadow-Ford	0	clutch on parade

STARTING GRID:

1	Jarier	13	Mass
2	Pace	14	Pryce
3	Reutemann	15	Watson
4	Lauda	16	Laffite
5	Fittipaldi,E.	17	Donohue
6	Hunt	18	Ickx
7	Regazzoni	19	Stommelen
8	Depailler	20	Merzario
9	Scheckter,J.	21	Hill,G.
10	Andretti,Mario	22	Wilds
11	Peterson	23	Fittipaldi,W.
12	Brambilla		

Brazilian

GRAND PRIX No:	252
DATE:	January 26, 1975
VENUE:	Interlagos
POLE LAP:	Jarier, 2m 29.88s
FASTEST LAP:	Jarier, 2m 34.16s

Pn	Driver	Car	Laps	Time/Reason
1	Pace	Brabham-Ford	40	1h 44m 41.17s
2	Fittipaldi,E.	McLaren-Ford	40	1h 44m 46.96s
3	Mass	McLaren-Ford	40	1h 45m 17.83s
4	Regazzoni	Ferrari	40	1h 45m 24.45s
5	Lauda	Ferrari	40	1h 45m 43.05s
6	Hunt	Hesketh-Ford	40	1h 45m 46.29s
7	Andretti,Mario	Parnelli-Ford	40	1h 45m 47.98s
8	Reutemann	Brabham-Ford	40	1h 46m 20.79s
9	Ickx	Lotus-Ford	40	1h 46m 33.01s
10	Watson	Surtees-Ford	40	1h 47m 10.77s
11	Laffite	Williams-Ford	39	
12	Hill,G.	Lola-Ford	39	
13	Fittipaldi,W.	Fittipaldi-Ford	39	
14	Stommelen	Lola-Ford	39	
15	Peterson	Lotus-Ford	38	
r	Jarier	Shadow-Ford	32	fuel system
r	Depailler	Tyrrell-Ford	31	accident
r	Pryce	Shadow-Ford	31	accident
r	Merzario	Williams-Ford	24	fuel system
r	Wilds	BRM	22	electrical
r	Donohue	Penske-Ford	22	handling
r	Scheckter,J.	Tyrrell-Ford	18	oil tank
r	Brambilla	March-Ford	1	engine

STARTING GRID:

1	Jarier	13	Watson
2	Fittipaldi,E.	14	Pryce
3	Reutemann	15	Donohue
4	Lauda	16	Peterson
5	Regazzoni	17	Brambilla
6	Pace	18	Andretti,Mario
7	Hunt	19	Laffite
8	Scheckter,J.	20	Hill,G.
9	Depailler	21	Fittipaldi,W.
10	Mass	22	Wilds
11	Merzario	23	Stommelen
12	Ickx		

South African

GRAND PRIX No:	253
DATE:	March 1, 1975
VENUE:	Kyalami
POLE LAP:	Pace, 1m 16.41s
FASTEST LAP:	Pace, 1m 17.20s

Pn	Driver	Car	Laps	Time/Reason
1	Scheckter,J.	Tyrrell-Ford	78	1h 43m 16.90s
2	Reutemann	Brabham-Ford	78	1h 43m 20.64s
3	Depailler	Tyrrell-Ford	78	1h 43m 33.82s
4	Pace	Brabham-Ford	78	1h 43m 34.21s
5	Lauda	Ferrari	78	1h 43m 45.54s
6	Mass	McLaren-Ford	78	1h 44m 20.24s
7	Stommelen	Lola-Ford	78	1h 44m 29.81s
8	Donohue	Penske-Ford	77	
9	Pryce	Shadow-Ford	77	
10	Peterson	Lotus-Ford	77	
11	Tunmer	Lotus-Ford	76	
12	Ickx	Lotus-Ford	76	
13	Keizan	Lotus-Ford	76	
14	Charlton	McLaren-Ford	76	
15	Evans	BRM	76	
16	Regazzoni	Ferrari	71	throttle
17	Andretti,Mario	Parnelli-Ford	70	driveshaft
uc	Laffite	Williams-Ford	69	
uc	Fittipaldi,E.	McLaren-Ford	65	
r	Scheckter,I.	Tyrrell-Ford	55	accident
r	Hunt	Hesketh-Ford	53	fuel system
r	Jarier	Shadow-Ford	37	engine
r	Lombardi	March-Ford	23	engine
r	Merzario	Williams-Ford	22	engine
r	Watson	Surtees-Ford	19	clutch
r	Brambilla	March-Ford	16	oil leak
dns	Hill,G.	Lola-Ford		accident

STARTING GRID:

1	Pace	11	Fittipaldi,E.
2	Reutemann	12	Hunt
3	Scheckter,J.	13	Jarier
4	Lauda	14	Stommelen
5	Depailler	15	Merzario
6	Andretti,Mario	16	Mass
7	Brambilla	17	Scheckter,I.
8	Peterson	18	Donohue
9	Regazzoni	19	Pryce
10	Watson	20	Charlton +

Spanish

GRAND PRIX No:	254
DATE:	April 27, 1975
VENUE:	Montjuich Park
POLE LAP:	Lauda, 1m 23.40s
FASTEST LAP:	Andretti,Mario, 1m 25.10s

Pn	Driver	Car	Laps	Time/Reason
1	Mass	McLaren-Ford	29	42m 53.7s
2	Ickx	Lotus-Ford	29	42m 54.8s
3	Reutemann	Brabham-Ford	28	42m 37.5s
4	Jarier	Shadow-Ford	28	43m 44.8s
5	Brambilla	March-Ford	28	
6	Lombardi	March-Ford	27	
7	Brise	Williams-Ford	27	
8	Watson	Surtees-Ford	26	
r	Stommelen	Hill-Ford	25	accident
r	Pace	Brabham-Ford	25	accident
uc	Regazzoni	Ferrari	25	
r	Peterson	Lotus-Ford	23	accident
r	Pryce	Shadow-Ford	23	accident
r	Wunderink	Ensign-Ford	20	driveshaft
uc	Migault	Hill-Ford	18	
r	Andretti,Mario	Parnelli-Ford	16	accident
r	Evans	BRM	7	fuel system
r	Hunt	Hesketh-Ford	6	accident
r	Scheckter,J.	Tyrrell-Ford	3	engine
r	Donohue	Penske-Ford	3	accident
r	Jones	Hesketh-Ford	3	accident
r	Depailler	Tyrrell-Ford	1	accident
r	Merzario	Williams-Ford	1	safety protest
r	Fittipaldi,W.	Fittipaldi-Ford	1	safety protest
r	Lauda	Ferrari	0	accident
dns	Fittipaldi,E.	McLaren-Ford		safety protest

STARTING GRID:

1	Lauda	12	Peterson
2	Regazzoni	13	Scheckter,J.
3	Hunt	14	Pace
4	Andretti,Mario	15	Reutemann
5	Brambilla	16	Ickx
6	Watson	17	Donohue
7	Depailler	18	Brise
8	Pryce	19	Wunderink
9	Stommelen	20	Jones
10	Jarier	21	Fittipaldi,W.
11	Mass	22	Migault +

Monaco

GRAND PRIX No:	255
DATE:	May 11, 1975
VENUE:	Monte Carlo
POLE LAP:	Lauda, 1m 26.40s
FASTEST LAP:	Depailler, 1m 28.67s

Pn	Driver	Car	Laps	Time/Reason
1	Lauda	Ferrari	75	2h 01m 21.31s
2	Fittipaldi,E.	McLaren-Ford	75	2h 01m 24.09s
3	Pace	Brabham-Ford	75	2h 01m 39.12s
4	Peterson	Lotus-Ford	75	2h 01m 59.76s
5	Depailler	Tyrrell-Ford	75	2h 02m 02.17s
6	Mass	McLaren-Ford	75	2h 02m 03.38s
7	Scheckter,J.	Tyrrell-Ford	74	
8	Ickx	Lotus-Ford	74	
9	Reutemann	Brabham-Ford	73	
r	Donohue	Penske-Ford	66	accident
r	Hunt	Hesketh-Ford	63	accident
r	Jones	Hesketh-Ford	61	lost wheel
r	Brambilla	March-Ford	48	accident
r	Pryce	Shadow-Ford	39	accident
r	Watson	Surtees-Ford	36	spun off
r	Regazzoni	Ferrari	36	accident
r	Andretti,Mario	Parnelli-Ford	9	fire
r	Jarier	Shadow-Ford	0	accident

STARTING GRID:

1	Lauda	10	Reutemann
2	Pryce	11	Hunt
3	Jarier	12	Depailler
4	Peterson	13	Andretti,Mario
5	Brambilla	14	Ickx
6	Regazzoni	15	Mass
7	Scheckter,J.	16	Donohue
8	Pace	17	Watson
9	Fittipaldi,E.	18	Jones

Belgian

GRAND PRIX No:	256
DATE:	May 25, 1975
VENUE:	Zolder
POLE LAP:	Lauda, 1m 25.43s
FASTEST LAP:	Regazzoni, 1m 26.76s

Pn	Driver	Car	Laps	Time/Reason
1	Lauda	Ferrari	70	1h 43m 53.98s
2	Scheckter,J.	Tyrrell-Ford	70	1h 44m 13.20s
3	Reutemann	Brabham-Ford	70	1h 44m 35.80s
4	Depailler	Tyrrell-Ford	70	1h 44m 54.06s
5	Regazzoni	Ferrari	70	1h 44m 57.84s
6	Pryce	Shadow-Ford	70	1h 45m 22.43s
7	Fittipaldi,E.	McLaren-Ford	69	
8	Pace	Brabham-Ford	69	
9	Evans	BRM	68	
10	Watson	Surtees-Ford	68	
11	Donohue	Penske-Ford	67	
12	Fittipaldi,W.	Fittipaldi-Ford	67	
r	Migault	Hill-Ford	57	suspension
r	Brambilla	March-Ford	54	brakes
r	Ickx	Lotus-Ford	52	brakes
r	Peterson	Lotus-Ford	36	accident
r	Lombardi	March-Ford	18	engine
r	Laffite	Williams-Ford	18	gearbox
r	Brise	Hill-Ford	17	engine
r	Hunt	Hesketh-Ford	15	gear linkage
r	Jarier	Shadow-Ford	13	spun off
r	Merzario	Williams-Ford	2	clutch
r	Jones	Hesketh-Ford	1	accident
r	Mass	McLaren-Ford	0	accident

STARTING GRID:

1	Lauda	13	Jones
2	Pace	14	Peterson
3	Brambilla	15	Mass
4	Regazzoni	16	Ickx
5	Pryce	17	Laffite
6	Reutemann	18	Watson
7	Brise	19	Merzario
8	Fittipaldi,E.	20	Evans
9	Scheckter,J.	21	Donohue
10	Jarier	22	Migault
11	Hunt	23	Lombardi
12	Depailler	24	Fittipaldi,W.

Swedish

GRAND PRIX No: 257
DATE: June 8, 1975
VENUE: Anderstorp
POLE LAP: Brambilla, 1m 24.630s
FASTEST LAP: Lauda, 1m 28.267s

Pn	Driver	Car	Laps	Time/Reason
1	Lauda	Ferrari	80	1h 59m 18.319s
2	Reutemann	Brabham-Ford	80	1h 59m 24.607s
3	Regazzoni	Ferrari	80	1h 59m 47.414s
4	Andretti,Mario	Parnelli-Ford	80	2h 00m 02.699s
5	Donohue	Penske-Ford	80	2h 00m 49.082s
6	Brise	Hill-Ford	79	
7	Scheckter,J.	Tyrrell-Ford	79	
8	Fittipaldi,E.	McLaren-Ford	79	
9	Peterson	Lotus-Ford	79	
10	Palm	Hesketh-Ford	78	out of fuel
11	Jones	Hesketh-Ford	78	
12	Depailler	Tyrrell-Ford	78	
13	Evans	BRM	78	
14	Magee	Williams-Ford	78	
15	Ickx	Lotus-Ford	77	
16	Watson	Surtees-Ford	77	
17	Fittipaldi,W.	Fittipaldi-Ford	74	
r	Pryce	Shadow-Ford	53	spun off
r	Scheckter,I.	Williams-Ford	49	accident
r	Schuppan	Hill-Ford	47	driveshaft
r	Pace	Brabham-Ford	41	accident
r	Jarier	Shadow-Ford	38	engine
r	Brambilla	March-Ford	36	transmission
r	Mass	McLaren-Ford	34	water leak
r	Hunt	Hesketh-Ford	21	brake fluid
r	Lombardi	March-Ford	10	fuel system

STARTING GRID:

1	Brambilla	12	Regazzoni
2	Depailler	13	Hunt
3	Jarier	14	Mass
4	Reutemann	15	Andretti,Mario
5	Lauda	16	Donohue
6	Pace	17	Brise
7	Pryce	18	Ickx
8	Scheckter,J.	19	Jones
9	Peterson	20	Scheckter,I.
10	Watson	21	Palm
11	Fittipaldi,E.	22	Magee +

Dutch

GRAND PRIX No: 258
DATE: June 22, 1975
VENUE: Zandvoort
POLE LAP: Lauda, 1m 20.29s
FASTEST LAP: Lauda, 1m 21.54s

Pn	Driver	Car	Laps	Time/Reason
1	Hunt	Hesketh-Ford	75	1h 46m 57.40s
2	Lauda	Ferrari	75	1h 46m 58.46s
3	Regazzoni	Ferrari	75	1h 47m 52.46s
4	Reutemann	Brabham-Ford	74	
5	Pace	Brabham-Ford	74	
6	Pryce	Shadow-Ford	74	
7	Brise	Hill-Ford	74	
8	Donohue	Penske-Ford	74	
9	Depailler	Tyrrell-Ford	73	
10	van Lennep	Ensign-Ford	71	
11	Fittipaldi,W.	Fittipaldi-Ford	71	
12	Scheckter,I.	Williams-Ford	70	
13	Jones	Hill-Ford	70	
14	Lombardi	March-Ford	70	
15	Peterson	Lotus-Ford	69	out of fuel
16	Scheckter,J.	Tyrrell-Ford	67	engine
r	Laffite	Williams-Ford	65	engine
r	Mass	McLaren-Ford	61	accident
r	Jarier	Shadow-Ford	44	accident
r	Watson	Surtees-Ford	43	vibration
r	Fittipaldi,E.	McLaren-Ford	40	engine
r	Evans	BRM	23	crownwheel/pinion
r	Ickx	Lotus-Ford	6	engine
r	Brambilla	March-Ford	0	accident
dns	Fushida	Maki-Ford		engine

STARTING GRID:

1	Lauda	13	Depailler
2	Regazzoni	14	Watson
3	Hunt	15	Laffite
4	Scheckter,J.	16	Peterson
5	Reutemann	17	Jones
6	Fittipaldi,E.	18	Donohue
7	Brise	19	Scheckter,I.
8	Mass	20	Evans
9	Pace	21	Ickx
10	Jarier	22	van Lennep
11	Brambilla	23	Lombardi
12	Pryce	24	Fittipaldi,W.
		25	Fushida

French

GRAND PRIX No:	259
DATE:	July 6, 1975
VENUE:	Paul Ricard
POLE LAP:	Lauda, 1m 47.82s
FASTEST LAP:	Mass, 1m 50.60s

Pn	Driver	Car	Laps	Time/Reason
1	Lauda	Ferrari	54	1h 40m 18.84s
2	Hunt	Hesketh-Ford	54	1h 40m 20.43s
3	Mass	McLaren-Ford	54	1h 40m 21.15s
4	Fittipaldi,E.	McLaren-Ford	54	1h 40m 58.61s
5	Andretti,Mario	Parnelli-Ford	54	1h 41m 20.92s
6	Depailler	Tyrrell-Ford	54	1h 41m 26.24s
7	Brise	Hill-Ford	54	1h 41m 28.45s
8	Jarier	Shadow-Ford	54	1h 41m 38.62s
9	Scheckter,J.	Tyrrell-Ford	54	1h 41m 50.52s
10	Peterson	Lotus-Ford	54	1h 41m 54.86s
11	Laffite	Williams-Ford	54	1h 41m 55.61s
12	Jabouille	Tyrrell-Ford	54	1h 41m 55.97s
13	Watson	Surtees-Ford	53	
14	Reutemann	Brabham-Ford	53	
15	van Lennep	Ensign-Ford	53	
16	Jones	Hill-Ford	53	
17	Evans	BRM	52	
18	Lombardi	March-Ford	50	
r	Pace	Brabham-Ford	26	driveshaft
r	Ickx	Lotus-Ford	17	brakes
r	Fittipaldi,W.	Fittipaldi-Ford	14	engine
r	Donohue	Penske-Ford	6	driveshaft
r	Brambilla	March-Ford	6	suspension
r	Regazzoni	Ferrari	6	engine
r	Pryce	Shadow-Ford	2	transmission
dns	Migault	Williams-Ford		engine

STARTING GRID:

1	Lauda	12	Brise
2	Scheckter,J.	13	Depailler
3	Pryce	14	Watson
4	Hunt	15	Andretti,Mario
5	Jarier	16	Laffite
6	Pace	17	Peterson
7	Mass	18	Donohue
8	Brambilla	19	Ickx
9	Regazzoni	20	Jones
10	Fittipaldi,E.	21	Jabouille
11	Reutemann	22	van Lennep +

British

GRAND PRIX No:	260
DATE:	July 19, 1975
VENUE:	Silverstone
POLE LAP:	Pryce, 1m 19.36s
FASTEST LAP:	Regazzoni, 1m 20.90s

Pn	Driver	Car	Laps	Time/Reason
1	Fittipaldi,E.	McLaren-Ford	56	1h 22m 05.00s
2	Pace	Brabham-Ford	55	accident
3	Scheckter,J.	Tyrrell-Ford	55	accident
4	Hunt	Hesketh-Ford	55	accident
5	Donohue	March-Ford	55	accident
6	Brambilla	March-Ford	55	
7	Mass	McLaren-Ford	55	accident
8	Lauda	Ferrari	54	
9	Depailler	Tyrrell-Ford	54	accident
10	Jones	Hill-Ford	54	
11	Watson	Surtees-Ford	54	accident
12	Andretti,Mario	Parnelli-Ford	54	
13	Regazzoni	Ferrari	54	
14	Jarier	Shadow-Ford	53	accident
15	Brise	Hill-Ford	53	accident
16	Henton	Lotus-Ford	53	accident
17	Nicholson	Lyncar-Ford	51	accident
18	Morgan	Surtees-Ford	50	accident
19	Fittipaldi,W.	Fittipaldi-Ford	50	accident
r	Stuck,H-J.	March-Ford	45	accident
r	Crawford,J.	Lotus-Ford	28	accident
r	Pryce	Shadow-Ford	20	accident
r	Lombardi	March-Ford	18	engine
r	Peterson	Lotus-Ford	7	engine
r	Laffite	Williams-Ford	5	gearbox
r	Reutemann	Brabham-Ford	4	engine

STARTING GRID:

1	Pryce	12	Andretti,Mario
2	Pace	13	Brise
3	Lauda	14	Stuck,H-J.
4	Regazzoni	15	Donohue
5	Brambilla	16	Peterson
6	Scheckter,J.	17	Depailler
7	Fittipaldi,E.	18	Watson
8	Reutemann	19	Laffite
9	Hunt	20	Jones
10	Mass	21	Henton
11	Jarier	22	Lombardi +

German

GRAND PRIX No: 261
DATE: August 3, 1975
VENUE: Nurburgring
POLE LAP: Lauda, 6m 58.60s
FASTEST LAP: Regazzoni, 7m 06.40s

Pn	Driver	Car	Laps	Time/Reason
1	Reutemann	Brabham-Ford	14	1h 41m 14.1s
2	Laffite	Williams-Ford	14	1h 42m 51.8s
3	Lauda	Ferrari	14	1h 43m 37.4s
4	Pryce	Shadow-Ford	14	1h 44m 45.5s
5	Jones	Hill-Ford	14	1h 45m 04.4s
6	van Lennep	Ensign-Ford	14	1h 46m 19.6s
7	Lombardi	March-Ford	14	1h 48m 44.5s
8	Ertl	Hesketh-Ford	14	1h 48m 55.0s
9	Depailler	Tyrrell-Ford	13	
10	Andretti,Mario	Parnelli-Ford	12	out of fuel
r	Hunt	Hesketh-Ford	10	transmission
r	Regazzoni	Ferrari	9	engine
r	Brise	Hill-Ford	9	accident
r	Scheckter,J.	Tyrrell-Ford	7	accident
r	Jarier	Shadow-Ford	7	puncture
r	Pace	Brabham-Ford	5	suspension
r	Fittipaldi,W.	Fittipaldi-Ford	4	engine
r	Fittipaldi,E.	McLaren-Ford	3	suspension
r	Stuck,H-J.	March-Ford	3	engine
r	Brambilla	March-Ford	3	suspension
r	Watson	Lotus-Ford	2	suspension
r	Peterson	Lotus-Ford	1	clutch
r	Donohue	March-Ford	1	puncture
r	Mass	McLaren-Ford	0	accident
dns	Ashley	Williams-Ford		injured

STARTING GRID:

1	Lauda	14	Watson
2	Pace	15	Laffite
3	Scheckter,J.	16	Pryce
4	Depailler	17	Brise
5	Regazzoni	18	Peterson
6	Mass	19	Donohue
7	Stuck,H-J.	20	Ashley
8	Fittipaldi,E.	21	Jones
9	Hunt	22	Fittipaldi,W.
10	Reutemann	23	Ertl
11	Brambilla	24	van Lennep
12	Jarier	25	Lombardi
13	Andretti,Mario		

Austrian

GRAND PRIX No: 262
DATE: August 17, 1975
VENUE: Osterreichring
POLE LAP: Lauda, 1m 34.85s
FASTEST LAP: Brambilla, 1m 53.90s

Pn	Driver	Car	Laps	Time/Reason
1	Brambilla	March-Ford	29	57m 56.69s
2	Hunt	Hesketh-Ford	29	58m 23.72s
3	Pryce	Shadow-Ford	29	58m 31.54s
4	Mass	McLaren-Ford	29	59m 09.35s
5	Peterson	Lotus-Ford	29	59m 20.02s
6	Lauda	Ferrari	29	59m 26.97s
7	Regazzoni	Ferrari	29	59m 35.76s
8	Scheckter,J.	Tyrrell-Ford	28	
9	Fittipaldi,E.	McLaren-Ford	28	
10	Watson	Surtees-Ford	28	
11	Depailler	Tyrrell-Ford	28	
12	Amon	Ensign-Ford	28	
13	Lunger	Hesketh-Ford	28	
14	Reutemann	Brabham-Ford	28	
15	Brise	Hill-Ford	28	
16	Stommelen	Hill-Ford	27	
17	Lombardi	March-Ford	26	
uc	Wunderink	Ensign-Ford	25	
r	Ertl	Hesketh-Ford	23	electrical
r	Laffite	Williams-Ford	21	handling
r	Pace	Brabham-Ford	17	engine
r	Vonlanthen	Williams-Ford	14	engine
r	Stuck,H-J.	March-Ford	10	accident
r	Jarier	Shadow-Matra	10	fuel system
r	Evans	BRM	2	engine
r	Andretti,Mario	Parnelli-Ford	1	spun off
dns	Fittipaldi,W.	Fittipaldi-Ford		injured
dns	Donohue	March-Ford		fatal accident
dns	Henton	Lotus-Ford		accident

STARTING GRID:

1	Lauda	9	Scheckter,J.
2	Fittipaldi,E.	10	Reutemann
3	Stuck,H-J.	11	Hunt
4	Regazzoni	12	Laffite
5	Pace	13	Peterson
6	Depailler	14	Jarier
7	Brambilla	15	Pryce
8	Mass	16	Brise

+

Italian

GRAND PRIX No:	263
DATE:	September 7, 1975
VENUE:	Monza
POLE LAP:	Lauda, 1m 32.24s
FASTEST LAP:	Regazzoni, 1m 33.10s

Pn	Driver	Car	Laps	Time/Reason
1	Regazzoni	Ferrari	52	1h 22m 42.6s
2	Fittipaldi,E.	McLaren-Ford	52	1h 22m 59.2s
3	Lauda	Ferrari	52	1h 23m 05.8s
4	Reutemann	Brabham-Ford	52	1h 23m 37.7s
5	Hunt	Hesketh-Ford	52	1h 23m 39.7s
6	Pryce	Shadow-Ford	52	1h 23m 58.5s
7	Depailler	Tyrrell-Ford	51	
8	Scheckter,J.	Tyrrell-Ford	51	
9	Ertl	Hesketh-Ford	51	
10	Lunger	Hesketh-Ford	50	
11	Merzario	Fittipaldi-Ford	48	
12	Amon	Ensign-Ford	48	
13	Crawford,J.	Lotus-Ford	46	
14	Zorzi	Williams-Ford	46	
r	Jarier	Shadow-Matra	32	fuel pump
r	Lombardi	March-Ford	21	accident
r	Stuck,H-J.	March-Ford	15	accident
r	Laffite	Williams-Ford	7	gearbox
r	Pace	Brabham-Ford	6	throttle linkage
r	Stommelen	Hill-Ford	3	accident
r	Mass	McLaren-Ford	2	accident
r	Brambilla	March-Ford	1	clutch
r	Andretti,Mario	Parnelli-Ford	1	accident
r	Brise	Hill-Ford	1	accident
r	Peterson	Lotus-Ford	1	engine
r	Evans	BRM	0	electrical

STARTING GRID:

1	Lauda	12	Depailler
2	Regazzoni	13	Jarier
3	Fittipaldi,E.	14	Pryce
4	Scheckter,J.	15	Andretti,Mario
5	Mass	16	Stuck,H-J.
6	Brise	17	Ertl
7	Reutemann	18	Laffite
8	Hunt	19	Amon
9	Brambilla	20	Evans
10	Pace	21	Lunger
11	Peterson	22	Zorzi +

US

GRAND PRIX No:	264
DATE:	October 5, 1975
VENUE:	Watkins Glen
POLE LAP:	Lauda, 1m 42.003s
FASTEST LAP:	Fittipaldi,E., 1m 43.374s

Pn	Driver	Car	Laps	Time/Reason
1	Lauda	Ferrari	59	1h 42m 58.175s
2	Fittipaldi,E.	McLaren-Ford	59	1h 43m 03.118s
3	Mass	McLaren-Ford	59	1h 43m 45.812s
4	Hunt	Hesketh-Ford	59	1h 43m 47.650s
5	Peterson	Lotus-Ford	59	1h 43m 48.161s
6	Scheckter,J.	Tyrrell-Ford	59	1h 43m 48.496s
7	Brambilla	March-Ford	59	1h 44m 42.206s
8	Stuck,H-J.	March-Ford	58	
9	Watson	Penske-Ford	57	
10	Fittipaldi,W.	Fittipaldi-Ford	55	
r	Pryce	Shadow-Ford	52	
r	Henton	Lotus-Ford	49	
r	Lunger	Hesketh-Ford	46	accident
r	Wunderink	Ensign-Ford	41	gearbox
r	Regazzoni	Ferrari	28	withdrew
r	Jarier	Shadow-Ford	19	wheel bearing
r	Reutemann	Brabham-Ford	9	engine
r	Andretti,Mario	Parnelli-Ford	9	suspension
r	Brise	Hill-Ford	5	accident
r	Leclere	Tyrrell-Ford	5	engine
r	Depailler	Tyrrell-Ford	2	accident
r	Pace	Brabham-Ford	2	accident
dns	Laffite	Williams-Ford		injured
dns	Lombardi	Williams-Ford		ignition

STARTING GRID:

1	Lauda	13	Stuck,H-J.
2	Fittipaldi,E.	14	Peterson
3	Reutemann	15	Hunt
4	Jarier	16	Pace
5	Andretti,Mario	17	Brise
6	Brambilla	18	Lunger
7	Pryce	19	Henton
8	Depailler	20	Leclere
9	Mass	21	Wunderink
10	Scheckter,J.	22	Laffite
11	Regazzoni	23	Fittipaldi,W.
12	Watson	24	Lombardi

Brazilian

GRAND PRIX No: 265
DATE: January 25, 1976
VENUE: Interlagos
POLE LAP: Hunt, 2m 32.50s
FASTEST LAP: Jarier, 2m 35.07s

Pn	Driver	Car	Laps	Time/Reason
1	Lauda	Ferrari	40	1h 45m 16.78s
2	Depailler	Tyrrell-Ford	40	1h 45m 38.25s
3	Pryce	Shadow-Ford	40	1h 45m 40.62s
4	Stuck,H-J.	March-Ford	40	1h 46m 44.95s
5	Scheckter,J.	Tyrrell-Ford	40	1h 47m 13.24s
6	Mass	McLaren-Ford	40	1h 47m 15.05s
7	Regazzoni	Ferrari	40	1h 47m 32.02s
8	Ickx	Williams-Ford	39	
9	Zorzi	Williams-Ford	39	
10	Pace	Brabham-Alfa	39	
11	Hoffman	Fittipaldi-Ford	39	
12	Reutemann	Brabham-Alfa	37	out of fuel
13	Fittipaldi,E.	Fittipaldi-Ford	37	
14	Lombardi	March-Ford	36	
r	Jarier	Shadow-Ford	33	accident
r	Hunt	McLaren-Ford	32	accident
r	Brambilla	March-Ford	15	oil leak
r	Laffite	Ligier-Matra	14	gear linkage
r	Peterson	Lotus-Ford	10	accident
r	Andretti,Mario	Lotus-Ford	6	accident
r	Watson	Penske-Ford	2	fire
r	Ashley	BRM	2	oil pump

STARTING GRID:

1	Hunt	12	Pryce
2	Lauda	13	Scheckter,J.
3	Jarier	14	Stuck,H-J.
4	Regazzoni	15	Reutemann
5	Fittipaldi,E.	16	Andretti,Mario
6	Mass	17	Zorzi
7	Brambilla	18	Peterson
8	Watson	19	Ickx
9	Depailler	20	Hoffman
10	Pace	21	Ashley
11	Laffite	22	Lombardi

South African

GRAND PRIX No: 266
DATE: March 6, 1976
VENUE: Kyalami
POLE LAP: Hunt, 1m 16.10s
FASTEST LAP: Lauda, 1m 17.97s

Pn	Driver	Car	Laps	Time/Reason
1	Lauda	Ferrari	78	1h 42m 18.4s
2	Hunt	McLaren-Ford	78	1h 42m 19.7s
3	Mass	McLaren-Ford	78	1h 43m 04.3s
4	Scheckter,J.	Tyrrell-Ford	78	1h 43m 26.8s
5	Watson	Penske-Ford	77	
6	Andretti,Mario	Parnelli-Ford	77	
7	Pryce	Shadow-Ford	77	
8	Brambilla	March-Ford	77	
9	Depailler	Tyrrell-Ford	77	
10	Evans	Lotus-Ford	77	
11	Lunger	Surtees-Ford	77	
12	Stuck,H-J.	March-Ford	76	
13	Leclere	Williams-Ford	76	
14	Amon	Ensign-Ford	76	
15	Ertl	Hesketh-Ford	74	
16	Ickx	Williams-Ford	73	
17	Fittipaldi,E.	Fittipaldi-Ford	70	engine
r	Regazzoni	Ferrari	52	engine
r	Laffite	Ligier-Matra	49	engine
r	Jarier	Shadow-Ford	28	radiator
r	Pace	Brabham-Alfa	22	engine
r	Nilsson	Lotus-Ford	18	clutch
r	Reutemann	Brabham-Alfa	16	engine
r	Peterson	March-Ford	15	accident
r	Scheckter,I.	Tyrrell-Ford	0	accident

STARTING GRID:

1	Lauda	13	Andretti,Mario
2	Hunt	14	Pace
3	Watson	15	Jarier
4	Mass	16	Scheckter,I.
5	Brambilla	17	Stuck,H-J.
6	Depailler	18	Amon
7	Pryce	19	Ickx
8	Laffite	20	Lunger
9	Regazzoni	21	Fittipaldi,E.
10	Peterson	22	Leclere
11	Reutemann	23	Evans
12	Scheckter,J.	24	Ertl
		25	Nilsson

US West

GRAND PRIX No:	267
DATE:	March 28, 1976
VENUE:	Long Beach
POLE LAP:	Regazzoni, 1m 23.099s
FASTEST LAP:	Regazzoni, 1m 23.076s

Pn	Driver	Car	Laps	Time/Reason
1	Regazzoni	Ferrari	80	1h 53m 18.5s
2	Lauda	Ferrari	80	1h 54m 00.9s
3	Depailler	Tyrrell-Ford	80	1h 54m 08.4s
4	Laffite	Ligier-Matra	80	1h 54m 31.3s
5	Mass	McLaren-Ford	80	1h 54m 40.8s
6	Fittipaldi,E.	Fittipaldi-Ford	79	
7	Jarier	Shadow-Ford	79	
8	Amon	Ensign-Ford	78	
9	Pace	Brabham-Alfa	77	
10	Peterson	March-Ford	77	
uc	Jones	Surtees-Ford	70	
uc	Watson	Penske-Ford	69	
r	Scheckter,J.	Tyrrell-Ford	34	suspension
r	Pryce	Shadow-Ford	32	driveshaft
r	Andretti,Mario	Parnelli-Ford	15	water leak
r	Hunt	McLaren-Ford	3	accident
r	Stuck,H-J.	March-Ford	2	accident
r	Nilsson	Lotus-Ford	0	accident
r	Reutemann	Brabham-Alfa	0	accident
r	Brambilla	March-Ford	0	accident

STARTING GRID:

1	Regazzoni	11	Scheckter,J.
2	Depailler	12	Laffite
3	Hunt	13	Pace
4	Lauda	14	Mass
5	Pryce	15	Andretti,Mario
6	Peterson	16	Fittipaldi,E.
7	Jarier	17	Amon
8	Brambilla	18	Stuck,H-J.
9	Watson	19	Jones
10	Reutemann	20	Nilsson

Spanish

GRAND PRIX No:	268
DATE:	May 2, 1976
VENUE:	Jarama
POLE LAP:	Hunt, 1m 18.52s
FASTEST LAP:	Mass, 1m 20.93s

Pn	Driver	Car	Laps	Time/Reason
1	Hunt	McLaren-Ford	75	1h 42m 20.43s
2	Lauda	Ferrari	75	1h 42m 51.40s
3	Nilsson	Lotus-Ford	75	1h 43m 08.45s
4	Reutemann	Brabham-Alfa	74	
5	Amon	Ensign-Ford	74	
6	Pace	Brabham-Alfa	74	
7	Ickx	Williams-Ford	74	
8	Pryce	Shadow-Ford	74	
9	Jones	Surtees-Ford	74	
10	Leclere	Williams-Ford	73	
11	Regazzoni	Ferrari	72	
12	Laffite	Ligier-Matra	72	
13	Perkins	Boro-Ford	72	
r	Mass	McLaren-Ford	65	engine
r	Jarier	Shadow-Ford	61	electrical
r	Scheckter,J.	Tyrrell-Ford	53	engine
r	Watson	Penske-Ford	51	engine
r	Merzario	March-Ford	36	gear linkage
r	Andretti,Mario	Lotus-Ford	34	gearbox
r	Depailler	Tyrrell-Ford	25	accident
r	Brambilla	March-Ford	21	accident
r	Stuck,H-J.	March-Ford	16	gearbox
r	Peterson	March-Ford	11	transmission
r	Fittipaldi,E.	Fittipaldi-Ford	3	gear linkage

STARTING GRID:

1	Hunt	13	Watson
2	Lauda	14	Scheckter,J.
3	Depailler	15	Jarier
4	Mass	16	Peterson
5	Regazzoni	17	Stuck,H-J.
6	Brambilla	18	Merzario
7	Nilsson	19	Fittipaldi,E.
8	Laffite	20	Jones
9	Andretti,Mario	21	Ickx
10	Amon	22	Pryce
11	Pace	23	Leclere
12	Reutemann	24	Perkins

Belgian

GRAND PRIX No:	269
DATE:	May 16, 1976
VENUE:	Zolder
POLE LAP:	Lauda, 1m 26.55s
FASTEST LAP:	Lauda, 1m 25.98s

Pn	Driver	Car	Laps	Time/Reason
1	Lauda	Ferrari	70	1h 42m 53.23s
2	Regazzoni	Ferrari	70	1h 42m 56.69s
3	Laffite	Ligier-Matra	70	1h 43m 28.61s
4	Scheckter,J.	Tyrrell-Ford	70	1h 44m 24.31s
5	Jones	Surtees-Ford	69	
6	Mass	McLaren-Ford	69	
7	Watson	Penske-Ford	69	
8	Perkins	Boro-Ford	69	
9	Jarier	Shadow-Ford	69	
10	Pryce	Shadow-Ford	68	
11	Leclere	Williams-Ford	68	
12	Kessel	Brabham-Ford	63	
r	Lunger	Surtees-Ford	62	electrical
r	Pace	Brabham-Alfa	58	electrical
r	Amon	Ensign-Ford	51	lost wheel
r	Hunt	McLaren-Ford	35	transmission
r	Stuck,H-J.	March-Ford	33	suspension
r	Ertl	Hesketh-Ford	31	engine
r	Depailler	Tyrrell-Ford	29	engine
r	Andretti,Mario	Lotus-Ford	28	driveshaft
r	Neve	Brabham-Ford	24	driveshaft
r	Merzario	March-Ford	21	engine
r	Reutemann	Brabham-Alfa	17	engine
r	Peterson	March-Ford	16	accident
r	Nilsson	Lotus-Ford	7	accident
r	Brambilla	March-Ford	6	driveshaft

STARTING GRID:

1	Lauda	12	Reutemann
2	Regazzoni	13	Pryce
3	Hunt	14	Jarier
4	Depailler	15	Stuck,H-J.
5	Brambilla	16	Jones
6	Laffite	17	Watson
7	Scheckter,J.	18	Mass
8	Amon	19	Neve
9	Pace	20	Perkins
10	Peterson	21	Merzario
11	Andretti,Mario	22	Nilsson

Monaco

GRAND PRIX No:	270
DATE:	May 30, 1976
VENUE:	Monte Carlo
POLE LAP:	Lauda, 1m 29.65s
FASTEST LAP:	Regazzoni, 1m 30.28s

Pn	Driver	Car	Laps	Time/Reason
1	Lauda	Ferrari	78	1h 59m 51.47s
2	Scheckter,J.	Tyrrell-Ford	78	2h 00m 02.60s
3	Depailler	Tyrrell-Ford	78	2h 00m 56.31s
4	Stuck,H-J.	March-Ford	77	
5	Mass	McLaren-Ford	77	
6	Fittipaldi,E.	Fittipaldi-Ford	77	
7	Pryce	Shadow-Ford	77	
8	Jarier	Shadow-Ford	76	
9	Pace	Brabham-Alfa	76	
10	Watson	Penske-Ford	76	
11	Leclere	Williams-Ford	76	
12	Laffite	Ligier-Matra	75	accident
13	Amon	Ensign-Ford	74	
r	Regazzoni	Ferrari	73	accident
r	Nilsson	Lotus-Ford	39	engine
r	Peterson	March-Ford	26	accident
r	Hunt	McLaren-Ford	24	engine
r	Brambilla	March-Ford	9	suspension
r	Jones	Surtees-Ford	1	accident
r	Reutemann	Brabham-Alfa	0	accident

STARTING GRID:

1	Lauda	11	Mass
2	Regazzoni	12	Amon
3	Peterson	13	Pace
4	Depailler	14	Hunt
5	Scheckter,J.	15	Pryce
6	Stuck,H-J.	16	Nilsson
7	Fittipaldi,E.	17	Watson
8	Laffite	18	Leclere
9	Brambilla	19	Jones
10	Jarier	20	Reutemann

Swedish

GRAND PRIX No: 271

DATE: June 13, 1976

VENUE: Anderstorp

POLE LAP: Scheckter,J., 1m 25.659s

FASTEST LAP: Andretti,Mario, 1m 28.002s

Pn	Driver	Car	Laps	Time/Reason
1	Scheckter,J.	Tyrrell-Ford	72	1h 46m 53.73s
2	Depailler	Tyrrell-Ford	72	1h 47m 13.50s
3	Lauda	Ferrari	72	1h 47m 27.60s
4	Laffite	Ligier-Matra	72	1h 47m 49.55s
5	Hunt	McLaren-Ford	72	1h 47m 53.21s
6	Regazzoni	Ferrari	72	1h 47m 54.10s
7	Peterson	March-Ford	72	1h 47m 57.22s
8	Pace	Brabham-Alfa	72	1h 48m 05.34s
9	Pryce	Shadow-Ford	71	
10	Brambilla	March-Ford	71	
11	Mass	McLaren-Ford	71	
12	Jarier	Shadow-Ford	71	
13	Jones	Surtees-Ford	71	
14	Merzario	March-Ford	70	engine
15	Lunger	Surtees-Ford	70	
r	Ertl	Hesketh-Ford	54	spun off
r	Stuck,H-J.	March-Ford	52	engine
r	Andretti,Mario	Lotus-Ford	45	engine
r	Amon	Ensign-Ford	38	accident
r	Leclere	Williams-Ford	20	engine
r	Perkins	Boro-Ford	18	engine
r	Fittipaldi,E.	Fittipaldi-Ford	10	handling
r	Kessel	Brabham-Ford	5	accident
r	Nilsson	Lotus-Ford	2	accident
r	Reutemann	Brabham-Alfa	2	engine
r	Watson	Penske-Ford	0	accident

STARTING GRID:

1	Scheckter,J.	11	Regazzoni
2	Andretti,Mario	12	Pryce
3	Amon	13	Mass
4	Depailler	14	Jarier
5	Lauda	15	Brambilla
6	Nilsson	16	Reutemann
7	Laffite	17	Watson
8	Hunt	18	Jones
9	Peterson	19	Merzario
10	Pace	20	Stuck,H-J.

French

GRAND PRIX No: 272

DATE: July 4, 1976

VENUE: Paul Ricard

POLE LAP: Hunt, 1m 47.89s

FASTEST LAP: Lauda, 1m 51.00s

Pn	Driver	Car	Laps	Time/Reason
1	Hunt	McLaren-Ford	54	1h 40m 58.60s
2	Depailler	Tyrrell-Ford	54	1h 41m 11.30s
3	Watson	Penske-Ford	54	1h 41m 22.15s
4	Pace	Brabham-Alfa	54	1h 41m 23.42s
5	Andretti,Mario	Lotus-Ford	54	1h 41m 42.52s
6	Scheckter,J.	Tyrrell-Ford	54	1h 41m 53.67s
7	Stuck,H-J.	March-Ford	54	1h 42m 20.15s
8	Pryce	Shadow-Ford	54	1h 42m 29.27s
9	Merzario	March-Ford	54	1h 42m 52.17s
10	Ickx	Williams-Ford	53	
11	Reutemann	Brabham-Alfa	53	
12	Jarier	Shadow-Ford	53	
13	Leclere	Williams-Ford	53	
14	Laffite	Ligier-Matra	53	
15	Mass	McLaren-Ford	53	
16	Lunger	Surtees-Ford	53	
17	Edwards	Hesketh-Ford	53	
18	Neve	Ensign-Ford	53	
19	Peterson	March-Ford	51	fuel system
r	Jones	Surtees-Ford	44	suspension
r	Brambilla	March-Ford	28	engine
r	Fittipaldi,E.	Fittipaldi-Ford	21	engine
r	Pescarolo	Surtees-Ford	19	suspension
r	Regazzoni	Ferrari	17	engine
r	Lauda	Ferrari	8	engine
r	Nilsson	Lotus-Ford	8	transmission
dq	Ertl	Hesketh-Ford	4	illegal start

STARTING GRID:

1	Hunt	11	Brambilla
2	Lauda	12	Nilsson
3	Depailler	13	Laffite
4	Regazzoni	14	Mass
5	Pace	15	Jarier
6	Peterson	16	Pryce
7	Andretti,Mario	17	Stuck,H-J.
8	Watson	18	Jones
9	Scheckter,J.	19	Ickx
10	Reutemann	20	Merzario +

British

GRAND PRIX No: 273
DATE: July 18, 1976
VENUE: Brands Hatch
POLE LAP: Lauda, 1m 19.35s
FASTEST LAP: Lauda, 1m 19.91s

Pn	Driver	Car	Laps	Time/Reason
dq	Hunt	McLaren-Ford	76	tech infringement
1	Lauda	Ferrari	76	1h 44m 19.66s
2	Scheckter,J.	Tyrrell-Ford	76	1h 44m 35.84s
3	Watson	Penske-Ford	75	
4	Pryce	Shadow-Ford	75	
5	Jones	Surtees-Ford	75	
6	Fittipaldi,E.	Fittipaldi-Ford	74	
7	Ertl	Hesketh-Ford	73	
8	Pace	Brabham-Alfa	73	
9	Jarier	Shadow-Ford	70	
r	Nilsson	Lotus-Ford	67	engine
r	Peterson	March-Ford	60	engine
r	Lunger	Surtees-Ford	55	gearbox
r	Depailler	Tyrrell-Ford	47	engine
r	Reutemann	Brabham-Alfa	46	engine
r	Merzario	March-Ford	39	engine
dq	Regazzoni	Ferrari	36	engine
dq	Laffite	Ligier-Matra	31	suspension
r	Evans	Brabham-Ford	24	gearbox
r	Brambilla	March-Ford	22	suspension
r	Pescarolo	Surtees-Ford	16	engine
r	Amon	Ensign-Ford	8	engine
r	Andretti,Mario	Lotus-Ford	4	engine
r	Mass	McLaren-Ford	1	clutch
r	Stuck,H-J.	March-Ford	0	accident
r	Edwards	Hesketh-Ford	0	accident

STARTING GRID:

1	Lauda	12	Mass
2	Hunt	13	Laffite
3	Andretti,Mario	14	Nilsson
4	Regazzoni	15	Reutemann
5	Depailler	16	Pace
6	Amon	17	Stuck,H-J.
7	Peterson	18	Lunger
8	Scheckter,J.	19	Jones
9	Merzario	20	Pryce
10	Brambilla	21	Fittipaldi,E.
11	Watson	22	Evans +

German

GRAND PRIX No: 274
DATE: August 1, 1976
VENUE: Nurburgring
POLE LAP: Hunt, 7m 06.5s
FASTEST LAP: Scheckter,J., 7m 10.8s

Pn	Driver	Car	Laps	Time/Reason
1	Hunt	McLaren-Ford	14	1h 41m 42.7s
2	Scheckter,J.	Tyrrell-Ford	14	1h 42m 10.4s
3	Mass	McLaren-Ford	14	1h 42m 35.1s
4	Pace	Brabham-Alfa	14	1h 42m 36.9s
5	Nilsson	Lotus-Ford	14	1h 43m 40.0s
6	Stommelen	Brabham-Alfa	14	1h 44m 13.0s
7	Watson	Penske-Ford	14	1h 44m 16.6s
8	Pryce	Shadow-Ford	14	1h 44m 30.9s
9	Regazzoni	Ferrari	14	1h 45m 28.7s
10	Jones	Surtees-Ford	14	1h 45m 30.0s
11	Jarier	Shadow-Ford	14	1h 46m 34.4s
12	Andretti,Mario	Lotus-Ford	14	1h 46m 40.8s
13	Fittipaldi,E.	Fittipaldi-Ford	14	1h 47m 07.9s
14	Pesenti-Rossi	Tyrrell-Ford	13	
15	Edwards	Hesketh-Ford	13	
r	Merzario	Williams-Ford	3	brakes
r	Brambilla	March-Ford	1	accident
r	Depailler	Tyrrell-Ford	0	accident
r	Reutemann	Brabham-Alfa	0	engine
r	Peterson	March-Ford	0	accident
r	Lauda	Ferrari	0	accident
r	Lunger	Surtees-Ford	0	accident
r	Ertl	Hesketh-Ford	0	accident
r	Stuck,H-J.	March-Ford	0	clutch
r	Laffite	Ligier-Matra	0	gearbox
r	Amon	Ensign-Ford	0	withdrew at start

STARTING GRID:

1	Hunt	12	Andretti,Mario
2	Lauda	13	Brambilla
3	Depailler	14	Jones
4	Stuck,H-J.	15	Stommelen
5	Regazzoni	16	Nilsson
6	Laffite	17	Amon
7	Pace	18	Pryce
8	Scheckter,J.	19	Watson
9	Mass	20	Fittipaldi,E.
10	Reutemann	21	Merzario
11	Peterson	22	Ertl +

Austrian

GRAND PRIX No:	275
DATE:	August 15, 1976
VENUE:	Osterreichring
POLE LAP:	Hunt, 1m 35.02s
FASTEST LAP:	Hunt, 1m 35.91s

Pn	Driver	Car	Laps	Time/Reason
1	Watson	Penske-Ford	54	1h 30m 07.86s
2	Laffite	Ligier-Matra	54	1h 30m 18.65s
3	Nilsson	Lotus-Ford	54	1h 30m 19.84s
4	Hunt	McLaren-Ford	54	1h 30m 20.30s
5	Andretti,Mario	Ford	54	1h 30m 29.35s
6	Peterson	March-Ford	54	1h 30m 42.20s
7	Mass	McLaren-Ford	54	1h 31m 07.31s
8	Ertl	Hesketh-Ford	53	
9	Pescarolo	Surtees-Ford	52	
10	Lunger	Surtees-Ford	51	accident
11	Pesenti-Rossi	Tyrrell-Ford	51	
12	Lombardi	Brabham-Ford	50	
r	Binder	Ensign-Ford	47	throttle
r	Kessel	Brabham-Ford	44	
r	Brambilla	March-Ford	43	accident
r	Fittipaldi,E.	Fittipaldi-Ford	43	accident
r	Jarier	Shadow-Ford	40	fuel pump
r	Pace	Brabham-Alfa	40	accident
r	Jones	Surtees-Ford	40	accident
r	Stuck,H-J.	March-Ford	26	fuel pressure
r	Depailler	Tyrrell-Ford	24	suspension
r	Merzario	Williams-Ford	17	accident
r	Pryce	Shadow-Ford	14	brakes
r	Scheckter,J.	Tyrrell-Ford	14	accident
r	Reutemann	Brabham-Alfa	0	clutch

STARTING GRID:

1	Hunt	14	Reutemann
2	Watson	15	Jones
3	Peterson	16	Lunger
4	Nilsson	17	Fittipaldi,E.
5	Laffite	18	Jarier
6	Pryce	19	Binder
7	Brambilla	20	Ertl
8	Pace	21	Merzario
9	Andretti,Mario	22	Pescarolo
10	Scheckter,J.	23	Pesenti-Rossi
11	Stuck,H-J.	24	Lombardi
12	Mass	25	Kessel
13	Depailler		

Dutch

GRAND PRIX No:	276
DATE:	August 29, 1976
VENUE:	Zandvoort
POLE LAP:	Peterson, 1m 21.31s
FASTEST LAP:	Regazzoni, 1m 25.59s

Pn	Driver	Car	Laps	Time/Reason
1	Hunt	McLaren-Ford	75	1h 44m 52.09s
2	Regazzoni	Ferrari	75	1h 44m 53.01s
3	Andretti,Mario	Lotus-Ford	75	1h 44m 54.18s
4	Pryce	Shadow-Ford	75	1h 44m 59.03s
5	Scheckter,J.	Tyrrell-Ford	75	1h 45m 14.55s
6	Brambilla	March-Ford	75	1h 45m 37.12s
7	Depailler	Tyrrell-Ford	75	1h 45m 48.37s
8	Jones	Surtees-Ford	74	
9	Mass	McLaren-Ford	74	
10	Jarier	Shadow-Ford	74	
11	Pescarolo	Surtees-Ford	74	
12	Stommelen	Hesketh-Ford	72	
r	Ickx	Ensign-Ford	66	electrical
r	Hayje	Penske-Ford	63	driveshaft
r	Pace	Brabham-Alfa	53	oil leak
r	Laffite	Ligier-Matra	53	engine
r	Peterson	March-Ford	52	engine
r	Ertl	Hesketh-Ford	49	spun off
r	Watson	Penske-Ford	47	gearbox
r	Perkins	Boro-Ford	44	accident
r	Fittipaldi,E.	Fittipaldi-Ford	40	electrical
r	Reutemann	Brabham-Alfa	11	clutch
r	Nilsson	Lotus-Ford	10	accident
r	Andersson	Surtees-Ford	9	engine
r	Stuck,H-J.	March-Ford	9	engine
r	Merzario	Williams-Ford	5	accident

STARTING GRID:

1	Peterson	12	Reutemann
2	Hunt	13	Nilsson
3	Pryce	14	Depailler
4	Watson	15	Mass
5	Regazzoni	16	Jones
6	Andretti,Mario	17	Fittipaldi,E.
7	Brambilla	18	Stuck,H-J.
8	Scheckter,J.	19	Perkins
9	Pace	20	Jarier
10	Laffite	21	Hayje
11	Ickx	22	Pescarolo +

Italian

GRAND PRIX No:	277
DATE:	September 12, 1976
VENUE:	Monza
POLE LAP:	Laffite, 1m 41.35s
FASTEST LAP:	Peterson, 1m 41.30s

Pn	Driver	Car	Laps	Time/Reason
1	Peterson	March-Ford	52	1h 30m 35.6s
2	Regazzoni	Ferrari	52	1h 30m 37.9s
3	Laffite	Ligier-Matra	52	1h 30m 38.6s
4	Lauda	Ferrari	52	1h 30m 55.0s
5	Scheckter,J.	Tyrrell-Ford	52	1h 30m 55.1s
6	Depailler	Tyrrell-Ford	52	1h 31m 11.3s
7	Brambilla	March-Ford	52	1h 31m 19.5s
8	Pryce	Shadow-Ford	52	1h 31m 28.5s
9	Reutemann	Ferrari	52	1h 31m 33.1s
10	Ickx	Ensign-Ford	52	1h 31m 48.0s
11	Watson	Penske-Ford	52	1h 32m 17.8s
12	Jones	Surtees-Ford	51	
13	Nilsson	Lotus-Ford	51	
14	Lunger	Surtees-Ford	50	
15	Fittipaldi,E.	Fittipaldi-Ford	50	
16	Ertl	Hesketh-Ford	49	driveshaft
17	Pescarolo	Surtees-Ford	49	
18	Pesenti-Rossi	Tyrrell-Ford	49	
19	Jarier	Shadow-Ford	47	
r	Stommelen	Brabham-Alfa	41	engine
r	Stuck,H-J.	March-Ford	23	accident
r	Andretti,Mario	Lotus-Ford	23	accident
r	Hunt	McLaren-Ford	11	spun off
r	Perkins	Boro-Ford	8	engine
r	Pace	Brabham-Alfa	4	engine
r	Mass	McLaren-Ford	2	engine
dns	Merzario	Williams-Ford		withdrew
dns	Stuppacher	Tyrrell-Ford		did not show up

STARTING GRID:

1	Laffite	10	Ickx
2	Scheckter,J.	11	Stommelen
3	Pace	12	Nilsson
4	Depailler	13	Perkins
5	Lauda	14	Andretti,Mario
6	Stuck,H-J.	15	Pryce
7	Reutemann	16	Brambilla
8	Peterson	17	Jarier
9	Regazzoni	18	Jones +

Canadian

GRAND PRIX No:	278
DATE:	October 3, 1976
VENUE:	Mosport Park
POLE LAP:	Hunt, 1m 12.389s
FASTEST LAP:	Depailler, 1m 13.817s

Pn	Driver	Car	Laps	Time/Reason
1	Hunt	McLaren-Ford	80	1h 40m 09.626s
2	Depailler	Tyrrell-Ford	80	1h 40m 15.957s
3	Andretti,Mario	Lotus-Ford	80	1h 40m 19.992s
4	Scheckter,J.	Tyrrell-Ford	80	1h 40m 29.371s
5	Mass	McLaren-Ford	80	1h 40m 51.437s
6	Regazzoni	Ferrari	80	1h 40m 55.882s
7	Pace	Brabham-Alfa	80	1h 40m 56.098s
8	Lauda	Ferrari	80	1h 41m 22.583s
9	Peterson	March-Ford	79	
10	Watson	Penske-Ford	79	
11	Pryce	Shadow-Ford	79	
12	Nilsson	Lotus-Ford	79	
13	Ickx	Ensign-Ford	79	
14	Brambilla	March-Ford	79	
15	Lunger	Surtees-Ford	78	
16	Jones	Surtees-Ford	78	
17	Perkins	Brabham-Alfa	78	
18	Jarier	Shadow-Ford	77	
19	Pescarolo	Surtees-Ford	77	
20	Edwards	Hesketh-Ford	75	
r	Laffite	Ligier-Matra	43	engine
r	Fittipaldi,E.	Fittipaldi-Ford	41	exhaust
r	Stuck,H-J.	March-Ford	36	handling
r	Merzario	Williams-Ford	11	spun off
dns	Ertl	Hesketh-Ford		accident
dns	Amon	Williams-Ford		accident

STARTING GRID:

1	Hunt	12	Regazzoni
2	Peterson	13	Pryce
3	Brambilla	14	Watson
4	Depailler	15	Nilsson
5	Andretti,Mario	16	Ickx
6	Lauda	17	Fittipaldi,E.
7	Scheckter,J.	18	Jarier
8	Stuck,H-J.	19	Perkins
9	Laffite	20	Jones
10	Pace	21	Pescarolo
11	Mass	22	Lunger +

US East

GRAND PRIX No:	279
DATE:	October 10, 1976
VENUE:	Watkins Glen
POLE LAP:	Hunt, 1m 43.622s
FASTEST LAP:	Hunt, 1m 42.851s

Pn	Driver	Car	Laps	Time/Reason
1	Hunt	McLaren-Ford	59	1h 42m 40.741s
2	Scheckter,J.	Tyrrell-Ford	59	1h 42m 48.771s
3	Lauda	Ferrari	59	1h 43m 43.065s
4	Mass	McLaren-Ford	59	1h 43m 43.199s
5	Stuck,H-J.	March-Ford	59	1h 43m 48.719s
6	Watson	Penske-Ford	59	1h 43m 48.931s
7	Regazzoni	Ferrari	58	
8	Jones	Surtees-Ford	58	
9	Fittipaldi,E.	Fittipaldi-Ford	57	
10	Jarier	Shadow-Ford	57	
11	Lunger	Surtees-Ford	57	
12	Ribeiro	Hesketh-Ford	57	
13	Ertl	Hesketh-Ford	54	
14	Brown,Warwick	Williams-Ford	54	
uc	Pescarolo	Surtees-Ford	48	
r	Pryce	Shadow-Ford	45	engine
r	Laffite	Ligier-Matra	34	burst tyre
r	Brambilla	March-Ford	34	burst tyre
r	Pace	Brabham-Alfa	31	accident
r	Perkins	Brabham-Alfa	30	suspension
r	Andretti,Mario	Lotus-Ford	23	suspension
r	Ickx	Ensign-Ford	14	accident
r	Nilsson	Lotus-Ford	13	engine
r	Peterson	March-Ford	12	suspension
r	Merzario	Williams-Ford	9	spun off
r	Depailler	Tyrrell-Ford	7	fuel line

STARTING GRID:

1	Hunt	12	Laffite
2	Scheckter,J.	13	Perkins
3	Peterson	14	Regazzoni
4	Brambilla	15	Fittipaldi,E.
5	Lauda	16	Jarier
6	Stuck,H-J.	17	Mass
7	Depailler	18	Jones
8	Watson	19	Ickx
9	Pryce	20	Nilsson
10	Pace	21	Ertl
11	Andretti,Mario	22	Ribeiro +

Japanese

GRAND PRIX No:	280
DATE:	October 24, 1976
VENUE:	Fuji
POLE LAP:	Andretti,Mario, 1m 12.77s
FASTEST LAP:	Hasemi, 1m 18.23s

Pn	Driver	Car	Laps	Time/Reason
1	Andretti,Mario	Lotus-Ford	73	1h 43m 58.86s
2	Depailler	Tyrrell-Ford	72	1h 43m 59.14s
3	Hunt	McLaren-Ford	72	1h 44m 00.06s
4	Jones	Surtees-Ford	72	1h 44m 12.07s
5	Regazzoni	Ferrari	72	1h 44m 18.76s
6	Nilsson	Lotus-Ford	72	1h 44m 18.92s
7	Laffite	Ligier-Matra	72	
8	Ertl	Hesketh-Ford	72	
9	Takahara	Surtees-Ford	70	
10	Jarier	Shadow-Ford	69	
11	Hasemi	Kojima-Ford	66	
r	Scheckter,J.	Tyrrell-Ford	58	overheating
r	Binder	Williams-Ford	49	wheel bearing
r	Pryce	Shadow-Ford	46	engine
r	Brambilla	March-Ford	38	engine
r	Stuck,H-J.	March-Ford	37	electrical
r	Mass	McLaren-Ford	35	accident
r	Watson	Penske-Ford	33	engine
r	Hoshino	Tyrrell-Ford	27	tyres
r	Merzario	Williams-Ford	23	gearbox
r	Fittipaldi,E.	Fittipaldi-Ford	9	withdrew
r	Pace	Brabham-Alfa	7	withdrew
r	Lauda	Ferrari	2	withdrew
r	Perkins	Brabham-Alfa	1	withdrew
r	Peterson	March-Ford	0	engine
dns	Kawashima	Williams-Ford		engine

STARTING GRID:

1	Andretti,Mario	12	Mass
2	Hunt	13	Depailler
3	Lauda	14	Pryce
4	Watson	15	Jarier
5	Scheckter,J.	16	Nilsson
6	Pace	17	Perkins
7	Regazzoni	18	Stuck,H-J.
8	Brambilla	19	Merzario
9	Peterson	20	Jones
10	Hasemi	21	Hoshino
11	Laffite	22	Ertl +

Argentine

GRAND PRIX No: 281
DATE: January 9, 1977
VENUE: Buenos Aires
POLE LAP: Hunt, 1m 48.68s
FASTEST LAP: Hunt, 1m 51.06s

Pn	Driver	Car	Laps	Time/Reason
1	Scheckter,J.	Wolf-Ford	53	1h 40m 11.19s
2	Pace	Brabham-Alfa	53	1h 40m 54.43s
3	Reutemann	Ferrari	53	1h 40m 57.21s
4	Fittipaldi,E.	Fittipaldi-Ford	53	1h 41m 06.67s
5	Andretti,Mario	Lotus-Ford	51	wheel bearing
6	Regazzoni	Ensign-Ford	51	
7	Brambilla	Surtees-Ford	48	fuel system
r	Scheckter,I.	March-Ford	45	battery
uc	Pryce	Shadow-Ford	45	
r	Watson	Brabham-Alfa	41	handling
r	Ribeiro	March-Ford	39	gear lever
uc	Laffite	Ligier-Matra	37	
r	Depailler	Tyrrell-Ford	32	overheating
r	Hunt	McLaren-Ford	31	suspension
r	Mass	McLaren-Ford	28	engine
r	Peterson	Tyrrell-Ford	28	spun off
r	Hoffman	Fittipaldi-Ford	22	engine
r	Lauda	Ferrari	20	fuel system
r	Binder	Surtees-Ford	18	nose
r	Zorzi	Shadow-Ford	2	gearbox

STARTING GRID:

1	Hunt	11	Regazzoni
2	Watson	12	Brambilla
3	Depailler	13	Peterson
4	Lauda	14	Laffite
5	Mass	15	Fittipaldi,E.
6	Pace	16	Scheckter,I.
7	Reutemann	17	Binder
8	Andretti,Mario	18	Hoffman
9	Pryce	19	Ribeiro
10	Scheckter,J.	20	Zorzi

Brazilian

GRAND PRIX No: 282
DATE: January 23, 1977
VENUE: Interlagos
POLE LAP: Hunt, 2m 30.11s
FASTEST LAP: Hunt, 2m 34.55s

Pn	Driver	Car	Laps	Time/Reason
1	Reutemann	Ferrari	40	1h 45m 07.72s
2	Hunt	McLaren-Ford	40	1h 45m 18.43s
3	Lauda	Ferrari	40	1h 46m 55.23s
4	Fittipaldi,E.	Fittipaldi-Ford	39	
5	Nilsson	Lotus-Ford	39	
6	Zorzi	Shadow-Ford	39	
7	Hoffman	Fittipaldi-Ford	38	
r	Pryce	Shadow-Ford	33	engine
r	Pace	Brabham-Alfa	33	accident
r	Binder	Surtees-Ford	32	suspension
r	Watson	Brabham-Alfa	30	accident
r	Laffite	Ligier-Matra	26	accident
r	Depailler	Tyrrell-Ford	23	accident
r	Andretti,Mario	Lotus-Ford	19	electrical
r	Ribeiro	March-Ford	16	engine
r	Mass	McLaren-Ford	12	accident
r	Regazzoni	Ensign-Ford	12	accident
r	Peterson	Tyrrell-Ford	12	accident
r	Scheckter,J.	Wolf-Ford	11	engine
r	Brambilla	Surtees-Ford	11	accident
r	Scheckter,I.	March-Ford	1	transmission
r	Perkins	BRM	1	engine

STARTING GRID:

1	Hunt	12	Pryce
2	Reutemann	13	Lauda
3	Andretti,Mario	14	Laffite
4	Mass	15	Scheckter,J.
5	Pace	16	Fittipaldi,E.
6	Depailler	17	Scheckter,I.
7	Watson	18	Zorzi
8	Peterson	19	Hoffman
9	Regazzoni	20	Binder
10	Nilsson	21	Ribeiro
11	Brambilla	22	Perkins

South African

GRAND PRIX No:	283
DATE:	March 5, 1977
VENUE:	Kyalami
POLE LAP:	Hunt, 1m 15.96s
FASTEST LAP:	Watson, 1m 17.63s

Pn	Driver	Car	Laps	Time/Reason
1	Lauda	Ferrari	78	1h 42m 21.6s
2	Scheckter,J.	Wolf-Ford	78	1h 42m 26.8s
3	Depailler	Tyrrell-Ford	78	1h 42m 27.3s
4	Hunt	McLaren-Ford	78	1h 42m 31.1s
5	Mass	McLaren-Ford	78	1h 42m 41.5s
6	Watson	Brabham-Alfa	78	1h 42m 41.8s
7	Brambilla	Surtees-Ford	78	1h 42m 45.2s
8	Reutemann	Ferrari	78	1h 42m 48.3s
9	Regazzoni	Ensign-Ford	78	1h 43m 07.8s
10	Fittipaldi,E.	Fittipaldi-Ford	78	1h 43m 33.3s
11	Binder	Surtees-Ford	77	
12	Nilsson	Lotus-Ford	77	
13	Pace	Brabham-Alfa	76	
14	Lunger	March-Ford	76	
15	Perkins	BRM	73	
r	Ribeiro	March-Ford	66	engine
r	Stuck,H-J.	March-Ford	55	engine
r	Andretti,Mario	Lotus-Ford	43	suspension
r	Hayje	March-Ford	33	gearbox
r	Pryce	Shadow-Ford	22	fatal accident
r	Laffite	Ligier-Matra	22	accident
r	Zorzi	Shadow-Ford	21	engine
r	Peterson	Tyrrell-Ford	5	fuel pressure

STARTING GRID:

1	Hunt	13	Mass
2	Pace	14	Brambilla
3	Lauda	15	Pryce
4	Depailler	16	Regazzoni
5	Scheckter,J.	17	Ribeiro
6	Andretti,Mario	18	Stuck,H-J.
7	Peterson	19	Binder
8	Reutemann	20	Zorzi
9	Fittipaldi,E.	21	Hayje
10	Nilsson	22	Perkins
11	Watson	23	Lunger
12	Laffite		

US West

GRAND PRIX No:	284
DATE:	April 3, 1977
VENUE:	Long Beach
POLE LAP:	Lauda, 1m 21.630s
FASTEST LAP:	Lauda, 1m 22.753s

Pn	Driver	Car	Laps	Time/Reason
1	Andretti,Mario	Lotus-Ford	80	1h 51m 35.470s
2	Lauda	Ferrari	80	1h 51m 36.243s
3	Scheckter,J.	Wolf-Ford	80	1h 51m 40.327s
4	Depailler	Tyrrell-Ford	80	1h 52m 49.957s
5	Fittipaldi,E.	Fittipaldi-Ford	80	1h 52m 56.378s
6	Jarier	Penske-Ford	79	
7	Hunt	McLaren-Ford	79	
8	Nilsson	Lotus-Ford	79	
9	Laffite	Ligier-Matra	78	electrical
10	Henton	March-Ford	77	
11	Binder	Surtees-Ford	77	
r	Peterson	Tyrrell-Ford	62	fuel line
r	Regazzoni	Ensign-Ford	57	gearbox
r	Stuck,H-J.	Brabham-Alfa	53	brakes
r	Jones	Shadow-Ford	40	gearbox
r	Mass	McLaren-Ford	39	vibration
dq	Watson	Brabham-Alfa	33	push start
r	Zorzi	Shadow-Ford	27	gearbox
r	Ribeiro	March-Ford	15	gearbox
r	Reutemann	Ferrari	5	accident
r	Lunger	March-Ford	4	accident
r	Brambilla	Surtees-Ford	0	accident

STARTING GRID:

1	Lauda	12	Depailler
2	Andretti,Mario	13	Regazzoni
3	Scheckter,J.	14	Jones
4	Reutemann	15	Mass
5	Laffite	16	Nilsson
6	Watson	17	Stuck,H-J.
7	Fittipaldi,E.	18	Henton
8	Hunt	19	Binder
9	Jarier	20	Zorzi
10	Peterson	21	Lunger
11	Brambilla	22	Ribeiro

Spanish

GRAND PRIX No: 285
DATE: May 8, 1977
VENUE: Jarama
POLE LAP: Andretti,Mario, 1m 18.70s
FASTEST LAP: Laffite, 1m 20.81s

Pn	Driver	Car	Laps	Time/Reason
1	Andretti,Mario	Lotus-Ford	75	1h 42m 52.22s
2	Reutemann	Ferrari	75	1h 43m 08.07s
3	Scheckter,J.	Wolf-Ford	75	1h 43m 16.73s
4	Mass	McLaren-Ford	75	1h 43m 17.09s
5	Nilsson	Lotus-Ford	75	1h 43m 58.05s
6	Stuck,H-J.	Brabham-Alfa	74	
7	Laffite	Ligier-Matra	74	
8	Peterson	Tyrrell-Ford	74	
9	Binder	Surtees-Ford	73	
10	Lunger	March-Ford	72	
11	Scheckter,I.	March-Ford	72	
12	Neve	March-Ford	71	
13	Villota	McLaren-Ford	70	
14	Fittipaldi,E.	Fittipaldi-Ford	70	
r	Watson	Brabham-Alfa	64	fuel system
r	Jones	Shadow-Ford	56	accident
r	Keegan	Hesketh-Ford	32	accident
r	Ertl	Hesketh-Ford	29	radiator
r	Zorzi	Shadow-Ford	25	engine
r	Merzario	March-Ford	16	suspension
r	Depailler	Tyrrell-Ford	12	engine
r	Hunt	McLaren-Ford	10	engine
r	Regazzoni	Ensign-Ford	9	accident
r	Brambilla	Surtees-Ford	9	accident
dns	Lauda	Ferrari		injury

STARTING GRID:

1	Andretti,Mario	14	Jones
2	Laffite	15	Peterson
3	Lauda	16	Keegan
4	Reutemann	17	Scheckter,I.
5	Scheckter,J.	18	Ertl
6	Watson	19	Fittipaldi,E.
7	Hunt	20	Binder
8	Regazzoni	21	Merzario
9	Mass	22	Neve
10	Depailler	23	Villota
11	Brambilla	24	Zorzi
12	Nilsson	25	Lunger
13	Stuck,H-J.		

Monaco

GRAND PRIX No: 286
DATE: May 22, 1977
VENUE: Monte Carlo
POLE LAP: Watson, 1m 29.86s
FASTEST LAP: Scheckter,J., 1m 31.07s

Pn	Driver	Car	Laps	Time/Reason
1	Scheckter,J.	Wolf-Ford	76	1h 57m 52.77s
2	Lauda	Ferrari	76	1h 57m 53.66s
3	Reutemann	Ferrari	76	1h 58m 25.57s
4	Mass	McLaren-Ford	76	1h 58m 27.37s
5	Andretti,Mario	Lotus-Ford	76	1h 58m 28.32s
6	Jones	Shadow-Ford	76	1h 58m 29.38s
7	Laffite	Ligier-Matra	76	1h 58m 57.21s
8	Brambilla	Surtees-Ford	76	1h 59m 01.41s
9	Patrese	Shadow-Ford	75	
10	Ickx	Ensign-Ford	75	
11	Jarier	Penske-Ford	74	
12	Keegan	Hesketh-Ford	73	
r	Nilsson	Lotus-Ford	51	gearbox
r	Watson	Brabham-Alfa	48	gearbox
r	Depailler	Tyrrell-Ford	46	gearbox
r	Binder	Surtees-Ford	41	fuel injection
r	Fittipaldi,E.	Fittipaldi-Ford	37	engine
r	Hunt	McLaren-Ford	25	engine
r	Stuck,H-J.	Brabham-Alfa	19	fire
r	Peterson	Tyrrell-Ford	10	brakes

STARTING GRID:

1	Watson	11	Jones
2	Scheckter,J.	12	Jarier
3	Reutemann	13	Nilsson
4	Peterson	14	Brambilla
5	Stuck,H-J.	15	Patrese
6	Lauda	16	Laffite
7	Hunt	17	Ickx
8	Depailler	18	Fittipaldi,E.
9	Mass	19	Binder
10	Andretti,Mario	20	Keegan

Belgian

GRAND PRIX No:	287
DATE:	June 5, 1977
VENUE:	Zolder
POLE LAP:	Andretti,Mario, 1m 24.64s
FASTEST LAP:	Nilsson, 1m 27.36s

Pn	Driver	Car	Laps	Time/Reason
1	Nilsson	Lotus-Ford	70	1h 55m 05.71s
2	Lauda	Ferrari	70	1h 55m 19.90s
3	Peterson	Tyrrell-Ford	70	1h 55m 25.66s
4	Brambilla	Surtees-Ford	70	1h 55m 30.69s
5	Jones	Shadow-Ford	70	1h 56m 21.18s
6	Stuck,H-J.	Brabham-Alfa	69	
7	Hunt	McLaren-Ford	69	
8	Depailler	Tyrrell-Ford	69	
9	Ertl	Hesketh-Ford	69	
10	Neve	March-Ford	68	
11	Jarier	Penske-Ford	68	
12	Perkins	Surtees-Ford	67	
13	Purley	Lec-Ford	67	
14	Merzario	March-Ford	65	
15	Hayje	March-Ford	63	
r	Scheckter,J.	Wolf-Ford	62	engine
r	Mass	McLaren-Ford	39	accident
r	Laffite	Ligier-Matra	32	engine
r	Regazzoni	Ensign-Ford	29	engine
r	Keegan	Hesketh-Ford	14	accident
r	Reutemann	Ferrari	14	accident
r	Patrese	Shadow-Ford	12	accident
r	Scheckter,I.	March-Ford	8	accident
r	Fittipaldi,E.	Fittipaldi-Ford	2	electrical
r	Andretti,Mario	Lotus-Ford	0	accident
r	Watson	Brabham-Alfa	0	accident
dns	Lunger	McLaren-Ford		car not ready

STARTING GRID:

1	Andretti,Mario	11	Lauda
2	Watson	12	Brambilla
3	Nilsson	13	Regazzoni
4	Scheckter,J.	14	Merzario
5	Depailler	15	Patrese
6	Mass	16	Fittipaldi,E.
7	Reutemann	17	Jones
8	Peterson	18	Stuck,H-J.
9	Hunt	19	Keegan
10	Laffite	20	Purley +

Swedish

GRAND PRIX No:	288
DATE:	19 June, 1977
VENUE:	Anderstorp
POLE LAP:	Andretti,Mario, 1m 25.404s
FASTEST LAP:	Andretti,Mario, 1m 27.607s

Pn	Driver	Car	Laps	Time/Reason
1	Laffite	Ligier-Matra	72	1h 46m 55.520s
2	Mass	McLaren-Ford	72	1h 47m 03.969s
3	Reutemann	Ferrari	72	1h 47m 09.889s
4	Depailler	Tyrrell-Ford	72	1h 47m 11.828s
5	Watson	Brabham-Alfa	72	1h 47m 14.255s
6	Andretti,Mario	Lotus-Ford	72	1h 47m 20.797s
7	Regazzoni	Ensign-Ford	72	1h 47m 26.786s
8	Jarier	Penske-Ford	72	1h 48m 00.086s
9	Oliver	Shadow-Ford	72	1h 48m 17.999s
10	Stuck,H-J.	Brabham-Alfa	71	
11	Lunger	McLaren-Ford	71	
12	Hunt	McLaren-Ford	71	
13	Keegan	Hesketh-Ford	71	
14	Purley	Lec-Ford	70	
15	Neve	March-Ford	69	
16	Ertl	Hesketh-Ford	68	
17	Jones	Shadow-Ford	67	
18	Fittipaldi,E.	Fittipaldi-Ford	66	
19	Nilsson	Lotus-Ford	64	wheel bearing
r	Scheckter,I.	March-Ford	61	driveshaft
r	Brambilla	Surtees-Ford	52	fuel pressure
r	Lauda	Ferrari	47	handling
r	Scheckter,J.	Wolf-Ford	29	accident
r	Peterson	Tyrrell-Ford	7	ignition

STARTING GRID:

1	Andretti,Mario	13	Reutemann
2	Watson	14	Brambilla
3	Lunger	15	Regazzoni
4	Hunt	16	Lauda
5	Scheckter,J.	17	Oliver
6	Stuck,H-J.	18	Jarier
7	Depailler	19	Fittipaldi,E.
8	Nilsson	20	Purley
9	Laffite	21	Neve
10	Mass	22	Scheckter,I.
11	Peterson	23	Ertl
12	Jones	24	Keegan

French

GRAND PRIX No:	289
DATE:	July 3, 1977
VENUE:	Dijon
POLE LAP:	Andretti,Mario, 1m 12.210s
FASTEST LAP:	Andretti,Mario, 1m 13.75s

Pn	Driver	Car	Laps	Time/Reason
1	Andretti,Mario	Lotus-Ford	80	1h 39m 40.13s
2	Watson	Brabham-Alfa	80	1h 39m 41.68s
3	Hunt	McLaren-Ford	80	1h 40m 14.00s
4	Nilsson	Lotus-Ford	80	1h 40m 51.21s
5	Lauda	Ferrari	80	1h 40m 54.58s
6	Reutemann	Ferrari	79	
7	Regazzoni	Ensign-Ford	79	
8	Laffite	Ligier-Matra	78	
9	Mass	McLaren-Ford	78	
10	Keegan	Hesketh-Ford	78	
11	Fittipaldi,E.	Fittipaldi-Ford	77	
12	Peterson	Tyrrell-Ford	77	
13	Brambilla	Surtees-Ford	77	
uc	Scheckter,I.	March-Ford	69	
r	Scheckter,J.	Wolf-Ford	66	accident
r	Stuck,H-J.	Brabham-Alfa	64	accident
r	Jones	Shadow-Ford	60	driveshaft
r	Merzario	March-Ford	27	gearbox
r	Depailler	Tyrrell-Ford	21	accident
r	Patrese	Shadow-Ford	6	engine
r	Purley	Lec-Ford	5	accident
r	Jarier	Penske-Ford	4	accident

STARTING GRID:

1	Andretti,Mario	12	Depailler
2	Hunt	13	Stuck,H-J.
3	Nilsson	14	Keegan
4	Watson	15	Regazzoni
5	Laffite	15	Patrese
6	Reutemann	17	Peterson
7	Mass	18	Merzario
8	Scheckter,J.	19	Jarier
9	Lauda	20	Scheckter,I.
10	Jones	21	Purley
11	Brambilla	22	Fittipaldi,E.

British

GRAND PRIX No:	290
DATE:	July 16, 1977
VENUE:	Silverstone
POLE LAP:	Hunt, 1m 18.49s
FASTEST LAP:	Hunt, 1m 19.60s

Pn	Driver	Car	Laps	Time/Reason
1	Hunt	McLaren-Ford	68	1h 31m 46.06s
2	Lauda	Ferrari	68	1h 32m 04.37s
3	Nilsson	Lotus-Ford	68	1h 32m 05.63s
4	Mass	McLaren-Ford	68	1h 32m 33.82s
5	Stuck,H-J.	Brabham-Alfa	68	1h 32m 57.79s
6	Laffite	Ligier-Matra	67	
7	Jones	Shadow-Ford	67	
8	Brambilla	Surtees-Ford	67	
9	Jarier	Penske-Ford	67	
10	Neve	March-Ford	66	
11	Villeneuve,G.	McLaren-Ford	66	
12	Schuppan	Surtees-Ford	66	
13	Lunger	McLaren-Ford	64	
14	Andretti,Mario	Lotus-Ford	62	engine
15	Reutemann	Ferrari	62	
r	Watson	Brabham-Alfa	60	engine
r	Scheckter,J.	Wolf-Ford	59	engine
r	Fittipaldi,E.	Fittipaldi-Ford	42	engine
r	Merzario	March-Ford	28	driveshaft
r	Patrese	Shadow-Ford	20	fuel pressure
r	Depailler	Tyrrell-Ford	16	accident
r	Jabouille	Renault	16	turbocharger
r	Scheckter,I.	March-Ford	6	accident
r	Tambay	Ensign-Ford	3	electrical
r	Peterson	Tyrrell-Ford	3	engine
r	Keegan	Hesketh-Ford	0	accident

STARTING GRID:

1	Hunt	12	Jones
2	Watson	13	Keegan
3	Lauda	14	Reutemann
4	Mass	15	Laffite
5	Scheckter,J.	16	Tambay
6	Nilsson	17	Merzario
7	Andretti,Mario	18	Depailler
8	Stuck,H-J.	19	Lunger
9	Brambilla	20	Jarier
10	Villeneuve,G.	21	Jabouille
11	Peterson	22	Fittipaldi,E. +

German

GRAND PRIX No:	291
DATE:	July 31, 1977
VENUE:	Hockenheim
POLE LAP:	Scheckter,J., 1m 53.07s
FASTEST LAP:	Lauda, 1m 55.99s

Pn	Driver	Car	Laps	Time/Reason
1	Lauda	Ferrari	47	1h 31m 48.62s
2	Scheckter,J.	Wolf-Ford	47	1h 32m 02.95s
3	Stuck,H-J.	Brabham-Alfa	47	1h 32m 09.52s
4	Reutemann	Ferrari	47	1h 32m 48.89s
5	Brambilla	Surtees-Ford	47	1h 33m 15.99s
6	Tambay	Ensign-Ford	47	1h 33m 18.43s
7	Schuppan	Surtees-Ford	46	
8	Ribeiro	March-Ford	46	
9	Peterson	Tyrrell-Ford	42	engine
10	Patrese	Shadow-Ford	42	lost wheel
r	Keegan	Hesketh-Ford	40	accident
r	Andretti,Mario	Lotus-Ford	34	engine
r	Hunt	McLaren-Ford	32	fuel pump
r	Nilsson	Lotus-Ford	31	engine
r	Mass	McLaren-Ford	26	gearbox
r	Depailler	Tyrrell-Ford	22	engine
r	Laffite	Ligier-Matra	21	engine
r	Rebaque	Hesketh-Ford	20	battery
r	Lunger	McLaren-Ford	14	accident
r	Scheckter,I.	March-Ford	9	clutch
r	Watson	Brabham-Alfa	8	engine
r	Jarier	Penske-Ford	5	accident
r	Jones	Shadow-Ford	0	accident
r	Regazzoni	Ensign-Ford	0	accident

STARTING GRID:

1	Scheckter,J.	13	Mass
2	Watson	14	Peterson
3	Lauda	15	Depailler
4	Hunt	16	Patrese
5	Stuck,H-J.	17	Jones
6	Laffite	18	Scheckter,I.
7	Andretti,Mario	19	Schuppan
8	Reutemann	20	Ribeiro
9	Nilsson	21	Lunger
10	Brambilla	22	Regazzoni
11	Tambay	23	Keegan
12	Jarier	24	Rebaque

Austrian

GRAND PRIX No:	292
DATE:	August 14, 1977
VENUE:	Osterreichring
POLE LAP:	Lauda, 1m 39.32s
FASTEST LAP:	Watson, 1m 40.96s

Pn	Driver	Car	Laps	Time/Reason
1	Jones	Shadow-Ford	54	1h 37m 16.49s
2	Lauda	Ferrari	54	1h 37m 36.62s
3	Stuck,H-J.	Brabham-Alfa	54	1h 37m 50.99s
4	Reutemann	Ferrari	54	1h 37m 51.24s
5	Peterson	Tyrrell-Ford	54	1h 38m 18.58s
6	Mass	McLaren-Ford	53	
7	Keegan	Hesketh-Ford	53	
8	Watson	Brabham-Alfa	53	
9	Neve	March-Ford	53	
10	Lunger	McLaren-Ford	53	
11	Fittipaldi,E.	Fittipaldi-Ford	53	
12	Binder	Penske-Ford	53	
13	Depailler	Tyrrell-Ford	53	
14	Jarier	Penske-Ford	52	
15	Brambilla	Surtees-Ford	52	
16	Schuppan	Surtees-Ford	52	
17	Villota	McLaren-Ford	50	accident
r	Scheckter,J.	Wolf-Ford	45	spun off
r	Hunt	McLaren-Ford	43	engine
r	Tambay	Ensign-Ford	41	engine
r	Nilsson	Lotus-Ford	38	engine
r	Merzario	Shadow-Ford	29	gear-change
r	Laffite	Ligier-Matra	21	oil leak
r	Andretti,Mario	Lotus-Ford	11	engine
r	Scheckter,I.	March-Ford	2	accident
r	Regazzoni	Ensign-Ford	0	accident

STARTING GRID:

1	Lauda	12	Watson
2	Hunt	13	Brambilla
3	Andretti,Mario	14	Jones
4	Stuck,H-J.	15	Peterson
5	Reutemann	16	Nilsson
6	Laffite	17	Lunger
7	Tambay	18	Jarier
8	Scheckter,J.	19	Binder
9	Mass	20	Keegan
10	Depailler	21	Merzario
11	Regazzoni	22	Neve

+

Dutch

GRAND PRIX No:	293
DATE:	August 28, 1977
VENUE:	Zandvoort
POLE LAP:	Andretti,Mario, 1m 18.65s
FASTEST LAP:	Lauda, 1m 19.99s

Pn	Driver	Car	Laps	Time/Reason
1	Lauda	Ferrari	75	1h 41m 45.93s
2	Laffite	Ligier-Matra	75	1h 41m 47.82s
3	Scheckter,J.	Wolf-Ford	74	
4	Fittipaldi,E.	Fittipaldi-Ford	74	
5	Tambay	Ensign-Ford	73	out of fuel
6	Reutemann	Ferrari	73	
7	Stuck,H-J.	Brabham-Alfa	73	
8	Binder	Penske-Ford	73	
9	Lunger	McLaren-Ford	73	
10	Scheckter,I.	March-Ford	73	
11	Ribeiro	March-Ford	72	
12	Brambilla	Surtees-Ford	67	accident
13	Patrese	Shadow-Ford	67	
dq	Henton	Ensign-Ford	52	push start
r	Jabouille	Renault	39	suspension
r	Nilsson	Lotus-Ford	34	accident
r	Jones	Shadow-Ford	32	engine
r	Depailler	Tyrrell-Ford	31	engine
r	Peterson	Tyrrell-Ford	18	ignition
r	Regazzoni	Ensign-Ford	17	throttle
r	Andretti,Mario	Lotus-Ford	14	engine
r	Keegan	Hesketh-Ford	8	accident
r	Hunt	McLaren-Ford	5	accident
r	Jarier	Penske-Ford	4	engine
r	Watson	Brabham-Alfa	2	engine
r	Mass	McLaren-Ford	0	accident

STARTING GRID:

1	Andretti,Mario	12	Tambay
2	Laffite	13	Jones
3	Hunt	14	Mass
4	Lauda	15	Scheckter,J.
5	Nilsson	16	Patrese
6	Reutemann	17	Fittipaldi,E.
7	Peterson	18	Binder
8	Watson	19	Stuck,H-J.
9	Regazzoni	20	Lunger
10	Jabouille	21	Jarier
11	Depailler	22	Brambilla +

Italian

GRAND PRIX No:	294
DATE:	September 11, 1977
VENUE:	Monza
POLE LAP:	Hunt, 1m 38.08s
FASTEST LAP:	Andretti,Mario, 1m 39.10s

Pn	Driver	Car	Laps	Time/Reason
1	Andretti,Mario	Lotus-Ford	52	1h 27m 50.30s
2	Lauda	Ferrari	52	1h 28m 07.26s
3	Jones	Shadow-Ford	52	1h 28m 13.93s
4	Mass	McLaren-Ford	52	1h 28m 18.78s
5	Regazzoni	Ensign-Ford	52	1h 28m 21.41s
6	Peterson	Tyrrell-Ford	52	1h 29m 09.52s
7	Neve	March-Ford	50	
8	Laffite	Ligier-Matra	50	
9	Keegan	Hesketh-Ford	48	
r	Scheckter,I.	March-Ford	41	transmission
r	Reutemann	Ferrari	39	accident
r	Giacomelli	McLaren-Ford	38	engine
r	Patrese	Shadow-Ford	38	accident
r	Stuck,H-J.	Brabham-Alfa	31	engine
r	Hunt	McLaren-Ford	26	spun off
r	Depailler	Tyrrell-Ford	24	engine
r	Scheckter,J.	Wolf-Ford	23	engine
r	Jabouille	Renault	23	engine
r	Jarier	Penske-Ford	19	engine
r	Brambilla	Surtees-Ford	5	radiator
r	Tambay	Ensign-Ford	9	engine
r	Lunger	McLaren-Ford	4	engine
r	Nilsson	Lotus-Ford	4	suspension
r	Watson	Brabham-Alfa	3	accident

STARTING GRID:

1	Hunt	13	Depailler
2	Reutemann	14	Watson
3	Scheckter,J.	15	Giacomelli
4	Andretti,Mario	16	Jones
5	Lauda	17	Scheckter,I.
6	Patrese	18	Jarier
7	Regazzoni	19	Nilsson
8	Laffite	20	Jabouille
9	Mass	21	Tambay
10	Brambilla	22	Lunger
11	Stuck,H-J.	23	Keegan
12	Peterson	24	Neve

US East

GRAND PRIX No:	295
DATE:	October 2, 1977
VENUE:	Watkins Glen
POLE LAP:	Hunt, 1m 40.863s
FASTEST LAP:	Peterson, 1m 51.854s

Pn	Driver	Car	Laps	Time/Reason
1	Hunt	McLaren-Ford	59	1h 58m 23.267s
2	Andretti,Mario	Lotus-Ford	59	1h 58m 25.293s
3	Scheckter,J.	Wolf-Ford	59	1h 59m 42.146s
4	Lauda	Ferrari	59	2h 00m 03.882s
5	Regazzoni	Ensign-Ford	59	2h 00m 11.405s
6	Reutemann	Ferrari	58	
7	Laffite	Ligier-Matra	58	
8	Keegan	Hesketh-Ford	58	
9	Jarier	Shadow-Ford	58	
10	Lunger	McLaren-Ford	57	
11	Binder	Surtees-Ford	57	
12	Watson	Brabham-Alfa	57	
13	Fittipaldi,E.	Fittipaldi-Ford	57	
14	Depailler	Tyrrell-Ford	56	
15	Ribeiro	March-Ford	56	
16	Peterson	Tyrrell-Ford	56	
17	Ashley	Hesketh-Ford	55	
18	Neve	March-Ford	55	
19	Brambilla	Surtees-Ford	54	
r	Jabouille	Renault	30	alternator
r	Nilsson	Lotus-Ford	17	accident
r	Stuck,H-J.	Brabham-Alfa	14	accident
r	Scheckter,I.	March-Ford	10	accident
r	Mass	McLaren-Ford	8	fuel pump
r	Ongais	Penske-Ford	6	accident
r	Jones	Shadow-Ford	3	accident

STARTING GRID:

1	Hunt	12	Nilsson
2	Stuck,H-J.	13	Jones
3	Watson	14	Jabouille
4	Andretti,Mario	15	Mass
5	Peterson	16	Jarier
6	Reutemann	17	Lunger
7	Lauda	18	Fittipaldi,E.
8	Depailler	19	Regazzoni
9	Scheckter,J.	20	Keegan
10	Laffite	21	Scheckter,I.
11	Brambilla	22	Ashley +

Canadian

GRAND PRIX No:	296
DATE:	October 9, 1977
VENUE:	Mosport Park
POLE LAP:	Andretti,Mario, 1m 11.385s
FASTEST LAP:	Andretti,Mario, 1m 13.299s

Pn	Driver	Car	Laps	Time/Reason
1	Scheckter,J.	Wolf-Ford	80	1h 40m 00.00s
2	Depailler	Tyrrell-Ford	80	1h 40m 06.77s
3	Mass	McLaren-Ford	80	1h 40m 15.76s
4	Jones	Shadow-Ford	80	1h 40m 46.69s
5	Tambay	Ensign-Ford	80	1h 41m 03.26s
6	Brambilla	Surtees-Ford	78	accident
7	Ongais	Penske-Ford	78	
8	Ribeiro	March-Ford	78	
9	Andretti,Mario	Lotus-Ford	77	engine
10	Patrese	Shadow-Ford	76	accident
11	Lunger	McLaren-Ford	76	engine
12	Villeneuve,G.	Ferrari	76	driveshaft
r	Hunt	McLaren-Ford	61	accident
r	Neve	March-Ford	56	engine
r	Peterson	Tyrrell-Ford	34	fuel leak
r	Keegan	Hesketh-Ford	32	accident
r	Binder	Surtees-Ford	31	accident
r	Fittipaldi,E.	Fittipaldi-Ford	29	engine
r	Scheckter,I.	March-Ford	29	engine
r	Reutemann	Ferrari	20	fuel pressure
r	Stuck,H-J.	Brabham-Alfa	19	engine
r	Nilsson	Lotus-Ford	17	accident
r	Laffite	Ligier-Matra	12	driveshaft
r	Watson	Brabham-Alfa	1	accident
r	Regazzoni	Ensign-Ford	0	accident
dns	Ashley	Hesketh-Ford		injured

STARTING GRID:

1	Andretti,Mario	12	Reutemann
2	Hunt	13	Stuck,H-J.
3	Peterson	14	Regazzoni
4	Nilsson	15	Brambilla
5	Mass	16	Tambay
6	Depailler	17	Villeneuve,G.
7	Jones	18	Scheckter,I.
8	Patrese	19	Fittipaldi,E.
9	Scheckter,J.	20	Lunger
10	Watson	21	Neve
11	Laffite	22	Ongais +

Japanese

GRAND PRIX No:	297
DATE:	October 23, 1977
VENUE:	Fuji
POLE LAP:	Andretti,Mario, 1m 12.23s
FASTEST LAP:	Scheckter,J., 1m 14.30s

Pn	Driver	Car	Laps	Time/Reason
1	Hunt	McLaren-Ford	73	1h 31m 51.68s
2	Reutemann	Ferrari	73	1h 32m 54.13s
3	Depailler	Tyrrell-Ford	73	1h 32m 58.07s
4	Jones	Shadow-Ford	73	1h 32m 58.29s
5	Laffite	Ligier-Matra	72	out of fuel
6	Patrese	Shadow-Ford	72	
7	Stuck,H-J.	Brabham-Alfa	72	
8	Brambilla	Surtees-Ford	71	
9	Takahashi	Tyrrell-Ford	71	
10	Scheckter,J.	Wolf-Ford	71	
11	Hoshino	Kojima-Ford	71	
12	Ribeiro	March-Ford	69	
r	Nilsson	Lotus-Ford	63	gearbox
r	Regazzoni	Ensign-Ford	43	engine
r	Watson	Brabham-Alfa	29	gearbox
r	Mass	McLaren-Ford	28	engine
r	Tambay	Ensign-Ford	14	engine
r	Peterson	Tyrrell-Ford	5	accident
r	Villeneuve,G.	Ferrari	5	accident
r	Jarier	Ligier-Matra	3	engine
r	Binder	Surtees-Ford	1	accident
r	Takahara	Kojima-Ford	1	accident
r	Andretti,Mario	Lotus-Ford	1	accident

STARTING GRID:

1	Andretti,Mario	13	Patrese
2	Hunt	14	Nilsson
3	Watson	15	Depailler
4	Stuck,H-J.	16	Tambay
5	Laffite	17	Jarier
6	Scheckter,J.	18	Peterson
7	Reutemann	19	Takahara
8	Mass	20	Villeneuve,G.
9	Brambilla	21	Binder
10	Regazzoni	22	Takahashi
11	Hoshino	23	Ribeiro
12	Jones		

Argentine

GRAND PRIX No:	298
DATE:	January 15, 1978
VENUE:	Buenos Aires
POLE LAP:	Andretti,Mario, 1m 47.75s
FASTEST LAP:	Villeneuve,G., 1m 49.76s

Pn	Driver	Car	Laps	Time/Reason
1	Andretti,Mario	Lotus-Ford	52	1h 37m 04.47s
2	Lauda	Brabham-Alfa	52	1h 37m 17.68s
3	Depailler	Tyrrell-Ford	52	1h 37m 18.11s
4	Hunt	McLaren-Ford	52	1h 37m 20.52s
5	Peterson	Lotus-Ford	52	1h 38m 19.32s
6	Tambay	McLaren-Ford	52	1h 38m 24.37s
7	Reutemann	Ferrari	52	1h 38m 27.07s
8	Villeneuve,G.	Ferrari	52	1h 38m 43.35s
9	Fittipaldi,E.	Fittipaldi-Ford	52	1h 38m 45.07s
10	Scheckter,J.	Wolf-Ford	52	1h 38m 47.97s
11	Mass	ATS-Ford	52	1h 38m 53.54s
12	Jarier	ATS-Ford	51	
13	Lunger	McLaren-Ford	51	
14	Pironi	Tyrrell-Ford	51	
15	Regazzoni	Shadow-Ford	51	
16	Laffite	Ligier-Matra	50	engine
17	Stuck,H-J.	Shadow-Ford	50	
18	Brambilla	Surtees-Ford	50	
r	Watson	Brabham-Alfa	41	engine
r	Jones	Williams-Ford	36	fuel vaporisation
r	Ongais	Ensign-Ford	35	rotor arm
r	Leoni	Ensign-Ford	28	engine
r	Merzario	Merzario-Ford	9	differential
r	Keegan	Surtees-Ford	4	overheating

STARTING GRID:

1	Andretti,Mario	13	Mass
2	Reutemann	14	Jones
3	Peterson	15	Scheckter,J.
4	Watson	16	Regazzoni
5	Lauda	17	Fittipaldi,E.
6	Hunt	18	Stuck,H-J.
7	Villeneuve,G.	19	Keegan
8	Laffite	20	Merzario
9	Tambay	21	Ongais
10	Depailler	22	Leoni
11	Jarier	23	Pironi
12	Brambilla	24	Lunger

Brazilian

GRAND PRIX No: 299
DATE: January 29, 1978
VENUE: Rio de Janeiro
POLE LAP: Peterson, 1m 40.45s
FASTEST LAP: Reutemann, 1m 43.07s

Pn	Driver	Car	Laps	Time/Reason
1	Reutemann	Ferrari	63	1h 49m 59.86s
2	Fittipaldi,E.	Fittipaldi-Ford	63	1h 50m 48.99s
3	Lauda	Brabham-Alfa	63	1h 50m 56.88s
4	Andretti,Mario	Lotus-Ford	63	1h 51m 32.98s
5	Regazzoni	Shadow-Ford	62	
6	Pironi	Tyrrell-Ford	62	
7	Mass	ATS-Ford	62	
8	Watson	Brabham-Alfa	61	
9	Laffite	Ligier-Matra	61	
10	Patrese	Arrows-Ford	59	
11	Jones	Williams-Ford	58	
r	Rebaque	Lotus-Ford	40	driver tired
r	Villeneuve,G.	Ferrari	35	accident
r	Tambay	McLaren-Ford	34	accident
r	Stuck,H-J.	Shadow-Ford	25	fuel pump
r	Hunt	McLaren-Ford	25	accident
r	Scheckter,J.	Wolf-Ford	16	suspension
r	Peterson	Lotus-Ford	15	suspension
r	Ongais	Ensign-Ford	13	brakes
r	Lunger	McLaren-Ford	11	overheating
r	Depailler	Tyrrell-Ford	8	accident
r	Keegan	Surtees-Ford	5	accident

STARTING GRID:

1	Peterson	12	Scheckter,J.
2	Hunt	13	Lunger
3	Andretti,Mario	14	Laffite
4	Reutemann	15	Regazzoni
5	Tambay	16	Patrese
6	Villeneuve,G.	17	Pironi
7	Fittipaldi,E.	18	Mass
8	Jones	19	Watson
9	Stuck,H-J.	20	Rebaque
10	Lauda	21	Ongais
11	Depailler	22	Keegan

South African

GRAND PRIX No: 300
DATE: March 4, 1978
VENUE: Kyalami
POLE LAP: Lauda, 1m 14.65s
FASTEST LAP: Andretti,Mario, 1m 17.09s

Pn	Driver	Car	Laps	Time/Reason
1	Peterson	Lotus-Ford	78	1h 42m 15.767s
2	Depailler	Tyrrell-Ford	78	1h 42m 16.233s
3	Watson	Brabham-Alfa	78	1h 42m 20.209s
4	Jones	Williams-Ford	78	1h 42m 54.753s
5	Laffite	Ligier-Matra	78	1h 43m 24.985s
6	Pironi	Tyrrell-Ford	77	
7	Andretti,Mario	Lotus-Ford	77	
8	Jarier	ATS-Ford	77	
9	Stommelen	Arrows-Ford	77	
10	Rebaque	Lotus-Ford	77	
11	Lunger	McLaren-Ford	76	
12	Brambilla	Surtees-Ford	76	
r	Patrese	Arrows-Ford	63	engine
r	Scheckter,J.	Wolf-Ford	59	accident
r	Tambay	McLaren-Ford	56	accident
r	Reutemann	Ferrari	55	accident
r	Villeneuve,G.	Ferrari	55	oil leak
r	Keegan	Surtees-Ford	52	engine
r	Lauda	Brabham-Alfa	52	engine
r	Mass	ATS-Ford	43	engine
r	Merzario	Merzario-Ford	39	suspension
r	Jabouille	Renault	38	engine
r	Rosberg	Theodore-Ford	14	clutch
r	Fittipaldi,E.	Fittipaldi-Ford	8	transmission
r	Cheever	Hesketh-Ford	8	engine
r	Hunt	McLaren-Ford	5	engine

STARTING GRID:

1	Lauda	12	Peterson
2	Andretti,Mario	13	Laffite
3	Hunt	14	Pironi
4	Tambay	15	Mass
5	Scheckter,J.	16	Fittipaldi,E.
6	Jabouille	17	Jarier
7	Patrese	18	Jones
8	Villeneuve,G.	19	Brambilla
9	Reutemann	20	Lunger
10	Watson	21	Rebaque
11	Depailler	22	Stommelen +

US West

GRAND PRIX No: 301
DATE: April 2, 1978
VENUE: Long Beach
POLE LAP: Reutemann, 1m 20.636s
FASTEST LAP: Jones, 1m 22.215s

Pn	Driver	Car	Laps	Time/Reason
1	Reutemann	Ferrari	80	1h 52m 01.301s
2	Andretti,Mario	Lotus-Ford	80	1h 52m 12.362s
3	Depailler	Tyrrell-Ford	80	1h 52m 30.252s
4	Peterson	Lotus-Ford	80	1h 52m 46.904s
5	Laffite	Ligier-Matra	80	1h 53m 24.185s
6	Patrese	Arrows-Ford	79	
7	Jones	Williams-Ford	79	
8	Fittipaldi,E.	Fittipaldi-Ford	79	
9	Stommelen	Arrows-Ford	79	
10	Regazzoni	Shadow-Ford	79	
11	Jarier	ATS-Ford	75	
12	Tambay	McLaren-Ford	74	accident
r	Scheckter,J.	Wolf-Ford	59	accident
r	Brambilla	Surtees-Ford	50	crownwheel and pinion
r	Jabouille	Renault	43	turbocharger
r	Villeneuve,G.	Ferrari	38	accident
r	Lauda	Brabham-Alfa	27	ignition
r	Pironi	Tyrrell-Ford	25	gearbox
r	Merzario	Merzario-Ford	17	gearbox
r	Mass	ATS-Ford	11	brakes
r	Watson	Brabham-Alfa	9	oil tank
r	Hunt	McLaren-Ford	5	accident
dns	Keegan	Surtees-Ford		accident
dns	Stuck,H-J.	Shadow-Ford		accident

STARTING GRID:

1	Reutemann	13	Jabouille
2	Villeneuve,G.	14	Laffite
3	Lauda	15	Fittipaldi,E.
4	Andretti,Mario	16	Mass
5	Watson	17	Brambilla
6	Peterson	18	Stommelen
7	Hunt	19	Jarier
8	Jones	20	Regazzoni
9	Patrese	21	Merzario
10	Scheckter,J.	22	Keegan
11	Tambay	23	Stuck,H-J.
12	Depailler	24	Pironi

Monaco

GRAND PRIX No: 302
DATE: May 7, 1978
VENUE: Monte Carlo
POLE LAP: Reutemann, 1m 28.34s
FASTEST LAP: Lauda, 1m 28.65s

Pn	Driver	Car	Laps	Time/Reason
1	Depailler	Tyrrell-Ford	75	1h 55m 14.66s
2	Lauda	Brabham-Alfa	75	1h 55m 37.11s
3	Scheckter,J.	Wolf-Ford	75	1h 55m 46.95s
4	Watson	Brabham-Alfa	75	1h 55m 48.19s
5	Pironi	Tyrrell-Ford	75	1h 56m 22.72s
6	Patrese	Arrows-Ford	75	1h 56m 23.42s
7	Tambay	McLaren-Ford	74	
8	Reutemann	Ferrari	74	
9	Fittipaldi,E.	Fittipaldi-Ford	74	
10	Jabouille	Renault	71	
11	Andretti,Mario	Lotus-Ford	69	
r	Villeneuve,G.	Ferrari	62	accident
r	Peterson	Lotus-Ford	56	gearbox
r	Hunt	McLaren-Ford	43	anti-roll bar
r	Stommelen	Arrows-Ford	38	driver unwell
r	Jones	Williams-Ford	29	oil leak
r	Ickx	Ensign-Ford	27	brakes
r	Stuck,H-J.	Shadow-Ford	24	steering
r	Laffite	Ligier-Matra	13	gearbox
r	Keegan	Surtees-Ford	8	crownwheel and pinion

STARTING GRID:

1	Reutemann	11	Tambay
2	Watson	12	Jabouille
3	Lauda	13	Pironi
4	Andretti,Mario	14	Patrese
5	Depailler	15	Laffite
6	Hunt	16	Ickx
7	Peterson	17	Stuck,H-J.
8	Villeneuve,G.	18	Keegan
9	Scheckter,J.	19	Stommelen
10	Jones	20	Fittipaldi,E.

Belgian

GRAND PRIX No: 303
DATE: May 21, 1978
VENUE: Zolder
POLE LAP: Andretti,Mario, 1m 20.90s
FASTEST LAP: Peterson, 1m 23.13s

Pn	Driver	Car	Laps	Time/Reason
1	Andretti,Mario	Lotus-Ford	70	1h 39m 52.02s
2	Peterson	Lotus-Ford	70	1h 40m 01.92s
3	Reutemann	Ferrari	70	1h 40m 16.36s
4	Villeneuve,G.	Ferrari	70	1h 40m 39.06s
5	Laffite	Ligier-Matra	69	accident
6	Pironi	Tyrrell-Ford	69	
7	Lunger	McLaren-Ford	69	
8	Giacomelli	McLaren-Ford	69	
9	Arnoux	Martini-Ford	68	
10	Jones	Williams-Ford	68	
11	Mass	ATS-Ford	68	
12	Ickx	Ensign-Ford	64	
13	Brambilla	Surtees-Ford	63	engine
r	Stuck,H-J.	Shadow-Ford	56	spun off
uc	Jabouille	Renault	56	
r	Scheckter,J.	Wolf-Ford	53	accident
r	Depailler	Tyrrell-Ford	51	gearbox
r	Regazzoni	Shadow-Ford	40	differential
r	Patrese	Arrows-Ford	31	suspension
r	Stommelen	Arrows-Ford	26	accident
r	Watson	Brabham-Alfa	18	accident
r	Fittipaldi,E.	Fittipaldi-Ford	0	accident
r	Hunt	McLaren-Ford	0	accident
r	Lauda	Brabham-Alfa	0	accident

STARTING GRID:

1	Andretti,Mario	13	Depailler
2	Reutemann	14	Laffite
3	Lauda	15	Fittipaldi,E.
4	Villeneuve,G.	16	Mass
5	Scheckter,J.	17	Stommelen
6	Hunt	18	Regazzoni
7	Peterson	19	Arnoux
8	Patrese	20	Stuck,H-J.
9	Watson	21	Giacomelli
10	Jabouille	22	Ickx
11	Jones	23	Pironi
12	Brambilla	24	Lunger

Spanish

GRAND PRIX No: 304
DATE: June 4, 1978
VENUE: Jarama
POLE LAP: Andretti,Mario, 1m 16.39s
FASTEST LAP: Andretti,Mario, 1m 20.06s

Pn	Driver	Car	Laps	Time/Reason
1	Andretti,Mario	Lotus-Ford	75	1h 41m 47.06s
2	Peterson	Lotus-Ford	75	1h 42m 06.62s
3	Laffite	Ligier-Matra	75	1h 42m 24.30s
4	Scheckter,J.	Wolf-Ford	75	1h 42m 47.12s
5	Watson	Brabham-Alfa	75	1h 42m 52.98s
6	Hunt	McLaren-Ford	74	
7	Brambilla	Surtees-Ford	74	
8	Jones	Williams-Ford	74	
9	Mass	ATS-Ford	74	
10	Villeneuve,G.	Ferrari	74	
11	Keegan	Surtees-Ford	73	
12	Pironi	Tyrrell-Ford	71	
13	Jabouille	Renault	71	
14	Stommelen	Arrows-Ford	71	
15	Regazzoni	Shadow-Ford	67	fuel system
r	Ickx	Ensign-Ford	64	engine
r	Fittipaldi,E.	Fittipaldi-Ford	62	throttle
r	Reutemann	Ferrari	57	accident
r	Lauda	Brabham-Alfa	56	engine
r	Depailler	Tyrrell-Ford	51	engine
r	Stuck,H-J.	Shadow-Ford	45	suspension
r	Rebaque	Lotus-Ford	21	exhaust
r	Patrese	Arrows-Ford	21	engine
r	Tambay	McLaren-Ford	16	spun off

STARTING GRID:

1	Andretti,Mario	13	Pironi
2	Peterson	14	Tambay
3	Reutemann	15	Fittipaldi,E.
4	Hunt	16	Brambilla
5	Villeneuve,G.	17	Mass
6	Lauda	18	Jones
7	Watson	19	Stommelen
8	Patrese	20	Rebaque
9	Scheckter,J.	21	Ickx
10	Laffite	22	Regazzoni
11	Jabouille	23	Keegan
12	Depailler	24	Stuck,H-J.

Swedish

GRAND PRIX No:	305
DATE:	June 17, 1978
VENUE:	Anderstorp
POLE LAP:	Andretti,Mario, 1m 22.058s
FASTEST LAP:	Lauda, 1m 24.836s

Pn	Driver	Car	Laps	Time/Reason
1	Lauda	Brabham-Alfa	70	1h 41m 00.606s
2	Patrese	Arrows-Ford	70	1h 41m 34.625s
3	Peterson	Lotus-Ford	70	1h 41m 34.711s
4	Tambay	McLaren-Ford	69	
5	Regazzoni	Shadow-Ford	69	
6	Fittipaldi,E.	Fittipaldi-Ford	69	
7	Laffite	Ligier-Matra	69	
8	Hunt	McLaren-Ford	69	
9	Villeneuve,G.	Ferrari	69	
10	Reutemann	Ferrari	69	
11	Stuck,H-J.	Shadow-Ford	68	
12	Rebaque	Lotus-Ford	68	
13	Mass	ATS-Ford	68	
14	Stommelen	Arrows-Ford	67	
15	Rosberg	ATS-Ford	63	
uc	Merzario	Merzario-Ford	62	
r	Andretti,Mario	Lotus-Ford	46	engine
r	Jones	Williams-Ford	46	wheel bearing
r	Depailler	Tyrrell-Ford	42	suspension
r	Jabouille	Renault	28	engine
r	Watson	Brabham-Alfa	19	throttle
r	Scheckter,J.	Wolf-Ford	16	overheating
r	Pironi	Tyrrell-Ford	8	accident
r	Brambilla	Surtees-Ford	7	accident

STARTING GRID:

1	Andretti,Mario	13	Fittipaldi,E.
2	Watson	14	Hunt
3	Lauda	15	Tambay
4	Peterson	16	Regazzoni
5	Patrese	17	Pironi
6	Scheckter,J.	18	Brambilla
7	Villeneuve,G.	19	Mass
8	Reutemann	20	Stuck,H-J.
9	Jones	21	Rebaque
10	Jabouille	22	Merzario
11	Laffite	23	Rosberg
12	Depailler	24	Stommelen

French

GRAND PRIX No:	306
DATE:	July 2, 1978
VENUE:	Paul Ricard
POLE LAP:	Watson, 1m 44.41s
FASTEST LAP:	Reutemann, 1m 48.56s

Pn	Driver	Car	Laps	Time/Reason
1	Andretti,Mario	Lotus-Ford	54	1h 38m 51.92s
2	Peterson	Lotus-Ford	54	1h 38m 54.85s
3	Hunt	McLaren-Ford	54	1h 39m 11.72s
4	Watson	Brabham-Alfa	54	1h 39m 28.80s
5	Jones	Williams-Ford	54	1h 39m 33.73s
6	Scheckter,J.	Wolf-Ford	54	1h 39m 46.45s
7	Laffite	Ligier-Matra	54	1h 39m 46.66s
8	Patrese	Arrows-Ford	54	1h 40m 16.80s
9	Tambay	McLaren-Ford	54	1h 40m 18.98s
10	Pironi	Tyrrell-Ford	54	1h 40m 21.90s
11	Stuck,H-J.	Shadow-Ford	53	
12	Villeneuve,G.	Ferrari	53	
13	Mass	ATS-Ford	53	
14	Arnoux	Martini-Ford	53	
15	Stommelen	Arrows-Ford	53	
16	Rosberg	ATS-Ford	52	
17	Brambilla	Surtees-Ford	52	
18	Reutemann	Ferrari	49	
r	Lunger	McLaren-Ford	45	engine
r	Fittipaldi,E.	Fittipaldi-Ford	43	suspension
r	Keegan	Surtees-Ford	40	engine
r	Giacomelli	McLaren-Ford	28	engine
r	Depailler	Tyrrell-Ford	10	engine
r	Lauda	Brabham-Alfa	10	engine
r	Regazzoni	Shadow-Ford	4	electrical
r	Jabouille	Renault	1	engine

STARTING GRID:

1	Watson	12	Patrese
2	Andretti,Mario	13	Depailler
3	Lauda	14	Jones
4	Hunt	15	Fittipaldi,E.
5	Peterson	16	Pironi
6	Tambay	17	Regazzoni
7	Scheckter,J.	18	Arnoux
8	Reutemann	19	Brambilla
9	Villeneuve,G.	20	Stuck,H-J.
10	Laffite	21	Stommelen
11	Jabouille	22	Giacomelli +

British

GRAND PRIX No:	307
DATE:	July 16, 1978
VENUE:	Brands Hatch
POLE LAP:	Peterson, 1m 16.80s
FASTEST LAP:	Lauda, 1m 18.60s

Pn	Driver	Car	Laps	Time/Reason
1	Reutemann	Ferrari	76	1h 42m 12.39s
2	Lauda	Brabham-Alfa	76	1h 42m 13.62s
3	Watson	Brabham-Alfa	76	1h 42m 49.64s
4	Depailler	Tyrrell-Ford	76	1h 43m 25.66s
5	Stuck,H-J.	Shadow-Ford	75	
6	Tambay	McLaren-Ford	75	
7	Giacomelli	McLaren-Ford	75	
8	Lunger	McLaren-Ford	75	
9	Brambilla	Surtees-Ford	75	
10	Laffite	Ligier-Matra	73	
uc	Mass	ATS-Ford	66	
r	Rosberg	ATS-Ford	59	suspension
r	Regazzoni	Shadow-Ford	49	gearbox
r	Jabouille	Renault	46	engine
r	Patrese	Arrows-Ford	40	suspension
r	Pironi	Tyrrell-Ford	40	gearbox
r	Scheckter,J.	Wolf-Ford	36	gearbox
r	Fittipaldi,E.	Fittipaldi-Ford	32	engine
r	Merzario	Merzario-Ford	32	fuel pump
r	Daly	Ensign-Ford	30	lost wheel
r	Andretti,Mario	Lotus-Ford	28	engine
r	Jones	Williams-Ford	26	driveshaft
r	Villeneuve,G.	Ferrari	19	driveshaft
r	Rebaque	Lotus-Ford	15	gearbox
r	Hunt	McLaren-Ford	7	accident
r	Peterson	Lotus-Ford	6	fuel leak

STARTING GRID:

1	Peterson	12	Jabouille
2	Andretti,Mario	13	Villeneuve,G.
3	Scheckter,J.	14	Hunt
4	Lauda	15	Daly
5	Patrese	16	Giacomelli
6	Jones	17	Regazzoni
7	Laffite	18	Stuck,H-J.
8	Reutemann	19	Pironi
9	Watson	20	Tambay
10	Depailler	21	Rebaque
11	Fittipaldi,E.	22	Rosberg +

German

GRAND PRIX No:	308
DATE:	July 30, 1978
VENUE:	Hockenheim
POLE LAP:	Andretti,Mario, 1m 51.90s
FASTEST LAP:	Peterson, 1m 55.62s

Pn	Driver	Car	Laps	Time/Reason
1	Andretti,Mario	Lotus-Ford	45	1h 28m 00.90s
2	Scheckter,J.	Wolf-Ford	45	1h 28m 16.25s
3	Laffite	Ligier-Matra	45	1h 28m 28.91s
4	Fittipaldi,E.	Fittipaldi-Ford	45	1h 28m 37.78s
5	Pironi	Tyrrell-Ford	45	1h 28m 58.16s
6	Rebaque	Lotus-Ford	45	1h 29m 38.76s
7	Watson	Brabham-Alfa	45	1h 29m 40.43s
8	Villeneuve,G.	Ferrari	45	1h 29m 57.77s
9	Patrese	Arrows-Ford	44	
10	Rosberg	Wolf-Ford	42	
dq	Stommelen	Arrows-Ford	42	wrong way to pits
11	Ertl	Ensign-Ford	41	engine
r	Peterson	Lotus-Ford	36	gearbox
dq	Hunt	McLaren-Ford	34	wrong way to pits
r	Jones	Williams-Ford	31	fuel vaporisation
r	Piquet	Ensign-Ford	31	engine
r	Brambilla	Surtees-Ford	24	fuel vaporisation
r	Tambay	McLaren-Ford	16	puncture
r	Reutemann	Ferrari	14	fuel vaporisation
r	Lauda	Brabham-Alfa	11	engine
r	Jabouille	Renault	5	engine
r	Stuck,H-J.	Shadow-Ford	1	accident
r	Mass	ATS-Ford	1	accident
r	Depailler	Tyrrell-Ford	0	accident

STARTING GRID:

1	Andretti,Mario	13	Depailler
2	Peterson	14	Patrese
3	Lauda	15	Villeneuve,G.
4	Scheckter,J.	16	Pironi
5	Watson	17	Stommelen
6	Jones	18	Rebaque
7	Laffite	19	Rosberg
8	Hunt	20	Brambilla
9	Jabouille	21	Piquet
10	Fittipaldi,E.	22	Mass
11	Tambay	23	Ertl
12	Reutemann	24	Stuck,H-J.

Austrian

GRAND PRIX No: 309
DATE: August 13, 1978
VENUE: Osterreichring
POLE LAP: Peterson, 1m 37.71s
FASTEST LAP: Peterson, 1m 43.12s

Pn	Driver	Car	Laps	Time/Reason
1	Peterson	Lotus-Ford	54	1h 41m 21.57s
2	Depailler	Tyrrell-Ford	54	1h 42m 09.01s
3	Villeneuve,G.	Ferrari	54	1h 43m 01.33s
4	Fittipaldi,E.	Fittipaldi-Ford	53	
5	Laffite	Ligier-Matra	53	
6	Brambilla	Surtees-Ford	53	
7	Watson	Brabham-Alfa	53	
8	Lunger	McLaren-Ford	52	
9	Arnoux	Martini-Ford	52	
uc	Rosberg	Wolf-Ford	47	
uc	Regazzoni	Shadow-Ford	47	
dq	Daly	Ensign-Ford	43	push start
r	Tambay	McLaren-Ford	40	accident
r	Stuck,H-J.	Shadow-Ford	33	accident
r	Jabouille	Renault	31	gearbox
r	Lauda	Brabham-Alfa	28	accident
dq	Reutemann	Ferrari	27	push start
r	Pironi	Tyrrell-Ford	20	accident
r	Hunt	McLaren-Ford	8	accident
r	Jones	Williams-Ford	7	accident
r	Ertl	Ensign-Ford	6	accident
r	Patrese	Arrows-Ford	6	accident
r	Scheckter,J.	Wolf-Ford	3	accident
r	Rebaque	Lotus-Ford	1	clutch
r	Piquet	McLaren-Ford	2	accident
r	Andretti,Mario	Lotus-Ford	0	accident

STARTING GRID:

1	Peterson	11	Villeneuve,G.
2	Andretti,Mario	12	Lauda
3	Jabouille	13	Depailler
4	Reutemann	14	Tambay
5	Laffite	15	Jones
6	Fittipaldi,E.	16	Patrese
7	Scheckter,J.	17	Lunger
8	Hunt	18	Rebaque
9	Pironi	19	Daly
10	Watson	20	Piquet +

Dutch

GRAND PRIX No: 310
DATE: August 27, 1978
VENUE: Zandvoort
POLE LAP: Andretti,Mario, 1m 16.36s
FASTEST LAP: Lauda, 1m 19.57s

Pn	Driver	Car	Laps	Time/Reason
1	Andretti,Mario	Lotus-Ford	75	1h 41m 04.23s
2	Peterson	Lotus-Ford	75	1h 41m 04.55s
3	Lauda	Brabham-Alfa	75	1h 41m 16.44s
4	Watson	Brabham-Alfa	75	1h 41m 25.15s
5	Fittipaldi,E.	Fittipaldi-Ford	75	1h 41m 25.73s
6	Villeneuve,G.	Ferrari	75	1h 41m 50.18s
7	Reutemann	Ferrari	75	1h 42m 04.73s
8	Laffite	Ligier-Matra	74	
9	Tambay	McLaren-Ford	74	
10	Hunt	McLaren-Ford	74	
11	Rebaque	Lotus-Ford	74	
12	Scheckter,J.	Wolf-Ford	73	
r	Giacomelli	McLaren-Ford	60	spun off
r	Stuck,H-J.	Shadow-Ford	56	differential
r	Arnoux	Martini-Ford	40	rear wing
r	Merzario	Merzario-Ford	40	engine
dq	Brambilla	Surtees-Ford	37	push start
r	Jabouille	Renault	35	engine
r	Lunger	McLaren-Ford	35	engine
r	Rosberg	Wolf-Ford	21	throttle
r	Jones	Williams-Ford	17	throttle cable
r	Piquet	McLaren-Ford	16	driveshaft
r	Depailler	Tyrrell-Ford	13	engine
r	Daly	Ensign-Ford	10	driveshaft
r	Patrese	Arrows-Ford	0	accident
r	Pironi	Tyrrell-Ford	0	accident
dns	Keegan	Surtees-Ford		broken hand

STARTING GRID:

1	Andretti,Mario	11	Jones
2	Peterson	12	Depailler
3	Lauda	13	Patrese
4	Reutemann	14	Tambay
5	Villeneuve,G.	15	Scheckter,J.
6	Laffite	16	Daly
7	Hunt	17	Pironi
8	Watson	18	Stuck,H-J.
9	Jabouille	19	Giacomelli
10	Fittipaldi,E.	20	Rebaque +

Italian

GRAND PRIX No:	311
DATE:	September 10, 1978
VENUE:	Monza
POLE LAP:	Andretti,Mario, 1m 37.520s
FASTEST LAP:	Andretti,Mario, 1m 38.230s

Pn	Driver	Car	Laps	Time/Reason
1	Lauda	Brabham-Alfa	40	1h 07m 04.53s
2	Watson	Brabham-Alfa	40	1h 07m 06.02s
3	Reutemann	Ferrari	40	1h 07m 25.01s
4	Laffite	Ligier-Matra	40	1h 07m 42.07s
5	Tambay	McLaren-Ford	40	1h 07m 44.93s
6	Andretti,Mario	Lotus-Ford	40	1h 07m 50.87s *
7	Villeneuve,G.	Ferrari	40	1h 07m 53.02s *
8	Fittipaldi,E.	Fittipaldi-Ford	40	1h 07m 59.78s
9	Piquet	McLaren-Ford	40	1h 08m 11.37s
10	Daly	Ensign-Ford	40	1h 08m 13.65s
11	Depailler	Tyrrell-Ford	40	1h 08m 21.11s
12	Scheckter,J.	Wolf-Ford	39	
13	Jones	Williams-Ford	39	
14	Giacomelli	McLaren-Ford	39	
uc	Regazzoni	Shadow-Ford	33	
r	Patrese	Arrows-Ford	29	engine
r	Hunt	McLaren-Ford	19	distributor
r	Merzario	Merzario-Ford	14	engine
r	Jabouille	Renault	6	engine
r	Brambilla	Surtees-Ford	0	accident
r	Lunger	McLaren-Ford	0	accident
r	Peterson	Lotus-Ford	0	fatal accident
r	Pironi	Tyrrell-Ford	0	accident
r	Stuck,H-J.	Shadow-Ford	0	accident

STARTING GRID:

1	Andretti,Mario	13	Fittipaldi,E.
2	Villeneuve,G.	14	Pironi
3	Jabouille	15	Regazzoni
4	Lauda	16	Depailler
5	Peterson	17	Stuck,H-J.
6	Jones	18	Daly
7	Watson	19	Tambay
8	Laffite	20	Giacomelli
9	Scheckter,J.	21	Lunger
10	Hunt	22	Merzario
11	Reutemann	23	Brambilla
12	Patrese	24	Piquet

US East

GRAND PRIX No:	312
DATE:	October 1, 1978
VENUE:	Watkins Glen
POLE LAP:	Andretti,Mario, 1m 38.114s
FASTEST LAP:	Jarier, 1m 39.557s

Pn	Driver	Car	Laps	Time/Reason
1	Reutemann	Ferrari	59	1h 40m 48.800s
2	Jones	Williams-Ford	59	1h 41m 08.539s
3	Scheckter,J.	Wolf-Ford	59	1h 41m 34.501s
4	Jabouille	Renault	59	1h 42m 13.807s
5	Fittipaldi,E.	Fittipaldi-Ford	59	1h 42m 16.889s
6	Tambay	McLaren-Ford	59	1h 42m 30.010s
7	Hunt	McLaren-Ford	58	
8	Daly	Ensign-Ford	58	
9	Arnoux	Surtees-Ford	58	
10	Pironi	Tyrrell-Ford	58	
11	Laffite	Ligier-Matra	58	
12	Rahal	Wolf-Ford	58	
13	Lunger	Ensign-Ford	58	
14	Regazzoni	Shadow-Ford	56	
15	Jarier	Lotus-Ford	55	out of fuel
16	Stommelen	Arrows-Ford	54	
r	Merzario	Merzario-Ford	46	gearbox
r	Bleekemolen	ATS-Ford	43	oil pump
r	Lauda	Brabham-Alfa	28	engine
r	Andretti,Mario	Lotus-Ford	27	engine
r	Watson	Brabham-Alfa	25	engine
r	Depailler	Tyrrell-Ford	23	wheel
r	Villeneuve,G.	Ferrari	22	engine
r	Rosberg	ATS-Ford	21	gear linkage
r	Stuck,H-J.	Shadow-Ford	1	fuel pump
r	Rebaque	Lotus-Ford	0	clutch

STARTING GRID:

1	Andretti,Mario	12	Depailler
2	Reutemann	13	Fittipaldi,E.
3	Jones	14	Stuck,H-J.
4	Villeneuve,G.	15	Rosberg
5	Lauda	16	Pironi
6	Hunt	17	Regazzoni
7	Watson	18	Tambay
8	Jarier	19	Daly
9	Jabouille	20	Rahal
10	Laffite	21	Arnoux
11	Scheckter,J.	22	Stommelen +

Canadian

GRAND PRIX No:	313
DATE:	October 8, 1978
VENUE:	Montreal
POLE LAP:	Jarier, 1m 38.015s
FASTEST LAP:	Jones, 1m 38.072s

Pn	Driver	Car	Laps	Time/Reason
1	Villeneuve,G.	Ferrari	70	1h 57m 49.196s
2	Scheckter,J.	Wolf-Ford	70	1h 58m 02.568s
3	Reutemann	Ferrari	70	1h 58m 08.604s
4	Patrese	Arrows-Ford	70	1h 58m 13.863s
5	Depailler	Tyrrell-Ford	70	1h 58m 17.754s
6	Daly	Ensign-Ford	70	1h 58m 43.672s
7	Pironi	Tyrrell-Ford	70	1h 59m 10.446s
8	Tambay	McLaren-Ford	70	1h 59m 15.756s
9	Jones	Williams-Ford	70	1h 59m 18.138s
10	Andretti,Mario	Lotus-Ford	69	
11	Piquet	Brabham-Alfa	69	
12	Jabouille	Renault	65	
uc	Rosberg	ATS-Ford	58	
r	Laffite	Ligier-Matra	52	transmission
r	Hunt	McLaren-Ford	51	accident
r	Jarier	Lotus-Ford	49	cooler
r	Arnoux	Surtees-Ford	37	engine
r	Rahal	Wolf-Ford	16	fuel system
r	Watson	Brabham-Alfa	8	accident
r	Lauda	Brabham-Alfa	5	accident
r	Stuck,H-J.	Shadow-Ford	1	accident
r	Fittipaldi,E.	Fittipaldi-Ford	0	accident

STARTING GRID:

1	Jarier	12	Patrese
2	Scheckter,J.	13	Depailler
3	Villeneuve,G.	14	Piquet
4	Watson	15	Daly
5	Jones	16	Arnoux
6	Fittipaldi,E.	17	Tambay
7	Lauda	18	Pironi
8	Stuck,H-J.	19	Hunt
9	Andretti,Mario	20	Rahal
10	Laffite	21	Rosberg
11	Reutemann	22	Jabouille

Argentine

GRAND PRIX No:	314
DATE:	January 21, 1979
VENUE:	Buenos Aires
POLE LAP:	Laffite, 1m 44.20s
FASTEST LAP:	Laffite, 1m 46.91s

Pn	Driver	Car	Laps	Time/Reason
1	Laffite	Ligier-Ford	53	1h 36m 03.21s
2	Reutemann	Lotus-Ford	53	1h 36m 18.15s
3	Watson	McLaren-Ford	53	1h 37m 32.02s
4	Depailler	Ligier-Ford	53	1h 37m 44.93s
5	Andretti,Mario	Lotus-Ford	52	
6	Fittipaldi,E.	Fittipaldi-Ford	52	
7	de Angelis	Shadow-Ford	52	
8	Mass	Arrows-Ford	51	
9	Jones	Williams-Ford	51	
10	Regazzoni	Williams-Ford	51	
11	Daly	Ensign-Ford	51	
12	Villeneuve,G.	Ferrari	48	engine
r	Rebaque	Lotus-Ford	46	suspension
r	Lammers	Shadow-Ford	42	broken cv joint
r	Hunt	Wolf-Ford	41	electrical
r	Jarier	Tyrrell-Ford	15	engine
r	Jabouille	Renault	15	engine
r	Lauda	Brabham-Alfa	8	fuel pressure
r	Arnoux	Renault	6	engine
r	Scheckter,J.	Ferrari	0	accident
r	Pironi	Tyrrell-Ford	0	accident
r	Tambay	McLaren-Ford	0	accident
r	Piquet	Brabham-Alfa	0	accident
r	Merzario	Merzario-Ford	0	accident

STARTING GRID:

1	Laffite	13	Mass
2	Depailler	14	Jones
3	Reutemann	15	de Angelis
4	Jarier	16	Regazzoni
5	Scheckter,J.	17	Hunt
6	Watson	18	Rebaque
7	Andretti,Mario	19	Piquet
8	Pironi	20	Lammers
9	Tambay	21	Merzario
10	Villeneuve,G.	22	Lauda
11	Fittipaldi,E.	23	Daly
12	Jabouille	24	Arnoux

Brazilian

GRAND PRIX No: 315
DATE: February 4, 1979
VENUE: Interlagos
POLE LAP: Laffite, 2m 23.07s
FASTEST LAP: Laffite, 2m 28.76s

Pn	Driver	Car	Laps	Time/Reason
1	Laffite	Ligier-Ford	40	1h 40m 09.64s
2	Depailler	Ligier-Ford	40	1h 40m 14.92s
3	Reutemann	Lotus-Ford	40	1h 40m 53.78s
4	Pironi	Tyrrell-Ford	40	1h 41m 35.52s
5	Villeneuve,G.	Ferrari	39	
6	Scheckter,J.	Ferrari	39	
7	Mass	Arrows-Ford	39	
8	Watson	McLaren-Ford	39	
9	Patrese	Arrows-Ford	39	
10	Jabouille	Renault	39	
11	Fittipaldi,E.	Fittipaldi-Ford	39	
12	de Angelis	Shadow-Ford	39	
13	Daly	Ensign-Ford	39	
14	Lammers	Shadow-Ford	39	
15	Regazzoni	Williams-Ford	38	
r	Jones	Williams-Ford	33	fuel pressure
r	Stuck,H-J.	ATS-Ford	31	steering wheel
r	Arnoux	Renault	28	spun off
r	Tambay	McLaren-Ford	7	accident
r	Hunt	Wolf-Ford	7	steering rack
r	Piquet	Brabham-Alfa	5	accident
r	Lauda	Brabham-Alfa	5	gear linkage
r	Andretti,Mario	Lotus-Ford	2	misfiring
dns	Jarier	Tyrrell-Ford		electrical

STARTING GRID:

1	Laffite	13	Jones
2	Depailler	14	Watson
3	Reutemann	15	Jarier
4	Andretti,Mario	16	Patrese
5	Villeneuve,G.	17	Regazzoni
6	Scheckter,J.	18	Tambay
7	Jabouille	19	Mass
8	Pironi	20	de Angelis
9	Fittipaldi,E.	21	Lammers
10	Hunt	22	Piquet
11	Arnoux	23	Daly
12	Lauda	24	Stuck,H-J.

South African

GRAND PRIX No: 316
DATE: March 3, 1979
VENUE: Kyalami
POLE LAP: Jabouille, 1m 11.800s
FASTEST LAP: Villeneuve,G., 1m 14.412s

Pn	Driver	Car	Laps	Time/Reason
1	Villeneuve,G.	Ferrari	78	1h 41m 49.96s
2	Scheckter,J.	Ferrari	78	1h 41m 53.38s
3	Jarier	Tyrrell-Ford	78	1h 42m 12.07s
4	Andretti,Mario	Lotus-Ford	78	1h 42m 17.84s
5	Reutemann	Lotus-Ford	78	1h 42m 56.93s
6	Lauda	Brabham-Alfa	77	
7	Piquet	Brabham-Alfa	77	
8	Hunt	Wolf-Ford	77	
9	Regazzoni	Williams-Ford	76	
10	Tambay	McLaren-Ford	75	
11	Patrese	Arrows-Ford	75	
12	Mass	Arrows-Ford	74	
13	Fittipaldi,E.	Fittipaldi-Ford	74	
14	Rebaque	Lotus-Ford	71	engine
r	Arnoux	Renault	67	puncture
r	Jones	Williams-Ford	63	suspension
r	Watson	McLaren-Ford	61	ignition
r	Stuck,H-J.	ATS-Ford	57	accident
r	Jabouille	Renault	47	engine
r	Laffite	Ligier-Ford	45	accident
r	Pironi	Tyrrell-Ford	25	throttle
r	de Angelis	Shadow-Ford	16	accident
r	Depailler	Ligier-Ford	4	accident
r	Lammers	Shadow-Ford	2	accident

STARTING GRID:

1	Jabouille	13	Hunt
2	Scheckter,J.	14	Watson
3	Villeneuve,G.	15	de Angelis
4	Lauda	16	Patrese
5	Depailler	17	Tambay
6	Laffite	18	Fittipaldi,E.
7	Pironi	19	Jones
8	Andretti,Mario	20	Mass
9	Jarier	21	Lammers
10	Arnoux	22	Regazzoni
11	Reutemann	23	Rebaque
12	Piquet	24	Stuck,H-J.

US West

GRAND PRIX No: 317
DATE: April 8, 1979
VENUE: Long Beach
POLE LAP: Villeneuve,G., 1m 18.825s
FASTEST LAP: Villeneuve,G., 1m 21.200s

Pn	Driver	Car	Laps	Time/Reason
1	Villeneuve,G.	Ferrari	80	1h 50m 25.40s
2	Scheckter,J.	Ferrari	80	1h 50m 54.78s
3	Jones	Williams-Ford	80	1h 51m 25.09s
4	Andretti,Mario	Lotus-Ford	80	1h 51m 29.73s
5	Depailler	Ligier-Ford	80	1h 51m 48.92s
6	Jarier	Tyrrell-Ford	79	
7	de Angelis	Shadow-Ford	78	
8	Piquet	Brabham-Alfa	78	
9	Mass	Arrows-Ford	78	
dq	Pironi	Tyrrell-Ford	72	push start
r	Rebaque	Lotus-Ford	71	accident
r	Daly	Ensign-Ford	69	accident
r	Watson	McLaren-Ford	62	injection
dq	Stuck,H-J.	ATS-Ford	49	push start
r	Regazzoni	Williams-Ford	48	engine
r	Lammers	Shadow-Ford	47	suspension
r	Patrese	Arrows-Ford	40	brakes
r	Reutemann	Lotus-Ford	21	driveshaft
r	Fittipaldi,E.	Fittipaldi-Ford	19	driveshaft
r	Merzario	Merzario-Ford	13	engine
r	Laffite	Ligier-Ford	8	brakes
r	Hunt	Wolf-Ford	0	driveshaft
r	Lauda	Brabham-Alfa	0	accident
r	Tambay	McLaren-Ford	0	accident
dns	Jabouille	Renault		injured
dns	Arnoux	Renault		withdrew

STARTING GRID:

1	Villeneuve,G.	12	Piquet
2	Reutemann	13	Mass
3	Scheckter,J.	14	Lammers
4	Depailler	15	Regazzoni
5	Laffite	16	Fittipaldi,E.
6	Andretti,Mario	17	Pironi
7	Jarier	18	Watson
8	Hunt	19	Tambay
9	Patrese	20	Jabouille
10	Jones	21	Stuck,H-J.
11	Lauda	22	Arnoux +

Spanish

GRAND PRIX No: 318
DATE: April 29, 1979
VENUE: Jarama
POLE LAP: Laffite, 1m 14.50s
FASTEST LAP: Villeneuve,G., 1m 16.44s

Pn	Driver	Car	Laps	Time/Reason
1	Depailler	Ligier-Ford	75	1h 39m 11.84s
2	Reutemann	Lotus-Ford	75	1h 39m 32.78s
3	Andretti,Mario	Lotus-Ford	75	1h 39m 39.15s
4	Scheckter,J.	Ferrari	75	1h 39m 40.52s
5	Jarier	Tyrrell-Ford	75	1h 39m 42.23s
6	Pironi	Tyrrell-Ford	75	1h 40m 00.27s
7	Villeneuve,G.	Ferrari	75	1h 40m 04.15s
8	Mass	Arrows-Ford	75	1h 40m 26.68s
9	Arnoux	Renault	74	
10	Patrese	Arrows-Ford	74	
11	Fittipaldi,E.	Fittipaldi-Ford	74	
12	Lammers	Shadow-Ford	73	
13	Tambay	McLaren-Ford	72	
14	Stuck,H-J.	ATS-Ford	69	
r	Lauda	Brabham-Alfa	63	water leak
r	Rebaque	Lotus-Ford	58	engine
r	Jones	Williams-Ford	54	gear selection
r	de Angelis	Shadow-Ford	52	engine
r	Regazzoni	Williams-Ford	32	engine
r	Hunt	Wolf-Ford	26	brakes
r	Watson	McLaren-Ford	21	engine
r	Jabouille	Renault	21	turbo
r	Laffite	Ligier-Ford	15	engine
r	Piquet	Brabham-Alfa	15	fuel metering

STARTING GRID:

1	Laffite	13	Jones
2	Depailler	14	Regazzoni
3	Villeneuve,G.	15	Hunt
4	Andretti,Mario	16	Patrese
5	Scheckter,J.	17	Mass
6	Lauda	18	Watson
7	Piquet	19	Fittipaldi,E.
8	Reutemann	20	Tambay
9	Jabouille	21	Stuck,H-J.
10	Pironi	22	de Angelis
11	Arnoux	23	Rebaque
12	Jarier	24	Lammers

Belgian

GRAND PRIX No: 319
DATE: May 13, 1979
VENUE: Zolder
POLE LAP: Laffite, 1m 21.13s
FASTEST LAP: Villeneuve,G., 1m 23.09s

Pn	Driver	Car	Laps	Time/Reason
1	Scheckter,J.	Ferrari	70	1h 39m 59.53s
2	Laffite	Ligier-Ford	70	1h 40m 14.89s
3	Pironi	Tyrrell-Ford	70	1h 40m 34.70s
4	Reutemann	Lotus-Ford	70	1h 40m 46.02s
5	Patrese	Arrows-Ford	70	1h 41m 03.84s
6	Watson	McLaren-Ford	70	1h 41m 05.38s
7	Villeneuve,G.	Ferrari	69	
8	Stuck,H-J.	ATS-Ford	69	
9	Fittipaldi,E.	Fittipaldi-Ford	68	
10	Lammers	Shadow-Ford	68	
11	Jarier	Tyrrell-Ford	67	
r	Depailler	Ligier-Ford	46	accident
r	Hunt	Wolf-Ford	40	accident
r	Jones	Williams-Ford	39	electrical
r	Andretti,Mario	Lotus-Ford	27	brakes
r	Piquet	Brabham-Alfa	23	engine
r	Lauda	Brabham-Alfa	23	engine
r	Arnoux	Renault	22	turbocharger
r	Giacomelli	Alfa Romeo	21	accident
r	de Angelis	Shadow-Ford	21	accident
r	Mass	Arrows-Ford	17	spun off
r	Rebaque	Lotus-Ford	13	driveshaft
r	Jabouille	Renault	13	turbocharger
r	Regazzoni	Williams-Ford	1	accident

STARTING GRID:

1	Laffite	13	Lauda
2	Depailler	14	Giacomelli
3	Piquet	15	Rebaque
4	Jones	16	Patrese
5	Andretti,Mario	17	Jabouille
6	Villeneuve,G.	18	Arnoux
7	Scheckter,J.	19	Watson
8	Regazzoni	20	Stuck,H-J.
9	Hunt	21	Lammers
10	Reutemann	22	Mass
11	Jarier	23	Fittipaldi,E.
12	Pironi	24	de Angelis

Monaco

GRAND PRIX No: 320
DATE: May 27, 1979
VENUE: Monte Carlo
POLE LAP: Scheckter,J., 1m 26.45s
FASTEST LAP: Depailler, 1m 28.82s

Pn	Driver	Car	Laps	Time/Reason
1	Scheckter,J.	Ferrari	76	1h 55m 22.48s
2	Regazzoni	Williams-Ford	76	1h 55m 22.92s
3	Reutemann	Lotus-Ford	76	1h 55m 31.05s
4	Watson	McLaren-Ford	76	1h 56m 03.79s
5	Depailler	Ligier-Ford	74	engine
6	Mass	Arrows-Ford	69	
7	Piquet	Brabham-Alfa	68	transmission
8	Jabouille	Renault	68	
r	Laffite	Ligier-Ford	55	gearbox
r	Villeneuve,G.	Ferrari	54	transmission
r	Jones	Williams-Ford	43	accident
r	Jarier	Tyrrell-Ford	34	suspension
r	Stuck,H-J.	ATS-Ford	30	wheel
r	Lauda	Brabham-Alfa	21	accident
r	Pironi	Tyrrell-Ford	21	accident
r	Andretti,Mario	Lotus-Ford	21	suspension
r	Fittipaldi,E.	Fittipaldi-Ford	17	engine
r	Arnoux	Renault	8	accident
r	Hunt	Wolf-Ford	4	transmission
r	Patrese	Arrows-Ford	4	suspension

STARTING GRID:

1	Scheckter,J.	11	Reutemann
2	Villeneuve,G.	12	Stuck,H-J.
3	Depailler	13	Andretti,Mario
4	Lauda	14	Watson
5	Laffite	15	Patrese
6	Jarier	16	Regazzoni
7	Pironi	17	Fittipaldi,E.
8	Mass	18	Piquet
9	Jones	19	Arnoux
10	Hunt	20	Jabouille

French

GRAND PRIX No: 321
DATE: July 1, 1979
VENUE: Dijon
POLE LAP: Jabouille, 1m 07.19s
FASTEST LAP: Arnoux, 1m 09.16s

Pn	Driver	Car	Laps	Time/Reason
1	Jabouille	Renault	80	1h 35m 20.42s
2	Villeneuve,G.	Ferrari	80	1h 35m 35.01s
3	Arnoux	Renault	80	1h 35m 35.25s
4	Jones	Williams-Ford	80	1h 35m 57.03s
5	Jarier	Tyrrell-Ford	80	1h 36m 24.93s
6	Regazzoni	Williams-Ford	80	1h 36m 25.93s
7	Scheckter,J.	Ferrari	79	
8	Laffite	Ligier-Ford	79	
9	Rosberg	Wolf-Ford	79	
10	Tambay	McLaren-Ford	78	
11	Watson	McLaren-Ford	78	
12	Rebaque	Lotus-Ford	78	
13	Reutemann	Lotus-Ford	77	accident
14	Patrese	Arrows-Ford	77	
15	Mass	Arrows-Ford	75	
16	de Angelis	Shadow-Ford	75	
17	Giacomelli	Alfa Romeo	75	
18	Lammers	Shadow-Ford	73	
r	Pironi	Tyrrell-Ford	71	suspension
r	Fittipaldi,E.	Fittipaldi-Ford	53	engine
r	Piquet	Brabham-Alfa	52	accident
r	Andretti,Mario	Lotus-Ford	51	brakes
r	Ickx	Ligier-Ford	45	engine
r	Lauda	Brabham-Alfa	23	spun off
dns	Stuck,H-J.	ATS-Ford		dispute

STARTING GRID:

1	Jabouille	14	Ickx
2	Arnoux	15	Watson
3	Villeneuve,G.	16	Rosberg
4	Piquet	17	Giacomelli
5	Scheckter,J.	18	Fittipaldi,E.
6	Lauda	19	Patrese
7	Jones	20	Tambay
8	Laffite	21	Lammers
9	Regazzoni	22	Mass
10	Jarier	23	Stuck,H-J.
11	Pironi	24	Rebaque
12	Andretti,Mario	25	de Angelis
13	Reutemann		

British

GRAND PRIX No: 322
DATE: July 14, 1979
VENUE: Silverstone
POLE LAP: Jones, 1m 11.88s
FASTEST LAP: Regazzoni, 1m 14.40s

Pn	Driver	Car	Laps	Time/Reason
1	Regazzoni	Williams-Ford	68	1h 26m 11.17s
2	Arnoux	Renault	68	1h 26m 35.45s
3	Jarier	Tyrrell-Ford	67	
4	Watson	McLaren-Ford	67	
5	Scheckter,J.	Ferrari	67	
6	Ickx	Ligier-Ford	67	
7	Tambay	McLaren-Ford	66	out of fuel
8	Reutemann	Lotus-Ford	66	
9	Rebaque	Lotus-Ford	66	
10	Pironi	Tyrrell-Ford	66	
11	Lammers	Shadow-Ford	65	
12	de Angelis	Shadow-Ford	65	
13	Gaillard	Ensign-Ford	65	
14	Villeneuve,G.	Ferrari	63	fuel vaporisation
r	Mass	Arrows-Ford	36	gearbox
r	Patrese	Arrows-Ford	45	gearbox
r	Rosberg	Wolf-Ford	44	fuel system
r	Laffite	Ligier-Ford	44	engine
r	Jones	Williams-Ford	38	water pump
r	Fittipaldi,E.	Fittipaldi-Ford	25	engine
r	Jabouille	Renault	21	engine
r	Lauda	Brabham-Alfa	12	brakes
r	Andretti,Mario	Lotus-Ford	3	wheel
r	Piquet	Brabham-Alfa	1	spun off

STARTING GRID:

1	Jones	13	Villeneuve,G.
2	Jabouille	14	Rosberg
3	Piquet	15	Pironi
4	Regazzoni	16	Jarier
5	Arnoux	17	Ickx
6	Lauda	18	Tambay
7	Watson	19	Patrese
8	Reutemann	20	Mass
9	Andretti,Mario	21	Lammers
10	Laffite	22	Fittipaldi,E.
11	Scheckter,J.	23	Gaillard
12	de Angelis	24	Rebaque

German

GRAND PRIX No: 323
DATE: July 29, 1979
VENUE: Hockenheim
POLE LAP: Jabouille, 1m 48.48s
FASTEST LAP: Villeneuve,G., 1m 51.89s

Pn	Driver	Car	Laps	Time/Reason
1	Jones	Williams-Ford	45	1h 24m 48.83s
2	Regazzoni	Williams-Ford	45	1h 24m 51.74s
3	Laffite	Ligier-Ford	45	1h 25m 07.22s
4	Scheckter,J.	Ferrari	45	1h 25m 20.03s
5	Watson	McLaren-Ford	45	1h 26m 26.63s
6	Mass	Arrows-Ford	44	
7	Lees	Tyrrell-Ford	44	
8	Villeneuve,G.	Ferrari	44	
9	Pironi	Tyrrell-Ford	44	
10	Lammers	Shadow-Ford	44	
11	de Angelis	Shadow-Ford	43	
12	Piquet	Brabham-Alfa	42	engine
r	Patrese	Arrows-Ford	34	puncture
r	Tambay	McLaren-Ford	30	suspension
r	Rosberg	Wolf-Ford	29	engine
r	Lauda	Brabham-Alfa	27	engine
r	Ickx	Ligier-Ford	24	puncture
r	Rebaque	Lotus-Ford	22	handling
r	Andretti,Mario	Lotus-Ford	16	cv joint
r	Arnoux	Renault	9	puncture
r	Jabouille	Renault	7	spun off
r	Fittipaldi,E.	Fittipaldi-Ford	4	electrical
r	Reutemann	Lotus-Ford	1	accident
r	Stuck,H-J.	ATS-Ford	0	suspension

STARTING GRID:

1	Jabouille	13	Reutemann
2	Jones	14	Ickx
3	Laffite	15	Tambay
4	Piquet	16	Lees
5	Scheckter,J.	17	Rosberg
6	Regazzoni	18	Mass
7	Lauda	19	Patrese
8	Pironi	20	Lammers
9	Villeneuve,G.	21	de Angelis
10	Arnoux	22	Fittipaldi,E.
11	Andretti,Mario	23	Stuck,H-J.
12	Watson	24	Rebaque

Austrian

GRAND PRIX No: 324
DATE: August 12, 1979
VENUE: Osterreichring
POLE LAP: Arnoux, 1m 34.07s
FASTEST LAP: Arnoux, 1m 35.77s

Pn	Driver	Car	Laps	Time/Reason
1	Jones	Williams-Ford	54	1h 27m 38.01s
2	Villeneuve,G.	Ferrari	54	1h 28m 14.06s
3	Laffite	Ligier-Ford	54	1h 28m 24.78s
4	Scheckter,J.	Ferrari	54	1h 28m 25.22s
5	Regazzoni	Williams-Ford	54	1h 28m 26.93s
6	Arnoux	Renault	53	
7	Pironi	Tyrrell-Ford	53	
8	Daly	Tyrrell-Ford	53	
9	Watson	McLaren-Ford	53	
10	Tambay	McLaren-Ford	53	
r	Lauda	Brabham-Alfa	45	oil pressure
r	Gaillard	Ensign-Ford	42	suspension
r	de Angelis	Shadow-Ford	34	engine
r	Patrese	Arrows-Ford	34	suspension
r	Piquet	Brabham-Alfa	32	engine
r	Stuck,H-J.	ATS-Ford	28	engine
r	Ickx	Ligier-Ford	26	engine
r	Reutemann	Lotus-Ford	22	handling
r	Jabouille	Renault	16	transmission
r	Fittipaldi,E.	Fittipaldi-Ford	15	brakes
r	Rosberg	Wolf-Ford	15	electrical
r	Lammers	Shadow-Ford	3	accident
r	Mass	Arrows-Ford	1	engine
r	Andretti,Mario	Lotus-Ford	0	clutch

STARTING GRID:

1	Arnoux	13	Patrese
2	Jones	14	Tambay
3	Jabouille	15	Andretti,Mario
4	Lauda	16	Watson
5	Villeneuve,G.	17	Reutemann
6	Regazzoni	18	Stuck,H-J.
7	Piquet	19	Fittipaldi,E.
8	Laffite	20	Mass
9	Scheckter,J.	21	Ickx
10	Pironi	22	de Angelis
11	Daly	23	Lammers
12	Rosberg	24	Gaillard

Dutch

GRAND PRIX No:	325
DATE:	August 26, 1979
VENUE:	Zandvoort
POLE LAP:	Arnoux, 1m 15.461s
FASTEST LAP:	Villeneuve,G., 1m 19.438s

Pn	Driver	Car	Laps	Time/Reason
1	Jones	Williams-Ford	75	1h 41m 19.775s
2	Scheckter,J.	Ferrari	75	1h 41m 41.558s
3	Laffite	Ligier-Ford	75	1h 42m 23.028s
4	Piquet	Brabham-Alfa	74	
5	Ickx	Ligier-Ford	74	
6	Mass	Arrows-Ford	73	
7	Rebaque	Lotus-Ford	73	
r	Pironi	Tyrrell-Ford	51	suspension
r	Villeneuve,G.	Ferrari	49	suspension
r	de Angelis	Shadow-Ford	40	driveshaft
r	Rosberg	Wolf-Ford	33	engine
r	Jabouille	Renault	26	clutch
r	Watson	McLaren-Ford	22	engine
r	Jarier	Tyrrell-Ford	20	spun off
r	Stuck,H-J.	ATS-Ford	19	driveshaft
r	Lammers	Shadow-Ford	12	gearbox
r	Andretti,Mario	Lotus-Ford	9	suspension
r	Patrese	Arrows-Ford	7	accident
r	Tambay	McLaren-Ford	6	engine
r	Lauda	Brabham-Alfa	4	withdrew
r	Fittipaldi,E.	Fittipaldi-Ford	2	electrical
r	Reutemann	Lotus-Ford	1	accident
r	Arnoux	Renault	1	accident
r	Regazzoni	Williams-Ford	0	accident

STARTING GRID:

1	Arnoux	13	Reutemann
2	Jones	14	Tambay
3	Regazzoni	15	Stuck,H-J.
4	Jabouille	16	Jarier
5	Scheckter,J.	17	Andretti,Mario
6	Villeneuve,G.	18	Mass
7	Laffite	19	Patrese
8	Rosberg	20	Ickx
9	Lauda	21	Fittipaldi,E.
10	Pironi	22	de Angelis
11	Piquet	23	Lammers
12	Watson	24	Rebaque

Italian

GRAND PRIX No:	326
DATE:	September 9, 1979
VENUE:	Monza
POLE LAP:	Jabouille, 1m 34.580s
FASTEST LAP:	Regazzoni, 1m 35.600s

Pn	Driver	Car	Laps	Time/Reason
1	Scheckter,J.	Ferrari	50	1h 22m 00.22s
2	Villeneuve,G.	Ferrari	50	1h 22m 00.68s
3	Regazzoni	Williams-Ford	50	1h 22m 05.00s
4	Lauda	Brabham-Alfa	50	1h 22m 54.62s
5	Andretti,Mario	Lotus-Ford	50	1h 22m 59.92s
6	Jarier	Tyrrell-Ford	50	1h 23m 01.77s
7	Reutemann	Lotus-Ford	50	1h 23m 24.36s
8	Fittipaldi,E.	Fittipaldi-Ford	49	
9	Jones	Williams-Ford	49	
10	Pironi	Tyrrell-Ford	49	
11	Stuck,H-J.	ATS-Ford	49	
12	Brambilla	Alfa Romeo	49	
13	Patrese	Arrows-Ford	47	
14	Jabouille	Renault	45	engine
r	Laffite	Ligier-Ford	41	engine
r	Rosberg	Wolf-Ford	41	engine
r	Ickx	Ligier-Ford	40	engine
r	de Angelis	Shadow-Ford	33	clutch
r	Giacomelli	Alfa Romeo	28	spun off
r	Watson	McLaren-Ford	13	accident
r	Arnoux	Renault	13	misfiring
r	Tambay	McLaren-Ford	3	engine
r	Mass	Arrows-Ford	3	suspension
r	Piquet	Brabham-Alfa	1	accident

STARTING GRID:

1	Jabouille	13	Reutemann
2	Arnoux	14	Tambay
3	Scheckter,J.	15	Stuck,H-J.
4	Jones	16	Jarier
5	Villeneuve,G.	17	Patrese
6	Regazzoni	18	Giacomelli
7	Laffite	19	Watson
8	Piquet	20	Fittipaldi,E.
9	Lauda	21	Mass
10	Andretti,Mario	22	Brambilla
11	Ickx	23	Rosberg
12	Pironi	24	de Angelis

Canadian

GRAND PRIX No: 327
DATE: September 30, 1979
VENUE: Montreal
POLE LAP: Jones, 1m 29.892s
FASTEST LAP: Jones, 1m 31.272s

Pn	Driver	Car	Laps	Time/Reason
1	Jones	Williams-Ford	72	1h 52m 06.892s
2	Villeneuve,G.	Ferrari	72	1h 52m 07.972s
3	Regazzoni	Williams-Ford	72	1h 53m 20.548s
4	Scheckter,J.	Ferrari	71	
5	Pironi	Tyrrell-Ford	71	
6	Watson	McLaren-Ford	70	
7	Zunino	Brabham-Ford	68	
8	Fittipaldi,E.	Fittipaldi-Ford	67	
9	Lammers	Shadow-Ford	67	
10	Andretti,Mario	Lotus-Ford	66	out of fuel
r	Piquet	Brabham-Ford	61	gearbox
r	Brambilla	Alfa Romeo	52	fuel metering
r	Ickx	Ligier-Ford	47	gearbox
r	Jarier	Tyrrell-Ford	33	engine
r	Daly	Tyrrell-Ford	28	engine
r	Rebaque	Rebaque-Ford	26	engine
r	de Angelis	Shadow-Ford	24	rotor arm
r	Jabouille	Renault	24	brakes
r	Reutemann	Lotus-Ford	23	suspension
r	Patrese	Arrows-Ford	20	spun off
r	Tambay	McLaren-Ford	19	engine
r	Arnoux	Renault	14	accident
r	Stuck,H-J.	ATS-Ford	14	accident
r	Laffite	Ligier-Ford	10	engine

STARTING GRID:

1	Jones	13	Jarier
2	Villeneuve,G.	14	Patrese
3	Regazzoni	15	Fittipaldi,E.
4	Piquet	16	Ickx
5	Laffite	17	Watson
6	Pironi	18	Brambilla
7	Jabouille	19	Zunino
8	Arnoux	20	Tambay
9	Scheckter,J.	21	Lammers
10	Andretti,Mario	22	Rebaque
11	Reutemann	23	de Angelis
12	Stuck,H-J.	24	Daly

US East

GRAND PRIX No: 328
DATE: October 7, 1979
VENUE: Watkins Glen
POLE LAP: Jones, 1m 36.615s
FASTEST LAP: Piquet, 1m 40.054s

Pn	Driver	Car	Laps	Time/Reason
1	Villeneuve,G.	Ferrari	59	1h 52m 17.734s
2	Arnoux	Renault	59	1h 53m 06.521s
3	Pironi	Tyrrell-Ford	59	1h 53m 10.933s
4	de Angelis	Shadow-Ford	59	1h 53m 48.246s
5	Stuck,H-J.	ATS-Ford	59	1h 53m 58.993s
6	Watson	McLaren-Ford	58	
7	Fittipaldi,E.	Fittipaldi-Ford	54	
8	Piquet	Brabham-Ford	53	driveshaft
r	Daly	Tyrrell-Ford	52	accident
r	Scheckter,J.	Ferrari	48	burst tyre
r	Patrese	Arrows-Ford	44	suspension
r	Jones	Williams-Ford	36	lost wheel
r	Surer	Ensign-Ford	32	engine
r	Regazzoni	Williams-Ford	29	accident
r	Zunino	Brabham-Ford	25	accident
r	Jabouille	Renault	24	camshaft
r	Tambay	McLaren-Ford	20	engine
r	Rosberg	Wolf-Ford	20	accident
r	Jarier	Tyrrell-Ford	18	accident
r	Andretti,Mario	Lotus-Ford	16	gearbox
r	Reutemann	Lotus-Ford	6	accident
r	Laffite	Ligier-Ford	3	accident
r	Ickx	Ligier-Ford	2	accident
r	Giacomelli	Alfa Romeo	0	accident

STARTING GRID:

1	Jones	13	Watson
2	Piquet	14	Stuck,H-J.
3	Villeneuve,G.	15	Daly
4	Laffite	16	Scheckter,J.
5	Regazzoni	17	Andretti,Mario
6	Reutemann	18	Giacomelli
7	Arnoux	19	Patrese
8	Jabouille	20	de Angelis
9	Zunino	21	Surer
10	Pironi	22	Tambay
11	Jarier	23	Fittipaldi,E.
12	Rosberg	24	Ickx

Argentine

GRAND PRIX No:	329
DATE:	January 13, 1980
VENUE:	Buenos Aires
POLE LAP:	Jones, 1m 44.17s
FASTEST LAP:	Jones, 1m 50.45s

Pn	Driver	Car	Laps	Time/Reason
1	Jones	Williams-Ford	53	1h 43m 24.38s
2	Piquet	Brabham-Ford	53	1h 43m 48.97s
3	Rosberg	Fittipaldi-Ford	53	1h 44m 43.02s
4	Daly	Tyrrell-Ford	53	1h 44m 47.86s
5	Giacomelli	Alfa Romeo	52	
6	Prost	McLaren-Ford	52	
7	Zunino	Brabham-Ford	51	
uc	Regazzoni	Ensign-Ford	44	
uc	Fittipaldi,E.	Fittipaldi-Ford	37	
r	Depailler	Alfa Romeo	46	engine
r	Scheckter,J.	Ferrari	45	engine
r	Villeneuve,G.	Ferrari	36	accident
r	Laffite	Ligier-Ford	30	engine
r	Surer	ATS-Ford	27	fire
r	Patrese	Arrows-Ford	27	engine
r	Mass	Arrows-Ford	20	gearbox
r	Andretti,Mario	Lotus-Ford	20	fuel system
r	Reutemann	Williams-Ford	12	engine
r	de Angelis	Lotus-Ford	7	suspension
r	Watson	McLaren-Ford	5	gearbox
r	Jabouille	Renault	3	clutch
r	Arnoux	Renault	2	suspenson
r	Pironi	Ligier-Ford	1	engine
r	Jarier	Tyrrell-Ford	1	accident

STARTING GRID:

1	Jones	13	Rosberg
2	Laffite	14	Mass
3	Pironi	15	Regazzoni
4	Piquet	16	Zunino
5	de Angelis	17	Watson
6	Andretti,Mario	18	Jarier
7	Patrese	19	Arnoux
8	Villeneuve,G.	20	Giacomelli
9	Jabouille	21	Surer
10	Reutemann	22	Daly
11	Scheckter,J.	23	Depailler
12	Prost	24	Fittipaldi,E.

Brazilian

GRAND PRIX No:	330
DATE:	January 27, 1980
VENUE:	Interlagos
POLE LAP:	Jabouille, 2m 21.40s
FASTEST LAP:	Arnoux, 2m 27.31s

Pn	Driver	Car	Laps	Time/Reason
1	Arnoux	Renault	40	1h 40m 01.33s
2	de Angelis	Lotus-Ford	40	1h 40m 23.19s
3	Jones	Williams-Ford	40	1h 41m 07.44s
4	Pironi	Ligier-Ford	40	1h 41m 41.46s
5	Prost	McLaren-Ford	40	1h 42m 26.74s
6	Patrese	Arrows-Ford	39	
7	Surer	ATS-Ford	39	
8	Zunino	Brabham-Ford	39	
9	Rosberg	Fittipaldi-Ford	39	
10	Mass	Arrows-Ford	39	
11	Watson	McLaren-Ford	39	
12	Jarier	Tyrrell-Ford	39	
13	Giacomelli	Alfa Romeo	39	
14	Daly	Tyrrell-Ford	38	
15	Fittipaldi,E.	Fittipaldi-Ford	38	
16	Villeneuve,G.	Ferrari	36	throttle
r	Depailler	Alfa Romeo	33	electrical
r	Jabouille	Renault	25	turbo
r	Piquet	Brabham-Ford	14	accident
r	Regazzoni	Ensign-Ford	13	handling
r	Laffite	Ligier-Ford	13	electrical
r	Scheckter,J.	Ferrari	10	engine
r	Reutemann	Williams-Ford	1	driveshaft
r	Andretti,Mario	Lotus-Ford	1	spun off

STARTING GRID:

1	Jabouille	13	Prost
2	Pironi	14	Patrese
3	Villeneuve,G.	15	Rosberg
4	Reutemann	16	Mass
5	Laffite	17	Giacomelli
6	Arnoux	18	Zunino
7	de Angelis	19	Fittipaldi,E.
8	Scheckter,J.	20	Surer
9	Piquet	21	Depailler
10	Jones	22	Jarier
11	Andretti,Mario	23	Watson
12	Regazzoni	24	Daly

South African

GRAND PRIX No: 331
DATE: March 1, 1980
VENUE: Kyalami
POLE LAP: Jabouille, 1m 10.00s
FASTEST LAP: Arnoux, 1m 13.15s

Pn	Driver	Car	Laps	Time/Reason
1	Arnoux	Renault	78	1h 36m 52.54s
2	Laffite	Ligier-Ford	78	1h 37m 26.61s
3	Pironi	Ligier-Ford	78	1h 37m 45.03s
4	Piquet	Brabham-Ford	78	1h 37m 53.56s
5	Reutemann	Williams-Ford	77	
6	Mass	Arrows-Ford	77	
7	Jarier	Tyrrell-Ford	77	
8	Fittipaldi,E.	Fittipaldi-Ford	77	
9	Regazzoni	Ensign-Ford	77	
10	Zunino	Brabham-Ford	77	
11	Watson	McLaren-Ford	76	
12	Andretti,Mario	Lotus-Ford	76	
13	Lees	Shadow-Ford	70	accident
r	Giacomelli	Alfa Romeo	69	engine
r	Jabouille	Renault	61	puncture
r	Daly	Tyrrell-Ford	61	puncture
r	Rosberg	Fittipaldi-Ford	58	accident
uc	Depailler	Alfa Romeo	53	
r	Jones	Williams-Ford	34	gearbox
r	Villeneuve,G.	Ferrari	31	transmission
r	Scheckter,J.	Ferrari	14	engine
r	Patrese	Arrows-Ford	10	accident
r	Cheever	Osella-Ford	8	accident
r	de Angelis	Lotus-Ford	1	accident
dns	Prost	McLaren-Ford		injured

STARTING GRID:

1	Jabouille	14	de Angelis
2	Arnoux	15	Andretti,Mario
3	Piquet	16	Daly
4	Laffite	17	Zunino
5	Pironi	18	Fittipaldi,E.
6	Reutemann	19	Mass
7	Depailler	20	Regazzoni
8	Jones	21	Watson
9	Scheckter,J.	22	Prost
10	Villeneuve,G.	23	Cheever
11	Patrese	24	Rosberg
12	Giacomelli	25	Lees
13	Jarier		

US West

GRAND PRIX No: 332
DATE: March 30, 1982
VENUE: Long Beach
POLE LAP: Piquet, 1m 17.694s
FASTEST LAP: Piquet, 1m 19.830s

Pn	Driver	Car	Laps	Time/Reason
1	Piquet	Brabham-Ford	80	1h 50m 18.550s
2	Patrese	Arrows-Ford	80	1h 51m 07.762s
3	Fittipaldi,E.	Fittipaldi-Ford	80	1h 51m 37.113s
4	Watson	McLaren-Ford	79	
5	Scheckter,J.	Ferrari	79	
6	Pironi	Ligier-Ford	79	
7	Mass	Arrows-Ford	79	
8	Daly	Tyrrell-Ford	79	
9	Arnoux	Renault	78	
10	Jabouille	Renault	71	
r	Rosberg	Fittipaldi-Ford	58	engine
r	Regazzoni	Ensign-Ford	50	accident
r	Giacomelli	Alfa Romeo	49	accident
r	Jones	Williams-Ford	47	accident
r	Villeneuve,G.	Ferrari	46	driveshaft
r	Depailler	Alfa Romeo	40	suspension
r	Laffite	Ligier-Ford	36	puncture
r	Cheever	Osella-Ford	11	driveshaft
r	Reutemann	Williams-Ford	3	driveshaft
r	Jarier	Tyrrell-Ford	3	accident
r	de Angelis	Lotus-Ford	3	accident
r	Zunino	Brabham-Ford	0	accident
r	Andretti,Mario	Lotus-Ford	0	accident
r	Lammers	ATS-Ford	0	driveshaft

STARTING GRID:

1	Piquet	13	Laffite
2	Arnoux	14	Daly
3	Depailler	15	Andretti,Mario
4	Lammers	16	Scheckter,J.
5	Jones	17	Mass
6	Giacomelli	18	Zunino
7	Reutemann	19	Cheever
8	Patrese	20	de Angelis
9	Pironi	21	Watson
10	Villeneuve,G.	22	Rosberg
11	Jabouille	23	Regazzoni
12	Jarier	24	Fittipaldi,E.

Belgian

GRAND PRIX No: 333
DATE: May 4, 1980
VENUE: Zolder
POLE LAP: Jones, 1m 19.12s
FASTEST LAP: Laffite, 1m 20.88s

Pn	Driver	Car	Laps	Time/Reason
1	Pironi	Ligier-Ford	72	1h 38m 46.51s
2	Jones	Williams-Ford	72	1h 39m 33.88s
3	Reutemann	Williams-Ford	72	1h 40m 10.63s
4	Arnoux	Renault	71	
5	Jarier	Tyrrell-Ford	71	
6	Villeneuve,G.	Ferrari	71	
7	Rosberg	Fittipaldi-Ford	71	
8	Scheckter,J.	Ferrari	70	
9	Daly	Tyrrell-Ford	70	
10	de Angelis	Lotus-Ford	69	accident
11	Laffite	Ligier-Ford	68	
r	Lammers	ATS-Ford	64	engine
uc	Watson	McLaren-Ford	61	
r	Patrese	Arrows-Ford	58	accident
r	Andretti,Mario	Lotus-Ford	41	gear linkage
r	Depailler	Alfa Romeo	38	exhaust
r	Piquet	Brabham-Ford	32	accident
r	Prost	McLaren-Ford	29	transmission
r	Fittipaldi,E.	Fittipaldi-Ford	16	electrical
r	Needell	Ensign-Ford	12	engine
r	Giacomelli	Alfa Romeo	11	suspension
r	Zunino	Brabham-Ford	5	clutch
r	Jabouille	Renault	1	clutch
r	Mass	Arrows-Ford	1	accident

STARTING GRID:

1	Jones	13	Mass
2	Pironi	14	Scheckter,J.
3	Laffite	15	Lammers
4	Reutemann	16	Patrese
5	Jabouille	17	Andretti,Mario
6	Arnoux	18	Giacomelli
7	Piquet	19	Prost
8	de Angelis	20	Watson
9	Jarier	21	Rosberg
10	Depailler	22	Zunino
11	Daly	23	Needell
12	Villeneuve,G.	24	Fittipaldi,E.

Monaco

GRAND PRIX No: 334
DATE: May 18, 1980
VENUE: Monte Carlo
POLE LAP: Pironi, 1m 24.813s
FASTEST LAP: Reutemann, 1m 27.418s

Pn	Driver	Car	Laps	Time/Reason
1	Reutemann	Williams-Ford	76	1h 55m 34.365s
2	Laffite	Ligier-Ford	76	1h 56m 47.994s
3	Piquet	Brabham-Ford	76	1h 56m 52.091s
4	Mass	Arrows-Ford	75	
5	Villeneuve,G.	Ferrari	75	
6	Fittipaldi,E.	Fittipaldi-Ford	74	
7	Andretti,Mario	Lotus-Ford	73	
8	Patrese	Arrows-Ford	73	
9	de Angelis	Lotus-Ford	68	accident
uc	Lammers	ATS-Ford	64	
r	Pironi	Ligier-Ford	54	accident
r	Arnoux	Renault	53	accident
r	Depailler	Alfa Romeo	50	engine
r	Scheckter,J.	Ferrari	27	handling
r	Jabouille	Renault	25	gearbox
r	Jones	Williams-Ford	24	differential
r	Jarier	Tyrrell-Ford	0	accident
r	Giacomelli	Alfa Romeo	0	accident
r	Prost	McLaren-Ford	0	accident
r	Daly	Tyrrell-Ford	0	accident

STARTING GRID:

1	Pironi	11	Patrese
2	Reutemann	12	Daly
3	Jones	13	Lammers
4	Piquet	14	de Angelis
5	Laffite	15	Mass
6	Villeneuve,G.	16	Jabouille
7	Depailler	17	Scheckter,J.
8	Giacomelli	18	Fittipaldi,E.
9	Jarier	19	Andretti,Mario
10	Prost	20	Arnoux

French

GRAND PRIX No:	335
DATE:	June 29, 1980
VENUE:	Paul Ricard
POLE LAP:	Laffite, 1m 38.88s
FASTEST LAP:	Jones, 1m 41.45s

Pn	Driver	Car	Laps	Time/Reason
1	Jones	Williams-Ford	54	1h 32m 43.42s
2	Pironi	Ligier-Ford	54	1h 32m 47.94s
3	Laffite	Ligier-Ford	54	1h 33m 13.68s
4	Piquet	Brabham-Ford	54	1h 33m 58.30s
5	Arnoux	Renault	54	1h 33m 59.57s
6	Reutemann	Williams-Ford	54	1h 34m 00.16s
7	Watson	McLaren-Ford	53	
8	Villeneuve,G.	Ferrari	53	
9	Patrese	Arrows-Ford	53	
10	Mass	Arrows-Ford	53	
11	Daly	Tyrrell-Ford	52	
12	Scheckter,J.	Ferrari	52	
13	Fittipaldi,E.	Fittipaldi-Ford	50	
14	Jarier	Tyrrell-Ford	50	
r	Cheever	Osella-Ford	43	engine
r	Surer	ATS-Ford	26	gearbox
r	Depailler	Alfa Romeo	25	handling
r	Andretti,Mario	Lotus-Ford	18	gearbox
r	Rosberg	Fittipaldi-Ford	8	accident
r	Giacomelli	Alfa Romeo	8	handling
r	Prost	McLaren-Ford	6	transmission
r	de Angelis	Lotus-Ford	3	clutch
r	Zunino	Brabham-Ford	0	clutch
r	Jabouille	Renault	0	transmission

STARTING GRID:

1	Laffite	13	Watson
2	Arnoux	14	de Angelis
3	Pironi	15	Mass
4	Jones	16	Jarier
5	Reutemann	17	Villeneuve,G.
6	Jabouille	18	Patrese
7	Prost	19	Scheckter,J.
8	Piquet	20	Daly
9	Giacomelli	21	Cheever
10	Depailler	22	Zunino
11	Surer	23	Rosberg
12	Andretti,Mario	24	Fittipaldi,E.

British

GRAND PRIX No:	336
DATE:	July 13, 1980
VENUE:	Brands Hatch
POLE LAP:	Pironi, 1m 11.004s
FASTEST LAP:	Pironi, 1m 12.368s

Pn	Driver	Car	Laps	Time/Reason
1	Jones	Williams-Ford	76	1h 34m 49.228s
2	Piquet	Brabham-Ford	76	1h 35m 00.235s
3	Reutemann	Williams-Ford	76	1h 35m 02.513s
4	Daly	Tyrrell-Ford	75	
5	Jarier	Tyrrell-Ford	75	
6	Prost	McLaren-Ford	75	
7	Rebaque	Brabham-Ford	74	
8	Watson	McLaren-Ford	74	
9	Patrese	Arrows-Ford	73	
10	Scheckter,J.	Ferrari	73	
11	Keegan	Williams-Ford	73	
12	Fittipaldi,E.	Fittipaldi-Ford	72	
13	Mass	Arrows-Ford	69	
uc	Arnoux	Renault	67	
r	Pironi	Ligier-Ford	63	wheel
r	Surer	ATS-Ford	59	engine
r	Andretti,Mario	Lotus-Ford	57	gearbox
r	Giacomelli	Alfa Romeo	42	accident
r	Villeneuve,G.	Ferrari	35	engine
r	Laffite	Ligier-Ford	30	accident
r	Depailler	Alfa Romeo	27	engine
r	Cheever	Osella-Ford	17	suspension
r	de Angelis	Lotus-Ford	16	suspension
r	Jabouille	Renault	6	engine

STARTING GRID:

1	Pironi	13	Jabouille
2	Laffite	14	de Angelis
3	Jones	15	Surer
4	Reutemann	16	Arnoux
5	Piquet	17	Rebaque
6	Giacomelli	18	Keegan
7	Prost	19	Villeneuve,G.
8	Depailler	20	Cheever
9	Andretti,Mario	21	Patrese
10	Daly	22	Fittipaldi,E.
11	Jarier	23	Scheckter,J.
12	Watson	24	Mass

German

GRAND PRIX No:	337
DATE:	August 10, 1980
VENUE:	Hockenheim
POLE LAP:	Jones, 1m 45.85s
FASTEST LAP:	Jones, 1m 48.49s

Pn	Driver	Car	Laps	Time/Reason
1	Laffite	Ligier-Ford	45	1h 22m 59.73s
2	Reutemann	Williams-Ford	45	1h 23m 02.92s
3	Jones	Williams-Ford	45	1h 23m 43.26s
4	Piquet	Brabham-Ford	45	1h 23m 44.21s
5	Giacomelli	Alfa Romeo	45	1h 24m 16.22s
6	Villeneuve,G.	Ferrari	45	1h 24m 28.45s
7	Andretti,Mario	Lotus-Ford	45	1h 24m 32.74s
8	Mass	Arrows-Ford	45	1h 24m 47.48s
9	Patrese	Arrows-Ford	44	
10	Daly	Tyrrell-Ford	44	
11	Prost	McLaren-Ford	44	
12	Surer	ATS-Ford	44	
13	Scheckter,J.	Ferrari	44	
14	Lammers	Ensign-Ford	44	
15	Jarier	Tyrrell-Ford	44	
16	de Angelis	Lotus-Ford	43	wheel bearing
r	Watson	McLaren-Ford	39	engine
r	Jabouille	Renault	27	engine
r	Arnoux	Renault	26	engine
r	Cheever	Osella-Ford	23	gearbox
r	Pironi	Ligier-Ford	18	driveshaft
r	Fittipaldi,E.	Fittipaldi-Ford	18	broken skirt
r	Rosberg	Fittipaldi-Ford	8	wheel bearing
r	Rebaque	Brabham-Ford	4	gearbox

STARTING GRID:

1	Jones	13	Surer
2	Jabouille	14	Prost
3	Arnoux	15	Rebaque
4	Reutemann	16	Villeneuve,G.
5	Laffite	17	Mass
6	Piquet	18	Cheever
7	Pironi	19	Giacomelli
8	Rosberg	20	Watson
9	Andretti,Mario	21	Scheckter,J.
10	Patrese	22	Daly
11	de Angelis	23	Jarier
12	Fittipaldi,E.	24	Lammers

Austrian

GRAND PRIX No:	338
DATE:	August 17, 1980
VENUE:	Osterreichring
POLE LAP:	Arnoux, 1m 30.27s
FASTEST LAP:	Arnoux, 1m 32.53s

Pn	Driver	Car	Laps	Time/Reason
1	Jabouille	Renault	54	1h 26m 15.73s
2	Jones	Williams-Ford	54	1h 26m 16.55s
3	Reutemann	Williams-Ford	54	1h 26m 35.09s
4	Laffite	Ligier-Ford	54	1h 26m 57.75s
5	Piquet	Brabham-Ford	54	1h 27m 18.54s
6	de Angelis	Lotus-Ford	54	1h 27m 30.70s
7	Prost	McLaren-Ford	54	1h 27m 49.14s
8	Villeneuve,G.	Ferrari	53	
9	Arnoux	Renault	53	
10	Rebaque	Brabham-Ford	53	
11	Fittipaldi,E.	Fittipaldi-Ford	53	
12	Surer	ATS-Ford	53	
13	Scheckter,J.	Ferrari	53	
14	Patrese	Arrows-Ford	53	
15	Keegan	Williams-Ford	52	
16	Rosberg	Fittipaldi-Ford	52	
r	Mansell	Lotus-Ford	40	engine
r	Watson	McLaren-Ford	34	engine
r	Giacomelli	Alfa Romeo	28	suspension
r	Jarier	Tyrrell-Ford	25	engine
r	Pironi	Ligier-Ford	25	handling
r	Cheever	Osella-Ford	23	wheel bearing
r	Daly	Tyrrell-Ford	12	brakes
r	Andretti,Mario	Lotus-Ford	6	engine

STARTING GRID:

1	Arnoux	13	Jarier
2	Jabouille	14	Rebaque
3	Jones	15	Villeneuve,G.
4	Reutemann	16	Surer
5	Laffite	17	Andretti,Mario
6	Pironi	18	Patrese
7	Piquet	19	Cheever
8	Giacomelli	20	Keegan
9	de Angelis	21	Watson
10	Daly	22	Scheckter,J.
11	Rosberg	23	Fittipaldi,E.
12	Prost	24	Mansell

Dutch

GRAND PRIX No:	339
DATE:	August 31, 1980
VENUE:	Zandvoort
POLE LAP:	Arnoux, 1m 17.44s
FASTEST LAP:	Arnoux, 1m 19.35s

Pn	Driver	Car	Laps	Time/Reason
1	Piquet	Brabham-Ford	72	1h 38m 13.83s
2	Arnoux	Renault	72	1h 38m 26.76s
3	Laffite	Ligier-Ford	72	1h 38m 27.26s
4	Reutemann	Williams-Ford	72	1h 38m 29.12s
5	Jarier	Tyrrell-Ford	72	1h 39m 13.85s
6	Prost	McLaren-Ford	72	1h 39m 36.45s
7	Villeneuve,G.	Ferrari	71	
8	Andretti,Mario	Lotus-Ford	70	out of fuel
9	Scheckter,J.	Ferrari	70	
10	Surer	ATS-Ford	69	
11	Jones	Williams-Ford	69	
r	Daly	Tyrrell-Ford	60	brakes
r	Giacomelli	Alfa Romeo	58	damaged skirt
r	Cheever	Osella-Ford	38	engine
r	Patrese	Arrows-Ford	29	engine
r	Jabouille	Renault	23	handling
r	Lees	Ensign-Ford	21	accident
r	Brambilla	Alfa Romeo	21	accident
r	Watson	McLaren-Ford	18	engine
r	Fittipaldi,E.	Fittipaldi-Ford	16	brakes
r	Mansell	Lotus-Ford	15	brakes
r	Pironi	Ligier-Ford	2	accident
r	de Angelis	Lotus-Ford	2	accident
r	Rebaque	Brabham-Ford	1	gearbox

STARTING GRID:

1	Arnoux	13	Rebaque
2	Jabouille	14	Patrese
3	Reutemann	15	Pironi
4	Jones	16	Mansell
5	Piquet	17	Jarier
6	Laffite	18	Prost
7	Villeneuve,G.	19	Cheever
8	Giacomelli	20	Surer
9	Watson	21	Fittipaldi,E.
10	Andretti,Mario	22	Brambilla
11	de Angelis	23	Daly
12	Scheckter,J.	24	Lees

Italian

GRAND PRIX No:	340
DATE:	September 14, 1980
VENUE:	Imola
POLE LAP:	Arnoux, 1m 33.988s
FASTEST LAP:	Jones, 1m 36.089s

Pn	Driver	Car	Laps	Time/Reason
1	Piquet	Brabham-Ford	60	1h 38m 07.52s
2	Jones	Williams-Ford	60	1h 38m 36.45s
3	Reutemann	Williams-Ford	60	1h 39m 21.19s
4	de Angelis	Lotus-Ford	59	
5	Rosberg	Fittipaldi-Ford	59	
6	Pironi	Ligier-Ford	59	
7	Prost	McLaren-Ford	59	
8	Scheckter,J.	Ferrari	59	
9	Laffite	Ligier-Ford	59	
10	Arnoux	Renault	58	
11	Keegan	Williams-Ford	58	
12	Cheever	Osella-Ford	57	
13	Jarier	Tyrrell-Ford	54	brakes
r	Jabouille	Renault	53	gearbox
r	Surer	ATS-Ford	45	engine
r	Andretti,Mario	Lotus-Ford	40	engine
r	Patrese	Arrows-Ford	38	engine
r	Daly	Tyrrell-Ford	33	accident
r	Watson	McLaren-Ford	20	brakes
r	Rebaque	Brabham-Ford	18	suspension
r	Fittipaldi,E.	Fittipaldi-Ford	17	accident
r	Villeneuve,G.	Ferrari	5	accident
r	Giacomelli	Alfa Romeo	5	accident
r	Brambilla	Alfa Romeo	4	accident

STARTING GRID:

1	Arnoux	13	Pironi
2	Jabouille	14	Watson
3	Reutemann	15	Fittipaldi,E.
4	Giacomelli	16	Scheckter,J.
5	Piquet	17	Cheever
6	Jones	18	de Angelis
7	Patrese	19	Brambilla
8	Villeneuve,G.	20	Laffite
9	Rebaque	21	Keegan
10	Andretti,Mario	22	Daly
11	Rosberg	23	Surer
12	Jarier	24	Prost

Canadian

GRAND PRIX No:	341
DATE:	September 28, 1980
VENUE:	Montreal
POLE LAP:	Piquet, 1m 27.328s
FASTEST LAP:	Pironi, 1m 28.769s

Pn	Driver	Car	Laps	Time/Reason
1	Jones	Williams-Ford	70	1h 46m 45.53s
2	Reutemann	Williams-Ford	70	1h 47m 01.07s
3	Pironi	Ligier-Ford	70	1h 47m 04.60s
4	Watson	McLaren-Ford	70	1h 47m 16.51s
5	Villeneuve,G.	Ferrari	70	1h 47m 40.76s
6	Rebaque	Brabham-Ford	69	
7	Jarier	Tyrrell-Ford	69	
8	Laffite	Ligier-Ford	68	out of fuel
9	Rosberg	Fittipaldi-Ford	68	
10	de Angelis	Lotus-Ford	68	
11	Mass	Arrows-Ford	67	
12	Lammers	Ensign-Ford	66	
r	Prost	McLaren-Ford	41	accident
r	Arnoux	Renault	39	brakes
r	Jabouille	Renault	25	accident
r	Piquet	Brabham-Ford	23	engine
r	Andretti,Mario	Lotus-Ford	11	engine
r	de Cesaris	Alfa Romeo	8	engine
r	Cheever	Osella-Ford	8	fuel pressure
r	Fittipaldi,E.	Fittipaldi-Ford	8	gearbox
r	Giacomelli	Alfa Romeo	7	damaged skirt
r	Patrese	Arrows-Ford	6	accident
r	Daly	Tyrrell-Ford	0	accident at first
r	Thackwell	Tyrrell-Ford	0	accident at first

STARTING GRID:

1	Piquet	13	Jabouille
2	Jones	14	Cheever
3	Pironi	15	Jarier
4	Giacomelli	16	Fittipaldi,E.
5	Reutemann	17	de Angelis
6	Rosberg	18	Andretti,Mario
7	Watson	19	Lammers
8	de Cesaris	20	Daly
9	Laffite	21	Mass
10	Rebaque	22	Villeneuve,G.
11	Patrese	23	Arnoux
12	Prost	24	Thackwell

US East

GRAND PRIX No:	342
DATE:	October 5, 1980
VENUE:	Watkins Glen
POLE LAP:	Giacomelli, 1m 33.291s
FASTEST LAP:	Jones, 1m 34.068s

Pn	Driver	Car	Laps	Time/Reason
1	Jones	Williams-Ford	59	1h 34m 36.05s
2	Reutemann	Williams-Ford	59	1h 34m 40.26s
3	Pironi	Ligier-Ford	59	1h 34m 48.62s
4	de Angelis	Lotus-Ford	59	1h 35m 05.74s
5	Laffite	Ligier-Ford	58	
6	Andretti,Mario	Lotus-Ford	58	
7	Arnoux	Renault	58	
8	Surer	ATS-Ford	57	
9	Keegan	Williams-Ford	57	
10	Rosberg	Fittipaldi-Ford	57	
11	Scheckter,J.	Ferrari	56	
uc	Watson	McLaren-Ford	50	
r	Villeneuve,G.	Ferrari	49	accident
uc	Jarier	Tyrrell-Ford	40	
r	Mass	Arrows-Ford	36	driveshaft
r	Giacomelli	Alfa Romeo	31	electrical
r	Piquet	Brabham-Ford	25	spun off
r	Cheever	Osella-Ford	21	suspension
r	Rebaque	Brabham-Ford	20	engine
r	Patrese	Arrows-Ford	16	accident
r	Lammers	Ensign-Ford	16	steering
r	Fittipaldi,E.	Fittipaldi-Ford	15	suspension
r	Daly	Tyrrell-Ford	3	accident
r	de Cesaris	Alfa Romeo	2	accident
dns	Prost	Tyrrell-Ford		injured

STARTING GRID:

1	Giacomelli	13	Prost
2	Piquet	14	Rosberg
3	Reutemann	15	Keegan
4	de Angelis	16	Cheever
5	Jones	17	Surer
6	Arnoux	18	Villeneuve,G.
7	Pironi	19	Fittipaldi,E.
8	Rebaque	20	Patrese
9	Watson	21	Daly
10	de Cesaris	22	Jarier
11	Andretti,Mario	23	Scheckter,J.
12	Laffite	24	Mass
		25	Lammers

US West

GRAND PRIX No:	343
DATE:	March 15, 1981
VENUE:	Long Beach
POLE LAP:	Patrese, 1m 19.390s
FASTEST LAP:	Jones, 1m 20.901s

Pn	Driver	Car	Laps	Time/Reason
1	Jones	Williams-Ford	80	1h 50m 41.33s
2	Reutemann	Williams-Ford	80	1h 50m 50.52s
3	Piquet	Brabham-Ford	80	1h 51m 16.25s
4	Andretti,Mario	Alfa Romeo	80	1h 51m 30.64s
5	Cheever	Tyrrell-Ford	80	1h 51m 48.03s
6	Tambay	Theodore-Ford	79	
7	Serra	Fittipaldi-Ford	78	
8	Arnoux	Renault	77	
r	Surer	Ensign-Ford	70	electrical
r	Pironi	Ferrari	67	engine
r	Jarier	Ligier-Matra	64	fuel pump
r	Rebaque	Brabham-Ford	49	accident
r	Laffite	Ligier-Matra	41	accident
r	Giacomelli	Alfa Romeo	41	accident
r	Lammers	ATS-Ford	41	accident
r	Rosberg	Fittipaldi-Ford	41	distributor
r	Patrese	Arrows-Ford	33	fuel filter
r	Gabbiani	Osella-Ford	26	accident
r	Mansell	Lotus-Ford	25	accident
r	Villeneuve,G.	Ferrari	17	driveshaft
r	Watson	McLaren-Ford	16	engine
r	de Angelis	Lotus-Ford	13	accident
r	Prost	Renault	0	accident
r	de Cesaris	McLaren-Ford	0	accident

STARTING GRID:

1	Patrese	13	de Angelis
2	Jones	14	Prost
3	Reutemann	15	Rebaque
4	Piquet	16	Rosberg
5	Villeneuve,G.	17	Tambay
6	Andretti,Mario	18	Serra
7	Mansell	19	Surer
8	Cheever	20	Arnoux
9	Giacomelli	21	Lammers
10	Jarier	22	de Cesaris
11	Pironi	23	Watson
12	Laffite	24	Gabbiani

Brazilian

GRAND PRIX No:	344
DATE:	March 29, 1981
VENUE:	Rio de Janeiro
POLE LAP:	Piquet, 1m 35.079s
FASTEST LAP:	Surer, 1m 54.302s

Pn	Driver	Car	Laps	Time/Reason
1	Reutemann	Williams-Ford	62	2h 00m 23.66s
2	Jones	Williams-Ford	62	2h 00m 28.10s
3	Patrese	Arrows-Ford	62	2h 01m 26.74s
4	Surer	Ensign-Ford	62	2h 01m 40.69s
5	de Angelis	Lotus-Ford	62	2h 01m 50.08s
6	Laffite	Ligier-Matra	62	2h 01m 50.49s
7	Jarier	Ligier-Matra	62	2h 01m 53.91s
8	Watson	McLaren-Ford	61	
9	Rosberg	Fittipaldi-Ford	61	
10	Tambay	Theodore-Ford	61	
11	Mansell	Lotus-Ford	61	
12	Piquet	Brabham-Ford	60	
13	Zunino	Tyrrell-Ford	57	
uc	Cheever	Tyrrell-Ford	49	
r	Giacomelli	Alfa Romeo	40	electrical
r	Villeneuve,G.	Ferrari	25	turbo
r	Rebaque	Brabham-Ford	22	suspension
r	Stohr	Arrows-Ford	20	accident
r	Prost	Renault	20	accident
r	Pironi	Ferrari	19	accident
r	de Cesaris	McLaren-Ford	9	electrical
r	Serra	Fittipaldi-Ford	0	accident
r	Arnoux	Renault	0	accident
r	Andretti,Mario	Alfa Romeo	0	accident

STARTING GRID:

1	Piquet	13	Mansell
2	Reutemann	14	Cheever
3	Jones	15	Watson
4	Patrese	16	Laffite
5	Prost	17	Pironi
6	Giacomelli	18	Surer
7	Villeneuve,G.	19	Tambay
8	Arnoux	20	de Cesaris
9	Andretti,Mario	21	Stohr
10	de Angelis	22	Serra
11	Rebaque	23	Jarier
12	Rosberg	24	Zunino

Argentine

GRAND PRIX No:	345
DATE:	April 12, 1981
VENUE:	Buenos Aires
POLE LAP:	Piquet, 1m 42.665s
FASTEST LAP:	Piquet, 1m 45.287s

Pn	Driver	Car	Laps	Time/Reason
1	Piquet	Brabham-Ford	53	1h 34m 32.74s
2	Reutemann	Williams-Ford	53	1h 34m 59.35s
3	Prost	Renault	53	1h 35m 22.72s
4	Jones	Williams-Ford	53	1h 35m 40.62s
5	Arnoux	Renault	53	1h 36m 04.59s
6	de Angelis	Lotus-Ford	52	
7	Patrese	Arrows-Ford	52	
8	Andretti,Mario	Alfa Romeo	52	
9	Stohr	Arrows-Ford	52	
10	Giacomelli	Alfa Romeo	51	out of fuel
11	de Cesaris	McLaren-Ford	51	
12	Lammers	ATS-Ford	51	
13	Zunino	Tyrrell-Ford	51	
r	Villeneuve,G.	Ferrari	40	driveshaft
r	Tambay	Theodore-Ford	36	engine
r	Watson	McLaren-Ford	36	crownwheel/pinion
r	Rebaque	Brabham-Ford	32	distributor
r	Serra	Fittipaldi-Ford	28	gearbox
r	Laffite	Ligier-Matra	19	handling
r	Surer	Ensign-Ford	14	engine
r	Rosberg	Fittipaldi-Ford	4	fuel pump
r	Mansell	Lotus-Ford	3	engine
r	Pironi	Ferrari	3	engine
r	Cheever	Tyrrell-Ford	1	clutch

STARTING GRID:

1	Piquet	13	Cheever
2	Prost	14	Tambay
3	Jones	15	Mansell
4	Reutemann	16	Surer
5	Arnoux	17	Andretti,Mario
6	Rebaque	18	de Cesaris
7	Villeneuve,G.	19	Stohr
8	Rosberg	20	Serra
9	Patrese	21	Laffite
10	de Angelis	22	Giacomelli
11	Watson	23	Lammers
12	Pironi	24	Zunino

San Marino

GRAND PRIX No:	346
DATE:	May 3, 1981
VENUE:	Imola
POLE LAP:	Villeneuve,G., 1m 34.523s
FASTEST LAP:	Villeneuve,G., 1m 48.064s

Pn	Driver	Car	Laps	Time/Reason
1	Piquet	Brabham-Ford	60	1h 51m 23.97s
2	Patrese	Arrows-Ford	60	1h 51m 28.55s
3	Reutemann	Williams-Ford	60	1h 51m 30.31s
4	Rebaque	Brabham-Ford	60	1h 51m 46.86s
5	Pironi	Ferrari	60	1h 51m 49.84s
6	de Cesaris	McLaren-Ford	60	1h 52m 30.58s
7	Villeneuve,G.	Ferrari	60	1h 53m 05.94s
8	Arnoux	Renault	59	
9	Surer	Ensign-Ford	59	
10	Watson	McLaren-Ford	58	
11	Tambay	Theodore-Ford	58	
12	Jones	Williams-Ford	58	
13	Borgudd	ATS-Ford	57	
uc	Jabouille	Ligier-Matra	45	
r	Salazar	March-Ford	38	oil pressure
r	Alboreto	Tyrrell-Ford	31	accident
r	Gabbiani	Osella-Ford	31	accident
r	Giacomelli	Alfa Romeo	28	accident
r	Cheever	Tyrrell-Ford	28	accident
r	Andretti,Mario	Alfa Romeo	26	gearbox
r	Rosberg	Fittipaldi-Ford	14	engine
r	Laffite	Ligier-Matra	7	accident
r	Prost	Renault	3	gearbox
r	Guerra	Osella-Ford	0	accident

STARTING GRID:

1	Villeneuve,G.	13	Rebaque
2	Reutemann	14	de Cesaris
3	Arnoux	15	Rosberg
4	Prost	16	Tambay
5	Piquet	17	Alboreto
6	Pironi	18	Jabouille
7	Watson	19	Cheever
8	Jones	20	Gabbiani
9	Patrese	21	Surer
10	Laffite	22	Guerra
11	Giacomelli	23	Salazar
12	Andretti,Mario	24	Borgudd

Belgian

GRAND PRIX No: 347
DATE: May 17, 1981
VENUE: Zolder
POLE LAP: Reutemann, 1m 22.28s
FASTEST LAP: Reutemann, 1m 23.30s

Pn	Driver	Car	Laps	Time/Reason
1	Reutemann	Williams-Ford	54	1h 16m 31.61s
2	Laffite	Ligier-Matra	54	1h 17m 07.67s
3	Mansell	Lotus-Ford	54	1h 17m 15.30s
4	Villeneuve,G.	Ferrari	54	1h 17m 19.25s
5	de Angelis	Lotus-Ford	54	1h 17m 20.81s
6	Cheever	Tyrrell-Ford	54	1h 17m 24.12s
7	Watson	McLaren-Ford	54	1h 17m 33.27s
8	Pironi	Ferrari	54	1h 18m 03.65s
9	Giacomelli	Alfa Romeo	54	1h 18m 07.19s
10	Andretti,Mario	Alfa Romeo	53	
11	Surer	Ensign-Ford	52	
12	Alboreto	Tyrrell-Ford	52	
13	Ghinzani	Osella-Ford	50	
r	Rebaque	Brabham-Ford	39	accident
r	Jabouille	Ligier-Matra	35	transmission
r	Serra	Fittipaldi-Ford	29	engine
r	Gabbiani	Osella-Ford	22	engine
r	Jones	Williams-Ford	19	accident
r	de Cesaris	McLaren-Ford	11	gearbox
r	Piquet	Brabham-Ford	10	accident
r	Rosberg	Fittipaldi-Ford	10	gear-lever
r	Prost	Renault	2	clutch
r	Stohr	Arrows-Ford	0	accident
r	Patrese	Arrows-Ford	0	accident

STARTING GRID:

1	Reutemann	13	Stohr
2	Piquet	14	de Angelis
3	Pironi	15	Surer
4	Patrese	16	Jabouille
5	Watson	17	Giacomelli
6	Jones	18	Andretti,Mario
7	Villeneuve,G.	19	Alboreto
8	Cheever	20	Serra
9	Laffite	21	Rebaque
10	Mansell	22	Gabbiani
11	Rosberg	23	de Cesaris
12	Prost	24	Ghinzani

Monaco

GRAND PRIX No: 348
DATE: May 31, 1981
VENUE: Monte Carlo
POLE LAP: Piquet, 1m 25.71s
FASTEST LAP: Jones, 1m 27.47s

Pn	Driver	Car	Laps	Time/Reason
1	Villeneuve,G.	Ferrari	76	1h 54m 23.38s
2	Jones	Williams-Ford	76	1h 55m 03.29s
3	Laffite	Ligier-Matra	76	1h 55m 52.62s
4	Pironi	Ferrari	75	
5	Cheever	Tyrrell-Ford	74	
6	Surer	Ensign-Ford	74	
7	Tambay	Theodore-Ford	72	
r	Piquet	Brabham-Ford	53	accident
r	Watson	McLaren-Ford	53	engine
r	Alboreto	Tyrrell-Ford	50	spun off
r	Giacomelli	Alfa Romeo	50	accident
r	Prost	Renault	45	engine
r	Reutemann	Williams-Ford	34	gearbox
r	Arnoux	Renault	32	accident
r	de Angelis	Lotus-Ford	32	engine
r	Patrese	Arrows-Ford	29	gearbox
r	Mansell	Lotus-Ford	16	suspension
r	Stohr	Arrows-Ford	15	electrical
r	de Cesaris	McLaren-Ford	0	accident
r	Andretti,Mario	Alfa Romeo	0	accident

STARTING GRID:

1	Piquet	11	de Cesaris
2	Villeneuve,G.	12	Andretti,Mario
3	Mansell	13	Arnoux
4	Reutemann	14	Stohr
5	Patrese	15	Cheever
6	de Angelis	16	Tambay
7	Jones	17	Pironi
8	Laffite	18	Giacomelli
9	Prost	19	Surer
10	Watson	20	Alboreto

Spanish

GRAND PRIX No:	349
DATE:	June 21, 1981
VENUE:	Jarama
POLE LAP:	Laffite, 1m 13.754s
FASTEST LAP:	Jones, 1m 17.818s

Pn	Driver	Car	Laps	Time/Reason
1	Villeneuve,G.	Ferrari	80	1h 46m 35.01s
2	Laffite	Ligier-Matra	80	1h 46m 35.23s
3	Watson	McLaren-Ford	80	1h 46m 35.59s
4	Reutemann	Williams-Ford	80	1h 46m 36.02s
5	de Angelis	Lotus-Ford	80	1h 46m 36.25s
6	Mansell	Lotus-Ford	80	1h 47m 03.59s
7	Jones	Williams-Ford	80	1h 47m 31.59s
8	Andretti,Mario	Alfa Romeo	80	1h 47m 35.81s
9	Arnoux	Renault	80	1h 47m 42.09s
10	Giacomelli	Alfa Romeo	80	1h 47m 48.66s
11	Serra	Fittipaldi-Ford	79	
12	Rosberg	Fittipaldi-Ford	78	
13	Tambay	Theodore-Ford	78	
14	Salazar	Ensign-Ford	77	
15	Pironi	Ferrari	76	
16	Daly	March-Ford	75	
uc	Cheever	Tyrrell-Ford	61	
r	Jabouille	Ligier-Matra	52	brakes
r	Rebaque	Brabham-Ford	46	gearbox
r	Piquet	Brabham-Ford	43	accident
r	Stohr	Arrows-Ford	43	engine
r	Prost	Renault	28	accident
r	Patrese	Arrows-Ford	21	engine
r	de Cesaris	McLaren-Ford	9	accident

STARTING GRID:

1 Laffite	13 Pironi
2 Jones	14 de Cesaris
3 Reutemann	15 Rosberg
4 Watson	16 Tambay
5 Prost	17 Arnoux
6 Giacomelli	18 Rebaque
7 Villeneuve,G.	19 Jabouille
8 Andretti,Mario	20 Cheever
9 Piquet	21 Serra
10 de Angelis	22 Daly
11 Mansell	23 Stohr
12 Patrese	24 Salazar

French

GRAND PRIX No:	350
DATE:	July 5, 1981
VENUE:	Dijon
POLE LAP:	Arnoux, 1m 05.95s
FASTEST LAP:	Prost, 1m 09.14s

Pn	Driver	Car	Laps	Time/Reason
1	Prost	Renault	80	1h 35m 48.13s
2	Watson	McLaren-Ford	80	1h 35m 50.42s
3	Piquet	Brabham-Ford	80	1h 36m 12.35s
4	Arnoux	Renault	80	1h 36m 30.43s
5	Pironi	Ferrari	79	
6	de Angelis	Lotus-Ford	79	
7	Mansell	Lotus-Ford	79	
8	Andretti,Mario	Alfa Romeo	79	
9	Rebaque	Brabham-Ford	78	
10	Reutemann	Williams-Ford	78	
11	de Cesaris	McLaren-Ford	78	
12	Surer	Theodore-Ford	78	
13	Cheever	Tyrrell-Ford	77	
14	Patrese	Arrows-Ford	77	
15	Giacomelli	Alfa Romeo	77	
16	Alboreto	Tyrrell-Ford	77	
17	Jones	Williams-Ford	76	
r	Laffite	Ligier-Matra	57	suspension
r	Daly	March-Ford	55	engine
r	Villeneuve,G.	Ferrari	41	electrical
r	Tambay	Theodore-Ford	30	wheel bearing
r	Rosberg	Fittipaldi-Ford	11	suspension
r	Salazar	Ensign-Ford	6	suspension
dns	Serra	Fittipaldi-Ford		accident

STARTING GRID:

1 Arnoux	13 Mansell
2 Watson	14 Pironi
3 Prost	15 Rebaque
4 Piquet	16 Tambay
5 de Cesaris	17 Rosberg
6 Laffite	18 Patrese
7 Reutemann	19 Cheever
8 de Angelis	20 Daly
9 Jones	21 Surer
10 Andretti,Mario	22 Salazar
11 Villeneuve,G.	23 Alboreto
12 Giacomelli	24 Serra

British

GRAND PRIX No: 351
DATE: July 18, 1981
VENUE: Silverstone
POLE LAP: Arnoux, 1m 11.000s
FASTEST LAP: Arnoux, 1m 15.067s

Pn	Driver	Car	Laps	Time/Reason
1	Watson	McLaren-Ford	68	1h 26m 54.80s
2	Reutemann	Williams-Ford	68	1h 27m 35.45s
3	Laffite	Ligier-Matra	67	
4	Cheever	Tyrrell-Ford	67	
5	Rebaque	Brabham-Ford	67	
6	Borgudd	ATS-Ford	67	
7	Daly	March-Ford	66	
8	Jarier	Osella-Ford	65	
9	Arnoux	Renault	64	engine
10	Patrese	Arrows-Ford	64	engine
11	Surer	Theodore-Ford	61	out of fuel
r	Andretti,Mario	Alfa Romeo	59	throttle
r	Rosberg	Fittipaldi-Ford	56	suspension
r	de Angelis	Lotus-Ford	25	black flagged
r	Prost	Renault	17	engine
r	Tambay	Ligier-Matra	15	ignition
r	Pironi	Ferrari	13	engine
r	Piquet	Brabham-Ford	11	accident
r	Giacomelli	Alfa Romeo	5	gearbox
r	Villeneuve,G.	Ferrari	4	accident
r	Jones	Williams-Ford	3	accident
r	de Cesaris	McLaren-Ford	3	accident
r	Alboreto	Tyrrell-Ford	0	clutch
r	Stohr	Arrows-Ford	0	accident

STARTING GRID:

1	Arnoux	13	Rebaque
2	Prost	14	Laffite
3	Piquet	15	Tambay
4	Pironi	16	Rosberg
5	Watson	17	Daly
6	de Cesaris	18	Stohr
7	Jones	19	Alboreto
8	Villeneuve,G.	20	Jarier
9	Reutemann	21	Borgudd
10	Patrese	22	de Angelis
11	Andretti,Mario	23	Cheever
12	Giacomelli	24	Surer

German

GRAND PRIX No: 352
DATE: August 2, 1981
VENUE: Hockenheim
POLE LAP: Prost, 1m 47.50s
FASTEST LAP: Jones, 1m 52.42s

Pn	Driver	Car	Laps	Time/Reason
1	Piquet	Brabham-Ford	45	1h 25m 55.60s
2	Prost	Renault	45	1h 26m 07.12s
3	Laffite	Ligier-Matra	45	1h 27m 00.20s
4	Rebaque	Brabham-Ford	45	1h 27m 35.29s
5	Cheever	Tyrrell-Ford	45	1h 27m 46.12s
6	Watson	McLaren-Ford	44	
7	de Angelis	Lotus-Ford	44	
8	Jarier	Osella-Ford	44	
9	Andretti,Mario	Alfa Romeo	44	
10	Villeneuve,G.	Ferrari	44	
11	Jones	Williams-Ford	44	
12	Stohr	Arrows-Ford	44	
13	Arnoux	Renault	44	
14	Surer	Theodore-Ford	43	
15	Giacomelli	Alfa Romeo	43	
uc	Salazar	Ensign-Ford	39	
r	Borgudd	ATS-Ford	35	engine
r	Reutemann	Williams-Ford	27	engine
r	Patrese	Arrows-Ford	27	engine
r	Tambay	Ligier-Matra	27	wheel
r	Daly	March-Ford	15	steering
r	Mansell	Lotus-Ford	12	fuel leak
r	de Cesaris	McLaren-Ford	4	spun off
r	Pironi	Ferrari	1	engine

STARTING GRID:

1	Prost	13	Patrese
2	Arnoux	14	de Angelis
3	Reutemann	15	Mansell
4	Jones	16	Rebaque
5	Pironi	17	Jarier
6	Piquet	18	Cheever
7	Laffite	19	Giacomelli
8	Villeneuve,G.	20	Borgudd
9	Watson	21	Daly
10	de Cesaris	22	Surer
11	Tambay	23	Salazar
12	Andretti,Mario	24	Stohr

Austrian

GRAND PRIX No: 353
DATE: August 16, 1981
VENUE: Osterreichring
POLE LAP: Arnoux, 1m 32.018s
FASTEST LAP: Laffite, 1m 37.620s

Pn	Driver	Car	Laps	Time/Reason
1	Laffite	Ligier-Matra	53	1h 27m 36.47s
2	Arnoux	Renault	53	1h 27m 41.64s
3	Piquet	Brabham-Ford	53	1h 27m 43.81s
4	Jones	Williams-Ford	53	1h 27m 48.51s
5	Reutemann	Williams-Ford	53	1h 28m 08.32s
6	Watson	McLaren-Ford	53	1h 29m 07.61s
7	de Angelis	Lotus-Ford	52	
8	de Cesaris	McLaren-Ford	52	
9	Pironi	Ferrari	52	
10	Jarier	Osella-Ford	51	
11	Daly	March-Ford	47	
r	Andretti,Mario	Alfa Romeo	46	engine
r	Borgudd	ATS-Ford	44	brakes
r	Patrese	Arrows-Ford	43	engine
r	Salazar	Ensign-Ford	43	engine
r	Alboreto	Tyrrell-Ford	40	engine
r	Giacomelli	Alfa Romeo	35	engine
r	Rebaque	Brabham-Ford	31	clutch
r	Stohr	Arrows-Ford	27	spun off
r	Prost	Renault	26	suspension
r	Tambay	Ligier-Matra	26	engine
r	Mansell	Lotus-Ford	23	engine
r	Villeneuve,G.	Ferrari	11	accident
r	Surer	Theodore-Ford	0	distributor

STARTING GRID:

1	Arnoux	13	Andretti,Mario
2	Prost	14	Jarier
3	Villeneuve,G.	15	Rebaque
4	Laffite	16	Giacomelli
5	Reutemann	17	Tambay
6	Jones	18	de Cesaris
7	Piquet	19	Daly
8	Pironi	20	Salazar
9	de Angelis	21	Borgudd
10	Patrese	22	Alboreto
11	Mansell	23	Surer
12	Watson	24	Stohr

Dutch

GRAND PRIX No: 354
DATE: August 30, 1981
VENUE: Zandvoort
POLE LAP: Prost, 1m 18.176s
FASTEST LAP: Jones, 1m 21.830s

Pn	Driver	Car	Laps	Time/Reason
1	Prost	Renault	72	1h 40m 22.43s
2	Piquet	Brabham-Ford	72	1h 40m 30.67s
3	Jones	Williams-Ford	72	1h 40m 57.93s
4	Rebaque	Brabham-Ford	71	
5	de Angelis	Lotus-Ford	71	
6	Salazar	Ensign-Ford	70	
7	Stohr	Arrows-Ford	69	
8	Surer	Theodore-Ford	69	
9	Alboreto	Tyrrell-Ford	68	engine
10	Borgudd	ATS-Ford	68	
r	Andretti,Mario	Alfa Romeo	62	accident
r	Watson	McLaren-Ford	50	electrical
r	Cheever	Tyrrell-Ford	46	accident
r	Jarier	Osella-Ford	29	gearbox
r	Arnoux	Renault	21	accident
r	Giacomelli	Alfa Romeo	19	accident
r	Laffite	Ligier-Matra	18	accident
r	Reutemann	Williams-Ford	18	accident
r	Patrese	Arrows-Ford	16	suspension
r	Daly	March-Ford	5	suspension
r	Pironi	Ferrari	4	accident
r	Mansell	Lotus-Ford	1	electrical
r	Tambay	Ligier-Matra	0	accident
r	Villeneuve,G.	Ferrari	0	accident

STARTING GRID:

1	Prost	13	Giacomelli
2	Arnoux	14	Rebaque
3	Piquet	15	Villeneuve,G.
4	Jones	16	Mansell
5	Reutemann	17	Jarier
6	Laffite	18	Daly
7	Andretti,Mario	19	Surer
8	Watson	20	Stohr
9	de Angelis	21	Cheever
10	Patrese	22	Borgudd
11	Tambay	23	Salazar
12	Pironi	24	Alboreto

Italian

GRAND PRIX No: 355
DATE: September 13, 1981
VENUE: Monza
POLE LAP: Arnoux, 1m 33.467s
FASTEST LAP: Reutemann, 1m 37.528s

Pn	Driver	Car	Laps	Time/Reason
1	Prost	Renault	52	1h 26m 33.897s
2	Jones	Williams-Ford	52	1h 26m 56.072s
3	Reutemann	Williams-Ford	52	1h 27m 24.484s
4	de Angelis	Lotus-Ford	52	1h 28m 06.799s
5	Pironi	Ferrari	52	1h 28m 08.419s
6	Piquet	Brabham-Ford	51	engine
7	de Cesaris	McLaren-Ford	51	accident
8	Giacomelli	Alfa Romeo	50	
9	Jarier	Osella-Ford	50	
10	Henton	Toleman-Hart	49	
r	Andretti,Mario	Alfa Romeo	41	engine
r	Daly	March-Ford	37	gearbox
r	Tambay	Ligier-Matra	22	puncture
r	Mansell	Lotus-Ford	21	handling
r	Watson	McLaren-Ford	19	accident
r	Patrese	Arrows-Ford	19	gearbox
r	Alboreto	Tyrrell-Ford	16	accident
r	Salazar	Ensign-Ford	13	burst tyre
r	Arnoux	Renault	12	accident
r	Cheever	Tyrrell-Ford	11	spun off
r	Laffite	Ligier-Matra	11	puncture
r	Borgudd	ATS-Ford	10	spun off
r	Villeneuve,G.	Ferrari	6	turbo
r	Rebaque	Brabham-Ford	0	electrical

STARTING GRID:

1	Arnoux	13	Andretti,Mario
2	Reutemann	14	Rebaque
3	Prost	15	Tambay
4	Laffite	16	de Cesaris
5	Jones	17	Cheever
6	Piquet	18	Jarier
7	Watson	19	Daly
8	Pironi	20	Patrese
9	Villeneuve,G.	21	Borgudd
10	Giacomelli	22	Alboreto
11	de Angelis	23	Henton
12	Mansell	24	Salazar

Canadian

GRAND PRIX No: 356
DATE: September 27, 1981
VENUE: Montreal
POLE LAP: Piquet, 1m 29.211s
FASTEST LAP: Watson, 1m 49.475s

Pn	Driver	Car	Laps	Time/Reason
1	Laffite	Ligier-Matra	63	2h 01m 25.205s
2	Watson	McLaren-Ford	63	2h 01m 31.438s
3	Villeneuve,G.	Ferrari	63	2h 03m 15.480s
4	Giacomelli	Alfa Romeo	62	
5	Piquet	Brabham-Ford	62	
6	de Angelis	Lotus-Ford	62	
7	Andretti,Mario	Alfa Romeo	62	
8	Daly	March-Ford	61	
9	Surer	Theodore-Ford	61	
10	Reutemann	Williams-Ford	60	
11	Alboreto	Tyrrell-Ford	59	
12	Cheever	Tyrrell-Ford	56	engine
r	de Cesaris	McLaren-Ford	51	spun off
r	Prost	Renault	48	accident
r	Mansell	Lotus-Ford	45	accident
r	Borgudd	ATS-Ford	39	spun off
r	Rebaque	Brabham-Ford	35	spun off
r	Jarier	Osella-Ford	26	accident
r	Pironi	Ferrari	24	engine
r	Jones	Williams-Ford	24	handling
r	Salazar	Ensign-Ford	8	spun off
r	Tambay	Ligier-Matra	6	spun off
r	Patrese	Arrows-Ford	6	spun off
r	Arnoux	Renault	0	accident

STARTING GRID:

1	Piquet	13	de Cesaris
2	Reutemann	14	Cheever
3	Jones	15	Giacomelli
4	Prost	16	Andretti,Mario
5	Mansell	17	Tambay
6	Rebaque	18	Patrese
7	de Angelis	19	Surer
8	Arnoux	20	Daly
9	Watson	21	Borgudd
10	Laffite	22	Alboreto
11	Villeneuve,G.	23	Jarier
12	Pironi	24	Salazar

Caesar's Palace

GRAND PRIX No:	357
DATE:	October 17, 1981
VENUE:	Las Vegas
POLE LAP:	Reutemann, 1m 17.821s
FASTEST LAP:	Pironi, 1m 20.156s

Pn	Driver	Car	Laps	Time/Reason
1	Jones	Williams-Ford	75	1h 44m 09.077s
2	Prost	Renault	75	1h 44m 29.125s
3	Giacomelli	Alfa Romeo	75	1h 44m 29 505s
4	Mansell	Lotus-Ford	75	1h 44m 56.550s
5	Piquet	Brabham-Ford	75	1h 45m 25.515s
6	Laffite	Ligier-Matra	75	1h 45m 27 252s
7	Watson	McLaren-Ford	75	1h 45m 27.574s
8	Reutemann	Williams-Ford	74	
9	Pironi	Ferrari	73	
10	Rosberg	Fittipaldi-Ford	73	
11	Patrese	Arrows-Ford	71	
12	de Cesaris	McLaren-Ford	69	
13	Alboreto	Tyrrell-Ford	67	
uc	Salazar	Ensign-Ford	61	
r	Warwick	Toleman-Hart	43	gearbox
r	Andretti,Mario	Alfa Romeo	29	suspension
dq	Villeneuve,G.	Ferrari	22	illegal start
r	Rebaque	Brabham-Ford	20	spun off
r	Surer	Theodore-Ford	19	suspension
r	Cheever	Tyrrell-Ford	10	engine
r	Arnoux	Renault	10	electrical
r	Tambay	Ligier-Matra	2	accident
r	de Angelis	Lotus-Ford	2	water leak
r	Jarier	Osella-Ford	0	transmission

STARTING GRID:

1	Reutemann	13	Arnoux
2	Jones	14	de Cesaris
3	Villeneuve,G.	15	de Angelis
4	Piquet	16	Rebaque
5	Prost	17	Alboreto
6	Watson	18	Pironi
7	Tambay	19	Cheever
8	Giacomelli	20	Rosberg
9	Mansell	21	Jarier
10	Andretti,Mario	22	Warwick
11	Patrese	23	Surer
12	Laffite	24	Salazar +

South African

GRAND PRIX No:	358
DATE:	January 23, 1982
VENUE:	Kyalami
POLE LAP:	Arnoux, 1m 06.351s
FASTEST LAP:	Prost, 1m 08.278s

Pn	Driver	Car	Laps	Time/Reason
1	Prost	Renault	77	1h 32m 08.401s
2	Reutemann	Williams-Ford	77	1h 32m 23.347s
3	Arnoux	Renault	77	1h 32m 36.301s
4	Lauda	McLaren-Ford	77	1h 32m 40.514s
5	Rosberg	Williams-Ford	77	1h 32m 54.540s
6	Watson	McLaren-Ford	77	1h 32m 59.394s
7	Alboreto	Tyrrell-Ford	76	
8	de Angelis	Lotus-Ford	76	
9	Salazar	ATS-Ford	75	
10	Winkelhock	ATS-Ford	75	
11	Giacomelli	Alfa Romeo	74	
12	Mass	March-Ford	74	
13	de Cesaris	Alfa Romeo	73	
14	Daly	Theodore-Ford	73	
15	Boesel	March-Ford	72	
16	Borgudd	Tyrrell-Ford	72	
17	Serra	Fittipaldi-Ford	72	
18	Pironi	Ferrari	71	
r	Laffite	Ligier-Matra	54	fuel system
r	Warwick	Toleman-Hart	43	accident
r	Patrese	Brabham-BMW	18	turbo
r	Cheever	Ligier-Matra	11	fuel system
r	Villeneuve,G.	Ferrari	6	turbo
r	Piquet	Brabham-BMW	3	accident
r	Mansell	Lotus-Ford	0	electrical
r	Jarier	Osella-Ford	0	accident

STARTING GRID:

1	Arnoux	12	Salazar
2	Piquet	13	Lauda
3	Villeneuve,G.	14	Warwick
4	Patrese	15	de Angelis
5	Prost	16	de Cesaris
6	Pironi	17	Cheever
7	Rosberg	18	Mansell
8	Reutemann	19	Giacomelli
9	Watson	20	Winkelhock
10	Alboreto	21	Boesel
11	Laffite	22	Mass +

Brazilian

GRAND PRIX No: 359
DATE: March 21, 1982
VENUE: Rio de Janeiro
POLE LAP: Prost, 1m 28.808s
FASTEST LAP: Prost, 1m 37.016s

Pn	Driver	Car	Laps	Time/Reason
dq	Piquet	Brabham-Ford	63	underweight
dq	Rosberg	Williams-Ford	63	underweight
1	Prost	Renault	63	1h 44m 33.134s
2	Watson	McLaren-Ford	63	1h 44m 36.124s
3	Mansell	Lotus-Ford	63	1h 45m 09.993s
4	Alboreto	Tyrrell-Ford	63	1h 45m 23.895s
5	Winkelhock	ATS-Ford	62	
6	Pironi	Ferrari	62	
7	Borgudd	Tyrrell-Ford	61	
8	Mass	March-Ford	61	
9	Jarier	Osella-Ford	60	
10	Baldi	Arrows-Ford	59	
r	Salazar	ATS-Ford	38	engine
r	Serra	Fittipaldi-Ford	36	accident
r	Patrese	Brabham-Ford	33	driver tired
r	Villeneuve,G.	Ferrari	29	spun off
r	Lauda	McLaren-Ford	22	accident
r	Arnoux	Renault	21	accident
r	Reutemann	Williams-Ford	21	accident
r	de Angelis	Lotus-Ford	21	accident
r	Cheever	Ligier-Matra	19	water leak
r	Giacomelli	Alfa Romeo	16	engine
r	Laffite	Ligier-Matra	15	engine
r	de Cesaris	Alfa Romeo	14	undertray
r	Daly	Theodore-Ford	12	spun off
r	Boesel	March-Ford	11	accident

STARTING GRID:

1	Prost	12	Watson
2	Villeneuve,G.	13	Alboreto
3	Rosberg	14	Mansell
4	Arnoux	15	Winkelhock
5	Lauda	16	Giacomelli
6	Reutemann	17	Boesel
7	Piquet	18	Salazar
8	Pironi	19	Baldi
9	Patrese	20	Daly
10	de Cesaris	21	Borgudd
11	de Angelis	22	Mass

+

US West

GRAND PRIX No: 360
DATE: April 4, 1982
VENUE: Long Beach
POLE LAP: de Cesaris, 1m 27.316s
FASTEST LAP: Lauda, 1m 30.831s

Pn	Driver	Car	Laps	Time/Reason
1	Lauda	McLaren-Ford	75	1h 58m 25.318s
2	Rosberg	Williams-Ford	75	1h 58m 39.978s
dq	Villeneuve,G.	Ferrari	75	illegal wing
3	Patrese	Brabham-Ford	75	1h 59m 44.461s
4	Alboreto	Tyrrell-Ford	75	1h 59m 46.265s
5	de Angelis	Lotus-Ford	74	
6	Watson	McLaren-Ford	74	
7	Mansell	Lotus-Ford	73	
8	Mass	March-Ford	73	
9	Boesel	March-Ford	70	
10	Borgudd	Tyrrell-Ford	68	
r	Cheever	Ligier-Matra	58	gearbox
r	de Cesaris	Alfa Romeo	33	accident
r	Henton	Arrows-Ford	32	accident
r	Guerrero	Ensign-Ford	27	accident
r	Laffite	Ligier-Matra	26	spun off
r	Jarier	Osella-Ford	26	transmission
r	Piquet	Brabham-Ford	25	accident
r	Daly	Theodore-Ford	22	accident
r	Andretti,Mario	Williams-Ford	19	accident
r	Prost	Renault	10	accident
r	Pironi	Ferrari	6	accident
r	Arnoux	Renault	5	accident
r	Giacomelli	Alfa Romeo	5	accident
r	Salazar	ATS-Ford	3	accident
r	Winkelhock	ATS-Ford	1	accident

STARTING GRID:

1	de Cesaris	12	Alboreto
2	Lauda	13	Cheever
3	Arnoux	14	Andretti,Mario
4	Prost	15	Laffite
5	Giacomelli	16	de Angelis
6	Piquet	17	Mansell
7	Villeneuve,G.	18	Patrese
8	Rosberg	19	Guerrero
9	Pironi	20	Henton
10	Jarier	21	Mass
11	Watson	22	Daly

+

San Marino

GRAND PRIX No: 361
DATE: April 25, 1982
VENUE: Imola
POLE LAP: Arnoux, 1m 29.765s
FASTEST LAP: Pironi, 1m 35.036s

Pn	Driver	Car	Laps	Time/Reason
1	Pironi	Ferrari	60	1h 36m 38.887s
2	Villeneuve,G.	Ferrari	60	1h 36m 39.253s
3	Alboreto	Tyrrell-Ford	60	1h 37m 46.571s
4	Jarier	Osella-Ford	59	
5	Salazar	ATS-Ford	57	
dq	Winkelhock	ATS-Ford	54	underweight
uc	Fabi,T.	Toleman-Hart	52	
r	Arnoux	Renault	44	engine
r	Giacomelli	Alfa Romeo	24	engine
r	Paletti	Osella-Ford	7	suspension
r	Prost	Renault	6	engine
r	de Cesaris	Alfa Romeo	4	fuel system
r	Henton	Tyrrell-Ford	0	transmission

STARTING GRID:

1 Arnoux
2 Prost
3 Villeneuve,G.
4 Pironi
5 Alboreto
6 Giacomelli
7 de Cesaris
8 Jarier
9 Fabi,T.
10 Henton
11 Winkelhock
12 Paletti
13 Salazar

Belgian

GRAND PRIX No: 362
DATE: May 9, 1982
VENUE: Zolder
POLE LAP: Prost, 1m 15.701s
FASTEST LAP: Watson, 1m 20.214s

Pn	Driver	Car	Laps	Time/Reason
1	Watson	McLaren-Ford	70	1h 35m 41.995s
2	Rosberg	Williams-Ford	70	1h 35m 49.263s
dq	Lauda	McLaren-Ford	70	underweight
3	Cheever	Ligier-Matra	69	
4	de Angelis	Lotus-Ford	68	
5	Piquet	Brabham-BMW	67	
6	Serra	Fittipaldi-Ford	67	
7	Surer	Arrows-Ford	66	
8	Boesel	March-Ford	66	
9	Laffite	Ligier-Matra	66	
r	Daly	Williams-Ford	60	accident
r	Mass	March-Ford	60	engine
r	Prost	Renault	59	spun off
r	Patrese	Brabham-BMW	52	accident
r	Baldi	Arrows-Ford	51	throttle
r	Jarier	Osella-Ford	37	rear wing
r	de Cesaris	Alfa Romeo	34	gearbox
r	Henton	Tyrrell-Ford	33	engine
r	Alboreto	Tyrrell-Ford	29	engine
r	Warwick	Toleman-Hart	29	transmission
r	Fabi,T.	Toleman-Hart	13	brakes
r	Mansell	Lotus-Ford	9	gearbox
r	Arnoux	Renault	7	turbo
r	Winkelhock	ATS-Ford	0	clutch
r	Salazar	ATS-Ford	0	accident
r	Giacomelli	Alfa Romeo	0	accident
dns	Pironi	Ferrari		death of GV
dns	Villeneuve,G.	Ferrari		fatal accident

STARTING GRID:

1 Prost
2 Arnoux
3 Rosberg
4 Lauda
5 Alboreto
6 Pironi
7 de Cesaris
8 Villeneuve,G.
9 Mansell
10 Piquet
11 Patrese
12 Watson
13 de Angelis
14 Winkelhock
15 Daly
16 Cheever
17 Giacomelli
18 Jarier +

Monaco

GRAND PRIX No:	363
DATE:	May 23, 1982
VENUE:	Monte Carlo
POLE LAP:	Arnoux, 1m 23.281s
FASTEST LAP:	Patrese, 1m 26.354s

Pn	Driver	Car	Laps	Time/Reason
1	Patrese	Brabham-Ford	76	1h 54m 11.259s
2	Pironi	Ferrari	75	electrical
3	de Cesaris	Alfa Romeo	75	out of fuel
4	Mansell	Lotus-Ford	75	
5	de Angelis	Lotus-Ford	75	
6	Daly	Williams-Ford	74	accident
7	Prost	Renault	73	accident
8	Henton	Tyrrell-Ford	72	
9	Surer	Arrows-Ford	70	
10	Alboreto	Tyrrell-Ford	69	suspension
r	Rosberg	Williams-Ford	64	accident
r	Lauda	McLaren-Ford	56	engine
r	Piquet	Brabham-BMW	49	gearbox
r	Watson	McLaren-Ford	35	electrical
r	Winkelhock	ATS-Ford	31	transmission
r	Laffite	Ligier-Matra	29	handling
r	Cheever	Ligier-Matra	27	engine
r	Salazar	ATS-Ford	22	fire extinguisher
r	Arnoux	Renault	14	spun off
r	Giacomelli	Alfa Romeo	4	transmission

STARTING GRID:

1	Arnoux	11	Mansell
2	Patrese	12	Lauda
3	Giacomelli	13	Piquet
4	Prost	14	Winkelhock
5	Pironi	15	de Angelis
6	Rosberg	16	Cheever
7	de Cesaris	17	Henton
8	Daly	18	Laffite
9	Alboreto	19	Surer
10	Watson	20	Salazar

US

GRAND PRIX No:	364
DATE:	June 6, 1982
VENUE:	Detroit
POLE LAP:	Prost, 1m 48.537s
FASTEST LAP:	Prost, 1m 50.438s

Pn	Driver	Car	Laps	Time/Reason
1	Watson	McLaren-Ford	62	1h 58m 41.043s
2	Cheever	Ligier-Matra	62	1h 58m 56.769s
3	Pironi	Ferrari	62	1h 59m 09.120s
4	Rosberg	Williams-Ford	62	1h 59m 53.019s
5	Daly	Williams-Ford	62	2h 00m 04.800s
6	Laffite	Ligier-Matra	61	
7	Mass	March-Ford	61	
8	Surer	Arrows-Ford	61	
9	Henton	Tyrrell-Ford	60	
10	Arnoux	Renault	59	
11	Serra	Fittipaldi-Ford	59	
uc	Prost	Renault	54	
r	Mansell	Lotus-Ford	44	engine
r	Lauda	McLaren-Ford	40	accident
r	Alboreto	Tyrrell-Ford	40	accident
r	Giacomelli	Alfa Romeo	30	accident
r	de Angelis	Lotus-Ford	17	gearbox
r	Salazar	ATS-Ford	13	accident
r	Guerrero	Ensign-Ford	6	accident
r	Patrese	Brabham-Ford	6	accident
r	de Cesaris	Alfa Romeo	2	transmission
r	Jarier	Osella-Ford	2	engine
r	Winkelhock	ATS-Ford	1	accident
r	Boesel	March-Ford	0	accident
r	Baldi	Arrows-Ford	0	accident
dns	Paletti	Osella-Ford		accident

STARTING GRID:

1	Prost	12	Daly
2	de Cesaris	13	Laffite
3	Rosberg	14	Patrese
4	Pironi	15	Arnoux
5	Winkelhock	16	Alboreto
6	Giacomelli	17	Watson
7	Mansell	18	Mass
8	de Angelis	19	Surer
9	Cheever	20	Henton
10	Lauda	21	Boesel
11	Guerrero	22	Jarier

+

Canadian

GRAND PRIX No:	365
DATE:	June 13, 1982
VENUE:	Montreal
POLE LAP:	Pironi, 1m 27.509s
FASTEST LAP:	Pironi, 1m 28.323s

Pn	Driver	Car	Laps	Time/Reason
1	Piquet	Brabham-BMW	70	1h 46m 39.577s
2	Patrese	Brabham-Ford	70	1h 46m 53.376s
3	Watson	McLaren-Ford	70	1h 47m 41.413s
4	de Angelis	Lotus-Ford	69	
5	Surer	Arrows-Ford	69	
6	de Cesaris	Alfa Romeo	68	out of fuel
7	Daly	Williams-Ford	68	out of fuel
8	Baldi	Arrows-Ford	68	
9	Pironi	Ferrari	67	
10	Cheever	Ligier-Matra	66	out of fuel
11	Mass	March-Ford	66	
r	Henton	Tyrrell-Ford	59	
r	Rosberg	Williams-Ford	52	gearbox
r	Boesel	March-Ford	47	engine
r	Alboreto	Tyrrell-Ford	41	gearbox
r	Prost	Renault	30	engine
r	Arnoux	Renault	28	spun off
r	Salazar	ATS-Ford	20	engine
r	Lauda	McLaren-Ford	17	clutch
r	Laffite	Ligier-Matra	8	fuel system
r	Guerrero	Ensign-Ford	2	clutch
r	Giacomelli	Alfa Romeo	1	accident
r	Mansell	Lotus-Ford	1	accident
r	Lees	Theodore-Ford	0	accident
r	Jarier	Osella-Ford	0	withdrew
r	Paletti	Osella-Ford	0	fatal accident

STARTING GRID:

1	Pironi	12	Cheever
2	Arnoux	13	Daly
3	Prost	14	Mansell
4	Piquet	15	Alboreto
5	Giacomelli	16	Surer
6	Watson	17	Baldi
7	Rosberg	18	Jarier
8	Patrese	19	Laffite
9	de Cesaris	20	Guerrero
10	de Angelis	21	Boesel
11	Lauda	22	Mass

Dutch

GRAND PRIX No:	366
DATE:	July 3, 1982
VENUE:	Zandvoort
POLE LAP:	Arnoux, 1m 14.233s
FASTEST LAP:	Warwick, 1m 19.780s

Pn	Driver	Car	Laps	Time/Reason
1	Pironi	Ferrari	72	1h 38m 03.254s
2	Piquet	Brabham-BMW	72	1h 38m 24.903s
3	Rosberg	Williams-Ford	72	1h 38m 25.619s
4	Lauda	McLaren-Ford	71	
5	Daly	Williams-Ford	71	
6	Baldi	Arrows-Ford	71	
7	Alboreto	Tyrrell-Ford	71	
8	Tambay	Ferrari	71	
9	Watson	McLaren-Ford	71	
10	Surer	Arrows-Ford	71	
11	Giacomelli	Alfa Romeo	70	
12	Winkelhock	ATS-Ford	70	
13	Salazar	ATS-Ford	70	
14	Jarier	Osella-Ford	69	
15	Patrese	Brabham-BMW	69	
r	Mass	March-Ford	60	engine
r	Lammers	Theodore-Ford	41	engine
r	de Angelis	Lotus-Ford	40	handling
r	de Cesaris	Alfa Romeo	35	electrical
r	Prost	Renault	33	engine
r	Arnoux	Renault	21	accident
r	Henton	Tyrrell-Ford	21	throttle
r	Boesel	March-Ford	21	engine
r	Serra	Fittipaldi-Ford	18	fuel system
r	Warwick	Toleman-Hart	15	oil leak
r	Laffite	Ligier-Matra	5	handling

STARTING GRID:

1	Arnoux	12	Daly
2	Prost	13	Warwick
3	Piquet	14	Alboreto
4	Pironi	15	de Angelis
5	Lauda	16	Baldi
6	Tambay	17	Surer
7	Rosberg	18	Winkelhock
8	Giacomelli	19	Serra
9	de Cesaris	20	Henton
10	Patrese	21	Laffite
11	Watson	22	Boesel

British

GRAND PRIX No:	367
DATE:	July 18, 1982
VENUE:	Brands Hatch
POLE LAP:	Rosberg, 1m 09.540s
FASTEST LAP:	Henton, 1m 13.028s

Pn	Driver	Car	Laps	Time/Reason
1	Lauda	McLaren-Ford	76	1h 35m 33.812s
2	Pironi	Ferrari	76	1h 35m 59.538s
3	Tambay	Ferrari	76	1h 36m 12.248s
4	de Angelis	Lotus-Ford	76	1h 36m 15.054s
5	Daly	Williams-Ford	76	1h 36m 15.242s
6	Prost	Renault	76	1h 36m 15.448s
7	Giacomelli	Alfa Romeo	75	
8	Henton	Tyrrell-Ford	75	
9	Baldi	Arrows-Ford	74	
10	Mass	March-Ford	73	
r	de Cesaris	Alfa Romeo	66	electrical
r	Cheever	Ligier-Matra	60	engine
r	Surer	Arrows-Ford	59	mechanical
r	Rosberg	Williams-Ford	50	fuel pressure
uc	Alboreto	Tyrrell-Ford	44	
r	Laffite	Ligier-Matra	41	gearbox
r	Warwick	Toleman-Hart	40	transmission
r	Mansell	Lotus-Ford	29	handling
r	Piquet	Brabham-BMW	9	fuel system
r	Guerrero	Ensign-Ford	3	engine
r	Jarier	Osella-Ford	2	accident
r	Serra	Fittipaldi-Ford	2	accident
r	Watson	McLaren-Ford	2	spun off
r	Fabi,T.	Toleman-Hart	0	accident
r	Arnoux	Renault	0	accident
r	Patrese	Brabham-BMW	0	accident

STARTING GRID:

1	Rosberg	9	Alboreto
2	Patrese	10	Daly
3	Piquet	11	de Cesaris
4	Pironi	12	Watson
5	Lauda	13	Tambay
6	Arnoux	14	Giacomelli
7	de Angelis	15	Fabi,T.
8	Prost	16	Warwick +

French

GRAND PRIX No:	368
DATE:	July 25, 1982
VENUE:	Paul Ricard
POLE LAP:	Arnoux, 1m 34.406s
FASTEST LAP:	Patrese, 1m 40.075s

Pn	Driver	Car	Laps	Time/Reason
1	Arnoux	Renault	54	1h 33m 33.217s
2	Prost	Renault	54	1h 33m 50.525s
3	Pironi	Ferrari	54	1h 34m 15.345s
4	Tambay	Ferrari	54	1h 34m 49.458s
5	Rosberg	Williams-Ford	54	1h 35m 04.211s
6	Alboreto	Tyrrell-Ford	54	1h 35m 05.556s
7	Daly	Williams-Ford	53	
8	Lauda	McLaren-Ford	53	
9	Giacomelli	Alfa Romeo	53	
10	Henton	Tyrrell-Ford	53	
11	Winkelhock	ATS-Ford	52	
12	Lees	Lotus-Ford	52	
13	Surer	Arrows-Ford	52	
14	Laffite	Ligier-Matra	51	
15	Warwick	Toleman-Hart	50	
16	Cheever	Ligier-Matra	49	
r	de Cesaris	Alfa Romeo	25	accident
r	Piquet	Brabham-BMW	23	engine
r	de Angelis	Lotus-Ford	17	fuel pressure
r	Watson	McLaren-Ford	13	electrical
r	Mass	March-Ford	10	accident
r	Baldi	Arrows-Ford	10	accident
r	Patrese	Brabham-BMW	9	engine
r	Salazar	ATS-Ford	2	accident
r	Fabi,T.	Toleman-Hart	0	oil pressure
r	Jarier	Osella-Ford	0	transmission

STARTING GRID:

1	Arnoux	12	Watson
2	Prost	13	de Angelis
3	Pironi	14	Warwick
4	Patrese	15	Alboreto
5	Tambay	16	Laffite
6	Piquet	17	Jarier
7	de Cesaris	18	Winkelhock
8	Giacomelli	19	Cheever
9	Lauda	20	Surer
10	Rosberg	21	Fabi,T.
11	Daly	22	Salazar +

German

GRAND PRIX No: 369
DATE: August 8, 1982
VENUE: Hockenheim
POLE LAP: Pironi, 1m 47.947s
FASTEST LAP: Piquet, 1m 54.035s

Pn	Driver	Car	Laps	Time/Reason
1	Tambay	Ferrari	45	1h 27m 25.178s
2	Arnoux	Renault	45	1h 27m 41.557s
3	Rosberg	Williams-Ford	44	
4	Alboreto	Tyrrell-Ford	44	
5	Giacomelli	Alfa Romeo	44	
6	Surer	Arrows-Ford	44	
7	Henton	Tyrrell-Ford	44	
8	Guerrero	Ensign-Ford	44	
9	Mansell	Lotus-Ford	43	
10	Warwick	Toleman-Hart	43	
11	Serra	Fittipaldi-Ford	43	
r	Watson	McLaren-Ford	36	suspension
r	Laffite	Ligier-Matra	36	handling
r	Daly	Williams-Ford	25	engine
r	Boesel	March-Ford	22	puncture
r	de Angelis	Lotus-Ford	21	driver ill
r	Piquet	Brabham-BMW	18	accident
r	Salazar	ATS-Ford	17	accident
r	Prost	Renault	14	electrical
r	Patrese	Brabham-BMW	13	engine
r	de Cesaris	Alfa Romeo	9	accident
r	Cheever	Ligier-Matra	8	handling
r	Baldi	Arrows-Ford	6	engine
r	Jarier	Osella-Ford	3	suspension
r	Winkelhock	ATS-Ford	3	transmission
dns	Pironi	Ferrari		injured
dns	Lauda	McLaren-Ford		injured

STARTING GRID:

1 Pironi
2 Prost
3 Arnoux
4 Piquet
5 Tambay
6 Patrese
7 Alboreto
8 Lauda
9 de Cesaris
10 Rosberg
11 Watson
12 Giacomelli
13 Cheever
14 de Angelis
15 Warwick
16 Laffite
17 Winkelhock
18 Henton
19 Mansell
20 Daly +

Austrian

GRAND PRIX No: 370
DATE: August 15, 1982
VENUE: Osterreichring
POLE LAP: Piquet, 1m 27.612s
FASTEST LAP: Piquet, 1m 33.699s

Pn	Driver	Car	Laps	Time/Reason
1	de Angelis	Lotus-Ford	53	1h 25m 02.212s
2	Rosberg	Williams-Ford	53	1h 25m 02.262s
3	Laffite	Ligier-Matra	52	
4	Tambay	Ferrari	52	
5	Lauda	McLaren-Ford	52	
6	Baldi	Arrows-Ford	52	
7	Serra	Fittipaldi-Ford	51	
8	Prost	Renault	48	fuel injection
r	Watson	McLaren-Ford	44	engine
r	Henton	Tyrrell-Ford	32	engine
r	Piquet	Brabham-BMW	31	engine
r	Byrne	Theodore-Ford	28	spun off
r	Surer	Arrows-Ford	28	engine
r	Patrese	Brabham-BMW	27	engine
r	Cheever	Ligier-Matra	22	engine
r	Mansell	Lotus-Ford	17	engine
r	Arnoux	Renault	16	engine
r	Winkelhock	ATS-Ford	15	engine
r	Warwick	Toleman-Hart	7	suspension
r	Fabi,T.	Toleman-Hart	7	transmission
r	Guerrero	Ensign-Ford	6	transmission
r	Alboreto	Tyrrell-Ford	1	accident
r	Keegan	March-Ford	1	accident
r	de Cesaris	Alfa Romeo	0	accident
r	Daly	Williams-Ford	0	accident
r	Giacomelli	Alfa Romeo	0	accident

STARTING GRID:

1 Piquet
2 Patrese
3 Prost
4 Tambay
5 Arnoux
6 Rosberg
7 de Angelis
8 Alboreto
9 Daly
10 Lauda
11 de Cesaris
12 Mansell
13 Giacomelli
14 Laffite
15 Warwick
16 Guerrero
17 Fabi,T.
18 Watson
19 Henton
20 Serra
21 Surer
22 Cheever +

Swiss

GRAND PRIX No:	371
DATE:	August 29, 1982
VENUE:	Dijon-Prenois
POLE LAP:	Prost, 1m 01.380s
FASTEST LAP:	Prost, 1m 07.477s

Pn	Driver	Car	Laps	Time/Reason
1	Rosberg	Williams-Ford	80	1h 32m 41.087s
2	Prost	Renault	80	1h 32m 45.529s
3	Lauda	McLaren-Ford	80	1h 33m 41.430s
4	Piquet	Brabham-BMW	79	
5	Patrese	Brabham-BMW	79	
6	de Angelis	Lotus-Ford	79	
7	Alboreto	Tyrrell-Ford	79	
8	Mansell	Lotus-Ford	79	
9	Daly	Williams-Ford	79	
10	de Cesaris	Alfa Romeo	78	
11	Henton	Tyrrell-Ford	78	
12	Giacomelli	Alfa Romeo	78	
13	Watson	McLaren-Ford	77	
14	Salazar	ATS-Ford	77	
15	Surer	Arrows-Ford	76	
r	Arnoux	Renault	75	fuel injection
uc	Cheever	Ligier-Matra	70	
r	Winkelhock	ATS-Ford	55	engine
r	Jarier	Osella-Ford	44	engine
r	Laffite	Ligier-Matra	33	handling
r	Fabi,T.	Toleman-Hart	31	overheating
r	Boesel	March-Ford	31	clutch
r	Keegan	March-Ford	25	spun off
r	Warwick	Toleman-Hart	24	engine
r	Guerrero	Ensign-Ford	4	engine
dns	Tambay	Ferrari		injured

STARTING GRID:

1	Prost	12	Alboreto
2	Arnoux	13	Laffite
3	Patrese	14	Surer
4	Lauda	15	de Angelis
5	de Cesaris	16	Cheever
6	Piquet	17	Jarier
7	Daly	18	Henton
8	Rosberg	19	Guerrero
9	Giacomelli	20	Winkelhock
10	Tambay	21	Warwick
11	Watson	22	Keegan +

Italian

GRAND PRIX No:	372
DATE:	September 12, 1982
VENUE:	Monza
POLE LAP:	Andretti,Mario, 1m 28.473s
FASTEST LAP:	Arnoux, 1m 33.619s

Pn	Driver	Car	Laps	Time/Reason
1	Arnoux	Renault	52	1h 22m 25.734s
2	Tambay	Ferrari	52	1h 22m 39.798s
3	Andretti,Mario	Ferrari	52	1h 23m 14.186s
4	Watson	McLaren-Ford	52	1h 23m 53.579s
5	Alboreto	Tyrrell-Ford	51	
6	Cheever	Ligier-Matra	51	
7	Mansell	Lotus-Ford	51	
8	Rosberg	Williams-Ford	50	
9	Salazar	ATS-Ford	50	
10	de Cesaris	Alfa Romeo	50	
11	Serra	Fittipaldi-Ford	49	
12	Baldi	Arrows-Ford	49	
uc	Guerrero	Ensign-Ford	40	
r	de Angelis	Lotus-Ford	33	throttle
r	Giacomelli	Alfa Romeo	32	handling
r	Surer	Arrows-Ford	28	ignition
r	Prost	Renault	27	fuel injection
r	Lauda	McLaren-Ford	21	handling
r	Jarier	Osella-Ford	10	lost wheel
r	Piquet	Brabham-BMW	7	clutch
r	Patrese	Brabham-BMW	6	clutch
r	Laffite	Ligier-Matra	5	gearbox
r	Fabi,T.	Toleman-Hart	2	engine
r	Daly	Williams-Ford	0	accident
r	Warwick	Toleman-Hart	0	accident
r	Henton	Tyrrell-Ford	0	accident

STARTING GRID:

1	Andretti,Mario	12	Watson
2	Piquet	13	Daly
3	Tambay	14	Cheever
4	Patrese	15	Jarier
5	Prost	16	Warwick
6	Arnoux	17	de Angelis
7	Rosberg	18	Guerrero
8	Giacomelli	19	Surer
9	de Cesaris	20	Henton
10	Lauda	21	Laffite
11	Alboreto	22	Fabi,T. +

Caesar's Palace

GRAND PRIX No: 373
DATE: September 25, 1982
VENUE: Las Vegas
POLE LAP: Prost, 1m 16.356s
FASTEST LAP: Alboreto, 1m 19.639s

Pn	Driver	Car	Laps	Time/Reason
1	Alboreto	Tyrrell-Ford	75	1h 41m 56.888s
2	Watson	McLaren-Ford	75	1h 42m 24.180s
3	Cheever	Ligier-Matra	75	1h 42m 53.338s
4	Prost	Renault	75	1h 43m 05.536s
5	Rosberg	Williams-Ford	75	1h 43m 08.263s
6	Daly	Williams-Ford	74	
7	Surer	Arrows-Ford	74	
8	Henton	Tyrrell-Ford	74	
9	de Cesaris	Alfa Romeo	73	
10	Giacomelli	Alfa Romeo	73	
11	Baldi	Arrows-Ford	73	
12	Keegan	March-Ford	73	
13	Boesel	March-Ford	69	
uc	Winkelhock	ATS-Ford	62	
r	Lauda	McLaren-Ford	53	engine
r	Byrne	Theodore-Ford	39	spun off
r	Warwick	Toleman-Hart	32	ignition
r	de Angelis	Lotus-Ford	28	engine
r	Andretti,Mario	Ferrari	26	suspension
r	Piquet	Brabham-BMW	26	engine
r	Arnoux	Renault	20	engine
r	Patrese	Brabham-BMW	17	clutch
r	Mansell	Lotus-Ford	8	accident
r	Laffite	Ligier-Matra	5	engine
dns	Tambay	Ferrari		injured
dns	Guerrero	Ensign-Ford		engine
dns	Jarier	Osella-Ford		accident

STARTING GRID:

1	Prost	11	Laffite
2	Arnoux	12	Piquet
3	Alboreto	13	Lauda
4	Cheever	14	Daly
5	Patrese	15	Guerrero
6	Rosberg	16	Giacomelli
7	Andretti,Mario	17	Surer
8	Tambay	18	de Cesaris
9	Watson	19	Henton
10	Warwick	20	de Angelis +

Brazilian

GRAND PRIX No: 374
DATE: March 13, 1983
VENUE: Rio de Janeiro
POLE LAP: Rosberg, 1m 34.526s
FASTEST LAP: Piquet, 1m 39.829s

Pn	Driver	Car	Laps	Time/Reason
1	Piquet	Brabham-BMW	63	1h 48m 27.731s
dq	Rosberg	Williams-Ford	63	push start
2	Lauda	McLaren-Ford	63	1h 49m 19.614s
3	Laffite	Williams-Ford	63	1h 49m 41.682s
4	Tambay	Ferrari	63	1h 49m 45.848s
5	Surer	Arrows-Ford	63	1h 49m 45.939s
6	Prost	Renault	62	
7	Warwick	Toleman-Hart	62	
8	Serra	Arrows-Ford	62	
9	Arnoux	Ferrari	62	
10	Sullivan	Tyrrell-Ford	62	
11	Mansell	Lotus-Ford	61	
dq	de Angelis	Lotus-Ford	60	changed car before start
12	Cecotto	Theodore-Ford	60	
13	Salazar	RAM-Ford	59	
14	Winkelhock	ATS-BMW	59	
uc	Guerrero	Theodore-Ford	53	
r	Cheever	Renault	41	turbo
r	Watson	McLaren-Ford	34	engine
r	Boesel	Ligier-Ford	25	electrical
r	Baldi	Alfa Romeo	23	accident
r	Jarier	Ligier-Ford	22	suspension
r	Patrese	Brabham-BMW	19	exhaust
r	Fabi,C.	Osella-Ford	17	engine
r	Giacomelli	Toleman-Hart	16	spun off
r	Alboreto	Tyrrell-Ford	7	accident

STARTING GRID:

1	Rosberg	11	Alboreto
2	Prost	12	Jarier
3	Tambay	13	de Angelis
4	Piquet	14	Guerrero
5	Warwick	15	Giacomelli
6	Arnoux	16	Watson
7	Patrese	17	Boesel
8	Cheever	18	Laffite
9	Lauda	19	Cecotto
10	Baldi	20	Surer +

US West

GRAND PRIX No: 375
DATE: March 27, 1983
VENUE: Long Beach
POLE LAP: Tambay, 1m 26.117s
FASTEST LAP: Lauda, 1m 28.330s

Pn	Driver	Car	Laps	Time/Reason
1	Watson	McLaren-Ford	75	1h 53m 34.889s
2	Lauda	McLaren-Ford	75	1h 54m 02.882s
3	Arnoux	Ferrari	75	1h 54m 48.527s
4	Laffite	Williams-Ford	74	
5	Surer	Arrows-Ford	74	
6	Cecotto	Theodore-Ford	74	
7	Boesel	Ligier-Ford	73	
8	Sullivan	Tyrrell-Ford	73	
9	Alboreto	Tyrrell-Ford	73	
10	Patrese	Brabham-BMW	72	distributor
11	Prost	Renault	72	
12	Mansell	Lotus-Ford	72	
r	Cheever	Renault	67	gearbox
r	Jones	Arrows-Ford	58	driver discomfort
r	Piquet	Brabham-BMW	51	throttle
r	de Cesaris	Alfa Romeo	48	gearbox
r	de Angelis	Lotus-Renault	29	tyres
r	Guerrero	Theodore-Ford	27	gearbox
r	Jarier	Ligier-Ford	26	accident
r	Giacomelli	Toleman-Hart	26	battery
r	Baldi	Alfa Romeo	26	accident
r	Tambay	Ferrari	25	accident
r	Rosberg	Williams-Ford	25	accident
r	Salazar	RAM-Ford	25	gearbox
r	Warwick	Toleman-Hart	11	accident
r	Winkelhock	ATS-BMW	3	accident

STARTING GRID:

1	Tambay	12	Jones
2	Arnoux	13	Mansell
3	Rosberg	14	Giacomelli
4	Laffite	15	Cheever
5	de Angelis	16	Surer
6	Warwick	17	Cecotto
7	Alboreto	18	Guerrero
8	Prost	19	de Cesaris
9	Sullivan	20	Piquet
10	Jarier	21	Baldi
11	Patrese	22	Watson +

French

GRAND PRIX No: 376
DATE: April 17, 1983
VENUE: Paul Ricard
POLE LAP: Prost, 1m 36.672s
FASTEST LAP: Prost, 1m 42.695s

Pn	Driver	Car	Laps	Time/Reason
1	Prost	Renault	54	1h 34m 13.913s
2	Piquet	Brabham-BMW	54	1h 34m 43.633s
3	Cheever	Renault	54	1h 34m 54.145s
4	Tambay	Ferrari	54	1h 35m 20.793s
5	Rosberg	Williams-Ford	53	
6	Laffite	Williams-Ford	53	
7	Arnoux	Ferrari	53	
8	Alboreto	Tyrrell-Ford	53	
9	Jarier	Ligier-Ford	53	
10	Surer	Arrows-Ford	53	
11	Cecotto	Theodore-Ford	52	
12	de Cesaris	Alfa Romeo	50	
13	Giacomelli	Toleman-Hart	49	gearbox
r	Boesel	Ligier-Ford	47	engine
r	Fabi,C.	Osella-Ford	36	engine
r	Winkelhock	ATS-BMW	36	engine
r	Lauda	McLaren-Ford	29	wheel bearing
r	Baldi	Alfa Romeo	28	accident
r	Serra	Arrows-Ford	26	gearbox
r	Guerrero	Theodore-Ford	23	engine
r	Sullivan	Tyrrell-Ford	21	clutch
r	de Angelis	Lotus-Renault	20	electrical
r	Patrese	Brabham-BMW	19	overheating
r	Warwick	Toleman-Hart	14	engine
r	Mansell	Lotus-Ford	6	handling
r	Watson	McLaren-Ford	3	throttle

STARTING GRID:

1	Prost	12	Lauda
2	Cheever	13	Giacomelli
3	Patrese	14	Watson
4	Arnoux	15	Alboreto
5	de Angelis	16	Rosberg
6	Piquet	17	Cecotto
7	de Cesaris	18	Mansell
8	Baldi	19	Laffite
9	Warwick	20	Jarier
10	Winkelhock	21	Surer
11	Tambay	22	Guerrero +

San Marino

GRAND PRIX No: 377
DATE: May 1, 1983
VENUE: Imola
POLE LAP: Arnoux, 1m 31.238s
FASTEST LAP: Patrese, 1m 34.437s

Pn	Driver	Car	Laps	Time/Reason
1	Tambay	Ferrari	60	1h 37m 52.460s
2	Prost	Renault	60	1h 38m 41.241s
3	Arnoux	Ferrari	59	
4	Rosberg	Williams-Ford	59	
5	Watson	McLaren-Ford	59	
6	Surer	Arrows-Ford	59	
7	Laffite	Williams-Ford	59	
8	Serra	Arrows-Ford	58	
9	Boesel	Ligier-Ford	58	
10	Baldi	Alfa Romeo	57	engine
11	Winkelhock	ATS-BMW	57	
12	Mansell	Lotus-Ford	56	accident
13	Patrese	Brabham-BMW	54	accident
r	de Cesaris	Alfa Romeo	46	distributor
r	de Angelis	Lotus-Renault	44	handling
r	Piquet	Brabham-BMW	42	engine
r	Jarier	Ligier-Ford	40	radiator
r	Sullivan	Tyrrell-Ford	37	accident
r	Warwick	Toleman-Hart	27	accident
r	Fabi,C.	Osella-Ford	20	accident
r	Giacomelli	Toleman-Hart	21	suspension
r	Lauda	McLaren-Ford	11	accident
r	Cecotto	Theodore-Ford	11	accident
r	Alboreto	Tyrrell-Ford	10	accident
r	Guerrero	Theodore-Ford	3	accident
r	Cheever	Renault	2	turbo

STARTING GRID:

1	Arnoux	12	Surer
2	Piquet	13	Alboreto
3	Tambay	14	Warwick
4	Prost	15	Mansell
5	Patrese	16	Laffite
6	Cheever	17	Giacomelli
7	Winkelhock	18	Lauda
8	de Cesaris	19	Jarier
9	de Angelis	20	Serra
10	Baldi	21	Guerrero
11	Rosberg	22	Sullivan

+

Monaco

GRAND PRIX No: 378
DATE: May 15, 1983
VENUE: Monte Carlo
POLE LAP: Prost, 1m 24.840s
FASTEST LAP: Piquet, 1m 27.283s

Pn	Driver	Car	Laps	Time/Reason
1	Rosberg	Williams-Ford	76	1h 56m 38.121s
2	Piquet	Brabham-BMW	76	1h 56m 56.596s
3	Prost	Renault	76	1h 57m 09.487s
4	Tambay	Ferrari	76	1h 57m 42.418s
5	Sullivan	Tyrrell-Ford	74	
6	Baldi	Alfa Romeo	74	
7	Serra	Arrows-Ford	74	
r	Patrese	Brabham-BMW	64	electrical
r	Laffite	Williams-Ford	54	gearbox
r	Warwick	Toleman-Hart	50	accident
r	de Angelis	Lotus-Renault	50	driveshaft
r	Surer	Arrows-Ford	49	accident
r	Jarier	Ligier-Ford	33	suspension
r	Cheever	Renault	30	engine
r	de Cesaris	Alfa Romeo	14	gearbox
r	Arnoux	Ferrari	6	accident
r	Boesel	Ligier-Ford	3	accident
r	Winkelhock	ATS-BMW	3	accident
r	Alboreto	Tyrrell-Ford	0	accident
r	Mansell	Lotus-Ford	0	accident

STARTING GRID:

1	Prost	11	Alboreto
2	Arnoux	12	Surer
3	Cheever	13	Baldi
4	Tambay	14	Mansell
5	Rosberg	15	Serra
6	Piquet	16	Winkelhock
7	de Cesaris	17	Patrese
8	Laffite	18	Boesel
9	Jarier	19	de Angelis
10	Warwick	20	Sullivan

Belgian

GRAND PRIX No: 379
DATE: May 22, 1983
VENUE: Spa-Francorchamps
POLE LAP: Prost, 2m 04.615s
FASTEST LAP: de Cesaris, 2m 07.493s

Pn	Driver	Car	Laps	Time/Reason
1	Prost	Renault	40	1h 27m 11.502s
2	Tambay	Ferrari	40	1h 27m 34.684s
3	Cheever	Renault	40	1h 27m 51.371s
4	Piquet	Brabham-BMW	40	1h 27m 53.797s
5	Rosberg	Williams-Ford	40	1h 28m 01.982s
6	Laffite	Williams-Ford	40	1h 28m 44.609s
7	Warwick	Toleman-Hart	40	1h 29m 10.041s
8	Giacomelli	Toleman-Hart	40	1h 29m 49.775s
9	de Angelis	Lotus-Renault	39	
10	Cecotto	Theodore-Ford	39	
11	Surer	Arrows-Ford	39	
12	Sullivan	Tyrrell-Ford	39	
13	Boesel	Ligier-Ford	39	
14	Alboreto	Tyrrell-Ford	38	
r	Lauda	McLaren-Ford	33	engine
r	Mansell	Lotus-Ford	30	gearbox
r	de Cesaris	Alfa Romeo	25	engine
r	Guerrero	Theodore-Ford	23	engine
r	Arnoux	Ferrari	22	engine
r	Fabi,C.	Osella-Ford	19	suspension
r	Winkelhock	ATS-BMW	18	wheel
r	Watson	McLaren-Ford	8	accident
r	Jarier	Ligier-Ford	8	accident
r	Boutsen	Arrows-Ford	4	suspension
r	Baldi	Alfa Romeo	3	throttle
r	Patrese	Brabham-BMW	0	engine

STARTING GRID:

1	Prost	12	Baldi
2	Tambay	13	de Angelis
3	de Cesaris	14	Guerrero
4	Piquet	15	Lauda
5	Arnoux	16	Giacomelli
6	Patrese	17	Alboreto
7	Winkelhock	18	Boutsen
8	Cheever	19	Mansell
9	Rosberg	20	Watson
10	Surer	21	Jarier
11	Laffite	22	Warwick +

US

GRAND PRIX No: 380
DATE: June 5, 1983
VENUE: Detroit
POLE LAP: Arnoux, 1m 44.734s
FASTEST LAP: Watson, 1m 47.668s

Pn	Driver	Car	Laps	Time/Reason
1	Alboreto	Tyrrell-Ford	60	1h 50m 53.669s
2	Rosberg	Williams-Ford	60	1h 51m 01.371s
3	Watson	McLaren-Ford	60	1h 51m 02.952s
4	Piquet	Brabham-BMW	60	1h 52m 05.854s
5	Laffite	Williams-Ford	60	1h 52m 26.272s
6	Mansell	Lotus-Ford	59	
7	Boutsen	Arrows-Ford	59	
8	Prost	Renault	59	
9	Giacomelli	Toleman-Hart	59	
10	Boesel	Ligier-Ford	58	
11	Surer	Arrows-Ford	58	
12	Baldi	Alfa Romeo	56	
r	Lauda	McLaren-Ford	49	shock absorber
uc	Guerrero	Theodore-Ford	38	
r	Cecotto	Theodore-Ford	34	gearbox
r	de Cesaris	Alfa Romeo	33	turbo
r	Arnoux	Ferrari	31	electrical
r	Sullivan	Tyrrell-Ford	30	electrical
r	Jarier	Ligier-Ford	29	wheel
r	Winkelhock	ATS-BMW	26	accident
r	Warwick	Toleman-Hart	25	engine
r	Patrese	Brabham-BMW	24	brakes
r	de Angelis	Lotus-Renault	5	transmission
r	Cheever	Renault	4	distributor
r	Ghinzani	Osella-Alfa	4	overheating
r	Tambay	Ferrari	0	stalled

STARTING GRID:

1	Arnoux	12	Rosberg
2	Piquet	13	Prost
3	Tambay	14	Mansell
4	de Angelis	15	Patrese
5	Surer	16	Sullivan
6	Alboreto	17	Giacomelli
7	Cheever	18	Lauda
8	de Cesaris	19	Jarier
9	Warwick	20	Laffite
10	Boutsen	21	Watson
11	Guerrero	22	Winkelhock +

Canadian

GRAND PRIX No: 381
DATE: June 12, 1983
VENUE: Montreal
POLE LAP: Arnoux, 1m 28.729s
FASTEST LAP: Tambay, 1m 30.851s

Pn	Driver	Car	Laps	Time/Reason
1	Arnoux	Ferrari	70	1h 48m 31.838s
2	Cheever	Renault	70	1h 49m 13.867s
3	Tambay	Ferrari	70	1h 49m 24.448s
4	Rosberg	Williams-Ford	70	1h 49m 48.886s
5	Prost	Renault	69	
6	Watson	McLaren-Ford	69	
7	Boutsen	Arrows-Ford	69	
8	Alboreto	Tyrrell-Ford	68	
dq	Sullivan	Tyrrell-Ford	68	underweight
9	Winkelhock	ATS-BMW	67	
10	Baldi	Alfa Romeo	67	
r	Patrese	Brabham-BMW	57	gearbox
r	Warwick	Toleman-Hart	47	
r	Giacomelli	Toleman-Hart	43	
r	Mansell	Lotus-Ford	43	handling
r	de Cesaris	Alfa Romeo	43	engine
r	Laffite	Williams-Ford	38	gearbox
r	Boesel	Ligier-Ford	32	wheel
r	Guerrero	Theodore-Ford	27	engine
r	Fabi,C.	Osella-Ford	27	engine
r	Cecotto	Theodore-Ford	18	crownwheel/pinion
r	Piquet	Brabham-BMW	16	throttle
r	Lauda	McLaren-Ford	11	spun off
r	de Angelis	Lotus-Renault	2	throttle
r	Jarier	Ligier-Ford	1	gearbox
r	Surer	Arrows-Ford	1	transmission

STARTING GRID:

1	Arnoux	12	Warwick
2	Prost	13	Laffite
3	Piquet	14	Surer
4	Tambay	15	Boutsen
5	Patrese	16	Jarier
6	Cheever	17	Alboreto
7	Winkelhock	18	Mansell
8	de Cesaris	19	Lauda
9	Rosberg	20	Watson
10	Giacomelli	21	Guerrero
11	de Angelis	22	Sullivan +

British

GRAND PRIX No: 382
DATE: July 16, 1983
VENUE: Silverstone
POLE LAP: Arnoux, 1m 09.462s
FASTEST LAP: Prost, 1m 14.212s

Pn	Driver	Car	Laps	Time/Reason
1	Prost	Renault	67	1h 24m 39.780s
2	Piquet	Brabham-BMW	67	1h 24m 58.941s
3	Tambay	Ferrari	67	1h 25m 06.026s
4	Mansell	Lotus-Renault	67	1h 25m 18.732s
5	Arnoux	Ferrari	67	1h 25m 38.654s
6	Lauda	McLaren-Ford	66	
7	Baldi	Alfa Romeo	66	
8	de Cesaris	Alfa Romeo	66	
9	Watson	McLaren-Ford	66	
10	Jarier	Ligier-Ford	65	
11	Rosberg	Williams-Ford	65	
12	Laffite	Williams-Ford	65	
13	Alboreto	Tyrrell-Ford	65	
14	Sullivan	Tyrrell-Ford	65	
15	Boutsen	Arrows-Ford	65	
16	Guerrero	Theodore-Ford	64	
17	Surer	Arrows-Ford	64	
r	Winkelhock	ATS-BMW	49	overheating
r	Boesel	Ligier-Ford	48	suspension
r	Ghinzani	Osella-Alfa	46	fuel pressure
r	Warwick	Toleman-Hart	27	gearbox
r	Patrese	Brabham-BMW	9	turbo
r	Johansson	Spirit-Honda	5	fuel pump
r	Cheever	Renault	3	engine
r	Giacomelli	Toleman-Hart	3	turbo
r	de Angelis	Lotus-Renault	1	distributor

STARTING GRID:

1	Arnoux	12	Giacomelli
2	Tambay	13	Rosberg
3	Prost	14	Johansson
4	de Angelis	15	Lauda
5	Patrese	16	Alboreto
6	Piquet	17	Boutsen
7	Cheever	18	Mansell
8	Winkelhock	19	Surer
9	de Cesaris	20	Laffite
10	Warwick	21	Guerrero
11	Baldi	22	Boesel +

German

GRAND PRIX No: 383

DATE: August 7, 1983

VENUE: Hockenheim

POLE LAP: Tambay, 1m 49.328s

FASTEST LAP: Arnoux, 1m 53.938s

Pn	Driver	Car	Laps	Time/Reason
1	Arnoux	Ferrari	45	1h 27m 10.319s
2	de Cesaris	Alfa Romeo	45	1h 28m 20.971s
3	Patrese	Brabham-BMW	45	1h 28m 54.412s
4	Prost	Renault	45	1h 29m 11.069s
dq	Lauda	McLaren-Ford	44	reversed in pits
5	Watson	McLaren-Ford	44	
6	Laffite	Williams-Ford	44	
7	Surer	Arrows-Ford	44	
8	Jarier	Ligier-Ford	44	
9	Boutsen	Arrows-Ford	44	
10	Rosberg	Williams-Ford	44	
11	Cecotto	Theodore-Ford	44	
12	Sullivan	Tyrrell-Ford	43	
13	Piquet	Brabham-BMW	42	fire
r	Cheever	Renault	38	fuel injection
r	Ghinzani	Osella-Alfa	34	engine
r	Boesel	Ligier-Ford	27	engine
r	Baldi	Alfa Romeo	24	engine
r	Giacomelli	Toleman-Hart	19	turbo
r	Warwick	Toleman-Hart	17	engine
r	Johansson	Spirit-Honda	11	engine
r	Tambay	Ferrari	11	engine
r	de Angelis	Lotus-Renault	10	overheating
r	Alboreto	Tyrrell-Ford	4	fuel pump
r	Mansell	Lotus-Renault	1	engine
r	Guerrero	Theodore-Ford	0	engine

STARTING GRID:

1	Tambay	12	Rosberg
2	Arnoux	13	Johansson
3	de Cesaris	14	Boutsen
4	Piquet	15	Laffite
5	Prost	16	Alboreto
6	Cheever	17	Mansell
7	Baldi	18	Lauda
8	Patrese	19	Jarier
9	Warwick	20	Surer
10	Giacomelli	21	Sullivan
11	de Angelis	22	Cecotto +

Austrian

GRAND PRIX No: 384

DATE: August 14, 1983

VENUE: Osterreichring

POLE LAP: Tambay, 1m 29.871s

FASTEST LAP: Prost, 1m 33.961s

Pn	Driver	Car	Laps	Time/Reason
1	Prost	Renault	53	1h 24m 32.745s
2	Arnoux	Ferrari	53	1h 24m 39.580s
3	Piquet	Brabham-BMW	53	1h 25m 00.404s
4	Cheever	Renault	53	1h 25m 01.140s
5	Mansell	Lotus-Renault	52	
6	Lauda	McLaren-Ford	51	
7	Jarier	Ligier-Ford	51	
8	Rosberg	Williams-Ford	51	
9	Watson	McLaren-Ford	51	
10	Fabi,C.	Osella-Alfa	50	
11	Ghinzani	Osella-Alfa	49	
12	Johansson	Spirit-Honda	48	
13	Boutsen	Arrows-Ford	48	
r	Winkelhock	ATS-BMW	33	overheating
r	de Cesaris	Alfa Romeo	31	out of fuel
r	Tambay	Ferrari	30	engine
r	Patrese	Brabham-BMW	29	overheating
r	Guerrero	Theodore-Ford	25	gearbox
r	Laffite	Williams-Ford	21	handling
r	Baldi	Alfa Romeo	13	engine
r	Alboreto	Tyrrell-Ford	8	accident
r	Warwick	Toleman-Hart	2	turbo
r	Giacomelli	Toleman-Hart	1	accident
r	Sullivan	Tyrrell-Ford	0	accident
r	Surer	Arrows-Ford	0	accident
r	de Angelis	Lotus-Renault	0	accident

STARTING GRID:

1	Tambay	12	de Angelis
2	Arnoux	13	Winkelhock
3	Mansell	14	Lauda
4	Piquet	15	Rosberg
5	Prost	16	Johansson
6	Patrese	17	Watson
7	Giacomelli	18	Alboreto
8	Cheever	19	Boutsen
9	Baldi	20	Jarier
10	Warwick	21	Guerrero
11	de Cesaris	22	Surer +

Dutch

GRAND PRIX No:	385
DATE:	August 28, 1983
VENUE:	Zandvoort
POLE LAP:	Piquet, 1m 15.630s
FASTEST LAP:	Arnoux, 1m 19.863s

Pn	Driver	Car	Laps	Time/Reason
1	Arnoux	Ferrari	72	1h 38m 41.950s
2	Tambay	Ferrari	72	1h 39m 02.789s
3	Watson	McLaren-Ford	72	1h 39m 25.691s
4	Warwick	Toleman-Hart	72	1h 39m 58.789s
5	Baldi	Alfa Romeo	72	1h 40m 06.242s
6	Alboreto	Tyrrell-Ford	71	
7	Johansson	Spirit-Honda	70	
8	Surer	Arrows-Ford	70	
9	Patrese	Brabham-BMW	70	
10	Boesel	Ligier-Ford	70	
11	Fabi,C.	Osella-Alfa	68	engine
12	Guerrero	Theodore-Ford	68	
13	Giacomelli	Toleman-Hart	68	
14	Boutsen	Arrows-Ford	68	engine
r	Rosberg	Williams-Ford	53	misfiring
dq	Winkelhock	ATS-BMW	50	overtook parade
r	Piquet	Brabham-BMW	41	accident
r	Prost	Renault	41	accident
r	Cheever	Renault	39	turbo
r	Laffite	Williams-Ford	37	tyres
r	Mansell	Lotus-Renault	26	spun off
r	Lauda	McLaren-TAG	25	brakes
r	Sullivan	Tyrrell-Ford	20	engine
r	de Angelis	Lotus-Renault	12	fuel metering
r	de Cesaris	Alfa Romeo	5	engine
r	Jarier	Ligier-Ford	3	suspension

STARTING GRID:

1	Piquet	12	Baldi
2	Tambay	13	Giacomelli
3	de Angelis	14	Surer
4	Prost	15	Watson
5	Mansell	16	Johansson
6	Patrese	17	Laffite
7	Warwick	18	Alboreto
8	de Cesaris	19	Lauda
9	Winkelhock	20	Guerrero
10	Arnoux	21	Boutsen
11	Cheever	22	Jarier

Italian

GRAND PRIX No:	386
DATE:	September 11, 1983
VENUE:	Monza
POLE LAP:	Patrese, 1m 29.122s
FASTEST LAP:	Piquet, 1m 34.431s

Pn	Driver	Car	Laps	Time/Reason
1	Piquet	Brabham-BMW	52	1h 23m 10.880s
2	Arnoux	Ferrari	52	1h 23m 21.092s
3	Cheever	Renault	52	1h 23m 29.492s
4	Tambay	Ferrari	52	1h 23m 39.903s
5	de Angelis	Lotus-Renault	52	1h 24m 04.560s
6	Warwick	Toleman-Hart	52	1h 24m 24.228s
7	Giacomelli	Toleman-Hart	52	1h 24m 44.802s
8	Mansell	Lotus-Renault	52	1h 24m 46.915s
9	Jarier	Ligier-Ford	51	
10	Surer	Arrows-Ford	51	
11	Rosberg	Williams-Ford	51	
12	Cecotto	Theodore-Ford	50	
13	Guerrero	Theodore-Ford	50	
r	Fabi,C.	Osella-Alfa	46	oil union
r	Sullivan	Tyrrell-Ford	44	fuel pump
r	Boutsen	Arrows-Ford	42	engine
r	Winkelhock	ATS-BMW	35	exhaust
r	Alboreto	Tyrrell-Ford	29	clutch
r	Prost	Renault	26	turbo
r	Lauda	McLaren-TAG	24	electrical
r	Watson	McLaren-TAG	13	engine
r	Ghinzani	Osella-Alfa	10	gearbox
r	Baldi	Alfa Romeo	5	turbo
r	Johansson	Spirit-Honda	4	distributor
r	Patrese	Brabham-BMW	3	electrical
r	de Cesaris	Alfa Romeo	2	spun off

STARTING GRID:

1	Patrese	12	Warwick
2	Tambay	13	Lauda
3	Arnoux	14	Giacomelli
4	Piquet	15	Watson
5	Prost	16	Rosberg
6	de Cesaris	17	Johansson
7	Cheever	18	Boutsen
8	de Angelis	19	Jarier
9	Winkelhock	20	Surer
10	Baldi	21	Guerrero
11	Mansell	22	Sullivan

European

GRAND PRIX No:	387
DATE:	September 25, 1983
VENUE:	Brands Hatch
POLE LAP:	de Angelis, 1m 12.092s
FASTEST LAP:	Mansell, 1m 14.342s

Pn	Driver	Car	Laps	Time/Reason
1	Piquet	Brabham-BMW	76	1h 36m 45.865s
2	Prost	Renault	76	1h 36m 52.436s
3	Mansell	Lotus-Renault	76	1h 37m 16.180s
4	de Cesaris	Alfa Romeo	76	1h 37m 20.261s
5	Warwick	Toleman-Hart	76	1h 37m 30.780s
6	Giacomelli	Toleman-Hart	76	1h 37m 38.055s
7	Patrese	Brabham-BMW	76	1h 37m 58.549s
8	Winkelhock	ATS-BMW	75	
9	Arnoux	Ferrari	75	
10	Cheever	Renault	75	
11	Boutsen	Arrows-Ford	75	
12	Guerrero	Theodore-Ford	75	
13	Palmer	Williams-Ford	74	
14	Johansson	Spirit-Honda	74	
15	Boesel	Ligier-Ford	73	
r	Tambay	Ferrari	67	accident
r	Alboreto	Tyrrell-Ford	65	engine
uc	Ghinzani	Osella-Alfa	63	
r	Surer	Arrows-Ford	51	engine
r	Rosberg	Williams-Ford	43	engine
r	Baldi	Alfa Romeo	39	clutch
r	Watson	McLaren-TAG	36	accident
r	Sullivan	Tyrrell-Ford	27	fire
r	Lauda	McLaren-TAG	26	engine
r	de Angelis	Lotus-Renault	13	engine
r	Jarier	Ligier-Ford	0	transmission

STARTING GRID:

1	de Angelis	12	Giacomelli
2	Patrese	13	Lauda
3	Mansell	14	de Cesaris
4	Piquet	15	Baldi
5	Arnoux	16	Rosberg
6	Tambay	17	Surer
7	Cheever	18	Boutsen
8	Prost	19	Johansson
9	Winkelhock	20	Sullivan
10	Watson	21	Guerrero
11	Warwick	22	Jarier

+

South African

GRAND PRIX No:	388
DATE:	October 15, 1983
VENUE:	Kyalami
POLE LAP:	Tambay, 1m 06.554s
FASTEST LAP:	Piquet, 1m 09.948s

Pn	Driver	Car	Laps	Time/Reason
1	Patrese	Brabham-BMW	77	1h 33m 25.708s
2	de Cesaris	Alfa Romeo	77	1h 33m 35.027s
3	Piquet	Brabham-BMW	77	1h 33m 47.677s
4	Warwick	Toleman-Hart	76	
5	Rosberg	Williams-Honda	76	
6	Cheever	Renault	76	
7	Sullivan	Tyrrell-Ford	75	
8	Surer	Arrows-Ford	75	
9	Boutsen	Arrows-Ford	74	
10	Jarier	Ligier-Ford	73	
11	Lauda	McLaren-TAG	71	electrical
12	Acheson	RAM-Ford	71	
uc	Mansell	Lotus-Renault	68	
uc	Boesel	Ligier-Ford	66	
r	Alboreto	Tyrrell-Ford	60	engine
r	Tambay	Ferrari	56	turbo
r	Giacomelli	Toleman-Hart	56	turbo
r	Prost	Renault	35	turbo
r	Fabi,C.	Osella-Alfa	28	engine
r	de Angelis	Lotus-Renault	20	engine
dq	Watson	McLaren-TAG	18	overtook parade
r	Arnoux	Ferrari	9	engine
r	Baldi	Alfa Romeo	5	engine
r	Ghinzani	Osella-Alfa	1	engine
r	Winkelhock	ATS-BMW	1	engine
r	Laffite	Williams-Honda	1	accident

STARTING GRID:

1	Tambay	12	Lauda
2	Piquet	13	Warwick
3	Patrese	14	Cheever
4	Arnoux	15	Watson
5	Prost	16	Giacomelli
6	Rosberg	17	Baldi
7	Mansell	18	Alboreto
8	Winkelhock	19	Sullivan
9	de Cesaris	20	Boutsen
10	Laffite	21	Jarier
11	de Angelis	22	Surer

+

Brazilian

GRAND PRIX No:	389
DATE:	March 25, 1984
VENUE:	Rio de Janeiro
POLE LAP:	de Angelis, 1m 28.932s
FASTEST LAP:	Prost, 1m 36.499s

Pn	Driver	Car	Laps	Time/Reason
1	Prost	McLaren-TAG	61	1h 42m 34.492s
2	Rosberg	Williams-Honda	61	1h 43m 15.006s
3	de Angelis	Lotus-Renault	61	1h 43m 33.620s
4	Cheever	Alfa Romeo	60	
dq	Brundle	Tyrrell-Ford	60	see race notes
5	Tambay	Renault	59	out of fuel
6	Boutsen	Arrows-Ford	59	
7	Surer	Arrows-Ford	59	
8	Palmer	RAM-Hart	58	
r	Warwick	Renault	51	suspension
r	de Cesaris	Ligier-Renault	42	gearbox
r	Patrese	Alfa Romeo	41	gearbox
r	Lauda	McLaren-TAG	38	electrical
r	Mansell	Lotus-Renault	35	accident
r	Piquet	Brabham-BMW	32	engine
r	Fabi,T.	Brabham-BMW	32	turbo
r	Arnoux	Ferrari	30	battery
r	Ghinzani	Osella-Alfa	28	gearbox
r	Hesnault	Ligier-Renault	25	overheating
r	Alliot	RAM-Hart	24	battery
r	Cecotto	Toleman-Hart	18	turbo
r	Laffite	Williams-Honda	15	electrical
r	Alboreto	Ferrari	14	brakes
r	Baldi	Spirit-Hart	12	distributor
dq	Bellof	Tyrrell-Ford	11	see race notes
r	Senna	Toleman-Hart	8	turbo
dns	Winkelhock	ATS-BMW		pushed in pit

STARTING GRID:

1 de Angelis	11 Patrese
2 Alboreto	12 Cheever
3 Warwick	13 Laffite
4 Prost	14 de Cesaris
5 Mansell	15 Winkelhock
6 Lauda	16 Fabi,T.
7 Piquet	17 Senna
8 Tambay	18 Cecotto
9 Rosberg	19 Brundle
10 Arnoux	20 Hesnault +

South African

GRAND PRIX No:	390
DATE:	April 7, 1984
VENUE:	Kyalami
POLE LAP:	Piquet, 1m 04.871s
FASTEST LAP:	Tambay, 1m 08.877s

Pn	Driver	Car	Laps	Time/Reason
1	Lauda	McLaren-TAG	75	1h 29m 23.430s
2	Prost	McLaren-TAG	75	1h 30m 29.380s
3	Warwick	Renault	74	
4	Patrese	Alfa Romeo	73	
5	de Cesaris	Ligier-Renault	73	
6	Senna	Toleman-Hart	72	
7	de Angelis	Lotus-Renault	71	
8	Baldi	Spirit-Hart	71	
9	Surer	Arrows-Ford	71	
10	Hesnault	Ligier-Renault	71	
dq	Brundle	Tyrrell-Ford	71	see race notes
11	Alboreto	Ferrari	70	ignition
12	Boutsen	Arrows-Ford	70	
r	Tambay	Renault	66	fuel system
r	Laffite	Williams-Honda	60	cv joint
dq	Bellof	Tyrrell-Ford	60	see race notes
r	Winkelhock	ATS-BMW	53	battery
r	Rosberg	Williams-Honda	51	lost wheel
r	Mansell	Lotus-Renault	51	turbo
r	Arnoux	Ferrari	40	fuel injection
r	Piquet	Brabham-BMW	29	turbo
r	Cecotto	Toleman-Hart	26	burst tyre
r	Alliot	RAM-Hart	24	water leak
r	Palmer	RAM-Hart	22	gearbox
r	Fabi,T.	Brabham-BMW	18	turbo
r	Cheever	Alfa Romeo	4	radiator
dns	Ghinzani	Osella-Alfa R.		injured

STARTING GRID:

1 Piquet	11 Laffite
2 Rosberg	12 Winkelhock
3 Mansell	13 Senna
4 Tambay	14 de Cesaris
5 Prost	15 Arnoux
6 Fabi,T.	16 Cheever
7 de Angelis	17 Hesnault
8 Lauda	18 Patrese
9 Warwick	19 Cecotto
10 Alboreto	20 Ghinzani +

Belgian

GRAND PRIX No: 391
DATE: April 29, 1984
VENUE: Zolder
POLE LAP: Alboreto, 1m 14.846s
FASTEST LAP: Arnoux, 1m 19.294s

Pn	Driver	Car	Laps	Time/Reason
1	Alboreto	Ferrari	70	1h 36m 32.048s
2	Warwick	Renault	70	1h 37m 14.434s
3	Arnoux	Ferrari	70	1h 37m 41.851s
4	Rosberg	Williams-Honda	69	out of fuel
5	de Angelis	Lotus-Renault	69	
dq	Bellof	Tyrrell-Ford	69	see race notes
6	Senna	Toleman-Hart	68	
7	Tambay	Renault	68	
8	Surer	Arrows-Ford	68	
9	Piquet	Brabham-BMW	66	engine
10	Palmer	RAM-Hart	64	
r	Baldi	Spirit-Hart	53	suspension
dq	Brundle	Tyrrell-Ford	51	see race notes
r	Fabi,T.	Brabham-BMW	42	spun off
r	de Cesaris	Ligier-Renault	42	accident
r	Winkelhock	ATS-BMW	39	exhaust
r	Lauda	McLaren-TAG	35	water pump
r	Cheever	Alfa Romeo	28	engine
r	Laffite	Williams-Honda	15	electrical
r	Hesnault	Ligier-Renault	15	radiator
r	Boutsen	Arrows-BMW	15	misfiring
r	Ghinzani	Osella-Alfa	14	transmission
r	Mansell	Lotus-Renault	14	clutch
r	Prost	McLaren-TAG	5	distributor
r	Patrese	Alfa Romeo	2	ignition
r	Cecotto	Toleman-Hart	1	clutch

STARTING GRID:

1	Alboreto	12	Tambay
2	Arnoux	13	de Cesaris
3	Rosberg	14	Lauda
4	Warwick	15	Laffite
5	de Angelis	16	Cecotto
6	Winkelhock	17	Boutsen
7	Patrese	18	Fabi,T.
8	Prost	19	Senna
9	Piquet	20	Ghinzani
10	Mansell	21	Bellof
11	Cheever	22	Brundle +

San Marino

GRAND PRIX No: 392
DATE: May 6, 1984
VENUE: Imola
POLE LAP: Piquet, 1m 28.517s
FASTEST LAP: Piquet, 1m 33.275s

Pn	Driver	Car	Laps	Time/Reason
1	Prost	McLaren-TAG	60	1h 36m 53.579s
2	Arnoux	Ferrari	60	1h 37m 07.095s
3	de Angelis	Lotus-Renault	59	out of fuel
4	Warwick	Renault	59	
dq	Bellof	Tyrrell-Ford	59	see race notes
5	Boutsen	Arrows-Ford	59	
6	de Cesaris	Ligier-Renault	58	out of fuel
7	Cheever	Alfa Romeo	58	out of fuel
8	Baldi	Spirit-Hart	58	
9	Palmer	RAM-Hart	57	
dq	Brundle	Tyrrell-Ford	55	see race notes
10	Alliot	RAM-Hart	53	engine
uc	Cecotto	Toleman-Hart	52	
r	Piquet	Brabham-BMW	48	turbo
r	Fabi,T.	Brabham-BMW	48	turbo
r	Gartner	Osella-Alfa	46	engine
r	Surer	Arrows-BMW	40	turbo
r	Winkelhock	ATS-BMW	31	turbo
r	Alboreto	Ferrari	23	exhaust
r	Lauda	McLaren-TAG	15	engine
r	Laffite	Williams-Honda	11	engine
r	Patrese	Alfa Romeo	6	electrical
r	Mansell	Lotus-Renault	2	spun off
r	Rosberg	Williams-Honda	2	electrical
r	Tambay	Renault	0	accident
r	Hesnault	Ligier-Renault	0	accident

STARTING GRID:

1	Piquet	12	de Cesaris
2	Prost	13	Alboreto
3	Rosberg	14	Tambay
4	Warwick	15	Laffite
5	Lauda	16	Surer
6	Arnoux	17	Hesnault
7	Winkelhock	18	Mansell
8	Cheever	19	Cecotto
9	Fabi,T.	20	Boutsen
10	Patrese	21	Bellof
11	de Angelis	22	Brundle +

French

GRAND PRIX No:	393
DATE:	May 20, 1984
VENUE:	Dijon
POLE LAP:	Tambay, 1m 02.200s
FASTEST LAP:	Prost, 1m 05.257s

Pn	Driver	Car	Laps	Time/Reason
1	Lauda	McLaren-TAG	79	1h 31m 11.951s
2	Tambay	Renault	79	1h 31m 19.105s
3	Mansell	Lotus-Renault	79	1h 31m 35.920s
4	Arnoux	Ferrari	79	1h 31m 55.657s
5	de Angelis	Lotus-Renault	79	1h 32m 18.076s
6	Rosberg	Williams-Honda	78	
7	Prost	McLaren-TAG	78	
8	Laffite	Williams-Honda	78	
9	Fabi,T.	Brabham-BMW	78	
10	de Cesaris	Ligier-Renault	77	
11	Boutsen	Arrows-BMW	77	
dq	Brundle	Tyrrell-Ford	76	see race notes
12	Ghinzani	Osella-Alfa	74	
13	Palmer	RAM-Hart	72	
r	Baldi	Spirit-Hart	61	engine
r	Warwick	Renault	53	accident
r	Surer	Arrows-Ford	51	accident
r	Cheever	Alfa Romeo	51	engine
r	Senna	Toleman-Hart	35	turbo
r	Alboreto	Ferrari	33	engine
r	Cecotto	Toleman-Hart	22	turbo
r	Patrese	Alfa Romeo	15	engine
r	Piquet	Brabham-BMW	11	turbo
dq	Bellof	Tyrrell-Ford	11	see race notes
r	Winkelhock	ATS-BMW	5	clutch
r	Alliot	RAM-Hart	4	electrical

STARTING GRID:

1	Tambay	12	Laffite
2	de Angelis	13	Senna
3	Piquet	14	Boutsen
4	Rosberg	15	Patrese
5	Prost	16	Cheever
6	Mansell	17	Fabi,T.
7	Warwick	18	Cecotto
8	Winkelhock	19	Surer
9	Lauda	20	Bellof
10	Alboreto	21	Palmer
11	Arnoux	22	Alliot

Monaco

GRAND PRIX No:	394
DATE:	June 3, 1984
VENUE:	Monte Carlo
POLE LAP:	Prost, 1m 22.661s
FASTEST LAP:	Senna, 1m 54.334s

Pn	Driver	Car	Laps	Time/Reason
1	Prost	McLaren-TAG	31	1h 01m 07.740s
2	Senna	Toleman-Hart	31	1h 01m 15.186s
dq	Bellof	Tyrrell-Ford	31	see race notes
3	Arnoux	Ferrari	31	1h 01m 36.817s
4	Rosberg	Williams-Honda	31	1h 01m 42.986s
5	de Angelis	Lotus-Renault	31	1h 01m 52.179s
6	Alboreto	Ferrari	30	
7	Ghinzani	Osella-Alfa	30	
8	Laffite	Williams-Honda	30	
r	Patrese	Alfa Romeo	24	steering
r	Lauda	McLaren-TAG	23	spun off
r	Winkelhock	ATS-BMW	22	spun off
r	Mansell	Lotus-Renault	15	accident
r	Piquet	Brabham-BMW	14	electrical
r	Hesnault	Ligier-Renault	12	electrical
r	Fabi,C.	Brabham-BMW	9	spun off
r	Cecotto	Toleman-Hart	1	spun off
r	de Cesaris	Ligier-Renault	1	accident
r	Warwick	Renault	0	accident
r	Tambay	Renault	0	accident

STARTING GRID:

1	Prost	11	de Angelis
2	Mansell	12	Winkelhock
3	Arnoux	13	Senna
4	Alboreto	14	Patrese
5	Warwick	15	Fabi,C.
6	Tambay	16	Laffite
7	de Cesaris	17	Hesnault
8	Lauda	18	Cecotto
9	Piquet	19	Ghinzani
10	Rosberg	20	Bellof

Canadian

GRAND PRIX No: 395
DATE: June 17, 1984
VENUE: Montreal
POLE LAP: Piquet, 1m 25.442s
FASTEST LAP: Piquet, 1m 28.763s

Pn	Driver	Car	Laps	Time/Reason
1	Piquet	Brabham-BMW	70	1h 46m 23.748s
2	Lauda	McLaren-TAG	70	1h 46m 26.360s
3	Prost	McLaren-TAG	70	1h 47m 51.780s
4	de Angelis	Lotus-Renault	69	
5	Arnoux	Ferrari	68	
6	Mansell	Lotus-Renault	68	
7	Senna	Toleman-Hart	68	
8	Winkelhock	ATS-BMW	68	
9	Cecotto	Toleman-Hart	68	
dq	Brundle	Tyrrell-Ford	68	see race notes
10	Alliot	RAM-Hart	65	
11	Cheever	Alfa Romeo	63	out of fuel
r	Surer	Arrows-Ford	59	engine
r	Warwick	Renault	57	underbody
uc	Rothengatter	Spirit-Hart	56	
r	Bellof	Tyrrell-Ford	52	driveshaft
r	de Cesaris	Ligier-Renault	40	brakes
r	Fabi,C.	Brabham-BMW	39	turbo
r	Boutsen	Arrows-BMW	38	engine
r	Patrese	Alfa Romeo	37	accident
r	Rosberg	Williams-Honda	32	fuel system
r	Laffite	Williams-Honda	31	turbo
r	Thackwell	RAM-Hart	29	turbo
r	Ghinzani	Osella-Alfa	11	gearbox
r	Alboreto	Ferrari	10	engine
r	Hesnault	Ligier-Renault	7	turbo

STARTING GRID:

1	Piquet	12	Winkelhock
2	Prost	13	Hesnault
3	de Angelis	14	Patrese
4	Warwick	15	Rosberg
5	Arnoux	16	Fabi,C.
6	Alboreto	17	Laffite
7	Mansell	18	Boutsen
8	Lauda	19	Ghinzani
9	Senna	20	Cecotto
10	de Cesaris	21	Brundle
11	Cheever	22	Bellof

+

Detroit

GRAND PRIX No: 396
DATE: June 24, 1984
VENUE: Detroit
POLE LAP: Piquet, 1m 40.980s
FASTEST LAP: Warwick, 1m 46.221s

Pn	Driver	Car	Laps	Time/Reason
1	Piquet	Brabham-BMW	63	1h 55m 41.842s
dq	Brundle	Tyrrell-Ford	63	see race notes
2	de Angelis	Lotus-Renault	63	1h 56m 14.480s
3	Fabi,T.	Brabham-BMW	63	1h 57m 08.370s
4	Prost	McLaren-TAG	63	1h 57m 37.100s
5	Laffite	Williams-Honda	62	
r	Alboreto	Ferrari	49	engine
r	Rosberg	Williams-Honda	47	exhaust
r	Warwick	Renault	40	gearbox
dq	Bellof	Tyrrell-Ford	33	see race notes
r	Tambay	Renault	33	transmission
r	Alliot	RAM-Hart	33	brakes
r	Lauda	McLaren-TAG	33	electrical
r	Mansell	Lotus-Renault	27	gearbox
r	Boutsen	Arrows-BMW	27	engine
r	de Cesaris	Ligier-Renault	24	overheating
r	Cecotto	Toleman-Hart	23	clutch
r	Cheever	Alfa Romeo	21	engine
r	Senna	Toleman-Hart	21	accident
r	Patrese	Alfa Romeo	20	spun off
r	Hesnault	Ligier-Renault	3	accident
r	Ghinzani	Osella-Alfa	3	accident
r	Arnoux	Ferrari	2	accident
r	Palmer	RAM-Hart	2	accident
r	Winkelhock	ATS-BMW	0	accident
r	Surer	Arrows-Ford	0	accident

STARTING GRID:

1	Piquet	12	de Cesaris
2	Prost	13	Boutsen
3	Mansell	14	Winkelhock
4	Alboreto	15	Arnoux
5	de Angelis	16	Bellof
6	Warwick	17	Cecotto
7	Senna	18	Hesnault
8	Cheever	19	Laffite
9	Tambay	20	Alliot
10	Lauda	21	Rosberg
11	Brundle	22	Surer

+

Dallas

GRAND PRIX No:	397
DATE:	July 8, 1984
VENUE:	Dallas
POLE LAP:	Mansell, 1m 37.041s
FASTEST LAP:	Lauda, 1m 45.353s

Pn	Driver	Car	Laps	Time/Reason
1	Rosberg	Williams-Honda	67	2h 01m 22.617s
2	Arnoux	Ferrari	67	2h 01m 45.081s
3	de Angelis	Lotus-Renault	66	
4	Laffite	Williams-Honda	65	
5	Ghinzani	Osella-Alfa	65	
6	Mansell	Lotus-Renault	64	gearbox
7	Fabi,C.	Brabham-BMW	64	
8	Winkelhock	ATS-BMW	64	
r	Lauda	McLaren-TAG	60	accident
r	Prost	McLaren-TAG	56	accident
r	Boutsen	Arrows-BMW	55	accident
r	Alboreto	Ferrari	54	accident
r	Surer	Arrows-BMW	54	accident
r	Senna	Toleman-Hart	47	driveshaft
r	Palmer	RAM-Hart	46	electrical
r	Piquet	Brabham-BMW	45	accident
r	Tambay	Renault	25	accident
r	Cecotto	Toleman-Hart	25	accident
r	de Cesaris	Ligier-Renault	15	accident
r	Rothengatter	Spirit-Hart	15	fuel leak
r	Patrese	Alfa Romeo	12	accident
r	Warwick	Renault	10	spun off
dq	Bellof	Tyrrell-Ford	9	see race notes
r	Cheever	Alfa Romeo	8	accident
r	Hesnault	Ligier-Renault	0	accident
dns	Alliot	RAM-Hart		accident

STARTING GRID:

1	Mansell	12	Piquet
2	de Angelis	13	Winkelhock
3	Warwick	14	Cheever
4	Arnoux	15	Cecotto
5	Lauda	16	de Cesaris
6	Senna	17	Bellof
7	Prost	18	Ghinzani
8	Rosberg	19	Hesnault
9	Alboreto	20	Boutsen
10	Tambay	21	Patrese
11	Fabi,C.	22	Surer

+

British

GRAND PRIX No:	398
DATE:	July 22, 1984
VENUE:	Brands Hatch
POLE LAP:	Piquet, 1m 10.869s
FASTEST LAP:	Lauda, 1m 13.191s

Pn	Driver	Car	Laps	Time/Reason
1	Lauda	McLaren-TAG	71	1h 29m 28.532s
2	Warwick	Renault	71	1h 30m 10.655s
3	Senna	Toleman-Hart	71	1h 30m 31.860s
4	de Angelis	Lotus-Renault	70	
5	Alboreto	Ferrari	70	
6	Arnoux	Ferrari	70	
7	Piquet	Brabham-BMW	70	
8	Tambay	Renault	69	turbo
9	Ghinzani	Osella-Alfa	68	
10	de Cesaris	Ligier-Renault	68	
dq	Bellof	Tyrrell-Ford	68	see race notes
11	Surer	Arrows-BMW	67	
12	Patrese	Alfa Romeo	66	
uc	Rothengatter	Spirit-Hart	62	
r	Hesnault	Ligier-Renault	43	electrical
r	Prost	McLaren-TAG	37	gearbox
r	Mansell	Lotus-Renault	24	gearbox
r	Boutsen	Arrows-BMW	24	electrical
r	Laffite	Williams-Honda	14	water pump
r	Palmer	RAM-Hart	10	steering
r	Fabi,T.	Brabham-BMW	9	electrical
r	Winkelhock	ATS-BMW	8	spun off
r	Rosberg	Williams-Honda	5	turbo
r	Cheever	Alfa Romeo	1	accident
dq	Johansson	Tyrrell-Ford	1	see race notes
r	Alliot	RAM-Hart	0	accident
r	Gartner	Osella-Alfa	0	accident

STARTING GRID:

1	Piquet	11	Winkelhock
2	Prost	12	Boutsen
3	Lauda	13	Arnoux
4	de Angelis	14	Fabi,T.
5	Rosberg	15	Surer
6	Warwick	16	Laffite
7	Senna	17	Patrese
8	Mansell	18	Cheever
9	Alboreto	19	de Cesaris
10	Tambay	20	Hesnault

+

German

GRAND PRIX No: 399
DATE: August 5, 1984
VENUE: Hockenheim
POLE LAP: Prost, 1m 47.012s
FASTEST LAP: Prost, 1m 53.538s

Pn	Driver	Car	Laps	Time/Reason
1	Prost	McLaren-TAG	44	1h 24m 43.210s
2	Lauda	McLaren-TAG	44	1h 24m 46.359s
3	Warwick	Renault	44	1h 25m 19.633s
4	Mansell	Lotus-Renault	44	1h 25m 34.873s
5	Tambay	Renault	44	1h 25m 55.159s
6	Arnoux	Ferrari	43	
7	de Cesaris	Ligier-Renault	43	
8	Hesnault	Ligier-Renault	43	
dq	Johansson	Tyrrell-Ford	42	see race notes
9	Rothengatter	Spirit-Hart	40	
r	Winkelhock	ATS-BMW	31	turbo
r	Cheever	Alfa Romeo	29	engine
r	Fabi,T.	Brabham-BMW	28	turbo
r	Piquet	Brabham-BMW	23	gearbox
r	Patrese	Alfa Romeo	16	fuel metering unit
r	Ghinzani	Osella-Alfa	14	electrical
r	Gartner	Osella-Alfa	13	turbo
r	Alboreto	Ferrari	13	engine
r	Palmer	RAM-Hart	11	turbo
r	Rosberg	Williams-Honda	10	electrical
r	Laffite	Williams-Honda	10	engine
r	Boutsen	Arrows-BMW	8	oil pressure
r	de Angelis	Lotus-Renault	8	turbo
r	Alliot	RAM-Hart	7	overheating
r	Senna	Toleman-Hart	4	accident
r	Surer	Arrows-BMW	1	turbo

STARTING GRID:

1	Prost	12	Laffite
2	de Angelis	13	Winkelhock
3	Warwick	14	Surer
4	Tambay	15	Boutsen
5	Piquet	16	Mansell
6	Alboreto	17	Hesnault
7	Lauda	18	Cheever
8	Fabi,T.	19	Rosberg
9	Senna	20	Patrese
10	Arnoux	21	Ghinzani
11	de Cesaris	22	Alliot +

Austrian

GRAND PRIX No: 400
DATE: August 19, 1984
VENUE: Osterreichring
POLE LAP: Piquet, 1m 26.173s
FASTEST LAP: Lauda, 1m 32.882s

Pn	Driver	Car	Laps	Time/Reason
1	Lauda	McLaren-TAG	51	1h 21m 12.851s
2	Piquet	Brabham-BMW	51	1h 21m 36.376s
3	Alboreto	Ferrari	51	1h 22m 01.849s
4	Fabi,T.	Brabham-BMW	51	1h 22m 09.163s
5	Boutsen	Arrows-BMW	50	
6	Surer	Arrows-BMW	50	
7	Arnoux	Ferrari	50	
8	Hesnault	Ligier-Renault	49	
9	Palmer	RAM-Hart	49	
10	Patrese	Alfa Romeo	48	out of fuel
11	Alliot	RAM-Hart	48	
12	Berger,G.	ATS-BMW	48	gearbox
r	Tambay	Renault	42	engine
r	Senna	Toleman-Hart	35	oil pressure
r	Mansell	Lotus-Renault	32	engine
r	Prost	McLaren-TAG	28	spun off
r	de Angelis	Lotus-Renault	28	engine
uc	Rothengatter	Spirit-Hart	23	
r	Cheever	Alfa Romeo	18	engine
r	Warwick	Renault	17	engine
r	de Cesaris	Ligier-Renault	15	fuel injection
r	Rosberg	Williams-Honda	15	handling
r	Laffite	Williams-Honda	12	engine
r	Gartner	Osella-Alfa	6	engine
r	Ghinzani	Osella-Alfa	4	gearbox
dns	Winkelhock	ATS-BMW		gearbox

STARTING GRID:

1	Piquet	12	Alboreto
2	Prost	13	Patrese
3	de Angelis	14	Winkelhock
4	Lauda	15	Arnoux
5	Tambay	16	Cheever
6	Warwick	17	Boutsen
7	Fabi,T.	18	de Cesaris
8	Mansell	19	Surer
9	Rosberg	20	Berger,G.
10	Senna	21	Hesnault
11	Laffite	22	Gartner +

Dutch

GRAND PRIX No: 401
DATE: August 26, 1984
VENUE: Zandvoort
POLE LAP: Prost, 1m 13.567s
FASTEST LAP: Arnoux, 1m 19.465s

Pn	Driver	Car	Laps	Time/Reason
1	Prost	McLaren-TAG	71	1h 37m 21.468s
2	Lauda	McLaren-TAG	71	1h 37m 31.751s
3	Mansell	Lotus-Renault	71	1h 38m 41.012s
4	de Angelis	Lotus-Renault	70	
5	Fabi,T.	Brabham-BMW	70	
6	Tambay	Renault	70	
7	Hesnault	Ligier-Renault	69	
dq	Johansson	Tyrrell-Ford	69	see race notes
dq	Bellof	Tyrrell-Ford	69	see race notes
8	Rosberg	Williams-Honda	68	out of fuel
9	Palmer	RAM-Hart	67	
10	Alliot	RAM-Hart	67	
11	Arnoux	Ferrari	66	electrical
12	Gartner	Osella-Alfa	66	
13	Cheever	Alfa Romeo	65	out of fuel
r	Boutsen	Arrows-BMW	59	accident
r	Rothengatter	Spirit-Hart	53	throttle
r	Patrese	Alfa Romeo	51	engine
r	de Cesaris	Ligier-Renault	31	engine
r	Laffite	Williams-Honda	23	engine
r	Warwick	Renault	23	spun off
r	Winkelhock	ATS-BMW	22	spun off
r	Senna	Toleman-Hart	19	engine
r	Surer	Arrows-BMW	17	wheel
r	Piquet	Brabham-BMW	10	oil pressure
r	Ghinzani	Osella-Alfa	8	fuel pump
r	Alboreto	Ferrari	7	engine

STARTING GRID:

1	Prost	11	Boutsen
2	Piquet	12	Mansell
3	de Angelis	13	Senna
4	Warwick	14	de Cesaris
5	Tambay	15	Arnoux
6	Lauda	16	Winkelhock
7	Rosberg	17	Cheever
8	Laffite	18	Patrese
9	Alboreto	19	Surer
10	Fabi,T.	20	Hesnault +

Italian

GRAND PRIX No: 402
DATE: September 9, 1984
VENUE: Monza
POLE LAP: Piquet, 1m 26.584s
FASTEST LAP: Lauda, 1m 31.912s

Pn	Driver	Car	Laps	Time/Reason
1	Lauda	McLaren-TAG	51	1h 20m 29.065s
2	Alboreto	Ferrari	51	1h 20m 53.314s
3	Patrese	Alfa Romeo	50	
4	Johansson	Toleman-Hart	49	
5	Gartner	Osella-Alfa	49	
6	Berger,G.	ATS-BMW	49	
7	Ghinzani	Osella-Alfa	48	out of fuel
8	Rothengatter	Spirit-Hart	48	
9	Cheever	Alfa Romeo	45	out of fuel
10	Boutsen	Arrows-BMW	45	
r	Tambay	Renault	43	throttle
r	Fabi,T.	Brabham-BMW	43	engine
r	Surer	Arrows-BMW	43	engine
r	Warwick	Renault	31	oil pressure
r	Palmer	RAM-Hart	20	oil pressure
r	Piquet	Brabham-BMW	15	engine
r	de Angelis	Lotus-Renault	14	gearbox
r	Mansell	Lotus-Renault	13	spun off
r	Laffite	Williams-Honda	10	turbo
r	Rosberg	Williams-Honda	8	engine
r	de Cesaris	Ligier-Renault	7	engine
r	Hesnault	Ligier-Renault	7	spun off
r	Alliot	RAM-Hart	6	electrical
r	Arnoux	Ferrari	5	gearbox
r	Prost	McLaren-TAG	4	engine

STARTING GRID:

1	Piquet	13	Laffite
2	Prost	14	Arnoux
3	de Angelis	15	Surer
4	Lauda	16	de Cesaris
5	Fabi,T.	17	Johansson
6	Rosberg	18	Hesnault
7	Mansell	19	Boutsen
8	Tambay	20	Berger,G.
9	Patrese	21	Ghinzani
10	Cheever	22	Alliot
11	Alboreto	23	Gartner
12	Warwick	24	Rothengatter
		25	Palmer

European

GRAND PRIX No:	403
DATE:	October 7, 1984
VENUE:	Nurburgring
POLE LAP:	Piquet, 1m 18.871s
FASTEST LAP:	Alboreto & Piquet, 1m 23.146s

Pn	Driver	Car	Laps	Time/Reason
1	Prost	McLaren-TAG	67	1h 35m 13.284s
2	Alboreto	Ferrari	67	1h 35m 37.195s
3	Piquet	Brabham-BMW	67	1h 35m 38.206s
4	Lauda	McLaren-TAG	67	1h 35m 56.370s
5	Arnoux	Ferrari	67	1h 36m 14.714s
6	Patrese	Alfa Romeo	66	
7	de Cesaris	Ligier-Renault	65	
8	Baldi	Spirit-Hart	65	
9	Boutsen	Arrows-BMW	64	electrical
10	Hesnault	Ligier-Renault	64	
11	Warwick	Renault	61	overheating
12	Gartner	Osella-Alfa	60	fuel system
r	Fabi,T.	Brabham-BMW	57	gearbox
r	Mansell	Lotus-Renault	51	engine
r	Tambay	Renault	47	fuel system
r	Cheever	Alfa Romeo	37	fuel pump
r	Alliot	RAM-Hart	37	turbo
r	Palmer	RAM-Hart	35	turbo
r	Laffite	Williams-Honda	27	engine
r	de Angelis	Lotus-Renault	25	turbo
r	Johansson	Toleman-Hart	17	overheating
r	Rosberg	Williams-Honda	0	accident
r	Berger,G.	ATS-BMW	0	accident
r	Surer	Arrows-BMW	0	accident
r	Ghinzani	Osella-Alfa	0	accident
r	Senna	Toleman-Hart	0	accident

STARTING GRID:

1	Piquet	12	Senna
2	Prost	13	Cheever
3	Tambay	14	Laffite
4	Rosberg	15	Lauda
5	Alboreto	16	Surer
6	Arnoux	17	de Cesaris
7	Warwick	18	Berger,G.
8	Mansell	19	Hesnault
9	Patrese	20	Ghinzani
10	Fabi,T.	21	Palmer
11	Boutsen	22	Gartner +

Portuguese

GRAND PRIX No:	404
DATE:	October 21, 1984
VENUE:	Estoril
POLE LAP:	Piquet, 1m 21.703s
FASTEST LAP:	Lauda, 1m 22.996s

Pn	Driver	Car	Laps	Time/Reason
1	Prost	McLaren-TAG	70	1h 41m 11.753s
2	Lauda	McLaren-TAG	70	1h 41m 25.178s
3	Senna	Toleman-Hart	70	1h 41m 31.795s
4	Alboreto	Ferrari	70	1h 41m 32.070s
5	de Angelis	Lotus-Renault	70	1h 42m 43.922s
6	Piquet	Brabham-BMW	69	
7	Tambay	Renault	69	
8	Patrese	Alfa Romeo	69	
9	Arnoux	Ferrari	69	
10	Winkelhock	Brabham-BMW	69	
11	Johansson	Toleman-Hart	69	
12	de Cesaris	Ligier-Renault	69	
13	Berger,G.	ATS-BMW	68	
14	Laffite	Williams-Honda	67	
15	Baldi	Spirit-Hart	66	
16	Gartner	Osella-Alfa	65	out of fuel
17	Cheever	Alfa Romeo	64	
r	Ghinzani	Osella-Alfa	60	engine
r	Mansell	Lotus-Renault	52	spun off
r	Warwick	Renault	51	gearbox
r	Streiff	Renault	48	driveshaft
r	Rosberg	Williams-Honda	39	engine
r	Hesnault	Ligier-Renault	31	electrical
r	Boutsen	Arrows-BMW	24	driveshaft
r	Palmer	RAM-Hart	19	gearbox
r	Surer	Arrows-BMW	8	electrical
r	Alliot	RAM-Hart	2	engine

STARTING GRID:

1	Piquet	11	Lauda
2	Prost	12	Patrese
3	Senna	13	Streiff
4	Rosberg	14	Cheever
5	de Angelis	15	Laffite
6	Mansell	16	Surer
7	Tambay	17	Arnoux
8	Alboreto	18	Boutsen
9	Warwick	19	Winkelhock
10	Johansson	20	de Cesaris +

Brazilian

GRAND PRIX No: 405
DATE: April 7, 1985
VENUE: Rio de Janeiro
POLE LAP: Alboreto, 1m 27.768s
FASTEST LAP: Prost, 1m 36.702s

Pn	Driver	Car	Laps	Time/Reason
1	Prost	McLaren-TAG	61	1h 41m 26.115s
2	Alboreto	Ferrari	61	1h 41m 29.374s
3	de Angelis	Lotus-Renault	60	
4	Arnoux	Ferrari	59	
5	Tambay	Renault	59	
6	Laffite	Ligier-Renault	59	
7	Johansson	Tyrrell-Ford	58	
8	Brundle	Tyrrell-Ford	58	
9	Alliot	RAM-Hart	58	
10	Warwick	Renault	57	
11	Boutsen	Arrows-BMW	57	
12	Ghinzani	Osella-Alfa	57	
13	Winkelhock	RAM-Hart	57	
r	Berger,G.	Arrows-BMW	51	suspension
r	Senna	Lotus-Renault	48	electrical
r	Cheever	Alfa Romeo	42	engine
r	Martini	Minardi-Ford	41	engine
r	Lauda	McLaren-TAG	27	fuel system
r	de Cesaris	Ligier-Renault	26	accident
r	Patrese	Alfa Romeo	20	puncture
r	Rosberg	Williams-Honda	10	turbo
r	Hesnault	Brabham-BMW	9	accident
r	Mansell	Williams-Honda	8	exhaust
r	Baldi	Spirit-Hart	7	turbo
r	Piquet	Brabham-BMW	2	transmission

STARTING GRID:

1	Alboreto	14	Patrese
2	Rosberg	15	Laffite
3	de Angelis	16	Winkelhock
4	Senna	17	Hesnault
5	Mansell	18	Cheever
6	Prost	19	Berger,G.
7	Arnoux	20	Alliot
8	Piquet	21	Brundle
9	Lauda	22	Ghinzani
10	Warwick	23	Johansson
11	Tambay	24	Baldi
12	Boutsen	25	Martini
13	de Cesaris		

Portuguese

GRAND PRIX No: 406
DATE: April 21, 1985
VENUE: Estoril
POLE LAP: Senna, 1m 21.007s
FASTEST LAP: Senna, 1m 44.121s

Pn	Driver	Car	Laps	Time/Reason
1	Senna	Lotus-Renault	67	2h 00m 28.006s
2	Alboreto	Ferrari	67	2h 01m 30.984s
3	Tambay	Renault	66	
4	de Angelis	Lotus-Renault	66	
5	Mansell	Williams-Honda	65	
6	Bellof	Tyrrell-Ford	65	
7	Warwick	Renault	65	
8	Johansson	Ferrari	62	
9	Ghinzani	Osella-Alfa	61	
uc	Winkelhock	RAM-Hart	50	
r	Lauda	McLaren-TAG	49	engine
r	Cheever	Alfa Romeo	36	engine
r	Prost	McLaren-TAG	30	spun off
r	de Cesaris	Ligier-Renault	29	handling
r	Boutsen	Arrows-BMW	28	engine
r	Piquet	Brabham-BMW	28	handling
r	Brundle	Tyrrell-Ford	20	gear
r	Baldi	Spirit-Hart	19	spun off
r	Rosberg	Williams-Honda	16	spun off
r	Laffite	Ligier-Renault	15	handling
r	Berger,G.	Arrows-BMW	12	spun off
r	Martini	Minardi-Ford	12	spun off
r	Patrese	Alfa Romeo	4	spun off
r	Alliot	RAM-Hart	3	spun off
r	Hesnault	Brabham-BMW	3	electrical
r	Palmer	Zakspeed	2	suspension

STARTING GRID:

1	Senna	12	Tambay
2	Prost	13	Patrese
3	Rosberg	14	Cheever
4	de Angelis	15	Winkelhock
5	Alboreto	16	Boutsen
6	Warwick	17	Berger,G.
7	Lauda	18	Laffite
8	de Cesaris	19	Hesnault
9	Mansell	20	Alliot
10	Piquet	21	Bellof
11	Johansson	22	Brundle

San Marino

GRAND PRIX No: 407
DATE: May 5, 1985
VENUE: Imola
POLE LAP: Senna, 1m 27.327s
FASTEST LAP: Alboreto, 1m 30.961s

Pn	Driver	Car	Laps	Time/Reason
dq	Prost	McLaren-TAG	60	underweight
1	de Angelis	Lotus-Renault	60	1h 34m 35.955s
2	Boutsen	Arrows-BMW	59	
3	Tambay	Renault	59	
4	Lauda	McLaren-TAG	59	
5	Mansell	Williams-Honda	58	
6	Johansson	Ferrari	57	out of fuel
7	Senna	Lotus-Renault	57	out of fuel
8	Piquet	Brabham-BMW	57	
9	Brundle	Tyrrell-Ford	56	
10	Warwick	Renault	56	
r	Cheever	Alfa Romeo	50	engine
uc	Ghinzani	Osella-Alfa	46	
r	Alboreto	Ferrari	29	electrical
r	Winkelhock	RAM-Hart	27	engine
r	Alliot	RAM-Hart	24	engine
r	Rosberg	Williams-Honda	23	throttle
r	Laffite	Ligier-Renault	22	turbo
r	Martini	Minardi-MM	14	turbo
r	de Cesaris	Ligier-Renault	11	spun off
r	Baldi	Spirit-Hart	9	electrical
r	Hesnault	Brabham-BMW	5	engine
r	Bellof	Tyrrell-Ford	5	engine
r	Berger,G.	Arrows-BMW	4	electrical
r	Patrese	Alfa Romeo	4	engine

STARTING GRID:

1 Senna
2 Rosberg
3 de Angelis
4 Alboreto
5 Boutsen
6 Prost
7 Mansell
8 Lauda
9 Piquet
10 Berger,G.
11 Tambay
12 Cheever
13 de Cesaris
14 Warwick
15 Johansson
16 Laffite
17 Patrese
18 Martini
19 Hesnault
20 Alliot
21 Ghinzani
22 Winkelhock
23 Bellof
24 Brundle
25 Baldi

Monaco

GRAND PRIX No: 408
DATE: May 19, 1985
VENUE: Monte Carlo
POLE LAP: Senna, 1m 20.450s
FASTEST LAP: Alboreto, 1m 22.637s

Pn	Driver	Car	Laps	Time/Reason
1	Prost	McLaren-TAG	78	1h 51m 58.034s
2	Alboreto	Ferrari	78	1h 52m 05.575s
3	de Angelis	Lotus-Renault	78	1h 53m 25.205s
4	de Cesaris	Ligier-Renault	77	
5	Warwick	Renault	77	
6	Laffite	Ligier-Renault	77	
7	Mansell	Williams-Honda	77	
8	Rosberg	Williams-Honda	76	
9	Boutsen	Arrows-BMW	76	
10	Brundle	Tyrrell-Ford	74	
11	Palmer	Zakspeed	74	
r	Lauda	McLaren-TAG	17	spun off
r	Patrese	Alfa Romeo	16	accident
r	Piquet	Brabham-BMW	16	accident
r	Fabi,T.	Toleman-Hart	16	turbo
r	Senna	Lotus-Renault	13	engine
r	Cheever	Alfa Romeo	10	alternator
r	Johansson	Ferrari	1	accident
r	Tambay	Renault	0	accident
r	Berger,G.	Arrows-BMW	0	accident

STARTING GRID:

1 Senna
2 Mansell
3 Alboreto
4 Cheever
5 Prost
6 Boutsen
7 Rosberg
8 de Cesaris
9 de Angelis
10 Warwick
11 Berger,G.
12 Patrese
13 Piquet
14 Lauda
15 Johansson
16 Laffite
17 Tambay
18 Brundle
19 Palmer
20 Fabi,T.

Canadian

GRAND PRIX No: 409
DATE: June 16, 1985
VENUE: Montreal
POLE LAP: de Angelis, 1m 24.567s
FASTEST LAP: Senna, 1m 27.445s

Pn	Driver	Car	Laps	Time/Reason
1	Alboreto	Ferrari	70	1h 46m 01.813s
2	Johansson	Ferrari	70	1h 46m 03.770s
3	Prost	McLaren-TAG	70	1h 46m 06.154s
4	Rosberg	Williams-Honda	70	1h 46m 29.634s
5	de Angelis	Lotus-Renault	70	1h 46m 45.162s
6	Mansell	Williams-Honda	70	1h 47m 19.691s
7	Tambay	Renault	69	
8	Laffite	Ligier-Renault	69	
9	Boutsen	Arrows-BMW	68	
10	Patrese	Alfa Romeo	68	
11	Bellof	Tyrrell-Ford	68	
12	Brundle	Tyrrell-Ford	68	
13	Berger,G.	Arrows-BMW	67	
14	de Cesaris	Ligier-Renault	67	
15	Surer	Brabham-BMW	67	
16	Senna	Lotus-Renault	65	
17	Cheever	Alfa Romeo	64	
r	Martini	Minardi-MM	57	accident
r	Lauda	McLaren-TAG	37	engine
r	Ghinzani	Osella-Alfa	35	engine
r	Alliot	RAM-Hart	28	accident
r	Warwick	Renault	25	accident
r	Winkelhock	RAM-Hart	5	accident
r	Fabi,T.	Toleman-Hart	3	turbo
r	Piquet	Brabham-BMW	0	transmission

STARTING GRID:

1 de Angelis
2 Senna
3 Alboreto
4 Johansson
5 Prost
6 Warwick
7 Boutsen
8 Rosberg
9 Piquet
10 Tambay
11 Cheever
12 Berger,G.
13 Patrese
14 Winkelhock
15 de Cesaris
16 Mansell
17 Lauda
18 Fabi,T.
19 Laffite
20 Surer
21 Alliot
22 Ghinzani
23 Bellof
24 Brundle
25 Martini

US

GRAND PRIX No: 410
DATE: June 23, 1985
VENUE: Detroit
POLE LAP: Senna, 1m 42.051s
FASTEST LAP: Senna, 1m 45.612s

Pn	Driver	Car	Laps	Time/Reason
1	Rosberg	Williams-Honda	63	1h 55m 39.851s
2	Johansson	Ferrari	63	1h 56m 37.400s
3	Alboreto	Ferrari	63	1h 56m 43.021s
4	Bellof	Tyrrell-Ford	63	1h 56m 45.076s
5	de Angelis	Lotus-Renault	63	1h 57m 06.817s
6	Piquet	Brabham-BMW	62	
7	Boutsen	Arrows-BMW	62	
8	Surer	Brabham-BMW	62	
9	Cheever	Alfa Romeo	61	
10	de Cesaris	Ligier-Renault	61	
11	Berger,G.	Arrows-BMW	60	
12	Laffite	Ligier-Renault	58	
r	Senna	Lotus-Renault	51	accident
r	Brundle	Tyrrell-Ford	30	accident
r	Alliot	RAM-Hart	27	accident
r	Mansell	Williams-Honda	26	accident
r	Prost	McLaren-TAG	19	brakes
r	Patrese	Alfa Romeo	19	electrical
r	Warwick	Renault	18	transmission
r	Tambay	Renault	15	accident
r	Martini	Minardi-MM	11	engine
r	Lauda	McLaren-TAG	10	brakes
r	Fabi,T.	Toleman-Hart	4	clutch
r	Winkelhock	RAM-Hart	3	turbo
r	Ghinzani	Osella-Alfa	0	accident

STARTING GRID:

1 Senna
2 Mansell
3 Alboreto
4 Prost
5 Rosberg
6 Warwick
7 Cheever
8 de Angelis
9 Johansson
10 Piquet
11 Surer
12 Lauda
13 Fabi,T.
14 Patrese
15 Tambay
16 Laffite
17 de Cesaris
18 Brundle
19 Bellof
20 Winkelhock
21 Boutsen
22 Ghinzani
23 Alliot
24 Berger,G.
25 Martini

French

GRAND PRIX No: 411

DATE: July 7, 1985

VENUE: Paul Ricard

POLE LAP: Rosberg, 1m 32.462s

FASTEST LAP: Rosberg, 1m 39.914s

Pn	Driver	Car	Laps	Time/Reason
1	Piquet	Brabham-BMW	53	1h 31m 46.266s
2	Rosberg	Williams-Honda	53	1h 31m 52.926s
3	Prost	McLaren-TAG	53	1h 31m 55.551s
4	Johansson	Ferrari	53	1h 32m 39.757s
5	de Angelis	Lotus-Renault	53	1h 32m 39.956s
6	Tambay	Renault	53	1h 33m 01.433s
7	Warwick	Renault	53	1h 33m 30.478s
8	Surer	Brabham-BMW	52	
9	Boutsen	Arrows-BMW	52	
10	Cheever	Alfa Romeo	52	
11	Patrese	Alfa Romeo	52	
12	Winkelhock	RAM-Hart	50	
13	Bellof	Tyrrell-Ford	50	
14	Fabi,T.	Toleman-Hart	49	fuel pressure
15	Ghinzani	Osella-Alfa	49	
r	Brundle	Tyrrell-Renault	32	gearbox
r	Lauda	McLaren-TAG	30	gearbox
r	Senna	Lotus-Renault	26	engine
r	Berger,G.	Arrows-BMW	20	accident
r	Martini	Minardi-MM	19	accident
r	Alliot	RAM-Hart	8	fuel pressure
r	Palmer	Zakspeed	6	engine
r	Alboreto	Ferrari	5	turbo
r	de Cesaris	Ligier-Renault	4	driveshaft
r	Laffite	Ligier-Renault	2	turbo
dns	Mansell	Williams-Honda		injured

STARTING GRID:

1	Rosberg	12	Boutsen
2	Senna	13	de Cesaris
3	Alboreto	14	Surer
4	Prost	15	Laffite
5	Piquet	16	Johansson
6	Lauda	17	Patrese
7	de Angelis	18	Cheever
8	Mansell	19	Fabi,T.
9	Berger,G.	20	Winkelhock
10	Tambay	21	Brundle
11	Warwick	22	Palmer +

British

GRAND PRIX No: 412

DATE: July 21, 1985

VENUE: Silverstone

POLE LAP: Rosberg, 1m 05.591s

FASTEST LAP: Prost, 1m 09.886s

Pn	Driver	Car	Laps	Time/Reason
1	Prost	McLaren-TAG	65	1h 18m 10.436s
2	Alboreto	Ferrari	64	
3	Laffite	Ligier-Renault	64	
4	Piquet	Brabham-BMW	64	
5	Warwick	Renault	64	
6	Surer	Brabham-BMW	63	
7	Brundle	Tyrrell-Renault	63	
8	Berger,G.	Arrows-BMW	63	
9	Patrese	Alfa Romeo	62	
10	Senna	Lotus-Renault	60	fuel injection
11	Bellof	Tyrrell-Ford	59	
r	Lauda	McLaren-TAG	57	electrical
r	Boutsen	Arrows-BMW	57	spun off
r	de Cesaris	Ligier-Renault	41	clutch
r	Martini	Minardi-MM	38	transmission
uc	de Angelis	Lotus-Renault	37	
r	Winkelhock	RAM-Hart	28	turbo
r	Rosberg	Williams-Honda	21	exhaust
r	Mansell	Williams-Honda	17	clutch
r	Cheever	Alfa Romeo	17	turbo
r	Palmer	Zakspeed	6	
r	Fabi,T.	Toleman-Hart	4	crownwheel/pinion
r	Johansson	Ferrari	1	accident
r	Tambay	Renault	0	spun off
r	Alliot	RAM-Hart	0	accident
r	Ghinzani	Osella-Alfa	0	accident

STARTING GRID:

1	Rosberg	12	Warwick
2	Piquet	13	Tambay
3	Prost	14	Patrese
4	Senna	15	Surer
5	Mansell	16	Laffite
6	Alboreto	17	Berger,G.
7	de Cesaris	18	Winkelhock
8	de Angelis	19	Boutsen
9	Fabi,T.	20	Brundle
10	Lauda	21	Alliot
11	Johansson	22	Cheever +

German

GRAND PRIX No:	413
DATE:	August 4, 1985
VENUE:	Nurburgring
POLE LAP:	Fabi,T., 1m 17.429s
FASTEST LAP:	Lauda, 1m 22.806s

Pn	Driver	Car	Laps	Time/Reason
1	Alboreto	Ferrari	67	1h 35m 31.337s
2	Prost	McLaren-TAG	67	1h 35m 42.998s
3	Laffite	Ligier-Renault	67	1h 36m 22.491s
4	Boutsen	Arrows-BMW	67	1h 36m 26.616s
5	Lauda	McLaren-TAG	67	1h 36m 45.309s
6	Mansell	Williams-Honda	67	1h 36m 48.157s
7	Berger,G.	Arrows-BMW	66	
8	Bellof	Tyrrell-Renault	66	
9	Johansson	Ferrari	66	
10	Brundle	Tyrrell-Renault	63	
11	Martini	Minardi-MM	62	engine
12	Rosberg	Williams-Honda	61	brakes
r	Cheever	Alfa Romeo	45	turbo
r	de Angelis	Lotus-Renault	40	engine
r	Rothengatter	Osella-Alfa	32	gearbox
r	Fabi,T.	Toleman-Hart	29	clutch
r	Senna	Lotus-Renault	27	cv joint
r	Warwick	Renault	25	ignition
r	Piquet	Brabham-BMW	23	turbo
r	Tambay	Renault	19	spun off
r	Surer	Brabham-BMW	12	engine
r	Winkelhock	RAM-Hart	8	engine
r	Patrese	Alfa Romeo	8	gearbox
r	Hesnault	Renault	8	clutch
r	Alliot	RAM-Hart	8	oil pressure
r	Palmer	Zakspeed	7	alternator
r	de Cesaris	Ligier-Renault	0	steering

STARTING GRID:

1	Fabi,T.	11	Surer
2	Johansson	12	Lauda
3	Prost	13	Laffite
4	Rosberg	14	de Cesaris
5	Senna	15	Boutsen
6	Piquet	16	Tambay
7	de Angelis	17	Berger,G.
8	Alboreto	18	Cheever
9	Patrese	19	Bellof
10	Mansell	20	Warwick +

Austrian

GRAND PRIX No:	414
DATE:	August 18, 1985
VENUE:	Osterreichring
POLE LAP:	Prost, 1m 25.490s
FASTEST LAP:	Prost, 1m 29.241s

Pn	Driver	Car	Laps	Time/Reason
1	Prost	McLaren-TAG	52	1h 20m 12.583s
2	Senna	Lotus-Renault	52	1h 20m 42.585s
3	Alboreto	Ferrari	52	1h 20m 46.939s
4	Johansson	Ferrari	52	1h 20m 51.656s
5	de Angelis	Lotus-Renault	52	1h 21m 34.675s
6	Surer	Brabham-BMW	51	
7	Bellof	Tyrrell-Renault	49	out of fuel
8	Boutsen	Arrows-BMW	49	
9	Rothengatter	Osella-Alfa	48	
10	Tambay	Renault	46	engine
r	Laffite	Ligier-Renault	43	accident
r	Martini	Minardi-MM	40	suspension
r	Lauda	McLaren-TAG	39	engine
r	Berger,G.	Arrows-BMW	32	turbo
r	Fabi,T.	Toleman-Hart	31	electrical
r	Warwick	Renault	29	engine
r	Acheson	RAM-Hart	28	engine
r	Piquet	Brabham-BMW	26	exhaust
r	Mansell	Williams-Honda	25	engine
r	Patrese	Alfa Romeo	25	engine
r	Palmer	Zakspeed	17	engine
r	Alliot	RAM-Hart	16	turbo
r	de Cesaris	Ligier-Renault	13	accident
r	Cheever	Alfa Romeo	6	turbo
r	Rosberg	Williams-Honda	4	engine
r	Ghinzani	Toleman-Hart	0	engine

STARTING GRID:

1	Prost	12	Johansson
2	Mansell	13	Warwick
3	Lauda	14	Senna
4	Rosberg	15	Laffite
5	Piquet	16	Boutsen
6	Fabi,T.	17	Berger,G.
7	de Angelis	18	de Cesaris
8	Tambay	19	Ghinzani
9	Alboreto	20	Cheever
10	Patrese	21	Alliot
11	Surer	22	Bellof +

Dutch

GRAND PRIX No: 415
DATE: August 25, 1985
VENUE: Zandvoort
POLE LAP: Piquet, 1m 11.074s
FASTEST LAP: Prost, 1m 16.538s

Pn	Driver	Car	Laps	Time/Reason
1	Lauda	McLaren-TAG	70	1h 32m 29.263s
2	Prost	McLaren-TAG	70	1h 32m 29.495s
3	Senna	Lotus-Renault	70	1h 33m 17.754s
4	Alboreto	Ferrari	70	1h 33m 18.100s
5	de Angelis	Lotus-Renault	69	
6	Mansell	Williams-Honda	69	
7	Brundle	Tyrrell-Renault	69	
8	Piquet	Brabham-BMW	69	
9	Berger,G.	Arrows-BMW	68	
10	Surer	Brabham-BMW	65	exhaust
uc	Rothengatter	Osella-Alfa	46	
r	Boutsen	Arrows-BMW	44	suspension
r	Alliot	RAM-Hart	42	engine
r	Bellof	Tyrrell-Renault	39	engine
r	Warwick	Renault	37	gearbox
r	de Cesaris	Ligier-Renault	35	turbo
r	Tambay	Renault	32	transmission
r	Rosberg	Williams-Honda	20	engine
r	Fabi,T.	Toleman-Hart	18	wheel
r	Laffite	Ligier-Renault	17	electrical
r	Palmer	Zakspeed	13	oil pressure
r	Ghinzani	Toleman-Hart	12	engine
r	Johansson	Ferrari	9	engine
r	Martini	Minardi-MM	1	accident
r	Cheever	Alfa Romeo	1	turbo
r	Patrese	Alfa Romeo	1	turbo

STARTING GRID:

1	Piquet	11	de Angelis
2	Bellof	12	Warwick
2	Rosberg	13	Laffite
3	Prost	14	Berger,G.
4	Senna	15	Ghinzani
5	Fabi,T.	16	Alboreto
6	Tambay	17	Johansson
7	Mansell	18	de Cesaris
8	Boutsen	19	Patrese
9	Surer	20	Cheever
10	Lauda	21	Brundle +

Italian

GRAND PRIX No: 416
DATE: September 8, 1985
VENUE: Monza
POLE LAP: Senna, 1m 25.084s
FASTEST LAP: Mansell, 1m 28.283s

Pn	Driver	Car	Laps	Time/Reason
1	Prost	McLaren-TAG	51	1h 17m 59.451s
2	Piquet	Brabham-BMW	51	1h 18m 51.086s
3	Senna	Lotus-Renault	51	1h 18m 59.841s
4	Surer	Brabham-BMW	51	1h 19m 00.060s
5	Johansson	Ferrari	50	
6	de Angelis	Lotus-Renault	50	
7	Tambay	Renault	50	
8	Brundle	Tyrrell-Renault	50	
9	Boutsen	Arrows-BMW	50	
10	Streiff	Ligier-Renault	49	
11	Mansell	Williams-Honda	47	engine
12	Fabi,T.	Toleman-Hart	47	
13	Alboreto	Ferrari	45	engine
r	Rosberg	Williams-Honda	44	engine
r	Laffite	Ligier-Renault	40	engine
r	Lauda	McLaren-TAG	33	transmission
r	Patrese	Alfa Romeo	31	exhaust
r	Rothengatter	Osella-Alfa	26	engine
r	Alliot	RAM-Hart	19	turbo
r	Berger,G.	Arrows-BMW	13	engine
r	Warwick	Renault	9	transmission
r	Jones	Lola-Hart	6	distributor
r	Cheever	Alfa Romeo	3	engine
r	Acheson	RAM-Hart	2	clutch
r	Martini	Minardi-MM	0	fuel pump
r	Ghinzani	Toleman-Hart	0	stalled

STARTING GRID:

1	Senna	12	Warwick
2	Rosberg	13	Patrese
3	Mansell	14	Boutsen
4	Piquet	15	Fabi,T.
5	Prost	16	Lauda
6	de Angelis	17	Cheever
7	Alboreto	18	Brundle
8	Tambay	19	Streiff
9	Surer	20	Laffite
10	Johansson	21	Ghinzani
11	Berger,G.	22	Rothengatter +

Belgian

GRAND PRIX No: 417
DATE: September 15, 1985
VENUE: Spa-Francorchamps
POLE LAP: Prost, 1m 55.306s
FASTEST LAP: Prost, 2m 01.730s

Pn	Driver	Car	Laps	Time/Reason
1	Senna	Lotus-Renault	43	1h 34m 19.893s
2	Mansell	Williams-Honda	43	1h 34m 48.315s
3	Prost	McLaren-TAG	43	1h 35m 15.002s
4	Rosberg	Williams-Honda	43	1h 35m 35.183s
5	Piquet	Brabham-BMW	42	
6	Warwick	Renault	42	
7	Berger,G.	Arrows-BMW	42	
8	Surer	Brabham-BMW	42	
9	Streiff	Ligier-Renault	42	
10	Boutsen	Arrows-BMW	40	
11	Laffite	Ligier-Renault	38	accident
12	Martini	Minardi-MM	38	
13	Brundle	Tyrrell-Renault	38	
uc	Rothengatter	Osella-Alfa	37	
r	Patrese	Alfa Romeo	31	engine
r	Cheever	Alfa Romeo	26	gearbox
r	Tambay	Renault	24	gearbox
r	Fabi,T.	Toleman-Hart	23	throttle
r	de Angelis	Lotus-Renault	19	turbo
r	Danner	Zakspeed	16	gearbox
r	Alliot	RAM-Hart	10	accident
r	Johansson	Ferrari	7	engine
r	Ghinzani	Toleman-Hart	7	accident
r	Alboreto	Ferrari	3	clutch

STARTING GRID:

1	Prost	13	Tambay
2	Senna	14	Warwick
3	Piquet	15	Patrese
4	Alboreto	16	Ghinzani
5	Johansson	17	Laffite
6	Boutsen	18	Streiff
7	Mansell	19	Cheever
8	Berger,G.	20	Alliot
9	de Angelis	21	Brundle
10	Rosberg	22	Danner
11	Fabi,T.	23	Rothengatter
12	Surer	24	Martini

European

GRAND PRIX No: 418
DATE: October 6, 1985
VENUE: Brands Hatch
POLE LAP: Senna, 1m 07.169s
FASTEST LAP: Laffite, 1m 11.526s

Pn	Driver	Car	Laps	Time/Reason
1	Mansell	Williams-Honda	75	1h 32m38.109s
2	Senna	Lotus-Renault	75	1h 33m 19.505s
3	Rosberg	Williams-Honda	75	1h 33m 56.642s
4	Prost	McLaren-TAG	75	1h 34m 04.230s
5	de Angelis	Lotus-Renault	74	
6	Boutsen	Arrows-BMW	73	
7	Watson	McLaren-TAG	73	
8	Streiff	Ligier-Renault	73	
9	Patrese	Alfa Romeo	73	
10	Berger,G.	Arrows-BMW	73	
11	Cheever	Alfa Romeo	73	
12	Tambay	Renault	72	
r	Surer	Brabham-BMW	62	turbo
r	Johansson	Ferrari	59	electrical
r	Laffite	Ligier-Renault	58	engine
r	Danner	Zakspeed	50	engine
r	Capelli	Tyrrell-Renault	44	accident
r	Brundle	Tyrrell-Renault	40	water pipe
r	Fabi,T.	Toleman-Hart	33	engine
r	Alliot	RAM-Hart	31	engine
r	Ghinzani	Toleman-Hart	16	engine
r	Jones	Lola-Hart	13	radiator
r	Alboreto	Ferrari	13	turbo
r	Piquet	Brabham-BMW	6	accident
r	Warwick	Renault	4	fuel injection
r	Martini	Minardi-MM	3	accident

STARTING GRID:

1	Senna	12	Boutsen
2	Piquet	13	Johansson
3	Mansell	14	Ghinzani
4	Rosberg	15	Alboreto
5	Streiff	16	Brundle
6	Prost	17	Tambay
7	Surer	18	Cheever
8	Warwick	19	Berger,G.
9	de Angelis	20	Fabi,T.
10	Laffite	21	Watson
11	Patrese	22	Jones

+

South African

GRAND PRIX No: 419
DATE: October 19, 1985
VENUE: Kyalami
POLE LAP: Mansell, 1m 02.366s
FASTEST LAP: Rosberg, 1m 08.149s

Pn	Driver	Car	Laps	Time/Reason
1	Mansell	Williams-Honda	75	1h 28m 22.866s
2	Rosberg	Williams-Honda	75	1h 28m 30.438s
3	Prost	McLaren-TAG	75	1h 30m 14.700s
4	Johansson	Ferrari	74	
5	Berger,G.	Arrows-BMW	74	
6	Boutsen	Arrows-BMW	74	
7	Brundle	Tyrrell-Renault	73	
r	de Angelis	Lotus-Renault	52	engine
r	Martini	Minardi-MM	45	radiator
r	Lauda	McLaren-TAG	37	turbo
r	Streiff	Tyrrell-Renault	16	accident
r	Senna	Lotus-Renault	8	engine
r	Alboreto	Ferrari	8	turbo
r	Piquet	Brabham-BMW	6	engine
r	Ghinzani	Toleman-Hart	4	engine
r	Fabi,T.	Toleman-Hart	3	engine
r	Surer	Brabham-BMW	3	engine
r	Rothengatter	Osella-Alfa	1	electrical
r	Cheever	Alfa Romeo	0	accident
r	Patrese	Alfa Romeo	0	accident
dns	Jones	Lola-Hart		unwell

STARTING GRID:

1	Mansell	12	Patrese
2	Piquet	13	Ghinzani
3	Rosberg	14	Cheever
4	Senna	15	Alboreto
5	Surer	16	Johansson
6	de Angelis	17	Brundle
7	Fabi,T.	18	Jones
8	Lauda	19	Streiff
9	Prost	20	Martini
10	Boutsen	21	Rothengatter
11	Berger,G.		

Australian

GRAND PRIX No: 420
DATE: November 3, 1985
VENUE: Adelaide
POLE LAP: Senna, 1m 19.843s
FASTEST LAP: Rosberg, 1m 23.758s

Pn	Driver	Car	Laps	Time/Reason
1	Rosberg	Williams-Honda	82	2h 00m 40.473s
2	Laffite	Ligier-Renault	82	2h 01m 26.603s
3	Streiff	Ligier-Renault	82	2h 02m 09.009s
4	Capelli	Tyrrell-Renault	81	
5	Johansson	Ferrari	81	
6	Berger,G.	Arrows-BMW	81	
7	Rothengatter	Osella-Alfa	78	
8	Martini	Minardi-MM	78	
r	Senna	Lotus-Renault	62	engine
r	Alboreto	Ferrari	61	gearbox
r	Lauda	McLaren-TAG	57	accident
r	Warwick	Renault	57	transmission
uc	Brundle	Tyrrell-Renault	49	
r	Surer	Brabham-BMW	42	engine
r	Patrese	Alfa Romeo	42	exhaust
r	Fabi,T.	Toleman-Hart	40	engine
r	Boutsen	Arrows-BMW	37	oil leak
r	Ghinzani	Toleman-Hart	28	clutch
r	Prost	McLaren-TAG	26	engine
r	Tambay	Renault	20	transmission
r	Jones	Lola-Hart	20	electrical
dq	de Angelis	Lotus-Renault	17	illegal start
r	Piquet	Brabham-BMW	14	electrical fire
r	Cheever	Alfa Romeo	5	engine
r	Mansell	Williams-Honda	1	transmission

STARTING GRID:

1	Senna	13	Cheever
2	Mansell	14	Patrese
3	Rosberg	15	Johansson
4	Prost	16	Lauda
5	Alboreto	17	Brundle
6	Surer	18	Streiff
7	Berger,G.	19	Jones
8	Tambay	20	Laffite
9	Piquet	21	Ghinzani
10	de Angelis	22	Capelli
11	Boutsen	23	Martini
12	Warwick	24	Fabi,T.
		25	Rothengatter

Brazilian

GRAND PRIX No: 421
DATE: March 23, 1986
VENUE: Rio de Janeiro
POLE LAP: Senna, 1m 25.501s
FASTEST LAP: Piquet, 1m 33.546s

Pn	Driver	Car	Laps	Time/Reason
1	Piquet	Williams-Honda	61	1h 39m 32.583s
2	Senna	Lotus-Renault	61	1h 40m 07.410s
3	Laffite	Ligier-Renault	61	1h 40m 32.342s
4	Arnoux	Ligier-Renault	61	1h 41m 01.012s
5	Brundle	Tyrrell-Renault	60	
6	Berger,G.	Benetton-BMW	59	
7	Streiff	Tyrrell-Renault	59	
8	de Angelis	Brabham-BMW	58	
9	Dumfries	Lotus-Renault	58	
10	Fabi,T.	Benetton-BMW	56	
r	Boutsen	Arrows-BMW	37	exhaust
r	Alboreto	Ferrari	35	fuel pump
r	Prost	McLaren-TAG	30	engine
r	Danner	Osella-Alfa	29	engine
r	Johansson	Ferrari	26	brakes
r	Tambay	Lola-Hart	24	alternator
r	Patrese	Brabham-BMW	21	water pipe
r	Palmer	Zakspeed	20	airbox
r	Surer	Arrows-BMW	19	overheating
r	Nannini	Minardi-MM	18	oil leak
r	de Cesaris	Minardi-MM	16	gearbox
r	Ghinzani	Osella-Alfa	16	engine
r	Rosberg	McLaren-TAG	6	engine
r	Jones	Lola-Hart	5	rotor arm
r	Mansell	Williams-Honda	0	accident

STARTING GRID:

1 Senna
2 Piquet
3 Mansell
4 Arnoux
5 Laffite
6 Alboreto
7 Rosberg
8 Johansson
9 Prost
10 Patrese
11 Dumfries
12 Fabi,T.
13 Tambay
14 de Angelis
15 Boutsen
16 Berger,G.
17 Brundle
18 Streiff
19 Jones
20 Surer
21 Palmer
22 de Cesaris
23 Ghinzani
24 Danner
25 Nannini

Spanish

GRAND PRIX No: 422
DATE: April 13, 1986
VENUE: Jerez
POLE LAP: Senna, 1m 21.605s
FASTEST LAP: Mansell, 1m 27.176s

Pn	Driver	Car	Laps	Time/Reason
1	Senna	Lotus-Renault	72	1h 48m 47.735s
2	Mansell	Williams-Honda	72	1h 48m 47.749s
3	Prost	McLaren-TAG	72	1h 49m 09.287s
4	Rosberg	McLaren-TAG	71	
5	Fabi,T.	Benetton-BMW	71	
6	Berger,G.	Benetton-BMW	71	
7	Boutsen	Arrows-BMW	68	
8	Tambay	Lola-Hart	66	
r	Dumfries	Lotus-Renault	52	gearbox
r	Brundle	Tyrrell-Renault	41	oil leak
r	Laffite	Ligier-Renault	40	transmission
r	Piquet	Williams-Honda	39	overheating
r	Surer	Arrows-BMW	39	fuel leak
r	de Angelis	Brabham-BMW	29	gearbox
r	Arnoux	Ligier-Renault	29	transmission
r	Alboreto	Ferrari	22	wheel
r	Streiff	Tyrrell-Renault	22	oil leak
r	Danner	Osella-Alfa	14	engine
r	Johansson	Ferrari	11	brakes
r	Ghinzani	Osella-Alfa	10	engine
r	Patrese	Brabham-BMW	8	gearbox
r	de Cesaris	Minardi-MM	1	transmission
r	Palmer	Zakspeed	0	accident
r	Jones	Lola-Hart	0	accident
r	Nannini	Minardi-MM	0	transmission

STARTING GRID:

1 Senna
2 Piquet
3 Mansell
4 Prost
5 Rosberg
6 Arnoux
7 Berger,G.
8 Laffite
9 Fabi,T.
10 Dumfries
11 Johansson
12 Brundle
13 Alboreto
14 Patrese
15 de Angelis
16 Palmer
17 Jones
18 Tambay
19 Boutsen
20 Streiff
21 Ghinzani
22 Surer
23 Danner
24 de Cesaris
25 Nannini

San Marino

GRAND PRIX No:	423
DATE:	April 27, 1986
VENUE:	Imola
POLE LAP:	Senna, 1m 25.050s
FASTEST LAP:	Piquet, 1m 28.667s

Pn	Driver	Car	Laps	Time/Reason
1	Prost	McLaren-TAG	60	1h 32m 28.408s
2	Piquet	Williams-Honda	60	1h 32m 36.053s
3	Berger,G.	Benetton-BMW	59	
4	Johansson	Ferrari	59	
5	Rosberg	McLaren-TAG	58	out of fuel
6	Patrese	Brabham-BMW	58	out of fuel
7	Boutsen	Arrows-BMW	58	
8	Brundle	Tyrrell-Renault	58	
9	Surer	Arrows-BMW	57	out of fuel
10	Alboreto	Ferrari	56	turbo
r	Ghinzani	Osella-Alfa	52	out of fuel
r	Arnoux	Ligier-Renault	46	wheel
r	Streiff	Tyrrell-Renault	41	transmission
r	Fabi,T.	Benetton-BMW	39	engine
r	Palmer	Zakspeed	38	brakes
r	Danner	Osella-Alfa	31	turbo
r	Jones	Lola-Ford	28	overheating
r	de Cesaris	Minardi-MM	20	engine
r	de Angelis	Brabham-BMW	19	engine
r	Laffite	Ligier-Renault	14	turbo
r	Senna	Lotus-Renault	11	wheel
r	Mansell	Williams-Honda	8	engine
r	Dumfries	Lotus-Renault	8	wheel
r	Rothengatter	Zakspeed	7	turbo
r	Tambay	Lola-Hart	5	engine
r	Nannini	Minardi-MM	0	accident

STARTING GRID:

1	Senna	12	Boutsen
2	Piquet	13	Brundle
3	Mansell	14	Laffite
4	Prost	15	Surer
5	Alboreto	16	Patrese
6	Rosberg	17	Dumfries
7	Johansson	18	Nannini
8	Arnoux	19	de Angelis
9	Berger,G.	20	Palmer
10	Fabi,T.	21	Jones
11	Tambay	22	Streiff +

Monaco

GRAND PRIX No:	424
DATE:	May 11, 1986
VENUE:	Monte Carlo
POLE LAP:	Prost, 1m 22.627s
FASTEST LAP:	Prost, 1m 26.607s

Pn	Driver	Car	Laps	Time/Reason
1	Prost	McLaren-TAG	78	1h 55m 41.060s
2	Rosberg	McLaren-TAG	78	1h 56m 06.082s
3	Senna	Lotus-Renault	78	1h 56m 34.706s
4	Mansell	Williams-Honda	78	1h 56m 52.462s
5	Arnoux	Ligier-Renault	77	
6	Laffite	Ligier-Renault	77	
7	Piquet	Williams-Honda	77	
8	Boutsen	Arrows-BMW	75	
9	Surer	Arrows-BMW	75	
10	Johansson	Ferrari	75	
11	Streiff	Tyrrell-Renault	74	
12	Palmer	Zakspeed	74	
r	Brundle	Tyrrell-Renault	67	accident
r	Tambay	Lola-Ford	67	accident
r	Berger,G.	Benetton-BMW	42	transmission
r	Alboreto	Ferrari	38	turbo
r	Patrese	Brabham-BMW	38	engine
r	de Angelis	Brabham-BMW	31	intercooler
r	Fabi,T.	Benetton-BMW	17	brakes
r	Jones	Lola-Ford	2	spun off

STARTING GRID:

1	Prost	11	Piquet
2	Mansell	12	Arnoux
3	Senna	13	Streiff
4	Alboreto	14	Boutsen
5	Berger,G.	15	Johansson
6	Patrese	16	Fabi,T.
7	Laffite	17	Surer
8	Tambay	18	Jones
9	Rosberg	19	Palmer
10	Brundle	20	de Angelis

Belgian

GRAND PRIX No:	425
DATE:	May 25, 1986
VENUE:	Spa-Francorchamps
POLE LAP:	Piquet, 1m 54.331s
FASTEST LAP:	Prost, 1m 59.282s

Pn	Driver	Car	Laps	Time/Reason
1	Mansell	Williams-Honda	43	1h 27m 57.925s
2	Senna	Lotus-Renault	43	1h 28m 17.752s
3	Johansson	Ferrari	43	1h 28m 24.517s
4	Alboreto	Ferrari	43	1h 28m 27.559s
5	Laffite	Ligier-Renault	43	1h 29m 08.615s
6	Prost	McLaren-TAG	43	1h 30m 15.697s
7	Fabi,T.	Benetton-BMW	42	
8	Patrese	Brabham-BMW	42	
9	Surer	Arrows-BMW	41	fuel pump
10	Berger,G.	Benetton-BMW	41	
11	Jones	Lola-Ford	40	out of fuel
12	Streiff	Tyrrell-Renault	40	
r	Palmer	Zakspeed	37	electrical
r	de Cesaris	Minardi-MM	35	out of fuel
r	Brundle	Tyrrell-Renault	25	gearbox
r	Rothengatter	Zakspeed	25	electrical
r	Nannini	Minardi-MM	24	gearbox
r	Arnoux	Ligier-Renault	23	engine
r	Piquet	Williams-Honda	16	turbo
r	Boutsen	Arrows-BMW	7	electrical
r	Dumfries	Lotus-Renault	7	accident
r	Rosberg	McLaren-TAG	6	engine
r	Ghinzani	Osella-Alfa	3	engine
r	Danner	Osella-Alfa	2	engine
r	Tambay	Lola-Ford	0	accident

STARTING GRID:

1	Piquet	14	Boutsen
2	Berger,G.	15	Patrese
3	Prost	16	Jones
4	Senna	17	Laffite
5	Mansell	18	Streiff
6	Fabi,T.	19	de Cesaris
7	Arnoux	20	Palmer
8	Rosberg	21	Surer
9	Alboreto	22	Nannini
10	Tambay	23	Rothengatter
11	Johansson	24	Ghinzani
12	Brundle	25	Danner
13	Dumfries		

Canadian

GRAND PRIX No:	426
DATE:	June 15, 1986
VENUE:	Montreal
POLE LAP:	Mansell, 1m 24.118s
FASTEST LAP:	Piquet, 1m 25.443s

Pn	Driver	Car	Laps	Time/Reason
1	Mansell	Williams-Honda	69	1h 42m 26.415s
2	Prost	McLaren-TAG	69	1h 42m 47.074s
3	Piquet	Williams-Honda	69	1h 43m 02.677s
4	Rosberg	McLaren-TAG	69	1h 44m 02.088s
5	Senna	Lotus-Renault	68	
6	Arnoux	Ligier-Renault	68	
7	Laffite	Ligier-Renault	68	
8	Alboreto	Ferrari	68	
9	Brundle	Tyrrell-Renault	67	
10	Jones	Lola-Ford	66	
11	Streiff	Tyrrell-Renault	65	
12	Rothengatter	Zakspeed	63	
r	Patrese	Brabham-BMW	44	turbo
r	Ghinzani	Osella-Alfa	43	gearbox
r	de Cesaris	Minardi-MM	40	gearbox
r	Boutsen	Arrows-BMW	38	electrical
r	Berger,G.	Benetton-BMW	34	throttle
r	Johansson	Ferrari	29	accident
r	Dumfries	Lotus-Renault	28	accident
r	Palmer	Zakspeed	24	engine
r	Warwick	Brabham-BMW	20	engine
r	Nannini	Minardi-MM	17	turbo
r	Fabi,T.	Benetton-BMW	13	battery
r	Danner	Osella-Alfa	6	turbo
dns	Tambay	Lola-Ford		injured

STARTING GRID:

1	Mansell	13	Jones
2	Senna	14	Tambay
3	Piquet	15	Fabi,T.
4	Prost	16	Dumfries
5	Arnoux	17	Streiff
6	Rosberg	18	Johansson
7	Berger,G.	19	Brundle
8	Laffite	20	Nannini
9	Patrese	21	de Cesaris
10	Warwick	22	Palmer
11	Alboreto	23	Ghinzani
12	Boutsen	24	Rothengatter
		25	Danner

US

GRAND PRIX No:	427
DATE:	June 22, 1986
VENUE:	Detroit
POLE LAP:	Senna, 1m 38.301s
FASTEST LAP:	Piquet, 1m 41.233s

Pn	Driver	Car	Laps	Time/Reason
1	Senna	Lotus-Renault	63	1h 51m 12.847s
2	Laffite	Ligier-Renault	63	1h 51m 43.864s
3	Prost	McLaren-TAG	63	1h 51m 44.671s
4	Alboreto	Ferrari	63	1h 52m 43.783s
5	Mansell	Williams-Honda	62	
6	Patrese	Brabham-BMW	62	
7	Dumfries	Lotus-Renault	61	
8	Palmer	Zakspeed	61	
9	Streiff	Tyrrell-Renault	61	
10	Warwick	Brabham-BMW	60	
r	Danner	Arrows-BMW	51	fuel pump
r	Arnoux	Ligier-Renault	46	accident
r	Boutsen	Arrows-BMW	44	accident
r	de Cesaris	Minardi-MM	43	differential
r	Piquet	Williams-Honda	41	accident
r	Johansson	Ferrari	40	electrical
r	Fabi,T.	Benetton-BMW	38	clutch
r	Cheever	Lola-Ford	37	transmission
r	Jones	Lola-Ford	33	transmission
r	Berg	Osella-Alfa	28	electrical
r	Brundle	Tyrrell-Renault	15	electrical
r	Ghinzani	Osella-Alfa	14	turbo
r	Rosberg	McLaren-TAG	12	gearbox
r	Berger,G.	Benetton-BMW	8	ignition
r	Nannini	Minardi-MM	3	turbo

STARTING GRID:

1	Senna	14	Dumfries
2	Mansell	15	Warwick
3	Piquet	16	Brundle
4	Arnoux	17	Fabi,T.
5	Johansson	18	Streiff
6	Laffite	19	Danner
7	Prost	20	Palmer
8	Patrese	21	Jones
9	Rosberg	22	Ghinzani
10	Cheever	23	de Cesaris
11	Alboreto	24	Nannini
12	Berger,G.	25	Berg
13	Boutsen		

French

GRAND PRIX No:	428
DATE:	July 6, 1986
VENUE:	Paul Ricard
POLE LAP:	Senna, 1m 06.526s
FASTEST LAP:	Mansell, 1m 09.993s

Pn	Driver	Car	Laps	Time/Reason
1	Mansell	Williams-Honda	80	1h 37m 19.272s
2	Prost	McLaren-TAG	80	1h 37m 36.400s
3	Piquet	Williams-Honda	80	1h 37m 56.817s
4	Rosberg	McLaren-TAG	80	1h 38m 07.795s
5	Arnoux	Ligier-Renault	79	
6	Laffite	Ligier-Renault	79	
7	Patrese	Brabham-BMW	78	
8	Alboreto	Ferrari	78	
9	Warwick	Brabham-BMW	77	
10	Brundle	Tyrrell-Renault	77	
11	Danner	Arrows-BMW	76	
uc	Boutsen	Arrows-BMW	67	
r	Tambay	Lola-Ford	64	brake
r	Dumfries	Lotus-Renault	56	engine
r	Palmer	Zakspeed	46	engine
r	Streiff	Tyrrell-Renault	43	fuel injection
r	Rothengatter	Zakspeed	32	accident
r	Berg	Osella-Alfa	25	turbo
r	Berger,G.	Benetton-BMW	22	accident
r	Fabi,T.	Benetton-BMW	7	engine
r	Johansson	Ferrari	5	throttle
r	Senna	Lotus-Renault	3	accident
r	Ghinzani	Osella-Alfa	3	accident
r	Nannini	Minardi-MM	3	accident
r	de Cesaris	Minardi-MM	3	turbo
r	Jones	Lola-Ford	2	accident

STARTING GRID:

1	Senna	12	Dumfries
2	Mansell	13	Tambay
3	Piquet	14	Warwick
4	Arnoux	15	Brundle
5	Prost	16	Patrese
6	Alboreto	17	Streiff
7	Rosberg	18	Danner
8	Berger,G.	19	Nannini
9	Fabi,T.	20	Jones
10	Johansson	21	Boutsen
11	Laffite	22	Palmer

British

GRAND PRIX No: 429
DATE: July 13, 1986
VENUE: Brands Hatch
POLE LAP: Piquet, 1m 06.961s
FASTEST LAP: Mansell, 1m 09.593s

Pn	Driver	Car	Laps	Time/Reason
1	Mansell	Williams-Honda	75	1h 30m 38.471s
2	Piquet	Williams-Honda	75	1h 30m 44.405s
3	Prost	McLaren-TAG	74	
4	Arnoux	Ligier-Renault	73	
5	Brundle	Tyrrell-Renault	72	
6	Streiff	Tyrrell-Renault	72	
7	Dumfries	Lotus-Renault	72	
8	Warwick	Brabham-BMW	72	
9	Palmer	Zakspeed	69	
uc	Boutsen	Arrows-BMW	62	
r	Tambay	Lola-Ford	60	gearbox
r	Alboreto	Ferrari	51	turbo
r	Nannini	Minardi-MM	50	cv joint
r	Fabi,T.	Benetton-BMW	45	fuel line
r	Patrese	Brabham-BMW	39	engine
r	Senna	Lotus-Renault	27	gearbox
r	Rothengatter	Zakspeed	24	engine
r	de Cesaris	Minardi-MM	23	alternator
r	Berger,G.	Benetton-BMW	22	electrical
r	Jones	Lola-Ford	22	throttle
r	Johansson	Ferrari	20	radiator
r	Rosberg	McLaren-TAG	7	gearbox
r	Danner	Arrows-BMW	0	accident
r	Ghinzani	Osella-Alfa	0	accident
r	Berg	Osella-Alfa	0	accident
r	Laffite	Ligier-Renault	0	accident

STARTING GRID:

1	Piquet	12	Alboreto
2	Mansell	13	Boutsen
3	Senna	14	Jones
4	Berger,G.	15	Patrese
5	Rosberg	16	Streiff
6	Prost	17	Tambay
7	Fabi,T.	18	Johansson
8	Arnoux	19	Laffite
9	Warwick	20	Nannini
10	Dumfries	21	de Cesaris
11	Brundle	22	Palmer +

German

GRAND PRIX No: 430
DATE: July 27, 1986
VENUE: Hockenheim
POLE LAP: Rosberg, 1m 42.013s
FASTEST LAP: Berger,G., 1m 46.604s

Pn	Driver	Car	Laps	Time/Reason
1	Piquet	Williams-Honda	44	1h 22m 08.263s
2	Senna	Lotus-Renault	44	1h 22m 23.700s
3	Mansell	Williams-Honda	44	1h 22m 52.843s
4	Arnoux	Ligier-Renault	44	1h 23m 23.439s
5	Rosberg	McLaren-TAG	43	out of fuel
6	Prost	McLaren-TAG	43	out of fuel
7	Warwick	Brabham-BMW	43	
8	Tambay	Lola-Ford	43	
9	Jones	Lola-Ford	42	
10	Berger,G.	Benetton-BMW	42	
11	Johansson	Ferrari	41	rear wing
12	Berg	Osella-Alfa	40	
r	Danner	Arrows-BMW	38	turbo
r	Rothengatter	Zakspeed	38	gearbox
r	Palmer	Zakspeed	37	engine
r	Brundle	Tyrrell-Renault	34	engine
r	Patrese	Brabham-BMW	22	spark plugs
r	de Cesaris	Minardi-MM	20	gearbox
r	Nannini	Minardi-MM	19	overheating
r	Dumfries	Lotus-Renault	17	radiator
r	Boutsen	Arrows-BMW	13	turbo
r	Alliot	Ligier-Renault	11	engine
r	Ghinzani	Osella-Alfa	10	turbo
r	Streiff	Tyrrell-Renault	7	engine
r	Alboreto	Ferrari	6	transmission
r	Fabi,T.	Benetton-BMW	0	accident

STARTING GRID:

1	Rosberg	12	Dumfries
2	Prost	13	Tambay
3	Senna	14	Alliot
4	Berger,G.	15	Brundle
5	Piquet	16	Palmer
6	Mansell	17	Danner
7	Patrese	18	Streiff
8	Arnoux	19	Jones
9	Fabi,T.	20	Warwick
10	Alboreto	21	Boutsen
11	Johansson	22	Nannini +

Hungarian

GRAND PRIX No:	431
DATE:	August 10, 1986
VENUE:	Hungaroring
POLE LAP:	Senna, 1m 29.450s
FASTEST LAP:	Piquet, 1m 31.001s

Pn	Driver	Car	Laps	Time/Reason
1	Piquet	Williams-Honda	76	2h 00m 34.508s
2	Senna	Lotus-Renault	76	2h 00m 52.181s
3	Mansell	Williams-Honda	75	
4	Johansson	Ferrari	75	
5	Dumfries	Lotus-Renault	74	
6	Brundle	Tyrrell-Renault	74	
7	Tambay	Lola-Ford	74	
8	Streiff	Tyrrell-Renault	74	
9	Alliot	Ligier-Renault	73	
10	Palmer	Zakspeed	70	
r	Arnoux	Ligier-Renault	48	engine
r	Jones	Lola-Ford	46	transmission
r	Berger,G.	Benetton-BMW	44	transmission
r	Boutsen	Arrows-BMW	40	fuel metering unit
r	Rosberg	McLaren-TAG	34	suspension
r	Fabi,T.	Benetton-BMW	32	transmission
r	Nannini	Minardi-MM	30	engine
r	Alboreto	Ferrari	29	accident
r	Warwick	Brabham-BMW	28	accident
r	Prost	McLaren-TAG	23	accident
r	Ghinzani	Osella-Alfa	15	suspension
r	Danner	Arrows-BMW	7	suspension
r	Patrese	Brabham-BMW	5	accident
r	de Cesaris	Minardi-MM	5	engine
r	Rothengatter	Zakspeed	2	accident
r	Berg	Osella-Alfa	1	turbo

STARTING GRID:

1	Senna	12	Alliot
2	Piquet	13	Fabi,T.
3	Prost	14	Patrese
4	Mansell	15	Alboreto
5	Rosberg	16	Brundle
6	Tambay	17	Nannini
7	Johansson	18	Streiff
8	Dumfries	19	Warwick
9	Arnoux	20	de Cesaris
10	Jones	21	Danner
11	Berger,G.	22	Boutsen +

Austrian

GRAND PRIX No:	432
DATE:	August 17, 1986
VENUE:	Osterreichring
POLE LAP:	Fabi,T., 1m 23.549s
FASTEST LAP:	Berger,G., 1m 29.444s

Pn	Driver	Car	Laps	Time/Reason
1	Prost	McLaren-TAG	52	1h 21m 22.531s
2	Alboreto	Ferrari	51	
3	Johansson	Ferrari	50	
4	Jones	Lola-Ford	50	
5	Tambay	Lola-Ford	50	
6	Danner	Arrows-BMW	49	
7	Berger,G.	Benetton-BMW	49	
8	Rothengatter	Zakspeed	48	out of fuel
9	Rosberg	McLaren-TAG	47	electrical
10	Arnoux	Ligier-Renault	47	
11	Ghinzani	Osella-Alfa	46	
r	Mansell	Williams-Honda	32	cv joint
r	Piquet	Williams-Honda	29	overheating
r	Boutsen	Arrows-BMW	25	turbo
r	Fabi,T.	Benetton-BMW	17	engine
r	Alliot	Ligier-Renault	16	engine
r	Nannini	Minardi-MM	13	suspension
r	de Cesaris	Minardi-MM	13	driveshaft
r	Senna	Lotus-Renault	13	misfiring
r	Brundle	Tyrrell-Renault	12	engine
r	Streiff	Tyrrell-Renault	10	engine
r	Dumfries	Lotus-Renault	9	engine
r	Palmer	Zakspeed	8	engine
r	Berg	Osella-Alfa	6	electrical
r	Patrese	Brabham-BMW	2	engine

STARTING GRID:

1	Fabi,T.	13	Johansson
2	Berger,G.	14	Dumfries
3	Rosberg	15	Jones
4	Patrese	16	Brundle
5	Prost	17	Boutsen
6	Mansell	18	Nannini
7	Piquet	19	Streiff
8	Senna	20	Palmer
9	Alboreto	21	Danner
10	Alliot	22	de Cesaris
11	Arnoux	23	Rothengatter
12	Tambay	24	Ghinzani
		25	Berg

Italian

GRAND PRIX No: 433
DATE: September 7, 1986
VENUE: Monza
POLE LAP: Fabi,T., 1m 24.078s
FASTEST LAP: Fabi,T., 1m 28.099s

Pn	Driver	Car	Laps	Time/Reason
1	Piquet	Williams-Honda	51	1h 17m 42.889s
2	Mansell	Williams-Honda	51	1h 17m 52.717s
3	Johansson	Ferrari	51	1h 18m 05.804s
4	Rosberg	McLaren-TAG	51	1h 18m 36.698s
5	Berger,G.	Benetton-BMW	50	out of fuel
6	Jones	Lola-Ford	49	
7	Boutsen	Arrows-BMW	49	
8	Danner	Arrows-BMW	49	
9	Streiff	Tyrrell-Renault	49	
10	Brundle	Tyrrell-Renault	49	
11	Caffi	Osella-Alfa	45	
r	Fabi,T.	Benetton-BMW	44	puncture
r	Alboreto	Ferrari	33	engine
r	de Cesaris	Minardi-MM	33	engine
r	Capelli	AGS-MM	31	puncture
r	Arnoux	Ligier-Renault	30	gearbox
dq	Prost	McLaren-TAG	27	changed to spare car
r	Palmer	Zakspeed	27	alternator
r	Alliot	Ligier-Renault	22	engine
r	Dumfries	Lotus-Renault	18	gearbox
r	Warwick	Brabham-BMW	16	brakes
r	Nannini	Minardi-MM	15	alternator
r	Ghinzani	Osella-Alfa	12	accident
r	Tambay	Lola-Ford	2	accident
r	Patrese	Brabham-BMW	2	accident
r	Rothengatter	Zakspeed	1	electrical
r	Senna	Lotus-Renault	0	clutch

STARTING GRID:

1	Fabi,T.	10	Patrese
2	Prost	11	Arnoux
3	Mansell	12	Johansson
4	Berger,G.	13	Boutsen
5	Senna	14	Alliot
6	Piquet	15	Tambay
7	Warwick	16	Danner
8	Rosberg	17	Dumfries
9	Alboreto	18	Jones +

Portuguese

GRAND PRIX No: 434
DATE: September 21, 1986
VENUE: Estoril
POLE LAP: Senna, 1m 16.673s
FASTEST LAP: Mansell, 1m 20.943s

Pn	Driver	Car	Laps	Time/Reason
1	Mansell	Williams-Honda	70	1h 37m 21.900s
2	Prost	McLaren-TAG	70	1h 37m 40.672s
3	Piquet	Williams-Honda	70	1h 38m 11.174s
4	Senna	Lotus-Renault	69	out of fuel
5	Alboreto	Ferrari	69	
6	Johansson	Ferrari	69	
7	Arnoux	Ligier-Renault	69	
8	Fabi,T.	Benetton-BMW	68	out of fuel
9	Dumfries	Lotus-Renault	68	
10	Boutsen	Arrows-BMW	67	
11	Danner	Arrows-BMW	67	
12	Palmer	Zakspeed	67	
13	Berg	Osella-Alfa	63	
r	Patrese	Brabham-BMW	62	engine
uc	Tambay	Lola-Ford	62	
r	Nannini	Minardi-MM	60	gearbox
r	Berger,G.	Benetton-BMW	44	accident
r	de Cesaris	Minardi-MM	43	suspension
r	Rosberg	McLaren-TAG	41	engine
r	Warwick	Brabham-BMW	41	engine
r	Alliot	Ligier-Renault	39	engine
r	Streiff	Tyrrell-Renault	28	engine
r	Brundle	Tyrrell-Renault	18	engine
r	Jones	Lola-Ford	10	spun off
r	Rothengatter	Zakspeed	9	crownwheel/pinion
r	Ghinzani	Osella-Alfa	8	engine
r	Capelli	AGS-MM	6	gearbox

STARTING GRID:

1	Senna	11	Alliot
2	Mansell	12	Warwick
3	Prost	13	Alboreto
4	Berger,G.	14	Tambay
5	Fabi,T.	15	Dumfries
6	Piquet	16	de Cesaris
7	Rosberg	17	Jones
8	Johansson	18	Nannini
9	Patrese	19	Brundle
10	Arnoux	20	Palmer +

Mexican

GRAND PRIX No:	435
DATE:	October 12, 1986
VENUE:	Mexico City
POLE LAP:	Senna, 1m 16.990s
FASTEST LAP:	Piquet, 1m 19.360s

Pn	Driver	Car	Laps	Time/Reason
1	Berger,G.	Benetton-BMW	68	1h 33m 18.700s
2	Prost	McLaren-TAG	68	1h 33m 44.138s
3	Senna	Lotus-Renault	68	1h 34m 11.213s
4	Piquet	Williams-Honda	67	
5	Mansell	Williams-Honda	67	
6	Alliot	Ligier-Renault	67	
7	Boutsen	Arrows-BMW	66	
8	de Cesaris	Minardi-MM	66	
9	Danner	Arrows-BMW	66	
10	Palmer	Zakspeed	65	out of fuel
11	Brundle	Tyrrell-Renault	65	
12	Johansson	Ferrari	64	turbo
13	Patrese	Brabham-BMW	64	accident
14	Nannini	Minardi-MM	64	
15	Arnoux	Ligier-Renault	63	engine
16	Berg	Osella-Alfa	61	
r	Dumfries	Lotus-Renault	53	battery
r	Warwick	Brabham-BMW	37	engine
r	Jones	Lola-Ford	35	gearbox
r	Rosberg	McLaren-TAG	32	puncture
r	Alboreto	Ferrari	10	engine
r	Streiff	Tyrrell-Renault	8	turbo
r	Ghinzani	Osella-Alfa	8	engine
r	Fabi,T.	Benetton-BMW	4	engine
r	Tambay	Lola-Ford	0	accident
dns	Rothengatter	Zakspeed		accident

STARTING GRID:

1	Senna	12	Alboreto
2	Piquet	13	Arnoux
3	Mansell	14	Johansson
4	Berger,G.	15	Jones
5	Patrese	16	Brundle
6	Prost	17	Dumfries
7	Warwick	18	Palmer
8	Tambay	19	Streiff
9	Fabi,T.	20	Danner
10	Alliot	21	Boutsen
11	Rosberg	22	de Cesaris +

Australian

GRAND PRIX No:	436
DATE:	October 26, 1986
VENUE:	Adelaide
POLE LAP:	Mansell, 1m 18.403s
FASTEST LAP:	Piquet, 1m 20.787s

Pn	Driver	Car	Laps	Time/Reason
1	Prost	McLaren-TAG	82	1h 54m 20.388s
2	Piquet	Williams-Honda	82	1h 54m 24.593s
3	Johansson	Ferrari	81	
4	Brundle	Tyrrell-Renault	81	
5	Streiff	Tyrrell-Renault	80	out of fuel
6	Dumfries	Lotus-Renault	80	
7	Arnoux	Ligier-Renault	79	
8	Alliot	Ligier-Renault	79	
9	Palmer	Zakspeed	77	
10	Fabi,T.	Benetton-BMW	77	
uc	Tambay	Lola-Ford	70	
r	Mansell	Williams-Honda	63	burst tyre
r	Patrese	Brabham-BMW	63	electrical
r	Rosberg	McLaren-TAG	62	burst tyre
uc	Berg	Osella-Alfa	61	
r	Warwick	Brabham-BMW	57	brakes
r	Danner	Arrows-BMW	52	engine
r	Boutsen	Arrows-BMW	50	throttle
r	Senna	Lotus-Renault	43	engine
r	Berger,G.	Benetton-BMW	40	clutch
r	de Cesaris	Minardi-MM	40	extinguisher
r	Rothengatter	Zakspeed	32	suspension
r	Jones	Lola-Ford	16	engine
r	Nannini	Minardi-MM	10	accident
r	Ghinzani	Osella-Alfa	2	crownwheel/pinion
r	Alboreto	Ferrari	0	accident

STARTING GRID:

1	Mansell	12	Johansson
2	Piquet	13	Fabi,T.
3	Senna	14	Dumfries
4	Prost	15	Jones
5	Arnoux	16	Brundle
6	Berger,G.	17	Tambay
7	Rosberg	18	Nannini
8	Alliot	19	Patrese
9	Alboreto	20	Warwick
10	Streiff	21	Palmer
11	de Cesaris	22	Boutsen +

Brazilian

GRAND PRIX No: 437
DATE: April 12, 1987
VENUE: Rio de Janeiro
POLE LAP: Mansell, 1m 26.128s
FASTEST LAP: Piquet, 1m 33.861s

Pn	Driver	Car	Laps	Time/Reason
1	Prost	McLaren-TAG	61	1h 39m 45.141s
2	Piquet	Williams-Honda	61	1h 40m 25.688s
3	Johansson	McLaren-TAG	61	1h 40m 41.899s
4	Berger,G.	Ferrari	61	1h 41m 24.376s
5	Boutsen	Benetton-Ford	60	
6	Mansell	Williams-Honda	60	
7	Nakajima	Lotus-Honda	59	
8	Alboreto	Ferrari	58	underbody
9	Danner	Zakspeed	58	
10	Palmer	Tyrrell-Ford	58	
11	Streiff	Tyrrell-Ford	57	
12	Fabre	AGS-Ford	55	
r	Cheever	Arrows-Mega.	52	engine
r	Senna	Lotus-Honda	50	engine
r	Patrese	Brabham-BMW	48	electrical
r	de Cesaris	Brabham-BMW	21	gearbox
r	Warwick	Arrows-Mega.	20	overheating
r	Caffi	Osella-Alfa R.	20	driver tired
r	Nannini	Minardi-MM	17	suspension
r	Brundle	Zakspeed	15	engine
r	Fabi,T.	Benetton-Ford	9	misfiring
dq	Campos	Minardi-MM	3	illegal start
dns	Capelli	March-Ford		no engine

STARTING GRID:

1	Mansell	13	de Cesaris
2	Piquet	14	Cheever
3	Senna	15	Nannini
4	Fabi,T.	16	Campos
5	Prost	17	Danner
6	Boutsen	18	Palmer
7	Berger,G.	19	Brundle
8	Warwick	20	Streiff
9	Alboreto	21	Caffi
10	Johansson	22	Fabre
11	Patrese	23	Capelli
12	Nakajima		

San Marino

GRAND PRIX No: 438
DATE: May 3, 1987
VENUE: Imola
POLE LAP: Senna, 1m 25.826s
FASTEST LAP: Fabi,T., 1m 29.246s

Pn	Driver	Car	Laps	Time/Reason
1	Mansell	Williams-Honda	59	1h 31m 24.076s
2	Senna	Lotus-Honda	59	1h 31m 51.621s
3	Alboreto	Ferrari	59	1h 32m 03.220s
4	Johansson	McLaren-TAG	59	1h 32m 24.664s
5	Brundle	Zakspeed	57	
6	Nakajima	Lotus-Honda	57	
7	Danner	Zakspeed	57	
8	Streiff	Tyrrell-Ford	57	
9	Patrese	Brabham-BMW	57	
10	Alliot	Lola-Ford	56	
11	Warwick	Arrows-Mega.	55	out of fuel
12	Caffi	Osella-Alfa	54	out of fuel
13	Fabre	AGS-Ford	53	
r	Fabi,T.	Benetton-Ford	51	engine
r	Boutsen	Benetton-Ford	48	engine
r	Cheever	Arrows-Mega.	48	overheating
r	Palmer	Tyrrell-Ford	48	electrical
r	de Cesaris	Brabham-BMW	39	spun off
r	Campos	Minardi-MM	30	gearbox
r	Tarquini	Osella-Alfa	26	electrical
r	Nannini	Minardi-MM	25	engine
r	Capelli	March-Ford	18	rotor arm
r	Berger,G.	Ferrari	16	black box
r	Prost	McLaren-TAG	15	alternator
r	Ghinzani	Ligier-Megatron	7	withdrew
dns	Piquet	Williams-Honda		injured
dns	Arnoux	Ligier-Megatron		suspension

STARTING GRID:

1	Senna	11	Warwick
2	Mansell	12	Boutsen
3	Piquet	13	Nakajima
4	Prost	14	Arnoux
5	Fabi,T.	15	de Cesaris
6	Berger,G.	16	Brundle
7	Alboreto	17	Nannini
8	Patrese	18	Campos
9	Johansson	19	Danner
10	Cheever	20	Ghinzani +

Belgian

GRAND PRIX No: 439
DATE: May 17, 1987
VENUE: Spa-Francorchamps
POLE LAP: Mansell, 1m 52.026s
FASTEST LAP: Prost, 1m 57.153s

Pn	Driver	Car	Laps	Time/Reason
1	Prost	McLaren-TAG	43	1h 27m 03.217s
2	Johansson	McLaren-TAG	43	1h 27m 27.981s
3	de Cesaris	Brabham-BMW	42	out of fuel
4	Cheever	Arrows-Mega.	42	
5	Nakajima	Lotus-Honda	42	
6	Arnoux	Ligier-Megatron	41	
7	Ghinzani	Ligier-Megatron	40	out of fuel
8	Alliot	Lola-Ford	40	
9	Streiff	Tyrrell-Ford	39	
10	Fabre	AGS-Ford	38	electrical
r	Fabi,T.	Benetton-BMW	34	engine
r	Brundle	Zakspeed	19	engine
r	Boutsen	Benetton-BMW	18	wheel bearing
r	Mansell	Williams-Honda	17	underbody
r	Capelli	March-Ford	14	oil pressure
r	Piquet	Williams-Honda	11	turbo
r	Caffi	Osella-Alfa	11	engine
r	Alboreto	Ferrari	9	transmission
r	Danner	Zakspeed	9	brakes
r	Warwick	Arrows-Mega.	8	water hose
r	Patrese	Brabham-BMW	5	clutch
r	Berger,G.	Ferrari	2	engine
r	Nannini	Minardi-MM	1	engine
r	Senna	Lotus-Honda	0	accident
r	Campos	Minardi-MM	0	gearbox
r	Palmer	Tyrrell-Ford	0	accident at first

STARTING GRID:

1	Mansell	12	Warwick
2	Piquet	13	de Cesaris
3	Senna	14	Nannini
4	Berger,G.	15	Nakajima
5	Alboreto	16	Arnoux
6	Prost	17	Ghinzani
7	Boutsen	18	Brundle
8	Patrese	19	Campos
9	Fabi,T.	20	Danner
10	Johansson	21	Capelli
11	Cheever	22	Alliot +

Monaco

GRAND PRIX No: 440
DATE: May 30, 1987
VENUE: Monte Carlo
POLE LAP: Mansell, 1m 23.039s
FASTEST LAP: Senna, 1m 27.685s

Pn	Driver	Car	Laps	Time/Reason
1	Senna	Lotus-Honda	78	1h 57m 54.085s
2	Piquet	Williams-Honda	78	1h 58m 27.297s
3	Alboreto	Ferrari	78	1h 59m 06.924s
4	Berger,G.	Ferrari	77	
5	Palmer	Tyrrell-Ford	76	
6	Capelli	March-Ford	76	
7	Brundle	Zakspeed	76	
8	Fabi,T.	Benetton-Ford	76	
9	Prost	McLaren-TAG	75	engine
10	Nakajima	Lotus-Honda	75	
11	Arnoux	Ligier-Megatron	74	
12	Ghinzani	Ligier-Megatron	74	
13	Fabre	AGS-Ford	71	
r	Cheever	Arrows-Mega.	59	overheating
r	Warwick	Arrows-Mega.	58	gear selector
r	Johansson	McLaren-TAG	57	engine
r	Alliot	Lola-Ford	42	engine
r	Patrese	Brabham-BMW	41	electrical
r	Caffi	Osella-Alfa	39	electrical
r	de Cesaris	Brabham-BMW	38	suspension
r	Mansell	Williams-Honda	29	exhaust
r	Nannini	Minardi-MM	21	electrical
r	Streiff	Tyrrell-Ford	9	accident
r	Boutsen	Benetton-Ford	5	cv joint
dns	Campos	Minardi-MM		injured

STARTING GRID:

1	Mansell	13	Nannini
2	Senna	14	Brundle
3	Piquet	15	Palmer
4	Prost	16	Caffi
5	Alboreto	17	Nakajima
6	Cheever	18	Alliot
7	Johansson	19	Capelli
8	Berger,G.	20	Ghinzani
9	Boutsen	21	de Cesaris
10	Patrese	22	Arnoux
11	Warwick	23	Streiff
12	Fabi,T.	24	Fabre
		25	Campos

US

GRAND PRIX No:	441
DATE:	June 21, 1987
VENUE:	Detroit
POLE LAP:	Mansell, 1m 39.264s
FASTEST LAP:	Senna, 1m 40.464s

Pn	Driver	Car	Laps	Time/Reason
1	Senna	Lotus-Honda	63	1h 50m 16.358s
2	Piquet	Williams-Honda	63	1h 50m 50.177s
3	Prost	McLaren-TAG	63	1h 51m 01.685s
4	Berger,G.	Ferrari	63	1h 51m 18.959s
5	Mansell	Williams-Honda	62	
6	Cheever	Arrows-Mega.	60	out of fuel
7	Johansson	McLaren-TAG	60	
8	Danner	Zakspeed	60	
9	Patrese	Brabham-BMW	60	
10	Arnoux	Ligier-Megatron	60	
11	Palmer	Tyrrell-Ford	60	
12	Fabre	AGS-Ford	58	
r	Boutsen	Benetton-Ford	52	brake disc
r	Ghinzani	Ligier-Megatron	51	
r	Streiff	Tyrrell-Ford	44	lost wheel
r	Alliot	Lola-Ford	38	accident
r	Alboreto	Ferrari	25	gearbox
r	Nannini	Minardi-MM	22	engine
r	Brundle	Zakspeed	16	turbo
r	Warwick	Arrows-Mega.	12	accident
r	Capelli	March-Ford	9	electrical
r	Fabi,T.	Benetton-Ford	6	accident
r	Caffi	Osella-Alfa	3	gearbox
r	de Cesaris	Brabham-BMW	2	gearbox
r	Campos	Minardi-MM	1	accident
r	Nakajima	Lotus-Honda	0	accident

STARTING GRID:

1	Mansell	12	Berger,G.
2	Senna	13	Palmer
3	Piquet	14	Streiff
4	Boutsen	15	Brundle
5	Prost	16	Danner
6	Cheever	17	de Cesaris
7	Alboreto	18	Nannini
8	Fabi,T.	19	Caffi
9	Patrese	20	Alliot
10	Warwick	21	Arnoux
11	Johansson	22	Capelli +

French

GRAND PRIX No:	442
DATE:	July 5, 1987
VENUE:	Paul Ricard
POLE LAP:	Mansell, 1m 06.454s
FASTEST LAP:	Piquet, 1m 09.548s

Pn	Driver	Car	Laps	Time/Reason
1	Mansell	Williams-Honda	80	1h 37m 03.839s
2	Piquet	Williams-Honda	80	1h 37m 11.550s
3	Prost	McLaren-TAG	80	1h 37m 59.094s
4	Senna	Lotus-Honda	79	
5	Fabi,T.	Benetton-Ford	77	driveshaft
6	Streiff	Tyrrell-Ford	76	
7	Palmer	Tyrrell-Ford	76	
8	Johansson	McLaren-TAG	74	alternator
9	Fabre	AGS-Ford	74	
r	Berger,G.	Ferrari	71	suspension
uc	Nakajima	Lotus-Honda	71	
r	Alboreto	Ferrari	64	engine
r	Warwick	Arrows-Mega.	62	turbo
r	Alliot	Lola-Ford	57	transmission
r	Capelli	March-Ford	52	engine
r	Campos	Minardi-MM	52	turbo
r	Arnoux	Ligier-Megatron	33	exhaust
r	Boutsen	Benetton-Ford	31	engine
r	Danner	Zakspeed	26	overheating
r	Ghinzani	Ligier-Megatron	24	engine
r	Nannini	Minardi-MM	23	turbo
r	Patrese	Brabham-BMW	19	differential
r	Brundle	Zakspeed	18	lost wheel
r	Caffi	Osella-Alfa	11	gearbox
r	de Cesaris	Brabham-BMW	2	oil leak/fire
r	Cheever	Arrows-Mega.	0	master switch

STARTING GRID:

1	Mansell	12	Patrese
2	Prost	13	Arnoux
3	Senna	14	Cheever
4	Piquet	15	Nannini
5	Boutsen	16	Nakajima
6	Berger,G.	17	Ghinzani
7	Fabi,T.	18	Brundle
8	Alboreto	19	Danner
9	Johansson	20	Caffi
10	Warwick	21	Campos
11	de Cesaris	22	Capelli +

British

GRAND PRIX No: 443

DATE: July 12, 1987

VENUE: Silverstone

POLE LAP: Piquet, 1m 07.110s

FASTEST LAP: Mansell, 1m 09.832s

Pn	Driver	Car	Laps	Time/Reason
1	Mansell	Williams-Honda	65	1h 19m 11.780s
2	Piquet	Williams-Honda	65	1h 19m 13.698s
3	Senna	Lotus-Honda	64	
4	Nakajima	Lotus-Honda	63	
5	Warwick	Arrows-Mega.	63	
6	Fabi,T.	Benetton-Ford	63	
7	Boutsen	Benetton-Ford	62	
8	Palmer	Tyrrell-Ford	60	
9	Fabre	AGS-Ford	59	
r	Streiff	Tyrrell-Ford	57	engine
r	Brundle	Zakspeed	54	
r	Prost	McLaren-TAG	53	clutch/engine
r	Alboreto	Ferrari	52	suspension
r	Cheever	Arrows-Mega.	45	overheating
r	Campos	Minardi-MM	34	electrical
r	Caffi	Osella-Alfa	32	turbo
r	Danner	Zakspeed	32	gearbox
r	Patrese	Brabham-BMW	28	fuel metering unit
r	Johansson	McLaren-TAG	18	engine
r	Nannini	Minardi-MM	10	engine
r	de Cesaris	Brabham-BMW	8	fuel pipe/fire
r	Berger,G.	Ferrari	7	accident
r	Alliot	Lola-Ford	7	gearbox
r	Arnoux	Ligier-Megatron	3	electrical
r	Capelli	March-Ford	3	accident

STARTING GRID:

1	Piquet	14	Cheever
2	Mansell	15	Nannini
3	Senna	16	Arnoux
4	Prost	17	Brundle
5	Boutsen	18	Danner
6	Fabi,T.	19	Campos
7	Alboreto	20	Caffi
8	Berger,G.	21	Alliot
9	de Cesaris	22	Streiff
10	Johansson	23	Palmer
11	Patrese	24	Capelli
12	Nakajima	25	Fabre
13	Warwick		

German

GRAND PRIX No: 444

DATE: July 26, 1987

VENUE: Hockenheim

POLE LAP: Mansell, 1m 42.616s

FASTEST LAP: Mansell, 1m 45.716s

Pn	Driver	Car	Laps	Time/Reason
1	Piquet	Williams-Honda	44	1h 21m 25.091s
2	Johansson	McLaren-TAG	44	1h 23m 04.682s
3	Senna	Lotus-Honda	43	
4	Streiff	Tyrrell-Ford	43	
5	Palmer	Tyrrell-Ford	43	
6	Alliot	Lola-Ford	42	
7	Prost	McLaren-TAG	39	alternator
uc	Brundle	Zakspeed	34	
r	Ghinzani	Ligier-Megatron	32	engine
r	Campos	Minardi-MM	28	engine
r	Boutsen	Benetton-Ford	26	engine
r	Mansell	Williams-Honda	25	engine
r	Nannini	Minardi-MM	25	engine
r	Warwick	Arrows-Mega.	23	turbo
r	Danner	Zakspeed	21	input shaft
r	Berger,G.	Ferrari	19	turbo
r	Fabi,T.	Benetton-Ford	18	engine
r	Caffi	Osella-Alfa	17	turbo
r	de Cesaris	Brabham-BMW	12	engine
r	Alboreto	Ferrari	10	turbo
r	Fabre	AGS-Ford	10	valve
r	Cheever	Arrows-Mega.	9	turbo
r	Nakajima	LOWS-Honda	9	suspension
r	Capelli	March-Ford	7	rotor arm
r	Arnoux	Ligier-Megatron	6	electrical
r	Patrese	Brabham-BMW	5	ignition

STARTING GRID:

1	Mansell	12	Arnoux
2	Senna	13	Warwick
3	Prost	14	Nakajima
4	Piquet	15	Cheever
5	Alboreto	16	Nannini
6	Boutsen	17	Ghinzani
7	de Cesaris	18	Campos
8	Johansson	19	Brundle
9	Fabi,T.	20	Danner
10	Berger,G.	21	Alliot
11	Patrese	22	Streiff

+

Hungarian

GRAND PRIX No: 445
DATE: August 9, 1987
VENUE: Hungaroring
POLE LAP: Mansell, 1m 28.047s
FASTEST LAP: Piquet, 1m 30.149s

Pn	Driver	Car	Laps	Time/Reason
1	Piquet	Williams-Honda	76	1h 59m 26.793s
2	Senna	Lotus-Honda	76	2h 00m 04.520s
3	Prost	McLaren-TAG	76	2h 00m 54.249s
4	Boutsen	Benetton-Ford	75	
5	Patrese	Brabham-BMW	75	
6	Warwick	Arrows-Mega.	74	
7	Palmer	Tyrrell-Ford	74	
8	Cheever	Arrows-Mega.	74	
9	Streiff	Tyrrell-Ford	74	
10	Capelli	March-Ford	74	
11	Nannini	Minardi-MM	73	
12	Ghinzani	Ligier-Megatron	73	
13	Fabre	AGS-Ford	71	
14	Mansell	Williams-Honda	70	wheel
r	Caffi	Osella-Alfa	64	electrical
r	Arnoux	Ligier-Megatron	57	electrical
r	Alliot	Lola-Ford	48	accident
r	Brundle	Zakspeed	45	turbo
r	Alboreto	Ferrari	43	engine
r	de Cesaris	Brabham-BMW	43	gearbox
r	Johansson	McLaren-TAG	14	gearbox
r	Fabi,T.	Benetton-Ford	14	engine
r	Campos	Minardi-MM	14	accident
r	Berger,G.	Ferrari	13	cv joint
r	Danner	Zakspeed	3	electrical
r	Nakajima	Lotus-Honda	1	driveshaft

STARTING GRID:

1	Mansell	12	Fabi,T.
2	Berger,G.	13	de Cesaris
3	Piquet	14	Streiff
4	Prost	15	Alliot
5	Alboreto	16	Palmer
6	Senna	17	Nakajima
7	Boutsen	18	Capelli
8	Johansson	19	Arnoux
9	Warwick	20	Nannini
10	Patrese	21	Caffi
11	Cheever	22	Brundle +

Austrian

GRAND PRIX No: 446
DATE: August 16, 1987
VENUE: Osterreichring
POLE LAP: Piquet, 1m 23.357s
FASTEST LAP: Mansell, 1m 28.318s

Pn	Driver	Car	Laps	Time/Reason
1	Mansell	Williams-Honda	52	1h 18m 44.898s
2	Piquet	Williams-Honda	52	1h 19m 40.602s
3	Fabi,T.	Benetton-Ford	51	
4	Boutsen	Benetton-Ford	51	
5	Senna	Lotus-Honda	50	
6	Prost	McLaren-TAG	50	
7	Johansson	McLaren-TAG	50	
8	Ghinzani	Ligier-Megatron	50	
9	Danner	Zakspeed	49	
10	Arnoux	Ligier-Megatron	49	
11	Capelli	March-Ford	49	
12	Alliot	Lola-Ford	49	
13	Nakajima	Lotus-Honda	49	
dq	Brundle	Zakspeed	48	illegal wing
14	Palmer	Tyrrell-Ford	47	
uc	Fabre	AGS-Ford	45	
r	Patrese	Brabham-BMW	43	engine
r	Alboreto	Ferrari	42	exhaust
r	de Cesaris	Brabham-BMW	35	engine
r	Warwick	Arrows-Mega.	35	engine
r	Cheever	Arrows-Mega.	31	puncture
r	Berger,G.	Ferrari	5	engine
r	Campos	Minardi-MM	3	distributor belt
r	Nannini	Minardi-MM	1	engine
r	Caffi	Osella-Alfa	0	electrical
r	Streiff	Tyrrell-Ford	0	accident

STARTING GRID:

1	Piquet	12	Cheever
2	Mansell	13	Nakajima
3	Berger,G.	14	Johansson
4	Boutsen	15	Nannini
5	Fabi,T.	16	Arnoux
6	Alboreto	17	Brundle
7	Senna	18	Ghinzani
8	Patrese	19	Campos
9	Prost	20	Danner
10	de Cesaris	21	Caffi
11	Warwick	22	Alliot +

Italian

GRAND PRIX No:	447
DATE:	September 6, 1987
VENUE:	Monza
POLE LAP:	Piquet, 1m 23.460s
FASTEST LAP:	Senna, 1m 26.796s

Pn	Driver	Car	Laps	Time/Reason
1	Piquet	Williams-Honda	50	1h 14m 47.707s
2	Senna	Lotus-Honda	50	1h 14m 49.513s
3	Mansell	Williams-Honda	50	1h 15m 36.743s
4	Berger,G.	Ferrari	50	1h 15m 45.686s
5	Boutsen	Benetton-Ford	50	1h 16m 09.026s
6	Johansson	McLaren-TAG	50	1h 16m 16.494s
7	Fabi,T.	Benetton-Ford	49	
8	Ghinzani	Ligier-Megatron	48	
9	Danner	Zakspeed	48	
10	Arnoux	Ligier-Megatron	48	
11	Nakajima	Lotus-Honda	47	
12	Streiff	Tyrrell-Ford	47	
13	Capelli	March-Lotus	47	
14	Palmer	Tyrrell-Ford	47	
15	Prost	McLaren-TAG	46	
16	Nannini	Minardi-MM	45	out of fuel
r	Brundle	Zakspeed	43	gearbox
r	Alliot	Lola-Ford	37	accident
r	Campos	Minardi-MM	34	fuel filter fire
r	Cheever	Arrows-Mega.	27	cv joint
r	Forini	Osella-Alfa	27	turbo
r	Caffi	Osella-Alfa	16	wheel
r	Alboreto	Ferrari	13	turbo
r	Warwick	Arrows-Mega.	9	fuel metering unit
r	de Cesaris	Brabham-BMW	7	suspension
r	Patrese	Brabham-BMW	5	engine

STARTING GRID:

1	Piquet	12	Warwick
2	Mansell	13	Cheever
3	Berger,G.	14	Nakajima
4	Senna	15	Arnoux
5	Prost	16	Danner
6	Boutsen	17	Brundle
7	Fabi,T.	18	Nannini
8	Alboreto	19	Ghinzani
9	Patrese	20	Campos
10	de Cesaris	21	Caffi
11	Johansson	22	Palmer +

Portuguese

GRAND PRIX No:	448
DATE:	September 20, 1987
VENUE:	Estoril
POLE LAP:	Berger,G., 1m 17.620s
FASTEST LAP:	Berger,G., 1m 19.282s

Pn	Driver	Car	Laps	Time/Reason
1	Prost	McLaren-TAG	70	1h 37m 03.906s
2	Berger,G.	Ferrari	70	1h 37m 24.399s
3	Piquet	Williams-Honda	70	1h 38m 07.201s
4	Fabi,T.	Benetton-Ford	69	
5	Johansson	McLaren-TAG	69	
6	Cheever	Arrows-Mega.	68	
7	Senna	Lotus-Honda	68	
8	Nakajima	Lotus-Honda	68	
9	Capelli	March-Ford	67	
10	Palmer	Tyrrell-Ford	67	
11	Nannini	Minardi-MM	66	out of fuel
12	Streiff	Tyrrell-Ford	66	
13	Warwick	Arrows-Mega.	66	
14	Boutsen	Benetton-Ford	64	
r	de Cesaris	Brabham-BMW	54	injector pipe
r	Alboreto	Ferrari	38	gear linkage
r	Brundle	Zakspeed	35	gearbox
r	Forini	Osella-Alfa	32	turbo
r	Alliot	Lola-Ford	31	electrical
r	Arnoux	Ligier-Megatron	29	radiator
r	Caffi	Osella-Alfa	27	turbo
r	Ghinzani	Ligier-Megatron	24	ignition
r	Campos	Minardi-MM	24	accident
r	Mansell	Williams-Honda	13	electrical
r	Patrese	Brabham-BMW	13	engine
r	Danner	Zakspeed	0	accident

STARTING GRID:

1	Berger,G.	12	Warwick
2	Mansell	13	de Cesaris
3	Prost	14	Nannini
4	Piquet	15	Nakajima
5	Senna	16	Danner
6	Alboreto	17	Brundle
7	Patrese	18	Arnoux
8	Johansson	19	Alliot
9	Boutsen	20	Campos
10	Fabi,T.	21	Streiff
11	Cheever	22	Capelli +

Spanish

GRAND PRIX No: 449
DATE: September 27, 1987
VENUE: Jerez
POLE LAP: Piquet, 1m 22.461s
FASTEST LAP: Berger,G., 1m 26.986s

Pn	Driver	Car	Laps	Time/Reason
1	Mansell	Williams-Honda	72	1h 49m 12.692s
2	Prost	McLaren-TAG	72	1h 49m 34.917s
3	Johansson	McLaren-TAG	72	1h 49m 43.510s
4	Piquet	Williams-Honda	72	1h 49m 44.142s
5	Senna	Lotus-Honda	72	1h 50m 26.199s
6	Alliot	Lola-Ford	71	
7	Streiff	Tyrrell-Ford	71	
8	Cheever	Arrows-Mega.	70	out of fuel
9	Nakajima	Zakspeed	70	
10	Warwick	Arrows-Mega.	70	
11	Brundle	Zakspeed	70	
12	Capelli	March-Ford	70	
13	Patrese	Brabham-BMW	68	
14	Campos	Minardi-MM	68	
15	Alboreto	Ferrari	67	engine
16	Boutsen	Benetton-BMW	66	brakes
r	Berger,G.	Ferrari	62	engine
r	Palmer	Tyrrell-Ford	55	accident
r	Arnoux	Ligier-Megatron	55	engine
r	Danner	Zakspeed	50	gearbox
r	Nannini	Minardi-MM	45	turbo
r	Fabi,T.	Benetton-BMW	40	engine
r	de Cesaris	Brabham-BMW	26	gearbox
r	Ghinzani	Ligier-Megatron	24	ignition
r	Fabre	AGS-Ford	10	clutch
r	Larini	Coloni-Ford	8	suspension

STARTING GRID:

1	Piquet	12	Warwick
2	Mansell	13	Cheever
3	Berger,G.	14	Arnoux
4	Alboreto	15	Streiff
5	Senna	16	Palmer
6	Fabi,T.	17	Alliot
7	Prost	18	Nakajima
8	Boutsen	19	Capelli
9	Patrese	20	Brundle
10	de Cesaris	21	Nannini
11	Johansson	22	Danner +

Mexican

GRAND PRIX No: 450
DATE: October 18, 1987
VENUE: Mexico City
POLE LAP: Mansell, 1m 18.383s
FASTEST LAP: Piquet, 1m 19.132s

Pn	Driver	Car	Laps	Time/Reason
1	Mansell	Williams-Honda	63	1h 26m 24.207s
2	Piquet	Williams-Honda	63	1h 26m 50.383s
3	Patrese	Brabham-BMW	63	1h 27m 51.086s
4	Cheever	Arrows-Mega.	63	1h 28m 05.559s
5	Fabi,T.	Benetton-Ford	61	
6	Alliot	Lola-Ford	60	
7	Palmer	Tyrrell-Ford	60	
8	Streiff	Tyrrell-Ford	60	
9	Dalmas	Lola-Ford	59	
r	Senna	Lotus-Honda	54	spun off
r	Capelli	March-Ford	51	engine
r	Caffi	Osella-Alfa	50	engine
r	Ghinzani	Ligier-Megatron	43	overheating
r	Campos	Minardi-MM	32	gear linkage
r	Arnoux	Ligier-Megatron	29	ignition
r	Warwick	Arrows-Mega.	26	accident
r	de Cesaris	Brabham-BMW	22	spun off
r	Berger,G.	Ferrari	20	engine
r	Boutsen	Benetton-Ford	15	electrical
r	Nannini	Minardi-MM	13	turbo
r	Alboreto	Ferrari	12	engine
r	Brundle	Zakspeed	3	engine
r	Johansson	McLaren-TAG	1	accident
r	Nakajima	Lotus-Honda	1	accident
r	Danner	Zakspeed	1	accident
r	Prost	McLaren-TAG	0	accident

STARTING GRID:

1	Mansell	12	Cheever
2	Berger,G.	13	Brundle
3	Piquet	14	Nannini
4	Boutsen	15	Johansson
5	Prost	16	Nakajima
6	Fabi,T.	17	Danner
7	Senna	18	Arnoux
8	Patrese	19	Campos
9	Alboreto	20	Capelli
10	de Cesaris	21	Ghinzani
11	Warwick	22	Palmer +

Japanese

GRAND PRIX No:	451
DATE:	November 1, 1987
VENUE:	Suzuka
POLE LAP:	Berger,G., 1m 40.042s
FASTEST LAP:	Prost, 1m 43.844s

Pn	Driver	Car	Laps	Time/Reason
1	Berger,G.	Ferrari	51	1h 32m 58.072s
2	Senna	Lotus-Honda	51	1h 33m 15.456s
3	Johansson	McLaren-TAG	51	1h 33m 15.766s
4	Alboreto	Ferrari	51	1h 34m 18.513s
5	Boutsen	Benetton-Ford	51	1h 34m 23.648s
6	Nakajima	Lotus-Honda	51	1h 34m 34.551s
7	Prost	McLaren-TAG	50	
8	Palmer	Tyrrell-Ford	50	
9	Cheever	Arrows-Mega.	50	
10	Warwick	Arrows-Mega.	50	
11	Patrese	Brabham-BMW	49	engine
12	Streiff	Tyrrell-Ford	49	
13	Ghinzani	Ligier-Megatron	48	out of fuel
14	Dalmas	Lola-Ford	47	electrical
15	Piquet	Williams-Honda	46	engine
r	Arnoux	Ligier-Megatron	44	out of fuel
r	Caffi	Osella-Alfa	43	out of fuel
r	Moreno	AGS-Ford	38	injection
r	Nannini	Minardi-MM	35	engine
r	Brundle	Zakspeed	32	overheating
r	de Cesaris	Brabham-BMW	26	engine
r	Fabi,T.	Benetton-Ford	16	engine
r	Danner	Zakspeed	13	engine
r	Capelli	March-Ford	13	accident
r	Campos	Minardi-MM	2	engine
r	Alliot	Lola-Ford	0	accident
dns	Mansell	Williams-Honda		injured

STARTING GRID:

1	Berger,G.	11	de Cesaris
2	Prost	12	Nakajima
3	Boutsen	13	Cheever
4	Alboreto	14	Alliot
5	Piquet	15	Warwick
6	Fabi,T.	16	Nannini
7	Mansell	17	Brundle
8	Senna	18	Danner
9	Patrese	19	Arnoux
10	Johansson	20	Palmer +

Australian

GRAND PRIX No:	452
DATE:	November 15, 1987
VENUE:	Adelaide
POLE LAP:	Berger,G., 1m 17.267s
FASTEST LAP:	Berger,G., 1m 20.416s

Pn	Driver	Car	Laps	Time/Reason
1	Berger,G.	Ferrari	82	1h 52m 56.144s
dq	Senna	Lotus-Honda	82	illegal ducts
2	Alboreto	Ferrari	82	1h 54m 04.028s
3	Boutsen	Benetton-Ford	81	
4	Palmer	Tyrrell-Ford	80	
5	Dalmas	Lola-Ford	79	
6	Moreno	AGS-Ford	79	
7	Danner	Zakspeed	79	
8	de Cesaris	Brabham-BMW	78	
9	Patrese	Williams-Honda	76	
r	Piquet	Williams-Honda	58	gearbox
r	Capelli	March-Ford	58	spun off
r	Prost	McLaren-TAG	53	brakes
r	Cheever	Arrows-Mega.	53	overheating
r	Johansson	McLaren-TAG	48	brakes
r	Fabi,T.	Benetton-Ford	46	brakes
r	Campos	Minardi-MM	46	gearbox
r	Alliot	Lola-Ford	45	electrical
r	Arnoux	Ligier-Megatron	41	electrical
r	Modena	Brabham-BMW	31	driver tired
r	Ghinzani	Ligier-Megatron	26	turbo
r	Nakajima	Lotus-Honda	22	suspension
r	Warwick	Arrows-Mega.	19	transmission
r	Brundle	Zakspeed	18	gear lever
r	Streiff	Tyrrell-Ford	6	spun off
r	Nannini	Minardi-MM	0	accident

STARTING GRID:

1	Berger,G.	12	Warwick
2	Prost	13	Nannini
3	Piquet	14	Nakajima
4	Senna	15	Modena
5	Boutsen	16	Brundle
6	Alboreto	17	Alliot
7	Patrese	18	Streiff
8	Johansson	19	Palmer
9	Fabi,T.	20	Arnoux
10	de Cesaris	21	Dalmas
11	Cheever	22	Ghinzani +

Brazilian

GRAND PRIX No:	453
DATE:	April 3, 1988
VENUE:	Rio de Janeiro
POLE LAP:	Senna, 1m 28.096s
FASTEST LAP:	Berger,G., 1m 32.943s

Pn	Driver	Car	Laps	Time/Reason
1	Prost	McLaren-Honda	60	1h 36m 06.587s
2	Berger,G.	Ferrari	60	1h 36m 16.730s
3	Piquet	Lotus-Honda	60	1h 37m 15.438s
4	Warwick	Arrows-Mega.	60	1h 37m 20.205s
5	Alboreto	Ferrari	60	1h 37m 21.413s
6	Nakajima	Lotus-Honda	59	
7	Boutsen	Benetton-Ford	59	
8	Cheever	Arrows-Mega.	59	
9	Johansson	Ligier-Judd	57	
r	de Cesaris	Rial-Ford	53	engine
r	Palmer	Tyrrell-Ford	47	driveshaft
r	Sala	Minardi-Ford	46	rear wing
r	Alliot	Lola-Ford	40	suspension
r	Tarquini	Coloni-Ford	35	suspension
r	Streiff	AGS-Ford	35	brakes
r	Dalmas	Lola-Ford	32	engine
dq	Senna	McLaren-Honda	31	changed car
r	Arnoux	Ligier-Judd	23	clutch
r	Modena	EuroBrun-Ford	20	engine
r	Mansell	Williams-Judd	18	overheating
r	Nannini	Benetton-Ford	7	overheating
r	Patrese	Williams-Judd	6	overheating
r	Capelli	March-Judd	6	overheating
r	Campos	Minardi-Ford	5	rear wing
r	Gugelmin	March-Judd	0	transmission
r	Larrauri	EuroBrun-Ford	0	engine

STARTING GRID:

1	Senna	12	Nannini
2	Mansell	13	Gugelmin
3	Prost	14	de Cesaris
4	Berger,G.	15	Cheever
5	Piquet	16	Dalmas
6	Alboreto	17	Alliot
7	Boutsen	18	Arnoux
8	Patrese	19	Streiff
9	Capelli	20	Sala
10	Nakajima	21	Johansson
11	Warwick	22	Palmer +

San Marino

GRAND PRIX No:	454
DATE:	May 1, 1988
VENUE:	Imola
POLE LAP:	Senna, 1m 27.148s
FASTEST LAP:	Prost, 1m 29.685s

Pn	Driver	Car	Laps	Time/Reason
1	Senna	McLaren-Honda	60	1h 32m 41.264s
2	Prost	McLaren-Honda	60	1h 32m 43.598s
3	Piquet	Lotus-Honda	59	
4	Boutsen	Benetton-Ford	59	
5	Berger,G.	Ferrari	59	
6	Nannini	Benetton-Ford	59	
7	Cheever	Arrows-Mega.	59	
8	Nakajima	Lotus-Honda	59	
9	Warwick	Arrows-Mega.	58	
10	Streiff	AGS-Ford	58	
11	Sala	Minardi-Ford	58	
12	Dalmas	Lola-Ford	58	
13	Patrese	Williams-Judd	58	
14	Palmer	Tyrrell-Ford	58	
15	Gugelmin	March-Judd	58	
16	Campos	Minardi-Ford	57	
17	Alliot	Lola-Ford	57	
18	Alboreto	Ferrari	54	engine
uc	Modena	EuroBrun-Ford	52	
r	Bailey	Tyrrell-Ford	48	gearbox
r	Mansell	Williams-Judd	42	electrical
r	Tarquini	Coloni-Ford	40	throttle
r	Caffi	Dallara-Ford	18	gearbox
r	Ghinzani	Zakspeed	16	electrical
r	Capelli	March-Judd	2	gearbox
r	de Cesaris	Rial-Ford	0	suspension

STARTING GRID:

1	Senna	12	Nakajima
2	Prost	13	Streiff
3	Piquet	14	Warwick
4	Nannini	15	Alliot
5	Berger,G.	16	de Cesaris
6	Patrese	17	Tarquini
7	Cheever	18	Sala
8	Boutsen	19	Dalmas
9	Capelli	20	Gugelmin
10	Alboreto	21	Bailey
11	Mansell	22	Campos +

Monaco

GRAND PRIX No:	455
DATE:	May 15, 1988
VENUE:	Monte Carlo
POLE LAP:	Senna, 1m 23.998s
FASTEST LAP:	Senna, 1m 26.321s

Pn	Driver	Car	Laps	Time/Reason
1	Prost	McLaren-Honda	78	1h 57m 17.077s
2	Berger,G.	Ferrari	78	1h 57m 37.530s
3	Alboreto	Ferrari	78	1h 57m 58.306s
4	Warwick	Arrows-Mega.	77	
5	Palmer	Tyrrell-Ford	77	
6	Patrese	Williams-Judd	77	
7	Dalmas	Lola-Ford	77	
8	Boutsen	Benetton-Ford	76	
9	Larini	Osella-Alfa	75	
10	Capelli	March-Judd	72	
r	Senna	McLaren-Honda	66	accident
r	Alliot	Lola-Ford	50	accident
r	Gugelmin	March-Judd	45	fuel pump
r	Ghinzani	Zakspeed	43	gearbox
r	Nannini	Benetton-Ford	38	accident
r	Sala	Minardi-Ford	36	driveshaft
r	Mansell	Williams-Judd	32	accident
r	de Cesaris	Rial-Ford	28	engine
r	Arnoux	Ligier-Judd	17	engine
r	Larrauri	EuroBrun-Ford	14	accident
r	Cheever	Arrows-Mega.	8	electrical
r	Johansson	Ligier-Judd	6	engine
r	Tarquini	Coloni-Ford	5	engine
r	Piquet	Lotus-Honda	0	accident
r	Caffi	Dallara-Ford	0	accident
r	Streiff	AGS-Ford	0	throttle

STARTING GRID:

1	Senna	12	Streiff
2	Prost	13	Alliot
3	Berger,G.	14	Gugelmin
4	Alboreto	15	Sala
5	Mansell	16	Boutsen
6	Nannini	17	Caffi
7	Warwick	18	Larrauri
8	Patrese	19	de Cesaris
9	Cheever	20	Arnoux
10	Palmer	21	Dalmas
11	Piquet	22	Capelli

+

Mexican

GRAND PRIX No:	456
DATE:	May 29, 1988
VENUE:	Mexico City
POLE LAP:	Senna, 1m 17.468s
FASTEST LAP:	Prost, 1m 18.608s

Pn	Driver	Car	Laps	Time/Reason
1	Prost	McLaren-Honda	67	1h 30m 15.737s
2	Senna	McLaren-Honda	67	1h 30m 22.841s
3	Berger,G.	Ferrari	67	1h 31m 13.051s
4	Alboreto	Ferrari	66	
5	Warwick	Arrows-Mega.	66	
6	Cheever	Arrows-Mega.	66	
7	Nannini	Benetton-Ford	65	
8	Boutsen	Benetton-Ford	64	
9	Dalmas	Lola-Ford	64	
10	Johansson	Ligier-Judd	63	
11	Sala	Minardi-Ford	63	
12	Streiff	AGS-Ford	63	
13	Larrauri	EuroBrun-Ford	63	
14	Tarquini	Coloni-Ford	62	
15	Ghinzani	Zakspeed	61	
16	Capelli	March-Judd	61	
r	Piquet	Lotus-Honda	58	engine
r	de Cesaris	Rial-Ford	52	transmission
r	Nakajima	Lotus-Honda	27	turbo
r	Mansell	Williams-Judd	20	engine
r	Schneider	Zakspeed	16	engine
r	Patrese	Williams-Judd	16	engine
r	Arnoux	Ligier-Judd	13	accident
r	Caffi	Dallara-Ford	13	accident
r	Gugelmin	March-Judd	10	engine
r	Alliot	Lola-Ford	0	handling

STARTING GRID:

1	Senna	12	de Cesaris
2	Prost	13	Alliot
3	Berger,G.	14	Mansell
4	Piquet	15	Schneider
5	Alboreto	16	Gugelmin
6	Nakajima	17	Patrese
7	Cheever	18	Ghinzani
8	Nannini	19	Streiff
9	Warwick	20	Arnoux
10	Capelli	21	Tarquini
11	Boutsen	22	Dalmas

+

Canadian

GRAND PRIX No: 457
DATE: June 12, 1988
VENUE: Montreal
POLE LAP: Senna, 1m 21.681s
FASTEST LAP: Senna, 1m 24.973s

Pn	Driver	Car	Laps	Time/Reason
1	Senna	McLaren-Honda	69	1h 39m 46.6128s
2	Prost	McLaren-Honda	69	1h 39m 52.552s
3	Boutsen	Benetton-Ford	69	1h 40m 38.027s
4	Piquet	Lotus-Honda	68	
5	Capelli	March-Judd	68	
6	Palmer	Tyrrell-Ford	67	
7	Warwick	Arrows-Mega.	67	
8	Tarquini	Coloni-Ford	67	
9	de Cesaris	Rial-Ford	66	
10	Alliot	Lola-Ford	66	
11	Nakajima	Lotus-Honda	66	
12	Modena	EuroBrun-Ford	66	
13	Sala	Minardi-Ford	64	
14	Ghinzani	Zakspeed	63	
r	Gugelmin	March-Judd	54	gearbox
r	Streiff	AGS-Ford	41	suspension
r	Arnoux	Ligier-Judd	36	gearbox
r	Alboreto	Ferrari	33	engine
r	Patrese	Williams-Judd	32	engine
r	Cheever	Arrows-Mega.	31	throttle
r	Mansell	Williams-Judd	28	engine
r	Johansson	Ligier-Judd	24	engine
r	Berger,G.	Ferrari	22	ignition
r	Nannini	Benetton-Ford	15	ignition
r	Larrauri	EuroBrun-Ford	8	accident
r	Bailey	Tyrrell-Ford	0	accident

STARTING GRID:

1	Senna	12	de Cesaris
2	Prost	13	Nakajima
3	Berger,G.	14	Capelli
4	Alboreto	15	Modena
5	Nannini	16	Warwick
6	Piquet	17	Alliot
7	Boutsen	18	Gugelmin
8	Cheever	19	Palmer
9	Mansell	20	Arnoux
10	Streiff	21	Sala
11	Patrese	22	Ghinzani

+

US

GRAND PRIX No: 458
DATE: June 19, 1988
VENUE: Detroit
POLE LAP: Senna, 1m 40.606s
FASTEST LAP: Prost, 1m 44.836s

Pn	Driver	Car	Laps	Time/Reason
1	Senna	McLaren-Honda	63	1h 54m 56.035s
2	Prost	McLaren-Honda	63	1h 55m 34.748s
3	Boutsen	Benetton-Ford	62	
4	de Cesaris	Rial-Ford	62	
5	Palmer	Tyrrell-Ford	62	
6	Martini	Minardi-Ford	62	
7	Dalmas	Lola-Ford	61	
8	Caffi	Dallara-Ford	61	
9	Bailey	Tyrrell-Ford	59	accident
r	Sala	Minardi-Ford	54	transmission
r	Alliot	Lola-Ford	46	gearbox
r	Modena	EuroBrun-Ford	46	accident
r	Alboreto	Ferrari	45	spun off
r	Arnoux	Ligier-Judd	45	engine
r	Gugelmin	March-Judd	34	engine
r	Patrese	Williams-Judd	26	electrical
r	Piquet	Lotus-Honda	26	accident
r	Larrauri	EuroBrun-Ford	26	gearbox
r	Warwick	Arrows-Mega.	24	accident
r	Mansell	Williams-Judd	18	electrical
r	Streiff	AGS-Ford	15	suspension
r	Nannini	Benetton-Ford	14	suspension
r	Cheever	Arrows-Mega.	14	electrical
r	Larini	Osella-Alfa	7	engine
r	Berger,G.	Ferrari	6	puncture
r	Johansson	Ligier-Judd	2	engine
dns	Capelli	March-Judd		injured

STARTING GRID:

1	Senna	11	Streiff
2	Berger,G.	12	de Cesaris
3	Alboreto	13	Gugelmin
4	Prost	14	Alliot
5	Boutsen	15	Cheever
6	Mansell	16	Martini
7	Nannini	17	Palmer
8	Piquet	18	Johansson
9	Warwick	19	Modena
10	Patrese	20	Arnoux

+

French

GRAND PRIX No: 459
DATE: July 3, 1988
VENUE: Paul Ricard
POLE LAP: Prost, 1m 07.589s
FASTEST LAP: Prost, 1m 11.737s

Pn	Driver	Car	Laps	Time/Reason
1	Prost	McLaren-Honda	80	1h 37m 37.328s
2	Senna	McLaren-Honda	80	1h 38m 09.080s
3	Alboreto	Ferrari	80	1h 38m 43.833s
4	Berger,G.	Ferrari	79	
5	Piquet	Lotus-Honda	79	
6	Nannini	Benetton-Ford	79	
7	Nakajima	Lotus-Honda	79	
8	Gugelmin	March-Judd	79	
9	Capelli	March-Judd	79	
10	de Cesaris	Rial-Ford	78	
11	Cheever	Arrows-Mega.	78	
12	Caffi	Dallara-Ford	78	
13	Dalmas	Lola-Ford	78	
14	Modena	EuroBrun-Ford	77	
15	Martini	Minardi-Ford	77	
uc	Sala	Minardi-Ford	70	
r	Larrauri	EuroBrun-Ford	64	clutch
r	Larini	Osella-Alfa	56	driveshaft
r	Schneider	Zakspeed	55	gearbox
r	Mansell	Williams-Judd	48	suspension
r	Alliot	Lola-Ford	46	electrical
r	Palmer	Tyrrell-Ford	40	engine
r	Patrese	Williams-Judd	35	brakes
r	Boutsen	Benetton-Ford	28	engine
r	Streiff	AGS-Ford	20	fuel leak
r	Warwick	Arrows-Mega.	11	spun off
dns	Ghinzani	Zakspeed		Excluded-missed weight check

STARTING GRID:

1	Prost	10	Capelli
2	Senna	11	Warwick
3	Berger,G.	12	de Cesaris
4	Alboreto	13	Cheever
5	Boutsen	14	Caffi
6	Nannini	15	Patrese
7	Piquet	16	Gugelmin
8	Nakajima	17	Streiff
9	Mansell	18	Alliot +

British

GRAND PRIX No: 460
DATE: July 10, 1988
VENUE: Silverstone
POLE LAP: Berger,G., 1m 10.133s
FASTEST LAP: Mansell, 1m 23.308s

Pn	Driver	Car	Laps	Time/Reason
1	Senna	McLaren-Honda	65	1h 33m 16.367s
2	Mansell	Williams-Judd	65	1h 33m 39.711s
3	Nannini	Benetton-Ford	65	1h 34m 07.581s
4	Gugelmin	March-Judd	65	1h 34m 27.745s
5	Piquet	Lotus-Honda	65	1h 34m 37.202s
6	Warwick	Arrows-Mega.	64	
7	Cheever	Arrows-Mega.	64	
8	Patrese	Williams-Judd	64	
9	Berger,G.	Ferrari	64	
10	Nakajima	Lotus-Honda	64	
11	Caffi	Dallara-Ford	64	
12	Modena	EuroBrun-Ford	64	
13	Dalmas	Lola-Ford	63	
14	Alliot	Lola-Ford	63	
15	Martini	Minardi-Ford	63	
16	Bailey	Tyrrell-Ford	63	
17	Alboreto	Ferrari	62	out of fuel
18	Arnoux	Ligier-Judd	62	
19	Larini	Osella-Alfa	60	out of fuel
r	Boutsen	Benetton-Ford	38	gearbox
r	Capelli	March-Judd	34	alternator
r	Prost	McLaren-Honda	24	handling
r	Palmer	Tyrrell-Ford	14	transmission
r	de Cesaris	Rial-Ford	9	transmission
r	Streiff	AGS-Ford	8	accident
r	Sala	Minardi-Ford	0	accident

STARTING GRID:

1	Berger,G.	12	Boutsen
2	Alboreto	13	Cheever
3	Senna	14	de Cesaris
4	Prost	15	Patrese
5	Gugelmin	16	Streiff
6	Capelli	17	Palmer
7	Piquet	18	Sala
8	Nannini	19	Martini
9	Warwick	20	Modena
10	Nakajima	21	Caffi
11	Mansell	22	Alliot +

German

GRAND PRIX No: 461
DATE: July 24, 1988
VENUE: Hockenheim
POLE LAP: Senna, 1m 44.596s
FASTEST LAP: Nannini, 2m 03.032s

Pn	Driver	Car	Laps	Time/Reason
1	Senna	McLaren-Honda	44	1h 32m 54.188s
2	Prost	McLaren-Honda	44	1h 33m 07.797s
3	Berger,G.	Ferrari	44	1h 33m 46.283s
4	Alboreto	Ferrari	44	1h 34m 35.100s
5	Capelli	March-Judd	44	1h 34m 43.794s
6	Boutsen	Benetton-Ford	43	
7	Warwick	Arrows-Mega.	43	
8	Gugelmin	March-Judd	43	
9	Nakajima	Lotus-Honda	43	
10	Cheever	Arrows-Mega.	43	
11	Palmer	Tyrrell-Ford	43	
12	Schneider	Zakspeed	43	
13	de Cesaris	Rial-Ford	42	
14	Ghinzani	Zakspeed	42	
15	Caffi	Dallara-Ford	42	
16	Larrauri	EuroBrun-Ford	42	
17	Arnoux	Ligier-Judd	41	
18	Nannini	Benetton-Ford	40	
r	Dalmas	Lola-Ford	38	throttle
r	Streiff	AGS-Ford	38	accelerator
r	Patrese	Williams-Judd	34	accident
r	Larini	Osella-Alfa	27	fuel line
r	Mansell	Williams-Judd	16	accident
r	Modena	EuroBrun-Ford	15	engine
r	Alliot	Lola-Ford	8	accident
r	Piquet	Lotus-Honda	1	accident

STARTING GRID:

1	Senna	12	Warwick
2	Prost	13	Patrese
3	Berger,G.	14	de Cesaris
4	Alboreto	15	Cheever
5	Piquet	16	Streiff
6	Nannini	17	Arnoux
7	Capelli	18	Larini
8	Nakajima	19	Caffi
9	Boutsen	20	Alliot
10	Gugelmin	21	Dalmas
11	Mansell	22	Schneider +

Hungarian

GRAND PRIX No: 462
DATE: August 7, 1988
VENUE: Hungaroring
POLE LAP: Senna, 1m 27.635s
FASTEST LAP: Prost, 1m 30.639s

Pn	Driver	Car	Laps	Time/Reason
1	Senna	McLaren-Honda	76	1h 57m 47.081s
2	Prost	McLaren-Honda	76	1h 57m 47.610s
3	Boutsen	Benetton-Ford	76	1h 58m 18.491s
4	Berger,G.	Ferrari	76	1h 59m 15.751s
5	Gugelmin	March-Judd	75	
6	Patrese	Williams-Judd	75	
7	Nakajima	Lotus-Honda	73	
8	Piquet	Lotus-Honda	73	
9	Dalmas	Lola-Ford	73	
10	Sala	Minardi-Ford	72	
11	Modena	EuroBrun-Ford	72	
12	Alliot	Lola-Ford	72	
13	Tarquini	Coloni-Ford	71	
r	Warwick	Arrows-Mega.	65	brakes
r	Mansell	Williams-Judd	60	driver tired
r	Cheever	Arrows-Mega.	55	brakes
r	Alboreto	Ferrari	40	engine
r	Arnoux	Ligier-Judd	32	engine
r	de Cesaris	Rial-Ford	28	cv joint
r	Nannini	Benetton-Ford	24	water pipe
r	Caffi	Dallara-Ford	22	engine
r	Johansson	Ligier-Judd	19	throttle
r	Martini	Minardi-Ford	8	accident
r	Streiff	AGS-Ford	8	suspension
r	Capelli	March-Judd	5	misfiring
r	Palmer	Tyrrell-Ford	3	engine

STARTING GRID:

1	Senna	12	Warwick
2	Mansell	13	Piquet
3	Boutsen	14	Cheever
4	Capelli	15	Alboreto
5	Nannini	16	Martini
6	Patrese	17	Dalmas
7	Prost	18	de Cesaris
8	Gugelmin	19	Nakajima
9	Berger,G.	20	Alliot
10	Caffi	21	Palmer
11	Sala	22	Tarquini +

Belgian

GRAND PRIX No: 463
DATE: August 28, 1988
VENUE: Spa-Francorchamps
POLE LAP: Senna, 1m 53.718s
FASTEST LAP: Berger,G., 2m 00.772s

Pn	Driver	Car	Laps	Time/Reason
1	Senna	McLaren-Honda	43	1h 28m 00.549s
2	Prost	McLaren-Honda	43	1h 28m 31.019s
dq	Boutsen	Benetton-Ford	43	fuel illegal
dq	Nannini	Benetton-Ford	43	fuel illegal
3	Capelli	March-Judd	43	1h 29m 16.317s
4	Piquet	Lotus-Honda	43	1h 29m 24.177s
5	Warwick	Arrows-Mega.	43	1h 29m 25.904s
6	Cheever	Arrows-Mega.	42	
7	Brundle	Williams-Judd	42	
8	Caffi	Dallara-Ford	42	
9	Alliot	Lola-Ford	42	
10	Streiff	AGS-Ford	42	
11	Johansson	Ligier-Judd	39	engine
12	Palmer	Tyrrell-Ford	39	throttle
13	Schneider	Zakspeed	38	gearbox
uc	Tarquini	Coloni-Ford	36	
r	Alboreto	Ferrari	35	engine
r	Patrese	Williams-Judd	30	engine
r	Gugelmin	March-Judd	29	accident
r	Ghinzani	Zakspeed	25	oil line
r	Nakajima	Lotus-Honda	21	engine
r	Larini	Osella-Alfa	14	fuel pump
r	Berger,G.	Ferrari	11	engine
r	Dalmas	Lola-Ford	9	engine
r	de Cesaris	Rial-Ford	2	accident
r	Arnoux	Ligier-Judd	2	accident

STARTING GRID:

1	Senna	12	Brundle
2	Prost	13	Gugelmin
3	Berger,G.	14	Capelli
4	Alboreto	15	Caffi
5	Patrese	16	Alliot
6	Boutsen	17	Arnoux
7	Nannini	18	Streiff
8	Nakajima	19	de Cesaris
9	Piquet	20	Johansson
10	Warwick	21	Palmer
11	Cheever	22	Tarquini +

Italian

GRAND PRIX No: 464
DATE: September 11, 1988
VENUE: Monza
POLE LAP: Senna, 1m 25.974s
FASTEST LAP: Alboreto, 1m 29.070s

Pn	Driver	Car	Laps	Time/Reason
1	Berger,G.	Ferrari	51	1h 17m 39.744s
2	Alboreto	Ferrari	51	1h 17m 40.246s
3	Cheever	Arrows-Mega.	51	1h 18m 15.276s
4	Warwick	Arrows-Mega.	51	1h 18m 15.858s
5	Capelli	March-Judd	51	1h 18m 32.266s
6	Boutsen	Benetton-Ford	51	1h 18m 39.622s
7	Patrese	Williams-Judd	51	1h 18m 54.487s
8	Gugelmin	March-Judd	51	1h 19m 12.310s
9	Nannini	Benetton-Ford	50	
10	Senna	McLaren-Honda	49	accident
11	Schlesser,J-L	Williams-Judd	49	
12	Bailey	Tyrrell-Ford	49	
13	Arnoux	Ligier-Judd	49	
r	Prost	McLaren-Honda	34	engine
r	Alliot	Lola-Ford	32	engine
r	Streiff	AGS-Ford	31	gearbox
r	Schneider	Zakspeed	28	engine
r	de Cesaris	Rial-Ford	27	handling
r	Ghinzani	Zakspeed	25	engine
r	Caffi	Dallara-Ford	24	electrical
r	Dalmas	Lola-Ford	17	oil tank
r	Martini	Minardi-Ford	15	engine
r	Nakajima	Lotus-Honda	14	engine
r	Sala	Minardi-Ford	12	gearbox
r	Piquet	Lotus-Honda	11	accident
r	Larini	Osella-Alfa	2	engine

STARTING GRID:

1	Senna	12	Nakajima
2	Prost	13	Gugelmin
3	Berger,G.	14	Martini
4	Alboreto	15	Schneider
5	Cheever	16	Ghinzani
6	Warwick	17	Larini
7	Piquet	18	de Cesaris
8	Boutsen	19	Sala
9	Nannini	20	Alliot
10	Patrese	21	Caffi
11	Capelli	22	Schlesser,J-L +

Portuguese

GRAND PRIX No: 465
DATE: September 25, 1988
VENUE: Estoril
POLE LAP: Prost, 1m 17.411s
FASTEST LAP: Berger,G., 1m 21.961s

Pn	Driver	Car	Laps	Time/Reason
1	Prost	McLaren-Honda	70	1h 37m 04.958s
2	Capelli	March-Judd	70	1h 37m 50.511s
3	Boutsen	Benetton-Ford	70	1h 38m 25.577s
4	Warwick	Arrows-Mega.	70	1h 38m 48.377s
5	Alboreto	Ferrari	70	1h 38m 52.842s
6	Senna	McLaren-Honda	70	1h 38m 59.227s
7	Caffi	Dallara-Ford	69	
8	Sala	Minardi-Ford	68	
9	Streiff	AGS-Ford	68	
10	Arnoux	Ligier-Judd	68	
11	Tarquini	Coloni-Ford	65	
12	Larini	Osella-Alfa	63	
r	Gugelmin	March-Judd	59	engine
r	Mansell	Williams-Judd	54	accident
r	Palmer	Tyrrell-Ford	53	engine
r	Nannini	Benetton-Ford	52	vibration
r	Berger,G.	Ferrari	35	accident
r	Piquet	Lotus-Honda	34	clutch
r	Patrese	Williams-Judd	29	overheating
r	Martini	Minardi-Ford	27	engine
r	Dalmas	Lola-Ford	20	alternator
r	Nakajima	Lotus-Honda	16	accident
r	de Cesaris	Rial-Ford	11	driveshaft
r	Cheever	Arrows-Mega.	10	turbo
r	Alliot	Lola-Ford	7	engine
r	Johansson	Ligier-Judd	4	engine

STARTING GRID:

1	Prost	12	de Cesaris
2	Senna	13	Boutsen
3	Capelli	14	Martini
4	Berger,G.	15	Dalmas
5	Gugelmin	16	Nakajima
6	Mansell	17	Caffi
7	Alboreto	18	Cheever
8	Piquet	19	Sala
9	Nannini	20	Alliot
10	Warwick	21	Streiff
11	Patrese	22	Palmer +

Spanish

GRAND PRIX No: 466
DATE: October 2, 1988
VENUE: Jerez
POLE LAP: Senna, 1m 24.067s
FASTEST LAP: Prost, 1m 27.845s

Pn	Driver	Car	Laps	Time/Reason
1	Prost	McLaren-Honda	72	1h 48m 43.851s
2	Mansell	Williams-Judd	72	1h 49m 10.083s
3	Nannini	Benetton-Ford	72	1h 49m 19.297s
4	Senna	McLaren-Honda	72	1h 49m 30.561s
5	Patrese	Williams-Judd	72	1h 49m 31.281s
6	Berger,G.	Ferrari	72	1h 49m 35.664s
7	Gugelmin	March-Judd	72	1h 49m 39.815s
8	Piquet	Lotus-Honda	72	1h 50m 01.160s
9	Boutsen	Benetton-Ford	72	1h 50m 01.506s
10	Caffi	Dallara-Ford	71	
11	Dalmas	Lola-Ford	71	
12	Sala	Minardi-Ford	70	
13	Modena	EuroBrun-Ford	70	
14	Alliot	Lola-Ford	69	
r	Johansson	Ligier-Judd	62	lost wheel
r	Cheever	Arrows-Mega.	60	handling
r	Capelli	March-Judd	45	engine
r	Warwick	Arrows-Mega.	41	accident
r	de Cesaris	Rial-Ford	37	engine
r	Streiff	AGS-Ford	16	engine
r	Alboreto	Ferrari	15	engine
r	Martini	Minardi-Ford	15	gearbox
r	Nakajima	Lotus-Honda	14	spun off
r	Larini	Osella-Alfa	9	suspension
r	Palmer	Tyrrell-Ford	4	accident
r	Arnoux	Ligier-Judd	0	throttle

STARTING GRID:

1	Senna	12	Alliot
2	Prost	13	Streiff
3	Mansell	14	Larini
4	Boutsen	15	Nakajima
5	Nannini	16	Dalmas
6	Capelli	17	Warwick
7	Patrese	18	Caffi
8	Berger,G.	19	Arnoux
9	Piquet	20	Martini
10	Alboreto	21	Johansson
11	Gugelmin	22	Palmer +

Japanese

GRAND PRIX No:	467
DATE:	October 30, 1988
VENUE:	Suzuka
POLE LAP:	Senna, 1m 41.853s
FASTEST LAP:	Senna, 1m 46.326s

Pn	Driver	Car	Laps	Time/Reason
1	Senna	McLaren-Honda	51	1h 33m 26.173s
2	Prost	McLaren-Honda	51	1h 33m 39.536s
3	Boutsen	Benetton-Ford	51	1h 34m 02.282s
4	Berger,G.	Ferrari	51	1h 34m 52.887s
5	Nannini	Benetton-Ford	51	1h 34m 56.776s
6	Patrese	Williams-Judd	51	1h 35m 03.788s
7	Nakajima	Lotus-Honda	50	
8	Streiff	AGS-Ford	50	
9	Alliot	Lola-Ford	50	
10	Gugelmin	March-Judd	50	
11	Alboreto	Ferrari	50	
12	Palmer	Tyrrell-Ford	50	
13	Martini	Minardi-Ford	49	
14	Bailey	Tyrrell-Ford	49	
15	Sala	Minardi-Ford	49	
16	Suzuki,A.	Lola-Ford	48	
17	Arnoux	Ligier-Judd	48	
r	de Cesaris	Rial-Ford	35	engine
r	Cheever	Arrows-Mega.	35	turbo
r	Larini	Osella-Alfa	34	lost wheel
r	Piquet	Lotus-Honda	34	driver unwell
r	Mansell	Williams-Judd	24	accident
r	Caffi	Dallara-Ford	22	accident
r	Capelli	March-Judd	19	engine
r	Warwick	Arrows-Mega.	16	accident
r	Schneider	Zakspeed	14	driver injury pain

STARTING GRID:

1	Senna	12	Nannini
2	Prost	13	Gugelmin
3	Berger,G.	14	de Cesaris
4	Capelli	15	Cheever
5	Piquet	16	Palmer
6	Nakajima	17	Martini
7	Warwick	18	Streiff
8	Mansell	19	Alliot
9	Alboreto	20	Suzuki,A.
10	Boutsen	21	Caffi
11	Patrese	22	Sala +

Australian

GRAND PRIX No:	468
DATE:	November 13, 1988
VENUE:	Adelaide
POLE LAP:	Senna, 1m 17.748s
FASTEST LAP:	Prost, 1m 21.216s

Pn	Driver	Car	Laps	Time/Reason
1	Prost	McLaren-Honda	82	1h 53m 14.676s
2	Senna	McLaren-Honda	82	1h 53m 51.463s
3	Piquet	Lotus-Honda	82	1h 54m 02.222s
4	Patrese	Williams-Judd	82	1h 54m 34.764s
5	Boutsen	Benetton-Ford	81	
6	Capelli	March-Judd	81	
7	Martini	Minardi-Ford	80	
8	de Cesaris	Rial-Ford	77	out of fuel
9	Johansson	Ligier-Judd	76	out of fuel
10	Alliot	Lola-Ford	75	electrical
11	Streiff	AGS-Ford	73	electrical
r	Ghinzani	Zakspeed	69	out of fuel
r	Mansell	Williams-Judd	65	accident
r	Nannini	Benetton-Ford	63	accident
r	Modena	EuroBrun-Ford	63	half-shaft
r	Warwick	Arrows-Mega.	52	throttle
r	Cheever	Arrows-Mega.	51	engine
r	Gugelmin	March-Judd	46	accident
r	Nakajima	Lotus-Honda	46	accident
r	Sala	Minardi-Ford	41	electrical
r	Caffi	Dallara-Ford	32	clutch
r	Berger,G.	Ferrari	25	accident
r	Arnoux	Ligier-Judd	24	accident
r	Palmer	Tyrrell-Ford	16	crownwheel/pinion
r	Larrauri	EuroBrun-Ford	12	half-shaft
r	Alboreto	Ferrari	0	accident

STARTING GRID:

1	Senna	12	Alboreto
2	Prost	13	Nakajima
3	Mansell	14	Martini
4	Berger,G.	15	de Cesaris
5	Piquet	16	Streiff
6	Patrese	17	Palmer
7	Warwick	18	Cheever
8	Nannini	19	Gugelmin
9	Capelli	20	Modena
10	Boutsen	21	Sala
11	Caffi	22	Johansson +

Brazilian

GRAND PRIX No:	469
DATE:	March 26, 1989
VENUE:	Rio de Janeiro
POLE LAP:	Senna, 1m 25.302s
FASTEST LAP:	Patrese, 1m 32.507s

Pn	Driver	Car	Laps	Time/Reason
1	Mansell	Ferrari	61	1h 38m 58.744s
2	Prost	McLaren-Honda	61	1h 39m 06.553s
3	Gugelmin	March-Judd	61	1h 39m 08.114s
4	Herbert	Benetton-Ford	61	1h 39m 09.237s
5	Warwick	Arrows-Ford	61	1h 39m 16.610s
6	Nannini	Benetton-Ford	61	1h 39m 16.985s
7	Palmer	Tyrrell-Ford	60	
8	Nakajima	Lotus-Judd	60	
9	Grouillard	Ligier-Judd	60	
10	Alboreto	Tyrrell-Ford	59	
11	Senna	McLaren-Honda	59	
12	Alliot	Lola-Lam.	58	
13	de Cesaris	Dallara-Ford	57	
14	Danner	Rial-Ford	56	
r	Patrese	Williams-Ren.	51	alternator
r	Cheever	Arrows-Ford	37	accident
r	Schneider	Zakspeed-Yam.	36	accident
r	Brundle	Brabham-Judd	27	engine
r	Capelli	March-Judd	22	suspension
r	Piquet	Lotus-Judd	10	fuel pump
dq	Larini	Osella-Ford	10	illegal start
r	Modena	Brabham-Judd	9	cv joint
r	Boutsen	Williams-Ren.	3	engine
r	Martini	Minardi-Ford	2	engine mount
r	Sala	Minardi-Ford	0	accident
r	Berger,G.	Ferrari	0	accident

STARTING GRID:

1	Senna	12	Gugelmin
2	Patrese	13	Brundle
3	Berger,G.	14	Modena
4	Boutsen	15	de Cesaris
5	Prost	16	Martini
6	Mansell	17	Danner
7	Capelli	18	Palmer
8	Warwick	19	Larini
9	Piquet	20	Alboreto
10	Herbert	21	Nakajima
11	Nannini	22	Grouillard

+

San Marino

GRAND PRIX No:	470
DATE:	April 23, 1989
VENUE:	Imola
POLE LAP:	Senna, 1m 26.010s
FASTEST LAP:	Prost, 1m 26.795s

Pn	Driver	Car	Laps	Time/Reason
1	Senna	McLaren-Honda	58	1h 26m 51.245s
2	Prost	McLaren-Honda	58	1h 27m 31.470s
3	Nannini	Benetton-Ford	57	
4	Boutsen	Williams-Ren.	57	
5	Warwick	Arrows-Ford	57	
6	Palmer	Tyrrell-Ford	57	
7	Caffi	Dallara-Ford	57	
8	Tarquini	AGS-Ford	57	
9	Cheever	Arrows-Ford	56	
10	de Cesaris	Dallara-Ford	56	
11	Herbert	Benetton-Ford	56	
12	Larini	Osella-Ford	52	
r	Brundle	Brabham-Judd	51	engine
r	Nakajima	Lotus-Judd	46	electrical
r	Sala	Minardi-Ford	43	spun off
r	Gugelmin	March-Judd	39	gearbox
r	Piquet	Lotus-Judd	29	engine
r	Mansell	Ferrari	23	gearbox
r	Patrese	Williams-Ren.	21	engine
r	Modena	Brabham-Judd	19	accident
r	Martini	Minardi-Ford	6	gearbox
dq	Grouillard	Ligier-Ford	4	illegal repairs
r	Berger,G.	Ferrari	3	accident
r	Capelli	March-Judd	1	spun off
r	Alliot	Lola-Lam.	0	fuel feed
dns	Dalmas	Lola-Lam.	0	stalled

STARTING GRID:

1	Senna	12	Warwick
2	Prost	13	Capelli
3	Mansell	14	Larini
4	Patrese	15	Sala
5	Berger,G.	16	de Cesaris
6	Boutsen	17	Modena
7	Nannini	18	Tarquini
8	Piquet	19	Gugelmin
9	Caffi	20	Alliot
10	Grouillard	21	Cheever
11	Martini	22	Brundle

+

Monaco

GRAND PRIX No:	471
DATE:	May 7, 1989
VENUE:	Monte Carlo
POLE LAP:	Senna, 1m 22.308s
FASTEST LAP:	Prost, 1m 25.501s

Pn	Driver	Car	Laps	Time/Reason
1	Senna	McLaren-Honda	77	1h 53m 33.251s
2	Prost	McLaren-Honda	77	1h 54m 23.780s
3	Modena	Brabham-Judd	76	
4	Caffi	Dallara-Ford	75	
5	Alboreto	Tyrrell-Ford	75	
6	Brundle	Brabham-Judd	75	
7	Cheever	Arrows-Ford	75	
8	Nannini	Benetton-Ford	74	
9	Palmer	Tyrrell-Ford	74	
10	Boutsen	Williams-Ren.	74	
11	Capelli	March-Judd	73	electrical
12	Arnoux	Ligier-Ford	73	
13	de Cesaris	Dallara-Ford	73	
14	Herbert	Benetton-Ford	73	
15	Patrese	Williams-Ren.	73	
r	Sala	Minardi-Ford	48	engine
r	Tarquini	AGS-Ford	46	
r	Moreno	Coloni-Ford	44	gearbox
r	Alliot	Lola-Lam.	38	engine
r	Gugelmin	March-Judd	36	engine
r	Piquet	Lotus-Judd	32	accident
r	Mansell	Ferrari	30	gearbox
r	Raphanel	Coloni-Ford	19	gearbox
r	Grouillard	Ligier-Ford	4	gearbox
r	Martini	Minardi-Ford	3	clutch
r	Warwick	Arrows-Ford	2	gearbox

STARTING GRID:

1	Senna	12	Alboreto
2	Prost	13	Tarquini
3	Boutsen	14	Gugelmin
4	Brundle	15	Nannini
5	Mansell	16	Grouillard
6	Warwick	17	Alliot
7	Patrese	18	Raphanel
8	Modena	19	Piquet
9	Caffi	20	Cheever
10	de Cesaris	21	Arnoux
11	Martini	22	Capelli

+

Mexican

GRAND PRIX No:	472
DATE:	May 28, 1989
VENUE:	Mexico City
POLE LAP:	Senna, 1m 17.876s
FASTEST LAP:	Mansell, 1m 20.420s

Pn	Driver	Car	Laps	Time/Reason
1	Senna	McLaren-Honda	69	1h 35m 21.431s
2	Patrese	Williams-Ren.	69	1h 35m 36.991s
3	Alboreto	Tyrrell-Ford	69	1h 35m 52.685s
4	Nannini	Benetton-Ford	69	1h 36m 06.926s
5	Prost	McLaren-Honda	69	1h 36m 17.544s
6	Tarquini	AGS-Ford	68	
7	Cheever	Arrows-Ford	68	
8	Grouillard	Ligier-Ford	68	
9	Brundle	Brabham-Judd	68	
10	Modena	Brabham-Judd	68	
11	Piquet	Lotus-Judd	68	
12	Danner	Rial-Ford	67	
13	Caffi	Dallara-Ford	67	
14	Arnoux	Ligier-Ford	66	
15	Herbert	Benetton-Ford	66	
r	Martini	Minardi-Ford	53	engine
r	Mansell	Ferrari	43	gearbox
r	Warwick	Arrows-Ford	35	electrical
r	Nakajima	Lotus-Judd	35	spun off
uc	Alliot	Lola-Lam.	28	
r	de Cesaris	Dallara-Ford	20	fuel pump
r	Berger,G.	Ferrari	16	gearbox
r	Johansson	Onyx-Ford	16	transmission
r	Boutsen	Williams-Ren.	15	electrical
r	Palmer	Tyrrell-Ford	9	throttle linkage
r	Capelli	March-Judd	6	gearbox

STARTING GRID:

1	Senna	12	de Cesaris
2	Prost	13	Nannini
3	Mansell	14	Palmer
4	Capelli	15	Nakajima
5	Patrese	16	Alliot
6	Berger,G.	17	Tarquini
7	Alboreto	18	Herbert
8	Boutsen	19	Caffi
9	Modena	20	Brundle
10	Warwick	21	Johansson
11	Grouillard	22	Martini

+

US

GRAND PRIX No: 473
DATE: June 4, 1989
VENUE: Phoenix
POLE LAP: Senna, 1m 30.108s
FASTEST LAP: Senna, 1m 33.969s

Pn	Driver	Car	Laps	Time/Reason
1	Prost	McLaren-Honda	75	2h 01m 33.133s
2	Patrese	Williams-Ren.	75	2h 02m 12.829s
3	Cheever	Arrows-Ford	75	2h 02m 16.343s
4	Danner	Rial-Ford	74	
5	Herbert	Benetton-Ford	74	
6	Boutsen	Williams-Ren.	74	
7	Tarquini	AGS-Ford	73	
8	de Cesaris	Dallara-Ford	70	
9	Palmer	Tyrrell-Ford	69	fuel injection
r	Berger,G.	Ferrari	61	alternator
r	Caffi	Dallara-Ford	52	accident
r	Piquet	Lotus-Judd	52	suspen/accident
r	Johansson	Onyx-Ford	50	suspension
r	Sala	Minardi-Ford	46	engine
r	Senna	McLaren-Honda	44	electrical
r	Brundle	Brabham-Judd	43	brakes
r	Modena	Brabham-Judd	37	brakes
r	Mansell	Ferrari	31	gearbox
r	Martini	Minardi-Ford	26	engine
r	Nakajima	Lotus-Judd	24	throttle cable
r	Capelli	March-Judd	22	gearbox
dq	Gugelmin	March-Judd	20	added brake fluid
r	Alboreto	Tyrrell-Ford	17	gearbox
r	Nannini	Benetton-Ford	10	driver ill
r	Warwick	Arrows-Ford	7	accident
r	Alliot	Lola-Lam.	3	engine

STARTING GRID:

1	Senna	12	Alliot
2	Prost	13	de Cesaris
3	Nannini	14	Patrese
4	Mansell	15	Martini
5	Brundle	16	Boutsen
6	Caffi	17	Cheever
7	Modena	18	Gugelmin
8	Berger,G.	19	Johansson
9	Alboreto	20	Sala
10	Warwick	21	Palmer
11	Capelli	22	Piquet

+

Canadian

GRAND PRIX No: 474
DATE: June 18, 1989
VENUE: Montreal
POLE LAP: Prost, 1m 20.973s
FASTEST LAP: Palmer, 1m 31.925s

Pn	Driver	Car	Laps	Time/Reason
1	Boutsen	Williams-Ren.	69	2h 01m 24.073s
2	Patrese	Williams-Ren.	69	2h 01m 54.080s
3	de Cesaris	Dallara-Ford	69	2h 03m 00.722s
4	Piquet	Lotus-Judd	69	2h 03m 05.557s
5	Arnoux	Ligier-Ford	68	
6	Caffi	Dallara-Ford	67	
7	Senna	McLaren-Honda	66	
8	Danner	Rial-Ford	66	
r	Moreno	Coloni-Ford	57	gearbox
r	Warwick	Arrows-Ford	40	engine
r	Palmer	Tyrrell-Ford	35	accident
r	Larini	Osella-Ford	33	electrical
r	Capelli	March-Judd	28	accident
r	Alliot	Lola-Lam.	26	accident
dq	Johansson	Onyx-Ford		black flag
r	Sala	Minardi-Ford	11	accident
r	Gugelmin	March-Judd	11	electrileal
r	Berger,G.	Ferrari	6	alternator
r	Tarquini	AGS-Ford	6	accident
r	Cheever	Arrows-Ford	3	electrical
r	Prost	McLaren-Honda	2	suspension
r	Alboreto	Tyrrell-Ford	0	gearbox
r	Modena	Brabham-Judd	0	accident
r	Martini	Minardi-Ford	0	accident
dq	Mansell	Ferrari		start in pitlane
dq	Nannini	Benetton-Ford		start in pitlane

STARTING GRID:

1	Prost	12	Warwick
2	Senna	13	Nannini
3	Patrese	14	Palmer
4	Berger,G.	15	Larini
5	Mansell	16	Cheever
6	Boutsen	17	Gugelmin
7	Modena	18	Johansson
8	Caffi	19	Piquet
9	de Cesaris	20	Alboreto
10	Alliot	21	Capelli
11	Martini	22	Arnoux

+

French

GRAND PRIX No:	475
DATE:	July 9, 1989
VENUE:	Paul Ricard
POLE LAP:	Prost, 1m 07.203s
FASTEST LAP:	Gugelmin, 1m 12.090s

Pn	Driver	Car	Laps	Time/Reason
1	Prost	McLaren-Honda	80	1h 38m 29.411s
2	Mansell	Ferrari	80	1h 39m 13.428s
3	Patrese	Williams-Ren.	80	1h 39m 36.332s
4	Alesi	Tyrrell-Ford	80	1h 39m 42.643s
5	Johansson	Onyx-Ford	79	
6	Grouillard	Ligier-Ford	79	
7	Cheever	Arrows-Ford	79	
8	Piquet	Lotus-Judd	78	
9	Pirro	Benetton-Ford	78	
10	Palmer	Tyrrell-Ford	78	
11	Bernard	Lola-Lam.	77	
12	Donnelly	Arrows-Ford	77	
13	Gachot	Onyx-Ford	76	
uc	Gugelmin	March-Judd	71	
r	Modena	Brabham-Judd	67	engine
r	Boutsen	Williams-Ren.	51	gearbox
r	Nakajima	Lotus-Judd	49	electrical
r	Capelli	March-Judd	43	engine
r	Nannini	Benetton-Ford	40	suspension
r	Martini	Minardi-Ford	31	oil pressure
r	Alliot	Lola-Lam.	30	engine
r	Tarquini	AGS-Ford	30	engine
r	Berger,G.	Ferrari	29	gearbox
r	Caffi	Dallara-Ford	27	clutch
r	Arnoux	Ligier-Ford	14	engine
r	Senna	McLaren-Honda	0	transmission

STARTING GRID:

1	Prost	12	Capelli
2	Senna	13	Johansson
3	Mansell	14	Donnelly
4	Nannini	15	Bernard
5	Boutsen	16	Alesi
6	Berger,G.	17	Grouillard
7	Alliot	18	Arnoux
8	Patrese	19	Nakajima
9	Palmer	20	Piquet
10	Gugelmin	21	Tarquini
11	Gachot	22	Modena +

British

GRAND PRIX No:	476
DATE:	July 16, 1989
VENUE:	Silverstone
POLE LAP:	Senna, 1m 09.099s
FASTEST LAP:	Mansell, 1m 12.017s

Pn	Driver	Car	Laps	Time/Reason
1	Prost	McLaren-Honda	64	1h 19m 22.131s
2	Mansell	Ferrari	64	1h 19m 41.500s
3	Nannini	Benetton-Ford	64	1h 20m 10.150s
4	Piquet	Lotus-Judd	64	1h 20m 28.866s
5	Martini	Minardi-Ford	63	
6	Sala	Minardi-Ford	63	
7	Grouillard	Ligier-Ford	63	
8	Nakajima	Lotus-Judd	63	
9	Warwick	Arrows-Ford	62	
10	Boutsen	Williams-Ren.	62	
11	Pirro	Benetton-Ford	62	
12	Gachot	Onyx-Ford	62	
r	Gugelmin	March-Judd	54	gearbox
r	Brundle	Brabham-Judd	49	engine
r	Berger,G.	Ferrari	49	gearbox
r	Bernard	Lola-Lam.	46	engine
r	Alliot	Lola-Lam.	39	engine
r	Palmer	Tyrrell-Ford	32	accident
r	Modena	Brabham-Judd	31	engine
r	Alesi	Tyrrell-Ford	28	accident
r	Larini	Osella-Ford	23	handling
r	Patrese	Williams-Ren.	19	accident
r	Capelli	March-Judd	15	transmission
r	de Cesaris	Dallara-Ford	14	engine
r	Senna	McLaren-Honda	11	gearbox
r	Moreno	Coloni-Ford	2	engine

STARTING GRID:

1	Senna	12	Alliot
2	Prost	13	Bernard
3	Mansell	14	Modena
4	Berger,G.	15	Sala
5	Patrese	16	Nakajima
6	Gugelmin	17	Larini
7	Boutsen	18	Palmer
8	Capelli	19	Warwick
9	Nannini	20	Brundle
10	Piquet	21	Gachot
11	Martini	22	Alesi +

German

GRAND PRIX No: 477
DATE: July 30, 1989
VENUE: Hockenheim
POLE LAP: Senna, 1m 42.300s
FASTEST LAP: Senna, 1m 45.884s

Pn	Driver	Car	Laps	Time/Reason
1	Senna	McLaren-Honda	45	1h 21m 43.302s
2	Prost	McLaren-Honda	45	1h 22m 01.453s
3	Mansell	Ferrari	45	1h 23m 06.656s
4	Patrese	Williams-Ren.	44	
5	Piquet	Lotus-Judd	44	
6	Warwick	Arrows-Ford	44	
7	de Cesaris	Dallara-Ford	44	
8	Brundle	Brabham-Judd	44	
9	Martini	Minardi-Ford	44	
10	Alesi	Tyrrell-Ford	43	
11	Arnoux	Ligier-Ford	42	
12	Cheever	Arrows-Ford	40	
r	Modena	Brabham-Judd	37	engine
r	Nakajima	Lotus-Judd	36	spun off
r	Capelli	March-Judd	32	engine
r	Gugelmin	March-Judd	28	transmission
r	Pirro	Benetton-Ford	26	accident
r	Alliot	Lola-Lam.	20	engine
r	Palmer	Tyrrell-Ford	16	throttle cable
r	Berger,G.	Ferrari	13	accident
r	Johansson	Onyx-Ford	8	wheel bearing
r	Nannini	Benetton-Ford	6	ignition
r	Boutsen	Williams-Ren.	4	accident
r	Caffi	Dallara-Ford	2	engine
r	Alboreto	Lola-Lam.	1	electrical
r	Grouillard	Ligier-Ford	0	transmission

STARTING GRID:

1	Senna	12	Brundle
2	Prost	13	Martini
3	Mansell	14	Gugelmin
4	Berger,G.	15	Alliot
5	Patrese	16	Modena
6	Boutsen	17	Warwick
7	Nannini	18	Nakajima
8	Piquet	19	Palmer
9	Pirro	20	Caffi
10	Alesi	21	de Cesaris
11	Grouillard	22	Capelli +

Hungarian

GRAND PRIX No: 478
DATE: August 13, 1989
VENUE: Hungaroring
POLE LAP: Patrese, 1m 19.726s
FASTEST LAP: Mansell, 1m 22.637s

Pn	Driver	Car	Laps	Time/Reason
1	Mansell	Ferrari	77	1h 49m 38.650s
2	Senna	McLaren-Honda	77	1h 50m 04.617s
3	Boutsen	Williams-Ren.	77	1h 50m 17.004s
4	Prost	McLaren-Honda	77	1h 50m 22.827s
5	Cheever	Arrows-Ford	77	1h 50m 23.756s
6	Piquet	Lotus-Judd	77	1h 50m 50.689s
7	Caffi	Dallara-Ford	77	1h 51m 02.875s
8	Pirro	Benetton-Ford	76	
9	Alesi	Tyrrell-Ford	76	
10	Warwick	Arrows-Ford	76	
11	Modena	Brabham-Judd	76	
12	Brundle	Brabham-Judd	75	
13	Palmer	Tyrrell-Ford	73	
r	Sala	Minardi-Ford	57	spun off
r	Berger,G.	Ferrari	56	gearbox
r	Patrese	Williams-Ren.	54	radiator
r	Johansson	Onyx-Ford	48	transmission
r	Nannini	Benetton-Ford	46	gearbox
r	Gachot	Onyx-Ford	38	transmission
r	Nakajima	Lotus-Judd	33	accident
r	Gugelmin	March-Judd	27	electrical
r	Capelli	March-Judd	26	wheel
r	Alboreto	Lola-Lam.	26	engine
r	Martini	Minardi-Ford	19	wheel
r	Ghinzani	Osella-Ford	19	electrical
r	de Cesaris	Dallara-Ford	0	clutch

STARTING GRID:

1	Patrese	12	Mansell
2	Senna	13	Gugelmin
3	Caffi	14	Capelli
4	Boutsen	15	Brundle
5	Prost	16	Cheever
6	Berger,G.	17	Piquet
7	Nannini	18	de Cesaris
8	Modena	19	Palmer
9	Warwick	20	Nakajima
10	Martini	21	Gachot
11	Alesi	22	Ghinzani +

Belgian

GRAND PRIX No: 479
DATE: August 27, 1989
VENUE: Spa-Francorchamps
POLE LAP: Senna, 1m 50.867s
FASTEST LAP: Prost, 2m 11.571s

Pn	Driver	Car	Laps	Time/Reason
1	Senna	McLaren-Honda	44	1h 40m 54.196s
2	Prost	McLaren-Honda	44	1h 40m 55.500s
3	Mansell	Ferrari	44	1h 40m 56.020s
4	Boutsen	Williams-Ren.	44	1h 41m 48.614s
5	Nannini	Benetton-Ford	44	1h 42m 03.001s
6	Warwick	Arrows-Ford	44	1h 42m 12.512s
7	Gugelmin	March-Judd	43	
8	Johansson	Onyx-Ford	43	
9	Martini	Minardi-Ford	43	
10	Pirro	Benetton-Ford	43	
11	de Cesaris	Dallara-Ford	43	
12	Capelli	March-Judd	43	
13	Grouillard	Ligier-Ford	43	
14	Palmer	Tyrrell-Ford	42	
15	Sala	Minardi-Ford	41	
16	Alliot	Lola-Lam.	39	
r	Cheever	Arrows-Ford	38	loose wheel
r	Gachot	Onyx-Ford	21	wheel bearing
r	Patrese	Williams-Ren.	20	accident
r	Alboreto	Lola-Lam.	19	accident
r	Caffi	Dallara-Ford	13	spun off
r	Brundle	Brabham-Judd	12	brakes
r	Berger,G.	Ferrari	9	spun off
r	Modena	Brabham-Judd	9	handling
r	Arnoux	Ligier-Ford	4	accident
r	Herbert	Tyrrell-Ford	3	spun off

STARTING GRID:

1	Senna	12	Caffi
2	Prost	13	Pirro
3	Berger,G.	14	Martini
4	Boutsen	15	Johansson
5	Patrese	16	Herbert
6	Mansell	17	Arnoux
7	Nannini	18	de Cesaris
8	Modena	19	Capelli
9	Gugelmin	20	Brundle
10	Warwick	21	Palmer
11	Alliot	22	Alboreto +

Italian

GRAND PRIX No: 480
DATE: September 10, 1989
VENUE: Monza
POLE LAP: Senna, 1m 23.720s
FASTEST LAP: Prost, 1m 28.107s

Pn	Driver	Car	Laps	Time/Reason
1	Prost	McLaren-Honda	53	1h 19m 27.550s
2	Berger,G.	Ferrari	53	1h 19m 34.876s
3	Boutsen	Williams-Ren.	53	1h 19m 42.525s
4	Patrese	Williams-Ren.	53	1h 20m 06.272s
5	Alesi	Tyrrell-Ford	52	
6	Brundle	Brabham-Judd	52	
7	Martini	Minardi-Ford	52	
8	Sala	Minardi-Ford	51	
9	Arnoux	Ligier-Ford	51	
10	Nakajima	Lotus-Judd	51	
11	Caffi	Dallara-Ford	47	
r	de Cesaris	Dallara-Ford	45	engine
r	Senna	McLaren-Honda	44	engine
r	Mansell	Ferrari	41	gearbox
r	Gachot	Onyx-Ford	38	overheating
r	Nannini	Benetton-Ford	33	brakes
r	Capelli	March-Judd	30	engine
r	Grouillard	Ligier-Ford	30	exhaust
r	Piquet	Lotus-Judd	23	spun off
r	Palmer	Tyrrell-Ford	18	engine
r	Warwick	Arrows-Ford	18	engine
r	Larini	Osella-Ford	16	gearbox
r	Alboreto	Lola-Lam.	14	engine
r	Gugelmin	March-Judd	14	throttle
r	Alliot	Lola-Lam.	1	throttle
r	Pirro	Benetton-Ford	0	gearbox

STARTING GRID:

1	Senna	12	Brundle
2	Berger,G.	13	Alboreto
3	Mansell	14	Palmer
4	Prost	15	Martini
5	Patrese	16	Warwick
6	Boutsen	17	de Cesaris
7	Alliot	18	Capelli
8	Nannini	19	Nakajima
9	Pirro	20	Caffi
10	Alesi	21	Grouillard
11	Piquet	22	Gachot +

Portuguese

GRAND PRIX No: 481
DATE: September 24, 1989
VENUE: Estoril
POLE LAP: Senna, 1m 15.468s
FASTEST LAP: Berger,G., 1m 18.986s

Pn	Driver	Car	Laps	Time/Reason
1	Berger,G.	Ferrari	71	1h 36m 48.546s
2	Prost	McLaren-Honda	71	1h 37m 21.183s
3	Johansson	Onyx-Ford	71	1h 37m 43.871s
4	Nannini	Benetton-Ford	71	1h 38m 10.915s
5	Martini	Minardi-Ford	70	
6	Palmer	Tyrrell-Ford	70	
7	Nakajima	Lotus-Judd	70	
8	Brundle	Brabham-Judd	70	
9	Alliot	Lola-Lam.	70	
10	Gugelmin	March-Judd	69	
11	Alboreto	Lola-Lam.	69	
12	Sala	Minardi-Ford	69	
13	Arnoux	Ligier-Ford	69	
14	Modena	Brabham-Judd	69	
r	Patrese	Williams-Ren.	60	radiator
r	Boutsen	Williams-Ren.	60	radiator
r	Senna	McLaren-Honda	48	accident
dq	Mansell	Ferrari	48	reversing in pits
r	Warwick	Arrows-Ford	37	accident
r	Piquet	Lotus-Judd	33	accident
r	Caffi	Dallara-Ford	33	accident
r	Pirro	Benetton-Ford	29	shock absorber
r	Capelli	March-Judd	25	engine
r	Cheever	Arrows-Ford	24	spun off
r	de Cesaris	Dallara-Ford	17	electrical
r	Moreno	Coloni-Ford	11	electrical

STARTING GRID:

1	Senna	12	Johansson
2	Berger,G.	13	Nannini
3	Mansell	14	Gugelmin
4	Prost	15	Moreno
5	Martini	16	Pirro
6	Patrese	17	Alliot
7	Caffi	18	Palmer
8	Boutsen	19	de Cesaris
9	Sala	20	Piquet
10	Brundle	21	Alboreto
11	Modena	22	Warwick

+

Spanish

GRAND PRIX No: 482
DATE: October 1, 1989
VENUE: Jerez
POLE LAP: Senna, 1m 20.291s
FASTEST LAP: Senna, 1m 25.779s

Pn	Driver	Car	Laps	Time/Reason
1	Senna	McLaren-Honda	73	1h 47m 48.264s
2	Berger,G.	Ferrari	73	1h 48m 15.315s
3	Prost	McLaren-Honda	73	1h 48m 42.052s
4	Alesi	Tyrrell-Ford	72	
5	Patrese	Williams-Ren.	72	
6	Alliot	Lola-Lam.	72	
7	de Cesaris	Dallara-Ford	72	
8	Piquet	Lotus-Judd	71	
9	Warwick	Arrows-Ford	71	
10	Palmer	Tyrrell-Ford	71	
r	Cheever	Arrows-Ford	61	engine
r	Pirro	Benetton-Ford	59	spun off
r	Caffi	Dallara-Ford	55	engine
r	Brundle	Brabham-Judd	51	exhaust
r	Gugelmin	March-Judd	47	accident
r	Sala	Minardi-Ford	47	accident
r	Boutsen	Williams-Ren.	40	fuel pump
r	Grouillard	Ligier-Ford	34	engine
r	Martini	Minardi-Ford	27	stalled
r	Capelli	March-Judd	23	transmission
r	Lehto	Onyx-Ford	20	gearbox
r	Ghinzani	Osella-Ford	17	gearbox
r	Nannini	Benetton-Ford	14	spun off
r	Modena	Brabham-Judd	11	engine
r	Larini	Osella-Ford	6	accident
r	Nakajima	Lotus-Judd	0	accident

STARTING GRID:

1	Senna	12	Modena
2	Berger,G.	13	Palmer
3	Prost	14	Nannini
4	Martini	15	de Cesaris
5	Alliot	16	Warwick
6	Patrese	17	Lehto
7	Piquet	18	Nakajima
8	Brundle	19	Capelli
9	Alesi	20	Sala
10	Pirro	21	Boutsen
11	Larini	22	Cheever

+

Japanese

GRAND PRIX No:	483
DATE:	October 22, 1989
VENUE:	Suzuka
POLE LAP:	Senna, 1m 38.041s
FASTEST LAP:	Prost, 1m 43.506s

Pn	Driver	Car	Laps	Time/Reason
dq	Senna	McLaren-Honda	53	cut chicane
1	Nannini	Benetton-Ford	53	1h 35m 06.277s
2	Patrese	Williams-Ren.	53	1h 35in 18.181s
3	Boutsen	Williams-Ren.	53	1h 35m 19.723s
4	Piquet	Lotus-Judd	53	1h 36m 50.502s
5	Brundle	Brabham-Judd	52	
6	Warwick	Arrows-Ford	52	
7	Gugelmin	March-Judd	52	
8	Cheever	Arrows-Ford	52	
9	Caffi	Dallara-Ford	52	
10	de Cesaris	Dallara-Ford	51	
r	Prost	McLaren-Honda	46	accident
r	Modena	Brabham-Judd	46	alternator
r	Mansell	Ferrari	43	engine
r	Nakajima	Lotus-Judd	41	engine
r	Alesi	Tyrrell-Ford	37	gearbox
r	Alliot	Lola-Lam.	36	engine
r	Berger,G.	Ferrari	34	transmission
r	Pirro	Benetton-Ford	33	accident
r	Grouillard	Ligier-Ford	31	engine
r	Capelli	March-Judd	27	suspension
r	Larini	Osella-Ford	21	brakes
r	Palmer	Tyrrell-Ford	20	fuel leak
r	Schneider	Zakspeed-Yam.	1	driveshaft
r	Barilla	Minardi-Ford	0	clutch
r	Sala	Minardi-Ford	0	accident

STARTING GRID:

1	Senna	12	Nakajima
2	Prost	13	Brundle
3	Berger,G.	14	Sala
4	Mansell	15	Caffi
5	Patrese	16	de Cesaris
6	Nannini	17	Capelli
7	Boutsen	18	Alesi
8	Alliot	19	Barilla
9	Modena	20	Gugelmin
10	Larini	21	Schneider
11	Piquet	22	Pirro

+

Australian

GRAND PRIX No:	484
DATE:	November 5, 1989
VENUE:	Adelaide
POLE LAP:	Senna, 1m 16.665s
FASTEST LAP:	Nakajima, 1m 38.480s

Pn	Driver	Car	Laps	Time/Reason
1	Boutsen	Williams-Ren.	70	2h 00m 17.421s
2	Nannini	Benetton-Ford	70	2h 00m 46.079s
3	Patrese	Williams-Ren.	70	2h 00m 55.104s
4	Nakajima	Lotus-Judd	70	2h 00m 59.752s
5	Pirro	Benetton-Ford	68	
6	Martini	Minardi-Ford	67	
7	Gugelmin	March-Judd	66	
8	Modena	Brabham-Judd	64	
r	Cheever	Arrows-Ford	42	stalled
r	Lehto	Onyx-Ford	27	engine
r	Grouillard	Ligier-Ford	22	accident
r	Piquet	Lotus-Judd	19	accident
r	Ghinzani	Osella-Ford	18	accident
r	Mansell	Ferrari	17	accident
r	Senna	McLaren-Honda	13	accident
r	Caffi	Dallara-Ford	13	accident
r	Capelli	March-Judd	13	radiator
r	de Cesaris	Dallara-Ford	12	accident
r	Brundle	Brabham-Judd	12	accident
r	Warwick	Arrows-Ford	7	accident
r	Berger,G.	Ferrari	6	accident
r	Alliot	Lola-Lam.	6	accident
r	Alesi	Tyrrell-Ford	5	spun off
r	Arnoux	Ligier-Ford	5	accident
r	Prost	McLaren-Honda	2	withdrew
r	Larini	Osella-Ford	0	stalled

STARTING GRID:

1	Senna	12	Brundle
2	Prost	13	Pirro
3	Martini	14	Berger,G.
4	Nannini	15	Alesi
5	Boutsen	16	Capelli
6	Patrese	17	Lehto
7	Mansell	18	Piquet
8	Modena	19	Alliot
9	de Cesaris	20	Warwick
10	Caffi	21	Ghinzani
11	Larini	22	Cheever

+

US

GRAND PRIX No:	485
DATE:	March 11, 1990
VENUE:	Phoenix
POLE LAP:	Berger,G., 1m 28.664s
FASTEST LAP:	Berger,G., 1m 31.050s

Pn	Driver	Car	Laps	Time/Reason
1	Senna	McLaren-Honda	72	1h 52m 32.829s
2	Alesi	Tyrrell-Ford	72	1h 52m 41.514s
3	Boutsen	Williams-Ren.	72	1h 53m 26.909s
4	Piquet	Benetton-Ford	72	1h 53m 41.187s
5	Modena	Brabham-Judd	72	1h 53m 42.332s
6	Nakajima	Tyrrell-Ford	71	
7	Martini	Minardi-Ford	71	
8	Bernard	Lola-Lam.	71	
9	Patrese	Williams-Ren.	71	
10	Alboreto	Arrows-Ford	70	
11	Nannini	Benetton-Ford	70	
12	Schneider	Arrows-Ford	70	
13	Moreno	EuroBrun-Judd	67	
14	Gugelmin	Leyton H.-Judd	66	
r	Barilla	Minardi-Ford	54	driver cramp
r	Suzuki,A.	Lola-Lam.	53	brakes
r	Mansell	Ferrari	49	clutch
r	Berger,G.	McLaren-Honda	44	clutch
r	Foitek	Brabham-Judd	39	accident
r	Grouillard	Osella-Ford	39	accident
r	de Cesaris	Dallara-Ford	25	engine
r	Prost	Ferrari	21	gearbox
r	Capelli	Leyton H.-Judd	20	electrical
r	Warwick	Lotus-Lam.	6	suspension
r	Larini	Ligier-Ford	4	throttle
r	Donnelly	Lotus-Lam.	0	gearbox

STARTING GRID:

1	Berger,G.	12	Patrese
2	Martini	13	Larini
3	de Cesaris	14	Barilla
4	Alesi	15	Bernard
5	Senna	16	Moreno
6	Piquet	17	Mansell
7	Prost	18	Suzuki,A.
8	Grouillard	19	Donnelly
9	Boutsen	20	Schneider
10	Modena	21	Alboreto
11	Nakajima	22	Nannini +

Brazilian

GRAND PRIX No:	486
DATE:	March 25, 1990
VENUE:	Interlagos
POLE LAP:	Senna, 1m 17.277s
FASTEST LAP:	Berger,G., 1m 19.899s

Pn	Driver	Car	Laps	Time/Reason
1	Prost	Ferrari	71	1h 37m 21.258s
2	Berger,G.	McLaren-Honda	71	1h 37m 34.822s
3	Senna	McLaren-Honda	71	1h 37m 58.980s
4	Mansell	Ferrari	71	1h 38m 08.524s
5	Boutsen	Williams-Ren.	70	
6	Piquet	Benetton-Ford	70	
7	Alesi	Tyrrell-Ford	70	
8	Nakajima	Tyrrell-Ford	70	
9	Martini	Minardi-Ford	69	
10	Nannini	Benetton-Ford	68	
11	Larini	Ligier-Ford	68	
12	Alliot	Ligier-Ford	68	
13	Patrese	Williams-Ren.	65	oil leak
14	Morbidelli	Dallara-Ford	64	
r	Caffi	Arrows-Ford	49	driver tired
r	Donnelly	Lotus-Lam.	43	spun off
r	Modena	Brabham-Judd	39	spun off
r	Barilla	Minardi-Ford	38	valve
r	Dalmas	AGS-Ford	28	suspension
r	Warwick	Lotus-Lam.	25	electrical
r	Suzuki,A.	Lola-Lam.	24	accident
r	Alboreto	Arrows-Ford	24	suspension
r	Foitek	Brabham-Judd	14	clutch
r	Bernard	Lola-Lam.	13	gearbox
r	Grouillard	Osella-Ford	8	accident
r	de Cesaris	Dallara-Ford	0	accident

STARTING GRID:

1	Senna	12	Modena
2	Berger,G.	13	Piquet
3	Boutsen	14	Donnelly
4	Patrese	15	Nannini
5	Mansell	16	Morbidelli
6	Prost	17	Barilla
7	Alesi	18	Suzuki,A.
8	Martini	19	Nakajima
9	de Cesaris	20	Larini
10	Alliot	21	Grouillard
11	Bernard	22	Foitek +

San Marino

GRAND PRIX No:	487
DATE:	May 13, 1990
VENUE:	Imola
POLE LAP:	Senna, 1m 23.220s
FASTEST LAP:	Nannini, 1m 27.156s

Pn	Driver	Car	Laps	Time/Reason
1	Patrese	Williams-Ren.	61	1h 30m 55.478s
2	Berger,G.	McLaren-Honda	61	1h 31m 00.595s
3	Nannini	Benetton-Ford	61	1h 31m 01.718s
4	Prost	Ferrari	61	1h 31m 02.321s
5	Piquet	Benetton-Ford	61	1h 31m 48.590s
6	Alesi	Tyrrell-Ford	60	
7	Warwick	Lola-Lam.	60	
8	Donnelly	Lotus-Lam.	60	
9	Alliot	Ligier-Ford	60	
10	Larini	Ligier-Ford	59	
11	Barilla	Minardi-Ford	59	
12	Lehto	Onyx-Ford	59	
13	Bernard	Lola-Lam.	56	gearbox
r	Grouillard	Osella-Ford	52	suspension
r	Mansell	Ferrari	38	engine
r	Foitek	Onyx-Ford	35	engine
r	Modena	Brabham-Judd	31	brakes
r	de Cesaris	Dallara-Ford	29	wheel
r	Gugelmin	Leyton H.-Judd	24	electrical
r	Boutsen	Williams-Ren.	17	engine
r	Suzuki,A.	Lola-Lam.	17	clutch
r	Senna	McLaren-Honda	3	wheel
r	Pirro	Dallara-Ford	2	electrical
r	Capelli	Leyton H.-Judd	0	accident
r	Nakajima	Tyrrell-Ford	0	accident
r	Moreno	EuroBrun-Judd	0	throttle
dns	Martini	Minardi-Ford		injured

STARTING GRID:

1	Senna	11	Warwick
2	Berger,G.	12	Donnelly
3	Patrese	13	Gugelmin
4	Boutsen	14	Bernard
5	Mansell	15	Modena
6	Prost	16	Suzuki,A.
7	Alesi	17	Alliot
8	Piquet	18	de Cesaris
9	Nannini	19	Capelli
10	Martini	20	Nakajima +

Monaco

GRAND PRIX No:	488
DATE:	May 27, 1990
VENUE:	Monte Carlo
POLE LAP:	Senna, 1m 21.314s
FASTEST LAP:	Senna, 1m 24.468s

Pn	Driver	Car	Laps	Time/Reason
1	Senna	McLaren-Honda	78	1h 52m 46.982s
2	Alesi	Tyrrell-Ford	78	1h 52m 48.069s
3	Berger,G.	McLaren-Honda	78	1h 52m 49.055s
4	Boutsen	Williams-Ren.	77	
5	Caffi	Arrows-Ford	76	
6	Bernard	Lola-Lam.	76	
7	Foitek	Onyx-Ford	72	
r	Warwick	Lotus-Lam.	66	brakes
r	Mansell	Ferrari	63	battery
r	Barilla	Minardi-Ford	52	gearbox
r	Lehto	Onyx-Ford	52	gearbox
r	Alliot	Ligier-Ford	47	gearbox
r	Patrese	Williams-Ren.	41	valve
r	de Cesaris	Dallara-Ford	38	accelerator
r	Nakajima	Tyrrell-Ford	36	spun off
dq	Piquet	Benetton-Ford	33	push start
r	Prost	Ferrari	30	battery
r	Nannini	Benetton-Ford	20	engine
r	Brabham,D.	Brabham-Judd	16	cv joint
r	Capelli	Leyton H.-Judd	13	brakes
r	Larini	Ligier-Ford	12	gearbox
r	Suzuki,A.	Lola-Lam.	11	electrical
r	Martini	Minardi-Ford	7	electrical
r	Donnelly	Lotus-Lam.	6	cv joint
r	Modena	Brabham-Judd	3	gearbox
r	Pirro	Dallara-Ford	0	vapour lock

STARTING GRID:

1	Senna	12	de Cesaris
2	Prost	13	Warwick
3	Alesi	14	Modena
4	Patrese	15	Suzuki,A.
5	Berger,G.	16	Nannini
6	Boutsen	17	Larini
7	Mansell	18	Alliot
8	Martini	19	Barilla
9	Pirro	20	Foitek
10	Piquet	21	Nakajima
11	Donnelly	22	Caffi +

Canadian

GRAND PRIX No:	489
DATE:	June 10, 1990
VENUE:	Montreal
POLE LAP:	Senna, 1m 20.399s
FASTEST LAP:	Berger,G., 1m 22.077s

Pn	Driver	Car	Laps	Time/Reason
1	Senna	McLaren-Honda	70	1h 42m 56.400s
2	Piquet	Benetton-Ford	70	1h 43m 06.897s
3	Mansell	Ferrari	70	1h 43m 09.785
4	Berger,G.	McLaren-Honda	70	1h 43m 11.254s
5	Prost	Ferrari	70	1h 43m 12.220s
6	Warwick	Lotus-Lam.	68	
7	Modena	Brabham-Judd	68	
8	Caffi	Arrows-Ford	68	
9	Bernard	Lola-Lam.	67	
10	Capelli	Leyton H.-Judd	67	
11	Nakajima	Tyrrell-Ford	67	
12	Suzuki,A.	Lola-Lam.	66	
13	Grouillard	Osella-Ford	65	
r	Donnelly	Lotus-Lam.	57	engine
r	Foitek	Onyx-Ford	53	valve
r	de Cesaris	Dallara-Ford	50	input shaft
r	Lehto	Onyx-Ford	46	misfiring
r	Patrese	Williams-Ren.	44	brakes
r	Alliot	Ligier-Ford	34	engine
r	Alesi	Tyrrell-Ford	26	accident
r	Nannini	Benetton-Ford	21	accident
r	Boutsen	Williams-Ren.	19	accident
r	Larini	Ligier-Ford	18	accident
r	Pirro	Dallara-Ford	11	accident
r	Alboreto	Arrows-Ford	11	accident
r	Martini	Minardi-Ford	0	spun off

STARTING GRID:

1	Senna	12	Donnelly
2	Berger,G.	13	Nakajima
3	Prost	14	Alboreto
4	Nannini	15	Grouillard
5	Piquet	16	Martini
6	Boutsen	17	Alliot
7	Mansell	18	Suzuki,A.
8	Alesi	19	Pirro
9	Patrese	20	Larini
10	Modena	21	Foitek
11	Warwick	22	Lehto

+

Mexican

GRAND PRIX No:	490
DATE:	June 24, 1990
VENUE:	Mexico City
POLE LAP:	Berger,G., 1m 17.277s
FASTEST LAP:	Prost, 1m 17.958s

Pn	Driver	Car	Laps	Time/Reason
1	Prost	Ferrari	69	1h 32m 35.783s
2	Mansell	Ferrari	69	1h 33m 01.134s
3	Berger,G.	McLaren-Honda	69	1h 33m 01.313s
4	Nannini	Benetton-Ford	69	1h 33m 16.882s
5	Boutsen	Williams-Ren.	69	1h 33m 22.452s
6	Piquet	Benetton-Ford	69	1h 33m 22.726s
7	Alesi	Tyrrell-Ford	69	1h 33m 24.860s
8	Donnelly	Lotus-Lam.	69	1h 33m 41.925s
9	Patrese	Williams-Ren.	69	1h 33m 45.701s
10	Warwick	Lotus-Lam.	68	
11	Modena	Brabham-Judd	68	
12	Martini	Minardi-Ford	68	
13	de Cesaris	Dallara-Ford	68	
14	Barilla	Minardi-Ford	67	
15	Foitek	Onyx-Ford	67	
16	Larini	Ligier-Ford	67	
17	Alboreto	Arrows-Ford	66	
18	Alliot	Ligier-Ford	66	
19	Grouillard	Osella-Ford	65	
20	Senna	McLaren-Honda	63	puncture
r	Lehto	Onyx-Ford	26	engine
r	Bernard	Lola-Lam.	12	wheel
r	Suzuki,A.	Lola-Lam.	11	accident
r	Nakajima	Tyrrell-Ford	11	accident
r	Brabham,D.	Brabham-Judd	11	electrical
r	Pirro	Dallara-Ford	10	engine
dns	Moreno	EuroBrun-Judd		push start

STARTING GRID:

1	Berger,G.	11	Warwick
2	Patrese	12	Donnelly
3	Senna	13	Prost
4	Mansell	14	Nannini
5	Boutsen	15	de Cesaris
6	Alesi	16	Barilla
7	Martini	17	Alboreto
8	Piquet	18	Pirro
9	Nakajima	19	Suzuki,A.
10	Modena	20	Grouillard

+

French

GRAND PRIX No:	491
DATE:	July 8, 1990
VENUE:	Paul Ricard
POLE LAP:	Mansell, 1m 04.402s
FASTEST LAP:	Mansell, 1m 08.012s

Pn	Driver	Car	Laps	Time/Reason
1	Prost	Ferrari	80	1h 33m 29.606s
2	Capelli	Leyton H.-Judd	80	1h 33m 38.232s
3	Senna	McLaren-Honda	80	1h 33m 41.212s
4	Piquet	Benetton-Ford	80	1h 34m 10.813s
5	Berger,G.	McLaren-Honda	80	1h 34m 11.825s
6	Patrese	Williams-Ren.	80	1h 34m 38.957s
7	Suzuki,A.	Lola-Lam.	79	
8	Bernard	Lola-Lam.	79	
9	Alliot	Ligier-Ford	79	
10	Alboreto	Arrows-Ford	79	
11	Warwick	Lotus-Lam.	79	
12	Donnelly	Lotus-Lam.	79	
13	Modena	Brabham-Judd	78	
14	Larini	Ligier-Ford	78	
15	Brabham,D.	Brabham-Judd	77	
dq	de Cesaris	Dallara-Ford	77	underweight
16	Nannini	Benetton-Ford	75	electrical
17	Dalmas	AGS-Ford	75	
18	Mansell	Ferrari	72	engine
r	Nakajima	Tyrrell-Ford	63	gearbox
r	Gugelmin	Leyton H.-Judd	58	fuel system
r	Martini	Minardi-Ford	40	electrical
r	Alesi	Tyrrell-Ford	23	driveshaft
r	Caffi	Arrows-Ford	22	suspension
r	Boutsen	Williams-Ren.	8	engine
r	Pirro	Dallara-Ford	7	brakes

STARTING GRID:

1	Mansell	12	Alliot
2	Berger,G.	13	Alesi
3	Senna	14	Suzuki,A.
4	Prost	15	Nakajima
5	Nannini	16	Warwick
6	Patrese	17	Donnelly
7	Capelli	18	Alboreto
8	Boutsen	19	Larini
9	Piquet	20	Modena
10	Gugelmin	21	de Cesaris
11	Bernard	22	Caffi

+

British

GRAND PRIX No:	492
DATE:	July 15, 1990
VENUE:	Silverstone
POLE LAP:	Mansell, 1m 07.428s
FASTEST LAP:	Mansell, 1m 11.291s

Pn	Driver	Car	Laps	Time/Reason
1	Prost	Ferrari	64	1h 18m 30.999s
2	Boutsen	Williams-Ren.	64	1h 19m 10.091s
3	Senna	McLaren-Honda	64	1h 19m 14.087s
4	Bernard	Lola-Lam.	64	1h 19m 46.301s
5	Piquet	Benetton-Ford	64	1h 19m 55.002s
6	Suzuki,A.	Lola-Lam.	63	
7	Caffi	Arrows-Ford	63	
8	Alesi	Tyrrell-Ford	63	
9	Modena	Brabham-Judd	62	
10	Larini	Ligier-Ford	62	
11	Pirro	Dallara-Ford	62	
12	Barilla	Minardi-Ford	62	
13	Alliot	Ligier-Ford	61	
14	Berger,G.	McLaren-Honda	60	throttle
r	Mansell	Ferrari	55	gearbox
r	Capelli	Leyton H.-Judd	48	fuel system
r	Donnelly	Lotus-Lam.	48	engine
r	Warwick	Lotus-Lam.	46	engine
r	Tarquini	AGS-Ford	41	engine
r	Alboreto	Arrows-Ford	37	electrical
r	Patrese	Williams-Ren.	26	accident
r	Nakajima	Tyrrell-Ford	20	electrical
r	Nannini	Benetton-Ford	15	accident
r	de Cesaris	Dallara-Ford	12	gearbox
r	Martini	Minardi-Ford	31	alternator
dns	Gugelmin	Leyton H.-Judd		fuel pump

STARTING GRID:

1	Mansell	12	Nakajima
2	Senna	13	Nannini
3	Berger,G.	14	Donnelly
4	Boutsen	15	Gugelmin
5	Prost	16	Warwick
6	Alesi	17	Caffi
7	Patrese	18	Martini
8	Bernard	19	Pirro
9	Suzuki,A.	20	Modena
10	Capelli	21	Larini
11	Piquet	22	Alliot

+

German

GRAND PRIX No: 493
DATE: July 29, 1990
VENUE: Hockenheim
POLE LAP: Senna, 1m 40.198s
FASTEST LAP: Boutsen, 1m 45.602s

Pn	Driver	Car	Laps	Time/Reason
1	Senna	McLaren-Honda	45	1h 20m 47.164s
2	Nannini	Benetton-Ford	45	1h 20m 53.684s
3	Berger,G.	McLaren-Honda	45	1h 20m 55.717s
4	Prost	Ferrari	45	1h 21m 32.434s
5	Patrese	Williams-Honda	45	1h 21m 35.192s
6	Boutsen	Williams-Honda	45	1h 22m 08.655s
7	Capelli	Leyton H.-Judd	44	
8	Warwick	Lotus-Lam.	44	
9	Caffi	Arrows-Ford	44	
10	Larini	Ligier-Ford	43	
11	Alesi	Tyrrell-Ford	40	cv joint
r	Lehto	Onyx-Ford	39	
r	Bernard	Lola-Lam.	35	electrical
r	Suzuki,A.	Lola-Lam.	33	clutch
r	Nakajima	Tyrrell-Ford	24	electrical
r	Piquet	Benetton-Ford	23	engine
r	Martini	Minardi-Ford	20	engine
r	Foitek	Onyx-Ford	19	spun off
dq	Alliot	Ligier-Ford	16	push start
r	Mansell	Ferrari	15	undertray
r	Gugelmin	Leyton H.-Judd	12	engine
r	Brabham,D.	Brabham-Judd	12	valve
r	Alboreto	Arrows-Ford	10	engine
r	Donnelly	Lotus-Lam.	1	clutch
r	Pirro	Dallara-Ford	0	accident
r	Modena	Brabham-Judd	0	clutch

STARTING GRID:

1	Senna	12	Bernard
2	Berger,G.	13	Nakajima
3	Prost	14	Gugelmin
4	Mansell	15	Martini
5	Patrese	16	Warwick
6	Boutsen	17	Modena
7	Piquet	18	Caffi
8	Alesi	19	Alboreto
9	Nannini	20	Donnelly
10	Capelli	21	Brabham,D.
11	Suzuki,A.	22	Larini

+

Hungarian

GRAND PRIX No: 494
DATE: August 12, 1990
VENUE: Hungaroring
POLE LAP: Boutsen, 1m 17.919s
FASTEST LAP: Patrese, 1m 22.058s

Pn	Driver	Car	Laps	Time/Reason
1	Boutsen	Williams-Ren.	77	1h 49m 30.597s
2	Senna	McLaren-Honda	77	1h 49m 30.885s
3	Piquet	Benetton-Ford	77	1h 49m 58.490s
4	Patrese	Williams-Ren.	77	1h 50m 02.430s
5	Warwick	Lotus-Lam.	77	1h 50m 44.841s
6	Bernard	Lola-Lam.	77	1h 50m 54.905s
7	Donnelly	Lotus-Lam.	76	
8	Gugelmin	Leyton H.-Judd	76	
9	Caffi	Arrows-Ford	76	
10	Pirro	Dallara-Ford	76	
11	Larini	Ligier-Ford	76	
12	Alboreto	Arrows-Ford	75	
13	Tarquini	AGS-Ford	74	
14	Alliot	Ligier-Ford	74	
15	Barilla	Minardi-Ford	74	
16	Berger,G.	McLaren-Honda	72	accident
17	Mansell	Ferrari	71	accident
r	Nannini	Benetton-Ford	64	accident
r	Capelli	Leyton H.-Judd	56	gearbox
r	Suzuki,A.	Lola-Lam.	37	oil filter
r	Prost	Ferrari	36	gearbox
r	Alesi	Tyrrell-Ford	36	accident
r	Modena	Brabham-Judd	35	engine
r	Martini	Minardi-Ford	35	accident
r	de Cesaris	Dallara-Ford	22	engine
r	Nakajima	Tyrrell-Ford	9	spun off

STARTING GRID:

1	Boutsen	12	Bernard
2	Patrese	13	Pirro
3	Berger,G.	14	Martini
4	Senna	15	Nakajima
5	Mansell	16	Capelli
6	Alesi	17	Gugelmin
7	Nannini	18	Donnelly
8	Prost	19	Suzuki,A.
9	Piquet	20	Modena
10	de Cesaris	21	Alliot
11	Warwick	22	Alboreto

+

Belgian

GRAND PRIX No: 495
DATE: August 26, 1990
VENUE: Spa-Francorchamps
POLE LAP: Senna, 1m 50.365s
FASTEST LAP: Prost, 1m 55.087s

Pn	Driver	Car	Laps	Time/Reason
1	Senna	McLaren-Honda	44	1h 26m 31.997s
2	Prost	Ferrari	44	1h 26m 35.547s
3	Berger,G.	McLaren-Honda	44	1h 27m 00.459s
4	Nannini	Benetton-Ford	44	1h 27m 21.334s
5	Piquet	Benetton-Ford	44	1h 28m 01.647s
6	Gugelmin	Leyton H.-Judd	44	1h 28m 20.848s
7	Capelli	Leyton H.-Judd	43	
8	Alesi	Tyrrell-Ford	43	
9	Bernard	Lola-Lam.	43	
10	Caffi	Arrows-Ford	43	
11	Warwick	Lotus-Lam.	43	
12	Donnelly	Lola-Lam.	43	
13	Alboreto	Arrows-Ford	43	
14	Larini	Ligier-Ford	42	
15	Martini	Minardi-Ford	42	
16	Grouillard	Osella-Ford	42	
17	Modena	Brabham-Judd	39	engine
r	Brabham,D.	Brabham-Judd	36	electrical
r	de Cesaris	Dallara-Ford	27	water leak
r	Boutsen	Williams-Ren.	21	transmission
r	Mansell	Ferrari	19	handling
r	Patrese	Williams-Ren.	18	gearbox
r	Pirro	Dallara-Ford	5	water pipe
r	Nakajima	Tyrrell-Ford	4	engine
r	Barilla	Minardi-Ford	0	accident
r	Suzuki,A.	Lola-Lam.	0	suspension

STARTING GRID:

1	Senna	12	Capelli
2	Berger,G.	13	Modena
3	Prost	14	Gugelmin
4	Boutsen	15	Bernard
5	Mansell	16	Martini
6	Nannini	17	Pirro
7	Patrese	18	Warwick
8	Piquet	19	Caffi
9	Alesi	20	de Cesaris
10	Nakajima	21	Larini
11	Suzuki,A.	22	Donnelly +

Italian

GRAND PRIX No: 496
DATE: September 9, 1990
VENUE: Monza
POLE LAP: Senna, 1m 22.533s
FASTEST LAP: Senna, 1m 26.254s

Pn	Driver	Car	Laps	Time/Reason
1	Senna	McLaren-Honda	53	1h 17m 57.878s
2	Prost	Ferrari	53	1h 18m 03.932s
3	Berger,G.	McLaren-Honda	53	1h 18m 05.282s
4	Mansell	Ferrari	53	1h 18m 54.097s
5	Patrese	Williams-Ren.	53	1h 19m 23.152s
6	Nakajima	Tyrrell-Ford	52	
7	Piquet	Benetton-Ford	52	
8	Nannini	Benetton-Ford	52	
9	Caffi	Arrows-Ford	51	
10	de Cesaris	Dallara-Ford	51	
11	Larini	Ligier-Ford	51	
12	Alboreto	Arrows-Ford	50	spun off
13	Alliot	Ligier-Ford	50	
uc	Dalmas	AGS-Ford	45	
r	Capelli	Leyton H.-Judd	35	fuel pump
r	Suzuki,A.	Lola-Lam.	36	electrical
r	Grouillard	Osella-Ford	27	wheel bearing
r	Gugelmin	Leyton H.-Judd	24	engine
r	Modena	Brabham-Judd	21	valve
r	Boutsen	Williams-Ren.	18	suspension
r	Warwick	Lotus-Lam.	15	clutch
r	Pirro	Dallara-Ford	14	gearbox
r	Donnelly	Lotus-Lam.	13	engine
r	Bernard	Lola-Lam.	10	gearbox
r	Martini	Minardi-Ford	7	suspension
r	Alesi	Tyrrell-Ford	4	spun off

STARTING GRID:

1	Senna	12	Warwick
2	Prost	13	Bernard
3	Berger,G.	14	Nakajima
4	Mansell	15	Martini
5	Alesi	16	Capelli
6	Boutsen	17	Modena
7	Patrese	18	Suzuki,A.
8	Nannini	19	Pirro
9	Piquet	20	Alliot
10	Gugelmin	21	Caffi
11	Donnelly	22	Alboreto +

Portuguese

GRAND PRIX No: 497
DATE: September 23, 1990
VENUE: Estoril
POLE LAP: Mansell, 1m 13.557s
FASTEST LAP: Patrese, 1m 18.306s

Pn	Driver	Car	Laps	Time/Reason
1	Mansell	Ferrari	61	1h 22m 11.014s
2	Senna	McLaren-Honda	61	1h 22m 13.822s
3	Prost	Ferrari	61	1h 22m 15.203s
4	Berger,G.	McLaren-Honda	61	1h 22m 16.910s
5	Piquet	Benetton-Ford	61	1h 23m 08.432s
6	Nannini	Benetton-Ford	61	1h 23m 09.263s
7	Patrese	Williams-Ren.	60	
8	Alesi	Tyrrell-Ford	60	
9	Alboreto	Arrows-Ford	60	
10	Larini	Ligier-Ford	59	
11	Martini	Minardi-Ford	59	
12	Gugelmin	Leyton H.-Judd	59	
13	Caffi	Arrows-Ford	58	accident
14	Suzuki,A.	Lola-Lam.	58	accident
15	Pirro	Dallara-Ford	58	
r	Alliot	Ligier-Ford	52	accident
r	Brabham,D.	Brabham-Judd	52	gearbox
r	Capelli	Leyton H.-Judd	51	engine
r	Boutsen	Williams-Ren.	30	gearbox
r	Bernard	Lola-Lam.	24	gearbox
r	Modena	Brabham-Judd	21	gearbox
r	Donnelly	Lotus-Lam.	14	alternator
r	Warwick	Lotus-Lam.	5	throttle
r	Dalmas	AGS-Ford	3	driveshaft
r	de Cesaris	Dallara-Ford	0	throttle
dns	Nakajima	Tyrrell-Ford		driver ill

STARTING GRID:

1	Mansell	12	Capelli
2	Prost	13	Pirro
3	Senna	14	Gugelmin
4	Berger,G.	15	Donnelly
5	Patrese	16	Martini
6	Piquet	17	Caffi
7	Boutsen	18	de Cesaris
8	Alesi	19	Alboreto
9	Nannini	20	Nakajima
10	Bernard	21	Alliot
11	Suzuki,A.	22	Warwick +

Spanish

GRAND PRIX No: 498
DATE: September 30, 1990
VENUE: Jerez
POLE LAP: Senna, 1m 18.387s
FASTEST LAP: Patrese, 1m 24.513s

Pn	Driver	Car	Laps	Time/Reason
1	Prost	Ferrari	73	1h 48m 01.461s
2	Mansell	Ferrari	73	1h 48m 23.525s
3	Nannini	Benetton-Ford	73	1h 48m 36.335s
4	Boutsen	Williams-Ren.	73	1h 48m 44.757s
5	Patrese	Williams-Ren.	73	1h 48m 58.991s
6	Suzuki,A.	Lola-Lam.	73	1h 49m 05.189s
7	Larini	Ligier-Ford	72	
8	Gugelmin	Leyton H.-Judd	72	
9	Dalmas	AGS-Ford	72	
10	Alboreto	Arrows-Ford	71	
r	Warwick	Lotus-Lam.	63	gearbox
r	Capelli	Leyton H.-Judd	59	driver cramp
r	Berger,G.	McLaren-Honda	56	accident
r	Senna	McLaren-Honda	53	engine
r	Piquet	Benetton-Ford	47	alternator
r	de Cesaris	Dallara-Ford	47	engine
r	Grouillard	Osella-Ford	45	wheel
r	Martini	Minardi-Ford	41	wheel
r	Alliot	Ligier-Ford	22	spun off
r	Bernard	Lola-Lam.	20	clutch
r	Nakajima	Tyrrell-Ford	13	spun off
r	Tarquini	AGS-Ford	5	accident
r	Modena	Brabham-Judd	5	spun off
r	Pirro	Dallara-Ford	0	throttle
r	Alesi	Tyrrell-Ford	0	spun off
dns	Donnelly	Lotus-Lam.		injured

STARTING GRID:

1	Senna	12	Gugelmin
2	Prost	13	Alliot
3	Mansell	14	Nakajima
4	Alesi	15	Suzuki,A.
5	Berger,G.	16	Pirro
6	Patrese	17	de Cesaris
7	Boutsen	18	Bernard
8	Piquet	19	Capelli
9	Nannini	20	Larini
10	Warwick	21	Grouillard
11	Martini	22	Tarquini +

Japanese

GRAND PRIX No:	499
DATE:	October 21, 1990
VENUE:	Suzuka
POLE LAP:	Senna, 1m 36.996s
FASTEST LAP:	Patrese, 1m 44.233s

Pn	Driver	Car	Laps	Time/Reason
1	Piquet	Benetton-Ford	53	1h 34m 36.824s
2	Moreno	Benetton-Ford	53	1h 34m 44.047s
3	Suzuki,A.	Lola-Lam.	53	1h 34m 59.293s
4	Patrese	Williams-Ren.	53	1h 35m 13.082s
5	Boutsen	Williams-Ren.	53	1h 35m 23.708s
6	Nakajima	Tyrrell-Ford	53	1h 35m 49.174s
7	Larini	Ligier-Ford	52	
8	Martini	Minardi-Ford	52	
9	Caffi	Arrows-Ford	52	
10	Alliot	Ligier-Ford	52	
r	Warwick	Lotus-Lam.	38	gearbox
r	Herbert	Lotus-Lam.	31	engine
r	Alboreto	Arrows-Ford	28	engine
r	Mansell	Ferrari	26	driveshaft
r	Pirro	Dallara-Ford	24	alternator
r	Bernard	Lola-Lam.	24	oil leak
r	Morbidelli	Minardi-Ford	18	spun off
r	Capelli	Leyton H.-Judd	16	misfiring
r	de Cesaris	Dallara-Ford	13	spun off
r	Gugelmin	Leyton H.-Judd	5	engine
r	Brabham,D.	Brabham-Judd	2	suspension
r	Berger,G.	McLaren-Honda	1	spun off
r	Modena	Brabham-Judd	0	accident
r	Prost	Ferrari	0	accident
r	Senna	McLaren-Honda	0	accident
dns	Alesi	Tyrrell-Ford		injured

STARTING GRID:

1	Senna	12	Warwick
2	Prost	13	Capelli
3	Mansell	14	Nakajima
4	Berger,G.	15	Herbert
5	Boutsen	16	Gugelmin
6	Piquet	17	Bernard
7	Alesi	18	Larini
8	Patrese	19	Pirro
9	Moreno	20	Morbidelli
10	Suzuki,A.	21	Alliot
11	Martini	22	Brabham,D. +

Australian

GRAND PRIX No:	500
DATE:	November 4, 1990
VENUE:	Adelaide
POLE LAP:	Senna, 1m 15.671s
FASTEST LAP:	Mansell, 1m 18.203s

Pn	Driver	Car	Laps	Time/Reason
1	Piquet	Benetton-Ford	81	1h 49m 44.570s
2	Mansell	Ferrari	81	1h 49m 47.699s
3	Prost	Ferrari	81	1h 50m 21.829s
4	Berger,G.	McLaren-Honda	81	1h 50m 31.432s
5	Boutsen	Williams-Ren.	81	1h 51m 35.730s
6	Patrese	Williams-Ren.	80	
7	Moreno	Benetton-Ford	80	
8	Alesi	Tyrrell-Ford	80	
9	Martini	Minardi-Ford	79	
10	Larini	Ligier-Ford	79	
11	Alliot	Ligier-Ford	78	
12	Modena	Brabham-Judd	77	
13	Grouillard	Osella-Ford	74	
r	Pirro	Dallara-Ford	68	engine
r	Senna	McLaren-Honda	61	accident
r	Tarquini	AGS-Ford	58	oil fire
r	Herbert	Lotus-Lam.	57	stalled
r	Nakajima	Tyrrell-Ford	53	spun off
r	Capelli	Leyton H.-Judd	46	throttle
r	Warwick	Lotus-Lam.	43	gearbox
r	Gugelmin	Leyton H.-Judd	27	brakes
r	de Cesaris	Dallara-Ford	23	electrical
r	Bernard	Lola-Lam.	21	gearbox
r	Morbidelli	Minardi-Ford	20	gearbox
r	Brabham,D.	Brabham-Judd	18	spun off
r	Suzuki,A.	Lola-Lam.	6	differential

STARTING GRID:

1	Senna	12	Larini
2	Berger,G.	13	Nakajima
3	Mansell	14	Capelli
4	Prost	15	de Cesaris
5	Alesi	16	Gugelmin
6	Patrese	17	Modena
7	Piquet	18	Herbert
8	Moreno	19	Alliot
9	Boutsen	20	Morbidelli
10	Martini	21	Pirro
11	Warwick	22	Grouillard +

US

GRAND PRIX No:	501
DATE:	March 10, 1991
VENUE:	Phoenix
POLE LAP:	Senna, 1m 21.434s
FASTEST LAP:	Alesi, 1m 26.758s

Pn	Driver	Car	Laps	Time/Reason
1	Senna	McLaren-Honda	81	2h 00m 47.626s
2	Prost	Ferrari	81	2h 01m 04.150s
3	Piquet	Benetton-Ford	81	2h 01m 05.204s
4	Modena	Tyrrell-Honda	81	
5	Nakajima	Tyrrell-Honda	80	
6	Suzuki,A.	Lola-Ford	79	
7	Larini	Lamborghini	78	
8	Tarquini	AGS-Ford	77	
9	Martini	Minardi-Ferrari	75	
10	Gachot	Jordan-Ford	75	
11	Brundle	Brabham-Yam.	73	
12	Alesi	Ferrari	72	
r	Hakkinen	Lotus-Judd	60	engine
r	Patrese	Williams-Ren.	50	accident
r	Moreno	Benetton-Ford	50	accident
r	Alboreto	Footwork-Porsche	42	gearbox
r	Capelli	Leyton H.-Ilmor	41	gearbox
r	Boutsen	Ligier-Lam.	41	electrical
r	Berger,G.	McLaren-Honda	37	fuel pressure
r	Mansell	Williams-Ren.	36	gearbox
r	Gugelmin	Leyton H.-Ilmor	45	gearbox
r	Blundell	Brabham-Yam.	35	accident
r	Pirro	Dallara-Judd	17	gearbox
r	Morbidelli	Minardi-Ferrari	16	gearbox
r	Lehto	Dallara-Judd	13	clutch
r	Bernard	Lola-Ford	5	engine

STARTING GRID:

1	Senna	12	Brundle
2	Prost	13	Hakkinen
3	Patrese	14	Gachot
4	Mansell	15	Martini
5	Piquet	16	Nakajima
6	Alesi	17	Larini
7	Berger,G.	18	Capelli
8	Moreno	19	Bernard
9	Pirro	20	Boutsen
10	Lehto	21	Suzuki,A.
11	Modena	22	Tarquini +

Brazilian

GRAND PRIX No:	502
DATE:	March 24, 1991
VENUE:	Interlagos
POLE LAP:	Senna, 1m 16.392s
FASTEST LAP:	Mansell, 1m 20.436s

Pn	Driver	Car	Laps	Time/Reason
1	Senna	McLaren-Honda	71	1h 38m 28.128s
2	Patrese	Williams-Ren.	71	1h 38m 31.119s
3	Berger,G.	McLaren-Honda	71	1h 38m 33.544s
4	Prost	Ferrari	71	1h 38m 47.497s
5	Piquet	Benetton-Ford	71	1h 38m 50.088s
6	Alesi	Ferrari	71	1h 38m 51.769s
7	Moreno	Benetton-Ford	70	
8	Morbidelli	Minardi-Ferrari	69	
9	Hakkinen	Lotus-Judd	68	
10	Boutsen	Ligier-Lam.	68	
11	Pirro	Dallara-Judd	68	
12	Brundle	Brabham-Yam.	67	
13	Gachot	Jordan-Ford	63	fuel system
r	Mansell	Williams-Ren.	59	gearbox
r	Comas	Ligier-Lam.	50	engine
r	Martini	Minardi-Ferrari	47	spun off
r	Blundell	Brabham-Yam.	34	engine
r	Bernard	Lola-Ford	33	clutch
r	Lehto	Dallara-Judd	22	alternator
r	de Cesaris	Jordan-Ford	20	accident
r	Modena	Tyrrell-Honda	19	gear change
r	Capelli	Leyton H.-Ilmor	16	engine
r	Nakajima	Tyrrell-Honda	12	accident
r	Gugelmin	Leyton H.-Ilmor	9	driver unwell
r	Tarquini	AGS-Ford	0	accident
dns	Suzuki,A.	Lola-Ford		fuel pump

STARTING GRID:

1	Senna	12	Pirro
2	Patrese	13	de Cesaris
3	Mansell	14	Moreno
4	Berger,G.	15	Capelli
5	Alesi	16	Nakajima
6	Prost	17	Suzuki,A.
7	Piquet	18	Boutsen
8	Gugelmin	19	Lehto
9	Modena	20	Martini
10	Gachot	21	Morbidelli
11	Bernard	22	Hakkinen +

San Marino

GRAND PRIX No:	503
DATE:	April 28, 1991
VENUE:	Imola
POLE LAP:	Senna, 1m 21.877s
FASTEST LAP:	Berger,G., 1m 26.531s

Pn	Driver	Car	Laps	Time/Reason
1	Senna	McLaren-Honda	61	1h 35m 14.750s
2	Berger,G.	McLaren-Honda	61	1h 35m 16.425s
3	Lehto	Dallara-Judd	60	
4	Martini	Minardi-Ferrari	59	
5	Hakkinen	Lotus-Judd	58	
6	Bailey	Lotus-Judd	58	
7	Boutsen	Ligier-Lam.	58	
8	Blundell	Brabham-Yam.	58	
9	Van de Poele	Lamborghini	57	engine
10	Comas	Ligier-Lam.	57	
11	Brundle	Brabham-Yam.	57	
12	Gugelmin	Leyton H.-Ilmor	55	engine
13	Moreno	Benetton-Ford	54	engine
r	Modena	Tyrrell-Honda	41	transmission
r	de Cesaris	Jordan-Ford	37	gear linkage
r	Gachot	Jordan-Ford	37	suspension
r	Capelli	Leyton H.-Ilmor	24	spun off
r	Bernard	Lola-Ford	17	engine
r	Patrese	Williams-Ren.	17	engine
r	Nakajima	Tyrrell-Honda	15	transmission
r	Morbidelli	Minardi-Ferrari	10	gearbox
r	Alesi	Ferrari	2	spun off
r	Suzuki,A.	Lola-Ford	2	spun off
r	Piquet	Benetton-Ford	1	spun off
r	Mansell	Williams-Ren.	0	accident
dns	Prost	Ferrari	0	spun off parade

STARTING GRID:

1	Senna	12	Gachot
2	Patrese	13	Moreno
3	Mansell	14	Piquet
4	Prost	15	Gugelmin
5	Berger,G.	16	Lehto
6	Modena	17	Bernard
7	Alesi	18	Brundle
8	Morbidelli	19	Comas
9	Martini	20	Suzuki,A.
10	Nakajima	21	Van de Poele
11	de Cesaris	22	Capelli

Monaco

GRAND PRIX No:	504
DATE:	May 12, 1991
VENUE:	Monte Carlo
POLE LAP:	Senna, 1m 20.344s
FASTEST LAP:	Prost, 1m 24.368s

Pn	Driver	Car	Laps	Time/Reason
1	Senna	McLaren-Honda	78	1h 53m 02.344s
2	Mansell	Williams-Ren.	78	1h 53m 20.682s
3	Alesi	Ferrari	78	1h 53m 49.789s
4	Moreno	Benetton-Ford	77	
5	Prost	Ferrari	77	
6	Pirro	Dallara-Judd	77	
7	Boutsen	Ligier-Lam.	76	
8	Gachot	Jordan-Ford	76	
9	Bernard	Lola-Ford	76	
10	Comas	Ligier-Lam.	76	
11	Lehto	Dallara-Judd	75	
12	Martini	Minardi-Ferrari	72	
r	Hakkinen	Lotus-Judd	64	fire
r	Morbidelli	Minardi-Ferrari	49	gearbox
r	Gugelmin	Leyton H.-Ilmor	43	throttle
r	Modena	Tyrrell-Honda	42	engine
r	Patrese	Williams-Ren.	42	accident
r	Blundell	Brabham-Yam.	41	accident
r	Alboreto	Footwork-Porsche	39	engine
r	Nakajima	Tyrrell-Honda	35	accident
r	Suzuki,A.	Lola-Ford	24	brakes
r	de Cesaris	Jordan-Ford	21	throttle
r	Capelli	Leyton H.-Ilmor	12	brakes
r	Tarquini	AGS-Ford	9	gearbox
r	Berger,G.	McLaren-Honda	9	accident
r	Piquet	Benetton-Ford	0	accident

STARTING GRID:

1	Senna	12	Pirro
2	Modena	13	Lehto
3	Patrese	14	Martini
4	Mansell	15	Gugelmin
4	Piquet	16	Boutsen
6	Berger,G.	17	Morbidelli
7	Prost	18	Capelli
8	Moreno	19	Suzuki,A.
9	Alesi	20	Tarquini
10	de Cesaris	21	Bernard
11	Nakajima	22	Blundell

Canadian

GRAND PRIX No: 505
DATE: June 2, 1991
VENUE: Montreal
POLE LAP: Patrese, 1m 19.837s
FASTEST LAP: Mansell, 1m 22.385s

Pn	Driver	Car	Laps	Time/Reason
1	Piquet	Benetton-Ford	69	1h 38m 51.490s
2	Modena	Tyrrell-Ford	69	1h 39m 23.322s
3	Patrese	Williams-Ren.	69	1h 39m 33.707s
4	de Cesaris	Jordan-Ford	69	1h 40m 11.700s
5	Gachot	Jordan-Ford	69	1h 40m 13.841s
6	Mansell	Williams-Ren.	68	gearbox
7	Martini	Minardi-Ferrari	68	
8	Comas	Ligier-Lam.	68	
9	Pirro	Dallara-Judd	68	
10	Nakajima	Tyrrell-Ford	67	
r	Gugelmin	Leyton H.-Ilmor	61	engine
r	Lehto	Dallara-Judd	50	engine
r	Johansson	Footwork-Porsche	48	brakes
r	Capelli	Leyton H.-Ilmor	42	engine
r	Alesi	Ferrari	34	engine
r	Bernard	Lola-Ford	29	transmission
r	Prost	Ferrari	27	gearbox
r	Boutsen	Ligier-Lam.	27	engine
r	Senna	McLaren-Honda	25	electrical
r	Hakkinen	Lotus-Judd	21	spun off
r	Brundle	Brabham-Yam.	21	engine
r	Morbidelli	Minardi-Ferrari	20	spun off
r	Moreno	Benetton-Ford	10	accident
r	Berger,G.	McLaren-Honda	4	electrical
r	Suzuki,A.	Lola-Ford	3	fire
r	Alboreto	Footwork-Porsche	2	throttle

STARTING GRID:

1	Patrese	12	Nakajima
2	Mansell	13	Capelli
3	Senna	14	Gachot
4	Prost	15	Morbidelli
5	Moreno	16	Boutsen
6	Berger,G.	17	Lehto
7	Alesi	18	Martini
8	Piquet	19	Bernard
9	Modena	20	Brundle
10	Pirro	21	Alboreto
11	de Cesaris	22	Suzuki,A.

+

Mexican

GRAND PRIX No: 506
DATE: June 16, 1991
VENUE: Mexico City
POLE LAP: Patrese, 1m 16.696s
FASTEST LAP: Mansell, 1m 16.788s

Pn	Driver	Car	Laps	Time/Reason
1	Patrese	Williams-Ren.	67	1h 29m 23.322s
2	Mansell	Williams-Ren.	67	1h 29m 53.541s
3	Senna	McLaren-Honda	67	1h 30m 49.561s
4	de Cesaris	Jordan-Ford	66	
5	Moreno	Benetton-Ford	66	
6	Bernard	Lola-Ford	66	
7	Morbidelli	Minardi-Ferrari	66	
8	Boutsen	Ligier-Lam.	65	
9	Hakkinen	Lotus-Judd	65	
10	Herbert	Lotus-Judd	65	
11	Modena	Tyrrell-Honda	64	
12	Nakajima	Tyrrell-Honda	64	
r	Blundell	Brabham-Yam.	54	engine
r	Gachot	Jordan-Ford	51	spun off
r	Suzuki,A.	Lola-Ford	48	gearbox
r	Piquet	Benetton-Ford	44	wheel-bearing
r	Alesi	Ferrari	42	clutch
r	Lehto	Dallara-Judd	30	engine
r	Alboreto	Footwork-Porsche	24	oil pressure
r	Brundle	Brabham-Yam.	20	lost wheel
r	Capelli	Leyton H.-Ilmor	19	engine
r	Prost	Ferrari	16	misfiring
r	Gugelmin	Leyton H.-Ilmor	16	engine
r	Grouillard	Fondmetal-Ford	13	oil leak
r	Berger,G.	McLaren-Honda	5	engine
r	Martini	Minardi-Ferrari	4	accident

STARTING GRID:

1	Patrese	12	Blundell
2	Mansell	13	Nakajima
3	Senna	14	Boutsen
4	Alesi	15	Martini
5	Berger,G.	16	Lehto
6	Piquet	17	Brundle
7	Prost	18	Bernard
8	Modena	19	Suzuki,A.
9	Moreno	20	Gachot
10	Grouillard	21	Gugelmin
11	de Cesaris	22	Capelli

+

French

GRAND PRIX No:	507
DATE:	July 7, 1991
VENUE:	Magny-Cours
POLE LAP:	Patrese, 1m 14.559s
FASTEST LAP:	Mansell, 1m 19.168s

Pn	Driver	Car	Laps	Time/Reason
1	Mansell	Williams-Ren.	72	1h 38m 00.056s
2	Prost	Ferrari	72	1h 38m 05.059s
3	Senna	McLaren-Honda	72	1h 38m 34.990s
4	Alesi	Ferrari	72	1h 38m 35.976s
5	Patrese	Williams-Ren.	71	
6	de Cesaris	Jordan-Ford	71	
7	Gugelmin	Leyton H.-Ilmor	70	
8	Piquet	Benetton-Ford	70	
9	Martini	Minardi-Ferrari	70	
10	Herbert	Lotus-Judd	70	
11	Comas	Ligier-Lam.	70	
12	Boutsen	Ligier-Lam.	69	
r	Moreno	Benetton-Ford	63	driver unwell
r	Modena	Tyrrell-Honda	57	gearbox
r	Grouillard	Fondmetal-Ford	47	oil leak
r	Bernard	Lola-Ford	43	transmission
r	Lehto	Dallara-Judd	39	puncture
r	Blundell	Brabham-Yam.	36	accident
r	Suzuki,A.	Lola-Ford	32	transmission
r	Alboreto	Footwork-Porsche	31	gearbox
r	Brundle	Brabham-Yam.	21	gearbox
r	Nakajima	Tyrrell-Honda	12	spun off
r	Morbidelli	Minardi-Ferrari	8	accident
r	Capelli	Leyton H.-Ilmor	7	spun off
r	Berger,G.	McLaren-Honda	6	engine
r	Gachot	Jordan-Ford	0	accident

STARTING GRID:

1	Patrese	12	de Cesaris
2	Prost	13	Martini
3	Senna	14	Comas
4	Mansell	15	Capelli
5	Berger,G.	16	Boutsen
6	Alesi	17	Blundell
7	Piquet	18	Nakajima
8	Moreno	19	Gachot
9	Gugelmin	20	Herbert
10	Morbidelli	21	Grouillard
11	Modena	22	Suzuki,A. +

British

GRAND PRIX No:	508
DATE:	July 14, 1991
VENUE:	Silverstone
POLE LAP:	Mansell, 1m 20.939s
FASTEST LAP:	Mansell, 1m 26.379s

Pn	Driver	Car	Laps	Time/Reason
1	Mansell	Williams-Ren.	59	1h 27m 35.479s
2	Berger,G.	McLaren-Honda	59	1h 28m 17.772s
3	Prost	Ferrari	59	1h 28m 35.629s
4	Senna	McLaren-Honda	58	fuel pressure
5	Piquet	Benetton-Ford	58	
6	Gachot	Jordan-Ford	58	
7	Modena	Tyrrell-Honda	58	
8	Nakajima	Tyrrell-Honda	58	
9	Martini	Minardi-Ferrari	58	
10	Pirro	Dallara-Judd	57	
11	Morbidelli	Minardi-Ferrari	57	
12	Hakkinen	Lotus-Judd	57	
13	Lehto	Dallara-Judd	56	
14	Herbert	Lotus-Judd	55	
r	Blundell	Brabham-Yam.	52	engine
r	de Cesaris	Jordan-Ford	41	accident
r	Alesi	Ferrari	31	accident
r	Suzuki,A.	Lola-Ford	29	accident
r	Boutsen	Ligier-Lam.	29	engine
r	Brundle	Brabham-Yam.	28	throttle
r	Alboreto	Footwork-Ford	25	gearbox
r	Gugelmin	Leyton H.-Ilmor	24	vibration
r	Moreno	Benetton-Ford	21	gearbox
r	Bernard	Lola-Ford	21	crownwheel/pinion
r	Capelli	Leyton H.-Ilmor	16	spun off
r	Patrese	Williams-Ren.	0	accident

STARTING GRID:

1	Mansell	12	Blundell
2	Senna	13	de Cesaris
3	Patrese	14	Brundle
4	Berger,G.	15	Nakajima
5	Prost	16	Capelli
6	Alesi	17	Gachot
7	Moreno	18	Pirro
8	Piquet	19	Boutsen
9	Gugelmin	20	Morbidelli
10	Modena	21	Bernard
11	Lehto	22	Suzuki,A. +

German

GRAND PRIX No:	509
DATE:	July 28, 1991
VENUE:	Hockenheim
POLE LAP:	Mansell, 1m 37.087s
FASTEST LAP:	Patrese, 1m 43.569s

Pn	Driver	Car	Laps	Time/Reason
1	Mansell	Williams-Ren.	45	1h 19m 29.661s
2	Patrese	Williams-Ren.	45	1h 19m 43.440s
3	Alesi	Ferrari	45	1h 19m 47.279s
4	Berger,G.	McLaren-Honda	45	1h 20m 02.312s
5	de Cesaris	Jordan-Ford	45	1h 20m 47.198s
6	Gachot	Jordan-Ford	45	1h 21m 10.226s
7	Senna	McLaren-Honda	44	out of fuel
8	Moreno	Benetton-Ford	44	
9	Boutsen	Ligier-Lam.	44	
10	Pirro	Dallara-Judd	44	
11	Brundle	Brabham-Yam.	43	
12	Blundell	Brabham-Yam.	43	
13	Modena	Tyrrell-Honda	41	
r	Prost	Ferrari	37	accident
r	Capelli	Leyton H.-Ilmor	36	misfiring
r	Lehto	Dallara-Judd	35	engine
r	Piquet	Benetton-Ford	27	gearbox
r	Nakajima	Tyrrell-Honda	26	gearbox
r	Comas	Ligier-Lam.	22	engine
r	Gugelmin	Leyton H.-Ilmor	21	gearbox
r	Hakkinen	Lotus-Judd	19	engine
r	Suzuki,A.	Lola-Ford	15	engine
r	Morbidelli	Minardi-Ferrari	14	differential
r	Martini	Minardi-Ferrari	11	engine
r	Bernard	Lola-Ford	9	crownwheel/pinion
r	Larini	Lamborghini	0	spun off

STARTING GRID:

1	Mansell	12	Capelli
2	Senna	13	Nakajima
3	Berger,G.	14	Modena
4	Patrese	15	Brundle
5	Prost	16	Gugelmin
6	Alesi	17	Boutsen
7	de Cesaris	18	Pirro
8	Piquet	19	Morbidelli
9	Moreno	20	Lehto
10	Martini	21	Blundell
11	Gachot	22	Suzuki,A. +

Hungarian

GRAND PRIX No:	510
DATE:	August 11, 1991
VENUE:	Hungaroring
POLE LAP:	Senna, 1m 16.147s
FASTEST LAP:	Gachot, 1m 21.547s

Pn	Driver	Car	Laps	Time/Reason
1	Senna	McLaren-Honda	77	1h 49m 12.796s
2	Mansell	Williams-Ren.	77	1h 49m 17.395s
3	Patrese	Williams-Ren.	77	1h 49m 28.390s
4	Berger,G.	McLaren-Honda	77	1h 49m 34.652s
5	Alesi	Ferrari	77	1h 49m 44.185s
6	Capelli	Leyton H.-Ilmor	76	
7	de Cesaris	Jordan-Ford	76	
8	Moreno	Benetton-Ford	76	
9	Gachot	Jordan-Ford	75	
10	Comas	Ligier-Lam.	75	
11	Gugelmin	Leyton H.-Ilmor	75	
12	Modena	Tyrrell-Ford	75	
13	Morbidelli	Minardi-Ferrari	75	
14	Hakkinen	Lotus-Judd	74	
15	Nakajima	Tyrrell-Honda	74	
16	Larini	Lamborghini	74	
17	Boutsen	Ligier-Lam.	71	engine
r	Martini	Minardi-Ferrari	65	engine
r	Blundell	Brabham-Yam.	62	spun off
r	Brundle	Brabham-Yam.	59	driver cramp
r	Lehto	Dallara-Judd	49	oil pressure
r	Piquet	Benetton-Ford	38	gearbox
r	Bernard	Lola-Ford	38	electrical
r	Suzuki,A.	Lola-Ford	38	electrical
r	Pirro	Dallara-Judd	37	oil pressure
r	Prost	Ferrari	28	engine

STARTING GRID:

1	Senna	12	Lehto
2	Patrese	13	Gugelmin
3	Mansell	14	Nakajima
4	Prost	15	Moreno
5	Berger,G.	16	Gachot
6	Alesi	17	de Cesaris
7	Pirro	18	Martini
8	Modena	19	Boutsen
9	Capelli	20	Blundell
10	Brundle	21	Bernard
11	Piquet	22	Suzuki,A. +

Belgian

GRAND PRIX No:	511
DATE:	August 25, 1991
VENUE:	Spa-Francorchamps
POLE LAP:	Senna, 1m 47.811s
FASTEST LAP:	Moreno, 1m 55.161s

Pn	Driver	Car	Laps	Time/Reason
1	Senna	McLaren-Honda	44	1h 27m 17.669s
2	Berger,G.	McLaren-Honda	44	1h 27m 19.750s
3	Piquet	Benetton-Ford	44	1h 27m 49.845s
4	Moreno	Benetton-Ford	44	1h 27m 54.979s
5	Patrese	Williams-Ren.	44	1h 28m 14.856s
6	Blundell	Brabham-Yam.	44	1h 28m 57.704s
7	Herbert	Lotus-Judd	44	1h 29m 02.268s
8	Pirro	Dallara-Judd	43	
9	Brundle	Brabham-Yam.	43	
10	Grouillard	Fondmetal-Ford	43	
11	Boutsen	Ligier-Lam.	43	
12	Martini	Minardi-Ferrari	42	
13	de Cesaris	Jordan-Ford	41	engine
r	Modena	Tyrrell-Honda	33	oil fire
r	Lehto	Dallara-Judd	33	engine
r	Alesi	Ferrari	30	engine
r	Morbidelli	Minardi-Ferrari	29	clutch
r	Hakkinen	Lotus-Judd	25	engine
r	Comas	Ligier-Lam.	25	crankshaft
r	Mansell	Williams-Ren.	22	electrical
r	Bernard	Lola-Ford	21	engine
r	Capelli	Leyton H.-Ilmor	13	engine
r	Nakajima	Tyrrell-Honda	7	accident
r	Prost	Ferrari	2	engine
r	Gugelmin	Leyton H.-Ilmor	1	engine
r	Schumacher,M.	Jordan-Ford	0	clutch

STARTING GRID:

1	Senna	12	Capelli
2	Prost	13	Blundell
3	Mansell	14	Lehto
4	Berger,G.	15	Gugelmin
5	Alesi	16	Brundle
6	Piquet	17	Patrese
7	Schumacher,M.	18	Boutsen
8	Moreno	19	Morbidelli
9	Martini	20	Bernard
10	Modena	21	Herbert
11	de Cesaris	22	Nakajima

+

Italian

GRAND PRIX No:	512
DATE:	September 8, 1991
VENUE:	Monza
POLE LAP:	Senna, 1m 21.114s
FASTEST LAP:	Senna, 1m 26.061s

Pn	Driver	Car	Laps	Time/Reason
1	Mansell	Williams-Ren.	53	1h 17m 54.319s
2	Senna	McLaren-Honda	53	1h 18m 10.581s
3	Prost	Ferrari	53	1h 18m 11.148s
4	Berger,G.	McLaren-Honda	53	1h 18m 22.038s
5	Schumacher,M.	Benetton-Ford	53	1h 18m 28.782s
6	Piquet	Benetton-Ford	53	1h 18m 39.919s
7	de Cesaris	Jordan-Ford	53	1h 18m 45.455s
8	Capelli	Leyton H.-Ilmor	53	1h 19m 09.338s
9	Morbidelli	Minardi-Ferrari	52	
10	Pirro	Dallara-Judd	52	
11	Comas	Ligier-Lam.	52	
12	Blundell	Brabham-Yam.	52	
13	Brundle	Brabham-Yam.	52	
14	Hakkinen	Lotus-Judd	49	
15	Gugelmin	Leyton H.-Ilmor	49	
16	Larini	Lamborghini	48	
r	Grouillard	Fondmetal-Ford	46	engine
r	Lehto	Dallara-Judd	35	suspension
r	Modena	Tyrrell-Ford	32	engine
r	Alesi	Ferrari	29	engine
r	Patrese	Williams-Ren.	27	gearbox
r	Nakajima	Tyrrell-Honda	24	throttle
r	Bernard	Lola-Ford	21	engine
r	Martini	Minardi-Ferrari	8	spun off
r	Moreno	Jordan-Ford	2	spun off
r	Boutsen	Ligier-Lam.	1	spun off

STARTING GRID:

1	Senna	12	Capelli
2	Mansell	13	Modena
3	Berger,G.	14	de Cesaris
4	Patrese	15	Grouillard
5	Prost	16	Nakajima
6	Alesi	17	Pirro
7	Schumacher,M.	18	Morbidelli
8	Piquet	19	Gugelmin
9	Moreno	20	Brundle
10	Martini	21	Lehto
11	Blundell	22	Boutsen

+

Portuguese

GRAND PRIX No: 513
DATE: September 22, 1991
VENUE: Estoril
POLE LAP: Patrese, 1m 13.001s
FASTEST LAP: Mansell, 1m 18.179s

Pn	Driver	Car	Laps	Time/Reason
1	Patrese	Williams-Ren.	71	1h 35m 42.304s
2	Senna	McLaren-Honda	71	1h 36m 03.245s
3	Alesi	Ferrari	71	1h 36m 35.858s
4	Martini	Minardi-Ferrari	71	1h 36m 45.802s
5	Piquet	Benetton-Ford	71	1h 36m 52.337s
6	Schumacher,M.	Benetton-Ford	71	1h 36m 58.886s
7	Gugelmin	Leyton H.-Ilmor	70	
8	de Cesaris	Jordan-Ford	70	
9	Morbidelli	Minardi-Ferrari	70	
10	Moreno	Jordan-Ford	70	
11	Comas	Ligier-Lam.	70	
12	Brundle	Brabham-Yam.	69	
13	Nakajima	Tyrrell-Honda	68	
14	Hakkinen	Lotus-Judd	68	
15	Alboreto	Footwork-Ford	68	
16	Boutsen	Ligier-Lam.	68	
17	Capelli	Leyton H.-Ilmor	64	nose
r	Modena	Tyrrell-Honda	56	engine
dq	Mansell	Williams-Ren.	56	illegal pit stop
r	Suzuki,A.	Lola-Ford	40	gearbox
r	Prost	Ferrari	39	engine
r	Berger,G.	McLaren-Honda	37	engine
r	Pirro	Dallara-Judd	18	engine
r	Lehto	Dallara-Judd	14	gear lever
r	Blundell	Brabham-Yam.	12	suspension
r	Herbert	Lotus-Judd	1	engine

STARTING GRID:

1	Patrese	12	Modena
2	Berger,G.	13	Morbidelli
3	Senna	14	de Cesaris
4	Mansell	15	Blundell
5	Prost	16	Moreno
6	Alesi	17	Pirro
7	Gugelmin	18	Lehto
8	Martini	19	Brundle
9	Capelli	20	Boutsen
10	Schumacher,M.	21	Nakajima
11	Piquet	22	Herbert

+

Spanish

GRAND PRIX No: 514
DATE: September 29, 1991
VENUE: Barcelona
POLE LAP: Berger,G., 1m 18.751s
FASTEST LAP: Patrese, 1m 22.837s

Pn	Driver	Car	Laps	Time/Reason
1	Mansell	Williams-Ren.	65	1h 38m 41.541s
2	Prost	Ferrari	65	1h 38m 52.872s
3	Patrese	Williams-Ren.	65	1h 38m 57.450s
4	Alesi	Ferrari	65	1h 39m 04.313s
5	Senna	McLaren-Honda	65	1h 39m 43.943s
6	Schumacher,M.	Benetton-Ford	65	1h 40m 01.009s
7	Gugelmin	Leyton H.-Ilmor	64	
8	Lehto	Dallara-Judd	64	
9	Zanardi	Jordan-Ford	64	
10	Brundle	Brabham-Yam.	63	
11	Piquet	Benetton-Ford	63	
12	Tarquini	Fondmetal-Ford	63	
13	Martini	Minardi-Ferrari	63	
14	Morbidelli	Minardi-Ferrari	62	accident
15	Pirro	Dallara-Judd	62	
16	Modena	Tyrrell-Honda	62	
17	Nakajima	Tyrrell-Honda	62	
r	Blundell	Brabham-Yam.	49	engine
r	Comas	Ligier-Lam.	36	engine
r	Berger,G.	McLaren-Honda	33	engine
r	Alboreto	Footwork-Ford	23	engine
r	de Cesaris	Jordan-Ford	22	electrical
r	Hakkinen	Lotus-Judd	5	accident
r	Capelli	Leyton H.-Ilmor	1	accident
r	Bernard	Lola-Ford	0	accident
r	Boutsen	Ligier-Lam.	0	accident

STARTING GRID:

1	Berger,G.	12	Blundell
2	Mansell	13	Gugelmin
3	Senna	14	Modena
4	Patrese	15	Lehto
5	Schumacher,M.	16	Morbidelli
6	Prost	17	de Cesaris
7	Alesi	18	Nakajima
8	Capelli	19	Martini
9	Pirro	20	Zanardi
10	Piquet	21	Hakkinen
11	Brundle	22	Tarquini

+

Japanese

GRAND PRIX No:	515
DATE:	October 20, 1991
VENUE:	Suzuka
POLE LAP:	Berger,G., 1m 34.700s
FASTEST LAP:	Senna, 1m 41.532s

Pn	Driver	Car	Laps	Time/Reason
1	Berger,G.	McLaren-Honda	53	1h 32m 10.695s
2	Senna	McLaren-Honda	53	1h 32m 11.039s
3	Patrese	Williams-Ren.	53	1h 33m 07.426s
4	Prost	Ferrari	53	1h 33m 31.456s
5	Brundle	Brabham-Yam.	52	
6	Modena	Tyrrell-Honda	52	
7	Piquet	Benetton-Ford	52	
8	Gugelmin	Leyton H.-Ilmor	52	
9	Boutsen	Ligier-Lam.	52	
10	Caffi	Footwork-Ford	51	
11	Tarquini	Fondmetal-Ford	50	
r	Comas	Ligier-Lam.	41	engine
r	Martini	Minardi-Ferrari	39	electrical
r	Schumacher,M.	Benetton-Ford	34	engine
r	Herbert	Lotus-Judd	31	engine
r	Nakajima	Tyrrell-Honda	30	accident
r	Suzuki,A.	Lola-Ford	26	engine
r	Morbidelli	Minardi-Ferrari	15	wheel bearing
r	Mansell	Williams-Ren.	9	accident
r	Zanardi	Jordan-Ford	7	gearbox
r	Hakkinen	Lotus-Judd	4	spun off
r	de Cesaris	Jordan-Ford	1	accident
r	Lehto	Dallara-Judd	1	accident
r	Pirro	Dallara-Judd	1	accident
r	Wendlinger	Leyton H.-Ilmor	1	accident
r	Alesi	Ferrari	0	engine

STARTING GRID:

1	Berger,G.	12	Zanardi
2	Senna	13	Modena
3	Mansell	14	Nakajima
4	Prost	15	Pirro
5	Patrese	16	Boutsen
6	Alesi	17	Gugelmin
7	Martini	18	Brundle
8	Morbidelli	19	Comas
9	Schumacher,M.	20	Hakkinen
10	de Cesaris	21	Wendlinger
11	Lehto	22	Herbert

+

Australian

GRAND PRIX No:	516
DATE:	November 3, 1991
VENUE:	Adelaide
POLE LAP:	Senna, 1m 14.041s
FASTEST LAP:	Berger,G., 1m 41.141s

Pn	Driver	Car	Laps	Time/Reason
1	Senna	McLaren-Honda	14	24m 34.889s
2	Mansell	Williams-Ren.	14	24m 36.158s
3	Berger,G.	McLaren-Honda	14	24m 40.019s
4	Piquet	Benetton-Ford	14	25m 05.002s
5	Patrese	Williams-Ren.	14	25m 25.436s
6	Morbidelli	Ferrari	14	25m 25.968s
7	Pirro	Dallara-Judd	14	25m 27.260s
8	de Cesaris	Jordan-Ford	14	25m 35.330s
9	Zanardi	Jordan-Ford	14	25m 50.466s
10	Modena	Tyrrell-Honda	14	25m 55.269s
11	Herbert	Lotus-Judd	14	25m 56.972s
12	Lehto	Dallara-Judd	14	26m 13.418s
13	Alboreto	Footwork-Ford	14	26m 14.202s
14	Gugelmin	Leyton H.-Ilmor	13	
15	Caffi	Footwork-Ford	13	
16	Moreno	Minardi-Ferrari	13	
17	Blundell	Brabham-Yam.	13	
18	Comas	Ligier-Lam.	13	
19	Hakkinen	Lotus-Judd	13	
20	Wendlinger	Leyton H.-Ilmor	12	
r	Martini	Minardi-Ferrari	8	accident
r	Schumacher,M.	Benetton-Ford	5	accident
r	Alesi	Ferrari	5	accident
r	Larini	Lamborghini	5	accident
r	Boutsen	Ligier-Lam.	5	accident
r	Nakajima	Tyrrell-Honda	4	accident

STARTING GRID:

1	Senna	12	de Cesaris
2	Berger,G.	13	Pirro
3	Mansell	14	Gugelmin
4	Patrese	15	Alboreto
5	Piquet	16	Zanardi
6	Schumacher,M.	17	Blundell
7	Alesi	18	Moreno
8	Morbidelli	19	Larini
9	Modena	20	Boutsen
10	Martini	21	Herbert
11	Lehto	22	Comas

+

South African

GRAND PRIX No:	517
DATE:	March 1, 1992
VENUE:	Kyalami
POLE LAP:	Mansell, 1m 15.486s
FASTEST LAP:	Mansell, 1m 17.578s

Pn	Driver	Car	Laps	Time/Reason
1	Mansell	Williams-Ren.	72	1h 36m 45.320s
2	Patrese	Williams-Ren.	72	1h 37m 09.680s
3	Senna	McLaren-Honda	72	1h 37m 29.995s
4	Schumacher,M.	Benetton-Ford	72	1h 37m 33.183s
5	Berger,G.	McLaren-Honda	72	1h 37m 58.954s
6	Herbert	Lotus-Ford	71	
7	Comas	Ligier-Renault	71	
8	Suzuki,A.	Footwork-MH	70	
9	Hakkinen	Lotus-Ford	70	
10	Alboreto	Footwork-MH	70	
11	Gugelmin	Jordan-Yamaha	70	
12	Katayama	Larrousse-Lam.	68	
13	Van de Poele	Brabham-Judd	68	
r	Grouillard	Tyrrell-Ilmor	62	clutch
r	Boutsen	Ligier-Renault	60	engine
r	Martini	Dallara-Ferrari	56	clutch
r	Morbidelli	Minardi-Lam.	55	engine
r	Lehto	Dallara-Ferrari	46	transmission
r	Fittipaldi,C.	Minardi-Lam.	43	electrical
r	de Cesaris	Tyrrell-Ilmor	41	engine
r	Alesi	Ferrari	40	engine
r	Capelli	Ferrari	28	engine
r	Tarquini	Fondmetal-Ford	23	engine
r	Wendlinger	March-Ilmor	13	overheating
r	Gachot	Larrousse-Lam.	8	suspension
r	Brundle	Benetton-Ford	1	clutch

STARTING GRID:

1	Mansell	12	Grouillard
2	Senna	13	Comas
3	Berger,G.	14	Boutsen
4	Patrese	15	Tarquini
5	Alesi	16	Suzuki,A.
6	Schumacher,M.	17	Alboreto
7	Wendlinger	18	Katayama
8	Brundle	19	Morbidelli
9	Capelli	20	Fittipaldi,C.
10	de Cesaris	21	Hakkinen
11	Herbert	22	Gachot +

Mexican

GRAND PRIX No:	518
DATE:	March 22, 1992
VENUE:	Mexico City
POLE LAP:	Mansell, 1m 16.346s
FASTEST LAP:	Berger,G., 1m 17.711s

Pn	Driver	Car	Laps	Time/Reason
1	Mansell	Williams-Ren.	69	1h 31m 53.587s
2	Patrese	Williams-Ren.	69	1h 32m 06.558s
3	Schumacher,M.	Benetton-Ford	69	1h 32m 15.016s
4	Berger,G.	McLaren-Honda	69	1h 32m 26.934s
5	de Cesaris	Tyrrell-Ilmor	68	
6	Hakkinen	Lotus-Ford	68	
7	Herbert	Lotus-Ford	68	
8	Lehto	Dallara-Ferrari	68	
9	Comas	Ligier-Renault	67	
10	Boutsen	Ligier-Renault	67	
11	Gachot	Larrousse-Lam.	66	
12	Katayama	Larrousse-Lam.	66	
13	Alboreto	Footwork-MH	65	
r	Brundle	Benetton-Ford	47	overheating
r	Tarquini	Fondmetal-Ford	45	clutch
r	Chiesa	Fondmetal-Ford	37	spun off
r	Martini	Dallara-Ferrari	36	handling
r	Alesi	Ferrari	31	engine
r	Morbidelli	Minardi-Lam.	29	spun off
r	Modena	Jordan-Yamaha	17	gearbox
r	Grouillard	Tyrrell-Ilmor	12	engine
r	Senna	McLaren-Honda	11	transmission
r	Fittipaldi,C.	Minardi-Lam.	2	spun off
r	Gugelmin	Jordan-Yamaha	0	engine
r	Capelli	Ferrari	0	accident
r	Wendlinger	March-Ilmor	0	accident

STARTING GRID:

1	Mansell	12	Herbert
2	Patrese	13	Gachot
3	Schumacher,M.	14	Tarquini
4	Brundle	15	Modena
5	Berger,G.	16	Grouillard
6	Senna	17	Fittipaldi,C.
7	Lehto	18	Hakkinen
8	Gugelmin	19	Wendlinger
9	Martini	20	Capelli
10	Alesi	21	Morbidelli
11	de Cesaris	22	Boutsen +

Brazilian

GRAND PRIX No:	519
DATE:	April 5, 1992
VENUE:	Interlagos
POLE LAP:	Mansell, 1m 15.703s
FASTEST LAP:	Patrese, 1m 19.490s

Pn	Driver	Car	Laps	Time/Reason
1	Mansell	Williams-Ren.	71	1h 36m 51.856s
2	Patrese	Williams-Ren.	71	1h 37m 21.186s
3	Schumacher,M.	Benetton-Ford	70	
4	Alesi	Ferrari	70	
5	Capelli	Ferrari	70	
6	Alboreto	Footwork-MH	70	
7	Morbidelli	Minardi-Lam.	69	
8	Lehto	Dallara-Ferrari	69	
9	Katayama	Larrousse-Lam.	68	
10	Hakkinen	Lotus-Ford	67	
r	Tarquini	Fondmetal-Ford	62	engine
r	Wendlinger	March-Ilmor	56	clutch
r	Fittipaldi,C.	Minardi-Lam.	55	gearbox
r	Grouillard	Tyrrell-Ilmor	53	engine
r	Comas	Ligier-Renault	43	engine
r	Herbert	Lotus-Ford	37	accident
r	Boutsen	Ligier-Renault	37	accident
r	Gugelmin	Jordan-Yamaha	37	gearbox
r	Brundle	Benetton-Ford	31	accident
r	Martini	Dallara-Ferrari	25	clutch
r	Gachot	Larrousse-Lam.	24	supension
r	de Cesaris	Tyrrell-Ilmor	22	electrical
r	Senna	McLaren-Honda	18	electrical
r	Berger,G.	McLaren-Honda	4	overheating
r	Suzuki,A.	Footwork-MH	3	engine
r	Modena	Jordan-Yamaha	1	gearbox

STARTING GRID:

1	Mansell	12	Modena
2	Patrese	13	de Cesaris
3	Senna	14	Alboreto
4	Berger,G.	15	Comas
5	Schumacher,M.	16	Lehto
6	Alesi	17	Grouillard
7	Brundle	18	Gachot
8	Martini	19	Tarquini
9	Wendlinger	20	Fittipaldi,C.
10	Boutsen	21	Gugelmin
11	Capelli	22	Suzuki,A. +

Spanish

GRAND PRIX No:	520
DATE:	May 3, 1992
VENUE:	Barcelona
POLE LAP:	Mansell, 1m 20.190s
FASTEST LAP:	Mansell, 1m 42.503s

Pn	Driver	Car	Laps	Time/Reason
1	Mansell	Williams-Ren.	65	1h 56m 10.674s
2	Schumacher,M.	Benetton-Ford	65	1h 56m 34.588s
3	Alesi	Ferrari	65	1h 56m 37.136s
4	Berger,G.	McLaren-Honda	65	1h 57m 31.321s
5	Alboreto	Footwork-MH	64	
6	Martini	Dallara-Ferrari	63	
7	Suzuki,A.	Footwork-MH	63	
8	Wendlinger	March-Ilmor	63	
9	Senna	McLaren-Honda	62	spun off
10	Capelli	Ferrari	62	spun off
11	Fittipaldi,C.	Minardi-Lam.	61	
12	Belmondo	March-Ilmor	61	
r	Lehto	Dallara-Ferrari	56	spun off
r	Tarquini	Fondmetal-Ford	56	spun off
r	Hakkinen	Lotus-Ford	56	spun off
r	Comas	Ligier-Renault	55	spun off
r	Gachot	Larrousse-Lam.	35	engine
r	Grouillard	Tyrrell-Ilmor	30	spun off
r	Morbidelli	Minardi-Lam.	26	handling
r	Gugelmin	Jordan-Yamaha	24	spun off
r	Chiesa	Fondmetal-Ford	22	spun off
r	Patrese	Williams-Ren.	20	spun off
r	Herbert	Lotus-Ford	13	spun off
r	Boutsen	Ligier-Renault	11	engine
r	Brundle	Benetton-Ford	4	spun off
r	de Cesaris	Tyrrell-Ilmor	2	spun off

STARTING GRID:

1	Mansell	12	Lehto
2	Schumacher,M.	13	Martini
3	Senna	14	Boutsen
4	Patrese	15	Grouillard
5	Capelli	16	Alboreto
6	Brundle	17	Gugelmin
7	Berger,G.	18	Tarquini
8	Alesi	19	Suzuki,A.
9	Wendlinger	20	Chiesa
10	Comas	21	Hakkinen
11	de Cesaris	22	Fittipaldi,C. +

San Marino

GRAND PRIX No: 521
DATE: May 17, 1992
VENUE: Imola
POLE LAP: Mansell, 1m 21.842s
FASTEST LAP: Patrese, 1m 26.100s

Pn	Driver	Car	Laps	Time/Reason
1	Mansell	Williams-Ren.	60	1h 28m 40.927s
2	Patrese	Williams-Ren.	60	1h 28m 50.378s
3	Senna	McLaren-Honda	60	1h 29m 29.911s
4	Brundle	Benetton-Ford	60	1h 29m 33.934s
5	Alboreto	Footwork-MH	59	
6	Martini	Dallara-Ferrari	59	
7	Gugelmin	Jordan-Yamaha	58	
8	Grouillard	Tyrrell-Ilmor	58	
9	Comas	Ligier-Renault	58	
10	Suzuki,A.	Footwork-MH	58	
11	Lehto	Dallara-Ferrari	57	overheating
12	Wendlinger	March-Ilmor	57	
13	Belmondo	March-Ilmor	57	
14	de Cesaris	Tyrrell-Ilmor	55	fuel pressure
r	Katayama	Larrousse-Lam.	40	spun off
r	Alesi	Ferrari	39	accident
r	Berger,G.	McLaren-Honda	39	accident
r	Gachot	Larrousse-Lam.	32	spun off
r	Boutsen	Ligier-Renault	29	engine
r	Modena	Jordan-Yamaha	25	gearbox
r	Morbidelli	Minardi-Lam.	24	transmission
r	Tarquini	Fondmetal-Ford	24	overheating
r	Schumacher,M.	Benetton-Ford	20	spun off
r	Capelli	Ferrari	11	spun off
r	Fittipaldi,C.	Minardi-Lam.	8	transmission
r	Herbert	Lotus-Ford	8	gearbox

STARTING GRID:

1	Mansell	12	Wendlinger
2	Patrese	13	Comas
3	Senna	14	de Cesaris
4	Berger,G.	15	Martini
5	Schumacher,M.	16	Lehto
6	Brundle	17	Katayama
7	Alesi	18	Gugelmin
8	Capelli	19	Gachot
9	Alboreto	20	Grouillard
10	Boutsen	21	Morbidelli
11	Suzuki,A.	22	Tarquini +

Monaco

GRAND PRIX No: 522
DATE: May 31, 1992
VENUE: Monte Carlo
POLE LAP: Mansell, 1m 19.495s
FASTEST LAP: Mansell, 1m 21.598s

Pn	Driver	Car	Laps	Time/Reason
1	Senna	McLaren-Honda	78	1h 50m 59.372s
2	Mansell	Williams-Ren.	78	1h 50m 59.587s
3	Patrese	Williams-Ren.	78	1h 51m 31.215s
4	Schumacher,M.	Benetton-Ford	78	1h 51m 38.666s
5	Brundle	Benetton-Ford	78	1h 52m 20.719s
6	Gachot	Larrousse-Lam.	77	
7	Alboreto	Footwork-MH	77	
8	Fittipaldi,C.	Minardi-Lam.	77	
9	Lehto	Dallara-Ferrari	76	
10	Comas	Ligier-Renault	76	
11	Suzuki,A.	Footwork-MH	76	
12	Boutsen	Ligier-Renault	75	
r	Capelli	Ferrari	60	accident
r	Berger,G.	McLaren-Honda	32	gearbox
r	Hakkinen	Lotus-Ford	30	gearbox
r	Alesi	Ferrari	28	electrical
r	Gugelmin	Jordan-Yamaha	18	transmission
r	Herbert	Lotus-Ford	17	accident
r	Moreno	Andrea MJ	11	engine
r	de Cesaris	Tyrrell-Ilmor	9	gearbox
r	Tarquini	Fondmetal-Ford	9	engine
r	Modena	Jordan-Yamaha	6	accident
r	Grouillard	Tyrrell-Ilmor	4	transmission
r	Wendlinger	March-Ilmor	1	gearbox
r	Morbidelli	Minardi-Lam.	1	transmission
r	Martini	Dallara-Ferrari	0	accident

STARTING GRID:

1	Mansell	12	Morbidelli
2	Patrese	13	Gugelmin
3	Senna	14	Hakkinen
4	Alesi	15	Gachot
5	Berger,G.	16	Fittipaldi,C.
6	Schumacher,M.	17	Martini
7	Brundle	18	Suzuki,A.
8	Capelli	19	Lehto
9	Herbert	20	Wendlinger
10	de Cesaris	21	Modena
11	Alboreto	22	Boutsen +

Canadian

GRAND PRIX No: 523
DATE: June 14, 1992
VENUE: Montreal
POLE LAP: Senna, 1m 19.775s
FASTEST LAP: Berger,G., 1m 22.325s

Pn	Driver	Car	Laps	Time/Reason
1	Berger,G.	McLaren-Honda	69	1h 37m 08.299s
2	Schumacher,M.	Benetton-Ford	69	1h 37m 20.700s
3	Alesi	Ferrari	69	1h 38m 15.626s
4	Wendlinger	March-Ilmor	68	
5	de Cesaris	Tyrrell-Ilmor	68	
6	Comas	Ligier-Renault	68	
7	Alboreto	Footwork-MH	68	
8	Martini	Dallara-Ferrari	68	
9	Lehto	Dallara-Ferrari	68	
10	Boutsen	Ligier-Renault	67	
11	Morbidelli	Minardi-Lam.	67	
12	Grouillard	Tyrrell-Ilmor	67	
13	Fittipaldi,C.	Minardi-Lam.	65	gearbox
14	Belmondo	March-Ilmor	64	
r	Katayama	Larrousse-Lam.	61	engine
r	Brundle	Benetton-Ford	45	transmission
r	Patrese	Williams-Ren.	43	gearbox
r	Senna	McLaren-Honda	37	electrical
r	Modena	Jordan-Yamaha	36	transmission
r	Hakkinen	Lotus-Ford	35	gearbox
r	Herbert	Lotus-Ford	34	clutch
r	Capelli	Ferrari	18	accident
r	Mansell	Williams-Ren.	14	accident
r	Gugelmin	Jordan-Yamaha	14	transmission
dq	Gachot	Larrousse-Lam.	14	push start
r	Tarquini	Fondmetal-Ford	0	gearbox

STARTING GRID:

1	Senna	12	Wendlinger
2	Patrese	13	Morbidelli
3	Mansell	14	de Cesaris
4	Berger,G.	15	Martini
5	Schumacher,M.	16	Alboreto
6	Herbert	17	Modena
7	Brundle	18	Tarquini
8	Alesi	19	Gachot
9	Capelli	20	Belmondo
10	Hakkinen	21	Boutsen
11	Katayama	22	Comas +

French

GRAND PRIX No: 524
DATE: July 5, 1992
VENUE: Magny-Cours
POLE LAP: Mansell, 1m 13.864s
FASTEST LAP: Mansell, 1m 17.070s

Pn	Driver	Car	Laps	Time/Reason
1	Mansell	Williams-Ren.	69	1h 38m 08.459s
2	Patrese	Williams-Ren.	69	1h 38m 54.906s
3	Brundle	Benetton-Ford	69	1h 39m 21.038s
4	Hakkinen	Lotus-Ford	68	
5	Comas	Ligier-Renault	68	
6	Herbert	Lotus-Ford	68	
7	Alboreto	Footwork-MH	68	
8	Morbidelli	Minardi-Lam.	68	
9	Lehto	Dallara-Ferrari	67	
10	Martini	Dallara-Ferrari	67	
11	Grouillard	Tyrrell-Ilmor	67	
r	Alesi	Ferrari	61	engine
r	de Cesaris	Tyrrell-Ilmor	51	spun off
r	Katayama	Larrousse-Lam.	49	engine
r	Boutsen	Ligier-Renault	46	spun off
r	Capelli	Ferrari	38	electrical
r	Wendlinger	March-Ilmor	33	gearbox
r	Modena	Jordan-Yamaha	25	engine
r	Suzuki,A.	Footwork-MH	20	spun off
r	Schumacher,M.	Benetton-Ford	17	accident
r	Berger,G.	McLaren-Honda	10	engine
r	Tarquini	Fondmetal-Ford	6	throttle
r	Gugelmin	Jordan-Yamaha	0	accident
r	Gachot	Larrousse-Lam.	0	accident
r	Chiesa	Fondmetal-Ford	0	accident
r	Senna	McLaren-Honda	0	accident

STARTING GRID:

1	Mansell	12	Herbert
2	Patrese	13	Gachot
3	Senna	14	Alboreto
4	Berger,G.	15	Suzuki,A.
5	Schumacher,M.	16	Morbidelli
6	Alesi	17	Lehto
7	Brundle	18	Katayama
8	Capelli	19	de Cesaris
9	Boutsen	20	Modena
10	Comas	21	Wendlinger
11	Hakkinen	22	Grouillard +

British

GRAND PRIX No: 525

DATE: July 12, 1992

VENUE: Silverstone

POLE LAP: Mansell, 1m 18.965s

FASTEST LAP: Mansell, 1m 22.539s

Pn	Driver	Car	Laps	Time/Reason
1	Mansell	Williams-Ren.	59	1h 25m 42.991s
2	Patrese	Williams-Ren.	59	1h 26m 22.085s
3	Brundle	Benetton-Ford	59	1h 26m 31.386s
4	Schumacher,M.	Benetton-Ford	59	1h 26m 36.258s
5	Berger,G.	McLaren-Honda	59	1h 26m 38.786s
6	Hakkinen	Lotus-Ford	59	1h 27m 03.129s
7	Alboreto	Footwork-MH	58	
8	Comas	Ligier-Renault	58	
9	Capelli	Ferrari	58	
10	Boutsen	Ligier-Renault	57	
11	Grouillard	Tyrrell-Ilmor	57	
12	Suzuki,A.	Footwork-MH	57	
13	Lehto	Dallara-Ferrari	57	
14	Tarquini	Fondmetal-Ford	57	
15	Martini	Dallara-Ferrari	56	
16	Hill,D.	Brabham-Judd	55	
17	Morbidelli	Minardi-Lam.	53	oil pressure
r	Senna	McLaren-Honda	52	gearbox
r	de Cesaris	Tyrrell-Ilmor	46	spun off
r	Alesi	Ferrari	43	fire extinguisher
r	Modena	Jordan-Yamaha	43	engine
r	Gugelmin	Jordan-Yamaha	37	engine
r	Gachot	Larrousse-Lam.	32	wheel bearing
r	Herbert	Lotus-Ford	31	gearbox
r	Wendlinger	March-Ilmor	27	gearbox
r	Katayama	Larrousse-Lam.	27	clutch

STARTING GRID:

1	Mansell	12	Alboreto
2	Patrese	13	Boutsen
3	Senna	14	Capelli
4	Schumacher,M.	15	Tarquini
5	Berger,G.	16	Katayama
6	Brundle	17	Suzuki,A.
7	Herbert	18	de Cesaris
8	Alesi	19	Lehto
9	Hakkinen	20	Grouillard
10	Comas	21	Wendlinger
11	Gachot	22	Martini +

German

GRAND PRIX No: 526

DATE: July 26, 1992

VENUE: Hockenheim

POLE LAP: Mansell, 1m 37.960s

FASTEST LAP: Patrese, 1m 41.591s

Pn	Driver	Car	Laps	Time/Reason
1	Mansell	Williams-Ren.	45	1h 18m 22.032s
2	Senna	McLaren-Honda	45	1h 18m 26.532s
3	Schumacher,M.	Benetton-Ford	45	1h 18m 56.494s
4	Brundle	Benetton-Ford	45	1h 18m 58.991s
5	Alesi	Ferrari	45	1h 19m 34.639s
6	Comas	Ligier-Renault	45	1h 19m 58.530s
7	Boutsen	Ligier-Renault	45	1h 19m 59.212s
8	Patrese	Williams-Ren.	44	spun off
9	Alboreto	Footwork-MH	44	
10	Lehto	Dallara-Ferrari	44	
11	Martini	Dallara-Ferrari	44	
12	Morbidelli	Minardi-Lam.	44	
13	Belmondo	March-Ilmor	44	
14	Gachot	Larrousse-Lam.	44	
15	Gugelmin	Jordan-Yamaha	43	
16	Wendlinger	March-Ilmor	42	
r	Tarquini	Fondmetal-Ford	33	engine
r	de Cesaris	Tyrrell-Ilmor	25	engine
r	Herbert	Lotus-Ford	23	engine
r	Capelli	Ferrari	21	engine
r	Hakkinen	Lotus-Ford	21	engine
r	Berger,G.	McLaren-Honda	16	engine
r	Grouillard	Tyrrell-Ilmor	8	engine
r	Katayama	Larrousse-Lam.	8	spun off
r	Suzuki,A.	Footwork-MH	1	spun off
r	Zanardi	Minardi-Lam.	1	clutch

STARTING GRID:

1	Mansell	12	Capelli
2	Patrese	13	Hakkinen
3	Senna	14	Grouillard
4	Berger,G.	15	Suzuki,A.
5	Alesi	16	Katayama
6	Schumacher,M.	17	Alboreto
7	Comas	18	Martini
8	Boutsen	19	Tarquini
9	Brundle	20	de Cesaris
10	Wendlinger	21	Lehto
11	Herbert	22	Belmondo +

Hungarian

GRAND PRIX No: 527
DATE: August 16, 1992
VENUE: Hungaroring
POLE LAP: Patrese, 1m 15.476s
FASTEST LAP: Mansell, 1m 18.308s

Pn	Driver	Car	Laps	Time/Reason
1	Senna	McLaren-Honda	77	1h 46m 19.216s
2	Mansell	Williams-Ren.	77	1h 46m 59.355s
3	Berger,G.	McLaren-Honda	77	1h 47m 09.998s
4	Hakkinen	Lotus-Ford	77	1h 47m 13.529s
5	Brundle	Benetton-Ford	77	1h 47m 16.714s
6	Capelli	Ferrari	76	
7	Alboreto	Footwork-MH	75	
8	de Cesaris	Tyrrell-Ilmor	75	
9	Belmondo	March-Ilmor	74	
10	Gugelmin	Jordan-Yamaha	73	
11	Hill,D.	Brabham-Judd	73	
r	Schumacher,M.	Benetton-Ford	63	accident
r	Patrese	Williams-Ren.	55	engine
r	Martini	Dallara-Ferrari	40	gearbox
r	Katayama	Larrousse-Lam.	35	engine
r	Alesi	Ferrari	14	spun off
r	Gachot	Larrousse-Lam.	13	accident
r	Suzuki,A.	Footwork-MH	13	accident
r	Grouillard	Tyrrell-Ilmor	13	engine
r	Wendlinger	March-Ilmor	13	accident
r	Modena	Jordan-Yamaha	13	accident
r	Van de Poele	Fondmetal-Ford	2	accident
r	Tarquini	Fondmetal-Ford	0	accident
r	Herbert	Lotus-Ford	0	accident
r	Comas	Ligier-Renault	0	accident
r	Boutsen	Ligier-Renault	0	accident

STARTING GRID:

1	Patrese	12	Tarquini
2	Mansell	13	Herbert
3	Senna	14	Suzuki,A.
4	Schumacher,M.	15	Gachot
5	Berger,G.	16	Hakkinen
6	Brundle	17	Belmondo
7	Alboreto	18	Van de Poele
8	Comas	19	de Cesaris
9	Alesi	20	Katayama
10	Capelli	21	Gugelmin
11	Boutsen	22	Grouillard +

Belgian

GRAND PRIX No: 528
DATE: August 30, 1992
VENUE: Spa-Francorchamps
POLE LAP: Mansell, 1m 50.454s
FASTEST LAP: Schumacher,M., 1m 53.791s

Pn	Driver	Car	Laps	Time/Reason
1	Schumacher,M.	Benetton-Ford	44	1h 36m 10.721s
2	Mansell	Williams-Ren.	44	1h 36m 47.316s
3	Patrese	Williams-Ren.	44	1h 36m 54.618s
4	Brundle	Benetton-Ford	44	1h 36m 56.780s
5	Senna	McLaren-Honda	44	1h 37m 19.090s
6	Hakkinen	Lotus-Ford	44	1h 37m 20.751s
7	Lehto	Dallara-Ferrari	44	1h 37m 48.958s
8	de Cesaris	Tyrrell-Ilmor	43	
9	Suzuki,A.	Footwork-MH	43	
10	Van de Poele	Fondmetal-Ford	43	
11	Wendlinger	March-Ilmor	43	
12	Naspetti	March-Ilmor	43	
13	Herbert	Lotus-Ford	42	engine
14	Gugelmin	Jordan-Yamaha	42	
15	Modena	Jordan-Yamaha	42	
16	Morbidelli	Minardi-Lam.	42	
17	Katayama	Larrousse-Lam.	42	
18	Gachot	Larrousse-Lam.	40	accident
r	Boutsen	Ligier-Renault	27	accident
r	Capelli	Ferrari	25	engine
r	Tarquini	Fondmetal-Ford	25	engine
r	Alboreto	Footwork-MH	20	gearbox
r	Alesi	Ferrari	7	spun off
r	Grouillard	Tyrrell-Ilmor	1	accident
r	Martini	Dallara-Ferrari	0	spun off
r	Berger,G.	McLaren-Honda	0	clutch

STARTING GRID:

1	Mansell	12	Capelli
2	Senna	13	de Cesaris
3	Schumacher,M.	14	Alboreto
4	Patrese	15	Van de Poele
5	Alesi	16	Lehto
6	Berger,G.	17	Modena
7	Boutsen	18	Martini
8	Hakkinen	19	Wendlinger
9	Brundle	20	Gachot
10	Herbert	21	Naspetti
11	Tarquini	22	Grouillard +

Italian

GRAND PRIX No:	529
DATE:	September 13, 1992
VENUE:	Monza
POLE LAP:	Mansell, 1m 22.221s
FASTEST LAP:	Mansell, 1m 26.119s

Pn	Driver	Car	Laps	Time/Reason
1	Senna	McLaren-Honda	53	1h 18m 15.349s
2	Brundle	Benetton-Ford	53	1h 18m 32.399s
3	Schumacher,M.	Benetton-Ford	53	1h 18m 39.722s
4	Berger,G.	McLaren-Honda	53	1h 19m 40.839s
5	Patrese	Williams-Ren.	53	1h 19m 48.507s
6	de Cesaris	Tyrrell-Ilmor	52	
7	Alboreto	Footwork-MH	52	
8	Martini	Dallara-Ferrari	52	
9	Katayama	Larrousse-Lam.	50	transmission
10	Wendlinger	March-Ilmor	50	
11	Lehto	Dallara-Ferrari	47	engine
r	Gugelmin	Jordan-Yamaha	46	transmission
r	Mansell	Williams-Ren.	46	hydraulics
r	Boutsen	Ligier-Renault	41	electrical
r	Comas	Ligier-Renault	35	accident
r	Tarquini	Fondmetal-Ford	30	gearbox
r	Grouillard	Tyrrell-Ilmor	26	engine
r	Herbert	Lotus-Ford	18	engine
r	Naspetti	March-Ilmor	17	spin
r	Alesi	Ferrari	12	engine
r	Capelli	Ferrari	12	spun off
r	Morbidelli	Minardi-Lam.	12	engine
r	Gachot	Larrousse-Lam.	11	engine
r	Hakkinen	Lotus-Ford	5	engine
r	Suzuki,A.	Footwork-MH	2	accident
r	Van de Poele	Fondmetal-Ford	0	clutch

STARTING GRID:

1	Mansell	12	Morbidelli
2	Senna	13	Herbert
3	Alesi	14	Lehto
4	Patrese	15	Comas
5	Berger,G.	16	Alboreto
6	Schumacher,M.	17	Wendlinger
7	Capelli	18	Grouillard
8	Boutsen	19	Suzuki,A.
9	Brundle	20	Tarquini
10	Gachot	21	de Cesaris
11	Hakkinen	22	Martini +

Portuguese

GRAND PRIX No:	530
DATE:	September 27, 1992
VENUE:	Estoril
POLE LAP:	Mansell, 1m 13.041s
FASTEST LAP:	Senna, 1m 16.272s

Pn	Driver	Car	Laps	Time/Reason
1	Mansell	Williams-Ren.	71	1h 34m 46.659s
2	Berger,G.	McLaren-Honda	71	1h 35m 24.192s
3	Senna	McLaren-Honda	70	
4	Brundle	Benetton-Ford	70	
5	Hakkinen	Lotus-Ford	70	
6	Alboreto	Footwork-MH	70	
7	Schumacher,M.	Benetton-Ford	69	
8	Boutsen	Ligier-Renault	69	
9	de Cesaris	Tyrrell-Ilmor	69	
10	Suzuki,A.	Footwork-MH	68	
11	Naspetti	March-Ilmor	68	
12	Fittipaldi,C.	Minardi-Lam.	68	
13	Modena	Jordan-Yamaha	68	
14	Morbidelli	Minardi-Lam.	68	
r	Lehto	Dallara-Ferrari	51	chassis
r	Wendlinger	March-Ilmor	48	gearbox
r	Comas	Ligier-Renault	47	engine
r	Katayama	Larrousse-Lam.	46	accident
r	Patrese	Williams-Ren.	43	accident
r	Martini	Dallara-Ferrari	43	puncture
r	Capelli	Ferrari	34	engine
r	Grouillard	Tyrrell-Ilmor	27	gearbox
r	Gachot	Larrousse-Lam.	25	fuel pressure
r	Gugelmin	Jordan-Yamaha	19	electrical
r	Alesi	Ferrari	12	spun off
r	Herbert	Lotus-Ford	2	accident

STARTING GRID:

1	Mansell	12	de Cesaris
2	Patrese	13	Gachot
3	Senna	14	Comas
4	Berger,G.	15	Grouillard
5	Schumacher,M.	16	Capelli
6	Brundle	17	Suzuki,A.
7	Hakkinen	18	Morbidelli
8	Alboreto	19	Lehto
9	Herbert	20	Gugelmin
10	Alesi	21	Martini
11	Boutsen	22	Wendlinger +

Japanese

GRAND PRIX No:	531
DATE:	October 25, 1992
VENUE:	Suzuka
POLE LAP:	Mansell, 1m 37.360s
FASTEST LAP:	Mansell, 1m 40.646s

Pn	Driver	Car	Laps	Time/Reason
1	Patrese	Williams-Ren.	53	1h 33m 09.553s
2	Berger,G.	McLaren-Honda	53	1h 33m 23.282s
3	Brundle	Benetton-Ford	53	1h 34m 25.056s
4	de Cesaris	Tyrrell-Ilmor	52	
5	Alesi	Ferrari	52	
6	Fittipaldi,C.	Minardi-Lam.	52	
7	Modena	Jordan-Yamaha	52	
8	Suzuki,A.	Footwork-MH	52	
9	Lehto	Dallara-Ferrari	52	
10	Martini	Dallara-Ferrari	52	
11	Katayama	Larrousse-Lam.	52	
12	Larini	Ferrari	52	
13	Naspetti	March-Ilmor	51	
14	Morbidelli	Minardi-Lam.	51	
15	Alboreto	Footwork-MH	51	
r	Mansell	Williams-Ren.	44	engine
r	Hakkinen	Lotus-Ford	44	engine
r	Gachot	Larrousse-Lam.	39	accident
r	Comas	Ligier-Renault	36	oil pressure
r	Lammers	March-Ilmor	27	gearbox
r	Gugelmin	Jordan-Yamaha	22	accident
r	Herbert	Lotus-Ford	15	transmission
r	Schumacher,M.	Benetton-Ford	13	gearbox
r	Grouillard	Tyrrell-Ilmor	6	accident
r	Boutsen	Ligier-Renault	3	gearbox
r	Senna	McLaren-Honda	2	engine

STARTING GRID:

1	Mansell	12	Fittipaldi,C.
2	Patrese	13	Brundle
3	Senna	14	Morbidelli
4	Berger,G.	15	Alesi
5	Schumacher,M.	16	Suzuki,A.
6	Herbert	17	Modena
7	Hakkinen	18	Gachot
8	Comas	19	Martini
9	de Cesaris	20	Katayama
10	Boutsen	21	Grouillard
11	Larini	22	Lehto

+

Australian

GRAND PRIX No:	532
DATE:	November 8, 1992
VENUE:	Adelaide
POLE LAP:	Mansell, 1m 13.732s
FASTEST LAP:	Schumacher,M., 1m 16.078s

Pn	Driver	Car	Laps	Time/Reason
1	Berger,G.	McLaren-Honda	81	1h 46m 54.786s
2	Schumacher,M.	Benetton-Ford	81	1h 46m 55.527s
3	Brundle	Benetton-Ford	81	1h 47m 48.942s
4	Alesi	Ferrari	80	
5	Boutsen	Ligier-Renault	80	
6	Modena	Jordan-Yamaha	80	
7	Hakkinen	Lotus-Ford	80	
8	Suzuki,A.	Footwork-MH	79	
9	Fittipaldi,C.	Minardi-Lam.	79	
10	Morbidelli	Minardi-Lam.	79	
11	Larini	Ferrari	79	
12	Lammers	March-Ilmor	78	
13	Herbert	Lotus-Ford	77	
r	Lehto	Dallara-Ferrari	70	transmission
r	Naspetti	March-Ilmor	55	gearbox
r	Gachot	Larrousse-Lam.	51	fuel pressure
r	Patrese	Williams-Ren.	50	electrical
r	Katayama	Larrousse-Lam.	35	differential
r	de Cesaris	Tyrrell-Ilmor	29	fire
r	Mansell	Williams-Ren.	18	accident
r	Senna	McLaren-Honda	18	accident
r	Gugelmin	Jordan-Yamaha	7	accident
r	Comas	Ligier-Renault	4	engine
r	Alboreto	Footwork-MH	0	accident
r	Grouillard	Tyrrell-Ilmor	0	accident
r	Martini	Dallara-Ferrari	0	accident

STARTING GRID:

1	Mansell	12	Herbert
2	Senna	13	Grouillard
3	Patrese	14	Martini
4	Berger,G.	15	Modena
5	Schumacher,M.	16	Morbidelli
6	Alesi	17	Fittipaldi,C.
7	de Cesaris	18	Suzuki,A.
8	Brundle	19	Larini
9	Comas	20	Gugelmin
10	Hakkinen	21	Gachot
11	Alboreto	22	Boutsen

+

South African

GRAND PRIX No:	533
DATE:	March 14, 1993
VENUE:	Kyalami
POLE LAP:	Prost, 1m 15.696s
FASTEST LAP:	Prost, 1m 19.492s

Pn	Driver	Car	Laps	Time/Reason
1	Prost	Williams-Ren.	72	1h 38m 45.082s
2	Senna	McLaren-Ford	72	1h 40m 04.906s
3	Blundell	Ligier-Renault	71	
4	Fittipaldi,C.	Minardi-Ford	71	
5	Lehto	Sauber-Ilmor	70	
6	Berger,G.	Ferrari	69	engine
7	Warwick	Footwork-MH	69	spun off
r	Brundle	Ligier-Renault	57	spun off
r	Alboreto	Lola-Ferrari	55	engine
r	Comas	Larrousse-Lam.	51	engine
r	Patrese	Benetton-Ford	46	spun off
r	Schumacher,M.	Benetton-Ford	39	accident
r	Herbert	Lotus-Ford	38	fuel pressure
r	Wendlinger	Sauber-Ilmor	33	electrical
r	Barrichello	Jordan-Hart	31	gearbox
r	Alesi	Ferrari	30	hydraulics
r	Alliot	Larrousse-Lam.	27	spun off
r	Barbazza	Minardi-Ford	21	accident
r	Suzuki,A.	Footwork-MH	21	accident
r	Badoer	Lola-Ferrari	20	gearbox
r	Hill,D.	Williams-Ren.	16	accident
r	Zanardi	Lotus-Ford	16	accident
r	Andretti,Michael	McLaren-Ford	4	accident
r	Capelli	Jordan-Hart	2	accident
r	Katayama	Tyrrell-Yamaha	1	transmission
r	de Cesaris	Tyrrell-Yamaha	0	transmission

STARTING GRID:

1	Prost	12	Brundle
2	Senna	13	Fittipaldi,C.
3	Schumacher,M.	14	Barrichello
4	Hill,D.	15	Berger,G.
5	Alesi	16	Zanardi
6	Lehto	17	Herbert
7	Patrese	18	Capelli
8	Blundell	19	Comas
9	Andretti,Michael	20	Suzuki,A.
10	Wendlinger	21	Katayama
11	Alliot	22	Warwick

+

Brazilian

GRAND PRIX No:	534
DATE:	March 28, 1993
VENUE:	Interlagos
POLE LAP:	Prost, 1m 15.866s
FASTEST LAP:	Schumacher,M., 1m 20.024s

Pn	Driver	Car	Laps	Time/Reason
1	Senna	McLaren-Ford	71	1h 51m 15.485s
2	Hill,D.	Williams-Ren.	71	1h 51m 32.110s
3	Schumacher,M.	Benetton-Ford	71	1h 52m 00.921s
4	Herbert	Lotus-Ford	71	1h 52m 02.042s
5	Blundell	Ligier-Renault	71	1h 52m 07.612s
6	Zanardi	Lotus-Ford	70	
7	Alliot	Larrousse-Lam.	70	
8	Alesi	Ferrari	70	
9	Warwick	Footwork-MH	69	
10	Comas	Larrousse-Lam.	69	
11	Alboreto	Lola-Ferrari	68	
12	Badoer	Lola-Ferrari	68	
r	Wendlinger	Sauber-Ilmor	61	engine
r	Lehto	Sauber-Ilmor	52	electrical
r	de Cesaris	Tyrrell-Yamaha	48	electrical
r	Prost	Williams-Ren.	29	accident
r	Fittipaldi,C.	Minardi-Ford	28	accident
r	Suzuki,A.	Footwork-MH	27	accident
r	Katayama	Tyrrell-Yamaha	26	accident
r	Barrichello	Jordan-Hart	13	gearbox
r	Patrese	Benetton-Ford	3	suspension
r	Brundle	Ligier-Renault	0	accident
r	Barbazza	Minardi-Ford	0	accident
r	Andretti,Michael	McLaren-Ford	0	accident
r	Berger,G.	Ferrari	0	accident

STARTING GRID:

1	Prost	12	Herbert
2	Hill,D.	13	Berger,G.
3	Senna	14	Barrichello
4	Schumacher,M.	15	Zanardi
5	Andretti,Michael	16	Brundle
6	Patrese	17	Comas
7	Lehto	18	Warwick
8	Wendlinger	19	Suzuki,A.
9	Alesi	20	Fittipaldi,C.
10	Blundell	21	Badoer
11	Alliot	22	Katayama

+

European

GRAND PRIX No: 535
DATE: April 11, 1993
VENUE: Donington Park
POLE LAP: Prost, 1m 10.458s
FASTEST LAP: Senna, 1m 18.029s

Pn	Driver	Car	Laps	Time/Reason
1	Senna	McLaren-Ford	76	1h 50m 46.570s
2	Hill,D.	Williams-Ren.	76	1h 52m 09.769s
3	Prost	Williams-Ren.	75	
4	Herbert	Lotus-Ford	75	
5	Patrese	Benetton-Ford	74	
6	Barbazza	Minardi-Ford	74	
7	Fittipaldi,C.	Minardi-Ford	73	
8	Zanardi	Lotus-Ford	72	
9	Comas	Larrousse-Lam.	72	
10	Barrichello	Jordan-Hart	70	fuel pressure
11	Alboreto	Lola-Ferrari	70	
r	Warwick	Footwork-MH	66	gearbox
r	Boutsen	Jordan-Hart	61	throttle
r	de Cesaris	Tyrrell-Yamaha	55	gearbox
r	Alesi	Ferrari	36	suspension
r	Suzuki,A.	Footwork-MH	29	gearbox
r	Alliot	Larrousse-Lam.	27	accident
r	Schumacher,M.	Benetton-Ford	22	accident
r	Blundell	Ligier-Renault	20	accident
r	Berger,G.	Ferrari	19	suspension
r	Lehto	Sauber-Ilmor	13	handling
r	Katayama	Tyrrell-Yamaha	11	clutch
r	Brundle	Ligier-Renault	7	accident
r	Andretti,Michael	McLaren-Ford	0	accident
r	Wendlinger	Sauber-Ilmor	0	accident

STARTING GRID:

1	Prost	12	Barrichello
2	Hill,D.	13	Zanardi
3	Schumacher,M.	14	Warwick
4	Senna	15	Alliot
5	Wendlinger	16	Fittipaldi,C.
6	Andretti,Michael	17	Comas
7	Lehto	18	Katayama
8	Berger,G.	19	Boutsen
9	Alesi	20	Barbazza
10	Patrese	21	Blundell
11	Herbert	22	Brundle +

San Marino

GRAND PRIX No: 536
DATE: April 25, 1993
VENUE: Imola
POLE LAP: Prost, 1m 22.070s
FASTEST LAP: Prost, 1m 26.128s

Pn	Driver	Car	Laps	Time/Reason
1	Prost	Williams-Ren.	61	1h 33m 20.413s
2	Schumacher,M.	Benetton-Ford	61	1h 33m 52.823s
3	Brundle	Ligier-Renault	60	
4	Lehto	Sauber-Ilmor	59	engine
5	Alliot	Larrousse-Lam.	59	
6	Barbazza	Minardi-Ford	59	
7	Badoer	Lola-Ferrari	58	
8	Herbert	Lotus-Ford	57	engine
9	Suzuki,A.	Footwork-MH	54	
r	Zanardi	Lotus-Ford	53	accident
r	Wendlinger	Sauber-Ilmor	48	engine
r	Senna	McLaren-Ford	42	hydraulics
r	Alesi	Ferrari	40	clutch
r	Fittipaldi,C.	Minardi-Ford	36	steering
r	Andretti,Michael	McLaren-Ford	32	spun off
r	Warwick	Footwork-MH	29	spun off
r	Katayama	Tyrrell-Yamaha	22	engine
r	Hill,D.	Williams-Ren.	20	spun off
r	Comas	Larrousse-Lam.	18	oil pressure
r	de Cesaris	Tyrrell-Yamaha	18	gearbox
r	Barrichello	Jordan-Hart	17	spun off
r	Berger,G.	Ferrari	8	gearbox
r	Boutsen	Jordan-Hart	1	gearbox
r	Patrese	Benetton-Ford	0	accident
r	Blundell	Ligier-Renault	0	accident

STARTING GRID:

1	Prost	12	Herbert
2	Hill,D.	13	Barrichello
3	Schumacher,M.	14	Alliot
4	Senna	15	Warwick
5	Wendlinger	16	Lehto
6	Andretti,Michael	17	Comas
7	Blundell	18	de Cesaris
8	Berger,G.	19	Boutsen
9	Alesi	20	Zanardi
10	Brundle	21	Suzuki,A.
11	Patrese	22	Katayama +

Spanish

GRAND PRIX No: 537
DATE: May 9, 1993
VENUE: Barcelona
POLE LAP: Prost, 1m 17.809s
FASTEST LAP: Schumacher,M., 1m 20.989s

Pn	Driver	Car	Laps	Time/Reason
1	Prost	Williams-Ren.	65	1h 32m 27.685s
2	Senna	McLaren-Ford	65	1h 32m 44.558s
3	Schumacher,M.	Benetton-Ford	65	1h 32m 54.810s
4	Patrese	Benetton-Ford	64	
5	Andretti,Michael	McLaren-Ford	64	
6	Berger,G.	Ferrari	63	
7	Blundell	Ligier-Renault	63	
8	Fittipaldi,C.	Minardi-Ford	63	
9	Comas	Larrousse-Lam.	63	
10	Suzuki,A.	Footwork-MH	63	
11	Boutsen	Jordan-Hart	62	
12	Barrichello	Jordan-Hart	62	
13	Warwick	Footwork-MH	62	
14	Zanardi	Lotus-Ford	60	engine
r	Lehto	Sauber-Ilmor	53	engine
r	Badoer	Lola-Ferrari	43	clutch
r	Wendlinger	Sauber-Ilmor	42	fuel pressure
dq	de Cesaris	Tyrrell-Yamaha	42	push start
r	Hill,D.	Williams-Ren.	41	engine
r	Alesi	Ferrari	40	engine
r	Barbazza	Minardi-Ford	37	accident
r	Alliot	Larrousse-Lam.	26	gearbox
r	Brundle	Ligier-Renault	11	accident
r	Katayama	Tyrrell-Yamaha	11	accident
r	Herbert	Lotus-Ford	2	suspension

STARTING GRID:

1	Prost	12	Blundell
2	Hill,D.	13	Alliot
3	Senna	14	Comas
4	Schumacher,M.	15	Zanardi
5	Patrese	16	Warwick
6	Wendlinger	17	Barrichello
7	Andretti,Michael	18	Brundle
8	Alesi	19	Suzuki,A.
9	Lehto	20	Fittipaldi,C.
10	Herbert	21	Boutsen
11	Berger,G.	22	Badoer +

Monaco

GRAND PRIX No: 538
DATE: May 23, 1993
VENUE: Monte Carlo
POLE LAP: Prost, 1m 20.557s
FASTEST LAP: Prost, 1m 23.604s

Pn	Driver	Car	Laps	Time/Reason
1	Senna	McLaren-Ford	78	1h 52m 10.947s
2	Hill,D.	Williams-Ren.	78	1h 53m 03.065s
3	Alesi	Ferrari	78	1h 53m 14.309s
4	Prost	Williams-Ren.	77	
5	Fittipaldi,C.	Minardi-Ford	76	
6	Brundle	Ligier-Renault	76	
7	Zanardi	Lotus-Ford	76	
8	Andretti,Michael	McLaren-Ford	76	
9	Barrichello	Jordan-Hart	76	
10	de Cesaris	Tyrrell-Yamaha	76	
11	Barbazza	Minardi-Ford	75	
12	Alliot	Larrousse-Lam.	75	
13	Wendlinger	Sauber-Ilmor	74	
14	Berger,G.	Ferrari	70	accident
r	Herbert	Lotus-Ford	61	accident
r	Patrese	Benetton-Ford	53	engine
r	Comas	Larrousse-Lam.	51	accident
r	Suzuki,A.	Footwork-MH	46	accident
r	Warwick	Footwork-MH	43	throttle
r	Schumacher,M.	Benetton-Ford	32	suspension
r	Katayama	Tyrrell-Yamaha	31	oil leak
r	Alboreto	Lola-Ferrari	28	gearbox
r	Lehto	Sauber-Ilmor	23	accident
r	Boutsen	Jordan-Hart	12	suspension
r	Blundell	Ligier-Renault	3	suspension

STARTING GRID:

1	Prost	12	Warwick
2	Schumacher,M.	13	Brundle
3	Senna	14	Herbert
4	Hill,D.	15	Alliot
5	Alesi	16	Barrichello
6	Patrese	17	Fittipaldi,C.
7	Berger,G.	18	Suzuki,A.
8	Wendlinger	19	de Cesaris
9	Andretti,Michael	20	Zanardi
10	Comas	21	Blundell
11	Lehto	22	Katayama +

Canadian

GRAND PRIX No:	539
DATE:	June 13, 1993
VENUE:	Montreal
POLE LAP:	Prost, 1m 18.987s
FASTEST LAP:	Schumacher,M., 1m 21.500s

Pn	Driver	Car	Laps	Time/Reason
1	Prost	Williams-Ren.	69	1h 36m 41.822s
2	Schumacher,M.	Benetton-Ford	69	1h 36m 56.349s
3	Hill,D.	Williams-Ren.	69	1h 37m 34.507s
4	Berger,G.	Ferrari	68	
5	Brundle	Ligier-Renault	68	
6	Wendlinger	Sauber-Ilmor	68	
7	Lehto	Sauber-Ilmor	68	
8	Comas	Larrousse-Lam.	68	
9	Fittipaldi,C.	Minardi-Ford	67	
10	Herbert	Lotus-Ford	67	
11	Zanardi	Lotus-Ford	67	
12	Boutsen	Jordan-Hart	67	
13	Suzuki,A.	Footwork-MH	66	
14	Andretti,Michael	McLaren-Ford	66	
15	Badoer	Lola-Ferrari	65	
16	Warwick	Footwork-MH	65	
17	Katayama	Tyrrell-Yamaha	64	
18	Senna	McLaren-Ford	62	alternator
r	Patrese	Benetton-Ford	52	cramp
r	de Cesaris	Tyrrell-Yamaha	45	accident
r	Barbazza	Minardi-Ford	33	gearbox
r	Alesi	Ferrari	23	engine
r	Blundell	Ligier-Renault	13	accident
r	Barrichello	Jordan-Hart	10	electrical
r	Alliot	Larrousse-Lam.	8	gear lever

STARTING GRID:

1	Prost	12	Andretti,Michael
2	Hill,D.	13	Comas
3	Schumacher,M.	14	Barrichello
4	Patrese	15	Alliot
5	Berger,G.	16	Suzuki,A.
6	Alesi	17	Fittipaldi,C.
7	Brundle	18	Warwick
8	Senna	19	de Cesaris
9	Wendlinger	20	Herbert
10	Blundell	21	Zanardi
11	Lehto	22	Katayama +

French

GRAND PRIX No:	540
DATE:	July 4, 1993
VENUE:	Magny-Cours
POLE LAP:	Hill,D., 1m 14.382s
FASTEST LAP:	Schumacher,M., 1m 19.256s

Pn	Driver	Car	Laps	Time/Reason
1	Prost	Williams-Ren.	72	1h 38m 35.241s
2	Hill,D.	Williams-Ren.	72	1h 38m 35.583s
3	Schumacher,M.	Benetton-Ford	72	1h 38m 56.450s
4	Senna	McLaren-Ford	72	1h 39m 07.646s
5	Brundle	Ligier-Renault	72	1h 39m 09.036s
6	Andretti,Michael	McLaren-Ford	71	
7	Barrichello	Jordan-Hart	71	
8	Fittipaldi,C.	Minardi-Ford	71	
9	Alliot	Larrousse-Lam.	70	
10	Patrese	Benetton-Ford	70	
11	Boutsen	Jordan-Hart	70	
12	Suzuki,A.	Footwork-MH	70	
13	Warwick	Footwork-MH	70	
14	Berger,G.	Ferrari	70	
15	de Cesaris	Tyrrell-Yamaha	68	
16	Comas	Larrousse-Lam.	66	gearbox
r	Alesi	Ferrari	47	engine
r	Badoer	Lola-Ferrari	28	suspension
r	Wendlinger	Sauber-Ilmor	25	gearbox
r	Lehto	Sauber-Ilmor	22	gearbox
r	Blundell	Ligier-Renault	20	spun off
r	Herbert	Lotus-Ford	16	spun off
r	Barbazza	Minardi-Ford	16	gearbox
r	Katayama	Tyrrell-Yamaha	9	oil leak
r	Zanardi	Lotus-Ford	3	suspension

STARTING GRID:

1	Hill,D.	12	Patrese
2	Prost	13	Suzuki,A.
3	Brundle	14	Berger,G.
4	Blundell	15	Warwick
5	Senna	16	Andretti,Michael
6	Alesi	17	Zanardi
7	Schumacher,M.	18	Lehto
8	Barrichello	19	Herbert
9	Comas	20	Boutsen
10	Alliot	21	Katayama
11	Wendlinger	22	Badoer +

British

GRAND PRIX No: 541
DATE: July 11, 1993
VENUE: Silverstone
POLE LAP: Prost, 1m 19.006s
FASTEST LAP: Hill,D., 1m 22.515s

Pn	Driver	Car	Laps	Time/Reason
1	Prost	Williams-Ren.	59	1h 25m 38.189s
2	Schumacher,M.	Benetton-Ford	59	1h 25m 45.849s
3	Patrese	Benetton-Ford	59	1h 26m 55.671s
4	Herbert	Lotus-Ford	59	1h 26m 56.596s
5	Senna	McLaren-Ford	58	out of fuel
6	Warwick	Footwork-MH	58	
7	Blundell	Ligier-Renault	58	
8	Lehto	Sauber-Ilmor	58	
9	Alesi	Ferrari	58	
10	Barrichello	Jordan-Hart	58	
11	Alliot	Larrousse-Lam.	57	
12	Fittipaldi,C.	Minardi-Ford	56	gearbox
13	Katayama	Tyrrell-Yamaha	55	
14	Brundle	Ligier-Renault	53	gearbox
uc	de Cesaris	Tyrrell-Yamaha	43	
r	Hill,D.	Williams-Ren.	41	engine
r	Zanardi	Lotus-Ford	41	engine
r	Boutsen	Jordan-Hart	41	spun off
r	Badoer	Lola-Ferrari	32	wheel
r	Martini	Minardi-Ford	31	driver discomfort
r	Wendlinger	Sauber-Ilmor	24	accident
r	Berger,G.	Ferrari	10	suspension
r	Suzuki,A.	Footwork-MH	8	spun off
r	Andretti,Michael	McLaren-Ford	0	spun off
r	Comas	Larrousse-Lam.	0	transmission

STARTING GRID:

1	Prost	12	Alesi
2	Hill,D.	13	Berger,G.
3	Schumacher,M.	14	Zanardi
4	Senna	15	Barrichello
5	Patrese	16	Lehto
6	Brundle	17	Comas
7	Herbert	18	Wendlinger
8	Warwick	19	Fittipaldi,C.
9	Blundell	20	Martini
10	Suzuki,A.	21	de Cesaris
11	Andretti,Michael	22	Katayama +

German

GRAND PRIX No: 542
DATE: July 25, 1993
VENUE: Hockenheim
POLE LAP: Prost, 1m 38.748s
FASTEST LAP: Schumacher,M., 1m 41.859s

Pn	Driver	Car	Laps	Time/Reason
1	Prost	Williams-Ren.	45	1h 18m 40.885s
2	Schumacher,M.	Benetton-Ford	45	1h 18m 57.549s
3	Blundell	Ligier-Renault	45	1h 19m 40.234s
4	Senna	McLaren-Ford	45	1h 19m 49.114s
5	Patrese	Benetton-Ford	45	1h 20m 12.401s
6	Berger,G.	Ferrari	45	1h 20m 15.639s
7	Alesi	Ferrari	45	1h 20m 16.726s
8	Brundle	Ligier-Renault	44	
9	Wendlinger	Sauber-Ilmor	44	
10	Herbert	Lotus-Ford	44	
11	Fittipaldi,C.	Minardi-Ford	44	
12	Alliot	Larrousse-Lam.	44	
13	Boutsen	Jordan-Hart	44	
14	Martini	Minardi-Ford	44	
15	Hill,D.	Williams-Ren.	43	puncture
16	Alboreto	Lola-Ferrari	43	
17	Warwick	Footwork-MH	43	
r	Barrichello	Jordan-Hart	34	wheel
r	Katayama	Tyrrell-Yamaha	28	spun off
r	Lehto	Sauber-Ilmor	22	throttle
r	Zanardi	Lotus-Ford	19	spun off
r	Suzuki,A.	Footwork-MH	9	gearbox
r	Andretti,Michael	McLaren-Ford	4	accident
r	Badoer	Lola-Ferrari	4	suspension
r	de Cesaris	Tyrrell-Yamaha	1	gearbox
r	Comas	Larrousse-Lam.	0	clutch

STARTING GRID:

1	Prost	12	Andretti,Michael
2	Hill,D.	13	Herbert
3	Schumacher,M.	14	Wendlinger
4	Senna	15	Zanardi
5	Blundell	16	Comas
6	Brundle	17	Barrichello
7	Patrese	18	Lehto
8	Suzuki,A.	19	de Cesaris
9	Berger,G.	20	Fittipaldi,C.
10	Alesi	21	Katayama
11	Warwick	22	Martini +

Hungarian

GRAND PRIX No: 543
DATE: August 15, 1993
VENUE: Hungaroring
POLE LAP: Prost, 1m 14.631s
FASTEST LAP: Prost, 1m 19.633s

Pn	Driver	Car	Laps	Time/Reason
1	Hill,D.	Williams-Ren.	77	1h 47m 39.098s
2	Patrese	Benetton-Ford	77	1h 48m 51.013s
3	Berger,G.	Ferrari	77	1h 48m 57.140s
4	Warwick	Footwork-MH	76	
5	Brundle	Ligier-Renault	76	
6	Wendlinger	Sauber-Ilmor	76	
7	Blundell	Ligier-Renault	76	
8	Alliot	Larrousse-Lam.	75	
9	Boutsen	Jordan-Hart	75	
10	Katayama	Tyrrell-Yamaha	73	
11	de Cesaris	Tyrrell-Yamaha	72	
12	Prost	Williams-Ren.	70	
r	Martini	Minardi-Ford	59	accident
r	Comas	Larrousse-Lam.	54	oil leak
r	Zanardi	Lotus-Ford	45	gearbox
r	Suzuki,A.	Footwork-MH	41	spun off
r	Alboreto	Lola-Ferrari	39	engine
r	Herbert	Lotus-Ford	38	spun off
r	Badoer	Lola-Ferrari	37	spun off
r	Schumacher,M.	Benetton-Ford	26	spun off
r	Fittipaldi,C.	Minardi-Ford	22	accident
r	Alesi	Ferrari	22	accident
r	Lehto	Sauber-Ilmor	18	engine
r	Senna	McLaren-Ford	17	throttle
r	Andretti,Michael	McLaren-Ford	15	throttle
r	Barrichello	Jordan-Hart	0	accident

STARTING GRID:

1	Prost	12	Blundell
2	Hill,D.	13	Brundle
3	Schumacher,M.	14	Fittipaldi,C.
4	Senna	15	Lehto
5	Patrese	16	Barrichello
6	Berger,G.	17	Wendlinger
7	Martini	18	Comas
8	Alesi	19	Alliot
9	Warwick	20	Herbert
10	Suzuki,A.	21	Zanardi
11	Andretti,Michael	22	de Cesaris

Belgian

GRAND PRIX No: 544
DATE: August 29, 1993
VENUE: Spa-Francorchamps
POLE LAP: Prost, 1m 47.571s
FASTEST LAP: Prost, 1m 51.095s

Pn	Driver	Car	Laps	Time/Reason
1	Hill,D.	Williams-Ren.	44	1h 24m 32.124s
2	Schumacher,M.	Benetton-Ford	44	1h 24m 35.792s
3	Prost	Williams-Ren.	44	1h 24m 47.112s
4	Senna	McLaren-Ford	44	1h 26m 11.887s
5	Herbert	Lotus-Ford	43	
6	Patrese	Benetton-Ford	43	
7	Brundle	Ligier-Renault	43	
8	Andretti,Michael	McLaren-Ford	43	
9	Lehto	Sauber-Ilmor	43	
10	Berger,G.	Ferrari	42	accident
11	Blundell	Ligier-Renault	42	accident
12	Alliot	Larrousse-Lam.	42	
13	Badoer	Lola-Ferrari	42	
14	Alboreto	Lola-Ferrari	41	
15	Katayama	Tyrrell-Yamaha	40	
r	Comas	Larrousse-Lam.	37	fuel pump
r	Warwick	Footwork-MH	28	electrical
r	Wendlinger	Sauber-Ilmor	27	engine
r	de Cesaris	Tyrrell-Yamaha	24	engine
r	Fittipaldi,C.	Minardi-Ford	15	accident
r	Martini	Minardi-Ford	15	spun off
r	Suzuki,A.	Footwork-MH	14	suspension
r	Barrichello	Jordan-Hart	11	wheel
r	Alesi	Ferrari	4	suspension
r	Boutsen	Jordan-Hart	0	gearbox

STARTING GRID:

1	Prost	12	Wendlinger
2	Hill,D.	13	Barrichello
3	Schumacher,M.	14	Andretti,Michael
4	Alesi	15	Blundell
5	Senna	16	Berger,G.
6	Suzuki,A.	17	de Cesaris
7	Warwick	18	Alliot
8	Patrese	19	Comas
9	Lehto	20	Boutsen
10	Herbert	21	Martini
11	Brundle	22	Fittipaldi,C. +

Italian

GRAND PRIX No: 545
DATE: September 12, 1993
VENUE: Monza
POLE LAP: Prost, 1m 21.179s
FASTEST LAP: Hill,D., 1m 23.575s

Pn	Driver	Car	Laps	Time/Reason
1	Hill,D.	Williams-Ren.	53	1h 17m 07.509s
2	Alesi	Ferrari	53	1h 17m 47.521s
3	Andretti,Michael	McLaren-Ford	52	
4	Wendlinger	Sauber-Ilmor	52	
5	Patrese	Benetton-Ford	52	
6	Comas	Larrousse-Lam.	51	
7	Martini	Minardi-Ford	51	accident
8	Fittipaldi,C.	Minardi-Ford	51	accident
9	Alliot	Larrousse-Lam.	51	
10	Badoer	Lola-Ferrari	51	
11	Lamy	Lotus-Ford	49	engine
12	Prost	Williams-Ren.	48	engine
13	de Cesaris	Tyrrell-Yamaha	47	oil pressure
14	Katayama	Tyrrell-Yamaha	47	
r	Alboreto	Lola-Ferrari	23	suspension
r	Schumacher,M.	Benetton-Ford	21	engine
r	Blundell	Ligier-Renault	20	accident
r	Berger,G.	Ferrari	15	suspension
r	Herbert	Lotus-Ford	14	accident
r	Brundle	Ligier-Renault	8	accident
r	Senna	McLaren-Ford	8	accident
r	Suzuki,A.	Footwork-MH	0	accident
r	Warwick	Footwork-MH	0	accident
r	Lehto	Sauber-Ilmor	0	accident
r	Barrichello	Jordan-Hart	0	accident
r	Apicella	Jordan-Hart	0	accident

STARTING GRID:

1	Prost	12	Brundle
2	Hill,D.	13	Lehto
3	Alesi	14	Blundell
4	Senna	15	Wendlinger
5	Schumacher,M.	16	Alliot
6	Berger,G.	17	Katayama
7	Herbert	18	de Cesaris
8	Suzuki,A.	19	Barrichello
9	Andretti,Michael	20	Comas
10	Patrese	21	Alboreto
11	Warwick	22	Martini

+

Portuguese

GRAND PRIX No: 546
DATE: September 26, 1993
VENUE: Estoril
POLE LAP: Hill,D., 1m 11.494s
FASTEST LAP: Hill,D., 1m 14.859s

Pn	Driver	Car	Laps	Time/Reason
1	Schumacher,M.	Benetton-Ford	71	1h 32m 46.309s
2	Prost	Williams-Ren.	71	1h 32m 47.291s
3	Hill,D.	Williams-Ren.	71	1h 32m 54.515s
4	Alesi	Ferrari	71	1h 33m 53.914s
5	Wendlinger	Sauber-Ilmor	70	
6	Brundle	Ligier-Renault	70	
7	Lehto	Sauber-Ilmor	69	
8	Martini	Minardi-Ford	69	
9	Fittipaldi,C.	Minardi-Ford	69	
10	Alliot	Larrousse-Lam.	69	
11	Comas	Larrousse-Lam.	68	
12	de Cesaris	Tyrrell-Yamaha	68	
13	Barrichello	Jordan-Hart	68	
14	Badoer	Lola-Ferrari	68	
15	Warwick	Footwork-MH	63	accident
16	Patrese	Benetton-Ford	63	accident
r	Lamy	Lotus-Ford	61	accident
r	Herbert	Lotus-Ford	60	accident
r	Blundell	Ligier-Renault	51	accident
r	Alboreto	Lola-Ferrari	38	gearbox
r	Berger,G.	Ferrari	35	suspension
r	Hakkinen	McLaren-Ford	32	accident
r	Suzuki,A.	Footwork-MH	27	gearbox
r	Senna	McLaren-Ford	19	engine
r	Katayama	Tyrrell-Yamaha	12	accident
r	Naspetti	Jordan-Hart	8	engine

STARTING GRID:

1	Hill,D.	12	Lehto
2	Prost	13	Wendlinger
3	Hakkinen	14	Herbert
4	Senna	15	Barrichello
5	Alesi	16	Suzuki,A.
6	Schumacher,M.	17	de Cesaris
7	Patrese	18	Lamy
8	Berger,G.	19	Martini
9	Warwick	20	Alliot
10	Blundell	21	Katayama
11	Brundle	22	Comas

+

Japanese

GRAND PRIX No:	547
DATE:	October 24, 1993
VENUE:	Suzuka
POLE LAP:	Prost, 1m 37.154s
FASTEST LAP:	Prost, 1m 41.176s

Pn	Driver	Car	Laps	Time/Reason
1	Senna	McLaren-Ford	53	1h 40m 27.912s
2	Prost	Williams-Ren.	53	1h 40m 39.347s
3	Hakkinen	McLaren-Ford	53	1h 40m 54.041s
4	Hill,D.	Williams-Ren.	53	1h 41m 51.450s
5	Barrichello	Jordan-Hart	53	1h 42m 03.013s
6	Irvine	Jordan-Hart	53	1h 42m 14.333s
7	Blundell	Ligier-Renault	52	
8	Lehto	Sauber-Ilmor	52	
9	Brundle	Ligier-Renault	51	accident
10	Martini	Minardi-Ford	51	
11	Herbert	Lotus-Ford	51	
12	Suzuki,T.	Larrousse-Lam.	51	
13	Lamy	Lotus-Ford	49	accident
14	Warwick	Footwork-MH	48	accident
r	Patrese	Benetton-Ford	45	accident
r	Berger,G.	Ferrari	40	engine
r	Suzuki,A.	Footwork-MH	28	spun off
r	Katayama	Tyrrell-Yamaha	26	engine
r	Gounon	Minardi-Ford	26	withdrew
r	Wendlinger	Sauber-Ilmor	25	throttle
r	Comas	Larrousse-Lam.	17	engine
r	Schumacher,M.	Benetton-Ford	10	accident
r	Alesi	Ferrari	7	electrical
r	de Cesaris	Tyrrell-Yamaha	0	accident

STARTING GRID:

1	Prost	13	Katayama
2	Senna	14	Alesi
3	Hakkinen	15	Brundle
4	Schumacher,M.	16	Wendlinger
5	Berger,G.	17	Blundell
6	Hill,D.	18	de Cesaris
7	Warwick	19	Herbert
8	Irvine	20	Lamy
9	Suzuki,A.	21	Comas
10	Patrese	22	Martini
11	Lehto	23	Suzuki,T.
12	Barrichello	24	Gounon

Australian

GRAND PRIX No:	548
DATE:	November 7, 1993
VENUE:	Adelaide
POLE LAP:	Senna, 1m 13.371s
FASTEST LAP:	Hill,D., 1m 15.381s

Pn	Driver	Car	Laps	Time/Reason
1	Senna	McLaren-Ford	79	1h 43m 27.476s
2	Prost	Williams-Ren.	79	1h 43m 36.735s
3	Hill,D.	Williams-Ren.	79	1h 44m 01.378s
4	Alesi	Ferrari	78	
5	Berger,G.	Ferrari	78	
6	Brundle	Ligier-Renault	78	
7	Suzuki,A.	Footwork-MH	78	
8	Patrese	Benetton-Ford	77	fuel pressure
9	Blundell	Ligier-Renault	77	
10	Warwick	Footwork-MH	77	
11	Barrichello	Jordan-Hart	76	
12	Comas	Larrousse-Lam.	75	
13	de Cesaris	Tyrrell-Yamaha	74	
14	Suzuki,T.	Larrousse-Lam.	73	
15	Wendlinger	Sauber-Ilmor	56	brakes
r	Lehto	Sauber-Ilmor	34	throttle
r	Gounon	Minardi-Ford	28	spun off
r	Hakkinen	McLaren-Ford	19	brake
r	Schumacher,M.	Benetton-Ford	11	engine
r	Katayama	Tyrrell-Yamaha	10	accident
r	Irvine	Jordan-Hart	9	accident
r	Herbert	Lotus-Ford	5	suspension
r	Martini	Minardi-Ford	0	gearbox
r	Lamy	Lotus-Ford	0	accident

STARTING GRID:

1	Senna	13	Barrichello
2	Prost	14	Blundell
3	Hill,D.	15	de Cesaris
4	Schumacher,M.	16	Martini
5	Hakkinen	17	Warwick
6	Berger,G.	18	Katayama
7	Alesi	19	Irvine
8	Brundle	20	Herbert
9	Patrese	21	Comas
10	Suzuki,A.	22	Gounon
11	Wendlinger	23	Lamy
12	Lehto	24	Suzuki,T.

Brazilian

GRAND PRIX No: 549
DATE: March 27, 1994
VENUE: Interlagos
POLE LAP: Senna, 1m 15.962s
FASTEST LAP: Schumacher,M., 1m 18.455s

Pn	Driver	Car	Laps	Time/Reason
1	Schumacher,M.	Benetton-Ford	71	1h 35m 38.759s
2	Hill,D.	Williams-Ren.	70	
3	Alesi	Ferrari	70	
4	Barrichello	Jordan-Hart	70	
5	Katayama	Tyrrell-Yamaha	69	
6	Wendlinger	Sauber-Merc.	69	
7	Herbert	Lotus-MH	69	
8	Martini	Minardi-Ford	69	
9	Comas	Larrousse-Ford	68	
10	Lamy	Lotus-MH	68	
11	Panis	Ligier-Renault	68	
12	Brabham,D.	Simtek-Ford	67	
r	Senna	Williams-Ren.	55	spun off
r	Brundle	McLaren-Peug.	34	accident
r	Irvine	Jordan-Hart	34	accident
r	Verstappen	Benetton-Ford	34	accident
r	Bernard	Ligier-Renault	33	accident
r	Blundell	Tyrrell-Yamaha	21	accident
r	Fittipaldi,C.	Footwork-Ford	21	gearbox
r	Frentzen	Sauber-Merc.	15	spun off
r	Hakkinen	McLaren-Peug.	13	fire
r	Alboreto	Minardi-Ford	7	electrical
r	Morbidelli	Footwork-Ford	5	gearbox
r	Berger,G.	Ferrari	5	engine
r	Beretta	Larrousse-Ford	2	accident
r	Gachot	Pacific-Ilmor	1	accident

STARTING GRID:

1	Senna	12	Blundell
2	Schumacher,M.	13	Comas
3	Alesi	14	Barrichello
4	Hill,D.	15	Martini
5	Frentzen	16	Irvine
6	Morbidelli	17	Berger,G.
7	Wendlinger	18	Brundle
8	Hakkinen	19	Panis
9	Verstappen	20	Bernard
10	Katayama	21	Herbert
11	Fittipaldi,C.	22	Alboreto

+

Pacific

GRAND PRIX No: 550
DATE: April 17, 1994
VENUE: Aida
POLE LAP: Senna, 1m 10.218s
FASTEST LAP: Schumacher,M., 1m 14.023s

Pn	Driver	Car	Laps	Time/Reason
1	Schumacher,M.	Benetton-Ford	83	1h 47m 01.693s
2	Berger,G.	Ferrari	83	1h 47m 16.993s
3	Barrichello	Jordan-Hart	82	
4	Fittipaldi,C.	Footwork-Ford	82	
5	Frentzen	Sauber-Merc.	82	
6	Comas	Larrousse-Ford	80	
7	Herbert	Lotus-MH	80	
8	Lamy	Lotus-MH	79	
9	Panis	Ligier-Renault	78	
10	Bernard	Ligier-Renault	78	
11	Ratzenberger	Simtek-Ford	78	
r	Morbidelli	Footwork-Ford	69	engine
r	Wendlinger	Sauber-Merc.	69	accident
r	Alboreto	Minardi-Ford	69	accident
r	Brundle	McLaren-Peug.	67	engine
r	Martini	Minardi-Ford	63	brakes
r	Verstappen	Benetton-Ford	54	spun off
r	Hill,D.	Williams-Ren.	49	transmission
r	Suzuki,A.	Jordan-Hart	44	steering
r	Katayama	Tyrrell-Yamaha	42	engine
r	Hakkinen	McLaren-Peug.	19	gearbox
r	Beretta	Larrousse-Ford	14	electrical
r	Brabham,D.	Simtek-Ford	2	engine
r	Senna	Williams-Ren.	0	accident
r	Blundell	Tyrrell-Yamaha	0	accident
r	Larini	Ferrari	0	accident

STARTING GRID:

1	Senna	12	Blundell
2	Schumacher,M.	13	Morbidelli
3	Hill,D.	14	Katayama
4	Hakkinen	15	Alboreto
5	Berger,G.	16	Comas
6	Brundle	17	Martini
7	Larini	18	Bernard
8	Barrichello	19	Wendlinger
9	Fittipaldi,C.	20	Suzuki,A.
10	Verstappen	21	Beretta
11	Frentzen	22	Panis

+

San Marino

GRAND PRIX No: 551
DATE: May 1, 1994
VENUE: Imola
POLE LAP: Senna, 1m 21.548s
FASTEST LAP: Hill,D., 1m 24.335s

Pn	Driver	Car	Laps	Time/Reason
1	Schumacher,M.	Benetton-Ford	58	1h 28m 28.642s
2	Larini	Ferrari	58	1h 29m 23.584s
3	Hakkinen	McLaren-Peug.	58	1h 29m 39.321s
4	Wendlinger	Sauber-Merc.	58	1h 29m 42.300s
5	Katayama	Tyrrell-Yamaha	57	
6	Hill,D.	Williams-Ren.	57	
7	Frentzen	Sauber-Merc.	57	
8	Brundle	McLaren-Peug.	57	
9	Blundell	Tyrrell-Yamaha	56	
10	Herbert	Lotus-MH	56	
11	Panis	Ligier-Renault	56	
12	Bernard	Ligier-Renault	56	
13	Fittipaldi,C.	Footwork-Ford	54	brakes
r	de Cesaris	Jordan-Hart	49	accident
r	Alboreto	Minardi-Ford	44	wheel
r	Morbidelli	Footwork-Ford	40	engine
r	Martini	Minardi-Ford	37	spun off
r	Brabham,D.	Simtek-Ford	27	accident
r	Gachot	Pacific-Ilmor	23	oil pressure
r	Beretta	Larrousse-Ford	17	engine
r	Berger,G.	Ferrari	16	handling
r	Senna	Williams-Ren.	5	fatal accident
r	Comas	Larrousse-Ford	5	accident
r	Lehto	Benetton-Ford	0	accident
r	Lamy	Lotus-MH	0	accident

STARTING GRID:

1	Senna	14	Martini
2	Schumacher,M.	15	Alboreto
3	Berger,G.	16	Fittipaldi,C.
4	Hill,D.	17	Bernard
5	Lehto	18	Comas
6	Larini	19	Panis
7	Frentzen	20	Herbert
8	Hakkinen	21	de Cesaris
9	Katayama	22	Lamy
10	Wendlinger	23	Beretta
11	Morbidelli	24	Brabham,D.
12	Blundell	25	Gachot
13	Brundle		

Monaco

GRAND PRIX No: 552
DATE: May 15, 1994
VENUE: Monte Carlo
POLE LAP: Schumacher,M., 1m 18.560s
FASTEST LAP: Schumacher,M., 1m 21.076s

Pn	Driver	Car	Laps	Time/Reason
1	Schumacher,M.	Benetton-Ford	78	1h 49m 55.372s
2	Brundle	McLaren-Peug.	78	1h 50m 32.650s
3	Berger,G.	Ferrari	78	1h 51m 12.196s
4	de Cesaris	Jordan-Hart	77	
5	Alesi	Ferrari	77	
6	Alboreto	Minardi-Ford	77	
7	Lehto	Benetton-Ford	77	
8	Beretta	Larrousse-Ford	76	
9	Panis	Ligier-Renault	76	
10	Comas	Larrousse-Ford	75	
11	Lamy	Lotus-MH	73	
r	Herbert	Lotus-MH	68	gearbox
r	Belmondo	Pacific-Ilmor	53	spun off
r	Gachot	Pacific-Ilmor	49	gearbox
r	Fittipaldi,C.	Footwork-Ford	47	gearbox
r	Brabham,D.	Simtek-Ford	45	accident
r	Blundell	Tyrrell-Yamaha	40	engine
r	Katayama	Tyrrell-Yamaha	38	gearbox
r	Bernard	Ligier-Renault	34	spun off
r	Barrichello	Jordan-Hart	27	electrical
r	Hill,D.	Williams-Ren.	0	accident
r	Hakkinen	McLaren-Peug.	0	accident
r	Morbidelli	Footwork-Ford	0	accident
r	Martini	Minardi-Ford	0	accident
dns	Frentzen	Sauber-Merc.		withdrew
dns	Wendlinger	Sauber-Merc.		injured

STARTING GRID:

1	Schumacher,M.	12	Alboreto
2	Hakkinen	13	Comas
3	Berger,G.	14	de Cesaris
4	Hill,D.	15	Barrichello
5	Alesi	16	Herbert
6	Fittipaldi,C.	17	Lehto
7	Morbidelli	18	Beretta
8	Brundle	19	Lamy
9	Martini	20	Panis
10	Blundell	21	Bernard
11	Katayama	22	Brabham,D. +

Spanish

GRAND PRIX No: 553
DATE: May 29, 1994
VENUE: Barcelona
POLE LAP: Schumacher,M., 1m 21.908s
FASTEST LAP: Schumacher,M., 1m 25.155s

Pn	Driver	Car	Laps	Time/Reason
1	Hill,D.	Williams-Ren.	65	1h 36m 14.374s
2	Schumacher,M.	Benetton-Ford	65	1h 36m 38.540s
3	Blundell	Tyrrell-Yamaha	65	1h 37m 41.343s
4	Alesi	Ferrari	64	
5	Martini	Minardi-Ford	64	
6	Irvine	Jordan-Hart	64	
7	Panis	Ligier-Renault	63	
8	Bernard	Ligier-Renault	62	
9	Zanardi	Lotus-MH	62	
10	Brabham,D.	Simtek-Ford	61	
11	Brundle	McLaren-Peug.	59	transmission
r	Lehto	Benetton-Ford	53	engine
r	Hakkinen	McLaren-Peug.	48	engine
r	Herbert	Lotus-MH	41	spun off
r	Barrichello	Jordan-Hart	39	gearbox
r	Fittipaldi,C.	Footwork-Ford	35	engine
r	Coulthard	Williams-Ren.	32	electrical
r	Gachot	Pacific-Ilmor	32	rear wing
r	Berger,G.	Ferrari	27	gearbox
r	Morbidelli	Footwork-Ford	24	fuel system
r	Frentzen	Sauber-Merc.	21	gearbox
r	Comas	Larrousse-Ford	19	water leak
r	Katayama	Tyrrell-Yamaha	16	engine
r	Alboreto	Minardi-Ford	4	engine
r	Belmondo	Pacific-Ilmor	2	spun off
dns	Beretta	Larrousse-Ford	0	engine on parade

STARTING GRID:

1	Schumacher,M.	12	Frentzen
2	Hill,D.	13	Irvine
3	Hakkinen	14	Alboreto
4	Lehto	15	Morbidelli
5	Barrichello	16	Comas
6	Alesi	17	Beretta
7	Berger,G.	18	Martini
8	Brundle	19	Panis
9	Coulthard	20	Bernard
10	Katayama	21	Fittipaldi,C.
11	Blundell	22	Herbert

+

Canadian

GRAND PRIX No: 554
DATE: June 12, 1994
VENUE: Montreal
POLE LAP: Schumacher,M., 1m 26.178s
FASTEST LAP: Schumacher,M., 1m 28.927s

Pn	Driver	Car	Laps	Time/Reason
1	Schumacher,M.	Benetton-Ford	69	1h 44m 31.887s
2	Hill,D.	Williams-Ren.	69	1h 45m 11.547s
3	Alesi	Ferrari	69	1h 45m 45.275s
4	Berger,G.	Ferrari	69	1h 45m 47.496s
5	Coulthard	Williams-Ren.	68	
dq	Fittipaldi,C.	Footwork-Ford	68	underweight
6	Lehto	Benetton-Ford	68	
7	Barrichello	Jordan-Hart	68	
8	Herbert	Lotus-MH	68	
9	Martini	Minardi-Ford	68	
10	Blundell	Tyrrell-Yamaha	67	accident
11	Alboreto	Minardi-Ford	67	
12	Panis	Ligier-Renault	67	
13	Bernard	Ligier-Renault	66	
14	Brabham,D.	Simtek-Ford	65	
15	Zanardi	Lotus-MH	62	engine
r	Hakkinen	McLaren-Peug.	61	engine
r	Beretta	Larrousse-Ford	57	engine
r	Morbidelli	Footwork-Ford	50	gearbox
r	Gachot	Pacific-Ilmor	47	oil pressure
r	Comas	Larrousse-Ford	45	clutch
r	Katayama	Tyrrell-Yamaha	44	spun off
r	Irvine	Jordan-Hart	40	accident
r	de Cesaris	Sauber-Merc.	24	oil leak
r	Frentzen	Sauber-Merc.	5	accident
r	Brundle	McLaren-Peug.	3	electrical

STARTING GRID:

1	Schumacher,M.	12	Brundle
2	Alesi	13	Blundell
3	Berger,G.	14	de Cesaris
4	Hill,D.	15	Martini
5	Coulthard	16	Fittipaldi,C.
6	Barrichello	17	Herbert
7	Hakkinen	18	Alboreto
8	Irvine	19	Panis
9	Katayama	20	Lehto
10	Frentzen	21	Comas
11	Morbidelli	22	Beretta

+

French

GRAND PRIX No: 555
DATE: July 3, 1994
VENUE: Magny-Cours
POLE LAP: Hill,D., 1m 16.282s
FASTEST LAP: Hill,D., 1m 19.678s

Pn	Driver	Car	Laps	Time/Reason
1	Schumacher,M.	Benetton-Ford	72	1h 38m 35.704s
2	Hill,D.	Williams-Ren.	72	1h 38m 48.446s
3	Berger,G.	Ferrari	72	1h 39m 28.469s
4	Frentzen	Sauber-Merc.	71	
5	Martini	Minardi-Ford	70	
6	de Cesaris	Sauber-Merc.	70	
7	Herbert	Lotus-MH	70	
8	Fittipaldi,C.	Footwork-Ford	70	
9	Gounon	Simtek-Ford	68	
10	Blundell	Tyrrell-Yamaha	67	
11	Comas	Larrousse-Ford	66	engine
r	Katayama	Tyrrell-Yamaha	53	spun off
r	Hakkinen	McLaren-Peug.	48	engine
r	Mansell	Williams-Ren.	45	transmission
r	Alesi	Ferrari	41	accident
r	Barrichello	Jordan-Hart	41	accident
r	Bernard	Ligier-Renault	40	gearbox
r	Beretta	Larrousse-Ford	36	engine
r	Brundle	McLaren-Peug.	29	engine
r	Morbidelli	Footwork-Ford	28	accident
r	Panis	Ligier-Renault	28	accident
r	Brabham,D.	Simtek-Ford	28	engine
r	Verstappen	Benetton-Ford	25	spun off
r	Irvine	Jordan-Hart	24	spun off
r	Alboreto	Minardi-Ford	21	engine
r	Zanardi	Lotus-MH	20	engine

STARTING GRID:

1	Hill,D.	12	Brundle
2	Mansell	13	Panis
3	Schumacher,M.	14	Katayama
4	Alesi	15	Bernard
5	Berger,G.	16	Martini
6	Irvine	17	Blundell
7	Barrichello	18	Fittipaldi,C.
8	Verstappen	19	Herbert
9	Hakkinen	20	Comas
10	Frentzen	21	Alboreto
11	de Cesaris	22	Morbidelli +

British

GRAND PRIX No: 556
DATE: July 10, 1994
VENUE: Silverstone
POLE LAP: Hill,D., 1m 24.960s
FASTEST LAP: Hill,D., 1m 27.100s

Pn	Driver	Car	Laps	Time/Reason
1	Hill,D.	Williams-Ren.	60	1h 30m 03.640s
dq	Schumacher,M.	Benetton-Ford	60	overtook on parade
2	Alesi	Ferrari	60	1h 31m 11.768s
3	Hakkinen	McLaren-Peug.	60	1h 31m 44.299s
4	Barrichello	Jordan-Hart	60	1h 31m 45.391s
5	Coulthard	Williams-Ren.	59	
6	Katayama	Tyrrell-Yamaha	59	
7	Frentzen	Sauber-Merc.	59	
8	Verstappen	Benetton-Ford	59	
9	Fittipaldi,C.	Footwork-Ford	58	
10	Martini	Minardi-Ford	58	
11	Herbert	Lotus-Mug. Ho.	58	
12	Panis	Ligier-Renault	58	
13	Bernard	Ligier-Renault	58	
14	Beretta	Larrousse-Ford	58	
15	Brabham,D.	Simtek-Ford	57	
16	Gounon	Simtek-Ford	57	
r	Alboreto	Minardi-Ford	48	engine
r	Berger,G.	Ferrari	32	engine
r	Blundell	Tyrrell-Yamaha	20	gearbox
r	Comas	Larrousse-Ford	12	engine
r	de Cesaris	Sauber-Merc.	11	engine
r	Morbidelli	Footwork-Ford	5	fuel system
r	Zanardi	Lotus-Mug. Ho.	4	engine
r	Brundle	McLaren	0	engine
dns	Irvine	Jordan-Hart	0	engine parade lap

STARTING GRID:

1	Hill,D.	12	Irvine
2	Schumacher,M.	13	Frentzen
3	Berger,G.	14	Martini
4	Alesi	15	Panis
5	Hakkinen	16	Morbidelli
6	Barrichello	17	Alboreto
7	Coulthard	18	de Cesaris
8	Katayama	19	Zanardi
9	Brundle	20	Fittipaldi,C.
10	Verstappen	21	Herbert
11	Blundell	22	Comas +

German

GRAND PRIX No:	557
DATE:	July 31, 1994
VENUE:	Hockenheim
POLE LAP:	Berger,G., 1m 43.582s
FASTEST LAP:	Coulthard, 1m 46.211s

Pn	Driver	Car	Laps	Time/Reason
1	Berger,G.	Ferrari	45	1h 22m 37.272s
2	Panis	Ligier-Renault	45	1h 23m 32.051s
3	Bernard	Ligier-Renault	45	1h 23m 42.314s
4	Fittipaldi,C.	Footwork-Ford	45	1h 23m 58.881s
5	Morbidelli	Footwork-Ford	45	
6	Comas	Larrousse-Ford	45	
7	Beretta	Larrousse-Ford	44	
8	Hill,D.	Williams-Ren.	44	
r	Gounon	Simtek-Ford	39	gearbox
r	Brabham,D.	Simtek-Ford	37	clutch
r	Schumacher,M.	Benetton-Ford	20	engine
r	Brundle	McLaren-Peug.	19	engine
r	Coulthard	Williams-Ren.	17	electrical
r	Verstappen	Benetton-Ford	15	fire
r	Katayama	Tyrrell-Yamaha	6	throttle
r	Alesi	Ferrari	0	electrical
r	Frentzen	Sauber-Merc.	0	accident
r	Herbert	Lotus-MH	0	accident
r	Barrichello	Jordan-Hart	0	accident
r	Irvine	Jordan-Hart	0	accident
r	Blundell	Tyrrell-Yamaha	0	accident
r	Hakkinen	McLaren-Peug.	0	accident
r	Zanardi	Lotus-MH	0	accident
r	Martini	Minardi-Ford	0	accident
r	Alboreto	Minardi-Ford	0	accident
r	de Cesaris	Sauber-Merc.	0	accident

STARTING GRID:

1	Berger,G.	12	Panis
2	Alesi	13	Brundle
3	Hill,D.	14	Bernard
4	Schumacher,M.	15	Herbert
5	Katayama	16	Morbidelli
6	Coulthard	17	Fittipaldi,C.
7	Blundell	18	de Cesaris
8	Hakkinen	19	Verstappen
9	Frentzen	20	Martini
10	Irvine	21	Zanardi
11	Barrichello	22	Comas

+

Hungarian

GRAND PRIX No:	558
DATE:	August 14, 1994
VENUE:	Hungaroring
POLE LAP:	Schumacher,M., 1m 18.258s
FASTEST LAP:	Schumacher,M., 1m 20.881s

Pn	Driver	Car	Laps	Time/Reason
1	Schumacher,M.	Benetton-Ford	77	1h 48m 00.185s
2	Hill,D.	Williams-Ren.	77	1h 48m 21.012s
3	Verstappen	Benetton-Ford	77	1h 49m 10.514s
4	Brundle	McLaren-Peug.	76	electrical
5	Blundell	Tyrrell-Yamaha	76	
6	Panis	Ligier-Renault	76	
7	Alboreto	Minardi-Ford	75	
8	Comas	Larrousse-Ford	75	
9	Beretta	Larrousse-Ford	75	
10	Bernard	Ligier-Renault	75	
11	Brabham,D.	Simtek-Ford	74	
12	Berger,G.	Ferrari	72	
13	Zanardi	Lotus-MH	72	
14	Fittipaldi,C.	Footwork-Ford	69	gearbox
r	Coulthard	Williams-Ren.	59	accident
r	Alesi	Ferrari	58	gearbox
r	Martini	Minardi-Ford	58	spun off
r	Frentzen	Sauber-Merc.	39	gearbox
r	Herbert	Lotus-MH	34	electrical
r	de Cesaris	Sauber-Merc.	30	accident
r	Morbidelli	Footwork-Ford	30	accident
r	Alliot	McLaren-Peug.	21	water leak
r	Gounon	Simtek-Ford	9	handling
r	Katayama	Tyrrell-Yamaha	0	accident
r	Barrichello	Jordan-Hart	0	accident
r	Irvine	Jordan-Hart	0	accident

STARTING GRID:

1	Schumacher,M.	12	Verstappen
2	Hill,D.	13	Alesi
3	Coulthard	14	Alliot
4	Berger,G.	15	Martini
5	Katayama	16	Fittipaldi,C.
6	Brundle	17	de Cesaris
7	Irvine	18	Bernard
8	Frentzen	19	Morbidelli
9	Panis	20	Alboreto
10	Barrichello	21	Comas
11	Blundell	22	Zanardi

+

Belgian

GRAND PRIX No:	559
DATE:	August 28, 1994
VENUE:	Spa-Francorchamps
POLE LAP:	Barrichello, 2m 21.494s
FASTEST LAP:	Hill,D., 1m 57.117s

Pn	Driver	Car	Laps	Time/Reason
dq	Schumacher,M.	Benetton-Ford	44	illegal skidblock
1	Hill,D.	Williams-Ren.	44	1h 28m 33.508s
2	Hakkinen	McLaren-Peug.	44	1h 28m 47.170s
3	Verstappen	Benetton-Ford	44	1h 29m 38.551s
4	Coulthard	Williams-Ren.	44	1h 29m 57.623s
5	Blundell	Tyrrell-Yamaha	43	
6	Morbidelli	Footwork-Ford	43	
7	Panis	Ligier-Renault	43	
8	Martini	Minardi-Ford	43	
9	Alboreto	Minardi-Ford	43	
10	Bernard	Ligier-Renault	42	
11	Gounon	Simtek-Ford	42	
12	Herbert	Lotus-MH	41	
13	Irvine	Jordan-Hart	40	electrical
r	Fittipaldi,C.	Footwork-Ford	33	engine
r	Brabham,D.	Simtek-Ford	29	wheel
r	de Cesaris	Sauber-Merc.	27	throttle
r	Brundle	McLaren-Peug.	24	spun off
r	Barrichello	Jordan-Hart	19	spun off
r	Katayama	Tyrrell-Yamaha	18	engine
r	Adams	Lotus-MH	15	spun off
r	Berger,G.	Ferrari	11	engine
r	Alliot	Larrousse-Ford	11	engine
r	Frentzen	Sauber-Merc.	10	spun off
r	Comas	Larrousse-Ford	3	engine
r	Alesi	Ferrari	2	engine

STARTING GRID:

1	Barrichello	12	Blundell
2	Schumacher,M.	13	Brundle
3	Hill,D.	14	Morbidelli
4	Irvine	15	de Cesaris
5	Alesi	16	Bernard
6	Verstappen	17	Panis
7	Coulthard	18	Alboreto
8	Hakkinen	19	Alliot
9	Frentzen	20	Herbert
10	Martini	21	Brabham,D.
11	Berger,G.	22	Comas

+

Italian

GRAND PRIX No:	560
DATE:	September 11, 1994
VENUE:	Monza
POLE LAP:	Alesi, 1m 23.844s
FASTEST LAP:	Hill,D., 1m 25.930s

Pn	Driver	Car	Laps	Time/Reason
1	Hill,D.	Williams-Ren.	53	1h 18m 02.754s
2	Berger,G.	Ferrari	53	1h 18m 07.684s
3	Hakkinen	McLaren-Peug.	53	1h 18m 28.394s
4	Barrichello	Jordan-Hart	53	1h 18m 53.388s
5	Brundle	McLaren-Peug.	53	1h 19m 28.329s
6	Coulthard	Williams-Ren.	52	out of fuel
7	Bernard	Ligier-Renault	52	
8	Comas	Larrousse-Ford	52	
9	Lehto	Benetton-Ford	52	
10	Panis	Ligier-Renault	51	
r	Brabham,D.	Simtek-Ford	46	brakes
r	Katayama	Tyrrell-Yamaha	45	brakes
r	Fittipaldi,C.	Footwork-Ford	43	engine
r	Irvine	Jordan-Hart	41	engine
r	Blundell	Tyrrell-Yamaha	39	brakes
r	Martini	Minardi-Ford	30	spun off
r	Alboreto	Minardi-Ford	28	gearbox
r	Frentzen	Sauber-Merc.	22	engine
r	de Cesaris	Sauber-Merc.	20	engine
r	Gounon	Simtek-Ford	20	transmission
r	Dalmas	Larrousse-Ford	18	spun off
r	Alesi	Ferrari	14	gearbox
r	Herbert	Lotus-MH	13	engine
r	Verstappen	Benetton-Ford	0	puncture
r	Zanardi	Lotus-MH	0	accident
r	Morbidelli	Footwork-Ford	0	accident

STARTING GRID:

1	Alesi	12	Bernard
2	Berger,G.	13	Zanardi
3	Hill,D.	14	Katayama
4	Herbert	15	Brundle
5	Coulthard	16	Barrichello
6	Panis	17	Morbidelli
7	Hakkinen	18	Martini
8	de Cesaris	19	Fittipaldi,C.
9	Irvine	20	Lehto
10	Verstappen	21	Blundell
11	Frentzen	22	Alboreto

+

Portuguese

GRAND PRIX No:	561
DATE:	September 25, 1994
VENUE:	Estoril
POLE LAP:	Berger,G., 1m 20.608s
FASTEST LAP:	Coulthard, 1m 22.446s

Pn	Driver	Car	Laps	Time/Reason
1	Hill,D.	Williams-Ren.	71	1h 41m 10.165s
2	Coulthard	Williams-Ren.	71	1h 41m 10.768s
3	Hakkinen	McLaren-Peug.	71	1h 41m 30.358s
4	Barrichello	Jordan-Hart	71	1h 41m 38.168s
5	Verstappen	Benetton-Ford	71	1h 41m 39.550s
6	Brundle	McLaren-Peug.	71	1h 42m 02.867s
7	Irvine	Jordan-Hart	70	
8	Fittipaldi,C.	Footwork-Ford	70	
dq	Panis	Ligier-Renault	70	illegal skidblock
9	Morbidelli	Footwork-Ford	70	
10	Bernard	Ligier-Renault	70	
11	Herbert	Lotus-MH	70	
12	Martini	Minardi-Ford	69	
13	Alboreto	Minardi-Ford	69	
14	Dalmas	Larrousse-Ford	69	
15	Gounon	Simtek-Ford	67	
16	Adams	Lotus-MH	67	
r	Blundell	Tyrrell-Yamaha	61	engine
r	Lehto	Benetton-Ford	60	spun off
r	de Cesaris	Sauber-Merc.	54	spun off
r	Alesi	Ferrari	38	accident
r	Brabham,D.	Simtek-Ford	36	accident
r	Frentzen	Sauber-Merc.	31	transmission
r	Comas	Larrousse-Ford	27	accident
r	Katayama	Tyrrell-Yamaha	26	gearbox
r	Berger,G.	Ferrari	7	gearbox

STARTING GRID:

1	Berger,G.	12	Blundell
2	Hill,D.	13	Irvine
3	Coulthard	14	Lehto
4	Hakkinen	15	Panis
5	Alesi	16	Morbidelli
6	Katayama	17	de Cesaris
7	Brundle	18	Martini
8	Barrichello	19	Alboreto
9	Frentzen	20	Herbert
10	Verstappen	21	Bernard
11	Fittipaldi,C.	22	Comas +

European

GRAND PRIX No:	562
DATE:	October 16, 1994
VENUE:	Jerez
POLE LAP:	Schumacher,M., 1m 22.762s
FASTEST LAP:	Schumacher,M., 1m 25.040s

Pn	Driver	Car	Laps	Time/Reason
1	Schumacher,M.	Benetton-Ford	69	1h 40m 26.689s
2	Hill,D.	Williams-Ren.	69	1h 40m 51.378s
3	Hakkinen	McLaren-Peug.	69	1h 41m 36.337s
4	Irvine	Jordan-Hart	69	1h 41m 45.135s
5	Berger,G.	Ferrari	68	
6	Frentzen	Sauber-Merc.	68	
7	Katayama	Tyrrell-Yamaha	68	
8	Herbert	Ligier-Renault	68	
9	Panis	Ligier-Renault	68	
10	Alesi	Ferrari	68	
11	Morbidelli	Footwork-Ford	68	
12	Barrichello	Jordan-Hart	68	
13	Blundell	Tyrrell-Yamaha	68	
14	Alboreto	Minardi-Ford	67	
15	Martini	Minardi-Ford	67	
16	Zanardi	Lotus-MH	67	
17	Fittipaldi,C.	Footwork-Ford	66	
18	Bernard	Lotus-MH	66	
19	Schiattarella	Simtek-Ford	64	
r	Mansell	Williams-Ren.	47	spun off
r	Brabham,D.	Simtek-Ford	42	engine
r	de Cesaris	Sauber-Merc.	37	throttle
r	Comas	Larrousse-Ford	37	electrical
r	Verstappen	Benetton-Ford	15	spun off
r	Noda	Larrousse-Ford	10	gearbox
r	Brundle	McLaren-Peug.	8	engine

STARTING GRID:

1	Schumacher,M.	12	Verstappen
2	Hill,D.	13	Katayama
3	Mansell	14	Blundell
4	Frentzen	15	Brundle
5	Barrichello	16	Alesi
6	Berger,G.	17	Martini
7	Herbert	18	de Cesaris
8	Morbidelli	19	Fittipaldi,C.
9	Hakkinen	20	Alboreto
10	Irvine	21	Zanardi
11	Panis	22	Bernard +

Japanese

GRAND PRIX No: 563
DATE: November 6, 1994
VENUE: Suzuka
POLE LAP: Schumacher,M., 1m 37.209s
FASTEST LAP: Hill,D., 1m 56.597s

Pn	Driver	Car	Laps	Time/Reason
1	Hill,D.	Williams-Ren.	50	1h 55m 53.532s
2	Schumacher,M.	Benetton-Ford	50	1h 55m 56.897s
3	Alesi	Ferrari	50	1h 56m 45.577s
4	Mansell	Williams-Ren.	50	1h 56m 49.606s
5	Irvine	Jordan-Hart	50	1h 57m 35.639s
6	Frentzen	Sauber-Merc.	50	1h 57m 53.395s
7	Hakkinen	McLaren-Peug.	50	1h 57m 56.517s
8	Fittipaldi,C.	Footwork-Ford	49	
9	Comas	Larrousse-Ford	49	
10	Salo	Lotus-MH	49	
11	Panis	Ligier-Renault	49	
12	Brabham,D.	Simtek-Ford	48	
13	Zanardi	Lotus-MH	48	
r	Blundell	Tyrrell-Yamaha	26	engine
r	Barrichello	Jordan-Hart	16	gearbox
r	Brundle	McLaren-Peug.	13	accident
r	Morbidelli	Footwork-Ford	10	accident
r	Berger,G.	Ferrari	10	electrical
r	Lagorce	Ligier-Renault	10	accident
r	Martini	Minardi-Ford	10	accident
r	Alboreto	Minardi-Ford	3	spun off
r	Herbert	Benetton-Ford	3	spun off
r	Katayama	Tyrrell-Yamaha	3	accident
r	Inoue	Simtek-Ford	0	accident
r	Noda	Larrousse-Ford	0	fuel injection
r	Lehto	Sauber-Merc.	0	engine

STARTING GRID:

1	Schumacher,M.	12	Morbidelli
2	Hill,D.	13	Blundell
3	Frentzen	14	Katayama
4	Mansell	15	Lehto
5	Herbert	16	Martini
6	Irvine	17	Zanardi
7	Alesi	18	Fittipaldi,C.
8	Hakkinen	19	Panis
9	Brundle	20	Lagorce
10	Barrichello	21	Alboreto
11	Berger,G.	22	Comas

+

Australian

GRAND PRIX No: 564
DATE: November 13, 1994
VENUE: Adelaide
POLE LAP: Mansell, 1m 16.179s
FASTEST LAP: Schumacher,M., 1m 17.140s

Pn	Driver	Car	Laps	Time/Reason
1	Mansell	Williams-Ren.	81	1h 47m 51.480s
2	Berger,G.	Ferrari	81	1h 47m 53.991s
3	Brundle	McLaren-Peug.	81	1h 48m 43.967s
4	Barrichello	Jordan-Hart	81	1h 49m 02.010s
5	Panis	Ligier-Renault	80	
6	Alesi	Ferrari	80	
7	Frentzen	Sauber-Merc.	80	
8	Fittipaldi,C.	Footwork-Ford	80	
9	Martini	Minardi-Ford	79	
10	Lehto	Sauber-Merc.	79	
11	Lagorce	Ligier-Renault	79	
12	Hakkinen	McLaren-Peug.	76	brakes
r	Alboreto	Minardi-Ford	69	accident
r	Blundell	Tyrrell-Yamaha	66	accident
r	Deletraz	Larrousse-Ford	56	gearbox
r	Salo	Lotus-MH	49	electrical
r	Brabham,D.	Simtek-Ford	49	engine
r	Zanardi	Lotus-MH	40	throttle
r	Hill,D.	Williams-Ren.	35	accident
r	Schumacher,M.	Benetton-Ford	35	accident
r	Schiattarella	Simtek-Ford	21	gear lever
r	Katayama	Tyrrell-Yamaha	19	spun off
r	Noda	Larrousse-Ford	18	oil leak
r	Morbidelli	Footwork-Ford	17	oil leak
r	Irvine	Jordan-Hart	15	spun off
r	Herbert	Benetton-Ford	13	gearbox

STARTING GRID:

1	Mansell	12	Panis
2	Schumacher,M.	13	Blundell
3	Hill,D.	14	Zanardi
4	Hakkinen	15	Katayama
5	Barrichello	16	Alboreto
6	Irvine	17	Lehto
7	Herbert	18	Martini
8	Alesi	19	Fittipaldi,C.
9	Brundle	20	Lagorce
10	Frentzen	21	Morbidelli
11	Berger,G.	22	Salo

+

Brazilian

GRAND PRIX No: 565
DATE: March 26, 1995
VENUE: Interlagos
POLE LAP: Hill,D., 1m 20.081s
FASTEST LAP: Schumacher,M., 1m 20.921s

Pn	Driver	Car	Laps	Time/Reason
1	Schumacher,M.	Benetton-Ren.	71	1h 38m 34.154s
2	Coulthard	Williams-Ren.	71	1h 38m 42.214s
3	Berger,G.	Ferrari	70	
4	Hakkinen	McLaren-Merc.	70	
5	Alesi	Ferrari	70	
6	Blundell	McLaren-Merc.	70	
7	Salo	Tyrrell-Yamaha	69	
8	Suzuki,A.	Ligier-MH	69	
9	Montermini	Pacific-Ford	65	
10	Diniz	Forti-Ford	64	
r	Morbidelli	Footwork-Hart	62	fuel valve
r	Inoue	Footwork-Hart	48	fire
r	Badoer	Minardi-Ford	47	gearbox
r	Moreno	Forti-Ford	47	spun out
r	Wendlinger	Sauber-Ford	41	electrical
r	Hill,D.	Williams-Ren.	30	gearbox
r	Herbert	Benetton-Ren.	30	accident
r	Gachot	Pacific-Ford	23	gearbox
r	Barrichello	Jordan-Peugeot	16	gearbox
r	Verstappen	Simtek-Ford	16	clutch
r	Katayama	Tyrrell-Yamaha	15	spun out
r	Irvine	Jordan-Peugeot	15	gearbox
r	Schiattarella	Simtek-Ford	12	steering box
r	Frentzen	Sauber-Ford	10	electrical
r	Panis	Ligier-MH	0	spun out
dns	Martini	Minardi-Ford		gearbox

STARTING GRID:

1	Hill,D.	12	Salo
2	Schumacher,M.	13	Morbidelli
3	Coulthard	14	Frentzen
4	Herbert	15	Suzuki,A.
5	Berger,G.	16	Barrichello
6	Alesi	17	Martini
7	Hakkinen	18	Badoer
8	Irvine	19	Wendlinger
9	Blundell	20	Gachot
10	Panis	21	Inoue
11	Katayama	22	Montermini +

Argentine

GRAND PRIX No: 566
DATE: April 9, 1995
VENUE: Buenos Aires
POLE LAP: Coulthard, 1m 53.241s
FASTEST LAP: Schumacher,M., 1m 30.522s

Pn	Driver	Car	Laps	Time/Reason
1	Hill,D.	Williams-Ren.	72	1h 53m 14.532s
2	Alesi	Ferrari	72	1h 53m 20.939s
3	Schumacher,M.	Benetton-Ren.	72	1h 53m 47.908s
4	Herbert	Benetton-Ren.	71	
5	Frentzen	Sauber-Ford	70	
6	Berger,G.	Ferrari	70	
7	Panis	Ligier-MH	70	
8	Katayama	Tyrrell-Yamaha	69	
9	Schiattarella	Simtek-Ford	68	
uc	Diniz	Forti-Ford	63	
uc	Moreno	Forti-Ford	63	
r	Salo	Tyrrell-Yamaha	48	accident
r	Suzuki,A.	Ligier-MH	47	accident
r	Martini	Minardi-Ford	44	spun out
r	Morbidelli	Footwork-Hart	43	electrical
r	Inoue	Footwork-Hart	40	spun out
r	Barrichello	Jordan-Peugeot	33	engine
r	Verstappen	Simtek-Ford	23	gearbox
r	Coulthard	Williams-Ren.	16	engine
r	Blundell	McLaren-Merc.	9	oil cooler
r	Irvine	Jordan-Peugeot	6	engine
r	Montermini	Pacific-Ford	1	suspension
r	Hakkinen	McLaren-Merc.	0	accident
r	Gachot	Pacific-Ford	0	accident
r	Wendlinger	Sauber-Ford	0	accident
r	Badoer	Minardi-Ford	0	accident

STARTING GRID:

1	Coulthard	12	Morbidelli
2	Hill,D.	13	Badoer
3	Schumacher,M.	14	Verstappen
4	Irvine	15	Katayama
5	Hakkinen	16	Martini
6	Alesi	17	Blundell
7	Salo	18	Panis
8	Berger,G.	19	Suzuki,A.
9	Frentzen	20	Schiattarella
10	Barrichello	21	Wendlinger
11	Herbert	22	Montermini +

San Marino

GRAND PRIX No: 567
DATE: April 30, 1995
VENUE: Imola
POLE LAP: Schumacher,M., 1m 27.274s
FASTEST LAP: Berger,G., 1m 29.568s

Pn	Driver	Car	Laps	Time/Reason
1	Hill,D.	Williams-Ren.	63	1h 41m 42.552s
2	Alesi	Ferrari	63	1h 42m 01.062s
3	Berger,G.	Ferrari	63	1h 42m 25.668s
4	Coulthard	Williams-Ren.	63	1h 42m 34.442s
5	Hakkinen	McLaren-Merc.	62	
6	Frentzen	Sauber-Ford	62	
7	Herbert	Benetton-Ren.	61	
8	Irvine	Jordan-Peugeot	61	
9	Panis	Ligier-MH	61	
10	Mansell	McLaren-Merc.	61	
11	Suzuki,A.	Ligier-MH	60	
12	Martini	Minardi-Ford	59	
13	Morbidelli	Footwork-Hart	59	
14	Badoer	Minardi-Ford	59	
uc	Diniz	Forti-Ford	56	
uc	Moreno	Forti-Ford	56	
r	Wendlinger	Sauber-Ford	43	wheel nut stuck
r	Gachot	Pacific-Ford	36	hydraulics
r	Schiattarella	Simtek-Ford	35	suspension
r	Barrichello	Jordan-Peugeot	31	gearbox
r	Katayama	Tyrrell-Yamaha	23	spun out
r	Salo	Tyrrell-Yamaha	19	engine
r	Montermini	Pacific-Ford	15	hydraulics
r	Verstappen	Simtek-Ford	14	gearbox
r	Inoue	Footwork-Hart	12	accident
r	Schumacher,M.	Benetton-Ren.	10	accident

STARTING GRID:

1	Schumacher,M.	12	Panis
2	Berger,G.	13	Salo
3	Coulthard	14	Frentzen
4	Hill,D.	15	Katayama
5	Alesi	16	Suzuki,A.
6	Hakkinen	17	Verstappen
7	Irvine	18	Martini
8	Herbert	19	Inoue
9	Mansell	20	Badoer
10	Barrichello	21	Wendlinger
11	Morbidelli	22	Gachot +

Spanish

GRAND PRIX No: 568
DATE: May 14, 1995
VENUE: Barcelona
POLE LAP: Schumacher,M., 1m 21.452s
FASTEST LAP: Hill,D., 1m 24.531s

Pn	Driver	Car	Laps	Time/Reason
1	Schumacher,M.	Benetton-Ren.	65	1h 34m 20.507s
2	Herbert	Benetton-Ren.	65	1h 35m 12.495s
3	Berger,G.	Ferrari	65	1h 35m 25.744s
4	Hill,D.	Williams-Ren.	65	1h 36m 22.256s
5	Irvine	Jordan-Peugeot	64	
6	Panis	Ligier-MH	64	
7	Barrichello	Jordan-Peugeot	64	
8	Frentzen	Sauber-Ford	64	
9	Brundle	Ligier-MH	64	
10	Salo	Tyrrell-Yamaha	64	
11	Morbidelli	Footwork-Hart	63	
12	Verstappen	Simtek-Ford	63	
13	Wendlinger	Sauber-Ford	63	
14	Martini	Minardi-Ford	62	
15	Schiattarella	Simtek-Ford	61	
r	Katayama	Tyrrell-Yamaha	56	engine
r	Coulthard	Williams-Ren.	54	gearbox
r	Hakkinen	McLaren-Merc.	53	fuel pressure
r	Inoue	Footwork-Hart	43	engine
r	Gachot	Pacific-Ford	43	fire
r	Moreno	Forti-Ford	39	water pump
r	Alesi	Ferrari	25	engine
r	Badoer	Minardi-Ford	21	gearbox
r	Mansell	McLaren-Merc.	18	handling
r	Diniz	Forti-Ford	17	gearbox
dns	Montermini	Pacific-Ford	0	gearbox on grid

STARTING GRID:

1	Schumacher,M.	12	Mansell
2	Alesi	13	Morbidelli
3	Berger,G.	14	Frentzen
4	Coulthard	15	Katayama
5	Hill,D.	16	Salo
6	Irvine	17	Verstappen
7	Herbert	18	Wendlinger
8	Barrichello	19	Inoue
9	Hakkinen	20	Martini
10	Panis	21	Badoer
11	Brundle	22	Schiattarella +

Monaco

GRAND PRIX No: 569
DATE: May 28, 1995
VENUE: Monte Carlo
POLE LAP: Hill,D., 1m 21.952s
FASTEST LAP: Alesi, 1m 24.621s

Pn	Driver	Car	Laps	Time/Reason
1	Schumacher,M.	Benetton-Ren.	78	1h 53m 11.258s
2	Hill,D.	Williams-Ren.	78	1h 53m 46.705s
3	Berger,G.	Ferrari	78	1h 54m 22.705s
4	Herbert	Benetton-Ren.	77	
5	Blundell	McLaren-Merc.	77	
6	Frentzen	Sauber-Ford	76	
7	Martini	Minardi-Ford	76	
8	Boullion	Sauber-Ford	75	
9	Morbidelli	Footwork-Hart	74	
10	Diniz	Forti-Ford	72	
r	Badoer	Minardi-Ford	68	suspension
r	Salo	Tyrrell-Yamaha	65	accident
r	Panis	Ligier-MH	63	engine
r	Barrichello	Jordan-Peugeot	60	throttle
r	Gachot	Pacific-Ford	42	gearbox
r	Alesi	Ferrari	41	accident
r	Brundle	Ligier-MH	40	accident
r	Inoue	Footwork-Hart	27	gearbox
r	Katayama	Tyrrell-Yamaha	26	spun out
dq	Montermini	Pacific-Ford	23	did not pit for penalty
r	Irvine	Jordan-Peugeot	22	Wheel failure
r	Coulthard	Williams-Ren.	16	gearbox
r	Moreno	Forti-Ford	9	accident
r	Hakkinen	McLaren-Merc.	8	engine
r	Schiattarella	Simtek-Ford	0	accident
r	Verstappen	Simtek-Ford	0	gearbox

STARTING GRID:

1	Hill,D.	11	Barrichello
2	Schumacher,M.	12	Panis
3	Coulthard	13	Morbidelli
4	Berger,G.	14	Frentzen
5	Alesi	15	Katayama
6	Hakkinen	16	Badoer
7	Herbert	17	Salo
8	Brundle	18	Martini
9	Irvine	19	Boullion
10	Blundell	20	Schiattarella +

Canadian

GRAND PRIX No: 570
DATE: June 12, 1995
VENUE: Montreal
POLE LAP: Schumacher,M., 1m 27.661s
FASTEST LAP: Schumacher,M., 1m 29.174s

Pn	Driver	Car	Laps	Time/Reason
1	Alesi	Ferrari	69	1h 46m 31.131s
2	Barrichello	Jordan-Peugeot	69	1h 47m 03.020s
3	Irvine	Jordan-Peugeot	69	1h 47m 04.603s
4	Panis	Ligier-MH	69	1h 47m 07.839s
5	Schumacher,M.	Benetton-Ren.	69	1h 47m 08.393s
6	Morbidelli	Footwork-Hart	68	
7	Badoer	Minardi-Ford	68	
8	Salo	Tyrrell-Yamaha	68	
9	Inoue	Footwork-Hart	67	
r	Brundle	Ligier-MH	61	accident
r	Berger,G.	Ferrari	61	accident
r	Martini	Minardi-Ford	60	throttle
r	Moreno	Forti-Ford	54	fuel line
r	Hill,D.	Williams-Ren.	50	hydraulics
r	Blundell	McLaren-Merc.	47	engine
r	Katayama	Tyrrell-Yamaha	42	engine
r	Gachot	Pacific-Ford	36	battery
r	Frentzen	Sauber-Ford	26	engine
r	Diniz	Forti-Ford	26	gearbox
r	Boullion	Sauber-Ford	19	spun out
r	Montermini	Pacific-Ford	5	hydraulics
r	Coulthard	Williams-Ren.	1	spun out
r	Herbert	Benetton-Ren.	0	accident
r	Hakkinen	McLaren-Merc.	0	accident

STARTING GRID:

1	Schumacher,M.	13	Morbidelli
2	Hill,D.	14	Brundle
3	Coulthard	15	Salo
4	Berger,G.	16	Katayama
5	Alesi	17	Martini
6	Herbert	18	Boullion
7	Hakkinen	19	Badoer
8	Irvine	20	Gachot
9	Barrichello	21	Montermini
10	Blundell	22	Inoue
11	Panis	23	Moreno
12	Frentzen	24	Diniz

French

GRAND PRIX No:	571
DATE:	July 2, 1995
VENUE:	Magny-Cours
POLE LAP:	Hill,D., 1m 17.225s
FASTEST LAP:	Schumacher,M., 1m 20.218s

Pn	Driver	Car	Laps	Time/Reason
1	Schumacher,M.	Benetton-Ren.	72	1h 38m 28.429s
2	Hill,D.	Williams-Ren.	72	1h 38m 59.738s
3	Coulthard	Williams-Ren.	72	1h 39m 31.255s
4	Brundle	Ligier-MH	72	1h 39m 31.722s
5	Alesi	Ferrari	72	1h 39m 46.298s
6	Barrichello	Jordan-Peugeot	71	
7	Hakkinen	McLaren-Merc.	71	
8	Panis	Ligier-MH	71	
9	Irvine	Jordan-Peugeot	71	
10	Frentzen	Sauber-Ford	71	
11	Blundell	McLaren-Merc.	70	
12	Berger,G.	Ferrari	70	
13	Badoer	Minardi-Ford	69	
14	Morbidelli	Footwork-Hart	69	
15	Salo	Tyrrell-Yamaha	69	
16	Moreno	Forti-Ford	66	
uc	Montermini	Pacific-Ford	62	
r	Boullion	Sauber-Ford	48	transmission
r	Gachot	Pacific-Ford	24	gearbox
r	Martini	Minardi-Ford	23	gearbox
r	Herbert	Benetton-Ren.	2	accident
r	Katayama	Tyrrell-Yamaha	0	accident
r	Inoue	Footwork-Hart	0	accident
r	Diniz	Forti-Ford	0	accident

STARTING GRID:

1	Hill,D.	13	Blundell
2	Schumacher,M.	14	Salo
3	Coulthard	15	Boullion
4	Alesi	16	Morbidelli
5	Barrichello	17	Badoer
6	Panis	18	Inoue
7	Berger,G.	19	Katayama
8	Hakkinen	20	Martini
9	Brundle	21	Montermini
10	Herbert	22	Gachot
11	Irvine	23	Diniz
12	Frentzen	24	Moreno

British

GRAND PRIX No:	572
DATE:	July 10, 1995
VENUE:	Silverstone
POLE LAP:	Hill,D., 1m 28.124s
FASTEST LAP:	Hill,D., 1m 29.752s

Pn	Driver	Car	Laps	Time/Reason
1	Herbert	Benetton-Ren.	61	1h 34m 35.093s
2	Alesi	Ferrari	61	1h 34m 51.572s
3	Coulthard	Williams-Ren.	61	1h 34m 58.981s
4	Panis	Ligier-MH	61	1h 36m 08.261s
5	Blundell	McLaren-Merc.	61	1h 36m 23.265s
6	Frentzen	Sauber-Ford	60	
7	Martini	Minardi-Ford	60	
8	Salo	Tyrrell-Yamaha	60	
9	Boullion	Sauber-Ford	60	
10	Badoer	Minardi-Ford	60	
11	Barrichello	Jordan-Peugeot	59	accident
12	Gachot	Pacific-Ford	58	
r	Moreno	Forti-Ford	48	hydraulics
r	Schumacher,M.	Benetton-Ren.	45	accident
r	Hill,D.	Williams-Ren.	45	accident
r	Papis	Footwork-Hart	28	accident
r	Katayama	Tyrrell-Yamaha	22	fuel feed
r	Montermini	Pacific-Ford	21	spun out
r	Hakkinen	McLaren-Merc.	20	electrical
r	Berger,G.	Ferrari	20	loose wheel
r	Brundle	Ligier-MH	16	spun out
r	Inoue	Footwork-Hart	16	spun out
r	Diniz	Forti-Ford	13	gear selection
r	Irvine	Jordan-Peugeot	2	electrical

STARTING GRID:

1	Hill,D.	13	Panis
2	Schumacher,M.	14	Katayama
3	Coulthard	15	Martini
4	Berger,G.	16	Boullion
5	Herbert	17	Papis
6	Alesi	18	Badoer
7	Irvine	19	Inoue
8	Hakkinen	20	Diniz
9	Barrichello	21	Gachot
10	Blundell	22	Moreno
11	Brundle	23	Salo
12	Frentzen	24	Montermini

German

GRAND PRIX No: 573
DATE: July 30, 1995
VENUE: Hockenheim
POLE LAP: Hill,D., 1m 44.385s
FASTEST LAP: Schumacher,M., 1m 48.824s

Pn	Driver	Car	Laps	Time/Reason
1	Schumacher,M.	Benetton-Ren.	45	1h 22m 56.043s
2	Coulthard	Williams-Ren.	45	1h 23m 02.031s
3	Berger,G.	Ferrari	45	1h 24m 04.140s
4	Herbert	Benetton-Ren.	45	1h 24m 19.479s
5	Boullion	Sauber-Ford	44	
6	Suzuki,A.	Ligier-MH	44	
7	Katayama	Tyrrell-Yamaha	44	
8	Montermini	Pacific-Ford	42	
9	Irvine	Jordan-Peugeot	41	
r	Hakkinen	McLaren-Merc.	33	engine
r	Frentzen	Sauber-Ford	32	engine
r	Badoer	Minardi-Ford	28	gearbox
r	Lavaggi	Pacific-Ford	27	gearbox
r	Moreno	Forti-Ford	27	driveshaft
r	Barrichello	Jordan-Peugeot	20	engine
r	Blundell	McLaren-Merc.	17	engine
r	Panis	Ligier-MH	13	water leak
r	Alesi	Ferrari	12	engine
r	Martini	Minardi-Ford	11	engine
r	Inoue	Footwork-Hart	9	gearbox
r	Diniz	Forti-Ford	8	brakes
r	Hill,D.	Williams-Ren.	1	accident
r	Salo	Tyrrell-Yamaha	0	transmission
r	Papis	Footwork-Hart	0	gearbox

STARTING GRID:

1	Hill,D.	13	Salo
2	Schumacher,M.	14	Boullion
3	Coulthard	15	Papis
4	Berger,G.	16	Badoer
5	Barrichello	17	Katayama
6	Irvine	18	Suzuki,A.
7	Hakkinen	19	Inoue
8	Blundell	20	Martini
9	Herbert	21	Diniz
10	Alesi	22	Moreno
11	Frentzen	23	Montermini
12	Panis	24	Lavaggi

Hungarian

GRAND PRIX No: 574
DATE: August 13, 1995
VENUE: Hungaroring
POLE LAP: Hill,D., 1m 16.982s
FASTEST LAP: Hill,D., 1m 20.247s

Pn	Driver	Car	Laps	Time/Reason
1	Hill,D.	Williams-Ren.	77	1h 46m 25.271s
2	Coulthard	Williams-Ren.	77	1h 46m 59.119s
3	Berger,G.	Ferrari	76	
4	Herbert	Benetton-Ren.	76	
5	Frentzen	Sauber-Ford	76	
6	Panis	Ligier-MH	76	
7	Barrichello	Jordan-Peugeot	76	
8	Badoer	Minardi-Ford	75	
9	Lamy	Minardi-Ford	74	
10	Boullion	Sauber-Ford	74	
11	Schumacher,M.	Benetton-Ren.	73	fuel pump
12	Montermini	Pacific-Ford	73	
13	Irvine	Jordan-Peugeot	70	clutch
r	Brundle	Ligier-MH	67	engine
r	Salo	Tyrrell-Yamaha	58	throttle
r	Blundell	McLaren-Merc.	54	engine
r	Katayama	Tyrrell-Yamaha	46	accident
r	Papis	Footwork-Hart	45	brakes
r	Alesi	Ferrari	42	engine
r	Diniz	Forti-Ford	32	engine
r	Inoue	Footwork-Hart	13	engine
r	Moreno	Forti-Ford	8	gear lever
r	Lavaggi	Pacific-Ford	5	spun out
r	Hakkinen	McLaren-Merc.	3	engine

STARTING GRID:

1	Hill,D.	13	Blundell
2	Coulthard	14	Barrichello
3	Schumacher,M.	15	Lamy
4	Berger,G.	16	Salo
5	Hakkinen	17	Katayama
6	Alesi	18	Inoue
7	Irvine	19	Boullion
8	Brundle	20	Papis
9	Herbert	21	Moreno
10	Panis	22	Montermini
11	Frentzen	23	Diniz
12	Badoer	24	Lavaggi

Belgian

GRAND PRIX No:	575
DATE:	August 27, 1995
VENUE:	Spa-Francorchamps
POLE LAP:	Berger,G., 1m 54.392s
FASTEST LAP:	Coulthard, 1m 53.412s

Pn	Driver	Car	Laps	Time/Reason
1	Schumacher,M.	Benetton-Ren.	44	1h 36m 47.875s
2	Hill,D.	Williams-Ren.	44	1h 37m 07.368s
3	Brundle	Ligier-MH	44	1h 37m 12.873s
4	Frentzen	Sauber-Ford	44	1h 37m 14.847s
5	Blundell	McLaren-Merc.	44	1h 37m 21.647s
6	Barrichello	Jordan-Peugeot	44	1h 37m 27.549s
7	Herbert	Benetton-Ren.	44	1h 37m 41.923s
8	Salo	Tyrrell-Yamaha	44	1h 37m 42.423s
9	Panis	Ligier-MH	44	1h 37m 54.045s
10	Lamy	Minardi-Ford	44	1h 38m 07.664s
11	Boullion	Sauber-Ford	43	
12	Inoue	Footwork-Hart	43	
13	Diniz	Forti-Ford	42	
14	Moreno	Forti-Ford	42	
r	Katayama	Tyrrell-Yamaha	28	accident
r	Lavaggi	Pacific-Ford	27	gearbox
r	Badoer	Minardi-Ford	23	accident
r	Berger,G.	Ferrari	22	electrical
r	Irvine	Jordan-Peugeot	21	refuelling fire
r	Papis	Footwork-Hart	20	spun out
r	Montermini	Pacific-Ford	18	out of fuel
r	Coulthard	Williams-Ren.	13	gearbox
r	Alesi	Ferrari	4	suspension
r	Hakkinen	McLaren-Merc.	1	spun out

STARTING GRID:

1	Berger,G.	13	Brundle
2	Alesi	14	Boullion
3	Hakkinen	15	Katayama
4	Herbert	16	Schumacher,M.
5	Coulthard	17	Lamy
6	Blundell	18	Inoue
7	Irvine	19	Badoer
8	Hill,D.	20	Papis
9	Panis	21	Montermini
10	Frentzen	22	Moreno
11	Salo	23	Lavaggi
12	Barrichello	24	Diniz

Italian

GRAND PRIX No:	576
DATE:	September 10, 1995
VENUE:	Monza
POLE LAP:	Coulthard, 1m 24.462s
FASTEST LAP:	Berger,G., 1m 26.419s

Pn	Driver	Car	Laps	Time/Reason
1	Herbert	Benetton-Ren.	53	1h 18m 27.916s
2	Hakkinen	McLaren-Merc.	53	1h 18m 45.695s
3	Frentzen	Sauber-Ford	53	1h 18m 52.237s
4	Blundell	McLaren-Merc.	53	1h 18m 56.139s
5	Salo	Tyrrell-Yamaha	52	
6	Boullion	Sauber-Ford	52	
7	Papis	Footwork-Hart	52	
8	Inoue	Footwork-Hart	52	
9	Diniz	Forti-Ford	50	
uc	Katayama	Tyrrell-Yamaha	47	
r	Alesi	Ferrari	45	wheel bearings
r	Barrichello	Jordan-Peugeot	43	clutch
r	Irvine	Jordan-Peugeot	40	engine
r	Berger,G.	Ferrari	32	hit by camera
r	Badoer	Minardi-Ford	26	accident
r	Schumacher,M.	Benetton-Ren.	23	accident
r	Hill,D.	Williams-Ren.	23	accident
r	Panis	Ligier-MH	20	spun out
r	Coulthard	Williams-Ren.	13	wheel bearings
r	Brundle	Ligier-MH	10	puncture
r	Lavaggi	Pacific-Ford	6	spun out
r	Lamy	Minardi-Ford	0	differential
r	Moreno	Forti-Ford	0	accident
r	Montermini	Pacific-Ford	0	accident

STARTING GRID:

1	Coulthard	13	Panis
2	Schumacher,M.	14	Boullion
3	Berger,G.	15	Papis
4	Hill,D.	16	Salo
5	Alesi	17	Katayama
6	Barrichello	18	Badoer
7	Hakkinen	19	Lamy
8	Herbert	20	Inoue
9	Blundell	21	Montermini
10	Frentzen	22	Moreno
11	Brundle	23	Diniz
12	Irvine	24	Lavaggi

Portuguese

GRAND PRIX No: 577
DATE: September 24, 1995
VENUE: Estoril
POLE LAP: Coulthard, 1m 20.537s
FASTEST LAP: Coulthard, 1m 23.220s

Pn	Driver	Car	Laps	Time/Reason
1	Coulthard	Williams-Ren.	71	1h 41m 52.145s
2	Schumacher,M.	Benetton-Ren.	71	1h 41m 59.393s
3	Hill,D.	Williams-Ren.	71	1h 42m 14.266s
4	Berger,G.	Ferrari	71	1h 43m 17.024s
5	Alesi	Ferrari	71	1h 43m 17.574s
6	Frentzen	Sauber-Ford	70	
7	Herbert	Benetton-Ren.	70	
8	Brundle	Ligier-MH	70	
9	Blundell	McLaren-Merc.	70	
10	Irvine	Jordan-Peugeot	70	
11	Barrichello	Jordan-Peugeot	70	
12	Boullion	Sauber-Ford	70	
13	Salo	Tyrrell-Yamaha	69	
14	Badoer	Minardi-Ford	68	
15	Inoue	Footwork-Hart	68	
16	Diniz	Forti-Ford	66	
17	Moreno	Forti-Ford	64	
r	Montermini	Pacific-Ford	53	gearbox
r	Hakkinen	McLaren-Merc.	44	engine
r	Deletraz	Pacific-Ford	14	driver cramp
r	Panis	Ligier-MH	10	spun out
r	Lamy	Minardi-Ford	7	hydraulics
r	Katayama	Tyrrell-Yamaha	0	accident
r	Papis	Footwork-Hart	0	accident

STARTING GRID:

1	Coulthard	13	Hakkinen
2	Hill,D.	14	Boullion
3	Schumacher,M.	15	Salo
4	Berger,G.	16	Katayama
5	Frentzen	17	Lamy
6	Herbert	18	Badoer
7	Alesi	19	Inoue
8	Barrichello	20	Papis
9	Brundle	21	Montermini
10	Irvine	22	Diniz
11	Panis	23	Moreno
12	Blundell	24	Deletraz

European

GRAND PRIX No: 578
DATE: October 1, 1995
VENUE: Nurburgring
POLE LAP: Coulthard, 1m 18.738s
FASTEST LAP: Schumacher,M., 1m 21.180s

Pn	Driver	Car	Laps	Time/Reason
1	Schumacher,M.	Benetton-Ren.	67	1h 39m 59.044s
2	Alesi	Ferrari	67	1h 40m 01.728s
3	Coulthard	Williams-Ren.	67	1h 40m 34.426s
4	Barrichello	Jordan-Peugeot	66	
5	Herbert	Benetton-Ren.	66	
6	Irvine	Jordan-Peugeot	66	
7	Brundle	Ligier-MH	66	
8	Hakkinen	McLaren-Merc.	65	
9	Lamy	Minardi-Ford	64	
10	Salo	Tyrrell-Yamaha	64	
11	Badoer	Minardi-Ford	64	
12	Papis	Footwork-Hart	64	
13	Diniz	Forti-Ford	62	
14	Tarquini	Tyrrell-Yamaha	61	
15	Deletraz	Pacific-Ford	60	
r	Hill,D.	Williams-Ren.	58	accident
r	Montermini	Pacific-Ford	45	out of fuel
r	Boullion	Sauber-Ford	44	accident
r	Berger,G.	Ferrari	40	electrical
r	Moreno	Forti-Ford	22	gearbox
r	Frentzen	Sauber-Ford	17	accident
r	Panis	Ligier-MH	14	spun out
r	Blundell	McLaren-Merc.	14	accident
r	Inoue	Footwork-Hart	0	electrical

STARTING GRID:

1	Coulthard	13	Boullion
2	Hill,D.	14	Panis
3	Schumacher,M.	15	Salo
4	Berger,G.	16	Lamy
5	Irvine	17	Papis
6	Alesi	18	Badoer
7	Herbert	19	Tarquini
8	Frentzen	20	Montermini
9	Hakkinen	21	Inoue
10	Blundell	22	Diniz
11	Barrichello	23	Moreno
12	Brundle	24	Deletraz

Pacific

GRAND PRIX No:	579
DATE:	October 17, 1995
VENUE:	Aida
POLE LAP:	Coulthard, 1m 14.013s
FASTEST LAP:	Schumacher,M., 1m 16.374s

Pn	Driver	Car	Laps	Time/Reason
1	Schumacher,M.	Benetton-Ren.	83	1h 48m 49.972s
2	Coulthard	Williams-Ren.	83	1h 49m 04.892s
3	Hill,D.	Williams-Ren.	83	1h 49m 38.305s
4	Berger,G.	Ferrari	82	
5	Alesi	Ferrari	82	
6	Herbert	Benetton-Ren.	82	
7	Frentzen	Sauber-Ford	82	
8	Panis	Ligier-MH	81	
9	Blundell	McLaren-Merc.	81	
10	Magnussen	McLaren-Merc.	81	
11	Irvine	Jordan-Peugeot	81	
12	Salo	Tyrrell-Yamaha	80	
13	Lamy	Minardi-Ford	80	
14	Katayama	Tyrrell-Yamaha	80	
15	Badoer	Minardi-Ford	80	
16	Moreno	Forti-Ford	78	
17	Diniz	Forti-Ford	77	
r	Barrichello	Jordan-Peugeot	67	electrical
r	Morbidelli	Footwork-Hart	53	engine
r	Inoue	Footwork-Hart	38	engine
r	Montermini	Pacific-Ford	14	gearbox
r	Suzuki,A.	Ligier-MH	10	spun out
r	Boullion	Sauber-Ford	7	spun out
r	Gachot	Pacific-Ford	2	gearbox

STARTING GRID:

1	Coulthard	13	Suzuki,A.
2	Hill,D.	14	Lamy
3	Schumacher,M.	15	Boullion
4	Alesi	16	Badoer
5	Berger,G.	17	Katayama
6	Irvine	18	Salo
7	Herbert	19	Morbidelli
8	Frentzen	20	Inoue
9	Panis	21	Diniz
10	Blundell	22	Moreno
11	Barrichello	23	Montermini
12	Magnussen	24	Gachot

Japanese

GRAND PRIX No:	580
DATE:	October 29, 1995
VENUE:	Suzuka
POLE LAP:	Schumacher,M., 1m 38.023s
FASTEST LAP:	Schumacher,M., 1m 42.976s

Pn	Driver	Car	Laps	Time/Reason
1	Schumacher,M.	Benetton-Ren.	53	1h 36m 52.930s
2	Hakkinen	McLaren-Merc.	53	1h 37m 12.267s
3	Herbert	Benetton-Ren.	53	1h 38m 16.734s
4	Irvine	Jordan-Peugeot	53	1h 38m 35.066s
5	Panis	Ligier-MH	52	
6	Salo	Tyrrell-Yamaha	52	
7	Blundell	McLaren-Merc.	52	
8	Frentzen	Sauber-Ford	52	
9	Badoer	Minardi-Ford	51	
10	Wendlinger	Sauber-Ford	51	
11	Lamy	Minardi-Ford	51	
12	Inoue	Footwork-Hart	51	
r	Hill,D.	Williams-Ren.	40	spun out
r	Coulthard	Williams-Ren.	39	accident
r	Diniz	Forti-Ford	32	spun out
r	Alesi	Ferrari	24	gearbox
r	Montermini	Pacific-Ford	23	spun out
r	Berger,G.	Ferrari	16	engine
r	Barrichello	Jordan-Peugeot	15	accident
r	Katayama	Tyrrell-Yamaha	12	accident
r	Gachot	Pacific-Ford	6	driveshaft
r	Moreno	Forti-Ford	1	gearbox
r	Morbidelli	Footwork-Hart	0	spun out
dns	Suzuki,A.	Ligier-MH		injured

STARTING GRID:

1	Schumacher,M.	13	Suzuki,A.
2	Alesi	14	Katayama
3	Hakkinen	15	Morbidelli
4	Hill,D.	16	Wendlinger
5	Berger,G.	17	Lamy
6	Coulthard	18	Badoer
7	Irvine	19	Inoue
8	Frentzen	20	Montermini
9	Herbert	21	Diniz
10	Barrichello	22	Moreno
11	Panis	23	Gachot
12	Salo	24	Blundell

Australian

GRAND PRIX No:	581
DATE:	November 13, 1995
VENUE:	Adelaide
POLE LAP:	Hill,D., 1m 15.505s
FASTEST LAP:	Hill,D., 1m 17.493s

Pn	Driver	Car	Laps	Time/Reason
1	Hill,D.	Williams-Ren.	81	1h 49m 15.946s
2	Panis	Ligier-MH	79	1h 49m 17.711s
3	Morbidelli	Footwork-Hart	79	1h 49m 28.091s
4	Blundell	McLaren-Merc.	79	1h 49m 48.256s
5	Salo	Tyrrell-Yamaha	78	
6	Lamy	Minardi-Ford	78	
7	Diniz	Forti-Ford	77	
8	Gachot	Pacific-Ford	76	
r	Katayama	Tyrrell-Yamaha	70	oil line
r	Herbert	Benetton-Ren.	69	driveshaft
r	Irvine	Jordan-Peugeot	62	engine
r	Frentzen	Sauber-Ford	39	gearbox
r	Berger,G.	Ferrari	34	engine
r	Brundle	Ligier-MH	29	accident
r	Schumacher,M.	Benetton-Ren.	25	accident
r	Alesi	Ferrari	23	accident
r	Moreno	Forti-Ford	21	accident
r	Barrichello	Jordan-Peugeot	20	accident
r	Coulthard	Williams-Ren.	19	accident
r	Inoue	Footwork-Hart	15	spun out
r	Wendlinger	Sauber-Ford	8	withdrew
r	Montermini	Pacific-Ford	2	spun out
dns	Badoer	Minardi-Ford	0	electrical on grid

STARTING GRID:

1	Hill,D.	13	Morbidelli
2	Coulthard	14	Salo
3	Schumacher,M.	15	Badoer
4	Berger,G.	16	Katayama
5	Alesi	17	Lamy
6	Frentzen	18	Wendlinger
7	Barrichello	19	Inoue
8	Herbert	20	Moreno
9	Irvine	21	Diniz
10	Blundell	22	Montermini
11	Brundle	23	Gachot
12	Panis		

Australian

GRAND PRIX No:	582
DATE:	March 10, 1996
VENUE:	Melbourne
POLE LAP:	Villeneuve,J., 1m 32.371s
FASTEST LAP:	Villeneuve,J., 1m 33.241s

Pn	Driver	Car	Laps	Time/Reason
1	Hill,D.	Williams-Ren.	58	1h 32m 50.491s
2	Villeneuve,J.	Williams-Ren.	58	1h 32m 28.511s
3	Irvine	Ferrari	58	1h 33m 53.062s
4	Berger,G.	Benetton-Ren.	58	1h 34m 07.528s
5	Hakkinen	McLaren-Merc.	58	1h 34m 25.562s
6	Salo	Tyrrell-Yamaha	57	
7	Panis	Ligier-MH	57	
8	Frentzen	Sauber-Ford	57	
9	Rosset	Footwork-Hart	56	
10	Diniz	Ligier-MH	56	
11	Katayama	Tyrrell-Yamaha	55	
r	Lamy	Minardi-Ford	43	seat belt defect
r	Schumacher,M.	Ferrari	33	brake fluid
r	Fisichella	Minardi-Ford	33	clutch
r	Barrichello	Jordan-Peugeot	30	engine
r	Coulthard	McLaren-Merc.	25	throttle
r	Verstappen	Footwork-Hart	16	engine
r	Alesi	Benetton-Ren.	10	accident
r	Brundle	Jordan-Peugeot	2	spun out
dns	Herbert	Sauber-Ford	0	accident at start
dnq	Badoer	Forti-Ford		107% rule
dnq	Montermini	Forti-Ford		107% rule

STARTING GRID:

1	Villeneuve,J.	12	Verstappen
2	Hill,D.	13	Coulthard
3	Irvine	14	Herbert
4	Schumacher,M.	15	Katayama
5	Hakkinen	16	Fisichella
6	Alesi	17	Lamy
7	Berger,G.	18	Rosset
8	Barrichello	19	Brundle
9	Frentzen	20	Diniz
10	Salo	107	Badoer
11	Panis	107	Montermini

Brazilian

GRAND PRIX No:	583
DATE:	March 31, 1996
VENUE:	Interlagos
POLE LAP:	Hill,D., 1m 18.111s
FASTEST LAP:	Hill,D., 1m 21.547s

Pn	Driver	Car	Laps	Time/Reason
1	Hill,D.	Williams-Ren.	71	1h 49m 52.976s
2	Alesi	Benetton-Ren.	71	1h 50m 10.958s
3	Schumacher,M.	Ferrari	70	
4	Hakkinen	McLaren-Merc.	70	
5	Salo	Tyrrell-Yamaha	70	
6	Panis	Ligier-MH	70	
7	Irvine	Ferrari	70	
8	Diniz	Ligier-MH	69	
9	Katayama	Tyrrell-Yamaha	69	
10	Lamy	Minardi-Ford	68	
11	Badoer	Forti-Ford	67	
12	Brundle	Jordan-Peugeot	64	spun out
r	Barrichello	Jordan-Peugeot	59	spun out
r	Frentzen	Sauber-Ford	36	gearbox
r	Coulthard	McLaren-Merc.	29	spun out
r	Herbert	Sauber-Ford	28	electrical
r	Villeneuve,J.	Williams-Ren.	26	spun out
r	Berger,G.	Benetton-Ren.	26	suspension
r	Montermini	Forti-Ford	26	spun out
r	Rosset	Footwork-Hart	24	accident
r	Verstappen	Footwork-Hart	19	engine
r	Marques	Minardi-Ford	0	spun out

STARTING GRID:

1	Hill,D.	12	Herbert
2	Barrichello	13	Verstappen
3	Villeneuve,J.	14	Coulthard
4	Schumacher,M.	15	Panis
5	Alesi	16	Katayama
6	Brundle	17	Rosset
7	Hakkinen	18	Diniz
8	Berger,G.	19	Marques
9	Frentzen	20	Lamy
10	Irvine	21	Badoer
11	Salo	22	Montermini

Argentine

GRAND PRIX No:	584
DATE:	April 7, 1996
VENUE:	Beunos Aires
POLE LAP:	Hill,D., 1m 30.346s
FASTEST LAP:	Alesi, 1m 29.413s

Pn	Driver	Car	Laps	Time/Reason
1	Hill,D.	Williams-Ren.	72	1h 54m 55.322s
2	Villeneuve,J.	Williams-Ren.	72	1h 55m 07.489s
3	Alesi	Benetton-Ren.	72	1h 55m 10.076s
4	Barrichello	Jordan-Peugeot	72	1h 55m 50.453s
5	Irvine	Ferrari	72	1h 56m 00.313s
6	Verstappen	Footwork-Hart	72	1h 56m 04.235s
7	Coulthard	McLaren-Merc.	72	1h 56m 08.772s
8	Panis	Ligier-MH	72	1h 56m 09.617s
9	Herbert	Sauber-Ford	71	
10	Montermini	Forti-Ford	69	
r	Berger,G.	Benetton-Ren.	56	suspension
r	Schumacher,M.	Ferrari	46	rear wing
r	Lamy	Minardi-Ford	39	spun out
r	Salo	Tyrrell-Yamaha	36	throttle
r	Brundle	Jordan-Peugeot	34	accident
r	Marques	Minardi-Ford	33	spun out
r	Frentzen	Sauber-Ford	32	spun out
r	Diniz	Ligier-MH	29	fire
r	Katayama	Tyrrell-Yamaha	28	clutch
r	Rosset	Footwork-Hart	24	fuel pump
r	Badoer	Forti-Ford	24	accident
r	Hakkinen	McLaren-Merc.	19	throttle

STARTING GRID:

1	Hill,D.	12	Panis
2	Schumacher,M.	13	Katayama
3	Villeneuve,J.	14	Marques
4	Alesi	15	Brundle
5	Berger,G.	16	Salo
6	Barrichello	17	Herbert
7	Verstappen	18	Diniz
8	Hakkinen	19	Lamy
9	Coulthard	20	Rosset
10	Irvine	21	Badoer
11	Frentzen	22	Montermini

European

GRAND PRIX No: 585
DATE: April 28, 1996
VENUE: Nurburgring
POLE LAP: Hill,D., 1m 18.941s
FASTEST LAP: Hill,D., 1m 21.363s

Pn	Driver	Car	Laps	Time/Reason
1	Villeneuve,J.	Williams-Ren.	67	1h 33m 26.473s
2	Schumacher,M.	Ferrari	67	1h 33m 27.235s
3	Coulthard	McLaren-Merc.	67	1h 33m 59.307s
4	Hill,D.	Williams-Ren.	67	1h 33m 59.984s
5	Barrichello	Jordan-Peugeot	67	1h 34m 00.186s
6	Brundle	Jordan-Peugeot	67	1h 34m 22.040s
7	Herbert	Sauber-Ford	67	1h 34m 44.500s
8	Hakkinen	McLaren-Merc.	67	1h 34m 44.911s
9	Berger,G.	Benetton-Ren.	67	1h 34m 47.534s
dq	Salo	Tyrrell-Yamaha	66	underweight
10	Diniz	Ligier-MH	66	
dq	Katayama	Tyrrell-Yamaha	65	push start
11	Rosset	Footwork-Hart	65	
12	Lamy	Minardi-Ford	65	
13	Fisichella	Minardi-Ford	65	
r	Frentzen	Sauber-Ford	59	accident
r	Verstappen	Footwork-Hart	38	gearbox
r	Panis	Ligier-MH	6	accident
r	Irvine	Ferrari	6	misfire
r	Alesi	Benetton-Ren.	1	accident
dnq	Montermini	Forti-Ford		107% rule
dnq	Badoer	Forti-Ford		107% rule

STARTING GRID:

1	Hill,D.	12	Herbert
2	Villeneuve,J.	13	Verstappen
3	Schumacher,M.	14	Salo
4	Alesi	15	Panis
5	Barrichello	16	Katayama
6	Coulthard	17	Diniz
7	Irvine	18	Fisichella
8	Berger,G.	19	Lamy
9	Hakkinen	20	Rosset
10	Frentzen	107	Montermini
11	Brundle	107	Badoer

San Marino

GRAND PRIX No: 586
DATE: May 5, 1996
VENUE: Imola
POLE LAP: Schumacher,M., 1m 26.890s
FASTEST LAP: Hill,D., 1m 28.931s

Pn	Driver	Car	Laps	Time/Reason
1	Hill,D.	Williams-Ren.	63	1h 35m 26.156s
2	Schumacher,M.	Ferrari	63	1h 35m 42.616s
3	Berger,G.	Benetton-Ren.	63	1h 36m 13.047s
4	Irvine	Ferrari	63	1h 36m 27.739s
5	Barrichello	Jordan-Peugeot	63	1h 36m 44.646s
6	Alesi	Benetton-Ren.	62	
7	Diniz	Ligier-MH	62	
8	Hakkinen	McLaren-Merc.	61	
9	Lamy	Minardi-Ford	61	
10	Badoer	Forti-Ford	59	
11	Villeneuve,J.	Williams-Ren.	57	
r	Panis	Ligier-MH	54	gearbox
r	Katayama	Tyrrell-Yamaha	45	loss of drive
r	Coulthard	McLaren-Merc.	44	hydraulics
r	Rosset	Footwork-Hart	40	broken refuelling
r	Verstappen	Footwork-Hart	38	broken refuelling
r	Brundle	Jordan-Peugeot	36	spun out
r	Frentzen	Sauber-Ford	32	brakes
r	Fisichella	Minardi-Ford	30	engine
r	Herbert	Sauber-Ford	25	misfire
r	Salo	Tyrrell-Yamaha	23	engine
dnq	Montermini	Forti-Ford		107% rule

STARTING GRID:

1	Schumacher,M.	12	Brundle
2	Hill,D.	13	Panis
3	Villeneuve,J.	14	Verstappen
4	Coulthard	15	Herbert
5	Alesi	16	Katayama
6	Irvine	17	Diniz
7	Berger,G.	18	Lamy
8	Salo	19	Fisichella
9	Barrichello	20	Rosset
10	Frentzen	21	Badoer
11	Hakkinen	107	Montermini

Monaco

GRAND PRIX No:	587
DATE:	May 19, 1996
VENUE:	Monte Carlo
POLE LAP:	Schumacher,M., 1m 20.356s
FASTEST LAP:	Alesi, 1m 25.205s

Pn	Driver	Car	Laps	Time/Reason
1	Panis	Ligier-MH	75	2h 00m 45.629s
2	Coulthard	McLaren-Merc.	75	2h 00m 50.457s
3	Herbert	Sauber-Ford	75	2h 01m 23.132s
4	Frentzen	Sauber-Ford	74	
5	Salo	Tyrrell-Yamaha	70	accident
6	Hakkinen	McLaren-Merc.	70	accident
7	Irvine	Ferrari	68	accident
r	Villeneuve,J.	Williams-Ren.	66	accident
r	Alesi	Benetton-Ren.	60	suspension
r	Badoer	Forti-Ford	60	accident
r	Hill,D.	Williams-Ren.	40	engine
r	Brundle	Jordan-Peugeot	30	spun out
r	Berger,G.	Benetton-Ren.	9	gearbox sensor
r	Diniz	Ligier-MH	5	transmission
r	Rosset	Footwork-Hart	3	accident
r	Katayama	Tyrrell-Yamaha	2	throttle
r	Schumacher,M.	Ferrari	0	accident
r	Verstappen	Footwork-Hart	0	accident
r	Barrichello	Jordan-Peugeot	0	accident
r	Lamy	Minardi-Ford	0	accident
r	Fisichella	Minardi-Ford	0	accident
dns	Montermini	Forti-Ford	0	accident parade

STARTING GRID:

1	Schumacher,M.	12	Verstappen
2	Hill,D.	13	Herbert
3	Alesi	14	Panis
4	Berger,G.	15	Katayama
5	Coulthard	16	Brundle
6	Barrichello	17	Diniz
7	Irvine	18	Fisichella
8	Hakkinen	19	Lamy
9	Frentzen	20	Rosset
10	Villeneuve,J.	21	Badoer
11	Salo	22	Montermini

Spanish

GRAND PRIX No:	588
DATE:	June 2, 1996
VENUE:	Barcelona
POLE LAP:	Hill,D., 1m 20.650s
FASTEST LAP:	Schumacher,M., 1m 45.517s

Pn	Driver	Car	Laps	Time/Reason
1	Schumacher,M.	Ferrari	65	1h 59m 49.307s
2	Alesi	Benetton-Ren.	65	2h 00m 34.609s
3	Villeneuve,J.	Williams-Ren.	65	2h 00m 37.695s
4	Frentzen	Sauber-Ford	64	
5	Hakkinen	McLaren-Merc.	64	
6	Diniz	Ligier-MH	63	
r	Verstappen	Footwork-Hart	47	spun out
r	Barrichello	Jordan-Peugeot	45	transmission
r	Berger,G.	Benetton-Ren.	44	spun out
r	Herbert	Sauber-Ford	20	spun out
r	Brundle	Jordan-Peugeot	17	transmission
dq	Salo	Tyrrell-Yamaha	16	used spare car
r	Hill,D.	Williams-Ren.	10	accident
r	Katayama	Tyrrell-Yamaha	8	electrical
r	Irvine	Ferrari	1	spun out
r	Panis	Ligier-MH	1	accident damage
r	Fisichella	Minardi-Ford	1	accident damage
r	Coulthard	McLaren-Merc.	0	accident
r	Rosset	Footwork-Hart	0	accident
r	Lamy	Minardi-Ford	0	accident
dnq	Badoer	Forti-Ford		107% rule
dnq	Montermini	Forti-Ford		107% rule

STARTING GRID:

1	Hill,D.	12	Salo
2	Villeneuve,J.	13	Verstappen
3	Schumacher,M.	14	Coulthard
4	Alesi	15	Brundle
5	Berger,G.	16	Katayama
6	Irvine	17	Diniz
7	Barrichello	18	Lamy
8	Panis	19	Fisichella
9	Herbert	20	Rosset
10	Hakkinen	107	Badoer
11	Frentzen	107	Montermini

Canadian

GRAND PRIX No:	589
DATE:	June 16, 1996
VENUE:	Montreal
POLE LAP:	Hill,D., 1m 21.059s
FASTEST LAP:	Villeneuve,J., 1m 21.916s

Pn	Driver	Car	Laps	Time/Reason
1	Hill,D.	Williams-Ren.	69	1h 36m 03.465s
2	Villeneuve,J.	Williams-Ren.	69	1h 36m 07.648s
3	Alesi	Benetton-Ren.	69	1h 36m 58.121s
4	Coulthard	McLaren-Merc.	69	1h 37m 07.138s
5	Hakkinen	McLaren-Merc.	68	
6	Brundle	Jordan-Peugeot	68	
7	Herbert	Sauber-Ford	68	
8	Fisichella	Minardi-Ford	67	
r	Lamy	Minardi-Ford	44	accident
r	Badoer	Forti-Ford	44	gearbox
r	Berger,G.	Benetton-Ren.	42	spun out
r	Schumacher,M.	Ferrari	41	driveshaft
r	Panis	Ligier-MH	39	engine
r	Salo	Tyrrell-Yamaha	39	engine
r	Diniz	Ligier-MH	38	engine
r	Barrichello	Jordan-Peugeot	22	clutch
r	Montermini	Forti-Ford	22	loose ballast
r	Frentzen	Sauber-Ford	19	gearbox
r	Verstappen	Footwork-Hart	10	engine
r	Rosset	Footwork-Hart	6	accident
r	Katayama	Tyrrell-Yamaha	6	accident
r	Irvine	Ferrari	1	suspension

STARTING GRID:

1	Hill,D.	12	Frentzen
2	Villeneuve,J.	13	Verstappen
3	Schumacher,M.	14	Salo
4	Alesi	15	Herbert
5	Irvine	16	Fisichella
6	Hakkinen	17	Katayama
7	Berger,G.	18	Diniz
8	Barrichello	19	Lamy
9	Brundle	20	Badoer
10	Coulthard	21	Rosset
11	Panis	22	Montermini

French

GRAND PRIX No:	590
DATE:	June 30, 1996
VENUE:	Magny-Cours
POLE LAP:	Schumacher,M., 1m 15.989s
FASTEST LAP:	Villeneuve,J., 1m 18.610s

Pn	Driver	Car	Laps	Time/Reason
1	Hill,D.	Williams-Ren.	72	1h 36m 28.795s
2	Villeneuve,J.	Williams-Ren.	72	1h 36m 36.922s
3	Alesi	Benetton-Ren.	72	1h 37m 15.237s
4	Berger,G.	Benetton-Ren.	72	1h 37m 15.654s
5	Hakkinen	McLaren-Merc.	72	1h 37m 31.569s
6	Coulthard	McLaren-Merc.	71	
7	Panis	Ligier-MH	71	
8	Brundle	Jordan-Peugeot	71	
9	Barrichello	Jordan-Peugeot	71	
10	Salo	Tyrrell-Yamaha	70	
dq	Herbert	Sauber-Ford	70	illegal car body
11	Rosset	Footwork-Hart	69	
12	Lamy	Minardi-Ford	69	
r	Frentzen	Sauber-Ford	56	throttle
r	Katayama	Tyrrell-Yamaha	33	engine
r	Badoer	Forti-Ford	29	engine
r	Diniz	Ligier-MH	28	engine
r	Verstappen	Footwork-Hart	10	steering arm
r	Irvine	Ferrari	5	gearbox
r	Fisichella	Minardi-Ford	2	fuel pump
r	Montermini	Forti-Ford	2	engine
dns	Schumacher,M.	Ferrari	0	engine on parade

STARTING GRID:

1	Schumacher,M.	12	Frentzen
2	Hill,D.	13	Salo
3	Alesi	14	Katayama
4	Berger,G.	15	Verstappen
5	Hakkinen	16	Herbert
6	Villeneuve,J.	17	Fisichella
7	Coulthard	18	Lamy
8	Brundle	19	Rosset
9	Panis	20	Badoer
10	Barrichello	21	Montermini
11	Diniz	22	Irvine

British

GRAND PRIX No: 591
DATE: July 14, 1996
VENUE: Silverstone
POLE LAP: Hill,D., 1m 26.875s
FASTEST LAP: Villeneuve,J., 1m 29.288s

Pn	Driver	Car	Laps	Time/Reason
1	Villeneuve,J.	Williams-Ren.	61	1h 33m 00.874s
2	Berger,G.	Benetton-Ren.	61	1h 33m 19.900s
3	Hakkinen	McLaren-Merc.	61	1h 33m 51.704s
4	Barrichello	Jordan-Peugeot	61	1h 34m 07.590s
5	Coulthard	McLaren-Merc.	61	1h 34m 23.381s
6	Brundle	Jordan-Peugeot	60	
7	Salo	Tyrrell-Yamaha	60	
8	Frentzen	Sauber-Ford	60	
9	Herbert	Sauber-Ford	60	
10	Verstappen	Footwork-Hart	60	
11	Fisichella	Minardi-Ford	59	
r	Alesi	Benetton-Ren.	44	brakes
r	Panis	Ligier-MH	40	handling
r	Diniz	Ligier-MH	38	engine
r	Hill,D.	Williams-Ren.	26	loose wheel nut
r	Lamy	Minardi-Ford	21	gear selection
r	Rosset	Footwork-Hart	13	electrical
r	Katayama	Tyrrell-Yamaha	12	engine
r	Irvine	Ferrari	5	engine
r	Schumacher,M.	Ferrari	3	hydraulics
dnq	Montermini	Forti-Ford		107% rule
dnq	Badoer	Forti-Ford		107% rule

STARTING GRID:

1	Hill,D.	12	Katayama
2	Villeneuve,J.	13	Herbert
3	Schumacher,M.	14	Salo
4	Hakkinen	15	Verstappen
5	Alesi	16	Panis
6	Barrichello	17	Diniz
7	Berger,G.	18	Fisichella
8	Brundle	19	Lamy
9	Coulthard	20	Rosset
10	Irvine	107	Montermini
11	Frentzen	107	Badoer

German

GRAND PRIX No: 592
DATE: July 28, 1996
VENUE: Hockenheim
POLE LAP: Hill,D., 1m 43.912s
FASTEST LAP: Hill,D., 1m 46.504s

Pn	Driver	Car	Laps	Time/Reason
1	Hill,D.	Williams-Ren.	45	1h 21m 43.417s
2	Alesi	Benetton-Ren.	45	1h 21m 54.869s
3	Villeneuve,J.	Williams-Ren.	45	1h 22m 17.343s
4	Schumacher,M.	Ferrari	45	1h 22m 24.934s
5	Coulthard	McLaren-Merc.	45	1h 22m 25.613s
6	Barrichello	Jordan-Peugeot	45	1h 23m 25.516s
7	Panis	Ligier-MH	45	1h 23m 27.329s
8	Frentzen	Sauber-Ford	44	
9	Salo	Tyrrell-Yamaha	44	
10	Brundle	Jordan-Peugeot	44	
11	Rosset	Footwork-Hart	44	
12	Lamy	Minardi-Ford	43	
13	Berger,G.	Benetton-Ren.	42	engine
r	Irvine	Ferrari	34	gearbox
r	Herbert	Sauber-Ford	25	gearbox
r	Diniz	Ligier-MH	19	engine
r	Katayama	Tyrrell-Yamaha	19	accident
r	Hakkinen	McLaren-Merc.	13	gearbox
r	Verstappen	Footwork-Hart	0	accident
dnq	Lavaggi	Minardi-Ford		107% rule

STARTING GRID:

1	Hill,D.	11	Diniz
2	Berger,G.	12	Panis
3	Schumacher,M.	13	Frentzen
4	Hakkinen	14	Herbert
5	Alesi	15	Salo
6	Villeneuve,J.	16	Katayama
7	Coulthard	17	Verstappen
8	Irvine	18	Lamy
9	Barrichello	19	Rosset
10	Brundle	107	Lavaggi

Hungarian

GRAND PRIX No: 593
DATE: August 11, 1996
VENUE: Hungaroring
POLE LAP: Schumacher,M., 1m 17.129s
FASTEST LAP: Hill,D., 1m 20.093s

Pn	Driver	Car	Laps	Time/Reason
1	Villeneuve,J.	Williams-Ren.	77	1h 46m 21.134s
2	Hill,D.	Williams-Ren.	77	1h 46m 21.905s
3	Alesi	Benetton-Ren.	77	1h 47m 45.346s
4	Hakkinen	McLaren-Merc.	76	
5	Panis	Ligier-MH	76	
6	Barrichello	Jordan-Peugeot	75	
7	Katayama	Tyrrell-Yamaha	74	
8	Rosset	Footwork-Hart	74	
9	Schumacher,M.	Ferrari	70	
10	Lavaggi	Minardi-Ford	69	
r	Berger,G.	Benetton-Ren.	64	engine
r	Frentzen	Sauber-Ford	50	engine
r	Herbert	Sauber-Ford	35	engine
r	Irvine	Ferrari	31	gearbox
r	Lamy	Minardi-Ford	24	suspension
r	Coulthard	McLaren-Merc.	23	engine
r	Verstappen	Footwork-Hart	10	accident
r	Brundle	Jordan-Peugeot	5	accident
r	Diniz	Ligier-MH	1	accident
r	Salo	Tyrrell-Yamaha	0	accident

STARTING GRID:

1	Schumacher,M.	11	Panis
2	Hill,D.	12	Brundle
3	Villeneuve,J.	13	Barrichello
4	Irvine	14	Katayama
5	Alesi	15	Diniz
6	Berger,G.	16	Salo
7	Hakkinen	17	Verstappen
8	Herbert	18	Rosset
9	Coulthard	19	Lamy
10	Frentzen	20	Lavaggi

Belgian

GRAND PRIX No: 594
DATE: August 25, 1996
VENUE: Spa-Francorchamps
POLE LAP: Villeneuve,J., 1m 50.574s
FASTEST LAP: Berger,G., 1m 53.067s

Pn	Driver	Car	Laps	Time/Reason
1	Schumacher,M.	Ferrari	44	1h 28m 15.125s
2	Villeneuve,J.	Williams-Ren.	44	1h 28m 20.727s
3	Hakkinen	McLaren-Merc.	44	1h 28m 30.835s
4	Alesi	Benetton-Ren.	44	1h 28m 34.250s
5	Hill,D.	Williams-Ren.	44	1h 28m 44.304s
6	Berger,G.	Benetton-Ren.	44	1h 28m 45.021s
7	Salo	Tyrrell-Yamaha	44	1h 29m 15.879s
8	Katayama	Tyrrell-Yamaha	44	1h 29m 55.352s
9	Rosset	Footwork-Hart	43	
10	Lamy	Minardi-Ford	43	
r	Coulthard	McLaren-Merc.	37	accident
r	Brundle	Jordan-Peugeot	34	engine
r	Irvine	Ferrari	29	gearbox
r	Barrichello	Jordan-Peugeot	29	handling
r	Diniz	Ligier-MH	22	misfire
r	Verstappen	Footwork-Hart	11	accident
r	Panis	Ligier-MH	0	accident
r	Herbert	Sauber-Ford	0	accident
r	Frentzen	Sauber-Ford	0	accident
dnq	Lavaggi	Minardi-Ford		107% rule

STARTING GRID:

1	Villeneuve,J.	11	Frentzen
2	Hill,D.	12	Herbert
3	Schumacher,M.	13	Salo
4	Coulthard	14	Panis
5	Berger,G.	15	Diniz
6	Hakkinen	16	Verstappen
7	Alesi	17	Katayama
8	Brundle	18	Rosset
9	Irvine	19	Lamy
10	Barrichello	107	Lavaggi

Italian

GRAND PRIX No:	595
DATE:	September 8, 1996
VENUE:	Monza
POLE LAP:	Hill,D., 1m 24.204s
FASTEST LAP:	Schumacher,M., 1m 26.110s

Pn	Driver	Car	Laps	Time/Reason
1	Schumacher,M.	Ferrari	53	1h 17m 43.632s
2	Alesi	Benetton-Ren.	53	1h 18m 01.897s
3	Hakkinen	McLaren-Merc.	53	1h 18m 50.267s
4	Brundle	Jordan-Peugeot	53	1h 19m 08.849s
5	Barrichello	Jordan-Peugeot	53	1h 19m 09.107s
6	Diniz	Ligier-MH	52	
7	Villeneuve,J.	Williams-Ren.	52	
8	Verstappen	Footwork-Hart	52	
9	Herbert	Sauber-Ford	51	engine
10	Katayama	Tyrrell-Yamaha	51	
r	Rosset	Footwork-Hart	36	steering arm
r	Irvine	Ferrari	23	accident
r	Lamy	Minardi-Ford	12	engine
r	Salo	Tyrrell-Yamaha	9	engine
r	Frentzen	Sauber-Ford	7	accident
r	Hill,D.	Williams-Ren.	5	accident
r	Lavaggi	Minardi-Ford	5	engine
r	Berger,G.	Benetton-Ren.	4	gearbox
r	Panis	Ligier-MH	2	accident
r	Coulthard	McLaren-Merc.	1	accident

STARTING GRID:

1	Hill,D.	11	Panis
2	Villeneuve,J.	12	Herbert
3	Schumacher,M.	13	Frentzen
4	Hakkinen	14	Diniz
5	Coulthard	15	Verstappen
6	Alesi	16	Katayama
7	Irvine	17	Salo
8	Berger,G.	18	Lamy
9	Brundle	19	Rosset
10	Barrichello	20	Lavaggi

Portuguese

GRAND PRIX No:	596
DATE:	Septmber 22, 1996
VENUE:	Estoril
POLE LAP:	Hill,D., 1m 20.330s
FASTEST LAP:	Villeneuve,J., 1m 22.873s

Pn	Driver	Car	Laps	Time/Reason
1	Villeneuve,J.	Williams-Ren.	70	1h 40m 22.915s
2	Hill,D.	Williams-Ren.	70	1h 40m 42.881s
3	Schumacher,M.	Ferrari	70	1h 41m 16.860s
4	Alesi	Benetton-Ren.	70	1h 41m 18.024s
5	Irvine	Ferrari	70	1h 41m 50.304s
6	Berger,G.	Benetton-Ren.	70	1h 41m 56.056s
7	Frentzen	Sauber-Ford	69	
8	Herbert	Sauber-Ford	69	
9	Brundle	Jordan-Peugeot	69	
10	Panis	Ligier-MH	69	
11	Salo	Tyrrell-Yamaha	69	
12	Katayama	Tyrrell-Yamaha	68	
13	Coulthard	McLaren-Merc.	68	
14	Rosset	Footwork-Hart	68	
15	Lavaggi	Minardi-Ford	65	
16	Lamy	Minardi-Ford	65	
r	Hakkinen	McLaren-Merc.	52	accident damage
r	Verstappen	Footwork-Hart	47	engine
r	Diniz	Ligier-MH	46	spun out
r	Barrichello	Jordan-Peugeot	41	spun out

STARTING GRID:

1	Hill,D.	11	Frentzen
2	Villeneuve,J.	12	Herbert
3	Alesi	13	Salo
4	Schumacher,M.	14	Katayama
5	Berger,G.	15	Panis
6	Irvine	16	Verstappen
7	Hakkinen	17	Rosset
8	Coulthard	18	Diniz
9	Barrichello	19	Lamy
10	Brundle	20	Lavaggi

Japanese

GRAND PRIX No: 597
DATE: October 13, 1996
VENUE: Suzuka
POLE LAP: Villeneuve,J., 1m 38.909s
FASTEST LAP: Villeneuve,J., 1m 44.043s

Pn	Driver	Car	Laps	Time/Reason
1	Hill,D.	Williams-Ren.	52	1h 32m 33.791s
2	Schumacher,M.	Ferrari	52	1h 32m 35.674s
3	Hakkinen	McLaren-Merc.	52	1h 32m 37.003s
4	Berger,G.	Benetton-Ren.	52	1h 33m 00.317s
5	Brundle	Jordan-Peugeot	52	1h 33m 40.911s
6	Frentzen	Sauber-Ford	52	1h 33m 54.977s
7	Panis	Ligier-MH	52	1h 33m 56.301s
8	Coulthard	McLaren-Merc.	52	1h 33m 59.024s
9	Barrichello	Jordan-Peugeot	52	1h 34m 14.856s
10	Herbert	Sauber-Ford	52	1h 34m 15.590s
11	Verstappen	Footwork-Hart	51	
12	Lamy	Minardi-Ford	50	
13	Rosset	Footwork-Hart	50	
r	Irvine	Ferrari	39	accident
r	Katayama	Tyrrell-Yamaha	37	engine
r	Villeneuve,J.	Williams-Ren.	36	lost wheel
r	Salo	Tyrrell-Yamaha	20	engine
r	Diniz	Ligier-MH	13	spun out
r	Alesi	Benetton-Ren.	0	accident
dnq	Lavaggi	Minardi-Ford		107% rule

STARTING GRID:

1	Villeneuve,J.	11	Barrichello
2	Hill,D.	12	Panis
3	Schumacher,M.	13	Herbert
4	Berger,G.	14	Katayama
5	Hakkinen	15	Salo
6	Irvine	16	Diniz
7	Frentzen	17	Verstappen
8	Coulthard	18	Lamy
9	Alesi	19	Rosset
10	Brundle	107	Lavaggi

Australian

GRAND PRIX No: 598
DATE: March 9, 1997
VENUE: Melbourne
POLE LAP: Villeneuve,J., 1m 29.369s
FASTEST LAP: Frentzen, 1m 30.585s

Pn	Driver	Car	Laps	Time/Reason
1	Coulthard	McLaren-Merc.	58	1h 30m 28.718s
2	Schumacher,M.	Ferrari	58	1h 30m 48.764s
3	Hakkinen	McLaren-Merc.	58	1h 30m 50.895s
4	Berger,G.	Benetton-Ren.	58	1h 30m 51.559s
5	Panis	Prost-MH	58	1h 31m 29.026s
6	Larini	Sauber-Petronas	58	1h 32m 04.758s
7	Nakano	Prost-MH	56	
8	Frentzen	Williams-Ren.	55	brakes
9	Trulli	Minardi-Hart	55	
10	Diniz	Arrows-Yamaha	54	
r	Barrichello	Stewart-Ford	49	engine
r	Salo	Tyrrell-Ford	42	electrical
r	Magnussen	Stewart-Ford	36	suspension
r	Alesi	Benetton-Ren.	34	out of fuel
r	Katayama	Minardi-Hart	32	fuel feed
r	Fisichella	Jordan-Peugeot	14	accident
r	Verstappen	Tyrrell-Ford	2	accident
r	Schumacher,R.	Jordan-Peugeot	1	driveshaft
r	Irvine	Ferrari	0	accident damage
r	Villeneuve,J.	Williams-Ren.	0	accident
r	Herbert	Sauber-Petronas	0	accident
dns	Hill,D.	Arrows-Yamaha	0	throttle on parade
dnq	Sospiri	Lola-Ford		107% rule
dnq	Rosset	Lola-Ford		107% rule

STARTING GRID:

1	Villeneuve,J.	13	Larini
2	Frentzen	14	Fisichella
3	Schumacher,M.	15	Katayama
4	Coulthard	16	Nakano
5	Irvine	17	Trulli
6	Hakkinen	18	Salo
7	Herbert	19	Magnussen
8	Alesi	20	Hill,D.
9	Panis	21	Verstappen
10	Berger,G.	22	Diniz
11	Barrichello	107	Sospiri
12	Schumacher,R.	107	Rosset

Brazilian

GRAND PRIX No: 599
DATE: March 30, 1997
VENUE: Interlagos
POLE LAP: Villeneuve,J., 1m 16.004s
FASTEST LAP: Villeneuve,J., 1m 18.397s

Pn	Driver	Car	Laps	Time/Reason
1	Villeneuve,J.	Williams-Ren.	72	1h 36m 06.990s
2	Berger,G.	Benetton-Ren.	72	1h 36m 11.180s
3	Panis	Prost-MH	72	1h 36m 22.860s
4	Hakkinen	McLaren-Merc.	72	1h 36m 40.023s
5	Schumacher,M.	Ferrari	72	1h 36m 40.721s
6	Alesi	Benetton-Ren.	72	1h 36m 41.010s
7	Herbert	Sauber-Petronas	72	1h 36m 57.902s
8	Fisichella	Jordan-Peugeot	72	1h 37m 07.629s
9	Frentzen	Williams-Ren.	72	1h 37m 22.392s
10	Coulthard	McLaren-Merc.	71	
11	Larini	Sauber-Petronas	71	
12	Trulli	Minardi-Hart	71	
13	Salo	Tyrrell-Ford	71	
14	Nakano	Prost-MH	71	
15	Verstappen	Tyrrell-Ford	70	
16	Irvine	Ferrari	70	
17	Hill,D.	Arrows-Yamaha	68	
18	Katayama	Minardi-Hart	67	
r	Schumacher,R.	Jordan-Peugeot	52	electrical
r	Barrichello	Stewart-Ford	16	suspension
r	Diniz	Arrows-Yamaha	15	spun out
dns	Magnussen	Stewart-Ford	0	accident at start

STARTING GRID:

1	Villeneuve,J.	12	Coulthard
2	Schumacher,M.	13	Herbert
3	Berger,G.	14	Irvine
4	Hakkinen	15	Nakano
5	Panis	16	Diniz
6	Alesi	17	Trulli
7	Fisichella	18	Katayama
8	Frentzen	19	Larini
9	Hill,D.	20	Magnussen
10	Schumacher,R.	21	Verstappen
11	Barrichello	22	Salo

Argentine

GRAND PRIX No: 600
DATE: April 13, 1997
VENUE: Buenos Aires
POLE LAP: Villeneuve,J., 1m 24.473s
FASTEST LAP: Berger,G., 1m 27.981s

Pn	Driver	Car	Laps	Time/Reason
1	Villeneuve,J.	Williams-Ren.	72	1h 52m 01.715s
2	Irvine	Ferrari	72	1h 52m 02.694s
3	Schumacher,R.	Jordan-Peugeot	72	1h 52m 13.804s
4	Herbert	Sauber-Petronas	72	1h 52m 31.634s
5	Hakkinen	McLaren-Merc.	72	1h 52m 32.066s
6	Berger,G.	Benetton-Ren.	72	1h 52m 33.108s
7	Alesi	Benetton-Ren.	72	1h 52m 48.074s
8	Salo	Tyrrell-Ford	71	
9	Trulli	Minardi-Hart	71	
10	Magnussen	Stewart-Ford	66	
r	Larini	Sauber-Petronas	53	spun out
r	Diniz	Arrows-Yamaha	50	engine
r	Nakano	Prost-MH	49	engine
r	Verstappen	Tyrrell-Ford	43	engine
r	Katayama	Minardi-Hart	37	spun out
r	Hill,D.	Arrows-Yamaha	33	engine
r	Fisichella	Jordan-Peugeot	24	accident
r	Barrichello	Stewart-Ford	24	throttle
r	Panis	Prost-MH	16	hydraulics
r	Frentzen	Williams-Ren.	5	clutch
r	Schumacher,M.	Ferrari	0	accident
r	Coulthard	McLaren-Merc.	0	accident

STARTING GRID:

1	Villeneuve,J.	12	Berger,G.
2	Frentzen	13	Hill,D.
3	Panis	14	Larini
4	Schumacher,M.	15	Magnussen
5	Barrichello	16	Verstappen
6	Schumacher,R.	17	Hakkinen
7	Irvine	18	Trulli
8	Herbert	19	Salo
9	Fisichella	20	Nakano
10	Coulthard	21	Katayama
11	Alesi	22	Diniz

San Marino

GRAND PRIX No: 601
DATE: April 27, 1997
VENUE: Imola
POLE LAP: Villeneuve,J., 1m 23.303s
FASTEST LAP: Frentzen, 1m 25.531s

Pn	Driver	Car	Laps	Time/Reason
1	Frentzen	Williams-Ren.	62	1h 31m 00.673s
2	Schumacher,M.	Ferrari	62	1h 31m 01.910s
3	Irvine	Ferrari	62	1h 32m 19.016s
4	Fisichella	Jordan-Peugeot	62	1h 32m 24.061s
5	Alesi	Benetton-Ren.	61	
6	Hakkinen	McLaren-Merc.	61	
7	Larini	Sauber-Petronas	61	
8	Panis	Prost-MH	61	
9	Salo	Tyrrell-Ford	60	
10	Verstappen	Tyrrell-Ford	60	
11	Katayama	Minardi-Hart	59	
r	Diniz	Arrows-Yamaha	53	exhaust
r	Villeneuve,J.	Williams-Ren.	40	gearbox
r	Coulthard	McLaren-Merc.	38	engine
r	Barrichello	Stewart-Ford	32	engine
r	Herbert	Sauber-Petronas	18	electrical
r	Schumacher,R.	Jordan-Peugeot	17	driveshaft
r	Nakano	Prost-MH	11	accident
r	Hill,D.	Arrows-Yamaha	11	accident
r	Berger,G.	Benetton-Ren.	4	spun out
r	Magnussen	Stewart-Ford	2	spun out
dns	Trulli	Minardi-Hart	0	gearbox on grid

STARTING GRID:

1	Villeneuve,J.	12	Larini
2	Frentzen	13	Barrichello
3	Schumacher,M.	14	Alesi
4	Panis	15	Hill,D.
5	Schumacher,R.	16	Magnussen
6	Fisichella	17	Diniz
7	Herbert	18	Nakano
8	Hakkinen	19	Salo
9	Irvine	20	Trulli
10	Coulthard	21	Verstappen
11	Berger,G.	22	Katayama

Monaco

GRAND PRIX No: 602
DATE: May 11, 1997
VENUE: Monte Carlo
POLE LAP: Frentzen, 1m 18.216s
FASTEST LAP: Schumacher,M., 1m 53.315s

Pn	Driver	Car	Laps	Time/Reason
1	Schumacher,M.	Ferrari	62	2h 00m 05.654s
2	Barrichello	Stewart-Ford	62	2h 00m 58.960s
3	Irvine	Ferrari	62	2h 01m 27.762s
4	Panis	Prost-MH	62	2h 01m 50.056s
5	Salo	Tyrrell-Ford	61	
6	Fisichella	Jordan-Peugeot	61	
7	Magnussen	Stewart-Ford	61	
8	Verstappen	Tyrrell-Ford	60	
9	Berger,G.	Benetton-Ren.	60	
10	Katayama	Minardi-Hart	60	
r	Frentzen	Williams-Ren.	39	accident
r	Nakano	Prost-MH	36	accident
r	Larini	Sauber-Petronas	24	accident
r	Alesi	Benetton-Ren.	16	spun out
r	Villeneuve,J.	Williams-Ren.	16	accident damage
r	Schumacher,R.	Jordan-Peugeot	10	accident
r	Herbert	Sauber-Petronas	9	accident
r	Trulli	Minardi-Hart	7	accident
r	Coulthard	McLaren-Merc.	1	accident
r	Hakkinen	McLaren-Merc.	1	accident
r	Hill,D.	Arrows-Yamaha	1	accident
r	Diniz	Arrows-Yamaha	0	spun out

STARTING GRID:

1	Frentzen	12	Panis
2	Schumacher,M.	13	Hill,D.
3	Villeneuve,J.	14	Salo
4	Fisichella	15	Irvine
5	Coulthard	16	Diniz
6	Schumacher,R.	17	Berger,G.
7	Herbert	18	Trulli
8	Hakkinen	19	Magnussen
9	Alesi	20	Katayama
10	Barrichello	21	Nakano
11	Larini	22	Verstappen

Spanish

GRAND PRIX No: 603
DATE: May 25, 1997
VENUE: Barcelona
POLE LAP: Villeneuve,J., 1m 16.525s
FASTEST LAP: Fisichella, 1m 22.242s

Pn	Driver	Car	Laps	Time/Reason
1	Villeneuve,J.	Williams-Ren.	64	1h 30m 35.896s
2	Panis	Prost-MH	64	1h 30m 41.700s
3	Alesi	Benetton-Ren.	64	1h 30m 48.430s
4	Schumacher,M.	Ferrari	64	1h 30m 53.975s
5	Herbert	Sauber-Petronas	64	1h 31m 03.882s
6	Coulthard	McLaren-Merc.	64	1h 31m 05.640s
7	Hakkinen	McLaren-Merc.	64	1h 31m 24.681s
8	Frentzen	Williams-Ren.	64	1h 31m 40.035s
9	Fisichella	Jordan-Peugeot	64	1h 31m 40.663s
10	Berger,G.	Benetton-Ren.	64	1h 31m 41.568s
11	Verstappen	Tyrrell-Ford	63	
12	Irvine	Ferrari	63	
13	Magnussen	Stewart-Ford	63	
14	Morbidelli	Sauber-Petronas	62	
15	Trulli	Minardi-Hart	62	
r	Diniz	Arrows-Yamaha	53	engine
r	Schumacher,R.	Jordan-Peugeot	50	engine
r	Barrichello	Stewart-Ford	37	engine
r	Salo	Tyrrell-Ford	35	puncture
r	Nakano	Prost-MH	34	gearbox
r	Hill,D.	Arrows-Yamaha	18	engine
r	Katayama	Minardi-Hart	11	hydraulic pump

STARTING GRID:

1	Villeneuve,J.	12	Panis
2	Frentzen	13	Morbidelli
3	Coulthard	14	Salo
4	Alesi	15	Hill,D.
5	Hakkinen	16	Nakano
6	Berger,G.	17	Barrichello
7	Schumacher,M.	18	Trulli
8	Fisichella	19	Verstappen
9	Schumacher,R.	20	Katayama
10	Herbert	21	Diniz
11	Irvine	22	Magnussen

Canadian

GRAND PRIX No: 604
DATE: June 15, 1997
VENUE: Montreal
POLE LAP: Schumacher,M., 1m 18.095s
FASTEST LAP: Coulthard, 1m 19.635s

Pn	Driver	Car	Laps	Time/Reason
1	Schumacher,M.	Ferrari	54	1h 17m 40.646s
2	Alesi	Benetton-Ren.	54	1h 17m 43.211s
3	Fisichella	Jordan-Peugeot	54	1h 17m 43.865s
4	Frentzen	Williams-Ren.	54	1h 17m 44.414s
5	Herbert	Sauber-Petronas	54	1h 17m 45.362s
6	Nakano	Prost-MH	54	1h 18m 17.347s
7	Coulthard	McLaren-Merc.	54	1h 18m 18.399s
8	Diniz	Arrows-Yamaha	53	
9	Hill,D.	Arrows-Yamaha	53	
10	Morbidelli	Sauber-Petronas	53	
11	Panis	Prost-MH	51	
r	Salo	Tyrrell-Ford	46	engine
r	Verstappen	Tyrrell-Ford	42	gearbox
r	Wurz	Benetton-Ren.	35	transmission
r	Barrichello	Stewart-Ford	33	gearbox
r	Trulli	Minardi-Hart	32	engine
r	Schumacher,R.	Jordan-Peugeot	14	accident
r	Katayama	Minardi-Hart	5	accident
r	Villeneuve,J.	Williams-Ren.	1	accident
r	Irvine	Ferrari	0	accident damage
r	Hakkinen	McLaren-Merc.	0	accident
r	Magnussen	Stewart-Ford	0	accident

STARTING GRID:

1	Schumacher,M.	12	Irvine
2	Villeneuve,J.	13	Herbert
3	Barrichello	14	Verstappen
4	Frentzen	15	Hill,D.
5	Coulthard	16	Diniz
6	Fisichella	17	Salo
7	Schumacher,R.	18	Morbidelli
8	Alesi	19	Nakano
9	Hakkinen	20	Trulli
10	Panis	21	Magnussen
11	Wurz	22	Katayama

French

GRAND PRIX No: 605
DATE: June 29, 1997
VENUE: Magny-Cours
POLE LAP: Schumacher,M., 1m 14.454s
FASTEST LAP: Schumacher,M., 1m 17.910s

Pn	Driver	Car	Laps	Time/Reason
1	Schumacher,M.	Ferrari	72	1h 38m 50.492s
2	Frentzen	Williams-Ren.	72	1h 39m 14.029s
3	Irvine	Ferrari	72	1h 40m 05.293s
4	Villeneuve,J.	Williams-Ren.	72	1h 40m 12.276s
5	Alesi	Benetton-Ren.	72	1h 40m 13.227s
6	Schumacher,R.	Jordan-Peugeot	72	1h 40m 20.363s
7	Coulthard	McLaren-Merc.	71	
8	Herbert	Sauber-Petronas	71	
9	Fisichella	Jordan-Peugeot	71	
10	Trulli	Prost-MH	70	
11	Katayama	Minardi-Hart	70	
12	Hill,D.	Arrows-Yamaha	69	
r	Salo	Tyrrell-Ford	61	electrical
r	Wurz	Benetton-Ren.	60	spun out
r	Diniz	Arrows-Yamaha	58	spun out
r	Fontana	Sauber-Petronas	40	spun out
r	Barrichello	Stewart-Ford	36	engine
r	Magnussen	Stewart-Ford	33	brake duct
r	Hakkinen	McLaren-Merc.	18	engine
r	Verstappen	Tyrrell-Ford	15	throttle
r	Nakano	Prost-MH	7	spun out
r	Marques	Minardi-Hart	5	engine

STARTING GRID:

1	Schumacher,M.	12	Nakano
2	Frentzen	13	Barrichello
3	Schumacher,R.	14	Herbert
4	Villeneuve,J.	15	Magnussen
5	Irvine	16	Diniz
6	Trulli	17	Hill,D.
7	Wurz	18	Verstappen
8	Alesi	19	Salo
9	Coulthard	20	Fontana
10	Hakkinen	21	Katayama
11	Fisichella	22	Marques

British

GRAND PRIX No: 606
DATE: July 13, 1997
VENUE: Silverstone
POLE LAP: Villeneuve,J., 1m 21.598s
FASTEST LAP: Schumacher,M., 1m 24.475s

Pn	Driver	Car	Laps	Time/Reason
1	Villeneuve,J.	Williams-Ren.	59	1h 28m 01.665s
2	Alesi	Benetton-Ren.	59	1h 28m 11.870s
3	Wurz	Benetton-Ren.	59	1h 28m 12.961s
4	Coulthard	McLaren-Merc.	59	1h 28m 32.894s
5	Schumacher,R.	Jordan-Peugeot	59	1h 28m 33.545s
6	Hill,D.	Arrows-Yamaha	59	1h 29m 15.217s
7	Fisichella	Jordan-Peugeot	58	
8	Trulli	Prost-MH	58	
9	Fontana	Sauber-Petronas	58	
10	Marques	Minardi-Hart	58	
11	Nakano	Prost-MH	57	
r	Hakkinen	McLaren-Merc.	52	engine
r	Magnussen	Stewart-Ford	50	engine
r	Verstappen	Tyrrell-Ford	45	engine
r	Irvine	Ferrari	44	transmission
r	Salo	Tyrrell-Ford	44	engine
r	Herbert	Sauber-Petronas	42	electrical
r	Schumacher,M.	Ferrari	38	wheel bearings
r	Barrichello	Stewart-Ford	37	engine
r	Diniz	Arrows-Yamaha	29	engine
r	Frentzen	Williams-Ren.	0	accident
r	Katayama	Minardi-Hart	0	accident

STARTING GRID:

1	Villeneuve,J.	12	Hill,D.
2	Frentzen	13	Trulli
3	Hakkinen	14	Nakano
4	Schumacher,M.	15	Magnussen
5	Schumacher,R.	16	Diniz
6	Coulthard	17	Salo
7	Irvine	18	Katayama
8	Wurz	19	Verstappen
9	Herbert	20	Marques
10	Fisichella	21	Barrichello
11	Alesi	22	Fontana

German

GRAND PRIX No:	607
DATE:	July 27, 1997
VENUE:	Hockenheim
POLE LAP:	Berger,G., 1m 41.873s
FASTEST LAP:	Berger,G., 1m 45.747s

Pn	Driver	Car	Laps	Time/Reason
1	Berger,G.	Benetton-Ren.	45	1h 20m 59.046s
2	Schumacher,M.	Ferrari	45	1h 21m 16.573s
3	Hakkinen	McLaren-Merc.	45	1h 21m 23.816s
4	Trulli	Prost-MH	45	1h 21m 26.211s
5	Schumacher,R.	Jordan-Peugeot	45	1h 21m 29.041s
6	Alesi	Benetton-Ren.	45	1h 21m 33.763s
7	Nakano	Prost-MH	45	1h 22m 18.768s
8	Hill,D.	Arrows-Yamaha	44	
9	Fontana	Sauber-Petronas	44	
10	Verstappen	Tyrrell-Ford	44	
11	Fisichella	Jordan-Peugeot	40	
r	Villeneuve,J.	Williams-Ren.	33	spun out
r	Barrichello	Stewart-Ford	33	engine
r	Salo	Tyrrell-Ford	33	clutch
r	Magnussen	Stewart-Ford	27	engine
r	Katayama	Minardi-Hart	23	out of fuel
r	Herbert	Sauber-Petronas	8	accident
r	Diniz	Arrows-Yamaha	8	accident
r	Coulthard	McLaren-Merc.	1	accident
r	Frentzen	Williams-Ren.	1	damage
r	Irvine	Ferrari	1	damage
r	Marques	Minardi-Hart	0	transmission

STARTING GRID:

1	Berger,G.	12	Barrichello
2	Fisichella	13	Hill,D.
3	Hakkinen	14	Herbert
4	Schumacher,M.	15	Magnussen
5	Frentzen	16	Diniz
6	Alesi	17	Nakano
7	Schumacher,R.	18	Fontana
8	Coulthard	19	Salo
9	Villeneuve,J.	20	Verstappen
10	Irvine	21	Marques
11	Trulli	22	Katayama

Hungarian

GRAND PRIX No:	608
DATE:	August 10, 1997
VENUE:	Hungaroring
POLE LAP:	Schumacher,M., 1m 14.672s
FASTEST LAP:	Frentzen, 1m 18.372s

Pn	Driver	Car	Laps	Time/Reason
1	Villeneuve,J.	Williams-Ren.	77	1h 45m 47.149s
2	Hill,D.	Arrows-Yamaha	77	1h 45m 56.228s
3	Herbert	Sauber-Petronas	77	1h 46m 07.594s
4	Schumacher,M.	Ferrari	77	1h 46m 17.650s
5	Schumacher,R.	Jordan-Peugeot	77	1h 46m 17.864s
6	Nakano	Prost-MH	77	1h 46m 28.661s
7	Trulli	Prost-MH	77	1h 47m 02.701s
8	Berger,G.	Benetton-Ren.	77	1h 47m 03.558s
9	Irvine	Ferrari	76	
10	Katayama	Minardi-Hart	76	
11	Alesi	Benetton-Ren.	76	
12	Marques	Minardi-Hart	75	
13	Salo	Tyrrell-Ford	75	
r	Coulthard	McLaren-Merc.	65	electrical
r	Verstappen	Tyrrell-Ford	61	gearbox
r	Diniz	Arrows-Yamaha	53	electrical
r	Fisichella	Jordan-Peugeot	42	spun out
r	Frentzen	Williams-Ren.	29	fuel filter
r	Barrichello	Stewart-Ford	29	engine
r	Hakkinen	McLaren-Merc.	12	hydraulics
r	Morbidelli	Sauber-Petronas	7	engine
r	Magnussen	Stewart-Ford	5	steering

STARTING GRID:

1	Schumacher,M.	12	Trulli
2	Villeneuve,J.	13	Fisichella
3	Hill,D.	14	Schumacher,R.
4	Hakkinen	15	Morbidelli
5	Irvine	16	Nakano
6	Frentzen	17	Magnussen
7	Berger,G.	18	Verstappen
8	Coulthard	19	Diniz
9	Alesi	20	Katayama
10	Herbert	21	Salo
11	Barrichello	22	Marques

Belgian

GRAND PRIX No:	609
DATE:	August 24, 1997
VENUE:	Spa-Francorchamps
POLE LAP:	Villeneuve,J., 1m 49.450s
FASTEST LAP:	Villeneuve,J., 1m 52.692s

Pn	Driver	Car	Laps	Time/Reason
1	Schumacher,M.	Ferrari	44	1h 33m 46.717s
2	Fisichella	Jordan-Peugeot	44	1h 34m 13.470s
dq	Hakkinen	McLaren-Merc.	44	illegal fuel
3	Frentzen	Williams-Ren.	44	1h 34m 18.864s
4	Herbert	Sauber-Petronas	44	1h 34m 25.742s
5	Villeneuve,J.	Williams-Ren.	44	1h 34m 28.820s
6	Berger,G.	Benetton-Ren.	44	1h 34m 50.458s
7	Diniz	Arrows-Yamaha	44	1h 35m 12.648s
8	Alesi	Benetton-Ren.	44	1h 35m 28.725s
9	Morbidelli	Sauber-Petronas	44	1h 35m 29.299s
10	Irvine	Ferrari	43	
11	Salo	Tyrrell-Ford	43	
12	Magnussen	Stewart-Ford	43	
13	Hill,D.	Arrows-Yamaha	42	
14	Katayama	Minardi-Hart	42	
15	Trulli	Prost-MH	42	
16	Verstappen	Tyrrell-Ford	25	spun out
r	Schumacher,R.	Jordan-Peugeot	21	spun out
r	Coulthard	McLaren-Merc.	19	spun out
r	Marques	Minardi-Hart	18	spun out
r	Barrichello	Stewart-Ford	8	steering arm
r	Nakano	Prost-MH	5	electrical

STARTING GRID:

1	Villeneuve,J.	12	Barrichello
2	Alesi	13	Morbidelli
3	Schumacher,M.	14	Trulli
4	Fisichella	15	Berger,G.
5	Hakkinen	16	Nakano
6	Schumacher,R.	17	Irvine
7	Frentzen	18	Magnussen
8	Diniz	19	Salo
9	Hill,D.	20	Katayama
10	Coulthard	21	Verstappen
11	Herbert	22	Marques

Italian

GRAND PRIX No:	610
DATE:	September 7, 1997
VENUE:	Monza
POLE LAP:	Alesi, 1m 22.990s
FASTEST LAP:	Hakkinen, 1m 24.808s

Pn	Driver	Car	Laps	Time/Reason
1	Coulthard	McLaren-Merc.	53	1h 17m 04.609s
2	Alesi	Benetton-Ren.	53	1h 17m 06.546s
3	Frentzen	Williams-Ren.	53	1h 17m 08.952s
4	Fisichella	Jordan-Peugeot	53	1h 17m 10.480s
5	Villeneuve,J.	Williams-Ren.	53	1h 17m 11.025s
6	Schumacher,M.	Ferrari	53	1h 17m 16.090s
7	Berger,G.	Benetton-Ren.	53	1h 17m 17.080s
8	Irvine	Ferrari	53	1h 17m 22.248s
9	Hakkinen	McLaren-Merc.	53	1h 17m 53.982s
10	Trulli	Prost-MH	53	1h 18m 07.315s
11	Nakano	Prost-MH	53	1h 18m 07.936s
12	Morbidelli	Sauber-Petronas	52	
13	Barrichello	Stewart-Ford	52	
14	Marques	Minardi-Hart	50	
r	Hill,D.	Arrows-Yamaha	46	engine
r	Schumacher,R.	Jordan-Peugeot	39	damage
r	Herbert	Sauber-Petronas	38	accident
r	Salo	Tyrrell-Ford	33	engine
r	Magnussen	Stewart-Ford	31	transmission
r	Verstappen	Tyrrell-Ford	12	hydraulics
r	Katayama	Minardi-Hart	8	puncture
r	Diniz	Arrows-Yamaha	4	suspension

STARTING GRID:

1	Alesi	12	Herbert
2	Frentzen	13	Magnussen
3	Fisichella	14	Hill,D.
4	Villeneuve,J.	15	Nakano
5	Hakkinen	16	Trulli
6	Coulthard	17	Diniz
7	Berger,G.	18	Morbidelli
8	Schumacher,R.	19	Salo
9	Schumacher,M.	20	Verstappen
10	Irvine	21	Katayama
11	Barrichello	22	Marques

Austrian

GRAND PRIX No:	611
DATE:	September 21, 1997
VENUE:	A1-Ring
POLE LAP:	Villeneuve,J., 1m 10.304s
FASTEST LAP:	Villeneuve,J., 1m 11.814s

Pn	Driver	Car	Laps	Time/Reason
1	Villeneuve,J.	Williams-Ren.	71	1h 27m 35.999s
2	Coulthard	McLaren-Merc.	71	1h 27m 38.908s
3	Frentzen	Williams-Ren.	71	1h 27m 39.961s
4	Fisichella	Jordan-Peugeot	71	1h 27m 48.126s
5	Schumacher,R.	Jordan-Peugeot	71	1h 28m 07.858s
6	Schumacher,M.	Ferrari	71	1h 28m 09.409s
7	Hill,D.	Arrows-Yamaha	71	1h 28m 13.206s
8	Herbert	Sauber-Petronas	71	1h 28m 25.056s
9	Morbidelli	Sauber-Petronas	71	1h 28m 42.454s
10	Berger,G.	Benetton-Ren.	70	
11	Katayama	Minardi-Hart	69	
12	Verstappen	Tyrrell-Ford	69	
13	Diniz	Arrows-Yamaha	64	shock absorber
14	Barrichello	Stewart-Ford	67	accident
r	Trulli	Prost-MH	58	engine
r	Magnussen	Stewart-Ford	58	engine
r	Nakano	Prost-MH	57	engine
r	Salo	Tyrrell-Ford	48	gearbox
r	Irvine	Ferrari	38	accident
r	Alesi	Benetton-Ren.	37	accident
r	Hakkinen	McLaren-Merc.	1	engine

STARTING GRID:

1	Villeneuve,J.	12	Herbert
2	Hakkinen	13	Morbidelli
3	Trulli	14	Fisichella
4	Frentzen	15	Alesi
5	Barrichello	16	Nakano
6	Magnussen	17	Diniz
7	Hill,D.	18	Berger,G.
8	Irvine	19	Katayama
9	Schumacher,M.	20	Verstappen
10	Coulthard	21	Salo
11	Schumacher,R.		

Luxembourg

GRAND PRIX No:	612
DATE:	September 28, 1997
VENUE:	Nurburgring
POLE LAP:	Hakkinen, 1m 16.602s
FASTEST LAP:	Frentzen, 1m 18.805s

Pn	Driver	Car	Laps	Time/Reason
1	Villeneuve,J.	Williams-Ren.	67	1h 31m 27.843s
2	Alesi	Benetton-Ren.	67	1h 31m 39.613s
3	Frentzen	Williams-Ren.	67	1h 31m 41.323s
4	Berger,G.	Benetton-Ren.	67	1h 31m 44.259s
5	Diniz	Arrows-Yamaha	67	1h 32m 10.990s
6	Panis	Prost-MH	67	1h 32m 11.593s
7	Herbert	Sauber-Petronas	67	1h 32m 12.197s
8	Hill,D.	Arrows-Yamaha	67	1h 32m 12.620s
9	Morbidelli	Sauber-Petronas	66	
10	Salo	Tyrrell-Ford	66	
r	Verstappen	Tyrrell-Ford	50	engine
r	Hakkinen	McLaren-Merc.	43	engine
r	Barrichello	Stewart-Ford	43	hydraulics
r	Coulthard	McLaren-Merc.	42	engine
r	Magnussen	Stewart-Ford	40	driveshaft
r	Irvine	Ferrari	22	engine
r	Nakano	Prost-MH	16	engine
r	Schumacher,M.	Ferrari	2	suspension
r	Marques	Minardi-Hart	1	engine
r	Katayama	Minardi-Hart	1	damage
r	Schumacher,R.	Jordan-Peugeot	0	accident
r	Fisichella	Jordan-Peugeot	0	accident

STARTING GRID:

1	Hakkinen	12	Magnussen
2	Villeneuve,J.	13	Hill,D.
3	Frentzen	14	Irvine
4	Fisichella	15	Diniz
5	Schumacher,M.	16	Herbert
6	Coulthard	17	Nakano
7	Berger,G.	18	Marques
8	Schumacher,R.	19	Morbidelli
9	Barrichello	20	Salo
10	Alesi	21	Verstappen
11	Panis	22	Katayama

Japanese

GRAND PRIX No:	613
DATE:	October 12, 1997
VENUE:	Suzuka
POLE LAP:	Villeneuve,J., 1m 36.071s
FASTEST LAP:	Frentzen, 1m 38.942s

Pn	Driver	Car	Laps	Time/Reason
1	Schumacher,M.	Ferrari	53	1h 29m 48.446s
2	Frentzen	Williams-Ren.	53	1h 29m 49.824s
3	Irvine	Ferrari	53	1h 30m 14.830s
4	Hakkinen	McLaren-Merc.	53	1h 30m 15.575s
dq	Villeneuve,J.	Williams-Ren.	53	ignored yellow flag
5	Alesi	Benetton-Ren.	53	1h 30m 28.849s
6	Herbert	Sauber-Petronas	53	1h 30m 30.076s
7	Fisichella	Jordan-Peugeot	53	1h 30m 45.271s
8	Berger,G.	Benetton-Ren.	53	1h 30m 48.875s
9	Schumacher,R.	Jordan-Peugeot	53	1h 31m 10.482s
10	Coulthard	McLaren-Merc.	52	
11	Hill,D.	Arrows-Yamaha	52	
12	Diniz	Arrows-Yamaha	52	
13	Verstappen	Tyrrell-Ford	52	
r	Marques	Minardi-Hart	46	gearbox
r	Salo	Tyrrell-Ford	46	engine
r	Panis	Prost-MH	36	engine
r	Nakano	Prost-MH	22	wheel bearings
r	Katayama	Minardi-Hart	8	engine
r	Barrichello	Stewart-Ford	6	spun out
r	Magnussen	Stewart-Ford	3	spun out
dns	Morbidelli	Sauber-Petronas		accident prac.

STARTING GRID:

1	Villeneuve,J.	12	Barrichello
2	Schumacher,M.	13	Schumacher,R.
3	Irvine	14	Magnussen
4	Hakkinen	15	Nakano
5	Berger,G.	16	Diniz
6	Frentzen	17	Hill,D.
7	Alesi	18	Morbidelli
8	Herbert	19	Katayama
9	Fisichella	20	Marques
10	Panis	21	Verstappen
11	Coulthard	22	Salo

European

GRAND PRIX No:	614
DATE:	October 26, 1997
VENUE:	Jerez
POLE LAP:	Villeneuve,J., 1m 21.072s
FASTEST LAP:	Frentzen, 1m 23.135s

Pn	Driver	Car	Laps	Time/Reason
1	Hakkinen	McLaren-Merc.	69	1h 38m 57.771s
2	Coulthard	McLaren-Merc.	69	1h 38m 59.425s
3	Villeneuve,J.	Williams-Ren.	69	1h 38m 59.574s
4	Berger,G.	Benetton-Ren.	69	1h 38m 59.690s
5	Irvine	Ferrari	69	1h 39m 01.560s
6	Frentzen	Williams-Ren.	69	1h 39m 02.308s
7	Panis	Prost-MH	69	1h 40m 04.916s
8	Herbert	Sauber-Petronas	69	1h 40m 10.732s
9	Magnussen	Stewart-Ford	69	1h 40m 15.258s
10	Nakano	Prost-MH	69	1h 40m 15.986s
11	Fisichella	Jordan-Peugeot	68	
12	Salo	Tyrrell-Ford	68	
13	Alesi	Benetton-Ren.	68	
14	Fontana	Sauber-Petronas	68	
15	Marques	Minardi-Hart	68	
16	Verstappen	Tyrrell-Ford	68	
17	Katayama	Minardi-Hart	68	
r	Schumacher,M.	Ferrari	47	accident
r	Hill,D.	Arrows-Yamaha	47	gearbox
r	Schumacher,R.	Jordan-Peugeot	44	water leak
r	Barrichello	Stewart-Ford	30	gearbox
r	Diniz	Arrows-Yamaha	11	spun out

STARTING GRID:

1	Villeneuve,J.	12	Barrichello
2	Schumacher,M.	13	Diniz
3	Frentzen	14	Herbert
4	Hill,D.	15	Nakano
5	Hakkinen	16	Schumacher,R.
6	Coulthard	17	Fisichella
7	Irvine	18	Fontana
8	Berger,G.	19	Katayama
9	Panis	20	Marques
10	Alesi	21	Salo
11	Magnussen	22	Verstappen

Australian

GRAND PRIX No:	615
DATE:	March 8, 1998
VENUE:	Melbourne
POLE LAP:	Hakkinen, 1m 30.010s
FASTEST LAP:	Hakkinen, 1m 31.649s

Pn	Driver	Car	Laps	Time/Reason
1	Hakkinen	McLaren-Merc.	58	1h 31m 45.996s
2	Coulthard	McLaren-Merc.	58	1h 31m 46.698s
3	Frentzen	Williams-Meca.	57	
4	Irvine	Ferrari	57	
5	Villeneuve,J.	Williams-Meca.	57	
6	Herbert	Sauber-Petronas	57	
7	Wurz	Benetton-Play.	57	
8	Hill,D.	Jordan-MH	57	
9	Panis	Prost-Peugeot	57	
r	Fisichella	Benetton-Play.	43	rear wing
r	Alesi	Sauber-Petronas	41	engine
r	Trulli	Prost-Peugeot	26	gearbox
r	Rosset	Tyrrell-Ford	25	gear selection
r	Salo	Arrows	23	transmission
r	Tuero	Minardi-Ford	22	engine
r	Nakano	Minardi-Ford	8	transmission
r	Schumacher,M.	Ferrari	5	engine
r	Diniz	Arrows	2	hydraulics
r	Schumacher,R.	Jordan-MH	1	accident
r	Magnussen	Stewart-Ford	1	accident
r	Takagi	Tyrrell-Ford	1	spun out
r	Barrichello	Stewart-Ford	0	gearbox

STARTING GRID:

1	Hakkinen	12	Alesi
2	Coulthard	13	Takagi
3	Schumacher,M.	14	Barrichello
4	Villeneuve,J.	15	Trulli
5	Herbert	16	Salo
6	Frentzen	17	Tuero
7	Fisichella	18	Magnussen
8	Irvine	19	Rosset
9	Schumacher,R.	20	Diniz
10	Hill,D.	21	Panis
11	Wurz	22	Nakano

Brazilian

GRAND PRIX No:	616
DATE:	March 29, 1998
VENUE:	Interlagos
POLE LAP:	Hakkinen, 1m 17.092s
FASTEST LAP:	Hakkinen, 1m 19.337s

Pn	Driver	Car	Laps	Time/Reason
1	Hakkinen	McLaren-Merc.	72	1h 37m 11.747s
2	Coulthard	McLaren-Merc.	72	1h 37m 12.849s
3	Schumacher,M.	Ferrari	72	1h 38m 12.297s
4	Wurz	Benetton-Play.	72	1h 38m 19.200s
5	Frentzen	Williams-Meca.	71	
6	Fisichella	Benetton-Play.	71	
7	Villeneuve,J.	Williams-Meca.	71	
8	Irvine	Ferrari	71	
9	Alesi	Sauber-Petronas	71	
dq	Hill,D.	Jordan-MH	70	underweight
10	Magnussen	Stewart-Ford	70	
r	Herbert	Sauber-Petronas	67	driver neck injury
r	Panis	Prost-Peugeot	63	gearbox
r	Barrichello	Stewart-Ford	56	gearbox
r	Rosset	Tyrrell-Ford	52	gearbox
r	Tuero	Minardi-Ford	44	electrical
r	Diniz	Arrows	26	gearbox
r	Takagi	Tyrrell-Ford	19	engine
r	Salo	Arrows	18	engine
r	Trulli	Prost-Peugeot	17	fuel pressure
r	Nakano	Minardi-Ford	3	spun out
r	Schumacher,R.	Jordan-MH	0	spun out

STARTING GRID:

1	Hakkinen	12	Trulli
2	Coulthard	13	Barrichello
3	Frentzen	14	Herbert
4	Schumacher,M.	15	Alesi
5	Wurz	16	Magnussen
6	Irvine	17	Takagi
7	Fisichella	18	Nakano
8	Schumacher,R.	19	Tuero
9	Panis	20	Salo
10	Villeneuve,J.	21	Rosset
11	Hill,D.	22	Diniz

Argentine

GRAND PRIX No: 617
DATE: April 12, 1998
VENUE: Buenos Aires
POLE LAP: Coulthard, 1m 25.852s
FASTEST LAP: Wurz, 1m 28.178s

Pn	Driver	Car	Laps	Time/Reason
1	Schumacher,M.	Ferrari	72	1h 48m 36.175s
2	Hakkinen	McLaren-Merc.	72	1h 48m 59.173s
3	Irvine	Ferrari	72	1h 49m 33.920s
4	Wurz	Benetton-Play.	72	1h 49m 44.309s
5	Alesi	Sauber-Petronas	72	1h 49m 54.461s
6	Coulthard	McLaren-Merc.	72	1h 49m 55.826s
7	Fisichella	Benetton-Play.	72	1h 50m 04.612s
8	Hill,D.	Jordan-MH	71	
9	Frentzen	Williams-Meca.	71	
10	Barrichello	Stewart-Ford	70	
11	Trulli	Prost-Peugeot	70	
12	Takagi	Tyrrell-Ford	70	
13	Nakano	Minardi-Ford	69	
14	Rosset	Tyrrell-Ford	68	
15	Panis	Prost-Peugeot	65	engine
r	Tuero	Minardi-Ford	63	accident
r	Villeneuve,J.	Williams-Meca.	52	accident
r	Herbert	Sauber-Petronas	46	accident damage
r	Schumacher,R.	Jordan-MH	22	spun out
r	Salo	Arrows	18	gearbox
r	Magnussen	Stewart-Ford	17	transmission
r	Diniz	Arrows	13	gearbox

STARTING GRID:

1	Coulthard	12	Herbert
2	Schumacher,M.	13	Takagi
3	Hakkinen	14	Barrichello
4	Irvine	15	Panis
5	Schumacher,R.	16	Trulli
6	Frentzen	17	Salo
7	Villeneuve,J.	18	Diniz
8	Wurz	19	Nakano
9	Hill,D.	20	Tuero
10	Fisichella	21	Rosset
11	Alesi	22	Magnussen

San Marino

GRAND PRIX No: 618
DATE: April 26, 1998
VENUE: Imola
POLE LAP: Coulthard, 1m 25.973s
FASTEST LAP: Schumacher,M., 1m 29.345s

Pn	Driver	Car	Laps	Time/Reason
1	Coulthard	McLaren-Merc.	62	1h 34m 24.593s
2	Schumacher,M.	Ferrari	62	1h 34m 29.147s
3	Irvine	Ferrari	62	1h 35m 16.368s
4	Villeneuve,J.	Williams-Meca.	62	1h 35m 19.183s
5	Frentzen	Williams-Meca.	62	1h 35m 42.069s
6	Alesi	Sauber-Petronas	61	
7	Schumacher,R.	Jordan-MH	60	
8	Tuero	Minardi-Ford	60	
9	Salo	Arrows	60	
r	Hill,D.	Jordan-MH	57	engine
r	Panis	Prost-Peugeot	56	engine
r	Rosset	Tyrrell-Ford	48	engine
r	Takagi	Tyrrell-Ford	40	engine
r	Trulli	Prost-Peugeot	34	throttle
r	Nakano	Minardi-Ford	27	engine
r	Diniz	Arrows	18	engine
r	Hakkinen	McLaren-Merc.	17	gearbox
r	Fisichella	Benetton-Play.	17	accident
r	Wurz	Benetton-Play.	17	gearbox
r	Herbert	Sauber-Petronas	12	puncture
r	Magnussen	Stewart-Ford	8	gearbox
r	Barrichello	Stewart-Ford	0	accident

STARTING GRID:

1	Coulthard	12	Alesi
2	Hakkinen	13	Panis
3	Schumacher,M.	14	Salo
4	Irvine	15	Takagi
5	Wurz	16	Trulli
6	Villeneuve,J.	17	Barrichello
7	Hill,D.	18	Diniz
8	Frentzen	19	Tuero
9	Schumacher,R.	20	Magnussen
10	Fisichella	21	Nakano
11	Herbert	22	Rosset

Spanish

GRAND PRIX No: 619

DATE: May 10, 1998

VENUE: Barcelona

POLE LAP: Hakkinen, 1m 20.262s

FASTEST LAP: Hakkinen, 1m 24.275s

Pn	Driver	Car	Laps	Time/Reason
1	Hakkinen	McLaren-Merc.	65	1h 33m 37.621s
2	Coulthard	McLaren-Merc.	65	1h 33m 47.060s
3	Schumacher,M.	Ferrari	65	1h 34m 24.715s
4	Wurz	Benetton-Play.	65	1h 34m 40.159s
5	Barrichello	Stewart-Ford	64	
6	Villeneuve,J.	Williams-Meca.	64	
7	Herbert	Sauber-Petronas	64	
8	Frentzen	Williams-Meca.	63	
9	Trulli	Prost-Peugeot	63	
10	Alesi	Sauber-Petronas	63	
11	Schumacher,R.	Jordan-MH	63	
12	Magnussen	Stewart-Ford	63	
13	Takagi	Tyrrell-Ford	63	
14	Nakano	Minardi-Ford	63	
15	Tuero	Minardi-Ford	63	
16	Panis	Prost-Peugeot	60	engine
r	Hill,D.	Jordan-MH	46	engine
r	Irvine	Ferrari	28	accident
r	Fisichella	Benetton-Play.	28	accident
r	Salo	Arrows	21	engine
r	Diniz	Arrows	20	engine
dnq	Rosset	Tyrrell-Ford		107% rule

STARTING GRID:

1	Hakkinen	12	Panis
2	Coulthard	13	Frentzen
3	Schumacher,M.	14	Alesi
4	Fisichella	15	Diniz
5	Wurz	16	Trulli
6	Irvine	17	Salo
7	Herbert	18	Magnussen
8	Hill,D.	19	Tuero
9	Barrichello	20	Nakano
10	Villeneuve,J.	21	Takagi
11	Schumacher,R.	107	Rosset

Monaco

GRAND PRIX No: 620

DATE: May 24, 1998

VENUE: Monte Carlo

POLE LAP: Hakkinen, 1m 19.798s

FASTEST LAP: Hakkinen, 1m 22.948s

Pn	Driver	Car	Laps	Time/Reason
1	Hakkinen	McLaren-Merc.	78	1h 51m 23.595s
2	Fisichella	Benetton-Play.	78	1h 51m 35.070s
3	Irvine	Ferrari	78	1h 52m 04.973s
4	Salo	Arrows	78	1h 52m 23.958s
5	Villeneuve,J.	Williams-Meca.	77	
6	Diniz	Arrows	77	
7	Herbert	Sauber-Petronas	77	
8	Hill,D.	Jordan-MH	76	
9	Nakano	Minardi-Ford	76	
10	Schumacher,M.	Ferrari	76	
11	Takagi	Tyrrell-Ford	76	
12	Alesi	Sauber-Petronas	72	engine
r	Trulli	Prost-Peugeot	56	gearbox
r	Panis	Prost-Peugeot	49	loose wheel
r	Schumacher,R.	Jordan-MH	44	accident damage
r	Wurz	Benetton-Play.	42	accident
r	Magnussen	Stewart-Ford	30	suspension
r	Coulthard	McLaren-Merc.	17	accident
r	Barrichello	Stewart-Ford	11	suspension
r	Frentzen	Williams-Meca.	9	accident
r	Tuero	Minardi-Ford	0	accident
dnq	Rosset	Tyrrell-Ford		107% rule

STARTING GRID:

1	Hakkinen	12	Diniz
2	Coulthard	13	Villeneuve,J.
3	Fisichella	14	Barrichello
4	Schumacher,M.	15	Hill,D.
5	Frentzen	16	Schumacher,R.
6	Wurz	17	Magnussen
7	Irvine	18	Panis
8	Salo	19	Nakano
9	Herbert	20	Takagi
10	Trulli	21	Tuero
11	Alesi	107	Rosset

Canadian

GRAND PRIX No: 621
DATE: June 7, 1998
VENUE: Montreal
POLE LAP: Coulthard, 1m 18.213s
FASTEST LAP: Schumacher,M., 1m 19.379s

Pn	Driver	Car	Laps	Time/Reason
1	Schumacher,M.	Ferrari	69	1h 40m 57.355s
2	Fisichella	Benetton-Play.	69	1h 41m 14.071s
3	Irvine	Ferrari	69	1h 41m 57.414s
4	Wurz	Benetton-Play.	69	1h 42m 00.587s
5	Barrichello	Stewart-Ford	69	1h 42m 18.868s
6	Magnussen	Stewart-Ford	68	
7	Nakano	Minardi-Ford	68	
8	Rosset	Tyrrell-Ford	68	
9	Diniz	Arrows	68	
10	Villeneuve,J.	Williams-Meca.	63	
r	Tuero	Minardi-Ford	53	electrical
r	Hill,D.	Jordan-MH	42	electrical
r	Panis	Prost-Peugeot	39	engine
r	Frentzen	Williams-Meca.	20	accident
r	Coulthard	McLaren-Merc.	18	throttle
r	Herbert	Sauber-Petronas	18	spun out
r	Salo	Arrows	18	steering
r	Hakkinen	McLaren-Merc.	0	gearbox
r	Schumacher,R.	Jordan-MH	0	loss of drive
r	Alesi	Sauber-Petronas	0	accident
r	Trulli	Prost-Peugeot	0	accident
r	Takagi	Tyrrell-Ford	0	loss of drive

STARTING GRID:

1	Coulthard	12	Herbert
2	Hakkinen	13	Barrichello
3	Schumacher,M.	14	Trulli
4	Fisichella	15	Panis
5	Schumacher,R.	16	Takagi
6	Villeneuve,J.	17	Salo
7	Frentzen	18	Nakano
8	Irvine	19	Diniz
9	Alesi	20	Magnussen
10	Hill,D.	21	Tuero
11	Wurz	22	Rosset

French

GRAND PRIX No: 622
DATE: June 28, 1998
VENUE: Magny-Cours
POLE LAP: Hakkinen, 1m 14.929s
FASTEST LAP: Coulthard, 1m 17.523s

Pn	Driver	Car	Laps	Time/Reason
1	Schumacher,M.	Ferrari	71	1h 34m 45.026s
2	Irvine	Ferrari	71	1h 35m 04.601s
3	Hakkinen	McLaren-Merc.	71	1h 35m 04.773s
4	Villeneuve,J.	Williams-Meca.	71	1h 35m 51.991s
5	Wurz	Benetton-Play.	70	
6	Coulthard	McLaren-Merc.	70	
7	Alesi	Sauber-Petronas	70	
8	Herbert	Sauber-Petronas	70	
9	Fisichella	Benetton-Play.	70	
10	Barrichello	Stewart-Ford	69	
11	Panis	Prost-Peugeot	69	
12	Verstappen	Stewart-Ford	69	
13	Salo	Arrows	69	
14	Diniz	Arrows	69	
15	Frentzen	Williams-Meca.	68	accident damage
16	Schumacher,R.	Jordan-MH	68	
17	Nakano	Minardi-Ford	65	engine
r	Takagi	Tyrrell-Ford	60	engine
r	Trulli	Prost-Peugeot	55	spun out
r	Tuero	Minardi-Ford	41	gearbox
r	Hill,D.	Jordan-MH	19	hydraulics
r	Rosset	Tyrrell-Ford	16	engine

STARTING GRID:

1	Hakkinen	12	Trulli
2	Schumacher,M.	13	Herbert
3	Coulthard	14	Barrichello
4	Irvine	15	Verstappen
5	Villeneuve,J.	16	Panis
6	Schumacher,R.	17	Diniz
7	Hill,D.	18	Rosset
8	Frentzen	19	Salo
9	Fisichella	20	Takagi
10	Wurz	21	Nakano
11	Alesi	22	Tuero

British

GRAND PRIX No: 623
DATE: July 12, 1998
VENUE: Silverstone
POLE LAP: Hakkinen, 1m 23.271s
FASTEST LAP: Schumacher,M., 1m 35.704s

Pn	Driver	Car	Laps	Time/Reason
1	Schumacher,M.	Ferrari	60	1h 47m 12.450s
2	Hakkinen	McLaren-Merc.	60	1h 47m 24.915s
3	Irvine	Ferrari	60	1h 47m 31.649s
4	Wurz	Benetton-Play.	59	
5	Fisichella	Benetton-Play.	59	
6	Schumacher,R.	Jordan-MH	59	
7	Villeneuve,J.	Williams-Meca.	59	
8	Nakano	Minardi-Ford	58	
9	Takagi	Tyrrell-Ford	56	
r	Alesi	Sauber-Petronas	53	electrical
r	Diniz	Arrows	45	spun out
r	Panis	Prost-Peugeot	40	spun out
r	Barrichello	Stewart-Ford	39	spun out
r	Verstappen	Stewart-Ford	38	engine
r	Coulthard	McLaren-Merc.	37	spun out
r	Trulli	Prost-Peugeot	37	spun out
r	Rosset	Tyrrell-Ford	29	spun out
r	Tuero	Minardi-Ford	29	spun out
r	Herbert	Sauber-Petronas	27	spun out
r	Salo	Arrows	27	spun out
r	Frentzen	Williams-Meca.	15	spun out
r	Hill,D.	Jordan-MH	13	spun out

STARTING GRID:

1	Hakkinen	12	Diniz
2	Schumacher,M.	13	Salo
3	Villeneuve,J.	14	Trulli
4	Coulthard	15	Verstappen
5	Irvine	16	Barrichello
6	Frentzen	17	Takagi
7	Hill,D.	18	Tuero
8	Alesi	19	Nakano
9	Herbert	20	Rosset
10	Fisichella	21	Schumacher,R.
11	Wurz	22	Panis

Austrian

GRAND PRIX No: 624
DATE: July 26, 1998
VENUE: A1-Ring
POLE LAP: Fisichella, 1m 29.598s
FASTEST LAP: Coulthard, 1m 12.878s

Pn	Driver	Car	Laps	Time/Reason
1	Hakkinen	McLaren-Merc.	71	1h 30m 44.086s
2	Coulthard	McLaren-Merc.	71	1h 30m 49.375s
3	Schumacher,M.	Ferrari	71	1h 31m 23.178s
4	Irvine	Ferrari	71	1h 31m 28.062s
5	Schumacher,R.	Jordan-MH	71	1h 31m 34.740s
6	Villeneuve,J.	Williams-Meca.	71	1h 31m 37.288s
7	Hill,D.	Jordan-MH	71	1h 31m 57.710s
8	Herbert	Sauber-Petronas	70	
9	Wurz	Benetton-Play.	70	
10	Trulli	Prost-Peugeot	70	
11	Nakano	Minardi-Ford	70	
12	Rosset	Tyrrell-Ford	69	
r	Verstappen	Stewart-Ford	51	engine
r	Tuero	Minardi-Ford	30	spun out
r	Fisichella	Benetton-Play.	21	accident
r	Alesi	Sauber-Petronas	21	accident
r	Frentzen	Williams-Meca.	16	engine
r	Barrichello	Stewart-Ford	8	brakes
r	Diniz	Arrows	3	accident damage
r	Salo	Arrows	1	accident damage
r	Panis	Prost-Peugeot	0	clutch
r	Takagi	Tyrrell-Ford	0	spun out

STARTING GRID:

1	Fisichella	12	Verstappen
2	Alesi	13	Diniz
3	Hakkinen	14	Coulthard
4	Schumacher,M.	15	Hill,D.
5	Barrichello	16	Trulli
6	Salo	17	Wurz
7	Frentzen	18	Herbert
8	Irvine	19	Tuero
9	Schumacher,R.	20	Takagi
10	Panis	21	Nakano
11	Villeneuve,J.	22	Rosset

German

GRAND PRIX No:	625
DATE:	August 2, 1998
VENUE:	Hockenheim
POLE LAP:	Hakkinen, 1m 41.838s
FASTEST LAP:	Coulthard, 1m 46.116s

Pn	Driver	Car	Laps	Time/Reason
1	Hakkinen	McLaren-Merc.	45	1h 20m 47.984s
2	Coulthard	McLaren-Merc.	45	1h 20m 48.410s
3	Villeneuve,J.	Williams-Meca.	45	1h 20m 50.561s
4	Hill,D.	Jordan-MH	45	1h 20m 55.169s
5	Schumacher,M.	Ferrari	45	1h 21m 00.597s
6	Schumacher,R.	Jordan-MH	45	1h 21m 17.722s
7	Fisichella	Benetton-Play.	45	1h 21m 19.010s
8	Irvine	Ferrari	45	1h 21m 19.633s
9	Frentzen	Williams-Meca.	45	1h 21m 20.768s
10	Alesi	Sauber-Petronas	45	1h 21m 36.355s
11	Wurz	Benetton-Play.	45	1h 21m 45.978s
12	Trulli	Prost-Peugeot	44	
13	Takagi	Tyrrell-Ford	44	
14	Salo	Arrows	44	
15	Panis	Prost-Peugeot	44	
16	Tuero	Minardi-Ford	43	
r	Herbert	Sauber-Petronas	37	gearbox
r	Nakano	Minardi-Ford	36	gearbox
r	Barrichello	Stewart-Ford	27	gearbox
r	Verstappen	Stewart-Ford	24	transmission
r	Diniz	Arrows	2	throttle

STARTING GRID:

1	Hakkinen	12	Herbert
2	Coulthard	13	Barrichello
3	Villeneuve,J.	14	Trulli
4	Schumacher,R.	15	Takagi
5	Hill,D.	16	Panis
6	Irvine	17	Salo
7	Wurz	18	Diniz
8	Fisichella	19	Verstappen
9	Schumacher,M.	20	Nakano
10	Frentzen	21	Tuero
11	Alesi		

Hungarian

GRAND PRIX No:	626
DATE:	August 16, 1998
VENUE:	Hungaroring
POLE LAP:	Hakkinen, 1m 16.973s
FASTEST LAP:	Schumacher,M., 1m 19.286s

Pn	Driver	Car	Laps	Time/Reason
1	Schumacher,M.	Ferrari	77	1h 45m 25.550s
2	Coulthard	McLaren-Merc.	77	1h 45m 34.983s
3	Villeneuve,J.	Williams-Meca.	77	1h 46m 09.994s
4	Hill,D.	Jordan-MH	77	1h 46m 20.626s
5	Frentzen	Williams-Meca.	77	1h 46m 22.060s
6	Hakkinen	McLaren-Merc.	76	
7	Alesi	Sauber-Petronas	76	
8	Fisichella	Benetton-Play.	76	
9	Schumacher,R.	Jordan-MH	76	
10	Herbert	Sauber-Petronas	76	
11	Diniz	Arrows	74	
12	Panis	Prost-Peugeot	74	
13	Verstappen	Stewart-Ford	74	
14	Takagi	Tyrrell-Ford	74	
15	Nakano	Minardi-Ford	74	
16	Wurz	Benetton-Play.	69	gearbox
r	Barrichello	Stewart-Ford	54	gearbox
r	Trulli	Prost-Peugeot	28	engine
r	Salo	Arrows	18	gearbox
r	Irvine	Ferrari	13	gearbox
r	Tuero	Minardi-Ford	13	engine
dnq	Rosset	Tyrrell-Ford		107% rule

STARTING GRID:

1	Hakkinen	12	Diniz
2	Coulthard	13	Salo
3	Schumacher,M.	14	Barrichello
4	Hill,D.	15	Herbert
5	Irvine	16	Trulli
6	Villeneuve,J.	17	Verstappen
7	Frentzen	18	Takagi
8	Fisichella	19	Nakano
9	Wurz	20	Panis
10	Schumacher,R.	21	Tuero
11	Alesi	107	Rosset

Belgian

GRAND PRIX No: 627

DATE: August 30, 1998

VENUE: Spa-Francorchamps

POLE LAP: Hakkinen, 1m 48.682s

FASTEST LAP: Schumacher,M., 2m 03.766s

Pn	Driver	Car	Laps	Time/Reason
1	Hill,D.	Jordan-MH	44	1h 43m 47.407s
2	Schumacher,R.	Jordan-MH	44	1h 43m 48.339s
3	Alesi	Sauber-Petronas	44	1h 43m 54.647s
4	Frentzen	Williams-Meca.	44	1h 44m 19.650s
5	Diniz	Arrows	44	1h 44m 39.089s
6	Trulli	Prost-Peugeot	42	
7	Coulthard	McLaren-Merc.	39	
8	Nakano	Minardi-Ford	39	
r	Fisichella	Benetton-Play.	26	accident
r	Schumacher,M.	Ferrari	25	accident
r	Irvine	Ferrari	25	spun out
r	Tuero	Minardi-Ford	17	electrical
r	Villeneuve,J.	Williams-Meca.	16	accident
r	Takagi	Tyrrell-Ford	10	spun out
r	Verstappen	Stewart-Ford	8	engine
r	Hakkinen	McLaren-Merc.	0	accident
r	Wurz	Benetton-Play.	0	accident
r	Herbert	Sauber-Petronas	0	accident
dns	Panis	Prost-Peugeot	0	accident at start
dns	Barrichello	Stewart-Ford	0	accident at start
dns	Salo	Arrows	0	accident at start
dns	Rosset	Tyrrell-Ford	0	accident at start

STARTING GRID:

1	Hakkinen	12	Herbert
2	Coulthard	13	Trulli
3	Hill,D.	14	Barrichello
4	Schumacher,M.	15	Panis
5	Irvine	16	Diniz
6	Villeneuve,J.	17	Verstappen
7	Fisichella	18	Salo
8	Schumacher,R.	19	Takagi
9	Frentzen	20	Rosset
10	Alesi	21	Nakano
11	Wurz	22	Tuero

Italian

GRAND PRIX No: 628

DATE: September 13, 1998

VENUE: Monza

POLE LAP: Schumacher,M., 1m 25.298s

FASTEST LAP: Hakkinen, 1m 25.139s

Pn	Driver	Car	Laps	Time/Reason
1	Schumacher,M.	Ferrari	53	1h 17m 09.672s
2	Irvine	Ferrari	53	1h 17m 47.649s
3	Schumacher,R.	Jordan-MH	53	1h 17m 50.824s
4	Hakkinen	McLaren-Merc.	53	1h 18m 05.343s
5	Alesi	Sauber-Petronas	53	1h 18m 11.544s
6	Hill,D.	Jordan-MH	53	1h 18m 16.360s
7	Frentzen	Williams-Meca.	52	
8	Fisichella	Benetton-Play.	52	
9	Takagi	Tyrrell-Ford	52	
10	Barrichello	Stewart-Ford	52	
11	Tuero	Minardi-Ford	51	
12	Rosset	Tyrrell-Ford	51	
13	Trulli	Prost-Peugeot	50	
r	Verstappen	Stewart-Ford	39	gearbox
r	Villeneuve,J.	Williams-Meca.	37	spun out
r	Salo	Arrows	32	throttle
r	Wurz	Benetton-Play.	24	gearbox
r	Coulthard	McLaren-Merc.	16	engine
r	Panis	Prost-Peugeot	15	handling
r	Nakano	Minardi-Ford	13	engine
r	Herbert	Sauber-Petronas	12	spun out
r	Diniz	Arrows	10	spun out

STARTING GRID:

1	Schumacher,M.	12	Frentzen
2	Villeneuve,J.	13	Barrichello
3	Hakkinen	14	Hill,D.
4	Coulthard	15	Herbert
5	Irvine	16	Salo
6	Schumacher,R.	17	Verstappen
7	Wurz	18	Rosset
8	Alesi	19	Takagi
9	Panis	20	Diniz
10	Trulli	21	Nakano
11	Fisichella	22	Tuero

Luxembourg

GRAND PRIX No: 629
DATE: September 27, 1998
VENUE: Nurburgring
POLE LAP: Schumacher,M., 1m 18.561s
FASTEST LAP: Hakkinen, 1m 20.450s

Pn	Driver	Car	Laps	Time/Reason
1	Hakkinen	McLaren-Merc.	67	1h 32m 14.789s
2	Schumacher,M.	Ferrari	67	1h 32m 17.000s
3	Coulthard	McLaren-Merc.	67	1h 32m 48.952s
4	Irvine	Ferrari	67	1h 33m 12.971s
5	Frentzen	Williams-Meca.	67	1h 33m 15.036s
6	Fisichella	Benetton-Play.	67	1h 33m 16.148s
7	Wurz	Benetton-Play.	67	1h 33m 19.578s
8	Villeneuve,J.	Williams-Meca.	66	
9	Hill,D.	Jordan-MH	66	
10	Alesi	Sauber-Petronas	66	
11	Barrichello	Stewart-Ford	65	
12	Panis	Prost-Peugeot	65	
13	Verstappen	Stewart-Ford	65	
14	Salo	Arrows	65	
15	Nakano	Minardi-Ford	65	
16	Takagi	Tyrrell-Ford	65	
uc	Tuero	Minardi-Ford	56	
r	Schumacher,R.	Jordan-MH	53	brakes
r	Herbert	Sauber-Petronas	37	engine
r	Rosset	Tyrrell-Ford	36	engine
r	Trulli	Prost-Peugeot	6	transmission
r	Diniz	Arrows	6	hydraulics

STARTING GRID:

1	Schumacher,M.	12	Barrichello
2	Irvine	13	Herbert
3	Hakkinen	14	Trulli
4	Fisichella	15	Panis
5	Coulthard	16	Salo
6	Schumacher,R.	17	Diniz
7	Frentzen	18	Verstappen
8	Wurz	19	Takagi
9	Villeneuve,J.	20	Nakano
10	Hill,D.	21	Tuero
11	Alesi	22	Rosset

Japanese

GRAND PRIX No: 630
DATE: November 1, 1998
VENUE: Suzuka
POLE LAP: Schumacher,M., 1m 36.293s
FASTEST LAP: Schumacher,M., 1m 40.190s

Pn	Driver	Car	Laps	Time/Reason
1	Hakkinen	McLaren-Merc.	51	1h 27m 22.535s
2	Irvine	Ferrari	51	1h 27m 29.026s
3	Coulthard	McLaren-Merc.	51	1h 27m 50.197s
4	Hill,D.	Jordan-MH	51	1h 28m 36.026s
5	Frentzen	Williams-Meca.	51	1h 28m 36.392s
6	Villeneuve,J.	Williams-Meca.	51	1h 28m 38.402s
7	Alesi	Sauber-Petronas	51	1h 28m 58.588s
8	Fisichella	Benetton-Play.	51	1h 29m 03.837s
9	Wurz	Benetton-Play.	50	1h 27m 37.673s
10	Herbert	Sauber-Petronas	50	1h 27m 43.035s
11	Panis	Prost-Peugeot	50	1h 28m 20.327s
12	Trulli	Prost-Peugeot	48	
r	Nakano	Minardi-Ford	40	electrical
r	Schumacher,M.	Ferrari	31	puncture
r	Takagi	Tyrrell-Ford	28	accident
r	Tuero	Minardi-Ford	28	accident
r	Barrichello	Stewart-Ford	25	hydraulics
r	Verstappen	Stewart-Ford	21	gearbox
r	Salo	Arrows	14	hydraulics
r	Schumacher,R.	Jordan-MH	13	engine
r	Diniz	Arrows	2	spun out
dnq	Rosset	Tyrrell-Ford		107% rule

STARTING GRID:

1	Schumacher,M.	12	Alesi
2	Hakkinen	13	Panis
3	Coulthard	14	Trulli
4	Irvine	15	Salo
5	Frentzen	16	Barrichello
6	Villeneuve,J.	17	Takagi
7	Schumacher,R.	18	Diniz
8	Hill,D.	19	Verstappen
9	Wurz	20	Nakano
10	Fisichella	21	Tuero
11	Herbert	107	Rosset

Australian

GRAND PRIX No:	631
DATE:	March 7, 1999
VENUE:	Melbourne
POLE LAP:	Hakkinen, 1m 30.462s
FASTEST LAP:	Schumacher,M., 1m 32.112s

Pn	Driver	Car	Laps	Time/Reason
1	Irvine	Ferrari	57	1h 35m 01.659s
2	Frentzen	Jordan-MH	57	1h 35m 02.686s
3	Schumacher,R.	Williams-Super.	57	1h 35m 08.671s
4	Fisichella	Benetton-Play.	57	1h 35m 35.077s
5	Barrichello	Stewart-Ford	57	1h 35m 56.357s
6	de la Rosa	Arrows	57	1h 36m 25.976s
7	Takagi	Arrows	57	1h 36m 27.947s
8	Schumacher,M.	Ferrari	56	1h 35m 16.505s
r	Zonta	BAR-Supertec	48	overheating
r	Badoer	Minardi-Ford	42	gearbox
r	Wurz	Benetton-Play.	28	suspension
r	Diniz	Sauber-Petronas	27	gearbox
r	Gene	Minardi-Ford	25	spin
r	Trulli	Prost-Peugeot	25	accident
r	Panis	Prost-Peugeot	23	locked wheel nut
r	Hakkinen	McLaren-Merc.	21	throttle
r	Zanardi	Williams-Super.	20	accident
r	Coulthard	McLaren-Merc.	13	gear stuck
r	Villeneuve,J.	BAR-Supertec	13	rear wing failure
r	Hill,D.	Jordan-MH	0	accident
r	Alesi	Sauber-Petronas	0	transmission
dns	Herbert	Stewart-Ford		dns

STARTING GRID:

1	Hakkinen	12	Trulli
2	Coulthard	13	Herbert
3	Schumacher,M.	14	Diniz
4	Barrichello	15	Zanardi
5	Frentzen	16	Alesi
6	Irvine	17	Takagi
7	Fisichella	18	de la Rosa
8	Schumacher,R.	19	Zonta
9	Hill,D.	20	Panis
10	Wurz	21	Badoer
11	Villeneuve,J.	22	Gene

Brazilian

GRAND PRIX No:	632
DATE:	April 11, 1999
VENUE:	Interlagos
POLE LAP:	Hakkinen, 1m 16.568s
FASTEST LAP:	Hakkinen, 1m 18.448s

Pn	Driver	Car	Laps	Time/Reason
1	Hakkinen	McLaren-Merc.	72	1h 38m 03.765s
2	Schumacher,M.	Ferrari	72	1h 38m 08.710s
3	Frentzen	Jordan-MH	71	1h 35m 58.877s
4	Schumacher,R.	Williams-Super.	71	1h 36m 22.860s
5	Irvine	Ferrari	71	1h 35m 23.103s
6	Panis	Prost-Peugeot	71	1h 37m 13.388s
7	Wurz	Benetton-Play.	70	1h 36m 12.021s
8	Takagi	Arrows	69	1h 36m 10.072s
9	Gene	Minardi-Ford	69	1h 37m 02.116s
r	de la Rosa	Arrows	52	hydraulics
r	Villeneuve,J.	BAR-Supertec	49	hydraulics
r	Zanardi	Williams-Super.	43	differential
r	Barrichello	Stewart-Ford	42	engine
r	Diniz	Sauber-Petronas	42	accident
r	Fisichella	Benetton-Play.	38	clutch
r	Sarrazin	Minardi-Ford	31	accident
r	Alesi	Sauber-Petronas	27	gearbox
r	Coulthard	McLaren-Merc.	22	gearbox
r	Trulli	Prost-Peugeot	21	gearbox
r	Herbert	Stewart-Ford	15	hydraulics
r	Hill,D.	Jordan-MH	10	steering

STARTING GRID:

1	Hakkinen	12	Panis
2	Coulthard	13	Trulli
3	Barrichello	14	Alesi
4	Schumacher,M.	15	Diniz
5	Fisichella	16	Zanardi
6	Irvine	17	de la Rosa
7	Hill,D.	18	Sarrazin
8	Frentzen	19	Takagi
9	Wurz	20	Gene
10	Herbert	21	Villeneuve,J.
11	Schumacher,R.		

San Marino

GRAND PRIX No: 633
DATE: May 2, 1999
VENUE: Imola
POLE LAP: Hakkinen, 1m 26.362s
FASTEST LAP: Schumacher,M., 1m 28.547s

Pn	Driver	Car	Laps	Time/Reason
1	Schumacher,M.	Ferrari	62	1h 33m 44.792s
2	Coulthard	McLaren-Merc.	62	1h 33m 49.057s
3	Barrichello	Stewart-Ford	61	1h 33m 46.721s
4	Hill,D.	Jordan-MH	61	1h 33m 47.629s
5	Fisichella	Benetton-Play.	61	1h 34m 27.002s
6	Alesi	Sauber-Petronas	61	1h 34m 33.056s
7	Salo	BAR-Supertec	59	electrics
8	Badoer	Minardi-Ford	59	3 laps down
9	Gene	Minardi-Ford	59	3 laps down
10	Herbert	Stewart-Ford	58	engine
11	Zanardi	Williams-Super.	58	spin
r	Diniz	Sauber-Petronas	49	spin
r	Panis	Prost-Peugeot	48	engine
r	Irvine	Ferrari	46	engine
r	Frentzen	Jordan-MH	46	spin
r	Takagi	Arrows	29	hydraulics
r	Schumacher,R.	Williams-Super.	28	engine
r	Hakkinen	McLaren-Merc.	17	accident
r	de la Rosa	Arrows	5	suspension
r	Wurz	Benetton-Play.	5	accident
r	Trulli	Prost-Peugeot	0	accident
r	Villeneuve,J.	BAR-Supertec	0	gearbox

STARTING GRID:

1	Hakkinen	12	Herbert
2	Coulthard	13	Alesi
3	Schumacher,M.	14	Trulli
4	Irvine	15	Diniz
5	Villeneuve,J.	16	Fisichella
6	Barrichello	17	Wurz
7	Frentzen	18	de la Rosa
8	Hill,D.	19	Salo
9	Schumacher,R.	20	Takagi
10	Zanardi	21	Gene
11	Panis	22	Badoer

Monaco

GRAND PRIX No: 634
DATE: May 16, 1999
VENUE: Monte Carlo
POLE LAP: Hakkinen, 1m 20.547s
FASTEST LAP: Hakkinen, 1m 22.259s

Pn	Driver	Car	Laps	Time/Reason
1	Schumacher,M.	Ferrari	78	1h 49m 31.812s
2	Irvine	Ferrari	78	1h 50m 02.288s
3	Hakkinen	McLaren-Merc.	78	1h 50m 09.295s
4	Frentzen	Jordan-MH	78	1h 50m 25.821s
5	Fisichella	Benetton-Play.	77	1h 49m 32.705s
6	Wurz	Benetton-Play.	77	1h 49m 47.799s
7	Trulli	Prost-Peugeot	77	1h 50m 05.845s
8	Zanardi	Williams-Super.	76	1h 49m 49.514s
9	Barrichello	Stewart-Ford	71	suspension
r	Schumacher,R.	Williams-Super.	54	accident
r	Alesi	Sauber-Petronas	50	accident
r	Diniz	Sauber-Petronas	49	accident
r	Panis	Prost-Peugeot	40	engine
r	Coulthard	McLaren-Merc.	36	oil leak
r	Salo	BAR-Supertec	36	brakes
r	Takagi	Arrows	36	engine
r	Villeneuve,J.	BAR-Supertec	32	oil leak
r	Herbert	Stewart-Ford	32	suspension
r	de la Rosa	Arrows	30	gearbox
r	Gene	Minardi-Ford	24	accident
r	Badoer	Minardi-Ford	10	gearbox
r	Hill,D.	Jordan-MH	3	accident

STARTING GRID:

1	Hakkinen	12	Salo
2	Schumacher,M.	13	Herbert
3	Coulthard	14	Alesi
4	Irvine	15	Diniz
5	Barrichello	16	Schumacher,R.
6	Frentzen	17	Hill,D.
7	Trulli	18	Panis
8	Villeneuve,J.	19	Takagi
9	Fisichella	20	Badoer
10	Wurz	21	de la Rosa
11	Zanardi	22	Gene

Spanish

GRAND PRIX No:	635
DATE:	May 30, 1999
VENUE:	Barcelona
POLE LAP:	Hakkinen, 1m 22.088s
FASTEST LAP:	Schumacher,M., 1m 24.982s

Pn	Driver	Car	Laps	Time/Reason
1	Hakkinen	McLaren-Merc.	65	1h 34m 13.665s
2	Coulthard	McLaren-Merc.	65	1h 34m 19.903s
3	Schumacher,M.	Ferrari	65	1h 34m 24.510s
4	Irvine	Ferrari	65	1h 34m 43.847s
5	Schumacher,R.	Williams-Super.	65	1h 35m 40.873s
6	Trulli	Prost-Peugeot	64	1h 34m 24.028s
7	Hill,D.	Jordan-MH	64	1h 34m 25.044s
dq	Barrichello	Stewart-Ford		excluded (from 8th position)
8	Salo	BAR-Supertec	64	1h 35m 21.065s
9	Fisichella	Benetton-Play.	64	1h 35m 22.704s
10	Wurz	Benetton-Play.	64	1h 35m 29.548s
11	de la Rosa	Arrows	63	1h 34m 41.268s
12	Takagi	Arrows	62	1h 34m 38.929s
r	Badoer	Minardi-Ford	50	spin
r	Villeneuve,J.	BAR-Supertec	40	gearbox
r	Diniz	Sauber-Petronas	40	gearbox
r	Herbert	Stewart-Ford	40	transmission
r	Frentzen	Jordan-MH	35	differential
r	Alesi	Sauber-Petronas	27	electrics
r	Zanardi	Williams-Super.	24	gearbox
r	Panis	Prost-Peugeot	24	oil pressure
r	Gene	Minardi-Ford	0	gearbox

STARTING GRID:

1	Hakkinen	12	Diniz
2	Irvine	13	Fisichella
3	Coulthard	14	Herbert
4	Schumacher,M.	15	Panis
5	Alesi	16	Salo
6	Villeneuve,J.	17	Zanardi
7	Barrichello	18	Wurz
8	Frentzen	19	de la Rosa
9	Trulli	20	Takagi
10	Schumacher,R.	21	Gene
11	Hill,D.	22	Badoer

Canadian

GRAND PRIX No:	636
DATE:	June 13, 1999
VENUE:	Montreal
POLE LAP:	Schumacher,M., 1m 19.298s
FASTEST LAP:	Irvine, 1m 20.382s

Pn	Driver	Car	Laps	Time/Reason
1	Hakkinen	McLaren-Merc.	69	1h 41m 35.727s
2	Fisichella	Benetton-Play.	69	1h 41m 36.509s
3	Irvine	Ferrari	69	1h 41m 37.524s
4	Schumacher,R.	Williams-Super.	69	1h 41m 38.119s
5	Herbert	Stewart-Ford	69	1h 41m 38.532s
6	Diniz	Sauber-Petronas	69	1h 41m 39.438s
7	Coulthard	McLaren-Merc.	69	1h 41m 40.731s
8	Gene	Minardi-Ford	68	1 lap down
9	Panis	Prost-Peugeot	68	1 lap down
10	Badoer	Minardi-Ford	67	2 laps down
11	Frentzen	Jordan-MH	65	brakes
r	Zanardi	Williams-Super.	50	gearbox
r	Takagi	Arrows	41	transmission
r	Villeneuve,J.	BAR-Supertec	34	accident
r	Schumacher,M.	Ferrari	29	accident
r	de la Rosa	Arrows	22	transmission
r	Hill,D.	Jordan-MH	14	accident
r	Barrichello	Stewart-Ford	14	accident damage
r	Zonta	BAR-Supertec	2	accident
r	Alesi	Sauber-Petronas	0	accident
r	Trulli	Prost-Peugeot	0	accident
r	Wurz	Benetton-Play.	0	accident

STARTING GRID:

1	Schumacher,M.	12	Zanardi
2	Hakkinen	13	Schumacher,R.
3	Irvine	14	Hill,D.
4	Coulthard	15	Panis
5	Barrichello	16	Villeneuve,J.
6	Frentzen	17	Zonta
7	Fisichella	18	Diniz
8	Alesi	19	Takagi
9	Trulli	20	de la Rosa
10	Herbert	21	Badoer
11	Wurz	22	Gene

French

GRAND PRIX No: 637
DATE: June 27, 1999
VENUE: Magny-Cours
POLE LAP: Barrichello, 1m 38.441s
FASTEST LAP: Coulthard, 1m 19.227s

Pn	Driver	Car	Laps	Time/Reason
1	Frentzen	Jordan-MH	72	1h 58m 24.343s
2	Hakkinen	McLaren-Merc.	72	1h 58m 35.435s
3	Barrichello	Stewart-Ford	72	1h 59m 07.775s
4	Schumacher,R.	Williams-Super.	72	1h 59m 09.818s
5	Schumacher,M.	Ferrari	72	1h 59m 12.224s
6	Irvine	Ferrari	72	1h 59m 13.244s
7	Trulli	Prost-Peugeot	72	1h 59m 22.114s
8	Panis	Prost-Peugeot	72	1h 59m 22.874s
9	Zonta	BAR-Supertec	72	1h 59m 53.107s
10	Badoer	Minardi-Ford	71	1 lap down
11	de la Rosa	Arrows	71	1 lap down
r	Fisichella	Benetton-Play.	42	spin
r	Hill,D.	Jordan-MH	31	misfire
r	Zanardi	Williams-Super.	26	engine
r	Villeneuve,J.	BAR-Supertec	25	spin
r	Wurz	Benetton-Play.	25	spin
r	Gene	Minardi-Ford	25	spin
r	Alesi	Sauber-Petronas	24	spin
r	Coulthard	McLaren-Merc.	9	alternator
r	Diniz	Sauber-Petronas	5	driveshaft
r	Herbert	Stewart-Ford	4	gearbox
dq	Takagi	Arrows		illegal tyres

STARTING GRID:

1	Barrichello	12	Villeneuve,J.
2	Alesi	13	Wurz
3	Panis	14	Hakkinen
4	Coulthard	15	Zanardi
5	Frentzen	16	Schumacher,R.
6	Schumacher,M.	17	Irvine
7	Fisichella	18	Hill,D.
8	Trulli	19	Gene
9	Herbert	20	Badoer
10	Zonta	21	de la Rosa
11	Diniz	22	Takagi

British

GRAND PRIX No: 638
DATE: July 11, 1999
VENUE: Silverstone
POLE LAP: Hakkinen, 1m 24.804s
FASTEST LAP: Hakkinen, 1m 28.309s

Pn	Driver	Car	Laps	Time/Reason
1	Coulthard	McLaren-Merc.	60	1h 32m 30.144s
2	Irvine	Ferrari	60	1h 32m 31.973s
3	Schumacher,R.	Williams-Super.	60	1h 32m 57.555s
4	Frentzen	Jordan-MH	60	1h 32m 57.933s
5	Hill,D.	Jordan-MH	60	1h 33m 08.750s
6	Diniz	Sauber-Petronas	60	1h 33m 23.787s
7	Fisichella	Benetton-Play.	60	1h 33m 24.758s
8	Barrichello	Stewart-Ford	60	1h 33m 38.734s
9	Trulli	Prost-Peugeot	60	1h 33m 42.189s
10	Wurz	Benetton-Play.	60	1h 33m 42.267s
11	Zanardi	Williams-Super.	60	1h 33m 47.268s
12	Herbert	Stewart-Ford	60	1h 33m 47.853s
13	Panis	Prost-Peugeot	60	1h 33m 50.636s
14	Alesi	Sauber-Petronas	59	1 lap down
15	Gene	Minardi-Ford	58	2 laps down
16	Takagi	Arrows	58	2 laps down
r	Zonta	BAR-Supertec	41	suspension
r	Hakkinen	McLaren-Merc.	35	wheel hub
r	Villeneuve,J.	BAR-Supertec	29	gearbox
r	Badoer	Minardi-Ford	6	gearbox
r	de la Rosa	Arrows	0	gearbox
dns	Schumacher,M.	Ferrari		dns

STARTING GRID:

1	Hakkinen	12	Diniz
2	Schumacher,M.	13	Zanardi
3	Coulthard	14	Trulli
4	Irvine	15	Panis
5	Frentzen	16	Zonta
6	Hill,D.	17	Fisichella
7	Barrichello	18	Wurz
8	Schumacher,R.	19	Takagi
9	Villeneuve,J.	20	de la Rosa
10	Alesi	21	Badoer
11	Herbert	22	Gene

Austrian

GRAND PRIX No: 639
DATE: July 25, 1999
VENUE: A1-Ring
POLE LAP: Hakkinen, 1m 10.954s
FASTEST LAP: Hakkinen, 1m 12.107s

Pn	Driver	Car	Laps	Time/Reason
1	Irvine	Ferrari	71	1h 28m 12.438s
2	Coulthard	McLaren-Merc.	71	1h 28m 12.751s
3	Hakkinen	McLaren-Merc.	71	1h 28m 34.720s
4	Frentzen	Jordan-MH	71	1h 29m 05.241s
5	Wurz	Benetton-Play.	71	1h 29m 18.796s
6	Diniz	Sauber-Petronas	71	1h 29m 23.371s
7	Trulli	Prost-Peugeot	70	1 lap down
8	Hill,D.	Jordan-MH	70	1 lap down
9	Salo	Ferrari	70	1 lap down
10	Panis	Prost-Peugeot	70	1 lap down
11	Gene	Minardi-Ford	70	1 lap down
12	Fisichella	Benetton-Play.	68	3 laps down – engine
13	Badoer	Minardi-Ford	68	3 laps down
14	Herbert	Stewart-Ford	67	4 laps down
15	Zonta	BAR-Supertec	63	8 laps down dnf
r	Barrichello	Stewart-Ford	55	engine
r	Alesi	Sauber-Petronas	49	out of fuel
r	de la Rosa	Arrows	38	brakes
r	Zanardi	Williams-Super.	35	out of fuel
r	Villeneuve,J.	BAR-Supertec	34	driveshaft
r	Takagi	Arrows	25	engine
r	Schumacher,R.	Williams-Super.	8	spin

STARTING GRID:

1	Hakkinen	12	Fisichella
2	Coulthard	13	Trulli
3	Irvine	14	Zanardi
4	Frentzen	15	Zonta
5	Barrichello	16	Diniz
6	Herbert	17	Alesi
7	Salo	18	Panis
8	Schumacher,R.	19	Badoer
9	Villeneuve,J.	20	Takagi
10	Wurz	21	de la Rosa
11	Hill,D.	22	Gene

German

GRAND PRIX No: 640
DATE: August 1, 1999
VENUE: Hockenheim
POLE LAP: Hakkinen, 1m 42.950s
FASTEST LAP: Coulthard, 1m 45.270s

Pn	Driver	Car	Laps	Time/Reason
1	Irvine	Ferrari	45	1h 21m 58.594s
2	Salo	Ferrari	45	1h 21m 59.601s
3	Frentzen	Jordan-MH	45	1h 22m 03.789s
4	Schumacher,R.	Williams-Super.	45	1h 22m 11.403s
5	Coulthard	McLaren-Merc.	45	1h 22m 15.417s
6	Panis	Prost-Peugeot	45	1h 22m 28.473s
7	Wurz	Benetton-Play.	45	1h 22m 31.927s
8	Alesi	Sauber-Petronas	45	1h 23m 09.885s
9	Gene	Minardi-Ford	45	1h 23m 46.912s
10	Badoer	Minardi-Ford	44	1 lap down
11	Herbert	Stewart-Ford	40	gearbox
r	de la Rosa	Arrows	37	accident
r	Hakkinen	McLaren-Merc.	25	accident
r	Zanardi	Williams-Super.	21	differential
r	Zonta	BAR-Supertec	20	engine
r	Takagi	Arrows	15	engine
r	Hill,D.	Jordan-MH	13	brakes
r	Trulli	Prost-Peugeot	10	engine
r	Fisichella	Benetton-Play.	7	suspension
r	Barrichello	Stewart-Ford	6	hydraulics
r	Villeneuve,J.	BAR-Supertec	0	accident
r	Diniz	Sauber-Petronas	0	accident

STARTING GRID:

1	Hakkinen	12	Villeneuve,J.
2	Frentzen	13	Wurz
3	Coulthard	14	Zanardi
4	Salo	15	Gene
5	Irvine	16	Diniz
6	Barrichello	17	Herbert
7	Panis	18	Zonta
8	Hill,D.	19	Badoer
9	Trulli	20	de la Rosa
10	Fisichella	21	Alesi
11	Schumacher,R.	22	Takagi

Hungarian

GRAND PRIX No: 641
DATE: August 15, 1999
VENUE: Hungaroring
POLE LAP: Hakkinen, 1m 18.156s
FASTEST LAP: Coulthard, 1m 20.699s

Pn	Driver	Car	Laps	Time/Reason
1	Hakkinen	McLaren-Merc.	77	1h 46m 23.536s
2	Coulthard	McLaren-Merc.	77	1h 46m 33.242s
3	Irvine	Ferrari	77	1h 46m 50.784s
4	Frentzen	Jordan-MH	77	1h 46m 55.351s
5	Barrichello	Stewart-Ford	77	1h 47m 07.344s
6	Hill,D.	Jordan-MH	77	1h 47m 19.262s
7	Wurz	Benetton-Play.	77	1h 47m 24.548s
8	Trulli	Prost-Peugeot	76	1 lap down
9	Schumacher,R.	Williams-Super.	76	1 lap down
10	Panis	Prost-Peugeot	76	1 lap down
11	Herbert	Stewart-Ford	76	1 lap down
12	Salo	Ferrari	75	2 laps down
13	Zonta	BAR-Supertec	75	2 laps down
14	Badoer	Minardi-Ford	75	2 laps down
15	de la Rosa	Arrows	75	2 laps down
16	Alesi	Sauber-Petronas	74	out of fuel
17	Gene	Minardi-Ford	74	3 laps down
r	Villeneuve,J.	BAR-Supertec	60	clutch
r	Fisichella	Benetton-Play.	52	fuel pressure
r	Takagi	Arrows	26	driveshaft
r	Diniz	Sauber-Petronas	19	spin
r	Zanardi	Williams-Super.	10	differential

STARTING GRID:

1	Hakkinen	12	Diniz
2	Irvine	13	Trulli
3	Coulthard	14	Panis
4	Fisichella	15	Zanardi
5	Frentzen	16	Schumacher,R.
6	Hill,D.	17	Zonta
7	Wurz	18	Salo
8	Barrichello	19	Badoer
9	Villeneuve,J.	20	de la Rosa
10	Herbert	21	Takagi
11	Alesi	22	Gene

Belgian

GRAND PRIX No: 642
DATE: August 29, 1999
VENUE: Spa-Francorchamps
POLE LAP: Hakkinen, 1m 50.329s
FASTEST LAP: Hakkinen, 1m 53.955s

Pn	Driver	Car	Laps	Time/Reason
1	Coulthard	McLaren-Merc.	44	1h 25m 43.057s
2	Hakkinen	McLaren-Merc.	44	1h 25m 53.526s
3	Frentzen	Jordan-MH	44	1h 26m 16.490s
4	Irvine	Ferrari	44	1h 26m 28.005s
5	Schumacher,R.	Williams-Super.	44	1h 26m 31.124s
6	Hill,D.	Jordan-MH	44	1h 26m 37.973s
7	Salo	Ferrari	44	1h 26m 39.306s
8	Zanardi	Williams-Super.	44	1h 26m 50.079s
9	Alesi	Sauber-Petronas	44	1h 26m 56.905s
10	Barrichello	Stewart-Ford	44	1h 27m 03.799s
11	Fisichella	Benetton-Play.	44	1h 27m 15.252s
12	Trulli	Prost-Peugeot	44	1h 27m 19.211s
13	Panis	Prost-Peugeot	44	1h 27m 24.600s
14	Wurz	Benetton-Play.	44	1h 27m 40.802s
15	Villeneuve,J.	BAR-Supertec	43	1 lap down
16	Gene	Minardi-Ford	43	1 lap down
r	de la Rosa	Arrows	35	transmission
r	Badoer	Minardi-Ford	33	suspension
r	Zonta	BAR-Supertec	33	gearbox
r	Herbert	Stewart-Ford	27	brakes
r	Diniz	Sauber-Petronas	19	accident
r	Takagi	Arrows	0	clutch

STARTING GRID:

1	Hakkinen	12	Trulli
2	Coulthard	13	Fisichella
3	Frentzen	14	Zonta
4	Hill,D.	15	Wurz
5	Schumacher,R.	16	Alesi
6	Irvine	17	Panis
7	Barrichello	18	Diniz
8	Zanardi	19	Takagi
9	Salo	20	Badoer
10	Herbert	21	Gene
11	Villeneuve,J.	22	de la Rosa

Italian

GRAND PRIX No:	643
DATE:	September 12, 1999
VENUE:	Monza
POLE LAP:	Hakkinen, 1m 22.432s
FASTEST LAP:	Schumacher,R., 1m 25.579s

Pn	Driver	Car	Laps	Time/Reason
1	Frentzen	Jordan-MH	53	1h 17m 02.923s
2	Schumacher,R.	Williams-Super.	53	1h 17m 06.195s
3	Salo	Ferrari	53	1h 17m 14.855s
4	Barrichello	Stewart-Ford	53	1h 17m 20.553s
5	Coulthard	McLaren-Merc.	53	1h 17m 21.085s
6	Irvine	Ferrari	53	1h 17m 30.325s
7	Zanardi	Williams-Super.	53	1h 17m 30.970s
8	Villeneuve,J.	BAR-Supertec	53	1h 17m 44.720s
9	Alesi	Sauber-Petronas	53	1h 17m 45.121s
10	Hill,D.	Jordan-MH	53	1h 17m 59.182s
11	Panis	Prost-Peugeot	52	1 lap down
r	Herbert	Stewart-Ford	40	clutch
r	Takagi	Arrows	35	spin
r	de la Rosa	Arrows	35	accident damage
r	Hakkinen	McLaren-Merc.	29	spin
r	Trulli	Prost-Peugeot	29	gearbox
r	Zonta	BAR-Supertec	25	wheel bearing
r	Badoer	Minardi-Ford	23	accident
r	Wurz	Benetton-Play.	11	electronics
r	Diniz	Sauber-Petronas	1	spin
r	Fisichella	Benetton-Play.	1	accident
r	Gene	Minardi-Ford	0	accident

STARTING GRID:

1	Hakkinen	12	Trulli
2	Frentzen	13	Alesi
3	Coulthard	14	Wurz
4	Zanardi	15	Herbert
5	Schumacher,R.	16	Diniz
6	Salo	17	Fisichella
7	Barrichello	18	Zonta
8	Irvine	19	Badoer
9	Hill,D.	20	Gene
10	Panis	21	de la Rosa
11	Villeneuve,J.	22	Takagi

European

GRAND PRIX No:	644
DATE:	September 26, 1999
VENUE:	Nurburgring
POLE LAP:	Frentzen, 1m 19.910s
FASTEST LAP:	Hakkinen, 1m 21.282s

Pn	Driver	Car	Laps	Time/Reason
1	Herbert	Stewart-Ford	66	1h 41m 54.314s
2	Trulli	Prost-Peugeot	66	1h 42m 16.933s
3	Barrichello	Stewart-Ford	66	1h 42m 17.180s
4	Schumacher,R.	Williams-Super.	66	1h 42m 33.822s
5	Hakkinen	McLaren-Merc.	66	1h 42m 57.264s
6	Gene	Minardi-Ford	66	1h 42m 59.468s
7	Irvine	Ferrari	66	1h 43m 00.997s
8	Zonta	BAR-Supertec	65	1 lap down
9	Panis	Prost-Peugeot	65	1 lap down
10	Villeneuve,J.	BAR-Supertec	61	clutch
r	Badoer	Minardi-Ford	53	gearbox
r	de la Rosa	Arrows	52	gearbox
r	Fisichella	Benetton-Play.	48	spunout
r	Salo	Ferrari	44	spunout
r	Takagi	Arrows	42	accident
r	Coulthard	McLaren-Merc.	37	spunout
r	Alesi	Sauber-Petronas	35	transmission
r	Frentzen	Jordan-MH	32	electronics
r	Zanardi	Williams-Super.	10	accident
r	Hill,D.	Jordan-MH	0	electrics
r	Wurz	Benetton-Play.	0	accident
r	Diniz	Sauber-Petronas	0	accident

STARTING GRID:

1	Frentzen	12	Salo
2	Coulthard	13	Diniz
3	Hakkinen	14	Herbert
4	Schumacher,R.	15	Barrichello
5	Panis	16	Alesi
6	Fisichella	17	Zonta
7	Hill,D.	18	Zanardi
8	Villeneuve,J.	19	Badoer
9	Irvine	20	Gene
10	Trulli	21	Takagi
11	Wurz	22	de la Rosa

Malaysian

GRAND PRIX No: 645
DATE: October 17, 1999
VENUE: Sepang
POLE LAP: Schumacher,M., 1m 39.688s
FASTEST LAP: Schumacher,M., 1m 40.267s

Pn	Driver	Car	Laps	Time/Reason
1	Irvine	Ferrari	56	1h 36m 38.494s
2	Schumacher,M.	Ferrari	56	1h 36m 39.534s
3	Hakkinen	McLaren-Merc.	56	1h 36m 48.237s
4	Herbert	Stewart-Ford	56	1h 36m 56.032s
5	Barrichello	Stewart-Ford	56	1h 37m 10.790s
6	Frentzen	Jordan-MH	56	1h 37m 13.378s
7	Alesi	Sauber-Petronas	56	1h 37m 32.902s
8	Wurz	Benetton-Play.	56	1h 37m 39.428s
9	Gene	Minardi-Ford	55	1 lap down
10	Zanardi	Williams-Super.	55	1 lap down
11	Fisichella	Benetton-Play.	52	4 laps down
r	Villeneuve,J.	BAR-Supertec	48	hydraulics
r	Diniz	Sauber-Petronas	44	spunout
r	de la Rosa	Arrows	30	engine
r	Badoer	Minardi-Ford	15	overheating
r	Coulthard	McLaren-Merc.	14	fuel pressure
r	Schumacher,R.	Williams-Super.	7	spunout
r	Takagi	Arrows	7	driveshaft
r	Zonta	BAR-Supertec	6	water leak
r	Panis	Prost-Peugeot	5	engine
r	Hill,D.	Jordan-MH	0	accident
dns	Trulli	Prost-Peugeot		dns - engine on form lap

STARTING GRID:

1	Schumacher,M.	12	Panis
2	Irvine	13	Zonta
3	Coulthard	14	Frentzen
4	Hakkinen	15	Alesi
5	Herbert	16	Zanardi
6	Barrichello	17	Diniz
7	Wurz	18	Trulli
8	Schumacher,R.	19	Gene
9	Hill,D.	20	de la Rosa
10	Villeneuve,J.	21	Badoer
11	Fisichella	22	Takagi

Japanese

GRAND PRIX No: 646
DATE: October 31, 1999
VENUE: Suzuka
POLE LAP: Schumacher,M., 1m 37.470s
FASTEST LAP: Schumacher,M., 1m 41.319s

Pn	Driver	Car	Laps	Time/Reason
1	Hakkinen	McLaren-Merc.	53	1h 31m 18.785s
2	Schumacher,M.	Ferrari	53	1h 31m 23.800s
3	Irvine	Ferrari	53	1h 32m 54.473s
4	Frentzen	Jordan-MH	53	1h 32m 57.420s
5	Schumacher,R.	Williams-Super.	53	1h 32m 58.279s
6	Alesi	Sauber-Petronas	52	1 lap down
7	Herbert	Stewart-Ford	52	1 lap down
8	Barrichello	Stewart-Ford	52	1 lap down
9	Villeneuve,J.	BAR-Supertec	52	1 lap down
10	Wurz	Benetton-Play.	52	1 lap down
11	Diniz	Sauber-Petronas	52	1 lap down
12	Zonta	BAR-Supertec	52	1 lap down
13	de la Rosa	Arrows	51	2 laps down
14	Fisichella	Benetton-Play.	47	engine
r	Takagi	Arrows	43	gearbox
r	Badoer	Minardi-Ford	43	engine
r	Coulthard	McLaren-Merc.	39	hydraulics
r	Gene	Minardi-Ford	31	gearbox
r	Hill,D.	Jordan-MH	21	retired
r	Panis	Prost-Peugeot	19	gearbox
r	Trulli	Prost-Peugeot	3	engine
r	Zanardi	Williams-Super.	0	electrics

STARTING GRID:

1	Schumacher,M.	12	Hill,D.
2	Hakkinen	13	Barrichello
3	Coulthard	14	Fisichella
4	Frentzen	15	Wurz
5	Irvine	16	Zanardi
6	Panis	17	Diniz
7	Trulli	18	Zonta
8	Herbert	19	Takagi
9	Schumacher,R.	20	Gene
10	Alesi	21	de la Rosa
11	Villeneuve,J.	22	Badoer

These pages detail races where drivers shared cars (1950-61). This aspect of the early F1 races is detailed in the Introduction to this Record File on Page 6. Itemised immediately below are those drives where a driver took over a car that was already running in a race in which the driver taking over did not start, and for which it was his first drive. In the list below there are details of all shared drives, listing the races and the various sharing drivers.

Year	Details
1950	British: Brian Shawe-Taylor did not start race but replaced Joe Fry.
1952	French: Peter Hirt did not start the race but replaced Rudolf Fischer.
1953	Italian: Musso didn't start the race but replaced Mantonvani. This would have been Musso's first race.
1953	Argentine: Harry Schell did not start the race but replaced Maurice Trintignant.
1954	Spanish: Volonterio did not start the race but replaced de Graffenried.
1954	British: Ron Flockhart did not start the race but took over Bira's car.
1955	Monaco: Paul Fere did not start the race but took over from Taruffi.
1955	Argentine: Maglioli did not start the race but replaced Farina.
1955	British: Peter Walker did not start the race but replaced Rolt in the Connaught.
1956	Italian: Jo Bonner took over Villoresi's car. Bonner had not started the original race.
1956	Argentina: Gerino Gerini did not start the race but took over from Chico Landi. Oscar Gonzalez did not start the race but took over from Uria.
1956	Monaco: Andre Pilette did not start the race but replaced Elie Bayol.
1957	Italian: Volonterio did not startthe race but replaced Simon.
1957	Argentina: von Tripps did not start the race but replaced both Perdisa and then Collins in the Lancia-Ferrari.

Year	GP No	Grand Prix	Pos	1st Driver	2nd Driver	3rd/4th/5th Drivers
1950	1	British	10	Fry	Shawe-Taylor	
1950	1	British	r	Walker,P.	Rolt	
1950	3	Indianapolis 500	5	Chitwood	Bettenhausen	
1950	3	Indianapolis 500	25	Banks	Agabashian	
1950	3	Indianapolis 500	27	Levrett	Cantrell	
1950	6	French	5	Etancelin	Chaboud	
1950	6	French	6	Pozzi	Rosier	
1950	7	Italian	2	Sefafini	Ascari	
1950	7	Italian	r	Truffi	Fangio	
1951	9	Indianapolis 500	3	McGrath	Ayulo	
1951	11	French	1	Fagioli	Fangio	
1951	11	French	2	Gonzalez,F.	Ascari	
1951	14	Italian	3	Bonetto	Farina	
1952	16	Swiss	r	Simon	Farina	
1952	19	French	11	Fischer	Hirt	
1952	19	French	r	de Graffenried	Schell	
1952	22	Dutch	9	Landi	Flinterman	
1953	24	Argentine	7	Trintignant	Schell	
1953	25	Indianapolis 500	3	Hanks	Carter	
1953	25	Indianapolis 500	4	Agabashian	Russo,P.	
1953	25	Indianapolis 500	7	Rathmann,J.	Johnson,E.	
1953	25	Indianapolis 500	9	Bettenhausen	Stevenson	Hartley
1953	25	Indianapolis 500	12	Scarborough	Scott	
1953	25	Indianapolis 500	15	Holland	Rathmann,J.	
1953	25	Indianapolis 500	16	Ward	Linden	Dinsmore

Year	No	Grand Prix	Pos	1st Driver	2nd Driver	3rd/4th/5th Drivers
1953	25	Indianapolis 500	17	Faulkner	Mantz	
1953	25	Indianapolis 500	19	Webb	Thomson	Holmes
1953	25	Indianapolis 500	23	Hoyt	Stevenson	Linden
1953	26	Dutch	3	Bonetto	Gonzalez,J.	
1953	27	Belgian	r	Clares	Fangio	
1953	30	German	7	Villoresi	Ascari	
1953	31	Swiss	4	Fangio	Bonetto	
1953	31	Swiss	r	Bonetto	Fangio	
1953	32	Italian	8	Mantovani	Musso	
1954	34	Indianapolis 500	4	Ruttman	Carter	
1954	34	Indianapolis 500	8	Russo,P.	Hoyt	
1954	34	Indianapolis 500	11	Cross	Parsons	Hanks/Linden/Davies
1954	34	Indianapolis 500	12	Stevenson	Faulkner	
1954	34	Indianapolis 500	15	Carter	Teague	Jackson/Bettenhausen
1954	34	Indianapolis 500	18	Elisian	Scott	
1954	34	Indianapolis 500	19	Armi	Fonder	
1954	34	Indianapolis 500	20	Hanks	Davies	Rathmann,J.
1954	34	Indianapolis 500	22	Ward	Johnson,E.	
1954	34	Indianapolis 500	23	Hartley	Teague	
1954	34	Indianapolis 500	24	Thomson	Linden	Daywalt
1954	34	Indianapolis 500	25	Linden	Scott	
1954	34	Indianapolis 500	28	Rathmann,J.	Flaherty	
1954	34	Indianapolis 500	30	Webb	Kladis	
1954	34	Indianapolis 500	31	Duncan	Fonder	
1954	35	Belgian	4	Hawthorn	Gonzalez,J.	
1954	37	British	19	Bira	Flockhart	
1954	37	British	r	Villoresi	Ascari	
1954	38	German	2	Gonzalez,F.	Hawthorn	
1954	40	Italian	3	Magioli	Gonzalez,J.	
1954	41	Spanish	r	de Graffenried	Volonterio	
1955	42	Argentine	2	Gonzalez,F.	Trintignant	Farina
1955	42	Argentine	2	Farina	Maglioli	Trintignant
1955	42	Argentine	4	Herrmann	Kling	Moss
1955	42	Argentine	6	Schell	Behra	
1955	42	Argentine	7	Musso	Mantovani	Schell
1955	42	Argentine	r	Bucci	Schell	Menditeguy
1955	42	Argentine	r	Mantovani	Musso	Behra
1955	42	Argentine	r	Castellotti	Villoresi	
1955	43	Monaco	3	Behra	Perdisa	
1955	43	Monaco	8	Perdisa	Behra	
1955	43	Monaco	9	Taruffi	Frere	
1955	44	Indianapolis 500	2	Bettenhausen	Russo,P.	
1955	44	Indianapolis 500	5	Faulkner	Horneier	
1955	45	Belgian	5	Mieres	Behra	
1955	47	British	6	Hawthorn	Castellotti	
1955	47	British	9	Wharton	Schell	
1955	47	British	r	Rolt	Walker,P.	
1956	49	Argentine	1	Musso	Fangio	

Year	No	Grand Prix	Pos	1st Driver	2nd Driver	3rd/4th/5th Drivers
1956	49	Argentine	4	Landi	Gerini	
1956	49	Argentine	6	Uria	Gonzalez,O.	
1956	50	Monaco	2	Collins	Fangio	
1956	50	Monaco	4	Fangio	Castellotti	
1956	50	Monaco	6	Bayol	Pilette,A.	
1956	51	Indianapolis 500	23	Elisian	Russo,E.	
1956	52	Belgian	3	Perdisa	Moss	
1956	53	French	5	Perdisa	Moss	
1956	53	French	10	Hawthorn	Schell	
1956	54	British	2	de Portago	Collins	
1956	54	British	11	Castellotti	de Portago	
1956	55	German	r	de Portago	Collins	
1956	55	German	r	Musso	Castellotti	
1956	56	Italian	2	Collins	Fangio	
1956	56	Italian	9	Fangio	Castellotti	
1956	56	Italian	r	Magioli	Behra	
1956	56	Italian	r	Villoresi	Bonnier	
1957	57	Argentine	5	Gonzalez,J.	de Portago	
1957	57	Argentine	6	Perdisa	Collins	von Trips
1957	58	Monaco	r	von Trips	Hawthorn	
1957	58	Monaco	r	Scarlatti	Schell	
1957	57	French	7	McDowell	Brabham,J.	
1957	61	British	1	Brooks	Moss	
1957	61	British	4	Trintignant	Collins	
1957	61	British	r	Moss	Brooks	
1957	64	Italian	5	Scatlatti	Schell	
1957	64	Italian	11	Simon	Volonterio	
1958	70	French	13	Lewis-Evans	Brooks	
1958	74	Italian	4	Gregory	Shelby	
1960	85	Argentine	3	Trintignant	Moss	
1961	91	British	r	Fairman	Moss	
1961	94	United States	12	Gendebien	Gregory	

A handful of races ran with F2 cars. This was done mainly to increase the number of cars competing in the race. The main races to have these cars running concurrently were the 1958 Moroccan Grands Prix and the 1966, 1967 and 1969 German Grand Prix. Although their results did not count, they are credited with having started the races. The 1967 and 1969 races had the F2 cars starting from a separate grid and were also classified according to where they finished in relation to the other F2 cars. This classification is detailed here. The numbers in brackets after the drivers' names are their starting grid positions.

GRAND PRIX: 157 – German

DATE: August 6, 1967

VENUE: Nurburgring

Pn	Driver	Car	Laps	Time/Reason
1	Oliver (2)	Lotus-Ford	15	2h 12m 04.9s
2	Rees (3)	Brabham-Ford	15	2h 14m 43.6s
3	Hobbs (5)	Lola-BMW	13	
4	Hart (8)	Protos-Ford	12	
5	Ickx (1)	Matra-Ford	11	suspension
6	Ahrens (6)	Protos-Ford	4	radiator
7	Schlesser,J. (4)	Matra-Ford	2	clutch
8	Mitter (7)	Brabham-Ford	0	engine

GRAND PRIX: 180 – German

DATE: August 3, 1969

VENUE: Nurburgring

Pn	Driver	Car	Laps	Time/Reaso
1	Pescarolo (3)	Matra-Ford	14	1h 58m 06.5s
2	Attwood (6)	Brabham-Ford	13	
3	Ahrens (5)	Brabham-Ford	13	
4	Stommelen (7)	Lotus-Ford	13	
5	Westbury (4)	Brabham-Ford	13	
6	Perrot (8)	Brabham-Ford	13	
r	Cevert (2)	Tecno-Ford	9	suspension
r	Servoz-Gavin (1)	Matra-Ford	6	suspension

GRID CONTINUATIONS

As outlined previously, the following pages contain the final grid positions for a number of Grands Prixs where there was not enough room to place them on the original page. The number relates to the Grand Prix number of the original race.

No: 3

9 Chitwood
10 Holland
11 Flaherty
12 Green
13 Carter
14 Webb
15 Hoyt
16 Fohr
17 Levrett
18 Rathmann,D.
19 Russo,P.
20 Brown,Walt
21 Banks
22 Schindler
23 Wallard
24 Ruttman
25 Hanks
26 Hellings
27 Davies
28 Rathmann,J.
29 Ader
30 Holmes
31 Hartley
32 Jackson
33 McDowell,J.

No:17

9 Griffith
10 Rathmann,J.
11 Stevenson
12 Banks
13 Fonder
14 Connor
15 Schindler
16 James,Joe
17 Ball
18 Hartley
19 Ascari
20 Cross
21 Bryan
22 Ward
23 Reece
24 Johnson,E.
25 Scott
26 Rigsby
27 Miller
28 Ayulo
29 Webb
30 Bettenhausen
31 Parsons
32 Sweikert
33 McDowell,J.

No: 20

11 Hamilton
12 Whitehead,G.
13 Brown,A.
14 Collins
15 Fischer
16 Moss
17 McAlpine
18 Brandon
19 Salvadori
20 Whitehead,P.
21 Trintignant
22 Murray
23 Claes
24 Hirt
25 Crook
26 Gaze
27 Cantoni
28 Bianco
29 Macklin
30 Ashton
31 Schell
32 de Graffenried

No: 21

11 Behra
12 Riess
13 Frere
14 Gaze
15 Ulmen
16 Bianco
17 Laurent
18 Helfrich
19 Brudes
20 Peters
21 Aston
22 Niedermayr
23 Krause
24 Schoeller
25 Balsa
26 Cantoni
27 Carini
28 Krakau
29 Klodwig
30 Bechem
31 Fischer
32 Claes

No: 25

9 Hanks
10 Ward
11 Scott
12 Cross
13 Hartley
14 Faulkner
15 Freeland
16 Stevenson
17 Russo,P.
18 Webb
19 Scarborough
20 McCoy
21 Daywalt
22 Teague
23 Nazaruk
24 Flaherty
25 Rathmann,J.
26 Nalon
27 Carter
28 Holland
29 Sweikert
30 Niday
31 Bryan
32 Davies
33 Thomson

No: 29

17 Hamilton
18 Gerard
19 Bira
20 Stewart,Ian
21 Brown,A.
22 Behra
23 Collins
24 Rosier
25 Crook
26 de Graffenried
27 Fairman
28 Salvadori

No: 30

7 Bonetto
8 Marimon
9 Behra
10 Schell
11 de Graffenried
12 Moss
13 Salvadori
14 Herrmann
15 Bira
16 McAlpine
17 Brown,A.
18 Heeks
19 Swaters
20 Nuckey
21 Fitzau
22 Rosier
23 Stuck,H.
24 Barth
25 Claes
26 Krause
27 Adolff
28 Helfrich
29 Seidel
30 Bechem
31 Loof
32 Klodwig
33 Bauer
34 Karch

No: 32

13 Bayol
14 Salvadori
15 Schell
16 Mieres
17 Rosier
18 McAlpine
19 Wharton
20 Carini
21 Landi
22 Fairman
23 Bira
24 Brown,A.
25 Chiron
26 Fitch
27 Macklin
28 Giraud-Cabantous
29 Stuck,H.
30 Claes

No: 34

9 Sweikert
10 Hanks
11 Ruttman
12 O'Connor
13 Niday
14 Nazaruk
15 Parsons
16 Ward
17 Hartley
18 Homeier
19 Vukovich
20 McCoy
21 Bettenhausen
22 Ayulo
23 Linden
24 Agabashian
25 Crockett
26 Duncan
27 Cross
28 Rathmann,J.
29 Webb
30 Hoyt
31 Elisian
32 Russo,P.
33 Armi

No: 37

11 Collins
12 Pilette,A.
13 Bucci
14 Parnell,R.
15 Manzon
16 Schell
17 Beauman
18 Gerard

19 Whitehouse
20 Gould
21 Riseley-Prichard
22 Marr
23 Thorne
24 Whitehead,P.
25 Brandon
26 Brown,A.
27 Villoresi
28 Marimon
30 Ascari
31 Rosier
32 Mieres

No: 44

9 Niday
10 Davies
11 Bryan
12 Flaherty
13 Russo,E.
14 Sweikert
15 Reece
16 Herman
17 Daywalt
18 Carter
19 O'Connor
20 Rathmann,J.
21 Freeland
22 Keller
23 Crawford,R.
24 Cross
25 Weyant
26 Boyd
27 Parsons
28 Andrews
29 Elisian
30 Ward
31 Templeman
32 Johnson,E.
33 Thomson

No: 51

11 Ruttman
12 Boyd
13 Hanks
14 Elisian
15 Ward
16 Daywalt
17 Crawford,R.
18 Thomson
19 Bryan
20 Andrews
21 Reece
22 Hartley
23 Veith
24 Turner
25 Christie
26 Freeland
27 Herman
28 Keller
29 Garrett
30 Griffith
31 Tolan
32 Johnson,E.
33 Dinsmore

No: 54

19 Villoresi
20 Halford
21 Fairman
22 Gerard
23 Emery
24 Maglioli
25 Godia
26 da Silva Ramos
27 Rosier
28 Brabham,J.

No: 68

11 Ward
12 Foyt
13 Freeland
14 Russo,P.
15 Garrett
16 Goldsmith
17 Christie
18 Sachs
19 Larson
20 Rathmann,J.
21 Keller
22 Thomson
23 Templeman
24 Unser,J.
25 Amick,G.
26 Johnson,E.
27 Sutton
28 Bisch
29 Weyant
30 Tolan
31 Magill
32 Wilson,D.
33 Cheesbourg

No: 87

11 Freeland
12 Ruby
13 Boyd
14 Christie
15 Weiler
16 Foyt
17 Thomson
18 Bettenhausen
19 Templeman
20 Force
21 Grim
22 Amick,R.
23 Hurtubuise
24 Goldsmith
25 Hartley
26 Veith
27 Carter
28 Tinglestad
29 Russo,E.
30 Herman
31 Homeier
32 McWithey
33 Wilson,D.

No: 98

23 Trintignant
24 Burgess
25 Taylor,H.
26 Scarlatti

No: 99

17 Taylor,H.
18 de Beaufort
19 Baghelti
20 Fairman
21 Bandini
22 Seidel
23 Greene
24 Maggs
25 Burgess
26 Ashmore
27 Marsh
28 Natili
29 Parnell,T.
30 Bianchi

No: 100

25 Ashmore
26 Collomb

No: 101

11 Moss
12 Gurney
13 Brooks
14 McLaren
15 de Beaufort
16 Lewis
17 Gregory
18 Salvadori
19 Surtees
20 Vaccarella
21 Bandini
22 Naylor
23 Trintignant
24 Taylor,H.
25 Bussinello
26 Ashmore
27 Fairman
28 Parnell,T.
29 Seidel
30 Pirocchi
31 Starrabba
32 Lippi

No: 108

23 Maggs
24 Brabham,J.
25 Bianchi
26 Taylor,T.

No: 147

17 Ickx
18 Arundell
19 Beltoise
20 Schlesser,J.
21 Rodriguez,P.
22 Ahrens
23 Herrmann
24 Courage
25 Rees
26 Taylor,J.
27 Lawrence
28 Hahne
29 Moser

No: 207

21 Eaton
22 Beuttler
23 Stommelen
24 Barber,S.
25 Craft
26 Lovely
27 Pescarolo

No: 208

19 Revson
20 Pescarolo
21 Gethin
22 Hobbs
23 Nanni
24 Cannon
25 Barber,S.
26 de Adamich
27 Craft
28 Bonnier
29 Lovely

No: 210

21 Lauda
22 Pescarolo
23 Marko
24 Pace
25 Stommelen
26 Love
27 Ferguson

No: 214

18 Depailler
19 Reutemann
20 Wisell
21 Nanni
22 Gethin
23 Hill,G.
24 Lauda
25 Walker,D.
26 Beuttler
27 Bell
28 Charlton

No: 215

21 Hill,G.
22 Fittipaldi,W.
23 Beuttler
24 Charlton
25 Stommelen
26 Pescarolo
27 Migault

No: 216

21 Fittipaldi,W.
22 Merzario
23 Walker,D.

24 Lauda
25 Bell
26 Charlton
27 Beuttler

No: 217
23 Pescarolo
24 Nanni
25 Beuttler
26 Migault

No: 220
13 Fittipaldi,W.
14 Hailwood
15 Pace
16 Wisell
17 Ganley
18 Beltoise
19 de Adamich
20 Barber,S.
21 Beuttler
22 Pescarolo
23 Posey
24 Redman
25 Surtees
26 Lauda
27 Peterson
28 Hill,G.
29 Gethin
30 Bell
31 Walker,D.
32 Schenken

No: 226
23 Oliver
24 Purley
25 Hill,G.
26 de Adamich

No: 229
17 Beltoise
18 Ganley
19 Ickx
20 de Adamich
21 von Opel
22 Williamson
23 Watson
24 Beuttler
25 Follmer
26 Oliver
27 Hill,G.
28 McRae

29 Amon

No: 234
23 Jarier
24 Schenken
25 Gethin
26 von Opel

No: 235
21 Follmer
22 Lauda
23 Oliver
24 Ickx
25 Watson
26 Fittipaldi,W.
27 Beuttler
28 von Opel

No: 236
23 Jarier
24 Schenken
25 Gethin
26 von Opel

No:238
21 Pescarolo
22 Scheckter,I.
23 Robarts
24 Keizan
25 Migault
26 Driver
27 Belso

No: 239
23 Migault
24 Amon
25 Schenken
26 von Opel

No: 240
13 Hailwood
14 Schuppan
15 Pescarolo
16 Ickx
17 Jarier
18 Redman
19 Watson
20 Pryce
21 Edwards
22 von Opel
23 Schenken
24 Reutemann
25 Migault

26 Mass
27 Pilette,T.
28 Larrousse
29 Hill,G.
30 van Lennep
31 Brambilla

No: 241
23 Schenken
24 Schuppan
25 Edwards
26 Pescarolo

No: 242
23 Roos
24 Pace
25 Kinnunen
26 Merzario

No: 246
21 Laffite
22 Schuppan
23 Brambilla
24 Pescarolo
25 Bell
26 Ashley

No: 249
23 Stuck,H-J.
24 Donohue
25 Amon
26 Wietzes

No: 250
21 Stommelen
22 Wilds
23 Koinigg
24 Hill,G.
25 Brambilla
26 Dolhem
27 Schenken

No: 253
20 Charlton
21 Ickx
22 Keizan
23 Laffite
24 Evans
25 Tunmer
26 Lombardi
27 Hill,G.

No: 254
22 Migault

23 Evans
24 Lombardi
25 Merzario
26 Fittipaldi,E.

No: 257
23 Evans
24 Lombardi
25 Fittipaldi,W.
26 Schuppan

No: 259
23 Fittipaldi,W.
24 Migault
25 Evans
26 Lombardi

No: 260
23 Morgan
24 Fittipaldi,W.
25 Crawford,J.
26 Nicholson

No: 262
17 Lunger
18 Watson
19 Andretti,Mario
20 Fittipaldi,W.
21 Amon
22 Donohue
23 Lombardi
24 Stommelen
25 Henton
26 Evans
27 Ertl
28 Wunderink
29 Vonlanthen

No: 263
23 Stommelen
24 Lombardi
25 Crawford,J.
26 Merzario

No: 269
23 Kessel
24 Ertl
25 Leclere
26 Lunger

No: 271
22 Perkins
23 Ertl
24 Lunger

25 Leclere
26 Kessel

No: 272
21 Fittipaldi,E.
22 Leclere
23 Lunger
24 Pescarolo
25 Edwards
26 Neve
27 Ertl

No: 273
23 Ertl
24 Jarier
25 Edwards
26 Pescarolo

No: 274
23 Jarier
24 Lunger
25 Edwards
26 Pesenti-Rossi

No: 276
23 Merzario
24 Ertl
25 Stommelen
26 Andersson

No: 277
19 Ertl
20 Fittipaldi,E.
21 Pesenti-Rossi
22 Pescarolo
23 Lunger
24 Merzario
25 Stuppacher
26 Hunt
27 Mass
28 Watson

No: 278
23 Ertl
24 Edwards
25 Merzario
26 Amon

No: 279
23 Brown,Warwick
24 Lunger
25 Merzario
26 Pescarolo

No: 280
23 Fittipaldi,E.
24 Takahara
25 Binder
26 Kawashima

No: 287
21 Scheckter,I.
22 Lunger
23 Perkins
24 Neve
25 Ertl
26 Jarier
27 Hayje

No: 290
23 Schuppan
24 Scheckter,I.
25 Patrese
26 Neve

No: 292
23 Fittipaldi,E.
24 Scheckter,I.
25 Schuppan
26 Villota

No: 293
23 Henton
24 Ribeiro
25 Scheckter,I.
26 Keegan

No: 295
23 Ribeiro
24 Neve
25 Binder
26 Ongais

No: 296
23 Ribeiro
24 Binder
25 Ashley
26 Keegan

No: 300
23 Keegan
24 Rosberg
25 Cheever
26 Merzario

No: 306
23 Keegan
24 Lunger
25 Mass
26 Rosberg

No: 307
23 Merzario
24 Lunger
25 Brambilla
26 Mass

No: 309
21 Brambilla
22 Regazzoni
23 Stuck,H-J.
24 Ertl
25 Rosberg
26 Arnoux

No: 310
21 Lunger
22 Brambilla
23 Arnoux
24 Rosberg
25 Keegan
26 Piquet
27 Merzario

No: 312
23 Rebaque
24 Lunger
25 Bleekemolen
26 Merzario

No: 317
23 de Angelis
24 Merzario
25 Rebaque
26 Daly

No: 358
23 Borgudd
24 Daly
25 Serra
26 Jarier

No: 359
23 Jarier
24 Laffite
25 Serra
26 Cheever

No: 360
23 Boesel
24 Borgudd
25 Winkelhock
26 Salazar

No: 362
19 Laffite
20 Salazar
21 Warwick
22 Henton
23 Fabi,T.
24 Surer
25 Serra
26 Boesel
27 Mass
28 Baldi

No: 364
23 Paletti
24 Baldi
25 Salazar
26 Serra

No: 367
17 Henton
18 Jarier
19 Guerrero
20 Laffite
21 Serra
22 Surer
23 Mansell
24 Cheever
25 Mass
26 Baldi

No: 368
23 Henton
24 Lees
25 Baldi
26 Mass

No: 369
21 Jarier
22 Guerrero
23 Salazar
24 Baldi
25 Boesel
26 Serra
27 Surer

No: 370
23 Baldi
24 Keegan
25 Winkelhock
26 Byrne

No: 371
23 Fabi,T.
24 Boesel
25 Salazar
26 Mansell

No: 372
23 Mansell
24 Baldi
25 Salazar
26 Serra

No: 373
20 Jarier
21 Mansell
22 Winkelhock
23 Baldi
24 Boesel
25 Keegan
26 Byrne

No: 374
21 Sullivan
22 Mansell
23 Serra
24 Fabi,C.
25 Winkelhock
26 Salazar

No: 375
23 Lauda
24 Winkelhock
25 Salazar
26 Boesel

No: 376
23 Fabi,C.
24 Sullivan
25 Boesel
26 Serra

No: 377
23 Cecotto
24 Watson
25 Boesel
26 Fabi,C.

No: 379
23 Sullivan
24 Fabi,C.
25 Cecotto
26 Boesel

No: 380
23 Boesel
24 Ghinzani
25 Baldi
26 Cecotto

No: 381
23 Cecotto
24 Boesel
25 Fabi,C.
26 Baldi

No: 382
23 Sullivan
24 Watson
25 Jarier
26 Ghinzani

No: 383
23 Watson
24 Guerrero
25 Boesel
26 Ghinzani

No: 384
23 Sullivan
24 Laffite
25 Ghinzani
26 Fabi,C.

No: 387
23 Boesel
24 Ghinzani
25 Palmer
26 Alboreto

No: 388
23 Boesel
24 Acheson
25 Fabi,C.
26 Ghinzani

No: 389
21 Boutsen
22 Ghinzani
23 Bellof
24 Baldi
25 Surer
26 Alliot
27 Palmer

No: 390
21 Baldi

22 Palmer
23 Alliot
24 Surer
25 Bellof
26 Brundle
27 Boutsen

No: 391
23 Hesnault
24 Surer
25 Baldi
26 Palmer

No: 392
23 Alliot
24 Baldi
25 Palmer
26 Gartner

No: 393
23 Brundle
24 Baldi
25 Ghinzani
26 de Cesaris

No: 395
23 Surer
24 Rothengatter
25 Thackwell
26 Alliot

No: 396
23 Fabi,T.
24 Palmer
25 Patrese
26 Ghinzani

No: 397
23 Rothengatter
24 Alliot
25 Laffite
26 Palmer

No: 398
21 Ghinzani
22 Rothengatter
23 Palmer
24 Alliot
25 Johansson
26 Bellof
27 Gartner

No: 399
23 Gartner
24 Rothengatter
25 Palmer
26 Johansson

No: 400
23 Ghinzani
24 Palmer
25 Alliot
26 Rothengatter

No: 401
21 Ghinzani
22 Palmer
23 Gartner
24 Bellof
25 Johansson
26 Alliot
27 Rothengatter

No: 403
23 de Angelis
24 Baldi
25 Alliot
26 Johansson

No: 404
21 Hesnault
22 Ghinzani
23 Berger,G.
24 Gartner
25 Baldi
26 Palmer
27 Alliot

No: 406
23 Palmer
24 Baldi
25 Martini
26 Ghinzani

No: 411
23 Alliot
24 Ghinzani
25 Martini
26 Bellof

No: 412
23 Martini
24 Palmer
25 Ghinzani
26 Bellof

No: 413
21 Alliot
22 Winkelhock
23 Hesnault
24 Palmer
25 Rothengatter
26 Brundle
27 Martini

No: 414
23 Acheson
24 Rothengatter
25 Palmer
26 Martini

No: 415
23 Palmer
24 Martini
25 Alliot
26 Rothengatter

No: 416
23 Martini
24 Acheson
25 Jones
26 Alliot

No: 418
23 Alliot
24 Capelli
25 Danner
26 Martini

No: 423
23 de Cesaris
24 Rothengatter
25 Danner
26 Ghinzani

No: 428
23 de Cesaris
24 Rothengatter
25 Ghinzani
26 Berg

No: 429
23 Danner
24 Ghinzani
25 Rothengatter
26 Berg

No: 430
23 de Cesaris
24 Rothengatter
25 Ghinzani
26 Berg

No: 431
23 Ghinzani
24 Palmer
25 Rothengatter
26 Berg

No: 433
19 Nannini
20 Brundle
21 de Cesaris
22 Palmer
23 Streiff
24 Rothengatter
25 Capelli
26 Ghinzani
27 Caffi

No: 434
21 Boutsen
22 Danner
23 Streiff
24 Ghinzani
25 Capelli
26 Rothengatter
27 Berg

No: 435
23 Rothengatter
24 Nannini
25 Ghinzani
26 Berg

No: 436
23 Rothengatter
24 Danner
25 Ghinzani
26 Berg

No: 438
21 Caffi
22 Streiff
23 Alliot
24 Capelli
25 Palmer
26 Fabre
27 Tarquini

No: 439
23 Streiff
24 Palmer
25 Fabre
26 Caffi

No: 441
23 Ghinzani
24 Nakajima
25 Campos
26 Fabre

No: 442
23 Alliot
24 Palmer
25 Streiff
26 Fabre

No: 444
23 Palmer
24 Capelli
25 Fabre
26 Caffi

No: 445
23 Danner
24 Campos
25 Ghinzani
26 Fabre

No: 446
23 Capelli
24 Palmer
25 Streiff
26 Fabre

No: 447
23 Alliot
24 Streiff
25 Capelli
26 Forini

No: 448
23 Ghinzani
24 Palmer
25 Caffi
26 Forini

No: 449
23 Ghinzani
24 Campos
25 Fabre
26 Larini

No: 450
23 Dalmas
24 Alliot
25 Streiff
26 Caffi

No: 451
21 Capelli
22 Campos
23 Dalmas

24 Caffi
25 Ghinzani
26 Streiff
27 Moren

No: 452
23 Capelli
24 Danner
25 Moreno
26 Campos

No: 453
23 Campos
24 Modena
25 Tarquini
26 Larrauri

No: 454
23 Palmer
24 Caffi
25 Ghinzani
26 Modena

No: 455
23 Ghinzani
24 Tarquini
25 Larini
26 Johansson

No: 456
23 Caffi
24 Johansson
25 Sala
26 Larrauri

No: 457
23 Bailey
24 Larrauri
25 Johansson
26 Tarquini

No: 458
21 Capelli
22 Caffi
23 Bailey
24 Larrauri
25 Dalmas
26 Sala
27 Larini

No: 459
19 Dalmas
20 Modena
21 Schneider
22 Ghinzani
23 Martini
24 Palmer
25 Larini
26 Sala
27 Larrauri

No: 460
23 Dalmas
24 Bailey
25 Arnoux
26 Larini

No: 461
23 Ghinzani
24 Palmer
25 Modena
26 Larrauri

No: 462
23 Streiff
24 Johansson
25 Arnoux
26 Modena

No: 463
23 Dalmas
24 Ghinzani
25 Schneider
26 Larini

No: 464
23 Streiff
24 Arnoux
25 Dalmas
26 Bailey

No: 465
23 Arnoux
24 Johansson
25 Larini
26 Tarquini

No: 466
23 de Cesaris
24 Sala
25 Cheever
26 Modena

No: 467
23 Arnoux
24 Larini
25 Schneider
26 Bailey

No: 468
23 Arnoux
24 Alliot
25 Larrauri
26 Ghinzani

No: 469
23 Sala
24 Cheever
25 Schneider
26 Alliot

No: 470
23 Herbert
24 Nakajima
25 Palmer
26 Dalmas

No: 471
23 Palmer
24 Herbert
25 Moreno
26 Sala

No: 472
23 Danner
24 Cheever
25 Arnoux
26 Piquet

No: 473
23 Nakajima
24 Tarquini
25 Herbert
26 Danner

No: 474
23 Danner
24 Sala
25 Tarquini
26 Moreno

No: 475
23 Martini
24 Pirro
25 Cheever
26 Caffi

No: 476
23 Moreno
24 Grouillard
25 de Cesaris
26 Pirro

No: 477
23 Arnoux
24 Johansson
25 Cheever
26 Alboreto

No: 478
23 Sala
24 Johansson
25 Pirro
26 Alboreto

No: 479
23 Gachot
24 Cheever
25 Sala
26 Grouillard

No: 480
23 Arnoux
24 Larini
25 Gugelmin
26 Sala

No: 481
23 Arnoux
24 Capelli
25 Nakajima
26 Cheever

No: 482
23 Caffi
24 Grouillard
25 Ghinzani
26 Gugelmin

No: 483
23 Grouillard
24 Cheever
25 Warwick
26 Palmer

No: 484
23 Nakajima
24 Grouillard
25 Gugelmin
26 Arnoux

No: 485
23 Foitek
24 Warwick
25 Gugelmin
26 Capelli

No: 486
23 Alboreto
24 Warwick
25 Caffi
26 Dalmas

No: 487
21 Larini
22 Pirro
23 Grouillard
24 Foitek
25 Moreno
26 Lehto
27 Barilla

No: 488
23 Capelli
24 Bernard
25 Brabham,D.
26 Lehto

No: 489
23 Bernard
24 Capelli
25 de Cesaris
26 Caffi

No: 490
21 Brabham,D.
22 Alliot
23 Foitek
24 Larini
25 Moreno
26 Bernard
27 Lehto

No: 491
23 Martini
24 Pirro
25 Brabham,D.
26 Dalmas

No: 492
23 de Cesaris
24 Barilla
25 Alboreto
26 Tarquini

No: 493
23 Pirro
24 Alliot
25 Lehto
26 Foitek

No: 494
23 Barilla
24 Tarquini
25 Larini
26 Caffi

No: 495
23 Grouillard
24 Brabham,D.
25 Barilla
26 Alboreto

No: 496
23 Grouillard
24 Dalmas
25 de Cesaris
26 Larini

No: 497
23 Larini
24 Modena
25 Dalmas
26 Brabham,D.

No: 498
23 Donnelly
24 Dalmas
25 Modena
26 Alboreto

No: 499
23 Modena
24 Caffi
25 Alboreto
26 de Cesaris

No: 500
23 Bernard
24 Suzuki,A.
25 Brabham,D.
26 Tarquini

No: 501
23 Gugelmin
24 Blundell
25 Alboreto
26 Morbidelli

No: 502
23 Comas
24 Tarquini
25 Blundell
26 Brundle

No: 503
23 Blundell
24 Boutsen
25 Hakkinen
26 Bailey

No: 504
23 Comas
24 Gachot
25 Alboreto
26 Hakkinen

No: 505
23 Gugelmin
24 Hakkinen
25 Johansson
26 Comas

No: 506
23 Morbidelli
24 Hakkinen
25 Herbert
26 Alboreto

No: 507
23 Bernard
24 Brundle
25 Alboreto
26 Lehto

No: 508
23 Martini
24 Herbert
25 Hakkinen
26 Alboreto

No: 509
23 Hakkinen
24 Larini
25 Bernard
26 Comas

No: 510
23 Morbidelli
24 Larini
25 Comas
26 Hakkinen

No: 511
23 Grouillard
24 Hakkinen
25 Pirro
26 Comas

No: 512
23 Comas
24 Larini
25 Bernard
26 Hakkinen

No: 513
23 Comas
24 Alboreto
25 Suzuki,A.
26 Hakkinen

No: 514
23 Bernard
24 Alboreto
25 Comas
26 Boutsen

No: 515
23 Tarquini
24 Suzuki,A.
25 Caffi
26 Piquet

No: 516
23 Caffi
24 Nakajima
25 Hakkinen
26 Wendlinger

No: 517
23 Gugelmin
24 Lehto
25 Martini
26 Van de Poele

No: 518
23 Chiesa
24 Katayama
25 Alboreto
26 Comas

No: 519
23 Morbidelli
24 Hakkinen
25 Katayama
26 Herbert

No: 520
23 Belmondo
24 Gachot
25 Herbert
26 Morbidelli

No: 521
23 Modena
24 Belmondo
25 Fittipaldi,C.
26 Herbert

No: 522
23 Comas
24 Grouillard
25 Tarquini
26 Moreno

No: 523
23 Lehto
24 Gugelmin
25 Fittipaldi,C.
26 Grouillard

No: 524
23 Tarquini
24 Gugelmin
25 Martini
26 Chiesa

No: 525
23 Modena
24 Gugelmin
25 Morbidelli
26 Hill,D.

No: 526
23 Gugelmin
24 Zanardi
25 Gachot
26 Morbidelli

No: 527
23 Wendlinger
24 Modena
25 Hill,D.
26 Martini

No: 528
23 Morbidelli
24 Gugelmin
25 Suzuki,A.
26 Katayama

No: 529
23 Katayama
24 Naspetti
25 Van de Poele
26 Gugelmin

No: 530
23 Naspetti
24 Modena
25 Katayama
26 Fittipaldi,C

No: 531
23 Lammers
24 Alboreto
25 Gugelmin
26 Naspetti

No: 532
23 Naspetti
24 Lehto
25 Lammers
26 Katayama

No: 533
23 de Cesaris
24 Barbazza
25 Alboreto
26 Badoer

No: 534
23 de Cesaris
24 Barbazza
25 Alboreto

No: 535
23 Suzuki,A.
24 Alboreto
25 de Cesaris

No: 536
23 Fittipaldi,C.
24 Badoer
25 Barbazza

No: 537
23 Katayama
24 de Cesaris
25 Barbazza

No: 538
23 Boutsen
24 Alboreto
25 Barbazza

No: 539
23 Barbazza
24 Boutsen
25 Badoer

No: 540
23 Fittipaldi,C.

24 Barbazza
25 de Cesaris

No: 541
23 Boutsen
24 Alliot
25 Badoer

No: 542
23 Alliot
24 Boutsen
25 Badoer
26 Alboreto

No: 543
23 Katayama
24 Boutsen
25 Alboreto
26 Badoer

No: 544
23 Katayama
24 Badoer
25 Alboreto

No: 545
23 Apicella
24 Fittipaldi,C.
25 Badoer
26 Lamy

No: 546
23 Naspetti
24 Fittipaldi,C.
25 Alboreto
26 Badoer

No: 549
23 Beretta
24 Lamy
25 Gachot
26 Brabham,D.

No: 550
23 Herbert
24 Lamy
25 Brabham,D.
26 Ratzenberger

No: 552
23 Gachot
24 Belmondo
25 Frentzen
26 Wendlinger

No: 553
23 Zanardi
24 Brabham,D.
25 Gachot
26 Belmondo

No: 554
23 Zanardi
24 Bernard
25 Brabham,D.
26 Gachot

No: 555
23 Zanardi
24 Brabham,D.
25 Beretta
26 Gounon

No: 556
23 Bernard
24 Beretta
25 Brabham,D.
26 Gounon

No: 557
23 Alboreto
24 Beretta
25 Brabham,D.
26 Gounon

No: 558
23 Brabham,D.
24 Herbert
25 Beretta
26 Gounon

No: 559
23 Katayama
24 Fittipaldi,C.
25 Gounon
26 Adams

No: 560
23 Dalmas
24 Comas
25 Gounon
26 Brabham,D.

No: 561
23 Dalmas
24 Brabham,D.
25 Adams
26 Gounon

No: 562
23 Comas
24 Noda
25 Brabham,D.
26 Schiattarella

No: 563
23 Noda
24 Brabham,D.
25 Salo
26 Inoue

No: 564
23 Noda
24 Brabham,D.
25 Deletraz
26 Schiattarella

No: 565
23 Moreno
24 Verstappen
25 Diniz
26 Schiattarella

No: 566
23 Gachot
24 Moreno
25 Diniz
26 Inoue

No: 567
23 Schiattarella
24 Montermini
25 Moreno
26 Diniz

No: 568
23 Montermini
24 Gachot
25 Moreno
26 Diniz

No: 569
21 Gachot
22 Diniz
23 Verstappen
24 Moreno
25 Montermini
26 Inoue

THE
DRIVERS

INTRODUCTION

This section of the *Formula 1 Record File* contains comprehensive race details for all drivers to have started a Grand Prix from 1950 to 1999. It includes details of drivers who have competed in the Indy 500 races; however, it does not include drivers who have only recorded dns results at Grands Prix. For readers who are familiar with the *Formula 1 Pocket Annual,* the format will be familiar.

Drivers are arranged alphabetically by surname and each entry is divided into three sections, although not all sections may be applicable. The first section lists personal details, this includes:

COUNTRY: country of origin
BORN: date of birth
GP STARTS: number of races driver has started
WC POINTS: number of Drivers World Championship points accumulated. This figure represents those points that were accredited towards final placement in the championship table. If this differs from the total figure scored then this number is shown in brackets after the initial value.
WC RECORD: the Drivers World Championship record, listing year, final position in the table, and number of points scored. Thus, an entry such as 1989-9/8 would signify that in 1989 the driver finished 9th in the table and scored 8 points. If the driver has not scored championship points then this entry is omitted.

The second section lists the driver"s general landmark performances. It details wins, poles and fastest laps as follows:

1st: number of wins plus the year and Grands Prix where they occurred.
2nd: number of second-place finishes plus the year and Grands Prix where they occurred.
3rd: number of third-place finishes plus the year and Grands Prix where they occurred.
Pole: number of pole positions secured plus the year and Grands Prix where they occurred.
Fast: number of fastest laps recorded plus the year and Grands Prix where they occurred.

The third and final section details the driver's Grands Prix career on a year by year basis.

Year: the year.
Team: the team the driver drove for. Abbreviations are used extensively here and a list of these can be found below. However, they are generally self-explanitory. The first two letters relate to the team and the second two relate to the engine where applicable. For example, an entry of BeRe
would translate to Benetton-Renault.
Grands Prix: This is a list of races the driver competed in for that year and that team with the finishing positions listed as well. The Grands Prix abbreviations are as used throughout this book and detailed elsewhere. Thus, an entry such as SA r, Mon 3, Bra dq
would translate to: a retirement in South Africa, a third place in Monaco and a disqualification in Brazil.

ABBREVIATIONS

Abb.	Full Name	Abb.	Full Name
Ada	Adams	BhPo	Behra-Porsche
AFBM	AFM-BMW	BlFd	Bellasi-Ford
AFM	AFM	BMW	BMW
AGFd	AGS-Ford	BoFd	Boro-Ford
AGFd	AGS-Ford	BrAl	Brabham-Alfa
AGMM	AGS-MM	BrBM	Brabham-BMW
AlSp	Alfa Special	BrBR	Brabham-BRM
Alta	Alta	BrCl	Brabham-Climax
AM	Aston Martin	BRCl	BRM-Climax
AmFd	Amon-Ford	BrFd	Brabham-Ford
AMJu	Andrea Moda-Judd	BrJu	Brabham-Judd
		BRM	BRM
AR	Alfa Romeo	Bro	Bromme
Ar	Arrows	BrRe	Brabham-Repco
ArBM	Arrows-BMW	BrYa	Brabham-Yamaha
ArFd	Arrows-Ford	Chr	Christensen
ArMe	Arrows-Megatron	CiFd	Coloni-Ford
ArYa	Arrows-Yamaha	CoAl	Cooper-Alfa
AsBu	Aston-Butterworth	CoAT	Cooper-ATS
		CoBo	Cooper-Borgward
ATBM	ATS-BMW (Germany)	CoBr	Cooper-Bristol
		CoBR	Cooper-BRM
ATFd	ATS-Ford (Germany)	CoCl	Cooper-Climax
		CoFd	Cooper-Ford
ATFd	ATS-Ford Gery	CoFe	Cooper-Ferrari
AtsI	ATS Italy	CoJA	Cooper-JAP
BASu	BAR-Supertec	CoMa	Cooper-Maserati
BeBM	Benetton-BMW	Con	Connaught
BeFd	Benetton-Ford	CoOs	Cooper-Osca
BePl	Benetton-Playlife	CwFd	Connew-Ford
BeRe	Benetton-Renault	DaFd	Dallara-Ford
		DaFe	Dallara-Ferrari

Abb.	Full Name
DaJu	Dallara-Judd
De	Deidt
DR	Del Roy
dTCr	de Tomaso-Conrero
dTFd	de Tomaso-Ford
dTOs	de Tomaso-Osca
Dunn	Dunn
EaCl	Eagle-Climax
EaWe	Eagle-Weslake
EBFd	EuroBrun-Ford
EBJu	EuroBrun-Judd
Elder	Elder
Em	Emeryson
EmCl	Emeryson-Climax
EMW	EMW
EnFd	Ensign-Ford
Epp	Epperly
ERA	ERA
Ew	Ewing
Fe	Ferrari
FeCl	Ferguson-Climax
FeJa	Ferrari-Jaguar
FiFd	Fittipaldi-Ford
FiFd	Forti-Ford
FN	Frazer Nash
FnFd	Fondmetal-Ford
FtFd	Footwork-Ford
FtHt	Footwork-Hart
FtMH	Footwork-Mugen Honda
FtPo	Footwork-Porsche
GiBR	Gilby-BRM
GiCl	Gilby-Climax
Gor	Gordini
HeFd	Hesketh-Ford
HiFd	Hill-Ford
Ho	Honda
HWM	HWM
JBCl	JBW-Climax
JBMa	JBW-Maserati
JoFd	Jordan-Ford
JoFd	Jordan-Hart
JoMH	Jordan-Mugen Honda
JoPe	Jordan-Peugeot
JoYa	Jordan-Yamaha
KK	Kurtis Kraft
KlMr	Klenk-Meteor
KoFd	Kojima-Ford
Ku	Kuzma
La	Lancia
LaFd	Larrousse-Ford
LaFe	Lancia-Ferrari
LaLm	Larrousse-Lamborghini
Lan	Langley
LaTa	Lago-Talbot
LcFd	Lec-Ford
LDAl	LDS-Alfa
LDCl	LDS-Climax
LDRe	LDS-Repco
Les	Lesovsky
LHIl	Leyton House-Ilmor
LHJu	Leyton House-Judd
LiFd	Ligier-Ford
LiJu	Ligier-Judd
LiLm	Ligier-Lamborghini
LiMat	Ligier-Matra
LiMe	Ligier-Megatron
LiMH	Ligier-Mugen Honda
LiRe	Ligier-Renault
LlCl	Lola-Climax
LlHt	Lola-Hart
Lm	Lamborghini
LoBM	Lola-BMW
LoFd	Lola-Ford
LoFe	Lola-Ferrari
LoLm	Lola-Lamborghini
LoMH	Lotus-Mugen Honda
LtBR	Lotus-BRM
LtHo	Lotus-Honda
LtJu	Lotus-Judd
LtLm	Lotus-Lamborghini
LtMas	Lotus-Maserati
LtRe	Lotus-Renault
LtTu	Lotus-Turbine
LyFd	Lyncar-Ford
MaAl	March-Alfa
MaIl	March-Ilmor
MaJd	March-Judd
Mar	Marchese
Mas	Maserati
Mat	Matra
MatBR	Matra-BRM
MatFd	Matra-Ford
McHo	McLaren-Honda
McMe	McLaren-Mercedes
McPe	McLaren-Peugeot
McTG	McLaren-TAG
Me	Mercedes
MiFd	Minardi-Ford
MiFe	Minardi-Ferrari
MiHt	Minardi-Hart
MiLm	Minardi-Lamborghini
MiMM	Minardi-MM
Mk	Meskowski
MkFd	Maki-Ford
Moo	Moore
MrFd	March-Ford
MrFd	Merzario-Ford
MsMi	Maserati-Milan
MsPl	Maserati-Platé
Nic	Nichels
Olson	Olson
OnFd	Onyx-Ford
OsAl	Osella-Alfa
OSCA	OSCA
OsFd	Osella-Ford
PaFd	Pac-Ford
PaFd	Parnelli-Ford
PaIl	Pac-Ilmor
Pan	Pankratz
Pawl	Pawl
Ph	Phillips
PkFd	Penske-Ford
Por	Porsche
PrMH	Prost-Mugen Honda
PrPe	Prost-Peugeot
Rae	Rae
Re	Renault
RiFd	Rial-Ford
RmFd	RAM-Ford
RmHt	RAM-Hart
SaFd	Sauber-Ford
SaIl	Sauber-Ilmor
SaMe	Sauber-Mercedes
SaPe	Sauber-Petronas
Sb	Scarab
ScBR	Scirocco-BRM
ScCl	Scirocco-Climax
Sch	Schroeder
ShCl	Shannon-Climax
Sher	Sherman
ShFd	Shadow-Ford
SiFd	Simtek-Ford
SiGo	Simca-Gordini
Snow	Snowberger
SpHt	Spirit-Hart
SpHo	Spirit-Honda
Ste	Stevens
StFd	Stebro-Ford
StFd	Stewart-Ford
Sut	Sutton
Ta	Talbot
Tec	Tecno
ThFd	Theodore-Ford
TjFd	Trojan-Ford
ToFd	Token-Ford
ToHt	Toleman-Hart
Trevis	Trevis
Tur	Turner
TyFd	Tyrrell-Ford
TyIl	Tyrrell-Ilmor
TyRe	Tyrrell-Renault
TyYa	Tyrrell-Yamaha
Va	Vanwall
Ver	Veritas
Wa	Watson
Wet	Wetteroth
WiFd	Williams-Ford
WiHo	Williams-Honda
WiJu	Williams-Judd
WiMh	Williams-Mecachrome
WiRe	Williams-Renault
WiSu	Williams-Supertec
WoFd	Wolf-Ford
Za	Zakspeed
ZaYa	Zakspeed-Yamaha

ABECASSIS, George

COUNTRY: GB
BORN: March 21, 1913
GP STARTS: 2
WC POINTS: 0

Year	Team	Grand(s) Prix
1951	HWM	Swi r
1952	HWM	Swi r

ACHESON, Kenny

COUNTRY: GB
BORN: November 27, 1957
GP STARTS: 3
WC POINTS: 0

Year	Team	Grand(s) Prix
1983	RmFd	SA 12
1985	RmHt	Aut r, Ita r

ADAMS, Phillippe

COUNTRY: Belgium
BORN: November 19, 1969
GP STARTS: 2
WC POINTS: 0

Year	Team	Grand(s) Prix
1994	LoMH	Bel r, Por 16

ADER, Walt

COUNTRY: US
BORN: December 15, 1913
GP STARTS: 1
WC POINTS: 0

Year	Team	Grand(s) Prix
1950	Rae	Indy 22

ADOLFF, Kurt

COUNTRY: Germany
BORN: November 5, 1921
GP STARTS: 1
WC POINTS: 0

Year	Team	Grand(s) Prix
1953	Fe	Ger r

AGABASHIAN, Freddie

COUNTRY: US
BORN: August 21, 1913
GP STARTS: 8
WC POINTS: 1.5
WC RECORD: 1953-18/1.5

Psn	No	Grand(s) Prix
Pole:	1	1952 Indy

Year	Team	Grand(s) Prix
1950	KK	Indy r
1951	KK	Indy r
1952	KK	Indy r
1953	KK	Indy 4
1954	KK	Indy 6
1955	KK	Indy r
1956	KK	Indy 12
1957	KK	Indy r

AHERNS, Kurt

COUNTRY: Germany
BORN: April 19, 1940
GP STARTS: 2
WC POINTS: 0

Year	Team	Grand(s) Prix
1966	BrFd	Ger r
1968	BrRe	Ger 12

ALBORETO, Michele

COUNTRY: Italy
BORN: December 23, 1956
GP STARTS: 194
WC POINTS: 186.5
WC RECORD: 1982-7/25; 1983-12/10; 1984-4/30.5; 1985-2/53; 1986-8/14; 1987-7/17; 1988-5/24; 1989-11/6; 1992-10/6; 1994-24/1

Psn	No	Grand(s) Prix
1st:	5	1982 CP; 1983 US; 1984 Bel; 1985 Can, Ger
2nd:	9	1984 Ita, Eur; 1985 Bra, Por, Mon, GB; 1986 Aut; 1987 Aus; 1988 Ita
3rd:	9	1982 SM; 1984 Aut; 1985 US, Aut; 1987 SM, Mon; 1988 Mon, Fra; 1989 Mex
Pole:	2	1984 Bel; 1985 Bra
Fast:	5	1982 CP; 1984 Eur; 1985 SM, Mon; 1988 Ita

Year	Team	Grand(s) Prix
1981	TyFd	SM r, Bel 12, Mon r, Fra 16, GB r, Aut r, Hol 9, Ita r, Can 11, US 13
1982	TyFd	SA 7, Bra 4, USW 4, SM 3, Bel r, Mon 10, US r, Can r, Hol 7, GB uc, Fra 6, Ger 4, Aut r, Swi 7, Ita 5, CP 1
1983	TyFd	Bra r, USW 9, Fra 8, SM r, Mon r, Bel 14, US 1, Can 8, GB 13, Ger r, Aut r, Hol 6, Ita r, Eur r, SA r
1984	Fe	Bra r, SA 11, Bel 1, SM r, Fra r, Mon 6, Can r, Detroit r, Dallas r, GB 5, Ger r, Aut 3, Hol r, Ita 2, Eur 2, Por 4
1985	Fe	Bra 2, Por 2, SM r, Mon 2, Can 1, US 3, Fra r, GB 2, Ger 1, Aut 3, Hol 4, Ita 13, Bel r, Eur r, SA r, Aus r
1986	Fe	Bra r, Esp r, SM 10, Mon r, Bel 4, Can 8, US 4, Fra 8, GB r, Ger r, Hun r, Aut 2, Ita r, Por 5, Mex r, Aus r
1987	Fe	Bra 8, SM 3, Bel r, Mon 3, US r, Fra r, GB r, Ger r, Hun r, Aut r, Ita r, Por r, Esp 15, Mex r, Jap 4, Aus 2
1988	Fe	Bra 5, SM 18, Mon 3, Mex 4, Can r, US r, Fra 3, GB 17, Ger 4, Hun r, Bel r, Ita 2, Por 5, Esp r, Jap 11, Aus r
1989	TyFd	Bra 10, Mon 5, Mex 3, US r, Can r
1989	LoLm	Ger r, Hun r, Bel r, Ita r, Por 11
1990	ArFd	US 10, Bra r, Can r, Mex 17, Fra 10, GB r, Ger r, Hun 12, Bel 13, Ita 12, Por 9, Esp 10, Jap r
1991	FtPo	US r, Mon r, Can r, Mex r, Fra r
1991	FtFd	GB r, Por 15, Esp r, Aus 13
1992	FtMH	SA 10, Mex 13, Bra 6, Esp 5, SM 5, Mon 7, Can 7, Fra 7, GB 7, Ger 9, Hun 7, Bel r, Ita 7, Por 6, Jap 15, Aus r
1993	Ll-Fe	SA r, Bra 11, Eur 11, Mon r, Ger 16, Hun r, Bel 14, Ita r, Por r
1994	MiFd	Bra r, Pac r, SM r, Mon 6, Esp r, Can 11, Fra r, GB r, Ger r, Hun 7, Bel 9, Ita r, Por 13, Eur 14, Jap r, Aus r

ALESI, Jean

COUNTRY: France
BORN: June 11, 1964
GP STARTS: 167
WC POINTS: 236
WC RECORD: 1989-9/8; 1990-9/13; 1991-7/21; 1992-7/18; 1993-6/16; 1994-5/24; 1995-5/42; 1996-4/47; 1997-3/36; 1998-11/9; 1999-15/2

Psn	No	Grand(s) Prix
1st:	1	1995 Can,
2nd:	16	1990 US, Mon; 1993 Ita; 1994 GB; 1995 Arg, SM, GB, Eur; 1996 Bra, Esp, Ger, Ita; 1997 Can, GB, Ita, Lux,
3rd:	15	1991 Mon, Ger, Por; 1992 Esp, Can; 1993 Mon; 1994 Bra, Can, Jap; 1996 Arg, Can, Fra, Hun; 1997 Esp; 1998 Bel,
Pole:	2	1994 Ita; 1997 Ita,
Fast:	4	1991 US; 1995 Mon; 1996 Arg, Mon,

Year	Team	Grand(s) Prix
1989	TyFd	Fra 4, GB r, Ger 10, Hun 9, Ita 5, Esp 4, Jap r, Aus r
1990	TyFd	US 2, Bra 7, SM 6, Mon 2, Can r, Mex 7, Fra r, GB 8, Ger 11, Hun r, Bel 8, Ita r, Por 8, Esp r, Jap dns, Aus 8
1991	Fe	US 12, Bra 6, SM r, Mon 3, Can r, Mex r, Fra 4, GB r, Ger 3, Hun 5, Bel r, Ita r, Por 3, Esp 4, Jap r, Aus r
1992	Fe	SA r, Mex r, Bra 4, Esp 3, SM r, Mon r, Can 3, Fra r, GB r, Ger 5, Hun r, Bel r, Ita r, Por r, Jap 5, Aus 4
1993	Fe	SA r, Bra 8, Eur r, SM r, Esp r, Mon 3, Can r, Fra r, GB 9, Ger 7, Hun r, Bel r, Ita 2, Por 4, Jap r, Aus 4
1994	Fe	Bra 3, Mon 5, Esp 4, Can 3, Fra r, GB 2, Ger r, Hun r, Bel r, Ita r, Por r, Eur 10, Jap 3, Aus 6
1995	Fe	Bra 5, Arg 2, SM 2, Esp r, Mon r, Can 1, Fra 5, GB 2, Ger r, Hun r, Bel r, Ita r, Por 5, Eur 2, Pac 5, Jap r, Aus r
1996	BeRe	Aus r, Bra 2, Arg 3, Eur r, SM 6, Mon r, Esp 2, Can 3, Fra 3, GB r, Ger 2, Hun 3, Bel 4, Ita 2, Por 4, Jap r
1997	BeRe	Aus r, Bra 6, Arg 7, SM 5, Mon r, Esp 3, Can 2, Fra 5, GB 2, Ger 6, Hun 11, Bel 8, Ita 2, Aut r, Lux 2, Jap 5, Eur 13
1998	SaPe	Aus r, Bra 9, Arg 5, SM 6, Esp 10, Mon 12, Can r, Fra 7, GB r, Aut r, Ger 10, Hun 7, Bel 3, Ita 5, Lux 10, Jap 7
1999	SaPe	Aus r, Bra r, SM 6, Mon r, Esp r, Can r, Fra r, GB 14, Aut r, Ger 8, Hun 16, Bel 9, Ita 9, Eur r, Mal 7, Jap 6

ALLIOT, Phillippe

COUNTRY: France
BORN: July 27, 1954
GP STARTS: 109
WC POINTS: 7

WC RECORD: 1986-18/1; 1987-16/3; 1989-26/1; 1993-17/2

Year	Team	Grand(s) Prix
1984	RmHt	Bra r, SA r, SM 10, Fra r, Can 10, Detroit r, Dallas dns, GB r, Ger r, Aut 11, Hol 10, Ita r, Eur r, Por r
1985	RmHt	Bra 9, Por r, SM r, Can r, US r, Fra r, GB r, Ger r, Aut r, Hol r, Ita r, Bel r, Eur r
1986	LiRe	Ger r, Hun 9, Aut r, Ita r, Por r, Mex 6, Aus 8
1987	LoFd	SM 10, Bel 8, Mon r, US r, Fra r, GB r, Ger 6, Hun r, Aut 12, Ita r, Por r, Esp 6, Mex 6, Jap r, Aus r
1988	LoFd	Bra r, SM 17, Mon r, Mex r, Can 10, US r, Fra r, GB 14, Ger r, Hun 12, Bel 9, Ita r, Por r, Esp 14, Jap 9, Aus 10
1989	LoLm	Bra 12, SM r, Mon r, Mex uc, US r, Can r, Fra r, GB r, Ger r, Bel 16, Ita r, Por 9, Esp 6, Jap r, Aus r
1990	LiFd	Bra 12, SM 9, Mon r, Can r, Mex 18, Fra 9, GB 13, Ger dq, Hun 14, Ita 13, Por r, Esp r, Jap 10, Aus 11
1993	LaLm	SA r, Bra 7, Eur r, SM 5, Esp r, Mon 12, Can r, Fra 9, GB 11, Ger 12, Hun 8, Bel 12, Ita 9, Por 10
1994	McPe	Hun r
1994	LaFd	Bel r

ALLISON, Cliff

COUNTRY: GB
BORN: February 8, 1932
GP STARTS: 16
WC POINTS: 11
WC RECORD: 1958-18/3; 1959-17/2; 1960-12/6

Psn	No	Grand(s) Prix
2nd:	1	1960 Arg,

Year	Team	Grand(s) Prix
1958	LoCl	Mon 6, Hol 6, Bel 4, Fra r, GB r, Ger 10
1958	Mas	Por r
1958	LoCl	Ita 7, Mor 10
1959	Fe	Mon r, Hol 9, Ger r, Ita 5, US r
1960	Fe	Arg 2
1961	LoCl	Mon 8

AMICK, George

COUNTRY: US
BORN: October 24, 1924
GP STARTS: 1
WC POINTS: 6
WC RECORD: 1958-15/6

Psn	No	Grand(s) Prix
2nd:	1	1958 Indy,

Year	Team	Grand(s) Prix
1958	Epp	Indy 2

AMICK, Red

COUNTRY: US
BORN: July 20, 1943
GP STARTS: 2
WC POINTS: 0

Year	Team	Grand(s) Prix
1959	KK	Indy r
1960	Epp	Indy 11

AMON, Chris

COUNTRY: New Zealand
BORN: July 20, 1943
GP STARTS: 96
WC POINTS: 83
WC RECORD: 1964-16/2; 1967-4/20; 1968-10/10; 1969-12/4; 1970-7/23; 1971-9/9; 1972-9/12; 1973-19/1; 1976-18/2

Psn	No	Grand(s) Prix
2nd:	3	1968 GB; 1970 Bel, Fra,
3rd:	8	1967 Mon, Bel, GB, Ger; 1969 Hol; 1970 Can; 1971 Esp; 1972 Fra,
Pole:	5	1968 Esp, Bel, Hol; 1971 Ita; 1972 Fra,
Fast:	3	1970 Mon; 1972 Mon, Fra,

Year	Team	Grand(s) Prix
1963	LICl	Bel r, Hol r, Fra 7, GB 7, Ger r, Ita dns
1963	LtBR	Mex r
1964	LtBR	Hol 5, Bel r, Fra 10, GB r, Ger r
1964	LoCl	Aut r
1964	LtBR	US r, Mex r
1965	LtBR	Fra r, Ger r
1966	CoMa	Fra 8
1967	Fe	Mon 3, Hol 4, Bel 3, Fra r, GB 3, Ger 3, Can 6, Ita 7, US r, Mex 9
1968	Fe	SA 4, Esp r, Bel r, Hol 6, Fra 10, GB 2, Ger r, Ita r, Can r, US r, Mex r
1969	Fe	SA r, Esp r, Mon r, Hol 3, Fra r, GB r
1970	MrFd	SA r, Esp r, Mon r, Bel 2, Hol r, Fra 2, GB 5, Ger r, Aut 8, Ita 7, Can 3, US 5, Mex 4

1971	Mat	SA 5, Esp 3, Mon r, Hol r, Fra 5, GB r, Ger r, Ita 6, Can 10, US 12
1972	Mat	SA 15, Esp r, Mon 6, Bel 6, Fra 3, GB 4, Ger 15, Aut 5, Ita r, Can 6, US 15
1973	Tec	Bel 6, Mon r, GB r, Hol r, Aut dns
1973	TyFd	Can 10, US dns
1974	AmFd	Esp r
1974	BRM	Can uc, US 9
1975	EnFd	Aut 12, Ita 12
1976	EnFd	SA 14, USW 8, Esp 5, Bel r, Mon 13, Swe r, GB r, Ger r
1976	WiFd	Can dns

ANDERSON, Bob

COUNTRY: GB
BORN: May 19, 1931
GP STARTS: 25
WC POINTS: 8
WC RECORD: 1964-11/5; 1966-17/1; 1967-16/2

Psn	No	Grand(s) Prix
3rd:	1	1964 Aut

Year	Team	Grand(s) Prix
1963	LICl	GB 12, Ita 12
1964	BrCl	Mon 7, Hol 6, Bel dns, Fra 12, GB 7, Ger r, Aut 3, Ita 11
1965	BrCl	SA uc, Mon 9, Fra dns, Fra r, GB r, Hol r, Ger dns
1966	BrCl	Mon r, Fra 7, GB uc, Hol r, Ger r, Ita 6
1967	BrCl	SA 5, Hol 9, Bel 8, Fra r, GB r
1976	SuFd	Hol r

ANDERSSON, Conny

COUNTRY: Sweden
BORN: December 28, 1939
GP STARTS: 1
WC POINTS: 0

Year	Team	Grand(s) Prix
1976	SuFd	Hol r

ANDRETTI, Mario

COUNTRY: US
BORN: February 28, 1940
GP STARTS: 128
WC POINTS: 180
WC RECORD: 1970-15/4; 1971-8/12; 1972-12/4; 1975-14/5; 1976-6/22; 1977-3/47; 1978-1/64; 1979-10/14; 1980-20/1; 1981-17/3; 1982-19/4
WORLD CHAMPION: 1978

Psn	No	Grand(s) Prix
1st:	12	1971 SA; 1976 Jap; 1977 USW, Esp, Fra, Ita; 1978 Arg, Bel, Esp, Fra, Ger, Hol
2nd:	2	1977 USE; 1978 USW
3rd:	5	1970 Esp; 1976 Hol, Can; 1979 Esp; 1982 Ita,
Pole:	18	1968 US; 1976 Jap; 1977 Esp, Bel, Swe, Fra, Hol, Can, Jap; 1978 Arg, Bel, Esp, Swe, Ger, Hol, Ita, USE; 1982 Ita
Fast:	10	1971 SA; 1975 Esp; 1976 Swe; 1977 Swe, Fra, Ita, Can; 1978 SA, Esp, Ita

Year	Team	Grand(s) Prix
1968	LtFd	Ita dns, US r
1969	LtFd	SA r, Ger r, US r
1970	MrFd	SA r, Esp 3, GB r, Ger r, Aut r
1971	Fe	SA 1, Esp r, Hol r, Ger 4, Can 13
1972	Fe	Arg r, SA 4, Esp r, Ita 7, US 6
1974	PaFd	Can 7, US dq
1975	PaFd	Arg r, Bra 7, SA 17, Esp r, Mon r, Swe 4, Fra 5, GB 12, Ger 10, Aut r, Ita r, US r
1976	LtFd	Bra r
1976	PaFd	SA 6, USW r
1976	LtFd	Esp r, Bel r, Swe r, Fra 5, GB r, Ger 12
1976	Ford	Aut 5
1976	LtFd	Hol 3, Ita r, Can 3, USE r, Jap 1
1977	LtFd	Arg 5, Bra r, SA r, USW 1, Esp 1, Mon 5, Bel r, Swe 6, Fra 1, GB 14, Ger r, Aut r, Hol r, Ita 1, USE 2, Can 9, Jap r
1978	LtFd	Arg 1, Bra 4, SA 7, USW 2, Mon 11, Bel 1, Esp 1, Swe r, Fra 1, GB r, Ger 1, Aut r, Hol 1, Ita 6, USE r, Can 10
1979	LtFd	Arg 5, Bra r, SA 4, USW 4, Esp 3, Bel r, Mon r, Fra r, GB r, Ger r, Aut r, Hol r, Ita 5, Can 10, USE r
1980	LtFd	Arg r, Bra r, SA 12, USW r, Bel r, Mon 7, Fra r, GB r, Ger 7, Aut r, Hol 8, Ita r, Can r, USE 6
1981	AR	USW 4, Bra r, Arg 8, SM r, Bel 10, Mon r, Esp 8, Fra 8, GB r, Ger 9, Aut r, Hol r, Ita r, Can 7, US r
1982	WiFd	USW r
1982	Fe	Ita 3, CP r

ANDRETTI, Michael

COUNTRY: US
BORN: October 5, 1962
GP STARTS: 13
WC POINTS: 7
WC RECORD: 1993-11/7

Psn	No	Grand(s) Prix
3rd:	1	1993 Ita

Year	Team	Grand(s) Prix
1993	McFd	SA r, Bra r, Eur r, SM r, Esp 5, Mon 8, Can 14, Fra 6, GB r, Ger r, Hun r, Bel 8, Ita 3

ANDREWS, Keith

COUNTRY: US
BORN: June 15, 1920
GP STARTS: 2
WC POINTS: 0

Year	Team	Grand(s) Prix
1955	Sch	Indy r
1956	KK	Indy r

APICELLA, Marco

COUNTRY: Italy
BORN: October 7, 1965
GP STARTS: 1
WC POINTS: 0

Year	Team	Grand(s) Prix
1993	JoFd	Ita r

ARMI, Frank

COUNTRY: US
BORN: October 12, 1918
GP STARTS: 1
WC POINTS: 0

Year	Team	Grand(s) Prix
1954	KK	Indy 19

ARNOLD, Chuck

COUNTRY: US
BORN: May 30, 1926
GP STARTS: 1
WC POINTS: 0

Year	Team	Grand(s) Prix
1959	KK	Indy 15

ARNOUX, Rene

COUNTRY: France
BORN: July 4, 1948
GP STARTS: 149
WC POINTS: 181
WC RECORD: 1979-8/17; 1980-6/29; 1981-9/11; 1982-6/28; 1983-3/49; 1984-6/27; 1985-17/3; 1986-8/14; 1987-19/1; 1989-23/2

Psn	No	Grand(s) Prix
1st:	7	1980 Bra, SA; 1982 Fra, Ita; 1983 Can, Ger, Hol
2nd:	9	1979 GB, USE; 1980 Hol; 1981 Aut; 1982 Ger; 1983 Aut, Ita; 1984 SM, Dallas
3rd:	6	1979 Fra; 1982 SA; 1983 USW, SM; 1984 Bel, Mon
Pole:	18	1979 Aut, Hol; 1980 Aut, Hol, Ita; 1981 Fra, GB, Aut, Ita; 1982 SA, SM, Mon, Hol, Fra; 1983 SM, US, Can, GB
Fast:	12	1979 Fra, Aut; 1980 Bra, SA, Aut, Hol; 1981 GB; 1982 Ita; 1983 Ger, Hol; 1984 Bel, Hol

Year	Team	Grand(s) Prix
1978	MnFd	Bel 9, Fra 14, Aut 9, Hol r
1978	SuFd	USE 9, Can r
1979	Re	Arg r, Bra r, SA r, USW dns, Esp 9, Bel r, Mon r, Fra 3, GB 2, Ger r, Aut 6, Hol r, Ita r, Can r, USE 2
1980	Re	Arg r, Bra 1, SA 1, USW 9, Bel 4, Mon r, Fra 5, GB uc, Ger r, Aut 9, Hol 2, Ita 10, Can r, USE 7
1981	Re	USW 8, Bra r, Arg 5, SM 8, Mon r, Esp 9, Fra 4, GB 9, Ger 13, Aut 2, Hol r, Ita r, Can r, US r
1982	Re	SA 3, Bra r, USW r, SM r, Bel r, Mon r, US 10, Can r, Hol r, GB r, Fra 1, Ger 2, Aut r, Swi r, Ita 1, CP r
1983	Fe	Bra 10, USW 3, Fra 7, SM 3, Mon r, Bel r, US r, Can 1, GB 5, Ger 1, Aut 2, Hol 1, Ita 2, Eur 9, SA r
1984	Fe	Bra r, SA r, Bel 3, SM 2, Fra 4, Mon 3, Can 5, Detroit r, Dallas 2, GB 6, Ger 6, Aut 7, Hol 11, Ita r, Eur 5, Por 9
1985	Fe	Bra 4
1986	LiRe	Bra 4, Esp r, SM r, Mon 5, Bel r, Can 6, US r, Fra 5, GB 4, Ger 4, Hun r, Aut 10, Ita r, Por 7, Mex 15, Aus 7

1987	LiMe	SM dns, Bel 6, Mon 11, US 10, Fra r, GB r, Ger r, Hun r, Aut 10, Ita 10, Por r, Esp r, Mex r, Jap r, Aus r
1988	LiJu	Bra r, Mon r, Mex r, Can r, US r, GB 18, Ger 17, Hun r, Bel r, Ita 13, Por 10, Esp r, Jap 17, Aus r
1989	LiFd	Mon 12, Mex 14, Can 5, Fra r, Ger 11, Bel r, Ita 9, Por 13, Aus r

ARUNDELL, Peter

COUNTRY: GB
BORN: November 8, 1933
GP STARTS: 11
WC POINTS: 12
WC RECORD: 1964-8/11; 1966-17/1

Psn	No	Grand(s) Prix
3rd:	2	1964 Mon, Hol

Year	Team	Grand(s) Prix
1963	LoCl	Fra dns
1964	LoCl	Mon 3, Hol 3, Bel 9, Fra 4
1966	LtBR	Bel dns, Fra r, GB r, Hol r, Ger 12, Ita 8
1966	LoCl	US 6
1966	LtBR	Mex 7

ASCARI, Alberto

COUNTRY: Italy
BORN: July 13, 1918
GP STARTS: 32
WC POINTS: 107.64 (140.14)
WC RECORD: 1950-5/11; 1951-2/25; 1952-1/36; 1953-1/34.5; 1954-25/1.14
WORLD CHAMPION: 1952, 1953

Psn	No	Grand(s) Prix
1st:	13	1951 Ger, Ita; 1952 Bel , Fra, GB, Ger, Hol, Ita; 1953 Arg, Hol, Bel, GB, Swi
2nd:	2	1950 Mon; 1951 Bel
Pole:	14	1951 Ger, Esp; 1952 Bel , Fra, Ger, Hol, Ita; 1953 Arg, Hol, Fra, GB, Ger, Ita; 1953 Esp
Fast:	12	1952 Bel , Fra, GB, Ger, Hol, Ita; 1953 Arg, GB, Ger, Swi; 1953 GB, Esp

Year	Team	Grand(s) Prix
1950	Fe	Mon 2, Swi r, Bel 5, Ita r
1951	Fe	Swi 6, Bel 2, Fra r, GB r, Ger 1, Ita 1, Esp 4
1952	Fe	Indy r, Bel 1, Fra 1, GB 1, Ger 1, Hol 1, Ita 1
1953	Fe	Arg 1, Hol 1, Bel 1, Fra 4, GB 1, Ger 8, Swi 1, Ita uc
1954	Mas	Fra r, GB r
1954	Fe	Ita r
1954	La	Esp r
1955	La	Arg r, Mon r

ASHDOWN, Peter

COUNTRY: GB
BORN: October 16, 1934
GP STARTS: 1
WC POINTS: 0

Year	Team	Grand(s) Prix
1959	CoCl	GB 12

ASHLEY, Ian

COUNTRY: GB
BORN: October 26, 1947
GP STARTS: 4
WC POINTS: 0

Year	Team	Grand(s) Prix
1974	ToFd	Ger 14, Aut uc
1975	WiFd	Ger dns
1976	BRM	Bra r
1977	HeFd	USE 17, Can dns

ASHMORE, Gerry

COUNTRY: GB
BORN: July 25, 1936
GP STARTS: 3
WC POINTS: 0

Year	Team	Grand(s) Prix
1961	LoCl	GB r, Ger 17, Ita r

ASTON, Bill

COUNTRY: GB
BORN: March 29, 1900
GP STARTS: 1
WC POINTS: 0

Year	Team	Grand(s) Prix
1952	AsBu	GB dns, Ger r

ATTWOOD, Dickie

COUNTRY: GB
BORN: April 4, 1940
GP STARTS: 16

WC POINTS: 11
WC RECORD: 1965-14/2; 1968-13/6; 1969-13/3

Psn	No	Grand(s) Prix
2nd:	1	1968 Mon
Fast:	1	1968 Mon

Year	Team	Grand(s) Prix
1964	BRM	GB dns
1965	LtBR	Mon r, Bel r, GB 13, Hol 12, Ger r, Ita 6, US 10, Mex 6
1967	CoMa	Can 10
1968	BRM	Mon 2, Bel r, Hol 7, Fra 7, GB r, Ger 14
1969	LtFd	Mon 4

AYULO, Manny

COUNTRY: US
BORN: October 20, 1921
GP STARTS: 3
WC POINTS: 2
WC RECORD: 1951-15/2

Year	Team	Grand(s) Prix
1952	Les	Indy 20
1953	Ku	Indy 13
1954	Ku	Indy 13

BADOER, Luca

COUNTRY: Italy
BORN: January 25, 1971
GP STARTS: 49
WC POINTS: 0

Year	Team	Grand(s) Prix
1993	Ll-Fe	SA r, Bra 12, SM 7, Esp r, Can 15, Fra r, GB r, Ger r, Hun r, Bel 13, Ita 10, Por 14
1995	MiFd	Bra r, Arg r, SM 14, Esp r, Mon r, Can 7, Fra 13, GB 10, Ger r, Hun 8, Bel r, Ita r, Por 14, Eur 11, Pac 15, Jap 9, Aus dns
1996	FiFd	Aus dnq, Bra 11, Arg r, Eur dnq, SM 10, Mon r, Esp dnq, Can r, Fra r, GB dnq
1999	MiFd	Aus r, SM 8, Mon r, Esp r, Can 10, Fra 10, GB r, Aut 13, Ger 10, Hun 14, Bel r, Ita r, Eur r, Mal r, Jap r

BAGHELTI, Giancario

COUNTRY: Italy
BORN: December 25, 1934
GP STARTS: 21
WC POINTS: 0

Psn	No	Grand(s) Prix
1st:	1	1961 Fra
Fast:	1	1961 Ita

Year	Team	Grand(s) Prix
1961	Fe	Fra 1, GB r, Ita r
1962	Fe	Hol 4, Bel r, Ger 10, Ita 5
1963	Atsl	Bel r, Hol r, Ita uc, US r, Mex r
1964	BRM	Hol 10, Bel 8, GB 12, Ger r, Aut 7, Ita 8
1965	BrCl	Ita r
1966	Fe	Ita uc
1967	LtFd	Ita r

BAILEY, Julian

COUNTRY: GB
BORN: October 9, 1961
GP STARTS: 7
WC POINTS: 1
WC RECORD: 1991-18/1

Year	Team	Grand(s) Prix
1988	TyFd	SM r, Can r, US 9, GB 16, Ita 12, Jap 14
1991	TyFd	Sm 6

BALDI, Mauro

COUNTRY: Italy
BORN: January 31, 1954
GP STARTS: 36
WC POINTS: 5
WC RECORD: 1982-22/2; 1983-16/3

Year	Team	Grand(s) Prix
1982	ArFd	Bra 10, Bel r, US r, Can 8, Hol 6, GB 9, Fra r, Ger r, Aut 6, Ita 12, Caesar's Palace 11
1983	AR	Bra r, USW r, Fra r, SM 10, Mon 6, Bel r, US 12, Can 10, GB 7, Ger r, Aut r, Hol 5, Ita r, Eur r, SA r
1984	SpHt	Bra r, SA 8, Bel r, SM 8, Fra r, Eur 8, Por 15
1985	SpHt	Bra r, Por r, SM r

BALL, Bobby

COUNTRY: US
BORN: August 26, 1925
GP STARTS: 2
WC POINTS: 2
WC RECORD: 1951-15/2

Year	Team	Grand(s) Prix
1951	Sch	Indy 5
1952	Ste	Indy r

BALSA, Marcel

COUNTRY: France
BORN: January 1, 1909
GP STARTS: 1
WC POINTS: 0

Year	Team	Grand(s) Prix
1952	BMW	Ger r

BANDINI, Lorenzo

COUNTRY: Italy
BORN: December 21, 1935
GP STARTS: 42
WC POINTS: 58
WC RECORD: 1962-12/4; 1963-9/6; 1964-4/23; 1965-6/13; 1966-8/12

Psn	No	Grand(s) Prix
1st:	1	1964 Aut
2nd:	2	1965 Mon; 1966 Mon
3rd:	5	1962 Mon; 1964 Ger, Ita, Mex; 1966 Bel
Pole:	1	1966 Fra
Fast:	2	1966 Mon, Fra

Year	Team	Grand(s) Prix
1961	CoMa	Bel r, GB 12, Ger r, Ita 8
1962	Fe	Mon 3, Ger r, Ita 8
1963	BRM	Fra 10, GB 5, Ger r
1963	Fe	Ita r, US 5, Mex r, SA 5
1964	Fe	Mon r, Hol r, Bel r, Fra 9, GB 5, Ger 3, Aut 1, Ita 3, US r, Mex 3
1965	Fe	SA r, Mon 2, Bel 9, Fra 8, GB r, Hol 9, Ger 6, Ita 4, US 4, Mex 8
1966	Fe	Mon 2, Bel 3, Fra uc, Hol 6, Ger 6, Ita r, US r
1967	Fe	Mon r

BANKS, Henry

COUNTRY: US
BORN: June 14, 1913
GP STARTS: 3
WC POINTS: 0

Year	Team	Grand(s) Prix
1950	Mas	Indy r
1951	Moo	Indy 6
1952	Les	Indy 19

BARBAZZA, Fabrizio

COUNTRY: Italy
BORN: April 2, 1963
GP STARTS: 8
WC POINTS: 2
WC RECORD: 1993-17/2

Year	Team	Grand(s) Prix
1993	MiFd	SA r, Bra r, Eur 6, SM 6, Esp r, Mon 11, Can r, Fra r

BARBER, Johnny

COUNTRY: GB
BORN: 1929
GP STARTS: 1
WC POINTS: 0

Year	Team	Grand(s) Prix
1953	CoBr	Arg 8

BARBER, Skip

COUNTRY: US
BORN: November 16, 1936
GP STARTS: 5
WC POINTS: 0

Year	Team	Grand(s) Prix
1971	MrFd	Hol uc, Can r, US uc
1972	MrFd	Can uc, US 16

BARILLA, Paulo

COUNTRY: Italy
BORN: April 20, 1961
GP STARTS: 9
WC POINTS: 0

Year	Team	Grand(s) Prix
1989	MiFd	Jap r
1990	MiFd	US r, Bra r, SM 11, Mon r, Mex 14, GB 12, Hun 15, Bel r

BARRICHELLO, Rubens

COUNTRY: Brazil
BORN: May 23, 1972
GP STARTS: 112
WC POINTS: 77
WC RECORD: 1993-17/2; 1994-6/19; 1995-11/11; 1996-8/14; 1997-13/6; 1998-12/4; 1999-7/21

Psn	No	Grand(s) Prix
2nd:	2	1995 Can; 1997 Mon
3rd:	4	1994 Pac; 1999 SM, Fra, Eur
Pole:	2	1994 Bel; 1999 Fra

Year	Team	Grand(s) Prix
1993	JoFd	SA r, Bra r, Eur 10, SM r, Esp 12, Mon 9, Can r, Fra 7, GB 10, Ger r, Hun r, Bel r, Ita r, Por 13, Jap 5, Aus 11
1994	JoFd	Bra 4, Pac 3, Mon r, Esp r, Can 7, Fra r, GB 4, Ger r, Hun r, Bel r, Ita 4, Por 4, Eur 12, Jap r, Aus 4
1995	JoPe	Bra r, Arg r, SM r, Esp 7, Mon r, Can 2, Fra 6, GB 11, Ger r, Hun 7, Bel 6, Ita r, Por 11, Eur 4, Pac r, Jap r, Aus r
1996	JoPe	Aus r, Bra r, Arg 4, Eur 5, SM 5, Mon r, Esp r, Can r, Fra 9, GB 4, Ger 6, Hun 6, Bel r, Ita 5, Por r, Jap 9
1997	StFd	Aus r, Bra r, Arg r, SM r, Mon 2, Esp r, Can r, Fra r, GB r, Ger r, Hun r, Bel r, Ita 13, Aut 14, Lux r, Jap r, Eur r
1998	StFd	Aus r, Bra r, Arg 10, SM r, Esp 5, Mon r, Can 5, Fra 10, GB r, Aut r, Ger r, Hun r, Bel dns, Ita 10, Lux 11, Jap r
1999	StFd	Aus 5, Bra r, SM 3, Mon 9, Esp dq, Can r, Fra 3, GB 8, Aut r, Ger r, Hun 5, Bel 10, Ita 4, Eur 3, Mal 5, Jap 8

BARTH, Edgar

COUNTRY: Germany
BORN: January 26, 1917
GP STARTS: 5
WC POINTS: 0

Year	Team	Grand(s) Prix
1953	EMW	Ger r
1957	Por	Ger 12
1958	Por	Ger 6
1960	Por	Ita 7
1964	CoCl	Ger r

BASSI, Giorgio

COUNTRY: Italy
BORN: January 20, 1934
GP STARTS: 1
WC POINTS: 0

Year	Team	Grand(s) Prix
1965	BRM	Ita r

BAUER, Erwin

COUNTRY: Germany
BORN: July 17, 1912
GP STARTS: 1
WC POINTS: 0

Year	Team	Grand(s) Prix
1953	Ver	Ger r

BAYOL, Elle

COUNTRY: France
BORN: February 28, 1914
GP STARTS: 7
WC POINTS: 2
WC RECORD: 1954-18/2

Year	Team	Grand(s) Prix
1952	OSCA	Ita r
1953	OSCA	Fra r, Ita r
1954	Gor	Arg 5
1955	Gor	Arg r, Mon r
1956	Gor	Mon 6

BEAUMAN, Don

COUNTRY: GB
BORN: July 26, 1928
GP STARTS: 1
WC POINTS: 0

Year	Team	Grand(s) Prix
1954	Con	GB 11

BECHEM, Gunther

COUNTRY: Germany
BORN: December 21, 1921
GP STARTS: 2
WC POINTS: 0

Year	Team	Grand(s) Prix
1952	BMW	Ger r
1953	AFM	Ger r

BEHRA, Jean

COUNTRY: France
BORN: February 16, 1921
GP STARTS: 52
WC POINTS: 51.14

WC RECORD: 1952-10/6; 1954-26/.14; 1955-9/6; 1956-4/22; 1957-11/6; 1958-10/9; 1959-17/2

Psn	No	Grand(s) Prix
2nd:	2	1956 Arg; 1957 Arg
3rd:	7	1952 Swi; 1955 Mon; 1956 Mon, Fra, GB, Ger; 1958 Hol
Fast:	1	1954 GB

Year	Team	Grand(s) Prix
1952	Gor	Swi 3, Bel r, Fra 7, Ger 5, Hol r, Ita r
1953	Gor	Arg 6, Bel r, Fra 10, GB r, Ger r, Swi r
1954	Gor	Arg dq, Bel r, Fra 6, GB r, Ger 10, Swi r, Ita r, Esp r
1955	Mas	Arg r, Mon 3, Bel r, Hol 6, GB r, Ita 4
1956	Mas	Arg 2, Mon 3, Bel 7, Fra 3, GB 3, Ger 3, Ita r
1957	Mas	Arg 2, Fra 6, GB r, Ger 6, Pescara r, Ita r
1958	Mas	Arg 5
1958	BRM	Mon r, Hol 3, Bel r, Fra 11, GB r, Ger r, Por 4, Ita r, Moroccan r
1959	Fe	Mon r, Hol 5, Fra r

BELL, Derek

COUNTRY: GB
BORN: October 31, 1941
GP STARTS: 9
WC POINTS: 1
WC RECORD: 1970-22/1

Year	Team	Grand(s) Prix
1968	Fe	Ita r, US r
1969	McFd	GB r
1970	BrFd	Bel r
1970	SuFd	US 6
1971	SuFd	GB r
1972	Tec	Fra dns, Ger r, Can dns, US r
1974	SuFd	Ger 11

BELLOF, Stefan

COUNTRY: Germany
BORN: November 20, 1957
GP STARTS: 20
WC POINTS: 4
WC RECORD: 1985-15/4

Year	Team	Grand(s) Prix
1984	TyFd	Bra dq, SA dq, Bel dq, SM dq, Fra dq, Mon dq, Can r, Detroit dq, Dallas dq, GB dq, Hol dq
1985	TyFd	Por 6, SM r, Can 11, US 4, Fra 13, GB 11
1985	TyRe	Ger 8, Aut 7, Hol r

BELMONDO, Paul

COUNTRY: France
BORN: April 23, 1963
GP STARTS: 7
WC POINTS: 0

Year	Team	Grand(s) Prix
1992	Mall	Esp 12, SM 13, Can 14, Ger 13, Hun 9
1994	Pall	Mon r, Esp r

BELSO, Tom

COUNTRY: Denmark
BORN: August 27, 1942
GP STARTS: 2
WC POINTS: 0

Year	Team	Grand(s) Prix
1974	WiFd	SA r, Swe 8

BELTOISE, Jean-Pierre

COUNTRY: France
BORN: April 26, 1937
GP STARTS: 86
WC POINTS: 77
WC RECORD: 1968-9/11; 1969-5/21; 1970-9/16; 1971-22/1; 1972-11/9; 1973-10/9; 1974-13/10

Psn	No	Grand(s) Prix
1st:	1	1972 Mon
2nd:	3	1968 Hol; 1969 Fra; 1974 SA
3rd:	4	1969 Esp, Ita; 1970 Bel, Ita
Fast:	4	1968 Esp, Hol; 1969 Ita; 1972 Bel

Year	Team	Grand(s) Prix
1966	MatFd	Ger 8
1967	MatFd	US 7, Mex 7
1968	MatFd	SA 6
1968	MatFd	Esp 5
1968	Mat	Mon r, Bel 8, Hol 2, Fra 9, GB r, Ger r, Ita 5, Can r, US r, Mex r
1969	MatFd	SA 6, Esp 3, Mon r, Hol 8, Fra 2, GB 9, Ger 6, Ita 3, Can 4, US r, Mex 5
1970	Mat	SA 4, Esp r, Mon r, Bel 3, Hol 5, Fra 13, GB r, Ger r, Aut 6, Ita 3, Can 8, US r, Mex 5
1971	Mat	Esp 6, Mon r, Hol 9, Fra 7, GB 7, Can r, US 8

1972	BRM	SA r, Esp r, Mon 1, Bel r, Fra 15, GB 11, Ger 9, Aut 8, Ita 8, Can r, US r
1973	BRM	Arg r, Bra r, SA r, Esp 5, Bel r, Mon r, Swe r, Fra 11, GB r, Hol 5, Ger r, Aut 5, Ita 13, Can 4, US 9
1974	BRM	Arg 5, Bra 10, SA 2, Esp r, Bel 5, Mon r, Swe r, Hol r, Fra 10, GB 12, Ger r, Aut r, Ita r, Can uc

BERETTA, Olivier

COUNTRY: Monaco
BORN: November 23, 1969
GP STARTS: 9
WC POINTS: 0

Year	Team	Grand(s) Prix
1994	LaFd	Bra r, Pac r, SM r, Mon 8, Esp dns, Can r, Fra r, GB 14, Ger 7, Hun 9

BERG, Allen

COUNTRY: Canada
BORN: August 1, 1961
GP STARTS: 9
WC POINTS: 0

Year	Team	Grand(s) Prix
1986	OsAl	US r, Fra r, GB r, Ger 12, Hun r, Aut r, Por 13, Mex 16, Aus uc

BERGER, Gerhard

COUNTRY: Austria
BORN: August 27, 1959
GP STARTS: 210
WC POINTS: 385
WC RECORD: 1985-17/3; 1986-7/17; 1987-5/36; 1988-3/41; 1989-7/21; 1990-3/43; 1991-4/43; 1992-5/49; 1993-8/12; 1994-3/41; 1995-6/31; 1996-6/21; 1997-5/27

Psn	No	Grand(s) Prix
1st:	10	1986 Mex; 1987 Jap, Aus; 1988 Ita; 1989 Por; 1991 Jap; 1992 Can, Aus; 1994 Ger; 1997 Ger
2nd:	17	1987 Por; 1988 Bra, Mon; 1989 Ita, Esp; 1990 Bra, SM; 1991 SM, GB, Bel; 1992 Por, Jap; 1994 Pac, Ita, Aus; 1996 GB; 1997 Bra
3rd:	21	1986 SM; 1988 Mex, Ger; 1990 Mon, Mex, Ger, Bel, Ita; 1991 Bra, Aus; 1992 Hun; 1993 Hun; 1994 Mon, Fra; 1995 Bra, SM, Esp, Mon, Ger, Hun; 1996 SM
Pole:	12	1987 Por, Jap, Aus; 1988 GB; 1989 US, Mex; 1991 Esp, Jap; 1994 Ger, Por; 1995 Bel; 1997 Ger
Fast:	21	1986 Ger, Aut; 1987 Por, Esp, Aus; 1988 Bra, Bel, Por; 1989 Por; 1989 US, Bra, Can; 1991 SM, Aus; 1992 Mex, Can; 1995 SM, Ita; 1996 Bel; 1997 Arg, Ger

Year	Team	Grand(s) Prix
1984	ATBM	Aut 12, Ita 6, Eur r, Por 13
1985	ArBM	Bra r, Por r, SM r, Mon r, Can 13, US 11, Fra r, GB 8, Ger 7, Aut r, Hol 9, Ita r, Bel 7, Eur 10, SA 5, Aus 6
1986	BeBM	Bra 6, Esp 6, SM 3, Mon r, Bel 10, Can r, US r, Fra r, GB r, Ger 10, Hun r, Aut 7, Ita 5, Por r, Mex 1, Aus r
1987	Fe	Bra 4, SM r, Bel r, Mon 4, US 4, Fra r, GB r, Ger r, Hun r, Aut r, Ita 4, Por 2, Esp r, Mex r, Jap 1, Aus 1
1988	Fe	Bra 2, SM 5, Mon 2, Mex 3, Can r, US r, Fra 4, GB 9, Ger 3, Hun 4, Bel r, Ita 1, Por r, Esp 6, Jap 4, Aus r
1989	Fe	Bra r, SM r, Mex r, US r, Can r, Fra r, GB r, Ger r, Hun r, Bel r, Ita 2, Por 1, Esp 2, Jap r, Aus r
1990	McHo	US r, Bra 2, SM 2, Mon 3, Can 4, Mex 3, Fra 5, GB 14, Ger 3, Hun 16, Bel 3, Ita 3, Por 4, Esp r, Jap r, Aus 4
1991	McHo	US r, Bra 3, SM 2, Mon r, Can r, Mex r, Fra r, GB 2, Ger 4, Hun 4, Bel 2, Ita 4, Por r, Esp r, Jap 1, Aus 3
1992	McHo	SA 5, Mex 4, Bra r, Esp 4, SM r, Mon r, Can 1, Fra r, GB 5, Ger r, Hun 3, Bel r, Ita 4, Por 2, Jap 2, Aus 1
1993	Fe	SA 6, Bra r, Eur r, SM r, Esp 6, Mon 14, Can 4, Fra 14, GB r, Ger 6, Hun 3, Bel 10, Ita r, Por r, Jap r, Aus 5
1994	Fe	Bra r, Pac 2, SM r, Mon 3, Esp r, Can 4, Fra 3, GB r, Ger 1, Hun 12, Bel r, Ita 2, Por r, Eur 5, Jap r, Aus 2
1995	Fe	Bra 3, Arg 6, SM 3, Esp 3, Mon 3, Can r, Fra 12, GB r, Ger 3, Hun 3, Bel r, Ita r, Por 4, Eur r, Pac 4, Jap r, Aus r
1996	BeRe	Aus 4, Bra r, Arg r, Eur 9, SM 3, Mon r, Esp r, Can r, Fra 4, GB 2, Ger 13, Hun r, Bel 6, Ita r, Por 6, Jap 4

1997	BeRe	Aus 4, Bra 2, Arg 6, SM r, Mon 9, Esp 10, Ger 1, Hun 8, Bel 6, Ita 7, Aut 10, Lux 4, Jap 8, Eur 4

BERGER, Georges

COUNTRY: Belgium
BORN: September 14, 1918
GP STARTS: 2
WC POINTS: 0

Year	Team	Grand(s) Prix
1953	SiGo	Bel r
1954	Gor	Fra r

BERNARD, Eric

COUNTRY: France
BORN: August 28, 1964
GP STARTS: 45
WC POINTS: 10
WC RECORD: 1990-13/5; 1991-18/1; 1994-18/4

Psn	No	Grand(s) Prix
3rd:	1	1994 Ger

Year	Team	Grand(s) Prix
1989	LoLm	Fra 11, GB r
1990	LoLm	US 8, Bra r, SM 13, Mon 6, Can 9, Mex r, Fra 8, GB 4, Ger r, Hun 6, Bel 9, Ita r, Por r, Esp r, Jap r, Aus r
1991	LoFd	US r, Bra r, SM r, Mon 9, Can r, Mex 6, Fra r, GB r, Ger r, Hun r, Bel r, Ita r, Esp r
1994	LiRe	Bra r, Pac 10, SM 12, Mon r, Esp 8, Can 13, Fra r, GB 13, Ger 3, Hun 10, Bel 10, Ita 7, Por 10
1994	LoMH	Eur 18

BETTENHAUSEN, Tony

COUNTRY: US
BORN: September 12, 1916
GP STARTS: 11
WC POINTS: 11
WC RECORD: 1950-20/1; 1955-13/3; 1958-16/4; 1959-15/3

Psn	No	Grand(s) Prix
2nd:	1	1955 Indy
Fast:	1	1958 Indy

Year	Team	Grand(s) Prix
1950	De	Indy r
1951	De	Indy r
1952	De	Indy r
1953	Ku	Indy 9
1954	KK	Indy r
1955	KK	Indy 2
1956	KK	Indy r
1957	KK	Indy 15
1958	Epp	Indy 4
1959	Epp	Indy 4
1960	Wa	Indy r

BEUTTLER, Mike

COUNTRY: GB
BORN: April 13, 1940
GP STARTS: 28
WC POINTS: 0

Year	Team	Grand(s) Prix
1971	MrFd	GB r, Ger dq, Aut uc, Ita r, Can uc
1972	MrFd	Mon 13, Bel r, Fra r, GB 13, Ger 8, Aut r, Ita 10, Can uc, US 13
1973	MrFd	Arg 10, Bra r, SA uc, Esp 7, Bel 11, Mon r, Swe 8, GB 11, Hol r, Ger 16, Aut r, Ita r, Can r, US 10

BIANCHI, Lucien

COUNTRY: Belgium
BORN: November 10, 1934
GP STARTS: 17
WC POINTS: 6
WC RECORD: 1960-24/1; 1968-17/5

Psn	No	Grand(s) Prix
3rd:	1	1968 Mon

Year	Team	Grand(s) Prix
1960	CoCl	Bel 6, Fra r, GB r
1961	LoCl	Bel r, Fra r, GB r
1962	LoCl	Bel 9
1962	EBMas	Ger 16
1963	LICl	Bel r
1965	BRM	Bel 12
1968	CoBR	Mon 3, Bel 6, Hol r, Ger r, Can uc, US r, Mex r

BIANCO, Gino

COUNTRY: Brazil
BORN: July 22, 1916
GP STARTS: 4
WC POINTS: 0

Year	Team	Grand(s) Prix
1952	Mas	GB 18, Ger r, Hol r, Ita r

BINDER, Hans

COUNTRY: Austria
BORN: June 12, 1948
GP STARTS: 13
WC POINTS: 0

Year	Team	Grand(s) Prix
1976	EnFd	Aut r
1976	WiFd	Jap r
1977	SuFd	Arg r, Bra r, SA 11, USW 11, Esp 9, Mon r
1977	PkF	Aut 12, Hol 8
1977	SuFd	USE 11, Can r, Jap r

BIONDETTI, Clemente

COUNTRY: Italy
BORN: August 18, 1898
GP STARTS: 1
WC POINTS: 0

Year	Team	Grand(s) Prix
1950	FeJa	Ita r

BIRA, B

COUNTRY: Thailand
BORN: July 15, 1914
GP STARTS: 19
WC POINTS: 8
WC RECORD: 1950-8/5; 1954-17/3

Year	Team	Grand(s) Prix
1950	Mas	GB r, Mon 5, Swi 4, Ita r
1951	OSCA	Esp r
1952	SiGo	Swi r, Bel 10
1952	Gor	Fra r, GB 11
1953	Con	Fra r, GB 7, Ger r
1953	Mas	Ita 13
1954	Mas	Arg 7, Bel 6, Fra 4, GB r, Ger r, Esp 9

BIRGER, Pablo

COUNTRY: Argentina
BORN: January 6, 1924
GP STARTS: 2
WC POINTS: 0

Year	Team	Grand(s) Prix
1953	SiGo	Arg r
1955	Gor	Arg r

BISCH, Art

COUNTRY: US
BORN: November 10, 1926
GP STARTS: 1
WC POINTS: 0

Year	Team	Grand(s) Prix
1958	Ku	Indy r

BIANCHARD, Harry

COUNTRY: US
BORN: January 31, 1960
GP STARTS: 1
WC POINTS: 0

Year	Team	Grand(s) Prix
1959	Por	US 7

BLEEKEMOLEN, Michael

COUNTRY: Holland
BORN: October 2, 1949
GP STARTS: 1
WC POINTS: 0

Year	Team	Grand(s) Prix
1978	ATFd	USE r

BLOKDYK, Trevor

COUNTRY: South Africa
BORN: November 30, 1935
GP STARTS: 1
WC POINTS: 0

Year	Team	Grand(s) Prix
1963	CoMa	SA 12

BLUNDELL, Mark

COUNTRY: GB
BORN: April 8, 1966
GP STARTS: 61
WC POINTS: 32
WC RECORD: 1991-18/1; 1993-10/10; 1994-12/8; 1995-10/13

Psn	No	Grand(s) Prix
3rd:	3	1993 SA, Ger; 1994 Esp

Year	Team	Grand(s) Prix
1991	BrYa	US r, Bra r, SM 8, Mon r, Mex r, Fra r, GB r, Ger 12, Hun r, Bel 6, Ita 12, Por r, Esp r, Aus 17
1993	LiRe	SA 3, Bra 5, Eur r, SM r, Esp 7, Mon r, Can r, Fra r, GB 7, Ger 3, Hun 7, Bel 11, Ita r, Por r, Jap 7, Aus 9
1994	TyYa	Bra r, Pac r, SM 9, Mon r, Esp 3, Can 10, Fra 10, GB r, Ger r, Hun 5, Bel 5, Ita r, Por r, Eur 13, Jap r, Aus r
1995	McMe	Bra 6, Arg r, Mon 5, Can r, Fra 11, GB 5, Ger r, Hun r, Bel 5, Ita 4, Por 9, Eur r, Pac 9, Jap 7, Aus 4

BOESEL, Raul

COUNTRY: Brazil
BORN: December 4, 1957
GP STARTS: 23
WC POINTS: 0

Year	Team	Grand(s) Prix
1982	MrFd	SA 15, Bra r, USW 9, Bel 8, US r, Can r, Hol r, Ger r, Swi r, Caesar's Palace 13
1983	LiFd	Bra r, USW 7, Fra r, SM 9, Mon r, Bel 13, US 10, Can r, GB r, Ger r, Hol 10, Eur 15, SA uc

BONDURANT, Bob

COUNTRY: US
BORN: April 27, 1933
GP STARTS: 9
WC POINTS: 3
WC RECORD: 1966-14/3

Year	Team	Grand(s) Prix
1965	Fe	US 9
1965	LtBR	Mex r
1966	BRM	Mon 4, Bel r, GB 9, Ger r, Ita 7
1966	EaCl	US dq
1966	EaWe	Mex r

BONETTO, Felice

COUNTRY: Italy
BORN: June 9, 1903
GP STARTS: 15
WC POINTS: 17.5
WC RECORD: 1950-19/2; 1951-8/7; 1952-16/2; 1953-9/6.5

Psn	No	Grand(s) Prix
3rd:	2	1951 Ita; 1953 Hol

Year	Team	Grand(s) Prix
1950	MasMi	Swi 5, Fra r
1951	AR	GB 4, Ger r, Ita 3, Esp 5
1952	Mas	Ger dq, Ita 5
1953	Mas	Arg r, Hol 3, Fra r, GB 6, Ger 4, Swi r, Ita 6

BONNIER, Jo

COUNTRY: Sweden
BORN: January 31, 1930
GP STARTS: 103
WC POINTS: 39
WC RECORD: 1958-18/3; 1959-8/10; 1960-15/4; 1961-13/3; 1962-14/3; 1963-9/6; 1964-15/3; 1966-17/1; 1967-14/3; 1968-21/3

Psn	No	Grand(s) Prix
1st:	1	1959 Hol
Pole:	1	1959 Hol

Year	Team	Grand(s) Prix
1957	Mas	Arg 7, GB r, Pescara r, Ita r
1958	Mas	Mon r, Hol 10, Bel 9, Fra 8, GB r, Ger r, Por r
1958	BRM	Ita r, Moroccan 4
1959	BRM	Mon r, Hol 1, Fra r, GB r, Ger 5, Por r, Ita 8
1960	BRM	Arg 7, Mon 5, Hol r, Bel r, Fra r, GB r, Por r, US 5
1961	Por	Mon r, Hol 11, Bel 7, Fra 7, GB 5, Ger r, Ita r, US 6
1962	Por	Hol 7, Mon 5, Fra r, GB r, Ger 7, Ita 6, US 13
1963	CoCl	Mon 7, Bel 5, Hol uc, Fra uc, GB r, Ger 6, Ita 7, US 8, Mex 5, SA 6
1964	CoCl	Mon 5
1964	BrBR	Hol 9, Bel r, GB r, Ger r
1964	BrCl	Aut 6, Ita 12, US r, Mex r
1965	BrCl	SA r, Mon 7, Bel r, Fra r, GB 7, Hol r, Ger 7, Ita 7, US 8, Mex r
1966	CoMa	Mon uc, Bel r
1966	BrCl	Fra uc, GB r
1966	CoMa	Hol 7, Ger r, Ita r, US uc, Mex 6
1967	CoMa	SA r, Bel r, GB r, Ger 5, Can 8, Ita r, US 6, Mex 10
1968	CoMa	SA r
1968	McBR	Bel r, Hol 8, GB r, Ita 6, Can r, US r
1968	Ho	Mex 5
1969	LtFd	GB r, Ger r
1970	McFd	US r
1971	McFd	SA r, Aut dns, Ita 10, US 16

BONOMI, Roberto

COUNTRY: Argentina
BORN: September 30, 1946
GP STARTS: 1
WC POINTS: 0

Year	Team	Grand(s) Prix
1960	CoMa	Arg 11

BORGUDD, Slim

COUNTRY: Sweden
BORN: November 25, 1946
GP STARTS: 10
WC POINTS: 1
WC RECORD: 1981-18/1

Year	Team	Grand(s) Prix
1981	ATFd	SM 13, GB 6, Ger r, Aut r, Hol 10, Ita r, Can r
1982	TyFd	SA 16, Bra 7, USW 10

BOTHA, Luki

COUNTRY: South Africa
BORN: January 16, 1930
GP STARTS: 1
WC POINTS: 0

Year	Team	Grand(s) Prix
1967	BrCl	SA uc

BOULLION, Jean-Christophe

COUNTRY: France
BORN: December 27, 1969
GP STARTS: 11
WC POINTS: 3
WC RECORD: 1995-16/3

Year	Team	Grand(s) Prix
1995	SaFd	Mon 8, Can r, Fra r, GB 9, Ger 5, Hun 10, Bel 11, Ita 6, Por 12, Eur r, Pac r

BOUTSEN, Thierry

COUNTRY: Belgium
BORN: July 13, 1957
GP STARTS: 163
WC POINTS: 132
WC RECORD: 1984-14/5; 1985-11/11; 1987-8/16; 1988-4/27; 1989-5/37; 1990-6/34; 1992-14/2

Psn	No	Grand(s) Prix
1st:	3	1989 Can, Aus; 1990 Hun
2nd:	2	1985 SM; 1990 GB
3rd:	10	1987 Aus; 1988 Can, US, Hun, Por, Jap; 1989 Hun, Ita, Jap; 1990 US
Pole:	1	1990 Hun
Fast:	1	1990 Ger

Year	Team	Grand(s) Prix
1983	ArFd	Bel r, US 7, Can 7, GB 15, Ger 9, Aut 13, Hol 14, Ita r, Eur 11, SA 9
1984	ArFd	Bra 6, SA 12
1984	ArBM	Bel r
1984	ArFd	SM 5
1984	ArBM	Fra 11, Can r, Detroit r, Dallas r, GB r, Ger r, Aut 5, Hol r, Ita 10, Eur 9, Por r
1985	ArBM	Bra 11, Por r, SM 2, Mon 9, Can 9, US 7, Fra 9, GB r, Ger 4, Aut 8, Hol r, Ita 9, Bel 10, Eur 6, SA 6, Aus r
1986	ArBM	Bra r, Esp 7, SM 7, Mon 8, Bel r, Can r, US r, Fra uc, GB uc, Ger r, Hun r, Aut r, Ita 7, Por 10, Mex 7, Aus r
1987	BeFd	Bra 5, SM r
1987	BeBM	Bel r
1987	BeFd	Mon r, US r, Fra r, GB 7, Ger r, Hun 4, Aut 4, Ita 5, Por 14
1987	BeBM	Esp 16
1987	BeFd	Mex r, Jap 5, Aus 3
1988	BeFd	Bra 7, SM 4, Mon 8, Mex 8, Can 3, US 3, Fra r, GB r, Ger 6, Hun 3, Bel dq, Ita 6, Por 3, Esp 9, Jap 3, Aus 5
1989	WiRe	Bra r, SM 4, Mon 10, Mex r, US 6, Can 1, Fra r, GB 10, Ger r, Hun 3, Bel 4, Ita 3, Por r, Esp r, Jap 3, Aus 1
1990	WiRe	US 3, Bra 5, SM r, Mon 4, Can r, Mex 5, Fra r, GB 2
1990	WiHo	Ger 6
1990	WiRe	Hun 1, Bel r, Ita r, Por r, Esp 4, Jap 5, Aus 5
1991	LiLm	US r, Bra 10, SM 7, Mon 7, Can r, Mex 8, Fra 12, GB r, Ger 9, Hun 17, Bel 11, Ita r, Por 16, Esp r, Jap 9, Aus r
1992	LiRe	SA r, Mex 10, Bra r, Esp r, SM r, Mon 12, Can 10, Fra r, GB 10, Ger 7, Hun r, Bel r, Ita r, Por 8, Jap r, Aus 5
1993	JoFd	Eur r, SM r, Esp 11, Mon r, Can 12, Fra 11, GB r, Ger 13, Hun 9, Bel r

BOYD, Johnny

COUNTRY: US
BORN: August 19, 1926
GP STARTS: 6
WC POINTS: 4
WC RECORD: 1958-16/4

Psn	No	Grand(s) Prix
3rd:	1	1958 Indy

Year	Team	Grand(s) Prix
1955	KK	Indy r
1956	KK	Indy r
1957	KK	Indy 6
1958	KK	Indy 3
1959	Epp	Indy 6
1960	Epp	Indy r

BRABHAM, David

COUNTRY: Australia
BORN: September 5, 1965
GP STARTS: 24
WC POINTS: 0

Year	Team	Grand(s) Prix
1990	BrJu	Mon r, Mex r, Fra 15, Ger r, Bel r, Por r, Jap r, Aus r
1994	SiFd	Bra 12, Pac r, SM r, Mon r, Esp 10, Can 14, Fra r, GB 15, Ger r, Hun 11, Bel r, Ita r, Por r, Eur r, Jap 12, Aus r

BRABHAM, Jack

COUNTRY: Australia
BORN: April 2, 1926
GP STARTS: 126
WC POINTS: 253 (261)
WC RECORD: 1958-18/3; 1959-1/31; 1960-1/43; 1961-11/4; 1962-9/9; 1963-7/14; 1964-8/11; 1965-10/9; 1966-1/42; 1967-2/46; 1968-23/2; 1969-10/14; 1970-5/25
WORLD CHAMPION: 1959, 1960, 1966

Psn	No	Grand(s) Prix
1st:	14	1959 Mon, GB; 1960 Hol, Bel, Fra, GB, Por; 1966 Fra, GB, Hol, Ger; 1967 Fra, Can; 1970 SA
2nd:	10	1959 Hol; 1963 Mex; 1966 Mex; 1967 Hol, Ger, Ita, Mex; 1969 Can; 1970 Mon, GB
3rd:	7	1959 Fra, Ita; 1964 Bel, Fra; 1965 US; 1969 Mex; 1970 Fra
Pole:	13	1959 GB; 1960 Bel, Fra, GB; 1961 US; 1966 GB, Hol, US; 1967 SA, Mon; 1968 SA, Mex; 1970 Esp
Fast:	12	1959 Mon; 1960 Bel, Fra, US; 1961 US; 1964 Fra; 1966 GB; 1969 Can; 1970 SA, Esp, Fra, GB

Year	Team	Grand(s) Prix
1955	CoBr	GB r
1956	Mas	GB r
1957	CoCl	Mon 6, Fra r, GB r, Ger r, Pescara 7
1958	CoCl	Mon 4, Hol 8, Bel r, Fra 6, GB 6, Ger r, Por 7, Ita r, Moroccan 11
1959	CoCl	Mon 1, Hol 2, Fra 3, GB 1, Ger r, Por r, Ita 3, US 4
1960	CoCl	Arg r, Mon dq, Hol 1, Bel 1, Fra 1, GB 1, Por 1, US 4
1961	CoCl	Mon r, Hol 6, Bel r, Fra r, GB 4, Ger r, Ita r, US r
1962	LoCl	Hol r, Mon r, Bel 6, Fra r, GB 5
1962	BrCl	Ger r, US 4, SA 4
1963	LoCl	Mon r
1963	BrCl	Bel r, Hol r, Fra 4, GB r, Ger 7, Ita 5, US 4, Mex 2, SA r
1964	BrCl	Mon r, Hol r, Bel 3, Fra 3, GB 4, Ger r, Aut 9, Ita r, US r, Mex r
1965	BrCl	SA 8, Mon r, Bel 4, Ger 5, US 3, Mex r
1966	BrRe	Mon r, Bel 4, Fra 1, GB 1, Hol 1, Ger 1, Ita r, US r, Mex 2
1967	BrRe	SA 6, Mon r, Hol 2, Bel r, Fra 1, GB 4, Ger 2, Can 1, Ita 2, US 5, Mex 2
1968	BrRe	SA r, Esp dns, Mon r, Bel r, Hol r, Fra r, GB r, Ger 5, Ita r, Can r, US r, Mex 10
1969	BrFd	SA r, Esp r, Mon r, Hol 6, Ita r, Can 2, US 4, Mex 3
1970	BrFd	SA 1, Esp r, Mon 2, Bel r, Hol 11, Fra 3, GB 2, Ger r, Aut 13, Ita r, Can r, US 10, Mex r

BRACK, Bill

COUNTRY: Canada
BORN: December 26, 1935
GP STARTS: 3
WC POINTS: 0

Year	Team	Grand(s) Prix
1968	LtFd	Can r
1969	BRM	Can 8
1972	BRM	Can r

BRAMBILLA, Vittorio

COUNTRY: Italy
BORN: November 11, 1937
GP STARTS: 74
WC POINTS: 15.5
WC RECORD: 1974-18/1; 1975-11/6.5; 1976-19/1; 1977-15/6; 1978-19/1

Psn	No	Grand(s) Prix
1st:	1	1975 Aut
Pole:	1	1975 Swe
Fast:	1	1975 Aut

Year	Team	Grand(s) Prix
1974	MrFd	SA 10, Esp dns, Bel 9, Mon r, Swe 10, Hol 10, Fra 11, GB r, Ger 13, Aut 6, Ita r, US r
1975	MrFd	Arg 9, Bra r, SA r, Esp 5, Mon r, Bel r, Swe r, Hol r, Fra r, GB 6, Ger r, Aut 1, Ita r, US 7
1976	MrFd	Bra r, SA 8, USW r, Esp r, Bel r, Mon r, Swe 10, Fra r, GB r, Ger r, Aut r, Hol 6, Ita 7, Can 14, USE r, Jap r
1977	SuFd	Arg 7, Bra r, SA 7, USW r, Esp r, Mon 8, Bel 4, Swe r, Fra 13, GB 8, Ger 5, Aut 15, Hol 12, Ita r, USE 19, Can 6, Jap 8
1978	SuFd	Arg 18, SA 12, USW r, Bel 13, Esp 7, Swe r, Fra 17, GB 9, Ger r, Aut 6, Hol dq, Ita r
1979	AR	Ita 12, Can r
1980	AR	Hol r, Ita r

BRANCA, Toni

COUNTRY: Switzerland
BORN: September 15, 1916
GP STARTS: 3
WC POINTS: 0

Year	Team	Grand(s) Prix
1950	Mas	Swi 11, Bel 10
1951	Mas	Ger r

BRANDON, Eric

COUNTRY: GB
BORN: July 18, 1920
GP STARTS: 5
WC POINTS: 0

Year	Team	Grand(s) Prix
1952	CoBr	Swi 8, Bel 9, GB 20, Ita 13
1954	CoBr	GB r

BRANSON, Don

COUNTRY: US
BORN: June 6, 1920
GP STARTS: 2
WC POINTS: 3
WC RECORD: 1960-19/3

Year	Team	Grand(s) Prix
1959	Ph	Indy r
1960	Ph	Indy 4

BRIDGER, Tom

COUNTRY: GB
BORN: June 24, 1934
GP STARTS: 1
WC POINTS: 0

Year	Team	Grand(s) Prix
1958	CoCl	Mor r

BRISE, Tony

COUNTRY: GB
BORN: March 28, 1952
GP STARTS: 10
WC POINTS: 1
WC RECORD: 1975-19/1

Year	Team	Grand(s) Prix
1975	WiFd	Esp 7
1975	HiFd	Bel r, Swe 6, Hol 7, Fra 7, GB 15, Ger r, Aut 15, Ita r, US r

BRISTOW, Chris

COUNTRY: GB
BORN: December 2, 1937
GP STARTS: 4
WC POINTS: 0

Year	Team	Grand(s) Prix
1959	CoBo	GB 10
1960	CoCl	Mon r, Hol r, Bel r

BROEKER, Peter

COUNTRY: Canada
BORN: May 15, 1929
GP STARTS: 1
WC POINTS: 0

Year	Team	Grand(s) Prix
1963	StFd	US 7

BROOKS, Tony

COUNTRY: GB
BORN: February 25, 1932
GP STARTS: 38
WC POINTS: 75
WC RECORD: 1957-5/11; 1958-3/24; 1959-2/27; 1960-11/7; 1961-10/6

Psn	No	Grand(s) Prix
1st:	6	1957 GB; 1958 Bel, Ger, Ita; 1959 Fra, Ger
2nd:	2	1957 Mon; 1959 Mon
3rd:	2	1959 US; 1961 US
Pole:	3	1958 Mon; 1959 Fra, Ger
Fast:	3	1957 Ita; 1959 Ger; 1961 GB

Year	Team	Grand(s) Prix
1956	BRM	Mon dns, GB r
1957	Va	Mon 2, GB 1, Ger 9, Pescara r, Ita 7
1958	Va	Mon r, Hol r, Bel 1, Fra r, GB 7, Ger 1, Por r, Ita 1, Mor r
1959	Fe	Mon 2, Hol r, Fra 1
1959	Va	GB r
1959	Fe	Ger 1, Por 9, Ita r, US 3
1960	CoCl	Mon 4, Hol r, Bel r
1960	Va	Fra r
1960	CoCl	GB 5, Por 5, US r
1961	BRCl	Mon r, Hol 9, Bel 13, Fra r, GB 9, Ger r, Ita 5, US 3

BROWN, Alan

COUNTRY: GB
BORN: November 20, 1919
GP STARTS: 8
WC POINTS: 0

Year	Team	Grand(s) Prix
1952	CoBr	Swi 5, Bel 6, GB 23, Ita 15
1953	CoBr	Arg 9, GB r, Ger r, Ita 15
1954	CoBr	GB dns

BROWN, Walt

COUNTRY: US
BORN: December 30, 1911
GP STARTS: 2
WC POINTS: 0

Year	Team	Grand(s) Prix
1950	KK	Indy 19
1951	KK	Indy r

BROWN, Warwick

COUNTRY: Australia
BORN: December 24, 1949
GP STARTS: 1
WC POINTS: 0

Year	Team	Grand(s) Prix
1976	WiFd	USE 14

BRUDES, Adolf

COUNTRY: Germany
BORN: October 15, 1899
GP STARTS: 1
WC POINTS: 0

Year	Team	Grand(s) Prix
1952	Ver	Ger r

BRUNDLE, Martin

COUNTRY: GB
BORN: June 1, 1959
GP STARTS: 158
WC POINTS: 98
WC RECORD: 1986-11/8; 1987-18/2; 1989-16/4; 1991-15/2; 1992-6/38; 1993-7/13; 1994-7/16; 1995-13/7; 1996-11/8

Psn	No	Grand(s) Prix
2nd:	2	1992 Ita; 1994 Mon
3rd:	7	1992 Fra, GB, Jap, Aus; 1993 SM; 1994 Aus; 1995 Bel

Year	Team	Grand(s) Prix
1984	TyFd	Bra dq, SA dq, Bel dq, SM dq, Fra dq, Can dq, Detroit dq
1985	TyFd	Bra 8, Por r, SM 9, Mon 10, Can 12, US r
1985	TyRe	Fra r, GB 7, Ger 10, Hol 7, Ita 8, Bel 13, Eur r, SA 7, Aus uc
1986	TyRe	Bra 5, Esp r, SM 8, Mon r, Bel r, Can 9, US r, Fra 10, GB 5, Ger r, Hun 6, Aut r, Ita 10, Por r, Mex 11, Aus 4
1987	Za	Bra r, SM 5, Bel r, Mon 7, US r, Fra r, GB r, Ger uc, Hun r, Aut dq, Ita r, Por r, Esp 11, Mex r, Jap r, Aus r
1988	WiJu	Bel 7

Year	Team	Grand(s) Prix
1989	BrJu	Bra r, SM r, Mon 6, Mex 9, US r, GB r, Ger 8, Hun 12, Bel r, Ita 6, Por 8, Esp r, Jap 5, Aus r
1991	BrYa	US 11, Bra 12, SM 11, Can r, Mex r, Fra r, GB r, Ger 11, Hun r, Bel 9, Ita 13, Por 12, Esp 10, Jap 5
1992	BeFd	SA r, Mex r, Bra r, Esp r, SM 4, Mon 5, Can r, Fra 3, GB 3, Ger 4, Hun 5, Bel 4, Ita 2, Por 4, Jap 3, Aus 3
1993	LiRe	SA r, Bra r, Eur r, SM 3, Esp r, Mon 6, Can 5, Fra 5, GB 14, Ger 8, Hun 5, Bel 7, Ita r, Por 6, Jap 9, Aus 6
1994	McPe	Bra r, Pac r, SM 8, Mon 2, Esp 11, Can r, Fra r, GB r, Ger r, Hun 4, Bel r, Ita 5, Por 6, Eur r, Jap r, Aus 3
1995	LiMH	Esp 9, Mon r, Can r, Fra 4, GB r, Hun r, Bel 3, Ita r, Por 8, Eur 7, Aus r
1996	JoPe	Aus r, Bra 12, Arg r, Eur 6, SM r, Mon r, Esp r, Can 6, Fra 8, GB 6, Ger 10, Hun r, Bel r, Ita 4, Por 9, Jap 5

BRYAN, Jimmy

COUNTRY: US
BORN: January 28, 1927
GP STARTS: 9
WC POINTS: 18
WC RECORD: 1954-8/6; 1957-14/4; 1958-13/8

Psn	No	Grand(s) Prix
1st:	1	1958 Indy
2nd:	1	1954 Indy
3rd:	1	1957 Indy

Year	Team	Grand(s) Prix
1952	KK	Indy 6
1953	Sch	Indy 14
1954	Ku	Indy 2
1955	Ku	Indy r
1956	Ku	Indy 19
1957	Ku	Indy 3
1958	Epp	Indy 1
1959	Epp	Indy r
1960	Epp	Indy r

BUCCI, Clemar

COUNTRY: Argentina
BORN: September 4, 1920
GP STARTS: 5
WC POINTS: 0

Year	Team	Grand(s) Prix
1954	Gor	GB r, Ger r, Swi r, Ita r
1955	Mas	Arg r

BUCKNUM, Ronnie

COUNTRY: US
BORN: April 5, 1936
GP STARTS: 11
WC POINTS: 2
WC RECORD: 1965-14/2

Year	Team	Grand(s) Prix
1964	Ho	Ger r, Ita r, US r
1965	Ho	Mon r, Bel r, Fra r, Ita r, US 13, Mex 5
1966	Ho	US r, Mex 8

BUEB, Ivor

COUNTRY: GB
BORN: June 6, 1923
GP STARTS: 5
WC POINTS: 0

Year	Team	Grand(s) Prix
1957	Con	Mon r
1957	Mas	GB uc
1958	Con	GB r
1958	LoCl	Ger 11
1959	CoBo	GB 13

BUENO, Luis

COUNTRY: Brazil
BORN: January 16, 1937
GP STARTS: 1
WC POINTS: 0

Year	Team	Grand(s) Prix
1973	SuFd	Bra 12

BURGESS, Ian

COUNTRY: GB
BORN: July 6, 1930
GP STARTS: 16
WC POINTS: 0

Year	Team	Grand(s) Prix
1958	CoCl	GB r, Ger 7
1959	CoMa	Fra r, GB r, Ger 6, Ita 14
1960	CoMa	Fra 10, GB r, US r
1961	LoCl	Fra 14, GB 14

1961	CoCl	Ger 12
1962	CoCl	GB 12, Ger 11
1963	ScBR	GB r, Ger r

BUSSINELLO, Roberto

COUNTRY: Italy
BORN: October 4, 1927
GP STARTS: 2
WC POINTS: 0

Year	Team	Grand(s) Prix
1961	dTOs	Ita r
1965	BRM	Ita r

BYRNE, Tommy

COUNTRY: Ireland
BORN: May 6, 1958
GP STARTS: 2
WC POINTS: 0

Year	Team	Grand(s) Prix
1982	ThFd	Aut r, Caesar's Palace r

CABIANCA, Giulio

COUNTRY: Italy
BORN: February 19, 1923
GP STARTS: 3
WC POINTS: 3
WC RECORD: 1960-19/3

Year	Team	Grand(s) Prix
1958	Mas	Ita r
1959	Mas	Ita 15
1960	CoFe	Ita 4

CABRAL, Mario

COUNTRY: Portugal
BORN: January 15, 1934
GP STARTS: 4
WC POINTS: 0

Year	Team	Grand(s) Prix
1959	CoMa	Por 10
1960	CoMa	Por r
1963	CoCl	Ger r
1964	Atsl	Ita r

CAFFI, Alex

COUNTRY: Italy
BORN: March 18, 1964
GP STARTS: 56
WC POINTS: 6
WC RECORD: 1989-16/4; 1990-16/2

Year	Team	Grand(s) Prix
1986	OsAl	Ita 11
1987	OsAR	Bra r
1987	OsAl	SM 12, Bel r, Mon r, US r, Fra r, GB r, Ger r, Hun r, Aut r, Ita r, Por r, Mex r, Jap r
1988	DaFd	SM r, Mon r, Mex r, US 8, Fra 12, GB 11, Ger 15, Hun r, Bel 8, Ita r, Por 7, Esp 10, Jap r, Aus r
1989	DaFd	SM 7, Mon 4, Mex 13, US r, Can 6, Fra r, Ger r, Hun 7, Bel r, Ita 11, Por r, Esp r, Jap 9, Aus r
1990	ArFd	Bra r, Mon 5, Can 8, Fra r, GB 7, Ger 9, Hun 9, Bel 10, Ita 9, Por 13, Jap 9
1991	FtFd	Jap 10, Aus 15

CAMPBELL-JONES, John

COUNTRY: GB
BORN: January 21, 1930
GP STARTS: 2
WC POINTS: 0

Year	Team	Grand(s) Prix
1962	LoCl	Bel uc
1963	LICI	GB 13

CAMPOS, Adrian

COUNTRY: Spain
BORN: June 17, 1960
GP STARTS: 17
WC POINTS: 0

Year	Team	Grand(s) Prix
1987	MiMM	Bra dq, SM r, Bel r, Mon dns, US r, Fra r, GB r, Ger r, Hun r, Aut r, Ita r, Por r, Esp 14, Mex r, Jap r, Aus r
1988	MiFd	Bra r, SM 16

CANNON, John

COUNTRY: Canada
BORN: June 21, 1937
GP STARTS: 1
WC POINTS: 0

Year	Team	Grand(s) Prix
1971	BRM	US 14

CANTONI, Heitnel

COUNTRY: Uruguay
BORN: 1896
GP STARTS: 3
WC POINTS: 0

Year	Team	Grand(s) Prix
1952	Mas	GB r, Ger r, Ita 11

CANTRELL, Bill

COUNTRY: US
BORN: January 31, 1908
GP STARTS: 1
WC POINTS: 0

Year	Team	Grand(s) Prix
1950	Mas	Indy r (shared)

CAPELLI, Ivan

COUNTRY: Italy
BORN: May 24, 1963
GP STARTS: 93
WC POINTS: 31
WC RECORD: 1985-17/3; 1987-19/1; 1988-7/17; 1990-10/6; 1991-18/1; 1992-12/3

Year	Team	Grand(s) Prix
1985	TyRe	Eur r, Aus 4
1986	AGMM	Ita r, Por r
1987	MrFd	Bra dns, SM r, Bel r, Mon 6, US r, Fra r, GB r, Ger r, Hun 10, Aut 11
1987	MaLt	Ita 13
1987	MrFd	Por 9, Esp 12, Mex r, Jap r, Aus r
1988	MaJd	Bra r, SM r, Mon 10, Mex 16, Can 5, US dns, Fra 9, GB r, Ger 5, Hun r, Bel 3, Ita 5, Por 2, Esp r, Jap r, Aus 6
1989	MaJd	Bra r, SM r, Mon 11, Mex r, US r, Can r, Fra r, GB r, Ger r, Hun r, Bel 12, Ita r, Por r, Esp r, Jap r, Aus r
1990	LHJu	US r, SM r, Mon r, Can 10, Fra 2, GB r, Ger 7, Hun r, Bel 7, Ita r, Por r, Esp r, Jap r, Aus r
1991	LHIl	US r, Bra r, SM r, Mon r, Can r, Mex r, Fra r, GB r, Ger r, Hun 6, Bel r, Ita 8, Por 17, Esp r
1992	Fe	SA r, Mex r, Bra 5, Esp 10, SM r, Mon r, Can r, Fra r, GB 9, Ger r, Hun 6, Bel r, Ita r, Por r
1993	JoFd	SA r

CARINI, Piero

COUNTRY: Italy
BORN: May 6, 1921
GP STARTS: 3
WC POINTS: 0

Year	Team	Grand(s) Prix
1952	Fe	Fra r, Ger r
1953	Fe	Ita r

CARTER, Duane

COUNTRY: US
BORN: May 5, 1913
GP STARTS: 8
WC POINTS: 6
WC RECORD: 1952-13/3; 1953-13/2; 1954-23/1.5

Year	Team	Grand(s) Prix
1950	Ste	Indy 12
1951	De	Indy 8
1952	Les	Indy 4
1953	Les	Indy r
1954	KK	Indy 15
1955	Ku	Indy 11
1959	KK	Indy 7
1960	Ku	Indy 12

CASTELLOTTI, Eugenio

COUNTRY: Italy
BORN: October 10, 1930
GP STARTS: 14
WC POINTS: 19.5
WC RECORD: 1955-3/12; 1956-6/7.5

Psn	No	Grand(s) Prix
2nd:	2	1955 Mon; 1956 Fra
3rd:	1	1955 Ita
Pole:	1	1955 Bel

Year	Team	Grand(s) Prix
1955	La	Arg r, Mon 2, Bel r
1955	Fe	Hol 5, GB r, Ita 3
1956	La-Fe	Arg r, Mon r, Bel r, Fra 2, GB 11, Ger r, Ita r
1957	La-Fe	Arg r

CECOTTO, Johnny

COUNTRY: Venezuela
BORN: January 25, 1956
GP STARTS: 18
WC POINTS: 1
WC RECORD: 1983-19/1

Year	Team	Grand(s) Prix
1983	ThFd	Bra 14, USW 6, Fra 11, SM r, Bel 10, US r, Can r, Ger 11, Ita 12
1984	ToHt	Bra r, SA r, Bel r, SM uc, Fra r, Mon r, Can 9, Detroit r, Dallas r

CERVERT, Francois

COUNTRY: France
BORN: February 25, 1944
GP STARTS: 46
WC POINTS: 89
WC RECORD: 1970-22/1; 1971-3/26; 1972-6/15; 1973-4/47

Psn	No	Grand(s) Prix
1st:	1	1971 US
2nd:	10	1971 Fra, Ger; 1972 Bel, US; 1973 Arg, Esp, Bel, Fra, Hol, Ger
3rd:	2	1971 Ita; 1973 Swe
Fast:	2	1971 Ger; 1973 Bel

Year	Team	Grand(s) Prix
1970	MrFd	Hol r, Fra 11, GB 7, Ger 7, Aut r, Ita 6, Can 9, US r, Mex r
1971	TyFd	SA r, Esp 7, Mon r, Hol r, Fra 2, GB 10, Ger 2, Aut r, Ita 3, Can 6, US 1
1972	TyFd	Arg r, SA 9, Esp r, Mon uc, Bel 2, Fra 4, GB r, Ger 10, Aut 9, Ita r, Can r, US 2
1973	TyFd	Arg 2, Bra 10, SA uc, Esp 2, Bel 2, Mon 4, Swe 3, Fra 2, GB 5, Hol 2, Ger 2, Aut r, Ita 5, Can r, US dns

CHABOUD, Eugene

COUNTRY: France
BORN: April 12, 1907
GP STARTS: 2
WC POINTS: 1
WC RECORD: 1950-20/1

Year	Team	Grand(s) Prix
1950	Ta	Bel r
1950	LaTa	Fra dns
1951	Ta	Fra 8

CHAMBERLAIN, Jay

COUNTRY: US
BORN: December 29, 1925
GP STARTS: 1
WC POINTS: 0

Year	Team	Grand(s) Prix
1962	LoCl	GB 15

CHARLTON, Dave

COUNTRY: South Africa
BORN: October 27, 1936
GP STARTS: 11
WC POINTS: 0

Year	Team	Grand(s) Prix
1967	BrCl	SA uc
1968	BrRe	SA r
1970	LtFd	SA r
1971	BrFd	SA r
1971	LtFd	GB r
1972	LtFd	SA r, Fra dns, GB r, Ger r
1973	LtFd	SA r
1974	McFd	SA 19
1975	McFd	SA 14

CHEESBOURG, Bill

COUNTRY: US
BORN: June 12, 1927
GP STARTS: 3
WC POINTS: 0

Year	Team	Grand(s) Prix
1957	KK	Indy r
1958	KK	Indy 10
1959	Ku	Indy r

CHEEVER, Eddie

COUNTRY: US
BORN: January 10, 1958
GP STARTS: 132
WC POINTS: 70
WC RECORD: 1981-11/10; 1982-12/15; 1983-6/22; 1984-16/3; 1987-10/8; 1988-12/6; 1989-11/6

Psn	No	Grand(s) Prix
2nd:	2	1982 US; 1983 Can

3rd:	7	1982 Bel, Caesar's Palace; 1983 Fra, Bel, Ita; 1988 Ita; 1989 US

Year	Team	Grand(s) Prix
1978	HeFd	SA r
1980	OsFd	SA r, USW r, Fra r, GB r, Ger r, Aut r, Hol r, Ita 12, Can r, USE r
1981	TyFd	USW 5, Bra uc, Arg r, SM r, Bel 6, Mon 5, Esp uc, Fra 13, GB 4, Ger 5, Hol r, Ita r, Can 12, US r
1982	LiMat	SA r, Bra r, USW r, Bel 3, Mon r, US 2, Can 10, GB r, Fra 16, Ger r, Aut r, Swi uc, Ita 6, Caesar's Palace 3
1983	Re	Bra r, USW r, Fra 3, SM r, Mon r, Bel 3, US r, Can 2, GB r, Ger r, Aut 4, Hol r, Ita 3, Eur 10, SA 6
1984	AR	Bra 4, SA r, Bel r, SM 7, Fra r, Can 11, Detroit r, Dallas r, GB r, Ger r, Aut r, Hol 13, Ita 9, Eur r, Por 17
1985	AR	Bra r, Por r, SM r, Mon r, Can 17, US 9, Fra 10, GB r, Ger r, Aut r, Hol r, Ita r, Bel r, Eur 11, SA r, Aus r
1986	LoFd	US r
1987	ArMe	Bra r, SM r, Bel 4, Mon r, US 6, Fra r, GB r, Ger r, Hun 8, Aut r, Ita r, Por 6, Esp 8, Mex 4, Jap 9, Aus r
1988	ArMe	Bra 8, SM 7, Mon r, Mex 6, Can r, US r, Fra 11, GB 7, Ger 10, Hun r, Bel 6, Ita 3, Por r, Esp r, Jap r, Aus r
1989	ArFd	Bra r, SM 9, Mon 7, Mex 7, US 3, Can r, Fra 7, Ger 12, Hun 5, Bel r, Por r, Esp r, Jap 8, Aus r

CHIESA, Andrea

COUNTRY: Switzerland
BORN: May 6, 1964
GP STARTS: 3
WC POINTS: 0

Year	Team	Grand(s) Prix
1992	FnFd	Mex r, Esp r, Fra r

CHIMERI, Ettore

COUNTRY: Venezuela
BORN: June 4, 1921
GP STARTS: 1
WC POINTS: 0

Year	Team	Grand(s) Prix
1960	Mas	Arg r

CHIRON, Louis

COUNTRY: Mon
BORN: August 3, 1899
GP STARTS: 15
WC POINTS: 4
WC RECORD: 1950-9/4

Psn	No	Grand(s) Prix
3rd:	1	1950 Mon

Year	Team	Grand(s) Prix
1950	Mas	GB r, Mon 3, Swi 9, Fra r, Ita r
1951	Mas	Swi 7, Bel r
1951	Ta	Fra 6, GB r, Ger r, Ita r, Esp r
1953	OSCA	Fra 15, Ita 12
1955	La	Mon 6

CHITWOOD, Joie

COUNTRY: US
BORN: April 12, 1912
GP STARTS: 1
WC POINTS: 1
WC RECORD: 1950-20/1

Year	Team	Grand(s) Prix
1950	KK	Indy 5

CHRISTIE, Bob

COUNTRY: US
BORN: April 4, 1924
GP STARTS: 5
WC POINTS: 0

Year	Team	Grand(s) Prix
1956	KK	Indy 13
1957	KK	Indy 13
1958	KK	Indy r
1959	KK	Indy r
1960	KK	Indy 10

CLAES, Johnnie

COUNTRY: Belgium
BORN: August 11, 1916
GP STARTS: 23
WC POINTS: 0

Year	Team	Grand(s) Prix
1950	Ta	GB 11, Mon 7, Swi 10, Bel 8, Fra r, Ita r
1951	Ta	Swi 14, Bel 7, Fra r, GB 13, Ger 12, Ita r, Esp r

1952	SiGo	Bel 8, Fra r, GB 14
1952	HWM	Ger 10
1953	Con	Hol uc
1953	Ma	Bel r
1953	Con	Fra 12, Ger r, Ita r
1955	Mas	Bel dns
1955	Fe	Hol 11

CLARK, Jim

COUNTRY: GB
BORN: March 4, 1936
GP STARTS: 72
WC POINTS: 255 (274)
WC RECORD: 1960-8/8; 1961-7/11; 1962-2/30; 1963-1/54; 1964-3/32; 1965-1/54; 1966-6/16; 1967-3/41; 1968-11/9
WORLD CHAMPION: 1963, 1965

Psn	No	Grand(s) Prix
1st:	25	1962 Bel, GB, US; 1963 Bel, Hol, Fra, GB, Ita, Mex, SA; 1964 Hol, Bel, GB; 1965 SA, Bel, Fra, GB, Hol, Ger; 1966 US; 1967 Hol, GB, US, Mex; 1968 SA
2nd:	1	1963 Ger
3rd:	6	1960 Por; 1961 Hol, Fra; 1963 US; 1966 Hol; 1967 Ita
Pole:	33	1962 Mon, Fra, GB, Ita, US, SA; 1963 Mon, Hol, Fra, GB, Ger, Mex, SA; 1964 Mon, Fra, GB, US, Mex; 1965 SA, Fra, GB, Ger, Ita, Mex; 1965 Mon, Ger; 1967 Bel, GB, Ger, Can, Ita, Mex; 1968 SA
Fast:	28	1961 Hol; 1962 Mon, Bel, GB, US, SA; 1963 Bel, Hol, Fra, Ita, US, Mex; 1964 Hol, GB, US, Mex; 1965 SA, Bel, Fra, Hol, Ger, Ita; 1966 Mon, Hol, Can, Ita, Mex; 1968 SA

Year	Team	Grand(s) Prix
1960	LoCl	Hol r, Bel 5, Fra 5, GB 17, Por 3, US 16
1961	LoCl	Mon 10, Hol 3, Bel 12, Fra 3, GB r, Ger 4, Ita r, US 8
1962	LoCl	Hol 11, Mon r, Bel 1, Fra r, GB 1, Ger 4, Ita r, US 1, SA r
1963	LoCl	Mon r, Bel 1, Hol 1, Fra 1, GB 1, Ger 2, Ita 1, US 3, Mex 1, SA 1
1964	LoCl	Mon 4, Hol 1, Bel 1, Fra r, GB 1, Ger r, Aut r, Ita r, US r, Mex 5
1965	LoCl	SA 1, Bel 1, Fra 1, GB 1, Hol 1, Ger 1, Ita r, US r, Mex r
1966	LoCl	Mon r, Bel r, GB 4, Hol 3, Ger r
1966	LtBR	Ita r, US 1, Mex r
1967	LtBR	SA r
1967	LoCl	Mon r
1967	LtFd	Hol 1, Bel 6, Fra r, GB 1, Ger r, Can r, Ita 3, US 1, Mex 1
1968	LtFd	SA 1

COLLINS, Peter

COUNTRY: GB
BORN: November 6, 1931
GP STARTS: 32
WC POINTS: 48
WC RECORD: 1956-3/25; 1957-8/8; 1958-5/15

Psn	No	Grand(s) Prix
1st:	3	1956 Bel, Fra; 1958 GB
2nd:	2	1956 Mon, Ita
3rd:	3	1957 Fra, Ger; 1958 Mon

Year	Team	Grand(s) Prix
1952	HWM	Swi r, Bel r, Fra 6, GB 22
1953	HWM	Hol 8, Bel r, Fra 13, GB r
1954	Va	GB r, Ita 7
1955	Mas	GB r, Ita r
1956	LaFe	Arg r, Mon 2, Bel 1, Fra 1, GB r, Ger r, Ita 2
1957	LaFe	Arg r, Mon r, Fra 3, GB r, Ger 3, Ita r
1958	Fe	Arg r, Mon 3, Hol r, Bel r, Fra 5, GB 1, Ger r

COLLOMB, Bernard

COUNTRY: France
BORN: October 7, 1930
GP STARTS: 4
WC POINTS: 0

Year	Team	Grand(s) Prix
1961	CoCl	Fra r, Ger r
1962	CoCl	Ger r
1963	LoCl	Ger uc

COMAS, Erik

COUNTRY: France
BORN: September 28, 1963
GP STARTS: 59
WC POINTS: 7
WC RECORD: 1992-11/4; 1993-20/1; 1994-23/2

Year	Team	Grand(s) Prix
1991	LiLm	Bra r, SM 10, Mon 10, Can 8, Fra 11, Ger r, Hun 10, Bel r, Ita 11, Por 11, Esp r, Jap r, Aus 18

1992	LiRe	SA 7, Mex 9, Bra r, Esp r, SM 9, Mon 10, Can 6, Fra 5, GB 8, Ger 6, Hun r, Ita r, Por r, Jap r, Aus r
1993	LaLm	SA r, Bra 10, Eur 9, SM r, Esp 9, Mon r, Can 8, Fra 16, GB r, Ger r, Hun r, Bel r, Ita 6, Por 11, Jap r, Aus 12
1994	LaFd	Bra 9, Pac 6, SM r, Mon 10, Esp r, Can r, Fra 11, GB r, Ger 6, Hun 8, Bel r, Ita 8, Por r, Eur r, Jap 9

COMOTTI, Franco

COUNTRY: Italy
BORN: July 24, 1906
GP STARTS: 2
WC POINTS: 0

Year	Team	Grand(s) Prix
1950	MasMi	Ita r
1952	Fe	Fra 12

CONNOR, George

COUNTRY: US
BORN: August 16, 1908
GP STARTS: 3
WC POINTS: 0

Year	Team	Grand(s) Prix
1950	Les	Indy 8
1951	Les	Indy r
1952	KK	Indy 8

CONSTANTINE, George

COUNTRY: US
BORN: February 22, 1918
GP STARTS: 1
WC POINTS: 0

Year	Team	Grand(s) Prix
1959	CoCl	US r

CORDTS, John

COUNTRY: Canada
BORN: July 23, 1935
GP STARTS: 1
WC POINTS: 0

Year	Team	Grand(s) Prix
1969	BrCl	Can r

COULTHARD, David

COUNTRY: GB
BORN: March 27, 1971
GP STARTS: 90
WC POINTS: 221
WC RECORD: 1994-8/14; 1995-3/49; 1996-7/18; 1997-3/36; 1998-3/56; 1999-4/48

Psn	No	Grand(s) Prix
1st:	6	1995 Por; 1997 Aus, Ita; 1998 SM; 1999 GB, Bel
2nd:	18	1994 Por; 1995 Bra, Ger, Hun, Pac; 1996 Mon; 1997 Aut, Eur; 1998 Aus, Bra, Esp, Aut, Ger, Hun; 1999 SM, Esp, Aut, Hun
3rd:	6	1995 Fra, GB, Eur; 1996 Eur; 1998 Lux, Jap
Pole:	8	1995 Arg, Ita, Por, Eur, Pac; 1998 Arg, SM, Can
Fast:	11	1994 Ger, Por; 1995 Bel, Por; 1997 Can; 1998 Fra, Aut, Ger; 1999 Fra, Ger, Hun

Year	Team	Grand(s) Prix
1994	WiRe	Esp r, Can 5, GB 5, Ger r, Hun r, Bel 4, Ita 6, Por 2
1995	WiRe	Bra 2, Arg r, SM 4, Esp r, Mon r, Can r, Fra 3, GB 3, Ger 2, Hun 2, Bel r, Ita r, Por 1, Eur 3, Pac 2, Jap r, Aus r
1996	McMe	Aus r, Bra r, Arg 7, Eur 3, SM r, Mon 2, Esp r, Can 4, Fra 6, GB 5, Ger 5, Hun r, Bel r, Ita r, Por 13, Jap 8
1997	McMe	Aus 1, Bra 10, Arg r, SM r, Mon r, Esp 6, Can 7, Fra 7, GB 4, Ger r, Hun r, Bel r, Ita 1, Aut 2, Lux r, Jap 10, Eur 2
1998	McMe	Aus 2, Bra 2, Arg 6, SM 1, Esp 2, Mon r, Can r, Fra 6, GB r, Aut 2, Ger 2, Hun 2, Bel 7, Ita r, Lux 3, Jap 3
1999	McMe	Aus r, Bra r, SM 2, Mon r, Esp 2, Can 7, Fra r, GB 1, Aut 2, Ger 5, Hun 2, Bel 1, Ita 5, Eur r, Mal r, Jap r

COURAGE, Piers

COUNTRY: GB
BORN: May 27, 1942
GP STARTS: 28
WC POINTS: 20
WC RECORD: 1968-19/4; 1969-8/16

Psn	No	Grand(s) Prix
2nd:	2	1969 Mon, US

Year	Team	Grand(s) Prix
1966	LtFd	Ger r
1967	LtBR	SA r
1967	BRM	Mon r
1968	BRM	Esp r, Mon r, Bel r, Hol r, Fra 6, GB 8, Ger 8, Ita 4, Can r, US r, Mex r
1969	BrFd	Esp r, Mon 2, Hol r, Fra r, GB 5, Ger r, Ita 5, Can r, US 2, Mex 10
1970	dTFd	SA r, Esp dns, Mon uc, Bel r, Hol r

CRAFT, Chris

COUNTRY: GB
BORN: November 17, 1939
GP STARTS: 1
WC POINTS: 0

Year	Team	Grand(s) Prix
1971	BrFd	Can dns, US r

CRAWFORD, Jim

COUNTRY: GB
BORN: February 13, 1948
GP STARTS: 2
WC POINTS: 0

Year	Team	Grand(s) Prix
1975	LtFd	GB r, Ita 13

CRAWFORD, Ray

COUNTRY: US
BORN: October 26, 1915
GP STARTS: 3
WC POINTS: 0

Year	Team	Grand(s) Prix
1955	KK	Indy r
1956	KK	Indy r
1959	Elder	Indy r

CREUS, Antonio

COUNTRY: Spain
BORN: 1922
GP STARTS: 1
WC POINTS: 0

Year	Team	Grand(s) Prix
1960	Mas	Arg r

CROCKETT, Larry

COUNTRY: US
BORN: October 23, 1926
GP STARTS: 1
WC POINTS: 0

Year	Team	Grand(s) Prix
1954	KK	Indy 9

CROOK, Tony

COUNTRY: GB
BORN: February 16, 1920
GP STARTS: 2
WC POINTS: 0

Year	Team	Grand(s) Prix
1952	FN	GB 21
1953	CoBr	GB r

CROSS, Art

COUNTRY: US
BORN: January 24, 1918
GP STARTS: 4
WC POINTS: 8
WC RECORD: 1952-16/2; 1953-10/6

Psn	No	Grand(s) Prix
2nd:	1	1953 Indy

Year	Team	Grand(s) Prix
1952	KK	Indy 5
1953	KK	Indy 2
1954	KK	Indy 11
1955	KK	Indy r

CROSSLEY, Geoff

COUNTRY: GB
BORN: May 11, 1921
GP STARTS: 2
WC POINTS: 0

Year	Team	Grand(s) Prix
1950	Alta	GB r, Bel 9

DA SILVA RAMOS, Nano

COUNTRY: Brazil
BORN: December 7, 1925
GP STARTS: 7
WC POINTS: 2
WC RECORD: 1956-19/2

Year	Team	Grand(s) Prix
1955	Gor	Hol 8, GB r, Ita r
1956	Gor	Mon 5, Fra 8, GB r, Ita r

DAIGH, Chuck

COUNTRY: US
BORN: November 29, 1923
GP STARTS: 3
WC POINTS: 0

Year	Team	Grand(s) Prix
1960	Sb	Hol dns, Bel r
1960	CoCl	GB r
1960	Sb	US 10

DALMAS, Yannick

COUNTRY: France
BORN: July 28, 1961
GP STARTS: 23
WC POINTS: 0

Year	Team	Grand(s) Prix
1987	LoFd	Mex 9, Jap 14, Aus 5
1988	LoFd	Bra r, SM 12, Mon 7, Mex 9, US 7, Fra 13, GB 13, Ger r, Hun 9, Bel r, Ita r, Por r, Esp 11
1989	LoLm	SM dns
1990	AGFd	Bra r, Fra 17, Ita uc, Por r, Esp 9
1994	LaFd	Ita r, Por 14

DALY, Derek

COUNTRY: Ireland
BORN: March 11, 1953
GP STARTS: 49
WC POINTS: 15
WC RECORD: 1978-19/1; 1980-10/6; 1982-13/8

Year	Team	Grand(s) Prix
1978	EnFd	GB r, Aut dq, Hol r, Ita 10, USE 8, Can 6
1979	EnFd	Arg 11, Bra 13, USW r
1979	TyFd	Aut 8, Can r, USE r
1980	TyFd	Arg 4, Bra 14, SA r, USW 8, Bel 9, Mon r, Fra 11, GB 4, Ger 10, Aut r, Hol r, Ita r, Can r, USE r
1981	MrFd	Esp 16, Fra r, GB 7, Ger r, Aut 11, Hol r, Ita r, Can 8
1982	ThFd	SA 14, Bra r, USW r
1982	WiFd	Bel r, Mon 6, US 5, Can 7, Hol 5, GB 5, Fra 7, Ger r, Aut r, Swi 9, Ita r, Caesar's Palace 6

DANNER, Christian

COUNTRY: Germany
BORN: April 4, 1958
GP STARTS: 36
WC POINTS: 4
WC RECORD: 1986-18/1; 1989-21/3

Year	Team	Grand(s) Prix
1985	Za	Bel r, Eur r
1986	OsAl	Bra r, Esp r, SM r, Bel r, Can r
1986	ArBM	US r, Fra 11, GB r, Ger r, Hun r, Aut 6, Ita 8, Por 11, Mex 9, Aus r
1987	Za	Bra 9, SM 7, Bel r, US 8, Fra r, GB r, Ger r, Hun r, Aut 9, Ita 9, Por r, Esp r, Mex r, Jap r, Aus 7
1989	RiFd	Bra 14, Mex 12, US 4, Can 8

DAPONTE, Jorge

COUNTRY: Argentina
BORN: June 5, 1923
GP STARTS: 2
WC POINTS: 0

Year	Team	Grand(s) Prix
1954	Mas	Arg r, Ita 11

DAVIES, Jimmy

COUNTRY: US
BORN: August 8, 1923
GP STARTS: 4
WC POINTS: 4
WC RECORD: 1955-12/4

Psn	No	Grand(s) Prix
3rd:	1	1955 Indy

Year	Team	Grand(s) Prix
1950	We	Indy 17
1951	Pawl	Indy r
1953	KK	Indy 10
1955	KK	Indy 3

DAVIS, Colin

COUNTRY: GB
BORN: July 29, 1933
GP STARTS: 2
WC POINTS: 0

Year	Team	Grand(s) Prix
1959	CoMa	Fra r, Ita 11

DAYWALT, Jimmy

COUNTRY: US
BORN: August 28, 1924
GP STARTS: 6
WC POINTS: 0

Year	Team	Grand(s) Prix
1953	KK	Indy 6
1954	KK	Indy r
1955	KK	Indy 9
1956	KK	Indy r
1957	KK	Indy r
1959	KK	Indy 14

de ADAMICH, Andrea

COUNTRY: Italy
BORN: October 3, 1941
GP STARTS: 30
WC POINTS: 6
WC RECORD: 1972-16/3; 1973-15/3

Year	Team	Grand(s) Prix
1968	Fe	SA r
1970	McAl	Fra uc
1970	McAR	GB dns
1970	McAl	Aut 12, Ita 8, Can r
1971	MaAl	SA 13, Esp r, Fra r, GB uc, Ger r, Ita r, US 11
1972	SuFd	Arg r, SA uc, Esp 4, Mon 7, Bel r, Fra 14, GB r, Ger 13, Aut 14, Ita r, Can r, US r
1973	SuFd	SA 8
1973	BrFd	Esp r, Bel 4, Mon 7, Fra r, GB r

de ANGELIS, Elio

COUNTRY: Italy
BORN: March 26, 1958
GP STARTS: 108
WC POINTS: 122
WC RECORD: 1979-15/3; 1980-7/13; 1981-8/14; 1982-9/23; 1983-17/2; 1984-3/34; 1985-5/33

Psn	No	Grand(s) Prix
1st:	2	1982 Aut; 1985 SM
2nd:	2	1980 Bra; 1984 Detroit
3rd:	5	1984 Bra, SM, Dallas; 1985 Bra, Mon
Pole:	3	1983 Eur; 1984 Bra; 1985 Can

Year	Team	Grand(s) Prix
1979	ShFd	Arg 7, Bra 12, SA r, USW 7, Esp r, Bel r, Fra 16, GB 12, Ger 11, Aut r, Hol r, Ita r, Can r, USE 4
1980	LtFd	Arg r, Bra 2, SA r, USW r, Bel 10, Mon 9, Fra r, GB r, Ger 16, Aut 6, Hol r, Ita 4, Can 10, USE 4
1981	LtFd	USW r, Bra 5, Arg 6, Bel 5, Mon r, Esp 5, Fra 6, GB r, Ger 7, Aut 7, Hol 5, Ita 4, Can 6, US r
1982	LtFd	SA 8, Bra r, USW 5, Bel 4, Mon 5, US r, Can 4, Hol r, GB 4, Fra r, Ger r, Aut 1, Swi 6, Ita r, Caesar's Palace r
1983	LtFd	Bra dq
1983	LtRe	USW r, Fra r, SM r, Mon r, Bel 9, US r, Can r, GB r, Ger r, Aut r, Hol r, Ita 5, Eur r, SA r
1984	LtRe	Bra 3, SA 7, Bel 5, SM 3, Fra 5, Mon 5, Can 4, Detroit 2, Dallas 3, GB 4, Ger r, Aut r, Hol 4, Ita r, Eur r, Por 5
1985	LtRe	Bra 3, Por 4, SM 1, Mon 3, Can 5, US 5, Fra 5, GB uc, Ger r, Aut 5, Hol 5, Ita 6, Bel r, Eur 5, SA r, Aus dq
1986	BrBM	Bra 8, Esp r, SM r, Mon r

de BEAUFORT, Carel Godin

COUNTRY: Holland
BORN: April 10, 1934
GP STARTS: 28
WC POINTS: 4
WC RECORD: 1962-16/2; 1963-14/2;

Year	Team	Grand(s) Prix
1957	Por	Ger 14
1958	Por	Hol 11, Ger r
1959	Por	Hol 10
1959	Mas	Fra 9
1960	CoCl	Hol 8 (F2)
1961	Por	Hol 14, Bel 11, Fra r, GB 16, Ger 14, Ita 7
1962	Por	Hol 6, Bel 7, Fra 6, GB 14, Ger 13, Ita 10, US r, SA 11
1963	Por	Bel 6, Hol 9, GB 10, Ger r, US 6, Mex 10, SA 10
1964	Por	Hol r
1964	BrBR	Ger dns

de CESARIS, Andrea

COUNTRY: Italy
BORN: May 31, 1959
GP STARTS: 208
WC POINTS: 58
WC RECORD: 1981-18/1; 1982-17/5; 1983-8/15; 1984-16/3; 1985-17/3; 1987-14/4; 1988-15/3; 1989-16/3; 1991-9/9; 1992-9/8; 1994-18/4

Psn	No	Grand(s) Prix
2nd:	2	1983 Ger, SA
3rd:	3	1982 Mon; 1987 Bel; 1989 Can
Pole:	1	1982 USW
Fast:	1	1983 Bel

Year	Team	Grand(s) Prix
1980	AR	Can r, USE r
1981	McFd	USW r, Bra r, Arg 11, SM 6, Bel r, Mon r, Esp r, Fra 11, GB r, Ger r, Aut 8, Ita 7, Can r, US 12
1982	AR	SA 13, Bra r, USW r, SM r, Bel r, Mon 3, US r, Can 6, Hol r, GB r, Fra r, Ger r, Aut r, Swi 10, Ita 10, Caesar's Palace 9
1983	AR	USW r, Fra 12, SM r, Mon r, Bel r, US r, Can r, GB 8, Ger 2, Aut r, Hol r, Ita r, Eur 4, SA 2
1984	LiRe	Bra r, SA 5, Bel r, SM 6, Fra 10, Mon r, Can r, Detroit r, Dallas r, GB 10, Ger 7, Aut r, Hol r, Ita r, Eur 7, Por 12
1985	LiRe	Bra r, Por r, SM r, Mon 4, Can 14, US 10, Fra r, GB r, Ger r, Aut r, Hol r
1986	MiMM	Bra r, Esp r, SM r, Bel r, Can r, US r, Fra r, GB r, Ger r, Hun r, Aut r, Ita r, Por r, Mex 8, Aus r
1987	BrBM	Bra r, SM r, Bel 3, Mon r, US r, Fra r, GB r, Ger r, Hun r, Aut r, Ita r, Por r, Esp r, Mex r, Jap r, Aus 8
1988	RiFd	Bra r, SM r, Mon r, Mex r, Can 9, US 4, Fra 10, GB r, Ger 13, Hun r, Bel r, Ita r, Por r, Esp r, Jap r, Aus 8
1989	DaFd	Bra 13, SM 10, Mon 13, Mex r, US 8, Can 3, GB r, Ger 7, Hun r, Bel 11, Ita r, Por r, Esp 7, Jap 10, Aus r
1990	DaFd	US r, Bra r, SM r, Mon r, Can r, Mex 13, Fra dq, GB r, Hun r, Bel r, Ita 10, Por r, Esp r, Jap r, Aus r
1991	JoFd	Bra r, SM r, Mon r, Can 4, Mex 4, Fra 6, GB r, Ger 5, Hun 7, Bel 13, Ita 7, Por 8, Esp r, Jap r, Aus 8
1992	TyIl	SA r, Mex 5, Bra r, Esp r, SM 14, Mon r, Can 5, Fra r, GB r, Ger r, Hun 8, Bel 8, Ita 6, Por 9, Jap 4, Aus r
1993	TyYa	SA r, Bra r, Eur r, SM r, Esp dq, Mon 10, Can r, Fra 15, GB uc, Ger r, Hun 11, Bel r, Ita 13, Por 12, Jap r, Aus 13
1994	JoFd	SM r, Mon 4
1994	SaMe	Can r, Fra 6, GB r, Ger r, Hun r, Bel r, Ita r, Por r, Eur r

de FILIPPIS, Maria Teresa

COUNTRY: Italy
BORN: November 11, 1926
GP STARTS: 3
WC POINTS: 0

Year	Team	Grand(s) Prix
1958	Mas	Bel 10, Por r, Ita r

de GRAFFENRIED, Toulo

COUNTRY: Switzerland
BORN: May 18, 1914
GP STARTS: 22
WC POINTS: 9
WC RECORD: 1951-15/2; 1953-8/7

Year	Team	Grand(s) Prix
1950	Mas	GB r, Mon r, Swi 6, Ita 6
1951	AR	Swi 5
1951	Mas	Fra r, Ger r
1951	AR	Ita r, Esp 6
1952	MasPl	Swi 6, Fra r, GB 19
1953	Mas	Hol 5, Bel 4, Fra 7, GB r, Ger 5, Swi r, Ita 14
1954	Mas	Arg 8, Esp r
1956	Mas	Ita 8

de KLERK, Peter

COUNTRY: South Africa
BORN: March 16, 1935
GP STARTS: 4
WC POINTS: 0

Year	Team	Grand(s) Prix
1963	AlSp	SA r
1965	AlSp	SA 10
1969	BrRe	SA uc
1970	BrFd	SA 11

de la ROSA, Pedro

COUNTRY: SPAIN
BORN: February 24, 1971
GP STARTS: 16
WC POINTS: 1
WC RECORD: 1999-17/1

Year	Team	Grand(s) Prix
1999	Ar	Aus 6, Bra r, SM r, Mon r, Esp 11, Can r, Fra 11, GB r, Aut r, Ger r, Hun 15, Bel r, Ita r, Eur r, Mal r, Jap 13

de PORTAGO, Alfonso

COUNTRY: Spain
BORN: October 11, 1928
GP STARTS: 4
WC POINTS: 4
WC RECORD: 1956-15/3; 1957-21/1

Psn	No	Grand(s) Prix
2nd:	1	1956 GB

Year	Team	Grand(s) Prix
1956	LaFe	Fra r, GB 2, Ger r, Ita r
1957	LaFe	Arg 5 (shared)

de TERRA, Max

COUNTRY: Switzerland
BORN: October 6, 1918
GP STARTS: 2
WC POINTS: 0

Year	Team	Grand(s) Prix
1952	SiGo	Swi r
1953	Fe	Swi uc

de TOMASO, Alessandro

COUNTRY: Argentina
BORN: July 10, 1928
GP STARTS: 2
WC POINTS: 0

Year	Team	Grand(s) Prix
1957	Fe	Arg 9
1959	CoOs	US r

de TORNACO, Charles

COUNTRY: Belgium
BORN: June 7, 1927
GP STARTS: 2
WC POINTS: 0

Year	Team	Grand(s) Prix
1952	Fe	Bel 7, Hol r

DELETRAZ, Jean-Denis

COUNTRY: Switzerland
BORN: October 1, 1963
GP STARTS: 3
WC POINTS: 0

Year	Team	Grand(s) Prix
1994	LaFd	Aus r
1995	PaFd	Por r, Eur 15

DEPAILLER, Patrick

COUNTRY: France
BORN: August 9, 1944
GP STARTS: 95
WC POINTS: 139 (141)
WC RECORD: 1974-9/14; 1975-9/12; 1976-4/39; 1977-8/20; 1978-5/34; 1979-6/20

Psn	No	Grand(s) Prix
1st:	2	1978 Mon; 1979 Esp
2nd:	10	1974 Swe; 1976 Bra, Swe, Fra, Can, Jap; 1977 Can; 1978 SA, Aut; 1979 Bra
3rd:	7	1975 SA; 1976 USW, Mon; 1977 SA, Jap; 1978 Arg, USW
Pole:	1	1974 Swe
Fast:	4	1974 Swe; 1975 Mon; 1976 Can; 1979 Mon

Year	Team	Grand(s) Prix
1972	TyFd	Fra uc, US 7
1974	TyFd	Arg 6, Bra 8, SA 4, Esp 8, Bel r, Mon 9, Swe 2, Hol 6, Fra 8, GB r, Ger r, Aut r, Ita 11, Can 5, US 6
1975	TyFd	Arg 5, Bra r, SA 3, Esp r, Mon 5, Bel 4, Swe 12, Hol 9, Fra 6, GB 9, Ger 9, Aut 11, Ita 7, US r
1976	TyFd	Bra 2, SA 9, USW 3, Esp r, Bel r, Mon 3, Swe 2, Fra 2, GB r, Ger r, Aut r, Hol 7, Ita 6, Can 2, USE r, Jap 2
1977	TyFd	Arg r, Bra r, SA 3, USW 4, Esp r, Mon r, Bel 8, Swe 4, Fra r, GB r, Ger r, Aut 13, Hol r, Ita r, USE 14, Can 2, Jap 3
1978	TyFd	Arg 3, Bra r, SA 2, USW 3, Mon 1, Bel r, Esp r, Swe r, Fra r, GB 4, Ger r, Aut 2, Hol r, Ita 11, USE r, Can 5

1979	LiFd	Arg 4, Bra 2, SA r, USW 5, Esp 1, Bel r, Mon 5
1980	AR	Arg r, Bra r, SA uc, USW r, Bel r, Mon r, Fra r, GB r

DINIZ, Pedro

COUNTRY: Brazil
BORN: May 22, 1970
GP STARTS: 82
WC POINTS: 10
WC RECORD: 1996-15/2; 1997-16/2; 1998-13/3; 1999-13/3

Year	Team	Grand(s) Prix
1995	FiFd	Bra 10, Arg uc, SM uc, Esp r, Mon 10, Can r, Fra r, GB r, Ger r, Hun r, Bel 13, Ita 9, Por 16, Eur 13, Pac 17, Jap r, Aus 7
1996	LiMH	Aus 10, Bra 8, Arg r, Eur 10, SM 7, Mon r, Esp 6, Can r, Fra r, GB r, Ger r, Hun r, Bel r, Ita 6, Por r, Jap r
1997	ArYa	Aus 10, Bra r, Arg r, SM r, Mon r, Esp r, Can 8, Fra r, GB r, Ger r, Hun r, Bel 7, Ita r, Aut 13, Lux 5, Jap 12, Eur r
1998	Ar	Aus r, Bra r, Arg r, SM r, Esp r, Mon 6, Can 9, Fra 14, GB r, Aut r, Ger r, Hun 11, Bel 5, Ita r, Lux r, Jap r
1999	SaPe	Aus r, Bra r, SM r, Mon r, Esp r, Can 6, Fra r, GB 6, Aut 6, Ger r, Hun r, Bel r, Ita r, Eur r, Mal r, Jap 11

DINSMORE, Duke

COUNTRY: US
BORN: April 10, 1913
GP STARTS: 3
WC POINTS: 0

Year	Team	Grand(s) Prix
1950	KK	Indy r
1951	Sch	Indy r
1956	KK	Indy 17

DOLHEM, Jose

COUNTRY: France
BORN: April 26, 1944
GP STARTS: 1
WC POINTS: 0

Year	Team	Grand(s) Prix
1974	SuFd	US r

DONNELLY, Martin

COUNTRY: GB
BORN: March 26, 1964
GP STARTS: 14
WC POINTS: 0

Year	Team	Grand(s) Prix
1989	ArFd	Fra 12
1990	LtLm	US r, Bra r, SM 8, Mon r, Can r, Mex 8, Fra 12, GB r, Ger r, Hun 7
1990	LoLm	Bel 12
1990	LtLm	Ita r, Por r, Esp dns

DONOHUE, Mark

COUNTRY: US
BORN: March 18, 1937
GP STARTS: 14
WC POINTS: 8
WC RECORD: 1971-16/4; 1975-15/4

Psn	No	Grand(s) Prix
3rd:	1	1971 Can

Year	Team	Grand(s) Prix
1971	McFd	Can 3
1974	PkFd	Can 12, US r
1975	PkFd	Arg 7, Bra r, SA 8, Esp r, Mon r, Bel 11, Swe 5, Hol 8, Fra r
1975	MrFd	GB 5, Ger r, Aut dns

D'OREY, Fritz

COUNTRY: Brazil
BORN: March 25, 1938
GP STARTS: 3
WC POINTS: 0

Year	Team	Grand(s) Prix
1959	Mas	Fra 10, GB r
1959	TMMas	US r

DOWNING, Ken

COUNTRY: GB
BORN: December 5, 1917
GP STARTS: 2
WC POINTS: 0

Year	Team	Grand(s) Prix
1952	Con	GB 9, Hol r

DRAKE, Bob

COUNTRY: US
BORN: December 14, 1919
GP STARTS: 1
WC POINTS: 0

Year	Team	Grand(s) Prix
1960	Mas	US 13

DRIVER, Paddy

COUNTRY: South Africa
BORN: May 13, 1934
GP STARTS: 1
WC POINTS: 0

Year	Team	Grand(s) Prix
1974	LtFd	SA r

DROGO, Piero

COUNTRY: Venezuela
BORN: August 8, 1926
GP STARTS: 1
WC POINTS: 0

Year	Team	Grand(s) Prix
1960	CoCl	Ita 8

DUMFRIES, Johnny

COUNTRY: GB
BORN: April 26, 1958
GP STARTS: 15
WC POINTS: 3
WC RECORD: 1986-13/3

Year	Team	Grand(s) Prix
1986	LtRe	Bra 9, Esp r, SM r, Bel r, Can r, US 7, Fra r, GB 7, Ger r, Hun 5, Aut r, Ita r, Por 9, Mex r, Aus 6

DUNCAN , Len

COUNTRY: US
BORN: July 25, 1911
GP STARTS: 1
WC POINTS: 0

Year	Team	Grand(s) Prix
1954	Sch	Indy r

EATON, George

COUNTRY: Canada
BORN: November 12, 1945
GP STARTS: 11
WC POINTS: 0

Year	Team	Grand(s) Prix
1969	BRM	US r, Mex r
1970	BRM	SA r, Hol r, Fra 12, GB r, Aut 11, Ita r, Can 10, US r
1971	BRM	Can 15

EDMUNDS, Don

COUNTRY: US
BORN: September 23, 1930
GP STARTS: 1
WC POINTS: 0

Year	Team	Grand(s) Prix
1957	KK	Indy r

EDWARDS, Guy

COUNTRY: GB
BORN: December 30, 1942
GP STARTS: 11
WC POINTS: 0

Year	Team	Grand(s) Prix
1974	LoFd	Arg 11, Bra r, Bel 12, Mon 8, Swe 7, Hol r, Fra 15
1976	HeFd	Fra 17, GB r, Ger 15, Can 20

ELFORD, Vic

COUNTRY: GB
BORN: June 10, 1935
GP STARTS: 13
WC POINTS: 8
WC RECORD: 1968-17/5; 1969-13/3

Year	Team	Grand(s) Prix
1968	CoBR	Fra 4, GB r, Ger r, Ita r, Can 5, US r, Mex 8
1969	CoMa	Mon 7
1969	McFd	Hol 10, Fra 5, GB 6, Ger r
1971	BRM	Ger 11

ELISIAN, Ed

COUNTRY: US
BORN: December 9, 1926
GP STARTS: 5
WC POINTS: 0

Year	Team	Grand(s) Prix
1954	Ste	Indy 18
1955	KK	Indy r
1956	KK	Indy r
1957	KK	Indy r
1958	Wa	Indy r

EMERY, Paul

COUNTRY: GB
BORN: November 12, 1916
GP STARTS: 1
WC POINTS: 0

Year	Team	Grand(s) Prix
1956	Em	GB r

ENGLAND, Paul

COUNTRY: Australia
BORN: March 28, 1929
GP STARTS: 1
WC POINTS: 0

Year	Team	Grand(s) Prix
1957	CoCl	Ger r

ERTL, Harald

COUNTRY: Austria
BORN: August 31, 1948
GP STARTS: 19
WC POINTS: 0

Year	Team	Grand(s) Prix
1975	HeFd	Ger 8, Aut r, Ita 9
1976	HeFd	SA 15, Bel r, Swe r, Fra dq, GB 7, Ger r, Aut 8, Hol r, Ita 16, Can dns, USE 13, Jap 8
1977	HeFd	Esp r, Bel 9, Swe 16
1978	EnFd	Ger 11, Aut r

ESTEFANO, Nasif

COUNTRY: Argentina
BORN: November 18, 1932
GP STARTS: 1
WC POINTS: 0

Year	Team	Grand(s) Prix
1960	Mas	Arg 14

ETANCELIN, Phillippe

COUNTRY: France
BORN: December 28, 1896
GP STARTS: 12
WC POINTS: 3
WC RECORD: 1950-13/3

Year	Team	Grand(s) Prix
1950	Ta	GB 8, Mon r, Swi r, Bel r, Fra 5, Ita 5
1951	Ta	Swi 10, Bel r, Fra r, Ger r, Esp 8
1952	Mas	Fra 8

EVANS, Bob

COUNTRY: GB
BORN: June 11, 1947
GP STARTS: 10
WC POINTS: 0

Year	Team	Grand(s) Prix
1975	BRM	SA 15, Esp r, Bel 9, Swe 13, Hol r, Fra 17, Aut r, Ita r
1976	LtFd	SA 10
1976	BrFd	GB r

FABI, Corrado

COUNTRY: Italy
BORN: April 12, 1961
GP STARTS: 12
WC POINTS: 0

Year	Team	Grand(s) Prix
1983	OsFd	Bra r, Fra r, SM r, Bel r, Can r
1983	OsAl	Aut 10, Hol 11, Ita r, SA r
1984	BrBM	Mon r, Can r, Dallas 7

FABI, Teo

COUNTRY: Italy
BORN: March 9, 1955
GP STARTS: 64
WC POINTS: 23
WC RECORD: 1984-12/9; 1986-15/2; 1987-9/12

Psn	No	Grand(s) Prix
3rd:	2	1984 Detroit; 1987 Aut
Pole:	3	1985 Ger; 1986 Aut, Ita
Fast:	2	1986 Ita; 1987 SM

Year	Team	Grand(s) Prix
1982	ToHt	SM uc, Bel r, GB r, Fra r, Aut r, Swi r, Ita r
1984	BrBM	Bra r, SA r, Bel r, SM r, Fra 9, Detroit 3, GB r, Ger r, Aut 4, Hol 5, Ita r, Eur r
1985	ToHt	Mon r, Can r, US r, Fra 14, GB r, Ger r, Aut r, Hol r, Ita 12, Bel r, Eur r, SA r, Aus r
1986	BeBM	Bra 10, Esp 5, SM r, Mon r, Bel 7, Can r, US r, Fra r, GB r, Ger r, Hun r, Aut r, Ita r, Por 8, Mex r, Aus 10
1987	BeFd	Bra r, SM r, Bel r, Mon 8, US r, Fra 5, GB 6, Ger r, Hun r, Aut 3, Ita 7, Por 4, Esp r, Mex 5, Jap r, Aus r

FABRE, Pascal

COUNTRY: France
BORN: June 9, 1960
GP STARTS: 11
WC POINTS: 0

Year	Team	Grand(s) Prix
1987	AGFd	Bra 12, SM 13, Bel 10, Mon 13, US 12, Fra 9, GB 9, Ger r, Hun 13, Aut uc, Esp r

FAGIOLI, Luigi

COUNTRY: Italy
BORN: June 9, 1898
GP STARTS: 7
WC POINTS: 28 (32)
WC RECORD: 1950-3/24; 1951-11/4

Psn	No	Grand(s) Prix
1st:	1	1951 Fra
2nd:	4	1950 GB, Swi, Bel, Fra
3rd:	1	1950 Ita

Year	Team	Grand(s) Prix
1950	AR	GB 2, Mon r, Swi 2, Bel 2, Fra 2, Ita 3
1951	AR	Fra 1

FAIRMAN, Jack

COUNTRY: GB
BORN: March 15, 1913
GP STARTS: 12
WC POINTS: 5
WC RECORD: 1956-10/5

Year	Team	Grand(s) Prix
1953	HWM	GB r, Ita uc
1956	Con	GB 4, Ita 6
1957	BRM	GB r
1958	Con	GB r
1958	CoCl	Moroccan 8
1959	CoCl	GB r
1959	CoMa	Ita r
1960	CoCl	GB r
1961	FeCl	GB dq
1961	CoCl	Ita r

FANGIO, Juan Manuel

COUNTRY: Argentina
BORN: June 24, 1911
GP STARTS: 51
WC POINTS: 244.5 (277.14)
WC RECORD: 1950-2/27; 1951-1/31; 1953-2/27.5; 1954-1/42; 1955-1/40; 1956-1/30; 1957-1/40; 1958-14/7
WORLD CHAMPION: 1951, 1954, 1955, 1956, 1957

Psn	No	Grand(s) Prix
1st:	22	1950 Mon, Bel, Fra; 1951 Swi, Esp; 1953 Ita; 1954 Arg, Bel, Fra, Ger, Swi, Ita; 1955 Arg, Bel, Hol, Ita; 1956 GB, Ger; 1957 Arg, Mon, Fra, Ger
2nd:	8	1951 GB, Ger; 1953 Fra, GB, Ger; 1955 GB; 1957 Pescara, Ita
3rd:	1	1954 Esp
Pole:	29	1950 Mon, Swi, Fra, Ita; 1951 Swi, Bel, Fra, Ita; 1951 Bel, Swi; 1954 Bel, Fra, GB, Ger, Ita; 1955 Mon, Hol, Ita; 1955 Arg, Mon, Bel, Fra, Ger, Ita; 1957 Mon, Fra, Ger, Pescara; 1958 Arg
Fast:	23	1950 Mon, Fra, Ita; 1951 Swi, Bel, Fra, Ger, Esp; 1953 Fra, Ita; 1954 Bel, GB, Swi; 1955 Arg, Mon, Bel; 1955 Arg, Mon, Fra, Ger; 1957 Mon, Ger; 1958 Arg

Year	Team	Grand(s) Prix
1950	AR	GB 12, Mon 1, Swi r, Bel 1, Fra 1, Ita r
1951	AR	Swi 1, Bel 9, Fra 11, GB 2, Ger 2, Ita r, Esp 1
1953	Mas	Arg r, Hol r, Bel r, Fra 2, GB 2, Ger 2, Swi 4, Ita 1
1954	Mas	Arg 1, Bel 1
1954	Me	Fra 1, GB 4, Ger 1, Swi 1, Ita 1, Esp 3
1955	Me	Arg 1, Mon r, Bel 1, Hol 1, GB 2, Ita 1
1956	LaFe	Arg r, Mon 4, Bel r, Fra 4, GB 1, Ger 1, Ita 9
1957	Mas	Arg 1, Mon 1, Fra 1, GB r, Ger 1, Pescara 2, Ita 2
1958	Mas	Arg 4, Fra 4

FARINA, Nino

COUNTRY: Italy
BORN: October 30, 1906
GP STARTS: 33
WC POINTS: 115.33 (127.33)
WC RECORD: 1950-1/30; 1951-4/19; 1952-2/24; 1953-3/26; 1954-8/6; 1955-5/10.33
WORLD CHAMPION: 1950

Psn	No	Grand(s) Prix
1st:	5	1950 GB, Swi, Ita; 1951 Bel; 1953 Ger
2nd:	8	1952 Bel , Fra, Ger, Hol; 1953 Hol, Swi, Ita; 1954 Arg
3rd:	5	1951 Swi, Esp; 1953 GB; 1955 Arg, Bel
Pole:	5	1950 GB, Bel; 1952 Swi, GB; 1954 Arg
Fast:	5	1950 GB, Swi, Bel; 1951 GB, Ita

Year	Team	Grand(s) Prix
1950	AR	GB 1, Mon r, Swi 1, Bel 4, Fra 7, Ita 1
1951	AR	Swi 3, Bel 1, Fra 5, GB 14, Ger r, Ita r, Esp 3
1952	Fe	Swi r, Bel 2, Fra 2, GB 6, Ger 2, Hol 2, Ita 4
1953	Fe	Arg r, Hol 2, Bel r, Fra 5, GB 3, Ger 1, Swi 2, Ita 2
1954	Fe	Arg 2, Bel r
1955	Fe	Arg 3, Mon 4, Bel 3
1955	La	Ita dns

FAULKNER, Walt

COUNTRY: US
BORN: February 16, 1920
GP STARTS: 4
WC POINTS: 1
WC RECORD: 1955-22/1

Psn	No	Grand(s) Prix
Pole:	1	1950 Indy

Year	Team	Grand(s) Prix
1950	KK	Indy 7
1951	Ku	Indy r
1953	KK	Indy 17
1955	KK	Indy 5

FISCHER, Rudi

COUNTRY: Switzerland
BORN: April 19, 1912
GP STARTS: 7
WC POINTS: 10
WC RECORD: 1952-4/10

Psn	No	Grand(s) Prix
2nd:	1	1952 Swi
3rd:	1	1952 Ger

Year	Team	Grand(s) Prix
1951	Fe	Swi 11, Ger 6
1952	Fe	Swi 2, Fra 11, GB 13, Ger 3
1952	AFBM	Ger dns
1952	Fe	Ita r

FISHER, Mike

COUNTRY: US
BORN: March 13, 1943
GP STARTS: 1
WC POINTS: 0

Year	Team	Grand(s) Prix
1967	LtBR	Can 11

FISICHELLA, Giancario

COUNTRY: Italy
BORN: January 14, 1973
GP STARTS: 57
WC POINTS: 49
WC RECORD: 1997-8/20; 1998-9/16; 1999-9/13

Psn	No	Grand(s) Prix
2nd:	4	1997 Bel; 1998 Mon, Can; 1999 Can
3rd:	1	1997 Can
Pole:	1	1998 Aut
Fast:	1	1997 Esp

Year	Team	Grand(s) Prix
1996	MiFd	Aus r, Eur 13, SM r, Mon r, Esp r, Can 8, Fra r, GB 11
1997	JoPe	Aus r, Bra 8, Arg r, SM 4, Mon 6, Esp 9, Can 3, Fra 9, GB 7, Ger 11, Hun r, Bel 2, Ita 4, Aut 4, Lux r, Jap 7, Eur 11
1998	BePl	Aus r, Bra 6, Arg 7, SM r, Esp r, Mon 2, Can 2, Fra 9, GB 5, Aut r, Ger 7, Hun 8, Bel r, Ita 8, Lux 6, Jap 8
1999	BePl	Aus 4, Bra r, SM 5, Mon 5, Esp 9, Can 2, Fra r, GB 7, Aut 12, Ger r, Hun r, Bel 11, Ita r, Eur r, Mal 11, Jap 14

FITCH, John

COUNTRY: US
BORN: August 4, 1917
GP STARTS: 2
WC POINTS: 0

Year	Team	Grand(s) Prix
1953	HWM	Ita r
1955	Mas	Ita 9

FITTIPALDI, Christian

COUNTRY: Brazil
BORN: January 18, 1971
GP STARTS: 40
WC POINTS: 12
WC RECORD: 1992-17/1; 1993-13/5; 1994-14/6

Year	Team	Grand(s) Prix
1992	MiLm	SA r, Mex r, Bra r, Esp 11, SM r, Mon 8, Can 13, Por 12, Jap 6, Aus 9
1993	MiFd	SA 4, Bra r, Eur 7, SM r, Esp 8, Mon 5, Can 9, Fra 8, GB 12, Ger 11, Hun r, Bel r, Ita 8, Por 9
1994	FtFd	Bra r, Pac 4, SM 13, Mon r, Esp r, Can dq, Fra 8, GB 9, Ger 4, Hun 14, Bel r, Ita r, Por 8, Eur 17, Jap 8, Aus 8

FITTIPALDI, Emerson

COUNTRY: Brazil
BORN: December 12, 1946
GP STARTS: 144
WC POINTS: 281
WC RECORD: 1970-10/12; 1971-6/16; 1972-1/61; 1973-2/55; 1974-1/55; 1975-2/45; 1976-16/3; 1977-12/11; 1978-9/17; 1979-21/1; 1980-15/5
WORLD CHAMPION: 1972, 1974

Psn	No	Grand(s) Prix
1st:	14	1970 US; 1972 Esp, Bel, GB, Aut, Ita; 1973 Arg, Bra, Esp; 1974 Bra, Bel, Can; 1975 Arg, GB
2nd:	13	1971 Aut; 1972 SA, Fra; 1973 Mon, Ita, Can; 1974 GB, Ita; 1975 Bra, Mon, Ita, US; 1978 Bra
3rd:	8	1971 Fra, GB; 1972 Mon; 1973 SA, Bel; 1974 Esp, Hol; 1980 USW
Pole:	6	1972 Mon, Bel, Aut; 1973 Aut; 1974 Bra, Can
Fast:	6	1973 Arg, Bra, SA, Mon, Can; 1975 US

Year	Team	Grand(s) Prix
1970	LtFd	GB 8, Ger 4, Aut 15, Ita dns, US 1, Mex r
1971	LtFd	SA r, Esp r, Mon 5, Fra 3, GB 3, Ger r, Aut 2
1971	LtTu	Ita 8
1971	LtFd	Can 7, US uc
1972	LtFd	Arg r, SA 2, Esp 1, Mon 3, Bel 1, Fra 2, GB 1, Ger r, Aut 1, Ita 1, Can 11, US r
1973	LtFd	Arg 1, Bra 1, SA 3, Esp 1, Bel 3, Mon 2, Swe 12, Fra r, GB r, Hol r, Ger 6, Aut 11, Ita 2, Can 2, US 6
1974	McFd	Arg 10, Bra 1, SA 7, Esp 3, Bel 1, Mon 5, Swe 4, Hol 3, Fra r, GB 2, Ger r, Aut r, Ita 2, Can 1, US 4
1975	McFd	Arg 1, Bra 2, SA uc, Esp dns, Mon 2, Bel 7, Swe 8, Hol r, Fra 4, GB 1, Ger r, Aut 9, Ita 2, US 2
1976	FiFd	Bra 13, SA 17, USW 6, Esp r, Mon 6, Swe r, Fra r, GB 6, Ger 13, Aut r, Hol r, Ita 15, Can r, USE 9, Jap r
1977	FiFd	Arg 4, Bra 4, SA 10, USW 5, Esp 14, Mon r, Bel r, Swe 18, Fra 11, GB r, Aut 11, Hol 4, USE 13, Can r
1978	FiFd	Arg 9, Bra 2, SA r, USW 8, Mon 9, Bel r, Esp r, Swe 6, Fra r, GB r, Ger 4, Aut 4, Hol 5, Ita 8, USE 5, Can r
1979	FiFd	Arg 6, Bra 11, SA 13, USW r, Esp 11, Bel 9, Mon r, Fra r, GB r, Ger r, Aut r, Hol r, Ita 8, Can 8, USE 7
1980	FiFd	Arg uc, Bra 15, SA 8, USW 3, Bel r, Mon 6, Fra 13, GB 12, Ger r, Aut 11, Hol r, Ita r, Can r, USE r

FITTIPALDI, Wilson

COUNTRY: Brazil
BORN: December 25, 1943
GP STARTS: 35
WC POINTS: 3
WC RECORD: 1973-15/3

Year	Team	Grand(s) Prix
1972	BrFd	Esp 7, Mon 9, Bel r, Fra 8, GB 12, Ger 7, Aut r, Ita r, Can r, US r
1973	BrFd	Arg 6, Bra r, SA r, Esp 10, Bel r, Mon 11, Swe r, Fra 16, GB r, Hol r, Ger 5, Aut r, Ita r, Can 11, US uc
1975	FiFd	Arg r, Bra 13, Esp r, Bel 12, Swe 17, Hol 11, Fra r, GB 19, Ger r, Aut dns, US 10

FITZAU, Theo

COUNTRY: Germany
BORN: February 10, 1923
GP STARTS: 1
WC POINTS: 0

Year	Team	Grand(s) Prix
1953	AFM	Ger r

FLAHERTY, Pat

COUNTRY: US
BORN: January 6, 1926
GP STARTS: 5
WC POINTS: 8
WC RECORD: 1956-5/8

Psn	No	Grand(s) Prix
1st:	1	1956 Indy
Pole:	1	1956 Indy

Year	Team	Grand(s) Prix
1950	KK	Indy 10
1953	KK	Indy r
1955	KK	Indy 10
1956	Wa	Indy 1
1959	Wa	Indy r

FLINTERMAN, Jan

COUNTRY: Holland
BORN: October 2, 1919
GP STARTS: 1
WC POINTS: 0

Year	Team	Grand(s) Prix
1952	Mas	Hol r

FLOCKHART, Ron

COUNTRY: GB
BORN: June 16, 1923
GP STARTS: 12
WC POINTS: 5
WC RECORD: 1956-11/4; 1960-24/1

Psn	No	Grand(s) Prix
3rd:	1	1956 Ita

Year	Team	Grand(s) Prix
1956	BRM	GB r
1956	Con	Ita 3
1957	BRM	Mon r, Fra r
1958	BRM	Moroccan r
1959	BRM	Mon r, Fra 6, GB r, Por 7, Ita 13
1960	LoCl	Fra 6
1960	CoCl	US r

FOHR, Myron

COUNTRY: US
BORN: June 17, 1912
GP STARTS: 1
WC POINTS: 0

Year	Team	Grand(s) Prix
1950	Marchese	Indy 11

FOITEK, Gregor

COUNTRY: Switzerland
BORN: March 27, 1965
GP STARTS: 7
WC POINTS: 0

Year	Team	Grand(s) Prix
1990	BrJu	US r, Bra r
1990	OnFd	SM r, Mon 7, Can r, Mex 15, Ger r

FOLLMER, George

COUNTRY: US
BORN: January 27, 1934
GP STARTS: 12
WC POINTS: 5
WC RECORD: 1973-13/5

Psn	No	Grand(s) Prix
3rd:	1	1973 Esp

Year	Team	Grand(s) Prix
1973	ShFd	SA 6, Esp 3, Bel r, Mon dns, Swe 14, Fra r, GB r, Hol 10, Ger r, Aut r, Ita 10, Can 17, US 14

FONDER, George

COUNTRY: US
BORN: June 22, 1917
GP STARTS: 1
WC POINTS: 0

Year	Team	Grand(s) Prix
1952	Sherman	Indy 15

FONTANA, Norberto

COUNTRY: Argentina
BORN: January 20, 1975
GP STARTS: 4
WC POINTS: 0

Year	Team	Grand(s) Prix
1997	SaPe	Fra r, GB 9, Ger 9, Eur 14

FORBERG, Carl

COUNTRY: US
BORN: March 4, 1911
GP STARTS: 1
WC POINTS: 0

Year	Team	Grand(s) Prix
1951	KK	Indy 7

FORCE, Gene

COUNTRY: US
BORN: June 15, 1916
GP STARTS: 2
WC POINTS: 0

Year	Team	Grand(s) Prix
1951	KK	Indy r
1960	KK	Indy r

FORINI, Franco

COUNTRY: Switzerland
BORN: September 22, 1958
GP STARTS: 2
WC POINTS: 0

Year	Team	Grand(s) Prix
1987	OsAl	Ita r, Por r

FOTHERINGHAM-PARKER, Philip

COUNTRY: GB
BORN: September 22, 1907
GP STARTS: 1
WC POINTS: 0

Year	Team	Grand(s) Prix
1951	Mas	GB r

FOYT, AJ

COUNTRY: US
BORN: January 16, 1935
GP STARTS: 3
WC POINTS: 0

Year	Team	Grand(s) Prix
1958	Ku	Indy r
1959	Ku	Indy 10
1960	KK	Indy r

FREELAND, Don

COUNTRY: US
BORN: March 25, 1925
GP STARTS: 8
WC POINTS: 4
WC RECORD: 1956-11/4

Psn	No	Grand(s) Prix
3rd:	1	1956 Indy

Year	Team	Grand(s) Prix
1953	Wa	Indy r
1954	Ph	Indy 7
1955	Ph	Indy r
1956	Ph	Indy 3
1957	KK	Indy 17
1958	Ph	Indy 7
1959	KK	Indy r
1960	KK	Indy r

FRENTZEN, Heinz-Harald

COUNTRY: Germany
BORN: May 18, 1967
GP STARTS: 97
WC POINTS: 142
WC RECORD: 1994-13/7; 1995-9/15; 1996-12/7; 1997-2/42; 1998-7/17; 1999-3/54

Psn	No	Grand(s) Prix
1st:	3	1997 SM; 1999 Fra, Ita
2nd:	3	1997 Fra, Jap; 1999 Aus
3rd:	9	1995 Ita; 1997 Bel, Ita, Aut, Lux; 1998 Aus; 1999 Bra, Ger, Bel
Pole:	2	1997 Mon; 1999 Eur
Fast:	6	1997 Aus, SM, Hun, Lux, Jap, Eur

Year	Team	Grand(s) Prix
1994	SaMe	Bra r, Pac 5, SM 7, Mon dns, Esp r, Can r, Fra 4, GB 7, Ger r, Hun r, Bel r, Ita r, Por r, Eur 6, Jap 6, Aus 7
1995	SaFd	Bra r, Arg 5, SM 6, Esp 8, Mon 6, Can r, Fra 10, GB 6, Ger r, Hun 5, Bel 4, Ita 3, Por 6, Eur r, Pac 7, Jap 8, Aus r
1996	SaFd	Aus 8, Bra r, Arg r, Eur r, SM r, Mon 4, Esp 4, Can r, Fra r, GB 8, Ger 8, Hun r, Bel r, Ita r, Por 7, Jap 6
1997	WiRe	Aus 8, Bra 9, Arg r, SM 1, Mon r, Esp 8, Can 4, Fra 2, GB r, Ger r, Hun r, Bel 3, Ita 3, Aut 3, Lux 3, Jap 2, Eur 6

Year	Team	Grand(s) Prix
1998	WiMh	Aus 3, Bra 5, Arg 9, SM 5, Esp 8, Mon r, Can r, Fra 15, GB r, Aut r, Ger 9, Hun 5, Bel 4, Ita 7, Lux 5, Jap 5
1999	JoMH	Aus 2, Bra 3, SM r, Mon 4, Esp r, Can 11, Fra 1, GB 4, Aut 4, Ger 3, Hun 4, Bel 3, Ita 1, Eur r, Mal 6, Jap 4

FRERE, Paul

COUNTRY: Belgium
BORN: January 30, 1917
GP STARTS: 10
WC POINTS: 11
WC RECORD: 1952-16/2; 1955-13/3; 1956-7/6

Psn	No	Grand(s) Prix
2nd:	1	1956 Bel

Year	Team	Grand(s) Prix
1952	HWM	Bel 5, Ger r
1952	SiGo	Hol r
1953	HWM	Bel 10, Swi r
1954	Gor	Bel r, Fra r, Ger r
1955	Fe	Bel 4
1956	LaFe	Bel 2

FRY, Joe

COUNTRY: GB
BORN: October 26, 1915
GP STARTS: 1
WC POINTS: 0

Year	Team	Grand(s) Prix
1950	Mas	GB 10

GABBIANI, Bebe

COUNTRY: Italy
BORN: January 2, 1957
GP STARTS: 3
WC POINTS: 0

Year	Team	Grand(s) Prix
1981	OsFd	USW r, SM r, Bel r

GACHOT, Bertrand

COUNTRY: Belgium
BORN: December 23, 1962
GP STARTS: 47
WC POINTS: 5
WC RECORD: 1991-12/4; 1992-17/1

Psn	No	Grand(s) Prix
Fast:	1	1991 Hun

Year	Team	Grand(s) Prix
1989	OnFd	Fra 13, GB 12, Hun r, Bel r, Ita r
1991	JoFd	US 10, Bra 13, SM r, Mon 8, Can 5, Mex r, Fra r, GB 6, Ger 6, Hun 9
1992	LaLm	SA r, Mex 11, Bra r, Esp r, SM r, Mon 6, Can dq, Fra r, GB r, Ger 14, Hun r, Bel 18, Ita r, Por r, Jap r, Aus r
1994	Pall	Bra r, SM r, Mon r, Esp r, Can r
1995	PaFd	Bra r, Arg r, SM r, Esp r, Mon r, Can r, Fra r, GB 12, Pac r, Jap r, Aus 8

GAILLARD, Patrick

COUNTRY: France
BORN: February 12, 1952
GP STARTS: 2
WC POINTS: 0

Year	Team	Grand(s) Prix
1979	EnFd	GB 13, Aut r

GALVEZ, Oscar

COUNTRY: Argentina
BORN: August 17, 1913
GP STARTS: 1
WC POINTS: 2
WC RECORD: 1953-13/2

Year	Team	Grand(s) Prix
1953	Mas	Arg 5

GAMBLE, Fred

COUNTRY: US
BORN: March 17, 1932
GP STARTS: 1
WC POINTS: 0

Year	Team	Grand(s) Prix
1960	BhPor	Ita 10

GANLEY, Howden

COUNTRY: New Zealand
BORN: December 24, 1941
GP STARTS: 35
WC POINTS: 10
WC RECORD: 1971-14/5; 1972-12/4; 1973-19/1

Year	Team	Grand(s) Prix;
1971	BRM	SA r, Esp 10, Hol 7, Fra 10, GB 8, Ger r, Aut r, Ita 5, Can dns, US 4
1972	BRM	Arg 9, SA uc, Esp r, Mon r, Bel 8, Ger 4, Aut 6, Ita 11, Can 10, US r
1973	WiFd	Arg uc, Bra 7, SA 10, Esp r, Bel r, Mon r, Swe 11, Fra 14, GB 9, Hol 9, Ger dns, Aut uc, Ita uc, Can 6, US 12
1974	MrFd	Arg 8, Bra r

GARDNER, Frank

COUNTRY: Australia
BORN: October 1, 1930
GP STARTS: 8
WC POINTS: 0

Year	Team	Grand(s) Prix
1964	BrFd	GB r
1965	BrBR	SA 12, Mon r, Bel r, GB 8, Hol 11, Ger r, Ita r

GARRETT, Billy

COUNTRY: US
BORN: April 24, 1933
GP STARTS: 2
WC POINTS: 0

Year	Team	Grand(s) Prix
1956	Ku	Indy 16
1958	KK	Indy r

GARTNER, Jo

COUNTRY: Austria
BORN: January 24, 1954
GP STARTS: 8
WC POINTS: 0

Year	Team	Grand(s) Prix
1984	OsAl	SM r, GB r, Ger r, Aut r, Hol 12, Ita 5, Eur 12, Por 16

GAZE, Tony

COUNTRY: Australia
BORN: February 3, 1920
GP STARTS: 3
WC POINTS: 0

Year	Team	Grand(s) Prix
1952	HWM	Bel 15, GB r, Ger r

'GEKI' (Giacomo, Russo)

COUNTRY: Italy
BORN: October 23, 1937
GP STARTS: 2
WC POINTS: 0

Year	Team	Grand(s) Prix
1965	LoCl	Ita r
1966	LoCl	Ita 9

GENDEBIEN, Olivier

COUNTRY: Belgium
BORN: January 12, 1924
GP STARTS: 14
WC POINTS: 18
WC RECORD: 1956-19/2; 1959-15/3; 1960-6/10; 1961-13/3

Psn	No	Grand(s) Prix
2nd:	1	1960 Fra
3rd:	1	1960 Bel

Year	Team	Grand(s) Prix
1956	La-Fe	Arg 5, Fra r
1958	Fe	Bel 6, Ita r, Moroccan r
1959	Fe	Fra 4, Ita 6
1960	CoCl	Bel 3, Fra 2, GB 9, Por 7, US 12
1961	Fe	Bel 4
1961	LoCl	US 12

GENE, Marc

COUNTRY: Spain
BORN: March 29, 1974
GP STARTS: 16
WC POINTS: 1
WC RECORD: 1999-17/1

Year	Team	Grand(s) Prix
1999	MiFd	Aus r, Bra 9, SM 9, Mon r, Esp r, Can 8, Fra r, GB 15, Aut 11, Ger 9, Hun 17, Bel 16, Ita r, Eur 6, Mal 9, Jap r

GEORGE, Elmer

COUNTRY: US
BORN: July 15, 1928
GP STARTS: 1
WC POINTS: 0

Year	Team	Grand(s) Prix
1957	KK	Indy r

GERARD, Bob

COUNTRY: GB
BORN: January 19, 1914
GP STARTS: 8
WC POINTS: 0

Year	Team	Grand(s) Prix
1950	ERA	GB 6, Mon 6
1951	ERA	GB 11
1953	CoBr	Fra 11, GB r
1954	CoBr	GB 10
1956	CoBr	GB 12
1957	CoBr	GB 6

GERINI, Gerino

COUNTRY: Italy
BORN: August 10, 1928
GP STARTS: 5
WC POINTS: 1
WC RECORD: 1956-25/1.5

Year	Team	Grand(s) Prix
1956	Mas	Ita 11
1958	Mas	Fra 9, GB r, Ita r, Moroccan 13

GETHIN, Peter

COUNTRY: GB
BORN: February 21, 1940
GP STARTS: 30
WC POINTS: 11
WC RECORD: 1970-22/1; 1971-9/9; 1972-20/1

Psn	No	Grand(s) Prix
1st:	1	1971 Ita

Year	Team	Grand(s) Prix
1970	McFd	Hol r, Ger r, Aut 10, Ita uc, Can 6, US 14, Mex r
1971	McFd	SA r, Esp 8, Mon r, Hol uc, Fra 9, GB r, Ger r
1971	BRM	Aut 10, Ita 1, Can 14, US 9
1972	BRM	Arg r, SA uc, Esp r, Mon dq, Bel r, Fra dns, GB r, Aut 13, Ita 6, Can r, US r
1973	BRM	Can r
1974	LoFd	GB r

GHINZANI, Piercario

COUNTRY: Italy
BORN: January 16, 1952
GP STARTS: 76
WC POINTS: 2
WC RECORD: 1984-19/2

Year	Team	Grand(s) Prix
1981	OsFd	Bel 13
1983	OsAl	US r, GB r, Ger r, Aut 11, Ita r, Eur uc, SA r
1984	OsAl	Bra r
1984	OsAR	SA dns
1984	OsAl	Bel r, Fra 12, Mon 7, Can r, Detroit r, Dallas 5, GB 9, Ger r, Aut r, Hol r, Ita 7, Eur r, Por r
1985	OsAl	Bra 12, Por 9, SM uc, Can r, US r, Fra 15, GB r
1985	ToHt	Aut r, Hol r, Ita r, Bel r, Eur r, SA r, Aus r
1986	OsAl	Bra r, Esp r, SM r, Bel r, Can r, US r, Fra r, GB r, Ger r, Hun r, Aut 11, Ita r, Por r, Mex r, Aus r
1987	LiMe	SM r, Bel 7, Mon 12, US r, Fra r, Ger r, Hun 12, Aut 8, Ita 8, Por r, Esp r, Mex r, Jap 13, Aus r
1988	Za	SM r, Mon r, Mex 15, Can 14, Fra dns, Ger 14, Bel r, Ita r, Aus r
1989	OsFd	Hun r, Esp r, Aus r

GIACOMELLI, Bruno

COUNTRY: Italy
BORN: September 10, 1952
GP STARTS: 69
WC POINTS: 14
WC RECORD: 1980-17/4; 1981-15/7; 1982-22/2; 1983-19/1

Psn	No	Grand(s) Prix
3rd:	1	1981 US
Pole:	1	1980 USE

Year	Team	Grand(s) Prix
1977	McFd	Ita r
1978	McFd	Bel 8, Fra r, GB 7, Hol r, Ita 14
1979	AR	Bel r, Fra 17, Ita r, USE r
1980	AR	Arg 5, Bra 13, SA r, USW r, Bel r, Mon r, Fra r, GB r, Ger 5, Aut r, Hol r, Ita r, Can r, USE r
1981	AR	USW r, Bra r, Arg 10, SM r, Bel 9, Mon r, Esp 10, Fra 15, GB r, Ger 15, Aut r, Hol r, Ita 8, Can 4, US 3
1982	AR	SA 11, Bra r, USW r, SM r, Bel r, Mon r, US r, Can r, Hol 11, GB 7, Fra 9, Ger 5, Aut r, Swi 12, Ita r, Caesar's Palace 10
1983	ToHt	Bra r, USW r, Fra 13, SM r, Bel 8, US 9, Can r, GB r, Ger r, Aut r, Hol 13, Ita 7, Eur 6, SA r

GIBSON, Dick

COUNTRY: GB
BORN: April 16, 1918
GP STARTS: 2
WC POINTS: 0

Year	Team	Grand(s) Prix
1957	CoCl	Ger r
1958	CoCl	Ger r

GINTHER, Richie

COUNTRY: US
BORN: August 5, 1930
GP STARTS: 52
WC POINTS: 102 (107)
WC RECORD: 1960-8/8; 1961-5/16; 1962-8/10; 1963-3/29; 1964-4/23; 1965-7/11; 1966-11/5

Psn	No	Grand(s) Prix
1st:	1	1965 Mex
2nd:	8	1960 Ita; 1961 Mon; 1962 Ita; 1963 Mon, Ita, US; 1964 Mon, Aut
3rd:	5	1961 Bel, GB; 1962 Fra; 1963 Ger, Mex
Fast:	3	1961 Mon, Bel; 1966 Mex

Year	Team	Grand(s) Prix
1960	Fe	Mon 6, Hol 6
1960	Sb	Fra dns
1960	Fe	Ita 2
1961	Fe	Mon 2, Hol 5, Bel 3, Fra r, GB 3, Ger 8, Ita r
1962	BRM	Hol 9, Mon r, Bel r, Fra 3, GB 13, Ger 8, Ita 2, US r, SA 7
1963	BRM	Mon 2, Bel 4, Hol 5, Fra r, GB 4, Ger 3, Ita 2, US 2, Mex 3, SA r
1964	BRM	Mon 2, Hol 11, Bel 4, Fra 5, GB 8, Ger 7, Aut 2, Ita 4, US 4, Mex 8
1965	Ho	Mon r, Bel 6, Fra r, GB r, Hol 6, Ita r, US 7, Mex 1
1966	CoMa	Mon r, Bel 5
1966	Ho	Ita r, US uc, Mex 4

GIRAUD-CABANTOUS, Yves

COUNTRY: France
BORN: October 8, 1904
GP STARTS: 13
WC POINTS: 5
WC RECORD: 1950-13/3; 1951-15/2

Year	Team	Grand(s) Prix
1950	Ta	GB 4, Swi r, Bel r, Fra 8
1951	Ta	Swi r, Bel 5, Fra 7, Ger 11, Ita 8, Esp r
1952	HWM	Fra 10
1953	HWM	Fra 14, Ita uc

GIUNTI, Ignazio

COUNTRY: Italy
BORN: August 30, 1941
GP STARTS: 4
WC POINTS: 3
WC RECORD: 1970-17/3

Year	Team	Grand(s) Prix
1970	Fe	Bel 4, Fra 14, Aut 7, Ita r

GODIA, Francisco

COUNTRY: Spain
BORN: March 21, 1921
GP STARTS: 13
WC POINTS: 6
WC RECORD: 1956-7/6

Year	Team	Grand(s) Prix
1951	Mas	Esp 10
1954	Mas	Esp 6
1956	Mas	Bel r, Fra 7, GB 8, Ger 4, Ita 4
1957	Mas	Ger r, Pescara r, Ita 9
1958	Mas	Arg 8, Bel r, Fra r

GOETHAIS, Christian

COUNTRY: Belgium
BORN: August 4, 1928
GP STARTS: 1
WC POINTS: 0

Year	Team	Grand(s) Prix
1958	CoCl	Ger r

GOLDSMITH, Paul

COUNTRY: US
BORN: October 2, 1927
GP STARTS: 3
WC POINTS: 6
WC RECORD: 1959-17/2; 1960-15/4

Psn	No	Grand(s) Prix
3rd:	1	1960 Indy

Year	Team	Grand(s) Prix
1958	KK	Indy r
1959	Epp	Indy 5
1960	Epp	Indy 3

GONZALEZ, Jose Froilan

COUNTRY: Argentina
BORN: October 5, 1922
GP STARTS: 26
WC POINTS: 73.14 (78.64)
WC RECORD: 1951-3/24; 1952-9/6.5; 1953-6/13.5; 1954-2/25.14; 1955-17/2; 1957-19/2

Psn	No	Grand(s) Prix
1st:	2	1951 GB; 1954 GB
2nd:	7	1951 Fra, Ita, Esp; 1952 Ita; 1954 Ger, Swi; 1955 Arg
3rd:	4	1951 Ger; 1953 Arg, Fra; 1954 Arg
Pole:	3	1951 GB; 1954 Swi; 1955 Arg
Fast:	5	1952 Ita; 1953 Bel, GB; 1954 Arg, Ita

Year	Team	Grand(s) Prix
1950	Mas	Mon r, Fra r
1951	Ta	Swi r
1951	Fe	Fra 2, GB 1, Ger 3, Ita 2, Esp 2
1952	Mas	Ita 2
1953	Mas	Arg 3, Hol r, Bel r, Fra 3, GB 4
1954	Fe	Arg 3, Bel r, Fra r, GB 1, Ger 2, Swi 2, Ita r
1955	Fe	Arg 2
1956	Mas	Arg r
1956	Va	GB r
1957	LaFe	Arg 5
1960	Fe	Arg 10

GONZALEZ, Oscar

COUNTRY: URUGUAY
BORN:
GP STARTS (1)
GP POINTS: 0

Year	Team	Grand(s) Prix
1956	Mas	Arg (6) –Took over from Uria for finish

GORDINI, Aldo

COUNTRY: France
BORN: May 20, 1921
GP STARTS: 1
WC POINTS: 0

Year	Team	Grand(s) Prix
1951	SiGo	Fra r

GOULD, Horace

COUNTRY: GB
BORN: September 20, 1921
GP STARTS: 14
WC POINTS: 2
WC RECORD: 1956-19/2

Year	Team	Grand(s) Prix
1954	CoBr	GB uc
1955	Mas	Hol r, GB r, Ita r
1956	Mas	Mon 8, Bel r, GB 5, Ger r
1957	Mas	Mon r, Fra r, GB dns, Ger r, Pescara r, Ita 10
1958	Mas	Arg 9

GOUNON, Jean-Marc

COUNTRY: France
BORN: January 1, 1963
GP STARTS: 9
WC POINTS: 0

Year	Team	Grand(s) Prix
1993	MiFd	Jap r, Aus r
1994	SiFd	Fra 9, GB 16, Ger r, Hun r, Bel 11, Ita r, Por 15

GREEN, Cecil

COUNTRY: US
BORN: September 30, 1919
GP STARTS: 2
WC POINTS: 3
WC RECORD: 1950-13/3

Year	Team	Grand(s) Prix
1950	KK	Indy 4
1951	KK	Indy r

GREENE, Keith

COUNTRY: GB
BORN: January 5, 1938
GP STARTS: 3
WC POINTS: 0

Year	Team	Grand(s) Prix
1960	CoMa	GB r
1961	GiCl	GB 15
1962	GiBR	Ger r

GREGORY, Masten

COUNTRY: US
BORN: February 29, 1932
GP STARTS: 38
WC POINTS: 21
WC RECORD: 1957-6/10; 1959-8/10; 1962-18/1

Psn	No	Grand(s) Prix
2nd:	1	1959 Por
3rd:	2	1957 Mon; 1959 Hol

Year	Team	Grand(s) Prix
1957	Mas	Mon 3, Ger 8, Pescara 4, Ita 4
1958	Mas	Hol r, Bel r, Ita 4, Moroccan 6
1959	CoCl	Mon r, Hol 3, Fra r, GB 7, Ger r, Por 2
1960	BhPo	Arg 12 (F2)
1960	CoMa	Hol dns, Fra 9, GB 15, Por r
1961	CoCl	Bel 10, Fra 12, GB 11
1961	LoCl	Ita r, US r
1962	LoCl	Hol r
1962	LtBR	Bel r, Fra r
1962	LoCl	GB 7
1962	LtBR	Ita 12, US 6
1963	LtBR	Fra r, GB 11, Ita r
1963	LICl	US r, Mex r
1965	BRM	Bel r, GB 12, Ger 8, Ita r

GRIFFITH, Cliff

COUNTRY: US
BORN: February 6, 1916
GP STARTS: 3
WC POINTS: 0

Year	Team	Grand(s) Prix
1951	KK	Indy r
1952	KK	Indy 9
1956	Ste	Indy 10

GRIGNARD, Georges

COUNTRY: France
BORN: July 25, 1905
GP STARTS: 1
WC POINTS: 0

Year	Team	Grand(s) Prix
1951	Ta	Esp r

GRIM, Bobby

COUNTRY: US
BORN: September 4, 1924
GP STARTS: 2
WC POINTS: 0

Year	Team	Grand(s) Prix
1959	KK	Indy r
1960	Mes	Indy 16

GROUILLARD, Olivier

COUNTRY: France
BORN: September 2, 1958
GP STARTS: 41
WC POINTS: 1
WC RECORD: 1989-26/1

Year	Team	Grand(s) Prix
1989	LiJu	Bra 9
1989	LiFd	SM dq, Mon r, Mex 8, Fra 6, GB 7, Ger r, Bel 13, Ita r, Esp r, Jap r, Aus r
1990	OsFd	US r, Bra r, SM r, Can 13, Mex 19, Bel 16, Ita r, Esp r, Aus 13
1991	FnFd	Mex r, Fra r, Bel 10, Ita r
1992	TyII	SA r, Mex r, Bra r, Esp r, SM 8, Mon r, Can 12, Fra 11, GB 11, Ger r, Hun r, Bel r, Ita r, Por r, Jap r, Aus r

GUELFI, Andre

COUNTRY: France
BORN: May 6, 1919
GP STARTS: 1
WC POINTS: 0

Year	Team	Grand(s) Prix
1958	CoCl	Moroccan 15

GUERRA, Miguel-Angel

COUNTRY: Argentina
BORN: August 31, 1953
GP STARTS: 1
WC POINTS: 0

Year	Team	Grand(s) Prix
1981	OsFd	SM r

GUERRERO, Roberto

COUNTRY: Colombia

BORN: November 16, 1958
GP STARTS: 21
WC POINTS: 0

Year	Team	Grand(s) Prix
1982	EnFd	USW r, US r, Can r, GB r, Ger 8, Aut r, Swi r, Ita uc, Caesar's Palace dns
1983	ThFd	Bra uc, USW r, Fra r, SM r, Bel r, US uc, Can r, GB 16, Ger r, Aut r, Hol 12, Ita 13, Eur 12

GUGELMIN, Mauricio

COUNTRY: Brazil
BORN: April 20, 1963
GP STARTS: 74
WC POINTS: 10
WC RECORD: 1988-13/5; 1989-16/4; 1990-18/1

Psn	No	Grand(s) Prix
3rd:	1	1989 Bra
Fast:	1	1989 Fra

Year	Team	Grand(s) Prix
1988	MaJd	Bra r, SM 15, Mon r, Mex r, Can r, US r, Fra 8, GB 4, Ger 8, Hun 5, Bel r, Ita 8, Por r, Esp 7, Jap 10, Aus r
1989	MaJd	Bra 3, SM r, Mon r, US dq, Can r, Fra uc, GB r, Ger r, Hun r, Bel 7, Ita r, Por 10, Esp r, Jap 7, Aus 7
1990	LHJu	US 14, SM r, Fra r, GB dns, Ger r, Hun 8, Bel 6, Ita r, Por 12, Esp 8, Jap r, Aus r
1991	LHIl	US r, Bra r, SM 12, Mon r, Can r, Mex r, Fra 7, GB r, Ger r, Hun 11, Bel r, Ita 15, Por 7, Esp 7, Jap 8, Aus 14
1992	JoYa	SA 11, Mex r, Bra r, Esp r, SM 7, Mon r, Can r, Fra r, GB r, Ger 15, Hun 10, Bel 14, Ita r, Por r, Jap r, Aus r

GURNEY, Dan

COUNTRY: US
BORN: April 13, 1931
GP STARTS: 86
WC POINTS: 133
WC RECORD: 1959-7/13; 1961-3/21; 1962-5/15; 1963-5/19; 1964-6/19; 1965-4/25; 1966-12/4; 1967-8/13; 1968-21/3; 1970-22/1

Psn	No	Grand(s) Prix
1st:	4	1962 Fra; 1964 Fra, Mex; 1967 Bel
2nd:	8	1959 Ger; 1961 Fra, Ita, US; 1963 Hol, SA; 1965 US, Mex
3rd:	7	1959 Por; 1962 Ger; 1963 Bel; 1965 Hol, Ger, Ita; 1967 Can
Pole:	3	1962 Ger; 1963 Hol, Bel
Fast:	6	1963 SA; 1964 Bel, Aut; 1965 Mex; 1967 Bel, Ger

Year	Team	Grand(s) Prix
1959	Fe	Fra r, Ger 2, Por 3, Ita 4
1960	BRM	Mon r, Hol r, Bel r, Fra r, GB 10, Por r, US r
1961	Por	Mon 5, Hol 10, Bel 6, Fra 2, GB 7, Ger 7, Ita 2, US 2
1962	Por	Hol r, Mon r
1962	LtBR	Bel dns
1962	Por	Fra 1, GB 9, Ger 3, Ita r, US 5
1963	BrCl	Mon r, Bel 3, Hol 2, Fra 5, GB r, Ger r, Ita r, US r, Mex 6, SA 2
1964	BrCl	Mon r, Hol r, Bel 6, Fra 1, GB 13, Ger 10, Aut r, Ita 10, US r, Mex 1
1965	BrCl	SA r, Bel 10, Fra r, GB 6, Hol 3, Ger 3, Ita 3, US 2, Mex 2
1966	EaCl	Bel uc, Fra 5, GB r, Hol r, Ger 7
1966	EaWe	Ita r, US r
1966	EaCl	Mex 5
1967	EaCl	SA r
1967	EaWe	Mon r, Hol r, Bel 1, Fra r, GB r, Ger r, Can 3, Ita r, US r, Mex r
1968	EaWe	SA r, Mon r, Hol r, GB r, Ger 9, Ita r
1968	McFd	Can r, US 4, Mex r
1970	McFd	Hol r, Fra 6, GB r

HAHNE, Hubert

COUNTRY: Germany
BORN: March 28, 1935
GP STARTS: 3
WC POINTS: 0

Year	Team	Grand(s) Prix
1966	MatBR	Ger 9
1967	LIBM	Ger r
1968	LIBM	Ger 10
1969	BMW	Ger dns

HAILWOOD, Mike

COUNTRY: GB
BORN: April 2, 1940
GP STARTS: 50
WC POINTS: 29
WC RECORD: 1964-19/1; 1971-18/3; 1972-8/13; 1974-10/12

Psn	No	Grand(s) Prix
2nd:	1	1972 Ita
3rd:	1	1974 SA
Fast:	1	1972 SA

Year	Team	Grand(s) Prix
1963	LoCl	GB 8
1963	LICI	Ita 10
1964	LtBR	Mon 6, Hol r, Fra 8, GB r, Ger r, Aut 8, Ita r, US 8, Mex r
1965	LtBR	Mon r
1971	SuFd	Ita 4, US 15
1972	SuFd	SA r, Esp r, Mon r, Bel 4, Fra 6, GB r, Ger r, Aut 4, Ita 2, US 17
1973	SuFd	Arg r, Bra r, SA r, Esp r, Bel r, Mon 8, Swe r, Fra r, GB r, Hol r, Ger 14, Aut 10, Ita 7, Can 9, US r
1974	McFd	Arg 4, Bra 5, SA 3, Esp 9, Bel 7, Mon r, Swe r, Hol 4, Fra 7, GB r, Ger 15

HAKKINEN, Mika

COUNTRY: Finland
BORN: September 28, 1968
GP STARTS: 128
WC POINTS: 294
WC RECORD: 1991-15/2; 1992-8/11; 1993-15/4; 1994-4/26; 1995-7/17; 1996-5/31; 1997-5/27; 1998-1/100; 1999-1/76
WORLD CHAMPION: 1998, 1999

Psn	No	Grand(s) Prix
1st:	14	1997 Eur; 1998 Aus, Bra, Esp, Mon, Aut, Ger, Lux, Jap; 1999 Bra, Esp, Can, Hun, Jap
2nd:	7	1994 Bel; 1995 Ita, Jap; 1998 Arg, GB; 1999 Fra, Bel
3rd:	16	1993 Jap; 1994 SM, GB, Ita, Por, Eur; 1996 GB, Bel, Ita, Jap; 1997 Aus, Ger; 1998 Fra; 1999 Mon, Aut, Mal
Pole:	21	1997 Lux; 1998 Aus, Bra, Esp, Mon, Fra, GB, Ger, Hun, Bel; 1998 Aus, Bra, SM, Mon, Esp, GB, Aut, Ger, Hun, Bel, Ita
Fast:	13	1997 Ita; 1998 Aus, Bra, Esp, Mon, Ita, Lux; 1999 Bra, Mon, GB, Aut, Bel, Eur

Year	Team	Grand(s) Prix
1991	LtJu	US r, Bra 9, SM 5, Mon r, Can r, Mex 9, GB 12, Ger r, Hun 14, Bel r, Ita 14, Por 14, Esp r, Jap r, Aus 19
1992	LtFd	SA 9, Mex 6, Bra 10, Esp r, Mon r, Can r, Fra 4, GB 6, Ger r, Hun 4, Bel 6, Ita r, Por 5, Jap r, Aus 7
1993	McFd	Por r, Jap 3, Aus r
1994	McPe	Bra r, Pac r, SM 3, Mon r, Esp r, Can r, Fra r, GB 3, Ger r, Bel 2, Ita 3, Por 3, Eur 3, Jap 7, Aus 12
1995	McMe	Bra 4, Arg r, SM 5, Esp r, Mon r, Can r, Fra 7, GB r, Ger r, Hun r, Bel r, Ita 2, Por r, Eur 8, Jap 2
1996	McMe	Aus 5, Bra 4, Arg r, Eur 8, SM 8, Mon 6, Esp 5, Can 5, Fra 5, GB 3, Ger r, Hun 4, Bel 3, Ita 3, Por r, Jap 3
1997	McMe	Aus 3, Bra 4, Arg 5, SM 6, Mon r, Esp 7, Can r, Fra r, GB r, Ger 3, Hun r, Bel dq, Ita 9, Aut r, Lux r, Jap 4, Eur 1
1998	McMe	Aus 1, Bra 1, Arg 2, SM r, Esp 1, Mon 1, Can r, Fra 3, GB 2, Aut 1, Ger 1, Hun 6, Bel r, Ita 4, Lux 1, Jap 1
1999	McMe	Aus r, Bra 1, SM r, Mon 3, Esp 1, Can 1, Fra 2, GB r, Aut 3, Ger r, Hun 1, Bel 2, Ita r, Eur 5, Mal 3, Jap 1

HALFORD, Bruce

COUNTRY: GB
BORN: May 18, 1931
GP STARTS: 8
WC POINTS: 0

Year	Team	Grand(s) Prix
1956	Mas	GB r, Ger dq, Ita r
1957	Mass	Ger 11
1957	CoCl	Pescara r
1957	Mas	Ita r
1959	LoCl	Mon r
1960	CoCl	Fra 8

HALL, Jim

COUNTRY: US
BORN: July 23, 1935
GP STARTS: 11
WC POINTS: 3
WC RECORD: 1963-12/3

Year	Team	Grand(s) Prix
1960	LoCl	US 7
1961	LoCl	US r
1963	LtBR	Mon r, Bel r, Hol 8, Fra 11, GB 6, Ger 5, Ita 8, US r, Mex 8

HAMILTON, Duncan

COUNTRY: GB
BORN: April 30, 1920
GP STARTS: 5
WC POINTS: 0

Year	Team	Grand(s) Prix
1951	Ta	GB 12, Ger r
1952	HWM	GB r, Hol 7
1953	HWM	GB r

HAMPSHIRE, David

COUNTRY: GB
BORN: December 29, 1917
GP STARTS: 2
WC POINTS: 0

Year	Team	Grand(s) Prix
1950	Mas	GB 9, Fra r

HANKS, Sam

COUNTRY: US
BORN: July 13, 1914
GP STARTS: 8
WC POINTS: 20
WC RECORD: 1952-12/4; 1953-13/2; 1956-7/6; 1957-8/8

Psn	No	Grand(s) Prix
1st:	1	1957 Indy
2nd:	1	1956 Indy
3rd:	2	1952 Indy; 1953 Indy

Year	Team	Grand(s) Prix
1950	KK	Indy r
1951	KK	Indy r
1952	KK	Indy 3
1953	KK	Indy 3
1954	KK	Indy r
1955	KK	Indy r
1956	KK	Indy 2
1957	Epp	Indy 1

HANSGEN, Walt

COUNTRY: US
BORN: October 28, 1919
GP STARTS: 2
WC POINTS: 2
WC RECORD: 1964-16/2

Year	Team	Grand(s) Prix
1961	CoCl	US r
1964	LoCl	US 5

HARRIS, Mike

COUNTRY: Zimbabwe
BORN: May 25, 1939
GP STARTS: 1
WC POINTS: 0

Year	Team	Grand(s) Prix
1962	CoAl	SA r

HARRISON, TC

COUNTRY: GB
BORN: July 6, 1906
GP STARTS: 3
WC POINTS: 0

Year	Team	Grand(s) Prix
1950	ERA	GB 7, Mon r, Ita r

HART, Brian

COUNTRY: GB
BORN: September 7, 1936
GP STARTS: 1 (F2 Race)

Year	Team	Grand(s) Prix
1967		Ger 4

HARTLEY, Gene

COUNTRY: US
BORN: January 28, 1926
GP STARTS: 8
WC POINTS: 0

Year	Team	Grand(s) Prix
1950	Lang	Indy 16
1952	KK	Indy r
1953	KK	Indy r
1954	KK	Indy r
1956	Ku	Indy 11
1957	Les	Indy 10
1959	Ku	Indy 11
1960	KK	Indy 14

HASEMI, Masahiro

COUNTRY: Japan
BORN: November 13, 1945

GP STARTS: 1
WC POINTS: 0

Psn	No	Grand(s) Prix
Fast:	1	1976 Jap

Year	Team	Grand(s) Prix
1976	KoFd	Jap 11

HAWKINS, Paul

COUNTRY: Australia
BORN: October 12, 1937
GP STARTS: 3
WC POINTS: 0

Year	Team	Grand(s) Prix
1965	BrFd	SA 9, Mon r, Ger r

HAWTHORN, Mike

COUNTRY: GB
BORN: April 10, 1929
GP STARTS: 45
WC POINTS: 112.64 (127.64)
WC RECORD: 1952-4/10; 1953-4/19; 1954-3/24.64; 1956-11/4; 1957-4/13; 1958-1/42
WORLD CHAMPION: 1958

Psn	No	Grand(s) Prix
1st:	3	1953 Fra; 1954 Esp; 1958 Fra
2nd:	8	1954 GB, Ita; 1957 Ger; 1958 Bel, GB, Por, Ita, Moroccan
3rd:	6	1952 GB; 1953 Ger, Swi; 1956 Arg; 1957 GB; 1958 Arg
Pole:	4	1958 Bel, Fra, Ger, Moroccan
Fast:	6	1954 GB; 1958 Mon, Bel, Fra, GB, Por

Year	Team	Grand(s) Prix
1965	LoCl	Mon r, Ger r
1952	CoBr	Bel 4, Fra r, GB 3, Hol 4, Ita uc
1953	Fe	Arg 4, Hol 4, Bel 6, Fra 1, GB 5, Ger 3, Swi 3, Ita 4
1954	Fe	Arg dq, Bel 4, Fra r, GB 2, Ger r, Swi r, Ita 2, Esp 1
1955	Va	Mon r, Bel r
1955	Fe	Hol 7, GB 6, Ita r
1956	Mas	Arg 3
1956	BRM	Mon dns
1956	Mas	Bel dns
1956	Va	Fra 10
1956	BRM	GB r
1957	La-Fe	Arg r, Mon r, Fra 4, GB 3, Ger 2, Ita 6
1958	Fe	Arg 3, Mon r, Hol 5, Bel 2, Fra 1, GB 2, Ger r, Por 2, Ita 2, Moroccan 2

HAYJE, Boy

COUNTRY: Holland
BORN: May 3, 1949
GP STARTS: 3
WC POINTS: 0

Year	Team	Grand(s) Prix
1976	PkFd	Hol r
1977	MrFd	SA r, Bel 15

HEEKS, Willi

COUNTRY: Germany
BORN: February 13, 1922
GP STARTS: 2
WC POINTS: 0

Year	Team	Grand(s) Prix
1952	AFM	Ger r
1953	Ver	Ger r

HELFRICH, Theo

COUNTRY: Germany
BORN: May 13, 1913
GP STARTS: 3
WC POINTS: 0

Year	Team	Grand(s) Prix
1952	Ver	Ger r
1953	Ver	Ger 12
1954	KlMr	Ger r

HELLINGS, Mack

COUNTRY: US
BORN: September 14, 1917
GP STARTS: 2
WC POINTS: 0

Year	Team	Grand(s) Prix
1950	KK	Indy 13
1951	De	Indy r

HENTON, Brian

COUNTRY: GB
BORN: September 19, 1946
GP STARTS: 19
WC POINTS: 0

Psn	No	Grand(s) Prix
Fast:	1	1982 GB

Year	Team	Grand(s) Prix
1975	LtFd	GB 16, Aut dns, US r
1977	MrFd	USW 10
1977	EnFd	Hol dq
1981	ToHt	Ita 10
1982	ArFd	USW r
1982	TyFd	SM r, Bel r, Mon 8, US 9, Can r, Hol r, GB 8, Fra 10, Ger 7, Aut r, Swi 11, Ita r, Caesar's Palace 8

HERBERT, Johnny

COUNTRY: GB
BORN: June 25, 1964
GP STARTS: 143
WC POINTS: 98
WC RECORD: 1989-14/5; 1992-14/2; 1993-9/11; 1995-4/45; 1996-14/4; 1997-10/15; 1998-15/1; 1999-8/15

Psn	No	Grand(s) Prix
1st:	3	1995 GB, Ita; 1999 Eur
2nd:	1	1995 Esp
3rd:	3	1995 Jap; 1996 Mon; 1997 Hun

Year	Team	Grand(s) Prix
1989	BeFd	Bra 4, SM 11, Mon 14, Mex 15, US 5
1989	TyFd	Bel r
1990	LtLm	Jap r, Aus r
1991	LtJu	Mex 10, Fra 10, GB 14, Bel 7, Por r, Jap r, Aus 11
1992	LtFd	SA 6, Mex 7, Bra r, Esp r, SM r, Mon r, Can r, Fra 6, GB r, Ger r, Hun r, Bel 13, Ita r, Por r, Jap r, Aus 13
1993	LtFd	SA r, Bra 4, Eur 4, SM 8, Esp r, Mon r, Can 10, Fra r, GB 4, Ger 10, Hun r, Bel 5, Ita r, Por r, Jap 11, Aus r
1994	LoMH	Bra 7, Pac 7, SM 10, Mon r, Esp r, Can 8, Fra 7, GB 11, Ger r, Hun r, Bel 12, Ita r, Por 11
1994	LiRe	Eur 8
1994	BeFd	Jap r, Aus r
1995	BeRe	Bra r, Arg 4, SM 7, Esp 2, Mon 4, Can r, Fra r, GB 1, Ger 4, Hun 4, Bel 7, Ita 1, Por 7, Eur 5, Pac 6, Jap 3, Aus r
1996	SaFd	Aus dns, Bra r, Arg 9, Eur 7, SM r, Mon 3, Esp r, Can 7, Fra dq, GB 9, Ger r, Hun r, Bel r, Ita 9, Por 8, Jap 10
1997	SaPe	Aus r, Bra 7, Arg 4, SM r, Mon r, Esp 5, Can 5, Fra 8, GB r, Ger r, Hun 3, Bel 4, Ita r, Aut 8, Lux 7, Jap 6, Eur 8
1998	SaPe	Aus 6, Bra r, Arg r, SM r, Esp 7, Mon 7, Can r, Fra 8, GB r, Aut 8, Ger r, Hun 10, Bel r, Ita r, Lux r, Jap 10
1999	StFd	Aus dns, Bra r, SM 10, Mon r, Esp r, Can 5, Fra r, GB 12, Aut 14, Ger 11, Hun 11, Bel r, Ita r, Eur 1, Mal 4, Jap 7

HERMAN, Al

COUNTRY: US
BORN: March 15, 1927
GP STARTS: 5
WC POINTS: 0

Year	Team	Grand(s) Prix
1955	KK	Indy 7
1956	KK	Indy r
1957	Dunn	Indy r
1959	Dunn	Indy 13
1960	We	Indy r

HERRMANN, Hans

COUNTRY: Germany
BORN: February 23, 1928
GP STARTS: 18
WC POINTS: 2
WC RECORD: 1955-22/1; 1960-24/1

Psn	No	Grand(s) Prix
3rd:	1	1954 Swi
Fast:	1	1954 Fra

Year	Team	Grand(s) Prix
1953	Ver	Ger 9
1954	Me	Fra r, Ger r, Swi 3, Ita 4, Esp r
1955	Me	Arg 4
1957	Mas	Ger r
1958	Mas	Ger r, Ita r, Mor 9
1959	CoMa	GB r
1959	BRM	Ger r
1960	Por	Ita 6
1961	Por	Mon 9, Hol 15, Ger 13
1966	BrFd	Ger 11

HESNAULT, Francois

COUNTRY: France
BORN: December 30, 1956
GP STARTS: 19
WC POINTS: 0

Year	Team	Grand(s) Prix
1984	LiRe	Bra r, SA 10, Bel r, SM r, Mon r, Can r, Detroit r, Dallas r, GB r, Ger 8, Aut 8, Hol 7, Ita r, Eur 10, Por r
1985	BrBM	Bra r, Por r, SM r
1985	Re	Ger r

HILL, Damon

COUNTRY: GB
BORN: September 17, 1960
GP STARTS: 115
WC POINTS: 360
WC RECORD: 1993-3/69; 1994-2/91; 1995-2/69; 1996-1/97; 1997-12/7; 1998-6/20; 1999-11/7
WORLD CHAMPION: 1996

Psn	No	Grand(s) Prix
1st:	22	1993 Hun, Bel, Ita; 1994 Esp, GB, Bel, Ita, Por, Jap; 1995 Arg, SM, Hun, Aus; 1996 Aus, Bra, Arg, SM, Can, Fra, Ger, Jap; 1998 Bel
2nd:	15	1993 Bra, Eur, Mon, Fra; 1994 Bra, Can, Fra, Hun, Eur; 1995 Mon, Fra, Bel; 1996 Hun, Por; 1997 Hun
3rd:	5	1993 Can, Por, Aus; 1995 Por, Pac
Pole:	20	1993 Fra, Por; 1994 Fra, GB; 1994 Bra, Mon, Fra, GB, Ger, Hun, Aus; 1996 Bra, Arg, Eur, Esp, Can, GB, Ger, Ita, Por
Fast:	19	1993 GB, Ita, Por, Aus; 1994 SM, Fra, GB, Bel, Ita, Jap; 1995 Esp, GB, Hun, Aus; 1996 Bra, Eur, SM, Ger, Hun

Year	Team	Grand(s) Prix
1992	BrJu	GB 16, Hun 11
1993	WiRe	SA r, Bra 2, Eur 2, SM r, Esp r, Mon 2, Can 3, Fra 2, GB r, Ger 15, Hun 1, Bel 1, Ita 1, Por 3, Jap 4, Aus 3
1994	WiRe	Bra 2, Pac r, SM 6, Mon r, Esp 1, Can 2, Fra 2, GB 1, Ger 8, Hun 2, Bel 1, Ita 1, Por 1, Eur 2, Jap 1, Aus r
1995	WiRe	Bra r, Arg 1, SM 1, Esp 4, Mon 2, Can r, Fra 2, GB r, Ger r, Hun 1, Bel 2, Ita r, Por 3, Eur r, Pac 3, Jap r, Aus 1
1996	WiRe	Aus 1, Bra 1, Arg 1, Eur 4, SM 1, Mon r, Esp r, Can 1, Fra 1, GB r, Ger 1, Hun 2, Bel 5, Ita r, Por 2, Jap 1
1997	ArYa	Aus dns, Bra 17, Arg r, SM r, Mon r, Esp r, Can 9, Fra 12, GB 6, Ger 8, Hun 2, Bel 13, Ita r, Aut 7, Lux 8, Jap 11, Eur r
1998	JoMH	Aus 8, Bra dq, Arg 8, SM r, Esp r, Mon 8, Can r, Fra r, GB r, Aut 7, Ger 4, Hun 4, Bel 1, Ita 6, Lux 9, Jap 4
1999	JoMH	Aus r, Bra r, SM 4, Mon r, Esp 7, Can r, Fra r, GB 5, Aut 8, Ger r, Hun 6, Bel 6, Ita 10, Eur r, Mal r, Jap r

HILL, Graham

COUNTRY: GB
BORN: February 15, 1929
GP STARTS: 176
WC POINTS: 270 (287)
WC RECORD: 1960-15/4; 1961-13/3; 1962-1/42; 1963-2/29; 1964-2/39; 1965-2/40; 1966-5/17; 1967-6/15; 1968-1/48; 1969-7/19; 1970-13/7; 1971-21/2; 1972-12/4; 1974-18/1
WORLD CHAMPION: 1962, 1968

Psn	No	Grand(s) Prix
1st:	14	1962 Hol, Ger, Ita, SA; 1963 Mon, US; 1964 Mon, US; 1965 Mon, US; 1968 Esp, Mon, Mex; 1969 Mon
2nd:	15	1962 Bel, US; 1964 Fra, GB, Ger; 1965 GB, Ger, Ita; 1966 Hol; 1967 Mon, US; 1968 SA, Ger, US; 1969 SA
3rd:	7	1960 Hol; 1963 Fra, GB, SA; 1965 SA; 1966 Mon, GB
Pole:	13	1962 Bel; 1963 Bel, US; 1964 Aut; 1965 Mon, Bel, Hol, US; 1967 Hol, Fra, US; 1968 Mon, GB
Fast:	10	1960 GB; 1962 Fra, Ger, Ita; 1964 Mon; 1965 Mon, GB, US; 1967 Fra, US

Year	Team	Grand(s) Prix
1958	LoCl	Mon r, Hol r, Bel r, Fra r, GB r, Ger r, Por r, Ita 6, Mor 16
1959	LoCl	Mon r, Hol 7, Fra r, GB 9, Ger r, Por r, Ita r
1960	BRM	Arg r, Mon 7, Hol 3, Bel uc, Fra r, GB 14, Por r, US r
1961	BRCl	Mon r, Hol 8, Bel r, Fra 6, GB r, Ger r, Ita r, US 5
1962	BRM	Hol 1, Mon 6, Bel 2, Fra 9, GB 4, Ger 1, Ita 1, US 2, SA 1
1963	BRM	Mon 1, Bel r, Hol r, Fra 3, GB 3, Ger r, Ita r, US 1, Mex 4, SA 3
1964	BRM	Mon 1, Hol 4, Bel 5, Fra 2, GB 2, Ger 2, Aut r, Ita r, US 1, Mex 11
1965	BRM	SA 3, Mon 1, Bel 5, Fra 5, GB 2, Hol 4, Ger 2, Ita 2, US 1, Mex r

1966	BRM	Mon 3, Bel r, Fra r, GB 3, Hol 2, Ger 4, Ita r, US r, Mex r
1967	LtBR	SA r, Mon 2
1967	LtFd	Hol r, Bel r, Fra r, GB r, Ger r, Can 4, Ita r, US 2, Mex r
1968	LtFd	SA 2, Esp 1, Mon 1, Bel r, Hol 9, Fra r, GB r, Ger 2, Ita r, Can 4, US 2, Mex 1
1969	LtFd	SA 2, Esp r, Mon 1, Hol 7, Fra 6, GB 7, Ger 4, Ita 9, Can r, US r
1970	LtFd	SA 6, Esp 4, Mon 5, Bel r, Hol uc, Fra 10, GB 6, Ger r, Ita dns, Can uc, US r, Mex r
1971	BrFd	SA 9, Esp r, Mon r, Hol 10, Fra r, GB r, Ger 9, Aut 5, Ita r, Can r, US 7
1972	BrFd	Arg r, SA 6, Esp 10, Mon 12, Bel r, Fra 10, GB r, Ger 6, Aut r, Ita 5, Can 8, US 11
1973	ShFd	Esp r, Bel 9, Mon r, Swe r, Fra 10, GB r, Hol uc, Ger 13, Aut r, Ita 14, Can 16, US 13
1974	LoFd	Arg r, Bra 11, SA 12, Esp r, Bel 8, Mon 7, Swe 6, Hol r, Fra 13, GB 13, Ger 9, Aut 12, Ita 8, Can 14, US 8
1975	LoFd	Arg 10, Bra 12, SA dns

HILL, Phil

COUNTRY: US
BORN: April 20, 1927
GP STARTS: 48
WC POINTS: 94 (98)
WC RECORD: 1958-10/9; 1959-4/20; 1960-5/16; 1961-1/34; 1962-6/14; 1964-19/1
WORLD CHAMPION: 1961

Psn	No	Grand(s) Prix
1st:	3	1960 Ita; 1961 Bel, Ita
2nd:	5	1959 Fra, Ita; 1961 Hol, GB; 1962 Mon
3rd:	8	1958 Ita, Moroccan; 1959 Ger; 1960 Mon; 1961 Mon, Ger; 1962 Hol, Bel
Pole:	6	1960 Ita; 1961 Hol, Bel, Fra, GB, Ger
Fast:	6	1958 Ita; 1959 Ita; 1960 Bel, Ita; 1961 Fra, Ger

Year	Team	Grand(s) Prix
1958	Mas	Fra 7
1958	Fe	Ger 9, Ita 3, Moroccan 3
1959	Fe	Mon 4, Hol 6, Fra 2, Ger 3, Por r, Ita 2, US r
1960	Fe	Arg 8, Mon 3, Hol r, Bel 4, Fra r, GB 7, Por r, Ita 1
1960	CoCl	US 6
1961	Fe	Mon 3, Hol 2, Bel 1, Fra 9, GB 2, Ger 3, Ita 1
1962	Fe	Hol 3, Mon 2, Bel 3, GB r, Ger r, Ita 11
1963	Atsl	Bel r, Hol r
1963	LtBR	Fra uc
1963	Atsl	Ita 11, US r, Mex r
1964	CoCl	Mon r, Hol 8, Bel r, Fra 7, GB 6, Ger r, Aut r, US r, Mex 9

HIRT, Peter

COUNTRY: Switzerland
BORN: March 30, 1910
GP STARTS: 4
WC POINTS: 0

Year	Team	Grand(s) Prix
1951	Ver	Swi r
1952	Fe	Swi 7, GB r
1953	Fe	Swi r

HOBBS, David

COUNTRY: GB
BORN: June 9, 1939
GP STARTS: 6
WC POINTS: 0

Year	Team	Grand(s) Prix
1967	BRM	GB 8, Can 9
1968	Ho	Ita r
1971	McFd	US 10
1974	McFd	Aut 7, Ita 9

HOFFMAN, Ingo

COUNTRY: Brazil
BORN: February 18, 1953
GP STARTS: 3
WC POINTS: 0

Year	Team	Grand(s) Prix
1976	FiFd	Bra 11
1977	FiFd	Arg r, Bra 7

HOLLAND, Bill

COUNTRY: US
BORN: December 18, 1907
GP STARTS: 2
WC POINTS: 6
WC RECORD: 1950-7/6

Psn	No	Grand(s) Prix
2nd:	1	1950 Indy
Fast:	1	1950 Indy

Year	Team	Grand(s) Prix
1950	De	Indy 2
1953	KK	Indy 15

HOLMES, Jackie

COUNTRY: US
BORN: September 4, 1920
GP STARTS: 1
WC POINTS: 0

Year	Team	Grand(s) Prix
1950	Olson	Indy 23

HOMEIER, Bill

COUNTRY: US
BORN: August 31, 1918
GP STARTS: 2
WC POINTS: 1
WC RECORD: 1955-22/1

Year	Team	Grand(s) Prix
1954	KK	Indy r
1955	KK	Indy 5 (shared)
1960	Ku	Indy 13

HOSHINO, Kazuyoshi

COUNTRY: Japan
BORN: July 1, 1947
GP STARTS: 2
WC POINTS: 0

Year	Team	Grand(s) Prix
1976	TyFd	Jap r
1977	KoFd	Jap 11

HOYT, Jerry

COUNTRY: US
BORN: January 29, 1929
GP STARTS: 4
WC POINTS: 0

Psn	No	Grand(s) Prix
Pole:	1	1955 Indy

Year	Team	Grand(s) Prix
1950	KK	Indy 21
1953	KK	Indy r
1954	KK	Indy r
1955	Ste	Indy r

HULME, Denny

COUNTRY: New Zealand
BORN: June 18, 1936
GP STARTS: 112
WC POINTS: 248
WC RECORD: 1965-11/5; 1966-4/18; 1967-1/51; 1968-3/33; 1969-6/20; 1970-4/27; 1971-9/9; 1972-3/39; 1973-6/26; 1974-7/20
WORLD CHAMPION: 1967

Psn	No	Grand(s) Prix
1st:	8	1967 Mon, Ger; 1968 Ita, Can; 1969 Mex; 1972 SA; 1973 Swe; 1974 Arg
2nd:	9	1966 GB; 1967 Fra, GB, Can; 1968 Esp; 1970 SA; 1972 Arg, Aut; 1974 Aut
3rd:	16	1966 Fra, Ita, Mex; 1967 Hol, US, Mex; 1969 SA; 1970 GB, Ger, Mex; 1972 Bel, Ita, Can, US; 1973 Bra, GB
Pole:	1	1973 SA
Fast:	9	1966 Hol; 1967 SA, GB; 1971 Can; 1972 Aut; 1973 Bra, Swe, Fra; 1974 Bel

Year	Team	Grand(s) Prix
1965	BrCl	Mon 8, Fra 4, GB r, Hol 5, Ger r, Ita r
1966	BrCl	Mon r, Bel r
1966	BrRe	Fra 3, GB 2, Hol r, Ger r, Ita 3, US r, Mex 3
1967	BrRe	SA 4, Mon 1, Hol 3, Bel r, Fra 2, GB 2, Ger 1, Can 2, Ita r, US 3, Mex 3
1968	McBR	SA 5
1968	McFd	Esp 2, Mon 5, Bel r, Hol r, Fra 5, GB 4, Ger 7, Ita 1, Can 1, US r, Mex r
1969	McFd	SA 3, Esp 4, Mon 6, Hol 4, Fra 8, GB r, Ger r, Ita 7, Can r, US r, Mex 1
1970	McFd	SA 2, Esp r, Mon 4, Fra 4, GB 3, Ger 3, Aut r, Ita 4, Can r, US 7, Mex 3
1971	McFd	SA 6, Esp 5, Mon 4, Hol 12, Fra r, GB r, Ger r, Aut r, Can 4, US r
1972	McFd	Arg 2, SA 1, Esp r, Mon 15, Bel 3, Fra 7, GB 5, Ger r, Aut 2, Ita 3, Can 3, US 3
1973	McFd	Arg 5, Bra 3, SA 5, Esp 6, Bel 7, Mon 6, Swe 1, Fra 8, GB 3, Hol r, Ger 12, Aut 8, Ita 15, Can 13, US 4
1974	McFd	Arg 1, Bra 12, SA 9, Esp 6, Bel 6, Mon r, Swe r, Hol r, Fra 6, GB 7, Ger dq, Aut 2, Ita 6, Can 6, US r

HUNT, James

COUNTRY: GB
BORN: August 29, 1947
GP STARTS: 92
WC POINTS: 179
WC RECORD: 1973-8/14; 1974-8/15; 1975-4/33; 1976-1/69; 1977-5/40; 1978-13/8
WORLD CHAMPION: 1976

Psn	No	Grand(s) Prix
1st:	10	1975 Hol; 1976 Esp, Fra, Ger, Hol, Can, USE; 1977 GB, USE, Jap
2nd:	6	1973 US; 1975 Arg, Fra, Aut; 1976 SA; 1977 Bra
3rd:	7	1973 Hol; 1974 Swe, Aut, US; 1976 Jap; 1977 Fra; 1978 Fra
Pole:	14	1976 Bra, SA, Esp, Fra, Ger, Aut, Can, USE; 1977 Arg, Bra, SA, GB, Ita, USE
Fast:	8	1973 GB, US; 1975 Arg; 1976 Aut, USE; 1977 Arg, Bra, GB

Year	Team	Grand(s) Prix
1973	MrFd	Mon 9, Fra 6, GB 4, Hol 3, Aut r, Ita dns, Can 7, US 2
1974	MrFd	Arg r, Bra 9
1974	HeFd	SA r, Esp 10, Bel r, Mon r, Swe 3, Hol r, Fra r, GB r, Ger r, Aut 3, Ita r, Can 4, US 3
1975	HeFd	Arg 2, Bra 6, SA r, Esp r, Mon r, Bel r, Swe r, Hol 1, Fra 2, GB 4, Ger r, Aut 2, Ita 5, US 4
1976	McFd	Bra r, SA 2, USW r, Esp 1, Bel r, Mon r, Swe 5, Fra 1, GB dq, Ger 1, Aut 4, Hol 1, Ita r, Can 1, USE 1, Jap 3
1977	McFd	Arg r, Bra 2, SA 4, USW 7, Esp r, Mon r, Bel 7, Swe 12, Fra 3, GB 1, Ger r, Aut r, Hol r, Ita r, USE 1, Can r, Jap 1
1978	McFd	Arg 4, Bra r, SA r, USW r, Mon r, Bel r, Esp 6, Swe 8, Fra 3, GB r, Ger dq, Aut r, Hol 10, Ita r, USE 7, Can r
1979	WoFd	Arg r, Bra r, SA 8, USW r, Esp r, Bel r, Mon r

HURTUBUISE, Jim

COUNTRY: US
BORN: December 5, 1932
GP STARTS: 1
WC POINTS: 0

Year	Team	Grand(s) Prix
1960	Chr	Indy r

HUTCHINSON, Gus

COUNTRY: US
BORN: April 26, 1937
GP STARTS: 1
WC POINTS: 0

Year	Team	Grand(s) Prix
1970	BrFd	US r

ICKX, Jacky

COUNTRY: Belgium
BORN: January 1, 1945
GP STARTS: 116
WC POINTS: 181
WC RECORD: 1967-19/1; 1968-4/27; 1969–2/37; 1970-2/40; 1971-4/19; 1972-4/27; 1973-9/12; 1974-10/12; 1975-16/3; 1979-15/3

Psn	No	Grand(s) Prix
1st:	8	1968 Fra; 1969 Ger, Can; 1970 Aut, Can, Mex; 1971 Hol; 1972 Ger
2nd:	7	1969 GB, Mex; 1970 Ger; 1971 Esp; 1972 Esp, Mon; 1975 Esp
3rd:	10	1968 Bel, GB, Ita; 1969 Fra; 1970 Hol; 1971 Mon; 1972 Arg; 1973 Ger; 1974 Bra, GB
Pole:	13	1968 Ger; 1969 Ger, Can; 1970 Fra, Ger, Ita, US; 1971 Esp, Hol; 1972 Esp, GB, Ger, Ita
Fast:	14	1969 Ger, Can, Mex; 1970 Hol, Ger, Aut, US, Mex; 1971 Esp, Hol, US; 1972 Esp, Ger, Ita

Year	Team	Grand(s) Prix
1966	MatFd	Ger r
1967	CoMa	Ger (r–F2), Ita 6, US r
1968	Fe	SA r, Esp r, Bel 3, Hol 4, Fra 1, GB 3, Ger 4, Ita 3, Can dns, Mex r
1969	BrFd	SA r, Esp 6, Mon r, Hol 5, Fra 3, GB 2, Ger 1, Ita 10, Can 1, US r, Mex 2
1970	Fe	SA r, Esp r, Mon r, Bel 8, Hol 3, Fra r, GB r, Ger 2, Aut 1, Ita r, Can 1, US 4, Mex 1
1971	Fe	SA 8, Esp 2, Mon 3, Hol 1, Fra r, GB r, Ger r, Aut r, Ita r, Can 8, US r
1972	Fe	Arg 3, SA 8, Esp 2, Mon 2, Bel r, Fra 11, GB r, Ger 1, Aut r, Ita r, Can 12, US 5
1973	Fe	Arg 4, Bra 5, SA r, Esp 12, Bel r, Mon r, Swe 6, Fra 5, GB 8
1973	McFd	Ger 3
1973	Fe	Ita 8
1973	WiFd	US 7

1974	LtFd	Arg r, Bra 3, SA r, Esp r, Bel r, Mon r, Swe r, Hol 11, Fra 5, GB 3, Ger 5, Aut r, Ita r, Can 13, US r
1975	LtFd	Arg 8, Bra 9, SA 12, Esp 2, Mon 8, Bel r, Swe 15, Hol r, Fra r
1976	WiFd	Bra 8, SA 16, Esp 7, Fra 10
1976	EnFd	Hol r, Ita 10, Can 13, USE r
1977	EnFd	Mon 10
1978	EnFd	Mon r, Bel 12, Esp r
1979	LiFd	Fra r, GB 6, Ger r, Aut r, Hol 5, Ita r, Can r, USE r

IGLESIAS, Julio

COUNTRY: Argentina
BORN: February 22, 1922
GP STARTS: 1
WC POINTS: 0

Year	Team	Grand(s) Prix
1955	Gor	Arg r

INOUE, Taki

COUNTRY: Japan
BORN: September 5, 1963
GP STARTS: 18
WC POINTS: 0

Year	Team	Grand(s) Prix
1994	SiFd	Jap r
1995	FtHt	Bra r, Arg r, SM r, Esp r, Mon r, Can 9, Fra r, GB r, Ger r, Hun r, Bel 12, Ita 8, Por 15, Eur r, Pac r, Jap 12, Aus r

IRELAND, Innes

COUNTRY: GB
BORN: June 12, 1930
GP STARTS: 50
WC POINTS: 47
WC RECORD: 1959-12/5; 1960-4/18; 1961-6/12; 1962-16/2; 1963-9/6; 1964-12/4

Psn	No	Grand(s) Prix
1st:	1	1961 US
2nd:	2	1960 Hol, US
3rd:	1	1960 GB
Fast:	1	1960 Bel

Year	Team	Grand(s) Prix
1959	LoCl	Hol 4, Fra r, Ger r, Por r, Ita r, US 5
1960	LoCl	Arg 6, Mon 9, Hol 2, Bel r, Fra 7, GB 3, Por 6, US 2
1961	LoCl	Mon dns, Bel r, Fra 4, GB 10, Ger r, Ita r, US 1
1962	LoCl	Hol r, Mon r, Bel r, Fra r, GB 16, Ita r, US 8, SA 5
1963	LtBR	Mon r
1963	BRBR	Bel r, Hol 4, Fra 9, GB dq
1963	LtBR	Ger r
1963	BRBR	Ita 4
1964	LtBR	Mon dns
1964	BRBR	Bel 10, Fra r, GB 10, Aut 5, Ita 5, US r, Mex 12
1965	LtBR	Bel 13, Fra r, GB r, Hol 10, Ita 9, US r, Mex dns
1966	BRM	US r, Mex r

IRVINE, Eddie

COUNTRY: GB
BORN: November 10, 1965
GP STARTS: 96
WC POINTS: 173
WC RECORD: 1993-20/1; 1994-14/6; 1995-12/10; 1996-10/11; 1997-7/24; 1998-4/47; 1999-2/74

Psn	No	Grand(s) Prix
1st:	4	1999 Aus, Aut, Ger, Mal
2nd:	6	1997 Arg; 1998 Fra, Ita, Jap; 1999 Mon, GB
3rd:	14	1995 Can; 1996 Aus; 1997 SM, Mon, Fra, Jap; 1998 Arg, SM, Mon, Can, GB; 1999 Can, Hun, Jap
Fast:	1	1999 Can

Year	Team	Grand(s) Prix
1993	JoFd	Jap 6, Aus r
1994	JoFd	Bra r, Esp 6, Can r, Fra r, GB dns, Ger r, Hun r, Bel 13, Ita r, Por 7, Eur 4, Jap 5, Aus r
1995	JoPe	Bra r, Arg r, SM 8, Esp 5, Mon r, Can 3, Fra 9, GB r, Ger 9, Hun 13, Bel r, Ita r, Por 10, Eur 6, Pac 11, Jap 4, Aus r
1996	Fe	Aus 3, Bra 7, Arg 5, Eur r, SM 4, Mon 7, Esp r, Can r, Fra r, GB r, Ger r, Hun r, Bel r, Ita r, Por 5, Jap r
1997	Fe	Aus r, Bra 16, Arg 2, SM 3, Mon 3, Esp 12, Can r, Fra 3, GB r, Ger r, Hun 9, Bel 10, Ita 8, Aut r, Lux r, Jap 3, Eur 5
1998	Fe	Aus 4, Bra 8, Arg 3, SM 3, Esp r, Mon 3, Can 3, Fra 2, GB 3, Aut 4, Ger 8, Hun r, Bel r, Ita 2, Lux 4, Jap 2

1999	Fe	Aus 1, Bra 5, SM r, Mon 2, Esp 4, Can 3, Fra 6, GB 2, Aut 1, Ger 1, Hun 3, Bel 4, Ita 6, Eur 7, Mal 1, Jap 3

IRWIN, Chris

COUNTRY: GB
BORN: June 27, 1942
GP STARTS: 10
WC POINTS: 2
WC RECORD: 1967-16/2

Year	Team	Grand(s) Prix
1966	BrCl	GB 7
1967	LtBR	Hol 7
1967	BRM	Bel r, Fra 5, GB 7, Ger 7, Can r, Ita r, US r, Mex r

JABOUILLE, Jean-Pierre

COUNTRY: France
BORN: October 1, 1942
GP STARTS: 49
WC POINTS: 21
WC RECORD: 1978-17/3; 1979-13/9; 1980-8/9

Psn	No	Grand(s) Prix
1st:	2	1979 Fra; 1980 Aut
Pole:	6	1979 SA, Fra, Ger, Ita; 1980 Bra, SA

Year	Team	Grand(s) Prix
1975	TyFd	Fra 12
1977	Re	GB r, Hol r, Ita r, USE r
1978	Re	SA r, USW r, Mon 10, Bel uc, Esp 13, Swe r, Fra r, GB r, Ger r, Aut r, Hol r, Ita r, USE 4, Can 12
1979	Re	Arg r, Bra 10, SA r, USW dns, Esp r, Bel r, Mon 8, Fra 1, GB r, Ger r, Aut r, Hol r, Ita 14, Can r, USE r
1980	Re	Arg r, Bra r, SA r, USW 10, Bel r, Mon r, Fra r, GB r, Ger r, Aut 1, Hol r, Ita r, Can r
1981	LiMat	SM uc, Bel r, Esp r

JACKSON, Jimmy

COUNTRY: US
BORN: July 25, 1910
GP STARTS: 1
WC POINTS: 0

Year	Team	Grand(s) Prix
1950	KK	Indy r

JAMES, Joe

COUNTRY: US
BORN: May 23, 1925
GP STARTS: 2
WC POINTS: 0

Year	Team	Grand(s) Prix
1951	Wa	Indy r
1952	KK	Indy 13

JAMES, John

COUNTRY: GB
BORN: May 10, 1914
GP STARTS: 1
WC POINTS: 0

Year	Team	Grand(s) Prix
1951	Mas	GB r

JARIER, Jean-Pierre

COUNTRY: France
BORN: July 10, 1946
GP STARTS: 134
WC POINTS: 31.5
WC RECORD: 1974-14/6; 1975-18/1.5; 1977-19/1; 1979-10/14; 1980-10/6; 1982-20/3

Psn	No	Grand(s) Prix
3rd:	3	1974 Mon; 1979 SA, GB
Pole:	3	1975 Arg, Bra; 1978 Can
Fast:	3	1975 Bra; 1976 Bra; 1978 USE

Year	Team	Grand(s) Prix
1971	MrFd	Ita uc
1973	MrFd	Arg r, Bra r, SA uc, Bel r, Mon r, Swe r, Fra r, Aut r, Can uc, US 11
1974	ShFd	Arg r, Bra r, Esp uc, Bel 13, Mon 3, Swe 5, Hol r, Fra 12, GB r, Ger 8, Aut 8, Ita r, Can r, US 10
1975	ShFd	Arg dns, Bra r, SA r, Esp 4, Mon r, Bel r, Swe r, Hol r, Fra 8, GB 14, Ger r
1975	ShMat	Aut r, Ita r
1975	ShFd	US r
1976	ShFd	Bra r, SA r, USW 7, Esp r, Bel 9, Mon 8, Swe 12, Fra 12, GB 9, Ger 11, Aut r, Hol 10, Ita 19, Can 18, USE 10, Jap 10
1977	PkFt	USW 6, Mon 11, Bel 11, Swe 8, Fra r, GB 8, Ger r, Aut 14, Hol r, Ita r
1977	ShFdt	USE 9

1977	LiMat	Jap r
1978	ATFd	Arg 12, SA 8, USW 11
1978	LtFd	USE 15, Can r
1979	TyFd	Arg r, Bra dns, SA 3, USW 6, Esp 5, Bel 11, Mon r, Fra 5, GB 3, Hol r, Ita 6, Can r, USE r
1980	TyFd	Arg r, Bra 12, SA 7, USW r, Bel 5, Mon r, Fra 14, GB 5, Ger 15, Aut r, Hol 5, Ita 13, Can 7, USE uc
1981	LiMat	USW r, Bra 7
1981	OsFd	GB 8, Ger 8, Aut 10, Hol r, Ita 9, Can r, US r
1982	OsFd	SA r, Bra 9, USW r, SM 4, Bel r, US r, Can r, Hol 14, GB r, Fra r, Ger r, Swi r, Ita r, Caesar's Palace dns
1983	LiFd	Bra r, USW r, Fra 9, SM r, Mon r, Bel r, US r, Can r, GB 10, Ger 8, Aut 7, Hol r, Ita 9, Eur r, SA 10

JOHANSSON, Stefan

COUNTRY: Sweden
BORN: September 8, 1956
GP STARTS: 79
WC POINTS: 88
WC RECORD: 1984-16/3; 1985-7/26; 1986-5/23; 1987-6/30; 1989-11/6

Psn	No	Grand(s) Prix
2nd:	4	1985 Can, US; 1987 Bel, Ger
3rd:	8	1986 Bel, Aut, Ita, Aus; 1987 Bra, Esp, Jap; 1989 Por

Year	Team	Grand(s) Prix
1983	SpHo	GB r, Ger r, Aut 12, Hol 7, Ita r, Eur 14
1984	TyFd	GB dq, Ger dq, Hol dq
1984	ToHt	Ita 4, Eur r, Por 11
1985	TyFd	Bra 7
1985	Fe	Bra 7
1986	Fe	Bra r, Esp r, SM 4, Mon 10, Bel 3, Can r, US r, Fra r, GB r, Ger 11, Hun 4, Aut 3, Ita 3, Por 6, Mex 12, Aus 3
1987	McTG	Bra 3, SM 4, Bel 2, Mon r, US 7, Fra 8, GB r, Ger 2, Hun r, Aut 7, Ita 6, Por 5, Esp 3, Mex r, Jap 3, Aus r
1988	LiJu	Bra 9, Mon r, Mex 10, Can r, US r, Hun r, Bel 11, Por r, Esp r, Aus 9
1989	OnFd	Mex r, US r, Can dq, Fra 5, Ger r, Hun r, Bel 8, Por 3
1991	FtPo	Can r

JOHNSON, Eddie

COUNTRY: US
BORN: February 10, 1919
GP STARTS: 7
WC POINTS: 0

Year	Team	Grand(s) Prix
1952	Trevis	Indy 16
1955	Trevis	Indy 13
1956	Ku	Indy 15
1957	KK	Indy r
1958	KK	Indy 9
1959	KK	Indy 8
1960	Trevis	Indy 6

JOHNSON, Leslie

COUNTRY: GB
BORN: March 22, 1912
GP STARTS: 1
WC POINTS: 0

Year	Team	Grand(s) Prix
1950	ERA	GB r

JOHNSTONE, Bruce

COUNTRY: South Africa
BORN: January 30, 1937
GP STARTS: 1
WC POINTS: 0

Year	Team	Grand(s) Prix
1962	BRM	SA 9

JONES, Alan

COUNTRY: Australia
BORN: November 2, 1946
GP STARTS: 116
WC POINTS: 199 (206)
WC RECORD: 1975-17/2; 1976-14/7; 1977-7/22; 1978-11/11; 1979-3/40; 1980-1/67; 1981-3/46; 1986-12/4
WORLD CHAMPION: 1980

Psn	No	Grand(s) Prix
1st:	12	1977 Aut; 1979 Ger, Aut, Hol, Can; 1980 Arg, Fra, GB, Can, USE; 1981 USW, US
2nd:	7	1978 USE; 1980 Bel, Aut, Ita; 1981 Bra, Mon, Ita

3rd:	5	1977 Ita; 1979 USW; 1980 Bra, Ger; 1981 Hol
Pole:	6	1979 GB, Can, USE; 1980 Arg, Bel, Ger
Fast:	13	1978 USW, Can; 1979 Can; 1980 Arg, Fra, Ger, Ita, USE; 1981 USW, Mon, Esp, Ger, Hol

Year	Team	Grand(s) Prix
1975	HeFd	Esp r, Mon r, Bel r, Swe 11
1975	HiFd	Hol 13, Fra 16, GB 10, Ger 5
1976	SuFd	USW uc, Esp 9, Bel 5, Mon r, Swe 13, Fra r, GB 5, Ger 10, Aut r, Hol 8, Ita 12, Can 16, USE 8, Jap 4
1977	ShFd	USW r, Esp r, Mon 6, Bel 5, Swe 17, Fra r, GB 7, Ger r, Aut 1, Hol r, Ita 3, USE r, Can 4, Jap 4
1978	WiFd	Arg r, Bra 11, SA 4, USW 7, Mon r, Bel 10, Esp 8, Swe r, Fra 5, GB r, Ger r, Aut r, Hol r, Ita 13, USE 2, Can 9
1979	WiFd	Arg 9, Bra r, SA r, USW 3, Esp r, Bel r, Mon r, Fra 4, GB r, Ger 1, Aut 1, Hol 1, Ita 9, Can 1, USE r
1980	WiFd	Arg 1, Bra 3, SA r, USW r, Bel 2, Mon r, Fra 1, GB 1, Ger 3, Aut 2, Hol 11, Ita 2, Can 1, USE 1
1981	WiFd	USW 1, Bra 2, Arg 4, SM 12, Bel r, Mon 2, Esp 7, Fra 17, GB r, Ger 11, Aut 4, Hol 3, Ita 2, Can r, US 1
1983	ArFd	USW r
1985	LlHt	Ita r, Eur r, SA dns, Aus r
1986	LlHt	Bra r, Esp r
1986	LoFd	SM r, Mon r, Bel 11, Can 10, US r, Fra r, GB r, Ger 9, Hun r, Aut 4, Ita 6, Por r, Mex r, Aus r

KARCH, Oswald

COUNTRY: Germany
BORN: March 6, 1917
GP STARTS: 1
WC POINTS: 0

Year	Team	Grand(s) Prix
1953	Ver	Ger r

KATAYAMA, Ukyo

COUNTRY: Japan
BORN: May 29, 1963
GP STARTS: 95
WC POINTS: 5
WC RECORD: 1994-17/5

Year	Team	Grand(s) Prix
1992	LaLm	SA 12, Mex 12, Bra 9, SM r, Can r, Fra r, GB r, Ger r, Hun r, Bel 17, Ita 9, Por r, Jap 11, Aus r
1993	TyYa	SA r, Bra r, Eur r, SM r, Esp r, Mon r, Can 17, Fra r, GB 13, Ger r, Hun 10, Bel 15, Ita 14, Por r, Jap r, Aus r
1994	TyYa	Bra 5, Pac r, SM 5, Mon r, Esp r, Can r, Fra r, GB 6, Ger r, Hun r, Bel r, Ita r, Por r, Eur 7, Jap r, Aus r
1995	TyYa	Bra r, Arg 8, SM r, Esp r, Mon r, Can r, Fra r, GB r, Ger 7, Hun r, Bel r, Ita uc, Por r, Pac 14, Jap r, Aus r
1996	TyYa	Aus 11, Bra 9, Arg r, Eur dq, SM r, Mon r, Esp r, Can r, Fra r, GB r, Ger r, Hun 7, Bel 8, Ita 10, Por 12, Jap r
1997	MiHt	Aus r, Bra 18, Arg r, SM 11, Mon 10, Esp r, Can r, Fra 11, GB r, Ger r, Hun 10, Bel 14, Ita r, Aut 11, Lux r, Jap r, Eur 17

KAVANAGH, Ken

COUNTRY: Australia
BORN: December 12, 1923
GP STARTS: 1
WC POINTS: 0

Year	Team	Grand(s) Prix
1958	Mas	Bel r

KEEGAN, Rupert

COUNTRY: GB
BORN: February 25, 1955
GP STARTS: 25
WC POINTS: 0

Year	Team	Grand(s) Prix
1977	HeFd	Esp r, Mon 12, Bel r, Swe 13, Fra 10, GB r, Ger r, Aut 7, Hol r, Ita 9, USE 8, Can r
1978	SuFd	Arg r, Bra r, SA r, USW dns, Mon r, Esp 11, Fra r, Hol dns
1980	WiFd	GB 11, Aut 15, Ita 11, USE 9
1982	MrFd	Aut r, Swi r, Caesar's Palace 12

KEIZAN, Eddie

COUNTRY: South Africa
BORN: September 12, 1944
GP STARTS: 3
WC POINTS: 0

Year	Team	Grand(s) Prix
1973	TyFd	SA uc
1974	TyFd	SA 14
1975	LtFd	SA 13

KELLER, Al

COUNTRY: US
BORN: April 11, 1920
GP STARTS: 5
WC POINTS: 0

Year	Team	Grand(s) Prix
1955	KK	Indy r
1956	KK	Indy 14
1957	KK	Indy r
1958	KK	Indy 11
1959	Ku	Indy r

KELLY, Joe

COUNTRY: Ireland
BORN: March 13, 1913
GP STARTS: 2
WC POINTS: 0

Year	Team	Grand(s) Prix
1950	Alta	GB uc
1951	Alta	GB uc

KESSEL, Loris

COUNTRY: Switzerland
BORN: April 1, 1950
GP STARTS: 3
WC POINTS: 0

Year	Team	Grand(s) Prix
1976	BrFd	Bel 12, Swe r, Aut r

KINNUNEN, Leo

COUNTRY: Finland
BORN: August 5, 1943
GP STARTS: 1
WC POINTS: 0

Year	Team	Grand(s) Prix
1974	SuFd	Swe r

KLADIS, Danny

COUNTRY: US
BORN: February 10, 1917
GP STARTS: 1
WC POINTS: 0

Year	Team	Grand(s) Prix
1954	Indy r	

KLENK, Hans

COUNTRY: Germany
BORN: October 18, 1919
GP STARTS: 1
WC POINTS: 0

Year	Team	Grand(s) Prix
1952	Ver	Ger 11

KLING, Karl

COUNTRY: Germany
BORN: September 16, 1910
GP STARTS: 11
WC POINTS: 17
WC RECORD: 1954-5/12; 1955-11/5

Psn	No	Grand(s) Prix
2nd:	1	1954 Fra
3rd:	1	1955 GB
Fast:	1	1954 Ger

Year	Team	Grand(s) Prix
1954	Me	Fra 2, GB 7, Ger 4, Swi r, Ita r, Esp 5
1955	Me	Arg r, Bel r, Hol r, GB 3, Ita r

KLODWIG, Ernst

COUNTRY: Germany
BORN: May 23, 1903
GP STARTS: 2
WC POINTS: 0

Year	Team	Grand(s) Prix
1952	BMW	Ger 12
1953	BMW	Ger uc

KOINIGG, Helmut

COUNTRY: Austria
BORN: November 3, 1948
GP STARTS: 2
WC POINTS: 0

Year	Team	Grand(s) Prix
1974	SuFd	Can 10, US r

KRAUSE, Rudolf

COUNTRY: Germany
BORN: March 30, 1907
GP STARTS: 2
WC POINTS: 0

Year	Team	Grand(s) Prix
1952	BMW	Ger r
1953	BMW	Ger 14

la CAZE, Robert

COUNTRY: Morocco
BORN: February 26, 1917
GP STARTS: 1
WC POINTS: 0

Year	Team	Grand(s) Prix
1958	CoCl	Mor 14

LAFFITE, Jacques

COUNTRY: France
BORN: November 21, 1943
GP STARTS: 176
WC POINTS: 228
WC RECORD: 1975-12/6; 1976-7/20; 1977-10/18; 1978-8/19; 1979-4/36; 1980-4/34; 1981-4/44; 1982-17/5; 1983-11/11; 1984-14/5; 1985-9/16; 1986-8/14

Psn	No	Grand(s) Prix
1st:	6	1977 Swe; 1979 Arg, Bra; 1980 Ger; 1981 Aut, Can
2nd:	10	1975 Ger; 1976 Aut; 1977 Hol; 1979 Bel; 1980 SA, Mon; 1981 Bel, Esp; 1985 Aus; 1986 US
3rd:	16	1976 Bel, Ita; 1978 Esp, Ger; 1979 Ger, Aut, Hol; 1980 Fra, Hol; 1981 Mon, GB, Ger; 1982 Aut; 1985 GB, Ger; 1986 Bra
Pole:	7	1976 Ita; 1979 Arg, Bra, Esp, Bel; 1980 Fra; 1981 Esp
Fast:	6	1977 Esp; 1979 Arg, Bra; 1980 Bel; 1981 Aut; 1985 Eur

Year	Team	Grand(s) Prix
1974	WiFd	Ger r, Aut uc, Ita r, Can 15, US r
1975	WiFd	Arg r, Bra 11, SA uc, Bel r, Hol r, Fra 11, GB r, Ger 2, Aut r, Ita r, US dns
1976	LiMat	Bra r, SA r, USW 4, Esp 12, Bel 3, Mon 12, Swe 4, Fra 14, GB dq, Ger r, Aut 2, Hol r, Ita 3, Can r, USE r, Jap 7
1977	LiMat	Arg uc, Bra r, SA r, USW 9, Esp 7, Mon 7, Bel r, Swe 1, Fra 8, GB 6, Ger r, Aut r, Hol 2, Ita 8, USE 7, Can r, Jap 5
1978	LiMat	Arg 16, Bra 9, SA 5, USW 5, Mon r, Bel 5, Esp 3, Swe 7, Fra 7, GB 10, Ger 3, Aut 5, Hol 8, Ita 4, USE 11, Can r
1979	LiFd	Arg 1, Bra 1, SA r, USW r, Esp r, Bel 2, Mon r, Fra 8, GB r, Ger 3, Aut 3, Hol 3, Ita r, Can r, USE r
1980	LiFd	Arg r, Bra r, SA 2, USW r, Bel 11, Mon 2, Fra 3, GB r, Ger 1, Aut 4, Hol 3, Ita 9, Can 8, USE 5
1981	LiMat	USW r, Bra 6, Arg r, SM r, Bel 2, Mon 3, Esp 2, Fra r, GB 3, Ger 3, Aut 1, Hol r, Ita r, Can 1, US 6
1982	LiMat	SA r, Bra r, USW r, Bel 9, Mon r, US 6, Can r, Hol r, GB r, Fra 14, Ger r, Aut 3, Swi r, Ita r, Caesar's Palace r
1983	WiFd	Bra 4, USW 4, Fra 6, SM 7, Mon r, Bel 6, US 5, Can r, GB 12, Ger 6, Aut r, Hol r
1983	WiHo	SA r
1984	WiHo	Bra r, SA r, Bel r, SM r, Fra 8, Mon 8, Can r, Detroit 5, Dallas 4, GB r, Ger r, Aut r, Hol r, Ita r, Eur r, Por 14
1985	LiRe	Bra 6, Por r, SM r, Mon 6, Can 8, US 12, Fra r, GB 3, Ger 3, Aut r, Hol r, Ita r, Bel 11, Eur r, Aus 2
1986	LiRe	Bra 3, Esp r, SM r, Mon 6, Bel 5, Can 7, US 2, Fra 6, GB r

LAGORCE, Franck

COUNTRY: France
BORN: September 1, 1968
GP STARTS: 2
WC POINTS: 0

Year	Team	Grand(s) Prix
1994	LiRe	Jap r, Aus 11

LAMMERS, Jan

COUNTRY: Holland
BORN: June 6,1956
GP STARTS: 23
WC POINTS: 0

Year	Team	Grand(s) Prix
1979	ShFd	Arg r, Bra 14, SA r, USW r, Esp 12, Bel 10, Fra 18, GB 11, Ger 10, Aut r, Hol r, Can 9
1980	ATFd	USW r, Bel r, Mon uc
1980	EnFd	Ger 14, Can 12, USE r
1981	ATFd	USW r, Arg 12
1982	ThFd	Hol r
1992	Mall	Jap r, Aus 12

LAMY, Pedro

COUNTRY: Portugal
BORN: March 20, 1972
GP STARTS: 32
WC POINTS: 1
WC RECORD: 1995-17/1

Year	Team	Grand(s) Prix
1993	LtFd	Ita 11, Por r, Jap 13, Aus r
1994	LoMH	Bra 10, Pac 8, SM r, Mon 11
1995	MiFd	Hun 9, Bel 10, Ita r, Por r, Eur 9, Pac 13, Jap 11, Aus 6
1996	MiFd	Aus r, Bra 10, Arg r, Eur 12, SM 9, Mon r, Esp r, Can r, Fra 12, GB r, Ger 12, Hun r, Bel 10, Ita r, Por 16, Jap 12

LANDI, Chico

COUNTRY: Brazil
BORN: July 14, 1907
GP STARTS: 6
WC POINTS: 1.5
WC RECORD: 1956-25/1.5

Year	Team	Grand(s) Prix
1951	Fe	Ita r
1952	Mas	Hol 9, Ita 8
1953	Mas	Swi r, Ita r
1956	Mas	Arg 4

LANG, Hermann

COUNTRY: Germany
BORN: April 6, 1909
GP STARTS: 2
WC POINTS: 2
WC RECORD: 1953-13/2

Year	Team	Grand(s) Prix
1953	Mas	Swi 5
1954	Me	Ger r

LARINI, Nicola

COUNTRY: Italy
BORN: March 19, 1964
GP STARTS: 49
WC POINTS: 7
WC RECORD: 1994-14/6; 1997-19/1;

Psn	No	Grand(s) Prix
2nd:	1	1994 SM

Year	Team	Grand(s) Prix
1987	CiFd	Esp r
1988	OsAl	Mon 9, US r, Fra r, GB 19, Ger r, Bel r, Ita r, Por 12, Esp r, Jap r
1989	OsFd	Bra dq, SM 12, Can r, GB r, Ita r, Esp r, Jap r, Aus r
1990	LiFd	US r, Bra 11, SM 10, Mon r, Can r, Mex 16, Fra 14, GB 10, Ger 10, Hun 11, Bel 14, Ita 11, Por 10, Esp 7, Jap 7, Aus 10
1991	Lm	US 7, Ger r, Hun 16, Ita 16, Aus r
1992	Fe	Jap 12, Aus 11
1994	Fe	Pac r, SM 2
1997	SaPe	Aus 6, Bra 11, Arg r, SM 7, Mon r

LARRAURI, Oscar

COUNTRY: Argentina
BORN: August 19, 1954
GP STARTS: 8
WC POINTS: 0

Year	Team	Grand(s) Prix
1988	EBFd	Bra r, Mon r, Mex 13, Can r, US r, Fra r, Ger 16, Aus r

LARROUSSE, Gerard

COUNTRY: France
BORN: May 23, 1940
GP STARTS: 1
WC POINTS: 0

Year	Team	Grand(s) Prix
1974	BrFd	Bel r

LARSON, Jud

COUNTRY: US
BORN: January 21, 1923
GP STARTS: 2
WC POINTS: 0

Year	Team	Grand(s) Prix
1958	Wa	Indy 8
1959	KK	Indy r

LAUDA, Niki

COUNTRY: Austria
BORN: February 22, 1949
GP STARTS: 171
WC POINTS: 420.5
WC RECORD: 1973-17/2; 1974-4/38; 1975-1/64.5; 1976-2/68; 1977-1/72; 1978-4/44; 1979-14/4; 1982-5/30; 1983-10/12; 1984-1/72; 1985-10/14
WORLD CHAMPION: 1975, 1977, 1984

Psn	No	Grand(s) Prix
1st:	25	1974 Esp, Hol; 1975 Mon, Bel, Swe, Fra, US; 1976 Bra, SA, Bel, Mon, GB; 1977 SA, Ger, Hol; 1978 Swe, Ita; 1982 USW, GB; 1984 SA, Fra, GB, Aut, Ita; 1985 Hol
2nd:	20	1974 Arg, Bel, Fra; 1975 Hol; 1976 USW, Esp; 1977 USW, Mon, Bel, GB, Aut, Ita; 1978 Arg, Mon, GB; 1983 USW; 1984 Can, Ger, Hol, Por
3rd:	9	1975 Ger, Ita; 1976 Swe, USE; 1977 Bra; 1978 Bra, Hol; 1982 Swi; 1983 Bra
Pole:	24	1974 SA, Esp, Mon, Hol, Fra, GB, Ger, Aut, Ita; 1975 Esp, Mon, Bel, Hol, Fra, Ger, Aut, Ita, US; 1976 Bel, Mon, GB; 1977 USW, Aut; 1978 SA
Fast:	24	1974 Esp, GB, Can; 1975 Swe, Hol; 1976 SA, Bel, Fra, GB; 1977 USW, Ger, Hol; 1978 Mon, Swe, GB, Hol; 1982 USW; 1983 USW; 1984 Dallas, GB, Aut, Ita, Por; 1985 Ger

Year	Team	Grand(s) Prix
1971	MrFd	Aut r
1972	MrFd	Arg 11, SA 7, Esp r, Mon 16, Bel 12, Fra r, GB 9, Ger r, Aut 10, Ita 13, Can dq, US uc
1973	BRM	Arg r, Bra 8, SA r, Esp r, Bel 5, Mon r, Swe 13, Fra 9, GB 12, Hol r, Ger r, Aut dns, Ita r, Can r, US r
1974	Fe	Arg 2, Bra r, SA 16, Esp 1, Bel 2, Mon r, Swe r, Hol 1, Fra 2, GB 5, Ger r, Aut r, Ita r, Can r, US r
1975	Fe	Arg 6, Bra 5, SA 5, Esp r, Mon 1, Bel 1, Swe 1, Hol 2, Fra 1, GB 8, Ger 3, Aut 6, Ita 3, US 1
1976	Fe	Bra 1, SA 1, USW 2, Esp 2, Bel 1, Mon 1, Swe 3, Fra r, GB 1, Ger r, Ita 4, Can 8, USE 3, Jap r
1977	Fe	Arg r, Bra 3, SA 1, USW 2, Esp dns, Mon 2, Bel 2, Swe r, Fra 5, GB 2, Ger 1, Aut 2, Hol 1, Ita 2, USE 4
1978	BrAl	Arg 2, Bra 3, SA r, USW r, Mon 2, Bel r, Esp r, Swe 1, Fra r, GB 2, Ger r, Aut r, Hol 3, Ita 1, USE r, Can r
1979	BrAl	Arg r, Bra r, SA 6, USW r, Esp r, Bel r, Mon r, Fra r, GB r, Ger r, Aut r, Hol r, Ita 4
1982	McFd	SA 4, Bra r, USW 1, Bel dq, Mon r, US r, Can r, Hol 4, GB 1, Fra 8, Ger dns, Aut 5, Swi 3, Ita r, Caesar's Palace r
1983	McFd	Bra 3, USW 2, Fra r, SM r, Bel r, US r, Can r, GB 6, Ger dq, Aut 6
1983	McTG	Hol r, Ita r, Eur r, SA 11
1984	McTG	Bra r, SA 1, Bel r, SM r, Fra 1, Mon r, Can 2, Detroit r, Dallas r, GB 1, Ger 2, Aut 1, Hol 2, Ita 1, Eur 4, Por 2
1985	McTG	Bra r, Por r, SM 4, Mon r, Can r, US r, Fra r, GB r, Ger 5, Aut r, Hol 1, Ita r, SA r, Aus r

LAURENT, Roger

COUNTRY: Belgium
BORN: February 21, 1913
GP STARTS: 2
WC POINTS: 0

Year	Team	Grand(s) Prix
1952	HWM	Bel 12
1952	Fe	Ger 6

LAVAGGI, Giovanni

COUNTRY: Italy
BORN: February 18, 1958
GP STARTS: 7
WC POINTS: 0

Year	Team	Grand(s) Prix
1995	PaFd	Ger r, Hun r, Bel r, Ita r
1996	MiFd	Ger dnq, Hun 10, Bel dnq, Ita r, Por 15, Jap dnq

LAWRENCE, Chris

COUNTRY: GB
BORN: July 27, 1933
GP STARTS: 2
WC POINTS: 0

Year	Team	Grand(s) Prix
1966	CoFe	GB 11, Ger r

LECLERE, Michel

COUNTRY: France
BORN: March 18, 1946
GP STARTS: 7
WC POINTS: 0

Year	Team	Grand(s) Prix
1975	TyFd	US r
1976	WiFd	SA 13, Esp 10, Bel 11, Mon 11, Swe r, Fra 13
1962	LoCl	SA 6

LEDERLE, Neville

COUNTRY: South Africa
BORN: September 25, 1938
GP STARTS: 1
WC POINTS: 1
WC RECORD: 1962-18/1

Year	Team	Grand(s) Prix
1962	LoCl	SA 6

LEES, Geoff

COUNTRY: GB
BORN: May 1, 1951
GP STARTS: 5
WC POINTS: 0

Year	Team	Grand(s) Prix
1979	TyFd	Ger 7
1980	ShFd	SA 13
1980	EnFd	Hol r
1982	ThFd	Can r
1982	LtFd	Fra 12

LEGAT, Arthur

COUNTRY: Belgium
BORN: November 1, 1898
GP STARTS: 2
WC POINTS: 0

Year	Team	Grand(s) Prix
1952	Ver	Bel 13
1953	Ver	Bel r

LEHTO, JJ

COUNTRY: Finland
BORN: January 31, 1966
GP STARTS: 62
WC POINTS: 10
WC RECORD: 1991-12/4; 1993-13/5; 1994-24/1

Psn	No	Grand(s) Prix
3rd:	1	1991 SM

Year	Team	Grand(s) Prix
1989	OnFd	Esp r, Aus r
1990	OnFd	SM 12, Mon r, Can r, Mex r, Ger r
1991	DaJu	US r, Bra r, SM 3, Mon 11, Can r, Mex r, Fra r, GB 13, Ger r, Hun r, Bel r, Ita r, Por r, Esp 8, Jap r, Aus 12
1992	DaFe	SA r, Mex 8, Bra 8, Esp r, SM 11, Mon 9, Can 9, Fra 9, GB 13, Ger 10, Bel 7, Ita 11, Por r, Jap 9, Aus r
1993	SaIl	SA 5, Bra r, Eur r, SM 4, Esp r, Mon r, Can 7, Fra r, GB 8, Ger r, Hun r, Bel 9, Ita r, Por 7, Jap 8, Aus r
1994	BeFd	SM r, Mon 7, Esp r, Can 6, Ita 9, Por r
1994	SaMe	Jap r, Aus 10

LEONI, Lamberto

COUNTRY: Italy
BORN: May 24, 1953
GP STARTS: 1
WC POINTS: 0

Year	Team	Grand(s) Prix
1978	EnFd	Arg r

LESTON, Les

COUNTRY: GB
BORN: December 16, 1920
GP STARTS: 2
WC POINTS: 0

Year	Team	Grand(s) Prix
1956	Con	Ita r
1957	BRM	GB r

LEVEGH, Pierre

COUNTRY: France
BORN: December 22, 1905
GP STARTS: 6
WC POINTS: 0

Year	Team	Grand(s) Prix
1950	Ta	Bel 7, Fra r, Ita r
1951	Ta	Bel 8, Ger 9, Ita r

LEVRETT, Bayliss

COUNTRY: US
BORN: February 14, 1913
GP STARTS: 1
WC POINTS: 0

Year	Team	Grand(s) Prix
1950	Ada	Indy r

LEWIS, Jack

COUNTRY: GB
BORN: November 1, 1936
GP STARTS: 9
WC POINTS: 3
WC RECORD: 1961-13/3

Year	Team	Grand(s) Prix
1961	CoCl	Bel 9, Fra r, GB r, Ger 9, Ita 4
1962	CoCl	Hol 10, Fra r, GB 10, Ger r

LEWIS-EVANS , Stuart

COUNTRY: GB
BORN: April 20, 1930
GP STARTS: 14
WC POINTS: 16
WC RECORD: 1957-12/5; 1958-9/11

Psn	No	Grand(s) Prix
3rd:	2	1958 Bel, Por
Pole:	2	1957 Ita; 1958 Hol

Year	Team	Grand(s) Prix
1957	Con	Mon 4
1957	Va	Fra r, GB 7, Ger r, Pescara 5, Ita r
1958	Va	Mon r, Hol r, Bel 3, Fra 13, GB 4, Por 3, Ita r, Mor r

LIGIER, Guy

COUNTRY: France
BORN: July 12, 1930
GP STARTS: 12
WC POINTS: 1
WC RECORD: 1967-19/1

Year	Team	Grand(s) Prix
1966	CoMa	Mon uc, Bel uc, Fra uc, GB 10, Hol 9
1967	CoMa	Bel 10, Fra uc
1967	BrRe	GB 10, Ger 6, Ita r, US r, Mex 11

LINDEN, Andy

COUNTRY: US
BORN: April 5, 1922
GP STARTS: 7
WC POINTS: 6
WC RECORD: 1951-12/3; 1957-18/3

Year	Team	Grand(s) Prix
1951	Sher	Indy 4
1952	KK	Indy r
1953	Ste	Indy r
1954	Nich	Indy r
1955	KK	Indy 6
1956	KK	Indy r
1957	KK	Indy 5

LIPPI, Roberto

COUNTRY: Italy
BORN: October 17, 1926
GP STARTS: 1
WC POINTS: 0

Year	Team	Grand(s) Prix
1961	dTOs	Ita r

LOMBARDI, Lella

COUNTRY: Italy
BORN: March 26, 1943
GP STARTS: 12
WC POINTS: 0.5
WC RECORD: 1975-21/0.5

Year	Team	Grand(s) Prix
1975	MrFd	SA r, Esp 6, Bel r, Swe r, Hol 14, Fra 18, GB r, Ger 7, Aut 17, Ita r
1975	WiFd	US dns
1976	MrFd	Bra 14
1976	BrFd	Aut 12

LOOF, Ernst

COUNTRY: Germany
BORN: July 4, 1907
GP STARTS: 1
WC POINTS: 0

Year	Team	Grand(s) Prix
1953	Ver	Ger r

LOUVEAU, Henri

COUNTRY: France
BORN: January 25, 1910
GP STARTS: 2
WC POINTS: 0

Year	Team	Grand(s) Prix
1950	Ta	Ita r
1951	Ta	Swi r

LOVE, John

COUNTRY: Zimbabwe
BORN: December 7, 1924
GP STARTS: 9
WC POINTS: 6
WC RECORD: 1967-11/6

Psn	No	Grand(s) Prix
2nd:	1	1967 SA

Year	Team	Grand(s) Prix
1962	CoCl	SA 8
1963	CoCl	SA 9
1965	CoCl	SA r
1967	CoCl	SA 2
1968	BrRe	SA 9
1969	LtFd	SA r
1970	LtFd	SA 8
1971	MrFd	SA r
1972	SuFd	SA 16

LOVELY, Pete

COUNTRY: US
BORN: April 11, 1926
GP STARTS: 7
WC POINTS: 0

Year	Team	Grand(s) Prix
1960	CoFe	US 11
1969	LtFd	Can 7, US r, Mex 9
1970	LtFd	GB uc
1971	LtFd	Can uc, US uc

LOYER, Roger

COUNTRY: France
BORN: August 5, 1907
GP STARTS: 1
WC POINTS: 0

Year	Team	Grand(s) Prix
1954	Gor	Arg r

LUCAS, Jean

COUNTRY: France
BORN: April 25, 1917
GP STARTS: 1
WC POINTS: 0

Year	Team	Grand(s) Prix
1955	Gor	Ita r

LUNGER, Brett

COUNTRY: US
BORN: November 14, 1945
GP STARTS: 34
WC POINTS: 0

Year	Team	Grand(s) Prix
1975	HeFd	Aut 13, Ita 10, US r
1976	SuFd	SA 11, Bel r, Swe 15, Fra 16, GB r, Ger r, Aut 10, Ita 14, Can 15, USE 11
1977	MrFd	SA 14, USW r, Esp 10
1977	McFd	Bel dns, Swe 11, GB 13, Ger r, Aut 10, Hol 9, Ita r, USE 10, Can 11
1978	McFd	Arg 13, Bra r, SA 11, Bel 7, Fra r, GB 8, Aut 8, Hol r, Ita r
1978	EnFd	USE 13

MACDOWELL, Mike

COUNTRY: GB
BORN: September 13, 1932
GP STARTS: 1
WC POINTS: 0

Year	Team	Grand(s) Prix
1957	CoCl	Fra 7

MACKAY-FRASER, Herbert

COUNTRY: US
BORN: June 23, 1927
GP STARTS: 1
WC POINTS: 0

Year	Team	Grand(s) Prix
1957	BRM	Fra r

MACKEY, Bill

COUNTRY: US
BORN: December 15, 1927
GP STARTS: 1
WC POINTS: 0

Year	Team	Grand(s) Prix
1951	KK	Indy r

MACKLIN, Lance

COUNTRY: GB
BORN: September 2, 1919
GP STARTS: 13
WC POINTS: 0

Year	Team	Grand(s) Prix
1952	HWM	Swi r, Bel 11, Fra 9, GB 15, Hol 8
1953	HWM	Hol r, Bel r, Fra r, GB r, Swi r, Ita r
1954	HWM	Fra r
1955	Mas	GB 8

MAGEE, Damien

COUNTRY: GB
BORN: November 17, 1945
GP STARTS: 1
WC POINTS: 0

Year	Team	Grand(s) Prix
1975	WiFd	Swe 14

MAGGS, Tony

COUNTRY: South Africa
BORN: February 9, 1937
GP STARTS: 25
WC POINTS: 26
WC RECORD: 1962-7/13; 1963-8/9; 1964-12/4

Psn	No	Grand(s) Prix
2nd:	2	1962 Fra; 1963 Fra
3rd:	1	1962 SA

Year	Team	Grand(s) Prix
1961	LoCl	GB 13, Ger 11
1962	CoCl	Hol 5, Mon r, Bel r, Fra 2, GB 6, Ger 9, Ita 7, US 7, SA 3
1963	CoCl	Mon 5, Bel r, Hol r, Fra 2, GB 9, Ger r, Ita 6, US r, Mex r, SA 7
1964	BRM	Hol dns, Bel dns, GB r, Ger 6, Aut 4
1965	LtBR	SA 11

MAGILL, Mike

COUNTRY: US
BORN: February 18, 1920
GP STARTS: 3
WC POINTS: 0

Year	Team	Grand(s) Prix
1957	KK	Indy r
1958	KK	Indy r
1959	Sut	Indy r

MAGLIOLI, Umberto

COUNTRY: Italy
BORN: June 5, 1928
GP STARTS: 9
WC POINTS: 3.33
WC RECORD: 1954-18/2; 1955-21/1.33

Psn	No	Grand(s) Prix
3rd:	1	1954 Ita

Year	Team	Grand(s) Prix
1953	Fe	Ita 10
1954	Fe	Arg 9, Swi 7, Ita 3
1955	Fe	Ita 6
1956	Mas	GB r, Ger r, Ita r
1957	Por	Ger r

MAGNESSEN, Jan

COUNTRY: Denmark
BORN: July 4, 1973
GP STARTS: 24
WC POINTS: 1
WC RECORD: 1998-15/1

Year	Team	Grand(s) Prix
1995	McMe	Pac 10
1997	StFd	Aus r, Bra dns, Arg 10, SM r, Mon 7, Esp 13, Can r, Fra r, GB r, Ger r, Hun r, Bel 12, Ita r, Aut r, Lux r, Jap r, Eur 9
1998	StFd	Aus r, Bra 10, Arg r, SM r, Esp 12, Mon r, Can 6

MAIRESSE, Guy

COUNTRY: France
BORN: August 10, 1910
GP STARTS: 3
WC POINTS: 0

Year	Team	Grand(s) Prix
1950	Ta	Ita r
1951	Ta	Swi 15, Fra 9

MAIRESSE, Willy

COUNTRY: Belgium
BORN: October 1, 1928
GP STARTS: 12
WC POINTS: 0

Psn	No	Grand(s) Prix
3rd:	1	1960 Ita

Year	Team	Grand(s) Prix
1960	Fe	Bel r, Fra r, Ita 3
1961	LoCl	Bel r, Fra r
1961	Fe	Ger 16
1962	Fe	Mon 7, Bel r, Ita 4
1963	Fe	Mon r, Bel r, Ger r

MANTZ, Johnny

COUNTRY: US
BORN: September 18, 1918
GP STARTS: (1)

Year	Team	Grand(s) Prix
1953	KK	Indy 17 – Took over from Faulkner

MANSELL, Nigel

COUNTRY: GB
BORN: August 8, 1953
GP STARTS: 187
WC POINTS: 480 (482)
WC RECORD: 1981-14/8; 1982-14/7; 1983-12/10; 1984-9/13; 1985-6/31; 1986-2/70; 1987-2/61; 1988-9/12; 1989-4/38; 1990-5/37; 1991-2/72; 1992-1/108; 1994-9/13
WORLD CHAMPION: 1992

Psn	No	Grand(s) Prix
1st:	31	1985 Eur, SA; 1986 Bel, Can, Fra, GB, Por; 1987 SM, Fra, GB, Aut, Esp, Mex; 1989 Bra, Hun; 1990 Por; 1991 Fra, GB, Ger, Ita, Esp; 1992 SA, Mex, Bra, Esp, SM, Fra, GB, Ger, Por; 1994 Aus
2nd:	17	1985 Bel; 1986 Esp, Ita; 1988 GB, Esp; 1989 Fra, GB; 1990 Mex, Esp, Aus; 1991 Mon, Mex, Hun, Aus; 1992 Mon, Hun, Bel
3rd:	11	1981 Bel; 1982 Bra; 1983 Eur; 1984 Fra, Hol; 1986 Ger, Hun; 1987 Ita; 1989 Ger, Bel; 1990 Can
Pole:	32	1984 Dallas; 1985 SA; 1986 Can, Aus; 1987 Bra, Bel, Mon, US, Fra, Ger, Hun, Mex; 1990 Fra, GB, Por; 1991 GB, Ger; 1992 SA, Mex, Bra, Esp, SM, Mon, Fra, GB, Ger, Bel, Ita, Por, Jap, Aus; 1994 Aus
Fast:	30	1983 Eur; 1985 Ita; 1986 Esp, Fra, GB, Por; 1987 GB, Ger, Aut; 1988 GB; 1989 Mex, GB; Hun; 1990 Fra, GB, Aus; 1991 Bra, Can, Mex, Fra, GB, Por †; 1992 SA, Esp, Mon, Fra, GB, Hun, Ita, Jap

† Time at 1991 Por race set after Mansell had been disqualified; however, most records include his time as the fastest. See Patrese.

Year	Team	Grand(s) Prix
1980	LtFd	Aut r, Hol r
1981	LtFd	USW r, Bra 11, Arg r, Bel 3, Mon r, Esp 6, Fra 7, Ger r, Aut r, Hol r, Ita r, Can r, US 4
1982	LtFd	SA r, Bra 3, USW 7, Bel r, Mon 4, US r, Can r, GB r, Ger 9, Aut r, Swi 8, Ita 7, Caesar's Palace r
1983	LtFd	Bra 12, USW 12, Fra r, SM 12, Mon r, Bel r, US 6, Can r
1983	LtRe	GB 4, Ger r, Aut 5, Hol r, Ita 8, Eur 3, SA uc
1984	LtRe	Bra r, SA r, Bel r, SM r, Fra 3, Mon r, Can 6, Detroit r, Dallas 6, GB r, Ger 4, Aut r, Hol 3, Ita r, Eur r, Por r
1985	WiHo	Bra r, Por 5, SM 5, Mon 7, Can 6, US r, Fra dns, GB r, Ger 6, Aut r, Hol 6, Ita 11, Bel 2, Eur 1, SA 1, Aus r
1986	WiHo	Bra r, Esp 2, SM r, Mon 4, Bel 1, Can 1, US 5, Fra 1, GB 1, Ger 3, Hun 3, Aut r, Ita 2, Por 1, Mex 5, Aus r
1987	WiHo	Bra 6, SM 1, Bel r, Mon r, US 5, Fra 1, GB 1, Ger r, Hun 14, Aut 1, Ita 3, Por r, Esp 1, Mex 1, Jap dns
1988	WiJu	Bra r, SM r, Mon r, Mex r, Can r, US r, Fra r, GB 2, Ger r, Hun r, Por r, Esp 2, Jap r, Aus r
1989	Fe	Bra 1, SM r, Mon r, Mex r, US r, Can dq, Fra 2, GB 2, Ger 3, Hun 1, Bel 3, Ita r, Por dq, Jap r, Aus r
1990	Fe	US r, Bra 4, SM r, Mon r, Can 3, Mex 2, Fra 18, GB r, Ger r, Hun 17, Bel r, Ita 4, Por 1, Esp 2, Jap r, Aus 2
1991	WiRe	US r, Bra r, SM r, Mon 2, Can 6, Mex 2, Fra 1, GB 1, Ger 1, Hun 2, Bel r, Ita 1, Por dq, Esp 1, Jap r, Aus 2

1992	WiRe	SA 1, Mex 1, Bra 1, Esp 1, SM 1, Mon 2, Can r, Fra 1, GB 1, Ger 1, Hun 2, Bel 2, Ita r, Por 1, Jap r, Aus r
1994	WiRe	Fra r, Eur r, Jap 4, Aus 1
1995	McMe	SM 10, Esp r

MANTOVANI, Sergio

COUNTRY: Italy
BORN: May 22, 1929
GP STARTS: 7
WC POINTS: 4
WC RECORD: 1954-15/4

Year	Team	Grand(s) Prix
1953	Mas	Ita 8
1954	Mas	Bel 7, Ger 5, Swi 5, Ita 9, Esp r
1955	Mas	Arg r

MANZON, Robert

COUNTRY: France
BORN: April 12, 1917
GP STARTS: 28
WC POINTS: 16
WC RECORD: 1950-13/3; 1952-6/9; 1954-15/4

Psn	No	Grand(s) Prix
3rd:	2	1952 Bel ; 1954 Fra

Year	Team	Grand(s) Prix
1950	SiGo	Mon r, Fra 4, Ita r
1951	SiGo	Fra r, Ger 7, Ita r, Esp 9
1952	Gor	Swi r, Bel 3, Fra 4, GB r, Ger r, Hol 5, Ita 14
1953	Gor	Arg r
1954	Fe	Fra 3, GB r, Ger 9, Ita r, Esp r
1955	Gor	Mon r, Hol r, GB r
1956	Gor	Mon uc, Fra 9, GB 9, Ger r, Ita r

MARIMON, Onofre

COUNTRY: Argentina
BORN: December 19, 1923
GP STARTS: 11
WC POINTS: 8
WC RECORD: 1953-11/4; 1954-13/4.14

Psn	No	Grand(s) Prix
3rd:	2	1953 Bel; 1954 GB
Fast:	1	1954 GB

Year	Team	Grand(s) Prix
1951	MasMi	Fra r
1953	Mas	Bel 3, Fra 9, GB r, Ger r, Swi r, Ita 9
1954	Mas	Arg r, Bel r, Fra r, GB 3 Ger dns

MARKO, Helmut

COUNTRY: Austria
BORN: April 27, 1943
GP STARTS: 9
WC POINTS: 0

Year	Team	Grand(s) Prix
1971	BRM	Aut 11, Ita r, Can 12, US 13
1972	BRM	Arg 10, SA 14, Mon 8, Bel 10, Fra r

MARQUES, Tarso

COUNTRY: Brazil
BORN: January 19, 1976
GP STARTS: 11
WC POINTS: 0

Year	Team	Grand(s) Prix
1996	MiFd	Bra r, Arg r
1997	MiHt	Fra r, GB 10, Ger r, Hun 12, Bel r, Ita 14, Lux r, Jap r, Eur 15

MARR, Leslie

COUNTRY: GB
BORN: August 14, 1922
GP STARTS: 2
WC POINTS: 0

Year	Team	Grand(s) Prix
1954	Con	GB 13
1955	Con	GB r

MARSH, Tony

COUNTRY: GB
BORN: July 20, 1931
GP STARTS: 4
WC POINTS: 0

Year	Team	Grand(s) Prix
1957	CoCl	Ger 15
1958	CoCl	Ger 8
1961	LoCl	GB r, Ger 15

MARTIN, Eugene

COUNTRY: France
BORN: March 24, 1915
GP STARTS: 2
WC POINTS: 0

Year	Team	Grand(s) Prix
1950	Ta	GB r, Swi r

MARTINI, Pierluigi

COUNTRY: Italy
BORN: April 23, 1961
GP STARTS: 118
WC POINTS: 18
WC RECORD: 1988-16/1; 1989-14/5; 1991-11/6; 1992-14/2; 1994-18/4

Year	Team	Grand(s) Prix
1985	MiFd	Bra r, Por r
1985	MiMM	SM r, Can r, US r, Fra r, GB r, Ger 11, Aut r, Hol r, Ita r, Bel 12, Eur r, SA r, Aus 8
1988	MiFd	US 6, Fra 15, GB 15, Hun r, Ita r, Por r, Esp r, Jap 13, Aus 7
1989	MiFd	Bra r, SM r, Mon r, Mex r, US r, Can r, Fra r, GB 5, Ger 9, Hun r, Bel 9, Ita 7, Por 5, Esp r, Aus 6
1990	MiFd	US 7, Bra 9, SM dns, Mon r, Can r, Mex 12, Fra r, GB r, Ger r, Hun r, Bel 15, Ita r, Por 11, Esp r, Jap 8, Aus 9
1991	MiFe	US 9, Bra r, SM 4, Mon 12, Can 7, Mex r, Fra 9, GB 9, Ger r, Hun r, Bel 12, Ita r, Por 4, Esp 13, Jap r, Aus r
1992	DaFe	SA r, Mex r, Bra r, Esp 6, SM 6, Mon r, Can 8, Fra 10, GB 15, Ger 11, Hun r, Bel r, Ita 8, Por r, Jap 10, Aus r
1993	MiFd	GB r, Ger 14, Hun r, Bel r, Ita 7, Por 8, Jap 10, Aus r
1994	MiFd	Bra 8, Pac r, SM r, Mon r, Esp 5, Can 9, Fra 5, GB 10, Ger r, Hun r, Bel 8, Ita r, Por 12, Eur 15, Jap r, Aus 9
1995	MiFd	Bra dns, Arg r, SM 12, Esp 14, Mon 7, Can r, Fra r, GB 7, Ger r

MASS, Jochen

COUNTRY: Germany
BORN: September 30, 1946
GP STARTS: 105
WC POINTS: 71
WC RECORD: 1975-7/20; 1976-9/19; 1977-6/25; 1979-15/3; 1980-17/4

Psn	No	Grand(s) Prix
1st:	1	1975 Esp
2nd:	1	1977 Swe
3rd:	6	1975 Bra, Fra, US; 1976 SA, Ger; 1977 Can
Fast:	2	1975 Fra; 1976 Esp

Year	Team	Grand(s) Prix
1973	SuFd	GB r, Ger 7, US r
1974	SuFd	Arg r, Bra 17, SA r, Esp r, Bel r, Mon dns, Swe r, Hol r, Fra r, GB 14, Ger r, Can 16, US 7
1975	McFd	Arg 14, Bra 3, SA 6, Esp 1, Mon 6, Bel r, Swe r, Hol r, Fra 3, GB 7, Ger r, Aut 4, Ita r, US 3
1976	McFd	Bra 6, SA 3, USW 5, Esp r, Bel 6, Mon 5, Swe 11, Fra 15, GB r, Ger 3, Aut 7, Hol 9, Ita r, Can 5, USE 4, Jap r
1977	McFd	Arg r, Bra r, SA 5, USW r, Esp 4, Mon 4, Bel r, Swe 2, Fra 9, GB 4, Ger r, Aut 6, Hol r, Ita 4, USE r, Can 3, Jap r
1978	ATFd	Arg 11, Bra 7, SA r, USW r, Bel 11, Esp 9, Swe 13, Fra 13, GB uc, Ger r
1979	ArFd	Arg 8, Bra 7, SA 12, USW 9, Esp 8, Bel r, Mon 6, Fra 15, GB r, Ger 6, Aut r, Hol 6, Ita r
1980	ArFd	Arg r, Bra 10, SA 6, USW 7, Bel r, Mon 4, Fra 10, GB 13, Ger 8, Can 11, USE r
1982	MrFd	SA 12, Bra 8, USW 8, Bel r, US 7, Can 11, Hol r, GB 10, Fra r

MAX, Jean

COUNTRY: France
BORN: July 27, 1943
GP STARTS: 1
WC POINTS: 0

Year	Team	Grand(s) Prix
1971	MrFd	Fra uc

MAY, Michael

COUNTRY: Switzerland
BORN: August 18, 1934
GP STARTS: 2
WC POINTS: 0

Year	Team	Grand(s) Prix
1961	LoCl	Mon r, Fra 11

MAYER, Timmy

COUNTRY: US
BORN: February 22, 1938
GP STARTS: 1
WC POINTS: 0

Year	Team	Grand(s) Prix
1962	CoCl	US r

MAZET, Francois

COUNTRY: France
BORN: February 26, 1943
GP STARTS: 1
WC POINTS: 0

Year	Team	Grand(s) Prix
1971	MrFd	Fra 13

MCALPINE, Ken

COUNTRY: GB
BORN: September 21, 1920
GP STARTS: 7
WC POINTS: 0

Year	Team	Grand(s) Prix
1952	Con	GB 16, Ita r
1953	Con	Hol r, GB r, Ger 13, Ita uc
1955	Con	GB r

MCCOY, Ernie

COUNTRY: US
BORN: February 19, 1921
GP STARTS: 2
WC POINTS: 0

Year	Team	Grand(s) Prix
1953	Ste	Indy 8
1954	KK	Indy 16

MCDOWELL, Johnny

COUNTRY: US
BORN: January 29, 1915
GP STARTS: 3
WC POINTS: 0

Year	Team	Grand(s) Prix
1950	KK	Indy 18
1951	Mas	Indy r
1952	KK	Indy 21

MCGRATH, Jack

COUNTRY: US
BORN: October 8, 1919
GP STARTS: 6
WC POINTS: 9
WC RECORD: 1951-15/2; 1953-13/2; 1954-12/5

Psn	No	Grand(s) Prix
3rd:	2	1951 Indy; 1954 Indy
Pole:	1	1954 Indy
Fast:	1	1954 Indy

Year	Team	Grand(s) Prix
1950	KK	Indy 14
1951	KK	Indy 3
1952	KK	Indy 11
1953	KK	Indy 5
1954	KK	Indy 3
1955	KK	Indy r

MCLAREN, Bruce

COUNTRY: New Zealand
BORN: August 30, 1937
GP STARTS: 100
WC POINTS: 188.5 (196.5)
WC RECORD: 1959-6/16.5; 1960-2/34; 1961-7/11; 1962-3/27; 1963-6/17; 1964-7/13; 1965-8/10; 1966-14/3; 1967-14/3; 1968-5/22; 1969-3/26; 1970-14/6

Psn	No	Grand(s) Prix
1st:	4	1959 US; 1960 Arg; 1962 Mon; 1968 Bel
2nd:	11	1960 Mon, Bel, Por; 1962 SA; 1963 Bel; 1964 Bel, Ita; 1968 Can, Mex; 1969 Esp; 1970 Esp
3rd:	12	1959 GB; 1960 Fra, US; 1961 Ita; 1962 GB, Ita, US; 1963 Mon, Ita; 1965 Bel; 1969 GB, Ger
Fast:	3	1959 GB; 1960 Mon; 1962 Hol

Year	Team	Grand(s) Prix
1958	CoCl	Ger 5, Moroccan 12
1959	CoCl	Mon 5, Fra 5, GB 3, Ger r, Por r, Ita r, US 1
1960	CoCl	Arg 1, Mon 2, Hol r, Bel 2, Fra 3, GB 4, Por 2, US 3
1961	CoCl	Mon 6, Hol 12, Bel r, Fra 5, GB 8, Ger 6, Ita 3, US 4
1962	CoCl	Hol r, Mon 1, Bel r, Fra 4, GB 3, Ger 5, Ita 3, US 3, SA 2
1963	CoCl	Mon 3, Bel 2, Hol r, Fra r, GB r, Ger r, Ita 3, US r, Mex r, SA 4
1964	CoCl	Mon r, Hol 7, Bel 2, Fra 6, GB r, Ger r, Aut r, Ita 2, US r, Mex 7
1965	CoCl	SA 5, Mon 5, Bel 3, Fra r, GB 10, Hol r, Ger r, Ita 5, US r, Mex r
1966	McFd	Mon r
1966	McSe	Bel dns, GB 6, Hol dns
1966	McFd	US 5, Mex r
1967	McBR	Mon 4, Hol r
1967	EaWe	Fra r, GB r, Ger r

1967 McBR Can 7, Ita r, US r, Mex r
1968 McFd Esp r, Mon r, Bel 1, Hol r, Fra 8, GB 7, Ger 13, Ita r, Can 2, US 6, Mex 2
1969 McFd SA 5, Esp 2, Mon 5, Hol r, Fra 4, GB 3, Ger 3, Ita 4, Can 5, US dns
1970 McFd SA r, Esp 2, Mon r

MCRAE, Graham

COUNTRY: New Zealand
BORN: March 5, 1940
GP STARTS: 1
WC POINTS: 0

Year	Team	Grand(s) Prix
1973	WiFd	GB r

MCWITHEY, Jim

COUNTRY: US
BORN: July 4, 1927
GP STARTS: 2
WC POINTS: 0

Year	Team	Grand(s) Prix
1959	KK	Indy 16
1960	Epp	Indy r

MENDITEGUY, Carlos

COUNTRY: Argentina
BORN: August 10, 1915
GP STARTS: 10
WC POINTS: 9
WC RECORD: 1955-17/2; 1957-14/4; 1960-19/3

Psn	No	Grand(s) Prix
3rd:	1	1957 Arg

Year	Team	Grand(s) Prix
1953	Gor	Arg r
1954	Mas	Arg dns
1955	Mas	Arg r, Ita 5
1956	Mas	Arg r
1957	Mas	Arg 3, Mon r, Fra r, GB r
1958	Mas	Arg 7
1960	CoMa	Arg 4

MERZARIO, Arturo

COUNTRY: Italy
BORN: March 11, 1943
GP STARTS: 57
WC POINTS: 11
WC RECORD: 1972-20/1; 1973-12/6; 1974-17/4

Year	Team	Grand(s) Prix
1972	Fe	GB 6, Ger 12
1973	Fe	Arg 9, Bra 4, SA 4, Mon r, Fra 7, Aut 7, Ita r, Can 15, US 16
1974	WiFd	Arg r, Bra r, SA 6, Esp r, Bel r, Mon r, Swe dns, Hol r, Fra 9, GB r, Ger r, Aut r, Ita 4, Can r, US r
1975	WiFd	Arg r, Bra r, SA r, Esp r, Bel r
1975	FiFd	Ita 11
1976	MrFd	Esp r, Bel r, Swe 14, Fra 9, GB r
1976	WiFd	Ger r, Aut r, Hol r, Ita dns, Can r, USE r, Jap r
1977	MrFd	Esp r, Bel 14, Fra r, GB r
1977	ShFd	Aut r
1978	MrFd	Arg r, SA r, USW r, Swe uc, GB r, Hol r, Ita r, USE r
1979	MrFd	Arg r, USW r

MIERES, Roberto

COUNTRY: Argentina
BORN: December 3, 1924
GP STARTS: 17
WC POINTS: 13
WC RECORD: 1954-8/6; 1955-8/7

Psn	No	Grand(s) Prix
Fast:	1	1955 Hol

Year	Team	Grand(s) Prix
1953	Gor	Hol r, Fra r, Ita 7
1954	Mas	Arg r, Bel r, Fra r, GB 6, Ger r, Swi 4, Ita r, Esp 4
1955	Mas	Arg 5, Mon r, Bel 5, Hol 4, GB r, Ita 7

MIGAULT, Francois

COUNTRY: France
BORN: December 4, 1944
GP STARTS: 13
WC POINTS: 0

Year	Team	Grand(s) Prix
1972	CwFd	GB dns, Aut r
1974	BRM	Arg r, Bra 16, SA 15, Esp r, Bel 16, Mon r, Hol r, Fra 14, GB uc, Ita r
1975	HiFd	Esp uc, Bel r
1975	WiFd	Fra dns

MILES, John

COUNTRY: GB
BORN: June 14, 1943
GP STARTS: 12
WC POINTS: 2
WC RECORD: 1970-19/2

Year	Team	Grand(s) Prix
1969	LtFd	Fra r, GB 10, Ita r, Can r, Mex r
1970	LtFd	SA 5, Bel r, Hol 7, Fra 8, GB r, Ger r, Aut r, Ita dns

MILHOUX, Andre

COUNTRY: Belgium
BORN: December 9, 1928
GP STARTS: 1
WC POINTS: 0

Year	Team	Grand(s) Prix
1956	Gor	Ger r

MILLER, Chet

COUNTRY: US
BORN: July 19, 1902
GP STARTS: 2
WC POINTS: 0

Year	Team	Grand(s) Prix
1951	KK	Indy r
1952	KK	Indy r

MITTER, Gerhard

COUNTRY: Germany
BORN: August 30, 1935
GP STARTS: 4
WC POINTS: 3
WC RECORD: 1963-12/3

Year	Team	Grand(s) Prix
1963	Por	Hol r, Ger 4
1964	LoCl	Ger 9
1965	LoCl	Ger r
1966	LtFd	Ger dns
1969	BMW	Ger dns

MODENA, Stefano

COUNTRY: Italy
BORN: May 12, 1963
GP STARTS: 70
WC POINTS: 17
WC RECORD: 1989-16/4; 1990-16/2; 1991-8/10; 1992-17/1

Psn	No	Grand(s) Prix
2nd:	1	1991 Can
3rd:	1	1989 Mon

Year	Team	Grand(s) Prix
1987	BrBM	Aus r
1988	EBFd	Bra r, SM uc, Can 12, US r, Fra 14, GB 12, Ger r, Hun 11, Esp 13, Aus r
1989	BrJu	Bra r, SM r, Mon 3, Mex 10, US r, Can r, Fra r, GB r, Ger r, Hun 11, Bel r, Por 14, Esp r, Jap r, Aus 8
1990	BrJu	US 5, Bra r, SM r, Mon r, Can 7, Mex 11, Fra 13, GB 9, Ger r, Hun r, Bel 17, Ita r, Por r, Esp r, Jap r, Aus 12
1991	TyHo	US 4, Bra r, SM r, Mon r
1991	TyFd	Can 2
1991	TyHo	Mex 11, Fra r, GB 7, Ger 13
1991	TyFd	Hun 12
1991	TyHo	Bel r
1991	TyFd	Ita r
1991	TyHo	Por r, Esp 16, Jap 6, Aus 10
1992	JoYa	Mex r, Bra r, SM r, Mon r, Can r, Fra r, GB r, Hun r, Bel 15, Por 13, Jap 7, Aus 6

MONTERMINI, Andrea

COUNTRY: Italy
BORN: May 30, 1964
GP STARTS: 20
WC POINTS: 0

Year	Team	Grand(s) Prix
1995	PaFd	Bra 9, Arg r, SM r, Esp dns, Mon dq, Can r, Fra uc, GB r, Ger 8, Hun 12, Bel r, Ita r, Por r, Eur r, Pac r, Jap r, Aus r
1996	FiFd	Aus dnq, Bra r, Arg 10, Eur dnq, SM dnq, Mon dns, Esp dnq, Can r, Fra r, GB dnq

MONTGOMERIE-CHARRINGTON, Robin

COUNTRY: GB
BORN: June 22, 1915
GP STARTS: 1
WC POINTS: 0

Year	Team	Grand(s) Prix
1952	AsBu	Bel r

MORBIDELLI, Gianni

COUNTRY: Italy
BORN: January 13, 1968
GP STARTS: 67
WC POINTS: 8
WC RECORD: 1991-24/.5; 1994-22/3; 1995-14/5

Psn	No	Grand(s) Prix
3rd:	1	1995 Aus

Year	Team	Grand(s) Prix
1990	DaFd	Bra 14
1990	MiFd	Jap r, Aus r
1991	MiFe	US r, Bra 8, SM r, Mon r, Can r, Mex 7, Fra r, GB 11, Ger r, Hun 13, Bel r, Ita 9, Por 9, Esp 14, Jap r
1991	Fe	Aus 6
1992	MiLm	SA r, Mex r, Bra 7, Esp r, SM r, Mon r, Can 11, Fra 8, GB 17, Ger 12, Bel 16, Ita r, Por 14, Jap 14, Aus 10
1994	FtFd	Bra r, Pac r, SM r, Mon r, Esp r, Can r, Fra r, GB r, Ger 5, Hun r, Bel 6, Ita r, Por 9, Eur 11, Jap r, Aus r
1995	FtHt	Bra r, Arg r, SM 13, Esp 11, Mon 9, Can 6, Fra 14, Pac r, Jap r, Aus 3
1997	SaPe	Esp 14, Can 10, Hun r, Bel 9, Ita 12, Aut 9, Lux 9, Jap dns

MORENO, Roberto

COUNTRY: Brazil
BORN: February 11, 1959
GP STARTS: 42
WC POINTS: 15
WC RECORD: 1987-19/1; 1990-10/6; 1991-10/8

Psn	No	Grand(s) Prix
2nd:	1	1990 Jap
Fast:	1	1991 Bel

Year	Team	Grand(s) Prix
1987	AGFd	Jap r, Aus 6
1989	CiFd	Mon r, Can r, GB r, Por r
1990	EBJu	US 13, SM r, Mex dns
1990	BeFd	Jap 2, Aus 7
1991	BeFd	US r, Bra 7, SM 13, Mon 4, Can r, Mex 5, Fra r, GB r, Ger 8, Hun 8, Bel 4
1991	JoFd	Ita r, Por 10
1991	MiFe	Aus 16
1992	AMJu	Mon r
1995	FiFd	Bra r, Arg uc, SM uc, Esp r, Mon r, Can r, Fra 16, GB r, Ger r, Hun r, Bel 14, Ita r, Por 17, Eur r, Pac 16, Jap r, Aus r

MORGAN, Dave

COUNTRY: GB
BORN: August 7, 1944
GP STARTS: 1
WC POINTS: 0

Year	Team	Grand(s) Prix
1975	SuFd	GB 18

MOSER, Silvio

COUNTRY: Switzerland
BORN: April 24, 1941
GP STARTS: 12
WC POINTS: 3
WC RECORD: 1968-23/2; 1969-16/1

Year	Team	Grand(s) Prix
1966	BrFd	Ger dns
1967	CoAT	GB r
1968	BrRe	Hol 5, GB uc
1969	BrFd	Mon r, Hol r, Fra 7, Ita r, Can r, US 6, Mex 11
1970	BlFd	Aut r
1971	BlFd	Ita r

MOSS, Sterling

COUNTRY: GB
BORN: September 17, 1929
GP STARTS: 66
WC POINTS: 185.64 (186.64)
WC RECORD: 1954-13/4.14; 1955-2/23; 1956-2/27; 1957-2/25; 1958-2/41; 1959-3/25.5; 1960-3/19; 1961-3/21

Psn	No	Grand(s) Prix
1st:	16	1955 GB; 1956 Mon, Ita; 1957 GB (shared), Pescara, Ita; 1958 Arg, Hol, Por, Mor; 1959 Por, Ita; 1960 Mon, US; 1961 Mon, Ger
2nd:	5	1955 Bel, Hol; 1956 Ger; 1958 Fra; 1959 GB
3rd:	1	1954 Bel
Pole:	16	1955 GB; 1956 GB; 1957 Arg, GB; 1958 GB, Por, Ita; 1958 Mon, Por, Ita, US; 1959 Arg, Mon, Hol, US; 1961 Mon
Fast:	19	1954 GB; 1955 GB, Ita; 1956 Bel, GB, Ita; 1957 Arg, GB, Pescara; 1958 Hol, Ger, Mor;

1958 Hol, Fra, GB, Por; 1959 Arg, Hol; 1961 Mon

Year	Team	Grand(s) Prix
1951	HWM	Swi 8
1952	HWM	Swi r
1952	ERA	Bel r, GB r, Hol 11
1952	Con	Ita r
1953	Con	Hol 9
1953	CoAt	Fra r, Ger 6, Ita 16
1954	Mas	Bel 3, GB r, Ger r, Swi r, Ita 10, Esp r
1955	Me	Arg r, Mon r, Bel 2, Hol 2, GB 1, Ita r
1956	Mas	Arg r, Mon 1, Bel r, Fra r, GB 10, Ger 2, Ita 1
1957	Mas	Arg 8
1957	Va	Mon r, GB r, Ger 5, Pescara 1, Ita 1
1958	CoCl	Arg 1
1958	Va	Mon r, Hol 1, Bel r, Fra 2, GB r, Ger r, Por 1, Ita r, Mor 1
1959	CoCl	Mon r, Hol r
1959	BRM	Fra dq, GB 2r
1959	CoCl	Ger r, Por 1, Ita 1, US r
1960	CoCl	Arg r, Mon 1
1960	LoCl	Hol 4, Bel dns, Por dq, US 1
1961	LoCl	Mon 1, Hol 4, Bel 8, Fra r, GB r, Ger 1, Ita r, US r

MUNARON, Gino

COUNTRY: Italy
BORN: April 2, 1928
GP STARTS: 4
WC POINTS: 0

Year	Team	Grand(s) Prix
1960	Mas	Arg 13
1960	CoFe	Fra r, GB 16, Ita r

MURRAY, David

COUNTRY: GB
BORN: December 28, 1909
GP STARTS: 4
WC POINTS: 0

Year	Team	Grand(s) Prix
1950	Mas	GB r, Ita r
1951	Mas	GB r, Ger dns
1952	CoBr	GB r

MUSSO, Luigi

COUNTRY: Italy
BORN: July 29, 1924
GP STARTS: 23
WC POINTS: 44
WC RECORD: 1954-8/6; 1955-9/6; 1956-11/4; 1957-3/16; 1958-7/12

Psn	No	Grand(s) Prix
1st:	1	1956 Arg
2nd:	5	1954 Esp; 1957 Fra, GB; 1958 Arg, Mon
3rd:	1	1955 Hol
Fast:	1	1957 Fra

Year	Team	Grand(s) Prix
1954	Mas	Arg dns, Ita r, Esp 2
1955	Mas	Arg 7, Mon r, Bel 7, Hol 3, GB 5, Ita r
1956	LaFe	Arg 1, Mon r, Ger r, Ita 5
1957	LaFe	Arg r, Fra 2, GB 2, Ger 4, Pescara r, Ita 8
1958	Fe	Arg 2, Mon 2, Hol 7, Bel r, Fra r

NAKAJIMA, Satoru

COUNTRY: Japan
BORN: February 23, 1953
GP STARTS: 74
WC POINTS: 16
WC RECORD: 1987-11/7; 1988-16/1; 1989-21/3; 1990-14/3; 1991-15/2

Psn	No	Grand(s) Prix
Fast:	1	1989 Aus

Year	Team	Grand(s) Prix
1987	LtHo	Bra 7, SM 6, Bel 5, Mon 10, US r, Fra uc, GB 4
1987	LOHo	Ger r
1987	LtHo	Hun r, Aut 13, Ita 11, Por 8
1987	Za	Esp 9
1987	LtHo	Mex r, Jap 6, Aus r
1988	LtHo	Bra 6, SM 8, Mex r, Can 11, Fra 7, GB 10, Ger 9, Hun 7, Bel r, Ita r, Por r, Esp r, Jap 7, Aus r
1989	LtJu	Bra 8, SM r, Mex r, US r, Fra r, GB 8, Ger r, Hun r, Ita 10, Por 7, Esp r, Jap r, Aus 4
1990	TyFd	US 6, Bra 8, SM r, Mon r, Can 11, Mex r, Fra r, GB r, Ger r, Hun r, Bel r, Ita 6, Por dns, Esp r, Jap 6, Aus r
1991	TyHo	US 5, Bra r, SM r, Mon r
1991	TyFd	Can 10
1991	TyHo	Mex 12, Fra r, GB 8, Ger r, Hun 15, Bel r, Ita r, Por 13, Esp 17, Jap r, Aus r

NAKANO, Shinji

COUNTRY: Japan
BORN: April 1, 1971
GP STARTS: 33
WC POINTS: 2
WC RECORD: 1997-16/2

Year	Team	Grand(s) Prix
1997	PrMH	Aus 7, Bra 14, Arg r, SM r, Mon r, Esp r, Can 6, Fra r, GB 11, Ger 7, Hun 6, Bel r, Ita 11, Aut r, Lux r, Jap r, Eur 10
1998	MiFd	Aus r, Bra r, Arg 13, SM r, Esp 14, Mon 9, Can 7, Fra 17, GB 8, Aut 11, Ger r, Hun 15, Bel 8, Ita r, Lux 15, Jap r

NALON, Duke

COUNTRY: US
BORN: March 12, 1913
GP STARTS: 3
WC POINTS: 0

Psn	No	Grand(s) Prix
Pole:	1	1951 Indy

Year	Team	Grand(s) Prix
1951	KK	Indy r
1952	KK	Indy r
1953	KK	Indy 11

NANNI, Galli

COUNTRY: Italy
BORN: October 2, 1940
GP STARTS: 17
WC POINTS: 0

Year	Team	Grand(s) Prix
1971	MaAl	Hol r
1971	MrFd	GB 11
1971	MaAl	Ger 12, Aut 12, Ita r
1971	MrFd	Can 16, US r
1972	Tec	Bel r
1972	Fe	Fra 13
1972	Tec	GB r, Aut uc, Ita r
1973	WiFd	Arg r, Bra 9, Esp 11, Bel r, Mon r

NANNINI, Alessandro

COUNTRY: Italy
BORN: July 7, 1959
GP STARTS: 77
WC POINTS: 65
WC RECORD: 1988-9/12; 1989-6/32; 1990-8/21

Psn	No	Grand(s) Prix
1st:	1	1989 Jap
2nd:	2	1989 Aus; 1990 Ger
3rd:	6	1988 GB, Esp; 1989 SM, GB; 1990 SM, Esp
Fast:	2	1988 Ger; 1990 SM

Year	Team	Grand(s) Prix
1986	MiMM	Bra r, Esp r, SM r, Bel r, Can r, US r, Fra r, GB r, Ger r, Hun r, Aut r, Ita r, Por r, Mex 14, Aus r
1987	MiMM	Bra r, SM r, Bel r, Mon r, US r, Fra r, GB r, Ger r, Hun 11, Aut r, Ita 16, Por 11, Esp r, Mex r, Jap r, Aus r
1988	BeFd	Bra r, SM 6, Mon r, Mex 7, Can r, US r, Fra 6, GB 3, Ger 18, Hun r, Bel dq, Ita 9, Por r, Esp 3, Jap 5, Aus r
1989	BeFd	Bra 6, SM 3, Mon 8, Mex 4, US r, Can dq, Fra r, GB 3, Ger r, Hun r, Bel 5, Ita r, Por 4, Esp r, Jap 1, Aus 2
1990	BeFd	US 11, Bra 10, SM 3, Mon r, Can r, Mex 4, Fra 16, GB r, Ger 2, Hun r, Bel 4, Ita 8, Por 6, Esp 3

NASPETTI, Emanuele

COUNTRY: Italy
BORN: February 24, 1968
GP STARTS: 6
WC POINTS: 0

Year	Team	Grand(s) Prix
1992	Mall	Bel 12, Ita r, Por 11, Jap 13, Aus r
1993	JoFd	Por r

NATILI, Massimo

COUNTRY: Italy
BORN: July 28, 1935
GP STARTS: 1
WC POINTS: 0

Year	Team	Grand(s) Prix
1961	CoMa	GB r

NAYLOR, Brian

COUNTRY: GB
BORN: March 24, 1923
GP STARTS: 7
WC POINTS: 0

Year	Team	Grand(s) Prix
1957	CoCl	Ger 13
1958	CoCl	Ger r
1959	JBMas	GB r
1960	JBMas	GB 13, Ita r, US r
1961	JBCl	Ita r

NAZARUK, Mike

COUNTRY: US
BORN: October 2, 1921
GP STARTS: 3
WC POINTS: 8
WC RECORD: 1951-9/6; 1954-18/2

Psn	No	Grand(s) Prix
2nd:	1	1951 Indy

Year	Team	Grand(s) Prix
1951	KK	Indy 2
1953	Turner	Indy r
1954	KK	Indy 5

NEEDELL, Tiff

COUNTRY: GB
BORN: October 29, 1951
GP STARTS: 1
WC POINTS: 0

Year	Team	Grand(s) Prix
1980	EnFd	Bel r

NEVE, Patrick

COUNTRY: Belgium
BORN: October 13, 1949
GP STARTS: 10
WC POINTS: 0

Year	Team	Grand(s) Prix
1976	BrFd	Bel r
1976	EnFd	Fra 18
1977	MrFd	Esp 12, Bel 10, Swe 15, GB 10, Aut 9, Ita 7, USE 18, Can r

NICHOLSON, John

COUNTRY: New Zealand
BORN: October 6, 1941
GP STARTS: 1
WC POINTS: 0

Year	Team	Grand(s) Prix
1975	LyFd	GB 17

NIDAY, Cal

COUNTRY: US
BORN: April 29, 1916
GP STARTS: 3
WC POINTS: 0

Year	Team	Grand(s) Prix
1953	KK	Indy r
1954	Ste	Indy 10
1955	KK	Indy r

NIEDERMAYR, Helmut

COUNTRY: Germany
BORN: November 29, 1915
GP STARTS: 1
WC POINTS: 0

Year	Team	Grand(s) Prix
1952	AFM	Ger 9

NIEMANN, Brausch

COUNTRY: South Africa
BORN: January 7, 1939
GP STARTS: 1
WC POINTS: 0

Year	Team	Grand(s) Prix
1963	LtFd	SA uc

NILSSON, Gunnar

COUNTRY: Sweden
BORN: November 20, 1948
GP STARTS: 31
WC POINTS: 31
WC RECORD: 1976-10/11; 1977-8/20

Psn	No	Grand(s) Prix
1st:	1	1977 Bel
3rd:	3	1976 Esp, Aut; 1977 GB
Fast:	1	1977 Bel

Year	Team	Grand(s) Prix
1976	LtFd	SA r, USW r, Esp 3, Bel r, Mon r, Swe r, Fra r, GB r, Ger 5, Aut 3, Hol r, Ita 13, Can 12, USE r, Jap 6
1977	LtFd	Bra 5, SA 12, USW 8, Esp 5, Mon r, Bel 1, Swe 19, Fra 4, GB 3, Ger r, Aut r, Hol r, Ita r, USE r, Can r, Jap r

NODA, Hideki

COUNTRY: Japan
BORN: March 7, 1969
GP STARTS: 3
WC POINTS: 0

Year	Team	Grand(s) Prix
1994	LaFd	Eur r, Jap r, Aus r

NUCKEY, Hodney

COUNTRY: GB
BORN: June 26, 1929
GP STARTS: 1
WC POINTS: 0

Year	Team	Grand(s) Prix
1953	CoBr	Ger 11

O'BRIEN, Robert

COUNTRY: US
BORN:
GP STARTS: 1
WC POINTS: 0

Year	Team	Grand(s) Prix
1952	SiGo	Bel 14

O'CONNOR, Pat

COUNTRY: US
BORN: October 9, 1928
GP STARTS: 5
WC POINTS: 0

Psn	No	Grand(s) Prix
Pole:	1	1957 Indy

Year	Team	Grand(s) Prix
1954	KK	Indy r
1955	KK	Indy 8
1956	KK	Indy 18
1957	KK	Indy 8
1958	KK	Indy r

OLIVER, Jackie

COUNTRY: GB
BORN: August 14, 1942
GP STARTS: 49
WC POINTS: 13
WC RECORD: 1968-13/6; 1969-16/1; 1970-19/2; 1973-14/4

Psn	No	Grand(s) Prix
3rd:	2	1968 Mex; 1973 Can
Fast:	1	1968 Ita

Year	Team	Grand(s) Prix
1968	LtFd	Mon r, Bel 5, Hol uc, Fra dns, GB r, Ger 11, Ita r, Can r, US dns, Mex 3
1969	BRM	SA 7, Esp r, Mon r, Hol r, GB r, Ger r, Ita r, Can r, US r, Mex 6
1970	BRM	SA r, Esp r, Mon r, Bel r, Hol r, Fra r, GB r, Ger r, Aut 5, Ita r, Can uc, US r, Mex 7
1971	McFd	GB r, Aut 9, Ita 7
1972	BRM	GB r
1973	ShFd	SA r, Esp r, Bel r, Mon 10, Swe r, Fra r, GB r, Hol r, Ger 8, Aut r, Ita 11, Can 3, US 15
1977	ShFd	Swe 9

ONGAIS, Danny

COUNTRY: US
BORN: May 21, 1942
GP STARTS: 4
WC POINTS: 0

Year	Team	Grand(s) Prix
1977	PkFd	USE r, Can 7
1978	EnFd	Arg r, Bra r

OWEN, Arthur

COUNTRY: GB
BORN: March 23, 1915
GP STARTS: 1
WC POINTS: 0

Year	Team	Grand(s) Prix
1960	CoCl	Ita r

PACE, Carlos

COUNTRY: Brazil
BORN: October 6, 1944
GP STARTS: 72
WC POINTS: 58
WC RECORD: 1972-16/3; 1973-11/7; 1974-12/11; 1975-6/24; 1976-14/7; 1977-15/6

Psn	No	Grand(s) Prix
1st:	1	1975 Bra
2nd:	3	1974 US; 1975 GB; 1977 Arg
3rd:	2	1973 Aut; 1975 Mon

Pole: 1 1975 SA
Fast: 5 1973 Ger, Aut; 1974 Ita, US; 1975 SA

Year	Team	Grand(s) Prix
1972	MrFd	SA 17, Esp 6, Mon 17, Bel 5, Fra r, GB r, Ger uc, Aut uc, Ita r, Can 9, US r
1973	SuFd	Arg r, Bra r, SA r, Esp r, Bel 8, Mon r, Swe 10, Fra 13, GB r, Hol 7, Ger 4, Aut 3, Ita r, Can 18, US r
1974	SuFd	Arg r, Bra 4, SA 11, Esp 13, Bel r, Mon r, Swe r
1974	BrFd	GB 9, Ger 12, Aut r, Ita 5, Can 8, US 2
1975	BrFd	Arg r, Bra 1, SA 4, Esp r, Mon 3, Bel 8, Swe r, Hol 5, Fra r, GB 2, Ger r, Aut r, Ita r, US r
1976	BrAl	Bra 10, SA r, USW 9, Esp 6, Bel r, Mon 9, Swe 8, Fra 4, GB 8, Ger 4, Aut r, Hol r, Ita r, Can 7, USE r, Jap r
1977	BrAl	Arg 2, Bra r, SA 13

PAGANI, Nello

COUNTRY: Italy
BORN: October 11, 1911
GP STARTS: 1
WC POINTS: 0

Year	Team	Grand(s) Prix
1950	Mas	Swi 7

PALETTI, Riccardo

COUNTRY: Italy
BORN: June 15, 1958
GP STARTS: 2
WC POINTS: 0

Year	Team	Grand(s) Prix
1982	OsFd	SM r, US dns, Can r

PALM, Torsten

COUNTRY: Sweden
BORN: July 23, 1947
GP STARTS: 1
WC POINTS: 0

Year	Team	Grand(s) Prix
1975	HeFd	Swe 10

PALMER, Jonathan

COUNTRY: GB
BORN: November 7, 1956
GP STARTS: 83
WC POINTS: 14
WC RECORD: 1987-11/7; 1988-13/5; 1989-23/2

Psn	No	Grand(s) Prix
Fast:	1	1989 Can

Year	Team	Grand(s) Prix
1983	WiFd	Eur 13
1984	RmHt	Bra 8, SA r, Bel 10, SM 9, Fra 13, Detroit r, Dallas r, GB r, Ger r, Aut 9, Hol 9, Ita r, Eur r, Por r
1985	Za	Por r, Mon 11, Fra r, GB r, Ger r, Aut r, Hol r
1986	Za	Bra r, Esp r, SM r, Mon 12, Bel r, Can r, US 8, Fra r, GB 9, Ger r, Hun 10, Aut r, Ita r, Por 12, Mex 10, Aus 9
1987	TyFd	Bra 10, SM r, Bel r, Mon 5, US 11, Fra 7, GB 8, Ger 5, Hun 7, Aut 14, Ita 14, Por 10, Esp r, Mex 7, Jap 8, Aus 4
1988	TyFd	Bra r, SM 14, Mon 5, Can 6, US 5, Fra r, GB r, Ger 11, Hun r, Bel 12, Por r, Esp r, Jap 12, Aus r
1989	TyFd	Bra 7, SM 6, Mon 9, Mex r, US 9, Can r, Fra 10, GB r, Ger r, Hun 13, Bel 14, Ita r, Por 6, Esp 10, Jap r

PANIS, Olivier

COUNTRY: France
BORN: September 2, 1966
GP STARTS: 90
WC POINTS: 56
WC RECORD: 1994-11/9; 1995-8/16; 1996-9/13; 1997-9/16; 1999-15/2

Psn	No	Grand(s) Prix
1st:	1	1996 Mon
2nd:	3	1994 Ger; 1995 Aus; 1997 Esp
3rd:	1	1997 Bra

Year	Team	Grand(s) Prix
1994	LiRe	Bra 11, Pac 9, SM 11, Mon 9, Esp 7, Can 12, Fra r, GB 12, Ger 2, Hun 6, Bel 7, Ita 10, Por dq, Eur 9, Jap 11, Aus 5
1995	LiMH	Bra r, Arg 7, SM 9, Esp 6, Mon r, Can 4, Fra 8, GB 4, Ger r, Hun 6, Bel 9, Ita r, Por r, Eur r, Pac 8, Jap 5, Aus 2
1996	LiMH	Aus 7, Bra 6, Arg 8, Eur r, SM r, Mon 1, Esp r, Can r, Fra 7, GB r, Ger 7, Hun 5, Bel r, Ita r, Por 10, Jap 7
1997	PrMH	Aus 5, Bra 3, Arg r, SM 8, Mon 4, Esp 2, Can 11, Lux 6, Jap r, Eur 7

1998	PrPe	Aus 9, Bra r, Arg 15, SM r, Esp 16, Mon r, Can r, Fra 11, GB r, Aut r, Ger 15, Hun 12, Bel dns, Ita r, Lux 12, Jap 11
1999	PrPe	Aus r, Bra 6, SM r, Mon r, Esp r, Can 9, Fra 8, GB 13, Aut 10, Ger 6, Hun 10, Bel 13, Ita 11, Eur 9, Mal r, Jap r

PAPIS, Max

COUNTRY: Italy
BORN: October 3, 1969
GP STARTS: 7
WC POINTS: 0

Year	Team	Grand(s) Prix
1995	FtHt	GB r, Ger r, Hun r, Bel r, Ita 7, Por r, Eur 12

PARKES, Mike

COUNTRY: GB
BORN: September 24, 1931
GP STARTS: 6
WC POINTS: 14
WC RECORD: 1966-8/12; 1967-16/2

Psn	No	Grand(s) Prix
2nd:	2	1966 Fra, Ita
Pole:	1	1966 Ita

Year	Team	Grand(s) Prix
1966	Fe	Fra 2, Hol r, Ger r, Ita 2
1967	Fe	Hol 5, Bel r

PARNELL, Reg

COUNTRY: GB
BORN: July 2, 1911
GP STARTS: 6
WC POINTS: 0

Psn	No	Grand(s) Prix
3rd:	1	1950 GB

Year	Team	Grand(s) Prix
1950	AR	GB 3
1950	Mas	Fra r
1951	Fe	Fra 4
1951	BRM	GB 5, Ita dns
1952	CoBr	GB 7
1954	Fe	GB r

PARNELL, Tim

COUNTRY: GB
BORN: June 25, 1932
GP STARTS: 2
WC POINTS: 0

Year	Team	Grand(s) Prix
1961	LoCl	GB r, Ita 10

PARSONS, Johnnie

COUNTRY: US
BORN: July 4, 1918
GP STARTS: 9
WC POINTS: 11
WC RECORD: 1950-6/8; 1956-15/3

Psn	No	Grand(s) Prix
1st:	1	1950 Indy

Year	Team	Grand(s) Prix
1950	KK	Indy 1
1951	KK	Indy r
1952	KK	Indy 10
1953	KK	Indy r
1954	KK	Indy r
1955	KK	Indy r
1956	Ku	Indy 4
1957	KK	Indy 16
1958	KK	Indy 12

PATRESE, Riccardo

COUNTRY: Italy
BORN: April 17, 1954
GP STARTS: 256
WC POINTS: 281
WC RECORD: 1977-19/1; 1978-11/11; 1979-19/2; 1980-9/7; 1981-11/10; 1982-10/21; 1983-9/13; 1984-13/8; 1986-15/2; 1987-13/6; 1988-11/8; 1989-3/40; 1990-7/23; 1991-3/53; 1992-2/56; 1993-5/20

Psn	No	Grand(s) Prix
1st:	6	1982 Mon; 1983 SA; 1990 SM; 1991 Mex, Por; 1992 Jap
2nd:	17	1978 Swe; 1980 USW; 1981 SM; 1982 Can; 1989 Mex, US, Can, Jap; 1991 Bra, Ger; 1992 SA, Mex, Bra, SM, Fra, GB; 1993 Hun
3rd:	14	1981 Bra; 1982 USW; 1983 Ger; 1984 Ita; 1987 Mex; 1989 Fra, Aus; 1991 Can, Hun, Esp, Jap; 1992 Mon, Bel; 1993 GB

Pole:	8	1981 USW; 1983 Ita; 1989 Hun; 1991 Can, Mex, Fra, Por; 1992 Hun
Fast:	13	1982 Mon, Fra; 1983 SM; 1988 Bra; 1990 Hun, Por, Esp, Jap; 1991 Ger, (Por †), Esp; 1992 Bra, SM, Ger
		† Mansell recorded a faster time after he had been disqaulified. Records carry Mansell's time as the fastest, however.

Year	Team	Grand(s) Prix
1977	ShFd	Mon 9, Bel r, Fra r, GB r, Ger 10, Hol 13, Ita r, Can 10, Jap 6
1978	ArFd	Bra 10, SA r, USW 6, Mon 6, Bel r, Esp r, Swe 2, Fra 8, GB r, Ger 9, Aut r, Hol r, Ita r, Can 4
1979	ArFd	Bra 9, SA 11, USW r, Esp 10, Bel 5, Mon r, Fra 14, GB r, Ger r, Aut r, Hol r, Ita 13, Can r, USE r
1980	ArFd	Arg r, Bra 6, SA r, USW 2, Bel r, Mon 8, Fra 9, GB 9, Ger 9, Aut 14, Hol r, Ita r, Can r, USE r
1981	ArFd	USW r, Bra 3, Arg 7, SM 2, Bel r, Mon r, Esp r, Fra 14, GB 10, Ger r, Aut r, Hol r, Ita r, Can r, US 11
1982	BrBM	SA r
1982	BrFd	Bra r, USW 3
1982	BrBM	Bel r
1982	BrFd	Mon 1, US r, Can 2
1982	BrBM	Hol 15, GB r, Fra r, Ger r, Aut r, Swi 5, Ita r, Caesar's Palace r
1983	BrBM	Bra r, USW 10, Fra r, SM 13, Mon r, Bel r, US r, Can r, GB r, Ger 3, Aut r, Hol 9, Ita r, Eur 7, SA 1
1984	AR	Bra r, SA 4, Bel r, SM r, Fra r, Mon r, Can r, Detroit r, Dallas r, GB 12, Ger r, Aut 10, Hol r, Ita 3, Eur 6, Por 8
1985	AR	Bra r, Por r, SM r, Mon r, Can 10, US r, Fra 11, GB 9, Ger r, Aut r, Hol r, Ita r, Bel r, Eur 9, SA r, Aus r
1986	BrBM	Bra r, Esp r, SM 6, Mon r, Bel 8, Can r, US 6, Fra 7, GB r, Ger r, Hun r, Aut r, Ita r, Por r, Mex 13, Aus r
1987	BrBM	Bra r, SM 9, Bel r, Mon r, US 9, Fra r, GB r, Ger r, Hun 5, Aut r, Ita r, Por r, Esp 13, Mex 3, Jap 11
1987	WiHo	Aus 9
1988	WiJu	Bra r, SM 13, Mon 6, Mex r, Can r, US r, Fra r, GB 8, Ger r, Hun 6, Bel r, Ita 7, Por r, Esp 5, Jap 6, Aus 4
1989	WiRe	Bra r, SM r, Mon 15, Mex 2, US 2, Can 2, Fra 3, GB r, Ger 4, Hun r, Bel r, Ita 4, Por r, Esp 5, Jap 2, Aus 3
1990	WiRe	US 9, Bra 13, SM 1, Mon r, Can r, Mex 9, Fra 6, GB r
1990	WiHo	Ger 5
1990	WiRe	Hun 4, Bel r, Ita 5, Por 7, Esp 5, Jap 4, Aus 6
1991	WiRe	US r, Bra 2, SM r, Mon r, Can 3, Mex 1, Fra 5, GB r, Ger 2, Hun 3, Bel 5, Ita r, Por 1, Esp 3, Jap 3, Aus 5
1992	WiRe	SA 2, Mex 2, Bra 2, Esp r, SM 2, Mon 3, Can r, Fra 2, GB 2, Ger 8, Hun r, Bel 3, Ita 5, Por r, Jap 1, Aus r
1993	BeFd	SA r, Bra r, Eur 5, SM r, Esp 4, Mon r, Can r, Fra 10, GB 3, Ger 5, Hun 2, Bel 6, Ita 5, Por 16, Jap r, Aus 8

PEASE, Al

COUNTRY: Canada
BORN: October 15, 1921
GP STARTS: 2
WC POINTS: 0

Year	Team	Grand(s) Prix
1967	EaCl	Can uc
1968	EaCl	Can dns
1969	EaCl	Can dq

PENSKE, Roger

COUNTRY: US
BORN: February 20, 1937
GP STARTS: 2
WC POINTS: 0

Year	Team	Grand(s) Prix
1961	CoCl	US 9
1962	LoCl	US 9

PERDISA, Cesare

COUNTRY: Italy
BORN: October 21, 1932
GP STARTS: 7
WC POINTS: 5
WC RECORD: 1955-17/2; 1956-15/3

Psn	No	Grand(s) Prix
3rd:	1	1956 Bel

Year	Team	Grand(s) Prix
1955	Mas	Mon 8, Bel 8
1956	Mas	Mon 7, Bel 3, Fra 5, GB 7, Ger dns
1957	LaFe	Arg 6

PERKINS, Larry

COUNTRY: Australia
BORN: March 18, 1950
GP STARTS: 11
WC POINTS: 0

Year	Team	Grand(s) Prix
1976	BoFd	Esp 13, Bel 8, Swe r, Hol r, Ita r
1976	BrAl	Can 17, USE r, Jap r
1977	BRM	Bra r, SA 15
1977	SuFd	Bel 12

PERROT, Xavier

COUNTRY: Switzerland
BORN: February 1, 1932
GP STARTS: 1 (F2 Race)

Year	Team	Grand(s) Prix
1969		Ger 6

PESCAROLO, Henri

COUNTRY: France
BORN: September 25, 1942
GP STARTS: 56
WC POINTS: 12
WC RECORD: 1970-12/8; 1971-16/4

Psn	No	Grand(s) Prix
3rd:	1	1970 Mon
Fast:	1	1971 Ita

Year	Team	Grand(s) Prix
1968	Mat	Can r, US dns, Mex 9
1970	Mat	SA 7, Esp r, Mon 3, Bel 6, Hol 8, Fra 5, GB r, Ger 6, Aut 14, Ita r, Can 7, US 8, Mex 9
1971	MrFd	SA 11, Esp r, Mon 8, Hol uc, Fra r, GB 4, Ger r, Aut 6, Ita r, Can dns, US r
1972	MrFd	Arg 8, SA 11, Esp 11, Mon r, Bel uc, Fra dns
1972	WiFd	GB r
1972	MrFd	Ger r, dns dns, Can 13, US 14
1973	MrFd	Esp 8, Fra r, Ger 10
1974	BRM	Arg 9, Bra 14, SA 18, Esp 12, Bel r, Mon r, Swe r, Hol r, Fra r, GB r, Ger 10, Ita r
1976	SuFd	Fra r, GB r, Aut 9, Hol 11, Ita 17, Can 19, USE uc

PESENTI-ROSSI, Sandro

COUNTRY: Italy
BORN: August 31, 1942
GP STARTS: 3
WC POINTS: 0

Year	Team	Grand(s) Prix
1976	TyFd	Ger 14, Aut 11, Ita 18

PETERS, Josef

COUNTRY: Germany
BORN: September 16, 1914
GP STARTS: 1
WC POINTS: 0

Year	Team	Grand(s) Prix
1952	Ver	Ger r

PETERSON, Ronnie

COUNTRY: Sweden
BORN: February 14, 1944
GP STARTS: 123
WC POINTS: 206
WC RECORD: 1971-2/33; 1972-9/12; 1973-3/52; 1974-5/35; 1975-12/6; 1976-11/10; 1977-14/7; 1978-2/51

Psn	No	Grand(s) Prix
1st:	10	1973 Fra, Aut, Ita, US; 1974 Mon, Fra, Ita; 1976 Ita; 1978 SA, Aut
2nd:	10	1971 Mon, GB, Ita, Can; 1973 Swe, GB; 1978 Bel, Esp, Fra, Hol
3rd:	6	1971 US; 1972 Ger; 1973 Mon; 1974 Can; 1977 Bel; 1978 Swe
Pole:	14	1973 Bra, Esp, Bel, Swe, GB, Hol, Ita, Can, US; 1974 Arg; 1976 Hol; 1978 Bra, GB, Aut
Fast:	9	1973 Esp, Hol; 1974 Mon, Hol; 1976 Ita; 1977 USE; 1978 Bel, Ger, Aut

Year	Team	Grand(s) Prix
1970	MrFd	Mon 7, Bel uc, Hol 9, Fra r, GB 9, Ger r, Ita r, Can uc, US 11
1971	MrFd	SA 10, Esp r, Mon 2, Hol 4
1971	MaAl	Fra r
1971	MrFd	GB 2, Ger 5, Aut 8, Ita 2, Can 2, US 3
1972	MrFd	Arg 6, SA 5, Esp r, Mon 11, Bel 9, Fra 5, GB 7, Ger 3, Aut 12, Ita 9, Can dq, US 4
1973	LtFd	Arg r, Bra r, SA 11, Esp r, Bel r, Mon 3, Swe 2, Fra 1, GB 2, Hol 11, Ger r, Aut 1, Ita 1, Can r, US 1

Year	Team	Grand(s) Prix
1974	LtFd	Arg 13, Bra 6, SA r, Esp r, Bel r, Mon 1, Swe r, Hol 8, Fra 1, GB 10, Ger 4, Aut r, Ita 1, Can 3, US uc
1975	LtFd	Arg r, Bra 15, SA 10, Esp r, Mon 4, Bel r, Swe 9, Hol 15, Fra 10, GB r, Ger r, Aut 5, Ita r, US 5
1976	LtFd	Bra r
1976	MrFd	SA r, USW 10, Esp r, Bel r, Mon r, Swe 7, Fra 19, GB r, Ger r, Aut 6, Hol r, Ita 1, Can 9, USE r, Jap r
1977	TyFd	Arg r, Bra r, SA r, USW r, Esp 8, Mon r, Bel 3, Swe r, Fra 12, GB r, Ger 9, Aut 5, Hol r, Ita 6, USE 16, Can r, Jap r
1978	LtFd	Arg 5, Bra r, SA 1, USW 4, Mon r, Bel 2, Esp 2, Swe 3, Fra 2, GB r, Ger r, Aut 1, Hol 2, Ita r

PICARD, Francois

COUNTRY: France
BORN: April 26, 1921
GP STARTS: 1
WC POINTS: 0

Year	Team	Grand(s) Prix
1958	CoCl	Mor r

PIETERSE, Ernie

COUNTRY: South Africa
BORN: July 4, 1938
GP STARTS: 2
WC POINTS: 0

Year	Team	Grand(s) Prix
1962	LoCl	SA 10
1963	LoCl	SA r

PIETSCH, Paul

COUNTRY: Germany
BORN: June 20, 1911
GP STARTS: 3
WC POINTS: 0

Year	Team	Grand(s) Prix
1950	Mas	Ita r
1951	AR	Ger r
1952	Ver	Ger r

PILETTE, Andre

COUNTRY: Belgium
BORN: October 6, 1918
GP STARTS: 8
WC POINTS: 0

Year	Team	Grand(s) Prix
1951	Ta	Bel 6
1953	Con	Bel uc
1954	Gor	Bel 5, GB 9, Ger r
1956	LaFe	Bel 6
1956	Gor	Fra 11, Ger dns
1964	ScCl	Bel r

PILETTE, Teddy

COUNTRY: Belgium
BORN: July 26, 1942
GP STARTS: 1
WC POINTS: 0

Year	Team	Grand(s) Prix
1974	BrFd	Bel 17

PIOTTI, Luigi

COUNTRY: Italy
BORN: October 27, 1913
GP STARTS: 5
WC POINTS: 0

Year	Team	Grand(s) Prix
1956	Mas	Arg r, Ita 7
1957	Mas	Arg 10, Pescara r, Ita r

PIPER, David

COUNTRY: GB
BORN: December 2, 1930
GP STARTS: 2
WC POINTS: 0

Year	Team	Grand(s) Prix
1959	LoCl	GB r
1960	LoCl	GB 12

PIQUET, Nelson

COUNTRY: Brazil
BORN: August 17, 1952
GP STARTS: 204
WC POINTS: 481.5 (484.5)

WC RECORD: 1979-15/3; 1980-2/54; 1981-1/50; 1982-11/20; 1983-1/59; 1984-5/29; 1985-8/21; 1986-3/69; 1987-1/73; 1988-6/22; 1989-8/12; 1990-3/43; 1991-6/26.5

WORLD CHAMPION: 1981, 1983, 1987

Psn	No	Grand(s) Prix
1st:	23	1980 USW, Hol, Ita; 1981 Arg, SM, Ger; 1982 Can; 1983 Bra, Ita, Eur; 1984 Can, Detroit; 1985 Fra; 1986 Bra, Ger, Hun, Ita; 1987 Ger, Hun, Ita; 1990 Jap, Aus; 1991 Can
2nd:	20	1980 Arg, GB; 1981 Hol; 1982 Hol; 1983 Fra, Mon, GB; 1984 Aut; 1985 Ita; 1986 SM, GB, Aus; 1987 Bra, Mon, US, Fra, GB, Aut, Mex; 1990 Can
3rd:	17	1980 Mon; 1981 USW, Fra, Aut; 1983 Aut, SA; 1984 Eur; 1986 Can, Fra, Por; 1987 Por; 1988 Bra, SM, Aus; 1990 Hun; 1991 US, Bel
Pole:	24	1980 USW, Can; 1981 Bra, Arg, Mon, Can; 1982 Aut; 1983 Hol; 1983 SA, SM, Can, Detroit, GB, Aut, Ita, Eur, Por; 1985 Hol; 1986 Bel, GB; 1987 GB, Aut, Ita, Esp
Fast:	23	1979 USE; 1980 USW; 1981 Arg; 1982 Ger, Aut; 1983 Bra, Mon, Ita, SA; 1984 SM, Can, Eur; 1986 Bra, SM, Can, US, Hun, Mex, Aus; 1987 Bra, Fra, Hun, Mex

Year	Team	Grand(s) Prix
1978	EnFd	Ger r
1978	McFd	Aut r, Hol r, Ita 9
1978	BrAl	Can 11
1979	BrAl	Arg r, Bra r, SA 7, USW 8, Esp r, Bel r, Mon 7, Fra r, GB r, Ger 12, Aut r, Hol 4, Ita r
1979	BrFd	Can r, USE 8
1980	BrFd	Arg 2, Bra r, SA 4, USW 1, Bel r, Mon 3, Fra 4, GB 2, Ger 4, Aut 5, Hol 1, Ita 1, Can r, USE r
1981	BrFd	USW 3, Bra 12, Arg 1, SM 1, Bel r, Mon r, Esp r, Fra 3, GB r, Ger 1, Aut 3, Hol 2, Ita 6, Can 5, US 5
1982	BrBM	SA r
1982	BrFd	Bra dq, USW r
1982	BrBM	Bel 5, Mon r, Can 1, Hol 2, GB r, Fra r, Ger r, Aut r, Swi 4, Ita r, Caesar's Palace r
1983	BrBM	Bra 1, USW r, Fra 2, SM r, Mon 2, Bel 4, US 4, Can r, GB 2, Ger 13, Aut 3, Hol r, Ita 1, Eur 1, SA 3
1984	BrBM	Bra r, SA r, Bel 9, SM r, Fra r, Mon r, Can 1, Detroit 1, Dallas r, GB 7, Ger r, Aut 2, Hol r, Ita r, Eur 3, Por 6
1985	BrBM	Bra r, Por r, SM 8, Mon r, Can r, US 6, Fra 1, GB 4, Ger r, Aut r, Hol 8, Ita 2, Bel 5, Eur r, SA r, Aus r
1986	WiHo	Bra 1, Esp r, SM 2, Mon 7, Bel r, Can 3, US r, Fra 3, GB 2, Ger 1, Hun 1, Aut r, Ita 1, Por 3, Mex 4, Aus 2
1987	WiHo	Bra 2, SM dns, Bel r, Mon 2, US 2, Fra 2, GB 2, Ger 1, Hun 1, Aut 2, Ita 1, Por 3, Esp 4, Mex 2, Jap 15, Aus r
1988	LtHo	Bra 3, SM 3, Mon r, Mex r, Can 4, US r, Fra 5, GB 5, Ger r, Hun 8, Bel 4, Ita r, Por r, Esp 8, Jap r, Aus 3
1989	LtJu	Bra r, SM r, Mon r, Mex 11, US r, Can 4, Fra 8, GB 4, Ger 5, Hun 6, Ita r, Por r, Esp 8, Jap 4, Aus r
1990	BeFd	US 4, Bra 6, SM 5, Mon dq, Can 2, Mex 6, Fra 4, GB 5, Ger r, Hun 3, Bel 5, Ita 7, Por 5, Esp r, Jap 1, Aus 1
1991	BeFd	US 3, Bra 5, SM r, Mon r, Can 1, Mex r, Fra 8, GB 5, Ger r, Hun r, Bel 3, Ita 6, Por 5, Esp 11, Jap 7, Aus 4

PIROCCHI, Renato

COUNTRY: Italy
BORN: March 26, 1933
GP STARTS: 1
WC POINTS: 0

Year	Team	Grand(s) Prix
1961	CoMa	Ita 12

PIRONI, Didier

COUNTRY: France
BORN: March 26, 1952
GP STARTS: 70
WC POINTS: 101
WC RECORD: 1978-15/7; 1979-10/14; 1980-5/32; 1981-13/9; 1982-2/39

Psn	No	Grand(s) Prix
1st:	3	1980 Bel; 1982 SM, Hol
2nd:	3	1980 Fra; 1982 Mon, GB
3rd:	7	1979 Bel, USE; 1980 SA, Can, USE; 1982 US, Fra
Pole:	4	1980 Mon, GB; 1982 Can, Ger
Fast:	5	1980 GB, Can; 1981 US; 1982 SM, Can

Year	Team	Grand(s) Prix
1978	TyFd	Arg 14, Bra 6, SA 6, USW r, Mon 5, Bel 6, Esp 12, Swe r, Fra 10, GB r, Ger 5, Aut r, Hol r, Ita r, USE 10, Can 7
1979	TyFd	Arg r, Bra 4, SA r, USW dq, Esp 6, Bel 3, Mon r, Fra r, GB 10, Ger 9, Aut 7, Hol r, Ita 10, Can 5, USE 3
1980	LiFd	Arg r, Bra 4, SA 3, USW 6, Bel 1, Mon r, Fra 2, GB r, Ger r, Aut r, Hol r, Ita 6, Can 3, USE 3
1981	Fe	USW r, Bra r, Arg r, SM 5, Bel 8, Mon 4, Esp 15, Fra 5, GB r, Ger r, Aut 9, Hol r, Ita 5, Can r, US 9
1982	Fe	SA 18, Bra 6, USW r, SM 1, Bel dns, Mon 2, US 3, Can 9, Hol 1, GB 2, Fra 3, Ger dns

PIRRO, Emanuele

COUNTRY: Italy
BORN: January 12, 1962
GP STARTS: 37
WC POINTS: 3
WC RECORD: 1989-23/2; 1991-18/1

Year	Team	Grand(s) Prix
1989	BeFd	Fra 9, GB 11, Ger r, Hun 8, Bel 10, Ita r, Por r, Esp r, Jap r, Aus 5
1990	DaFd	SM r, Mon r, Can r, Mex r, Fra r, GB 11, Ger r, Hun 10, Bel r, Ita r, Por 15, Esp r, Jap r, Aus r
1991	DaJu	US r, Bra 11, Mon 6, Can 9, GB 10, Ger 10, Hun r, Bel 8, Ita 10, Por r, Esp 15, Jap r, Aus 7

POLLET, Jacques

COUNTRY: France
BORN: July 28, 1932
GP STARTS: 5
WC POINTS: 0

Year	Team	Grand(s) Prix
1954	Gor	Fra r, Esp r
1955	Gor	Mon 7, Hol 10, Ita r

PON, Ben

COUNTRY: Holland
BORN: December 9, 1936
GP STARTS: 1
WC POINTS: 0

Year	Team	Grand(s) Prix
1962	Por	Hol r

POORE, Dennis

COUNTRY: GB
BORN: August 19, 1916
GP STARTS: 2
WC POINTS: 3
WC RECORD: 1952-13/3

Year	Team	Grand(s) Prix
1952	Con	GB 4, Ita 12

POSEY, Sam

COUNTRY: US
BORN: May 26, 1944
GP STARTS: 2
WC POINTS: 0

Year	Team	Grand(s) Prix
1971	SuFd	US r
1972	SuFd	US 12

POZZI, Charles

COUNTRY: France
BORN: August 27, 1909
GP STARTS: 1
WC POINTS: 0

Year	Team	Grand(s) Prix
1950	Ta	Fra 6

PRETORIUS, Jackie

COUNTRY: South Africa
BORN: November 22, 1934
GP STARTS: 3
WC POINTS: 0

Year	Team	Grand(s) Prix
1968	BrCl	SA uc
1971	BrFd	SA r
1973	WiFd	SA r

PROPHET, David

COUNTRY: GB
BORN: October 9, 1937
GP STARTS: 2
WC POINTS: 0

Year	Team	Grand(s) Prix
1963	BrFd	SA r
1965	BrFd	SA 14

PROST, Alain

COUNTRY: France
BORN: February 24, 1955
GP STARTS: 199
WC POINTS: 768.5 (796.5)
WC RECORD: 1980-15/5; 1981-5/43; 1982-4/34; 1983-2/57; 1984-2/71.5; 1985-1/73; 1986-1/72; 1987-4/46; 1988-2/87; 1989-1/76; 1990-2/71; 1991-5/34; 1993-1/99
WORLD CHAMPION: 1985, 1986, 1989, 1993

Psn	No	Grand(s) Prix
1st:	51	1981 Fra, Hol, Ita; 1982 SA, Bra; 1983 Fra, Bel, GB, Aut; 1984 Bra, SM, Mon, Ger, Hol, Eur, Por; 1985 Bra, Mon, GB, Aut, Ita; 1986 SM, Mon, Aut, Aus; 1987 Bra, Bel, Por; 1988 Bra, Mon, Mex, Fra, Por, Esp, Aus; 1989 US, Fra, GB, Ita; 1990 Bra, Mex, Fra, GB, Esp; 1993 SA, SM, Esp, Can, Fra, GB, Ger,
2nd:	35	1981 Ger, US; 1982 Fra, Swi; 1983 SM, Eur; 1984 SA; 1985 Ger, Hol; 1986 Can, Fra, Por, Mex; 1987 Esp; 1988 SM, Can, US, Ger, Hun, Bel, Jap; 1989 Bra, SM, Mon, Ger, Bel, Por; 1990 Bel, Ita; 1991 US, Fra, Esp; 1993 Por, Jap, Aus
3rd:	20	1981 Arg; 1983 Mon; 1984 Can; 1985 Can, Fra, Bel, SA; 1986 Esp, US, GB; 1987 US, Fra, Hun; 1989 Esp; 1990 Por, Aus; 1991 GB, Ita; 1993 Eur, Bel
Pole:	33	1981 Ger, Hol; 1982 Bra, Bel, US, Swi, Caesar's Palace; 1983 Fra, Mon, Bel; 1984 Mon, Ger, Hol; 1985 Aut, Bel; 1986 Mon; 1988 Fra, Por; 1989 Can, Fra; 1993 SA, Bra, Eur, SM, Esp, Mon, Can, GB, Ger, Hun, Bel, Ita, Jap
Fast:	41	1981 Fra; 1982 SA, Bra, US, Swi; 1983 Fra, GB, Aut; 1984 Bra, Fra, Ger; 1985 Bra, GB, Aut, Hol, Bel; 1986 Mon, Bel; 1987 Bel, Jap; 1988 SM, Mex, US, Fra, Hun, Esp, Aus; 1989 SM, Mon, Bel, Ita, Jap; 1990 Mex, Bel; 1991 Mon; 1993 SA, SM, Mon, Hun, Bel, Jap

Year	Team	Grand(s) Prix
1980	McFd	Arg 6, Bra 5, SA dns, Bel r, Mon r, Fra r, GB 6, Ger 11, Aut 7, Hol 6, Ita 7, Can r
1980	TyFd	USE dns
1981	Re	USW r, Bra r, Arg 3, SM r, Bel r, Mon r, Esp r, Fra 1, GB r, Ger 2, Aut r, Hol 1, Ita 1, Can r, US 2
1982	Re	SA 1, Bra 1, USW r, SM r, Bel r, Mon 7, US uc, Can r, Hol r, GB 6, Fra 2, Ger r, Aut 8, Swi 2, Ita r, Caesar's Palace 4
1983	Re	Bra 7, USW 11, Fra 1, SM 2, Mon 3, Bel 1, US 8, Can 5, GB 1, Ger 4, Aut 1, Hol r, Ita r, Eur 2, SA r
1984	McTG	Bra 1, SA 2, Bel r, SM 1, Fra 7, Mon 1, Can 3, Detroit 4, Dallas r, GB r, Ger 1, Aut r, Hol 1, Ita r, Eur 1, Por 1
1985	McTG	Bra 1, Por r, SM dq, Mon 1, Can 3, US r, Fra 3, GB 1, Ger 2, Aut 1, Hol 2, Ita 1, Bel 3, Eur 4, SA 3, Aus r
1986	McTG	Bra r, Esp 3, SM 1, Mon 1, Bel 6, Can 2, US 3, Fra 2, GB 3, Ger 6, Hun r, Aut 1, Ita dq, Por 2, Mex 2, Aus 1
1987	McTG	Bra 1, SM r, Bel 1, Mon 9, US 3, Fra 3, GB r, Ger 7, Hun 3, Aut 6, Ita 15, Por 1, Esp 2, Mex r, Jap 7, Aus r
1988	McHo	Bra 1, SM 2, Mon 1, Mex 1, Can 2, US 2, Fra 1, GB r, Ger 2, Hun 2, Bel 2, Ita r, Por 1, Esp 1, Jap 2, Aus 1
1989	McHo	Bra 2, SM 2, Mon 2, Mex 5, US 1, Can r, Fra 1, GB 1, Ger 2, Hun 4, Bel 2, Ita 1, Por 2, Esp 3, Jap r, Aus r
1990	Fe	US r, Bra 1, SM 4, Mon r, Can 5, Mex 1, Fra 1, GB 1, Ger 4, Hun r, Bel 2, Ita 2, Por 3, Esp 1, Jap r, Aus 3
1991	Fe	US 2, Bra 4, SM dns, Mon 5, Can r, Mex r, Fra 2, GB 3, Ger r, Hun r, Bel r, Ita 3, Por r, Esp 2, Jap 4
1993	WiRe	SA 1, Bra r, Eur 3, SM 1, Esp 1, Mon 4, Can 1, Fra 1, GB 1, Ger 1, Hun 12, Bel 3, Ita 12, Por 2, Jap 2, Aus 2

PRYCE, Tom

COUNTRY: GB
BORN: June 11, 1949
GP STARTS: 42
WC POINTS: 19
WC RECORD: 1974-18/1; 1975-10/8; 1976-11/10

Psn	No	Grand(s) Prix
3rd:	2	1975 Aut; 1976 Bra
Pole:	1	1975 GB

Year	Team	Grand(s) Prix
1974	ToFd	Bel r
1974	ShFd	Hol r, Fra r, GB 8, Ger 6, Aut r, Ita 10, Can r, US uc
1975	ShFd	Arg 12, Bra r, SA 9, Esp r, Mon r, Bel 6, Swe r, Hol 6, Fra r, GB r, Ger 4, Aut 3, Ita 6, US r
1976	ShFd	Bra 3, SA 7, USW r, Esp 8, Bel 10, Mon 7, Swe 9, Fra 8, GB 4, Ger 8, Aut r, Hol 4, Ita 8, Can 11, USE r, Jap r
1977	ShFd	Arg uc, Bra r, SA r

PURLEY, David

COUNTRY: GB
BORN: January 26, 1945
GP STARTS: 7
WC POINTS: 0

Year	Team	Grand(s) Prix
1973	MrFd	Mon r, GB dns, Hol r, Ger 15, Ita 9
1977	LcFd	Bel 13, Swe 14, Fra r

QUESTER, Dieter

COUNTRY: Austria
BORN: May 30, 1939
GP STARTS: 1
WC POINTS: 0

Year	Team	Grand(s) Prix
1969	BMW	Ger dns
1974	SuFd	Aut 9

RABY, Ian

COUNTRY: GB
BORN: September 22, 1921
GP STARTS: 3
WC POINTS: 0

Year	Team	Grand(s) Prix
1963	GiBR	GB r
1964	BrBR	GB r
1965	BrBR	GB 11

RAHAL, Bobby

COUNTRY: US
BORN: January 10, 1953
GP STARTS: 2
WC POINTS: 0

Year	Team	Grand(s) Prix
1978	WoFd	USE 12, Can r

RAPHANEL, Pierre-Henri

COUNTRY: France
BORN: May 27, 1961
GP STARTS: 1
WC POINTS: 0

Year	Team	Grand(s) Prix
1989	CiFd	Mon r

RATHMANN, Dick

COUNTRY: US
BORN: January 6, 1926
GP STARTS: 5
WC POINTS: 2
WC RECORD: 1956-19/2

Psn	No	Grand(s) Prix
Pole:	1	1958 Indy

Year	Team	Grand(s) Prix
1950	Wa	Indy r
1956	KK	Indy 5
1958	Wa	Indy r
1959	Wa	Indy r
1960	Wa	Indy r

RATHMANN, Jim

COUNTRY: US
BORN: July 16, 1928
GP STARTS: 10
WC POINTS: 29
WC RECORD: 1952-10/6; 1957-10/7; 1958-21/2; 1959-11/6; 1960-8/8

Psn	No	Grand(s) Prix
1st:	1	1960 Indy
2nd:	3	1952 Indy; 1957 Indy; 1959 Indy
Fast:	2	1957 Indy; 1960 Indy

Year	Team	Grand(s) Prix
1950	Wet	Indy 24
1952	KK	Indy 2
1953	KK	Indy 7
1954	KK	Indy r
1955	Epp	Indy 14
1956	KK	Indy r
1957	Epp	Indy 2
1958	Epp	Indy 5
1959	Wa	Indy 2
1960	Wa	Indy 1

RATZENBERGER, Roland

COUNTRY: Austria
BORN: July 4, 1962
GP STARTS: 1
WC POINTS: 0

Year	Team	Grand(s) Prix
1994	SiFd	Pac 11

REBAQUE, Hector

COUNTRY: Mexico
BORN: February 5, 1956
GP STARTS: 41
WC POINTS: 13
WC RECORD: 1978-19/1; 1980-20/1; 1981-9/11

Year	Team	Grand(s) Prix
1977	HeFd	Ger r
1978	LtFd	Bra r, SA 10, Esp r, Swe 12, GB r, Ger 6, Aut r, Hol 11, USE r
1979	LtFd	Arg r, SA 14, USW r, Esp r, Bel r, Fra 12, GB 9, Ger r, Hol 7
1979	RqFd	Can r
1980	BrFd	GB 7, Ger r, Aut 10, Hol r, Ita r, Can 6, USE r
1981	BrFd	USW r, Bra r, Arg r, SM 4, Bel r, Esp r, Fra 9, GB 5, Ger 4, Aut r, Hol 4, Ita r, Can r, US r

REDMAN, Brian

COUNTRY: GB
BORN: March 9, 1937
GP STARTS: 12
WC POINTS: 8
WC RECORD: 1968-19/4; 1972-12/4

Psn	No	Grand(s) Prix
3rd:	1	1968 Esp

Year	Team	Grand(s) Prix
1968	CoMa	SA rr
1968	CoBR	Esp 3, Bel r
1970	dTFd	GB dns
1971	SuFd	SA 7
1972	McFd	Mon 5, Fra 9, Ger 5
1972	BRM	US r
1973	ShFd	US dq
1974	ShFd	Esp 7, Bel 18, Mon r

REECE, Jimmy

COUNTRY: US
BORN: November 17, 1929
GP STARTS: 6
WC POINTS: 0

Year	Team	Grand(s) Prix
1952	KK	Indy 7
1954	Pan	Indy 17
1955	Pan	Indy r
1956	Les	Indy 9
1957	KK	Indy r
1958	Wa	Indy 6

REES, Alan

COUNTRY: GB
BORN: January 12, 1938
GP STARTS: 2
WC POINTS: 0

Year	Team	Grand(s) Prix
1966	BrFd	Ger r
1967	CoMa	GB 9

REGAZZONI, Clay

COUNTRY: Switzerland
BORN: September 5, 1939
GP STARTS: 132
WC POINTS: 209 (212)
WC RECORD: 1970-3/33; 1971-7/13; 1972-6/15; 1973-17/2; 1974-2/52; 1975-5/25; 1976-5/31; 1977-17/5; 1978-16/4; 1979-5/29

Psn	No	Grand(s) Prix
1st:	5	1970 Ita; 1974 Ger; 1975 Ita; 1976 USW; 1979 GB
2nd:	13	1970 Aut, Can, Mex; 1972 Ger; 1974 Bra, Esp, Hol, Can; 1976 Bel, Hol, Ita; 1979 Mon, Ger
3rd:	10	1971 SA, Hol, Ger; 1972 Esp; 1974 Arg, Fra; 1975 Swe, Hol; 1979 Ita, Can
Pole:	5	1970 Mex; 1971 GB; 1973 Arg; 1974 Bel; 1976 USW
Fast:	15	1970 Aut, Ita, Can; 1974 Arg, Bra, Aut; 1975 Bel, GB, Ger, Ita; 1976 USW, Mon, Hol; 1979 GB, Ita

Year	Team	Grand(s) Prix
1970	Fe	Hol 4, GB 4, Ger r, Aut 2, Ita 1, Can 2, US 13, Mex 2
1971	Fe	SA 3, Esp r, Mon r, Hol 3, Fra r, GB r, Ger 3, Aut r, Ita r, Can r, US 6
1972	Fe	Arg 4, SA 12, Esp 3, Mon r, Bel r, Ger 2, Aut r, Ita r, Can 5, US 8
1973	BRM	Arg 7, Bra 6, SA r, Esp 9, Bel 10, Mon r, Swe 9, Fra 12, GB 7, Hol 8, Ger r, Aut 6, Ita r, US 8
1974	Fe	Arg 3, Bra 2, SA r, Esp 2, Bel 4, Mon 4, Swe r, Hol 2, Fra 3, GB 4, Ger 1, Aut 5, Ita r, Can 2, US 11
1975	Fe	Arg 4, Bra 4, SA 16, Esp uc, Mon r, Bel 5, Swe 3, Hol 3, Fra r, GB 13, Ger r, Aut 7, Ita 1, US r
1976	Fe	Bra 7, SA r, USW 1, Esp 11, Bel 2, Mon r, Swe 6, Fra r, GB dq, Ger 9, Hol 2, Ita 2, Can 6, USE 7, Jap 5
1977	EnFd	Arg 6, Bra r, SA 9, USW r, Esp r, Bel r, Swe 7, Fra 7, Ger r, Aut r, Hol r, Ita 5, USE 5, Can r, Jap r
1978	ShFd	Arg 15, Bra 5, USW 10, Bel r, Esp 15, Swe 5, Fra r, GB r, Aut uc, Ita uc, USE 14
1979	WiFd	Arg 10, Bra 15, SA 9, USW r, Esp r, Bel r, Mon 2, Fra 6, GB 1, Ger 2, Aut 5, Hol r, Ita 3, Can 3, USE r
1980	EnFd	Arg uc, Bra r, SA 9, USW r

REUTEMANN, Carlos

COUNTRY: Argentina
BORN: April 12, 1942
GP STARTS: 146
WC POINTS: 298 (310)
WC RECORD: 1972-16/3; 1973-7/16; 1974-6/32; 1975-3/37; 1976-16/3; 1977-4/42; 1978-3/48; 1979-7/20; 1980-3/42; 1981-2/49; 1982-15/6

Psn	No	Grand(s) Prix
1st:	12	1974 SA, Aut, US; 1975 Ger; 1977 Bra; 1978 Bra, USW, GB, USE; 1980 Mon; 1981 Bra, Bel
2nd:	13	1975 SA, Swe; 1977 Esp, Jap; 1979 Arg, Esp; 1980 Ger, Can, USE; 1981 USW, Arg, GB; 1982 SA
3rd:	20	1973 Fra, US; 1974 Ger; 1975 Arg, Esp, Bel; 1977 Arg, Mon, Swe; 1978 Bel, Ita, Can; 1979 Bra, Mon; 1980 Bel, GB, Aut, Ita; 1981 SM, Ita
Pole:	6	1972 Arg; 1974 US; 1978 USW, Mon; 1981 Bel, US
Fast:	6	1974 SA; 1978 Bra, Fra; 1980 Mon; 1981 Bel, Ita

Year	Team	Grand(s) Prix
1972	BrFd	Arg 7, SA r, Bel 13, Fra 12, GB 8, Ger r, Aut r, Ita r, Can 4, US r
1973	BrFd	Arg r, Bra 11, SA 7, Esp r, Bel r, Mon r, Swe 4, Fra 3, GB 6, Hol r, Ger r, Aut 4, Ita 6, Can 8, US 3
1974	BrFd	Arg 7, Bra 7, SA 1, Esp r, Bel r, Mon r, Swe r, Hol 12, Fra r, GB 6, Ger 3, Aut 1, Ita r, Can 9, US 1
1975	BrFd	Arg 3, Bra 8, SA 2, Esp 3, Mon 9, Bel 3, Swe 2, Hol 4, Fra 14, GB r, Ger 1, Aut 14, Ita 4, US r
1976	BrAl	Bra 12, SA r, USW r, Esp 4, Bel r, Mon r, Swe r, Fra 11, GB r, Ger r, Aut r, Hol r
1976	Fe	Ita 9
1977	Fe	Arg 3, Bra 1, SA 8, USW r, Esp 2, Mon 3, Bel r, Swe 3, Fra 6, GB 15, Ger 4, Aut 4, Hol 6, Ita r, USE 6, Can r, Jap 2
1978	Fe	Arg 7, Bra 1, SA r, USW 1, Mon 8, Bel 3, Esp r, Swe 10, Fra 18, GB 1, Ger r, Aut dq, Hol 7, Ita 3, USE 1, Can 3
1979	LtFd	Arg 2, Bra 3, SA 5, USW r, Esp 2, Bel 4, Mon 3, Fra 13, GB 8, Ger r, Aut r, Hol r, Ita 7, Can r, USE r
1980	WiFd	Arg r, Bra r, SA 5, USW r, Bel 3, Mon 1, Fra 6, GB 3, Ger 2, Aut 3, Hol 4, Ita 3, Can 2, USE 2
1981	WiFd	USW 2, Bra 1, Arg 2, SM 3, Bel 1, Mon r, Esp 4, Fra 10, GB 2, Ger r, Aut 5, Hol r, Ita 3, Can 10, US 8
1982	WiFd	SA 2, Bra r

REVENTLOW, Lance

COUNTRY: US
BORN: February 24, 1936
GP STARTS: 1
WC POINTS: 0

Year	Team	Grand(s) Prix
1960	Sb	Hol dns, Bel r

REVSON, Peter

COUNTRY: US
BORN: February 27, 1939
GP STARTS: 30
WC POINTS: 61
WC RECORD: 1972-5/23; 1973-5/38

Psn	No	Grand(s) Prix
1st:	2	1973 GB, Can
2nd:	2	1972 Can; 1973 SA
3rd:	4	1972 SA, GB, Aut; 1973 Ita
Pole:	1	1972 Can

Year	Team	Grand(s) Prix
1964	LtBR	Bel dq, GB r, Ger r, Ita 13
1971	TyFd	US r
1972	McFd	Arg r, SA 3, Esp 5, Bel 7, GB 3, Aut 3, Ita 4, Can 2, US 18
1973	McFd	Arg 8, Bra r, SA 2, Esp 4, Bel r, Mon 5, Swe 7, GB 1, Hol 4, Ger 9, Aut r, Ita 3, Can 1, US 5
1974	ShFd	Arg r, Bra r

RHODES, John

COUNTRY: GB
BORN: August 18, 1927
GP STARTS: 1
WC POINTS: 0

Year	Team	Grand(s) Prix
1965	CoCl	GB r

RIBEIRO, Alex

COUNTRY: Brazil
BORN: November 7, 1948
GP STARTS: 10
WC POINTS: 0

Year	Team	Grand(s) Prix
1976	HeFd	USE 12
1977	MrFd	Arg r, Bra r, SA r, USW r, Ger 8, Hol 11, USE 15, Can 8, Jap 12

RIESS, Fritz

COUNTRY: Germany
BORN: July 11, 1922
GP STARTS: 1
WC POINTS: 0

Year	Team	Grand(s) Prix
1952	Ver	Ger 7

RIGSBY, Jim

COUNTRY: US
BORN: June 6, 1923
GP STARTS: 1
WC POINTS: 0

Year	Team	Grand(s) Prix
1952	Wa	Indy 12

RINDT, Jochen

COUNTRY: Austria
BORN: April 18, 1942
GP STARTS: 60
WC POINTS: 107 (109)
WC RECORD: 1965-13/4; 1966-3/22; 1967-11/6; 1968-12/8; 1969-4/22; 1970-1/45
WORLD CHAMPION: 1970

Psn	No	Grand(s) Prix
1st:	6	1969 US; 1970 Mon, Hol, Fra, GB, Ger
2nd:	3	1966 Bel, US; 1969 Ita
3rd:	4	1966 Ger; 1968 SA, Ger; 1969 Can
Pole:	10	1968 Fra, Can; 1968 Esp, Hol, GB, Ita, US; 1970 Hol, GB, Aut
Fast:	3	1969 Esp, US; 1970 Bel

Year	Team	Grand(s) Prix
1964	BrBR	Aut r
1965	CoCl	SA r, Bel 11, Fra r, GB 14, Hol r, Ger 4, Ita 8, US 6, Mex r
1966	CoMa	Mon r, Bel 2, Fra 4, GB 5, Hol r, Ger 3, Ita 4, US 2, Mex r
1967	CoMa	SA r, Mon r, Hol r, Bel 4, Fra r, GB r, Ger r, Can r, Ita 4, US r
1968	BrRe	SA 3, Esp r, Mon r, Bel r, Hol r, Fra r, GB r, Ger 3, Ita r, Can r, US r, Mex r
1969	LtFd	SA r, Esp r, Hol r, Fra r, GB 4, Ger r, Ita 2, Can 3, US 1, Mex r
1970	LtFd	SA r, Esp r, Mon 1, Bel r, Hol 1, Fra 1, GB 1, Ger 1, Aut r, Ita dns

RISELEY-PRICHARD, John

COUNTRY: GB
BORN: January 17, 1924
GP STARTS: 1
WC POINTS: 0

Year	Team	Grand(s) Prix
1954	Con	GB r

ROBARTS, Richard

COUNTRY: GB
BORN: September 22, 1944
GP STARTS: 3
WC POINTS: 0

Year	Team	Grand(s) Prix
1974	BrFd	Arg r, Bra 15, SA 17

RODRIGUEZ LARRETA, Alberto

COUNTRY: Argentina
BORN: January 14, 1 934
GP STARTS: 1
WC POINTS: 0

Year	Team	Grand(s) Prix
1960	LoCl	Arg 9

RODRIGUEZ, Pedro

COUNTRY: Mexico
BORN: January 18, 1940
GP STARTS: 55
WC POINTS: 71
WC RECORD: 1964-19/1; 1965-14/2; 1967-6/15; 1968-6/18; 1969-13/3; 1970-7/23; 1971-9/9

Psn	No	Grand(s) Prix
1st:	2	1967 SA; 1970 Bel
2nd:	3	1968 Bel; 1970 US; 1971 Hol
3rd:	2	1968 Hol, Can
Fast:	1	1968 Fra

Year	Team	Grand(s) Prix
1963	LoCl	US r, Mex r
1964	Fe	Mex 6
1965	Fe	US 5, Mex 7
1966	LoCl	Fra r
1966	LtFd	Ger r
1966	LtBR	US r
1966	LoCl	Mex r
1967	CoMa	SA 1, Mon 5, Hol r, Bel 9, Fra 6, GB 5, Ger 8, Mex 6
1968	BRM	SA r, Esp r, Mon r, Bel 2, Hol 3, Fra uc, GB r, Ger 6, Ita r, Can 3, US r, Mex 4
1969	BRM	SA r, Esp r, Mon r
1969	Fe	GB r, Ita 6, Can r, US 5, Mex 7
1970	BRM	SA 9, Esp r, Mon 6, Bel 1, Hol 10, Fra r, GB r, Ger r, Aut 4, Ita r, Can 4, US 2, Mex 6
1971	BRM	SA r, Esp 4, Mon 9, Hol 2, Fra r

RODRIGUEZ, Ricardo

COUNTRY: Mexico
BORN: February 14, 1942
GP STARTS: 5
WC POINTS: 4
WC RECORD: 1962-12/4

Year	Team	Grand(s) Prix
1961	Fe	Ita r
1962	Fe	Hol 8, Bel 4, Ger 6, Ita r

ROL, Franco

COUNTRY: Italy
BORN: June 5, 1908
GP STARTS: 5
WC POINTS: 0

Year	Team	Grand(s) Prix
1950	Mas	Mon r, Fra r, Ita r
1951	OSCA	Ita 9
1952	Mas	Ita r

ROLT, Tony

COUNTRY: GB
BORN: October 16, 1918
GP STARTS: 2
WC POINTS: 0

Year	Team	Grand(s) Prix
1953	Con	GB r
1955	Con	GB r

ROOS, Bertil

COUNTRY: Sweden
BORN: October 12, 1943
GP STARTS: 1
WC POINTS: 0

Year	Team	Grand(s) Prix
1974	ShFd	Swe r

ROSBERG, Keke

COUNTRY: Finland
BORN: December 6, 1948
GP STARTS: 114

WC POINTS: 159.5
WC RECORD: 1980-10/6; 1982-1/44; 1983-5/27; 1984-8/20.5; 1985-3/40; 1986-6/22
WORLD CHAMPION: 1982

Psn	No	Grand(s) Prix
1st:	5	1982 Swi; 1983 Mon; 1984 Dallas; 1985 US, Aus
2nd:	8	1982 USW, Bel, Aut; 1983 US; 1984 Bra; 1985 Fra, SA; 1986 Mon
3rd:	4	1980 Arg; 1982 Hol, Ger; 1985 Eur
Pole:	5	1982 GB; 1982 Bra; 1985 Fra, GB; 1986 Ger
Fast:	3	1985 Fra, SA, Aus

Year	Team	Grand(s) Prix
1978	ThFd	SA r
1978	ATFd	Swe 15, Fra 16, GB r
1978	WoFd	Ger 10, Aut uc, Hol
1978	ATFd	USE r, Can uc
1979	WoFd	Fra 9, GB r, Ger r, Aut r, Hol r, Ita r, USE r
1980	FiFd	Arg 3, Bra 9, SA r, USW r, Bel 7, Fra r, Ger r, Aut 16, Ita 5, Can 9, USE 10
1981	FiFd	USW r, Bra 9, Arg r, SM r, Bel r, Esp 12, Fra r, GB r, US 10
1982	WiFd	SA 5, Bra dq, USW 2, Bel 2, Mon r, US 4, Can r, Hol 3, GB r, Fra 5, Ger 3, Aut 2, Swi 1, Ita 8, Caesar's Palace 5
1983	WiF	Bra dq, USW r, Fra 5, SM 4, Mon 1, Bel 5, US 2, Can 4, GB 11, Ger 10, Aut 8, Hol r, Ita 11, Eur r
1983	WiHo	SA 5
1984	WiHo	Bra 2, SA r, Bel 4, SM r, Fra 6, Mon 4, Can r, Detroit r, Dallas 1, GB r, Ger r, Aut r, Hol 8, Ita r, Eur r, Por r
1985	WiHo	Bra r, Por r, SM r, Mon 8, Can 4, US 1, Fra 2, GB r, Ger 12, Aut r, Hol r, Ita r, Bel 4, Eur 3, SA 2, Aus 1
1986	McTG	Bra r, Esp 4, SM 5, Mon 2, Bel r, Can 4, US r, Fra 4, GB r, Ger 5, Hun r, Aut 9, Ita 4, Por r, Mex r, Aus r

ROSE, Mauri

COUNTRY: US
BORN: May 26, 1906
GP STARTS: 2
WC POINTS: 4
WC RECORD: 1950-9/4

Psn	No	Grand(s) Prix
3rd:	1	1950 Indy

Year	Team	Grand(s) Prix
1950	De	Indy 3
1951	De	Indy r

ROSIER, Louis

COUNTRY: France
BORN: November 5, 1905
GP STARTS: 38
WC POINTS: 18
WC RECORD: 1950-4/13; 1951-12/3; 1956-19/2

Psn	No	Grand(s) Prix
3rd:	2	1950 Swi, Bel

Year	Team	Grand(s) Prix
1950	Ta	GB 5, Mon r, Swi 3, Bel 3, Fra r, Ita 4
1951	Ta	Swi 9, Bel 4, Fra r, GB 10, Ger 8, Ita 7, Esp 7
1952	Fe	Swi r, Bel r, Fra r, Ita 10
1953	Fe	Hol 7, Bel 8, Fra 8, GB 11, Ger 10, Swi r, Ita uc
1954	Fe	Arg r, Fra r, GB r, Ger 8
1954	Mas	Ita 8, Esp 7
1955	Mas	Mon r, Bel 9, Hol 9
1956	Mas	Mon r, Bel 8, Fra 6, GB r, Ger 5

ROSSET, Ricardo

COUNTRY: Brazil
BORN: July 27, 1968
GP STARTS: 26
WC POINTS: 0

Year	Team	Grand(s) Prix
1996	FtHt	Aus 9, Bra r, Arg r, Eur 11, SM r, Mon r, Esp r, Can r, Fra 11, GB r, Ger 11, Hun 8, Bel 9, Ita r, Por 14, Jap 13
1997	LoFd	Aus dnq
1998	TyFd	Aus r, Bra r, Arg 14, SM r, Esp dnq, Mon dnq, Can 8, Fra r, GB r, Aut 12, Hun dnq, Bel dns, Ita 12, Lux r, Jap dnq

ROTHENGATTER, Huub

COUNTRY: Holland
BORN: October 8, 1954
GP STARTS: 25
WC POINTS: 0

Year	Team	Grand(s) Prix
1984	SpHt	Can uc, Dallas r, GB uc, Ger 9, Aut uc, Hol r, Ita 8

1985	OsAl	Ger r, Aut 9, Hol uc, Ita r, Bel uc, SA r, Aus 7
1986	Za	SM r, Bel r, Can 12, Fra r, GB r, Ger r, Hun r, Aut 8, Ita r, Por r, Mex dns, Aus r

RUBY, Lloyd

COUNTRY: US
BORN: January 12, 1928
GP STARTS: 2
WC POINTS: 0

Year	Team	Grand(s) Prix
1960	Wa	Indy 7
1961	LoCl	US r

RUSSO, Eddie

COUNTRY: US
BORN: November 19, 1925
GP STARTS: 3
WC POINTS: 0

Year	Team	Grand(s) Prix
1955	Pawl	Indy r
1957	KK	Indy r
1960	KK	Indy r

RUSSO, Paul

COUNTRY: US
BORN: April 10, 1914
GP STARTS: 7
WC POINTS: 9.5
WC RECORD: 1953-18/1.5; 1955-13/3; 1956-27/1; 1957-14/4

Psn	No	Grand(s) Prix
Fast:	1	1956 Indy

Year	Team	Grand(s) Prix
1950	Nichels	Indy 9
1953	KK	Indy r
1954	KK	Indy 8
1956	KK	Indy r
1957	KK	Indy 4
1958	KK	Indy r
1959	KK	Indy 9

RUTTMAN, Troy

COUNTRY: US
BORN: March 11, 1930
GP STARTS: 8
WC POINTS: 9.5
WC RECORD: 1952-7/8; 1954-23/1.5

Psn	No	Grand(s) Prix
1st:	1	1952 Indy

Year	Team	Grand(s) Prix
1950	Les	Indy 15
1951	KK	Indy r
1952	Ku	Indy 1
1954	KK	Indy 4
1956	KK	Indy r
1957	Wa	Indy r
1958	Mas	Fra 10
1960	Wa	Indy r

RYAN, Peter

COUNTRY: Canada
BORN: June 10, 1940
GP STARTS: 1
WC POINTS: 0

Year	Team	Grand(s) Prix
1961	LoCl	US 10

SACHS, Eddie

COUNTRY: US
BORN: May 28, 1927
GP STARTS: 4
WC POINTS: 0

Psn	No	Grand(s) Prix
Pole:	1	1960 Indy

Year	Team	Grand(s) Prix
1957	Ku	Indy r
1958	Ku	Indy r
1959	Ku	Indy r
1960	We	Indy r

SAID, Bob

COUNTRY: US
BORN: May 5, 1932
GP STARTS: 1
WC POINTS: 0

Year	Team	Grand(s) Prix
1959	Con	US r

SALA, Luis

COUNTRY: Spain
BORN: May 15, 1959
GP STARTS: 26
WC POINTS: 1
WC RECORD: 1989-26/1

Year	Team	Grand(s) Prix
1988	MiFd	Bra r, SM 11, Mon r, Mex 11, Can 13, US r, Fra uc, GB r, Hun 10, Ita r, Por 8, Esp 12, Jap 15, Aus r
1989	MiFd	Bra r, SM r, Mon r, US r, Can r, GB 6, Hun r, Bel 15, Ita 8, Por 12, Esp r, Jap r

SALAZER, Eliseo

COUNTRY: Chile
BORN: November 14, 1954
GP STARTS: 24
WC POINTS: 3
WC RECORD: 1981-18/1; 1982-22/2

Year	Team	Grand(s) Prix
1981	MrFd	SM r
1981	EnFd	Esp 14, Fra r, Ger uc, Aut r, Hol 6, Ita r, Can r, US uc
1982	ATFd	SA 9, Bra r, USW r, SM 5, Bel r, Mon r, US r, Can r, Hol 13, Fra r, Ger r, Swi 14, Ita 9
1983	RmFd	Bra 15, USW r

SALO, Mika

COUNTRY: Finland
BORN: November 30, 1966
GP STARTS: 76
WC POINTS: 25
WC RECORD: 1995-14/5; 1996-13/5; 1997-16/2; 1998-13/3; 1999-10/10

Psn	No	Grand(s) Prix
2nd:	1	1999 Ger
3rd:	1	1999 Ita

Year	Team	Grand(s) Prix
1994	LoMH	Jap 10, Aus r
1995	TyYa	Bra 7, Arg r, SM r, Esp 10, Mon r, Can 8, Fra 15, GB 8, Ger r, Hun r, Bel 8, Ita 5, Por 13, Eur 10, Pac 12, Jap 6, Aus 5
1996	TyYa	Aus 6, Bra 5, Arg r, Eur dq, SM r, Mon 5, Esp dq, Can r, Fra 10, GB 7, Ger 9, Hun r, Bel 7, Ita r, Por 11, Jap r
1997	TyFd	Aus r, Bra 13, Arg 8, SM 9, Mon 5, Esp r, Can r, Fra r, GB r, Ger r, Hun 13, Bel 11, Ita r, Aut r, Lux 10, Jap r, Eur 12
1998	Ar	Aus r, Bra r, Arg r, SM 9, Esp r, Mon 4, Can r, Fra 13, GB r, Aut r, Ger 14, Hun r, Bel dns, Ita r, Lux 14, Jap r
1999	BASu	SM 7, Mon r, Esp 8
1999	Fe	Aut 9, Ger 2, Hun 12, Bel 7, Ita 3, Eur r

SALVADORI, Roy

COUNTRY: GB
BORN: May 12, 1922
GP STARTS: 47
WC POINTS: 18
WC RECORD: 1957-19/2; 1958-4/15; 1961-17/1

Psn	No	Grand(s) Prix
2nd:	1	1958 Ger
3rd:	1	1958 GB

Year	Team	Grand(s) Prix
1952	Fe	GB 8
1953	Con	Hol r, Fra r, GB r, Ger r, Ita r
1954	Mas	Fra r, GB r
1955	Mas	GB r
1956	Mas	GB r, Ger r, Ita uc
1957	Va	Fra r
1957	CoCl	GB 5, Ger r, Pescara r
1958	CoCl	Mon r, Hol 4, Bel 8, Fra uc, GB 3, Ger 2, Por 9, Ita 5, Mor 7
1959	CoMa	Mon r
1959	AM	Hol r
1959	CoMa	Fra r
1959	AM	GB 6, Por 6, Ita r
1959	CoMa	US r
1960	CoCl	Mon r
1960	AM	Hol dns, GB r
1960	CoCl	US 8
1961	CoCl	Fra 8, GB 6, Ger 10, Ita 6, US 7
1962	LICl	Hol r, Mon r, Fra r, GB r, Ger r, Ita r, SA r

SANESI, Consalvo

COUNTRY: Italy
BORN: March 28, 1911
GP STARTS: 5
WC POINTS: 3
WC RECORD: 1951-12/3

Year	Team	Grand(s) Prix
1950	AR	Ita r
1951	AR	Swi 4, Bel r, Fra 10, GB 6

SARRAZIN, Stephane

COUNTRY: France
BORN: November 2, 1974
GP STARTS: 1
WC POINTS: 0

Year	Team	Grand(s) Prix
1999	MiFd	Bra r

SCARBOROUGH, Carl

COUNTRY: US
BORN: July 3, 1914
GP STARTS: 2
WC POINTS: 0

Year	Team	Grand(s) Prix
1951	KK	Indy r
1953	KK	Indy 12

SCARFIOTTI, Ludovico

COUNTRY: Italy
BORN: October 18, 1933
GP STARTS: 10
WC POINTS: 17
WC RECORD: 1963-15/1; 1966-10/9; 1967-19/1; 1968-13/6

Psn	No	Grand(s) Prix
1st:	1	1966 Ita
Fast:	1	1966 Ita

Year	Team	Grand(s) Prix
1963	Fe	Hol 6, Fra dns
1964	Fe	Ita 9
1966	Fe	Ger r, Ita 1
1967	Fe	Hol 6, Bel uc
1967	EaWe	Ita r
1968	CoMa	SA r
1968	CoBR	Esp 4, Mon 4

SCARLATTI, Giorgio

COUNTRY: Italy
BORN: October 2, 1921
GP STARTS: 12
WC POINTS: 1
WC RECORD: 1957-21/1

Year	Team	Grand(s) Prix
1956	Fe	Ger r
1957	Mas	Mon r, Ger 10, Pescara 6, Ita 5
1958	Mas	Mon r, Hol r
1959	Mas	Fra 8
1959	CoCl	Ita 12
1960	Mas	Arg r
1960	CoMa	Ita r
1961	dTOs	Fra r

SCHECKTER, Ian

COUNTRY: South Africa
BORN: August 22, 1947
GP STARTS: 18
WC POINTS: 0

Year	Team	Grand(s) Prix
1974	LtFd	SA 13
1975	TyFd	SA r
1975	WiFd	Swe r, Hol 12
1976	TyFd	SA r
1977	MrFd	Arg r, Bra r, Esp 11, Bel r, Swe r, Fra uc, GB r, Ger r, Aut r, Hol 10, Ita r, USE r, Can r

SCHECKTER, Jody

COUNTRY: South Africa
BORN: January 29, 1950
GP STARTS: 112
WC POINTS: 246 (255)
WC RECORD: 1974-3/45; 1975-7/20; 1976-3/49; 1977-2/55; 1978-7/24; 1979-1/51; 1980-19/2
WORLD CHAMPION: 1979

Psn	No	Grand(s) Prix
1st:	10	1974 Swe, GB; 1975 SA; 1976 Swe; 1977 Arg, Mon, Can; 1979 Bel, Mon, Ita
2nd:	14	1974 Mon, Ger; 1975 Bel; 1976 Mon, GB, Ger, USE; 1977 SA, Ger; 1978 Ger, Can; 1979 SA, USW, Hol
3rd:	9	1974 Bel, Ita; 1975 GB; 1977 USW, Esp, Hol, USE; 1978 Mon, USE
Pole:	3	1976 Swe; 1977 Ger; 1979 Mon
Fast:	5	1974 Fra, Ger; 1976 Ger; 1977 Mon, Jap

Year	Team	Grand(s) Prix
1972	McFd	US 9
1973	McFd	SA 9, Fra r, GB r, Can r, US r
1974	TyFd	Arg r, Bra 13, SA 8, Esp 5, Bel 3, Mon 2, Swe 1, Hol 5, Fra 4, GB 1, Ger 2, Aut r, Ita 3, Can r, US r

1975 TyFd Arg 11, Bra r, SA 1, Esp r, Mon 7, Bel 2, Swe 7, Hol 16, Fra 9, GB 3, Ger r, Aut 8, Ita 8, US 6
1976 TyFd Bra 5, SA 4, USW r, Esp r, Bel 4, Mon 2, Swe 1, Fra 6, GB 2, Ger 2, Aut r, Hol 5, Ita 5, Can 4, USE 2, Jap r
1977 WoFd Arg 1, Bra r, SA 2, USW 3, Esp 3, Mon 1, Bel r, Swe r, Fra r, GB r, Ger 2, Aut r, Hol 3, Ita r, USE 3, Can 1, Jap 10
1978 WoFd Arg 10, Bra r, SA r, USW r, Mon 3, Bel r, Esp 4, Swe r, Fra 6, GB r, Ger 2, Aut r, Hol 12, Ita 12, USE 3, Can 2
1979 Fe Arg r, Bra 6, SA 2, USW 2, Esp 4, Bel 1, Mon 1, Fra 7, GB 5, Ger 4, Aut 4, Hol 2, Ita 1, Can 4, USE r
1980 Fe Arg r, Bra r, SA r, USW 5, Bel 8, Mon r, Fra 12, GB 10, Ger 13, Aut 13, Hol 9, Ita 8, USE 11

SCHELL, Harry

COUNTRY: US
BORN: July 29, 1921
GP STARTS: 55
WC POINTS: 32
WC RECORD: 1956-15/3; 1957-6/10; 1958-5/14; 1959-12/5

Psn	No	Grand(s) Prix
2nd:	1	1958 Hol
3rd:	1	1957 Pescara

Year	Team	Grand(s) Prix
1950	CoJA	Mon r
1950	Ta	Swi 8
1951	Mas	Swi 12, Fra r
1952	MaPl	Swi r, Fra r, GB 17
1953	Gor	Hol r, Bel 7, Fra r, GB r, Ger r, Ita 11
1954	Mas	Arg 6, Fra r, GB 12, Ger 7, Swi r, Esp r
1955	Mas	Arg 6
1955	Fe	Mon r
1955	Va	GB r, Ita r
1956	Va	Mon r, Bel 4, Fra r, GB r
1956	Mas	Ger r
1956	Va	Ita r
1957	Mas	Arg 4, Mon r, Fra 5, GB r, Ger 7, Pescara 3, Ita r
1958	Mas	Arg 6
1958	BRM	Mon 5, Hol 2, Bel 5, Fra 12, GB 5, Ger r, Por 6, Ita r, Moroccan 5
1959	BRM	Mon r, Hol r, Fra 7, GB 4, Ger uc, Por 5, Ita 7
1959	CoCl	US r
1960	CoCl	Arg r

SCHENKEN, Tim

COUNTRY: Australia
BORN: September 26, 1943
GP STARTS: 34
WC POINTS: 7
WC RECORD: 1971-14/5; 1972-19/2

Psn	No	Grand(s) Prix
3rd:	1	1971 Aut

Year	Team	Grand(s) Prix
1970	dTFd	Aut r, Ita r, Can uc, US r
1971	BrFd	Esp 9, Mon 10, Hol r, Fra 12, GB 12, Ger 6, Aut 3, Ita r, Can r, US r
1972	SuFd	Arg 5, SA r, Esp 8, Mon r, Bel r, Fra 17, GB r, Ger 14, Aut 11, Ita r, Can 7, US r
1973	WiFd	Can 14
1974	TjFd	Esp 14, Bel 10, Mon r, GB r, Aut 10, Ita r
1974	LtFd	US dq

SCHERRER, Albert

COUNTRY: Switzerland
BORN: February 28, 1908
GP STARTS: 1
WC POINTS: 0

Year	Team	Grand(s) Prix
1953	HWM	Swi uc

SCHIATTARELLA, Domenico

COUNTRY: Italy
BORN: November 17, 1967
GP STARTS: 7
WC POINTS: 0

Year	Team	Grand(s) Prix
1994	SiFd	Eur 19, Aus r
1995	SiFd	Bra r, Arg 9, SM r, Esp 15, Mon r

SCHILLER, Heinz

COUNTRY: Switzerland
BORN: January 25, 1930
GP STARTS: 1
WC POINTS: 0

Year	Team	Grand(s) Prix
1962	LtBR	Ger r

SCHINDLER, Bill

COUNTRY: US
BORN: March 6, 1909
GP STARTS: 3
WC POINTS: 0

Year	Team	Grand(s) Prix
1950	Snowberger	Indy r
1951	KK	Indy r
1952	Ste	Indy 14

SCHIESSER, Jo

COUNTRY: France
BORN: May 18, 1928
GP STARTS: 2
WC POINTS: 0

Year	Team	Grand(s) Prix
1966	MatFd	Ger 10
1968	Ho	Fra r

SCHIESSER, Jean-Louis

COUNTRY: France
BORN: September 12, 1948
GP STARTS: 1
WC POINTS: 0

Year	Team	Grand(s) Prix
1988	WiJu	Ita 11

SCHNEIDER, Bernd

COUNTRY: Germany
BORN: July 20, 1964
GP STARTS: 9
WC POINTS: 0

Year	Team	Grand(s) Prix
1988	Za	Mex r, Fra r, Ger 12, Bel 13, Ita r, Jap r
1989	ZaYa	Bra r, Jap r
1990	ArFd	US 12

SCHIELLER, Rudolf

COUNTRY: Switzerland
BORN: April 27, 1902
GP STARTS: 1
WC POINTS: 0

Year	Team	Grand(s) Prix
1952	Fe	Ger r

SCHROEDER, Rob

COUNTRY: US
BORN: May 11, 1926
GP STARTS: 1
WC POINTS: 0

Year	Team	Grand(s) Prix
1962	LoCl	US 10

SCHUMACHER, Michael

COUNTRY: Germany
BORN: January 3, 1969
GP STARTS: 126
WC POINTS: 570
WC RECORD: 1991-12/4; 1992-3/53; 1993-4/52; 1994-1/92; 1995-1/102; 1996-3/59; 1997-dq/78; 1998-2/86; 1999-5/44
WORLD CHAMPION: 1994, 1995

Psn	No	Grand(s) Prix
1st:	35	1992 Bel; 1993 Por; 1994 Bra, Pac, SM, Mon, Can, Fra, Hun, Eur; 1995 Bra, Esp, Mon, Fra, Ger, Bel, Eur, Pac, Jap; 1996 Esp, Bel, Ita; 1997 Mon, Can, Fra, Bel, Jap; 1998 Arg, Can, Fra, GB, Hun, Ita; 1999 SM, Mon
2nd:	22	1992 Esp, Can, Aus; 1993 SM, Can, GB, Ger, Bel; 1994 Esp, Jap; 1995 Por; 1996 Eur, SM, Jap; 1997 Aus, SM, Ger; 1998 SM, Lux; 1999 Bra, Mal, Jap
3rd:	14	1992 Mex, Bra, Ger, Ita; 1993 Bra, Esp, Fra; 1995 Arg; 1996 Bra, Por; 1998 Bra, Esp, Aut; 1999 Esp
Pole:	23	1994 Mon, Esp, Can, Hun, Eur, Jap; 1995 SM, Esp, Can, Jap; 1996 SM, Mon, Fra, Hun; 1997 Can, Fra, Hun; 1998 Ita, Lux, Jap; 1999 Can, Mal, Jap
Fast:	39	1992 Bel, Aus; 1993 Bra, Esp, Can, Fra, Ger; 1994 Bra, Pac, Mon, Esp, Can, Hun, Eur, Aus; 1995 Bra, Arg, Can, Fra, Ger, Eur, Pac, Jap; 1996 Esp, Ita; 1997 Mon, Fra, GB; 1998 SM, Can, GB, Hun, Bel, Jap; 1999 Aus, SM, Esp, Mal, Jap

Year	Team	Grand(s) Prix
1991	JoFd	Bel r
1991	BeFd	Ita 5, Por 6, Esp 6, Jap r, Aus r

1992	BeFd	SA 4, Mex 3, Bra 3, Esp 2, SM r, Mon 4, Can 2, Fra r, GB 4, Ger 3, Hun r, Bel 1, Ita 3, Por 7, Jap r, Aus 2
1993	BeFd	SA r, Bra 3, Eur r, SM 2, Esp 3, Mon r, Can 2, Fra 3, GB 2, Ger 2, Hun r, Bel 2, Ita r, Por 1, Jap r, Aus r
1994	BeFd	Bra 1, Pac 1, SM 1, Mon 1, Esp 2, Can 1, Fra 1, GB dq, Ger r, Hun 1, Bel dq, Eur 1, Jap 2, Aus r
1995	BeRe	Bra 1, Arg 3, SM r, Esp 1, Mon 1, Can 5, Fra 1, GB r, Ger 1, Hun 11, Bel 1, Ita r, Por 2, Eur 1, Pac 1, Jap 1, Aus r
1996	Fe	Aus r, Bra 3, Arg r, Eur 2, SM 2, Mon r, Esp 1, Can r, Fra dns, GB r, Ger 4, Hun 9, Bel 1, Ita 1, Por 3, Jap 2
1997	Fe	Aus 2, Bra 5, Arg r, SM 2, Mon 1, Esp 4, Can 1, Fra 1, GB r, Ger 2, Hun 4, Bel 1, Ita 6, Aut 6, Lux r, Jap 1, Eur r
1998	Fe	Aus r, Bra 3, Arg 1, SM 2, Esp 3, Mon 10, Can 1, Fra 1, GB 1, Aut 3, Ger 5, Hun 1, Bel r, Ita 1, Lux 2, Jap r
1999	Fe	Aus 8, Bra 2, SM 1, Mon 1, Esp 3, Can r, Fra 5, GB dns, Mal 2, Jap 2

SCHUMACHER, Ralf

COUNTRY: Germany
BORN: June 30, 1975
GP STARTS: 49
WC POINTS: 62
WC RECORD: 1997-11/13; 1998-10/14; 1999-6/35

Psn	No	Grand(s) Prix
2nd:	2	1998 Bel; 1999 Ita
3rd:	4	1997 Arg; 1998 Ita; 1999 Aus, GB
Fast:	1	1999 Ita

Year	Team	Grand(s) Prix
1997	JoPe	Aus r, Bra r, Arg 3, SM r, Mon r, Esp r, Can r, Fra 6, GB 5, Ger 5, Hun 5, Bel r, Ita r, Aut 5, Lux r, Jap 9, Eur r
1998	JoMH	Aus r, Bra r, Arg r, SM 7, Esp 11, Mon r, Can r, Fra 16, GB 6, Aut 5, Ger 6, Hun 9, Bel 2, Ita 3, Lux r, Jap r
1999	WiSu	Aus 3, Bra 4, SM r, Mon r, Esp 5, Can 4, Fra 4, GB 3, Aut r, Ger 4, Hun 9, Bel 5, Ita 2, Eur 4, Mal r, Jap 5

SCHUPPAN, Vern

COUNTRY: Australia
BORN: March 19, 1943
GP STARTS: 8
WC POINTS: 0

Year	Team	Grand(s) Prix
1974	EnFd	Bel 15, Mon r, Hol dq, Ger r
1975	HiFd	Swe r
1977	SuFd	GB 12, Ger 7, Aut 16

SCHWELM-CRUZ, Adolfo

COUNTRY: Argentina
BORN: June 28, 1923
GP STARTS: 1
WC POINTS: 0

Year	Team	Grand(s) Prix
1953	CoBr	Arg r

SCOTT, Bob

COUNTRY: US
BORN: October 4, 1928
GP STARTS: 2
WC POINTS: 0

Year	Team	Grand(s) Prix
1952	KK	Indy r
1953	Bro	Indy r

SCOTT-BROWN, Archie

COUNTRY: GB
BORN: May 13, 1927
GP STARTS: 1
WC POINTS: 0

Year	Team	Grand(s) Prix
1956	Con	GB r

SCOTTI, Piero

COUNTRY: Italy
BORN: November 11, 1909
GP STARTS: 1
WC POINTS: 0

Year	Team	Grand(s) Prix
1956	Con	Bel r

SEIDEL, Wolfgang

COUNTRY: Germany
BORN: July 4, 1926
GP STARTS: 10
WC POINTS: 0

Year	Team	Grand(s) Prix
1953	Ver	Ger uc
1958	Mas	Bel r
1958	CoCl	Ger r
1958	Mas	Mor r
1960	CoCl	Ita 9
1961	LoCl	GB uc, Ger r, Ita r
1962	EmCl	GB r
1962	LtBR	GB r

SENNA, Ayrton

COUNTRY: Brazil
BORN: March 21, 1960
GP STARTS: 161
WC POINTS: 610 (614)
WC RECORD: 1984-9/13; 1985-4/38; 1986-4/55; 1987-3/57; 1988-1/90; 1989-2/60; 1990-1/78; 1991-1/96; 1992-4/50; 1993-2/73
WORLD CHAMPION: 1988, 1990, 1991

Psn	No	Grand(s) Prix
1st:	41	1985 Por, Bel; 1986 Esp, US; 1987 Mon, US; 1988 SM, Can, US, GB, Ger, Hun, Bel, Jap; 1989 SM, Mon, Mex, Ger, Bel, Esp; 1990 US, Mon, Can, Ger, Bel, Ita; 1991 US, Bra, SM, Mon, Hun, Bel, Aus; 1992 Mon, Hun, Ita; 1993 Bra, Eur, Mon, Jap, Aus
2nd:	23	1984 Mon; 1985 Aut, Eur; 1986 Bra, Bel, Ger, Hun; 1987 SM, Hun, Ita, Jap; 1988 Mex, Fra, Aus; 1989 Hun; 1990 Hun, Por; 1991 Ita, Por, Jap; 1992 Ger; 1993 SA, Esp
3rd:	16	1984 GB, Por; 1985 Hol, Ita; 1986 Mon, Mex; 1987 GB, Ger; 1990 Bra, Fra, GB; 1991 Mex, Fra; 1992 SA, SM, Por
Pole:	65	1985 Por, SM, Mon, US, Ita, Eur, Aus; 1986 Bra, Esp, SM, US, Fra, Hun, Por, Mex; 1987 SM; 1987 Bra, SM, Mon, Mex, Can, US, Ger, Hun, Bel, Ita, Esp, Jap, Aus; 1989 Bra, SM, Mon, Mex, US, GB, Ger, Bel, Ita, Por, Esp, Jap, Aus; 1990 Bra, SM, Mon, Can, Ger, Bel, Ita, Esp, Jap, Aus; 1991 US, Bra, SM, Mon, Hun, Bel, Ita, Aus; 1992 Can; 1993 Aus; 1993 Bra, Pac, SM
Fast:	19	1984 Mon; 1985 Por, Can, US; 1987 Mon, US, Ita; 1988 Mon, Can, Jap; 1989 US, Ger, Esp; 1990 Mon, Ita; 1991 Ita, Jap; 1992 Por; 1993 Eur

Year	Team	Grand(s) Prix
1984	ToHt	Bra r, SA 6, Bel 6, Fra r, Mon 2, Can 7, Detroit r, Dallas r, GB 3, Ger r, Aut r, Hol r, Eur r, Por 3
1985	LtRe	Bra r, Por 1, SM 7, Mon r, Can 16, US r, Fra r, GB 10, Ger r, Aut 2, Hol 3, Ita 3, Bel 1, Eur 2, SA r, Aus r
1986	LtRe	Bra 2, Esp 1, SM r, Mon 3, Bel 2, Can 5, US 1, Fra r, GB r, Ger 2, Hun 2, Aut r, Ita r, Por 4, Mex 3, Aus r
1987	LtHo	Bra r, SM 2, Bel r, Mon 1, US 1, Fra 4, GB 3, Ger 3, Hun 2, Aut 5, Ita 2, Por 7, Esp 5, Mex r, Jap 2, Aus dq
1988	McHo	Bra dq, SM 1, Mon r, Mex 2, Can 1, US 1, Fra 2, GB 1, Ger 1, Hun 1, Bel 1, Ita 10, Por 6, Esp 4, Jap 1, Aus 2
1989	McHo	Bra 11, SM 1, Mon 1, Mex 1, US r, Can 7, Fra r, GB r, Ger 1, Hun 2, Bel 1, Ita r, Por r, Esp 1, Jap dq, Aus r
1990	McHo	US 1, Bra 3, SM r, Mon 1, Can 1, Mex 20, Fra 3, GB 3, Ger 1, Hun 2, Bel 1, Ita 1, Por 2, Esp r, Jap r, Aus r
1991	McHo	US 1, Bra 1, SM 1, Mon 1, Can r, Mex 3, Fra 3, GB 4, Ger 7, Hun 1, Bel 1, Ita 2, Por 2, Esp 5, Jap 2, Aus 1
1992	McHo	SA 3, Mex r, Bra r, Esp 9, SM 3, Mon 1, Can r, Fra r, GB r, Ger 2, Hun 1, Bel 5, Ita 1, Por 3, Jap r, Aus r
1993	McFd	SA 2, Bra 1, Eur 1, SM r, Esp 2, Mon 1, Can 18, Fra 4, GB 5, Ger 4, Hun r, Bel 4, Ita r, Por r, Jap 1, Aus 1
1994	WiRe	Bra r, Pac r, SM r

SERAFINI, Dorino

COUNTRY: Italy
BORN: July 22, 1909
GP STARTS: 1
WC POINTS: 3
WC RECORD: 1950-13/3

Psn	No	Grand(s) Prix
2nd:	1	1950 Ita

Year	Team	Grand(s) Prix
1950	Fe	Ita 2

SERRA, Chico

COUNTRY: Brazil
BORN: February 3, 1957
GP STARTS: 18
WC POINTS: 1
WC RECORD: 1982-26/1;

Year	Team	Grand(s) Prix
1981	FiFd	USW 7, Bra r, Arg r, Bel r, Esp 11, Fra dns
1982	FiFd	SA 17, Bra r, Bel 6, US 11, Hol r, GB r, Ger 11, Aut 7, Ita 11
1983	ArFd	Bra 9, Fra r, SM 8, Mon 7

SERRURIER, Doug

COUNTRY: South Africa
BORN: December 9, 1920
GP STARTS: 2
WC POINTS: 0

Year	Team	Grand(s) Prix
1962	LDAI	SA r
1963	LDAI	SA 11

SERVOZ-GAVIN, Johnny

COUNTRY: France
BORN: January 18, 1942
GP STARTS: 11
WC POINTS: 9
WC RECORD: 1968-13/6; 1969-16/1; 1970-19/2

Psn	No	Grand(s) Prix
2nd:	1	1968 Ita

Year	Team	Grand(s) Prix
1967	MatFd	Mon r
1968	MatFd	Mon r
1968	CoBR	Fra r
1968	MatFd	Ita 2, Can r, Mex r
1969	MatFd	Can 6, US uc, Mex 8
1970	MrFd	SA r, Esp 5

SETTEMBER, Tony

COUNTRY: US
BORN: April 13, 1905
GP STARTS: 6
WC POINTS: 0

Year	Team	Grand(s) Prix
1962	EmCl	GB 11, Ita r
1963	ScBR	Bel r, Fra r, GB r, Ger r

SHARP, Hap

COUNTRY: US
BORN: January 1, 1928
GP STARTS: 6
WC POINTS: 0

Year	Team	Grand(s) Prix
1961	CoCl	US 11
1962	CoCl	US 11
1963	LtBR	US r, Mex 7
1964	BrBR	US uc, Mex 13

SHAWE-TAYLOR, Brian

COUNTRY: GB
BORN: January 29, 1915
GP STARTS: 1
WC POINTS: 0

Year	Team	Grand(s) Prix
1951	ERA	GB 8

SHELBY, Carol

COUNTRY: US
BORN: January 11, 1923
GP STARTS: 8
WC POINTS: 0

Year	Team	Grand(s) Prix
1958	Mas	Fra r, GB 9, Por r, Ita r
1959	AM	Hol r, GB r, Por 8, Ita 10
1962	LoCl	GB r

SIFFERT, Jo

COUNTRY: Switzerland
BORN: July 7, 1936
GP STARTS: 96
WC POINTS: 68
WC RECORD: 1963-15/1; 1964-10/7; 1965-11/5; 1966-14/3; 1967-11/6; 1968-7/12; 1969-9/15; 1971-4/19

Psn	No	Grand(s) Prix
1st:	2	1968 GB; 1971 Aut
2nd:	2	1969 Hol; 1971 US
3rd:	2	1964 US; 1969 Mon

Pole: 2 1968 Mex; 1971 Aut
Fast: 4 1968 GB, Can, Mex; 1971 Aut

Year	Team	Grand(s) Prix
1962	LoCl	Bel 10
1962	LtBR	Fra r
1962	LoCl	Ger 12
1963	LtBR	Mon r, Bel r, Hol 7, Fra 6, GB r, Ger r, Ita r, US r, Mex 9
1964	LtBR	Mon 8
1964	BrBR	Hol uc, Bel r, Fra r, GB 11, Ger 4, Aut r, Ita 7, US 3, Mex r
1965	BrBR	SA 7, Mon 6, Bel 8, Fra 6, GB 9, Hol 13, Ger r, Ita r, US 11, Mex 4
1966	BrBR	Mon r
1966	CoMa	Bel r, Fra r, GB uc, Hol r, Ita r, US 4, Mex r
1967	CoMa	SA r, Mon r, Hol 10, Bel 7, Fra 4, GB r, Ger r, Can dns, Ita r, US 4, Mex 12
1968	CoMa	SA 7
1968	LtFd	Esp r, Mon r, Bel 7, Hol r, Fra 11, GB 1, Ger r, Ita r, Can r, US 5, Mex 6
1969	LtFd	SA 4, Esp r, Mon 3, Hol 2, Fra 9, GB 8, Ger 5, Ita 8, Can r, US r, Mex r
1970	MrFd	SA 10, Mon 8, Bel 7, Hol r, Fra r, GB r, Ger 8, Aut 9, Ita r, Can r, US 9, Mex r
1971	BRM	SA r, Esp r, Mon r, Hol 6, Fra 4, GB 9, Ger r, Aut 1, Ita 9, Can 9, US 2

SIMON, Andre

COUNTRY: France
BORN: January 5, 1920
GP STARTS: 11
WC POINTS: 0

Year	Team	Grand(s) Prix
1951	SiGo	Fra r, Ger r, Ita 6, Esp r
1952	Fe	Swi r, Ita 6
1955	Me	Mon r
1955	Mas	GB r
1956	Mas	Fra r
1956	Gor	Ita 10
1957	Mas	Ita 11

SOLANA, Moises

COUNTRY: Mexico
BORN: April 19, 1905
GP STARTS: 8
WC POINTS: 0

Year	Team	Grand(s) Prix
1963	BRM	Mex r
1964	LoCl	Mex 10
1965	LoCl	US 12, Mex r
1966	CoMa	Mex r
1967	LtFd	US r, Mex r
1968	LtFd	Mex r

SOLER-ROIG, Alex

COUNTRY: Spain
BORN: October 29, 1932
GP STARTS: 6
WC POINTS: 0

Year	Team	Grand(s) Prix
1971	MrFd	SA r, Esp r, Hol r, Fra r
1972	BRM	Arg r, Esp r

SOMMER, Raymond

COUNTRY: France
BORN: August 31, 1906
GP STARTS: 5
WC POINTS: 3
WC RECORD: 1950-13/3

Year	Team	Grand(s) Prix
1950	Fe/Ta	Mon 4, Swi r, Bel r, Fra r, Ita r

SPARKEN, Mike

COUNTRY: France
BORN: June 16, 1930
GP STARTS: 1
WC POINTS: 0

Year	Team	Grand(s) Prix
1955	Gor	GB 7

SPENCE, Mike

COUNTRY: GB
BORN: December 30, 1936
GP STARTS: 36
WC POINTS: 27
WC RECORD: 1964-12/4; 1965-8/10; 1966-12/4; 1967-10/9

Psn	No	Grand(s) Prix
3rd:	1	1965 Mex

Year	Team	Grand(s) Prix
1963	LoCl	Ita r

1964 LoCl GB 9, Ger 8, Aut r, Ita 6, US 7, Mex 4
1965 LoCl SA 4, Bel 7, Fra 7, GB 4, Hol 8, Ger r, Ita r, US r, Mex 3
1966 LtBR Mon r, Bel r, Fra r, GB r, Hol 5, Ger r, Ita 5, US r, Mex dns
1967 BRM SA r, Mon 6, Hol 8, Bel 5, Fra r, GB r, Ger r, Can 5, Ita 5, US r, Mex 5
1968 BRM SA r

STACEY, Alan

COUNTRY: GB
BORN: August 29, 1933
GP STARTS: 7
WC POINTS: 0

Year	Team	Grand(s) Prix
1958	LoCl	GB r
1959	LoCl	GB 8, US r
1960	LoCl	Arg r, Mon r, Hol r, Bel r

STARRABBA, Gaetano

COUNTRY: Italy
BORN: December 3, 1932
GP STARTS: 1
WC POINTS: 0

Year	Team	Grand(s) Prix
1961	LtMas	Ita r

STEVENSON, Chuck

COUNTRY: US
BORN: October 15, 1919
GP STARTS: 5
WC POINTS: 0

Year	Team	Grand(s) Prix
1951	Mar	Indy r
1952	KK	Indy 18
1953	Ku	Indy r
1954	Ku	Indy 12
1960	Wa	Indy 15

STEWART, Ian

COUNTRY: GB
BORN: July 15, 1929
GP STARTS: 1
WC POINTS: 0

Year	Team	Grand(s) Prix
1953	Con	GB r

STEWART, Jackie

COUNTRY: GB
BORN: June 11, 1939
GP STARTS: 99
WC POINTS: 359 (360)
WC RECORD: 1965-3/33; 1966-7/14; 1967-9/10; 1968-2/36; 1969-1/63; 1970-5/25; 1971-1/62; 1972-2/45; 1973-1/71
WORLD CHAMPION: 1969, 1971, 1973

Psn	No	Grand(s) Prix
1st:	27	1965 Ita; 1966 Mon; 1968 Hol, Ger, US; 1969 SA, Esp, Hol, Fra, GB, Ita; 1970 Esp; 1971 Esp, Mon, Fra, GB, Ger, Can; 1972 Arg, Fra, Can, US; 1973 SA, Bel, Mon, Hol, Ger
2nd:	11	1965 Bel, Fra, Hol; 1967 Bel; 1969 Ger; 1970 Hol, Ita; 1971 SA; 1972 GB; 1973 Bra, Aut
3rd:	5	1965 Mon; 1967 Fra; 1968 Fra; 1970 SA; 1973 Arg
Pole:	17	1969 Mon, Fra; 1970 SA, Mon, Bel, Can; 1971 SA, Mon, Fra, Ger, Can, US; 1972 SA, US; 1973 Mon, Fra, Ger
Fast:	15	1968 Ger, US; 1969 SA, Mon, Hol, Fra, GB; 1971 Mon, Fra, GB; 1972 Arg, GB, Can, US; 1973 Ita

Year	Team	Grand(s) Prix
1965	BRM	SA 6, Mon 3, Bel 2, Fra 2, GB 5, Hol 2, Ger r, Ita 1, US r, Mex r
1966	BRM	Mon 1, Bel r, GB r, Hol 4, Ger 5, Ita r, US r, Mex r
1967	BRM	SA r, Mon r, Hol r, Bel 2, Fra 3, GB r, Ger r, Can r, Ita r, US r, Mex r
1968	MatFd	SA r, Bel 4, Hol 1, Fra 3, GB 6, Ger 1, Ita r, Can 6, US 1, Mex 7
1969	MatFd	SA 1, Esp 1, Mon r, Hol 1, Fra 1, GB 1, Ger 2, Ita 1, Can r, US r, Mex 4
1970	MrFd	SA 3, Esp 1, Mon r, Bel r, Hol 2, Fra 9, GB r, Ger r, Aut r, Ita 2
1970	TyFd	Can r, US r, Mex r
1971	TyFd	SA 2, Esp 1, Mon 1, Hol 11, Fra 1, GB 1, Ger 1, Aut r, Ita r, Can 1, US 5
1972	TyFd	Arg 1, SA r, Esp r, Mon 4, Fra 1, GB 2, Ger 11, Aut 7, Ita r, Can 1, US 1
1973	TyFd	Arg 3, Bra 2, SA 1, Esp r, Bel 1, Mon 1, Swe 5, Fra 4, GB 10, Hol 1, Ger 1, Aut 2, Ita 4, Can 5, US dns

STEWART, Jimmy

COUNTRY: GB
BORN: March 6, 1931
GP STARTS: 1
WC POINTS: 0

Year	Team	Grand(s) Prix
1953	CoBr	GB 9

STOHR, Slegfried

COUNTRY: Italy
BORN: October 10, 1952
GP STARTS: 9
WC POINTS: 0

Year	Team	Grand(s) Prix
1981	ArFd	Bra r, Arg 9, Bel r, Mon r, Esp r, GB r, Ger 12, Aut r, Hol 7

STOMMELEN, Rolf

COUNTRY: Germany
BORN: July 11, 1943
GP STARTS: 53
WC POINTS: 14
WC RECORD: 1970-11/10; 1971-18/3; 1976-19/1

Psn	No	Grand(s) Prix
3rd:	1	1970 Aut

Year	Team	Grand(s) Prix
1970	BrFd	SA r, Esp r, Bel 5, Fra 7, GB dns, Ger 5, Aut 3, Ita 5, Can r, US 12, Mex r
1971	SuFd	SA 12, Esp r, Mon 6, Hol dq, Fra 11, GB 5, Ger 10, Aut 7, Ita dns, Can r
1972	MrFd	SA 13, Esp r, Mon 10, Bel 11, Fra 16, GB 10, Ger r, Aut 15
1973	BrFd	Ger 11, Aut r, Ita 12, Can 12
1974	LoFd	Aut r, Ita r, Can 11, US 12
1975	LoFd	Arg 13, Bra 14, SA 7
1975	HiFd	Esp r, Aut 16, Ita r
1976	BrAl	Ger 6
1976	HeFd	Hol 12
1976	BrAl	Ita r
1978	ArFd	SA 9, USW 9, Mon r, Bel r, Esp 14, Swe 14, Fra 15, Ger dq, USE 16

STREIFF, Phillippe

COUNTRY: France
BORN: June 26, 1955
GP STARTS: 54
WC POINTS: 11
WC RECORD: 1985-15/4; 1986-13/3; 1987-14/4

Psn	No	Grand(s) Prix
3rd:	1	1985 Aus

Year	Team	Grand(s) Prix
1984	Re	Por r
1985	LiRe	Ita 10, Bel 9, Eur 8
1985	TyRe	SA r
1985	LiRe	Aus 3
1986	TyRe	Bra 7, Esp r, SM r, Mon 11, Bel 12, Can 11, US 9, Fra r, GB 6, Ger r, Hun 8, Aut r, Ita 9, Por r, Mex r, Aus 5
1987	TyFd	Bra 11, SM 8, Bel 9, Mon r, US r, Fra 6, GB r, Ger 4, Hun 9, Aut r, Ita 12, Por 12, Esp 7, Mex 8, Jap 12, Aus r
1988	AGFd	Bra r, SM 10, Mon r, Mex 12, Can r, US r, Fra r, GB r, Ger r, Hun r, Bel 10, Ita r, Por 9, Esp r, Jap 8, Aus 11

STUCK, Hans

COUNTRY: Germany
BORN: December 27, 1900
GP STARTS: 3
WC POINTS: 0

Year	Team	Grand(s) Prix
1952	AFM	Swi r
1953	AFM	Ger r, Ita uc

STUCK, Hans-Joachim

COUNTRY: Germany
BORN: January 1, 1951
GP STARTS: 74
WC POINTS: 0

Psn	No	Grand(s) Prix
3rd:	2	1977 Ger, Aut

Year	Team	Grand(s) Prix
1974	MrFd	Arg r, Bra r, SA 5, Esp 4, Bel r, Mon r, Hol r, GB r, Ger 7, Aut 11, Ita r, Can r
1975	MrFd	GB r, Ger r, Aut r, Ita r, US 8
1976	MrFd	Bra 4, SA 12, USW r, Esp r, Bel r, Mon 4, Swe r, Fra 7, GB r, Ger r, Aut r, Hol r, Ita r, Can r, USE 5, Jap r

1977 MrFd SA r
1977 BrAl USW r, Esp 6, Mon r, Bel 6, Swe 10, Fra r, GB 5, Ger 3, Aut 3, Hol 7, Ita r, USE r, Can r, Jap 7
1978 ShFd Arg 17, Bra r, USW dns, Mon r, Bel r, Esp r, Swe 11, Fra 11, GB 5, Ger r, Aut r, Hol r, Ita r, USE r, Can r
1979 ATFd Bra r, SA r, USW dq, Esp 14, Bel 8, Mon r, Fra dns, Ger r, Aut r, Hol r, Ita 11, Can r, USE 5

SULLIVAN, Danny

COUNTRY: US
BORN: March 9, 1950
GP STARTS: 15
WC POINTS: 2
WC RECORD: 1983-17/2

Year	Team	Grand(s) Prix
1983	TyFd	Bra 11, USW 8, Fra r, SM r, Mon 5, Bel 12, US r, Can dq, GB 14, Ger 12, Aut r, Hol r, Ita r, Eur r, SA 7

SURER, Marc

COUNTRY: Switzerland
BORN: September 18, 1951
GP STARTS: 82
WC POINTS: 17
WC RECORD: 1981-16/4; 1982-20/3; 1983-15/4; 1984-20/1; 1985-13/5

Psn	No	Grand(s) Prix
Fast:	1	1981 Bra

Year	Team	Grand(s) Prix
1979	EnFd	USE r
1980	ATFd	Arg r, Bra 7, Fra r, GB r, Ger 12, Aut 12, Hol 10, Ita r, USE 8
1981	EnFd	USW r, Bra 4, Arg r, SM 9, Bel 11, Mon 6
1981	ThFd	Fra 12, GB 11, Ger 14, Aut r, Hol 8, Can 9, US r
1982	ArFd	Bel 7, Mon 9, US 8, Can 5, Hol 10, GB r, Fra 13, Ger 6, Aut r, Swi 15, Ita r, CP 7
1983	ArFd	Bra 6, USW 5, Fra 10, SM 6, Mon r, Bel 11, US 11, Can r, GB 17, Ger 7, Aut r, Hol 8, Ita 10, Eur r, SA 8
1984	ArFd	Bra 7, SA 9, Bel 8
1984	ArBM	SM r
1984	ArFd	Fra r, Can r, Detroit r
1984	ArBM	Dallas r, GB 11, Ger r, Aut 6, Hol r, Ita r, Eur r, Por r
1985	BrBM	Can 15, US 8, Fra 8, GB 6, Ger r, Aut 6, Hol 10, Ita 4, Bel 8, Eur r, SA r, Aus r
1986	ArBM	Bra r, Esp r, SM 9, Mon 9, Bel 9

SURTEES, John

COUNTRY: GB
BORN: February 11, 1934
GP STARTS: 111
WC POINTS: 180
WC RECORD: 1960-12/6; 1961-11/4; 1962-4/19; 1963-4/22; 1964-1/40; 1965-5/17; 1966-2/28; 1967-4/20; 1968-7/12; 1969-11/6; 1970-17/3; 1971-18/3
WORLD CHAMPION: 1964

Psn	No	Grand(s) Prix
1st:	6	1963 Ger; 1964 Ger, Ita; 1966 Bel, Mex; 1967 Ita
2nd:	10	1960 GB; 1962 GB, Ger; 1963 GB; 1964 Hol, US, Mex; 1965 SA; 1966 Ger; 1968 Fra
3rd:	8	1963 Hol; 1964 GB; 1965 Fra, GB; 1966 US; 1967 SA; 1968 US; 1969 US
Pole:	8	1960 Por; 1962 Hol; 1963 Ita; 1964 Ger, Ita; 1966 Bel, Mex; 1968 Ita
Fast:	11	1960 Por; 1963 Mon, GB, Ger; 1964 Ger, Ita; 1966 Bel, Ger, US; 1968 Bel; 1970 SA

Year	Team	Grand(s) Prix
1960	LoCl	Mon r, GB 2, Por r, US r
1961	CoCl	Mon r, Hol 7, Bel 5, Fra r, GB r, Ger 5, Ita r, US r
1962	LlCl	Hol r, Mon 4, Bel 5, Fra 5, GB 2, Ger 2, Ita r, US r, SA r
1963	Fe	Mon 4, Bel r, Hol 3, Fra r, GB 2, Ger 1, Ita r, US r, Mex dq, SA r
1964	Fe	Mon r, Hol 2, Bel r, Fra r, GB 3, Ger 1, Aut r, Ita 1, US 2, Mex 2
1965	Fe	SA 2, Mon 4, Bel r, Fra 3, GB 3, Hol 7, Ger r, Ita r
1966	Fe	Mon r, Bel 1
1966	CoMa	Fra r, GB r, Hol r, Ger 2, Ita r, US 3, Mex 1
1967	Ho	SA 3, Mon r, Hol r, Bel r, GB 6, Ger 4, Ita 1, US r, Mex 4
1968	Ho	SA 8, Esp r, Mon r, Bel r, Hol r, Fra 2, GB 5, Ger r, Ita r, Can r, US 3, Mex r
1969	BRM	SA r, Esp 5, Mon r, Hol 9, GB r, Ger dns, Ita uc, Can r, US 3, Mex r
1970	McFd	SA r, Esp r, Mon r, Hol 6
1970	SuFd	GB r, Ger 9, Aut r, Ita r, Can 5, US r, Mex 8

1971	SuFd	SA r, Esp 11, Mon 7, Hol 5, Fra 8, GB 6, Ger 7, Aut r, Ita r, Can 11, US 17
1972	SuFd	Ita r, US dns

SUTTON, Len

COUNTRY: US
BORN: August 9, 1925
GP STARTS: 3
WC POINTS: 0

Year	Team	Grand(s) Prix
1958	KK	Indy r
1959	Les	Indy r
1960	Wa	Indy r

SUZUKI, Aguri

COUNTRY: Japan
BORN: September 8, 1960
GP STARTS: 64
WC POINTS: 0

Psn	No	Grand(s) Prix
3rd:	1	1990 Jap

Year	Team	Grand(s) Prix
1988	LoFd	Jap 16
1990	LoLm	US r, Bra r, SM r, Mon r, Can 12, Mex r, Fra 7, GB 6, Ger r, Hun r, Bel r, Ita r, Por 14, Esp 6, Jap 3, Aus r
1991	LoFd	US 6, Bra dns, SM r, Mon r, Can r, Mex r, Fra r, GB r, Ger r, Hun r, Por r, Jap r
1992	FtMH	SA 8, Bra r, Esp 7, SM 10, Mon 11, Fra r, GB 12, Ger r, Hun r, Bel 9, Ita r, Por 10, Jap 8, Aus 8
1993	FtMH	SA r, Bra r, Eur r, SM 9, Esp 10, Mon r, Can 13, Fra 12, GB r, Ger r, Hun r, Bel r, Ita r, Por r, Jap r, Aus 7
1994	JoFd	Pac r
1995	LiMH	Bra 8, Arg r, SM 11, Ger 6, Pac r, Jap dns

SUZUKI, Toshio

COUNTRY: Japan
BORN: March 10, 1955
GP STARTS: 2
WC POINTS: 0

Year	Team	Grand(s) Prix
1993	LaLm	Jap 12, Aus 14

SWATERS, Jacques

COUNTRY: Belgium
BORN: October 30, 1926
GP STARTS: 7
WC POINTS: 0

Year	Team	Grand(s) Prix
1951	Ta	Ger 10, Ita r
1953	Fe	Ger 7, Swi r
1954	Fe	Bel r, Swi 8, Esp r

SWELKERT, Bob

COUNTRY: US
BORN: May 20, 1926
GP STARTS: 5
WC POINTS: 8
WC RECORD: 1955-7/8

Psn	No	Grand(s) Prix
1st:	1	1955 Indy

Year	Team	Grand(s) Prix
1952	KK	Indy r
1953	Ku	Indy r
1954	KK	Indy 14
1955	KK	Indy 1
1956	Ku	Indy 6

TAKAGI, Toranosuke

COUNTRY: Japan
BORN: February 12, 1974
GP STARTS: 32
WC POINTS: 0

Year	Team	Grand(s) Prix
1998	TyFd	Aus r, Bra r, Arg 12, SM r, Esp 13, Mon 11, Can r, Fra r, GB 9, Aut r, Ger 13, Hun 14, Bel r, Ita 9, Lux 16, Jap r
1999	Ar	Aus 7, Bra 8, SM r, Mon r, Esp 12, Can r, Fra dq, GB 16, Aut r, Ger r, Hun r, Bel r, Ita r, Eur r, Mal r, Jap r

TAKAHARA, Noratake

COUNTRY: Japan
BORN: June 6, 1951
GP STARTS: 2
WC POINTS: 0

Year	Team	Grand(s) Prix
1976	SuFd	Jap 9
1977	KoFd	Jap r

TAKAHASHI, Kunimitsu

COUNTRY: Japan
BORN: June 29, 1940
GP STARTS: 1
WC POINTS: 0

Year	Team	Grand(s) Prix
1977	TyFd	Jap 9

TAMBAY, Patrick

COUNTRY: France
BORN: June 25, 1949
GP STARTS: 114
WC POINTS: 103
WC RECORD: 1977-17/5; 1978-13/8; 1981-18/1; 1982-7/25; 1983-4/40; 1984-11/11; 1985-12/11; 1986-15/2

Psn	No	Grand(s) Prix
1st:	2	1982 Ger; 1983 SM
2nd:	4	1982 Ita; 1983 Bel, Hol; 1984 Fra
3rd:	5	1982 GB; 1983 Can, GB; 1985 Por, SM
Pole:	5	1983 USW, Ger, Aut, SA; 1984 Fra
Fast:	2	1983 Can; 1984 SA

Year	Team	Grand(s) Prix
1977	EnFd	GB r, Ger 6, Aut r, Hol 5, Ita r, Can 5, Jap r
1978	McFd	Arg 6, Bra r, SA r, USW 12, Mon 7, Esp r, Swe 4, Fra 9, GB 6, Ger r, Aut r, Hol 9, Ita 5, USE 6, Can 8
1979	McFd	Arg r, Bra r, SA 10, USW r, Esp 13, Fra 10, GB 7, Ger r, Aut 10, Hol r, Ita r, Can r, USE r
1981	ThFd	USW 6, Bra 10, Arg r, SM 11, Mon 7, Esp 13, Fra r
1981	LiMat	GB r, Ger r, Aut r, Hol r, Ita r, Can r, US r
1982	Fe	Hol 8, GB 3, Fra 4, Ger 1, Aut 4, Swi dns, Ita 2, CP dns
1983	Fe	Bra 5, USW r, Fra 4, SM 1, Mon 4, Bel 2, US r, Can 3, GB 3, Ger r, Aut r, Hol 2, Ita 4, Eur r, SA r
1984	Re	Bra 5, SA r, Bel 7, SM r, Fra 2, Mon r, Detroit r, Dallas r, GB 8, Ger 5, Aut r, Hol 6, Ita r, Eur r, Por 7
1985	Re	Bra 5, Por 3, SM 3, Mon r, Can 7, US r, Fra 6, GB r, Ger r, Aut 10, Hol r, Ita 7, Bel r, Eur 12, Aus r
1986	LlHt	Bra r, Esp 8, SM r
1986	LoFd	Mon r, Bel r, Can dns, Fra r, GB r, Ger 8, Hun 7, Aut 5, Ita r, Por uc, Mex r, Aus uc

TARQUINI, Gabriele

COUNTRY: Italy
BORN: March 2, 1962
GP STARTS: 38
WC POINTS: 1
WC RECORD: 1989-26/1

Year	Team	Grand(s) Prix
1987	OsAl	SM r
1988	CiFd	Bra r, SM r, Mon r, Mex 14, Can 8, Hun 13, Bel uc, Por 11
1989	AGFd	SM 8, Mon r, Mex 6, US 7, Can r, Fra r
1990	AGFd	GB r, Hun 13, Esp r, Aus r
1991	AGFd	US 8, Bra r, Mon r
1991	FnFd	Esp 12, Jap 11
1992	FnFd	SA r, Mex r, Bra r, Esp r, SM r, Mon r, Can r, Fra r, GB 14, Ger r, Hun r, Bel r, Ita r
1995	TyYa	Eur 14

TARUFFI, Piero

COUNTRY: Italy
BORN: October 12, 1906
GP STARTS: 18
WC POINTS: 41
WC RECORD: 1951-6/10; 1952-3/22; 1955-6/9

Psn	No	Grand(s) Prix
1st:	1	1952 Swi
2nd:	3	1951 Swi; 1952 GB; 1955 Ita
3rd:	1	1952 Fra
Fast:	1	1952 Swi

Year	Team	Grand(s) Prix
1950	AR	Ita r
1951	Fe	Swi 2, Bel r, Ger 5, Ita 5, Esp r
1952	Fe	Swi 1, Bel r, Fra 3, GB 2, Ger 4, Ita 7
1954	Fe	Ger 6
1955	Fe	Mon 9
1955	Me	GB 4, Ita 2
1956	Mas	Fra r
1956	Va	Ita r

TAYLOR, Henry

COUNTRY: GB
BORN: December 16, 1932
GP STARTS: 8

WC POINTS: 3
WC RECORD: 1960-19/3

Year	Team	Grand(s) Prix
1959	CoCl	GB 11
1960	CoCl	Hol 7, Fra 4, GB 8, US 14
1961	LoCl	Fra 10, GB r, Ita 11

TAYLOR, John

COUNTRY: GB
BORN: March 23, 1933
GP STARTS: 5
WC POINTS: 1
WC RECORD: 1966-17/1

Year	Team	Grand(s) Prix
1964	CoFd	GB 14
1966	BrBR	Fra 6, GB 8, Hol 8, Ger r

TAYLOR, Michael

COUNTRY: GB
BORN: April 24, 1934
GP STARTS: 1
WC POINTS: 0

Year	Team	Grand(s) Prix
1959	CoCl	GB r

TAYLOR, Trevor

COUNTRY: GB
BORN: December 26, 1936
GP STARTS: 27
WC POINTS: 8
WC RECORD: 1962-10/6; 1963-15/1; 1964-19/1

Psn	No	Grand(s) Prix
2nd:	1	1962 Hol

Year	Team	Grand(s) Prix
1961	LoCl	Hol 13
1962	LoCl	Hol 2, Mon r, Bel r, Fra 8, GB 8, Ger r, Ita r, US 12, SA r
1963	LoCl	Mon 6, Bel r, Hol uc, Fra r, GB dq, Ger 8, US r, Mex r, SA 8
1964	BrBR	Mon r, Bel 7, Fra r
1964	LtBR	GB r
1964	BRP-BRM	Aut r, US 6, Mex r
1966	ShCl	GB r

TEAGUE, Marshall

COUNTRY: US
BORN: May 22, 1921
GP STARTS: 2
WC POINTS: 0

Year	Team	Grand(s) Prix
1953	KK	Indy r
1957	KK	Indy 7

TEMPLEMAN, Shorty

COUNTRY: US
BORN: August 12, 1919
GP STARTS: 3
WC POINTS: 0

Year	Team	Grand(s) Prix
1955	Trevis	Indy r
1958	KK	Indy r
1960	KK	Indy 17

THACKWELL, Mike

COUNTRY: New Zealand
BORN: March 30, 1961
GP STARTS: 2
WC POINTS: 0

Year	Team	Grand(s) Prix
1980	TyFd	Can r
1984	RmHt	Can r

THIELE, Alfonso

COUNTRY: US
BORN: 1922
GP STARTS: 1
WC POINTS: 0

Year	Team	Grand(s) Prix
1960	CoMa	Ita r

THOMPSON, Eric

COUNTRY: GB
BORN: November 4, 1919
GP STARTS: 1
WC POINTS: 2
WC RECORD: 1952-16/2

Year	Team	Grand(s) Prix
1952	Con	GB 5

THOMSON, Johnny

COUNTRY: US
BORN: April 9, 1922
GP STARTS: 8
WC POINTS: 10
WC RECORD: 1955-13/3; 1959-12/5; 1960-23/2

Psn	No	Grand(s) Prix
3rd:	1	1959 Indy
Pole:	1	1959 Indy
Fast:	1	1959 Indy

Year	Team		Grand(s) Prix
1953	DR	1	Indy r
1954	Nic	1	Indy r
1955	Ku	1	Indy 4
1956	Ku	1	Indy r
1957	Ku	1	Indy 12
1958	KK	1	Indy r
1959	Les	1	Indy 3
1960	Les	1	Indy 5

THORNE, Leslie

COUNTRY: GB
BORN: June 23, 1916
GP STARTS: 1
WC POINTS: 0

Year	Team	Grand(s) Prix
1954	Con	GB uc

TINGLE, Sam

COUNTRY: Zimbabwe
BORN: August 24, 1921
GP STARTS: 5
WC POINTS: 0

Year	Team	Grand(s) Prix
1963	LDAl	SA r
1965	LDAl	SA 13
1967	LDCl	SA r
1968	LDRe	SA r
1969	BrRe	SA 8

TINGLESTAD, Bud

COUNTRY: US
BORN: April 4, 1928
GP STARTS: 1
WC POINTS: 0

Year	Team	Grand(s) Prix
1960	Trevis	Indy 9

TITTERINGTON, Desmond

COUNTRY: GB
BORN: May 1, 1928
GP STARTS: 1
WC POINTS: 0

Year	Team	Grand(s) Prix
1956	Con	GB r

TOLAN, Johnnie

COUNTRY: US
BORN: October 22, 1918
GP STARTS: 3
WC POINTS: 0

Year	Team	Grand(s) Prix
1956	KK	Indy r
1957	Ku	Indy r
1958	Ku	Indy 13

TRINTIGNANT, Maurice

COUNTRY: France
BORN: October 30, 1917
GP STARTS: 82
WC POINTS: 72.33
WC RECORD: 1952-16/2; 1953-11/4; 1954-4/17; 1955-4/11.33; 1957-12/5; 1958-7/12; 1959-5/19; 1964-16/2

Psn	No	Grand(s) Prix
1st:	2	1955 Mon; 1958 Mon
2nd:	2	1954 Bel; 1959 US
3rd:	4	1954 Ger; 1958 Ger; 1959 Mon; 1960 Arg
Fast:	1	1959 US

Year	Team	Grand(s) Prix
1950	SiGo	Mon r, Ita r
1951	SiGo	Fra r, Ger r, Ita r, Esp r
1952	Gor	Fra 5, GB r, Ger r, Hol 6, Ita r
1953	Gor	Arg 7, Hol 6, Bel 5, Fra r, GB r, Ger r, Swi r, Ita 5
1954	Fe	Arg 4, Bel 2, Fra r, GB 5, Ger 3, Swi r, Ita 5, Esp r
1955	Fe	Arg r, Mon 1, Bel 6, Hol r, GB r, Ita 8
1956	Va	Mon r, Bel r
1956	Bug	Fra r
1956	Va	GB r, Ita r

1957 LaFe Mon 5, Fra r, GB 4
1958 CoCl Mon 1, Hol 9
1958 Mas Bel 7
1958 BRM Fra r
1958 CoCl GB 8, Ger 3, Por 8, Ita r, Mor r
1959 CoCl Mon 3, Hol 8, Fra uc, GB 5, Ger 4, Por 4, Ita 9, US 2
1960 CoCl Arg 3
1960 CoMa Mon r, Hol r, Fra r
1960 AM GB 11
1960 CoMa US 15
1961 CoMa Mon 7, Bel r, Fra 13, Ger r, Ita 9
1962 LoCl Mon r, Bel 8, Fra 7, Ger r, Ita r, US r
1963 LICl Mon r
1963 LoCl Fra 8
1963 BRM Ita 9
1964 BRM Mon r, Fra 11, Ger 5, Ita r

TRULLI, Jarno

COUNTRY: Italy
BORN: July 13, 1973
GP STARTS: 44
WC POINTS: 11
WC RECORD: 1997-15/3; 1998-15/1; 1999-11/7

Psn	No	Grand(s) Prix
2nd:	1	1999 Eur

Year	Team	Grand(s) Prix
1997	MiHt	Aus 9, Bra 12, Arg 9, SM dns, Mon r, Esp 15, Can r
1997	PrMH	Fra 10, GB 8, Ger 4, Hun 7, Bel 15, Ita 10, Aut r
1998	PrPe	Aus r, Bra r, Arg 11, SM r, Esp 9, Mon r, Can r, Fra r, GB r, Aut 10, Ger 12, Hun r, Bel 6, Ita 13, Lux r, Jap 12
1999	PrPe	Aus r, Bra r, SM r, Mon 7, Esp 6, Can r, Fra 7, GB 9, Aut 7, Ger r, Hun 8, Bel 12, Ita r, Eur 2, Mal dns, Jap r

TUERO, Esterban

COUNTRY: Argentina
BORN: April 22, 1978
GP STARTS: 16
WC POINTS: 0

Year	Team	Grand(s) Prix
1998	MiFd	Aus r, Bra r, Arg r, SM 8, Esp 15, Mon r, Can r, Fra r, GB r, Aut r, Ger 16, Hun r, Bel r, Ita 11, Lux uc, Jap r

TUNMER, Guy

COUNTRY: South Africa
BORN: December 1, 1948
GP STARTS: 1
WC POINTS: 0

Year	Team	Grand(s) Prix
1975	LtFd	SA 11

TURNER, Jack

COUNTRY: US
BORN: February 12, 1920
GP STARTS: 4
WC POINTS: 0

Year	Team	Grand(s) Prix
1956	KK	Indy r
1957	KK	Indy 11
1958	Les	Indy r
1959	Chr	Indy r

ULMEN, Toni

COUNTRY: Germany
BORN: January 25, 1906
GP STARTS: 2
WC POINTS: 0

Year	Team	Grand(s) Prix
1952	Ver	Swi r, Ger 8

UNSER, Bobby

COUNTRY: US
BORN: February 20, 1934
GP STARTS: 1
WC POINTS: 0

Year	Team	Grand(s) Prix
1968	BRM	US r

UNSER, Jerry

COUNTRY: US
BORN: November 15, 1932
GP STARTS: 1
WC POINTS: 0

Year	Team	Grand(s) Prix
1958	KK	Indy r

URIA, Alberto

COUNTRY: Uruguay
BORN:
GP STARTS: 2
WC POINTS: 0

Year	Team	Grand(s) Prix
1955	Mas	Arg r
1956	Mas	Arg 6

VACCARELLA, Nino

COUNTRY: Italy
BORN: March 4, 1933
GP STARTS: 4
WC POINTS: 0

Year	Team	Grand(s) Prix
1961	dTCr	Ita r
1962	Por	Ger 15
1962	LoCl	Ita 9
1965	Fe	Ita r

VAN DE POELE, Eric

COUNTRY: Belgium
BORN: September 30, 1961
GP STARTS: 5
WC POINTS: 0

Year	Team	Grand(s) Prix
1991	Lm	SM 9
1992	BrJu	SA 13
1992	FnFd	Hun r, Bel 10, Ita r

VAN DER LOF, Dries

COUNTRY: Holland
BORN: August 23, 1919
GP STARTS: 1
WC POINTS: 0

Year	Team	Grand(s) Prix
1952	HWM	Hol uc

VAN LENNEP, Gijs

COUNTRY: Holland
BORN: March 16, 1942
GP STARTS: 8
WC POINTS: 2
WC RECORD: 1973-19/1; 1975-19/1

Year	Team	Grand(s) Prix
1971	SuFd	Hol 8
1973	WiFd	Hol 6, Aut 9, Ita r
1974	WiFd	Bel 14
1975	EnFd	Hol 10, Fra 15, Ger 6

VAN ROOYEN, Basil

COUNTRY: South Africa
BORN: April 19, 1938
GP STARTS: 2
WC POINTS: 0

Year	Team	Grand(s) Prix
1968	CoCl	SA r
1969	McFd	SA r

VEITH, Bob

COUNTRY: US
BORN: November 1, 1926
GP STARTS: 5
WC POINTS: 0

Year	Team	Grand(s) Prix
1956	KK	Indy 7
1957	Ph	Indy 9
1958	KK	Indy r
1959	Moo	Indy 12
1960	Mes	Indy 8

VERSTAPPEN, Jos

COUNTRY: Holland
BORN: March 4, 1972
GP STARTS: 57
WC POINTS: 11
WC RECORD: 1994-10/10; 1996-16/1

Psn	No	Grand(s) Prix
3rd:	2	1994 Hun, Bel

Year	Team	Grand(s) Prix
1994	BeFd	Bra r, Pac r, Fra r, GB 8, Ger r, Hun 3, Bel 3, Ita r, Por 5, Eur r
1995	SiFd	Bra r, Arg r, SM r, Esp 12, Mon r
1996	FtHt	Aus r, Bra r, Arg 6, Eur r, SM r, Mon r, Esp r, Can r, Fra r, GB 10, Ger r, Hun r, Bel r, Ita 8, Por r, Jap 11
1997	TyFd	Aus r, Bra 15, Arg r, SM 10, Mon 8, Esp 11, Can r, Fra r, GB r, Ger 10, Hun r, Bel 16, Ita r, Aut 12, Lux r, Jap 13, Eur 16

1998 StFd Fra 12, GB r, Aut r, Ger r, Hun 13, Bel r, Ita r, Lux 13, Jap r

VILLENEUVE, Gilles

COUNTRY: Canada
BORN: January 18, 1950
GP STARTS: 67
WC POINTS: 101 (107)
WC RECORD: 1978-9/17; 1979-2/47; 1980-10/6; 1981-7/25; 1982-15/6

Psn	No	Grand(s) Prix
1st:	6	1978 Can; 1979 SA, USW, USE; 1981 Mon, Esp
2nd:	5	1979 Fra, Aut, Ita, Can; 1982 SM
3rd:	2	1978 Aut; 1981 Can
Pole:	2	1979 USW; 1981 SM
Fast:	8	1978 Arg; 1979 SA, USW, Esp, Bel, Ger, Hol; 1981 SM

Year	Team	Grand(s) Prix
1977	McFd	GB 11
1977	Fe	Can 12, Jap r
1978	Fe	Arg 8, Bra r, SA r, USW r, Mon r, Bel 4, Esp 10, Swe 9, Fra 12, GB r, Ger 8, Aut 3, Hol 6, Ita 7, USE r, Can 1
1979	Fe	Arg 12, Bra 5, SA 1, USW 1, Esp 7, Bel 7, Mon r, Fra 2, GB 14, Ger 8, Aut 2, Hol r, Ita 2, Can 2, USE 1
1980	Fe	Arg r, Bra 16, SA r, USW r, Bel 6, Mon 5, Fra 8, GB r, Ger 6, Aut 8, Hol 7, Ita r, Can 5, USE r
1981	Fe	USW r, Bra r, Arg r, SM 7, Bel 4, Mon 1, Esp 1, Fra r, GB r, Ger 10, Aut r, Hol r, Ita r, Can 3, US dq
1982	Fe	SA r, Bra r, USW dq, SM 2, Bel dns

VILLENEUVE, Jacques

COUNTRY: Canada
BORN: April 9, 1971
GP STARTS: 65
WC POINTS: 180
WC RECORD: 1996-2/78; 1997-1/81; 1998-5/21
WORLD CHAMPION: 1997

Psn	No	Grand(s) Prix
1st:	11	1996 Eur, GB, Hun, Por; 1997 Bra, Arg, Esp, GB, Hun, Aut, Lux
2nd:	5	1996 Aus, Arg, Can, Fra, Bel
3rd:	5	1996 Esp, Ger; 1997 Eur; 1998 Ger, Hun
Pole:	13	1996 Aus, Bel, Jap; 1997 Aus, Bra, Arg, SM, Esp, GB, Bel, Aut, Jap, Eur
Fast:	9	1996 Aus, Can, Fra, GB, Por, Jap; 1997 Bra, Bel, Aut

Year	Team	Grand(s) Prix
1996	WiRe	Aus 2, Bra r, Arg 2, Eur 1, SM 11, Mon r, Esp 3, Can 2, Fra 2, GB 1, Ger 3, Hun 1, Bel 2, Ita 7, Por 1, Jap r
1997	WiRe	Aus r, Bra 1, Arg 1, SM r, Mon r, Esp 1, Can r, Fra 4, GB 1, Ger r, Hun 1, Bel 5, Ita 5, Aut 1, Lux 1, Jap dq, Eur 3
1998	WiMh	Aus 5, Bra 7, Arg r, SM 4, Esp 6, Mon 5, Can 10, Fra 4, GB 7, Aut 6, Ger 3, Hun 3, Bel r, Ita r, Lux 8, Jap 6
1999	BASu	Aus r, Bra r, SM r, Mon r, Esp r, Can r, Fra r, GB r, Aut r, Ger r, Hun r, Bel 15, Ita 8, Eur 10, Mal r, Jap 9

VILLORESI, Luigi

COUNTRY: Italy
BORN: May 16, 1909
GP STARTS: 31
WC POINTS: 46 (49)
WC RECORD: 1951-5/15; 1952-7/8; 1953-5/17; 1954-18/2; 1955-17/2; 1956-19/2

Psn	No	Grand(s) Prix
2nd:	2	1953 Arg, Bel
3rd:	6	1951 Bel, Fra, GB; 1952 Hol, Ita; 1953 Ita
Fast:	1	1953 Hol

Year	Team	Grand(s) Prix
1950	Fe	Mon r, Swi r, Bel 6
1951	Fe	Swi r, Bel 3, Fra 3, GB 3, Ger 4, Ita 4, Esp r
1952	Fe	Hol 3, Ita 3
1953	Fe	Arg 2, Hol r, Bel 2, Fra 6, GB r, Ger r, Swi 6, Ita 3
1954	Mas	Fra 5, GB r, Ger dns, Ita r
1954	La	Esp r
1955	La	Arg r, Mon 5, Ita dns
1956	Mas	Bel 5, Fra r, GB 6, Ger r, Ita r

VILLOTA, Emilio de

COUNTRY: Spain
BORN: July 26, 1946
GP STARTS: 2
WC POINTS: 0

Year	Team	Grand(s) Prix
1977	McFd	Esp 13, Aut 17

VOLONTERIO, Ottorino

COUNTRY: Switzerland
BORN: December 7, 1917
GP STARTS: 1
WC POINTS: 0

Year	Team	Grand(s) Prix
1956	Mas	Ger uc

VON OPEL, Rikky

COUNTRY: Liechtenstein
BORN: October 14, 1947
GP STARTS: 10
WC POINTS: 0

Year	Team	Grand(s) Prix
1973	EnFd	Fra 15, GB 13, Hol dns, Aut r, Ita r, Can uc, US r
1974	EnFd	Arg dns
1974	BrFd	Esp r, Bel r, Swe 9, Hol 9

VON TRIPS, Wolfgang

COUNTRY: Germany
BORN: May 4, 1928
GP STARTS: 26
WC POINTS: 56
WC RECORD: 1957-14/4; 1958-10/9; 1960-6/10; 1961-2/33

Psn	No	Grand(s) Prix
1st:	2	1961 Hol, GB
2nd:	2	1961 Bel, Ger
3rd:	2	1957 Ita; 1958 Fra
Pole:	1	1961 Ita

Year	Team	Grand(s) Prix
1956	LaFe	Ita dns
1957	LaFe	Mon r, Ita 3
1958	Fe	Mon r, Fra 3, GB r, Ger 4, Por 5, Ita r
1959	Por	Mon r
1959	Fe	US 6
1960	Fe	Arg 5, Mon 8, Hol 5, Bel r, Fra r, GB 6, Por 4, Ita 5
1960	CoMa	US 9
1961	Fe	Mon 4, Hol 1, Bel 2, Fra r, GB 1, Ger 2, Ita r

VONLANTHEN, Jo

COUNTRY: Switzerland
BORN: May 31, 1942
GP STARTS: 1
WC POINTS: 0

Year	Team	Grand(s) Prix
1975	WiFd	Aut r

VUKOVICH, Bill

COUNTRY: US
BORN: December 13, 1918
GP STARTS: 5
WC POINTS: 18
WC RECORD: 1952-20/1; 1953-7/8; 1954-6/8; 1955-22/1

Psn	No	Grand(s) Prix
1st:	2	1953 Indy; 1954 Indy
Pole:	1	1953 Indy
Fast:	3	1952 Indy; 1953 Indy; 1955 Indy

Year	Team	Grand(s) Prix
1951	Trevis	Indy r
1952	KK	Indy 17
1953	KK	Indy 1
1954	KK	Indy 1
1955	KK	Indy r

WACKER, Fred

COUNTRY: US
BORN: July 10, 1918
GP STARTS: 3
WC POINTS: 0

Year	Team	Grand(s) Prix
1953	Gor	Bel 9
1954	Gor	Swi r, Ita 6

WALKER, Dave

COUNTRY: Australia
BORN: June 10, 1941
GP STARTS: 11
WC POINTS: 0

Year	Team	Grand(s) Prix
1971	LtTu	Hol r
1972	LtFd	Arg dq, SA 10, Esp 9, Mon 14, Bel 14, Fra 18, GB r, Ger r, Aut r, US r

WALKER, Peter

COUNTRY: GB
BORN: December 7, 1912
GP STARTS: 3
WC POINTS: 0

Year	Team	Grand(s) Prix
1950	ERA	GB r
1951	BRM	GB 7
1955	Mas	Hol r

WALLARD, Lee

COUNTRY: US
BORN: September 7, 1910
GP STARTS: 2
WC POINTS: 8
WC RECORD: 1951-7/8

Psn	No	Grand(s) Prix
1st:	1	1951 Indy
Fast:	1	1951 Indy

Year	Team	Grand(s) Prix
1950	Moo	Indy 6
1951	KK	Indy 1

WALTER, Heini

COUNTRY: Switzerland
BORN: July 28, 1927
GP STARTS: 1
WC POINTS: 0

Year	Team	Grand(s) Prix
1962	Por	Ger 14

WARD, Rodger

COUNTRY: US
BORN: January 10, 1921
GP STARTS: 12
WC POINTS: 14
WC RECORD: 1959-10/8; 1960-12/6

Psn	No	Grand(s) Prix
1st:	1	1959 Indy
2nd:	1	1960 Indy

Year	Team	Grand(s) Prix
1951	Bro	Indy r
1952	KK	Indy r
1953	KK	Indy 16
1954	Pawl	Indy r
1955	Ku	Indy r
1956	KK	Indy 8
1957	Les	Indy r
1958	Les	Indy r
1959	Wa	Indy 1
1959	KK	US r
1960	Wa	Indy 2
1963	LtBR	US r

WARWICK, Derek

COUNTRY: GB
BORN: August 27, 1954
GP STARTS: 146
WC POINTS: 71
WC RECORD: 1983-14/9; 1984-7/23; 1985-13/5; 1987-16/3; 1988-7/17; 1989-10/7; 1990-14/3; 1993-15/4

Psn	No	Grand(s) Prix
2nd:	2	1984 Bel, GB
3rd:	2	1984 SA, Ger
Fast:	2	1982 Hol; 1984 Detroit

Year	Team	Grand(s) Prix
1981	ToHt	US r
1982	ToHt	SA r, Bel r, Hol r, GB r, Fra 15, Ger 10, Aut r, Swi r, Ita r, Caesar's Palace r
1983	ToHt	Bra 8, USW r, Fra r, SM r, Mon r, Bel 7, US r, Can r, GB r, Ger r, Aut r, Hol 4, Ita 6, Eur 5, SA 4
1984	Re	Bra r, SA 3, Bel 2, SM 4, Fra r, Mon r, Can r, Detroit r, Dallas r, GB 2, Ger 3, Aut r, Hol r, Ita r, Eur 11, Por r
1985	Re	Bra 10, Por 7, SM 10, Mon 5, Can r, US r, Fra 7, GB 5, Ger r, Aut r, Hol r, Ita r, Bel 6, Eur r, Aus r
1986	BrBM	Can r, US 10, Fra 9, GB 8, Ger 7, Hun r, Ita r, Por r, Mex r, Aus r
1987	ArMe	Bra r, SM 11, Bel r, Mon r, US r, Fra r, GB 5, Ger r, Hun 6, Aut r, Ita r, Por 13, Esp 10, Mex r, Jap 10, Aus r
1988	ArMe	Bra 4, SM 9, Mon 4, Mex 5, Can 7, US r, Fra r, GB 6, Ger 7, Hun r, Bel 5, Ita 4, Por 4, Esp r, Jap r, Aus r
1989	ArFd	Bra 5, SM 5, Mon r, Mex r, US r, Can r, GB 9, Ger 6, Hun 10, Bel 6, Ita r, Por r, Esp 9, Jap 6, Aus r
1990	LtLm	US r, Bra r
1990	LoLm	SM 7

1990 LtLm Mon r, Can 6, Mex 10, Fra 11, GB r, Ger 8, Hun 5, Bel 11, Ita r, Por r, Esp r, Jap r, Aus r
1993 FtMH SA 7, Bra 9, Eur r, SM r, Esp 13, Mon r, Can 16, Fra 13, GB 6, Ger 17, Hun 4, Bel r, Ita r, Por 15, Jap 14, Aus 10

WATSON, John

COUNTRY: GB
BORN: May 4, 1946
GP STARTS: 152
WC POINTS: 169
WC RECORD: 1974-14/6; 1976-7/20; 1977-13/9; 1978-6/25; 1979-9/15; 1980-10/6; 1981-6/27; 1982-2/39; 1983-6/22

Psn	No	Grand(s) Prix
1st:	5	1976 Aut; 1981 GB; 1982 Bel, US; 1983 USW
2nd:	6	1977 Fra; 1978 Ita; 1981 Fra, Can; 1982 Bra, Caesar's Palace
3rd:	9	1976 Fra, GB; 1978 SA, GB; 1979 Arg; 1981 Esp; 1982 Can; 1983 US, Hol
Pole:	2	1977 Mon; 1978 Fra
Fast:	5	1977 SA, Aut; 1981 Can; 1982 Bel; 1983 US

Year	Team	Grand(s) Prix
1973	BrFd	GB r, US r
1974	BrFd	Arg 12, Bra r, SA r, Esp 11, Bel 11, Mon 6, Swe 11, Hol 7, Fra 16, GB 11, Ger r, Aut 4, Ita 7, Can r, US 5
1975	SuFd	Arg dq, Bra 10, SA r, Esp 8, Mon r, Bel 10, Swe 16, Hol r, Fra 13, GB 11
1975	LtFd	Ger r
1975	SuFd	Aut 10
1975	PkFd	US 9
1976	PkFd	Bra r, SA 5, USW uc, Esp r, Bel 7, Mon 10, Swe r, Fra 3, GB 3, Ger 7, Aut 1, Hol r, Ita 11, Can 10, USE 6, Jap r
1977	BrAl	Arg r, Bra r, SA 6, USW dq, Esp r, Mon r, Bel r, Swe 5, Fra 2, GB r, Ger r, Aut 8, Hol r, Ita r, USE 12, Can r, Jap r
1978	BrAl	Arg r, Bra 8, SA 3, USW r, Mon 4, Bel r, Esp 5, Swe r, Fra 4, GB 3, Ger 7, Aut 7, Hol 4, Ita 2, USE r, Can r
1979	McFd	Arg 3, Bra 8, SA r, USW r, Esp r, Bel 6, Mon 4, Fra 11, GB 4, Ger 5, Aut 9, Hol r, Ita r, Can 6, USE 6
1980	McFd	Arg r, Bra 11, SA 11, USW 4, Bel uc, Fra 7, GB 8, Ger r, Aut r, Hol r, Ita r, Can 4, USE uc
1981	McFd	USW r, Bra 8, Arg r, SM 10, Bel 7, Mon r, Esp 3, Fra 2, GB 1, Ger 6, Aut 6, Hol r, Ita r, Can 2, US 7
1982	McFd	SA 6, Bra 2, USW 6, Bel 1, Mon r, US 1, Can 3, Hol 9, GB r, Fra r, Ger r, Aut r, Swi 13, Ita 4, Caesar's Palace 2
1983	McF	Bra r, USW 1, Fra r, SM 5, Bel r, US 3, Can 6, GB 9, Ger 5, Aut 9, Hol 3
1983	McTG	Ita r, Eur r, SA dq
1985	McTG	Eur 7

WEBB, Spider

COUNTRY: US
BORN: October 8, 1910
GP STARTS: 4
WC POINTS: 0

Year	Team	Grand(s) Prix
1950	Mas	Indy 20
1952	Bro	Indy r
1953	KK	Indy r
1954	Bro	Indy r

WEILER, Wayne

COUNTRY: US
BORN: December 9, 1934
GP STARTS: 1
WC POINTS: 0

Year	Team	Grand(s) Prix
1960	Epp	Indy r

WENDLINGER, Karl

COUNTRY: Austria
BORN: December 20, 1968
GP STARTS: 41
WC POINTS: 14
WC RECORD: 1992-12/3; 1993-11/7; 1994-18/4

Year	Team	Grand(s) Prix
1991	LHIl	Jap r, Aus 20
1992	MaIl	SA r, Mex r, Bra r, Esp 8, SM 12, Mon r, Can 4, Fra r, GB r, Ger 16, Hun r, Bel 11, Ita 10, Por r
1993	SaIl	SA r, Bra r, Eur r, SM r, Esp r, Mon 13, Can 6, Fra r, GB r, Ger 9, Hun 6, Bel r, Ita 4, Por 5, Jap r, Aus 15
1994	SaMe	Bra 6, Pac r, SM 4, Mon dns
1995	SaFd	Bra r, Arg r, SM r, Esp 13, Jap 10, Aus r

WESTBURY, Peter

COUNTRY: GB
BORN: May 26, 1938
GP STARTS: 1 (F2 Race)

Year	Team	Grand(s) Prix
1969		Ger 5

WEYANT, Chuck

COUNTRY: US
BORN: April 3, 1923
GP STARTS: 4
WC POINTS: 0

Year	Team	Grand(s) Prix
1955	KK	Indy 12
1957	Ku	Indy 14
1958	Dunn	Indy r
1959	KK	Indy r

WHARTON, Ken

COUNTRY: GB
BORN: March 21, 1916
GP STARTS: 15
WC POINTS: 3
WC RECORD: 1952-13/3

Year	Team	Grand(s) Prix
1952	FN	Swi 4, Bel r, Hol 10
1952	CoBr	Ita 9
1953	CoBr	Hol r, Fra r, GB 8, Swi 7, Ita uc
1954	Mas	Fra r, GB 8, Ger dns, Swi 6, Esp 8
1955	Va	GB 9, Ita r

WHITEHEAD, Graham

COUNTRY: GB
BORN: April 15, 1922
GP STARTS: 1
WC POINTS: 0

Year	Team	Grand(s) Prix
1952	Alta	GB 12

WHITEHEAD, Peter

COUNTRY: GB
BORN: November 12, 1914
GP STARTS: 10
WC POINTS: 0

Psn	No	Grand(s) Prix
3rd:	1	1950 Fra

Year	Team	Grand(s) Prix
1950	Fe	Mon dns, Fra 3, Ita 7
1951	Fe	Swi 13, Fra r, GB 9, Ita r
1952	Alta	Fra r
1952	Fe	GB 10
1953	CoAt	GB 10
1954	CoAt	GB r

WHITEHOUSE, Bill

COUNTRY: GB
BORN: April 1, 1909
GP STARTS: 1
WC POINTS: 0

Year	Team	Grand(s) Prix
1954	Con	GB r

WIDDOWS, Robin

COUNTRY: GB
BORN: May 27, 1942
GP STARTS: 1
WC POINTS: 0

Year	Team	Grand(s) Prix
1968	CoBR	GB r

WIETZES, Eppie

COUNTRY: Canada
BORN: May 28, 1938
GP STARTS: 2
WC POINTS: 0

Year	Team	Grand(s) Prix
1967	LtFd	Can r
1974	BrFd	Can r

WILDS, Mike

COUNTRY: GB
BORN: January 7, 1946
GP STARTS: 3
WC POINTS: 0

Year	Team	Grand(s) Prix
1974	EnFd	US uc
1975	BRM	Arg r, Bra r

WILLIAMS, Jonathan

COUNTRY: GB
BORN: October 26, 1942
GP STARTS: 1
WC POINTS: 0

Year	Team	Grand(s) Prix
1967	Fe	Mex 8

WILLIAMSON, Roger

COUNTRY: GB
BORN: February 2, 1948
GP STARTS: 2
WC POINTS: 0

Year	Team	Grand(s) Prix
1973	MrFd	GB r, Hol r

WILSON, Dempsey

COUNTRY: US
BORN: March 11, 1927
GP STARTS: 2
WC POINTS: 0

Year	Team	Grand(s) Prix
1958	Ku	Indy r
1960	KK	Indy r

WILSON, Vic

COUNTRY: South Africa
BORN: April 14, 1931
GP STARTS: 1
WC POINTS: 0

Year	Team	Grand(s) Prix
1960	CoCl	Ita r

WINKELHOCK, Manfred

COUNTRY: Germany
BORN: October 6, 1951
GP STARTS: 47
WC POINTS: 2
WC RECORD: 1982-22/2

Year	Team	Grand(s) Prix
1982	ATFd	SA 10, Bra 5, USW r, SM dq, Bel r, Mon r, US r, Hol 12, Fra 11, Ger r, Aut r, Swi r, CP uc
1983	ATBM	Bra 16, USW r, Fra r, SM 11, Mon r, Bel r, US r, Can 9, GB r, Aut r, Hol dq, Ita r, Eur 8, SA r
1984	ATBM	Bra dns, SA r, Bel r, SM r, Fra r, Mon r, Can 8, Detroit r, Dallas 8, GB r, Ger r, Aut dns, Hol r
1984	BrBM	Por 10
1985	RmHt	Bra 13, Por uc, SM r, Can r, US r, Fra 12, GB r, Ger r

WISELL, Reine

COUNTRY: Sweden
BORN: September 30, 1941
GP STARTS: 22
WC POINTS: 13
WC RECORD: 1970-15/4; 1971-9/9

Psn	No	Grand(s) Prix
3rd:	1	1970 US

Year	Team	Grand(s) Prix
1970	LtFd	US 3, Mex uc
1971	LtFd	SA 4, Esp uc, Mon r, Hol dq, Fra 6
1971	LtTu	GB uc
1971	LtFd	Ger 8, Aut 4, Can 5, US r
1972	BRM	Arg r, Esp r, Mon r, Fra r, Ger r, Ita 12
1972	LtFd	Can r, US 10
1973	MrFd	Swe dns, Fra r
1974	MrFd	Swe r

WUNDERINK, Roelof

COUNTRY: Holland
BORN: December 12, 1948
GP STARTS: 3
WC POINTS: 0

Year	Team	Grand(s) Prix
1975	EnFd	Esp r, Aut uc, US r

WURZ, Alex

COUNTRY: Austria
BORN: February 15, 1974
GP STARTS: 35
WC POINTS: 24
WC RECORD: 1997-14/4; 1998-7/17; 1999-13/3

Psn	No	Grand(s) Prix
3rd:	1	1997 GB
Fast:	1	1998 Arg

Year	Team	Grand(s) Prix
1997	BeRe	Can r, Fra r, GB 3
1998	BePl	Aus 7, Bra 4, Arg 4, SM r, Esp 4, Mon r, Can 4, Fra 5, GB 4, Aut 9, Ger 11, Hun 16, Bel r, Ita r, Lux 7, Jap 9
1999	BePl	Aus r, Bra 7, SM r, Mon 6, Esp 10, Can r, Fra r, GB 10, Aut 5, Ger 7, Hun 7, Bel 14, Ita r, Eur r, Mal 8, Jap 10

ZANARDI, Alessandro

COUNTRY: Italy
BORN: October 23, 1966
GP STARTS: 41
WC POINTS: 1
WC RECORD: 1993-20/1

Year	Team	Grand(s) Prix
1991	JoFd	Esp 9, Jap r, Aus 9
1992	MiLm	Ger r
1993	LtFd	SA r, Bra 6, Eur 8, SM r, Esp 14, Mon 7, Can 11, Fra r, GB r, Ger r, Hun r
1994	LoMH	Esp 9, Can 15, Fra r, GB r, Ger r, Hun 13, Ita r, Eur 16, Jap 13, Aus r
1999	WiSu	Aus r, Bra r, SM 11, Mon 8, Esp r, Can r, Fra r, GB 11, Aut r, Ger r, Hun r, Bel 8, Ita 7, Eur r, Mal 10, Jap r

ZONTA, Ricardo

COUNTRY: Brazil
BORN: March 23, 1976
GP STARTS: 12
WC POINTS: 0

Year	Team	Grand(s) Prix
1999	BASu	Aus r, Can r, Fra 9, GB r, Aut 15, Ger r, Hun 13, Bel r, Ita r, Eur 8, Mal r, Jap 12

ZORZI, Renzo

COUNTRY: Italy
BORN: December 12, 1946
GP STARTS: 7
WC POINTS: 1
WC RECORD: 1977-19/1

Year	Team	Grand(s) Prix
1975	WiFd	Ita 14
1976	WiFd	Bra 9
1977	ShFd	Arg r, Bra 6, SA r, USW r, Esp r

ZUNINO, Ricardo

COUNTRY: Argentina
BORN: April 13, 1949
GP STARTS: 10
WC POINTS: 0

Year	Team	Grand(s) Prix
1979	BrFd	Can 7, USE r
1980	BrFd	Arg 7, Bra 8, SA 10, USW r, Bel r, Fra r
1981	TyFd	Bra 13, Arg 13

WORLD CHAMPIONSHIP WINNERS 1950–1999

Year	Driver	Age	Country	Car	R	W	P	F
1950	Farina	44	Ita	Alfa Romeo	7	3	2	3
1951	Fangio	40	Arg	Alfa Romeo	8	3	4	5
1952	Ascari	34	Ita	Ferrari	8	6	5	5
1953	Ascari	35	Italy	Ferrari	9	5	6	4
1954	Fangio	43	Arg	Merc/Maserati	9	6	5	3
1955	Fangio	44	Arg	Mercedes	7	4	3	3
1956	Fangio	45	Arg	Lancia/Ferrari	8	3	5	3
1957	Fangio	46	Arg	Maserati	8	4	4	2
1958	Hawthorn	29	GB	Ferrari	11	1	4	5
1959	Brabham,J.	33	Aus	Cooper	9	2	1	1
1960	Brabham,J.	34	Aus	Cooper	10	5	3	3
1961	Hill,P.	34	USA	Ferrari	8	2	5	2
1962	Hill,G.	33	GB	BRM	9	4	1	3
1963	Clark	27	GB	Lotus	10	7	7	6
1964	Surtees	30	GB	Ferrari	10	2	2	2
1965	Clark	29	GB	Lotus	10	6	6	6
1966	Brabham,J.	40	Aus	Brabham	9	4	3	1
1967	Hulme	31	NZ	Brabham	11	2	0	2
1968	Hill,G.	39	GB	Lotus	12	3	2	0
1969	Stewart,Jack	30	GB	Matra	11	6	2	5
1970	Rindt	28	Aut	Lotus	13	5	3	1
1971	Stewart,Jack	32	GB	Tyrrell	11	6	6	3
1972	Fittipaldi,E.	26	Bra	Lotus	12	5	3	1
1973	Stewart,Jack	34	Bra	Tyrrell	15	5	3	1
1974	Fittipaldi,E.	28	Bra	McLaren	15	3	2	0
1975	Lauda	26	Aut	Ferrari	14	5	9	2
1976	Hunt	29	GB	McLaren	16	6	8	2
1977	Lauda	28	Aut	Ferrari	17	3	2	3
1978	Andretti,Mario	38	USA	Lotus	16	6	8	3
1979	Scheckter,J.	29	USA	Ferrari	15	3	1	1
1980	Jones	34	Aus	Williams	14	5	3	5
1981	Piquet	29	Bra	Brabham	15	3	4	1
1982	Rosberg	34	Fin	Williams	16	1	1	0
1983	Piquet	31	Bra	Brabham	15	3	1	4
1984	Lauda	35	Aut	McLaren	16	5	0	5
1985	Prost	30	Fra	McLaren	16	5	2	5
1986	Prost	31	Fra	McLaren	16	4	1	2
1987	Piquet	35	Bra	Williams	16	3	4	4
1988	Senna	28	Bra	McLaren	16	8	13	3
1989	Prost	34	Fra	McLaren	16	4	2	5
1990	Senna	30	Bra	McLaren	16	6	10	2
1991	Senna	31	Bra	McLaren	16	7	8	2
1992	Mansell	39	GB	Williams	16	9	14	8
1993	Prost	38	Fra	Williams	16	7	13	6
1994	Schumacher,M.	25	Ger	Benetton	16	8	6	8
1995	Schumacher,M.	26	Ger	Benetton	17	9	4	8
1996	Hill,D.	36	GB	Williams	16	8	9	5
1997	Villeneuve,J.	26	Can	Williams	17	7	11	3
1998	Hakkinen,M.	30	Fin	McLaren	16	9	10	7
1999	Hakkinen,M.	31	Fin	McLaren	16	5	11	6

R=Races, W=Wins, P=Poles, F=Fastest laps

CHAMPIONSHIP WINS BY NUMBER 1950–99

Titles	Driver	Country	Year
5	Fangio	Arg	1951, 1954, 1955, 1956, 1957
4	Prost	Fra	1985, 1986, 1989, 1993
3	Brabham,J.	Aus	1959, 1960, 1966
	Stewart,Jackie	GB	1969, 1971, 1973
	Lauda	Aut	1975, 1977, 1984
	Piquet	Bra	1981, 1983, 1987
	Senna	Bra	1988, 1990, 1991
2	Ascari	Ita	1952, 1953
	Hill,G.	GB	1962, 1968
	Clark	GB	1963, 1965
	Fittipaldi,E.	Bra	1972, 1974
	Schumacher,M.	Ger	1994, 1995
	Hakkinen,M.	Fin	1998, 1999
1	Farina	Italy	1950
	Hawthorn	GB	1958
	Hill,P.	USA	1961
	Surtees	GB	1964
	Hulme	NZ	1967
	Rindt	Aut	1970
	Hunt	GB	1976
	Andretti,Mario	USA	1978
	Scheckter,J.	USA	1979
	Jones	Aus	1980
	Rosberg	Fin	1982
	Mansell	GB	1992
	Hill,D.	GB	1996
	Villeneuve,J.	Can	1997

POINTS

The final tables for the Drivers World Championship can be found in the following pages. The tables are reasonably straightforward, however, there may be two sets of points listed for a driver or a constructor. The first number is the points obtained that counted towards the championship whereas a second score indicates the total number of points won. The difference arises because in some seasons only the best five or six results, for example, counted towards the championship total.

The number of points awarded has changed down the years. Here is a brief summary of the points awarded and races that counted towards results.

1950-59 Points awarded were 8, 6, 4, 3, 2 for 1st, 2nd, 3rd, 4th and 5th positions. The driver completing the fastest lap was awarded 1 point – if more than one driver shared the fastest lap then the single point was divided amongst them (thus the sometimes silly decimal points in the scores). Teams did not get a point for a fastest lap. Drivers sharing a car shared the points up to 1957 but only if it was deemed that they had completed enough laps of the race.

1960 Points awarded were 8, 6, 4, 3, 2, 1 for 1st, 2nd, 3rd, 4th, 5th and 6th positions.

1961-90 Points awarded were 9, 6, 4, 3, 2, 1 for 1st, 2nd, 3rd, 4th, 5th and 6th positions.

1991-99 Points awarded were 10, 6, 4, 3, 2, 1 for 1st, 2nd, 3rd, 4th, 5th and 6th positions.

Race results counted as follows down the years:

1950-53 Best four results were counted.
1954-57 Best five results were counted.
1958 Best six results were counted.
1959 Best five results were counted.
1960 Best six results were counted.
1961-62 Best five results were counted.
1963-65 Best six results were counted.
1966 Best five results were counted.
1967-78 Championship divided into two halves with worst result from each half discarded. If odd number of races, extra race included in first half.
1979 Best four results in each half were counted.
1980 Best fives results in each half were counted.
1981-90 Best eleven results were counted
1991-99 All results were counted.

1950

Pos	Driver	Team	Points
1	Farina	Alfa Romeo	30
2	Fangio	Alfa Romeo	27
3	Fagioli	Alfa Romeo	24 (28)
4	Rosier	Talbot	13
5	Ascari	Ferrari	11
6	Parsons	Kurtis Kraft	8
7	Holland	Deidt	6
8	Bira	Maserati	5
9	Chiron	Maserati	4
=	Parnell	Alfa Romeo	4
=	Rose	Deidt	4
=	Whitehead	Ferrari	4
13	Etancelin	Talbot	3
=	Giraud-Cabantous	Talbot	3
=	Green	Kurtis Kraft	3
=	Manzon	Simca Gordini	3
=	Serafini	Ferrari	3
=	Sommer	Ferrari	3
19	Bonetto	Maserati	2
20	Bettenhausen	Kurtis Kraft	1
=	Chaboud	Talbot	1
=	Chitwood	Kurtis Kraft	1

1951

Pos	Driver	Team	Points
1	Fangio	Alfa Romeo	31 (37)
2	Ascari	Ferrari	25 (28)
3	Gonzalez,J.	Ferrari	24 (27)
4	Farina	Alfa Romeo	19 (18)
5	Villoresi	Ferrari	15
6	Taruffi	Ferrari	10
7	Wallard	Kurtis Kraft	8
8	Bonetto	Alfa Romeo	7
9	Nazaruk	Kurtis Kraft	6
10	Parnell	Ferrari & BRM	5
11	Fagioli	Alfa Romeo	4
12	Linden	Sherman	3
=	Rosier	Talbot	3
=	Sanesi	Alfa Romeo	3
15	Ayulo	Kurtis Kraft	2
=	Ball	Schroeder	2
=	de Graffenried	Alfa Romeo	2
=	Giraud-Cabantous	Talbot	2
=	McGrath	Kurtis Kraft	2

1952

Pos	Driver	Team	Points
1	Ascari	Ferrari	36 (53.5)
2	Farina	Ferrari	24 (27)
3	Taruffi	Ferrari	22
4	Fischer	Ferrari	10
=	Hawthorn	Cooper	10
6	Manzon	Gordini	9
7	Ruttman	Kurtis Kraft	8
7	Villoresi	Ferrari	8
9	Gonzalez,J.	Maserati	6.5
10	Behra	Gordini	6
=	Rathmann,J.	Kurtis Kraft	6
12	Hanks	Kurtis Kraft	4
13	Carter	Lesovsky	3
=	Poore	Connaught	3
=	Wharton	Frazer Nash	3
16	Bonetto	Maserati	2
=	Brown	Cooper	2
=	Cross	Kurtis Kraft	2
=	Frere	HWM	2
=	Thompson	Connaught	2
=	Trintignant	Gordini	2
22	Vukovich	Kurtis Kraft	1

1953

Pos	Driver	Team	Points
1	Ascari	Ferrari	34.5 (46.5)
2	Fangio	Maserati	27.5 (29)
3	Farina	Ferrari	26 (32)
4	Hawthorn	Ferrari	19 (27)
5	Villoresi	Ferrari	17
6	Gonzalez,J.	Maserati	13.5 (14.5)
7	Vukovich	Kurtis Kraft	8
8	de Graffenried	Maserati	7
9	Bonetto	Maserati	6.5
10	Cross	Kurtis Kraft	6
11	Marimon	Maserati	4
=	Trintignant	Gordini	4
13	Carter	Kurtis Kraft	2
=	Galvez	Maserati	2
=	Hanks	Kurtis Kraft	2
=	Lang	Maserati	2
=	McGrath	Kurtis Kraft	2
18	Agabashian	Kurtis Kraft	1.5
=	Russo,P.	Kurtis Kraft	1.5

1954

Pos	Driver	Team	Points
1	Fangio	Maserati & Mercedes	42 (57.14)
2	Gonzalez,J.	Ferrari	25.14 (26.64)
3	Hawthorn	Ferrari	24.64
4	Trintignant	Ferrari	17
5	Kling	Mercedes	12
6	Vukovich	Kurtis Kraft	8
=	Hermann	Mercedes	8
8	Bryan	Kuzma	6
=	Farina	Ferrari	6
=	Musso	Maserati	6
=	Mieres	Maserati	6
12	McGrath	Kurtis Kraft	5
13	Marimon	Maserati	4.14
=	Moss	Maserati	4.14
15	Mantovani	Maserati	4
=	Manzon	Ferrari	4
17	Bira	Maserati	3
18	Bayol	Gordini	2
=	Maglioli	Ferrari	2
=	Nazaruk	Kurtis Kraft	2
=	Pilette	Gordini	2
=	Villoresi	Maserati	2
23	Carter	Kurtis Kraft	1.5
=	Ruttman	Kurtis Kraft	1.5
25	Ascari	Maserati & Lancia	1.14
26	Behra	Gordini	0.14

1955

Pos	Driver	Team	Points
1	Fangio	Mercedes	40 (41)
2	Moss	Mercedes	23
3	Castellotti	Lancia	12
4	Trintignant	Ferrari	11.33
5	Farina	Ferrari	10.33
6	Taruffi	Mercedes	9
7	Sweikert	Kurtis Kraft	8
8	Mieres	Maserati	7
9	Behra	Maserati	6
=	Musso	Maserati	6
11	Kling	Mercedes	5
12	Davies	Kurtis Kraft	4
13	Bettenhausen	Kurtis Kraft	3
=	Frere	Ferrari	3
=	Russo,P.	Kurtis Kraft	3
=	Thomson	Kuzma	3
17	Gonzalez,J.	Ferrari	2

=	Menditeguy	Maserati	2	
=	Perdisa	Maserati	2	
=	Villoresi	Lancia	2	
21	Maglioli	Ferrari	1.33	
22	Faulkner	Kurtis Kraft	1	
=	Herrmann	Mercedes	1	
=	Homeier	Kurtis Kraft	1	
=	Vukovich	Kurtis Kraft	1	

1956

Pos	Driver	Team	Points	
1	Fangio	Ferrari	30	(33)
2	Moss	Maserati	27	(28)
3	Collins	Ferrari	25	
4	Behra	Maserati	22	
5	Flaherty	Watson	8	
6	Castellotti	Ferrari	7.5	
7	Frere	Ferrari	6	
=	Godia	Maserati	6	
=	Hanks	Kurtis Kraft	6	
10	Fairman	Connaught	5	
11	Flockhart	Connaught	4	
=	Freeland	Phillips	4	
=	Hawthorn	Maserati	4	
=	Musso	Lancia	4	
15	Parsons	Kuzma	3	
=	Perdisa	Maserati	3	
=	de Portago	Lancia	3	
=	Schell	Vanwell	3	
19	Gendebien	Ferrari	2	
=	Gould	Maserati	2	
=	Rathmann,D.	Gordini	2	
=	Rosier	Kurtis Kraft	2	
=	da Silva Ramos	Maserati	2	
=	Villoresi	Maserati	2	
25	Gerini	Maserati	1.5	
=	Landi	Maserati	1.5	
27	Russo,P.	Kurtis Kraft	1	

1957

Pos	Driver	Team	Points	
1	Fangio	Maserati	40	(46)
2	Moss	Vanwell	25	
3	Musso	Ferrari	16	
4	Hawthorn	Ferrari	13	
5	Brooks	Vanwell	11	
6	Gregory	Maserati	10	
=	Schell	Maserati	10	
8	Collins	Ferrari	8	
=	Hanks	Epperly	8	
10	Rathmann,J.	Epperly	7	
11	Behra	Maserati	6	
12	Lewis-Evans	Connaught & Vanwell	5	
=	Trintignant	Lancia	5	
14	Bryan	Kuzma	4	
=	Menditeguy	Maserati	4	
=	von Trips	Kurtis Kraft	4	
=	Russo,P.	Ferrari	4	
18	Linden	Kurtis Kraft	3	
19	Gonzalez,J.	Lancia	2	
=	Salvadori	Cooper	2	
21	de Portago	Lancia	1	
=	Scarlatti	Maserati	1	

1958

Pos	Driver	Team	Points	
1	Hawthorn	Ferrari	42	(49)
2	Moss	Cooper & Vanwell	41	
3	Brooks	Vanwell	24	
4	Salvadori	Cooper	15	
5	Collins	Ferrari	15	
=	Schell	BRM	14	
7	Musso	Ferrari	12	
=	Trintignant	Cooper	12	
9	Lewis-Evans	Vanwell	11	
10	Behra	BRM	9	
=	Hill,P.	Ferrari	9	
=	von Trips	Ferrari	9	
13	Bryan	Epperly	8	
14	Fangio	Maserati	7	
15	Amick,G.	Epperly	6	
16	Bettenhausen	Epperly	4	
=	Boyd	Kurtis Kraft	4	
18	Allison	Lotus	3	
=	Bonnier	BRM	3	
=	Brabham,J.	Cooper	3	
21	Rathmann,J.	Epperly	2	

1959

Pos	Driver	Team	Points	
1	Brabham,J.	Cooper	31	(34)
2	Brooks	Ferrari	27	
3	Moss	BRM & Cooper	25.5	
4	Hill,P.	Ferrari	20	
5	Trintignant	Cooper	19	
6	McLaren	Cooper	16.5	
7	Gurney	Ferrari	13	
8	Bonnier	BRM	10	

Pos	Driver	Team	Points	
=	Gregory	Cooper	10	
10	Ward	Watson	8	
11	Rathmann,J.	Watson	6	
12	Ireland	Lotus	5	
=	Schell	BRM	5	
=	Thomson	Lesovsky	5	
15	Bettenhausen	Epperly	3	
=	Gendebien	Ferrari	3	
17	Allison	Ferrari	2	
=	Behra	Ferrari	2	
=	Goldsmith	Epperly	2	

1960

Pos	Driver	Team	Points	
1	Brabham,J.	Cooper	43	
2	McLaren	Cooper	34	(37)
3	Moss	Cooper & Lotus	19	
4	Ireland	Lotus	18	
5	Hill,P.	Ferrari	16	
6	Gendebien	Cooper	10	
=	von Trips	Ferrari	10	
8	Clark	Lotus	8	
=	Ginther	Ferrari	8	
=	Rathmann,J.	Watson	8	
11	Brooks	Cooper	7	
12	Allison	Ferrari	6	
=	Surtees	Lotus	6	
=	Ward	Watson	6	
15	Bonnier	BRM	4	
=	Goldsmith	Epperly	4	
=	Hill,G.	BRM	4	
=	Mairesse	Ferrari	4	
19	Branson	Phillips	3	
=	Cabianca	Cooper	3	
=	Menditeguy	Cooper	3	
=	Taylor,H.	Cooper	3	
23	Thomson	Lesovsky	2	
24	Bianchi	Cooper	1	
=	Flockhart	Lotus	1	
=	Herrmann	Porsche	1	
=	Johnson	Travis	1	

1961

Pos	Driver	Team	Points	
1	Hill,P.	Ferrari	34	(38)
2	von Trips	Ferrari	33	
3	Gurney	Porsche	21	
=	Moss	Lotus	21	
5	Ginther	Ferrari	16	
6	Ireland	Lotus	12	
7	Clark	Lotus	11	
=	McLaren	Cooper	11	
9	Baghetti	Ferrari	9	
10	Brooks	BRM	6	
11	Brabham,J.	Cooper	4	
=	Surtees	Cooper	4	
13	Bonnier	Porsche	3	
=	Gendebien	Ferrari	3	
=	Hill,G.	BRM	3	
=	Lewis	Cooper	3	
17	Salvadori	Cooper	1	

1962

Pos	Driver	Team	Points	
1	Hill,G.	BRM	42	(52)
2	Clark	Lotus	30	
3	McLaren	Cooper	27	(32)
4	Surtees	Lola	19	
5	Gurney	Porsche	15	
6	Hill,P.	Ferrari	14	
7	Maggs	Cooper	13	
8	Ginther	BRM	10	
9	Brabham,J.	Lotus & Brabham	9	
10	Taylor,T.	Lotus	6	
11	Baghetti	Ferrari	5	
12	Bandini	Ferrari	4	
=	Rodriguez,R.	Ferrari	4	
14	Bonnier	Porsche	3	
=	Mairesse	Ferrari	3	
16	de Beaufort	Porsche	2	
=	Ireland	Lotus	2	
18	Gregory	Lotus	1	
=	Lederle	Lotus	1	

1963

Pos	Driver	Team	Points	
1	Clark	Lotus	54	(73)
2	Hill,G.	BRM	29	
3	Ginther	BRM	29	(34)
4	Surtees	Ferrari	22	
5	Gurney	Brabham	19	
6	McLaren	Cooper	17	
7	Brabham,J.	Brabham	14	
8	Maggs	Cooper	9	
9	Bandini	Ferrari	6	
=	Bonnier	Cooper	6	
=	Ireland	BRP	6	
12	Hall	Lotus	3	

Pos	Driver	Team	Points	
=	Mitter	Porsche	3	
14	de Beaufort	Porsche	2	
15	Scarfiotti	Ferrari	1	
=	Siffert	Lotus	1	
=	Taylor,T.	Lotus	1	

1964

Pos	Driver	Team	Points	
1	Surtees	Ferrari	40	
2	Hill,G.	BRM	39	(41)
3	Clark	Lotus	32	
4	Bandini	Ferrari	23	
=	Ginther	BRM	23	
6	Gurney	Brabham	19	
7	McLaren	Cooper	13	
8	Arundell	Lotus	11	
=	Brabham,J.	Brabham	11	
10	Siffert	Brabham	7	
11	Anderson	Brabham	5	
12	Ireland	BRP	4	
=	Maggs	BRM	4	
=	Spence	Lotus	4	
15	Bonnier	Cooper & Brabham	3	
16	Amon	Lotus	2	
=	Hansgen	Lotus	2	
=	Trintignant	BRM	2	
19	Hailwood	Lotus	1	
=	Hill,P.	Cooper	1	
=	Rodriguez,P.	Ferrari	1	
=	Taylor,T.	BRP	1	

1965

Pos	Driver	Team	Points	
1	Clark	Lotus	54	
2	Hill,G.	BRM	40	(45)
3	Stewart,Jackie	BRM	33	(34)
4	Gurney	Brabham	25	
5	Surtees	Ferrari	17	
6	Bandini	Ferrari	13	
7	Ginther	Honda	11	
8	McLaren	Cooper	10	
=	Spence	Lotus	10	
10	Brabham,J.	Brabham	9	
11	Hulme	Brabham	5	
=	Siffert	Brabham	5	
13	Rindt	Cooper	4	
14	Attwood	Lotus	2	
=	Bucknum	Honda	2	
=	Rodriguez,P.	Ferrari	2	

1966

Pos	Driver	Team	Points	
1	Brabham,J.	Brabham	42	(45)
2	Surtees	Ferrari & Cooper	28	
3	Rindt	Cooper	22	(24)
4	Hulme	Brabham	18	
5	Hill,G.	BRM	17	
6	Clark	Lotus	16	
7	Stewart,Jackie	BRm	14	
8	Bandini	Ferrari	12	
=	Parkes	Ferrari	12	
10	Scarfiotti	Ferrari	9	
11	Ginther	Cooper & Honda	5	
12	Gurney	Eagle	4	
=	Spence	Lotus	4	
14	Bondurant	BRM	3	
=	McLaren	McLaren	3	
=	Siffert	Cooper	3	
17	Anderson	Brabham	1	
=	Arundell	Lotus	1	
=	Bonnier	Cooper	1	
=	Taylor,J.	Brabham	1	

1967

Pos	Driver	Team	Points	
1	Hulme	Brabham	51	
2	Brabham,J.	Brabham	46	(48)
3	Clark	Lotus	41	
4	Amon	Ferrari	20	
=	Surtees	Honda	20	
6	Hill,G.	Lotus	15	
=	Rodriguez,P.	Cooper	15	
8	Gurney	Eagle	13	
9	Stewart,Jackie	BRM	10	
10	Spence	BRM	9	
11	Love	Cooper	6	
=	Rindt	Cooper	6	
=	Siffert	Cooper	6	
14	Bonnier	Cooper	3	
=	McLaren	McLaren	3	
16	Anderson	Brabham	2	
=	Irwin	BRM	2	
=	Parkes	Ferrari	2	
19	Ickx	Cooper	1	
=	Ligier	Brabham	1	
=	Scarfiotti	Ferrari	1	

1968

Pos	Driver	Team	Points
1	Hill,G.	Lotus	48
2	Stewart,Jackie	Matra	36
3	Hulme	McLaren	33
4	Ickx	Ferrari	27
5	McLaren	McLaren	22
6	Rodriguez,P.	BRM	18
7	Siffert	Lotus	12
=	Surtees	Honda	12
9	Beltoise	Matra	11
10	Amon	Ferrari	10
11	Clark	Lotus	9
12	Rindt	Brabham	8
13	Attwood	BRM	6
=	Oliver	Lotus	6
=	Scarfiotti	Cooper	6
=	Servoz-Gavin	Matra	6
17	Bianchi	Cooper	5
=	Elford	Cooper	5
19	Courage	BRM	4
=	Redman	Cooper	4
21	Bonnier	McLaren & Honda	3
=	Gurney	McLaren	3
23	Brabham,J.	Brabham	2
=	Moser	Brabham	2

1969

Pos	Driver	Team	Points
1	Stewart,Jackie	Matra	63
2	Ickx	Brabham	37
3	McLaren	McLaren	26
4	Rindt	Lotus	22
5	Beltoise	Matra	21
6	Hulme	McLaren	20
7	Hill,G.	Lotus	19
8	Courage	Brabham	16
9	Siffert	Lotus	15
10	Brabham,J.	Brabham	14
11	Surtees	BRM	6
12	Amon	Ferrari	4
13	Attwood	Lotus	3
=	Elford	McLaren	3
=	Rodriguez,P.	Ferrari	3
16	Moser	Brabham	1
=	Oliver	BRM	1
=	Servoz-Gavin	Matra	1

1970

Pos	Driver	Team	Points
1	Rindt	Lotus	45
2	Ickx	Ferrari	40
3	Regazzoni	Ferrari	33
4	Hulme	McLaren	27
5	Brabham,J.	Brabham	25
=	Stewart,Jackie	March & Tyrrell	25
=	Amon	March & Tyrrell	23
7	Rodriguez,P.	BRM	23
9	Beltoise	Matra	16
10	Fittipaldi,E.	Lotus	12
11	Stommelen	Brabham	10
12	Pescarolo	Matra	8
13	Hill,G.	Lotus	7
14	McLaren	McLaren	6
15	Andretti,Mario	March	4
=	Wisell	Lotus	4
=	Giunti	Ferrari	3
=	Surtees	McLaren & Surtees	3
19	Miles	Lotus	2
=	Oliver	BRM	2
=	Servoz-Gavin	March	2
22	Bell	Surtees	1
=	Cevert	March	1
=	Gethin	McLaren	1
=	Gurney	McLaren	1

1971

Pos	Driver	Team	Points
1	Stewart,Jackie	Tyrrell	62
2	Peterson	March	33
3	Cevert	Tyrrell	26
4	Ickx	Ferrari	19
=	Siffert	BRM	19
6	Fittipaldi,E.	Lotus	16
7	Regazzoni	Ferrari	13
8	Andretti,Mario	Ferrari	12
9	Amon	Matra	9
=	Hulme	BRM	9
=	Gethin	McLaren	9
=	Rodriguez,P.	BRM	9
=	Wisell	Lotus	9
14	Ganley	BRM	5
=	Schenken	Brabham	5
16	Donohue	McLaren	4
=	Pescarolo	March	4
18	Hailwood	Surtees	3
=	Stommelen	Surtees	3

Pos	Driver	Team	Points
=	Surtees	Surtees	3
21	Hill,G.	Brabham	2
22	Beltoise	Matra	1

1972

Pos	Driver	Team	Points
1	Fittipaldi,E.	Lotus	61
2	Stewart,Jackie	Tyrrell	45
3	Hulme	McLaren	39
4	Ickx	Ferrari	27
5	Revson	McLaren	23
6	Cevert	Tyrrell	15
=	Regazzoni	Ferrari	15
8	Hailwood	Surtees	13
9	Amon	Matra	12
=	Peterson	March	12
11	Beltoise	BRM	9
12	Andretti,Mario	Ferrari	4
=	Ganley	BRM	4
=	Hill,G.	Brabham	4
=	Redman	McLaren	4
16	de Adamich	Surtees	3
=	Pace	March	3
=	Reutemann	Brabham	3
19	Schenken	Surtees	2
20	Gethin	BRM	1
=	Merzario	Ferrari	1

1973

Pos	Driver	Team	Points
1	Stewart,Jackie	Tyrrell	71
2	Fittipaldi,E.	Lotus	55
3	Peterson	Lotus	52
4	Cevert	Tyrrell	47
5	Revson	McLaren	38
6	Hulme	McLaren	26
7	Reutemann	McLaren	16
8	Hunt	March	14
9	Ickx	Ferrari	12
10	Beltoise	BRM	9
11	Pace	Surtees	7
12	Merzario	Ferrari	6
13	Follmer	Shadow	5
14	Oliver	Shadow	4
15	de Adamich	Brabham	3
=	Fittipaldi,W.	Brabham	3
17	Lauda	BRM	2
=	Regazzoni	BRM	2
19	Amon	Tecno	1
=	Ganley	Williams	1
=	van Lennep	Williams	1

1974

Pos	Driver	Team	Points
1	Fittipaldi,E.	McLaren	55
2	Regazzoni	Ferrari	52
3	Scheckter,J.	Tyrrell	45
4	Lauda	Ferrari	38
5	Peterson	Lotus	35
6	Reutemann	Brabham	32
7	Hulme	McLaren	20
8	Hunt	Hesketh	15
9	Depailler	Tyrrell	14
10	Hailwood	McLaren	12
=	Ickx	Lotus	12
12	Pace	Surtees & Brabham	11
13	Beltoise	BRM	10
14	Jarier	Shadow	6
=	Watson	Brabham	6
16	Stuck	March	5
17	Merzario	Williams	4
18	Brambilla	March	1
=	Hill,G.	Lola	1
=	Pryce	Shadow	1

1975

Pos	Driver	Team	Points
1	Lauda	Ferrari	64.5
2	Fittipaldi,E.	McLaren	45
3	Reutemann	Brabham	37
4	Hunt	Hesketh	33
5	Regazzoni	Ferrari	25
6	Pace	Brabham	24
7	Mass	McLaren	20
=	Scheckter,J.	Tyrrell	20
9	Depailler	Tyrrell	12
10	Pryce	Shadow	8
11	Brambilla	March	6.5
12	Laffite	Williams	6
=	Peterson	Lotus	6
14	Andretti,Mario	Parnelli	5
15	Donohue	Penske & March	4
16	Ickx	Lotus	3
17	Jones	Hill	2
18	Jarier	Shadow	1.5
19	Brise	Hill	1

=	van Lennep	Ensign	1
21	Lombardi	March	0.5

1976

Pos	Driver	Team	Points
1	Hunt	McLaren	69
2	Lauda	Ferrari	68
3	Scheckter,J.	Tyrrell	49
4	Depailler	Tyrrell	39
5	Regazzoni	Ferrari	31
6	Andretti,Mario	Parnelli & Lotus	22
7	Laffite	Ligier	20
=	Watson	Penske	20
9	Mass	McLaren	19
10	Nilsson	Lotus	11
11	Peterson	March	10
=	Pryce	Shadow	10
13	Stuck	March	8
14	Jones	Surtees	7
=	Pace	Brabham	7
16	Fittipaldi,E.	Fittipaldi	3
=	Reutemann	Brabham	3
18	Amon	Ensign	2
19	Brambilla	March	1
=	Stommelen	Brabham	1

1977

Pos	Driver	Team	Points
1	Lauda	Ferrari	72
2	Scheckter,J.	Wolf	55
3	Andretti,Mario	Lotus	47
4	Reutemann	Ferrari	42
5	Hunt	McLaren	40
6	Mass	McLaren	25
7	Jones	Shadow	22
8	Depailler	Tyrrell	20
=	Nilsson	Lotus	20
10	Laffite	Ligier	18
11	Stuck	Brabham	12
12	Fittipaldi,E.	Fittipaldi	11
13	Watson	Brabham	9
14	Peterson	Tyrrell	7
15	Brambilla	Surtees	6
=	Pace	Brabham	6
17	Regazzoni	Ensign	5
=	Tambay	Ensign	5
19	Jarier	Penske	1
=	Patrese	Shadow	1
=	Zorzi	Shadow	1

1978

Pos	Driver	Team	Points
1	Andretti,Mario	Lotus	64
2	Peterson	Lotus	51
3	Reutemann	Ferrari	48
4	Lauda	Brabham	44
5	Depailler	Tyrrell	34
6	Watson	Brabham	25
7	Scheckter,J.	Wolf	24
8	Laffite	Ligier	19
9	Fittipaldi,E.	Fittipaldi	17
=	Villeneuve,G.	Ferrari	17
11	Jones	Williams	11
=	Patrese	Arrows	11
13	Hunt	McLaren	8
=	Tambay	McLaren	8
15	Pironi	Tyrrell	7
16	Regazzoni	Shadow	4
17	Jabouille	Renault	3
18	Stuck,H-J	Shadow	2
19	Brambilla	Surtees	1
=	Daly	Ensign	1
=	Rebaque	Lotus	1

1979

Pos	Driver	Team	Points	
1	Scheckter,J.	Ferrari	51	(60)
2	Villeneuve,G.	Ferrari	47	(53)
3	Jones	Williams	40	(43)
4	Laffite	Ligier	36	
5	Regazzoni	Williams	29	(32)
6	Depailler	Ligier	20	(22)
7	Reutemann	Lotus	20	(25)
8	Arnoux	Renault	17	
9	Watson	McLaren	15	
10	Andretti,Mario	Lotus	14	
=	Jarier	Tyrrell	14	
=	Pironi	Tyrrell	14	
13	Jabouille	Renault	9	
14	Lauda	Brabham	4	
15	de Angelis	Shadow	3	
=	Ickx	Ligier	3	
=	Mass	Arrows	3	
=	Piquet	Brabham	3	
19	Patrese	Arrows	2	
=	Stuck,H-J	ATS	2	
21	Fittipaldi,E.	Fittipaldi	1	

1980

Pos	Driver	Team	Points	
1	Jones	Williams	67	(71)
2	Piquet	Brabham	54	
3	Reutemann	Williams	42	(49)
4	Laffite	Ligier	34	
5	Pironi	Ligier	32	
6	Arnoux	Renault	29	
7	de Angelis	Lotus	13	
8	Jabouille	Renault	9	
9	Patrese	Arrows	7	
10	Daly	Tyrrell	6	
=	Jarier	Tyrrell	6	
=	Rosberg	Fittipaldi	6	
=	Villeneuve,G.	Ferrari	6	
=	Watson	McLaren	6	
15	Fittipaldi,E.	Fittipaldi	5	
=	Prost	McLaren	5	
17	Giacomelli	Alfa Romeo	4	
=	Mass	Arrows	4	
19	Scheckter,J.	Ferrari	2	
20	Andretti,Mario	Lotus	1	
=	Rebaque	Brabham	1	

1981

Pos	Driver	Team	Points
1	Piquet	Brabham	50
2	Reutemann	Williams	49
3	Jones	Williams	46
4	Laffite	Ligier	44
5	Prost	Renault	43
6	Watson	McLaren	27
7	Villeneuve,G.	Ferrari	25
8	de Angelis	Lotus	14
9	Arnoux	Renault	11
=	Rebaque	Brabham	11
11	Cheever	Tyrrell	10
=	Patrese	Arrows	10
13	Pironi	Ferrari	9
14	Mansell	Lotus	8
15	Giacomelli	Alfa Romeo	7
16	Surer	Ensign	4
17	Andretti,Mario	Alfa Romeo	3
18	Borgudd	ATS	1
=	de Cesaris	McLaren	1
=	Salazar	Ensign	1
=	Tambay	Theodore	1

1982

Pos	Driver	Team	Points
1	Rosberg	Williams	44
2	Pironi	Ferrari	39
=	Watson	McLaren	39
4	Prost	Renault	34
5	Lauda	McLaren	30
6	Arnoux	Renault	28
7	Alboreto	Tyrrell	25
=	Tambay	Ferrari	25
9	de Angelis	Lotus	23
10	Patrese	Brabham	21
11	Piquet	Brabham	20
12	Cheever	Ligier	15
13	Daly	Williams	8
14	Mansell	Lotus	7
15	Reutemann	Williams	6
=	Villeneuve,G.	Ferrari	6
17	de Cesaris	Alfa Romeo	5
=	Laffite	Ligier	5
19	Andretti,Mario	Ferrari	4
20	Jarier	Osella	3
=	Surer	Arrows	3
22	Baldi	Arrows	2
=	Giacomelli	Alfa Romeo	2
=	Salazar	ATS	2
=	Winkelhock	ATS	2
26	Serra	Fittipaldi	1

1983

Pos	Driver	Team	Points
1	Piquet	Brabham	59
2	Prost	Renault	57
3	Arnoux	Ferrari	49
4	Tambay	Ferrari	40
5	Rosberg	Williams	27
6	Cheever	Renault	22
=	Watson	McLaren	22
8	de Cesaris	Alfa Romeo	15
9	Patrese	Brabham	13
10	Lauda	McLaren	12
11	Laffite	Williams	11
12	Alboreto	Tyrrell	10
=	Mansell	Lotus	10
14	Warwick	Toleman	9
15	Surer	Arrows	4
16	Baldi	Alfa Romeo	3
17	de Angelis	Lotus	2
=	Sullivan	Tyrrell	2

19	Cecotto	Theodore	1	
=	Giacomelli	Toleman	1	

1984

Pos	Driver	Team	Points
1	Lauda	McLaren	72
2	Prost	McLaren	71.5
3	de Angelis	Lotus	34
4	Alboreto	Ferrari	30.5
5	Piquet	Brabham	29
6	Arnoux	Ferrari	27
7	Warwick	Renault	23
8	Rosberg	Lotus	20.5
9	Senna	Toleman	13
=	Mansell	Ferrari	13
11	Tambay	Ferrari	11
12	Fabi,T.	Brabham	9
13	Patrese	Alfa Romeo	8
14	Boutsen	Arrows	5
=	Laffite	Williams	5
16	Cheever	Alfa Romeo	3
=	de Cesaris	Ligier	3
=	Johansson	Toleman	3
19	Ghinzani	Osella	2
20	Surer	Arrows	1

1985

Pos	Driver	Team	Points	
1	Prost	McLaren	73	(76)
2	Alboreto	Ferrari	53	
3	Rosberg	Williams	40	
4	Senna	Lotus	38	
5	de Angelis	Lotus	33	
6	Mansell	Williams	31	
7	Johansson	Ferrari	26	
8	Piquet	Brabham	21	
9	Laffite	Ligier	16	
10	Lauda	McLaren	14	
11	Boutsen	Arrows	11	
12	Tambay	Renault	11	
13	Surer	Brabham	5	
=	Warwick	Renault	5	
15	Bellof	Tyrrell	4	
=	Streiff	Ligier	4	
17	Arnoux	Ferrari	3	
=	Berger,G.	Arrows	3	
=	Capelli	Tyrrell	3	
=	de Cesaris	Ligier	3	

1986

Pos	Driver	Team	Points	
1	Prost	McLaren	72	(74)
2	Mansell	Williams	70	(72)
3	Piquet	Williams	69	
4	Senna	Lotus	55	
5	Johansson	Ferrari	23	
6	Rosberg	McLaren	22	
7	Berger,G.	Benetton	17	
8	Alboreto	Ferrari	14	
=	Arnoux	Ligier	14	
=	Laffite	Ligier	14	
11	Brundle	Tyrrell	8	
12	Jones	Lola	4	
13	Dumfries	Lotus	3	
=	Streiff	Tyrrell	3	
15	Fabi,T.	Benetton	2	
=	Patrese	Brabham	2	
=	Tambay	Lola	2	
18	Alliot	Ligier	1	
=	Danner	Arrows	1	

1987

Pos	Driver	Team	Points	
1	Piquet	Williams	73	(76)
2	Mansell	Williams	61	
3	Senna	Lotus	57	
4	Prost	McLaren	46	
5	Berger,G.	Ferrari	36	
6	Johansson	McLaren	30	
7	Alboreto	Ferrari	17	
8	Boutsen	Benetton	16	
9	Fabi,T.	Benetton	12	
10	Cheever	Arrows	8	
11	Nakajima	Lotus	7	
=	Palmer	Tyrrell	7	
13	Patrese	Brabham	6	
14	de Cesaris	Brabham	4	
=	Streiff	Tyrrell	4	
16	Alliot	Lola	3	
=	Warwick	Arrows	3	
18	Brundle	Zakspeed	2	
19	Arnoux	Ligier	1	
=	Capelli	March	1	
=	Moreno	AGS	1	

1988

Pos	Driver	Team	Points	
1	Senna	McLaren	90	(94)
2	Prost	McLaren	87	(105)
3	Berger,G.	Ferrari	41	
4	Boutsen	Benetton	27	
5	Alboreto	Ferrari	24	
6	Piquet	Lotus	22	
7	Capelli	March	17	
=	Warwick	Arrows	17	
9	Mansell	Williams	12	
=	Nannini	Benetton	12	
11	Patrese	Williams	8	
12	Cheever	Arrows	6	
13	Gugelmin	March	5	
=	Palmer	Tyrrell	5	
15	de Cesaris	Rial	3	
16	Martini	Minardi	1	
=	Nakajima	Lotus	1	

1989

Pos	Driver	Team	Points	
1	Prost	McLaren	76	(81)
2	Senna	McLaren	60	
3	Patrese	Williams	40	
4	Mansell	Ferrari	38	
5	Boutsen	Williams	37	
6	Nannini	Benetton	32	
7	Berger,G.	Ferrari	21	
8	Piquet	Lotus	12	
9	Alesi	Tyrrell	8	
10	Warwick	Arrows	7	
11	Alboreto	Tyrrell	6	
=	Cheever	Arrows	6	
=	Johansson	Onyx	6	
14	Herbert	Benetton	5	
=	Martini	Minardi	5	
16	Brundle	Brabham	4	
=	Caffi	Dallara	4	
=	de Cesaris	Dallara	4	
=	Gugelmin	March	4	
=	Modena	Brabham	4	
21	Danner	Rial	3	
=	Nakajima	Lotus	3	
23	Arnoux	Ligier	2	
=	Palmer	Tyrrell	2	
=	Pirro	Benetton	2	
26	Alliot	Lola	1	
=	Grouillard	Ligier	1	
=	Sala	Minardi	1	
=	Tarquini	AGS	1	

1990

Pos	Driver	Team	Points
1	Senna	McLaren	78
2	Prost	Ferrari	71
3	Berger,G.	McLaren	43
=	Piquet	Benetton	43
5	Mansell	Ferrari	37
6	Boutsen	Williams	34
7	Patrese	Williams	23
8	Nannini	Benetton	21
9	Alesi	Tyrrell	13
10	Capelli	Leyton House	6
=	Moreno	Benetton	6
=	Suzuki	Lola	6
13	Bernard	Lola	5
14	Nakajima	Tyrrell	3
=	Warwick	Lotus	3
16	Caffi	Arrows	2
=	Modena	Brabham	2
18	Gugelmin	Leyton House	1

1991

Pos	Driver	Team	Points
1	Senna	McLaren	96
2	Mansell	Williams	72
3	Patrese	Williams	53
4	Berger,G.	McLaren	43
5	Prost	Ferrari	34
6	Piquet	Benetton	26.5
7	Alesi	Ferrari	21
8	Modena	Tyrrell	10
9	de Cesaris	Jordan	9
10	Moreno	Benetton	8
11	Martini	Minardi	6
12	Gachot	Jordan	4
=	Lehto	Dallara	4
=	Schumacher,M.	Benetton	4
15	Brundle	Brabham	2
=	Hakkinen	Lotus	2
=	Nakajima	Tyrrell	2
18	Bailey	Lotus	1
=	Bernard	Larrousse	1
=	Blundell	Brabham	1
=	Capelli	Leyton House	1
=	Pirro	Dallara	1

=	Suzuki	Larrousse	1
24	Morbidelli	Ferrari	0.5

1992

Pos	Driver	Team	Points
1	Mansell	Williams	108
2	Patrese	Williams	56
3	Schumacher,M.	Benetton	53
4	Senna	McLaren	50
5	Berger,G.	McLaren	49
6	Brundle	Benetton	38
7	Alesi	Ferrari	18
8	Hakkinen	Lotus	11
9	de Cesaris	Tyrrell	8
10	Alboreto	Footwork	6
11	Comas	Ligier	4
12	Capelli	Ferrari	3
=	Wendlinger	March	3
14	Boutsen	Ligier	2
=	Herbert	Lotus	2
=	Martini	Dallara	2
17	Fittipaldi,C.	Minardi	1
=	Gachot	Larrousse	1
=	Modena	Jordan	1

1993

Pos	Driver	Team	Points
1	Prost	Williams	99
2	Senna	McLaren	73
3	Hill,D.	Williams	69
4	Schumacher,M.	Benetton	52
5	Patrese	Benetton	20
6	Alesi	Ferrari	16
7	Brundle	Ligier	13
8	Berger,G.	Ferrari	12
9	Herbert	Lotus	11
10	Blundell	Ligier	10
11	Andretti,Michael	McLaren	7
=	Wendlinger	Sauber	7
13	Fittipaldi,C.	Minardi	5
=	Lehto	Sauber	5
15	Hakkinen	McLaren	4
=	Warwick	Footwork	4
17	Alliot	Larrousse	2
=	Barbazza	Minardi	2
=	Barrichello	Jordan	2
20	Comas	Larrousse	1
=	Irvine	Jordan	1
=	Zanardi	Lotus	1

1994

Pos	Driver	Team	Points
1	Schumacher,M.	Benetton	92
2	Hill,D.	Williams	91
3	Berger,G.	Ferrari	41
4	Hakkinen	McLaren	26
5	Alesi	Ferrari	24
6	Barrichello	Jordan	19
7	Brundle	McLaren	16
8	Coulthard	Williams	14
9	Mansell	Williams	13
10	Verstappen	Benetton	10
11	Panis	Ligier	9
12	Blundell	Tyrrell	8
13	Frentzen	Sauber	7
14	Fittipaldi,C.	Footwork	6
=	Irvine	Jordan	6
=	Larini	Ferrari	6
17	Katayama	Tyrrell	5
18	Bernard	Ligier	4
=	de Cesaris	Jordan & Sauber	4
=	Martini	Minardi	4
=	Wendlinger	Sauber	4
22	Morbidelli	Footwork	3
23	Comas	Larrousse	2
24	Alboreto	Minardi	1
=	Lehto	Benetton	1

1995

Pos	Driver	Team	Points
1	Schumacher,M.	Benetton	102
2	Hill,D.	Williams	69
3	Coulthard	Williams	49
4	Herbert	Benetton	45
5	Alesi	Ferrari	42
6	Berger,G.	Ferrari	31
7	Hakkinen	McLaren	17
8	Panis	Ligier	16
9	Frentzen	Sauber	15
10	Blundell	McLaren	13
11	Barrichello	Jordan	11
12	Irvine	Jordan	10
13	Brundle	Ligier	7
14	Morbidelli	Footwork	5
=	Salo	Tyrrell	5
16	Boullion	Sauber	3
17	Lamy	Minardi	1
=	Suzuki	Ligier	1

1996

Pos	Driver	Team	Points
1	Hill,D.	Williams	97
2	Villeneuve,J.	Williams	78
3	Schumacher,M.	Ferrari	59
4	Alesi	Benetton	47
5	Hakkinen	McLaren	31
6	Berger,G.	Benetton	21
7	Coulthard	McLaren	18
8	Barrichello	Jordan	14
9	Panis	Ligier	13
10	Irvine	Ferrari	11
11	Brundle	Jordan	8
12	Frentzen	Sauber	7
13	Salo	Tyrrell	5
14	Herbert	Sauber	4
15	Diniz	Ligier	2
16	Verstappen	Footwork	1

1997

Pos	Driver	Team	Points
1	Villeneuve,J.	Williams	81
dq	Schumacher,M.	Ferrari	78
2	Frentzen	Williams	42
3	Alesi	Benetton	36
=	Coulthard	McLaren	36
5	Berger,G.	Benetton	27
=	Hakkinen	Benetton	27
7	Irvine	Ferrari	24
8	Fisichella	Jordan	20
9	Panis	Prost	16
10	Herbert	Sauber	15
11	Schumacher,R.	Jordan	13
12	Hill,D.	Arrows	7
13	Barrichello	Stewart	6
14	Wurz	Benetton	4
15	Trulli	Prost	3
16	Diniz	Arrows	2
=	Nakano	Prost	2
=	Salo	Tyrrell	2
19	Larini	Sauber	1

1998

Pos	Driver	Team	Points
1	Hakkinen	McLaren	100
2	Schumacher,M.	Ferrari	86
3	Coulthard	McLaren	56
4	Irvine	Ferrari	47
5	Villeneuve,J.	Williams	21
6	Hill,D.	Jordan	20
7	Frentzen	Williams	17
=	Wurz	Benetton	17
9	Fisichella	Benetton	16
10	Schumacher,R.	Jordan	14
11	Alesi	Sauber	9
12	Barrichello	Stewart	4
13	Diniz	Arrows	3
=	Salo	Arrows	3
15	Herbert	Sauber	1
=	Magnussen	Stewart	1
=	Trulli	Prost	1

1999

Pos	Driver	Team	Points
1	Hakkinen	McLaren	76
2	Irvine	Ferrari	74
3	Frentzen	Jordan	54
4	Coulthard	McLaren	48
5	Schumacher,M.	Ferrari	44
6	Schumacher,R.	Williams	35
7	Barrichello	Stewart	21
8	Herbert	Stewart	15
9	Fisichella	Benetton	13
10	Salo	BAR & Ferrari	10
11	Hill,D.	Jordan	7
=	Trulli	Prost	7
13	Diniz	Sauber	3
=	Wurz	Benetton	3
15	Alesi	Sauber	2
=	Panis	Prost	2
17	de la Rosa	Arrows	1
=	Gene	Minardi	1

MISCELLANEOUS DRIVER RECORDS

The RACE RECORDS section of this FactFile contains a variety of additional drivers' records, including all-time tables of wins, pole positions, fastest laps and much more.

THE
CONSTRUCTORS

CONSTRUCTOR NOTES

The following pages detail various statistics relating to the records of constructors and constructor-engine partnerships while competing in the first 50 years of the FIA Formula 1 Championship. Specific points relating to aspects of the material are detailed as they occur under the various headings. However, some overall notes as they apply globally are detailed here.

Contested: Listed under columns headed 'Const' are the number of GPs the constructor has taken part in. A count of one is applied for each Grand Prix regardless of the number of cars that the constructor may have competing in the race. The dns rules apply here. If a constructor fails to start a race due to all its cars recording dns then it has not been contested.

Car: This is the (total) number of cars that have taken part in the contested race(s).

Points: This is the total number of points scored in the Constructors' Cup championship. The championship did not start until 1958 and the points total therefore does not reflect championships prior to this.

NAME CHANGES

Down the years some constructors have changed names for a variety of reasons, the most common being change in ownership or change in sponsorship. This can lead to confusion with numbers. To account for this I have tried to list all the various figures and also produced combined totals for teams still in operation.

Andrea Moda: Bought Coloni in 1991.

Arrows: Was also known as Footwork – a major sponsor and shareholder from 1991, but renamed Arrows in 1998.

Benetton: Bought Toleman in 1986.

Ensign: Taken over by Theodore in 1983.

Ferrari: Stats include cars run as Lancia-Ferrari. Lancia cars were sold to Ferrari in 1955.

Fittipaldi: Bought by Wold in 1980.

Fondmetal: Bought Osella in 1991.

Leyton-House: Running name of March team in 1990-91.

March: During the 1990 and 1991 seasons the team was known as Leyton-House, a major sponsor of the team.

Osella: Bought by Fondmetal in 1991.

Theodore: Bought Ensign in 1983.

Toleman: Was bought by Benetton in 1986.

Wolf: Bought by Fittipaldi in 1980.

Constructor	Cont	Car	Win	Pole	Fast	Points
Adams	1	1	–	–	–	–
AFM	4	7	–	–	–	–
AGS	48	49	–	–	–	2
Alfa Romeo	110	234	10	12	14	50
Alfa Special	2	2	–	–	–	–
Alta	5	6	–	–	–	–
Amon	1	1	–	–	–	–
Andrea Moda	1	1	–	–	–	–
Arrows (Footwork)	337	633	–	1	–	157
Arrows	246	461	–	1	–	132
Aston	2	2	–	–	–	–
Aston Martin	5	10	–	–	–	–
ATS (Germany)	89	107	–	–	–	7
ATS (Italy)	6	11	–	–	–	–
BAR	16	31	–	–	–	–
Behra	2	2	–	–	–	–
Bellasi	2	2	–	–	–	–
Benetton (Toleman)	283	545	27	16	38	847.5
Benetton	226	451	27	15	36	821.5
BMW	2	6	–	–	–	–
Boro	5	5	–	–	–	–
Brabham	394	925	35	39	42	864
BRM	197	522	17	11	15	433
Bromme	4	4	–	–	–	–
BRP	13	18	–	–	–	11
Bugatti	1	1	–	–	–	–
Christensen	2	2	–	–	–	–
Coloni	13	14	–	–	–	–
Connaught	17	48	–	–	–	–
Connew	1	1	–	–	–	–
Cooper	129	501	16	11	14	342
Dallara	78	133	–	–	–	15
de Tomaso	10	12	–	–	–	–
Deidt	3	8	–	–	1	–
Del Roy	1	1	–	–	–	–
Dunn	3	3	–	–	–	–
Eagle	26	33	1	–	–	17
Elder	1	1	–	–	–	–
Emeryson	4	4	–	–	–	–
EMW	1	1	–	–	–	–
ENB	1	1	–	–	–	–
Ensign	98	110	–	–	1	19
Epperly	5	17	2	–	2	–
ERA	7	12	–	–	–	–
EuroBrun	14	20	–	–	–	–
Ewing	2	3	–	1	–	–
Ferguson	1	1	–	–	–	–
Ferrari (Lancia Fe.)	619	1426	125	127	139	2352.5

Constructor	Cont	Car	Win	Pole	Fast	Points
Fittipaldi	103	122	–	–	–	44
Fondmetal	19	25	–	–	–	–
Footwork	91	172	–	–	–	25
Ford	1	1	–	–	–	–
Forti	23	44	–	–	–	–
Frazer Nash	4	4	–	–	–	–
Gilby	3	3	–	–	–	–
Gordini (Simca)	40	127	–	–	1	–
Hesketh	52	73	1	–	1	48
Hill	10	19	–	–	–	3
Honda	35	46	2	1	2	48
HWM	14	44	–	–	–	–
JBW	5	5	–	–	–	–
Jordan	146	284	3	2	2	216
Klenk	1	1	–	–	–	–
Kojima	2	3	–	–	1	–
Kurtis Kraft	12	195	5	6	6	120
Kuzma	10	37	1	–	–	–
Lamborghini	6	6	–	–	–	–
Lancia	4	10	0	2	1	–
(Lancia–Ferrari)	12	59	5	6	5	–
Langley	1	1	–	–	–	–
Larrousse	48	93	–	–	–	6
LDS	5	6	–	–	–	–
Lec	3	3	–	–	–	–
Lesovsky	9	15	–	1	1	–
Leyton House	30	57	–	–	–	8
Ligier (see Prost)	326	577	9	9	9	388
Lola	149	246		1		43
Lotus	491	1227	79	107	71	1367
Lotus Turbine	3	3	–	–	–	–
LOWS	1	1	–	–	–	–
Lyncar	1	1	–	–	–	–
March	197	502	3	5	7	173.5
March (Leyton H.)	227	559	3	5	7	181.5
Marchese	2	2	–	–	–	–
Martini	4	4	–	–	–	–
Maserati	71	371	9	10	17	6
Matra (inc F2 cars)	62	116	9	4	12	163
McLaren	492	1036	123	103	89	2328.5
Mercedes	12	39	9	8	9	–
Merzario	10	10	–	–	–	–
Meskowski	1	2	–	–	–	–
Minardi	237	433	–	–	–	28
Moore	3	3	–	–	–	–
Nichels	2	3	–	–	–	–
Olson	1	1	–	–	–	–
Onyx	17	25	–	–	–	6

Constructor	Cont	Car	Win	Pole	Fast	Points
OSCA	5	7	–	–	–	–
Osella	132	166	–	–	–	5
Pacific	22	40	–	–	–	–
Pankratz	2	2	–	–	–	–
Parnelli	16	16	–	–	1	6
Pawl	3	3	–	–	–	–
Penske	40	43	1	–	–	23
Phillips	7	7	–	–	–	–
Porsche	32	71	1	1	–	47
Prost (Ligier)	375	673	9	9	9	419
Prost	49	96	–	–	–	31
Rae	1	1	–	–	–	–
RAM	31	54	–	–	–	–
Rebaque	1	1	–	–	–	–
Renault	123	227	15	31	18	312
Rial	20	20	–	–	–	6
Sauber	113	223	–	–	–	84
Scarab	2	3	–	–	–	–
Schroeder	4	5	–	–	–	–
Scirocco	5	7	–	–	–	–
Shadow	104	211	1	3	2	67.5
Shannon	1	1	–	–	–	–
Sherman	2	2	–	–	–	–
Simtek	21	37	–	–	–	–
Snowberger	1	1	–	–	–	–
Spirit	23	23	–	–	–	–
Stebro	1	1	–	–	–	–
Stevens	6	9	–	1	–	–
Stewart	49	95	1	1	–	47
Surtees	118	226	–	–	3	54
Sutton	1	1	–	–	–	–
Talbot	13	79	–	–	–	–
Tec Mec Maserati	1	1	–	–	–	–
Tecno	10	10	–	–	–	1
Theodore	34	44	–	–	–	2
Token	3	3	–	–	–	–
Toleman	57	94	–	1	2	26
Trevis	4	6	–	–	–	–
Trojan	6	6	–	–	–	–
Turner	1	1	–	–	–	–
Tyrrell	430	841	23	14	20	616
Vanwall	28	64	9	7	6	57
Veritas	6	18	–	–	–	–
Watson	9	22	3	2	1	–
Wetteroth	1	1	–	–	–	–
Williams	403	768	103	108	111	1989.5
Wolf	47	52	3	1	2	79
Zakspeed	53	84	–	–	–	2

Detailed below is a general finishing summary for each of the constructors. It lists the number of times a constructor has finished in the top six positions, the total number of races completed (C) and the total number of race retirements (r). Note that the numbers relate to total cars and a completion is defined as a car starting the race but not retiring.

Constructor	1	2	3	4	5	6	C	r
Adams	–	–	–	–	–	–	–	1
AFM	–	–	–	–	–	–	2	5
AGS	–	–	–	–	–	2	24	25
Alfa Romeo	10	8	8	8	7	5	100	134
Alfa Special	–	–	–	–	–	–	1	1
Alta	–	–	–	–	–	–	4	2
Amon	–	–	–	–	–	–	–	1
Andrea Moda	–	–	–	–	–	–	–	1
Arrows	–	5	3	10	15	30	242	219
Arrows +Footwork	–	5	4	13	18	36	325	308
Aston	–	–	–	–	–	–	–	2
Aston Martin	–	–	–	–	–	2	5	5
ATS (Germany)	–	–	–	–	3	2	49	58
ATS (Italy)	–	–	–	–	–	–	2	9
BAR	–	–	–	–	–	–	11	20
Behra	–	–	–	–	–	–	2	–
Bellasi	–	–	–	–	–	–	–	2
Benetton	27	31	40	40	37	27	297	154
Benetton +Toleman	27	32	42	43	38	31	325	220
BMW	–	–	–	–	–	–	3	3
Boro	–	–	–	–	–	–	2	3
Brabham	35	41	48	41	35	39	462	463
BRM	17	27	17	25	34	17	273	249
Bromme	–	–	–	–	–	–	–	4
BRP	–	–	–	2	2	1	11	7
Bugatti	–	–	–	–	–	–	–	1
Christensen	–	–	–	–	–	–	–	2
Coloni	–	–	–	–	–	–	5	9
Connaught	–	–	1	3	1	1	19	29
Connew	–	–	–	–	–	–	–	1
Cooper	16	18	24	29	27	27	290	210
Dallara	–	–	2	1	–	4	63	70
de Tomaso	–	–	–	–	–	–	2	10
Deidt	–	1	1	–	–	–	3	5
Del Roy	–	–	–	–	–	–	–	1
Dunn	–	–	–	–	–	–	1	2
Eagle	1	–	1	–	2	–	10	23

Constructor	1	2	3	4	5	6	C	r
Elder	–	–	–	–	–	–	–	1
Emeryson	–	–	–	–	–	–	2	2
EMW	–	–	–	–	–	–	–	1
ENB	–	–	–	–	–	–	1	–
Ensign	–	–	–	1	5	6	54	56
Epperly	2	2	1	2	2	1	12	5
ERA	–	–	–	–	–	2	6	6
EuroBrun	–	–	–	–	–	–	9	11
Ewing	–	–	–	–	–	–	1	2
Ferguson	–	–	–	–	–	–	1	–
Ferrari	125	162	149	117	78	67	1007	519
Fittipaldi	–	1	2	5	4	7	71	51
Fondmetal	–	–	–	–	–	–	5	20
Footwork	–	–	1	3	3	6	83	89
Ford	–	–	–	–	1	–	1	–
Forti	–	–	–	–	–	–	19	25
Frazer Nash	–	–	–	1	–	–	3	1
Gilby	–	–	–	–	–	–	1	2
Gordini	–	–	2	2	8	7	47	80
Hesketh	1	3	3	3	1	1	40	33
Hill	–	–	–	–	1	1	11	8
Honda	2	1	2	3	3	3	19	27
HWM	–	–	–	–	1	1	21	23
JBW	–	–	–	–	–	–	1	4
Jordan	3	4	8	26	15	22	152	132
Klenk	–	–	–	–	–	–	–	1
Kojima	–	–	–	–	–	–	2	1
Kurtis Kraft	5	5	6	4	7	5	95	100
Kuzma	1	1	1	2	–	1	22	15
Lago	–	–	–	–	–	–	–	–
Lamborghini	–	–	–	–	–	–	4	2
Lancia	–	1	–	–	1	1	3	7
Langley	–	–	–	–	–	–	1	–
Larrousse	–	–	–	–	1	4	44	49
LDS	–	–	–	–	–	–	2	4
Lec	–	–	–	–	–	–	2	1
Lesovsky	–	–	1	1	1	–	9	6
Leyton House	–	1	–	–	–	2	21	36
Ligier	9	14	27	13	23	29	317	260
Lola	–	2	1	3	4	12	109	137
Lotus	79	42	51	59	62	54	652	576
Lotus Turbine	–	–	–	–	–	–	2	1
LOWS	–	–	–	–	–	–	–	1
Lyncar	–	–	–	–	–	–	1	–
Maki	–	–	–	–	–	–	–	–
March	3	10	8	10	15	12	255	247
March +Leyton Hse	3	11	8	10	15	14	276	283

Constructor	1	2	3	4	5	6	C	r
Marchese	–	–	–	–	–	–	1	1
Martini	–	–	–	–	–	–	3	1
Maserati	9	10	18	19	21	20	189	182
Matra	9	4	8	5	9	14	79	35
McLaren	123	93	89	73	57	54	673	363
Mercedes	9	5	3	5	1	–	24	15
Merzario	–	–	–	–	–	–	1	9
Meskowski	–	–	–	–	–	–	2	–
Minardi	–	–	–	3	5	9	188	245
Moore	–	–	–	–	–	2	3	–
Nichels	–	–	–	–	–	–	1	2
Olson	–	–	–	–	–	–	1	–
Onyx	–	–	1	–	1	–	9	16
OSCA	–	–	–	–	–	–	3	4
Osella	–	–	–	1	2	–	46	120
Pacific	–	–	–	–	–	–	8	32
Pankratz	–	–	–	–	–	–	1	1
Parnelli	–	–	–	1	1	1	9	7
Pawl	–	–	–	–	–	–	–	3
Penske	1	–	2	–	2	2	27	16
Phillips	–	–	1	1	–	–	5	2
Porsche	1	3	1	1	4	9	54	17
Prost	–	2	1	2	1	7	55	41
Rae	–	–	–	–	–	–	1	–
RAM	–	–	–	–	–	–	16	38
Rebaque	–	–	–	–	–	–	–	1
Renault	15	15	11	7	8	6	101	126
Rial	–	–	–	2	–	–	9	11
Sauber	–	–	4	9	10	21	116	107
Scarab	–	–	–	–	–	–	1	2
Schroeder	–	–	–	–	1	–	2	3
Scirocco	–	–	–	–	–	–	–	7
Shadow	1	–	6	7	5	8	112	99
Shannon	–	–	–	–	–	–	–	1
Sherman	–	–	–	1	–	–	2	–
Simtek	–	–	–	–	–	–	15	22
Snowberger	–	–	–	–	–	–	–	1
Spirit	–	–	–	–	–	–	12	11
Stebro	–	–	–	–	–	–	1	–
Stevens	–	–	–	–	–	–	6	3
Stewart	1	1	3	2	6	1	41	54
Surtees	–	1	1	8	7	6	130	96
Sutton	–	–	–	–	–	–	–	1
Talbot	–	–	2	3	4	3	41	38
Tec Mec Maserati	–	–	–	–	–	–	–	1
Tecno	–	–	–	–	–	1	2	8
Theodore	–	–	–	–	–	2	23	21
Token	–	–	–	–	–	–	2	1
Toleman	–	1	2	3	1	4	28	66
Trevis	–	–	–	–	–	1	4	2
Trojan	–	–	–	–	–	–	3	3
Turner	–	–	–	–	–	–	–	1
Tyrrell	23	33	21	30	49	34	494	347
Vanwall	9	2	2	2	2	–	25	39
Veritas	–	–	–	–	–	–	7	11
Watson	3	2	–	–	–	1	10	12
Wetteroth	–	–	–	–	–	–	1	–
Williams	103	89	56	46	48	29	497	271
Wolf	3	4	6	1	–	1	24	28
Zakspeed	–	–	–		1	–	27	57

Introduction

This section identifies the performance of engines for each constructor. Under each constructor heading are listed the engine combinations used by the constructor. These are arranged alphabetically and do not indicate the order in which each was employed. The key to the seven columns is as follows:

Cars: total number of cars to have started Grands Prix
1-2-3: number of cars to have finished 1st, 2nd and 3rd
CC: number of cars to have completed races
CR: number of cars to have retired from race
Com%: completion percentage – Cars/CC

Constructor	Cars	1	2	3	CC	CR	Com%
Adams							
Adams	1	–	–	–	0	1	0.00
Total	*1*	–	–	–	*0*	*1*	*0.00*
AFM (Alex von Falkenhausen Motorenbau)							
AFM	7	–	–	–	2	5	28.57
Total	*7*	–	–	–	*4*	*5*	*57.14*
AGS (Automobiles Gonfaronaise Sportive)							
AGS-Ford	47	–	–	–	24	23	51.06
AGS-MM	2	–	–	–	0	2	0.00
Total	*49*	–	–	–	*24*	*25*	*48.98*
Alfa Romeo							
Alfa Romeo	234	10	8	8	100	134	42.74
Total	*234*	*10*	*8*	*8*	*100*	*134*	*42.74*
Alfa Special							
Alfa Special	2	–	–	–	1	1	50.00
Total	*2*	–	–	–	*1*	*1*	*50.00*
Alta							
Alta	6	–	–	–	4	2	66.67
Total	*6*	–	–	–	*4*	*2*	*66.67*
Amon							
Amon-Ford	1	–	–	–	0	1	0.00
Total	*1*	–	–	–	*0*	*1*	*0.00*
Andrea Moda							
Andrea Moda-Judd	1	–	–	–	0	1	0.00
Total	*1*	–	–	–	*0*	*1*	*0.00*
Arrows							
Arrows	63	–	–	–	21	43	33.33
Arrows-BMW	84	–	1	–	43	41	51.19
Arrows-Ford	217	–	3	2	132	85	60.83
Arrows-Megatron	64	–	–	1	31	33	48.44
Arrows-Yamaha	33	–	1	–	17	17	51.52
Total	*461*	–	*5*	*3*	*244*	*219*	*52.93*

Constructor	Cars	1	2	3	CC	CR	Com%
Arrows+Footwork							
Arrows Total	461	–	5	3	244	219	52.93
Footwork Total	172	–	–	1	83	89	48.26
Total	*633*	–	*5*	*4*	*327*	*308*	*51.49*
Aston							
Aston-Butterworth	2	–	–	–	1	2	50.00
Total	*2*	–	–	–	*1*	*2*	*50.00*
Aston Martin							
Aston Martin	10	–	–	–	6	5	60.00
Total	*10*	–	–	–	*6*	*5*	*60.00*
ATS (ATS Wheels – Germany)							
ATS-BMW	29	–	–	–	12	19	41.38
ATS-Ford	78	–	–	–	40	39	51.28
Total	*107*	–	–	–	*52*	*58*	*48.60*
ATS (Automobili Turismo e Sport – Italy)							
ATS (Italy)	11	–	–	–	2	9	18.18
Total	*11*	–	–	–	*2*	*9*	*18.18*
BAR (British American Racing)							
BAR-Supertec	31	–	–	–	11	20	35.48
Total	*31*	–	–	–	*11*	*20*	*35.48*
Behra							
Behra-Porsche	1	–	–	–	1	–	100.00
Behra-Porsche F2	1	–	–	–	1	–	100.00
Total	*2*	–	–	–	*2*	–	*100.00*
Bellasi							
Bellasi-Ford	2	–	–	–	0	2	0.00
Total	*2*	–	–	–	*0*	*2*	*0.00*
Benetton							
Benetton-BMW	36	1	–	1	14	22	38.89
Benetton-Ford	251	14	16	30	166	85	66.14
Benetton-Playlife	64	–	3	–	43	21	67.19
Benetton-Renault	100	12	12	9	74	26	74.00
Total	*451*	*27*	*31*	*40*	*297*	*154*	*65.85*
Benetton+Toleman							
Benetton Total	451	27	31	40	297	154	65.85
Toleman-Total	94	–	1	2	28	66	29.79
Total	*545*	*27*	*32*	*42*	*325*	*220*	*59.63*
BMW (Bayerische Motoren Werke)							
BMW	6	–	–	–	6	3	100.00
Total	*6*	–	–	–	*6*	*3*	*100.00*
Boro							
Boro-Ford	5	–	–	–	2	3	40.00
Total	*5*	–	–	–	*2*	*3*	*40.00*

Constructor	Cars	1	2	3	CC	CR	Com%
Brabham							
Brabham-Alfa	126	2	6	6	55	71	43.65
Brabham-BMW	177	8	6	7	69	108	38.98
Brabham-BRM	40	–	–	1	24	17	60.00
Brabham-Climax	110	2	5	8	65	48	59.09
Brabham-Ford	313	15	15	17	179	138	57.19
Brabham-Judd	58	–		1	23	35	39.66
Brabham-Repco	73	8	9	8	42	32	57.53
Brabham-Yamaha	28	–	–	–	14	14	50.00
Total	*925*	*35*	*41*	*48*	*471*	*463*	*50.92*
BRM (British Racing Motors)							
BRM	506	17	27	16	276	241	54.55
BRM-Climax	16	–	–	1	8	8	50.00
Total	*522*	*17*	*27*	*17*	*284*	*249*	*54.41*
Bromme							
Bromme	4	–	–	–	0	4	0.00
Total	*4*	–	–	–	*0*	*4*	*0.00*
BRP (British Racing Partnership)							
BRP-BRM	18	–	–	–	11	7	61.11
Total	*18*	–	–	–	*11*	*7*	*61.11*
Bugatti							
Bugatti	1	–	–	–	0	1	0.00
Total	*1*	–	–	–	*0*	*1*	*0.00*
Christensen							
Christensen	2	–	–	–	0	2	0.00
Total	*2*	–	–	–	*0*	*2*	*0.00*
Coloni							
Coloni-Ford	14	–	–	–	5	9	35.71
Total	*14*	–	–	–	*5*	*9*	*35.71*
Connaught							
Connaught	48	–	–	1	19	29	39.58
Total	*48*	–	–	*1*	*19*	*29*	*39.58*
Connew							
Connew-Ford	1	–	–	–	1	1	100.00
Total	*1*	–	–	–	*1*	*1*	*100.00*
Cooper							
Cooper-Alfa	1	–	–	–	0	1	0.00
Cooper-Alta	5	–	–	–	3	2	60.00
Cooper-ATS	1	–	–	–	0	1	0.00
Cooper-Borgward	2	–	–	–	2	–	100.00
Cooper-Bristol	38	–	–	1	28	11	73.68
Cooper-BRM	20	–	–	2	9	11	45.00
Cooper-Climax	295	14	15	19	179	117	60.68
Cooper-Climax F2	2	–	–	–	1	–	100.00
Cooper-Ferrari	7	–	–	–	4	3	57.14
Cooper-Ford	1	–	–	–	1	–	100.00
Cooper-JAP	1	–	–	–	0	1	0.00

Constructor	Cars	1	2	3	CC	CR	Com%
Cooper-Maserati	127	2	3	2	67	62	52.76
Cooper-Osca	1	–	–	–	0	1	0.00
Total	*501*	*16*	*18*	*24*	*294*	*210*	*58.80*
Dallara							
Dallara-Ferrari	31	–	–	–	19	12	61.29
Dallara-Ford	73	–	–	1	30	43	41.10
Dallara-Judd	29	–	–	1	14	15	48.28
Total	*133*	–	–	*2*	*63*	*70*	*47.37*
de Tomaso							
de Tomaso-Conrero	1	–	–	–	0	1	0.00
de Tomaso-Ford	8	–	–	–	4	6	50.00
de Tomaso-Osca	3	–	–	–	0	3	0.00
Total	*12*	–	–	–	*4*	*10*	*33.33*
Deidt							
Deidt	8	–	1	1	3	5	37.50
Total	*8*	–	*1*	*1*	*3*	*5*	*37.50*
Del Roy							
Del Roy	1	–	–	–	0	1	0.00
Total	*1*	–	–	–	*0*	*1*	*0.00*
Dunn							
Dunn	3	–	–	–	1	2	33.33
Total	*3*	–	–	–	*1*	*2*	*33.33*
Eagle							
Eagle-Climax	10	–	–	–	8	3	80.00
Eagle-Weslake	23	1	–	1	3	20	13.04
Total	*33*	*1*	–	*1*	*11*	*23*	*33.33*
Elder							
Elder	1	–	–	–	0	1	0.00
Total	*1*	–	–	–	*0*	*1*	*0.00*
Emeryson							
Emeryson	1	–	–	–	0	1	0.00
Emeryson-Climax	3	–	–	–	2	1	66.67
Total	*4*	–	–	–	*2*	*2*	*50.00*
EMW (Eisenacher Motoren Werke)							
EMW	1	–	–	–	0	1	0.00
Total	*1*	–	–	–	*0*	*1*	*0.00*
ENB (Ecurie Nationale Belge)							
ENB-Maserati	1	–	–	–	1	–	100.00
Total	*1*	–	–	–	*1*	–	*100.00*
Ensign							
Ensign-Ford	110	–	–	–	57	56	51.82
Total	*110*	–	–	–	*57*	*56*	*51.82*
Epperly							
Epperly	17	2	2	1	12	5	70.59
Total	*17*	*2*	*2*	*1*	*12*	*5*	*70.59*

Constructor	Cars	1	2	3	CC	CR	Com%
ERA (English Racing Automobiles)							
ERA	12	–	–	–	6	6	50.00
Total	*12*	–	–	–	*6*	*6*	*50.00*
EuroBrun							
EuroBrun-Ford	18	–	–	–	8	10	44.44
EuroBrun-Judd	2	–	–	–	2	1	100.00
Total	*20*	–	–	–	*10*	*11*	*50.00*
Ewing							
Ewing	3	–	–	–	1	2	33.33
Total	*3*	–	–	–	*1*	*2*	*33.33*
Ferguson							
Ferguson-Climax	1	–	–	–	1	–	100.00
Total	*1*	–	–	–	*1*	–	*100.00*
Ferrari							
Ferrari	1366	120	154	145	887	491	64.93
Lancia-Ferrari	59	5	8	4	33	27	55.93
Ferrari-Jaguar	1	–	–	–	0	1	0.00
Total	*1426*	*125*	*162*	*129*	*920*	*519*	*64.36*
Fittipaldi							
Fittipaldi-Ford	122	–	1	2	73	51	59.84
Total	*122*	–	*1*	*2*	*73*	*51*	*59.84*
Fondmetal							
Fondmetal-Ford	25	–	–	–	5	20	20.00
Total	*25*	–	–	–	*5*	*20*	*20.00*
Footwork							
Footwork-Ford	38	–	–	–	19	19	50.00
Footwork-Hart	66	–	–	1	25	41	37.88
Footwork-Mugen Honda	62	–	–	–	39	23	62.90
Footwork-Porsche	6	–	–	–	0	6	0.00
Total	*172*	–	–	*1*	*83*	*89*	*48.26*
Ford							
Ford	1	–	–	–	1	–	100.00
Total	*1*	–	–	–	*1*	–	*100.00*
Forti							
Forti-Ford	44	–	–	–	29	25	65.91
Total	*44*	–	–	–	*29*	*25*	*65.91*
Frazer Nash							
Frazer Nash	4	–	–	–	3	1	75.00
Total	*4*	–	–	–	*3*	*1*	*75.00*
Gilby							
Gilby-BRM	2	–	–	–	0	2	0.00
Gilby-Climax	1	–	–	–	1	–	100.00
Total	*3*	–	–	–	*1*	*2*	*33.33*

Constructor	Cars	1	2	3	CC	CR	Com%
Gordini							
Gordini	99	–	–	2	40	60	40.40
Simca-Gordini	28	–	–	–	8	20	28.57
Total	*127*	–	–	*2*	*48*	*80*	*37.80*
Hesketh							
Hesketh-Ford	73	1	3	3	42	33	57.53
Total	*73*	*1*	*3*	*3*	*42*	*33*	*57.53*
Hill							
Hill-Ford	19	–	–	–	11	8	57.89
Total	*19*	–	–	–	*11*	*8*	*57.89*
Honda							
Honda	46	2	1	2	19	27	41.30
Total	*46*	*2*	*1*	*2*	*19*	*27*	*41.30*
HWM							
HWM	44	–	–	–	21	23	47.73
Total	*44*	–	–	–	*21*	*23*	*47.73*
JBW (JB Wilkinson)							
JBW-Climax	1	–	–	–	0	1	0.00
JBW-Maserati	4	–	–	–	1	3	25.00
Total	*5*	–	–	–	*1*	*4*	*20.00*
Jordan							
Jordan-Ford	31	–	–	–	19	12	61.29
Jordan-Hart	61	–	–	1	29	33	47.54
Jordan-Mugen Honda	64	3	2	4	40	24	62.50
Jordan-Peugeot	100	–	2	3	56	44	56.00
Jordan-Yamaha	28	–	–	–	9	19	32.14
Total	*284*	*3*	*4*	*8*	*153*	*132*	*53.87*
Klenk							
Klenk-Meteor	1	–	–	–	0	1	0.00
Total	*1*	–	–	–	*0*	*1*	*0.00*
Kojima							
Kojima-Ford	3	–	–	–	2	1	66.67
Total	*3*	–	–	–	*2*	*1*	*66.67*
Kurtis Kraft							
Kurtis Kraft	195	5	5	6	95	100	48.72
Total	*195*	*5*	*5*	*6*	*95*	*100*	*48.72*
Kuzma							
Kuzma	37	1	1	1	22	15	59.46
Total	*37*	*1*	*1*	*1*	*22*	*15*	*59.46*
Lamborghini							
Lamborghini	6	–	–	–	4	2	66.67
Total	*6*	–	–	–	*4*	*2*	*66.67*
Lancia							
Lancia	10	–	1	–	5	7	50.00
Total	*10*	–	*1*	–	*5*	*7*	*50.00*

Constructor		1	2	3	CC	CR	Com%
Lancia-Ferra.							
Lancia-Ferrari	59	5	8	4	33	27	55.93
Total	*59*	*5*	*8*	*4*	*33*	*27*	*55.93*
Langley							
Langley	1	–	–	–	1	–	100.00
Total	*1*	–	–	–	*1*	–	*100.00*
Larrousse							
Larrousse-Ford	31	–	–	–	14	18	45.16
Larrousse-Lamborghini	62	–	–	–	31	31	50.00
Total	*93*	–	–	–	*45*	*49*	*48.39*
LDS (LD Serrurier)							
LDS-Alfa	3	–	–	–	2	1	66.67
LDS-Alfia	1	–	–	–	0	1	0.00
LDS-Climax	1	–	–	–	0	1	0.00
LDS-Repco	1	–	–	–	0	1	0.00
Total	*6*	–	–	–	*2*	*4*	*33.33*
Lec							
Lec-Ford	3	–	–	–	2	1	66.67
Total	3	–	–	–	2	1	66.67
Lesovsky							
Lesovsky	15	–	–	1	9	6	60.00
Total	*15*	–	–	*1*	*9*	*6*	*60.00*
Leyton House (March)							
L.House-Ilmor	32	–	–	–	12	20	37.50
L.House Judd	25	–	1	–	10	16	40.00
Total	*57*	–	*1*	–	*22*	*36*	*38.60*
Ligier (Prost							
Ligier-Ford	136	5	5	8	79	57	58.09
Ligier-Judd	25	–	–	–	10	15	40.00
Ligier-Lamborghini	29	–	–	–	18	11	62.07
Ligier-Matra	106	3	5	10	57	49	53.77
Ligier-Megatron	28	–	–	–	12	17	42.86
Ligier-Mugen Honda	65	1	1	1	35	31	53.85
Ligier-Renault	188	–	3	8	108	80	57.45
Total	*577*	*9*	*14*	*27*	*319*	*260*	*55.29*
Lola							
Lola-BMW	2	–	–	–	1	1	50.00
Lola-Climax	29	–	2	–	12	18	41.38
Lola-Ferrari	21	–	–	–	10	11	47.62
Lola-Ford	130	–	–	–	68	67	52.31
Lola-Hart	8	–	–	–	2	7	25.00
Lola-Lamborghini	56	–	–	1	24	33	42.86
Total	*246*	–	*2*	*1*	*117*	*137*	*47.56*

Constructor	Cars	1	2	3	CC	CR	Com%
Lotus							
Lotus-BRM	100	1	1	–	47	59	47.00
Lotus-Climax	255	24	5	9	144	114	56.47
Lotus-Ford	584	47	25	25	322	272	55.14
Lotus-Honda	60	2	4	5	40	20	66.67
Lotus-Judd	51	–	–	–	27	24	52.94
Lotus-Lamborghini	29	–	–	–	11	19	37.93
Lotus-Maserati	1	–	–	–	0	1	0.00
Lotus-Mugen Honda	32	–	–	–	19	13	59.38
Lotus-Renault	116	5	7	12	62	54	53.45
Total	*1228*	*79*	*42*	*51*	*673*	*576*	*54.80*
Lotus Turbine							
Lotus-Turbine	3	–	–	–	2	1	66.67
Total	*3*	–	–	–	*2*	*1*	*66.67*
LOWS							
LOWS-Honda	1	–	–	–	0	1	0.00
Total	*1*	–	–	–	*0*	*1*	*0.00*
Lyncar							
Lyncar-Ford	1	–	–	–	1	–	100.00
Total	*1*	–	–	–	*1*	–	*100.00*
March							
March-Alfa	12	–	–	–	5	7	41.67
March-Ford	401	3	9	6	216	193	53.87
March-Ilmor	26	–	–	–	15	11	57.69
March-Judd	62	–	1	2	27	36	43.55
March-Lotus	1	–	–	–	1	–	100.00
Total	*502*	*3*	*10*	*8*	*264*	*247*	*52.59*
March+Leyton House							
March Total	502	3	10	8	264	247	52.59
L.House Total	57	–	1	–	22	36	38.60
Total	*559*	*3*	*11*	*8*	*286*	*283*	*51.16*
Marchese							
Marchese	2	–	–	–	1	1	50.00
Total	*2*	–	–	–	*1*	*1*	*50.00*
Martini							
Martini-Ford	4	–	–	–	3	1	75.00
Total	*4*	–	–	–	*3*	*1*	*75.00*
Maserati							
Maserati	361	9	10	18	198	176	54.85
Maserati-Milan	4	–	–	–	1	3	25.00
Maserati-Plate	6	–	–	–	3	3	50.00
Total	*371*	*9*	*10*	*18*	*202*	*182*	*54.45*
Matra							
Matra	66	–	1	5	44	23	66.67
Matra-BRM	1	–	–	–	1	–	100.00

Constructor	Cars	1	2	3	CC	CR	Com%
Matra-Ford	43	9	3	3	32	11	74.42
Matra-Ford F2	4	–	–	–	3	1	75.00
Total	*114*	*9*	*4*	*8*	*80*	*35*	*70.18*
McLaren							
McLaren-Alfa	4	–	–	–	3	1	75.00
McLaren-Alfa Romeo	0	–	–	–	1	–	#DIV/0!
McLaren-BRM	13	–	–	–	5	8	38.46
McLaren-Ford	529	35	27	39	345	190	65.22
McLaren-Honda	160	44	30	17	120	40	75.00
McLaren-Mercedes	163	19	19	13	105	58	64.42
McLaren-Peugeot	32	–	2	6	15	17	46.88
McLaren-Serenissima	1	–	–	–	3	–	300.00
McLaren-TAG	134	25	15	14	85	49	63.43
Total	*1036*	*123*	*93*	*89*	*682*	*363*	*65.83*
Mercedes							
Mercedes	39	9	5	3	24	15	61.54
Total	*39*	*9*	*5*	*3*	*24*	*15*	*61.54*
Merzario							
Merzario-Ford	10	–	–	–	1	9	10.00
Total	*10*	–	–	–	*1*	*9*	*10.00*
Meskowski							
Meskowski	2	–	–	–	2	–	100.00
Total	*2*	–	–	–	*2*	–	*100.00*
Minardi							
Minardi-Ferrari	32	–	–	–	17	15	53.13
Minardi-Ford	269	–	–	–	136	139	50.56
Minardi-Hart	32	–	–	–	17	16	53.13
Minardi-Lamborghini	26	–	–	–	15	11	57.69
Minardi-MM	74	–	–	–	11	64	14.86
Total	*433*	–	–	–	*196*	*245*	*45.27*
Moore							
Moore	3	–	–	–	3	–	100.00
Total	*3*	–	–	–	*3*	–	*100.00*
Nichels							
Nichels	3	–	–	–	1	2	33.33
Total	*3*	–	–	–	*1*	*2*	*33.33*
Olson							
Olson	1	–	–	–	1	–	100.0
Total	*1*	–	–	–	*1*	–	*100.00*
Onyx							
Onyx-Ford	25	–	–	1	9	16	36.00
Total	*25*	–	–	*1*	*9*	*16*	*36.00*

Constructor	Cars	1	2	3	CC	CR	Com%
OSCA (Officine Specializate Construzione Automobili)							
OSCA	7	–	–	–	3	4	42.86
Total	*7*	–	–	–	*3*	*4*	*42.86*
Osella							
Osella-Alfa	103	–	–	–	31	72	30.10
Osella-Alfa Romeo	1	–	–	–	1	1	100.00
Osella-Ford	62	–	–	–	17	47	27.42
Total	*166*	–	–	–	*49*	*120*	*29.52*
Pacific							
Pacific-Ford	33	–	–	–	9	25	27.27
Pacific-Ilmor	7	–	–	–	0	7	0.00
Total	*40*	–	–	–	*9*	*32*	*22.50*
Pankratz							
Pankratz	2	–	–	–	1	1	50.00
Total	*2*	–	–	–	*1*	*1*	*50.00*
Parnelli							
Parnelli-Ford	16	–	–	–	9	7	56.25
Total	*16*	–	–	–	*9*	*7*	*56.25*
Pawl							
Pawl	3	–	–	–	0	3	0.00
Total	*3*	–	–	–	*0*	*3*	*0.00*
Penske							
Penske-Ford	43	1	–	2	27	16	62.79
Total	*43*	*1*	–	*2*	*27*	*16*	*62.79*
Phillips							
Phillips	7	–	–	1	5	2	71.43
Total	*7*	–	–	*1*	*5*	*2*	*71.43*
Porsche							
Porsche	71	1	3	1	54	17	76.06
Total	*71*	*1*	*3*	*1*	*54*	*17*	*76.06*
Prost							
Prost-M. Honda	34	–	1	1	22	12	64.71
Prost-Peugeot	62	–	1	–	35	29	56.45
Total	*96*	–	*2*	*1*	*57*	*41*	*59.38*
Prost+Ligier							
Prost Total	96	–	2	1	57	41	59.38
Ligier Total	577	9	14	27	319	260	55.29
Total	*673*	*9*	*16*	*28*	*376*	*301*	*55.87*
Rae							
Rae	1	–	–	–	1	–	100.00
Total	*1*	–	–	–	*1*	–	*100.00*
RAM							
RAM-Ford	3	–	–	–	2	1	66.67
RAM-Hart	51	–	–	–	15	37	29.41
Total	*54*	–	–	–	*17*	*38*	*31.48*

Constructor	Cars	1	2	3	CC	CR	Com%
Rebaque							
Rebaque-Ford	1	–	–	–	0	1	0.00
Total	*1*	–	–	–	*0*	*1*	*0.00*
Renault							
Renault	227	15	15	11	103	126	45.37
Total	*227*	*15*	*15*	*11*	*103*	*126*	*45.37*
Rial							
Rial-Ford	20	–	–	–	9	11	45.00
Total	*20*	–	–	–	*9*	*11*	*45.00*
Sauber							
Sauber-Ford	65	–	–	2	38	28	58.46
Sauber-Ilmor	32	–	–	–	14	18	43.75
Sauber-Mercedes	29	–	–	–	13	18	44.83
Sauber-Petronas	97	–	–	2	55	43	56.70
Total	*223*	–	–	*4*	*120*	*107*	*53.81*
Scarab							
Scarab	3	–	–	–	4	2	133.33
Total	*3*	–	–	–	*4*	*2*	*133.33*
Schroeder							
Schroeder	5	–	–	–	2	3	40.00
Total	*5*	–	–	–	*2*	*3*	*40.00*
Scirocco							
Scirocco-BRM	6	–	–	–	0	6	0.00
Scirocco-Climax	1	–	–	–	0	1	0.00
Total	*7*	–	–	–	*0*	*7*	*0.00*
Shadow							
Shadow-Ford	209	1	–	6	115	97	55.02
Shadow-Matra	2	–	–	–	0	2	0.00
Total	*211*	*1*	–	*6*	*115*	*99*	*54.50*
Shannon							
Shannon-Climax	1	–	–	–	0	1	0.00
Total	*1*	–	–	–	*0*	*1*	*0.00*
Sherman							
Sherman	2	–	–	–	2	–	100.00
Total	*2*	–	–	–	*2*	–	*100.00*
Simtek							
Simtek-Ford	37	–	–	–	15	22	40.54
Total	*37*	–	–	–	*15*	*22*	*40.54*
Snowberger							
Snowberger	1	–	–	–	0	1	0.00
Total	*1*	–	–	–	*0*	*1*	*0.00*
Spirit							
Spirit-Hart	17	–	–	–	9	8	52.94
Spirit-Honda	6	–	–	–	3	3	50.00
Total	*23*	–	–	–	*12*	*11*	*52.17*

Constructor	Cars	1	2	3	CC	CR	Com%
Stebro							
Stebro-Ford	1	–	–	–	1	–	100.00
Total	*1*	–	–	–	*1*	–	*100.00*
Stevens							
Stevens	9	–	–	–	6	3	66.67
Total	*9*	–	–	–	*6*	*3*	*66.67*
Stewart							
Stewart-Ford	95	1	1	3	44	54	46.32
Total	*95*	*1*	*1*	*3*	*44*	*54*	*46.32*
Surtees							
Surtees-Ford	226	–	1	1	135	96	59.73
Total	*226*	–	*1*	*1*	*135*	*96*	*59.73*
Sutton							
Sutton	1	–	–	–	0	1	0.00
Total	*1*	–	–	–	*0*	*1*	*0.00*
Talbot							
Talbot	79	–	–	2	41	38	51.90
Total	*79*	–	–	*2*	*41*	*38*	*51.90*
Tec Mec							
Tec Mec Maserati	1	–	–	–	0	1	0.00
Total	*1*	–	–	–	*0*	*1*	*0.00*
Tecno							
Tecno	10	–	–	–	5	8	50.00
Total	*10*	–	–	–	*5*	*8*	*50.00*
Theodore							
Theodore-Ford	44	–	–	–	23	21	52.27
Total	*44*	–	–	–	*23*	*21*	*52.27*
Token							
Token-Ford	3	–	–	–	2	1	66.67
Total	*3*	–	–	–	*2*	*1*	*66.67*
Toleman							
Toleman-Hart	94	–	1	2	28	66	29.79
Total	*94*	–	*1*	*2*	*28*	*66*	*29.79*
Trevis							
Trevis	6	–	–	–	4	2	66.67
Total	*6*	–	–	–	*4*	*2*	*66.67*
Trojan							
Trojan-Ford	6	–	–	–	3	3	50.00
Total	*6*	–	–	–	*3*	*3*	*50.00*
Turner							
Turner	1	–	–	–	0	1	0.00
Total	*1*	–	–	–	*0*	*1*	*0.00*

Constructor	Cars	1	2	3	CC	CR	Com%
Tyrrell							
Tyrrell-Ford	604	23	33	20	395	221	65.40
Tyrrell-Honda	28	–	–	–	13	15	46.43
Tyrrell-Ilmor	32	–	–	–	12	20	37.50
Tyrrell-Renault	47	–	–	–	28	19	59.57
Tyrrell-Yamaha	130	–		1	58	72	44.62
Total	*841*	*23*	*33*	*21*	*506*	*347*	*60.17*
Vanwall							
Vanwall	64	9	2	2	26	39	40.63
Total	*64*	*9*	*2*	*2*	*26*	*39*	*40.63*
Veritas							
Veritas	18	–	–	–	7	11	38.89
Total	*18*	–	–	–	*7*	*11*	*38.89*
Watson							
Watson	22	3	2	–	10	12	45.45
Total	*22*	*3*	*2*	–	*10*	*12*	*45.45*
Wetteroth							
Wetteroth	1	–	–	–	1	–	100.00
Total	*1*	–	–	–	*1*	–	*100.00*
Williams							
Williams-Ford	254	17	21	14	170	93	66.93
Williams-Honda	129	23	16	8	84	48	65.12
Williams-Judd	32	–	2	–	12	20	37.50
Williams-Mecachrome	32	–		3	25	7	78.13
Williams-Renault	289	63	49	29	200	89	69.20
Williams-Supertec	32	–	1	2	18	14	56.25
Total	*768*	*103*	*89*	*56*	*510*	*271*	*66.41*
Wolf							
Wolf-Ford	52	3	4	6	24	28	46.15
Total	*52*	*3*	*4*	*6*	*24*	*28*	*46.15*
Zakspeed							
Zakspeed	82	–	–	–	29	55	35.37
Zakspeed-Yamaha	2	–	–	–	0	2	0.00
Total	*84*	–	–	–	*29*	*57*	*34.52*

POINTS

The final tables for the Constructor's Cup (the Teams' Championship) can be found in the following pages. The tables are resonably straightforward. However, there may be two sets of points listed for a constructor. The first number is the points obtained that counted towards the championship whereas a second score indicates the total number of points won. The difference arises because in some seasons only the best five or six results, for example, counted towards the championship total.

The number of points awarded has changed down the years. Here is a brief summary of the points awarded and races that counted towards results. Note that the Constructors' Championship only came into being in 1958.

1958-59 Points awarded were 8, 6, 4, 3, 2 for 1st, 2nd, 3rd, 4th and 5th positions.
1960 Points awarded were 8, 6, 4, 3, 2, 1 for 1st, 2nd, 3rd, 4th, 5th and 6th positions.
1961-90 Points awarded were 9, 6, 4, 3, 2, 1 for 1st, 2nd, 3rd, 4th, 5th and 6th positions.
1991-99 Points awarded were 10, 6, 4, 3, 2, 1 for 1st, 2nd, 3rd, 4th, 5th and 6th positions.

Race results counted as follows down the years:

1950-53 Best four results were counted.
1954-57 Best five results were counted.
1958 Best six results were counted.
1959 Best five results were counted.
1960 Best six results were counted.
1961-62 Best five results were counted.
1963-65 Best six results were counted.
1966 Best five results were counted.
1967-78 Championship divided into two halves with worst result from each half discarded. If odd number of races, extra race included in first half.
1979 Best four results in each half were counted.
1979-99 All results were counted.

CONSTRUCTORS' CUP WINNERS 1958–1999

Year	Constructor	Engine	CC Pts	Tot Pts
1958	Vanwall	Vanwall	48	57
1959	Cooper	Climax	40	53
1960	Cooper	Climax	48	58
1961	Ferrari	Ferrari	40	52
1962	BRM	BRM	42	56
1963	Lotus	Climax	54	74
1964	Ferrari	Ferrari	45	49
1965	Lotus	Climax	54	58
1966	Brabham	Repco	42	49
1967	Brabham	Repco	63	67
1968	Lotus	Ford	62	62
1969	Matra	Ford	66	66
1970	Lotus	Ford	59	59
1971	Tyrrell	Ford	73	73
1972	Lotus	Ford	61	61
1973	Lotus	Ford	92	96
1974	McLaren	Ford	73	75
1975	Ferrari	Ferrari	72.5	72.5
1976	Ferrari	Ferrari	83	83
1977	Ferrari	Ferrari	95	97
1978	Lotus	Ford	86	86
1979	Ferrari	Ferrari	113	113
1980	Williams	Ford	120	120
1981	Williams	Ford	95	95
1982	Ferrari	Ferrari	74	74
1983	Ferrari	Ferrari	89	89
1984	McLaren	TAG Porsche	143.5	143.5
1985	McLaren	TAG	90	90
1986	Williams	Honda	135	135
1987	Williams	Honda	137	137
1988	McLaren	Honda	199	199
1989	McLaren	Honda	141	141
1990	McLaren	Honda	121	121
1991	McLaren	Honda	139	139
1992	Williams	Renault	164	164
1993	Williams	Renault	168	168
1994	Williams	Renault	118	118
1995	Benetton	Renault	137	137
1996	Williams	Renault	175	175
1997	Williams	Renault	123	123
1998	McLaren	Mercedes	156	156
1999	Ferrari	Ferrari	128	128

CONSTRUCTORS' CUP WINS

Titles	Car	Year(s)
9	Ferrari	1961, 1964, 1975, 1976, 1977, 1979, 1982, 1983 & 1999
9	Williams	1980, 1981, 1986, 1987, 1992, 1993, 1994, 1996 & 1997
8	McLaren	1974, 1984, 1985, 1988, 1989, 1990, 1991 & 1998
7	Lotus	1963, 1965, 1968, 1970, 1972, 1973 & 1978
2	Cooper	1959 & 1960
2	Brabham	1966 & 1967
1	Vanwall	1958
1	BRM	1962
1	Matra	1969
1	Tyrrell	1971
1	Benetton	1995

FINAL TABLES – YEAR BY YEAR

1958

Pos	Team	CC Points	Total
1	Vanwall	48	57
2	Ferrari	40	57
3	Cooper-Climax	31	
4	BRM	18	
5	Maserati	6	
6	Lotus-Climax	3	

1959

Pos	Team	CC Points	Total
1	Cooper-Climax	40	53
2	Ferrari	32	38
3	BRM	18	
4	Lotus-Climax	5	

1960

Pos	Team	CC Points	Total
1	Cooper-Climax	48	58
2	Lotus-Climax	34	37
3	Ferrari	26	27
4	BRM	8	
5	Cooper-Ferrari	3	
=	Cooper-Maserati	3	

1961

Pos	Team	CC Points	Total
1	Ferrari	40	52
2	Lotus-Climax	32	
3	Porsche	22	23
4	Cooper-Climax	14	18
5	BRM-Climax	7	

1962

Pos	Team	CC Points	Total
1	BRM	42	56
2	Lotus-Climax	36	38
3	Cooper-Climax	29	37
4	Lola-Climax	19	
5	Porsche	18	19
=	Ferrari	18	
7	Brabham-Climax	6	
8	Lotus-BRM	1	

1963

Pos	Team	CC Points	Total
1	Lotus-Climax	54	74
2	BRM	36	45
3	Brabham-Climax	28	30
4	Ferrari	26	
5	Cooper-Climax	25	26
6	BRP-BRM	6	
7	Porsche	5	
8	Lotus-BRM	4	

1964

Pos	Team	CC Points	Total
1	Ferrari	45	49
2	BRM	42	51
3	Lotus-Climax	37	40
4	Brabham-Climax	30	
5	Cooper-Climax	16	
6	Brabham-BRM	7	
7	BRP-BRM	5	
8	Lotus-BRM	3	

1965

Pos	Team	CC Points	Total
1	Lotus-Climax	54	58
2	BRM	45	61
3	Brabham-Climax	27	31
4	Ferrari	26	27
5	Cooper-Climax	14	

Pos	Team	CC Points	Total
6	Honda	11	
7	Brabham-BRM	5	
8	Lotus-BRM	2	

1966

Pos	Team	CC Points	Total
1	Brabham-Repco	42	49
2	Ferrari	31	32
3	Cooper-Maserati	30	35
4	BRM	22	
5	Lotus-BRM	13	
6	Lotus-Climax	8	
7	Eagle-Climax	4	
8	Honda	3	
9	McLaren-Ford	2	
10	Brabham-BRM	1	
=	Brabham-Climax	1	
=	McLaren-Serenissima	1	

1967

Pos	Team	CC Points	Total
1	Brabham-Repco	63	67
2	Lotus-Ford	44	
3	Cooper-Maserati	28	
4	Ferrari	20	
=	Honda	20	
6	BRM	17	
7	Eagle-Weslake	13	
8	Cooper-Climax	6	
=	Lotus-BRM	6	
10	McLaren-BRM	3	
11	Brabham-Climax	2	

1968

Pos	Team	CC Points	Total
1	Lotus-Ford	62	
2	McLaren-Ford	49	
3	Matra-Ford	45	
4	Ferrari	32	
5	BRM	28	
6	Cooper-BRM	14	
=	Honda	14	
8	Brabham-Repco	10	
9	Matra	8	
10	McLaren-BRM	3	

1969

Pos	Team	CC Points	Total
1	Matra-Ford	66	
2	Brabham-Ford	49	51
3	Lotus-Ford	47	
4	McLaren-Ford	38	40
5	BRM	7	
=	Ferrari	7	

1970

Pos	Team	CC Points	Total
1	Lotus-Ford	59	
2	Ferrari	52	55
3	March-Ford	48	
4	Brabham-Ford	35	
=	McLaren-Ford	35	
6	BRM	23	
=	Matra	23	
8	Surtees-Ford	3	

1971

Pos	Team	CC Points	Total
1	Tyrrell-Ford	73	
2	BRM	36	
3	March-Ford	33	34
=	Ferrari	33	
5	Lotus-Ford	21	
6	McLaren-Ford	10	
7	Matra	9	
8	Surtees-Ford	8	
9	Brabham-Ford	5	

1972

Pos	Team	CC Points	Total
1	Lotus-Ford	61	
2	Tyrrell-Ford	51	
3	McLaren-Ford	47	49
4	Ferrari	33	
5	Surtees-Ford	18	
6	March-Ford	15	
7	BRM	14	
8	Matra	12	
9	Brabham-Ford	7	

1973

Pos	Team	CC Points	Total
1	Lotus-Ford	92	96
2	Tyrrell-Ford	82	86
3	McLaren-Ford	58	
4	Brabham-Ford	22	
5	March-Ford	14	
6	BRM	12	
=	Ferrari	12	
8	Shadow-Ford	9	
9	Surtees-Ford	7	
10	Williams-Ford	2	
11	Tecno	1	

1974

Pos	Team	CC Points	Total
1	McLaren-Ford	73	75
2	Ferrari	65	
3	Tyrrell-Ford	52	
4	Lotus-Ford	42	
5	Brabham-Ford	35	
6	Hesketh-Ford	15	
7	BRM	10	
8	Shadow-Ford	7	
9	March-Ford	6	
10	Williams-Ford	4	
11	Surtees-Ford	3	
12	Lola-Ford	1	

1975

Pos	Team	CC Points	Total
1	Ferrari	72.5	
2	Brabham-Ford	54	56
3	McLaren-Ford	53	
4	Hesketh-Ford	33	
5	Tyrrell-Ford	25	
6	Shadow-Ford	9.5	
7	Lotus-Ford	9	
8	March-Ford	7.5	
9	Williams-Ford	6	
10	Parnelli-Ford	5	
11	Hill-Ford	3	
12	Penske-Ford	2	
13	Ensign-Ford	1	

1976

Pos	Team	CC Points	Total
1	Ferrari	83	
2	McLaren-Ford	74	75
3	Tyrrell-Ford	71	
4	Lotus-Ford	29	
5	Ligier-Matra	20	
=	Penske-Ford	20	
7	March-Ford	19	
8	Shadow-Ford	10	
9	Brabham-Alfa	9	
10	Surtees-Ford	7	
11	Fittipaldi-Ford	3	
12	Ensign-Ford	2	
13	Parnelli-Ford	1	

1977

Pos	Team	CC Points	Total
1	Ferrari	95	97
2	Lotus-Ford	62	
3	McLaren-Ford	60	
4	Wolf-Ford	55	
5	Brabham-Alfa	27	
=	Tyrrell-Ford	27	
7	Shadow-Ford	23	
8	Ligier-Matra	18	
9	Fittipaldi-Ford	11	
10	Ensign-Ford	10	
11	Surtees-Ford	6	
12	Penske-Ford	1	

1978

Pos	Team	CC Points	Total
1	Lotus-Ford	86	
2	Ferrari	58	
3	Brabham-Alfa	53	
4	Tyrrell-Ford	38	
5	Wolf-Ford	24	
6	Ligier-Matra	19	
7	Fittipaldi-Ford	17	
8	McLaren-Ford	15	
9	Arrows-Ford	11	
=	Williams-Ford	11	
11	Shadow-Ford	6	
12	Renault	3	
13	Surtees-Ford	1	
=	Ensign-Ford	1	

1979

Pos	Team	CC Points	Total
1	Ferrari	113	
2	Williams-Ford	75	
3	Ligier-Ford	61	
4	Lotus-Ford	39	
5	Tyrrell-Ford	28	
6	Renault	26	
7	McLaren-Ford	15	
8	Brabham-Alfa	7	
9	Arrows-Ford	5	
10	Shadow-Ford	3	
11	ATS-Ford	2	
12	Fittipaldi-Ford	1	

1980

Pos	Team	CC Points	Total
1	Williams-Ford	120	
2	Ligier-Ford	66	
3	Brabham-Ford	55	
4	Renault	38	
5	Lotus-Ford	14	
6	Tyrrell-Ford	12	
7	Arrows-Ford	11	
=	Fittipaldi-Ford	11	
=	McLaren-Ford	11	
10	Ferrari	8	
11	Alfa Romeo	4	

1981

Pos	Team	CC Points	Total
1	Williams-Ford	95	
2	Brabham-Ford	61	
3	Renault	54	
4	Ligier-Matra	44	
5	Ferrari	34	
6	McLaren-Ford	28	
7	Lotus-Ford	22	
8	Alfa Romeo	10	
=	Arrows-Ford	10	
=	Tyrrell-Ford	10	
11	Ensign-Ford	5	
12	ATS-Ford	1	
=	Theodore-Ford	1	

1982

Pos	Team	CC Points	Total
1	Ferrari	74	
2	McLaren-Ford	69	
3	Renault	62	
4	Williams-Ford	58	
5	Brabham-Ford/BMW	41	
6	Lotus-Ford	30	
7	Tyrrell-Ford	25	
8	Ligier-Matra	20	
9	Alfa Romeo	7	
10	Arrows-Ford	5	
11	ATS-Ford	4	
12	Osella-Ford	3	
13	Fittipaldi-Ford	1	

1983

Pos	Team	CC Points	Total
1	Ferrari	89	
2	Renault	79	
3	Brabham-BMW	72	
4	Williams-Ford/Honda	36	
5	McLaren-Ford/Porsche	34	
6	Alfa Romeo	18	
7	Tyrrell-Ford	12	
=	Lotus-Renault/Ford	12	
9	Toleman-Hart	10	
10	Arrows-Ford	4	
11	Williams-Honda	2	
12	Theodore-Ford	1	

1984

Pos	Team	CC Points	Total
1	McLaren-TAG Porsche	143.5	
2	Ferrari	57.5	
3	Lotus-Renault	47	
4	Brabham-BMW	38	
5	Renault	34	
6	Williams-Honda	25.5	
7	Toleman-Hart	16	
8	Alfa Romeo	11	
9	Arrows-Ford/BMW	6	
10	Ligier-Renault	3	
11	Osella-Alfa Romeo	2	

1985

Pos	Team	CC Points	Total
1	McLaren-TAG	90	
2	Ferrari	82	
3	Lotus-Renault	71	
=	Williams-Honda	71	
5	Brabham-BMW	26	
6	Ligier-Renault	23	
7	Renault	16	
8	Arrows-BMW	14	
9	Tyrrell-Ford/Renault	7	

1986

Pos	Team	CC Points	Total
1	Williams-Honda	135	
2	McLaren-TAG	87	
3	Lotus-Renault	57	
4	Ferrari	33	
5	Ligier-Renault	29	
6	Benetton-BMW	19	
7	Tyrrell-Renault	6	
=	Lola-Ford	6	
9	Brabham-BMW	2	
10	Arrows-BMW	1	

1987

Pos	Team	CC Points	Total
1	Williams-Honda	137	
2	McLaren-TAG	76	
3	Lotus-Honda	64	
4	Ferrari	53	
5	Benetton-Ford	28	
6	Arrows-Megatron	11	
=	Tyrrell-Ford	11	
8	Brabham-BMW	10	
9	Lola-Ford	3	
10	Zakspeed	2	
11	AGS-Ford	1	
=	Ligier-Megatron	1	
=	March-Ford	1	

1988

Pos	Team	CC Points	Total
1	McLaren-Honda	199	
2	Ferrari	65	
3	Benetton-Ford	39	
4	Arrows-Megatron	23	
=	Lotus-Honda	23	
6	March-Judd	22	
7	Williams-Judd	20	
8	Tyrrell-Ford	5	
9	Rial-Ford	3	
10	Minardi-Ford	1	

1989

Pos	Team	CC Points	Total
1	McLaren-Honda	141	
2	Williams-Renault	77	
3	Ferrari	59	
4	Benetton-Ford	39	
5	Tyrrell-Ford	16	
6	Lotus-Judd	15	
7	Arrows-Ford	13	
8	Brabham-Judd	8	
=	Dallara-Ford	8	
10	Minardi-Ford	6	
=	Onyx-Ford	6	
12	March-Judd	4	
13	Ligier-Ford	3	
=	Rial-Ford	3	
15	AGS-Ford	1	
=	Lola-Lamborghini	1	

1990

Pos	Team	CC Points	Total
1	McLaren-Honda	121	
2	Ferrari	110	
3	Benetton-Ford	71	
4	Williams-Renault	57	
5	Tyrrell-Ford	16	
6	Lola-Lamborghini	11	
7	Leyton House-Judd	7	
8	Lotus-Lamborghini	3	
9	Arrows-Ford	2	
=	Brabham-Judd	2	

1991

Pos	Team	CC Points	Total
1	McLaren-Honda	139	
2	Williams-Renault	125	
3	Ferrari	55.5	
4	Benetton-Ford	38.5	
5	Jordan-Ford	13	
6	Tyrrell-Honda	12	
7	Minardi-Ferrari	6	
8	Dallara-Judd	5	

9	Lotus-Judd	3	
=	Brabham-Yamaha	3	
11	Lola-Ford	2	
12	Leyton House-Ilmor	1	

1992

Pos	Team	CC Points	Total
1	Williams-Renault	164	
2	McLaren-Honda	99	
3	Benetton-Ford	91	
4	Ferrari	21	
5	Lotus-Ford	13	
6	Tyrrell-Ilmor	8	
7	Footwork-Mugen	6	
=	Ligier-Renault	6	
9	March-Ilmor	3	
10	Dallara-Ferrari	2	
11	Jordan-Yamaha	1	
=	Minardi-Lamborghini	1	
=	Larrousse-Lamborghini	1	

1993

Pos	Team	CC Points	Total
1	Williams-Renault	168	
2	McLaren-Ford	84	
3	Benetton-Ford	72	
4	Ferrari	28	
5	Ligier-Renault	23	
6	Lotus-Ford	12	
=	Sauber-Ilmor	12	
8	Minardi-Ford	7	
9	Footwork-Mugen	4	
10	Jordan-Hart	3	
=	Larrousse-Lamborghini	3	

1994

Pos	Team	CC Points	Total
1	Williams-Renault	118	
2	Benetton-Renault	103	
3	Ferrari	71	
4	McLaren-Peugeot	42	
5	Jordan-Hart	28	
6	Ligier-Renault	13	
=	Tyrrell-Yamaha	13	
8	Sauber-Mercedes	12	
9	Footwork-Ford	9	
10	Minardi-Ford	5	
11	Larrousse-Ford	2	

1995

Pos	Team	CC Points	Total
1	Benetton-Renault	137	
2	Williams-Renault	112	
3	Ferrari	73	
4	McLaren-Mercedes	30	
5	Ligier-Mugen Honda	24	
6	Jordan-Peugeot	21	
7	Sauber-Ford	18	
8	Tyrrell-Yamaha	5	
=	Footwork-Hart	5	
10	Minardi-Ford	1	

1996

Pos	Team	CC Points	Total
1	Williams-Renault	175	
2	Ferrari	70	
3	Benetton-Renault	68	
4	McLaren-Mercedes	49	
5	Jordan-Peugeot	22	
6	Ligier-Mugen Honda	15	
7	Sauber-Ford	11	
8	Tyrrell-Yamaha	5	
9	Footwork-Hart	1	

1997

Pos	Team	CC Points	Total
1	Williams-Renault	123	
2	Ferrari	102	
3	Benetton-Renault	67	
4	McLaren-Mercedes	63	
5	Jordan-Peugeot	33	
6	Prost-Mugen Honda	21	
7	Sauber-Petronas	16	
8	Arrows-Yamaha	9	
9	Stewart-Ford	6	
10	Tyrrell-Ford	2	

1998

Pos	Team	CC Points	Total
1	McLaren-Mercedes	156	
2	Ferrari	133	
3	Williams-Mecachrome	38	
4	Jordan-Mugen Honda	34	
5	Benetton-Playlife	33	
6	Sauber-Petronas	10	
7	Arrows	6	
8	Stewart-Ford	5	
9	Prost-Peugeot	1	

1999

Pos	Team	CC Points	Total
1	Ferrari	128	
2	McLaren-Mercedes	124	
3	Jordan-Mugen Honda	61	
4	Stewart-Ford	36	
5	Williams-Supertec	35	
6	Benetton-Playlife	16	
7	Prost-Peugeot	9	
8	Sauber-Petronas	5	
9	Arrows	1	
=	Minardi-Ford	1	

CONSTRUCTORS' CUP SUMMARY BY TEAM

Teams (constructors) are listed alphabetically and a year-by-year listing is given of the finishing position in the final Constructor's Cup table, followed by the points scored towards their Constructor Cup (CC) total and then the total points (TP) scored throughout the season. See previously for details on points scoring. Where a team may have changed name, this is indicated as appropriate. Only point scoring years are listed.

Year	Pos	CC	TP
AGS			
1987	11	1	1
1989	15	1	1
ALFA ROMEO			
1980	11	4	4
1981	8	10	10
1982	9	7	7
1983	6	18	18
1984	8	11	11
ARROWS / FOOTWORK†			
1978	9	11	11
1979	9	5	5
1980	7	11	11
1981	8	10	10
1982	10	5	5
1983	10	4	4
1984	9	6	6
1985	8	14	14
1986	10	1	1
1987	6	11	11
1988	4	23	23
1989	7	13	13
1990	9	2	2
1992 †	7	6	6
1993 †	9	4	4
1994 †	9	9	9
1995 †	8	5	5
1996 †	9	1	1
1997	8	9	9
1998	7	6	6
1999	9	1	1

Year	Pos	CC	TP
ATS			
1979	11	2	2
1981	12	1	1
1982	11	4	4
BENETTON			
1986	6	19	19
1987	5	28	28
1988	3	39	39
1989	4	39	39
1990	3	71	71
1991	4	38.5	38.5
1992	3	91	91
1993	3	72	72
1994	2	103	103
1995	1	137	137
1996	3	68	68
1997	3	67	67
1998	5	33	33
1999	6	16	16
(see also Toleman)			
BRABHAM			
1962	7	6	6
1963	3	28	30
1964	4	30	30
1964	6	7	7
1965	3	27	31
1965	7	5	5
1966	1	42	49
1966	10	1	1
1966	10	1	1
1967	1	63	67
1967	11	2	2
1968	8	10	10
1969	2	49	51

Year	Pos	CC	TP
1970	4	35	35
1971	9	5	5
1972	9	7	7
1973	4	22	22
1974	5	35	35
1975	2	54	56
1976	9	9	9
1977	5	27	27
1978	3	53	53
1979	8	7	7
1980	3	55	55
1981	2	61	61
1982	5	41	41
1983	3	72	72
1984	4	38	38
1985	5	26	26
1986	9	2	2
1987	8	10	10
1989	8	8	8
1990	9	2	2
1991	9	3	3
BRM			
1958	4	18	18
1959	3	18	18
1960	4	8	8
1961	5	7	7
1962	1	42	56
1963	2	36	45
1964	2	42	51
1965	2	45	61
1966	4	22	22
1967	6	17	17
1968	5	28	28
1969	5	7	7
1970	6	23	23
1971	2	36	36
1972	7	14	14
1973	6	12	12
1974	7	10	10
BRP			
1963	6	6	6
1964	7	5	5

Year	Pos	CC	TP
COOPER			
1958	3	31	31
1959	1	40	53
1960	1	48	58
1960	5	3	3
1960	5	3	3
1961	4	14	18
1962	3	29	37
1963	5	25	26
1964	5	16	16
1965	5	14	14
1966	3	30	35
1967	3	28	28
1967	8	6	6
1968	6	14	14
DALLARA			
1989	8	8	8
1991	8	5	5
1992	10	2	2
EAGLE			
1966	7	4	4
1967	7	13	13
ENSIGN			
1975	13	1	1
1976	12	2	2
1977	10	10	10
1978	13	1	1
1981	11	5	5
FERRARI			
1958	2	40	57
1959	2	32	38
1960	3	26	27
1961	1	40	52
1962	5	18	18
1963	4	26	26
1964	1	45	49
1965	4	26	27
1966	2	31	32
1967	4	20	20
1968	4	32	32

Year	Pos	CC	TP
1969	5	7	7
1970	2	52	55
1971	3	33	33
1972	4	33	33
1973	6	12	12
1974	2	65	65
1975	1	72.5	72.5
1976	1	83	83
1977	1	95	97
1978	2	58	58
1979	1	113	113
1980	10	8	8
1981	5	34	34
1982	1	74	74
1983	1	89	89
1984	2	57.5	57.5
1985	2	82	82
1986	4	33	33
1987	4	53	53
1988	2	65	65
1989	3	59	59
1990	2	110	110
1991	3	55.5	55.5
1992	4	21	21
1993	4	28	28
1994	3	71	71
1995	3	73	73
1996	2	70	70
1997	2	102	102
1998	2	133	133
1999	1	128	128

FITTIPALDI

1976	11	3	3
1977	9	11	11
1978	7	17	17
1979	12	1	1
1980	7	11	11
1982	13	1	1

FOOTWORK

1992	7	6	6
1993	9	4	4
1994	9	9	9
1995	8	5	5

Year	Pos	CC	TP
1996	9	1	1

(see also Arrows)

HESKETH

1974	6	15	15
1975	4	33	33

HILL

1975	11	3	3

HONDA

1965	6	11	11
1966	8	3	3
1967	4	20	20
1968	6	14	14

JORDAN

1991	5	13	13
1992	11	1	1
1993	10	3	3
1994	5	28	28
1995	6	21	21
1996	5	22	22
1997	5	33	33
1998	4	34	34
1999	3	61	61

LARROUSSE

1992	11	1	1
1993	10	3	3
1994	11	2	2

LEYTON HOUSE

1990	7	7	7
1991	12	1	1

(see March)

LIGIER

1976	5	20	20
1977	8	18	18
1978	6	19	19
1979	3	61	61
1980	2	66	66
1981	4	44	44
1982	8	20	20

Year	Pos	CC	TP
1984	10	3	3
1985	6	23	23
1986	5	29	29
1987	11	1	1
1989	13	3	3
1992	7	6	6
1993	5	23	23
1994	6	13	13
1995	5	24	24
1996	6	15	15

(see also Prost)

LOLA

1962	4	19	19
1974	12	1	1
1986	7	6	6
1987	9	3	3
1989	15	1	1
1990	6	11	11
1991	11	2	2

LOTUS

1958	6	3	3
1959	4	5	5
1960	2	34	37
1961	2	32	32
1962	2	36	38
1962	8	1	1
1963	1	54	74
1963	8	4	4
1964	3	37	40
1964	8	3	3
1965	1	54	58
1965	8	2	2
1966	5	13	13
1966	6	8	8
1967	2	44	44
1967	8	6	6
1968	1	62	62
1969	3	47	47
1970	1	59	59
1971	5	21	21
1972	1	61	61
1973	1	92	96
1974	4	42	42

Year	Pos	CC	TP
1975	7	9	9
1976	4	29	29
1977	2	62	62
1978	1	86	86
1979	4	39	39
1980	5	14	14
1981	7	22	22
1982	6	30	30
1983	7	12	12
1984	3	47	47
1985	3	71	71
1986	3	57	57
1987	3	64	64
1988	4	23	23
1989	6	15	15
1990	8	3	3
1991	9	3	3
1992	5	13	13
1993	6	12	12

MARCH

1970	3	48	48
1971	3	33	34
1972	6	15	15
1973	5	14	14
1974	9	6	6
1975	8	7.5	7.5
1976	7	19	19
1987	11	1	1
1988	6	22	22
1989	12	4	4
1990 †	7	7	7
1991 †	12	1	1
1992	9	3	3

(† run as Leyton House)

MASERATI

1958	5	6	6

MATRA

1968	3	45	45
1968	9	8	8
1969	1	66	66
1970	6	23	23
1971	7	9	9
1972	8	12	12

MCLAREN

Year	Pos	CC	TP
1966	9	2	2
1966	10	1	1
1967	10	3	3
1968	2	49	49
1968	10	3	3
1969	4	38	40
1970	4	35	35
1971	6	10	10
1972	3	47	49
1973	3	58	58
1974	1	73	75
1975	3	53	53
1976	2	74	75
1977	3	60	60
1978	8	15	15
1979	7	15	15
1980	7	11	11
1981	6	28	28
1982	2	69	69
1983	5	34	34
1984	1	143.5	143.5
1985	1	90	90
1986	2	87	87
1987	2	76	76
1988	1	199	199
1989	1	141	141
1990	1	121	121
1991	1	139	139
1992	2	99	99
1993	2	84	84
1994	4	42	42
1995	4	30	30
1996	4	49	49
1997	4	63	63
1998	1	156	156
1999	2	124	124

MINARDI

Year	Pos	CC	TP
1988	10	1	1
1989	10	6	6
1991	7	6	6
1992	11	1	1
1993	8	7	7
1994	10	5	5
1995	10	1	1
1999	9	1	1

ONYX

Year	Pos	CC	TP
1989	10	6	6

OSELLA

Year	Pos	CC	TP
1982	12	3	3
1984	11	2	2

PARNELLI

Year	Pos	CC	TP
1975	10	5	5
1976	13	1	1

PENSKE

Year	Pos	CC	TP
1975	12	2	2
1976	5	20	20
1977	12	1	1

PORSCHE

Year	Pos	CC	TP
1961	3	22	23
1962	5	18	19
1963	7	5	5

PROST

Year	Pos	CC	TP
1997	6	21	21
1998	9	1	1
1999	7	9	9

(see also Ligier)

RENAULT

Year	Pos	CC	TP
1978	12	3	3
1979	6	26	26
1980	4	38	38
1981	3	54	54
1982	3	62	62
1983	2	79	79
1984	5	34	34
1985	7	16	16

RIAL

Year	Pos	CC	TP
1988	9	3	3
1989	13	3	3

SAUBER

Year	Pos	CC	TP
1993	6	12	12
1994	8	12	12
1995	7	18	18
1996	7	11	11
1997	7	16	16
1998	6	10	10
1999	8	5	5

SHADOW

Year	Pos	CC	TP
1973	8	9	9
1974	8	7	7
1975	6	9.5	9.5
1976	8	10	10
1977	7	23	23
1978	11	6	6
1979	10	3	3

STEWART

Year	Pos	CC	TP
1997	9	6	6
1998	8	5	5
1999	4	36	36

SURTEES

Year	Pos	CC	TP
1970	8	3	3
1971	8	8	8
1972	5	18	18
1973	9	7	7
1974	11	3	3
1976	10	7	7
1977	11	6	6
1978	13	1	1

TECNO

Year	Pos	CC	TP
1973	11	1	1

THEODORE

Year	Pos	CC	TP
1981	12	1	1
1983	12	1	1

TOLEMAN

Year	Pos	CC	TP
1983	9	10	10
1984	7	16	16

(see also Benetton)

TYRRELL

Year	Pos	CC	TP
1971	1	73	73
1972	2	51	51
1973	2	82	86
1974	3	52	52
1975	5	25	25
1976	3	71	71
1977	5	27	27
1978	4	38	38
1979	5	28	28
1980	6	12	12
1981	8	10	10
1982	7	25	25
1983	7	12	12
1985	9	7	7
1986	7	6	6
1987	6	11	11
1988	8	5	5
1989	5	16	16
1990	5	16	16
1991	6	12	12
1992	6	8	8
1994	6	13	13
1995	8	5	5
1996	8	5	5
1997	10	2	2

VANWALL

Year	Pos	CC	TP
1958	1	48	57

WILLIAMS

Year	Pos	CC	TP
1973	10	2	2
1974	10	4	4
1975	9	6	6
1978	9	11	11
1979	2	75	75
1980	1	120	120
1981	1	95	95
1982	4	58	58
1983	4	36	36
1983	11	2	2
1984	6	25.5	25.5
1985	3	71	71
1986	1	135	135

Year	Pos	CC	TP
1987	1	137	137
1988	7	20	20
1989	2	77	77
1990	4	57	57
1991	2	125	125
1992	1	164	164
1993	1	168	168
1994	1	118	118
1995	2	112	112
1996	1	175	175
1997	1	123	123
1998	3	38	38
1999	5	35	35

WOLF

Year	Pos	CC	TP
1977	4	55	55
1978	5	24	24

ZAKSPEED

Year	Pos	CC	TP
1987	10	2	2

RACE DISQUALIFICATIONS BY CONSTRUCTOR

Car	Year	Grand Prix	Surname	Laps	Time/Reason
Arrows-Ford	1978	German	Stommelen	42	wrong way into pits
Arrows	1999	French	Takagi		use of illegal tyres
ATS-Ford (Germany)	1979	United States West	Stuck,H-J.	49	push start
ATS-Ford (Germany)	1982	San Marino	Winkelhock	54	underweight
ATS-BMW (Germany)	1983	Dutch	Winkelhock	50	overtook on parade lap
Benetton-Ford	1988	Belgian	Boutsen	43	fuel illegal
Benetton-Ford	1988	Belgian	Nannini	43	fuel illegal
Benetton-Ford	1989	Canadian	Nannini		illegal start in pitlane
Benetton-Ford	1990	Monaco	Piquet	33	push start
Benetton-Ford	1994	British	Schumacher,M.	60	overtook on parade lap
Benetton-Ford	1994	Belgian	Schumacher,M.	44	illegal skidblock
Brabham-Alfa	1977	United States West	Watson	33	push start
Brabham-Ford	1982	Brazilian	Piquet	63	underweight
BRM	1959	French	Moss	42	push start
BRM	1972	Monaco	Gethin	27	reversed into pits
BRP-BRM	1963	British	Ireland	26	push start
Cooper-Climax	1960	Monaco	Brabham,J.	40	push start
Dallara-Ford	1990	French	de Cesaris	77	underweight
Eagle-Climax	1966	United States	Bondurant	5	push start
Eagle-Climax	1969	Canadian	Pease	22	too slow
Ensign-Ford	1974	Dutch	Schuppan	68	illegal tyre change
Ensign-Ford	1977	Dutch	Henton	52	push start
Ensign-Ford	1978	Austrian	Daly	43	push start
Ferguson-Climax	1961	British	Fairman	56	push start
Ferrari	1954	Argentinian	Hawthorn		push start
Ferrari	1963	Mexican	Surtees	18	push start
Ferrari	1976	British	Regazzoni	36	engine
Ferrari	1978	Austrian	Reutemann	27	push start
Ferrari	1981	United States	Villeneuve,G.	22	illegal start
Ferrari	1982	United States West	Villeneuve,G.	75	illegal wing
Ferrari	1989	Canadian	Mansell		illegal start in pitlane
Ferrari	1989	Portuguese	Mansell	48	reversing in pits

Car	Year	Grand Prix	Surname	Laps	Reason
Footwork-Ford	1994	Canadian	Fittipaldi,C.	68	underweight
Gordini	1954	Argentinian	Behra		push start
Hesketh-Ford	1976	French	Ertl	4	driveshaft (illegal start)
Jordan-Mugen Honda	1998	Brazilian	Hill,D.	70	underweight
Larrousse-Lamborghini	1992	Canadian	Gachot	14	push start
Ligier-Matra	1976	British	Laffite	31	suspension
Ligier-Ford	1989	San Marino	Grouillard	4	illegal repairs
Ligier-Ford	1990	German	Alliot	16	push start
Ligier-Renault	1994	Portuguese	Panis	70	illegal skidblock
Lotus-Climax	1960	Portuguese	Moss	50	drove in wrong direction
Lotus-Climax	1963	British	Taylor,T.	23	push start
Lotus-BRM	1964	Belgian	Revson	27	push start
Lotus-Ford	1971	Dutch	Wisell	16	reversed into pits
Lotus-Ford	1972	Argentinian	Walker,D.	8	illegal repairs
Lotus-Ford	1974	United States	Schenken	6	started illegally
Lotus-Ford	1983	Brazilian	de Angelis	60	changed car before start
Lotus-Renault	1985	Australian	de Angelis	17	illegal start
Lotus-Honda	1987	Australian	Senna	82	illegal brake ducts
March-Ford	1971	German	Beuttler	3	wrong way into pits
March-Ford	1972	Canadian	Peterson	54	pushed car against traffic
March-Ford	1972	Canadian	Lauda	0	push start
March-Judd	1989	United States	Gugelmin	20	added brake fluid
Maserati	1952	German	Bonetto	1	push start
Maserati	1956	German	Halford	20	push start
McLaren-Ford	1974	German	Hulme	0	restarted in T-car after accident
McLaren-Ford	1976	British	Hunt	76	tech infringement
McLaren-Ford	1978	German	Hunt	34	wrong way into pits
McLaren-Ford	1982	Belgian	Lauda	70	underweight
McLaren-Ford	1983	German	Lauda	44	reversed in pits
McLaren-TAG	1983	South African	Watson	18	overtook on parade lap
McLaren-TAG	1985	San Marino	Prost	60	underweight
McLaren-TAG	1986	Italian	Prost	27	changed to spare car
McLaren-Honda	1988	Brazilian	Senna	31	changed car after parade lap
McLaren-Honda	1989	Japanese	Senna	53	cut across chicane
McLaren-Mercedes	1997	Belgian	Hakkinen	44	illegal fuel
Minardi-MM	1987	Brazilian	Campos	3	illegal start
Onyx-Ford	1989	Canadian	Johansson		ignored black flag
Osella-Ford	1989	Brazilian	Larini	10	illegal start
Pacific-Ford	1995	Monaco	Montermini	23	did not pit in time for Stop-Go penalty
Parnelli-Ford	1974	United States	Andretti,Mario	3	push start
Sauber-Ford	1996	French	Herbert	70	illegal car body
Shadow-Ford	1973	United States	Redman	5	push start
Stewart-Ford	1999	Spanish	Barrichello		plank fastening infringement
Surtees-Ford	1971	Dutch	Stommelen	18	push start
Surtees-Ford	1975	Argentinian	Watson	6	illegal repairs
Surtees-Ford	1978	Dutch	Brambilla	37	push start

Car	Year	Grand Prix	Surname	Laps	Reason
Tyrrell-Ford	1979	United States West	Pironi	72	push start
Tyrrell-Ford	1983	Canadian	Sullivan	68	underweight
Tyrrell-Ford	1984	Brazilian	Brundle	60	All Tyrrell cars were disqualified
Tyrrell-Ford	1984	Brazilian	Bellof	11	in 1984 when the team was found
Tyrrell-Ford	1984	South African	Brundle	71	to be guilty of using pit stops
Tyrrell-Ford	1984	South African	Bellof	60	to bring cars that were racing
Tyrrell-Ford	1984	Belgian	Bellof	69	underweight up to the required
Tyrrell-Ford	1984	Belgian	Brundle	51	weight
Tyrrell-Ford	1984	San Marino	Bellof	59	
Tyrrell-Ford	1984	San Marino	Brundle	55	
Tyrrell-Ford	1984	French	Brundle	76	
Tyrrell-Ford	1984	French	Bellof	11	
Tyrrell-Ford	1984	Monaco	Bellof	31	
Tyrrell-Ford	1984	Canadian	Brundle	68	
Tyrrell-Ford	1984	Detroit	Brundle	63	
Tyrrell-Ford	1984	Detroit	Bellof	33	
Tyrrell-Ford	1984	Dallas	Bellof	9	
Tyrrell-Ford	1984	British	Bellof	68	
Tyrrell-Ford	1984	British	Johansson	1	
Tyrrell-Ford	1984	German	Johansson	42	
Tyrrell-Ford	1984	Dutch	Johansson	69	
Tyrrell-Ford	1984	Dutch	Bellof	69	
Tyrrell-Yamaha	1993	Spanish	de Cesaris	42	push start
Tyrrell-Yamaha	1996	European	Salo	66	underweight
Tyrrell-Yamaha	1996	European	Katayama	65	push start
Tyrrell-Yamaha	1996	Spanish	Salo	16	used spare car
Williams-Ford	1982	Brazilian	Rosberg	63	underweight
Williams-Ford	1983	Brazilian	Rosberg	63	push start
Williams-Renault	1991	Portuguese	Mansell	56	illegal pit stop
Williams-Renault	1997	Japanese	Villeneuve,J.	53	ignored yellow flags
Zakspeed	1987	Austrian	Brundle	48	illegal wing

CONSTRUCTORS BY MOST DISQUALIFICATIONS

Team	dq
Tyrrell	26
McLaren	11
Lotus	9
Ferrari	8
Benetton	6
Benetton+Toleman	6
Ligier	4
March	4
March+Leyton House	4
Williams	4
ATS (Germany)	3
Ensign	3
Surtees	3
Arrows	2
Arrows+Footwork	2
Brabham	2
BRM	2
Eagle	2
Maserati	2
BRP	1
Cooper	1
Dallara	1
Ferguson	1
Footwork	1
Gordini	1
Hesketh	1
Jordan	1
Larrousse	1
Minardi	1
Onyx	1
Osella	1
Pacific	1
Parnelli	1
Sauber	1
Shadow	1
Stewart	1
Zakspeed	1

RACE
RECORDS

WINNERS BY GRANDS PRIX

ARGENTINE

1953	Ascari	Ferrari
1954	Fangio	Maserati
1955	Fangio	Mercedes
1956	Musso	Lancia-Ferrari
1957	Fangio	Maserati
1958	Moss	Cooper-Climax
1960	McLaren	Cooper-Climax
1972	Stewart,Jackie	Tyrrell-Ford
1973	Fittipaldi,E.	Lotus-Ford
1974	Hulme	McLaren-Ford
1975	Fittipaldi,E.	McLaren-Ford
1977	Scheckter,J.	Wolf-Ford
1978	Andretti,Mario	Lotus-Ford
1979	Laffite	Ligier-Ford
1980	Jones	Williams-Ford
1981	Piquet	Brabham-Ford
1995	Hill,D.	Williams-Renault
1996	Hill,D.	Williams-Renault
1997	Villeneuve,J.	Williams-Renault
1998	Schumacher,M.	Ferrari

AUSTRALIAN

1985	Rosberg	Williams-Honda
1986	Prost	McLaren-TAG
1987	Berger,G.	Ferrari
1988	Prost	McLaren-Honda
1989	Boutsen	Williams-Renault
1990	Piquet	Benetton-Ford
1991	Senna	McLaren-Honda
1992	Berger,G.	McLaren-Honda
1993	Senna	McLaren-Ford
1994	Mansell	Williams-Renault
1995	Hill,D.	Williams-Renault
1996	Hill,D.	Williams-Renault
1997	Coulthard	McLaren-Mercedes
1998	Hakkinen	McLaren-Mercedes
1999	Irvine	Ferrari

AUSTRIAN

1964	Bandini	Ferrari
1970	Ickx	Ferrari
1971	Siffert	BRM
1972	Fittipaldi,E.	Lotus-Ford
1973	Peterson	Lotus-Ford
1974	Reutemann	Brabham-Ford
1975	Brambilla	March-Ford
1976	Watson	Penske-Ford
1977	Jones	Shadow-Ford
1978	Peterson	Lotus-Ford
1979	Jones	Williams-Ford
1980	Jabouille	Renault
1981	Laffite	Ligier-Matra
1982	de Angelis	Lotus-Ford
1983	Prost	Renault
1984	Lauda	McLaren-TAG
1985	Prost	McLaren-TAG
1986	Prost	McLaren-TAG
1987	Mansell	Williams-Honda
1997	Villeneuve,J.	Williams-Renault
1998	Hakkinen	McLaren-Mercedes
1999	Irvine	Ferrari

BELGIAN

1950	Fangio	Alfa Romeo
1951	Farina	Alfa Romeo
1952	Ascari	Ferrari
1953	Ascari	Ferrari
1954	Fangio	Maserati
1955	Fangio	Mercedes
1956	Collins	Lancia-Ferrari
1958	Brooks	Vanwall
1960	Brabham,J.	Cooper-Climax
1961	Hill,P.	Ferrari
1962	Clark	Lotus-Climax
1963	Clark	Lotus-Climax
1964	Clark	Lotus-Climax
1965	Clark	Lotus-Climax
1966	Surtees	Ferrari
1967	Gurney	Eagle-Weslake
1968	McLaren	McLaren-Ford
1970	Rodriguez,P.	BRM
1972	Fittipaldi,E.	Lotus-Ford
1973	Stewart,Jackie	Tyrrell-Ford
1974	Fittipaldi,E.	McLaren-Ford
1975	Lauda	Ferrari
1976	Lauda	Ferrari
1977	Nilsson	Lotus-Ford
1978	Andretti,Mario	Lotus-Ford
1979	Scheckter,J.	Ferrari
1980	Pironi	Ligier-Ford
1981	Reutemann	Williams-Ford

1982	Watson	McLaren-Ford
1983	Prost	Renault
1984	Alboreto	Ferrari
1985	Senna	Lotus-Renault
1986	Mansell	Williams-Honda
1987	Prost	McLaren-TAG
1988	Senna	McLaren-Honda
1989	Senna	McLaren-Honda
1990	Senna	McLaren-Honda
1991	Senna	McLaren-Honda
1992	Schumacher,M.	Benetton-Ford
1993	Hill,D.	Williams-Renault
1994	Hill,D.	Williams-Renault
1995	Schumacher,M.	Benetton-Renault
1996	Schumacher,M.	Ferrari
1997	Schumacher,M.	Ferrari
1998	Hill,D.	Jordan-Mugen Honda
1999	Coulthard	McLaren-Mercedes

BRAZILIAN

1973	Fittipaldi,E.	Lotus-Ford
1974	Fittipaldi,E.	McLaren-Ford
1975	Pace	Brabham-Ford
1976	Lauda	Ferrari
1977	Reutemann	Ferrari
1978	Reutemann	Ferrari
1979	Laffite	Ligier-Ford
1980	Arnoux	Renault
1981	Reutemann	Williams-Ford
1982	Prost	Renault
1983	Piquet	Brabham-BMW
1984	Prost	McLaren-TAG
1985	Prost	McLaren-TAG
1986	Piquet	Williams-Honda
1987	Prost	McLaren-TAG
1988	Prost	McLaren-Honda
1989	Mansell	Ferrari
1990	Prost	Ferrari
1991	Senna	McLaren-Honda
1992	Mansell	Williams-Renault
1993	Senna	McLaren-Ford
1994	Schumacher,M.	Benetton-Ford
1995	Schumacher,M.	Benetton-Renault
1996	Hill,D.	Williams-Renault
1997	Villeneuve,J.	Williams-Renault
1998	Hakkinen	McLaren-Mercedes
1999	Hakkinen	McLaren-Mercedes

BRITISH

1950	Farina	Alfa Romeo
1951	Gonzalez,J.	Ferrari
1952	Ascari	Ferrari
1953	Ascari	Ferrari
1954	Gonzalez,J.	Ferrari
1955	Moss	Mercedes
1956	Fangio	Lancia-Ferrari
1957	Brooks	Vanwall
1958	Collins	Ferrari
1959	Brabham,J.	Cooper-Climax
1960	Brabham,J.	Cooper-Climax
1961	von Trips	Ferrari
1962	Clark	Lotus-Climax
1963	Clark	Lotus-Climax
1964	Clark	Lotus-Climax
1965	Clark	Lotus-Climax
1966	Brabham,J.	Brabham-Repco
1967	Clark	Lotus-Ford
1968	Siffert	Lotus-Ford
1969	Stewart,Jackie	Matra-Ford
1970	Rindt	Lotus-Ford
1971	Stewart,Jackie	Tyrrell-Ford
1972	Fittipaldi,E.	Lotus-Ford
1973	Revson	McLaren-Ford
1974	Scheckter,J.	Tyrrell-Ford
1975	Fittipaldi,E.	McLaren-Ford
1976	Lauda	Ferrari
1977	Hunt	McLaren-Ford
1978	Reutemann	Ferrari
1979	Regazzoni	Williams-Ford
1980	Jones	Williams-Ford
1981	Watson	McLaren-Ford
1982	Lauda	McLaren-Ford
1983	Prost	Renault
1984	Lauda	McLaren-TAG
1985	Prost	McLaren-TAG
1986	Mansell	Williams-Honda
1987	Mansell	Williams-Honda
1988	Senna	McLaren-Honda
1989	Prost	McLaren-Honda
1990	Prost	Ferrari
1991	Mansell	Williams-Renault
1992	Mansell	Williams-Renault
1993	Prost	Williams-Renault
1994	Hill,D.	Williams-Renault

1995	Herbert	Benetton-Renault
1996	Villeneuve,J.	Williams-Renault
1997	Villeneuve,J.	Williams-Renault
1998	Schumacher,M.	Ferrari
1999	Coulthard	McLaren-Mercedes

CAESAR'S PALACE

1981	Jones	Williams-Ford
1982	Alboreto	Tyrrell-Ford

CANADIAN

1967	Brabham,J.	Brabham-Repco
1968	Hulme	McLaren-Ford
1969	Ickx	Brabham-Ford
1970	Ickx	Ferrari
1971	Stewart,Jackie	Tyrrell-Ford
1972	Stewart,Jackie	Tyrrell-Ford
1973	Revson	McLaren-Ford
1974	Fittipaldi,E.	McLaren-Ford
1976	Hunt	McLaren-Ford
1977	Scheckter,J.	Wolf-Ford
1978	Villeneuve,G.	Ferrari
1979	Jones	Williams-Ford
1980	Jones	Williams-Ford
1981	Laffite	Ligier-Matra
1982	Piquet	Brabham-BMW
1983	Arnoux	Ferrari
1984	Piquet	Brabham-BMW
1985	Alboreto	Ferrari
1986	Mansell	Williams-Honda
1988	Senna	McLaren-Honda
1989	Boutsen	Williams-Renault
1990	Senna	McLaren-Honda
1991	Piquet	Benetton-Ford
1992	Berger,G.	McLaren-Honda
1993	Prost	Williams-Renault
1994	Schumacher,M.	Benetton-Ford
1995	Alesi	Ferrari
1996	Hill,D.	Williams-Renault
1997	Schumacher,M.	Ferrari
1998	Schumacher,M.	Ferrari
1999	Hakkinen	McLaren-Mercedes

DALLAS

1984	Rosberg	Williams-Honda

DETROIT

1984	Piquet	Brabham-BMW

DUTCH

1952	Ascari	Ferrari
1953	Ascari	Ferrari
1955	Fangio	Mercedes
1958	Moss	Vanwall
1959	Bonnier	BRM
1960	Brabham,J.	Cooper-Climax
1961	von Trips	Ferrari
1962	Hill,G.	BRM
1963	Clark	Lotus-Climax
1964	Clark	Lotus-Climax
1965	Clark	Lotus-Climax
1966	Brabham,J.	Brabham-Repco
1967	Clark	Lotus-Ford
1968	Stewart,Jackie	Matra-Ford
1969	Stewart,Jackie	Matra-Ford
1970	Rindt	Lotus-Ford
1971	Ickx	Ferrari
1973	Stewart,Jackie	Tyrrell-Ford
1974	Lauda	Ferrari
1975	Hunt	Hesketh-Ford
1976	Hunt	McLaren-Ford
1977	Lauda	Ferrari
1978	Andretti,Mario	Lotus-Ford
1979	Jones	Williams-Ford
1980	Piquet	Brabham-Ford
1981	Prost	Renault
1982	Pironi	Ferrari
1983	Arnoux	Ferrari
1984	Prost	McLaren-TAG
1985	Lauda	McLaren-TAG

EUROPEAN

1983	Piquet	Brabham-BMW
1984	Prost	McLaren-TAG
1985	Mansell	Williams-Honda
1993	Senna	McLaren-Ford
1994	Schumacher,M.	Benetton-Ford
1995	Schumacher,M.	Benetton-Renault
1996	Villeneuve,J.	Williams-Renault
1997	Hakkinen	McLaren-Mercedes
1999	Herbert	Stewart-Ford

FRENCH

1950	Fangio	Alfa Romeo
1951	Fagioli	Alfa Romeo
1952	Ascari	Ferrari
1953	Hawthorn	Ferrari
1954	Fangio	Mercedes
1956	Collins	Lancia-Ferrari
1957	Fangio	Maserati
1958	Hawthorn	Ferrari
1959	Brooks	Ferrari
1960	Brabham,J.	Cooper-Climax
1961	Baghelti	Ferrari
1962	Gurney	Porsche
1963	Clark	Lotus-Climax
1964	Gurney	Brabham-Climax
1965	Clark	Lotus-Climax
1966	Brabham,J.	Brabham-Repco
1967	Brabham,J.	Brabham-Repco
1968	Ickx	Ferrari
1969	Stewart,Jackie	Matra-Ford
1970	Rindt	Lotus-Ford
1971	Stewart,Jackie	Tyrrell-Ford
1972	Stewart,Jackie	Tyrrell-Ford
1973	Peterson	Lotus-Ford
1974	Peterson	Lotus-Ford
1975	Lauda	Ferrari
1976	Hunt	McLaren-Ford
1977	Andretti,Mario	Lotus-Ford
1978	Andretti,Mario	Lotus-Ford
1979	Jabouille	Renault
1980	Jones	Williams-Ford
1981	Prost	Renault
1982	Arnoux	Renault
1983	Prost	Renault
1984	Lauda	McLaren-TAG
1985	Piquet	Brabham-BMW
1986	Mansell	Williams-Honda
1987	Mansell	Williams-Honda
1988	Prost	McLaren-Honda
1989	Prost	McLaren-Honda
1990	Prost	Ferrari
1991	Mansell	Williams-Renault
1992	Mansell	Williams-Renault
1993	Prost	Williams-Renault
1994	Schumacher,M.	Benetton-Ford
1995	Schumacher,M.	Benetton-Renault
1996	Hill,D.	Williams-Renault
1997	Schumacher,M.	Ferrari
1998	Schumacher,M.	Ferrari
1999	Frentzen	Jordan-Mugen Honda

GERMAN

1951	Ascari	Ferrari
1952	Ascari	Ferrari
1953	Farina	Ferrari
1954	Fangio	Mercedes
1956	Fangio	Lancia-Ferrari
1957	Fangio	Maserati
1958	Brooks	Vanwall
1959	Brooks	Ferrari
1961	Moss	Lotus-Climax
1962	Hill,G.	BRM
1963	Surtees	Ferrari
1964	Surtees	Ferrari
1965	Clark	Lotus-Climax
1966	Brabham,J.	Brabham-Repco
1967	Hulme	Brabham-Repco
1968	Stewart,Jackie	Matra-Ford
1969	Ickx	Brabham-Ford
1970	Rindt	Lotus-Ford
1971	Stewart,Jackie	Tyrrell-Ford
1972	Ickx	Ferrari
1973	Stewart,Jackie	Tyrrell-Ford
1974	Regazzoni	Ferrari
1975	Reutemann	Brabham-Ford
1976	Hunt	McLaren-Ford
1977	Lauda	Ferrari
1978	Andretti,Mario	Lotus-Ford
1979	Jones	Williams-Ford
1980	Laffite	Ligier-Ford
1981	Piquet	Brabham-Ford
1982	Tambay	Ferrari
1983	Arnoux	Ferrari
1984	Prost	McLaren-TAG
1985	Alboreto	Ferrari
1986	Piquet	Williams-Honda
1987	Piquet	Williams-Honda
1988	Senna	McLaren-Honda
1989	Senna	McLaren-Honda
1990	Senna	McLaren-Honda
1991	Mansell	Williams-Renault
1992	Mansell	Williams-Renault

1993	Prost	Williams-Renault
1994	Berger,G.	Ferrari
1995	Schumacher,M.	Benetton-Renault
1996	Hill,D.	Williams-Renault
1997	Berger,G.	Benetton-Renault
1998	Hakkinen	McLaren-Mercedes
1999	Irvine	Ferrari

HUNGARIAN

1986	Piquet	Williams-Honda
1987	Piquet	Williams-Honda
1988	Senna	McLaren-Honda
1989	Mansell	Ferrari
1990	Boutsen	Williams-Renault
1991	Senna	McLaren-Honda
1992	Senna	McLaren-Honda
1993	Hill,D.	Williams-Renault
1994	Schumacher,M.	Benetton-Ford
1995	Hill,D.	Williams-Renault
1996	Villeneuve,J.	Williams-Renault
1997	Villeneuve,J.	Williams-Renault
1998	Schumacher,M.	Ferrari
1999	Hakkinen	McLaren-Mercedes

INDIANAPOLIS 500

1950	Parsons	Kurtis Kraft
1951	Wallard	Kurtis Kraft
1952	Ruttman	Kuzma
1953	Vukovich	Kurtis Kraft
1954	Vukovich	Kurtis Kraft
1955	Sweikert	Kurtis Kraft
1956	Flaherty	Watson
1957	Hanks	Epperly
1958	Bryan	Epperly
1959	Ward	Watson
1960	Rathmann,J.	Watson

ITALIAN

1950	Farina	Alfa Romeo
1951	Ascari	Ferrari
1952	Ascari	Ferrari
1953	Fangio	Maserati
1954	Fangio	Mercedes
1955	Fangio	Mercedes
1956	Moss	Maserati
1957	Moss	Vanwall
1958	Brooks	Vanwall
1959	Moss	Cooper-Climax
1960	Hill,P.	Ferrari
1961	Hill,P.	Ferrari
1962	Hill,G.	BRM
1963	Clark	Lotus-Climax
1964	Surtees	Ferrari
1965	Stewart,Jackie	BRM
1966	Scarfiotti	Ferrari
1967	Surtees	Honda
1968	Hulme	McLaren-Ford
1969	Stewart,Jackie	Matra-Ford
1970	Regazzoni	Ferrari
1971	Gethin	BRM
1972	Fittipaldi,E.	Lotus-Ford
1973	Peterson	Lotus-Ford
1974	Peterson	Lotus-Ford
1975	Regazzoni	Ferrari
1976	Peterson	March-Ford
1977	Andretti,Mario	Lotus-Ford
1978	Lauda	Brabham-Alfa
1979	Scheckter,J.	Ferrari
1980	Piquet	Brabham-Ford
1981	Prost	Renault
1982	Arnoux	Renault
1983	Piquet	Brabham-BMW
1984	Lauda	McLaren-TAG
1985	Prost	McLaren-TAG
1986	Piquet	Williams-Honda
1987	Piquet	Williams-Honda
1988	Berger,G.	Ferrari
1989	Prost	McLaren-Honda
1990	Senna	McLaren-Honda
1991	Mansell	Williams-Renault
1992	Senna	McLaren-Honda
1993	Hill,D.	Williams-Renault
1994	Hill,D.	Williams-Renault
1995	Herbert	Benetton-Renault
1996	Schumacher,M.	Ferrari
1997	Coulthard	McLaren-Mercedes
1998	Schumacher,M.	Ferrari
1999	Frentzen	Jordan-Mugen Honda

JAPANESE

1976	Andretti,Mario	Lotus-Ford
1977	Hunt	McLaren-Ford

1987	Berger,G.	Ferrari
1988	Senna	McLaren-Honda
1989	Nannini	Benetton-Ford
1990	Piquet	Benetton-Ford
1991	Berger,G.	McLaren-Honda
1992	Patrese	Williams-Renault
1993	Senna	McLaren-Ford
1994	Hill,D.	Williams-Renault
1995	Schumacher,M.	Benetton-Renault
1996	Hill,D.	Williams-Renault
1997	Schumacher,M.	Ferrari
1998	Hakkinen	McLaren-Mercedes
1999	Hakkinen	McLaren-Mercedes

LUXEMBOURG

1997	Villeneuve,J.	Williams-Renault
1998	Hakkinen	McLaren-Mercedes

MALAYSIAN

1999	Irvine	Ferrari

MEXICAN

1963	Clark	Lotus-Climax
1964	Gurney	Brabham-Climax
1965	Ginther	Honda
1966	Surtees	Cooper-Maserati
1967	Clark	Lotus-Ford
1968	Hill,G.	Lotus-Ford
1969	Hulme	McLaren-Ford
1970	Ickx	Ferrari
1986	Berger,G.	Benetton-BMW
1987	Mansell	Williams-Honda
1988	Prost	McLaren-Honda
1989	Senna	McLaren-Honda
1990	Prost	Ferrari
1991	Patrese	Williams-Renault
1992	Mansell	Williams-Renault

MONACO

1950	Fangio	Alfa Romeo
1955	Trintignant	Ferrari
1956	Moss	Maserati
1957	Fangio	Maserati
1958	Trintignant	Cooper-Climax
1959	Brabham,J.	Cooper-Climax
1960	Moss	Lotus-Climax
1961	Moss	Lotus-Climax
1962	McLaren	Cooper-Climax
1963	Hill,G.	BRM
1964	Hill,G.	BRM
1965	Hill,G.	BRM
1966	Stewart,Jackie	BRM
1967	Hulme	Brabham-Repco
1968	Hill,G.	Lotus-Ford
1969	Hill,G.	Lotus-Ford
1970	Rindt	Lotus-Ford
1971	Stewart,Jackie	Tyrrell-Ford
1972	Beltoise	BRM
1973	Stewart,Jackie	Tyrrell-Ford
1974	Peterson	Lotus-Ford
1975	Lauda	Ferrari
1976	Lauda	Ferrari
1977	Scheckter,J.	Wolf-Ford
1978	Depailler	Tyrrell-Ford
1979	Scheckter,J.	Ferrari
1980	Reutemann	Williams-Ford
1981	Villeneuve,G.	Ferrari
1982	Patrese	Brabham-Ford
1983	Rosberg	Williams-Ford
1984	Prost	McLaren-TAG
1985	Prost	McLaren-TAG
1986	Prost	McLaren-TAG
1987	Senna	Lotus-Honda
1988	Prost	McLaren-Honda
1989	Senna	McLaren-Honda
1990	Senna	McLaren-Honda
1991	Senna	McLaren-Honda
1992	Senna	McLaren-Honda
1993	Senna	McLaren-Ford
1994	Schumacher,M.	Benetton-Ford
1995	Schumacher,M.	Benetton-Renault
1996	Panis	Ligier-Mugen Honda
1997	Schumacher,M.	Ferrari
1998	Hakkinen	McLaren-Mercedes
1999	Schumacher,M.	Ferrari

MOROCCAN

1958	Moss	Vanwall

PACIFIC

1994	Schumacher,M.	Benetton-Ford
1995	Schumacher,M.	Benetton-Renault

PESCARA

1957	Moss	Vanwall

PORTUGUESE

1958	Moss	Vanwall
1959	Moss	Cooper-Climax
1960	Brabham,J.	Cooper-Climax
1984	Prost	McLaren-TAG
1985	Senna	Lotus-Renault
1986	Mansell	Williams-Honda
1987	Prost	McLaren-TAG
1988	Prost	McLaren-Honda
1989	Berger,G.	Ferrari
1990	Mansell	Ferrari
1991	Patrese	Williams-Renault
1992	Mansell	Williams-Renault
1993	Schumacher,M.	Benetton-Ford
1994	Hill,D.	Williams-Renault
1995	Coulthard	Williams-Renault
1996	Villeneuve,J.	Williams-Renault

SAN MARINO

1981	Piquet	Brabham-Ford
1982	Pironi	Ferrari
1983	Tambay	Ferrari
1984	Prost	McLaren-TAG
1985	de Angelis	Lotus-Renault
1986	Prost	McLaren-TAG
1987	Mansell	Williams-Honda
1988	Senna	McLaren-Honda
1989	Senna	McLaren-Honda
1990	Patrese	Williams-Renault
1991	Senna	McLaren-Honda
1992	Mansell	Williams-Renault
1993	Prost	Williams-Renault
1994	Schumacher,M.	Benetton-Ford
1995	Hill,D.	Williams-Renault
1996	Hill,D.	Williams-Renault
1997	Frentzen	Williams-Renault
1998	Coulthard	McLaren-Mercedes
1999	Schumacher,M.	Ferrari

SOUTH AFRICAN

1962	Hill,G.	BRM
1963	Clark	Lotus-Climax
1965	Clark	Lotus-Climax
1967	Rodriguez,P.	Cooper-Maserati
1968	Clark	Lotus-Ford
1969	Stewart,Jackie	Matra-Ford
1970	Brabham,J.	Brabham-Ford
1971	Andretti,Mario	Ferrari
1972	Hulme	McLaren-Ford
1973	Stewart,Jackie	Tyrrell-Ford
1974	Reutemann	Brabham-Ford
1975	Scheckter,J.	Tyrrell-Ford
1976	Lauda	Ferrari
1977	Lauda	Ferrari
1978	Peterson	Lotus-Ford
1979	Villeneuve,G.	Ferrari
1980	Arnoux	Renault
1982	Prost	Renault
1983	Patrese	Brabham-BMW
1984	Lauda	McLaren-TAG
1985	Mansell	Williams-Honda
1992	Mansell	Williams-Renault
1993	Prost	Williams-Renault

SPANISH

1951	Fangio	Alfa Romeo
1954	Hawthorn	Ferrari
1968	Hill,G.	Lotus-Ford
1969	Stewart,Jackie	Matra-Ford
1970	Stewart,Jackie	March-Ford
1971	Stewart,Jackie	Tyrrell-Ford
1972	Fittipaldi,E.	Lotus-Ford
1973	Fittipaldi,E.	Lotus-Ford
1974	Lauda	Ferrari
1975	Mass	McLaren-Ford
1976	Hunt	McLaren-Ford
1977	Andretti,Mario	Lotus-Ford
1978	Andretti,Mario	Lotus-Ford
1979	Depailler	Ligier-Ford
1981	Villeneuve,G.	Ferrari
1986	Senna	Lotus-Renault
1987	Mansell	Williams-Honda
1988	Prost	McLaren-Honda
1989	Senna	McLaren-Honda
1990	Prost	Ferrari
1991	Mansell	Williams-Renault
1992	Mansell	Williams-Renault
1993	Prost	Williams-Renault
1994	Hill,D.	Williams-Renault

1995	Schumacher,M.	Benetton-Renault
1996	Schumacher,M.	Ferrari
1997	Villeneuve,J.	Williams-Renault
1998	Hakkinen	McLaren-Mercedes
1999	Hakkinen	McLaren-Mercedes

SWEDISH

1973	Hulme	McLaren-Ford
1974	Scheckter,J.	Tyrrell-Ford
1975	Lauda	Ferrari
1976	Scheckter,J.	Tyrrell-Ford
1977	Laffite	Ligier-Matra
1978	Lauda	Brabham-Alfa

SWISS

1950	Farina	Alfa Romeo
1951	Fangio	Alfa Romeo
1952	Taruffi	Ferrari
1953	Ascari	Ferrari
1954	Fangio	Mercedes
1982	Rosberg	Williams-Ford

UNITED STATES

1959	McLaren	Cooper-Climax
1960	Moss	Lotus-Climax
1961	Ireland	Lotus-Climax
1962	Clark	Lotus-Climax
1963	Hill,G.	BRM
1964	Hill,G.	BRM
1965	Hill,G.	BRM
1966	Clark	Lotus-BRM
1967	Clark	Lotus-Ford
1968	Stewart,Jackie	Matra-Ford
1969	Rindt	Lotus-Ford
1970	Fittipaldi,E.	Lotus-Ford
1971	Cevert	Tyrrell-Ford
1972	Stewart,Jackie	Tyrrell-Ford
1973	Peterson	Lotus-Ford
1974	Reutemann	Brabham-Ford
1975	Lauda	Ferrari
1981	Jones	Williams-Ford
1982	Watson	McLaren-Ford
1983	Alboreto	Tyrrell-Ford
1985	Rosberg	Williams-Honda
1986	Senna	Lotus-Renault
1987	Senna	Lotus-Honda
1988	Senna	McLaren-Honda
1989	Prost	McLaren-Honda
1990	Senna	McLaren-Honda
1991	Senna	McLaren-Honda

UNITED STATES EAST

1976	Hunt	McLaren-Ford
1977	Hunt	McLaren-Ford
1978	Reutemann	Ferrari
1979	Villeneuve,G.	Ferrari
1980	Jones	Williams-Ford

UNITED STATES WEST

1976	Regazzoni	Ferrari
1977	Andretti,Mario	Lotus-Ford
1978	Reutemann	Ferrari
1979	Villeneuve,G.	Ferrari
1980	Piquet	Brabham-Ford
1981	Jones	Williams-Ford
1982	Lauda	McLaren-Ford
1983	Watson	McLaren-Ford

GRANDS PRIX – MOST WINS BY DRIVERS

ARGENTINE

Fangio	3	1954, 1955, 1957
Fittipaldi,E.	2	1973, 1975
Hill,D.	2	1995, 1996

AUSTRALIAN

Berger,Gerhard	2	1987, 1992
Hill,D.	2	1995, 1996
Prost	2	1986, 1988
Senna	2	1991, 1993

AUSTRIAN

Prost	3	1983, 1985, 1986
Jones	2	1977, 1979
Peterson	2	1973, 1978

BELGIAN

Senna	5	1985, 1988, 1989, 1990, 1991
Clark	4	1962, 1963, 1964, 1965
Schumacher,M.	4	1992, 1995, 1996, 1997
Fangio	3	1950, 1954, 1955
Hill,D.	3	1993, 1994, 1998

BRAZILIAN

Prost	6	1982, 1984, 1985, 1987, 1988, 1990
Reutemann	3	1977, 1978, 1981
Fittipaldi,E.	2	1973, 1974
Hakkinen	2	1998, 1999
Mansell	2	1989, 1992
Piquet	2	1983, 1986
Schumacher,M.	2	1994, 1995
Senna	2	1991, 1993

BRITISH

Clark	5	1962, 1963, 1964, 1965, 1967
Prost	5	1983, 1985, 1989, 1990, 1993
Mansell	4	1986, 1987, 1991, 1992
Lauda	3	1976, 1982, 1984
Brabham,J.	3	1959, 1960, 1966

CAESAR'S PALACE

Alboreto	1	1982
Jones	1	1981

CANADIAN

Piquet	3	1982, 1984, 1991
Schumacher,M.	3	1994, 1997, 1998
Ickx	2	1969, 1970
Jones	2	1979, 1980
Senna	2	1988, 1990
Stewart,Jackie	2	1971, 1972

DALLAS

Rosberg	1	1984

DETROIT

Piquet	1	1984

DUTCH

Clark	4	1963, 1964, 1965, 1967
Lauda	3	1974, 1977, 1985
Stewart,Jackie	3	1968, 1969, 1973

EUROPEAN

Schumacher,M.	2	1994, 1995

FRENCH

Prost	6	1981, 1983, 1988, 1989, 1990, 1993
Mansell	4	1986, 1987, 1991, 1992
Schumacher,M.	4	1994, 1995, 1997, 1998
Brabham,J.	3	1960, 1966, 1967
Fangio	3	1950, 1954, 1957
Stewart,Jackie	3	1969, 1971, 1972

GERMAN

Fangio	3	1954, 1956, 1957
Piquet	3	1981, 1986, 1987
Senna	3	1988, 1989, 1990
Stewart,Jackie	3	1968, 1971, 1973

HUNGARIAN

Senna	3	1988, 1991, 1992
Hill,D.	2	1993, 1995
Piquet	2	1986, 1987
Schumacher,M.	2	1994, 1998
Villeneuve,J.	2	1996, 1997

INDIANAPOLIS 500

Vukovich	2	1953, 1954

ITALIAN

Piquet	4	1980, 1983, 1986, 1987
Fangio	3	1953, 1954, 1955
Moss	3	1956, 1957, 1959
Peterson	3	1973, 1974, 1976
Prost	3	1981, 1985, 1989

JAPANESE

Berger,Gerhard	2	1987, 1991
Hakkinen	2	1998, 1999
Hill,D.	2	1994, 1996
Schumacher,M.	2	1995, 1997
Senna	2	1988, 1993

LUXEMBOURG

Hakkinen	1	1998
Villeneuve,J.	1	1997

MALAYSIAN

Irvine	1	1999

MEXICAN

Clark	2	1963, 1967
Mansell	2	1987, 1992
Prost	2	1988, 1990

MONACO

Senna	6	1987, 1989, 1990, 1991, 1992, 1993
Hill,G.	5	1963, 1964, 1965, 1968, 1969
Prost	4	1984, 1985, 1986, 1988
Schumacher,M.	4	1994, 1995, 1997, 1999
Moss	3	1956, 1960, 1961
Stewart,Jackie	3	1966, 1971, 1973

MOROCCAN

Moss	1	1958

PACIFIC

Schumacher,M.	2	1994, 1995

PESCARA

Moss	1	1957

PORTUGUESE

Mansell	3	1986, 1990, 1992
Prost	3	1984, 1987, 1988

SAN MARINO

Prost	3	1984, 1986, 1993
Senna	3	1988, 1989, 1991
Hill,D.	2	1995, 1996
Mansell	2	1987, 1992
Schumacher,M.	2	1994, 1999

SOUTH AFRICAN

Clark	3	1963, 1965, 1968
Lauda	3	1976, 1977, 1984
Mansell	2	1985, 1992
Prost	2	1982, 1993
Stewart,Jackie	2	1969, 1973

SPANISH

Mansell	3	1987, 1991, 1992
Prost	3	1988, 1990, 1993
Stewart,Jackie	3	1969, 1970, 1971
Andretti,Mario	2	1977, 1978
Fittipaldi,E.	2	1972, 1973
Hakkinen	2	1998, 1999
Schumacher,M.	2	1995, 1996
Senna	2	1986, 1989

SWEDISH

Lauda	2	1975, 1978
Scheckter,J.	2	1974. 1976
Hulme	1	1973
Laffite	1	1977

SWISS

Fangio	2	1951, 1954

US

Senna	5	1986, 1987, 1988, 1990, 1991
Clark	3	1962, 1966, 1967
Hill,G.	3	1963, 1964, 1965

US EAST

Hunt	2	1976, 1977

US WEST

Numerous drivers with one win.

A1-RING

Hakkinen	1	1998
Irvine	1	1999
Villeneuve,J.	1	1997

ADELAIDE

Berger,Gerhard	2	1987, 1992
Prost	2	1986, 1988
Senna	2	1991, 1993

AIDA

Schumacher,M.	2	1994, 1995

AINTREE

Brabham,J.	1	1959
Brooks/Moss	1	1957
Clark	1	1962
Moss	1	1955
von Trips	1	1961

ANDERSTORP

Lauda	2	1975, 1978
Scheckter,J.	2	1974, 1976

BARCELONA

Hakkinen	2	1998, 1999
Mansell	2	1991, 1992
Schumacher,M.	2	1995, 1996

BERLIN

Brooks	1	1959

BRANDS HATCH

Lauda	3	1976, 1982, 1984
Mansell	2	1985, 1986

BREMGARTEN

Fangio	2	1951, 1954

BUENOS AIRES

Fangio	3	1954, 1955, 1957
Fittipaldi,E.	2	1973, 1975
Hill,D.	2	1995, 1996

CASABLANCA

Moss	1	1958

CLERMONT-FERRAND

Stewart,Jackie	2	1969, 1972

DALLAS

Rosberg	1	1984

DETROIT

Senna	3	1986, 1987, 1988

DIJON

Andretti,Mario	1	1977
Jabouille	1	1979
Lauda	1	1984
Peterson	1	1974
Prost	1	1981
Rosberg	1	1982

DONINGTON PARK

Senna	1	1993

EAST LONDON

Clark	2	1963, 1965

ESTORIL

Mansell	3	1986, 1990, 1992
Prost	3	1984, 1987, 1988

FUJI

Andretti,Mario	1	1976
Hunt	1	1977

HOCKENHEIM

Piquet	3	1981, 1986, 1987
Senna	3	1988, 1989, 1990

HUNGARORING

Senna	3	1988, 1991, 1992

IMOLA

Prost	3	1984, 1986, 1993
Senna	3	1988, 1989, 1991

INDIANAPOLIS

Vukovich	2	1953, 1954

INTERLAGOS

Fittipaldi,E.	2	1973, 1974
Hakkinen	2	1998, 1999
Schumacher,M.	2	1994, 1995
Senna	2	1991, 1993

JARAMA

Andretti,Mario	2	1977, 1978

JEREZ

Prost	2	1988, 1990
Senna	2	1986, 1989

KYALAMI

Lauda	3	1976, 1977, 1984
Mansell	2	1985, 1992
Prost	2	1982, 1993
Stewart,Jackie	2	1969, 1973

LAS VEGAS

Alboreto	1	1982
Jones	1	1981

LE MANS

Brabham,J.	1	1967

LONG BEACH

Andretti,Mario	1	1977
Jones	1	1981
Lauda	1	1982
Piquet	1	1980
Regazzoni	1	1976
Reutemann	1	1978
Villeneuve,G.	1	1979
Watson	1	1983

MAGNY-COURS

Schumacher,M.	4	1994, 1995, 1997, 1998
Mansell	2	1991, 1992

MELBOURNE

Coulthard	1	1997
Hakkinen	1	1998
Hill,D.	1	1996
Irvine	1	1999

MEXICO CITY

Clark	2	1963, 1967
Mansell	2	1987, 1992
Prost	2	1988, 1990

MONSANTO

Moss	1	1959

MONTE CARLO

Senna	6	1987, 1989, 1990, 1991, 1992, 1993
Hill,G.	5	1963, 1964, 1965, 1968, 1969
Prost	4	1984, 1985, 1986, 1988
Schumacher,M.	4	1994, 1995, 1997, 1999

MONTJUICH PARK

Stewart,Jackie	2	1969, 1971

MONTREAL

Piquet	3	1982, 1984, 1991
Schumacher,M.	3	1994, 1997, 1998

MONZA

Fangio	3	1953, 1954, 1955
Moss	3	1956, 1957, 1959
Peterson	3	1973, 1974, 1976
Piquet	3	1983, 1986, 1987
Prost	3	1981, 1985, 1989

MOSPORT PARK

Stewart,Jackie	2	1971, 1972

NIVELLES

Fittipaldi,E.	2	1972, 1974

NURBURGRING

Fangio	3	1954, 1956, 1957
Stewart,Jackie	3	1968, 1971, 1973

OPORTO

Brabham,J.	1	1960
Moss	1	1958

OSTERREICHRING

Prost	3	1983, 1985, 1986
Jones	2	1977, 1979
Peterson	2	1973, 1978

PAUL RICARD

Prost	4	1983, 1988, 1989, 1990
Mansell	2	1986, 1987

PEDRABLES

Fangio	1	1951
Hawthorn	1	1954

PESCARA

Moss	1	1957

PHOENIX

Senna	2	1990, 1991

REIMS

Brabham,J.	2	1960, 1966
Fangio	2	1950, 1954
Hawthorn	2	1953, 1958

RIO DE JANEIRO

Prost	5	1982, 1984, 1985, 1987, 1988
Piquet	2	1983, 1986
Reutemann	2	1978, 1981

RIVERSIDE

Moss	1	1960

ROUEN

Gurney	2	1962, 1964

SEBRING

McLaren	1	1959

SEPANG

Irvine	1	1999

SILVERSTONE

Prost	5	1983, 1985, 1989, 1990, 1993
Clark	3	1963, 1965, 1967
Mansell	3	1987, 1991, 1992
Ascari	2	1952, 1953
Gonzalez,J.	2	1951, 1954
Stewart,Jackie	2	1969, 1971
Villeneuve,J.	2	1996, 1997

SPA-FRANCORCHAMPS

Senna	5	1985, 1988, 1989, 1990, 1991
Clark	4	1962, 1963, 1964, 1965
Schumacher,M.	4	1992, 1995, 1996, 1997
Fangio	3	1950, 1954, 1955
Hill,D.	3	1993, 1994, 1998

ST JOVITE

Hulme	1	1968
Ickx	1	1970

SUZUKA

Berger,Gerhard	2	1987, 1991
Hakkinen	2	1998, 1999
Hill,D.	2	1994, 1996
Schumacher,M.	2	1995, 1997
Senna	2	1988, 1993

WATKINS GLEN

Clark	3	1962, 1966, 1967
Hill,G.	3	1963, 1964, 1965
Hunt	2	1976, 1977
Reutemann	2	1974, 1978
Stewart,Jackie	2	1968, 1972

ZANDVOORT

Clark	4	1963, 1964, 1965, 1967
Lauda	3	1974, 1977, 1985
Stewart,Jackie	3	1968, 1969, 1973
Ascari	2	1952, 1953
Brabham,J.	2	1960, 1966
Hunt	2	1975, 1976
Prost	2	1981, 1984

ZELTWEG

Bandini	1	1964

ZOLDER

Lauda	2	1975, 1976

WORLD CHAMPIONSHIP LAST RACE DECIDERS

Year	GP	Circuit	Drivers
1950	Italian	Monza	Farina (30), Fangio (27), Fagioli (24)
1951	Spanish	Pedralbes	Fangio (31), Ascari (25)
1956	Italian	Monza	Fangio (30), Collins (25)*
1958	Moroccan	Casablanca	Hawthorn (42), Moss (41)
1959	USA	Sebring	Brabham (31), Brooks (27), Moss (25.5)
1962	S. African	E. London	G. Hill (42), Clark (30)
1964	Mexican	Mexico	Surtees (40), G. Hill (39), Clark (32)
1967	Mexican	Mexico	Hulme (51), Brabham (46)
1968	Mexican	Mexico	G. Hill (48), Stewart (36), Hulme (33)
1974	US	Watkins G.	E. Fittipaldi (55), Regazzoni (52), Scheckter (45)
1976	Japanese	Mount Fuji	Hunt (69), Lauda (68)
1981	C.Palace	Las Vegas	Piquet (50), Reutemann (49), Laffite (46)
1982	C.Palace	Las Vegas	Rosberg (44), Watson (39)†
1983	S. African	Kyalami	Piquet (59), Prost (57), Arnoux (49)
1984	Portugal	Estoril	Lauda (72), Prost (71.5)
1986	Australian	Adelaide	Prost (72), Mansell (70), Piquet (69)
1994	Australian	Adelaide	M. Schumacher (92), D. Hill (91)
1996	Japanese	Suzuka	D. Hill (97), J. Villeneuve (78)
1997	European	Jerez	J. Villeneuve (81), M. Schumacher (78)
1998	Japanese	Suzuka	Hakkinen (100), M. Schumacher (86)
1999	Japanese	Suzuka	M.Hakkinen (76), Irvine (74)

* Finished third in championship after Moss † Finished joint second with Pironi. Numbers in brackets are final points total.

GRANDS PRIX WITH DRIVER FATALITIES

Year	GP	Driver	Car	During
1954	German	O. Marimon	Maserati	P
1955	Indianapolis	B. Vukovich	Kurtis Kraft	R
1958	French	L. Musso	Ferrari	R
1958	German	P. Collins	Ferrari	R
1958	Moroccan	S. Lewis-Evans	Vanwall	R
1959	Indianapolis	J. Unser	Kurtis Kraft	R
		B. Cortner		R
1960	Belgian	C. Bristow	Cooper	R
		A. Stacey	Lotus	R
1961	Italian	Von Trips	Ferrari	R
1964	German	C. de Beaufort	Porsche	P
1966	German	J. Taylor	Brabham	R
1967	Monaco	L. Bandini	Ferrari	†R
1968	Frrench	J. Schlesser	Honda	R
1969	German	G. Mitter	BMW	P
1970	Dutch	P. Courage	De Tomaso	R
1970	Italian	J. Rindt	Lotus	P
1973	Dutch	R. Williamson	March	R
1973	US	F. Cevert	Tyrrell	P
1974	US	H. Koinigg	Surtees	R
1975	Austrian	M. Donohue	M-Penske	P
1977	South African	T. Pryce	Shadow	R
1978	Italian	R. Peterson	Lotus	*R
1982	Belgian	G. Villeneuve	Ferrari	P
1982	Canadian	R. Paletti	Osella Ford	R
1994	San Marino	R. Ratzenberger	Simtek	P
		A. Senna	Williams	R

P=Practice, R=Race

† Died three days after race from burns.

* Died the next day from injuries received during start of race.

DRIVERS – GENERAL RECORDS

DRIVERS BY NUMBER OF GRANDS PRIX STARTED

Driver	Starts	1st	2nd	3rd	Pole	FL
Patrese	256	6	17	14	8	13
Berger,G.	210	10	17	21	12	21
de Cesaris	208	–	2	3	1	1
Piquet	204	23	20	17	24	23
Prost	199	51	35	20	33	41
Alboreto	194	5	9	9	2	5
Mansell	187	31	17	11	32	30
Hill,G.	176	14	15	7	13	10
Laffite	176	6	10	16	7	6
Lauda	171	25	20	9	24	24
Alesi	167	1	16	15	2	4
Boutsen	163	3	2	10	1	1
Senna	161	41	23	16	65	19
Brundle	158	–	2	7	–	–
Watson	152	5	6	9	2	5
Arnoux	149	7	9	6	18	12
Reutemann	146	12	13	20	6	6
Warwick	146	–	2	2	–	2
Fittipaldi,E.	144	14	13	8	6	6
Herbert	143	3	1	3	–	–
Jarier	134	–	–	3	3	3
Cheever	132	–	2	7	–	–
Regazzoni	132	5	13	10	5	15
Andretti,Mario	128	12	2	5	18	10
Hakkinen	128	14	7	16	21	13
Brabham,J.	126	14	10	7	13	12
Schumacher,M.	126	35	22	14	23	39
Peterson	123	10	10	6	14	9
Martini	118	–	–	–	–	–
Ickx	116	8	7	10	13	14
Jones	116	12	7	5	6	13
Hill,D.	115	22	15	5	20	19
Rosberg	114	5	8	4	5	3
Tambay	114	2	4	5	5	2
Barrichello	112	–	2	4	2	–
Hulme	112	8	9	16	1	9
Scheckter,J.	112	10	14	9	3	5
Surtees	111	6	10	8	8	11
Alliot	109	–	–	–	–	–
de Angelis	108	2	2	5	3	–
Mass	105	1	1	6	–	2
Bonnier †	104	1	–	–	1	–
McLaren	100	4	11	12	–	3

† Including one shared drive

FL-Fastest Lap

DRIVERS BY NUMBER OF RACES WON

Driver	1st	Starts	2nd	3rd	Poles	FL
Prost	51	199	35	20	33	41
Senna	41	161	23	16	65	19
Schumacher,M.	35	126	22	14	23	39
Mansell	31	187	17	11	32	30
Stewart,Jackie	27	99	11	5	17	15
Clark	25	72	1	6	33	28
Lauda	25	171	20	9	24	24
Fangio †	24	51	8	1	29	23
Piquet	23	204	20	17	24	23
Hill,D.	22	115	15	5	20	19
Moss †	16	66	5	1	16	19
Brabham,J.	14	126	10	7	13	12
Fittipaldi,E.	14	144	13	8	6	6
Hakkinen	14	128	7	16	21	13
Hill,G.	14	176	15	7	13	10
Ascari †	13	32	4	–	14	12
Andretti,Mario	12	128	2	5	18	10
Jones	12	116	7	5	6	13
Reutemann	12	146	13	20	6	6
Villeneuve,J.	11	65	5	5	13	9
Berger,G.	10	210	17	21	12	21
Hunt	10	92	6	7	14	8
Peterson	10	123	10	6	14	9
Scheckter,J.	10	112	14	9	3	5
Hulme	8	112	9	16	1	9
Ickx	8	116	7	10	13	14
Arnoux	7	149	9	6	18	12
Brooks	6	38	2	2	3	3
Coulthard	6	90	18	6	8	11
Laffite	6	176	10	16	7	6
Patrese	6	256	17	14	8	13
Rindt	6	60	3	4	10	3
Surtees	6	111	10	8	8	11
Villeneuve,G.	6	67	5	2	2	8
Alboreto	5	194	9	9	2	5
Farina	5	33	8	5	5	5
Regazzoni	5	132	13	10	5	15
Rosberg	5	114	8	4	5	3
Watson	5	152	6	9	2	5

† Including shared drives/wins. Five wins minimum to be included.

DRIVERS TO HAVE WON THEIR FIRST GRAND PRIX

Drivers	Year	Grand Prix	Car	Grid
Baghelti	1961	French	Ferrari	12
Farina †	1950	British	Alfa Romeo	1
Parsons	1950	Indianapolis	Kurtis Kraft	5

† Farina also took pole and fastest lap – the only driver to do so in his first Grand Prix start!

DRIVERS TO HAVE COME SECOND IN THEIR FIRST GRAND PRIX

Drivers	Year	Grand Prix	Car	Grid
Amick,G.	1958	Indianapolis 500	Epperly	25
Ascari	1950	Monaco	Ferrari	7
Fagioli	1950	British	Alfa Romeo	2
Holland	1950	Indianapolis 500	Deidt	10
Kling	1954	French	Mercedes	2
Nazaruk	1951	Indianapolis 500	Kurtis Kraft	7
Parkes	1966	French	Ferrari	3
Serafini	1950	Italian	Ferrari	6
Villeneuve,J.	1996	Australian	Williams-Renault	1

DRIVERS WITH THREE OR MORE SUCCESSIVE GRAND PRIX WINS

Wins	Driver	Year(s)	Races
9	Ascari	1952/53	Bel, Fra, GB, Ger, Hol, Ita, Arg, Hol, Bel
5	Brabham	1960	Hol, Bel, Fra, GB, Por
	Clark	1965	Bel, Fra, GB, Hol, Ger
	Mansell	1992	SA, Mex, Bra, Esp, San
4	Senna	1988	GB, Ger, Hon, Bel
		1991	USA, Bra, San, Mon
	Fangio	1953/54	Ita/Arg, Bel, Fra
	Clark	1963	Bel, Hol, Fra, GB
	Brabham	1966	Fra, GB, Hol, Ger
	Rindt	1970	Hol, Fra, GB, Ger
	Prost	1993	Can, Fra, GB, Ger
	Schumacher,M.	1994	Bra, Pac, San, Mon
3	Fangio	1954	Ger, Sui, Ita
		1957	Arg, Mon, Fra
	Stewart	1969	Hol, Fra, GB
		1971	Fra, GB, Ger
	Lauda	1975	Mon, Bel, Swe
		1975/76	USA/Bra, SA
	Jones	1979	Ger, Aut, Hol
		1980/81	Can, USAE/USAW
	Prost	1984/85	Eur, Por/Bra
		1990	Mex, Fra, GB
	Mansell	1991	Fra, GB, Ger
		1992	Fra, GB, Ger
	Moss	1957/58	Pes, Ita/Arg
	Clark	1967/68	USA, Mex/SA
	Senna	1989	San, Mon, Mex
	Hill,D.	1993	Hun, Bel, Ita
		1994	Bel, Ita, Por
		1996	Aus, Bra, Arg
	Schumacher,M.	1995	Eur, Pac, Jap
		1998	Can, Fra, GB

DRIVERS TO WIN THEIR NATIONAL GRAND PRIX

Wins	Driver	Nat	Year(s)
6	Prost	French	1981, 1983, 1988, 1989, 1990, 1993
5	Clark	British	1962, 1963, 1964, 1965, 1967
4	Fangio	Argentine	1954, 1955, 1956, 1957
	Mansell	British	1986, 1987, 1991, 1992
2	Ascari	Italian	1951, 1952
	Moss	British	1955, 1957
	Stewart	British	1969, 1971
	Fittipaldi, E.	Brazilian	1973, 1974
	Piquet	Brazilian	1983, 1986
	Senna	Brazilian	1991, 1993
1	Farina	Italian	1950
	Collins	British	1958
	Scarfiotti	Italian	1966
	Pace	Brazilian	1975
	Scheckter	S. African	1975
	Andretti	American	1977
	Hunt	British	1977
	Villeneuve, G.	Canadian	1978
	Jabouille	French	1979
	Watson	British	1981
	Arnoux	French	1982
	Lauda	Austrian	1984
	Hill, Damon	British	1994
	Herbert	British	1995
	Schumacher, M.	German	1995
	Coulthard	British	1999

DRIVERS BY NUMBER OF POLE POSITIONS

Driver	Poles	Start	1st	2nd	3rd	Fast
Senna	65	161	41	23	16	19
Clark	33	72	25	1	6	28
Prost	33	199	51	35	20	41
Mansell	32	187	31	17	11	30

Driver	Poles	Start	1st	2nd	3rd	Fast
Fangio †	29	51	24	8	1	23
Lauda	24	171	25	20	9	24
Piquet	24	204	23	20	17	23
Schumacher,M.	23	126	35	22	14	39
Hakkinen	21	128	14	7	16	13
Hill,D.	20	115	22	15	5	19
Andretti,Mario	18	128	12	2	5	10
Arnoux	18	149	7	9	6	12
Stewart,Jackie	17	99	27	11	5	15
Moss †	16	66	16	5	1	19
Ascari †	14	32	13	4	–	12
Hunt	14	92	10	6	7	8
Peterson	14	123	10	10	6	9
Brabham,J.	13	126	14	10	7	12
Hill,G.	13	176	14	15	7	10
Ickx	13	116	8	7	10	14
Villeneuve,J.	13	65	11	5	5	9
Berger,G.	12	210	10	17	21	21
Rindt	10	60	6	3	4	3
Coulthard	8	90	6	18	6	11
Patrese	8	256	6	17	14	13
Surtees	8	111	6	10	8	11
Laffite	7	176	6	10	16	6
Fittipaldi,E.	6	144	14	13	8	6
Hill,P.	6	48	3	5	8	6
Jabouille	6	49	2	–	–	–
Jones	6	116	12	7	5	13
Reutemann	6	146	12	13	20	6
Amon	5	96	–	3	8	3
Farina	5	33	5	8	5	5
Regazzoni	5	132	5	13	10	15
Rosberg	5	114	5	8	4	3
Tambay	5	114	2	4	5	2

† Including shared drives. Five poles minimum to be included.

DRIVERS TO HAVE TAKEN POLE POSITION IN THEIR THEIR FIRST GRAND PRIX START

Drivers	Year	Grand Prix	Car	Pos
Andretti,Mario	1968	United States	Lotus-Ford	r
Farina	1950	British	Alfa Romeo	1
Faulkner	1950	Indianapolis 500	Kurtis Kraft	7
Nalon	1951	Indianapolis 500	Kurtis Kraft	r
Reutemann	1972	Argentinian	Brabham-Ford	7
Villeneuve,J.	1996	Australian	Williams-Renault	2

DRIVERS WITH MORE THAN FIVE POLE POSITIONS IN A SEASON

Poles	Races	Driver	Year(s)
14	16	Mansell	1992
13	16/16	Senna	1988 and 1989
	16	Prost	1993
11	16	Hakkinen	1999
10	16	Senna	1990
	17	Villeneuve, J.	1997
9	15/14	Lauda	1974 and 1975
	15	Peterson	1973
	16	Piquet	1984
	16	Hill, D.	1996
	16	Hakkinen	1998
8	16/16	Senna	1986 and 1991
	16	Hunt	1976
	16	Andretti	1978
	16	Mansell	1987
7	10	Clark	1963
	17	Andretti	1977
	16	Senna	1985
	17	Hill, D.	1995
6	9/10/11	Clark	1962, 1965 and 1967
	9	Ascari	1953
	11	Stewart	1971
	17	Hunt	1977
	16	Schumacher, M.	1994

DRIVERS BY NUMBER OF FASTEST LAPS

Driver	Fast	Start	1st	2nd	3rd	Poles
Prost	41	199	51	35	20	33
Schumacher,M.	39	126	35	22	14	23
Mansell	30	187	31	17	11	32
Clark	28	72	25	1	6	33
Lauda	24	171	25	20	9	24
Fangio †	23	51	24	8	1	29
Piquet	23	204	23	20	17	24
Berger,G.	21	210	10	17	21	12
Hill,D.	19	115	22	15	5	20
Moss †	19	66	16	5	1	16
Senna	19	161	41	23	16	65
Regazzoni	15	132	5	13	10	5
Stewart,Jackie	15	99	27	11	5	17
Ickx	14	116	8	7	10	13
Hakkinen	13	128	14	7	16	21
Jones	13	116	12	7	5	6
Patrese	13	256	6	17	14	8
Arnoux	12	149	7	9	6	18
Ascari †	12	32	13	4	–	14

Driver	Fast	Start	1st	2nd	3rd	Poles
Brabham,J.	12	126	14	10	7	13
Coulthard	11	90	6	18	6	8
Surtees	11	111	6	10	8	8
Andretti,Mario	10	128	12	2	5	18
Hill,G.	10	176	14	15	7	13
Hulme	9	112	8	9	16	1
Peterson	9	123	10	10	6	14
Villeneuve,J.	9	65	11	5	5	13
Hunt	8	92	10	6	7	14
Villeneuve,G.	8	67	6	5	2	2
Fittipaldi,E.	6	144	14	13	8	6
Frentzen	6	97	3	3	9	2
Gurney	6	86	4	8	7	3
Hawthorn	6	45	3	8	6	4
Hill,P.	6	48	3	5	8	6
Laffite	6	176	6	10	16	7
Reutemann	6	146	12	13	20	6
Alboreto	5	194	5	9	9	2
Farina	5	33	5	8	5	5
Gonzalez,J.	5	26	2	7	4	3
Pace	5	72	1	3	2	1
Pironi	5	70	3	3	7	4
Scheckter,J.	5	112	10	14	9	3
Watson	5	152	5	6	9	2

† Including shared drives. Five fastest laps minimum to be included.

DRIVERS TO HAVE TAKEN FASTEST LAP IN THEIR THEIR FIRST GRAND PRIX START

Drivers	Year	Grand Prix	Car	Pos
Farina	1950	British	Alfa Romeo	1
Hasemi	1976	Japanese	Kojima-Ford	11
Holland	1950	Indianapolis	Deidt	2
Villeneuve,J.	1996	Australian	Williams-Renault	2

DRIVERS BY MOST RACE COMPLETIONS

Driver	Comp	Start	Wins	Pole	Fast
Prost	146	199	51	33	41
Patrese	126	256	6	8	13
Piquet	126	204	23	24	23
Berger,G.	123	210	10	12	21
Senna	111	161	41	65	19
Hill,G.	106	176	14	13	10
Alboreto	103	194	5	2	5
Mansell	102	187	31	32	30
Boutsen	100	163	3	1	1
Fittipaldi,E.	99	144	14	6	6
Alesi	98	167	1	2	4
Laffite	98	176	6	7	6
Reutemann	98	146	12	6	6
Watson	95	152	5	2	5
Lauda	93	171	25	24	24
Schumacher,M.	93	126	35	23	39
Brundle	92	158	0	0	0
Regazzoni	87	132	5	5	15
Arnoux	82	149	7	18	12
Herbert	81	143	3	0	0
Hakkinen	79	128	14	21	13
Hulme	79	112	8	1	9
Hill,D.	77	115	22	20	19
Scheckter,J.	77	112	10	3	5
Peterson	75	123	10	14	9
de Cesaris	74	208	0	1	1

† Including shared drives. 70 completions minimum to be included.

DRIVERS BY MOST RACE RETIREMENTS

Driver	Retire	Start	Wins	Pole	Fast
de Cesaris	134	208	–	1	1
Patrese	130	256	6	8	13
Alboreto	91	194	5	2	5
Berger,G.	87	210	10	12	21
Mansell	85	187	31	32	30
Warwick	79	146	–	–	2
Laffite	78	176	6	7	6
Lauda	78	171	25	24	24
Piquet	78	204	23	24	23
Cheever	75	132	–	–	–
Hill,G.	70	176	14	13	10
Alesi	69	167	1	2	4
Arnoux	67	149	7	18	12
Brundle	66	158	–	–	–
Andretti,Mario	65	128	12	18	10
Jarier	65	134	–	3	3
Capelli	64	93	–	–	–
Boutsen	63	163	3	1	1
Martini	63	118	–	–	–
Alliot	62	109	–	–	–
Herbert	62	143	3	–	–
Katayama	61	95	–	–	–
Barrichello	58	112	–	2	–
Brabham,J.	58	126	14	13	12
Surtees	57	111	6	8	11
Watson	57	152	5	2	5
Tambay	55	114	2	5	2
Ghinzani	54	76	–	–	–
Prost	53	199	51	33	41

Driver	Retire	Start	Wins	Pole	Fast
Diniz	51	82	–	–	–
Rosberg	51	114	5	5	3
Bonnier †	50	104	1	1	–
Senna	50	161	41	65	19

† Including shared drives. 50 retirements minimum to be included.

DRIVERS BY MOST WORLD CHAMPIONSHIP POINTS

Driver	Country	WC Pts	Total Pts
Prost	France	768.5	796.5
Senna	Brazil	610	614
Schumacher,M.	Germany	570	570
Piquet	Brazil	481.5	484.5
Mansell	GB	480	482
Lauda	Austria	420.5	420.5
Berger,G.	Austria	385	385
Hill,D.	GB	360	360
Stewart,Jackie	GB	359	360
Reutemann	Argentina	298	310
Hakkinen	Finland	294	294
Fittipaldi,E.	Brazil	281	281
Patrese	Italy	281	281
Hill,G.	GB	270	287
Clark	GB	255	274
Brabham,J.	Australia	253	261
Hulme	New Zealand	248	248
Scheckter,J.	South Africa	246	255
Fangio	Argentina	244.5	277.14
Alesi	France	236	236
Laffite	France	228	228
Coulthard	GB	221	221
Regazzoni	Switzerland	209	212
Peterson	Sweden	206	206

List includes drivers to have score 200 points or more.

DRIVERS BY TOTAL POINTS SCORED

Driver	Country	WC Pts	Total Pts
Prost	France	768.5	796.5
Senna	Brazil	610	614
Schumacher,M.	Germany	570	570
Piquet	Brazil	481.5	484.5
Mansell	GB	480	482
Lauda	Austria	420.5	420.5
Berger,G.	Austria	385	385
Hill,D.	GB	360	360
Stewart,Jackie	GB	359	360
Reutemann	Argentina	298	310
Hakkinen	Finland	294	294
Hill,G.	GB	270	287
Fittipaldi,E.	Brazil	281	281
Patrese	Italy	281	281
Fangio	Argentina	244.5	277.14
Clark	GB	255	274
Brabham,J.	Australia	253	261
Scheckter,J.	South Africa	246	255
Hulme	New Zealand	248	248
Alesi	France	236	236
Laffite	France	228	228
Coulthard	GB	221	221
Regazzoni	Switzerland	209	212

List includes drivers to have score 200 points or more.

DRIVERS TO HAVE WON FROM POLE POSITION

Driver	Year	GP	Team
Alboreto	1984	Belgian	Ferrari
Andretti,Mario	1976	Japanese	Lotus-Ford
	1977	Spanish	Lotus-Ford
	1977	French	Lotus-Ford
	1978	Argentine	Lotus-Ford
	1978	Belgian	Lotus-Ford
	1978	Spanish	Lotus-Ford
	1978	German	Lotus-Ford
	1978	Dutch	Lotus-Ford
Arnoux	1982	French	Renault
	1983	Canadian	Ferrari
Ascari	1951	German	Ferrari
	1952	Belgian	Ferrari
	1952	French	Ferrari
	1952	German	Ferrari
	1952	Dutch	Ferrari
	1952	Italian	Ferrari
	1953	Argentine	Ferrari
	1953	Dutch	Ferrari
	1953	British	Ferrari
Berger,G.	1987	Japanese	Ferrari
	1987	Australian	Ferrari
	1991	Japanese	McLaren-Honda
	1994	German	Ferrari
	1997	German	Benetton-Renault
Bonnier	1959	Dutch	BRM
Boutsen	1990	Hungarian	Williams-Renault
Brabham,J.	1959	British	Cooper-Climax
	1960	Belgian	Cooper-Climax
	1960	French	Cooper-Climax
	1960	British	Cooper-Climax
	1966	British	Brabham-Repco
	1966	Dutch	Brabham-Repco

Driver	Year	GP	Team
Brooks	1959	French	Ferrari
	1959	German	Ferrari
Clark	1962	British	Lotus-Climax
	1962	United States	Lotus-Climax
	1963	Dutch	Lotus-Climax
	1963	French	Lotus-Climax
	1963	British	Lotus-Climax
	1963	Mexican	Lotus-Climax
	1963	South African	Lotus-Climax
	1964	British	Lotus-Climax
	1965	South African	Lotus-Climax
	1965	French	Lotus-Climax
	1965	British	Lotus-Climax
	1965	German	Lotus-Climax
	1967	British	Lotus-Ford
	1967	Mexican	Lotus-Ford
	1968	South African	Lotus-Ford
Coulthard	1995	Portuguese	Williams-Renault
	1998	San Marino	McLaren-Mercedes
Fangio	1950	Monaco	Alfa Romeo
	1950	French	Alfa Romeo
	1951	Swiss	Alfa Romeo
	1954	Belgian	Maserati
	1954	French	Mercedes
	1954	German	Mercedes
	1954	Italian	Mercedes
	1955	Dutch	Mercedes
	1955	Italian	Mercedes
	1956	German	Lancia-Ferrari
	1957	Monaco	Maserati
	1957	French	Maserati
	1957	German	Maserati
	1950	British	Alfa Romeo
Fittipaldi,E.	1972	Belgian	Lotus-Ford
	1972	Austrian	Lotus-Ford
	1974	Brazilian	McLaren-Ford
	1974	Canadian	McLaren-Ford
Flaherty	1956	Indianapolis	Watson
Gonzalez,J.	1951	British	Ferrari
Hakkinen	1998	Australian	McLaren-Mercedes
	1998	Brazilian	McLaren-Mercedes
	1998	Spanish	McLaren-Mercedes
	1998	Monaco	McLaren-Mercedes
	1998	German	McLaren-Mercedes
	1999	Brazilian	McLaren-Mercedes
	1999	Spanish	McLaren-Mercedes
	1999	Hungarian	McLaren-Mercedes
Hawthorn	1958	French	Ferrari

Driver	Year	GP	Team
Hill,D.	1994	British	Williams-Renault
	1995	Hungarian	Williams-Renault
	1995	Australian	Williams-Renault
	1996	Brazilian	Williams-Renault
	1996	Argentine	Williams-Renault
	1996	Canadian	Williams-Renault
	1996	German	Williams-Renault
Hill,G.	1963	US	BRM
	1965	Monaco	BRM
	1965	US	BRM
	1968	Monaco	Lotus-Ford
Hill,P.	1960	Italian	Ferrari
	1961	Belgian	Ferrari
Hunt	1976	Spanish	McLaren-Ford
	1976	French	McLaren-Ford
	1976	German	McLaren-Ford
	1976	Canadian	McLaren-Ford
	1976	US East	McLaren-Ford
	1977	British	McLaren-Ford
	1977	US East	McLaren-Ford
Ickx	1969	German	Brabham-Ford
	1969	Canadian	Brabham-Ford
	1971	Dutch	Ferrari
	1972	German	Ferrari
Jabouille	1979	French	Renault
Jones	1979	Canadian	Williams-Ford
	1980	Argentine	Williams-Ford
Laffite	1979	Argentine	Ligier-Ford
	1979	Brazilian	Ligier-Ford
Lauda	1974	Spanish	Ferrari
	1974	Dutch	Ferrari
	1975	Monaco	Ferrari
	1975	Belgian	Ferrari
	1975	French	Ferrari
	1975	US	Ferrari
	1976	Belgian	Ferrari
	1976	Monaco	Ferrari
	1976	British	Ferrari
Mansell	1985	South African	Williams-Honda
	1986	Canadian	Williams-Honda
	1987	French	Williams-Honda
	1987	Mexican	Williams-Honda
	1990	Portuguese	Ferrari
	1991	British	Williams-Renault
	1991	German	Williams-Renault
	1992	South African	Williams-Renault
	1992	Mexican	Williams-Renault
	1992	Brazilian	Williams-Renault

Driver	Year	GP	Team
	1992	Spanish	Williams-Renault
	1992	San Marino	Williams-Renault
	1992	French	Williams-Renault
	1992	British	Williams-Renault
	1992	German	Williams-Renault
	1992	Portuguese	Williams-Renault
	1994	Australian	Williams-Renault
Moss	1955	British	Mercedes
	1958	Portuguese	Vanwall
	1959	Portuguese	Cooper-Climax
	1959	Italian	Cooper-Climax
	1960	Monaco	Lotus-Climax
	1960	US	Lotus-Climax
	1961	Monaco	Lotus-Climax
Patrese	1991	Mexican	Williams-Renault
	1991	Portuguese	Williams-Renault
Peterson	1973	Italian	Lotus-Ford
	1973	US	Lotus-Ford
	1978	Austrian	Lotus-Ford
Piquet	1980	US West	Brabham-Ford
	1981	Argentine	Brabham-Ford
	1984	Canadian	Brabham-BMW
	1984	Detroit	Brabham-BMW
	1987	Italian	Williams-Honda
Prost	1981	Dutch	Renault
	1982	Brazilian	Renault
	1983	French	Renault
	1983	Belgian	Renault
	1984	Monaco	McLaren-TAG
	1984	German	McLaren-TAG
	1984	Dutch	McLaren-TAG
	1985	Austrian	McLaren-TAG
	1986	Monaco	McLaren-TAG
	1988	French	McLaren-Honda
	1988	Portuguese	McLaren-Honda
	1989	French	McLaren-Honda
	1993	South African	Williams-Renault
	1993	San Marino	Williams-Renault
	1993	Spanish	Williams-Renault
	1993	Canadian	Williams-Renault
	1993	British	Williams-Renault
	1993	German	Williams-Renault
Regazzoni	1976	US West	Ferrari
Reutemann	1974	US	Brabham-Ford
	1978	US West	Ferrari
	1981	Belgian	Williams-Ford
Rindt	1969	US	Lotus-Ford
	1970	Dutch	Lotus-Ford

Driver	Year	GP	Team
	1970	British	Lotus-Ford
Scheckter,J.	1976	Swedish	Tyrrell-Ford
	1979	Monaco	Ferrari
Schumacher,M.	1994	Monaco	Benetton-Ford
	1994	Canadian	Benetton-Ford
	1994	Hungarian	Benetton-Ford
	1994	European	Benetton-Ford
	1995	Spanish	Benetton-Renault
	1995	Japanese	Benetton-Renault
	1997	Canadian	Ferrari
	1997	French	Ferrari
	1998	Italian	Ferrari
Senna	1985	Portuguese	Lotus-Renault
	1986	Spanish	Lotus-Renault
	1986	United States	Lotus-Renault
	1988	San Marino	McLaren-Honda
	1988	Canadian	McLaren-Honda
	1988	United States	McLaren-Honda
	1988	German	McLaren-Honda
	1988	Hungarian	McLaren-Honda
	1988	Belgian	McLaren-Honda
	1988	Japanese	McLaren-Honda
	1989	San Marino	McLaren-Honda
	1989	Monaco	McLaren-Honda
	1989	Mexican	McLaren-Honda
	1989	German	McLaren-Honda
	1989	Belgian	McLaren-Honda
	1989	Spanish	McLaren-Honda
	1990	Monaco	McLaren-Honda
	1990	Canadian	McLaren-Honda
	1990	German	McLaren-Honda
	1990	Belgian	McLaren-Honda
	1990	Italian	McLaren-Honda
	1991	United States	McLaren-Honda
	1991	Brazilian	McLaren-Honda
	1991	San Marino	McLaren-Honda
	1991	Monaco	McLaren-Honda
	1991	Hungarian	McLaren-Honda
	1991	Belgian	McLaren-Honda
	1991	Australian	McLaren-Honda
	1993	Australian	McLaren-Ford
Siffert	1971	Austrian	BRM
Stewart,Jackie	1969	French	Matra-Ford
	1971	Monaco	Tyrrell-Ford
	1971	French	Tyrrell-Ford
	1971	German	Tyrrell-Ford
	1971	Canadian	Tyrrell-Ford
	1972	United States	Tyrrell-Ford

Driver	Year	GP	Team
	1973	Monaco	Tyrrell-Ford
	1973	German	Tyrrell-Ford
Surtees	1964	German	Ferrari
	1964	Italian	Ferrari
	1966	Belgian	Ferrari
	1966	Mexican	Cooper-Maserati
Villeneuve,G.	1979	US West	Ferrari
Villeneuve,J.	1997	Brazilian	Williams-Renault
	1997	Argentine	Williams-Renault
	1997	Spanish	Williams-Renault
	1997	British	Williams-Renault
	1997	Austrian	Williams-Renault
Vukovich	1953	Indy 500	Kurtis Kraft

DRIVERS BY TOTAL LAPS COMPLETED

Driver	Total	Driver	Total
Patrese	11299	Cheever	5491
Prost	10545	Rosberg	5303
Piquet	9870	Andretti,Mario	5276
Berger,G.	9793	Stewart,Jackie	5216
Alboreto	8767	McLaren	5071
Mansell	8761	Tambay	4989
Hill,G.	8754	Surtees	4976
Senna	8220	Barrichello	4943
Lauda	8146	Mass	4924
Boutsen	8042	Martini	4903
Alesi	8012	de Angelis	4757
Laffite	7999	Bonnier	4749
de Cesaris	7714	Frentzen	4738
Brundle	7553	Panis	4637
Watson	7389	Depailler	4634
Fittipaldi,E.	7282	Irvine	4574
Reutemann	6977	Amon	4555
Schumacher,M.	6710		
Arnoux	6612		
Regazzoni	6571		
Herbert	6570		
Warwick	6388		
Hulme	6227		
Brabham,J.	6110		
Hakkinen	6038		
Scheckter,J.	6034		
Hill,D.	5848		
Jarier	5744		
Peterson	5713		
Ickx	5639		
Jones	5565		

NB: 4500 laps minimum to be included.

DRIVERS TO HAVE FINISHED THEIR FIRST GRAND PRIX START

Driver	Year	GP	Pn
Acheson	1983	SA	12
Ader	1950	Indy	22
Alesi	1989	Fra	4
Allison	1958	Mon	6
Amick,G.	1958	Indy	2
Anderson	1963	GP	12
Armi	1954	Indy	19
Arnold	1959	Indy	15
Arnoux	1978	Bel	9
Arundell	1964	Mon	3
Ascari	1950	Mon	2
Ashdown	1959	GP	12
Ashley	1974	Ger	14
Ayulo	1952	Indy	20
Baghelti	1961	Fra	1
Baldi	1982	Bra	10
Ball	1951	Indy	5
Barber,J.	1953	Arg	8
Barber,S.	1971	Hol	uc
Beauman	1954	GP	11
Behra	1952	Swi	3
Belmondo	1992	Esp	12
Beltoise	1966	Ger	8
Berger,G.	1984	Aut	12
Bernard	1989	Fra	11
Bianchi	1960	Bel	6
Bianco	1952	GP	18
Blanchard	1959	US	7
Blokdyk	1963	SA	12
Boesel	1982	SA	15
Bondurant	1965	US	9
Bonetto	1950	Swi	5
Bonnier	1957	Arg	7
Bonomi	1960	Arg	11
Borgudd	1981	San	13
Botha	1967	SA	uc
Boullion	1995	Mon	8
Brambilla	1974	SA	10
Branca	1950	Swi	11
Brandon	1952	Swi	8
Brise	1975	Esp	7
Bristow	1959	GP	10
Broeker	1963	US	7
Brown,A.	1952	Swi	5
Brown,Walt	1950	Indy	19
Brown, Warwick	1976	USE	14
Brundle	1985	Bra	8
Bryan	1952	Indy	6
Bueno	1973	Bra	12
Cabral	1959	Por	10
Caffi	1986	Ita	11
Campbell-Jones	1962	Bel	uc
Cannon	1971	US	14
Carter	1950	Indy	12
Cecotto	1983	Bra	14
Chamberlain	1962	GP	15
Charlton	1967	SA	uc
Chitwood	1950	Indy	5
Christie	1956	Indy	13
Claes	1950	GP	11
Connor	1950	Indy	8
Crockett	1954	Indy	9
Crook	1952	GP	21
Cross	1952	Indy	5
da S.Ramos	1955	Hol	8
Dalmas	1987	Mex	9
Davies	1950	Indy	17
Daywalt	1953	Indy	6
de Angelis	1979	Arg	7
de Beaufort	1957	Ger	14
de Filippis	1958	Bel	10
de la Rosa	1999	Aus	6
de Tomaso	1957	Arg	9
de Tornaco	1952	Bel	7
Depailler	1972	Fra	uc
Diniz	1995	Bra	10
Donnelly	1989	Fra	12
Donohue	1971	Can	3
d'Orey	1959	Fra	10
Downing	1952	GP	9
Drake	1960	US	13
Drogo	1960	Ita	8
Dumfries	1986	Bra	9
Edwards	1974	Arg	11
Elford	1968	Fra	4
Elisian	1954	Indy	18
Ertl	1975	Ger	8
Estefano	1960	Arg	14

Driver	Year	GP	Pn
Etancelin	1950	GP	8
Evans	1975	SA	15
Fabi,T.	1982	San	uc
Fabre	1987	Bra	12
Fagioli	1950	GP	2
Fangio	1950	GP	12
Farina	1950	GP	1
Faulkner	1950	Indy	7
Fischer	1951	Swi	11
Fisher	1967	Can	11
Fittipaldi,E.	1970	GP	8
Fittipaldi,W.	1972	Esp	7
Flaherty	1950	Indy	10
Fohr	1950	Indy	11
Follmer	1973	SA	6
Fonder	1952	Indy	15
Forberg	1951	Indy	7
Frere	1952	Bel	5
Fry	1950	GP	10
Gachot	1989	Fra	13
Gaillard	1979	GP	13
Galvez	1953	Arg	5
Gamble	1960	Ita	10
Garrett	1956	Indy	16
Gaze	1952	Bel	15
Gendebien	1956	Arg	5
Gerard	1950	GP	6
Gerini	1956	Ita	11
Ghinzani	1981	Bel	13
Ginther	1960	Mon	6
Giraud-Cabantous	1950	GP	4
Giunti	1970	Bel	4
Godia	1951	Esp	10
Gould	1954	GP	uc
Green	1950	Indy	4
Gregory	1957	Mon	3
Grouillard	1989	Bra	9
Guelfi	1958	Mor	15
Hahne	1966	Ger	9
Hailwood	1963	GP	8
Hall	1960	US	7
Hamilton	1951	GP	12
Hampshire	1950	GP	9
Harrison	1950	GP	7
Hartley	1950	Indy	16
Hasemi	1976	Jap	11
Hawkins	1965	SA	9

Driver	Year	GP	Pn
Hawthorn	1952	Bel	4
Hellings	1950	Indy	13
Henton	1975	GP	16
Herbert	1989	Bra	4
Herman	1955	Indy	7
Herrmann	1953	Ger	9
Hill,D.	1992	GP	16
Hill,P.	1958	Fra	7
Hobbs	1967	GP	8
Hoffman	1976	Bra	11
Holland	1950	Indy	2
Holmes	1950	Indy	23
Hoyt	1950	Indy	21
Hulme	1965	Mon	8
Hunt	1973	Mon	9
Ireland	1959	Hol	4
Irvine	1993	Jap	6
Irwin	1966	GP	7
Jabouille	1975	Fra	12
Jarier	1971	Ita	uc
Johnson,E.	1952	Indy	16
Johnstone	1962	SA	9
Katayama	1992	SA	12
Keizan	1973	SA	uc
Kelly	1950	GP	uc
Kessel	1976	Bel	12
Klenk	1952	Ger	11
Kling	1954	Fra	2
Klodwig	1952	Ger	12
Koinigg	1974	Can	10
la Caze	1958	Mor	14
Lamy	1993	Ita	11
Lang	1953	Swi	5
Larson	1958	Indy	8
Laurent	1952	Bel	12
Lawrence	1966	GP	11
Lederle	1962	SA	6
Lees	1979	Ger	7
Legat	1952	Bel	13
Levegh	1950	Bel	7
Lewis	1961	Bel	9
Lewis-Evans	1957	Mon	4
Ligier	1966	Mon	uc
Linden	1951	Indy	4
Love	1962	SA	8
Lovely	1960	US	11
Lunger	1975	Aut	13

Driver	Year	GP	Pn
MacDowell,M.	1957	Fra	7
Magee	1975	Swe	14
Maggs	1961	GP	13
Maglioli	1953	Ita	10
Magnussen	1995	Pac	10
Mantovani	1953	Ita	8
Marko	1971	Aut	11
Marr	1954	GP	13
Marsh	1957	Ger	15
Max	1971	Fra	uc
Mazet	1971	Fra	13
McAlpine	1952	GP	16
McCoy	1953	Indy	8
McDowell,J.	1950	Indy	18
McGrath	1950	Indy	14
McLaren	1958	Ger	5
McWithey	1959	Indy	16
Merzario	1972	GP	6
Montermini	1995	Bra	9
Morbidelli	1990	Bra	14
Morgan	1975	GP	18
Moss	1951	Swi	8
Munaron	1960	Arg	13
Nakajima	1987	Bra	7
Nakano	1997	Aus	7
Naspetti	1992	Bel	12
Naylor	1957	Ger	13
Nazaruk	1951	Indy	2
Nicholson	1975	GP	17
Niedermayr	1952	Ger	9
Niemann	1963	SA	uc
Nuckey	1953	Ger	11
O'Brien	1952	Bel	14
Pace	1972	SA	17
Pagani	1950	Swi	7
Palm	1975	Swe	10
Palmer	1983	Eur	13
Panis	1994	Bra	11
Parkes	1966	Fra	2
Parnell,R.	1950	GP	3
Parsons	1950	Indy	1
Patrese	1977	Mon	9
Pease	1967	Can	uc
Penske	1961	US	9
Perdisa	1955	Mon	8
Perkins	1976	Esp	13

Driver	Year	GP	Pn
Pesenti-Rossi	1976	Ger	14
Peterson	1970	Mon	7
Pieterse	1962	SA	10
Pilette,A.	1951	Bel	6
Pilette,T.	1974	Bel	17
Pirocchi	1961	Ita	12
Pironi	1978	Arg	14
Pirro	1989	Fra	9
Poore	1952	GP	4
Pozzi	1950	Fra	6
Pretorius	1968	SA	uc
Prost	1980	Arg	6
Quester	1974	Aut	9
Rahal	1978	USE	12
Rathmann,J.	1950	Indy	24
Ratzenberger	1994	Pac	11
Reece	1952	Indy	7
Regazzoni	1970	Hol	4
Reutemann	1972	Arg	7
Ribeiro	1976	USE	12
Riess	1952	Ger	7
Rigsby	1952	Indy	12
Rodriguez Larreta	1960	Arg	9
Rose	1950	Indy	3
Rosier	1950	GP	5
Rosset	1996	Aus	9
Rothengatter	1984	Can	uc
Ruby	1960	Indy	7
Russo,P.	1950	Indy	9
Ruttman	1950	Indy	15
Ryan	1961	US	10
Salo	1994	Jap	10
Salvadori	1952	GP	8
Scarfiotti	1963	Hol	6
Scheckter,I.	1974	SA	13
Scheckter,J.	1972	US	9
Scherrer	1953	Swi	uc
Schiattarella	1994	Eur	19
Schlesser,J.	1966	Ger	10
Schlesser,J-L	1988	Ita	11

Driver	Year	GP	Pn
Schroeder	1962	US	10
Schuppan	1974	Bel	15
Seidel	1953	Ger	uc
Serafini	1950	Ita	2
Serra	1981	USW	7
Settember	1962	GP	11
Sharp	1961	US	11
Shawe-Taylor	1951	GP	8
Siffert	1962	Bel	10
Sommer	1950	Mon	4
Sparken	1955	GP	7
Stewart,Jackie	1965	SA	6
Stewart,Jimmy	1953	GP	9

Driver	Year	GP	Pn
Sullivan	1983	Bra	11
Suzuki,A.	1988	Jap	16
Suzuki,T.	1993	Jap	12
Swaters	1951	Ger	10
Takahara	1976	Jap	9
Takahashi	1977	Jap	9
Taylor,H.	1959	GP	11
Taylor,J.	1964	GP	14
Taylor,T.	1961	Hol	13
Thompson	1952	GP	5
Thorne	1954	GP	uc
Tinglestad	1960	Indy	9
Trulli	1997	Aus	9
Tunmer	1975	SA	11
Van de Poele	1991	San	9

Driver	Year	GP	Pn
Van der Lof	1952	Hol	uc
van Lennep	1971	Hol	8
Veith	1956	Indy	7
Villeneuve,G.	1977	GP	11
Villeneuve,J.	1996	Aus	2
Villota	1977	Esp	13
Volonterio	1956	Ger	uc
von Opel	1973	Fra	15
Wacker	1953	Bel	9
Wallard	1950	Indy	6
Walter	1962	Ger	14
Webb	1950	Indy	20
Weyant	1955	Indy	12
Wharton	1952	Swi	4

Driver	Year	GP	Pn
Whitehead,G.	1952	GP	12
Whitehead,P.	1950	Fra	3
Wilds	1974	US	uc
Williams	1967	Mex	8
Winkelhock	1982	SA	10
Wisell	1970	US	3
Zanardi	1991	Esp	9
Zorzi	1975	Ita	14

Out of 678 drivers to have recorded a Grand Prix start, 318 drivers have reached the finish line.

CONSTRUCTORS BY MOST RACES CONTESTED

Constructor	Cont	Win	Pole	Fast	Points
Ferrari	619	125	127	139	2352.5
McLaren	492	123	103	89	2328.5
Lotus	491	79	107	71	1367
Tyrrell	430	23	14	20	616
Williams	403	103	108	111	1989.5
Brabham	394	35	39	42	864
Prost + Ligier	375	9	9	9	419
Arrows + Footwork	337	–	1	–	157
Ligier	326	9	9	9	388
Benetton + Toleman	283	27	16	38	847.5
Arrows	246	–	1	–	132
Minardi	237	–	–	–	28
March + Leyton H.	227	3	5	7	181.5
Benetton	226	27	15	36	821.5
BRM	197	17	11	15	433
March	197	3	5	7	173.5
Lola	149	–	1	–	43
Jordan	146	3	2	2	216
Osella	132	–	–	–	5
Cooper	129	16	11	14	342
Renault	123	15	31	18	312
Surtees	118	–	–	3	54
Sauber	113	–	–	–	84
Alfa Romeo	110	10	12	14	50
Shadow	104	1	3	2	67.5
Fittipaldi	103	–	–	–	44
Ensign	98	–	–	1	19
Footwork	91	–	–	–	25
ATS (Germany)	89	–	–	–	7
Dallara	78	–	–	–	15
Maserati	71	9	10	17	6
Matra (inc F2 cars)	62	9	4	12	163
Toleman	57	–	1	2	26
Zakspeed	53	–	–	–	2
Hesketh	52	1	–	1	48
Prost	49	–	–	–	31
Stewart	49	1	1	–	47
AGS	48	–	–	–	2
Larrousse	48	–	–	–	6
Wolf	47	3	1	2	79
Gordini (Simca)	40	–	–	1	–
Penske	40	1	–	–	23

Minimum 40 Grands Prix to be included.

Points totals are total points scored, not just those awarded towards Constructors' Cup. This applies in these pages unless otherwise stated.

CONSTRUCTORS BY MOST CARS STARTING RACE

Constructor	Cars	Win	Pole	Fast	Points
Ferrari	1426	125	127	139	2352.5
Lotus	1227	79	107	71	1367
McLaren	1036	123	103	89	2328.5
Brabham	925	35	39	42	864
Tyrrell	841	23	14	20	616
Williams	768	103	108	111	1989.5
Prost + Ligier	673	9	9	9	419
Arrows + Footwork	633	–	1	–	157
Ligier	577	9	9	9	388
March + Leyton H.	559	3	5	7	181.5
Benetton + Toleman	545	27	16	38	847.5
BRM	522	17	11	15	433
March	502	3	5	7	173.5
Cooper	501	16	11	14	342
Arrows	461	–	1	–	132
Benetton	451	27	15	36	821.5
Minardi	433	–	–	–	28
Maserati	371	9	10	17	6
Jordan	284	3	2	2	216
Lola	246	–	1	–	43
Alfa Romeo	234	10	12	14	50
Renault	227	15	31	18	312
Surtees	226	–	–	3	54
Sauber	223	–	–	–	84
Shadow	211	1	3	2	67.5
Footwork	172	–	–	–	25
Osella	166	–	–	–	5
Dallara	133	–	–	–	15
Gordini (Simca)	127	–	–	1	–
Fittipaldi	122	–	–	–	44
Matra (inc F2 cars)	116	9	4	12	163
Ensign	110	–	–	1	19
ATS (Germany)	107	–	–	–	7
Prost	96	–	–	–	31
Stewart	95	1	1	–	47
Toleman	94	–	1	2	26
Larrousse	93	–	–	–	6
Zakspeed	84	–	–	–	2
Hesketh	73	1	–	1	48
Porsche	71	1	1	–	47
Vanwall	64	9	7	6	57

Minimum of 60 cars to be included.

CONSTRUCTORS BY MOST GRAND PRIX WINS

Constructor	Win	Cont	Pole	Fast	Points
Ferrari	125	619	127	139	2352.5
McLaren	123	492	103	89	2328.5
Williams	103	403	108	111	1989.5
Lotus	79	491	107	71	1367
Brabham	35	394	39	42	864
Benetton	27	226	15	36	821.5
Benetton + Toleman	27	283	16	38	847.5
Tyrrell	23	430	14	20	616
BRM	17	197	11	15	433
Cooper	16	129	11	14	342
Renault	15	123	31	18	312
Alfa Romeo	10	110	12	14	50
Ligier	9	326	9	9	388
Maserati	9	71	10	17	6
Matra (inc F2 cars)	9	62	4	12	163
Mercedes	9	12	8	9	0
Prost + Ligier	9	375	9	9	419
Vanwall	9	28	7	6	57
Kurtis Kraft	5	12	6	6	120
Jordan	3	146	2	2	216
March	3	197	5	7	173.5
March + Leyton H.	3	227	5	7	181.5
Watson	3	9	2	1	0
Wolf	3	47	1	2	79
Epperly	2	5	0	2	0
Honda	2	35	1	2	48
Eagle	1	26	0	0	17
Hesketh	1	52	0	1	48
Kuzma	1	10	0	0	0
Penske	1	40	0	0	23
Porsche	1	32	1	0	47
Shadow	1	104	3	2	67.5
Stewart	1	49	1	0	47

CONSTRUCTORS BY MOST WINS IN ONE SEASON

Wins	Constructor	Year
15	McLaren-Honda	1988
12	McLaren-Porsche	1984
	Williams-Renault	1996
11	Benetton-Renault	1995
10	McLaren-Honda	1989
	Williams-Renault	1992
	Williams-Honda	1987
9	McLaren-Mercedes	1998
	Williams-Honda	1986
	Williams-Honda	1987
8	Benetton-Ford	1994
	Lotus-Ford	1978
	McLaren-Honda	1991
	Williams-Honda	1987

CONSTRUCTORS BY MOST POLE POSITIONS

Constructor	Pole	Cont	Win	Fast	Points
Ferrari	127	619	125	139	2352.5
Williams	108	403	103	111	1989.5
Lotus	107	491	79	71	1367
McLaren	103	492	123	89	2328.5
Brabham	39	394	35	42	864
Renault	31	123	15	18	312
Benetton + Toleman	16	283	27	38	847.5
Benetton	15	226	27	36	821.5
Tyrrell	14	430	23	20	616
Alfa Romeo	12	110	10	14	50
BRM	11	197	17	15	433
Cooper	11	129	16	14	342
Maserati	10	71	9	17	6
Ligier	9	326	9	9	388
Prost + Ligier	9	375	9	9	419
Mercedes	8	12	9	9	–
Vanwall	7	28	9	6	57
Kurtis Kraft	6	12	5	6	120
March	5	197	3	7	173.5
March + Leyton H.	5	227	3	7	181.5
Matra (inc F2 cars)	4	62	9	12	163
Shadow	3	104	1	2	67.5
Jordan	2	146	3	2	216
Lancia	2	4	–	1	–
Watson	2	9	3	1	–
Arrows	1	246	–	–	132
Arrows + Footwork	1	337	–	–	157
Ewing	1	2	–	–	–
Honda	1	35	2	2	48
Lesovsky	1	9	–	1	–
Lola	1	149	–	–	43
Porsche	1	32	1	–	47
Stevens	1	6	–	–	–
Stewart	1	49	1	–	47
Toleman	1	57	–	2	26
Wolf	1	47	3	2	79

CONSTRUCTORS BY MOST POLES IN ONE SEASON

Poles	Constructor	Year
15	McLaren-Honda	1988
	McLaren-Honda	1989
	Williams-Renault	1992
	Williams-Renault	1993
12	Lotus-Ford	1978
	McLaren-Honda	1990
	McLaren-Mercedes	1998
	Williams-Honda	1987
	Williams-Renault	1995
	Williams-Renault	1996
11	McLaren-Mercedes	1999
	Williams-Renault	1997
10	Ferrari	1974
	Lotus-Ford	1973
	McLaren-Honda	1991
	Renault	1982

CONSTRUCTORS BY MOST FASTEST LAPS

Constructor	Fast	Cont	Win	Pole	Points
Ferrari	139	619	125	127	2352.5
Williams	111	403	103	108	1989.5
McLaren	89	492	123	103	2328.5
Lotus	71	491	79	107	1367
Brabham	42	394	35	39	864
Benetton + Toleman	38	283	27	16	847.5
Benetton	36	226	27	15	821.5
Tyrrell	20	430	23	14	616
Renault	18	123	15	31	312
Maserati	17	71	9	10	6
BRM	15	197	17	11	433
Alfa Romeo	14	110	10	12	50
Cooper	14	129	16	11	342
Matra (inc F2 cars)	12	62	9	4	163
Ligier	9	326	9	9	388
Mercedes	9	12	9	8	0
Prost + Ligier	9	375	9	9	419
March	7	197	3	5	173.5
March + Leyton H.	7	227	3	5	181.5
Kurtis Kraft	6	12	5	6	120
Vanwall	6	28	9	7	57
Honda	2	35	2	1	48
Jordan	2	146	3	2	216
Shadow	2	104	1	3	67.5
Toleman	2	57	0	1	26
Wolf	2	47	3	1	79
Lancia	1	4	0	2	0
Lesovsky	1	9	0	1	0
Watson	1	9	3	2	0

CONSTRUCTORS BY MOST FASTEST LAPS IN ONE SEASON

Fast	Constructor	Year
11	Williams-Honda	1986
	Williams-Renault	1992
	Williams-Renault	1996
10	McLaren-Honda	1988
	Williams-Renault	1993
	Williams-Renault	1997
9	McLaren-Mercedes	1998
	McLaren-Mercedes	1999
8	Benetton-Ford	1994
	Benetton-Renault	1995
	McLaren-Porsche	1984
	McLaren-Honda	1989
	Williams-Renault	1994

CONSTRUCTORS BY MOST CAR COMPLETIONS

Constructor	Comp	1st	2nd	3rd	Retire
Ferrari	907	125	162	149	519
McLaren	673	123	93	89	363
Lotus	652	79	42	51	576
Williams	497	103	89	56	271
Tyrrell	494	23	33	21	347
Brabham	462	35	41	48	463
Prost+Ligier	372	9	16	28	301
Arrows+Footwork	325	–	5	4	308
Benetton+Toleman	325	27	32	42	220
Ligier	317	9	14	27	260
Benetton	297	27	31	40	154
Cooper	290	16	18	24	210
March+Leyton House	276	3	11	8	283
BRM	273	17	27	17	249
March	255	3	10	8	247
Arrows	242	–	5	3	219
Maserati	189	9	10	18	182
Minardi	188	–	–	–	245
Jordan	152	3	4	8	132
Surtees	130	–	1	1	96
Sauber	116	–	–	4	107
Shadow	112	1	–	6	99
Lola	109	–	2	1	137
Renault	101	15	15	11	126
Alfa Romeo	100	10	8	8	134

Constructor	Comp	1st	2nd	3rd	Retire
Kurtis Kraft	95	5	5	6	100
Footwork	83	–	–	1	89
Matra	79	9	4	8	35
Fittipaldi	71	–	1	2	51
Dallara	63	–	–	2	70
Prost	55	–	2	1	41
Ensign	54	–	–	–	56
Porsche	54	1	3	1	17

CONSTRUCTORS BY MOST CAR RETIREMENTS

Constructor	Retire	1st	2nd	3rd	Comp
Lotus	576	79	42	51	652
Ferrari	519	125	162	149	907
Brabham	463	35	41	48	462
McLaren	363	123	93	89	673
Tyrrell	347	23	33	21	494
Arrows+Footwork	308	0	5	4	325
Prost+Ligier	301	9	16	28	372
March+Leyton House	283	3	11	8	276
Williams	271	103	89	56	497
Ligier	260	9	14	27	317
BRM	249	17	27	17	273
March	247	3	10	8	255
Minardi	245	–	–	–	188
Benetton+Toleman	220	27	32	42	325
Arrows	219	–	5	3	242
Cooper	210	16	18	24	290
Maserati	182	9	10	18	189
Benetton	154	27	31	40	297
Lola	137	–	2	1	109
Alfa Romeo	134	10	8	8	100
Jordan	132	3	4	8	152
Renault	126	15	15	11	101
Osella	120	–	–	–	46
Sauber	107	–	–	4	116
Kurtis Kraft	100	5	5	6	95
Shadow	99	1	–	6	112
Surtees	96	–	1	1	130
Footwork	89	–	–	1	83
Gordini	80	–	–	2	47
Dallara	70	–	–	2	63
Toleman	66	–	1	2	28
ATS (Germany)	58	–	–	–	49
Zakspeed	57	–	–	–	27
Ensign	56	–	–	–	54
Stewart	54	1	1	3	41
Fittipaldi	51	–	1	2	71

CONSTRUCTORS BY MOST WORLD CHAMPIONSHIP POINTS

Team	WC Pts	Grand Total
McLaren	2321.5	2328.5
Ferrari	2305.5	2352.5
Williams	1989.5	1989.5
Lotus	1331	1367
Benetton+Toleman	847.5	847.5
Brabham	843	864
Benetton	821.5	821.5
Tyrrell	612	616
Prost+Ligier	419	419
Ligier	388	388
BRM	385	433
Renault	312	312
Cooper	301	342
Jordan	216	216
March+Leyton House	180.5	181.5
March	172.5	173.5
Matra	163	163
Arrows+Footwork	157	157
Arrows	132	132
Sauber	84	84
Wolf	79	79
Shadow	67.5	67.5
Surtees	53	53
Alfa Romeo	50	50
Hesketh	48	48
Honda	48	48
Vanwall	48	57
Stewart	47	47
Porsche	45	47
Fittipaldi	44	44
Lola	43	43
Prost	31	31
Minardi	28	28
Toleman	26	26
Footwork	25	25
Penske	23	23
Ensign	19	19
Eagle	17	17
Dallara	15	15
BRP	11	11
Leyton House	8	8
ATS	7	7
Larrousse	6	6
Maserati	6	6
Onyx	6	6

Team	WC Pts	Grand Total
Parnelli	6	6
Rial	6	6
Osella	5	5
Hill	3	3
AGS	2	2
Theodore	2	2
Zakspeed	2	2
Tecno	1	1

CONSTRUCTORS BY MOST TOTAL POINTS

Team	WC Pts	Grand Total
Ferrari	2305.5	2352.5
McLaren	2321.5	2328.5
Williams	1989.5	1989.5
Lotus	1331	1367
Brabham	843	864
Benetton+Toleman	847.5	847.5
Benetton	821.5	821.5
Tyrrell	612	616
BRM	385	433
Prost+Ligier	419	419
Ligier	388	388
Cooper	301	342
Renault	312	312
Jordan	216	216
March+Leyton House	180.5	181.5
March	172.5	173.5
Matra	163	163
Arrows+Footwork	157	157
Arrows	132	132
Sauber	84	84
Wolf	79	79
Shadow	67.5	67.5
Vanwall	48	57
Surtees	53	53
Alfa Romeo	50	50
Hesketh	48	48
Honda	48	48
Porsche	45	47
Stewart	47	47
Fittipaldi	44	44
Lola	43	43
Prost	31	31
Minardi	28	28
Toleman	26	26
Footwork	25	25
Penske	23	23

Team	WC Pts	Grand Total
Ensign	19	19
Eagle	17	17
Dallara	15	15
BRP	11	11
Leyton House	8	8
ATS	7	7
Larrousse	6	6
Maserati	6	6
Onyx	6	6
Parnelli	6	6
Rial	6	6
Osella	5	5
Hill	3	3
AGS	2	2
Theodore	2	2
Zakspeed	2	2
Tecno	1	1

CONSTRUCTORS BY MOST LAPS COMPLETED

Team	Laps	Team	Laps
Ferrari	70563	Kuzma	5921
Lotus	55470	Dallara	5402
McLaren	51609	Fittipaldi	5343
Brabham	40989	Osella	4833
Tyrrell	39265	Prost	4469
Williams	38449	Gordini	4469
Arrows+Footwork	27954	Ensign	4432
Kurtis Kraft	26817	ATS (Germany)	4375
Ligier	26237	Larrousse	3961
Benetton+Toleman	25536	Stewart	3924
BRM	23694	Porsche	3305
March+Leyton H.	23507	Hesketh	3012
Cooper	22896	Zakspeed	2926
Benetton	22642	Toleman	2894
March	21316	Talbot	2792
Arrows	20813	Epperly	2784
Minardi	17398	Watson	2778
Maserati	16266	Wolf	2412
Jordan	12381	Leyton House	2191
Sauber	10055	Vanwall	2168
Lola	9959	Mercedes	2151
Surtees	9834	Penske	2137
Renault	9365	Honda	2074
Alfa Romeo	9164	Connaught	2053
Shadow	9114	AGS	2031
Footwork	7141		
Matra	6093		

Minimum of 2000 laps to be included in list.